What Great Paintings Say

Masterpieces in Detail

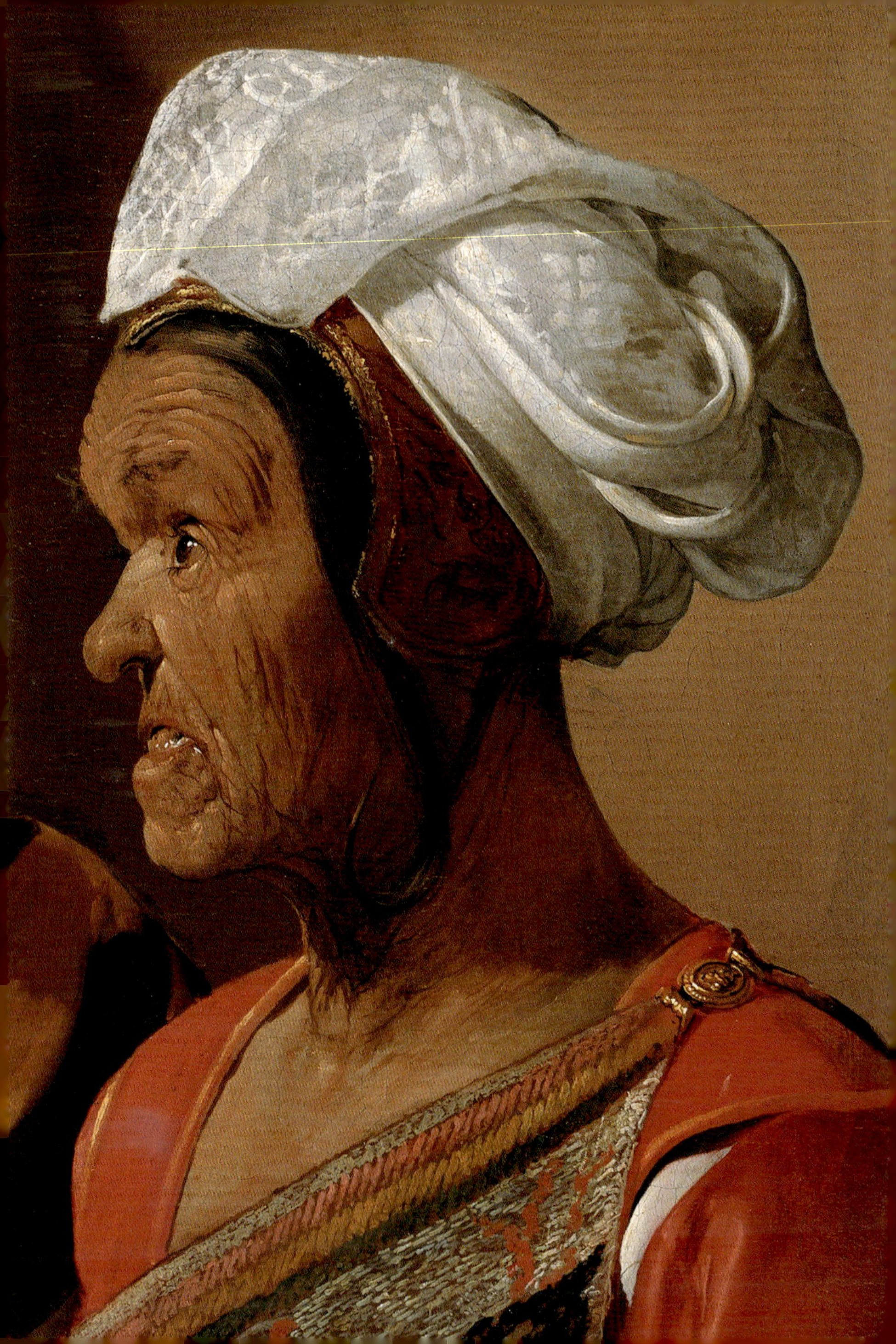

Rose-Marie & Rainer Hagen

What Great Paintings Say

Masterpieces in Detail

TASCHEN

Bibliotheca Universalis

Contents

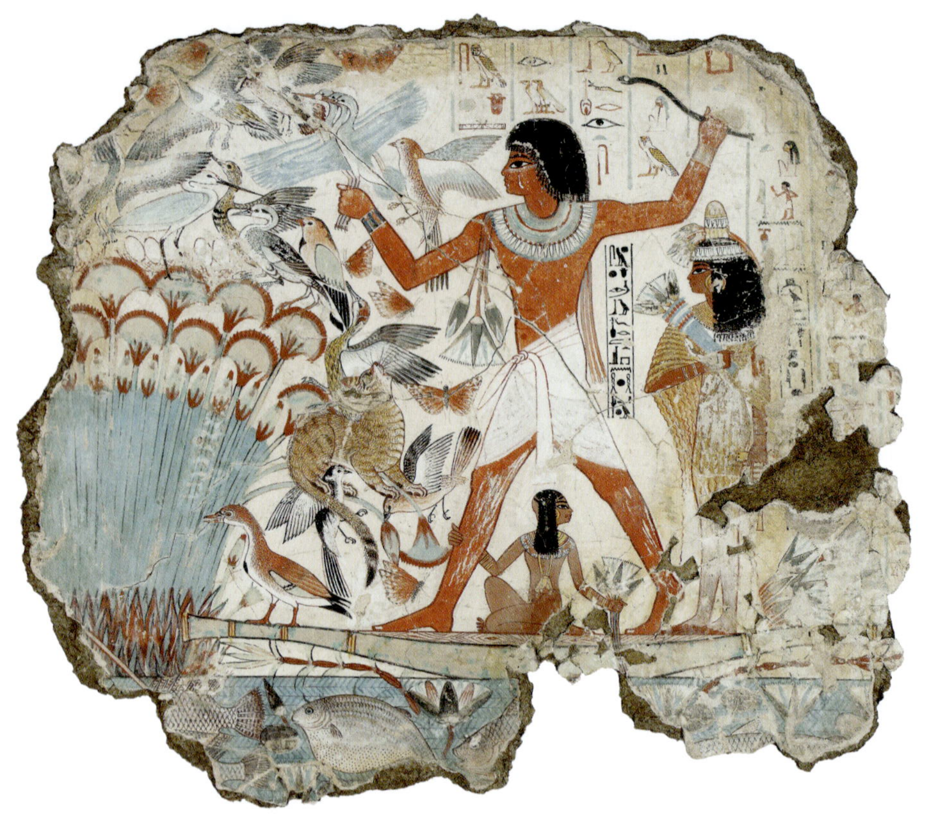

Anonymous

Bird hunt in the underworld

Fragment of a wall painting from the tomb of Nebamun,
Thebes, 18th Dynasty, before 1350 BC
83 x 98 cm, London, The British Museum

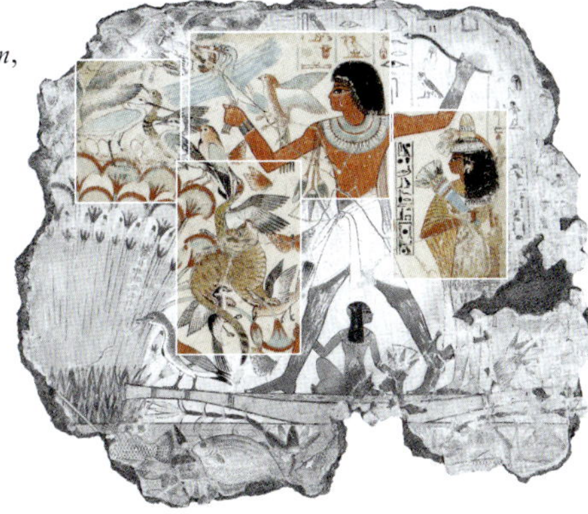

This fragment of a wall painting, so bright and cheerful in mood, belongs in the solitary seclusion of a tomb. It shows the deceased out hunting. He is swinging a throwing stick in his left hand and holding three birds firmly in his right. He stands on a flat boat of papyrus reeds, reinforced with wooden planks, that is altogether barely bigger than a surfboard. On the prow stands a Nile goose, and behind the deceased his wife; a daughter crouches between his legs. The air and bushes in front of him are full of birds: some appear to have been startled, others are shielding eggs in their nest.

Painted before 1350 BC, *Hunting in the Marshes* was not a new subject as such. Of the almost 200 examples uncovered to date, however, none offers such a wealth of bird species in such differentiated colours. We know from other wall paintings that a fowling scene of this kind is usually accompanied by a scene of the tomb owner fishing. In the case of the present fragment, this section no longer survives, but a length of spear can still be seen in the bottom left-hand corner, together with the tail end of the fish that the weapon has trapped.

The Egyptians believed in an existence after death, which was why they strove to preserve the body with their mummification techniques, performed daily rituals in which they supplied statues of the dead with food, and decorated their tombs with scenes from everyday life: lavishly spread tables, leafy vine bowers hung with bunches of grapes, excursions into the marshes and hunting in the papyrus thickets. The hieroglyphs beneath Nebamun's left shoulder tell us what pictures such as this fragment show, namely the deceased "enjoying himself and seeing beauty instead of a lifetime of eternal repetition". These scenes from life accompanied the dead and were infused with magical powers so that the deceased might fare as well in eternity as on earth. These powers were far more important than the aesthetic quality of the representation. This was true for all places of worship, for temples as for tombs. If the tomb-owners sit at tables piled high with haunches of beef and roast duck, for example, it is because these painted supplies of food will help ensure that the dead suffer no hunger for all eternity. For this reason artists and craftsmen muttered charms while working, the knowledge of which was passed – together with manual skills – from father to son. "I am the lord of mystery", boasted Iriirusen from the Middle Empire (*c.* 2040–1785 BC). "I have used all the power of magic" so that the paintings – created according to the correct conventions – might "live".

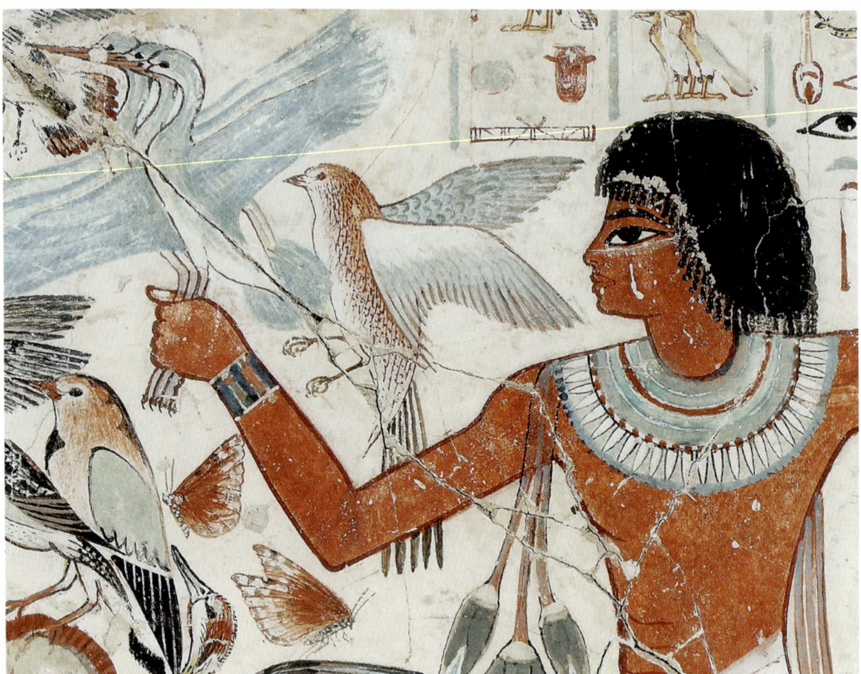

The tomb-owner remains forever young

One of the conventions of Ancient Egyptian painting and bas-relief was the representation of the human body from a combination of two angles: the head, torso and legs in side view, the eyes and shoulders from the front. Elements to which the Egyptians attached particular importance were to be clearly visible. Thus the width of the shoulders, for example, and the symbol of power held by kings in front of the breast, are better appreciated from the front. Striding legs, on the other hand, could not be shown from the front because the Egyptians were unfamiliar with spatial perspective. Individual body parts were painted without depth or modelling, but were laid down as a flat plane in one colour. The renunciation of the third dimension helped Egyptian art to achieve the clarity that we still admire in it today.

Its incisiveness and simplicity are also heightened by its renunciation of individuality. The tombowner was called Nebamun, but his face betrays nothing of his age or character and doesn't even register enjoyment of the hunt. The artist does not seek to capture a likeness but depicts only what we might call the core or the essence of the person – what remains when everything incidental and transient has been stripped away. The wig plaited into small braids and the wide collar tell us nothing about the personal tastes of the sitter, but were standard dress for men from the upper ranks of the Egyptian social hierarchy. Such men were identified only by their written name and title. Nebamun was a senior official and manager of a royal granary from the 18th Dynasty.

A more detailed representation of a bird hunt, found in a different tomb and dating from the Middle Empire, takes the form of a model boat. Manned by miniature oarsmen and paddlers, it includes men hurling spears tied to ropes (i.e. harpoons), high-ranking figures who are standing idly by, and a young woman stowing away the birds bagged by hunters. Documentary sources indicate that boats were normally bigger than the one Nebamun is standing on and had comfortable cabins for longer trips, as well as storage space for food and drink and the equipment and spoils of the hunt. Hunting in the marshes or in the desert was one of the sporting pursuits of the upper class. It required a degree of training, for example in how to use the throwing stick. These were slightly curved and broadened out at one end, which was often carved into the shape of a snake's head. In his other hand Nebamun is holding three decoys.

A fertile field for her lord

The wife is smaller than her husband, in line with the traditional pictorial hierarchy. Even if she had been taller in real life, in pictures her scale is reduced. It was social status, not reality, which counted. The royal official and granary manager ranked higher than his spouse and she higher than their daughter, who is holding her father's shin. These distinctions were valid not only within a family group but also wherever the Pharaoh or leading officials were depicted in the company of persons of lesser importance. It would be wrong to deduce from these relative proportions that strict subordination reigned within the family. A married woman was described as "mistress of the house" and in contrast to other Ancient societies, in which they were treated as minors and had to be represented in legal proceedings by a male relative, Egyptian women (at least in the New Empire from *c.* 1550 to 1075 BC) could go to court themselves. But that was probably just one side of the picture. The advice offered by Ptahhotep the sage (*c.* 2300 BC) to a married man is likely to be closer to the everyday reality of women's lives: "Fill her stomach and clothe her back, for she is a fertile field for her lord. Do not contend with her in a court of justice, but keep her from power and restrain her."

The high official's wife is festively attired: it is thus that the deceased should remember her and thus that she should accompany him into eternity. She wears a pleated dress with wide sleeves, through which the contours of her slender body can be seen. All women in tomb paintings have ideal figures. She is holding lotus blossoms in her arms and a scented cone sits on top of her head. Made of perfumed animal fat, the cone was worn on top of the wig on social occasions, causing the hair to shine and smell sweetly as it melted. Wigs were worn by both men and women of the upper class. Her hair was considered one of a woman's most important attractions,

even if it was not her own. "He found me alone," says the heroine of a fairytale of her admirer. "He said: 'Come, let us spend a while together. Let us go to bed, put on your wig.'"

Perfumes also played a major role in the perception of the Egyptians, and it is likely that people several thousand years ago could differentiate between scents to a greater degree than we can today. The proximity of the gods was signalled by a particular odour, called the "sweat of God". The hieroglyph for "joy" is a nose, and Ptahhotep the sage also advised the husband to provide his wife with perfumed ointments "as the remedy for her limbs" and thereby "gladden her heart as long as you live".

The depiction of married couples was characterized not only by their different sizes according to importance but also by their arrangement. The wife stands or walks behind the husband, as remains the custom in many regions of the Middle East and Africa even today. In adherence with another traditional convention of art, the wife has her feet close together as a sign of reticence while the husband strides out with energy and power.

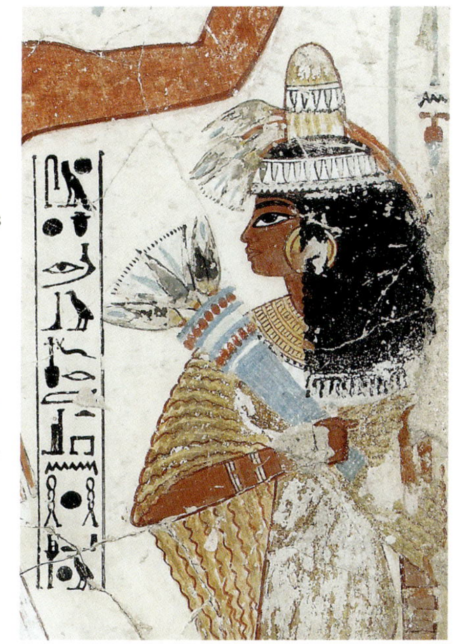

The cat as assistant hunter

Holding two birds in its claws and one in its teeth, the cat – like the people – has been idealized by the artist and portrayed as particularly handsome, large and clever. Whether it is retrieving the animals brought down by the throwing stick or hunting for itself is impossible to say.

Cats were popular companions on the hunt and in the home, where cats with brown and yellow stripes were preferred. One such Libyan wild cat is found in another tomb, painted lying under its master's chair and eating a fish. Gathered beneath the throne of a queen are three of her pets – a little monkey and a cat embracing a goose. Nebamun is also accompanied by a goose as well as a cat. A cat coffin elaborately decorated with reliefs has been found in Memphis, the Ancient capital: furnished with the usual protective female deities and spells, it resembles the sarcophagus of a small person. The mummified animal that lay inside was called Tamiat and belonged to Akhenaten's elder brother, who died before he could ascend to the throne. In a relief on one of the outer walls,

the cat Tamiat is seated at a table bearing food for all eternity.

The above examples date from the New Empire and are few in comparison to the Late Period, from which vast numbers of mummified bulls, dogs, birds and cats have come down to us. These vestiges of ancient animal cults also extend to magnificent statues of cats, in which the Egyptian feel for elegant line seems to have found a particularly welcome subject. The majority of these statues are cast in bronze and many are richly decorated, as in the bronze figure of a seated cat in the British Museum in London, which has gold rings in its nose and ears together with a wide ornamental collar and an eye amulet in front of its chest.

The proliferation in animal cults arose out of the belief that animals were embodiments of gods or at least possessed divine powers. Herodotus, the Greek, who travelled through Egypt in around 450 BC, wrote that the animals "in the country, whether domesticated or otherwise, are all regarded as sacred. If I were to explain why they are consecrated to the several gods, I should be led to speak of religious matters, which I particularly shrink from mentioning."

The goddess whom the Egyptians imagined as a cat was called Bastet. In the Old Kingdom (*c.* 2660–2190 BC) she had the shape of a lion, then she became a cat, then the lion goddess and cat goddess were combined. The Egyptian gods changed their attributes repeatedly over the course of the centuries and even embodied different powers from city to city, with the result that many of them appear to possess contradictory characteristics. This did not bother the Egyptians, for whom the true shape of a god remained an eternal mystery, independent of such metamorphoses. The cat goddess was held to be merry and boisterous, and feasts held in her honour were celebrated with copious amounts of alcohol, at least in the Late Period. She nevertheless retained something of the lion goddess, who embodied courage and the eagerness to fight and hunt. As a wild, frisky huntress, Nebamun's favourite cat accompanies her eternally young master.

The swamp as a mythical setting

Nebamun's tomb lay in the Theban Necropolis on the west bank of the Nile. The dead were almost always laid to rest to the west of cities, where the solar bark – the boat carrying the sun god – slipped

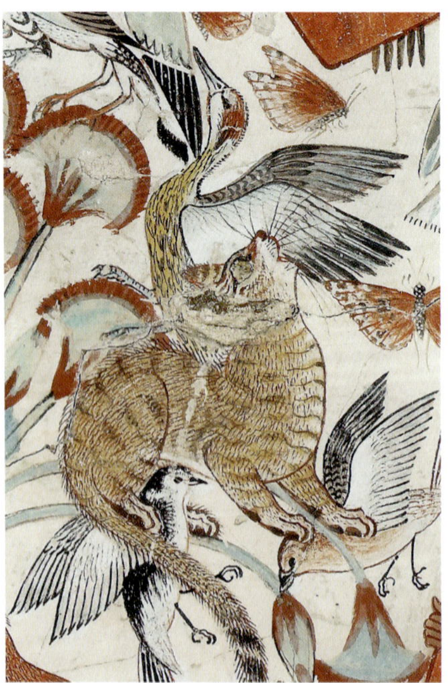

below the horizon at nightfall, having risen in the east and travelled across the sky during the day. In the underworld, on the primordial waters of Nun, it sails back to the east. It was the hope of the living to be able to join the bark of the gods after their death and to ascend with it back to the light. According to one theory, our pictorial motif is an encoded representation of precisely this journey by the dead: the hunt for fish in the water corresponds to the nocturnal passage across Nun, while the birds fluttering upwards embody the ascent into the heavens.

But our frequently painted subject also evokes associations of a quite different sort. These are connected with the behaviour of the Nile. Before the embankment dams were built, the Egyptians watched the waters rise every year and inundate large areas of the fertile countryside. The land was swallowed up and only reappeared once the great flood was over. This natural phenomenon reminded the Egyptians of the myth of the creation of the earth, which arose as something entirely new out of a material like the silt on the riverbank. Hence the thicket on the shore assumed a mythical aura of fertility and reproduction for the Egyptians, who made the lotus plant that grew in the swamp their symbol. The lotus flower closes at night and opens again in the morning. The marshes play a role in one of the legends of the gods. When Seth savagely tore Osiris to pieces, Isis – Osiris's wife – gathered up the dismembered parts of his body, fled to the marshes of the delta and used her magical powers to bring her dead husband back to life so he could impregnate her. She raised her son Horus in the shelter of the marshes until he was old enough to take up the struggle against his father's murderer.

Alongside the ascent into the heavens in the company of the birds, the Egyptians also associated the shores of the Nile with the idea of renewal. It is for this reason that the painter has made the bird's eggs so prominent, and that the tomb owner is accompanied by his wife and child – his wife dressed in her best clothes, unsuitable for a hunt but appropriate as a celebration of eternal regeneration. And all three carry lotus plants. The tomb owner carries them draped over his shoulder, the wife has them in her hand and on her wig, and the daughter is pulling a bunch out of the water.

The thicket could also be an out-of-the-way setting for erotic encounters, as implied by one anonymous poet: "My beloved, so that I may be alone

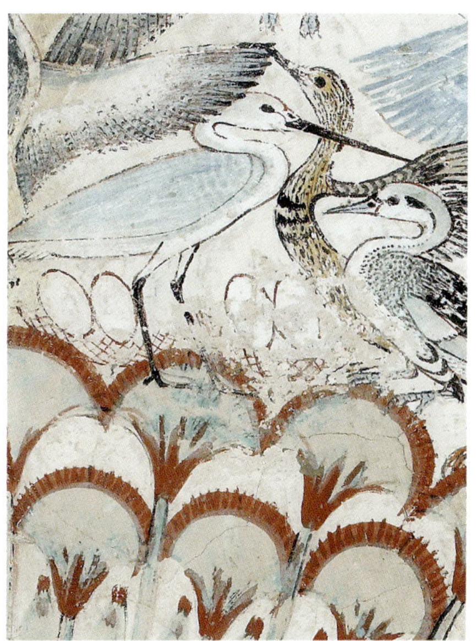

with you I have come bird catching, my snare in one hand, my net and my throwing stick in the other." In tomb paintings such things remain unspoken, not least because the spells cast by the painter meant the figures might come alive.

In Nebamun's day, only his family and friends had the opportunity to enjoy the wall paintings executed by the anonymous artist. The scenes that were to accompany the deceased were painted inside the tomb-chapel, which was only opened on feast days and for ritual purposes. As the centuries passed, the tombs were forgotten and their entrances became blocked. Only tomb robbers attempted to break in. The British Museum is today home to eleven fragments from the tomb of Nebamun, which were broken off the walls in a crude and careless manner. We owe the preservation of their delicate colours to the fact that they remained in the dark for millennia.

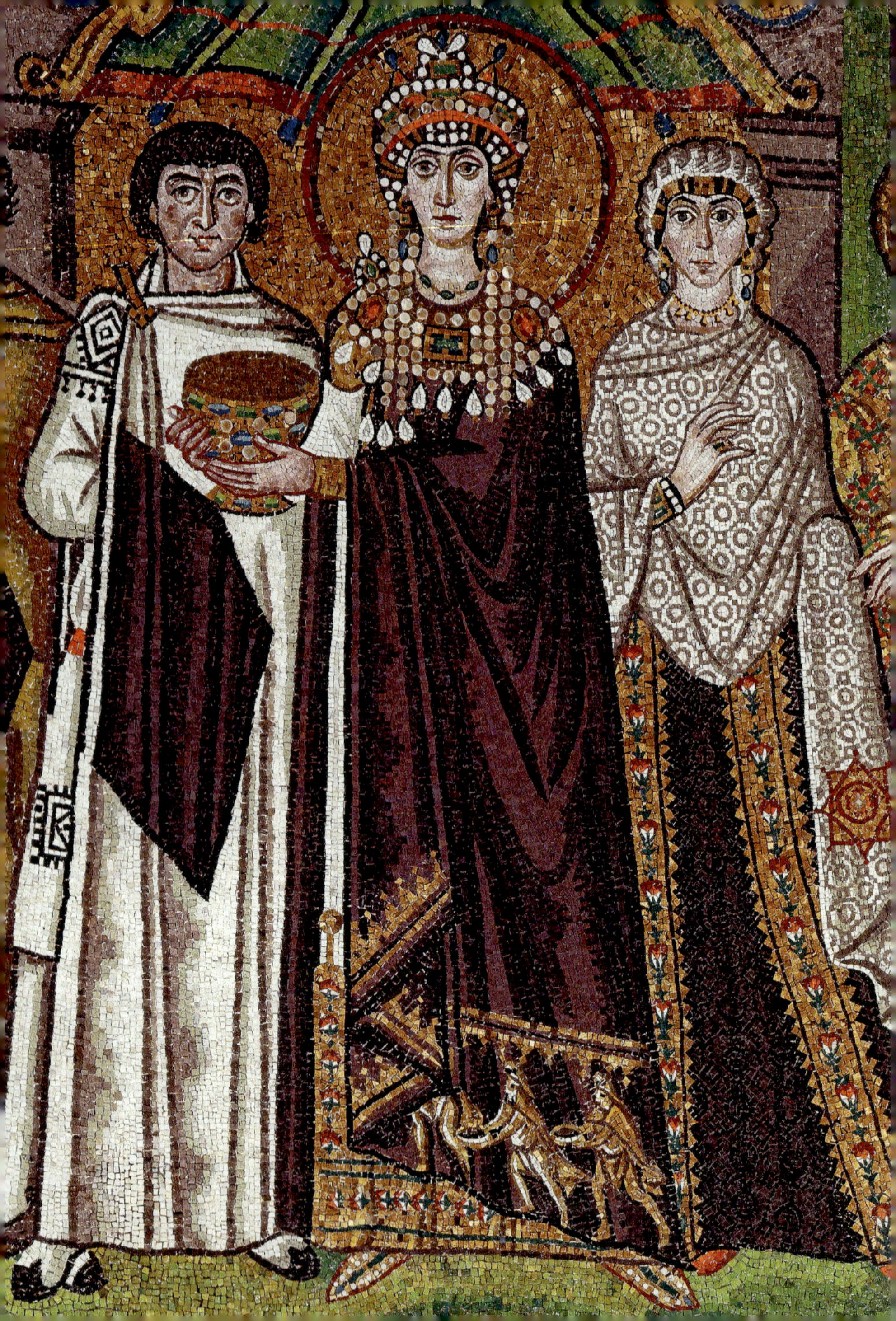

Anonymous

Group portrait with empress

The Empress Theodora with her Retinue, c. 547
Mosaic, Ravenna, Basilica di San Vitale

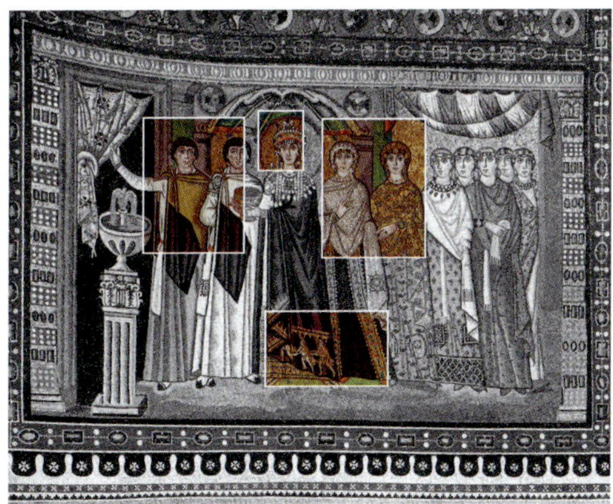

Whether we want to or not, we have to look up to Theodora, for her portrait is in a mosaic high over the heads of beholders in the church of San Vitale in Ravenna. From the opposite wall her husband, Justinian, emperor of the East Roman Empire, looks out across us. Theodora bears the insignia of power, clearly visible: the bejewelled triple diadem with the long chains of pearls, over a jewel-encrusted cap, and around her shoulders a cloak of imperial purple.

The empress is not aligned with her retinue; hers is the only figure over which no other overlaps. She is at the head of a procession and bears a communion chalice to the church. An official is pulling back the drape from a portal, and the dark opening contrasts with the golden brightness of the outdoor scene. The procession is moving across an area of greenery; a fountain is splashing; and over the ladies is a colourful awning. The empress is standing exactly underneath a baldachin borne on stone columns. Although accounts describe her as short and petite, Theodora dominates her court, thanks to her foreground position and her high headdress. Protocol dictated as much to the artists who worked on this mosaic in the mid-6th century.

The images of the imperial couple in Ravenna served a political purpose: they underlined the presence of the rulers in a city they had only recently reconquered for their empire. They were in a church because the emperor of the East Roman Empire was a religious leader and Christ's vicar upon earth. Hence the golden nimbus behind Theodora's head, a reflection of the light divine. This places her on a par with saints and apostles, quite a career for the daughter of a bear-tamer at the Constantinople hippodrome.

Eunuchs helped with the affairs of government
Meteoric careers were by no means unusual in mobile Byzantine society. The empress's closest confidant, Narses, probably shown here at her side, was born into slavery in Armenia in 480. Uneducated, and "a slight, to all appearances weakly man",

he made his way by his appetite for hard work and his expertise, both of which he exhibited in political and military positions. Rulers could rely on him. Narses is seen in the modest attitude prescribed by etiquette, both arms concealed beneath his cloak; for it was forbidden to approach the divine rulers with "impure hands".

Both of the men portrayed in the mosaic are dressed as Byzantine officials, in the uniform of the civil administration, which was organized along military lines. The officials' belt over the white tunic is almost concealed by the long cloak fastened at the right shoulder. The rank of the wearer was proclaimed by the colour of the cloak and the large rectangular piece of material sewn onto it. This was called a *tablion*; the emperor's was gold, that of Narses is the precious purple reserved for the most senior of the seven ranks of official.

Even the black and white footwear was part of the uniform. It was part of an official's salary and was presented to him by the emperor, together with his certificate of appointment. Many officials studied law and passed difficult examinations; others, such as Narses, had a background in hands-on work. Parents who wanted their sons to rise more easily to high office had them castrated at an early age. Narses too was a eunuch. Only eunuchs and priests could not become emperor in Byzantium – and so posed no threat to the ruler.

The East Roman emperors lived dangerously, in spite or maybe because of their seemingly infinite power. They went in fear of potential rivals in high office, for they were constantly beset with court intrigues, military conspiracies and popular uprisings. In theory the ruler was elected directly by the "people"; in practice, however, it was a small military clique that voted him in.

Thus in the late 5th century Justinian was a rural lad living in a village in Thrace, till his uncle, a dependable professional soldier, was unexpectedly

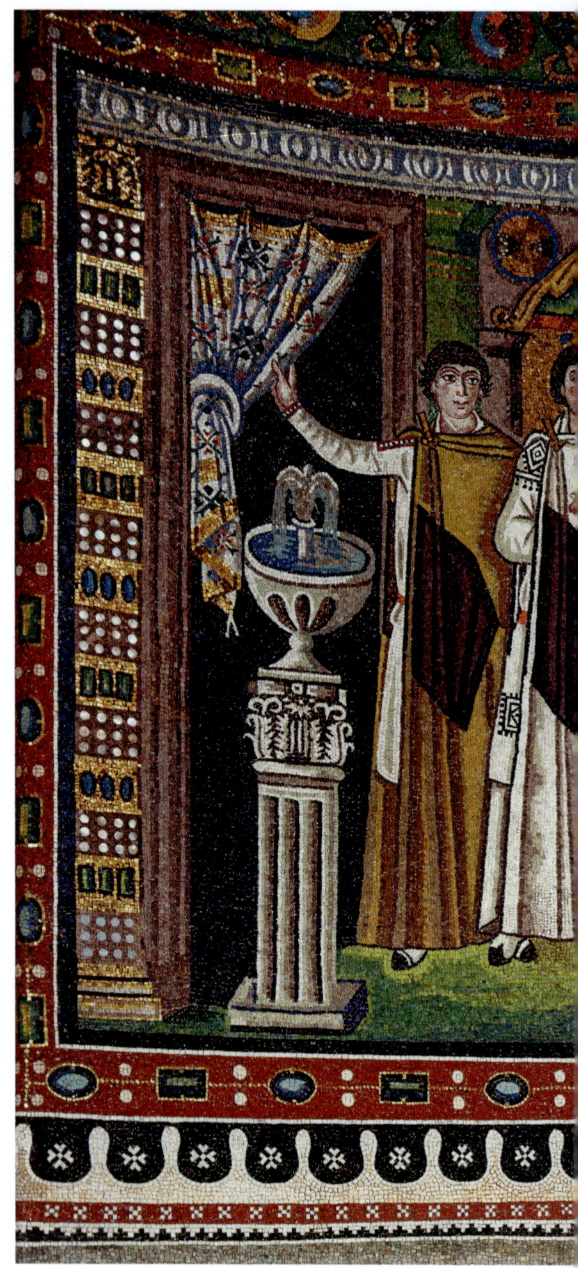

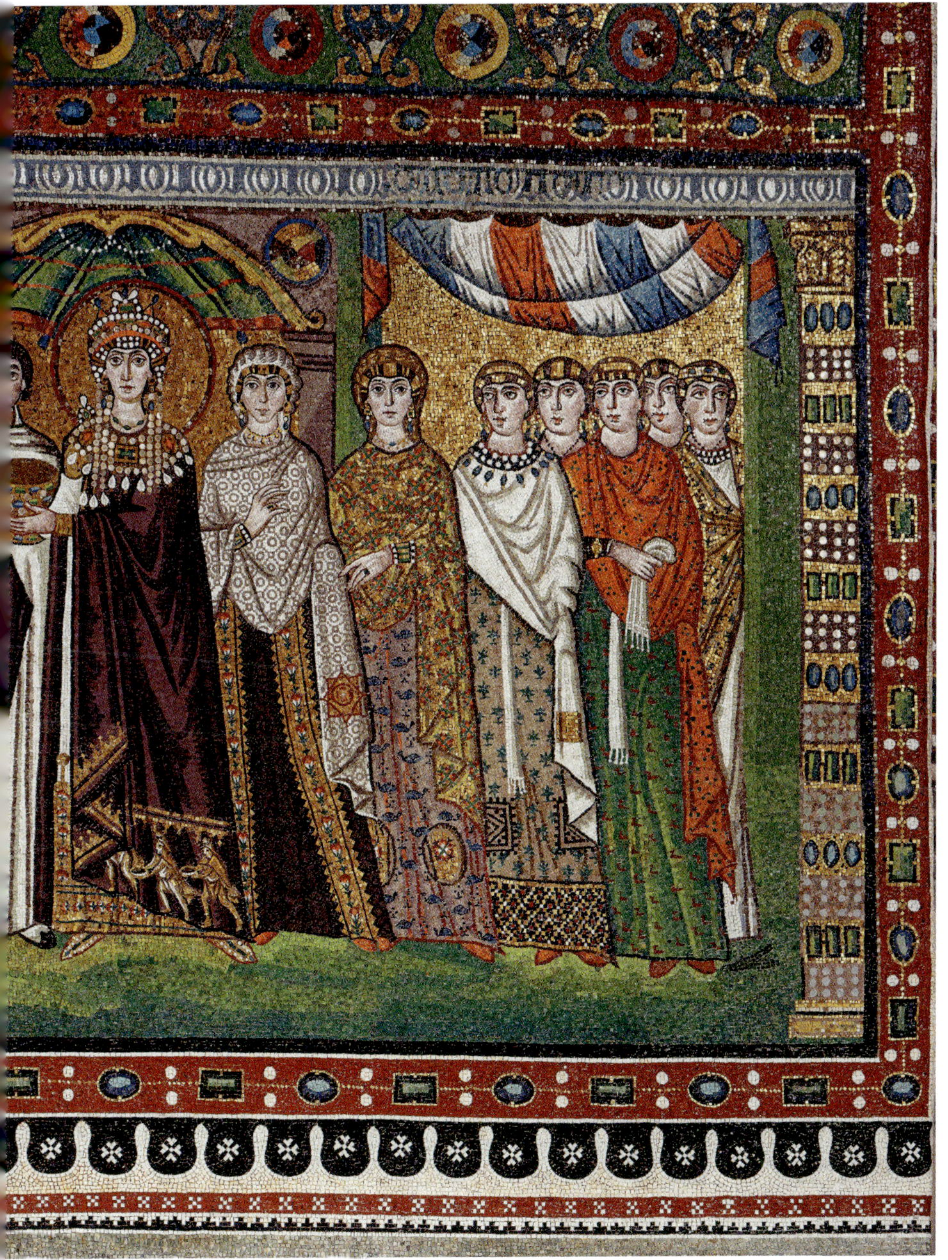

proclaimed emperor by the soldiery. Shortly afterwards, Justinian moved to the capital, Constantinople, where he received an excellent education and presently became the right-hand man of the ruler. This provided him with the means to assure himself of the throne. In 527, on the death of his uncle, Justinian became the official successor of Caesar and Augustus, the absolute overlord of an empire still known as "Roman" although for the past two centuries it had no longer been ruled from the banks of the Tiber but from the Bosporus. Rome's first Christian emperor, Constantine, had moved his capital there in dangerous times when tribes were on the move. Before the city was named after him, it was called Byzantium.

Justinian inherited a vast empire centred on the eastern Mediterranean, united only by the Christian religion and the person of the emperor. The western territories of the old Roman empire had fallen to barbarians. When Justinian came to the throne, the Ostrogoths ruled in Rome and Ravenna. The new emperor took as his great task in life the restoration of the old borders of the Roman Empire, and he succeeded; but the areas of North Africa and Italy that were conquered by his generals were lost once more after his death. The East Roman or Byzantine Empire, however, survived until 1453.

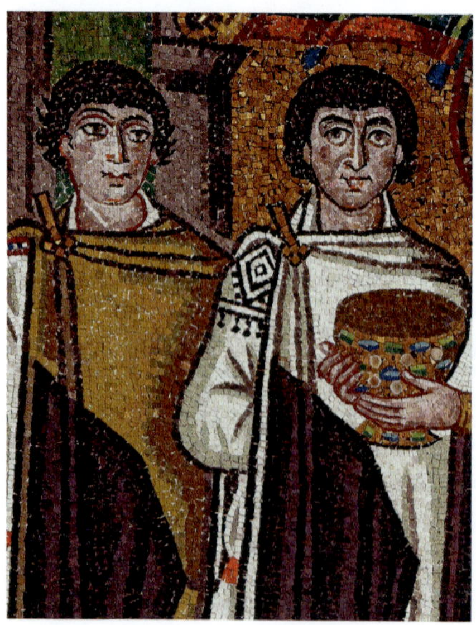

A woman well able to manage

The only certain likeness that we have of the empress Theodora is this one in Ravenna: large dark eyes, gazing from a narrow face. At this point she was no longer young, about fifty (we do not know when she was born). She died in 548, at about the same time as the church containing her image was consecrated. The portrait was copied from an original done in Constantinople, for in fact Theodora never set foot in Ravenna.

Theodora's features bear signs of illness (historians suspect cancer) or of the arduous toil of government affairs in an especially difficult time. About 540, plague spread through the East Roman Empire, taking a heavy toll on the population and ruining the economy. When Justinian too was stricken with the plague, the responsibility of government fell squarely upon Theodora. She proved well able to manage, pre-empting potential conspiracies and dealing with the administrative affairs of the empire as well as with military ventures – albeit not to the delight of the generals. This marked the peak of her power. For months, the empress was the absolute ruler in a patriarchal state that normally preferred her sex to be confined to the ladies' apartments. She was experienced in matters of government, since Justinian had involved her in them from the outset. This was envisaged neither by tradition nor by the constitution; but Justinian wished to share everything with the wife he worshipped his whole life long. He called her his "sweetest delight" or, from the literal meaning of her name in Greek, "the gift of God".

When he fell head over heels in love with Theodora, then a mere girl and twenty years younger than he, Justinian was already a counsellor to the emperor and in line for the throne. Theodora, by contrast, was from the lower classes. Since her early youth she had been performing on revue stages. "Fair of countenance, and graceful of form," she could neither dance nor sing, but nonetheless scored immense success with her comic striptease number. In a Leda burlesque she performed with a goose that was trained to pick out grains of corn from between her thighs whilst she writhed in transports of delight. In his *Secret History*, from which we know these things, Procopius (the contemporary who also wrote the official histories) described Theodora as "the sort of girl who if somebody walloped her or boxed her ears would make a jest of it and roar with laughter."

The bishop of Ephesus was even blunter: "Theodora was from a brothel."

No one, not even the church, raised any objection when the emperor's confidant fell so madly in love with this girl that he resolved to make her his lawful wife. Theodora was crowned empress at Justinian's side, and from that moment on even her arch-enemies (among them Procopius) could find not the slightest misdemeanour to accuse her of. She acquitted herself with dignity in her new role. She did not forget her earlier experiences, as is shown by an edict she promulgated against prostitution. Doubtless she owed her realism and tough will to the hard youth she spent in the hippodrome, the sleazy pleasure district of the capital: in 532, when whole quarters of the city were burnt to the ground in a popular uprising, and a mob besieged the palace, the emperor and his advisers were already debating flight, going into exile overseas, but Theodora, the one woman in a counsel of men, urged a fight and refused to flee. "I shall never take off the purple," she declared, "nor shall I ever see the day when those around me do not address me as the empress. The purple will make a good shroud." At her urging, Justinian's generals put down the insurrection. Some 40,000 were left dead. Sixteen years later, Theodora went to the grave in the imperial purple.

Intrigues in the holy palace

The two ladies immediately beside Theodora cannot be identified with certainty, but while the five companions in the background are all to a similar schematic design, these two have individualized features: the elder, with the high cheekbones, may be Antonina, the chatelaine of the palace and wife of the famous general Belisarius; the younger, who bears a resemblance to her, would then be Johannina, her daughter.

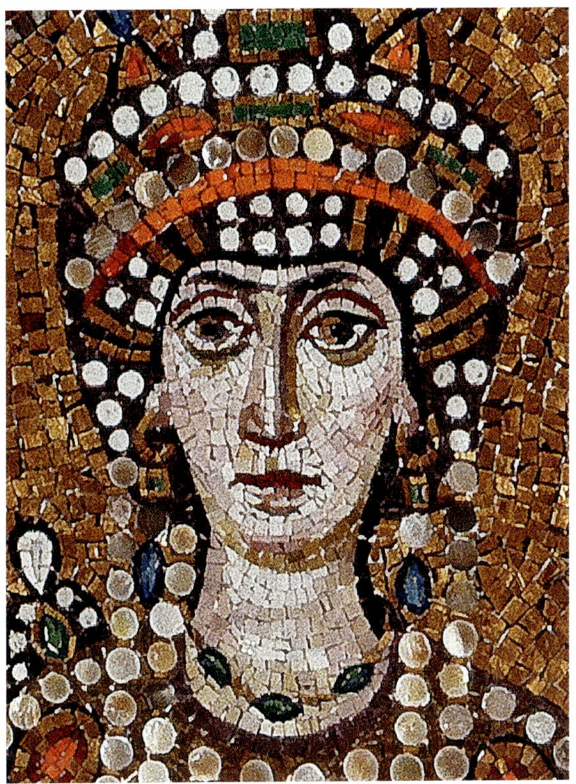

Like the empress, Antonina had had quite a career on the stage; both were strong-willed women who exerted a powerful influence on their partners, an influence that their contemporaries were at a loss to explain except by supposing them to use magic potions. Belisarius did indeed seem very much under his wife's thumb. Even on campaign he was inseparable from her; and time and again he turned a blind eye to her many blatant affairs.

If Theodora took her friend under her wing despite her scandalous lifestyle, it was not only out of loyal friendship. Through Antonina she had the popular general Belisarius, who might have been a dangerous rival for Justinian, where she wanted him. And in dealing with countless intrigues, the dependable Antonina proved her worth. In the "silken apartments of the holy palace", ably informed by a secret service organized by Narses, the two women deliberated strategies to put the empress's policies into effect and wipe out anyone who got in her way. For one powerful minister of finance, for instance, who had dared to bear tales about Theodora to Justinian, Antonina set a cunning trap: she led the unwary unfortunate to admit, with reliable witnesses listening in concealment, that he had his eyes on the throne. His fate was sealed.

It was also Antonina who carried out Theodora's plans in Italy in 537. She accompanied her husband there, persuading the reluctant Belisarius to depose the newly and lawfully elected Pope Silverius in Rome, on the orders of the empress. The Pope was replaced by force with a favourite of the empress's. Indeed, Silverius is said to have been first banished and then murdered, by a servant of Antonina's, at the empress's command.

But charges such as these were made by Procopius, the secretary of Belisarius, who hated Theodora, or by authors who disliked her policy on religion.

Her whole life long, the empress supported the Christian sect of the Monophysites, even hiding a persecuted bishop in her own apartments for years. The Monophysites were found chiefly in Egypt and Syria, and held that Christ had but one divine nature, and not an additional second, human nature, as the Orthodox Church taught. The Monophysites were persecuted as heretics, and that included the man concealed by the empress. Theodora's aim, which Justinian tolerated, was to place a Pope at the head of the Church who sympathized with her protégés. That end justified any means; and when the pontiff whom Belisarius had placed on St Peter's chair failed to satisfy her expectations too, she had him abducted from Rome and brought to Constantinople, where she could put pressure on him. Shortly before her death she seemed to be within sight of her goal: the Pope was yielding, and the Monophysites were rehabilitated. They praised the empress as "sent by God, to protect his persecuted people in the dangers of the tempest". But in fact the Orthodox Church was victorious in the long term. It was the Church that wrote the history books; and Theodora was not portrayed favourably in them.

Silk as a status symbol

The hem of Theodora's long cloak, worn over the bejewelled white robe, is adorned with figures embroidered in gold: the Three Kings bearing their gifts. The detail is minutely done, in coloured glass mosaic stones of various shapes. The number of pieces used for the two imperial mosaics in San Vitale is put at 322,560, many of them gold. A thousand years on, they still shine. Bedded upon an uneven ground of mortar, they still reflect the light in manifold ways.

We know neither who designed nor who made these works, for the masters who made mosaics did not sign their achievements. They may have been from Italy, where the Roman tradition was

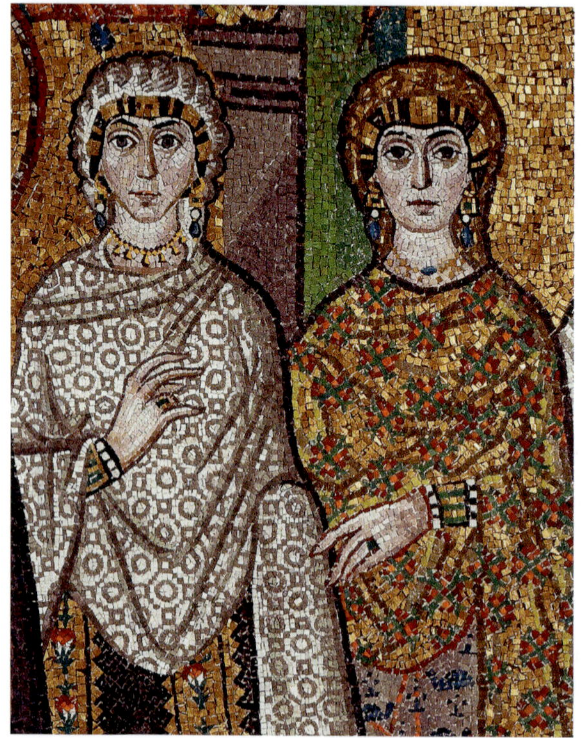

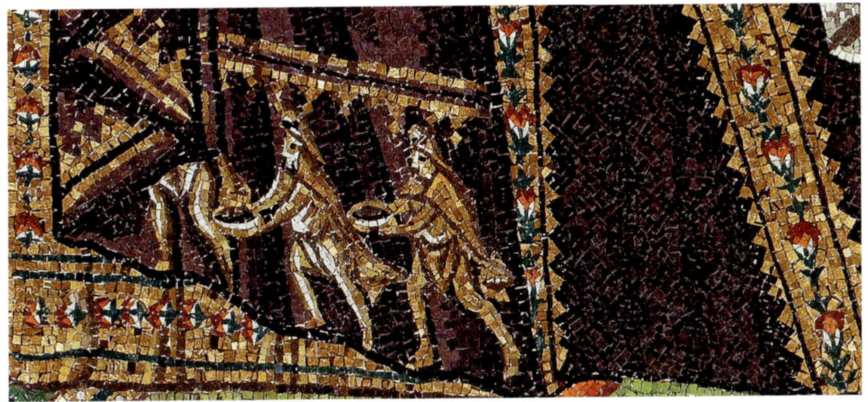

still alive, or equally from Constantinople. There were many outstanding Byzantine craftsmen, and throughout the Middle Ages Constantinople supplied Europe with luxury items: implements crafted of ivory, jewellery, and above all costly fabrics. Textiles were the most important sector of the Byzantine economy, assuming almost industrial proportions. But that splendorous workshop that was Byzantium produced not only for the export market (carefully monitored by customs); above all, their wares were produced for the imperial court. The exhibition of wealth was a deliberate act of policy.

"Through the beauty of its ceremonies," one Byzantine official noted, "imperial power appears a yet more splendid and magnificent thing. It makes as profound an impression on foreigners as it does on subjects of the empire." The emperor was good at the kind of show one might expect of God's vicar on earth. One contemporary poet described barbarians admitted to an audience supposing themselves already in heaven when they had barely crossed the threshold of the palace, so great was the splendour.

The protocol that set the emperor apart from mere mortals (and afforded him protection from them) extended to his clothing. Certain colour shades were reserved for the imperial family, and the death penalty could be inflicted on anyone who dared wear those shades. Tyrian purple in particular, the prized genuine purple from Tyre made from snails, was the colour of imperial garb. The shades it came in ranged from scarlet to the costliest brownish purple amethyst hue, which has been used to dye the silk we see Theodora wearing.

The fact that her neighbour is wearing a similar shade indicates her privileged status. Antonina and the other ladies of the court are furthermore wearing white patterned stoles of the latest Oriental fashion. All of them, on certain feast days, received their rich clothing from the hands of the empress; for silk fabrics were a state monopoly.

Silk came from remote China, on the caravan route that crossed Persia, where the trade might be interrupted at any time. Not until years after Theodora's death did wily Byzantine monks contrive to smuggle silkworms out of China in hollowed-out walking staffs. Byzantium likewise guarded the secret of silk well, and the material remained a status symbol.

The motif of the Three Kings embroidered onto the silk is found again in the mosaics of Ravenna, in Sant' Apollinare Nuovo. There we can see clearly what we can only guess at here: the biblical magi are not entitled to the imperial purple, nor are they assigned the aura of a halo – unlike the Empress Theodora.

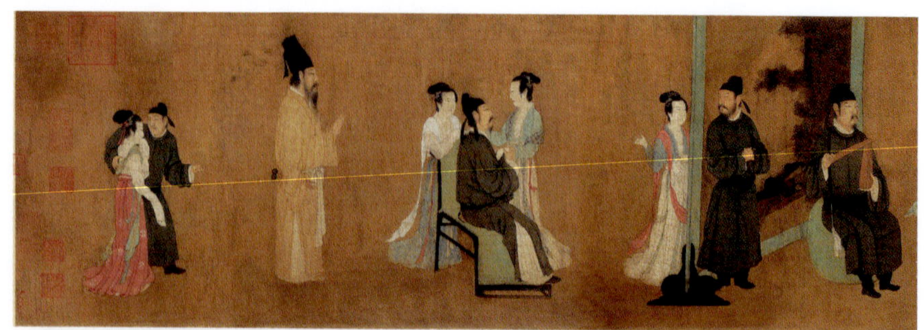

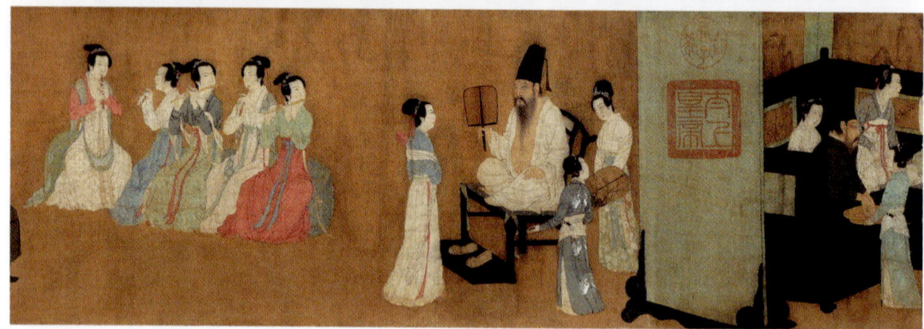

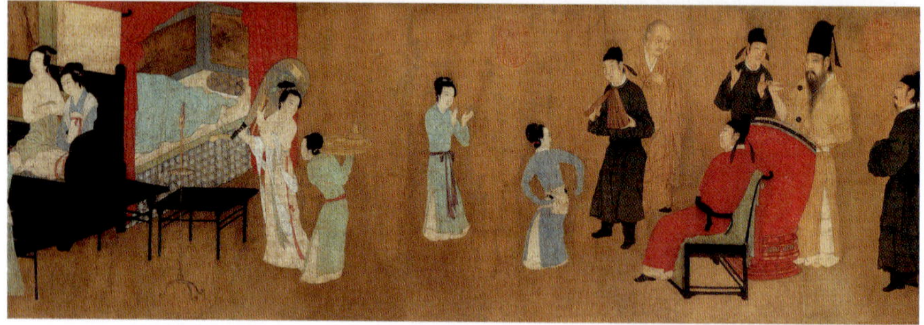

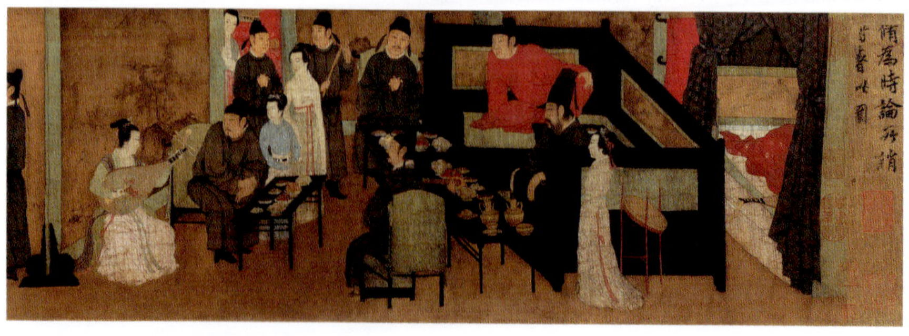
隋寫時論所消
景春映圖

Gu Hongzhong (*c.* AD 910–980)

Scenes from a wild party

The Night Revels of Han Xizai, c. 960
Scroll painting, 29 x 336 cm, Beijing, National Palace Museum

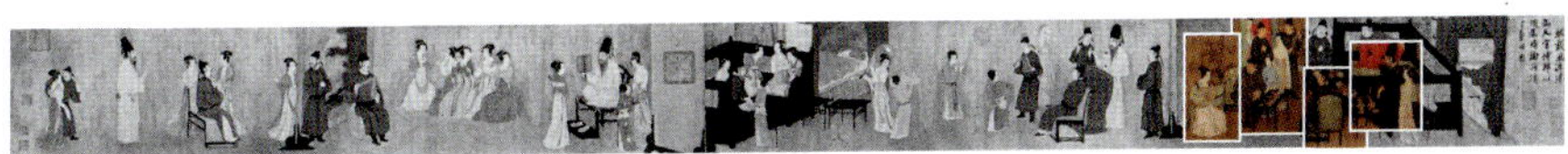

In order to check on the moral integrity of an official, a Chinese emperor used artists to spy on the nightly goings-on.

In order to keep tabs on the private lives of prominent individuals, today's tabloids send paparazzi with their cameras to nightclubs. In ancient China, so the story goes, an emperor dispatched one of his court painters to record with his brush what went on inside the home of a senior official. His motives weren't sensationalism, but reasons of state: the emperor had been planning to make the man his prime minister when it came to his ears that wild orgies were being held in the official's house every night.

The painter carried out his orders and delivered his report to his master – probably the first detective story in the history of art. It took the form of a silk handscroll some three metres in length, to be read as a horizontal strip from right to left, like Chinese writing. A work in this format was not hung on the wall but stored rolled up in a library. The owner could unfurl the scroll between two rods on a table and watch its scenes – separated only by painted wall screens – unfold in succession, like a very early forerunner of a film. The reportage takes us ever deeper inside the official's home, where as the night

progresses morals are gradually relaxed – albeit only to the extent of loosened clothing and discreet body contact, which appears fairly harmless to our eyes. In China, however, this must have been viewed much more sternly. In the opening scene at the far right-hand end of the handscroll (reproduced here in close-up), the atmosphere is still very formal. It is early evening and we are in the reception room; only on the right-hand edge of the picture, through curtains that have been drawn back, are we offered a glimpse of a bed with red covers. The bearded host and a man dressed in red, probably a guest of honour, are seated on a couch. Serious-faced men in dark robes are grouped around low tables and together with a number of ladies are listening to a female lute-player, who is seated on the far left in front of a tall screen.

A little night music, illustrated by the artist Gu Hongzhong, who lived from around AD 910 to 980, was a member of the imperial academy of art and bore the title of court painter. We know little else about him; his other works have vanished. As the owner of the *Night Revels*, the National Palace Museum in Beijing describes the scroll picture as original. A number of scholars, however, consider it to be a copy, albeit an excellent one, executed some 200 years later.

A luxury enclave amidst the chaos

Laid out on the low tables are dishes of rare delicacies and wine jugs made of precious metal. A banquet such as that described by a Chinese poet: "The purple meat of the camel's hump rises from roasting pots, glazed green, / the tender white fish are served on dishes of rock crystal. / To full, almost no one moves the chopsticks of rhinoceros horn, / in vain have knives hung with little bells carved all the food."

Luxury and abundance reign here. The participants in the night revels eat their fill and enjoy the music, while the rest of China is ruled by misery and famine and local war lords battle each other for power. Just one small empire in the fertile region south of the Yangtze River survived the collapse of the old order. It was to here that many members of the aristocracy fled, and it was here that they celebrated the lifestyle of the highly sophisticated Tang culture for a short while longer.

For almost 300 years the emperors of the Tang Dynasty had brought external and internal peace and prosperity to the whole of China. They had made of it not only the best governed but probably also the most civilized land in the world. In an epoch of openness and internationalism not dissimilar to the present, it traded with countries far away via the Silk Route. Eventually, however, incompetent leadership caused the Tang Dynasty to collapse in 907. The land was ravaged by civil wars until a general from the north finally succeeded in conquering all his rivals and founded a new, Song Dynasty that would in turn rule China for almost 300 years.

For some 40 years, the belligerent Song rulers left only the weak kingdom of the Southern Tang undisturbed. But Li Yu, the Southern Tang's last emperor and the one who commissioned our handscroll, lived in constant fear of them, well aware that his kingdom was in neither a financial nor a military position to withstand them. In 975 – only some fifteen years after the *Night Revels* was painted – the Song finally overran his capital of Jinling (modern-day Nanjing) without resistance and annexed his kingdom. Prior to being poisoned by the Song emperor at a banquet, Li Yu lived under house arrest in exile and wrote melancholy poems: "Spring flowers, autumn moon: where is their end? / The past: how much is known?" These verses are still sung to a popular melody even today.

Emperor Li Yu was a bad ruler but a committed patron of the arts, a connoisseur of music, calligraphy and painting who was himself famed as a poet and composer. He founded China's first academy of art, where he assembled many important painters who continued to work in the traditional style of the Tang period. Our artist, Gu Hongzhong, specialized in figural works and painted scenes from the lives of leisure led by courtiers and ladies-in-waiting, pictures that his imperial master sent north as tributes intended to placate the threatening Song.

Almost all documentary evidence of this epoch is lost. Emperor Li Yu had the records of his reign, both the written archives and his art collection, destroyed shortly before the enemy entered Jinling. For information about his kingdom, posterity must rely on second-hand sources, upon accounts that his victorious successors from the Song Dynasty compiled from oral traditions. All we know about the contents of Gu Hongzhong's handscroll is what we are told by later generations, namely by the authors of collections of anecdotes from the Song era and by the scroll's various owners, who – in line with Chinese custom – appended their own commentaries, interpretations and judgements to the work.

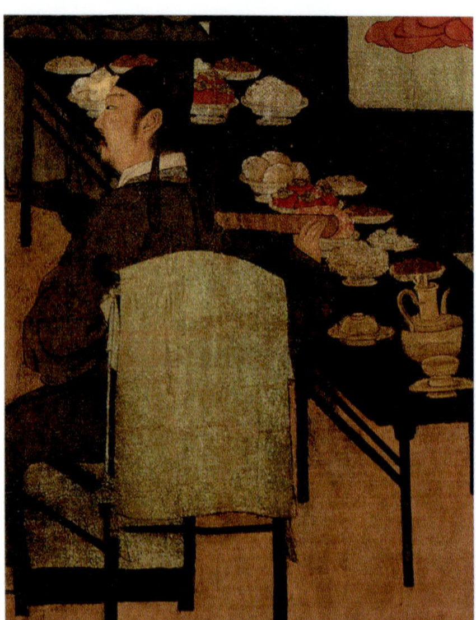

A worthy public servant?

The host of the *Night Revels*, Han Xizai (*c.* 911–970), is holding court on a raised dais which served as a seat during the day and as a bed at night. Like his guests, he is wearing dark robes together with a "scholar's cap" made out of black, reinforced gauze. This hat, with its two drooping, wing-like flaps, was the mark of Tang Dynasty officials and was only removed for sleeping. Han's rank in government can be judged from the height of his hat.

Han belonged to the elite class of scholar-officials, educated men who had passed a series of country-wide exams. After years of studying the Confucian classics, they governed China in the emperor's name as administrators, judges and ministers. In a hierarchical society in which, according to the teachings of Confucius, a person's first duty was to the common good, scholar-officials had to uphold the highest standards. They were expected to carry out their duties not only efficiently but also with the appropriate moral rectitude, and through their worthy conduct and virtuous lifestyle set an example to all. It was these strict regulations that the seemingly dignified Han Xizai proceeded to infringe.

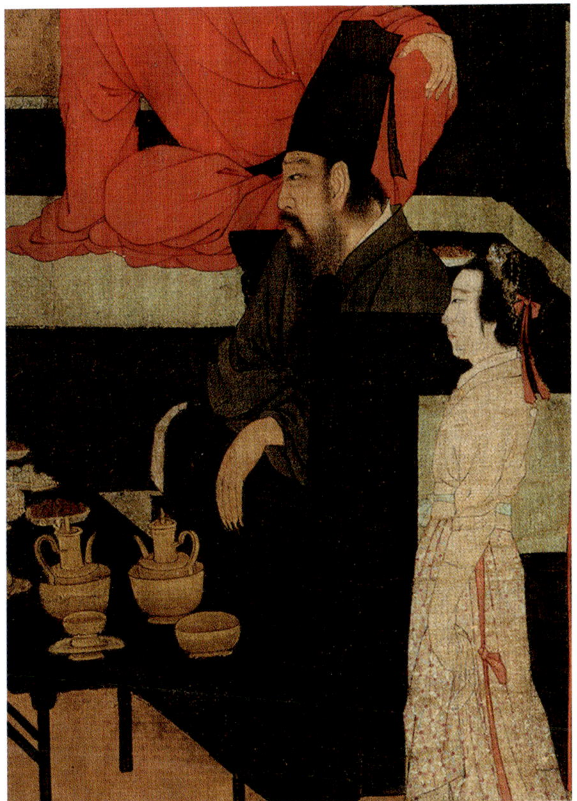

The *Night Revels* handscroll is first documented around 150 years after it was painted, when it is catalogued in the collection of one of the Song emperors, together by the following information: "Secretary of the Interior Han Xizai was obsessed with beautiful female singers and held endless parties at night. He imposed no restraints upon his guests and with wild cries they mingled with his ladies." None of this can be recognized in Gu Hongzhong's handscroll.

An anthology of anecdotes from the same period provides further details: Han Xizai is supposed to have kept up to 100 (!) maids and concubines, female singers and actresses in his home and squandered his entire family fortune on them. Since his official's salary "disappeared like the sound of a little bell" and was insufficient to cover his household expenses, Han Xizai begged for food from his ladies, disguised as a blind minstrel. The painter shows him at a later stage of the night's proceedings, beating a large drum that is standing on the right, near the dais, in the first scene.

What was the reason behind such offensive behaviour? The answer to this puzzling question is provided by one of the handscroll's later owners: "I don't want to go down in history as a fool!" Han Xizai is supposed to have confided to a friend, the Taoist monk Deming. Afraid that he was going to have to become the emperor's prime minister, he acted in this way "in order to avoid being appointed". Although the official, who was famed for his political foresight, died before the Tang Dynasty finally fell, he nevertheless saw it coming: "As soon as a true Son of Heaven appears on the great plain, this little southern empire will be vanquished in a second." He remained at court but avoided political responsibility by deliberately ruining his own reputation with orgies.

Emperor Li Yu regretted the fact – so we are informed by the above-mentioned catalogue of the imperial collection – that he was unable to see these famous parties with his own eyes. So he sent his court painter as a detective to Han Xizai's night revels, with the instructions to "reproduce from memory" everything he saw there.

There was a reason why the format of the horizontal handscroll was chosen for this confidential report. It was not destined for public viewing but reserved for the eyes of an individual. Winding the work from one rod onto the other, the owner could view one arm's length of pictures at a time, before

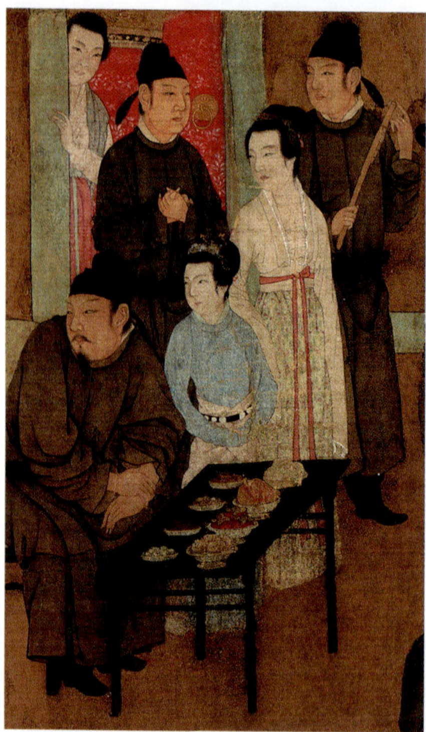

moving on to the next scene: private gratification for a curious ruler or voyeur.

Maids and concubines
The gentleman seen here sitting next to two ladies and looking across at the female lutenist was called (if we are to believe the sources) Li Jiaming. Under Emperor Li Yu, he was deputy director of the theatre and conservatoire of Jinling. The two young men in the background are probably students of the host, who are preparing for the highest state examinations under his instruction. Together with the guests, they form one of those select companies of literati who gathered ostensibly to exchange scholarly quotations or to recite improvised verse.

Contrasting with the solid, dark figures of the men – just one guest wears the red robes of the fifth-highest class of official – are slender young women in pale, partly see-through and low-cut dresses. They belong to the troupe of anonymous maids, courtesans, concubines and female artists for whom the host is supposed to have ruined himself. They served, entertained the guests and drank with them at the banquets that usually ended as alcoholic binges. What happened after that is discreetly suggested by the half curtained bed on the right behind the host, i.e. right at the start of the pictorial narrative. A woman appears to be hiding under the covers, ready for the "game of clouds and rain". The lute hanging over the edge of the mattress was employed as an erotic symbol.

The smallest of the girls, wearing a pale blue jacket, is supposed to have been the host's favourite singer. She was called Wang Wushan and belonged to the elevated category of female companions who were familiar with the classics, knew how to respond in an appropriate manner to a poem dedicated to them and in some cases even wrote poetry themselves. Occasionally they rose to become the concubine or even the powerful favourite of the emperor himself. In the second scene in the handscroll, Wang Wushan is dancing gracefully to the drum beat of the host.

A famous Chinese dancer known as Zhao Feiyan, "flying swallow", is said to have been so light-footed that she could dance on a strong man's palm. Emperor Li Yu, known as a great lover of dance, had a podium in the shape of an outsized lotus blossom built for his favourite to perform on. He commanded her to dance on the leaf with her feet bound in cloth in such as way as to resemble the pointed crescents of a moon. This novelty was so admired that the ladies of the court copied the dancer and thereby invented the custom of having tiny, crippled feet. Born of an imperial whim, these "lily feet" rapidly became an ideal of female beauty throughout the whole of China and the most powerful sexual attribute of women right up the beginning of the 20th century. It was impossible to dance on crippled feet, however, and women would from now on be mentioned only as singers and musicians. When Han Xizai's favourite performed at his party, it must have been as one of the last female dancers in China for centuries.

What a painted landscape betrays

The dancer's performance is followed in Gu Hongzhong's painted visual reportage by further scenes separated by wall screens: the host in more intimate conversation with girls on a bed, a flute concert by a female orchestra, a pair and a trio of figures hinting at growing intimacy, and lastly a guest departing with a tender farewell embrace.

Seated in front of one of the room dividers in the first scene is the female musician. She is playing the *pipa*, the four-stringed, pear-bodied Chinese lute. Her face matches the stereotype ideal of beauty in the Tang period and exhibits the "delicate and finely arching eyebrows" frequently praised in the literature. The viewer of the handscroll probably looked less closely at the facial features of the figures than at the representations of nature on the wall screens. These tell us much about the feelings and dreams of the owner.

Behind the female lutenist, gnarled trees rise from a precipitous rocky outcrop. Both are typical elements of traditional, stylized Chinese landscapes with their high mountains, distant rivers and tiny figures of hermits lost in their surroundings – landscapes for which many people living in a society regulated by Confucian morality must have yearned. A virtuous wise man, so Chinese intellectuals believed, should seek refuge in a hermitage if he found himself unable – like Han Xizai – to realize his goals. If this option was not available to him, however, he could also withdraw to his own garden or immerse himself in the contemplation of painted ideal landscapes – a sort of inner emigration.

The *Night Revels* – whether an original or a copy – passed through many collections over the course of

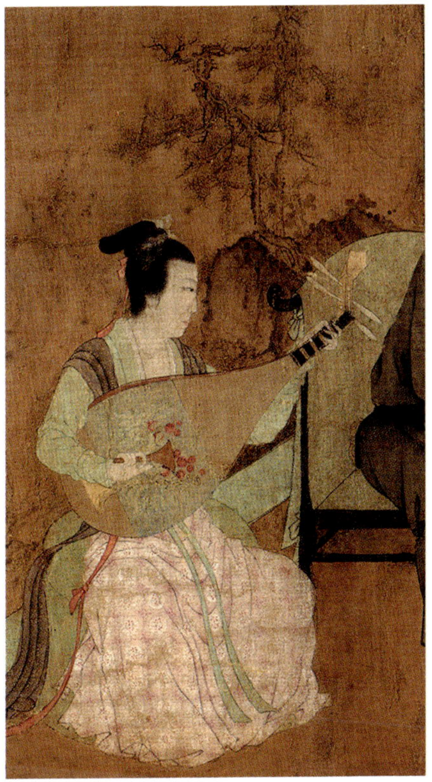

the centuries, at times disappearing amidst the upheavals of revolutions. China supposedly bought back the handscroll from British Hong Kong in the 1950s. For a long time even after this, however, memories of the feudalistic epochs in Chinese history were taboo, and only in the wake of the renewed acknowledgement of this past was the work placed on prominent display in a glass case in the National Palace Museum in Beijing. In China today, it is extremely popular: in 1990 scenes from the handscroll adorned a set of stamps, and in 2006 the film director Feng Xiaogang presented the orgies in Han Xizai's home to an international public on the cinema screen (*The Banquet*) – far less discreetly than in the painting by the artist Gu Hongzhong.

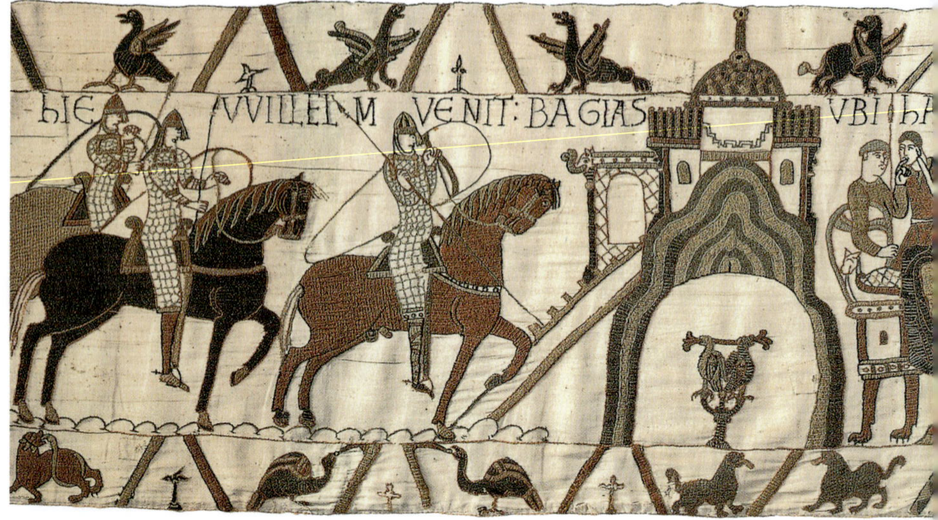

Anonymous

Propaganda on cloth

The Bayeux Tapestry, after 1066
0.5 x 70.34 m, Bayeux, Centre Guillaume Le Conquérant

First exhibited at Bayeux Cathedral in 1077, the tapestry marks a turning point in European history: it tells the story of William the Conqueror's victory over the English army at Hastings in 1066. The work now hangs in the Centre Guillaume Le Conquérant, Bayeux.

In 1025, at the Council of Arras in northern France, the clergy decided to embellish their churches with decorations of a new type. Historical events and figures were to be portrayed on cloth hangings to help educate the many illiterate members of the congregation. *The Bayeux Tapestry*, the most famous example of this form of medieval instruction, is *sans pareil*.

Consisting of several joined lengths of linen, the hanging is 50 cm wide and 70.34 metres long.

The final section of the work is missing, suggesting the original may have been several metres longer. The linen ground is embroidered in eight different colours of wool. It is not known who designed the cartoons or embroidered the cloth. The latter was probably the work of nuns. All that is known for sure is when and where the hanging was first exhibited: 14 July 1077, in the newly built cathedral at Bayeux, a small town in Normandy.

The town is depicted in the detail above. In fact, it is less "depicted" than reduced, in symbolic form, to two essential features: a hill – most towns in those days were built on high ground to facilitate their defence – and a large edifice, probably a church or castle. To preclude misinterpretation, occasional Latin inscriptions were added to identify scenes.

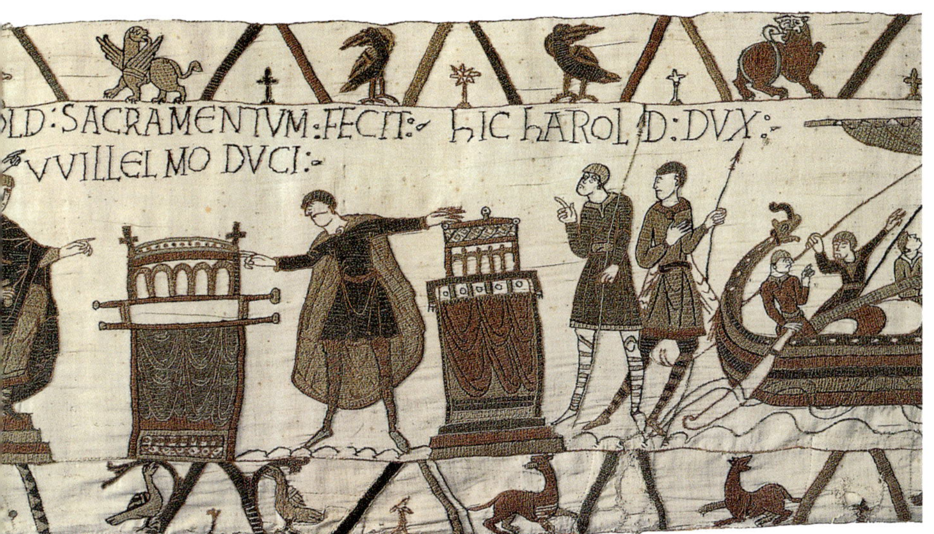

To the left of the town on the hill we read: "Here William arrives at Bayeux."

The narrative is framed above and below by a decorative border. Extending the entire length of the linen, these are filled with symbolic animals whose relation to the main action remains obscure. This is not always the case, however: the border under the battle scenes contains naked, mutilated corpses.

Notwithstanding its reductive symbolism, the hanging contains a wealth of documentary detail: the shape of the shields, the spores worn by cavalry, raised and reinforced bow props at the front and rear of saddles. The props provided support during battle, but they could also jeopardize the rider. In 1087 William was fatally injured when the pommel of his saddle ruptured his abdomen during a fall.

William is one of two main protagonists of the narrative. The story is told from his point of view: crossing the Channel as the Duke of Normandy in 1066, he routed his English opponents at the Battle of Hastings, was crowned King of England and entered history as William the Conqueror. The sole topic of the hanging is the representation and vindication of the victory won over England. Hung at Bayeux Cathedral, it served as an official declaration, as well as a means of religious and moral indoctrination.

An oath, extracted and broken

William, the Norman duke, sits to the right of the hill of Bayeux, his power symbolized by the sword resting on his shoulder. The second protagonist, the figure standing between two shrines, is the English King Harold. In 1063 Harold was cast ashore on the coast of France and held captive there. After paying ransom for him, William promised Harold his daughter in marriage. Here he is shown swearing allegiance to his new liege-lord. The shrines on which his hands are laid contain relics.

The significance of the oath, a ritual whose function was pivotal to contemporary society, was far from confined to the context of the *Bayeux* narrative. An individual was not the citizen of a state, but the vassal of a lord. Feudal society was constructed along the lines of a pyramid: the peasants took their tenures from knights or barons; the baron was invested with estate by a count; the count received his county as a fief from the duke, while the duke himself was given land by the king. To defend the country against aggressors the monarch needed the military and financial assistance of his nobles, who, in turn, required the service of their vassals. With few exceptions, feudal obligation was established not by

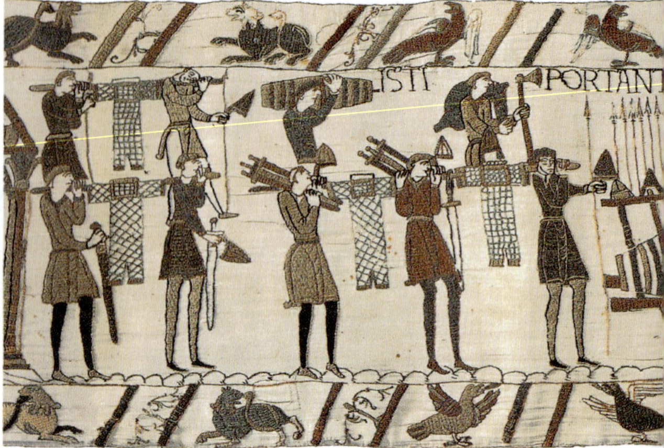

written contract, signed and sealed, but sworn in the form of an oath.

Oaths were sworn at a ceremony, with the procedure fairly strictly defined. Kneeling, the vassal recited a set formula by which he acknowledged homage to his superior. He would then stand and swear fealty to his new lord on the Holy Bible or on the authority of a relic. Following this, the lord granted his vassal a fief in the symbolic form of a branch, a staff or a ring.

The Bayeux Tapestry shows only the most important part of the ceremony: the oath sworn on the relics. This act had the force of conferring upon the church the office of official custodian. When Harold broke his oath, mounting the English throne in 1066, William sought the jurisdiction of the pope. Excommunicating the perjurious Harold, the pope placed a papal standard at William's disposal to accompany his Norman troops. William's campaign thus practically gained the status of a Holy War.

Things looked rather different from Harold's point of view. In swearing allegiance to William, he had not been a free man. By paying Harold's ransom, the Norman duke had become his superior. Harold's oath had acknowledged fealty to William, but without it, he presumably could never have left Normandy and returned to England. Furthermore, an English account of the event maintains that Harold's oath was sworn on a table under which relics were concealed – with Harold quite ignorant of the trap William had set for him.

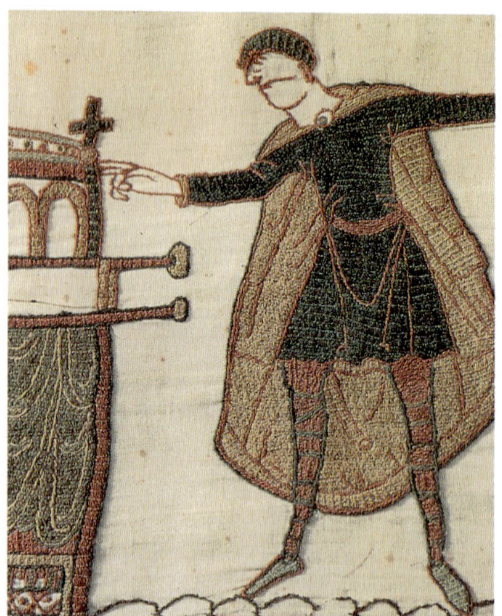

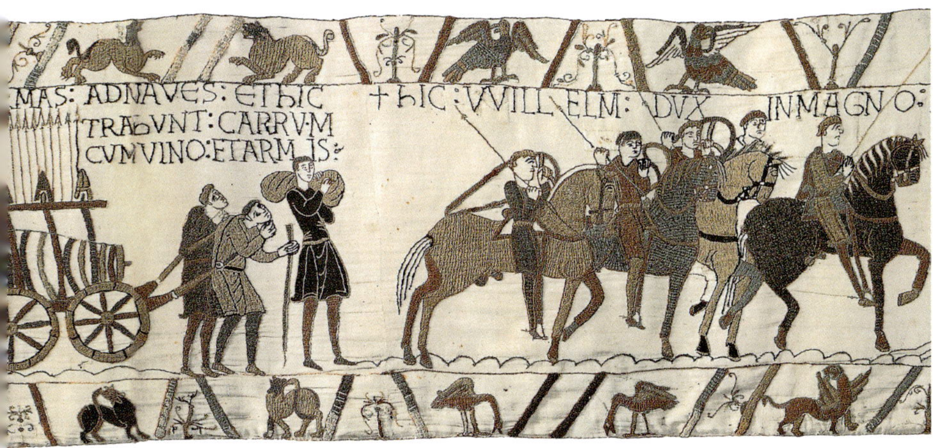

The previous king had promised the English throne to his cousin William. Harold knew this. He may have used his powerful allies to put pressure on the dying monarch. A contemporary chronicler cites the following dialogue: King: "It is known to you that I have taken steps to ensure my kingdom shall pass to William of Normandy after my death. Were it to pass to Harold, I do not think he would keep the peace." Harold: "Give it to me and I will look after it!" King: "Then you shall have my kingdom, but if I know William and his Normans, it will be the death of you."

To England with weapons and wine

William built a fleet and prepared it to carry his soldiers across the Channel to England. The hanging shows swords and a battle-axe being carried to the ships, a cart loaded with a row of twenty spears, helmets ranged on posts along the side of the wagon, following which three men carry suits of chain-mail, the typical armour of the day. The chain-mail consisted of connected links of thin iron covering the trunk and stretching to the elbows and knees, with slits at the front and back ensuring freedom of movement on horseback. In the centuries that followed, chain-mail was replaced by solid coats of armour, the spears by heavy lances. In the 11th century, however, soldiers were relatively lightly armed and still quite mobile.

The prominence given to wine indicates its relative importance as a provision: the embroidery shows a larger and smaller barrel, as well as a leather bottle slung over one bearer's shoulder. In peacetime, wine was imported to England by merchants; it was also produced in England as far north as the Scottish borders. The most important beverage of the age, wine was cherished less as a luxury than for its nutritional value. With no effective means of storage, however, it was generally drunk when little older than a year. Beer was more perishable still, and, what was more, impossible to transport. It could therefore be drunk solely in regions where it was produced.

Raising an army to conquer England proved something of a problem. Like all vassals, those bound to a duke were obliged to perform only certain clearly defined duties. William could set them smaller tasks – punitive expeditions against unruly neighbours, for example – as often as he wished, provided he did not require their services for longer than a week at a time. Only once a year at the most could he call upon his vassals to undertake a longer military campaign covering larger distances, though even the duration of these expeditions was limited to 40 days. All further services were seen as voluntary, requiring additional remuneration by the duke. Fighting which took them across the Channel was considered entirely beyond the call of duty.

William therefore had to use all his powers of persuasion, an undertaking whose success was undoubtedly facilitated by the pope's blessing. However, the main form of enticement at his disposal was the promise of enfeoffment: one of his followers was offered an English monastery, another a town, a

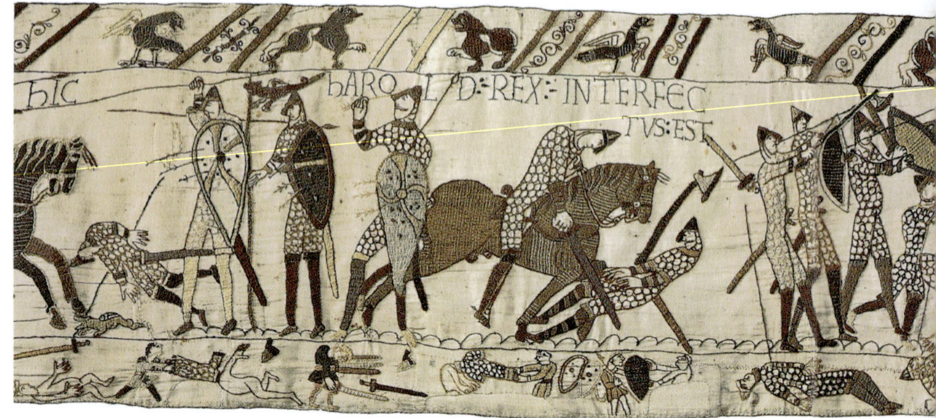

third might be lured with a whole county. William had to make promises on a grand scale, for the risks to which his vassals were putting their lives and livelihood were equally great. There was no way of predicting the outcome of the fighting.

Relatives were the most generous allies of all. At the time, power usually rested in the hands of an individual ruler, whose entire family profited as a result. In turn, it was in the family's best interest to support the ruler. William's brother, Bishop Odo of Bayeux, who took part in the campaign himself, provided financial backing for a hundred ships. Forbidden as a member of the clergy to wield a sword, he held a cudgel instead. William's other brother, Robert de Mortain, paid for a further 70 boats.

The ships were over 20 metres long and up to 5 metres wide. They had no deck, but planking drawn to a curve at prow and stern; amidships was a square sail, and a tiller was attached aft on the starboard side. This was the type of boat sailed by the Vikings, a reminder that the Normans themselves were originally Northmen. During the 9th and 10th centuries the Vikings had used such craft to occupy the coastal regions of Europe, founding new states of their own in England, Southern Italy and Normandy. To help him take England, William, himself a descendant of the Vikings, exploited the expansionist designs of the ruling Norwegian king, Harald Hardrada. He persuaded him to invade Northumberland, the most northerly county of today's England. The Norwegians landed and forced Harold to march north to meet them. The invading army was routed and the Norwegian king killed in the struggle.

King Harold falls in battle

Scarcely had Harold warded off the Norwegian attack when William landed south of Dover. Harold rode swiftly south, arriving with an army worn out after a hard-won battle and two forced marches. Taking up position on a ridge, he had ditches dug to thwart the Norman cavalry and waited for the onslaught. The Normans stormed the English position again and again, but could make no headway against the English shield-wall. Their principal obstacle was the English axemen, who cut down even their horses. One chronicle reports that "three horses were killed under William, one with a blow so great that the English axe, after severing his horse's head, cut deeply into the earth."

Realizing the ineffectiveness of frontal attack, William used cunning instead: making a pretence of retreat, he lured the English from their position. With their powerful formation broken, the English were no match for the Normans. Two brothers of Harold, both generals in his army, were killed. One of them had pleaded in vain with Harold to leave the fighting to them; for Harold, whether under coercion or not, had sworn allegiance to William, an oath that could not be broken lightly. Harold, too, fell in battle. The inscription in the detail reproduced above left reads: "King Harold is killed." The English king is shown with an arrow piercing one

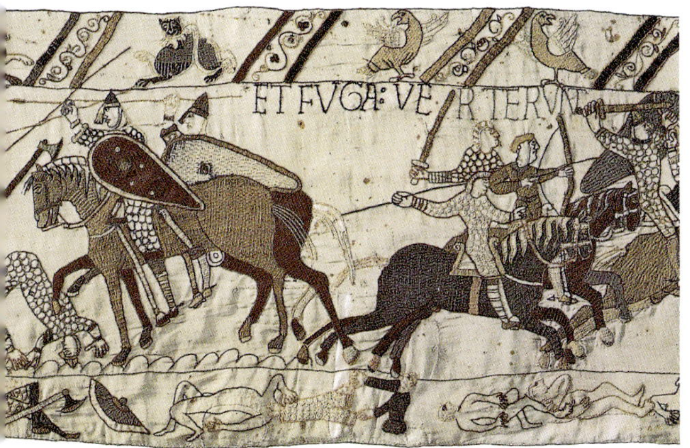

Hung in the church of a bishop who rose to power in the land of the vanquished, the embroidery served both to vindicate and to advertise. No less astonishing than the quality and scope of the work is the fact that it has survived for 900 years – despite the Hundred Years' War between England and France, the repeated destruction of the cathedral, the struggles between Calvinists and Catholics and the Revolution of 1789.

The hanging was to serve propaganda purposes on two further occasions. Contemplating an invasion of England at the beginning of the 19th century, Napoleon had the historic tapestry brought to Paris for six months in 1803 in order to rouse "the passions and general enthusiasm of the people". While Adolf Hitler was concocting plans for an invasion, a book on the tapestry appeared under the title: *A sword thrust against England*. But the Norman Duke William has remained the sole conqueror of the island kingdom.

eye. The hanging shows the maimed king struck down by a Norman cavalryman while attempting to extract the arrow. The cavalryman was later banished by William, according to one chronicle, for to kill a defenceless opponent constituted a breach of chivalrous conduct.

In fact, such battles involved relatively little slaughter. The corpses heaped in the lower border are an exaggeration. Vassals, fighting to advance the – more or less – private interests of their feudal lords, were inclined to see their own interests best served by maintaining a certain reticence in battle. In any case, it was less worth their while to kill an enemy than take him prisoner. Prisoners could be exchanged for a ransom: the more powerful the captive, the greater the sum that could be demanded for his release. The mutual obligations agreed by vassals and their lords usually foresaw the provision of ransom, should either party fall into enemy hands.

Fighting took place only at certain times. In winter, at night and in wet weather, swords remained in their sheaths. Furthermore, William's war was hardly a protracted affair: the Battle of Hastings, important as it was, was over in a day. By the evening of 14 October 1066 the last obstacle had been removed between William and London, where he was crowned on 25 December. Thus England and France began a period of common history that was to last 400 years.

And since history is always the history of the victor, the Normans provided a testimony to their conquest of England in the form of the *Bayeux Tapestry*.

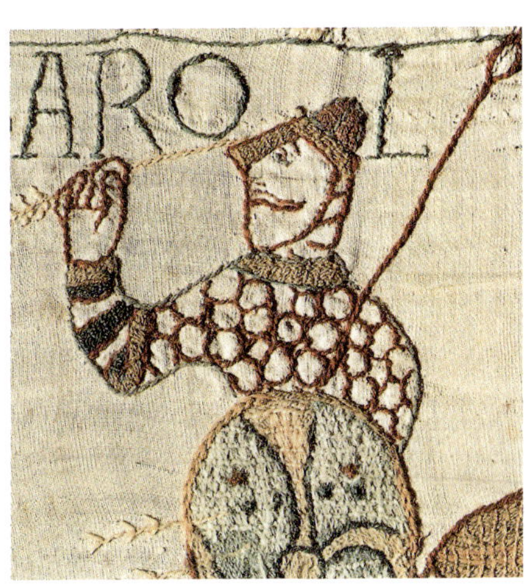

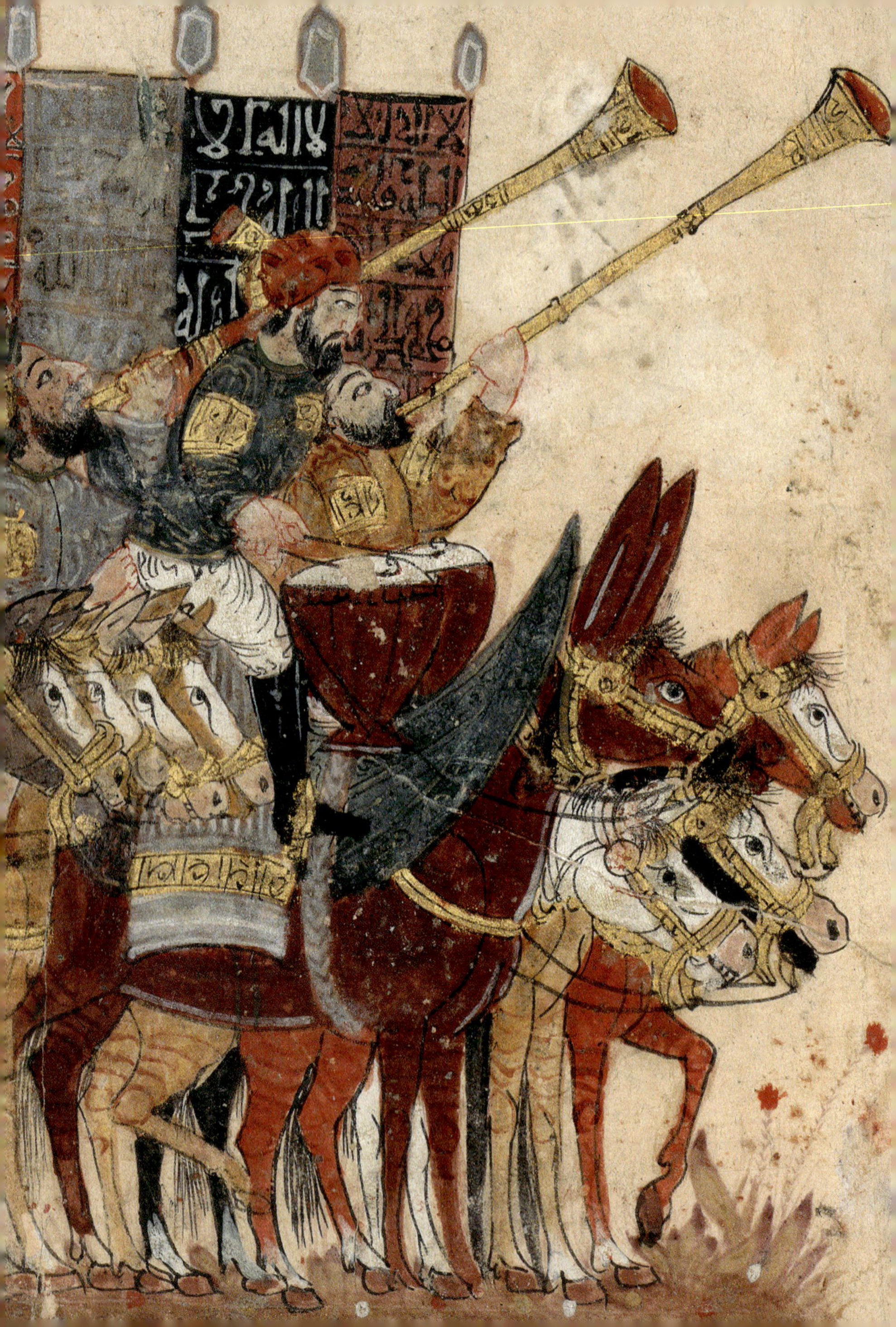

Al-Wasiti (13th century)

With drums and trumpets – the liar of Baghdad

Two miniatures from the Maqamat of al-Hariri, 1237
37 x 28 cm, Paris, Bibliothèque nationale de France

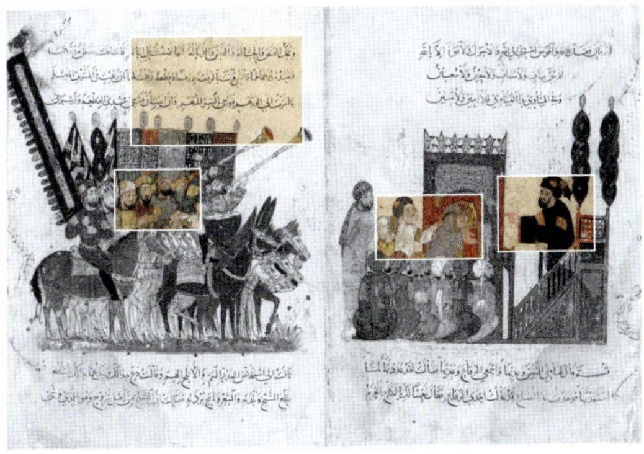

Riders with banners, drums and trumpets are celebrating the end of Ramadan. For a whole month, between the hours of sunrise and sunset they have been allowed neither to drink, nor eat, nor smoke, nor bathe and to attend only to the most necessary affairs. This period is now over. The pent-up vitality that is bursting forth after the month of fasting is conveyed through the colourful palette, the thronging horsemen and the implied noise of their instruments. Next to the street scene is a view into a mosque. The narrator of the story is standing on the left: having first watched the procession, he is now listening to the preacher and in the crowd of the faithful has spotted an old man who looks familiar. The man is accompanied by a woman, although women had no place in the part of the mosque reserved for men. The narrator has raised his hand to his mouth. The gesture has several meanings, but here it signals astonishment and curiosity.

The miniatures were painted in 1237 in Baghdad or within its sphere of influence. For centuries Baghdad had formed the centre of Islamic might, which extended from the borders of China

all the way to Spain. Fifty years previously, the Crusaders had been driven out of Jerusalem. Paris, with 250,000 inhabitants, was the largest city in Europe; Baghdad, with a population of 1.5 million, the largest city in the world.

Abu Zayd – itinerant beggar and virtuoso poet
The old man with the white beard has one hand on the woman's shoulder and is taking slips of paper out of his bag with the other. On these pieces of paper he begs for alms and claims that he is blind and has written the notes from memory. The narrator recognizes him as an old acquaintance and invites him and his female companion to dinner. After the meal, the old man asks for some scented water. The narrator leaves the room to fetch some, comes back and discovers that his two guests have absconded. The old man is called Abu Zayd and – between dashing heroes and beautiful women – was one of the most popular figures in the Ancient Arab world: a wandering beggar who scrounged a living by trickery and an extraordinary gift of the gab. The stories he told were a mixture of imagination

ويحل القفص والجبّة والقلنس والدلو بالغ أنها لضغثت على إبالة فانضاعت نصف مذبخها

فنشدت مذبخها فلما دانى وقفت بالرقعة درهما وقطعة وقلت لها ان رغبت في المستوف المعلم

واشرت الى الدرهم فوفى بالسرّ المبهم وإن أبيت أن تخرجي خذي القطعة وأبرزن

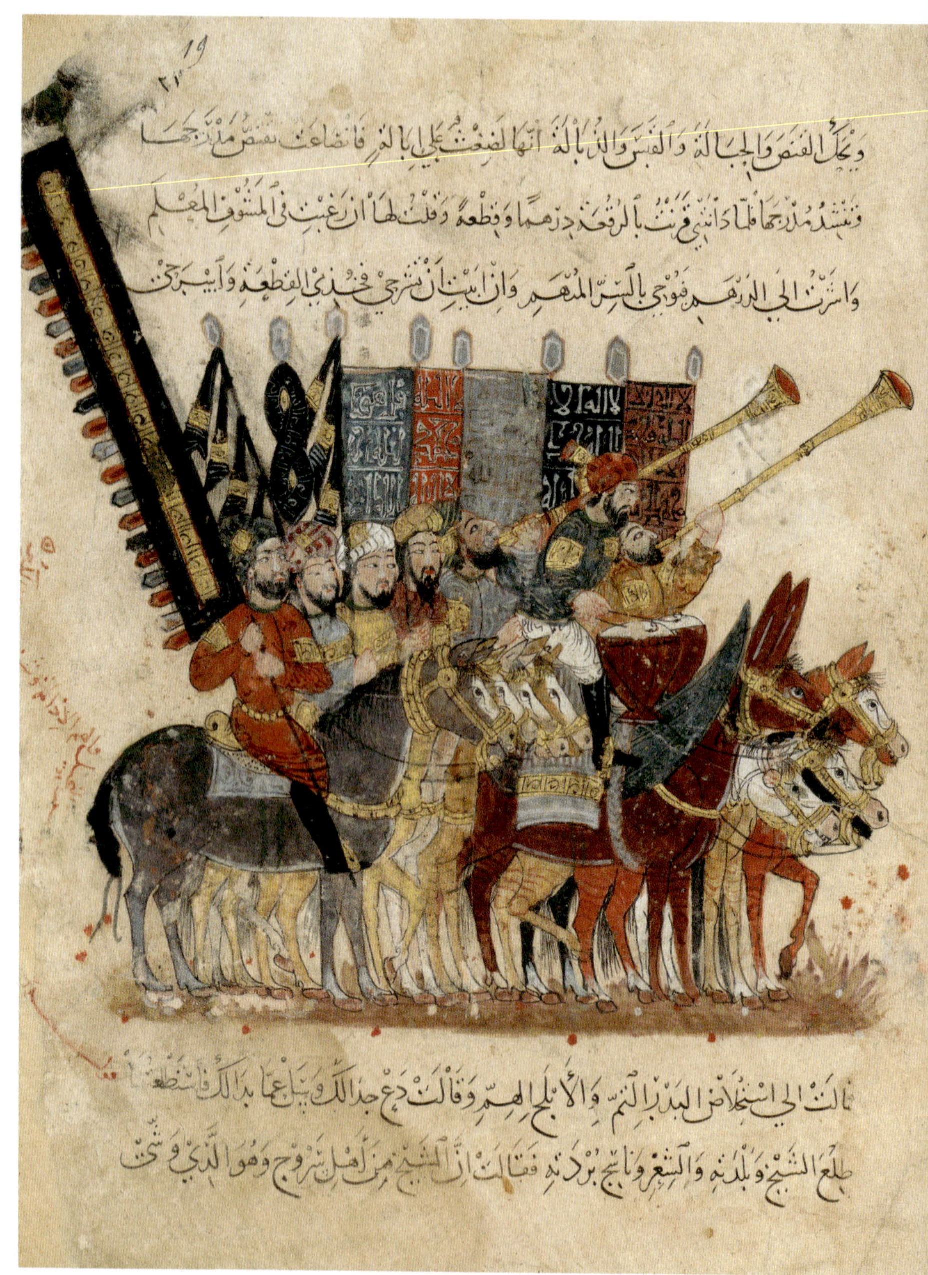

فألتفتت الى استخلاص البذر بالنثر والأبلج الهمّ وقلت دع جدالك وبلغ عما بدا لك فأسقطه

طلع الشيخ وبلده والشغر وأبرج بردته فقالت ان الشيخ من أهل سروج وهو الذي وشى

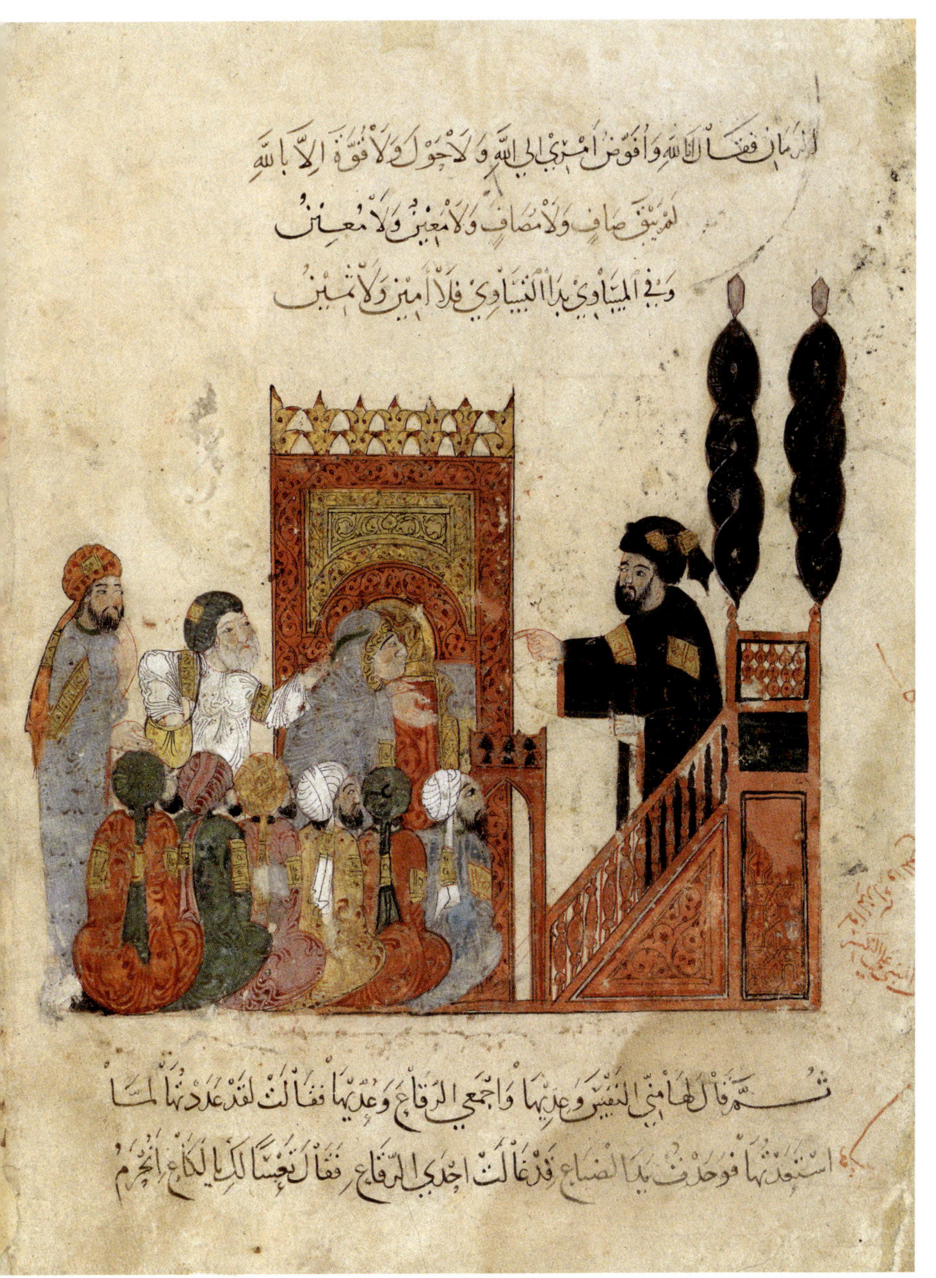

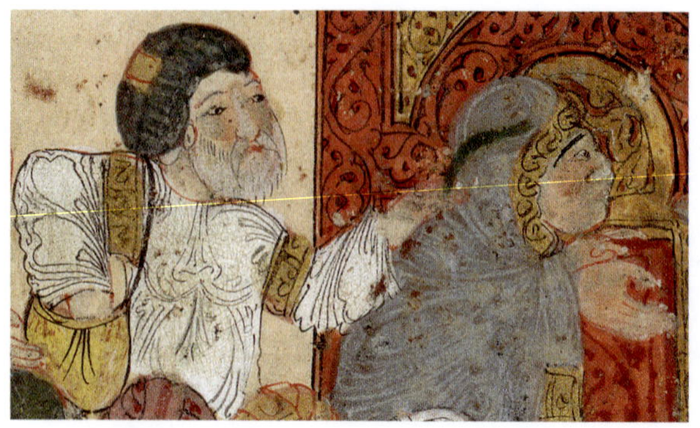

The literary figure of the itinerant beggar already existed, but experts agree that the extraordinary quality of al-Hariri's writing places his *Assemblies* amongst the finest works in the Arabic language. Al-Hariri composed his epic in rhyme, in line with a literary tradition confined not just to the *maqamat*: the suras of the Koran are also written in rhyme, potentates had their proclamations issued in rhyme, and Arabic is particularly rich in homonymic end syllables. Al-Hariri not only made dazzling use of these but ceaselessly invented metaphors and comparisons, made plays upon words and unleashed a torrent of language that sometimes swept the factual right out of sight. In this, he was assisted by the multiple meanings of Arabic words, something that is impossible to convey in the very much simpler language of English. Al-Hariri's *Maqamat* quickly become so popular that he was personally able to authorize over 700 copies. He died in 1122.

The Imam preaches to the faithful

Mosques have no altar and no pews. They are furnished with mats and carpets upon which the faithful sit and kneel. A tall, ornately decorated prayer niche in one wall indicates the direction of prayer – the direction of Mecca. To the right of this niche stands the pulpit, called the minbar, from where the Imam delivers his sermons. The minbar is traced back to Muhammad; the Prophet is supposed to have made himself two steps and a seat so that his listeners could see and understand him better. After his death, Muhammad's seat was raised ever higher and the number of steps grew to seventeen. The top step was frequently not used as it was considered to be reserved for the Prophet alone.

Al-Wasiti does not show the interior of the mosque, just the two characteristic features of its architecture – the prayer niche rising behind the faithful and the minbar. Unlike in Christian churches, the steps descend towards the congregation. The Imam decides how high he wishes to stand above his listeners. Al-Wasiti places him halfway up the stairs. In order to emphasize the importance of the pulpit and the steps, their access is marked

and untruths, but even when he was proved to have been lying, he was never punished because he had entertained his listeners so well. He was particularly good at arousing people's sympathy. Sometimes he played the blind man, at others he claimed to have seen his son but to have been unable to greet him out of shame at his own miserable state of dress. "Then he held up his garment, and coins rained down on it like sand." In another incident, he claimed that he couldn't say the letter R and delighted his audience with a long speech in which he cleverly avoided saying this one letter. The local official thereupon offered him a job, which Abu Zayd turned down, however, preferring "a place in a stable" to "being stabled in the same honorary post". He continued on his wanderings, the embodiment of a footloose existence and at the same time of the art – so highly valued in the Orient – of free speech, of story-telling, and the ability to inspire people with words.

The character of Abu Zayd was created around 1100 by a man called al-Hariri. He is the author and is not to be confused with the artist al-Wasiti, who copied out al-Hariri's text a good century later and illustrated it with 99 miniatures. We know that al-Hariri was a government official, owned a plantation of palm trees and wrote a poem on Arabic grammar and a book on the misuse of Arabic words and phrases. But it was his *Maqamat* that truly made him famous: 50 stories whose protagonist is always Abu Zayd. Translated into English as *The Assemblies of Al-Hariri*, the word *maqamat* can mean both the geographical location of an assembly and the actual assembly itself. In this case, *maqamat* describes the situation in which Abu Zayd becomes active.

by a doorway. Behind the preacher are two flags embroidered with the confession of faith and the name and title of the ruler. Images were forbidden, and the prayer niche and minbar were decorated instead with particularly lavish ornamentation.

A preacher was required to have not only a perfect knowledge of the Koran, but also a repertoire of expressive facial expressions and gestures. And he had to be a good orator, not too young and not too handsome, so as not to distract the faithful. In most miniatures, the gesture of the hand with the index finger extended simply means that he is speaking. Here, however, it may be pointing at the woman handing out the slips of paper, who does not belong among the men and who replies to the preacher by raising her palms upwards in a gesture of entreaty and apology – in other words, a suggestion of dialogue.

In 1160 the Spanish traveller Ibn Jubayr wrote from Baghdad of an Imam who "preached so skilfully and eloquently that I was utterly filled with admiration and astonishment". He, too, mentions pieces of paper: "After the sermon, assistants brought the Imam slips of paper on which they had written questions, and these he answered in a masterly fashion." Imam was the general name by which the leaders of Islamic communal prayer were known, and they were often highly educated men who also served in legal and diplomatic positions. In some sects of Islam, an Imam must be able to trace his genealogy back to the family or descendants of Muhammad. In al-Wasiti's miniature, the Imam is wearing black robes and a black turban. Both items of clothing are trimmed with gold braid, on which the confession of faith is probably embroidered.

For Muslims, letters are sacred signs

On the banners or standards behind the riders stands the Islamic confession of faith. And on the right-hand page – Arabic is written right to left – the text starts by praising Allah, who rules the fate of all. In this mosque, Abu Zayd was destined to receive only meagre alms – like scraps of food, as the text puts it. Only one unknown figure (who the reader knows to be the narrator) promises a larger coin, a dirham, if the woman will tell him who the beggar is.

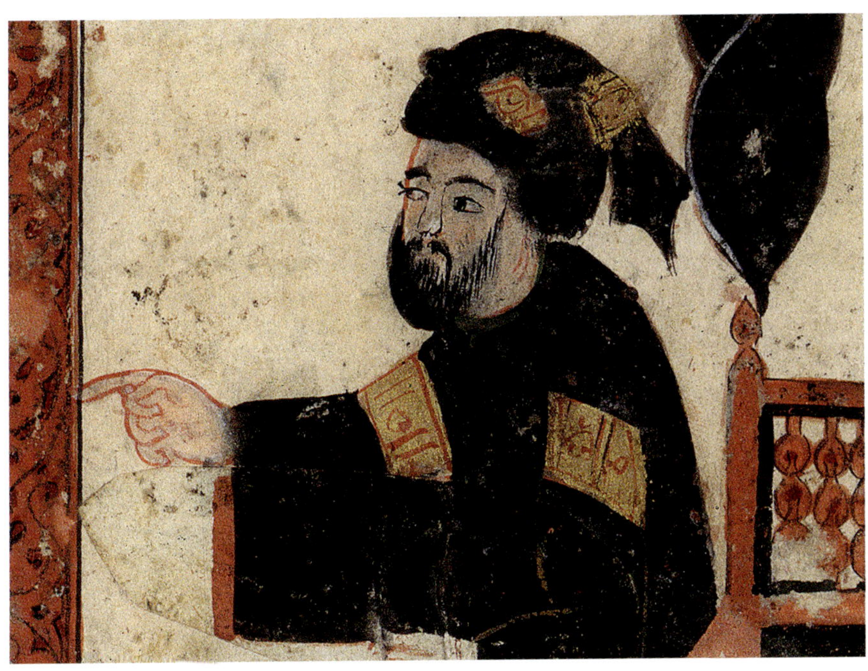

Writing and illustration were usually performed sitting cross-legged with a board across the knees. Paper was already in use here at a time when, in Europe, vellum was still the norm. The craft of paper-making reached the Western world via Chinese prisoners of war. In the 8th century Samarkand developed into the first Arab centre of paper manufacture. The raw material employed was hemp, whose fibres were separated and mashed to a pulp. Before it was finally ready for use, the paper had to be dyed by the scribe or one of his assistants and then rubbed smooth with a bone, frequently made of ivory. The guidelines necessary to ensure that the text was evenly spaced were not drawn on and then rubbed out, probably because this would have left marks. Instead, the calligraphers stretched threads across their board, laid the paper on top and pressed it down lightly onto this base: the lines could then be felt with the fingers and could be flattened out later.

The professions of calligrapher and copyist were highly regarded – for the very fact that they involved the written word. For Muslims, the letters of the alphabet are more than simply vehicles of information. When the Koran was set down in writing, something of its sacred character passed into the Arabic script. This semi-religious veneration was a contributing factor in the development of Islamic

calligraphy to such exquisite heights. Another factor was the ban on the representation of living creatures, and in particular humankind. Although images are not expressly forbidden in the Koran, the word for "to make pictures" can also signify "to create" – and no painter or sculptor should consider himself the equal of God the Creator. This ban was not always strictly upheld, but it channelled creative energies into the art of ornament and calligraphy and led to manuscripts of astonishing aesthetic quality. Books played a major role in civic society; many rulers were interested in the arts and sciences. Following their example, ordinary citizens assembled their own extensive libraries. Baghdad also had lending libraries, which in most cases were attached to schools. In 1233, i.e. four years before the production of the present manuscript, a library was founded in Baghdad as a repository of global thinking, with translations from the Chinese, Persian and Greek; a library whose holdings ran to several hundred thousand volumes and which would employ hundreds of librarians.

Copyists and calligraphers were not only highly regarded but also powerful, and they obstructed the introduction of printing presses. They were supported in this by those scholars whose job was to check all religious and legal transcripts, and whose income was thus also under threat. The veneration of the written word undoubtedly also

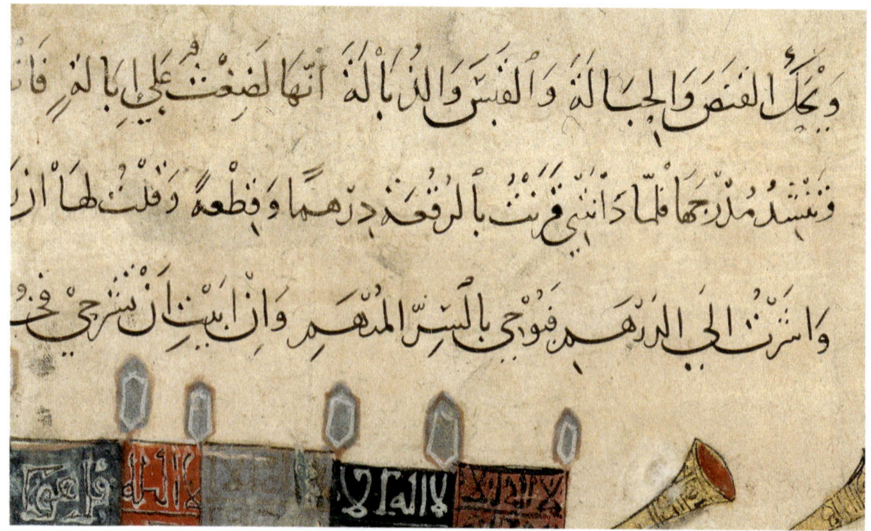

played a part. Thus it was that, although paper was introduced into the Islamic world several centuries earlier than in Europe, printing only arrived 300 years after Gutenberg. The first printed Koran was published in Venice in 1537/38; in the 18th century, several thousand scribes were still working in Constantinople.

… completed on 3 May 1237

The faces of al-Wasiti's riders are expressionless, and no emotions are displayed by the figures in his other miniatures, either. In this he was no different from painters in 13th-century Europe. Feelings were expressed, if

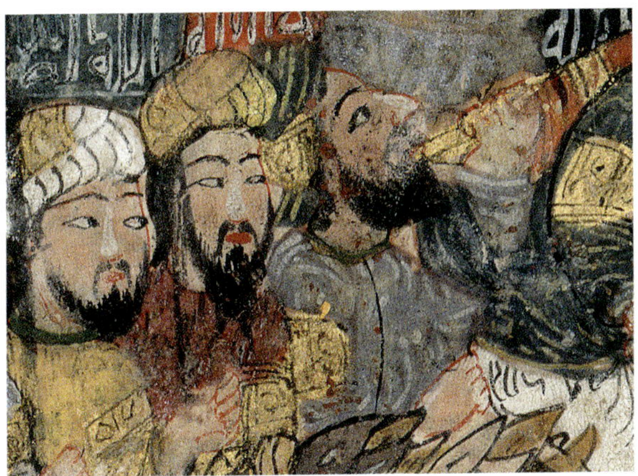

at all, through gestures; what was more important was to convey the origins and rank of the person portrayed. In Europe this was usually done by including their coat of arms. Al-Wasiti indicates via the shape of the eyes and nose that the riders with the banners are Asiatic, while the musicians are drawn from Semitic peoples. Nor does he forget that amongst the horses stands a mule.

This eye for detail was probably honed by studying the illustrations in scientific treatises, for example on horse medicine, botany and the stars. As in European painting of the 13th century, the use of perspective was not yet developed: spatial depth was indicated by partially concealing what lay behind – a technique that al-Wasiti also uses here to compress his men and animals into a small area. This mass of figures and movements is underpinned by a "grid" of horizontal and vertical lines, pierced by the diagonals of the flags and trumpets which depart at right angles.

Nothing is known of the life of al-Wasiti, the painter and calligrapher. That we are able to link his name with one of Arabic culture's most beautiful manuscripts is due solely to the fact that he has signed it. In a humble invocation to God, he wrote: "This manuscript, both text and pictures, was completed by the wretched slave of God, Yahya ibn Mahmud ibn Yahya ibn Abi al-Hasan ibn Kuwwarih al-Wasiti, who begs his Lord for mercy, for his forgiveness, his pardon, on the evening of the Saturday of the sixth day of the month of Ramadan in the

year 634 …" The sentence ends with a lengthy eulogy to God and his Prophet, the latter's family and companions. Translated from the Islamic calendar, the date corresponds to Saturday, 3 May 1237.

Thirteen illustrated *maqamat* manuscripts have survived, eleven of them from the 13th and early 14th century – one of the brief periods in which the prohibition of images was temporarily set aside in favour of their enjoyment. Later, some of these works would be harshly treated: the upper halves of the figures were smudged so as to render them unrecognizable or were symbolically killed with a fine line draw across their throat. When al-Wasiti illustrated the tales of Abu Zayd, Baghdad's greatest era was past. In 1258 a powerless government capitulated before the Mongols. It is estimated that the invaders slaughtered a million of the city's inhabitants, looted their homes and threw their libraries into the Tigris. "The books were heaped up on the river bed like a pontoon reaching from one shore to the other," recalled a contemporary. "Then they grew afraid that the river would burst its banks and preferred to burn the rest of the books.

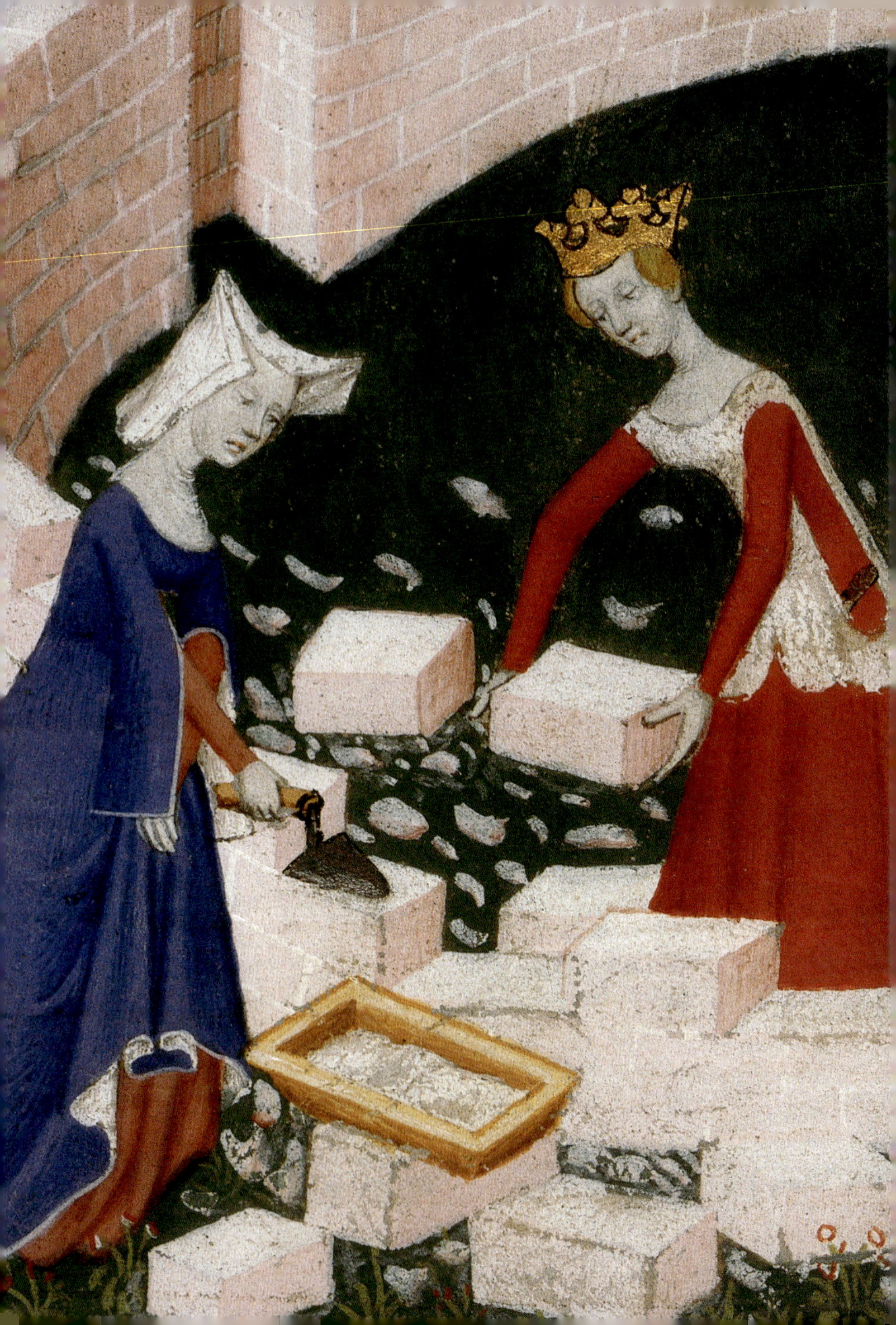

Anonymous

An early feminist at the end of the Middle Ages

Miniature from Christine de Pizan's "Book of the City of Ladies", c. 1405
Illumination on parchment, 12 x 18 cm, Paris, Bibliothèque nationale de France

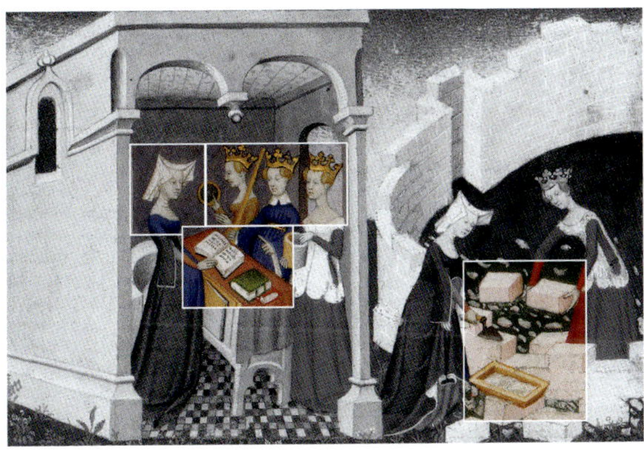

The first woman who was able to support herself and her family as a writer was called Christine de Pizan. She lived in France in an age of transition: the Middle Ages were drawing to a close and the Renaissance was already dawning. Around 1405 Christine was portrayed twice by a miniaturist in one of the illustrations to her *Book of the City of Ladies*. Christine is seen standing in her study as if in cross-section of a doll's house, wearing a blue dress and with one hand laid on a manuscript in front of her. She is receiving important guests: three crowned ladies. They would have been easy to identify in those days from the items they are carrying: Lady Reason holds a mirror, Lady Rectitude a rule and Lady Justice a measuring cup. The visitors command the authoress to fight discrimination against women. She is to write a book, as a stronghold for her sex: "Take the spade of your intelligence and dig deep… mix the mortar well in your inkpot and set to on the masonry work with great strokes of your pen."

The scene on the right shows Christine at work in the green Field of Letters, assisted by one of the ladies. With trowel and mortar the two are laying stone upon stone. A high wall is visible behind them. Such a protective wall was at that time no less desirable in real life, for while authoress and miniaturist were seated in their Paris study, France was caught up in the Hundred Years' War against England. Its king was insane and its princes were battling for power, igniting a civil war that would soon see the capital bathed in blood. Christine lived in terrible times.

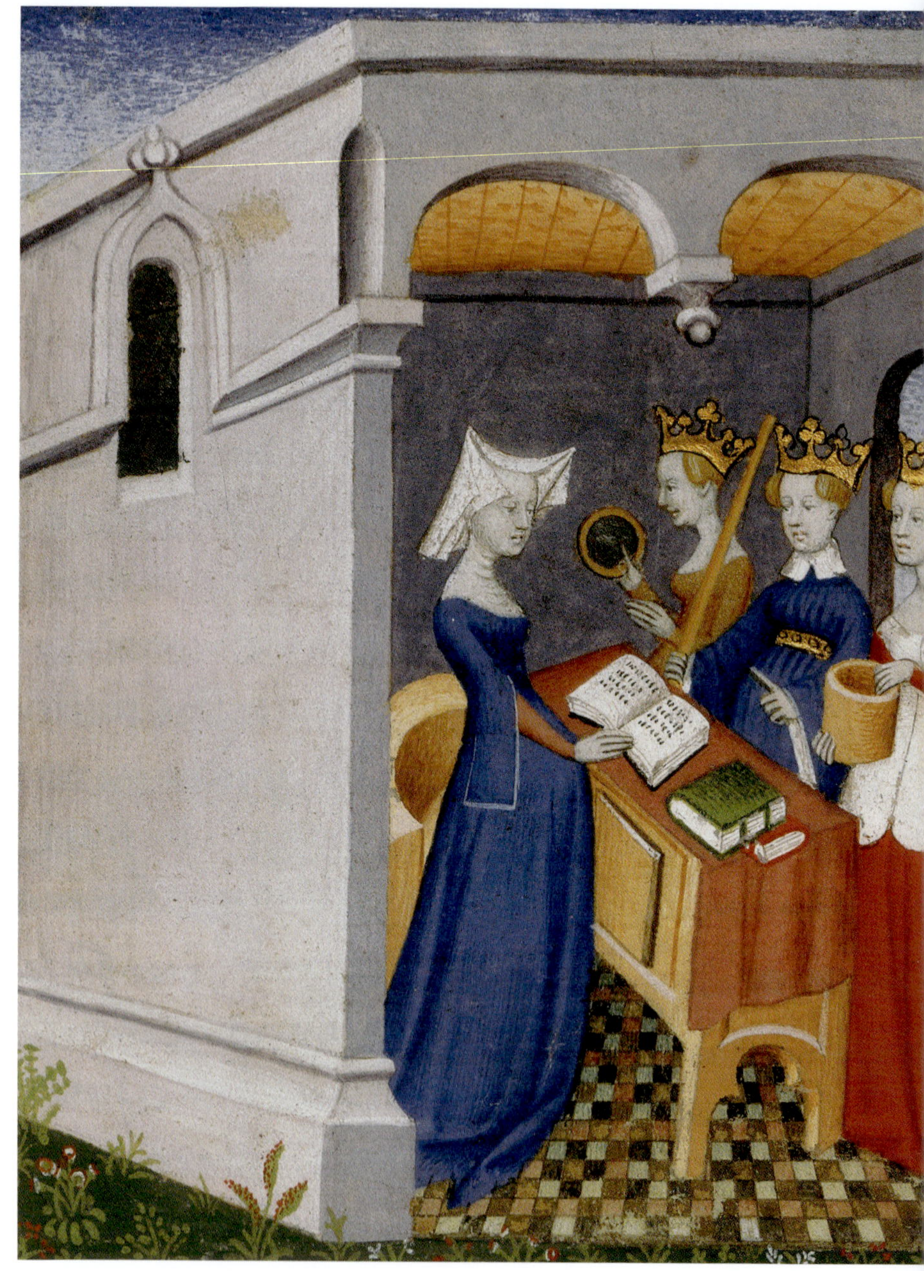

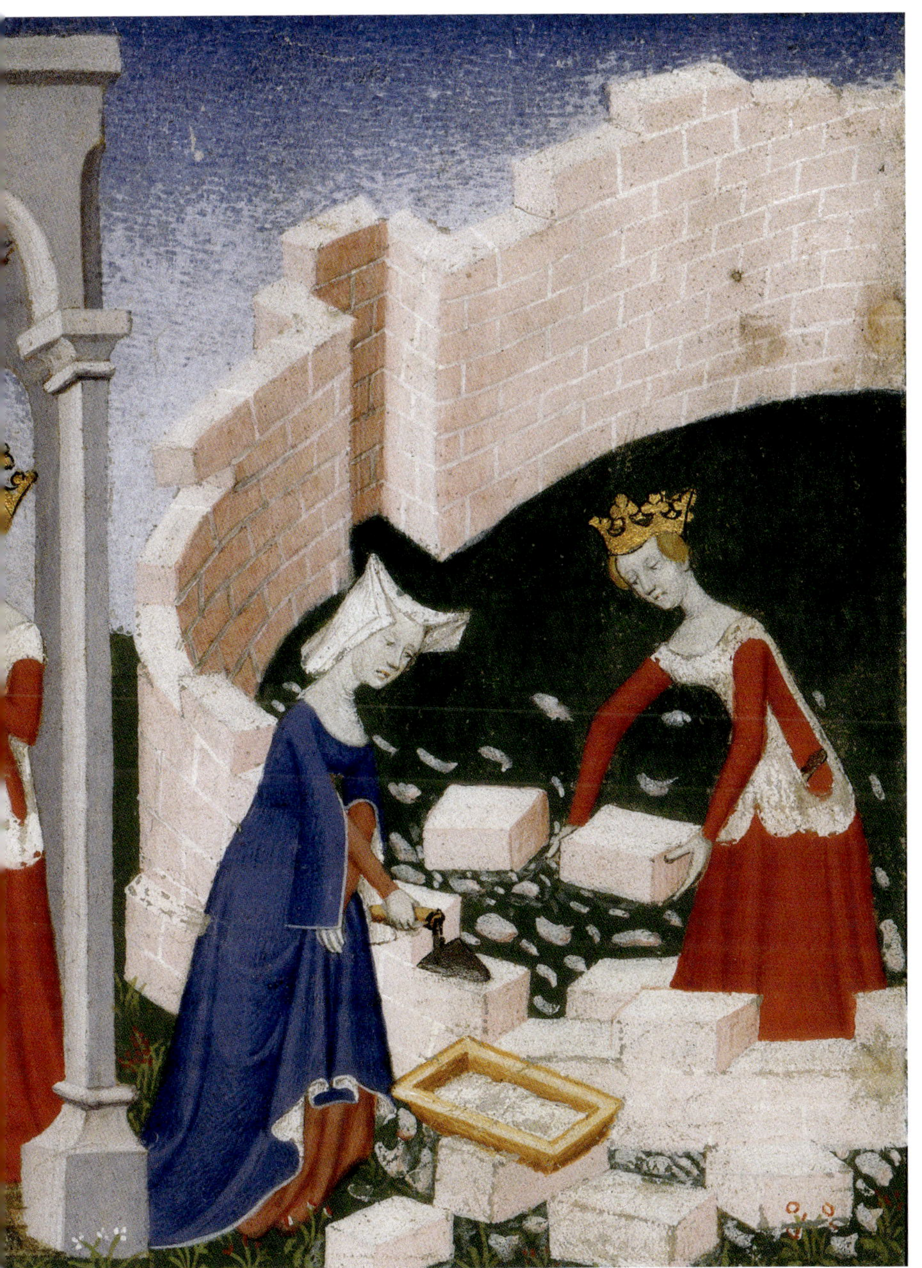

Her widow's veil hides her hair

Christine de Pizan can be identified in the miniatures by her plain blue dress and her white head covering, which also concealed her neck and breasts. This type of veil formed part of a widow's garb and was worn by the authoress for 40 years. She was 25 when she lost her husband and never married again. Sadness and loneliness run like leitmotifs through her work: "Alone I am and alone I wish to be / Alone my gentle friend has left me." Thus begins her most beautiful, and in France still her best-known poem.

The young woman was obliged to take charge of her life, something for which her background and education had not prepared her. Born in Venice around 1364, Christine moved with her family to Paris while she was still a child. Her scholarly father, who originated from Pizzano, a small town near Bologna, had been summoned to serve as personal physician and astrologer to King Charles V. Christine spent her youth in the sphere of the French court and at the age of fifteen was wed to the royal notary Etienne Castel. It appears to have been a very happy marriage. When he died suddenly in around 1389, Christine was left alone to care for three small children, her mother, two younger brothers and a niece. An income from the court was no longer forthcoming, for both her father and his protector, the king,

were dead. With no experience in business matters, the widow found herself involved in several court cases with her husband's clients and at the mercy of wily lawyers. "Oh God, why wasn't I born a male?" she lamented.

For fourteen long years she fought for her rights in court, gradually sold off what remained of her father's estate and probably worked as a copyist. This work not only brought in money but gave Christine the opportunity to further her education, for as a child, at her mother's wish, she had always been obliged to practise her spinning rather than attend the lessons given by her father to her brothers. Now, however, she withdrew to her chamber, closed the doors, and "surrounded by many books of different kinds" devoted herself to "the pursuit of knowledge". In this way, she developed talents of her own. As a young woman, she had already been permitted to recite her own verse in court competitions held within a small circle; now she composed in the strict forms and traditional genres of troubadour poetry and the pastoral idyll, which she infused with highly personal notes and which were evocative of her grief and loneliness. In 1399 she was able to present her friends with a collection of 100 ballads, and from now on she started voicing her opinions, in poetry and prose, on the current literary and political themes of her age. Altogether she composed some 40 works, prompting the French critic Gustave Lanson (1857–1934) to revile her as a "veritable bluestocking" and the "first of this insufferable lineage of women authors" who, all their life, "do nothing but multiply the proofs of their tireless facility, equalled only by their universal mediocrity".

In 1404 Christine was commissioned to write the biography of her father's protector, the dead King Charles V – by command of the Duke of Burgundy. Christine was undoubtedly helped in her career, at that time so unheard-of for a woman, by the fact that she came from an academic family, was close to the French court and was personally acquainted with the rich and powerful, to whose library she was granted free access. And she also seems to have had what Virginia Woolf, at the beginning of the 20th century, considered a writer's most vital – and for a woman, so rare – prerequisite: a room of her own. Gothic, sparsely furnished and with colourful tiles on the floor, Christine de Pizan's study is illustrated in several of her manuscripts. A little white dog sometimes keeps her company.

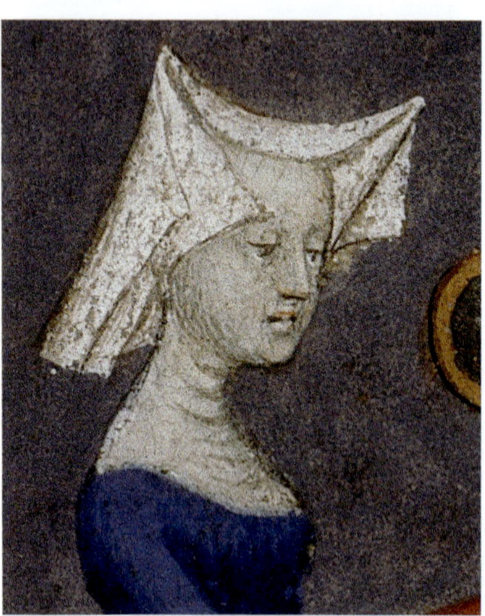

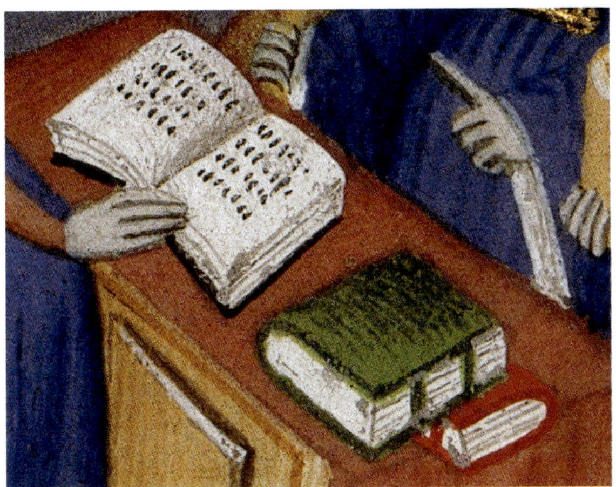

The first woman to earn a living by writing
Christine's first poems appeared in a modest volume on paper. Soon, however, she was able to have her texts copied onto expensive vellum, illustrated and sumptuously bound, like the manuscript lying on the table in front of her. Only four or five copies of each work were made, however. Half a century before the invention of the printing press, books, with their exquisite illuminations, had become luxury items. In France at that time, pictures were generally only found in churches, and hence illustrated manuscripts offered their owner a rare opportunity to admire non-religious motifs in a different style of representation. Book painting was in those days by no means considered a second-rate art.

The princes had replaced the Church as patrons of the arts. They commissioned tapestries, statues and objects of coloured glass or gold to demonstrate their might, and books for their personal enjoyment. Charles V installed a library of over 1,000 volumes on three floors of the Louvre – including not only prayer books and Books of Hours, but also illustrated translations of Aristotle, treatises on the art of hunting and the first known cookbook.

Christine seems to have closely supervised the manufacture of her manuscripts. A number of pages are even thought to contain corrections in her handwriting. The thrifty authoress thereby carefully masked flaws and holes in the parchment. She had them made not in monasteries, as had long been the convention, but in Paris workshops, where different specialists were responsible for the various stages of production. The parchment pages were sent in batches of eight at a time, first to the scribe, then to the rubricator, who inserted the headings and initials, and lastly to the miniaturist, who was responsible for the ornamentation and illustration of the text. The craftsmen were well paid and occasionally reproached by their employer Christine for their penchant for "excesses of luxury and love of the flesh".

The authoress has herself regularly portrayed in the illustrations to her manuscripts – just as she had a personal hand in the writing of the text. By contrast, her scribes and illuminators, who did not sign their work, remain anonymous. Only artists who were in the personal employ of a prince and are mentioned in their accounts, such as the Limburg brothers, are known to us by name. The head of the workshop whose style hallmarks most of Christine's manuscripts goes under the provisional name of the Master of the City of Ladies. He probably originated from Italy or Flanders, adopts stylistic elements of the Italian Trecento painters and the Netherlandish realists, experiments with spatial depth and perspective, and ranks with other colleagues amongst the founders of the new style that emerged around 1400 and which is today known as the International Gothic. For a brief, glittering period, these masters made Paris – so Christine declared – the "centre of the best illuminators in the world".

Building the City of Ladies stone by stone
Pieces of rubble and dusty footprints can be seen in the grass at the feet of the authoress. The miniaturist shows Christine spreading the mortar, which has been mixed in a wooden tray, with her trowel, while a crowned assistant passes her the next stone. They are working "literally" upon the construction of a City of Ladies, and Christine maintains this fiction throughout the whole book. As in the personifications of abstract concepts (Reason, Justice), she thereby adheres to medieval literary conventions. The famous *Romance of the Rose* begun by

Guillaume de Lorris in the 13th century was also laid out as an allegory: a knight's quest to win the love of an idealized, spotless lady is symbolized by a poetic search for a flower. The unfinished work was subsequently completed by a university professor, who turned it into a treatise full of attacks upon the wanton and false female sex and thereby sparked a dispute between the defenders of courtly love and the misogynists that would last for centuries. Christine was the first and only woman to enter the argument – in an open letter of 1402 and with her *City of Ladies*.

To refute the contemptuous theses of the professor and his supporters, Christine introduces her three ladies, Reason, Rectitude and Justice. As their "building blocks" they take famous women who have proved themselves the equal of men. Lady Reason cites the courageous Amazons and the heathen Queen Semiramis, who ruled a vast empire with a strong hand. Women "of superb intellect" and "great erudition" are also named, such as the "extremely fine poet and philosopher" Sappho. On the foundation of Reason, Lady Rectitude is able to build houses of virtuous women, faithful wives, respectable widows and good mothers.

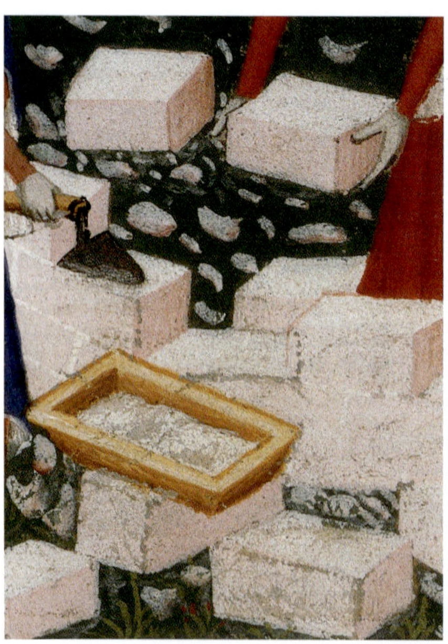

Lady Justice – responsible for higher affairs – adorns the City of Ladies with towers and turrets and oversees the ceremonial arrival of the Virgin Mary and her retinue of female saints to take up residence within them.

The authoress draws her examples from history, myth and legend – and amasses them in great numbers, because in medieval didactics the sheer volume of such *exempla* was considered proof of their veracity. Today this can sometimes be wearisome to read. What remains interesting, however, is Christine's pragmatic viewpoint: she does not sketch an ideal image of women such as is found in the medieval *Romance of the Rose*, but insists that by nature they are just as clever and gifted as men. Christine takes up the cause of widows and of wives beaten by their husbands, defends the female right to sensual pleasure and contradicts the arrogant assumption by men that woman want to be raped.

In the 20th century this earned her rediscovery by the feminists, who celebrate her as an early forerunner. But when Christine asks Lady Reason why women with able minds do not learn more so as to be able truly to hold their own in every sphere, the latter replies: "The answer, my dear girl, is that it's not necessary for the public good for women to go around doing what men are supposed to do… It's quite adequate that they perform the tasks for which they are fitted" (in the service of husband and family). Christine's utopia capitulates before social reality. In the period around 1400, no one could challenge the order supposedly ordained by God.

Reason, Rectitude and Justice
The success of Christine's works amongst her contemporaries was explained by the unheard-of fact that they stemmed from a woman's pen. The *City of Ladies* travelled as far afield as Milan and London. In view of the horrendous price of the manuscript and because only a dwindling minority of the population could actually read, its public was limited to the nobility or the wealthy urban middle classes (significantly, its title in French is *Cité des Dames*, i.e. *City of Ladies*, not *Women*). Its female readers could identify themselves with the three visitors of "great beauty", "majestic appearance" and "noble bearing".

Christine dedicated several of her works to Isabella of Bavaria (1371–1435), the wife of the insane Charles VI, and also had a copy of the *City of Ladies*

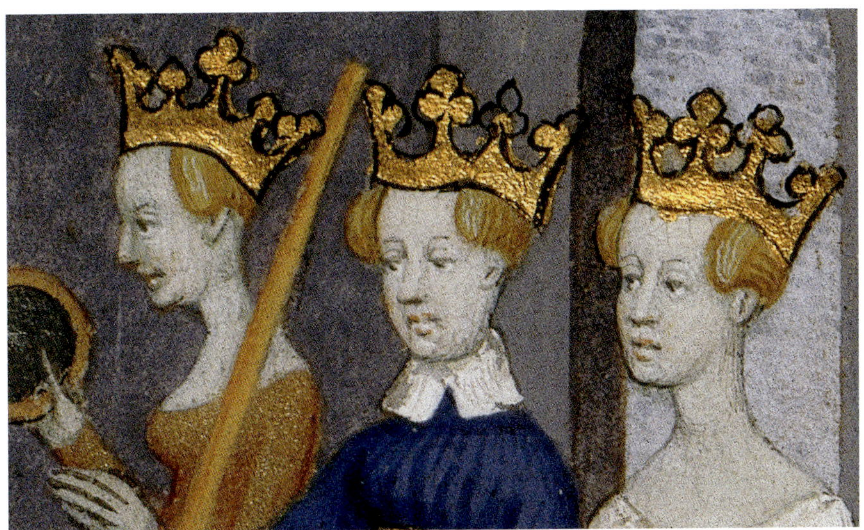

made for her. It is possible that it is Isabella who is helping to lay the blocks in the present miniature. In another illustration, the authoress is seen solemnly presenting the queen with a manuscript. Such books were not sold but were offered to a patron as a New Year gift, in return for which the patron would express his gratitude with allowances and lavish presents. The Duke of Burgundy who, like his brothers Charles V and the Duke of Berry, loved manuscripts, presented Christine with a silver goblet and made her son a page at his court. The person who actually commissioned the *City of Ladies* is thought to have been the Duke of Berry; despite his reputation for stinginess, he, too, probably expressed his appreciation towards Christine in an appropriate manner. Queen Isabella, on the other hand, had to be reminded several times before she eventually paid the authoress the money she had promised her. Isabella's profligate lifestyle and flagrant love affairs meant that she was reviled as a slut and detested by the people. In the struggle for power waged between the estranged Dukes of Burgundy and Berry and their supporters, Isabella intervened now for one party, now for the other, thinking only of her own advantage. In vain did the patriotic Christine implore the queen, in an "epistle" of 1411, to take steps towards resolving the conflict; in vain did she present the Duke of Berry

in 1413 with a *Book of Peace* – manuscripts devoid of illustrations or ornamentation, for the artists had emigrated and their patrons had other cares, were dying or being killed.

As the civil war escalated, Christine gave up writing and withdrew to the countryside, where for eleven years she remained within the protective walls of a nunnery – an institution not dissimilar to her ideal city of women. In the meantime, the warring French parties summoned the English enemy back to France and suffered catastrophic defeat at his hands. In 1420 the victorious English entered Paris, and Queen Isabella gave France and the hand of her daughter to Henry V of England. All seemed lost. In 1429, however, there filtered through the walls of Christine's nunnery the news that a French maid had wrested the city of Orléans from the hands of the enemy in battle and had crowned the Dauphin. Shortly before her death, Christine took up her pen one last time and composed a poem in Joan of Arc's honour. It must have given her particular pleasure to praise the heroic deeds of a brave woman who was one of her own contemporaries.

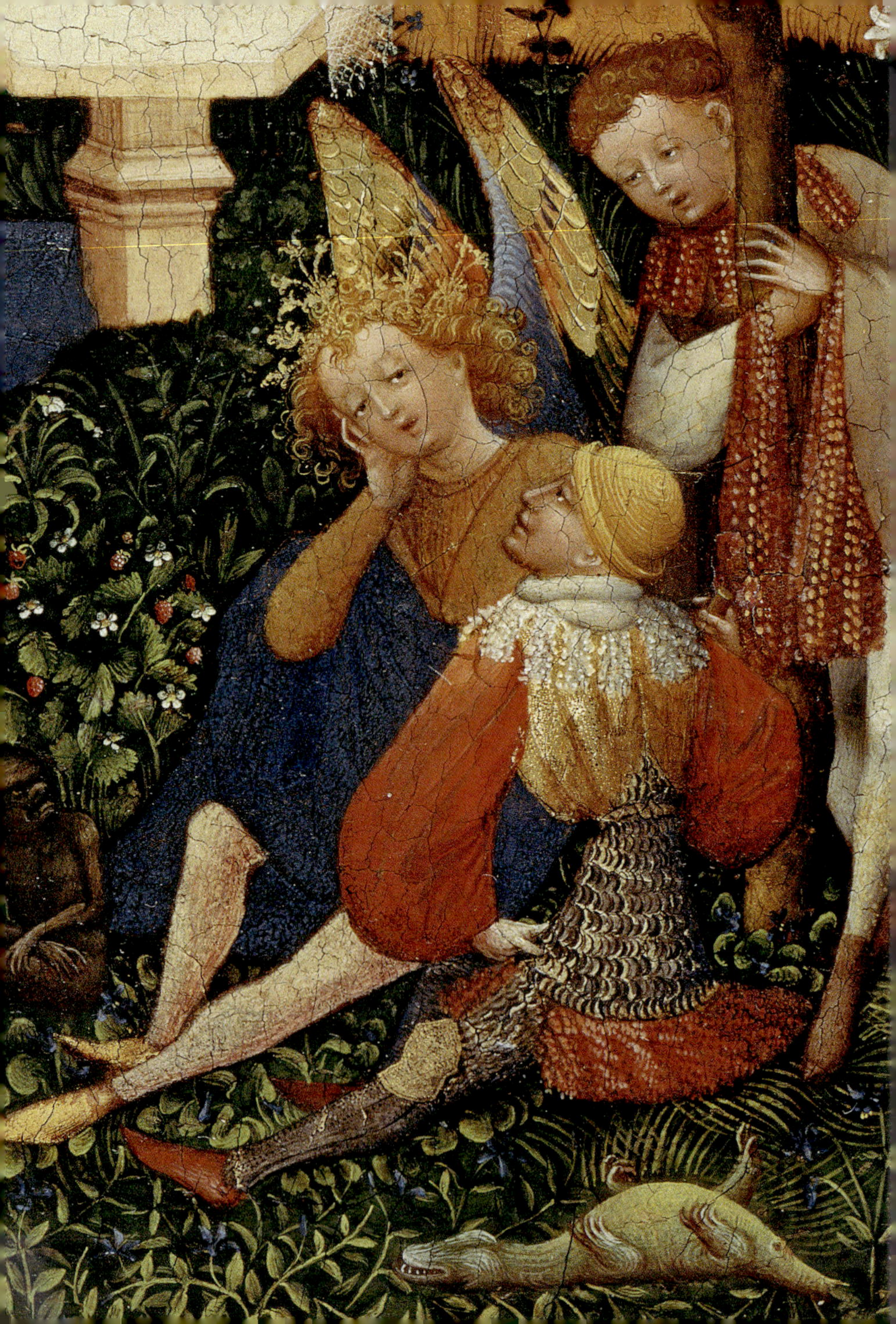

Upper Rhenish Master

"A garden inclosed is my spouse"

The Little Garden of Paradise, c. 1410
26.3 x 33.4 cm, Frankfurt, Städel Museum

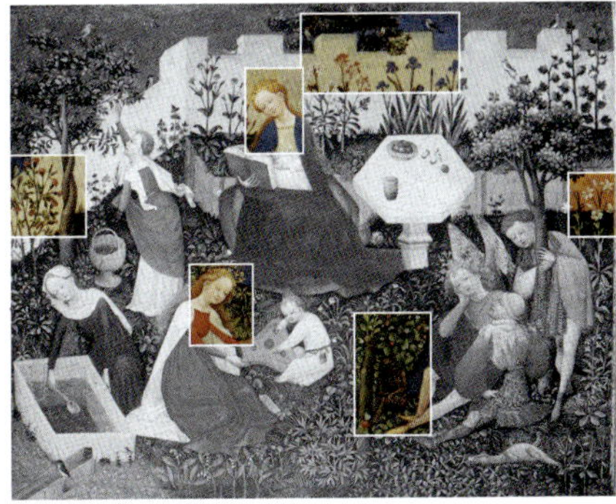

The painting, measuring 26.3 by 33.4 centimetres, is approximately the size of our reproduction on pages 52/53. The work dates from *c.* 1410, and is now in the Städel, Frankfurt. It shows a detail of a past world: the sequestered corner of a garden within a castle walls. The sole function of castles at that time was to provide protection. Conflicts between nobles were far less likely to be resolved by the emperor or his courts than by attack and defence. Fighting was a part of life at every level of society. The wall in the picture shields the peaceful garden scene from a violent world. The scene is also secluded from the confusion and discomforts of everyday life: excrement on the roads, stray dogs and pigs everywhere, the stench, cramped gloom and cold of the dwellings, the constant presence of sickness and poverty. The garden idyll shows a pictorial antidote to the hardships endured by the people of the time.

Gardens designed for pleasure were less common in 1410 than today. The first gardens in northern climes dated from the Roman occupation, but these disappeared with the collapse of the Roman Empire and the subsequent chaos of mass migration. With the spread of monastic life the idea of the garden again crossed the Alps, though the new horticulture was generally motivated by pragmatic rather than aesthetic considerations. Spices and medicinal herbs were grown in the cloister quadrangle, at whose centre stood a well. Part of the quadrangle was often set aside as a burial ground for the monks.

Monastic herb gardens soon expanded to include vegetables and fruit. The monasteries spread northward, bringing new agricultural techniques to the rural population and awakening their sympathy for Nature. There is a famous story about Abbot Walahfried, who, from 838, was head of Reichenau Abbey on Lake Constance: "When the seeds sprout tender shoots, Walahfried fetches fresh water in a large vessel and carefully waters the tiny shoots from the cupped palm of his hand so that the seeds are not hurt by a sudden gush of water ..."

Abbot Walahfried was mainly concerned with questions of labour and harvesting. It was not until 1200 that the garden was reinvented as a place of relaxation and enjoyment. Beauty emerged as a central criterion: the visitor was to spend his time in a pleasurable manner. Albertus Magnus (*c.* 1200–1280) of Cologne, a wise and learned father of the Church, was a passionate advocate of gardens, and much of his advice relating to their design is found on the

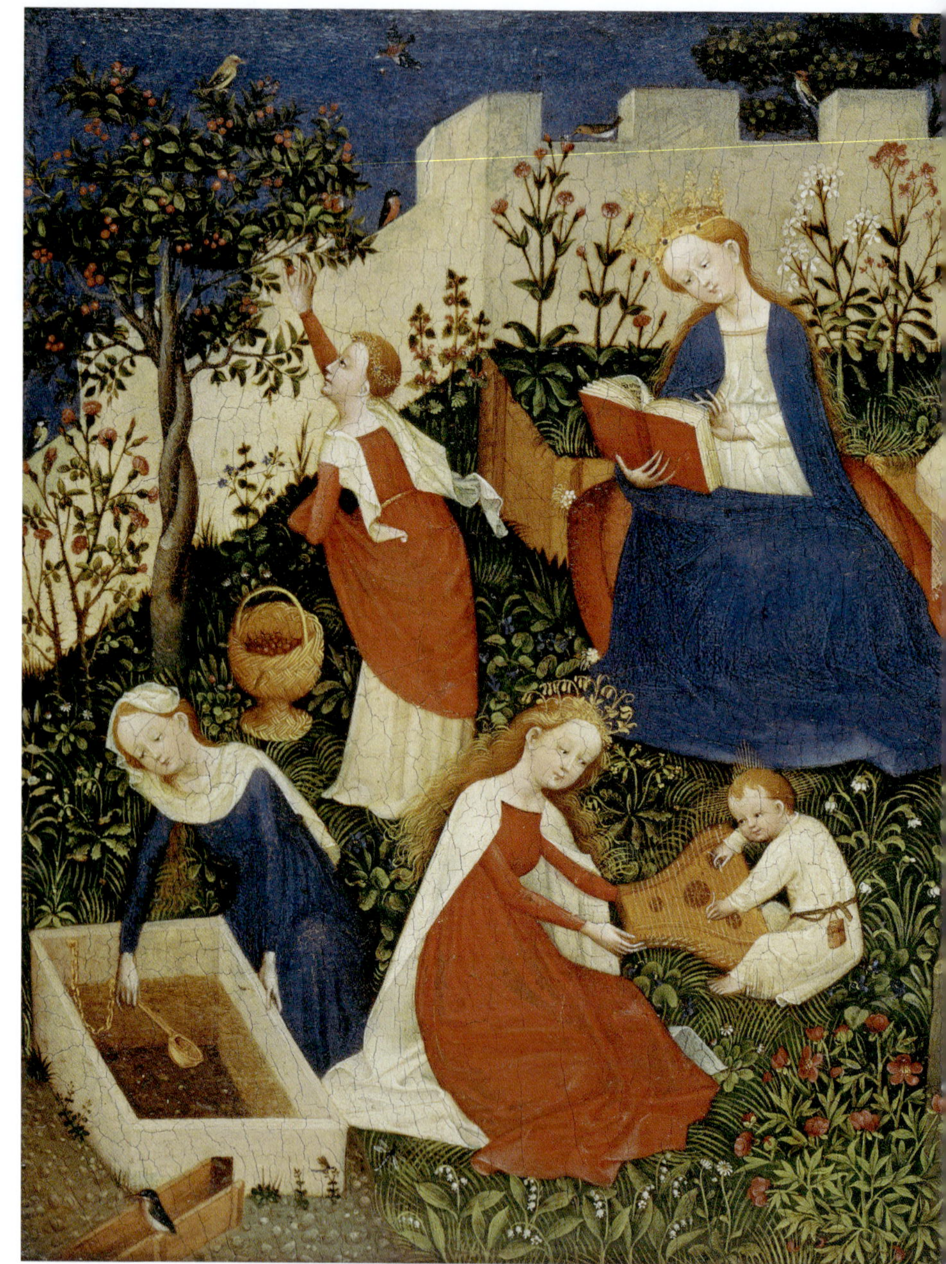

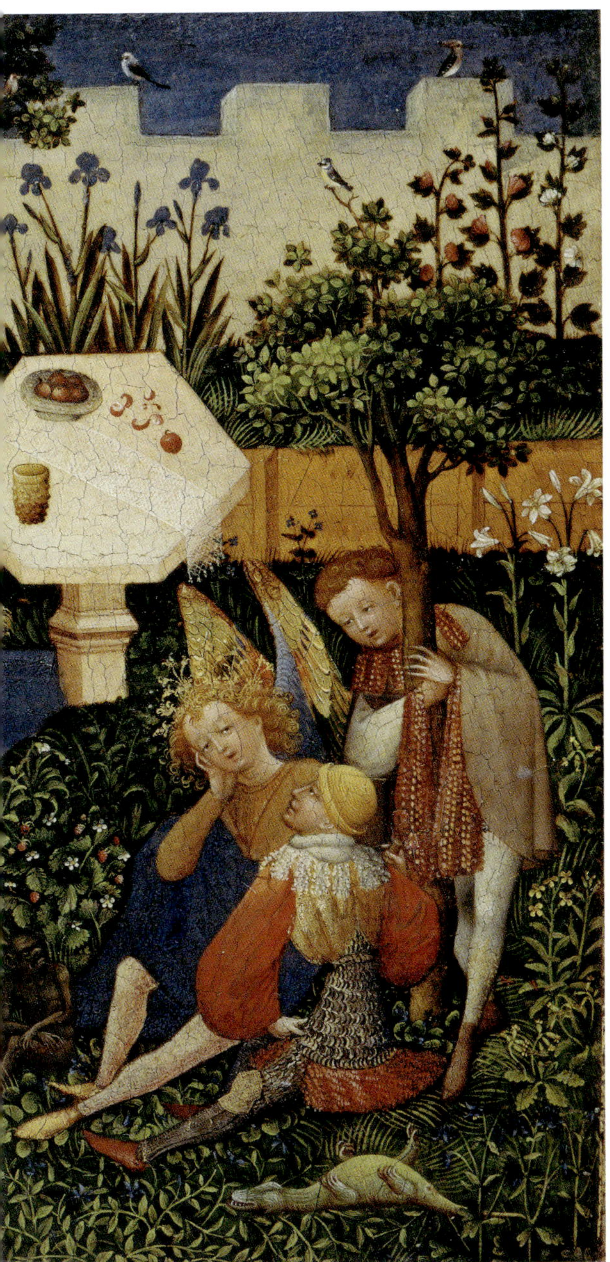

present panel. Entitled *The Little Garden of Paradise*, it was executed some 200 years later by an unknown Upper Rhenish master. According to the 13th-century sage, a garden should have "a raised sward, decked with pleasant flowers … suitable for sitting … and delightful repose". The trees were to stand well apart "for they may otherwise keep out the fresh breeze and thus impair our well-being". A "pleasure garden" should contain "a spring set in stone … for its purity will be a source of much delectation".

A legend for every saint

The artist has filled the castle garden with holy personages. The largest figure is Mary, wearing her heavenly crown and looking down at a book. She has no throne, but sits on a cushion in front of, and therefore below, the terraced part of the lawn. Contemporary spectators attributed significance to the relative height at which a figure sat. Though Mary was the Queen of Heaven, she was also humble and modest: "Behold the handmaid of the Lord."

Contemporaries of the Upper Rhenish master would have had little trouble naming the other women. They would not have identified them by their faces, however, to each of which the artist has lent the same gentle charm: small, very dark eyes, a small mouth with a spot of shadow under the lower lip.

Saints and other holy persons could be identified by the objects or activities attributed to them. St Dorothy, for example, is shown with a basket. According to legend, on her way to a martyr's death she was asked to send flowers and fruits from Heaven; she prayed before her execution, and immediately a boy appeared with the divine gift –

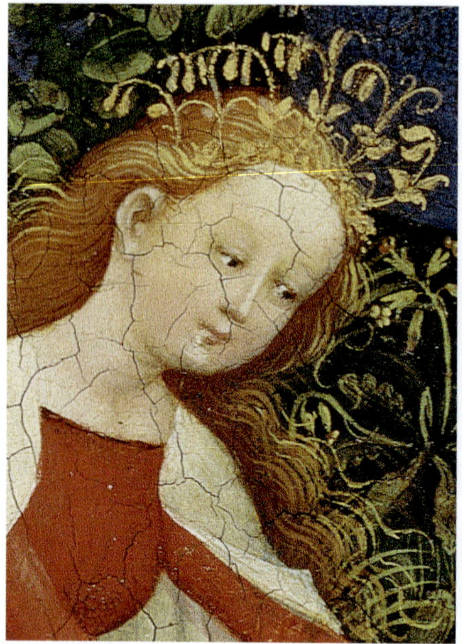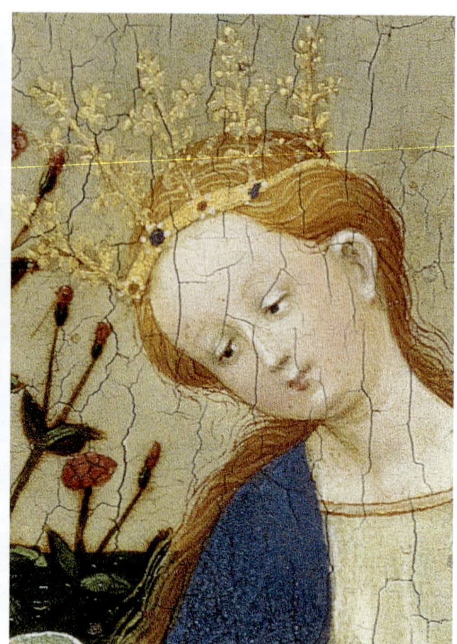

in a basket. Here, beyond the grave, she picks her cherries herself.

A legend was attributed to every saint, so a painting of this kind would have been full of stories to a contemporary spectator. However, some figures may have been more difficult to identify than St Dorothy. St Barbara, seen here drawing water from a spring, is shown without her usual attributes: a tower and chalice. Apparently, the artist could not find a place for them in his garden scene. Those who were acquainted with her legend, however, knew that her bones could work miracles, bringing water to dried-up rivers and ending droughts. In contrast to the verdant growth of the surrounding garden, the area around the well is dry and stony. A realist might infer that the grass around the well had been trodden down by the many people who came to draw water. However, a pious spectator would recognize the dry ground referred to in the legend, which the saint waters with a spoon on a chain to make it fertile.

The woman holding the medieval string instrument, a psaltery, for the child Jesus is probably St Catherine of Alexandria. It was said that Mary and Jesus appeared to her in a dream. Touching her

finger, Jesus told her he was wedded to her through faith. On waking, she found a ring on her finger. According to medieval belief St Catherine was closer to Jesus than any woman but Mary, which explains the position given to her by the artist.

Although the gospels make no reference to Jesus making music, medieval art often portrayed him as a musician. An illumination of *c.* 1300 shows him playing a violin, while an inscription reads: "Manifold joys Lord Jesus brings, to souls he is the sound of strings." Music was a sign of spiritual, or heavenly joy. The artist, unable to depict bliss by facial expression, chose a string instrument as a vehicle instead, a gesture understood by the contemporary spectator.

Red rose and white lily – flowers in praise of Mary
Like the string instrument, many details of *The Little Garden of Paradise* stand for something other than themselves. They are the signs and symbols of a pictorial language with which the majority of people in the Middle Ages were acquainted. Very few people could read at the time; in order to spread the faith, the church therefore needed a language of pictures, or, as we might call it today, a form of non-verbal communication.

Even the garden itself was a symbol, not merely the appropriate scene for a congregation of holy persons. Gardens were synonymous with paradise, presumably because of the Old Testament Garden of Eden. The unknown artist emphasizes the paradisial character of the garden by showing flowers in blossom which usually bloom in different seasons. He also avoids any sign of toil, to which Adam and Eve were condemned on their expulsion from the Garden of Eden.

A paradisial scene with a wall would be interpreted as a *hortus conclusus*, an enclosed garden. Walls do not usually have a place in paradise, but this one symbolizes Mary's virginity, underlining the special status of "Our Blessed Lady", for according to Christian belief Mary conceived without penetration. This pictorial symbol, too, derives from the Old Testament, from an image in the *Song of Solomon*: "A garden inclosed is my sister, my spouse ..."

Various superimposed layers of imagery interlace and merge in this painting; their independence is not painstakingly defined in the way we might wish it today. Thus paradise is represented not only by the garden but also by Mary herself: like paradise, where sexuality does not exist, Mary's immaculate conception places her in a permanently paradisial state. In a paean composed by the poet Conrad of

Würzburg, who died in 1287, Mary is "a living paradise filled with many noble flowers".

The table situated in Mary's immediate proximity emphasizes, like the height at which she sits, the Queen of Heaven's modesty, her status as the "handmaid" of God's divine purpose. In practice, the stone-carved hexagonal tables found in many paintings of the time were used for picnics and board-games.

Various flowers also characterize the Holy Virgin. In several parts of Germany the primrose – seen at the right edge of the painting – is still known as the *Himmelsschlüssel*, or "key to heaven"; for it was Mary who opened Man's door to heaven. The violets are another symbol of modesty, while the white lilies represent the Virgin's purity. The rose was a medieval symbol of the Holy Virgin and, indeed, of virginity in general; the branches with roses have no thorns.

The flowers in this garden would make up a veritable bouquet of virtues – gathered, of course, with the female spectators of the painting in mind.

These signs, allusions and symbols stand for something which eludes direct representation. Modern man has learned to distinguish clearly and coolly between the thing and the symbol. People 500 years ago saw one within the other: Mary was painted as a humble woman, an enclosed

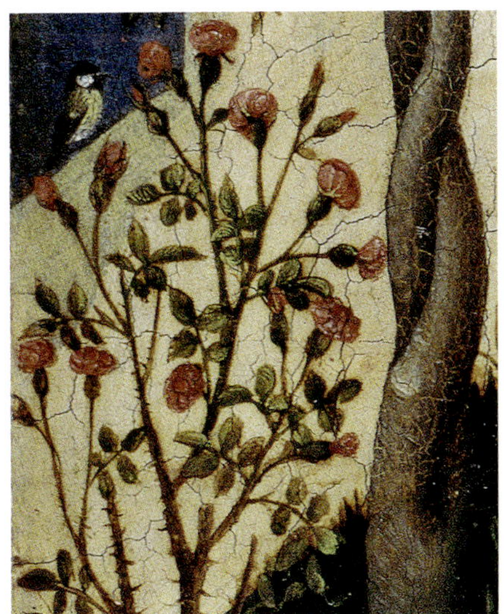

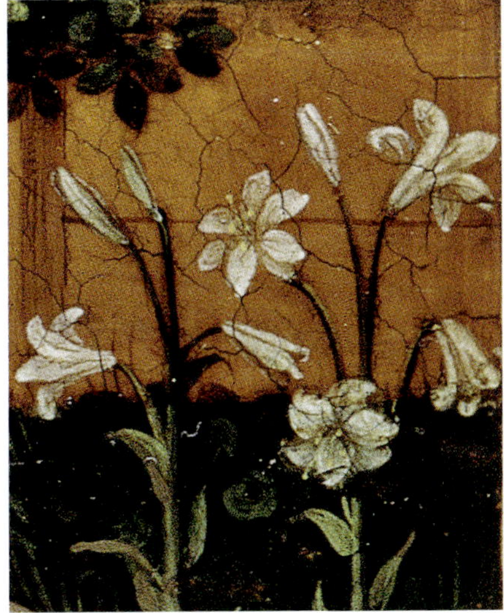

garden and a rose, her purity revered in the whiteness of the lily; thus God's history of salvation revealed itself through Nature. A painting of this kind was more than a theological treatise.

A tree stump stands for sinful humanity
How a sinless Madonna could possibly spring from a humanity burdened by original sin and expelled from paradise was a subject which gave rise to much racking of brains. The artist of *The Little Garden of Paradise* makes a contribution to the debate in the form of a tree stump from which grow two new shoots: which is as much as to say that even an old tree can bring forth new life.

To ensure spectators knew the tree stump stood for sinful humanity, the Upper Rhenish master painted a small devil next to it. To contend that devils, dead dragons or pollarded trees do not really belong in paradise would be to grant inappropriate weight to logic.

The fact that the three figures near the devil and dragon are male can be ascertained from the colour of their faces, which are darker in hue than those of the women. Apart from colour, however, their faces follow the same pattern as those of the women: men and women have the same eyes, the same mouths, and even the same tapering fingers.

Two of the three male figures are easily identified. The one wearing greaves and chain mail is St George, who liberated a virginal princess from the power of a dragon. Paintings that show George doing battle with the dragon generally make the mythical beast enormous and threatening; here it is shrunk to little more than a trademark. The angel with the headdress and the beautiful wings is Michael. He it was who hurled devils into the abyss, one of whom sits, well behaved, at his feet: dragons and devils are powerless in paradise.

The identity of the standing male figure remains obscure, with no hint of the artist's intention. If we look hard enough, however, we find a black bird just behind his knees. Black is the colour of death. Perhaps the panel was painted in memory of a young man who died. Its small format suggests it was intended for a private dwelling rather than a church. The tree around which the young man's arms are clasped appears to grow from his heart – an ancient symbol of eternal life.

On the other hand, it is possible that the young man was St Oswald. In Oswald's legend a raven acts as a divine messenger, carrying away the pious man's right arm when he falls in battle against the heathens. Yet another story! The spectator of 1410 would have found the picture full of stories combining religious teaching and entertainment. As an act of veneration dedicated to the Virgin Mary, the painting itself became an object of reverence, bringing solace to the faithful. It showed a better world in store for those who left this vale of tears. The artistic quality of the painting, so fascinating to today's museum visitor, was undoubtedly admired at the time. In terms of the panel's significance as a religious work, however, it meant relatively little.

Woodpecker, goldfinch and waxwing
Bliss in the life hereafter was not the only subject of paintings like this. Besides the garden of paradise there were also Gardens of Love, celebrations of worldly happiness. These did not depict sensuality in a crude manner, but harked back to the Arcadia of heathen antiquity, itself closely related to the idea of paradise. The effect was to show heaven on earth, so to speak.

As the subject of religious art, the garden of paradise did not last more than a few decades.

By the second half of the 15th century it had practically disappeared: a late blossom, embedded in a medieval language of symbols. The worldly Garden of Love, however, a more readily comprehensible topic, appeared again and again in a variety of different forms. Manet's *Le déjeuner sur l'herbe* is a more recent example.

The Garden of Love was a literary topos before it found its way into painting. The most well-known example today is Boccaccio's *Decameron*, written in Florence some 60 years before *The Little Garden of Paradise* was painted in the region of the Upper Rhine. The setting of these works is remarkably similar: the young Florentines tell each other stories in a garden "surrounded by walls", in the middle of which is a "lawn of fine grass adorned with a thousand brightly coloured flowers", where water gushes from a little fountain "gently splashing … into a wonderfully clear well". Here men and women did not sit apart on their best behaviour, for all who were present "strolled together, weaving the loveliest wreathes of manifold sprigs" and telling each other erotic tales.

The French *Romance of the Rose* predates the Italian *Decameron* by over a century. It also sings love's joys and complaints, is set in a garden and, like Boccaccio's *Decameron*, was read widely in Europe by the educated elite of the day. In both books, feelings of happiness are accompanied by birdsong. In the *Romance of the Rose* we read: "Their song was comparable to that of the angels in heaven." And only three sentences later: "One was inclined to believe it was not birdsong at all but the voices of sea sirens." Whether angels or sirens, divine messengers, or seductresses who were half beast, half human, whether Christian figures or those of antiquity, the example shows the essential ambiguity of all pictorial symbols at the time. Even spectators of a Christian garden of paradise would know that painted birds were there not only to sing God's praises.

The birds in *The Little Garden of Paradise* are rendered accurately. Zoologists have distinguished at least ten different species: great tit, oriole, bullfinch, chaffinch, robin, woodpecker, goldfinch, waxwing, hoopoe and blue tit. Had he been concerned solely with angelic music, the artist might have painted the birds as schematically as the faces of his saints. But he evidently wished to emphasize their variety, just as he did with the plants. He wanted to show what he saw; he wanted to be exact. The plants testify to this, with some twenty identifiable species.

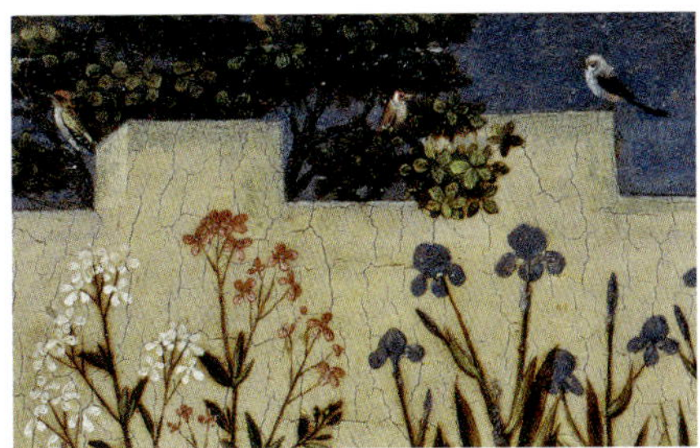

Exact zoological observation betrays an interest in natural science. This was new in a painting of *c.* 1410. While it is true that birds and flowers were frequently painted with some degree of accuracy, they had rarely been rendered with such a powerful inclination to catalogue empirical data. Medieval painting was usually dominated by religion. While this painting might appear to confirm the rule, it also illustrates a growing awareness of Nature; no longer mere adornment, the distinctive presence of a natural world is felt as strongly here as that of the holy figures. However, it was not until the next century that the first botanic gardens were created in Germany: at Leipzig in 1580, and at Heidelberg in 1597.

The discovery and scientific exploration of Nature were first steps on the long road to modernity. *The Little Garden of Paradise* lends visibility to that phase of intellectual history. However, the beauty of the painting also resides in the harmony, evidently still attainable, between religious and realistic views of the world: two types of experience which did not appear to present the dichotomy felt by Christians in the Western world today.

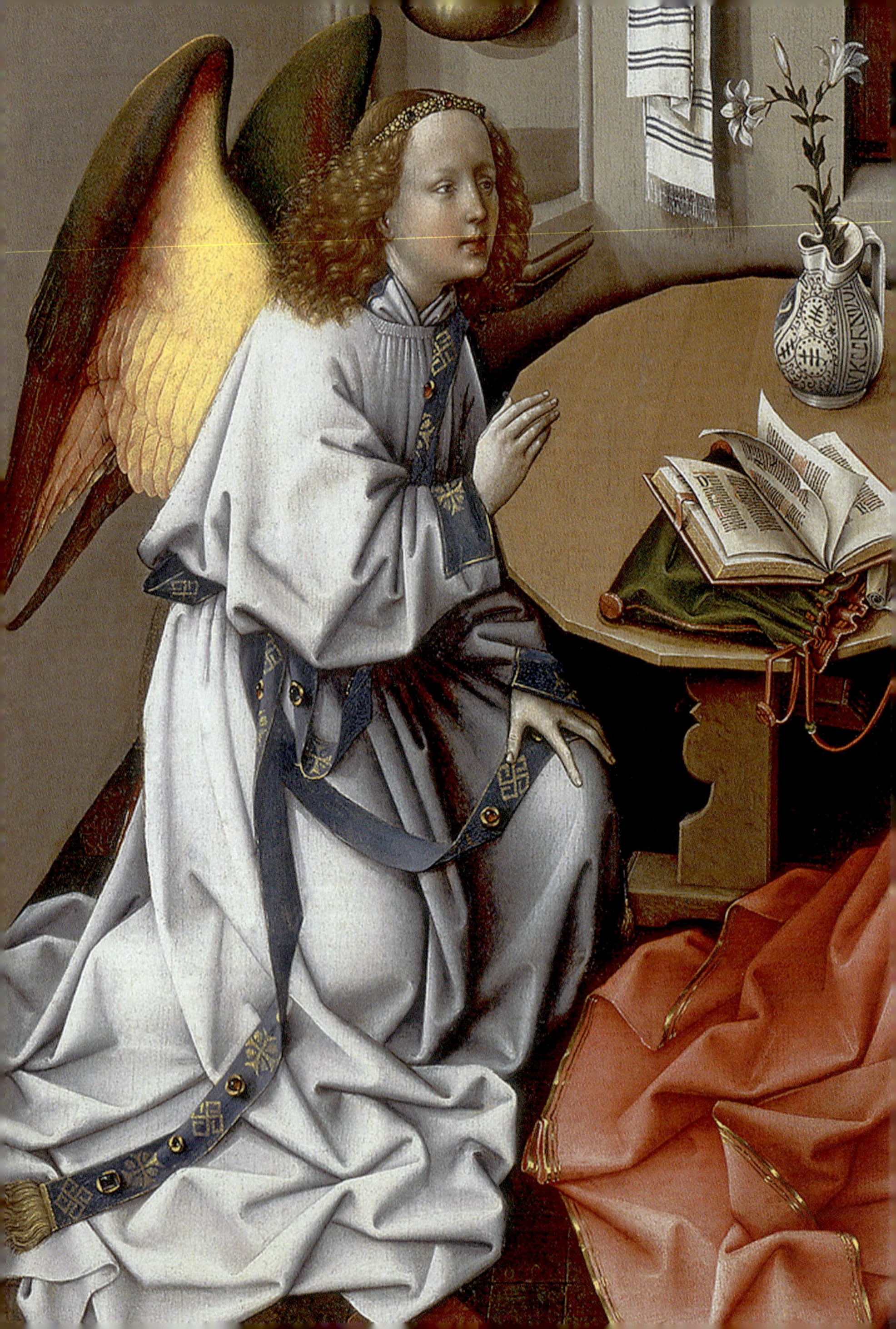

Robert Campin (*c*. 1375–1444)
(real name Guido di Pietro)

An angel in the living room

The Mérode Triptych
(Annunciation Triptych/Mérode Altarpiece, in which Joseph is seen making mousetraps), *c*. 1422/1430
64 x 120 cm, New York, The Metropolitan Museum of Art, The Cloisters Collection

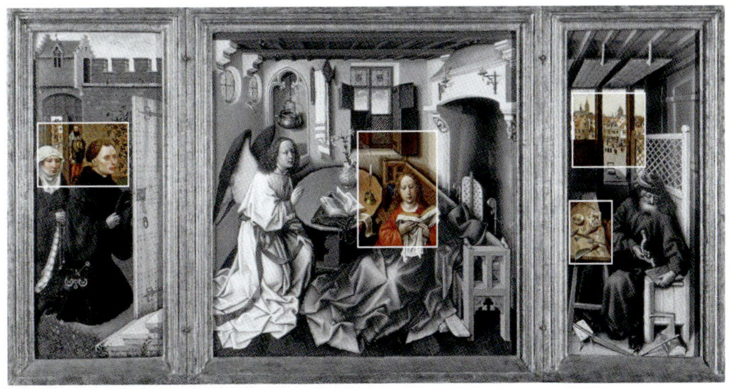

A living room, a workshop, a walled garden: interiors and nature, with glimpses of a city, its streets and squares. Seeing a reproduction, we might suppose this three-panelled painting to be large, but in fact it is relatively small, just 120 centimetres in total breadth and 64 centimetres high. It was intended not for a church but for a room rather like that in the centre portion, the Annunciation scene. The triptych served as a house altar, standing against or hanging on a wall, and the couple who endowed it would pray their daily *Ave Maria* before it. These words, meaning "Hail, Mary", were the Archangel Gabriel's words of greeting to the Virgin Mary when he came to tell her she would bear a son.

The Annunciation marks the beginning of the Christian story of salvation, and in order to underline the significance of the event, artists liked to relocate it to a church or palace. Until well into the Middle Ages they presented it, as they presented all biblical events, against a golden background. But in this version from the Netherlands, the Annunciation happens in an urban, middle-class setting.

The two figures in the centre panel are no ordinary burghers, but we perceive this (disregarding the angel's wings) only by comparing with the others in the two sides: the faces of Mary and the angel are less realistic and individual, and their garments far more splendid. The folds in the fabric alone constitute an entire chapter of art history.

Examination of the wood on which the triptych was painted has shown that the wood for the centre panel was felled around 1373 and that of the wing panels somewhat later. Art historians date the painter's work (though more than one may have worked on the picture) to between 1422 and 1430. And at that date an Annunciation set amongst the ordinary people was quite new.

The Holy Ghost snuffs the candle

Neither Mary nor the Archangel Gabriel, sent by God, has a halo. Apart from the wings of the angel, there is only one other indication that what is happening here is of a mystical, indeed divine nature: the tiny naked figure seen approaching Mary on seven golden rays from the round window nearer to us. This is Jesus, and the cross over his shoulder is

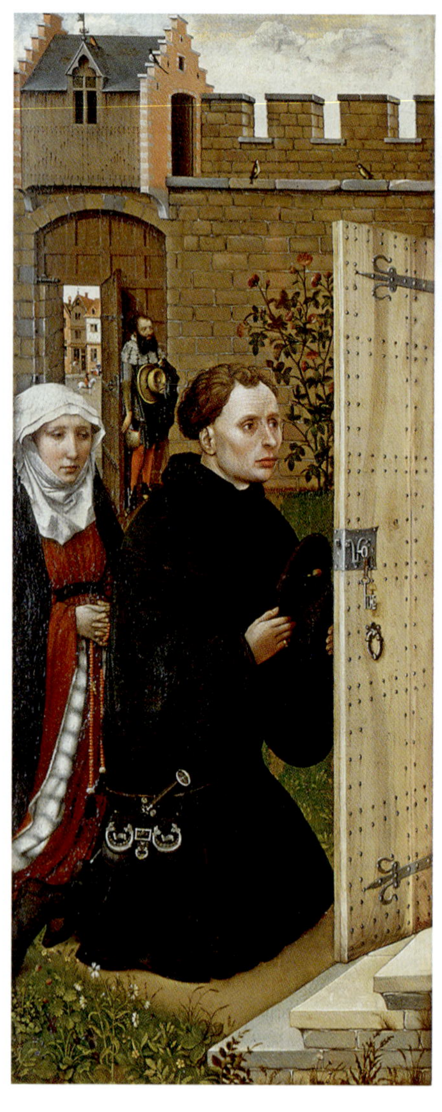

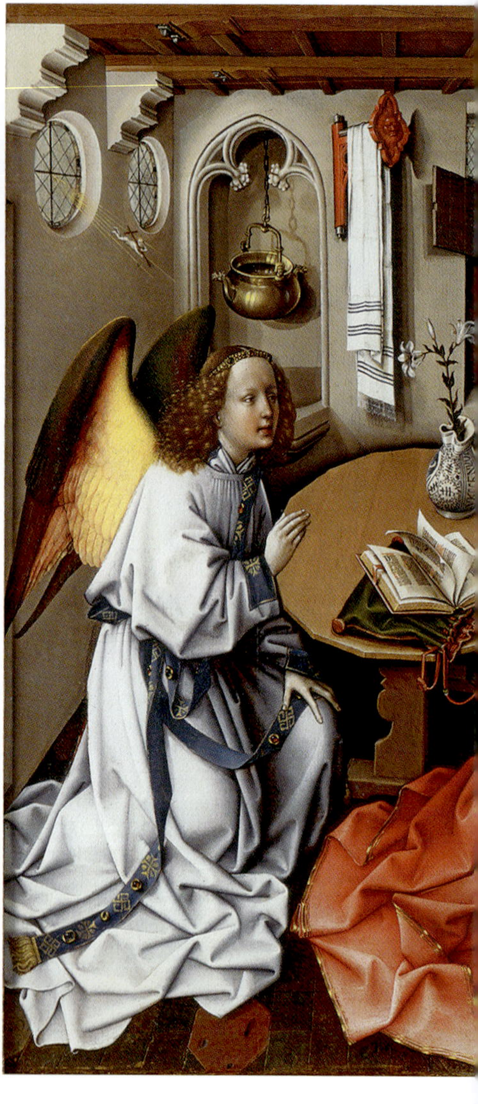

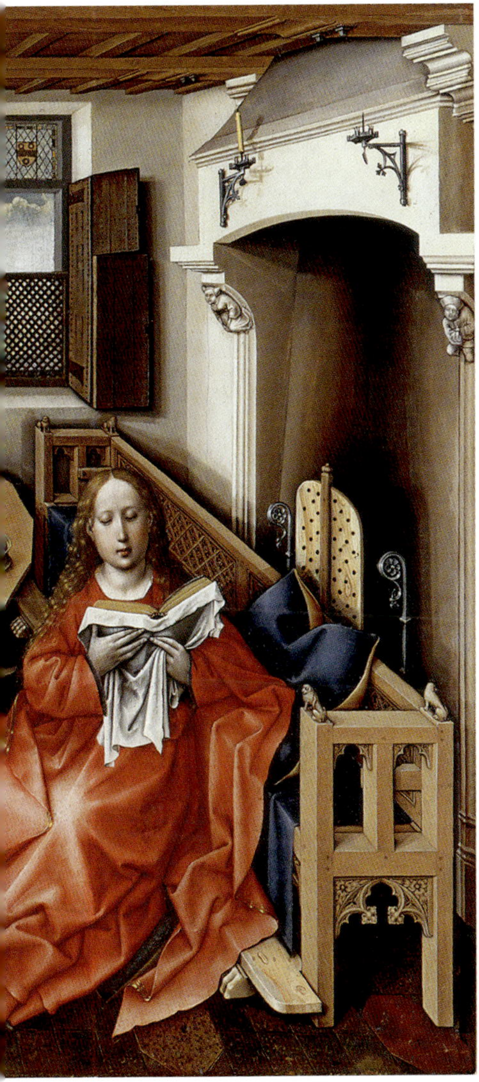

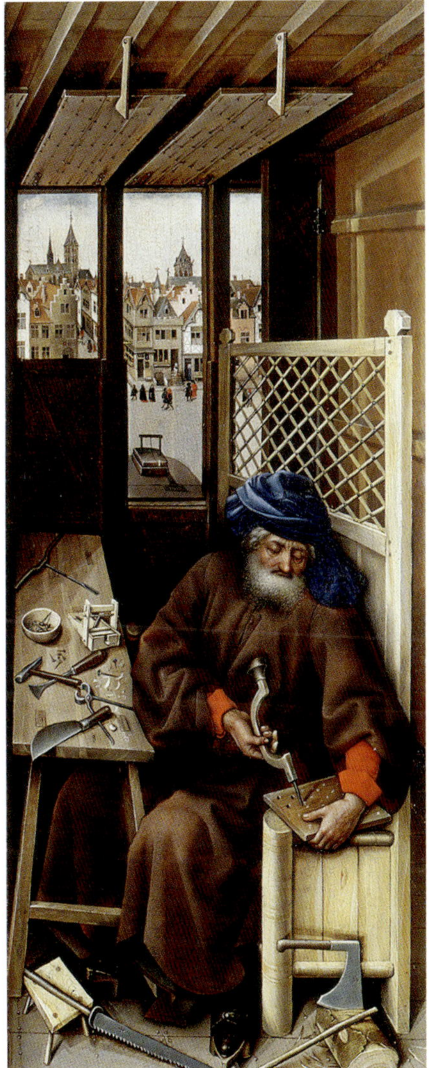

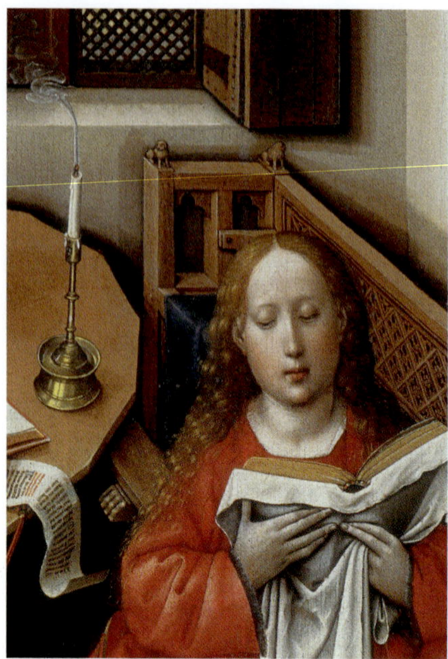

a reminder that his suffering will redeem humanity. Theologically, the Annunciation was equivalent to an act of conception, and God's seed was imagined as a miniature but fully formed body of Christ.

There are no haloes, no dove representing the Holy Ghost, no ecclesiastical or palace architecture, but instead a medium sized room with a table, a long seat, windows and a fireplace. The perspective is admittedly not quite faultless, but the individual objects, like the manner in which the ceiling and bench are constructed, have been faithfully recorded. At the far end of the bench we can even see a wooden pin, one of the pivots on which the backrest of the bench could be swung over to the other side. In winter, this meant one could sit cosily in front of the hearth.

The centre panel is one of the earliest pictorial representations of a room in an ordinary home. Even now we can still sense something of the relish with which the items of everyday life were taken note of and declared worthy of record in a painting.

One reason why the things of this world entered into Christian panel painting was the order that followed the rules formulated in 1223 by St Francis

of Assisi. This saint retains his popularity to this day; he preached to the birds, giving his attention to creatures in need, whether human or animal, rather than engaging in the dogmatic scholastic debates of the age. His mendicant followers were itinerant friars, and as they travelled they interpreted the Bible in terms of the reality their listeners lived in. Thus the Dutch preacher Geert Groote, for example, suggested in the late 14th century: "Let us imagine ourselves living in the same house as Christ and Mary." And that is exactly what our artist has done.

That said, many of the seemingly realistic details do in fact possess a theological significance. The white lilies in the majolica jug, the white towel, and the vessel of water, all illustrate Mary's immaculate purity; the half-closed windows and the absence of doors highlight the secluded retirement in which she lives. She is sitting not on the bench but in front of it, which betokens her humility. She is not touching the book she is reading with her hands but is holding it in a towel, demonstrating her respect for the sacred text. The lions on the bench armrest recall the throne of Solomon, and thus the wisdom of the Old Testament king. These are all symbols that can also be found in many an earlier painting of the Virgin.

The snuffed candle, however, is an unusual touch. It has only just been extinguished, as we can see from the smoke curling up from it. The painter was presumably aiming to show something that is not visible, a sudden draught of air: along with the angel and the divine seed, the Holy Ghost or the divine breath are also in the room. This is a moment beyond the human senses, registered in everyday terms.

The value of work

Joseph is always present in pictures of Christ's nativity, for as the future father who would raise Jesus he has an important role to play in the Holy Family. But he played no part in the conception, and was therefore normally absent from Annunciation scenes. The triptych breaks with this tradition – and, once again, it was probably through the Franciscan influence. The friars had elevated Joseph, often relegated to a supporting role and indeed a butt of ridicule in crude mystery plays, into a saint close to the people; in their version, Joseph had neither performed miracles nor suffered martyrdom, but he embodied the virtues of the believing and dutiful citizen. His was the example that might be followed in everyday life.

He is portrayed on the right wing panel as an artisan. The various precisely rendered tools, and Joseph's concentration as he positions his drill, suggest how important his occupation and station seemed to the artist, and to the man who commissioned the painting.

This was not something that could be taken for granted. As long as only the Church and the nobility commissioned paintings, little attention was paid to artisans. In the 14th and 15th centuries, however, as the cities grew, the power and self-confidence of the ordinary citizens increased as well. If they ordered a picture, they wanted to see their own world in it. Paintings were now commissioned by merchants making profits out of fine textiles traded afar, for example; or by master craftsmen whose large workshops had brought them prosperity.

A higher valuation has been placed upon Joseph, though at the same time the higher standing of Mary remains clear. His workshop is wooden, whereas Mary's room is stone-built. No door connects the two places. Joseph is excluded from the holy event.

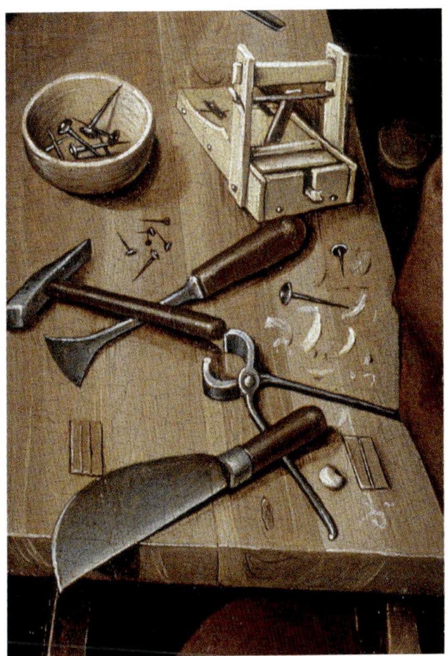

He does not know what is happening, and his concentration on his work could also be interpreted as a lack of awareness or imagination.

Along with his tools and nails there is a wooden box-like contraption on Joseph's table. This has been identified as a mouse-trap, and a reconstruction has demonstrated that it works. Why the mouse-trap is in the picture, though, is a moot point; indeed, its meaning has been debated so long that the triptych has sometimes been referred to as the "mouse-trap annunciation". Supposedly there are even two mouse-traps in the panel, the second being on the counter flap opened to the outside; this is said to be an older type of trap, but no one knows how it works. A theological explanation for the mouse-trap(s) was proposed by St Augustine, who described Christ as the *muscipula diaboli*, the devil's mouse-trap. By this he meant that Christ had saved the world and thus entrapped the devil.

But were the artist and the donor really familiar with this 4th-century analogy? It is possible, but not certain; and, looking at the painting, we may well wonder if those who seek symbols everywhere do not sometimes find more than the painter ever concealed in the first place. Would allusions to St Augustine really be in a picture meant for the everyday devotions of a family in business? Must high art really exclude all reference to banal everyday realities – such as the presence of mice in a house?

A city apparently peaceful, in troubled times
Through the half-opened windows in the Annunciation room we see a little sky, but in the background in the wing panels we see a city. In the religious part of the triptych, our gaze is directed upwards; to the right and left, we see the earthly home in which this great event is to be accommodated.

The different seasons are distinctly earthly and yet can only be interpreted through religion. On the left panel, roses and wild flowers are in bloom; on the right, there is a hint of snowfall. The Church calendar affords an explanation: the couple who endowed the painting are celebrating the Feast of the Annunciation on 25 March, and the painter is denoting springtime with flowers, whilst Joseph only enters into his paternal role with the birth of Christ, at Christmas.

Many attempts have been made to identify the city in the painting, but none has been definitive. Ghent and Liège have been proposed, but it might

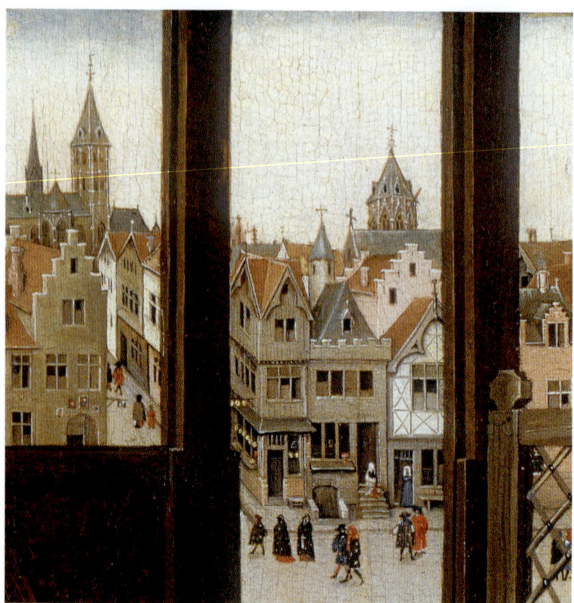

Campin (*c.* 1375–1444) had a large workshop in Tournai, several houses, and the respected office of city painter. He took the part of the insurgents, served as a member of one of their committees, and was sentenced, after the old oligarchy returned to power, to make a pilgrimage to Saint-Gilles in Provence. Probably, however, he paid a fine instead.

Three years later he was in court again, this time on a charge of adultery, though this may have been a pretext. His sentence of a year's banishment was suspended, but he left the city nonetheless, staying away for several years. Possibly he gave up his workshop before he left. Documents show that he discharged three men who had worked for him for many years, first ensuring that they were designated masters in their craft. One of them was Rogier van der Weyden, the co-founder with Campin and the van Eyck brothers of Netherlandish painting.

Van der Weyden may have done some work on the left wing of the triptych. X-rays have shown that both the woman and the man in the background were added later. This bearded man holding a straw hat has been identified as the Mechelen town herald.

A pious wish for a family

The woman was probably the wife of the man who commissioned the painting, and she was presumably added later because the triptych was painted before the marriage. The man who ordered the picture may have wanted it as a votive image, expressing a pious wish for a family. But this is speculation. The woman's hair and throat are chastely covered, as was customary then amongst married women. She is kneeling behind the man, holding a red coral rosary in her folded hands.

Research has focussed on the coats of arms in the windows on the centre panel in the attempt to identify the person who commissioned the triptych. The left one is uninformative, but the right points to a family named Ymbrecht or Inghelbrecht or Engelbrecht (names did not yet have the fixed writ-

equally be Tournai, where the artist lived, or Mechelen, which may have been where the man who commissioned the triptych lived. The buildings we can see were characteristic of northern France and Burgundy in the early 15th century. Some are half timber; some have stepped gables. Church towers are visible too. To the right may be a barber's shop, with three gleaming barber's basins in the window. All the figures in the right panel are warmly dressed, the women in black hooded cloaks over red skirts; the men have fashionably high headgear.

The impression is peaceful, but the times were troubled. The English had occupied large areas of France, and it was not until 1429 that Joan of Arc, the Maid of Orléans, led the French king to victory. The Duke of Burgundy, an uncle of the king, took advantage of his weakness in order to extend his own territory.

In addition to these wars there were civil wars. Europe was racked by a succession of urban revolts, in Florence (1378), in Paris (1418), in Bruges (1438), in Ghent (1451). In 1423, artisans and labourers seized power in Tournai and kept it till 1428. This was the city where Robert Campin was at work on his Annunciation.

ten forms they would have today). This name could be read as "angel brings", and it is conceivable that an Annunciation scene was ordered by way of allusion to the family name, as well as to the wish for a family. And perhaps what Gabriel has brought in this triptych is not only glad tidings but also Holy Scripture; the bag on the table may point to this. Still – an archangel descending from the throne of God to deliver a bag?

In terms of their dates, two men might have commissioned the triptych. Both lived in Mechelen, which is north of Brussels and about 100 kilometres from Tournai. The Metropolitan Museum of Art in New York, which now owns the work, believes that the donor was "probably" one Jan Engelbrecht, a well-to-do carrier or trader. German art historian Felix Thürlemann is adamant that it was Peter Inghelbrecht or Engelbrecht, who came from Cologne and had a cloth business in Mechelen; but the evidence advanced by Thürlemann is no more than probability.

The part played by the bearded herald is also open to debate. He occupies a prominent position, between the couple's heads, and his face, unlike that of the archangel, is so individual that it must be a portrait. Perhaps this man brought some important, good news.

The work is unsigned and takes its name, the *Mérode Triptych*, from its last private owners. The artist was long anonymous, and known as the Master of Flémalle from work he did in the Flemish monastery of Flémalle. Not until the early 20th century did Robert Campin emerge from the obscurity of this sobriquet. To what extent the triptych is indeed by his hand, however, and how much might have been by others in his workshop, is disputed.

Much as the triptych, with its plenitude of simple everyday things, is of this world, it nevertheless remains enigmatic. One puzzle is the wall separating Mary's room from the garden. On Mary's side there is no door in this wall, but on the side where the couple are kneeling there is. This inconsistency can be resolved on the symbolic level: the enclosed space in which we see the Virgin is intended to show that she leads a secluded, immaculate life, apart from the world. The donor is imagining that she has entered into his house. From without, he has opened the door; with his own eyes he beholds the Mother of God and petitions her for a family.

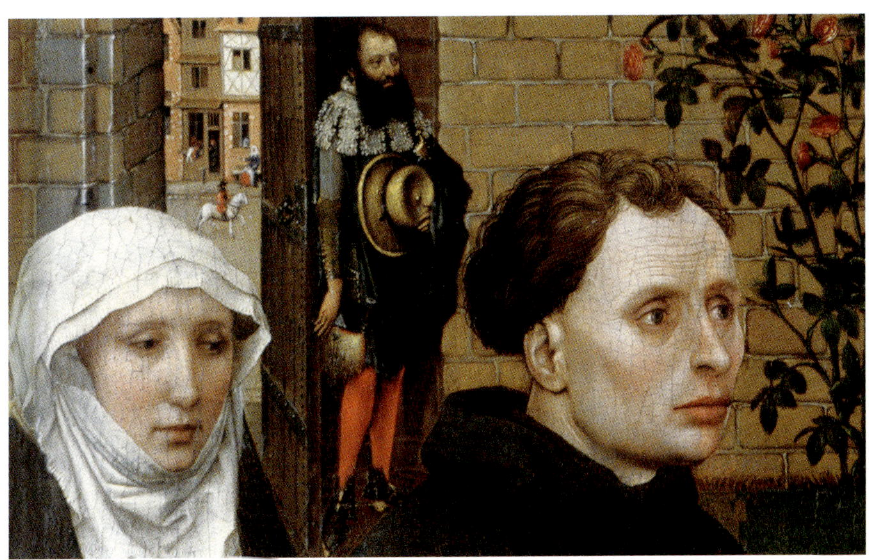

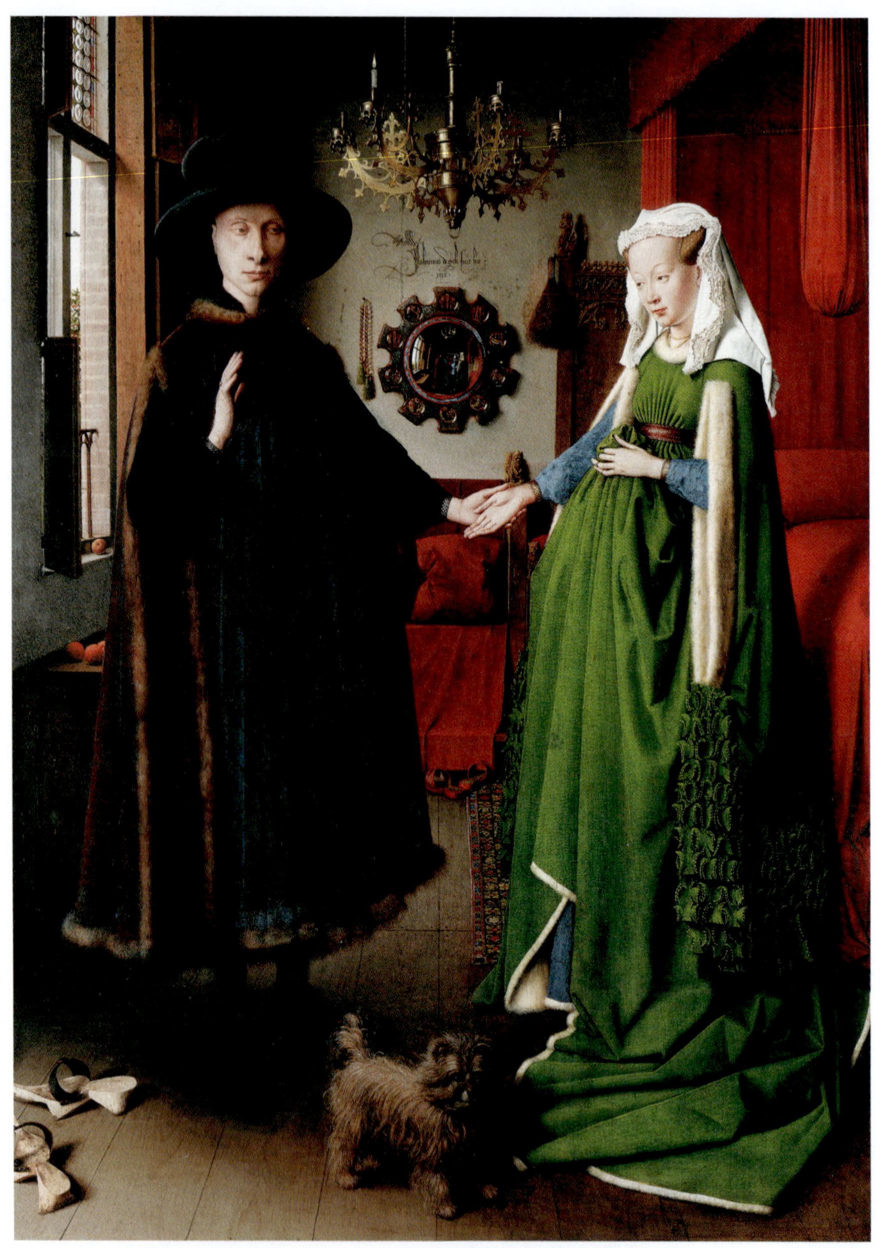

Jan van Eyck (*c.* 1390–1441)

An Italian in Bruges

The Arnolfini Marriage, 1434
82 x 60 cm, London, The National Gallery

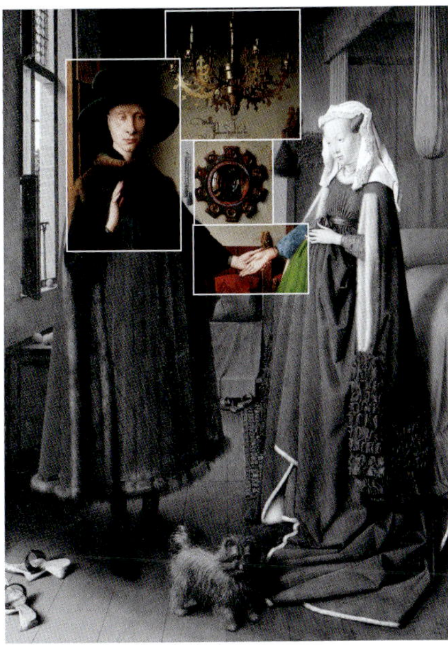

An aristocratically dressed couple in middle-class surroundings: slippers and clogs lie on the floor, and the woman's artfully pleated train tumbles not onto the gleaming marble tiles of some grand palace but onto plain floorboards. There is much that appears contradictory and mysterious in this panel.

It was executed in 1434 in Bruges, the leading centre of trade in northern Europe. Wood and furs arrived here from Russia and Scandinavia, silks, carpets and spices from merchants in Genoa and Venice, and lemons, figs and oranges from Spain and Portugal. Bruges was a wealthy place, "the most famous city in the world on account of the goods that are traded there and the merchants who live there", according to Philip the Good, Duke of Burgundy from 1419 to 1467. It was the chief port of his own duchy.

Burgundy stretched from the shores of the North Sea right down to the Swiss border, and for several decades was the most powerful political unit in Europe. Its dukes owned many palaces, including one in Bruges, and were lovers of luxury. Recognizing that Burgundy's might rested on the industriousness of its workforce, and in particular on the trading activities and textile industries of the Flemish towns, Philip the Good let his citizens improve their own standard of living and grow wealthy under Burgundian rule.

The couple in van Eyck's painting are undoubtedly rich. This is most evident in their clothing: the woman's outer garment, with its voluminous swathes of material, is trimmed with ermine. The folds at the bottom could only have been arranged so skilfully with the help of a maid, and the train, too, would have needed a second person to carry it

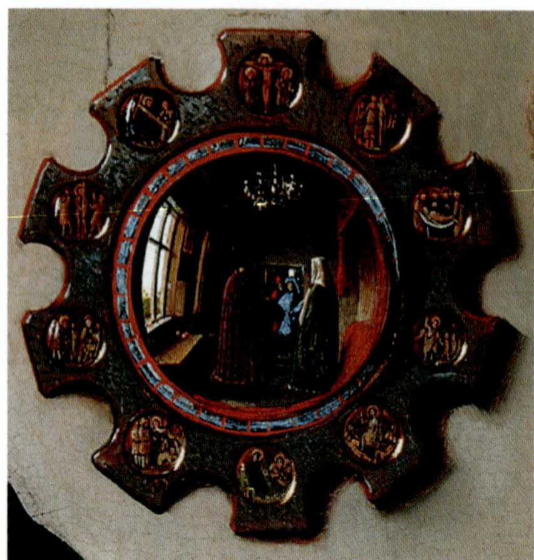

when moving about. To walk at all in such a dress presupposed a degree of practice normally only acquired in aristocratic circles.

The man is wearing a sumptuous velvet cloak trimmed or even lined with mink or sable. But the cloak is only calf length and is slit down the sides, allowing movement and activity. The fact that this man does not belong to the aristocracy is indicated by the wooden clogs in front of him, which were slipped on to avoid having to wade through the dirt in the streets. The high and mighty didn't need clogs – they travelled on horseback or were carried in litters.

Van Eyck gives no indication of the identity of his sitters either on the panel or in any other document, and it was only some 100 years after the work was executed that it was described in an inventory as: "A large panel painting, Hernoult le Fin with his wife in a room." Hernoult le Fin was the French version of the Italian surname Arnolfini. The Arnolfinis belonged to a family of merchants and bankers, originally from Lucca, who had opened an office in Bruges.

This foreign businessman was thus living in Bruges in aristocratic luxury. He owned Oriental carpets, chandeliers and mirrors; he had glazing in at least the top half of his windows; he could even afford expensive oranges. The room's cramped dimensions, however, are those of a middle-class home. As in all private chambers, the bed is dominant. During the day, the curtains were

tied up into a ball; people sat on the edge of the bed and even received visitors lying on top of the covers. At night, the curtains were drawn around the bed to create a new living space, a room within a room. In the Italian city-republics, the middle classes were permitted to live in their own palaces if they could afford it; in the Burgundy of van Eyck's day, however, that was uncommon. Only one man is said to have done it in Bruges – a Florentine compatriot of the Arnolfinis, the manager of the powerful Medici bank.

A mirror with magic properties

In the central axis of the composition, on the far wall of the room, hangs a mirror. Its frame is adorned with ten painted medallions containing scenes from the Passion of Christ. Glass mirrors in a middle-class home were unusual in van Eyck's day; people normally made do as best they could with polished metal. Only princely households could afford flat mirrors, which were considered a valuable rarity because they were so difficult to manufacture – the crystal base usually shattered when the hot liquid metal was poured over it. It would still be some time before a mixture of mercury and tin was invented which could be applied cold. Augsburg glass blowers, however, had arrived at an interim solution whereby they poured a metal mixture – evidently heated to not quite such a high temperature – into a glass sphere, and thereby obtained a convex mirror.

These curved mirrors were more affordable than flat ones. In French they were called *sorcières*, or "witches", because they magically expanded the viewer's field of vision. In this picture, we can see in the mirror the beams of the ceiling and a second window. Behind us, so to speak, we can see another room, and where we ourselves are standing the mirror shows us two figures just entering the room.

This effect was repeated 200 years later by the Spanish painter, Velázquez, in the flat mirror which appears in his large canvas *The Maid of Honour*. It is probable that van Eyck's *Arnolfini Marriage* was at that time part of the Spanish Royal Collection, of which Velázquez was the curator.

A very private ceremony

The woman lays her right hand carefully in the man's left. There is a solemnity to this joining of hands, which the artist places in almost the very centre of the composition and which is thereby lent particular significance. The two figures themselves adopt very formal poses within their everyday surroundings. The woman's train has been carefully arranged, and the man raises his right hand to take the oath. For van Eyck's contemporaries, the joining of hands and the gesture of oath-taking were sure indications that two people were pledging each other their troth.

In the 15th century, you needed neither a priest nor witnesses to enter into a Christian and legal marriage. A wedding could be performed anywhere, including – as here – in a private bedchamber. The sacrament of marriage was conducted not by priests but by husband and wife themselves. To officially announce their marriage, the newly-weds would attend Communion together the following morning, although even this was not compulsory.

Only at the Council of Trent a good century later did the Church succeed in making the attendance of a priest and two witnesses a necessary element of the marriage ceremony. It did so not for religious reasons, but in order to clamp down on the abuse and deception possible under the old system. Even after this, however, the ceremony still did not have to take place before the altar, but at most in front of a church door.

Although witnesses are not required at the Arnolfini wedding, two are nevertheless clearly visible in the mirror. They are needed for a different reason, namely to legalize a written contract of marriage. Such contracts were common where – as here – large amounts of money were involved; they regulated financial matters between the marriage partners and had to be signed by two witnesses.

It may well be that the financial agreement in the present case was particularly important, since this is clearly a "left-handed" marriage. The man takes the woman's hand in his left hand, not his right as was otherwise the convention. Such marriages were concluded between partners of unequal rank, and are still occasionally practised in ruling houses in our own times. More precisely, it was always the woman who came from the lower class. She had to relinquish all rights of inheritance for herself and her children and thus could not continue the family lineage,

but was guaranteed sufficient financial means to support herself in the event of widowhood. These means, or title deeds relating to them, were originally presented on the morning after the marriage. It is from the Low Latin *morganatica*, meaning a gift from a bridegroom to a bride, that we derive the term more politely given to this sort of union, namely a "morganatic" marriage.

The bride in this painting is not getting married in white – that would only become the convention in the second half of the 19th century – but in her most sumptuous Sunday best. Her bulging figure is not intended to indicate that she is pregnant, but like her small, high laced bosom illustrates the ideal of beauty held in the Late Gothic era. The copious folds of cloth which she carries with her also reflect the fashion and lavish style of the Burgundian empire – and elsewhere besides. Women dressed in such ample robes and often wearing large bonnets were compared by contemporary writers to ships under full sail, and an unkind French tongue commented that it was hard to distinguish the "empty" vessels from the pregnant ones.

The bride in van Eyck's picture must have been very young. The carved monster above her hand forms part of a seat standing against the back wall. It recalls the gargoyles which served as waterspouts on cathedral roofs. These, like the pose of the bride, were typical of the era which we call the Gothic.

An industrious banker

At the Burgundian court and amongst the social circles surrounding it, it was not just women's

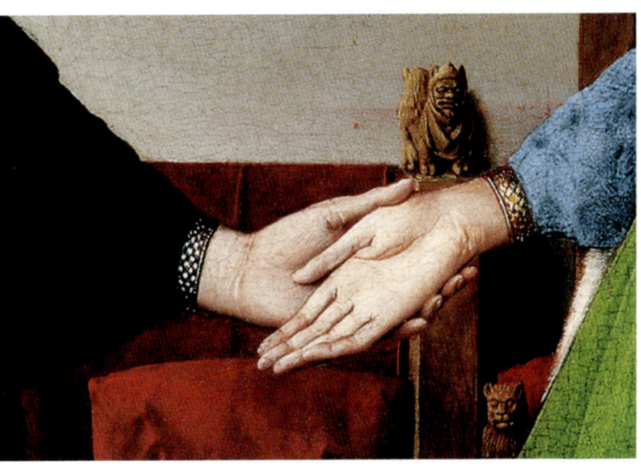

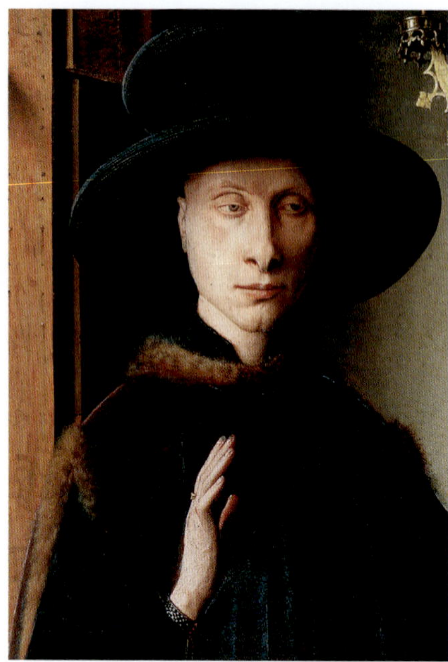

fashions that were extravagant – so, too, were the men's. They wore elaborately wound turbans or top hats of monstrous proportions. Philip the Good introduced dark colours for official occasions, as worn by Arnolfini here. These would later evolve into the black of Spanish court dress.

The bridegroom's hands are as white and well manicured as those of his bride. His narrow, sloping shoulders also indicate that he does not need physical strength to assert his position in society. Some see hints of a cool, calculating sophistication in his face. It is possible that the French version of his name, Hernoult le fin, is also intended to characterize him – as Hernoult the Refined, the Shrewd.

His forename is sadly missing from the inventory. Around 1434, however, at least two male members of the Arnolfini family were living in Bruges. The more prominent of them, Giovanni di Arrigo Arnolfini, was financial adviser to the Burgundian dukes and the French king, and wed an Italian banker's daughter, Giovanna Cenami, who inherited his estate after his death. This seems to rule out a morganatic marriage. It is possible, however, that his brother Michele made such a marriage, for we only know the first name of his wife. Perhaps he went against convention and married not a wealthy young woman from his home town, but a local Flemish girl. No document bothers to record her surname – evidently it was not worth mentioning.

The two Arnolfinis in Bruges dealt not just in goods, but also in money. In those days, Italians virtually had the monopoly on banking across the whole of Europe. Italy was the leading economic power and developed the techniques of banking, bills of exchange, letters of credit and even double-entry bookkeeping. Italian banks opened branches in all the major centres of trade. In Bruges, their representatives met daily with the city's merchants in the house of a Mr van der Burse. He would give his name to capitalism's most important institution: the bourse, or as we more familiarly know it, the stock exchange.

The customers of the Italian banks included not just businessmen, but also monarchs. The relationship between the bankers from Lucca, the city from which the Arnolfini brothers came, and the dukes of Burgundy was particularly close. One of the former had put up the enormous ransom needed to buy the freedom of a Burgundian heir imprisoned in the Orient. Lending money to rulers implied great honour, but also increased risk – they didn't always pay it back. Enforcement was out of the question. Every political defeat meant losses for the banks. Thus the death in battle in 1477 of the last Duke of Burgundy, Charles the Bold, also meant fatal losses for the Bruges branch of the Medici bank – the bank that had allowed itself to own a palace there. In the long term, the bank's ruin in Flanders probably also contributed to the fall of the Medici in Florence.

The secret language of everyday objects

Hanging above the couple's heads is an ornate chandelier of a kind manufactured in Flanders by art metalsmiths of the day. We know from records from the Bruges branch of the Medici bank that a similar chandelier was shipped in pieces to Italy.

A solitary candle burns in the chandelier. There is no obvious practical reason why just one flame should be lit; symbolically, however, it ties in with a popular medieval tradition, whereby a large burning candle was carried at the head of wedding processions or handed ceremonially by the bridegroom to the bride. The flame signified the all-seeing Christ, who is witness to the marriage vows. Earthly witnesses to the ceremony were thus not really required.

Visible beneath the right arm of the chandelier is a wooden figure forming part of the tall back of a chair. It represents St Margaret, the patroness of pregnant women, subduing the dragon. The chair stands directly beside the marriage bed. Like the candle and the carved chair decoration, most of the other objects in this room also have a hidden meaning. At the same time as giving us one of the earliest realistic portrayals of a middle-class interior, van Eyck also gives us symbols. For him, as for his contemporaries, objects carried a message. They spoke. Sadly, it is no longer always possible for us to decipher this secret language of objects.

A little dog, like the one between the bride and groom, for example, was a symbol of prosperity, but also of faithfulness. On tombstones of the day, a lion is frequently found at the feet of the husband, symbolizing strength and courage, and a dog at the feet of the wife. Fidelity in marriage was clearly only expected from the woman.

Several of the seemingly random objects in the room speak of the purity of the bride – the spotless mirror, for example, and the translucent beads of the rosary hanging beside it. These symbols are familiar from paintings of the Virgin and altarpieces. Indeed, it was in the churches of the Middle Ages that this type of imagery arose: a congregation which couldn't read needed "talking" images which it could contemplate and learn from.

Van Eyck himself painted a number of famous altarpieces, but he lived in a century in which devotional subjects began to be overtaken by secular images. *The Arnolfini Marriage* testifies to this process of transition: it uses the pictorial language of religious art to portray a domestic interior and a scene which, although it incorporates the presence of Christ, records not saints or martyrs but a banker and his wife.

Also to be understood symbolically are the slippers and clogs. Taken literally, they might indicate unseemly haste or an untidiness inappropriate for such a solemn ceremony. For van Eyck's contemporaries, however, they contained a reference to the Old Testament: "Do not come any closer. Take off your sandals, for you are standing on holy ground." Thus God spoke to Moses (Ex. 3:5). When a bride and groom administered the sacrament to each other, then even a simple wooden floor became "holy ground".

Van Eyck's painting illustrates the transition not just from sacred to secular art, but also from aristocratic to bourgeois subject matter. Portraits of the nobility had existed for a number of decades, some of them executed by van Eyck himself in his capacity as court painter. Philip the Good of Burgundy made him a chamberlain and occasionally also his envoy in confidential affairs. But Philip also allowed him to work for the middle classes, because he knew that his own power rested on their industriousness, their contribution to the economy and also their willingness to take financial risks.

Of particular significance in this painting is the signature of the artist. It is placed not modestly in the bottom right-hand corner, as was otherwise the convention, but prominently on the rear wall between the mirror and the chandelier. Even its formulation is unusual: instead of "Johann de Eyck fecit" (Jan van Eyck did this), it says "fuit hic" (was here). This inscription transforms the panel into a document. The artist signs not as the painter of the picture, but as a witness to the marriage. Perhaps the man who can be seen in the convex mirror, entering the room wearing a turban and a light blue gown, is in fact the artist himself.

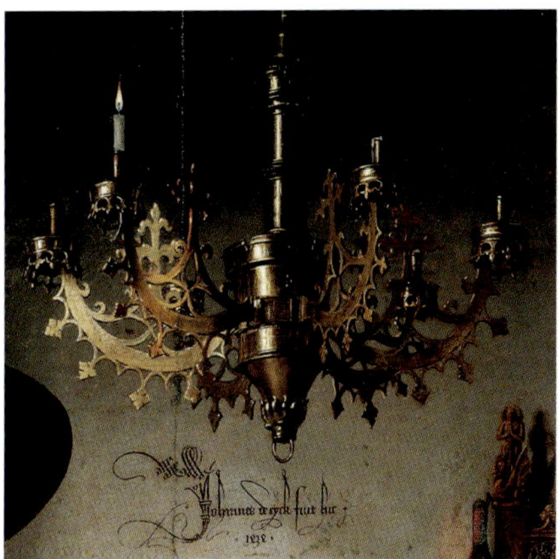

Paolo Uccello (1379–1475)

Monument to a military leader

The Battle of San Romano, c. 1435
182 x 319 cm, London, The National Gallery

The battle of San Romano was portrayed by Paolo Uccello in a cycle of three panels. Five centuries ago, all three hung together in the Medici Palace in Florence, in the large ground-floor room known as the Sala di Lorenzo. This we know from an inventory of 1492. Today, the panel discussed here hangs in the National Gallery in London, with the second in the Uffizi in Florence and the third in the Louvre in Paris.

We do not know the exact year in which Uccello executed his cycle of paintings, but we do know the date of the battle: 1 June 1432. San Romano is located halfway between Florence and Pisa. The battle itself represented a minor defeat by the Florentines of the Sienese and, were it not for Uccello, would have long been forgotten; it was one of the countless skirmishes which characterized the political situation in 15th-century Italy.

Italy differed from most of the rest of Europe at that time in lacking a central ruling power. Its nominal head, the Emperor, came only on brief visits from Germany; the Pope had no political authority, and no more or less power than any of Italy's other princes and cities. With no one above them to settle their disputes, these latter were constantly at war with one other, frequently switching their allegiances but usually with Milan on one side and Florence on the other.

It was during this period of permanent warfare that Renaissance culture experienced its greatest flowering – a culture which also infuses Uccello's panels. The fact that art and warfare flourished side by side shows that normal life in the cities and courts was largely unaffected by the many conflicts of the day. Nor did the citizens, courtiers or priests do any of the fighting themselves. They let others do that for them. As Niccolò Macchiavelli (1469–1527) would later write: "Italy thus found itself almost entirely in the hands of the Church and a few republics, but since neither priests nor civilians were accustomed to taking up arms, they began to hire armies."

The word for such a hire agreement was *condotta*, and the military commanders with whom they were signed were *condottieri*. These contracts set out what the employer had to pay weekly or monthly, how any spoils were to be divided, and the numbers of cavalry and infantry which the *condottiere* promised to supply. The *condottiere* guaranteed to fight on his employer's behalf as long as the money kept coming. Should the employer run out of funds, the contract immediately became void and the *condottiere* could hire himself and his troops out to another power. The *condottiere* was a professional soldier who feared only one thing: peace. A *condottiere* is once said to have tossed a coin to a beggar, who thereupon thanked him with the words "Peace be with you". Incensed, so the story goes, the *condottiere* turned around, shouted at the beggar and snatched back the money.

Uccello paints his *condottieri* with their troops. There were two reasons why the use of hired armies had become so widespread in Italy. Firstly, the absence of a central ruling dynasty also meant that Italian society lacked the class which was granted land by its lords and which raised armies for them

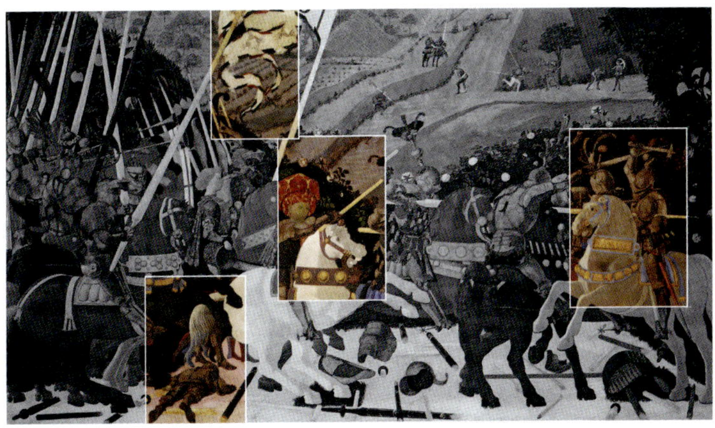

in return. Secondly, the growth of the mining industry in the 15th century had boosted the money supply across Europe, and much of this money found its way into the commercial centres of Italy. The city states were rich and could afford to pay for private armies.

The relationship between the warring republics and their *condottieri* was characterized by money and mistrust. For military power lay in the hands of the *condottieri*, not with the cities themselves. A city never allowed the army it was paying to pass through its own gates – only its commander. Wherever possible, the city fathers tried to keep back the wife or children of the *condottiere* as a sort of deposit. Or they employed several *condottieri* within the same army, in the hope that, in the event of attack, at least one of them would consider it to his advantage to defend the city. This naturally gave rise to issues of hierarchy amongst the various commanders.

Condottieri came from all classes of society. We know that the father of the *condottiere* in the Louvre panel was a peasant. All his sons became mercenaries; some of them rose up in the world, and the most famous of them produced a son who, as a *condottiere* in his own right, became Duke of Milan: Francesco Sforza. He was not the only one to rise up to become a ruling prince. In the words of one contemporary: "In our change-loving Italy, where nothing is set in stone and there is no long established ruling house, stable lads can easily become kings."

The chances of advancement were great, but so were the risks. The *condottiere* Carmagnola, for example, won an important battle for Venice, but subsequently upset his employers with his – to their minds – dwindling military zeal. The Venetians suspected that he was more eager to make pacts with the enemy than to fight for Venice's interests. So they instructed him to report to the Doge. Instead of being granted an audience, however, Carmagnola was imprisoned in the Doge's Palace and then beheaded. This took place on 5 May 1432, just a few weeks before the battle of San Romano. Macchiavelli is matter-of-fact about Carmagnola's fate: "As soon as they realized his commitment was waning, in other words that they were unlikely to profit further from him, but that they could not dismiss him, or they would lose what they had gained, they felt compelled to kill him for their own safety."

Lack of enthusiasm was an accusation levelled at many *condottieri*, but it arose directly out of the nature of their business: soldiers, horses and arms were their capital, and they naturally wanted to keep their assets more or less intact. And since they all felt the same way, they developed a certain professional etiquette: enemy horses were spared, and prisoners not killed but returned on payment of a ransom. Although Uccello portrays a terrifying war machine on two of his three panels, it seems that the battle of San Romano, like most others, was bloodless. There are no reports, at least, of any dead or injured. According to Macchiavelli, "The wars in Italy were begun without fear, fought without danger and finished without losses." They sooner resembled military ceremonies than real battles.

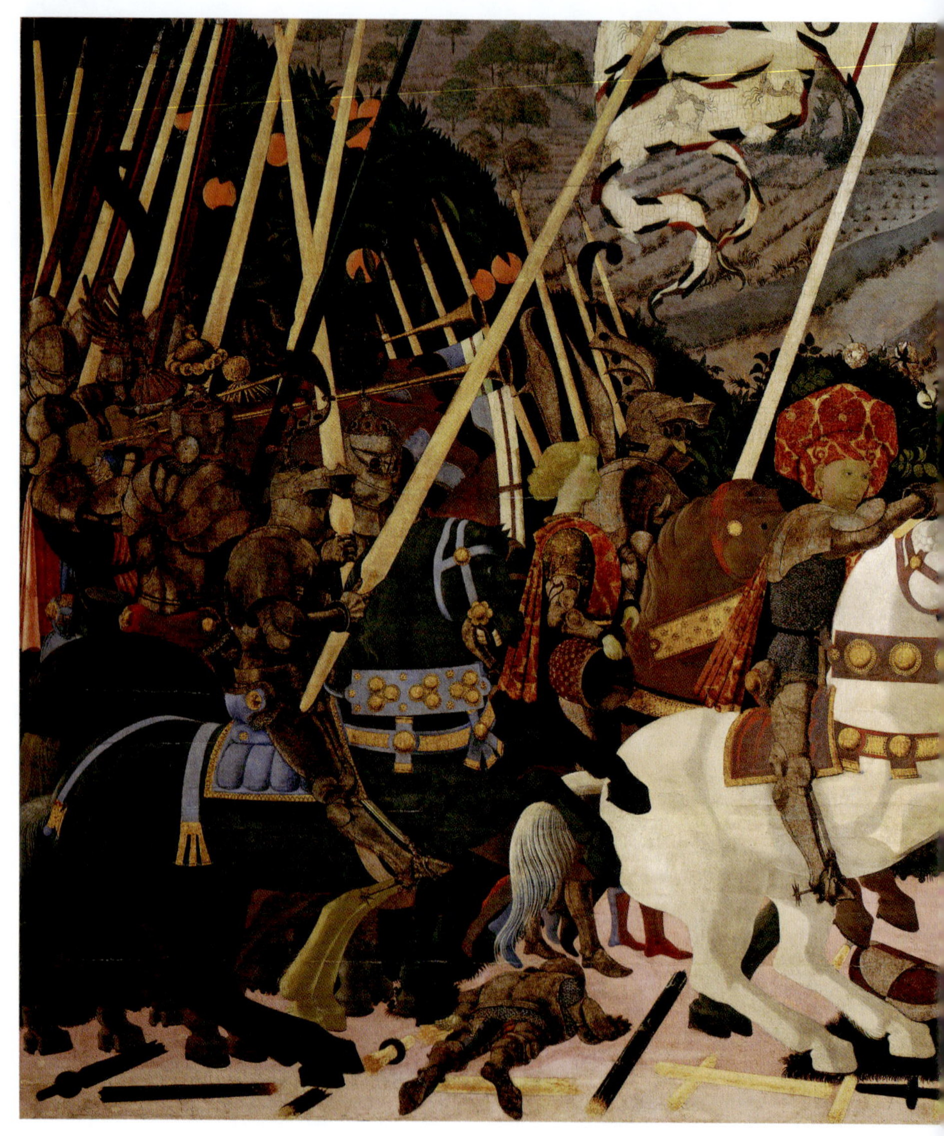

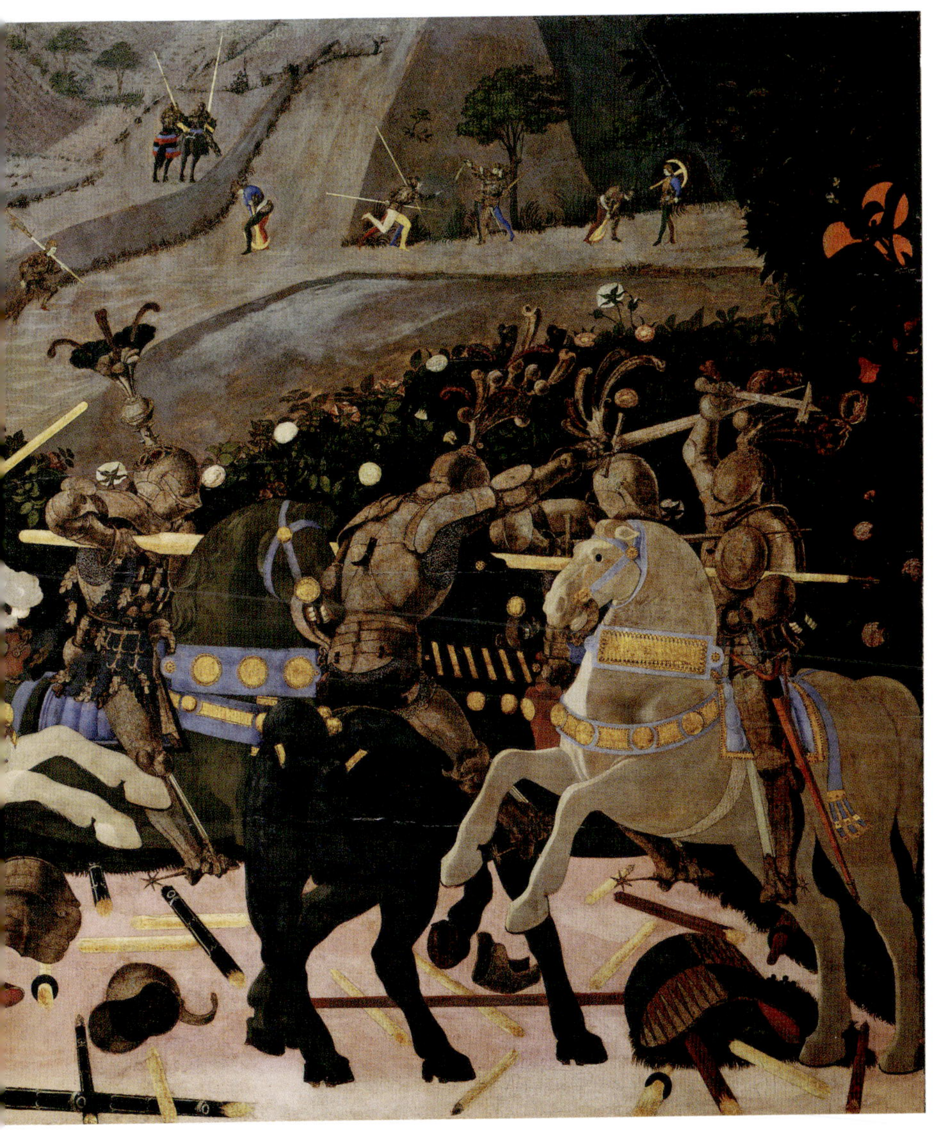

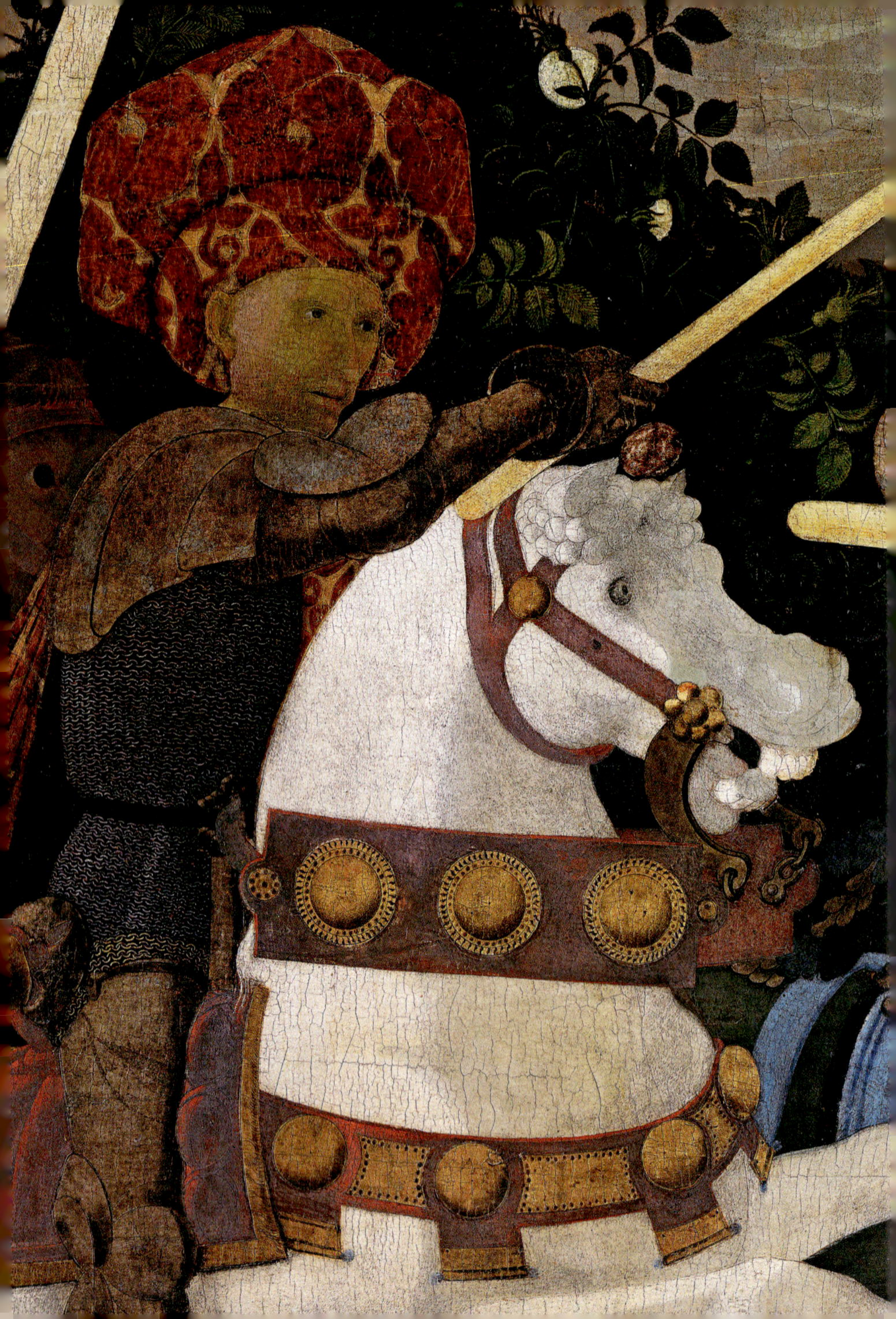

Death and transfiguration

Niccolò Mauruzi da Tolentino is the name of the *condottiere* with the general's staff. Uccello portrays him wearing a magnificent hat of red and gold velvet brocade. Tolentino might have worn such hats at official receptions or military parades, but certainly not on the battlefield. The page riding behind him is carrying his master's helmet, but this is itself too ostentatious for a real battle. Realism, however, was simply not on the agenda. All three paintings were intended to serve as visual propaganda and in particular to celebrate the feats of Niccolò Mauruzi da Tolentino.

The *condottiere's* praises had already been publicly sung a year after the battle of San Romano, when Florence's official speaker, Leonardo Bruni, declared that Tolentino possessed all the virtues of a great military leader: "courage in the midst of danger, perseverance, an overview of all operations and the gift of foresight".

Many Florentines held a quite different view, however. Giovanni Cavalcanti, for example, considered Tolentino a reckless fighter and a poor tactician. He describes how, at San Romano, Tolentino advanced too deep with a small unit of men and involuntarily embroiled them all in a fight. "When the battle went badly, Tolentino despaired and could hardly hold back his tears. He saw no escape until Micheletto [the *condottiere* in the Louvre panel] appeared and rescued us from the serious danger into which Niccolò had led us."

Matteo Palmieri (1406–1475) disagreed: Tolentino advanced so deep not out of recklessness, but in order to lure the enemy into a trap. The arrival of Micheletto had been a precisely planned outflanking manoeuvre, not a piece of good luck. What really happened, who won the battle of San Romano, we do not know; we have only conflicting reports, partisan commentaries.

Such partisanship arose out of the political situation in Florence. Cosimo de' Medici ruled the city via middlemen, but in 1433 was ousted and imprisoned by Rinaldo degli Albizzi. Cosimo had engaged Tolentino's services and lent him financial support, and his opponents now claimed that Cosimo was seeking to set himself up as absolute ruler with Tolentino's help. Rightly or wrongly, Tolentino was branded a member of the Medici camp. When the *condottiere* heard that Cosimo had been taken prisoner, he rode up to the city with his troops and only withdrew when he was told that Cosimo would be killed immediately if Tolentino attempted to force his way in.

Cosimo was spared execution but was exiled to Venice, while Rinaldo's men sent Tolentino north, as far from Florence as possible. On 28 August 1434 he was captured by the Milanese near Bologna. As his employer, Cosimo would normally have bought his release; in this case, however, Rinaldo didn't. With no prospect of fetching a ransom, Tolentino was of no value to the Milanese – he fell off his horse and died. To what extent he was pushed is unknown, but whatever the case, it was an inglorious end.

According to one anecdote from the period, the city fathers were discussing how best to get rid of a *condottiere* who had rendered good service but who had now grown dangerous. The solution: have him killed and then proclaim him one of the city's patron saints. Something similar happened to Niccolò Mauruzi da Tolentino. His inglorious end was followed by his apotheosis. After the Medici party had seized back the reins of power and Cosimo had returned from Venice, he had the *condottiere's* body brought back to Florence and buried in the cathedral, an uncommon honour for someone who was not a native Florentine. The service, which was held on 20 March 1435, was even attended by Pope Eugenius, freshly expelled from Rome.

Tolentino became a martyr for the Medici cause, but it is unlikely that this was the sole reason why Cosimo honoured his memory so publicly. Through the celebrations surrounding Tolentino, Cosimo celebrated himself. He showed himself a man who remained loyal to those who fought on his side, and reminded the world that the (supposedly) magnificent victory at San Romano was won for Florence under his rule. More propaganda, in other words. The fact that he commissioned no fewer than three paintings of the battle can probably be explained in the same way. Paintings, like commemorations of the dead, served to glorify the house of Medici. In 1456 Cosimo commissioned Andrea del Castagno to paint a fresco of Tolentino mounted on his horse in Florence cathedral. To be immortalized on horseback in a public place was evidently the wish of many *condottieri*, and in his eulogy Leonardo Bruni made discreet reference to the fact that the Ancient Romans also honoured their heroes with equestrian statues. This tradition had been forgotten in the Middle Ages but was

revived around 1450, when Donatello executed
the first equestrian statue of the Renaissance. It
was, moreover, dedicated to a *condottiere*, Erasmo
da Narni, known as Gattamelata, and stands in
Padua. Venice also erected an equestrian statue of
its *condottiere* Colleoni, although not – as the latter
had wished – on St Mark's Square. The Florentines,
economically minded as ever, held back; their
condottieri were commemorated not in bronze,
but in paint.

Flags as a means of orientation

Like most flags in the Middle Ages, Tolentino's
pennant is not rectangular, but ends in two long
tongues. The emblem of the mercenary leader is a
ring of rope with knots. He may have chosen this
himself, or it may have been awarded to him. Coats
of arms in those days could be made up of anything
and were constantly changing.

The *condottiere* Muzi Attendolo Sforza, for example, chose a quince as his emblem. He was then
granted permission to adopt the lion from the arms
of the prince employing him. He combined the two
by placing his quince on the paw of a lion, and later
added a dragon.

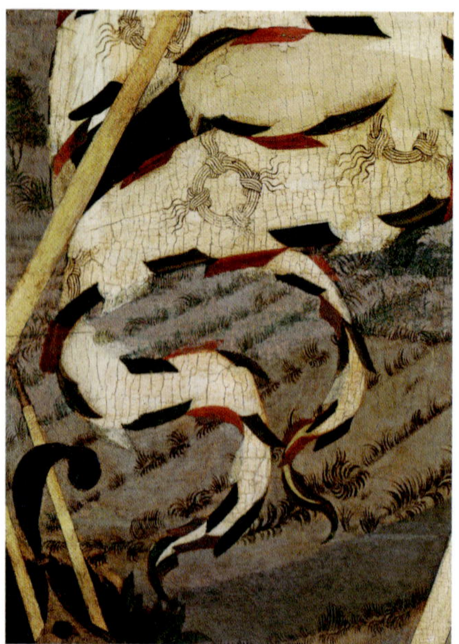

The practice of adopting a visual emblem had
established itself during the Crusades, when knights
from different countries and speaking different
languages had to fight in the same army. Flags, like
coats of arms, became particularly important following the introduction of visors. Since knights could
no longer be recognized by their faces, they needed
other forms of identification. *Condottieri* often omitted coats of arms from their shields, however, so as
not to attract their enemies' attention unnecessarily.
But flags showed friend and foe alike where everyone was. They acted, as one contemporary described
it, "like a torch in a room that lights everything up.
If, by some misfortune, they should go out, everyone
is left floundering in the dark and will be defeated."

The cavalry decide the battle

Tolentino is said to have had 2,000 cavalry and
1,500 infantry under his command, but only the
cavalry really counted. In attacks, the foot soldiers –
armed with pikes and crossbows – advanced
first. They cleared any obstacles for the horses,
shot their arrows from as close to as possible, and
then let themselves be overtaken by the cavalry.
After this they withdrew, usually to the side, to har-
rass the enemy from there. A few individuals stayed
with the riders in order to help them if they were
unseated. They were purely auxiliaries.

The *condottieri* skirmishes of the 15th century
were always decided by the cavalry. With their heavy
horses, they trotted towards each other at moderate
speed. The blow of a lance was not normally fatal,
but could lift a rider out of his saddle. Weighted
down by some 20 to 30 kg of armour, he was unable
to get back onto his feet unaided and was thus temporarily out of the fight.

After their lances, riders used maces or swords.
A sword could only wound or kill, however, if it
found a chink in the opponent's armour. As Uccello
illustrates, swords were forged with sharp tips so
as to better penetrate such chinks. A particularly
vulnerable part of the body was the armpit, and the
rider with the mace in Uccello's panel protects it
with a so-called "floating disk".

The discovery of perspective

The unhorsed riders and numerous pieces of broken
lance are precisely positioned along lines which
converge in the head of Tolentino's white mount
at the centre of the panel. But although the effect

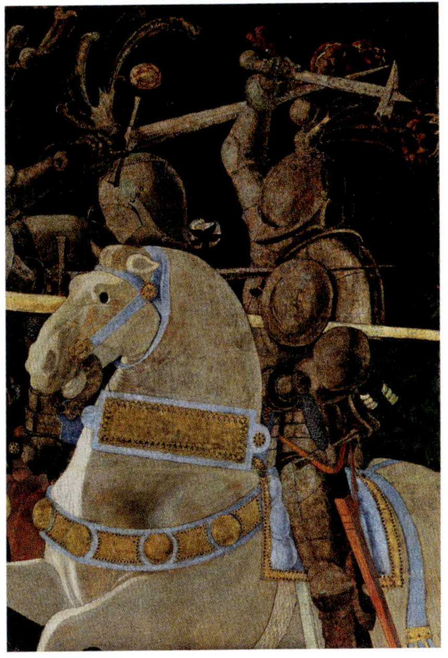

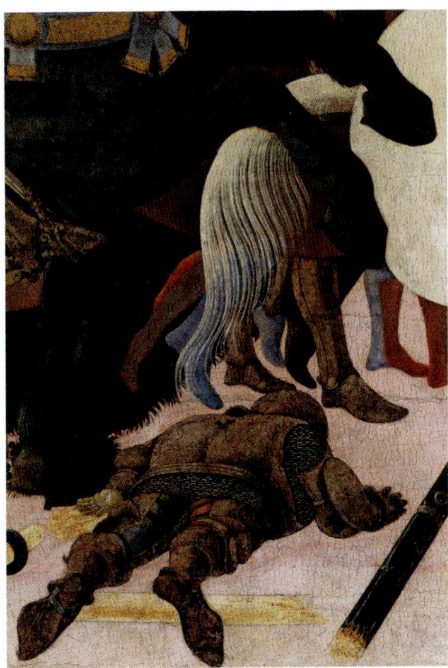

is almost academic, as if taken straight out of a textbook, Uccello was in fact here deploying something entirely new. He was one of the first artists to attempt the mathematical representation of space in painting. "Oh, what a lovely thing this perspective is!" he is said to have declared.

The perspective composition extends only as far as the hedge, however. The landscape behind fails to take up the receding lines of the foreground composition and remains spatially ill defined. It is impossible to tell just how far apart the fields, the trees and the soldiers drawing their crossbows are supposed to be. The composition thus falls into two parts. Perhaps Uccello was not yet capable of continuing into the background the perspective system which he achieves in the foreground. Perhaps he simply wasn't as interested in what was happening on the far side of the hedge. There are reasons why this might be so – and they arise out of 15th-century military tactics. Battles were decided by the cavalry, and the riders needed level terrain on which to attack. They couldn't fight uphill, nor could they jump obstacles. They needed firm ground to mount their charge. In front, therefore, we have the carefully

chosen – and mathematically idealized – battleground, and behind it the surrounding, militarily less important landscape.

The calculation of distances was important not just in art, but also in the burgeoning science of artillery. Gunners had to be able to use a plumb and square and, like painters, have a firm grasp of the basics of geometry. In 1453 Mohammed II destroyed the walls of Constantinople with his cannon; his biggest gun fired cannonballs almost a metre in diameter a distance of 1,600 metres. The advent of artillery signalled the end of the arms wielded by Uccello's *condottieri* – it arrived in the same century as perspective in painting.

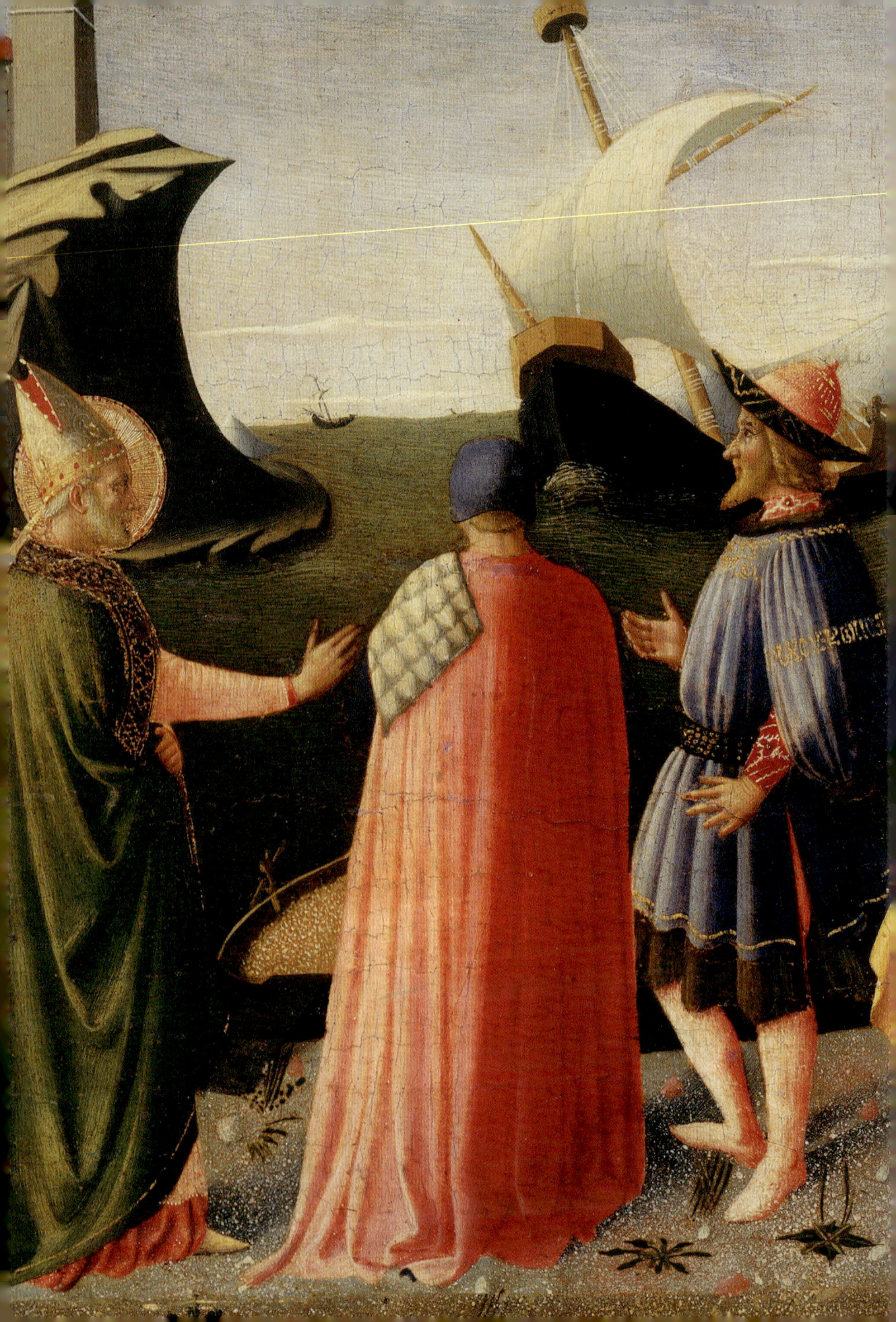

Fra Angelico (*c*. 1400–1455) (real name Guido di Pietro)

A saint with a practical turn of mind

St Nicholas of Bari, 1437
34 x 60 cm, Rome, Pinacoteca vaticana

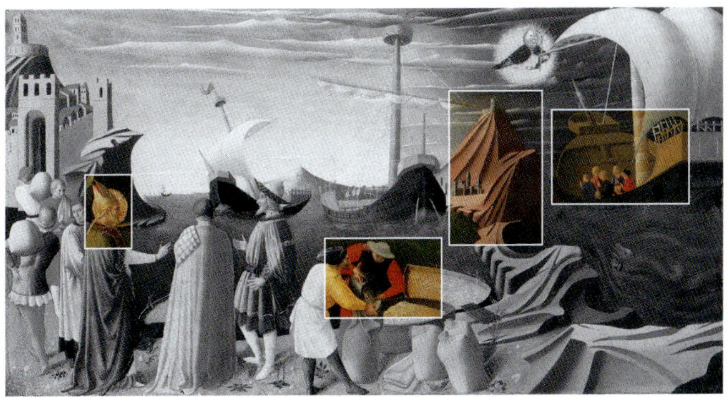

The life of St Nicholas, the popular patron saint of merchants and sailors, is surrounded by a wealth of legends. In Early Renaissance Florence, a monk by the name of Fra Angelico – Brother Angelic – portrayed a number of his miracles in paintings which "seem to have been made in heaven rather than in this world".

Two miracles associated with St Nicholas are depicted in this panel. The saint accordingly appears twice: in the Heavens, top right, he is helping ship-wrecked mariners in distress, while bottom left he is thanking a captain who has given him part of his consignment of grain. According to legend, St Nicholas miraculously caused the grain to multi-ply and thereby saved the inhabitants of the city of Myra from starvation.

The panel was originally flanked by two works identical to it in size and also depicting scenes from the life of St Nicholas. They each measured 34 by 60 centimetres and made up the front of a predella, a long, narrow plinth beneath an altarpiece. The three main panels above were each over 1 metre tall and showed the Madonna and Child with four saints in traditional, statuesque poses against a gold background. While these large paintings provided the centrepiece for worship, the St Nicholas scenes served as edifying entertainment in story form. In the 19th century the altar was broken up; two panels, including the one shown here, are today housed in the Vatican Museum in Rome, while the remaining parts are located in Perugia.

The altar was commissioned in 1437 for the Dominican Chapel of St Nicholas in Perugia. It was executed in Fiesole by a painter monk named Guido di Pietro (*c*. 1400–1455). He initially took the name Fra Giovanni upon entering the Dominican order, but later became known as Fra Angelico – "Brother Angelic". He painted the altar at a time of political as well as artistic upheaval: the mercantile magnate Cosimo de' Medici, already the dominant economic force in Florence, had just secured himself political power in the city republic. And just a year earlier, in 1436, the city's new cathedral had been consecrated; with its mighty cupola, it stood as the soaring sym-bol of a new movement – the Renaissance.

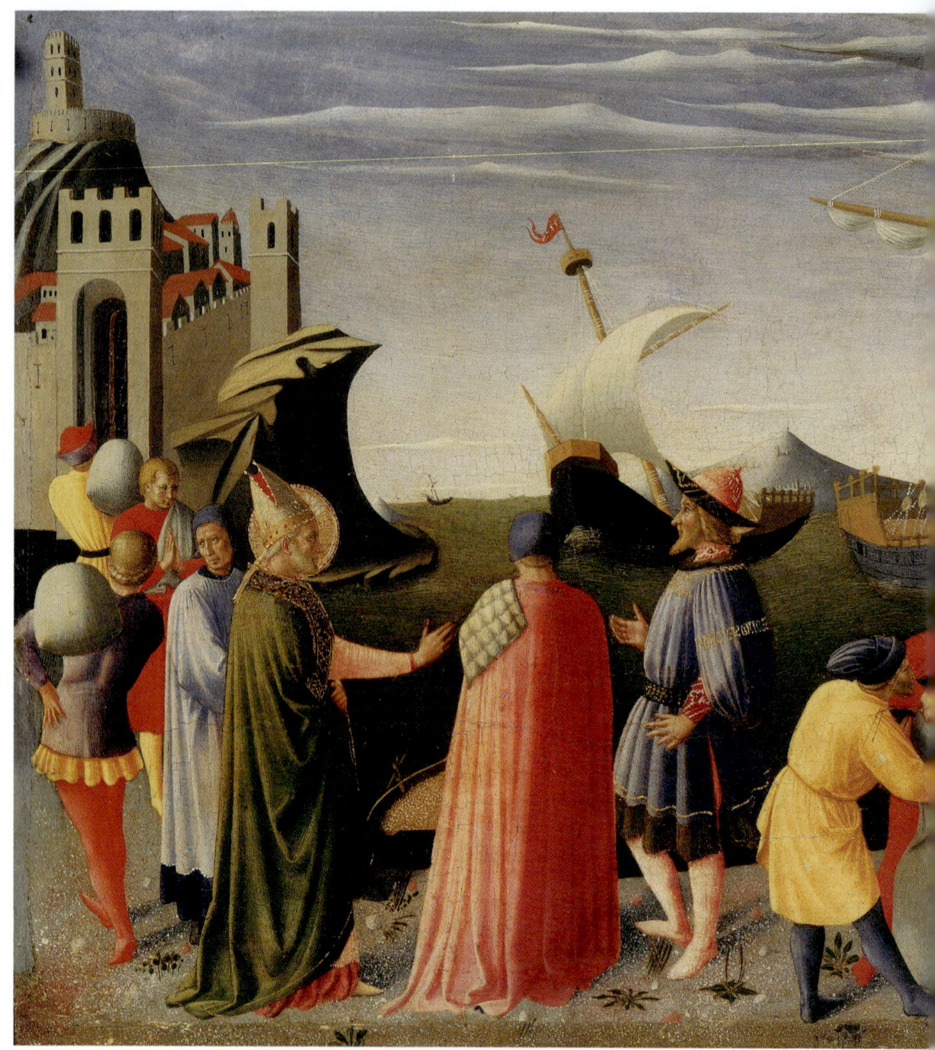

Successor to the ancient gods

At the time when Fra Angelico painted his altar, St Nicholas ranked amongst the most popular of the non-biblical saints. More than a dozen pious and miraculous acts were ascribed to him in the *Golden Legend*, the famous collection of readings on the saints compiled in the 13th century by Jacobus de Voragine. Over 2,000 monuments to his memory, dating from the years before 1500, have been recorded in Germany, the Netherlands and France alone.

Yet despite this, Nicholas was never officially beatified, and he probably never even existed. It is more likely that a number of different miracles were attributed to one name, which subsequently came to

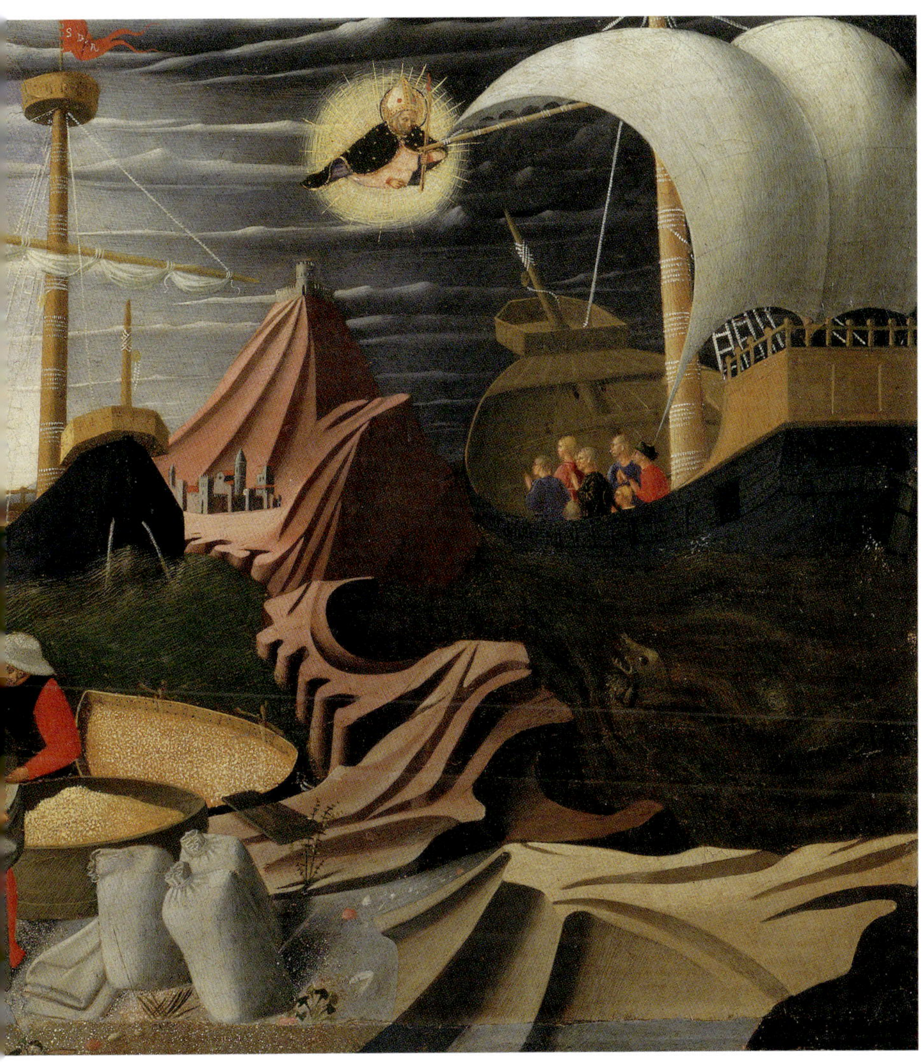

be associated with the real-life figure of Bishop Nicholas of Myra. The Golden Legend records that the bishop is supposed to have died in AD 343, on 6 December – St Nicholas' day.

The 6th of December was an important date even before the spread of Christianity. It is around this time that winter storms start to hit the Mediterranean, making seafaring more dangerous and the help of supernatural or submarine powers all the more important. The role formerly played by Poseidon and Neptune, the gods to whom the peoples of antiquity had addressed their prayers, was now assumed by St Nicholas, who become the patron saint of mariners.

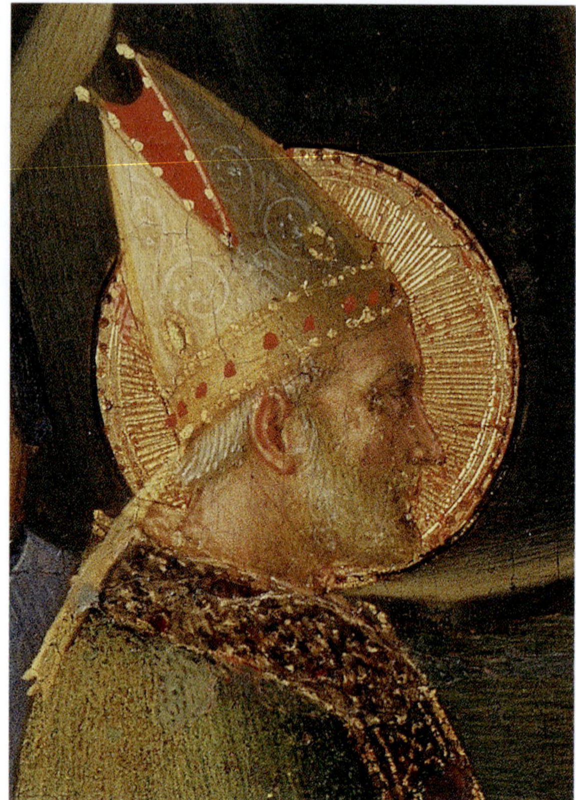

them "with the sails and ropes and other rigging of the ship, and the storm died down immediately". Fra Angelico sets a more specific scene: here, the ship has been driven against a rocky coastline in high seas and a sea-monster has reared its head out of the water. The miracle which St Nicholas is performing is to make the wind blow off the shore and cause the sails to billow towards the stern. In practical terms, this latter is impossible, since the yard, from which the sail is suspended, is attached to the front of the mast and cannot twist round to face the back. But the saint touches the yard with his bishop's staff, and the impossible happens.

Nicholas was initially popular in the Byzantine Empire. With the arrival of Islam, Italian ships abducted the saint's remains from Myra and took them to the port of Bari, where they remained until 1087. From there his fame was spread by mariners as far as northern Europe; he became the patron saint of the Hanseatic League and of what would later become New York. He is the only saint to have survived the Reformation in Protestant areas. Only Catholics have difficulties with him today, since he was never officially beatified. His halo is not legitimate.

There was a significance, too, in the fact that Nicholas came from Myra, located on the mountainous shores of the southern coast of modern day Turkey. From Myra, ships sailed for Alexandria. Instead of taking a coastal route, as was usual in those days, they steered directly south, with no landmarks from which to take their bearings. It seems understandable that sailors and captains setting off on such a perilous journey – a "voyage into the abyss", as it was called – should imagine their port of departure as the home of their patron saint.

The story of St Nicholas saving the seamen is one of the oldest of all the acts associated with his name, although in the *Golden Legend*, at least, we are given little information about the circumstances. The narrator is concerned only with telling us that the sailors prayed to St Nicholas, that he appeared, and assisted

Nicholas asked each ship for 100 measures of grain

According to the legend of St Nicholas and the famine, there were ships laden with wheat lying at harbour in Myra, preparing for their winter voyage. Nicholas "begged the ship's people to come to the aid of those who were starving, if only by allowing them 100 measures of wheat from each ship." The sailors replied: "Father, we dare not, because our cargo was measured at Alexandria and we must deliver it whole and entire to the emperor's granaries." Then Nicholas said: "Do what I tell you, and I promise you in God's power that the imperial customsmen will not find your cargo short." And so it was. Nicholas also multiplied the wheat thus donated to Myra, so that "not only did it suffice to feed the whole region for two whole years, but supplied enough for the sowing." It is a historical fact that grain consignments passed through Myra on their way from Alexandria to Constantinople. For many years grain served as a form of tax and as an important food staple for the imperial capital. Fra Angelico was not thinking of Constantinople, however, but of the capital of the Western Empire and his own Church. Thus one of the ship's pennants bears the letters "SPQR", the abbreviation for *Senatus Populusque Romanus* – the Senate and the People of Rome.

The object being used to pour the grain into the sacks is a measuring scoop, one of the most important pieces of equipment in the corn trade. Nicholas asks for 100 measures per ship, and the narrator emphasizes that the wheat has been measured out in Alexandria and will be measured again upon its arrival in Constantinople. A great deal of attention was paid to measuring, because different regions used different dry measures – something often exploited to make a profit.

The situation which prompted Nicholas' miracle was characteristic of the period from which it dates, and one which explains its enduring popularity – famine. Everyone was familiar with it, and most people suffered it. Wheat was the most important food source, and although the towns and cities practised stockpiling, two poor harvests in succession were sufficient to empty the granaries. There were few ways of importing food quickly, but those who succeeded could make up to 400 per cent profit.

Both bread and grain play a role in the legend of St Nicholas, and it is likely that early on the saint was assigned some of the functions of the pagan fertility gods. One of his attributes were three bread loaves, which were thrown overboard when a storm was brewing in the hope that they would appease the ocean.

In the days when famine was a constant threat, wheat became a symbol of prosperity and Nicholas a prosperity bringing saint. He was not only the patron saint of sailors, but also of merchants, especially corn merchants, shippers, weighers, millers, bakers and brewers. He offered protection against theft and loss of property, and he gave

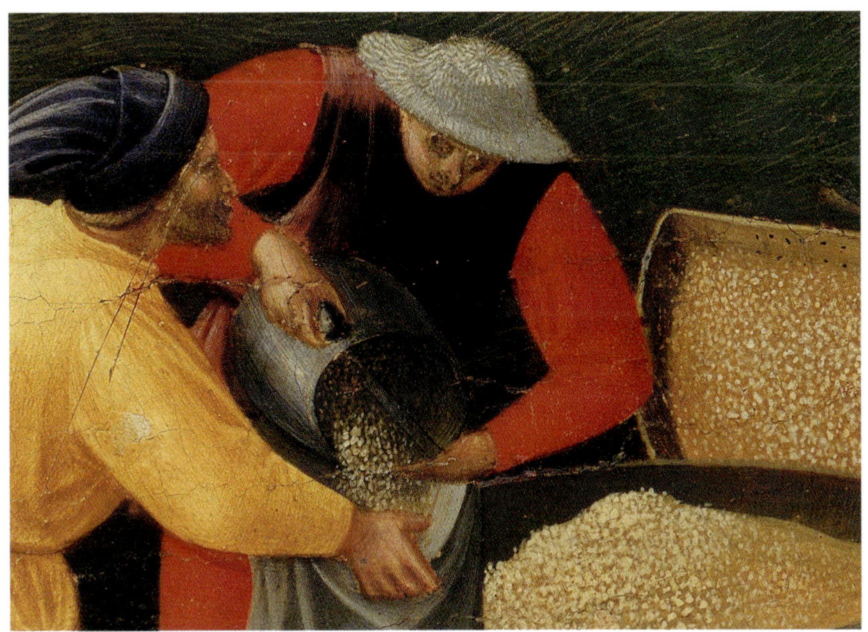

poor girls gold so that they could get married. The medieval Church, with its emphasis upon asceticism and the hereafter, no doubt needed a saint who didn't entirely disapprove of material happiness in order to enhance its popular appeal.

A cheque account for God
The present panel pays homage, not just to a popular saint, but also to seafaring and trade. Ships and goods occupy a large part of the picture. Mariners and merchants are depicted sailing across the seas in a threatening storm, while the captain facing the bishop is as large as the saint himself. Nicholas is thereby portrayed as a celestial fellow merchant.

This homage to trade, and in particular to international trade, reflects its crucial importance. It had undergone continuous expansion over the preceding century – in the shape of the Hanseatic League, for example – and had altered the balance of power within society. Cities of growing commercial and financial strength now rose up alongside the feudal lords of old, and within city republics such as Florence it was the bankers and merchants who held the reins of power. It was thanks to his banks and businesses that Cosimo de' Medici became political ruler of Florence, even if he never flouted his power in public. Like all Florentine merchants, he dressed in a plain red cloak and a simple black cap, like the man kneeling on the right in the group of supplicants.

Christian merchants had a problem, all the same: for a long time, their Church condemned all money trading as usury, as the deadly sin of avarice. This was punishable by excommunication and, after death,

the most excruciating torments of Hell. Even in the 12th century, the Canon Law of Gratian stated that: "The merchant cannot please God, or only with difficulty." In the 13th century Thomas Aquinas attempted to bring the Church's position up to date: "If we consider commerce from the point of view of the common weal, and if we wish to prevent a shortage of vital commodities, then profit, rather than being viewed as the goal, may be considered a due reward for effort."

Aquinas' dispensation was granted only to those goods essential to everyday living, and was thus strictly limited in its scope. Profit-oriented merchants continued to fall under suspicion of avarice. In order to avoid the torments of Hell (and often acting, too, out of a sense of social obligation), they became benefactors. Upon their foundation, Italian trading companies – metaphorically speaking – opened a cheque account especially to fund charitable works, and were not always paying mere lip service when they began their books and contracts with the words: "In the name of Our Lord Jesus Christ and the Blessed Virgin Mary …"

Most of their donations went to the Church or, via religious aid organizations, to the needy. Cosimo de' Medici endowed churches, chapels and monasteries, and for many years gave a home to Pope Eugene IV, who had enemies in Rome. In 1436 the Pope granted him permission to renovate a run-down building in Florence and to donate it to the Dominican monks in Fiesole as a monastery. Those monks included Fra Angelico, who was commissioned to decorate the new monastery. His frescos in San Marco are still one of the city's most important sights today.

From the point of view of eternity
A mountainous ridge separates the locations of the two miracles, but they are reunited by sea and sky, and appear to the viewer to be taking place at the same time. It was common practice in the Middle Ages to portray several events unfolding within one and the same painting. The Church sought to impart a sense of eternity, and *sub specie aeternitatis*

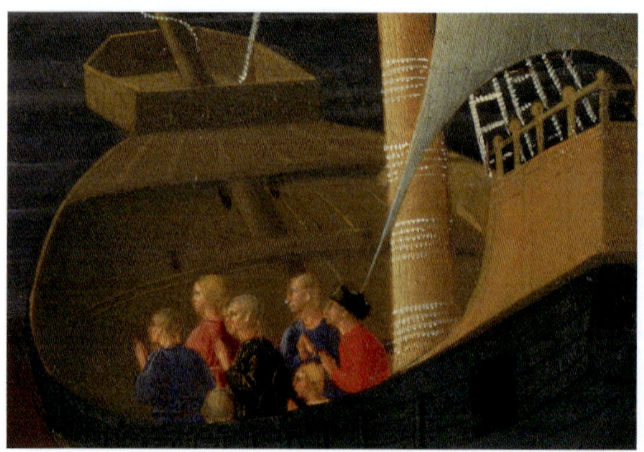

– from the point of view of eternity – differences in time and place were unimportant.

In the 15th century, however, real-life settings and real-life chronology began to command greater attention, also in art. Commissions were no longer awarded solely by the churches, but – with ever increasing frequency – by bankers and merchants. Their professions required them to think in terms of quarter days and trade routes; geography and elapsing time formed the bases upon which they made their calculations. Their sense of the reality of this life was strengthened by the rediscovery of the authors of antiquity. What we call the Renaissance was born.

An artist like Fra Angelico may have worked for the Church and his order, but his painting was financed over many years by Cosimo de' Medici, the most powerful merchant in Florence. Fra Angelico also painted the frescos in the cells in San Marco to which Cosimo withdrew to meditate, in order – or so his enemies said – to do penance for his greed.

The age in which the artist lived also influenced his art. Set against their gold backgrounds, the saints in Fra Angelico's main altarpiece are still entirely indebted to medieval tradition. In his predella panels, by contrast, the pious message is accompanied by a new attempt to invoke earthly reality in the picture and to lend depth to the whole through the use of perspective. In the chain of mountains rising up in the background, Fra Angelico was perhaps aiming to create an impression of three-dimensional space. He applied the laws of perspective only intermittently, however, as can be seen in the bowsprit of the middle ship, which seems to point vertically upwards rather than diagonally forwards, and in the ship on the left, whose front deck is portrayed from a different angle than its stern. And whereas the light – so important in the

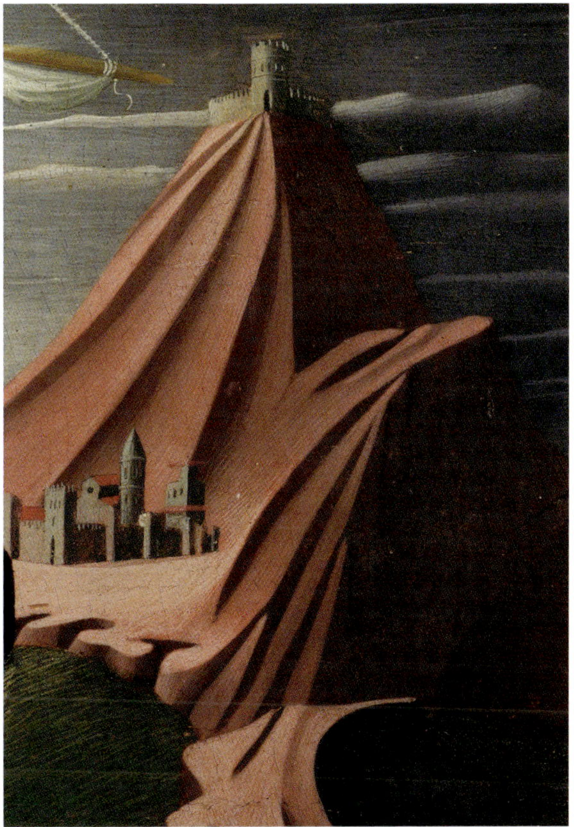

creation of spatial depth – strikes the mountains from the rear left, the figures in the foreground are illuminated from the front left. In yet another contradiction, the figures are observed in great detail, while the mountains and houses are portrayed in a strikingly simplified form.

What is so astonishing, not to say miraculous, about this panel is the fact that these contradictions cause absolutely no upset. It is as if we are looking at a scene from a dream, the portrayal of something supernatural taking place on our earth. Writing of Fra Angelico in the 16th century, the artist biographer Vasari observed that the monks' figures "are so exquisite that they really seem to be in Paradise".

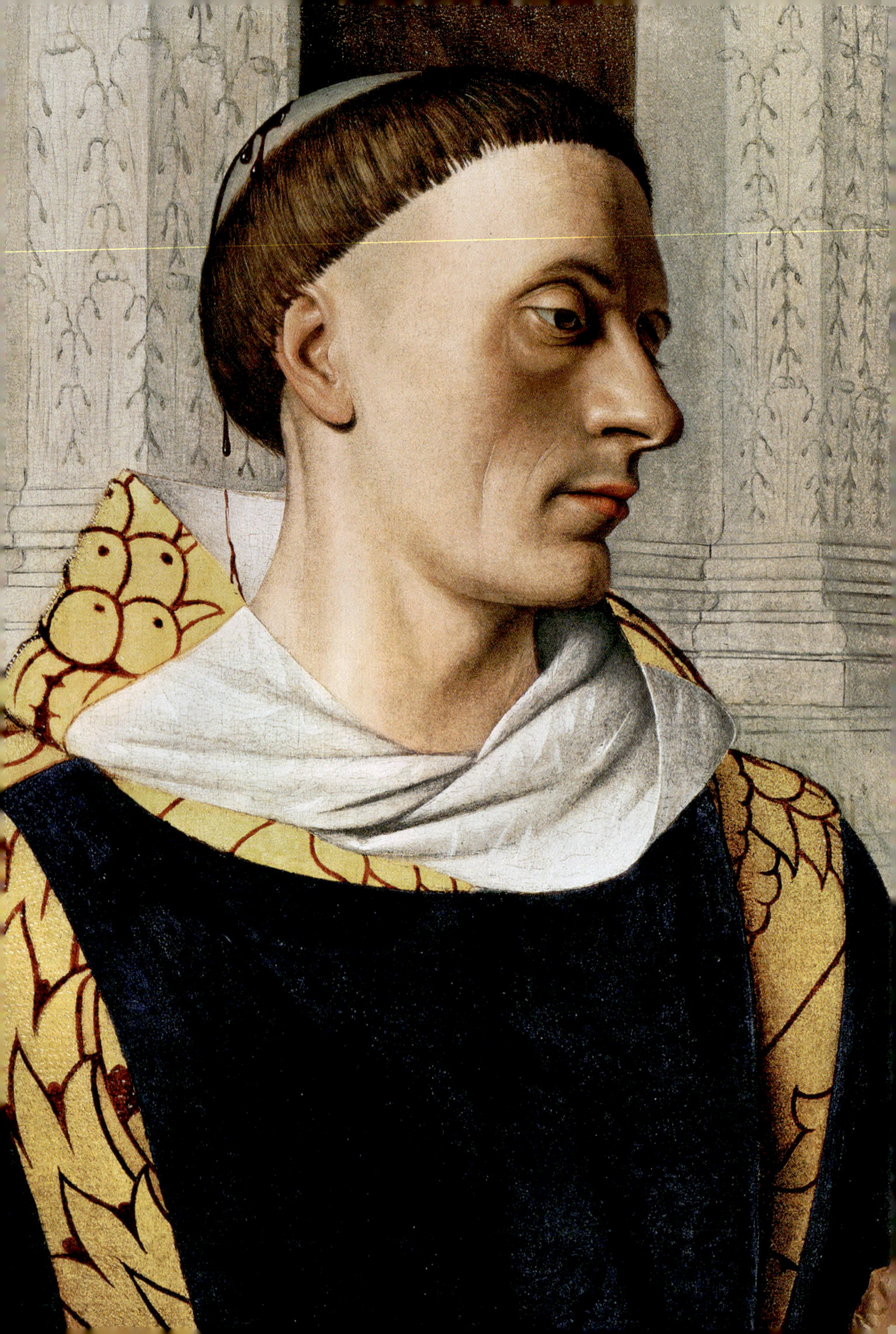

Jean Fouquet (1420–1481)

The King's mistress posing as the Virgin

The Melun Diptych, c. 1456

Left panel: *Étienne Chevalier and St Stephen*
93 x 85 cm, Berlin, Gemäldegalerie, Staatliche Museen zu Berlin
Right panel: *Virgin and Child*
91.8 x 83.3 cm, Antwerp, Koninklijk Museum
voor Schone Kunsten

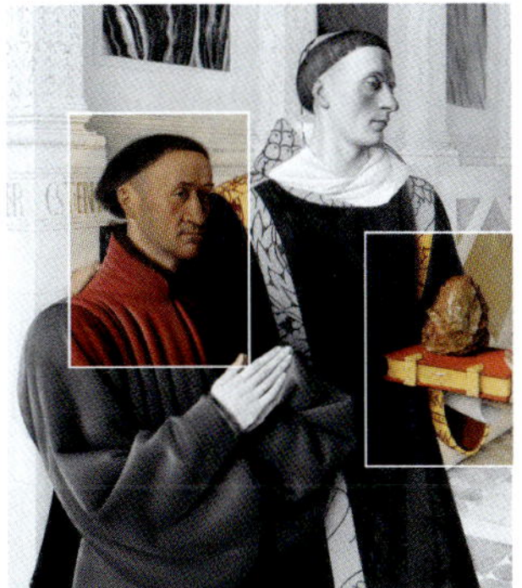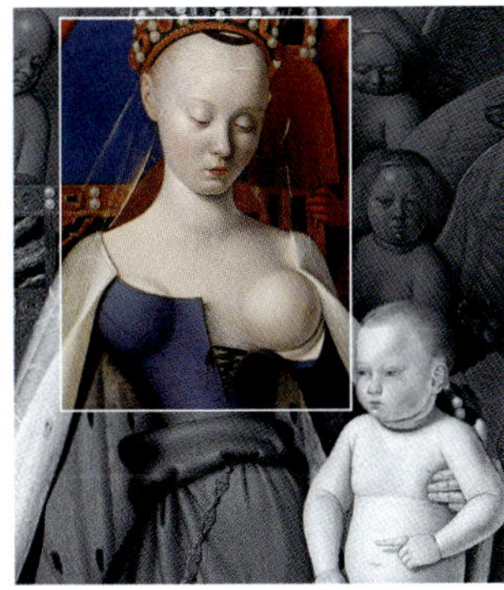

The work is in two parts, but today they appear together only in reproductions. In reality the two parts are in two different cities, the left panel in Berlin, the right in Antwerp.

Art historians had long suspected that they belonged together, but it was left to modern scientific examination of the wood on which they were painted to supply the evidence. Two boards of the Berlin panel and one in the Antwerp panel came from one and the same oak tree. It was felled, according to dendrochronological analysis, about 1446. Following the usual seasoning period of ten to fifteen years, the boards fetched up in the workshop of the French painter Jean Fouquet (1415/22–c. 1481), who painted a two-panel devotional picture, or diptych, on them, in about the year 1456.

The donor was Étienne Chevalier, the royal treasurer, and he is portrayed on the left panel, kneeling at prayer. Beside him stands St Stephen (Etienne in French), identifiable by his attributes: the Gospels, and one of the stones with which he was martyred. St Stephen's role is to intercede for Chevalier with the Virgin Mary, seen on the right panel, in the non terrestrial sphere, on a throne borne up by angels. One of the Virgin's breasts is exposed, and in her lap sits the infant Jesus, pointing a forefinger in the direction of the treasurer by way of indication that his prayer is heard and he may hope for divine clemency.

For centuries the diptych hung above Étienne Chevalier's tomb in the church of Notre Dame in the town of his birth, Melun, south of Paris. There it was intended to preserve the donor's memory "in perpetuity", together with the masses said every morning at six for the repose of his immortal soul.

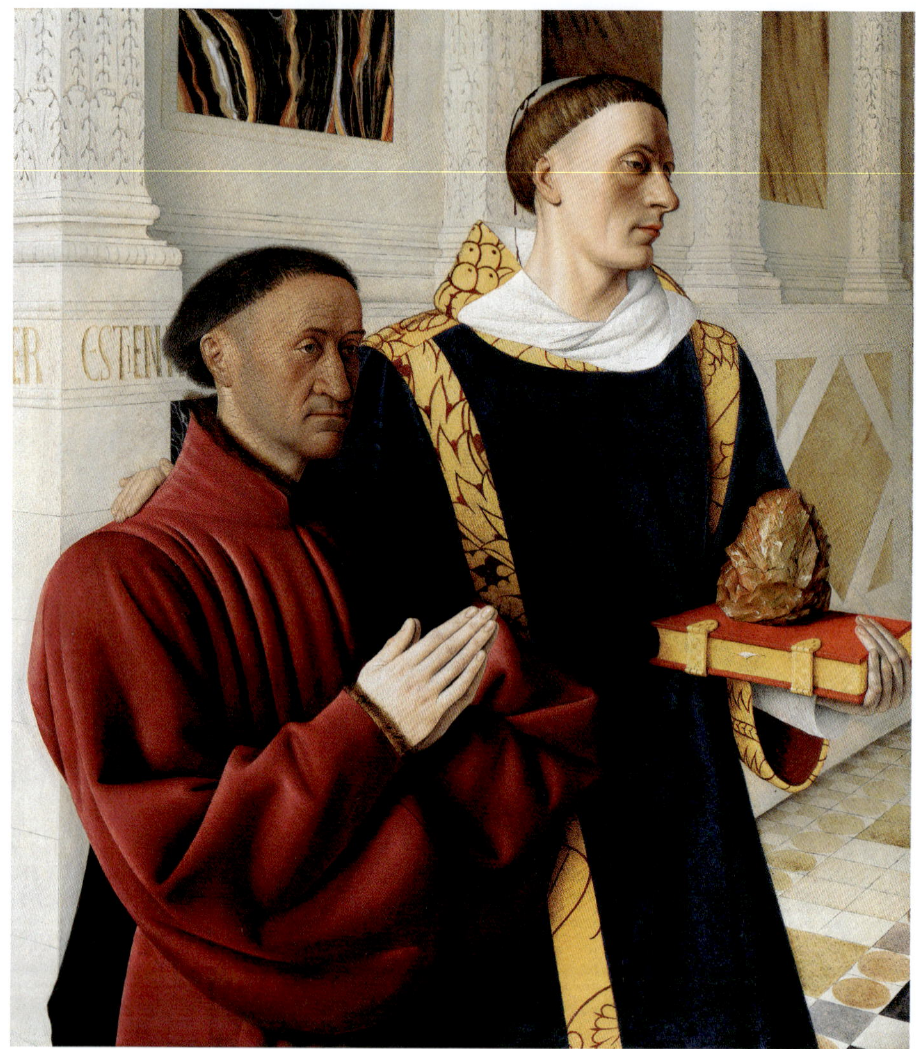

A trustworthy treasurer

The donor's name, "Estienne" (in the old spelling), is inscribed in the marble pillar behind him in gold letters. The treasurer is seen wearing a solemn maroon fur-lined robe – with the padded shoulders then in fashion and stiff pleats – and kneeling in a palatial hallway. Rooms of this kind, with marble walls and floors in the style of the Italian Renaissance, were uncommon in 15th-century Paris, but Chevalier's house in rue de la Verrerie was reputedly magnificent, with as many glass windows as there were days in the year. King Louis XI dined there in 1465, a high honour for an official, and a recognition of his services to France and the monarchy.

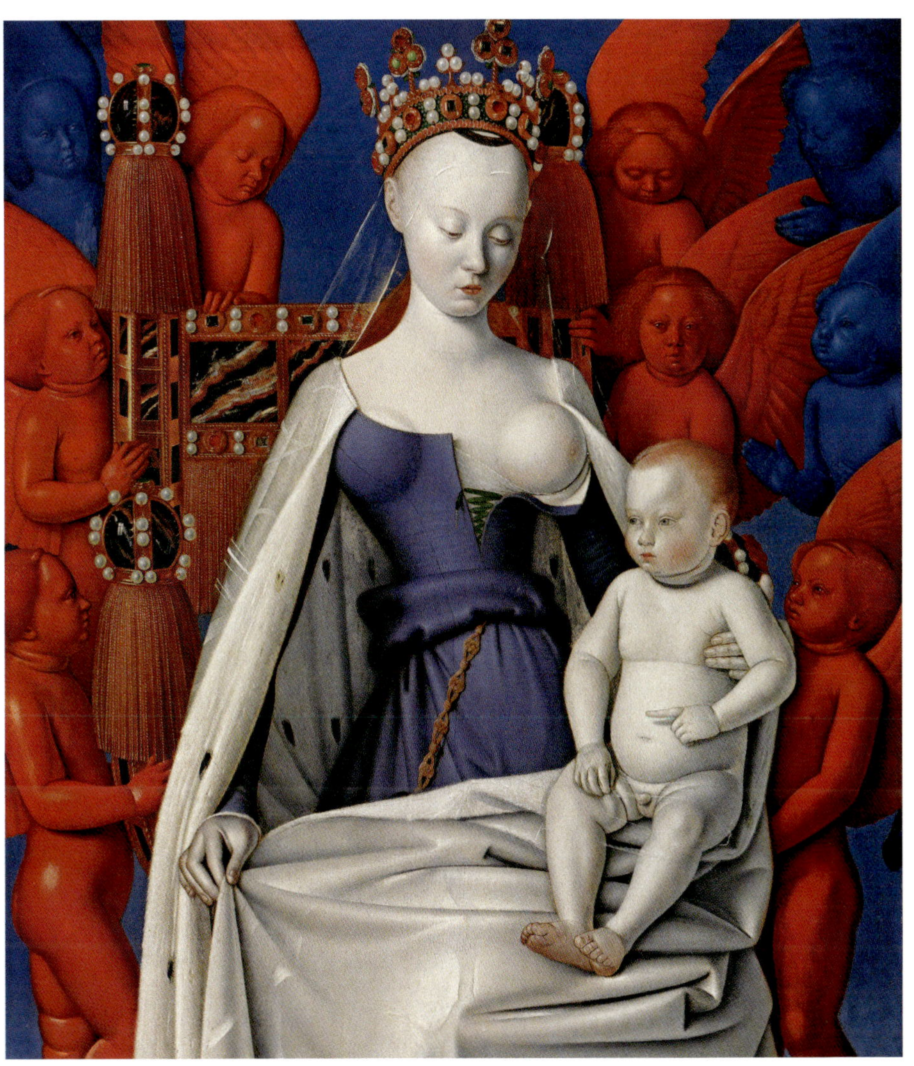

Chevalier's services were chiefly to Louis' father, Charles VII (1403–61). At his court, Chevalier (born around 1400) served as the royal secretary, notary and auditor in succession. Around mid-century he was the treasurer, responsible for the finances of the realm, with a seat in the royal council – that is to say, not merely in the larger, ceremonial council, but in the smaller privy council through which Charles VII conducted the daily affairs of government. The king liked to have non-aristocrats such as Chevalier about him, commoners who owed everything to him. They were the only ones on whom he could rely in the struggle against the nobility, a hotbed of ambition, intrigue and revolt.

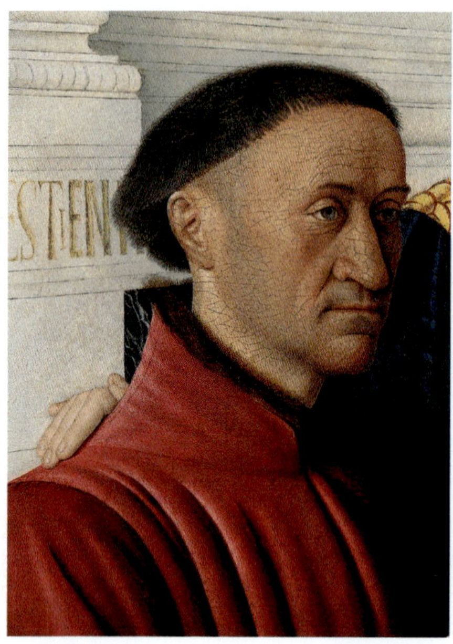

Towards the end of his reign, Charles had indeed managed to subdue the nobles. By concluding peace with his powerful cousin and enemy, the Duke of Burgundy, he had put an end to the civil war. And more: Charles VII has gone down in posterity as a weak king (dramatists from Schiller to Shaw portrayed him as an unfortunate or even ridiculous figure alongside Joan of Arc), yet it was he who brought to a victorious conclusion not only the civil war but also the Hundred Years' War. Little by little his forces drove out the English, who had occupied the larger part of France for almost 50 years. The invaders were obliged to yield province after province, until in 1453 they were finally driven to escape back across the sea. Charles VII (in another portrait by Fouquet) was justly celebrated as "the most victorious king".

The king owed his success to a group of hard-working officials in his service. One of these was Étienne Chevalier. It was he who procured the immense sums necessary to finance protracted military campaigns – and thus victory. Tax revenue came in very slowly indeed (not until 1444 had an assembly of the estates granted the king the right to levy taxes directly) and the royal coffers were forever lacking in ready cash to pay for the war. On one occasion, Chevalier himself made the king a personal loan of 1,100 livres. He had to wait years till the sum was repaid.

Of course a portion of the incoming revenue went to pay the servants of the state, and the treasurer was among those who amassed a fortune; but he appears to have been more cautious than others, for at court, where according to the contemporary chronicler Georges Chastellain "nobody tells the truth", the man with the stern features enjoyed the reputation of being incorruptible and trustworthy. It was no accident that the king's personal physician, the king's mistress, and even King Charles VII himself, appointed Chevalier the executor of their wills.

St Stephen's stone

A patron in heaven as powerful as St Stephen, depicted here in a blue dalmatic with gold braid standing supportively at the treasurer's side, could be of good use to a man in a prominent and vulnerable office at the intrigue-ridden court of Charles VII. The king was fickle in his favours, as two others in his service had discovered.

An enterprising merchant of Bourges, a commoner by the name of Jacques Coeur, had risen to become Master of the Privy Purse. But he became too wealthy. In 1451 Charles had him arrested without warning. Coeur was banished and his fortune confiscated and transferred to the coffers out of which the king paid for his war.

St Joan, too, was left in the lurch by Charles. She had lent assistance to the young heir to the throne when his fortunes were at their nadir, and had wrenched him out of his depressive, passive state. The English invaders, having inflicted a crushing defeat on the French at the battle of Agincourt in 1415, had occupied France and had nothing but scorn for Charles, who now held little more of France than the city of Bourges itself. Charles withdrew to that city, where he remained inactive and resigned to his fate until the warlike maid appeared in 1429. Joan declared that she had been sent by God. She took back the city of Orléans for France, and conducted Charles to Rheims, where he was crowned the rightful king.

Joan it was who restored courage to this despairing man and thus sparked the reconquest of his realm. But subsequently, when Joan fell into the hands of her enemies and was sentenced and burnt as a witch in 1431, the king never lifted a finger to help her.

More than twenty years were to pass before "the most victorious" Charles hesitantly started the process of appeal against that sentence – doubtless to counter the notion that he owed his successes at war to witchcraft. Not until 1456, the year in which Étienne Chevalier's diptych was painted by Fouquet, did a court rehabilitate Joan. She was nevertheless granted no place in official portraiture. A maid who had claimed to hear the voice of God was of necessity suspect in the eyes of the Church. It was not until 1920 that she was canonized.

St Stephen, on the other hand, was a recognized martyr, indeed the first. He was a patron from whom the treasurer might hope for efficacious help. And it was more than the name alone that linked them: the volume bound in red leather which the saint is holding, with its gold blocking and bookmark, was quite possibly from the treasurer's own library. For Chevalier was a collector of illuminated manuscript books, as were the king himself and his uncle, the Duke of Berry.

Chevalier had already ordered an illuminated book of hours from Jean Fouquet in 1448. This was a prayer book for the laity such as the great used at their private devotions, and in all probability it was not finished until about the same time as the diptych, since the work, both for the scribe who wrote the text and for the artist who illuminated the book, was long and arduous. All 47 of the miniatures which Jean Fouquet painted for Etienne Chevalier's magnificent book of hours have survived.

In certain scenes, whether biblical or depicting the lives of the saints, the treasurer can be seen – clad in black at the entombment of Christ, or in portrait style, as in the diptych, praying to the Virgin. In the book of hours too, his name or his imprese appears – a golden doubled 'e', the two letters tied by decorative love knots. These symbols, which evolved from traps for game, were taken (in contrast to wedding rings) to stand for an extramarital liaison.

Love knots of this kind apparently adorned the lost frame of the diptych.

The most beautiful woman in the world

The attractive Virgin poses conundrums. The great Dutch art historian and chronicler of the Middle Ages Johan Huizinga detected "a whiff of decadent godlessness" about her. Fouquet has not depicted her giving suck to the infant Jesus; indeed, her pert bosom is not one that prompts thoughts of breast feeding. Yet there is a theological justification for exposing the breast: just as Christ displays the wounds in his side to God the Father, so too Mary displays her breast, underlining her role as intercessor for humankind, on earth and in purgatory.

It is possible that this madonna bears the features of Katherine, the goodly wife of the donor, who died in 1452 and was buried beside him in Melun. More likely, however, is that this is a portrait of Agnès Sorel, a lady who had advanced Chevalier's career significantly and indeed may have meant even more to him, according to one persistent tradition. This rumour is even supported by an inscription on the reverse of the panel, dated 1775 and attested by notary: "The Holy Virgin, with the features of Agnès Sorel, mistress to King Charles VII of France, deceased 1450." To contemporaries, Agnès Sorel was quite simply "the most beautiful woman in the world". Barely had she appeared at the French court in 1443, aged about twenty, but the king, twice her age, was utterly captivated. We have this from Chastellain, the court chronicler of the Duke of Burgundy, and also from Enea Silvio Piccolomini, later Pope Pius II, who noted in his memoirs:

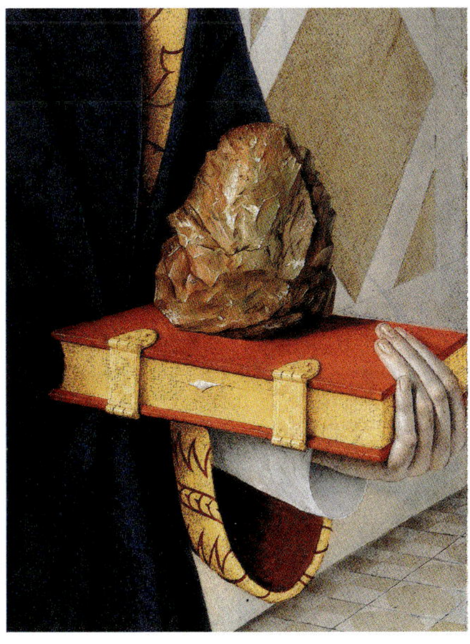

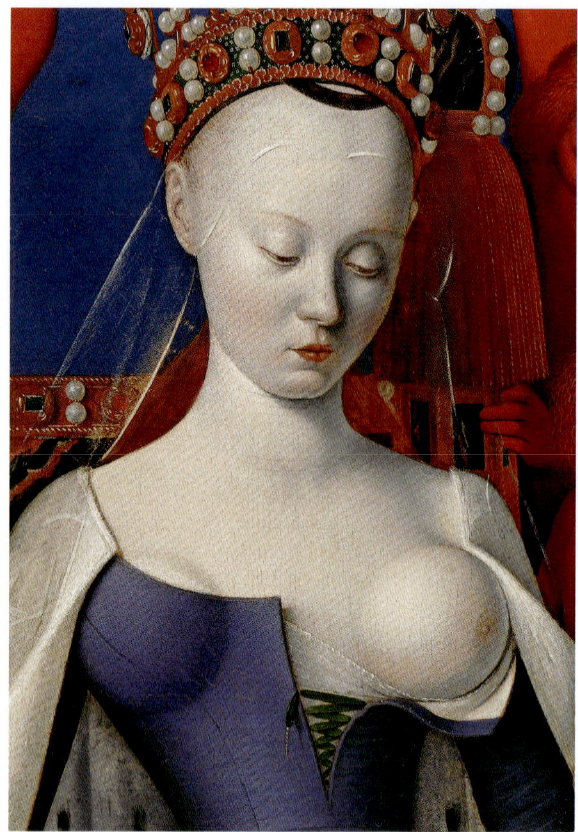

"Whether at table, in bed, or in the council chamber, she must needs be always at his side."

Charles' wife, Queen Marie, was fully occupied with raising her fourteen children. She was a devout woman, and, according to Chastellain, "had a face that would have struck fear even into the English".

The king's mistress, by contrast, was the only woman to appear before the court mounted on a stallion at a tournament, in gleaming silver armour studded with jewels. In church, we are told, she was good at exhibiting "a pretty anguish at her sins"; but while she was about it she held her head high and wore "the most monstrous" lace head dresses and trains, fully a third longer than any other princess had ever worn. She lowered her décolleté so far that a bishop made a complaint to the king about "cleavages that exposed the women's bosoms and nipples to view".

The influence of Agnès Sorel was felt not only in fashion but in politics. Like Joan of Arc fourteen years previously, she had the gift of arousing the king from the lethargy he recurrently subsided into. She inspired him with courage and the will to action, and motivated him to resume the fight against the English enemy after a lengthy period of inactivity.

The services rendered to France by this beautiful woman, who died young in childbirth, were later hymned by no less a personage than King Francis I (1494–1547), in lines of poetry that translate roughly as: "Her love deserves more praise, / since it brought about the revival of France, / than anything a nun may do in a convent / or a hermit in the wilderness."

To memorialize such a woman in a painting, as treasurer Chevalier did, seemed legitimate. At any rate, few would then have considered it blasphemous to portray and transfigure a presumed sinner, after her death, as the Virgin Mary. The monarch, anointed by God himself, was considered holy, and he conferred holiness on all he touched. So it was only right and proper that the left panel of the diptych should be entirely in red, white and blue, since these were the heraldic colours of the king.

A German Romantic identifies the donor

The artist, Jean Fouquet, was also in service with King Charles VII. He had painted his portrait – not very flatteringly, giving him a bulbous nose and pop eyes. Born in Tours between 1415 and 1422, Fouquet worked chiefly for the king, who resided mainly in the Loire Valley, and his courtiers. When Charles died in 1461, a rider bore his death mask from Bourges to Paris, where Fouquet was at the time, so that the artist might overpaint it for the obsequies, in which a royal likeness as true to life as possible played an important part.

Fouquet, like Chevalier the treasurer, was one of the few to remain in service under Charles' successor. In 1475, indeed, Fouquet was appointed court painter. But Louis XI was a power politician, with little time for art, and seems to have ordered mainly book illustrations from his painter.

We know nothing about the youth or training of the artist. Features of Dutch panel painting are apparent in his work: a psychological sensitivity in rendering the ascetic features of Chevalier, and a love of nature and of detail. It is possible that Fouquet had been apprenticed to a miniaturist.

What is certain is that from 1446 to 1448 he was in Italy, probably in the retinue of a legation of French churchmen. Be that as it may, he excited considerable attention with a portrait of Pope Eugenius IV. This painting is lost, but the Florentine Francesco Florio was still declaring in 1477 that the Frenchman "outdid the painters of every other century with his art".

We can assume that in Florence Fouquet enjoyed contact with Fra Angelico, Paolo Uccello and Masolino – and took the opportunity to learn perspective, spatiality, and a sense of the monumental, from these second-generation Renaissance artists. As well as the features of Italian architecture, the three-dimensionality of the protagonists in the Chevalier diptych betrays their influence.

We have another pointer to Fouquet's familiarity with the work of the Italians. Like Lorenzo Ghiberti (1378–1455), who had introduced a relief self-portrait into his bronze doors for the Florence Baptistery, Fouquet too immortalized himself in his own work. In the Louvre in Paris there is an enamel medal inscribed "Johes Fouquet", bearing a portrait which was evidently that of the artist, which was clearly forcibly broken out of the frame of the diptych.

Fouquet was famous in his day, and seen as the founder of a modern French school of painting, but now only a few of his panels have survived: the diptych, the portrait of the king (Paris), Gonella the court jester (Vienna), Chancellor Jouvenel des Ursins (Paris), and the pietà in the church at Nouans. Paradoxically, his fragile miniatures have stood the test of time better, being tucked away in folio volumes in the safe keeping of libraries.

The painter himself was forgotten. In 1775, when the cathedral chapter of Notre Dame in Melun needed to raise money for restoration purposes, the diptych was separated into two portions and sold, despite the express stipulations of the donor. After the French Revolution, the two halves appeared on the market separately. The right panel was bought in Paris by a lord mayor of Antwerp, and since 1840 it has been in the museum in that city.

The left panel was discovered at a dealer's in Basle, Switzerland, by the German poet Clemens Brentano (1 778 – 1842). Like many another Romantic, he was concerned to seek out and save the "countless doomed works of the most sublime art". The panel painting reminded him of the book of hours of Etienne Chevalier, which was in the possession of his brother, Georg Brentano, a Frankfurt banker. Only a short time previously the miniatures had been ascribed to Fouquet, of whom only the name was known. But the poet saw the similarity of the diptych figures to those in the book of hours, and this led in due course to the identification of the treasurer and his painter. Subsequently, in 1896, the painting joined the Berlin collection.

Comparative illustration:
Enamel medallion signed "Johes Fouquet" and Self-portrait, Paris, Musée du Louvre

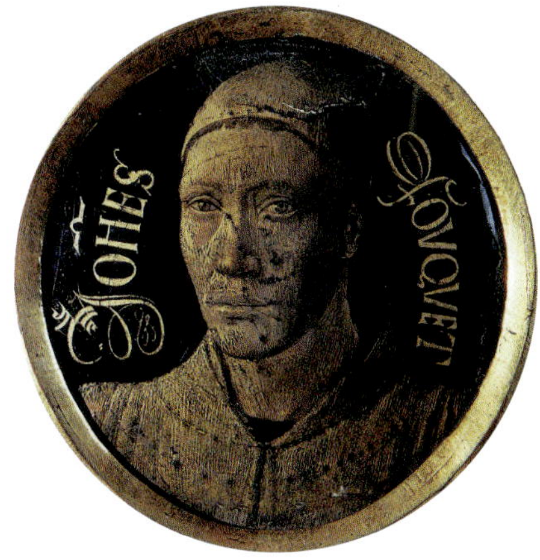

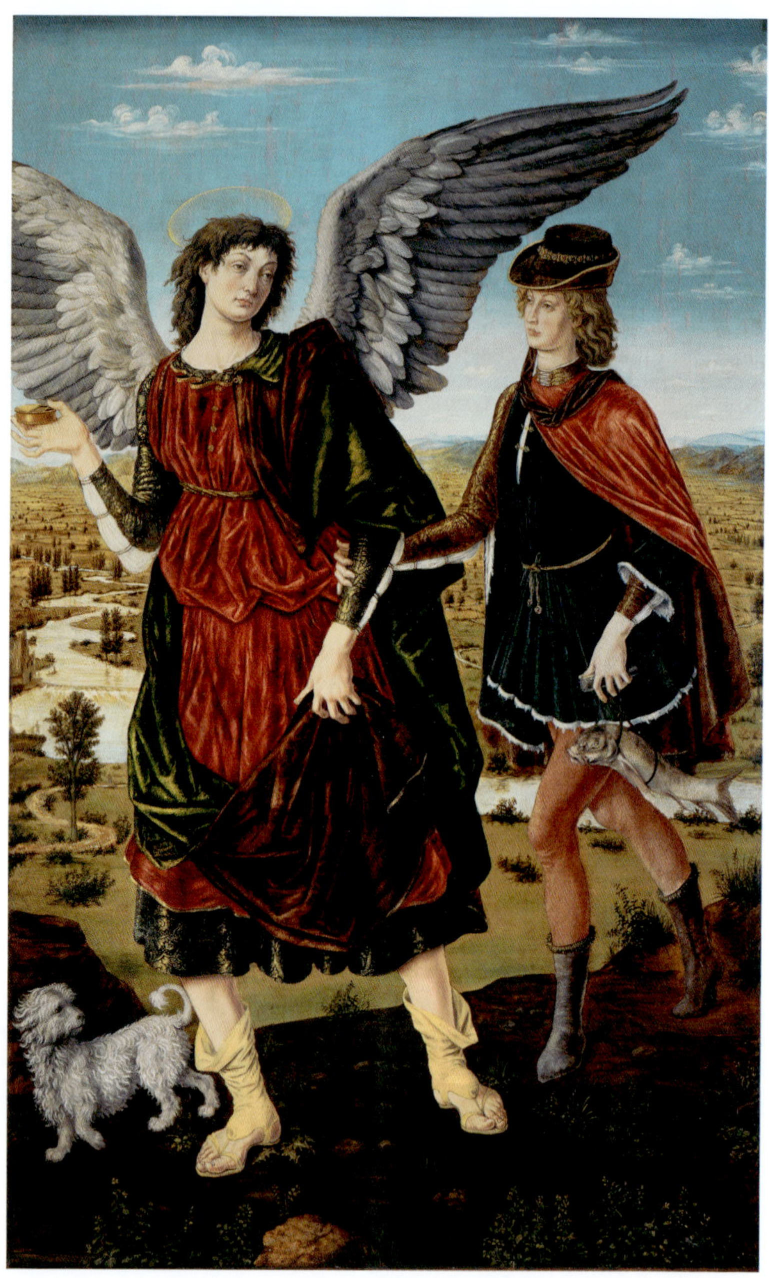

Antonio (1432–1498) and
Piero del Pollaiuolo (1441–1496)

An angel to watch over a son

Tobias and the Angel, c. 1469
188 x 119 cm, Turin, Galleria Sabauda

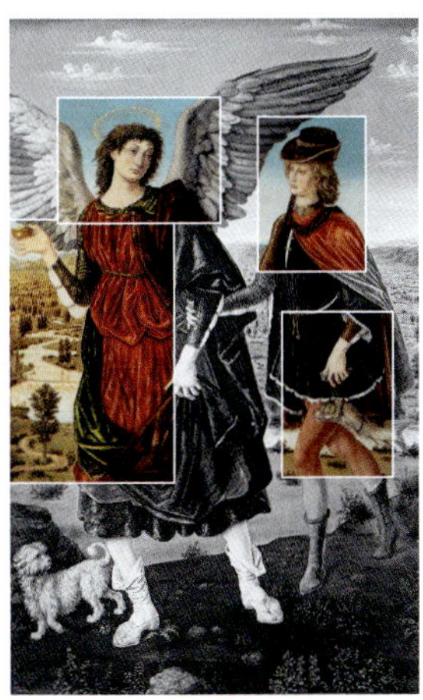

In the picture of Tobias and Archangel Raphael, the Pollaiuolo brothers take up a favourite motif amongst Florentine bankers – the dangerous travels of their sons.

A youth and an angel are travelling through a hilly river landscape. The youth is carrying a fish in a net, the angel a small tin. This motif appears in a striking number of Florentine paintings from between 1465 and 1485, the period of the Early Renaissance. It must have been particularly close to the hearts of the patrons for whom such pictures were executed, namely the bankers and merchants who governed Florence at that time. The young traveller is called Tobias and his story follows an archetypal pattern. A father sends his son to fulfil a challenge: he must find a treasure, slay a dragon and free a princess. It is a rite of initiation, and the youth must prove himself in order to become a man. He is frequently given a travelling companion and in this case it is Archangel Raphael, the forebear of all subsequent guardian-angel figures.

The story of Tobias and the Angel is found in the Book of Tobit, written around 100 BC. In the 15th century the Book of Tobit was a popular part of the Vulgate, the Latin translation of the Bible, but belongs neither to the Jewish nor the Protestant canon. It is set in Nineveh in the 7th century BC, amongst the Israelites who have been deported to Assyria. There the Jews are not permitted to live according to their own laws or to bury their dead.

A devout man, the elderly Tobit, bravely defies this ban. He goes blind, and his wife laments that mercy and righteousness bring no reward. But Tobit prays to God, who hears him and sends the Archangel to earth. The young Tobias is sent to collect a sum of money that his father has lent out in a distant city. Accompanied by his little dog, the youth sets off and is soon joined by Raphael. When they reach the River Tigris, a huge fish leaps out of the water and threatens to devour Tobias. Acting upon his companion's advice, Tobias seizes the fish, tosses it onto the bank and cuts out its heart, liver and gall bladder. The two then continue on to the house of a relative, whose daughter Sarah is in despair: seven men whom she wished to marry have been killed by a demon on their wedding night. At the angel's bidding, Tobias asks for her hand and drives the demon away by burning the fish's innards in their bridal chamber. Tobias marries Sarah and both return home, accompanied by the angel, who in the meantime has collected the outstanding debt. Tobias uses gall from the dead fish to restore his father's eyesight, but when the aged Tobit tries to pay his son's companion for his services, Raphael reveals his true identity and vanishes.

Devoutness and courage are rewarded, the "princess" is freed and the sick healed, and the youth becomes a man. Artists since the Middle Ages had portrayed episodes from the biblical narrative many times, but no scene was more popular than that of the two companions on their journey – even though

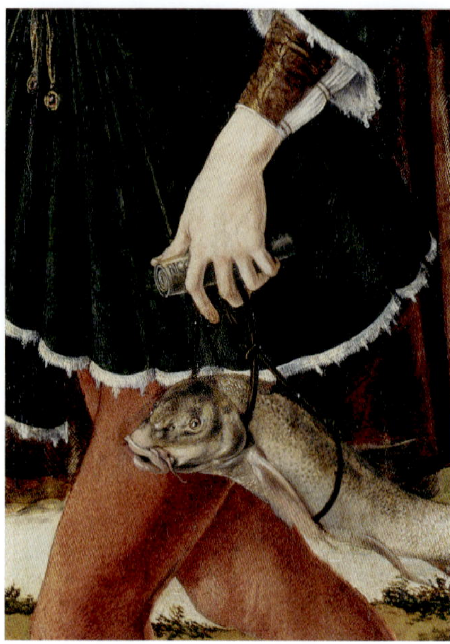

the Book of Tobit devotes only seven verses to this bit of the story. *Tobias and the Angel* was also painted by the Florentine artists Andrea del Verrocchio and Filippino Lippi in 1470 and 1480 respectively.

Demon or Christian symbol?

It is not known who commissioned the painting, today dated to around 1469, from the Pollaiuolo brothers. But a detail points to a circle of patrons from the Florentine world of finance: the small roll of parchment in Tobias's hand must be a bond or bill of exchange that he is to redeem for his father in the distant city. The bill of exchange, probably invented by Florentine bankers, offered a danger-free means of transferring sums of money between Florence, Avignon, Paris, London and Bruges – the cities where the Tuscan merchants of the day had their branch offices. Florence's wealth was based on its European trade in cloth and luxury goods: wool and raw cloth were imported cheaply from England, Flanders and Spain, processed, dyed and exported again at high prices. The financial transactions involved were handled by the large Florentine bank-ing houses. For centuries they had served kings and popes, and since 1435 the Medici family of bankers

had ruled discreetly but efficiently as "uncrowned kings" of the city on the Arno, which still called itself a republic.

A connection with the world of commerce may also be deduced from the information pro-vided by the painter Giorgio Vasari (1511–1574) in his biography of the Pollaiuolo brothers, written some 100 years after the execution of *Tobias and the Angel*. According to Vasari, "They also painted in oil on canvas on a pilaster of San Michele in Orto, an Angel Raphael with Tobias. " Although the work was not in fact painted on canvas but on six poplar panels (as revealed by its restoration around 1980), the location that Vasari gives is significant. The church of Orsanmichele, built between 1337 and 1404, lies in the heart of the city and was the centre of worship for the Florentine guilds, who since the Middle Ages had played a major role in Florence's economic and political affairs, architec-ture and arts. The large hall on the ground floor contained frescos, paintings, heraldic shields and banners. Statues and paintings of the patron saints of the guilds stood and hung on and beside its pillars. The monumental panel by the Pollaiuolo brothers almost seems designed to be installed at such a height.

Amongst the guilds that built and furnished Orsanmichele, the most important were the wool merchants, the cloth manufacturers and of course the bankers. The bankers' guild called itself the Arte del Cambio – the "guild of money changers". Since any financial operation that earned interest was prohibited by the Church, transactions had to take the guise of an exchange, with sums of money being converted in each case into other currencies and in other countries. That this nevertheless pricked the conscience of many a devout banker is evidenced by their wills, in which they bequeathed a large part of their profits to the poor or to the building of churches. "In the name of God and gain," they wrote on the first page of their ledgers, and it is significant that Tobias is carrying a fish – a tradi-tional Christian symbol – and a promissory note in the same hand. Although, in the incident by the river, the fish embodies a demon, it was also a symbol of the Christian faith, since the Greek word for fish can be read as an acrostic whose letters stand for "Jesus Christ, God's Son, Saviour". The fish appears in all representations of Tobias as his attribute and identifying feature.

A youth in fashionable travelling clothes

The fact that the work was destined for a house of God suggests that it was intended as a votive picture, a painted prayer to God or the saints: a prayer for succour or a token of gratitude for grace bestowed. Through it, the donor was able to invoke protection for family members who were in danger. In the Italy of the 15th century, such mostly small-format votive panels were produced in large quantities and were occasionally commissioned from workshops of high renown. In Italian texts, the hero of the biblical story is popularly known by the diminutive name of Tobiucciolo. Pollaiuolo's Tobias, with his smooth child's face beneath his small hat, is probably no more than fifteen or sixteen years old. This was the age in which the sons of Tuscan merchants left home to take up a post as an apprentice in the foreign branch of a bank or business. The journey was long – from Florence to Paris took 22 days – and perilous. There was the risk of being attacked by robbers and it was advisable to travel in a party or with an elder companion. At home, families prayed to St Christopher or to Archangel Raphael for a safe return.

Travelling abroad at an early age was something of a tradition in Florence: as early as 1421, twelve youths "from the city's first families" went as far as Alexandria in Egypt. They were sent to have a look around and open up branches of the family business. The venture was successful; Florence had soon overtaken the Orient in the manufacture of brocade and silver cloth and became, along with Venice, a marketplace for jewellery and luxury goods that supplied the whole of Europe. The young lads usually started out as errand boys in a local shop, while at the same time going to school to learn reading, writing and arithmetic. If it was found that they were lacking basic skills once they got abroad, they were sent straight back home, as happened to a novice in the Medici bank in Bruges in 1466. A hard life awaited the apprentices; they were beaten and had to sleep in the shop so that they could drive any thieves away. While their bosses ran the business from Florence, it was they who faced dangers and were the true heroes of their trade.

Our Tobias is wearing a magnificent set of clothes – not in the antique manner but in the latest Florentine fashion: tall leather boots: red hose, sleeves of gold brocade, a doublet lined with white fabric and a short, pleated skirt with a short cape on top. He lays his hand in a familiar manner on the

arm of his powerful companion, who is dressed in the longer robes of an adult. A youth who may have looked very like Tobias, named Piero Mazzei, set off for Barcelona at the start of the 15th century. His name is known to us through correspondence from the firm of Datini, which operated branches in Pisa, Genoa and Barcelona. The head of the company had himself once been a poor orphan and had started out with little more than a crimson jacket before he rose to become branch manager, shareholder and finally owner of the company. Piero is described in one letter as a "most delightful boy, as virtuous as a little virgin… and in all things as curious and solicitous as it is possible to be". When our picture was painted, Lorenzo de' Medici – himself barely twenty years of age – had just assumed power in Florence.

A heavenly double

The similarity between the faces of the two Florentine travellers recalls the pagan belief that each person has a double, created at the moment of their birth, who accompanies them through life. Christianity turned this "twin" into a guardian angel, whom the Pollaiuolo brothers have here

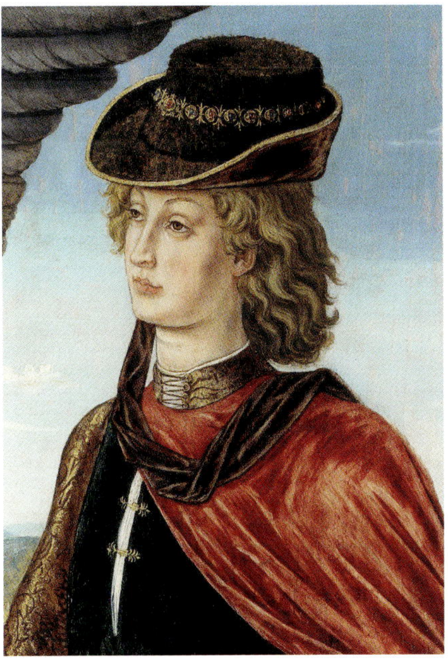

furnished with powerful, greyish-white feathered wings that span almost the full width of the painting. Many of their fellow Florentines were particularly active in their veneration of Archangel Raphael: he was the patron saint of two lay confraternities, one called La Scala after a hospital, the other the Compagnia dell'Arcangelo Raffaello, abbreviated to Il Raffa. These two associations commissioned numerous Raphael pictures that they gave away as gifts, exchanged or sold. In 1470 one of their members, the artist Francesco Botticini, painted an altarpiece in honour of the Archangel, and it is possible that the Pollaiuolos' *Tobias and the Angel* was also executed on their behalf.

Just as the city's economy was regulated by the guilds, society was structured by such confraternities. They organized its citizens into what we might today call "peer groups", based on geographical neighbourhood, mutual friendships and patronage. Within these associations, older "officers" and confessors ensured that unruly youths in particular were immersed in an atmosphere of "calm, purity and

peace" and kept busy with prayer, song and the organization of festivities. Even the ruling Medici belonged to the Charitable Company of the Magi and took part in their processions – immortalized in 1459 in frescos by Benozzo Gozzoli (1420–1497).

The Church, which has celestial aid workers for all eventualities, deployed Raphael in a number of roles. As the Angel of Safe Conduct, he protected pilgrims and travellers such as Tobias, even if he is not here carrying the pilgrim's staff and travel bag that are his usual attributes. Clearly visible is the tin in his right hand containing the fish's gall, the salve that cures blindness. Raphael's Hebrew name means "God has healed" or "God's healing", and as Raphael Medicinalis he was the patron of doctors and apothecaries. It was also his task to deliver to God the prayers of the righteous, such as those of the elderly Tobit and the despairing Sarah. In the hierarchy of the Roman Catholic Church, he belongs with Michael, Gabriel and Uriel to the four archangels, the highest of the angels. Byzantine icons show him beside Jesus and Mary as their bodyguard in

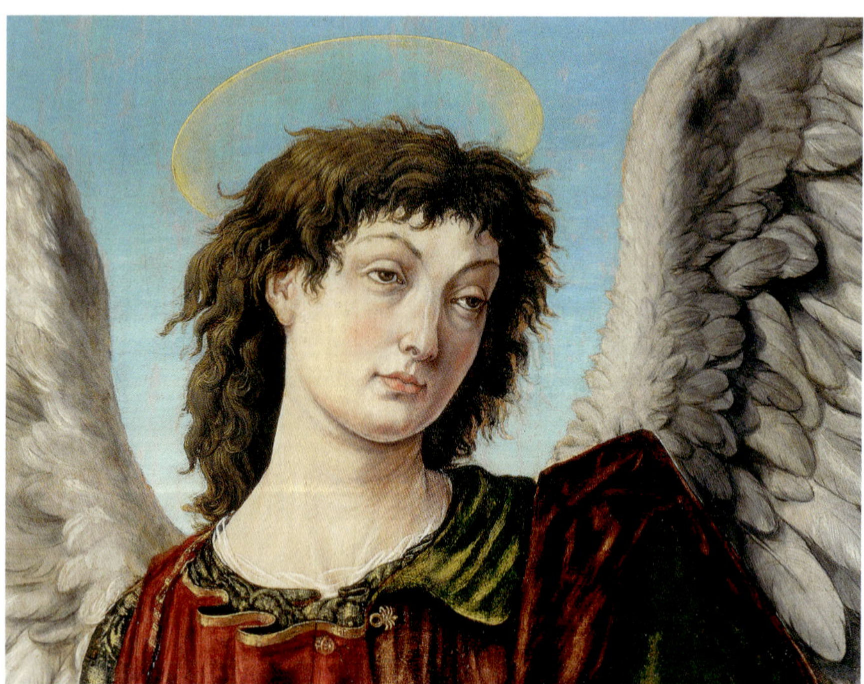

sumptuous court dress. The Pollaiuolo brothers also clothe Gabriel in fabrics of gold brocade, velvet and silk and use this wealth and the beauty of his figure to convey his high rank. It is almost impossible to recognize, in this powerful Gabriel, the forefather of the many female guardian angels in white night shirts who hung as colour prints over children's beds at the end of the 19th century.

Glittering with expensive fabrics and colours

It is not certain whether the Pollaiuolo brothers invented the motif of "Tobias and the Angel on their journey", but their votive picture, commissioned by an anxious family or devout confraternity, is one of the earliest examples of a type that served the needs of a mercantile society. The two artists ran one of the most successful and most innovative workshops of the Early Renaissance and one that was woven into the network of Florentine organizations. As a trained goldsmith, Antonio (1432–1498) joined the guild of silk weavers, for whom he designed liturgical vestments, but worked primarily as a sculptor, copperplate engraver and painter. Like his brother Piero (1441–1496), he also belonged to the Compagnia di San Luca painters' association. Their services were sought by the powerful: for the council chamber of the guild tribunal they painted representations of the Virtues, and for the Signoria – the city's nominal government – its patron saint, John the Baptist. The real ruler, Lorenzo de' Medici, also commissioned them to produce statues and pictures of Hercules, in the hope that he would be identified with this icon.

The brothers shared the tasks. Antonio, the head of the workshop, was particularly interested in anatomy and the movement of the body and assumed responsibility for the overall concept, drawing and design. Piero took over the execution, elongating the figures and giving them conventional, somewhat soporific faces but magnificent clothes. In a city that earned its wealth from dyeing fine cloth, particular attention was paid to the artist's use of colours. These were usually the most expensive part of a painting and were invoiced to the patron separately. The Pollaiuolos' protagonists wear dark malachite green and sought-after shades of red, ranging from the cinnabar, blood red and particularly precious scarlet of the angel's robes up to the almost black violet of the lining of his cloak. The restoration of the painting revealed that a number of different techniques were employed in its execu-

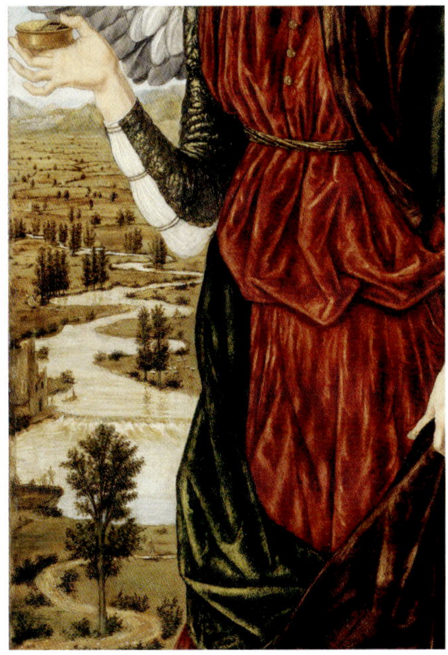

tion. New in Italy was the technique of oil painting, which the Pollaiuolos adopted from Netherlandish art and which permitted more translucent effects than traditional tempera. Oil paints and colourless varnish create the highlights on the velvet and silk of the clothes and also lend the landscape its diaphanous atmosphere. The brothers were probably the first to portray their immediate surroundings, in this case a sweeping view of the Arno Valley stretching away behind Tobias. As in their later pictures of *St Sebastian* and *The Annunciation*, the river can be seen snaking its way into the distance. The charm of the picture arises from the contrast between the poetic view of the background landscape and the two travellers looming so powerfully in the foreground. Towards the end of the 15th century the motif fell out of fashion; in the confusion that followed the death of Lorenzo and the expulsion of the Medici, the Florentines had other worries. Only a hundred years later would Tobias and Archangel Raphael reappear in pictures by the Rome based German artist Adam Elsheimer, but as small figures almost disappearing into Nature.

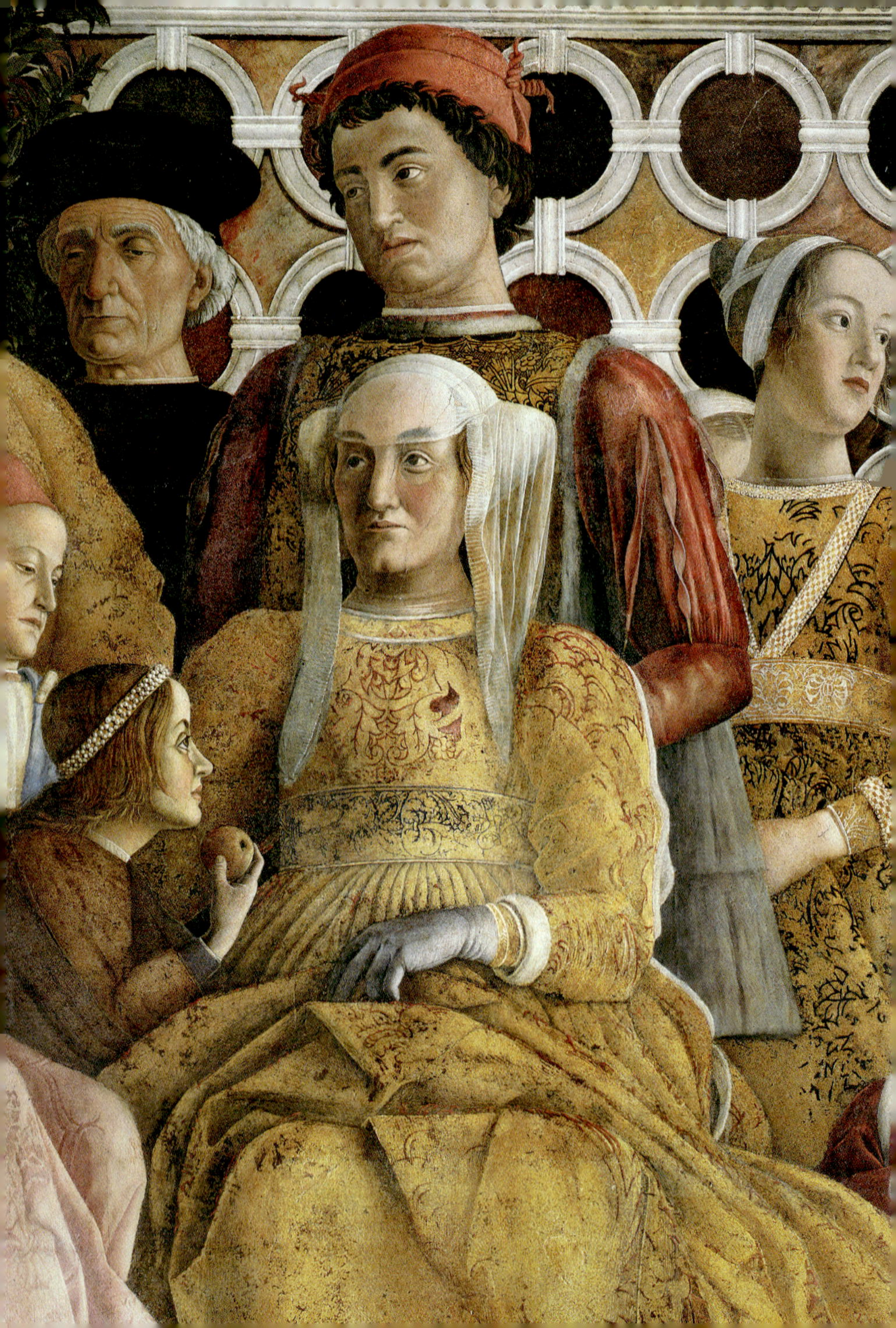

Andrea Mantegna (1431–1506)

The splendours of a small dynasty

Ludovico Gonzaga and His Family, c. 1470
600 x 807 cm, Mantua, Palazzo Ducale

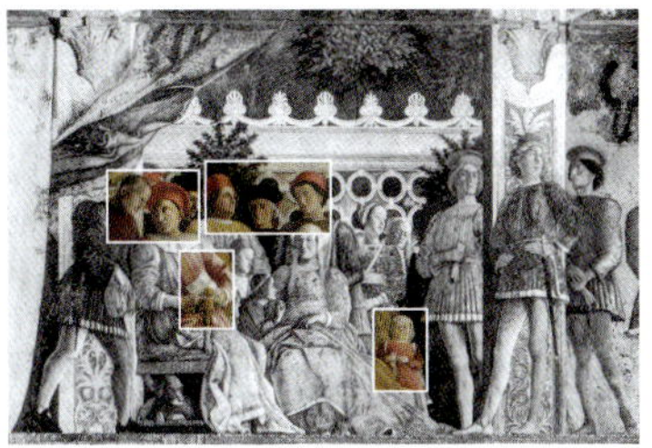

Their country was "marshy and unhealthy".
They suffered from gout, malaria, rickets and a
chronic shortage of cash. But the proud Gonzaga
commissioned their family portrait from the "most
modern" artist of their time. The fresco can still
be admired in the reception room of the Ducal
Palace in Mantua.

Gold embossed leather curtains are drawn back to
reveal a terrace. Here, a distinguished company is
gathered before a marble screen among the lemon
trees: the family and court of Marquis Ludovico
Gonzaga of Mantua, in northern Italy.

Only the reigning couple can be identified
beyond doubt. Ludovico is shown with a letter in
his hand, conferring with a secretary. Marchioness
Barbara of Brandenburg has a little daughter at
her knee; behind her may be one or two of her ten
children. The sombre officials in their dark clothes
contrast starkly with the arrogant-looking courtiers, possibly Gonzaga bastards, or masters of ceremonies. They wear stockings in the red-and-white
of the reigning house. Rubino, the marquis's dog,
and a dwarf complete the family portrait.

The Gonzaga, dressed in luxurious, gold spun
cloth and blessed with many children, present the
image of a confident, successful clan. In the middle
of the 15th century, the family had experienced a
sharp upturn in fortune.

In 1328, one of their predecessors, a simple but
nonetheless wealthy landowner, had risen to the
position of "Capitano" of the city of Mantua.
The family had succeeded in retaining its foothold,
amassing power and finally adding legitimacy to
its position through the purchase of a ducal title
from the emperor.

By the standards of the wealthy Florentine Medici,
the income of the Gonzaga was limited. Their small
territory on the Lombard plains was modest by
comparison with the powerful states of Venice or
Milan. Pope Pius II gave a bleak description of
Mantua in 1460: "Marshy and unhealthy … all
you could hear were the frogs." Ludovico Gonzaga
decided to find a remedy for this: he not only had
the marshes drained and the town squares paved
over, but did everything he could to attract the best
architects and artists to his court.

The architect and early Renaissance theorist Leon
Battista Alberti (1404–1472) designed churches for
the marquis in the very latest style – after the model
of antique temples.

In the Ducal Palace Mantegna's frescos transformed a relatively small reception room, later
called – for unknown reasons – the Camera degli
Sposi or Bridal Chamber; his illusionistic painting
appears to extend the real space of the room via
the ceiling into the sky, and through the walls on
either side into a terrace and landscape.

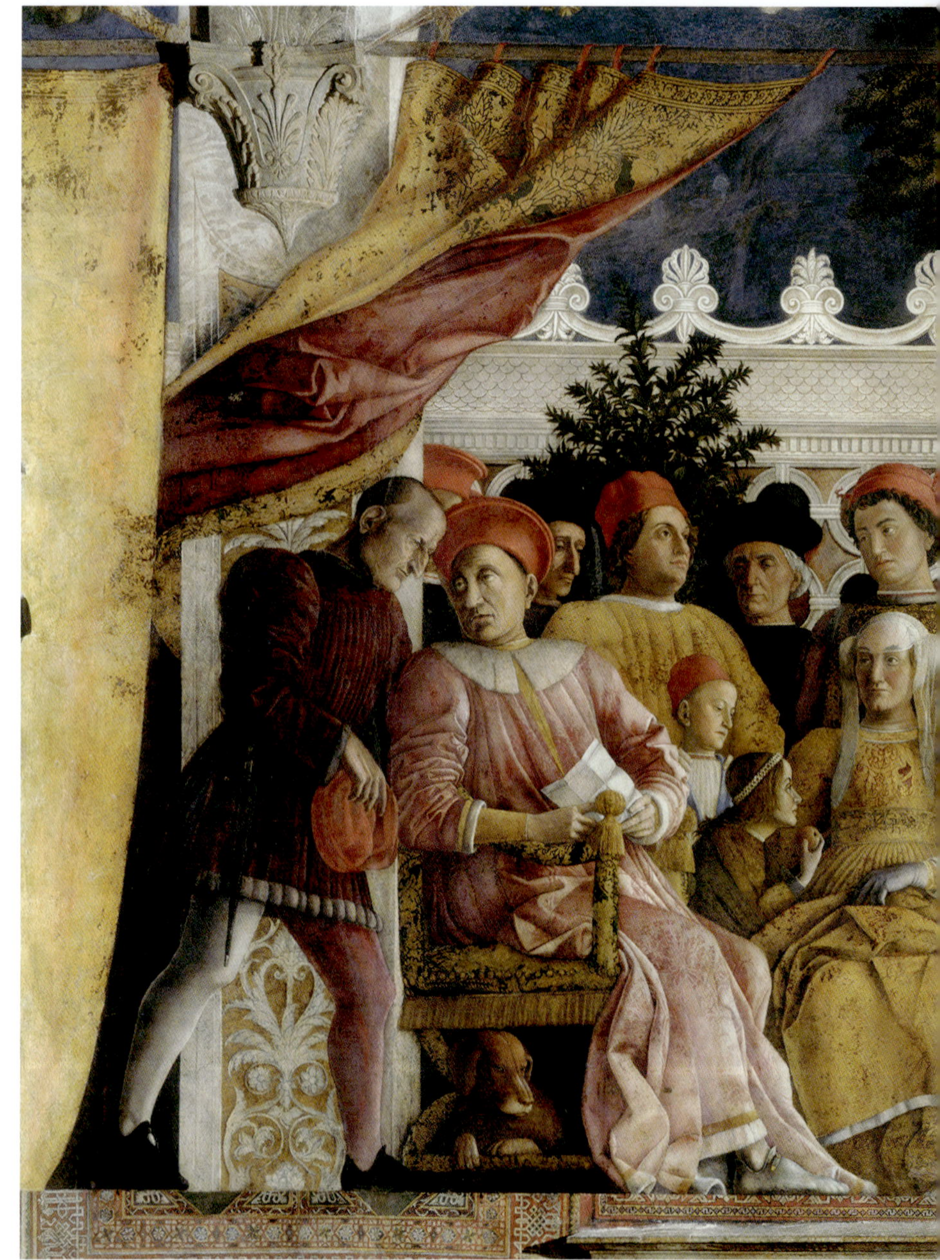

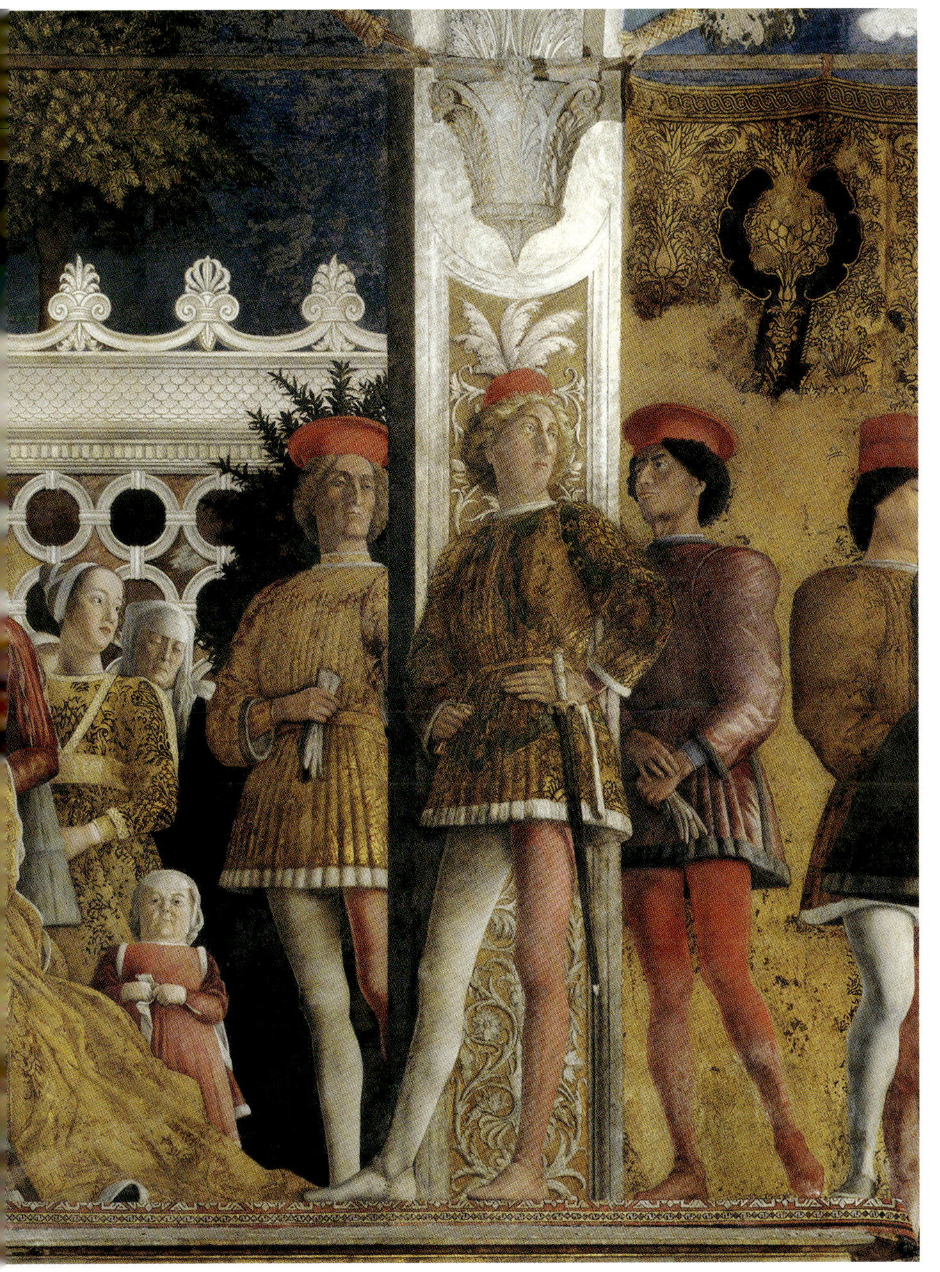

Three years to engage a painter

The writing on the sheet of paper held in Marquis Ludovico's hand could tell us something about the occasion for the group portrait, which was probably commissioned to commemorate a particularly significant event. Since it is impossible to decipher the letter, we can only speculate. What is certain, however, is that it bears testimony to a favourite pastime at the court of Mantua: the writing, reading and preservation of manuscripts. Owing to the work of countless clerks and secretaries, a huge archive and precise record of the most important events in Mantua has been passed on to posterity. The life of the painter Mantegna, who spent 46 years there, is thus more thoroughly documented than the life of any other artist of his time.

The documents begin in 1457 with the voluminous correspondence undertaken to attract the 26 year old painter to Mantua. Marquis Ludovico spent three years attempting to engage him. Andrea Mantegna (1431–1506) had made a name for himself with frescos in Padua. Their bold use of perspective and confident return to recently discovered antique models astonished his contemporaries. It was said that his portraits showed the sharply defined contours of Roman coins. Ludovico was determined to attract this

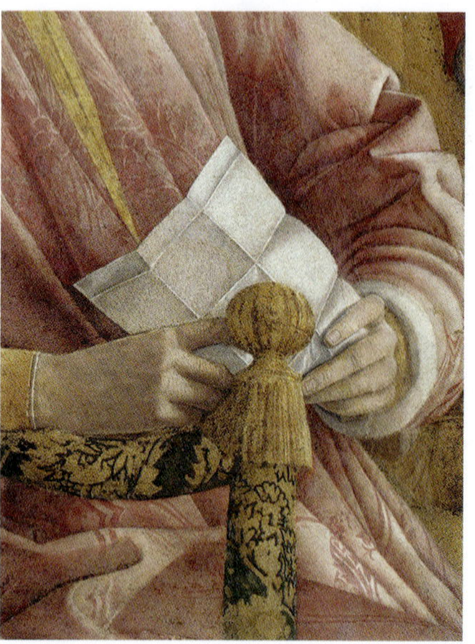

exciting, modern man to Mantua, which lacked its own artistic tradition at the time. At least he could boast the presence of one other innovator: the Florentine architect Leon Battista Alberti had recently been entrusted with the building of churches and palaces.

Mantegna was hesitant to assume the obligations that accompanied the position of court painter. These included a vast amount of time-consuming, routine work: the decoration of country houses, the planning and staging of court festivities. Moreover, if the testimony of the Pope could be believed, Mantua was hardly an attractive proposition. What could be used to entice Mantegna? For one thing, the sum, agreed by letter, of, "180 ducats per year, a house to live in, enough wheat for six persons and firewood". Owing to their chronic lack of money, the Gonzaga payments were often overdue (because of this, Mantegna was later forced to write countless reminders and requests for payment). The Lords of Mantua found it much easier to reward their ambitious painter with status symbols. In the course of the years, they conferred upon him the fine-sounding titles of Count Palatine and Knight of the Army of Gold.

The real reason for Mantegna's decision to go to Mantua in 1460 was probably the marquis's cultivated understanding of art, his ability to appreciate the innovations of the Renaissance and, not least, the solicitous attitude exhibited by this busy ruler towards the artists in his service, a quality also documented in the correspondence.

In 1465, for example, the marquis personally ordered "two cartloads of lime with which to paint our room in the castle": frescos were painted on a ground of fresh lime. In 1474 he sent for gold-leaf and lapis lazuli, paints so precious that they were usually added only as a final touch. These letters were separated by nine years, during which time Mantegna was evidently decorating the Camera Picta, or Painted Room, for the renovated palace. For in 1470 Ludovico complained about the slowness of the artist, "who started to paint the room so many years ago, and still has not completed half of it".

A cunning man of peace

Marquis Ludovico's stockingless foot wears a slipper, and his simple housecoat contrasts with the ostentatious gold thread of his family's dress. When Mantegna finally completed his frescos in 1474, the potentate was 62 years old, worn out by 30 years of government, and in ill health.

Ludovico had held highest military office. Initially serving the Venetians, he had eventually become general commander for the Dukes of Milan, a position he maintained for 28 years. His reliability and loyalty towards those he served contrasted favourably with the vast majority of *condottieri*, the mercenary generals paid by Italian princes to fight their wars. Unlike his peers, he was not interested in booty, nor in war as an art. Ludovico was a man of peace. He did not owe high military rank to martial prowess, but to the geographic and strategic position of his small state.

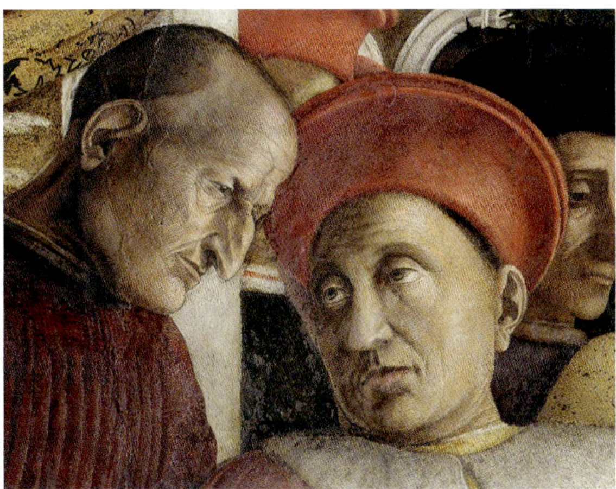

The River Po, used for transporting goods, flowed directly through the land of the Gonzaga. Mantua also controlled the approach to the Brenner Pass. Connecting Italy with the north, this was one of Europe's most important trading routes. Mantua, protected on all sides by water, was considered impregnable. The rival neighbouring powers of Venice and Milan therefore attempted to secure an alliance with the marquis, or at least his neutrality, and he was clever enough to play the two off against each other.

In order to achieve a certain degree of independence from both powers, the Gonzaga sought foreign support by marrying beyond the Alps. Ludovico was married to Barbara of Brandenburg, a relation of the emperor. For his heir, he himself chose a bride from the House of Wittelsbach. He maintained good neighbourly relations with Venice and Milan, and always commanded the army of whichever was prepared to pay him most. His wage as a *condottiere*, in reality a disguised reward for his alliance, was considerable – indeed it would occasionally exceed the income generated by his entire kingdom.

Without a separate, external income he could never have afforded such a lavish lifestyle at home. His princely suite would sometimes comprise more than 800 persons. He also had an expensive hobby: horse breeding. Of course, his Milanese ducats also permitted Ludovico to patronize the arts, to commission buildings and paintings. His investment proved worthwhile. Shortly after Ludovico's death, a man who was probably the greatest art expert among the Renaissance princes, Lorenzo de' Medici, also known as the Magnificent, travelled specially to Mantua to admire its paintings and collection of antiques. Out of a swamp where "all you could hear were the frogs" had arisen a town whose fame, within a mere twenty years, had spread far and wide.

A teacher who formed Renaissance Man

The white-haired man standing between two of Marquis Gonzaga's sons had been dead for some time when Mantegna came to paint his frescos. Vittorino da Feltre owed his place in this fresco to the gratitude of his former pupil. Without him, Ludovico Gonzaga would probably never have become quite such a remarkable ruler.

Vittorino da Feltre (1378–1446) came to Mantua as a teacher and court librarian. His pupils included not only Ludovico and his siblings, but also Ludovico's future wife, the German Barbara of Brandenburg, who had come to the Gonzaga court at the age of ten. With Vittorino's help this unattractive, but by all accounts clever girl became a ruling lady, fully capable of governing the state when her husband was away commanding foreign armies.

The reputation of Vittorino's "School for Princes" attracted pupils to Mantua from all over Italy, and many important figures of the Renaissance were educated there, among them Duke Federico of Urbino. All lived together, with 60 poor, but gifted pupils who received a scholarship from the Gonzaga, in Vittorino's "Ca' zoiosa", or "house of joy". The contrast between this more modern institution and the grim monastic schools of the Middle Ages, where pupils had lived under the rule of rote learning and the cane, was not solely atmospheric. Vittorino's educational ideas, derived from Classical models, were revolutionary for their time. He paid great attention to physical education, for example, and attempted to awaken in his pupils both a Christian sense of duty and a healthy respect for Classical virtues. His ideal was the *uomo universale*, combining vigour and spirit to form a harmonious whole.

Ludovico Gonzaga came very close to Vittorino's educational ideal. He was an intellectual of high artistic sensibility, and a man of action who was single minded in improving the fortunes of his family and town.

The marquis owed his political success to an inspired move: in 1459, following extensive preparations, he convened a conference of sovereign princes at Mantua, attended by the pope and dignitaries from both sides of the Alps. Although this plunged Ludovico into debt for many years, it gave him an opportunity to spin the threads of a cardinal's robe for his second son Francesco (1444–1483). Following Francesco's elevation to the rank of cardinal in 1462,

Ludovico greeted his son, according to one of his contemporaries, "with tears of joy"; it is possible that this was the triumphant occasion Mantegna's painting was intended to record. The paper in Ludovico's hand may be a letter of appointment bearing the papal seal.

Ludovico's two eldest sons, standing to the left and right of Vittorino da Feltre, although not educated by the great teacher himself, were brought up in his spirit. Cardinal Francesco, on the left, laid the foundations for a famous collection of Classical antiques. His older brother Federico, Ludovico's heir, despite spending the greater part of his few reigning years (1478–1484) on battlefields, was also a patron of the arts. Mantegna even worked under a third generation of Gonzaga. Ludovico's grandson, Francesco (1466–1519), had great respect for him: "an extraordinary painter, unequalled in our time." He, too, had learned that "a ruler becomes immortal by knowing how to honour great men." It was a lesson Vittorino da Feltre had taught Francesco's grandfather.

Gout, malaria, rickets: complaints of the Gonzaga
Dwarfs and other human freaks were much sought after as court fools; at some Renaissance courts they were systematically "bred", a practice otherwise

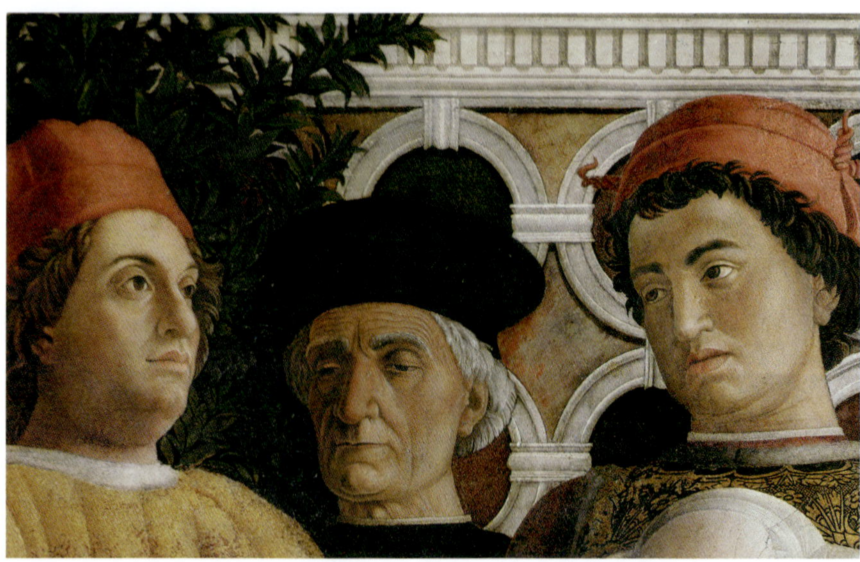

restricted to dogs and horses. Duchess Barbara is said to have kept two female dwarfs, Baby Beatricina and Maddelena the Midget, to entertain her. However, more malicious tongues have it that the dwarf in Mantegna's fresco was a daughter of the reigning couple. The proud ruling family of Mantua – according to retrospective medical diagnosis – not only suffered from gout and malaria, but also from arthritis and rickets, which often led to curvature of the spine.

The boy and girl at the duchess's knee look pale and thin; only two of ten children enjoyed perfect health. Two, including Cardinal Francesco, suffered from obesity; one had rickets, and four, among them Ludovico's heir Federico, had an unmistakably hunched back, although the fresco hides this. Since little is known of the remaining Gonzaga children, it cannot be excluded that they were dwarfs.

The defect probably entered the family through Ludovico's mother Paola Malatesta, who had come to Mantua from the renowned ruling house of Rimini. Two of her children were deformed, and even her eldest son Ludovico hardly demonstrated Vittorino da Feltre's ideal of a healthy mind in a healthy body. He suffered from obesity, and was often ill. It was possibly only the strict diet and regular exercise imposed on him by his teacher that prevented him from developing curvature of the spine as well. His heir Federico was not so lucky: he was described by one of his contemporaries as an "amiable, engaging man with a hump".

The Gonzaga bore their ailments with composure, accepting humiliation when necessary. In 1464 the Milanese heir, Galeazzo Maria Sforza, refused to marry Ludovico's daughter Dorotea with the words: "These women, born of the blood of hunchbacks, only give birth to new hunchbacks and other lepers." His first engagement, to Dorotea's elder sister Susanna, had been broken off at the first sign of her developing curvature of the spine. Susanna had thereupon entered a convent, leaving Dorotea to take her place as the Sforza heir's bride. But as soon as the opportunity of a more advantageous match arose – with an heiress from the house of Savoy – Sforza made public his feelings of disgust for the Gonzaga.

The insult threatened to cause a reversal of existing alliances, almost driving Ludovico into the service of Venice. In the end, however, the link with Milan proved stronger; over the years the marquis had become "like a son … like a brother" to successive

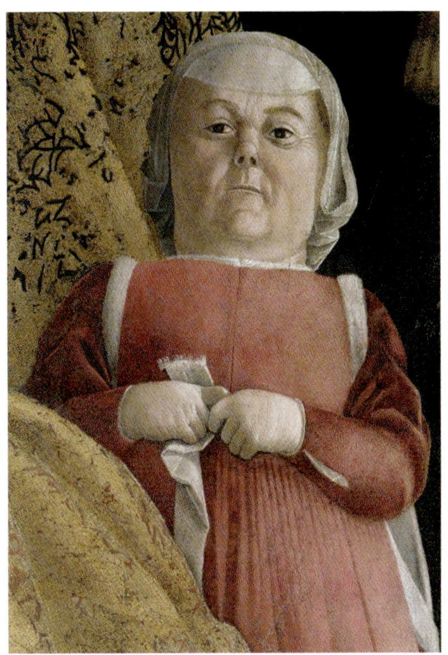

dukes: a true "guardian of the state of Milan". On three separate occasions, when the fate of the troubled house of Sforza lay in Ludovico's hands, the loyal general commander hurried to their immediate aid.

Perhaps Ludovico Gonzaga took secret revenge on the Sforza family by commissioning Andrea Mantegna to paint a fresco showing the moment of triumph when a missive containing a cry for help had reached him from the impertinent Milanese. Of course, he would not grant the Sforza name itself a place in the picture, for they were to have no part in the immortality which the lords of Mantua hoped to secure for themselves through Mantegna's art.

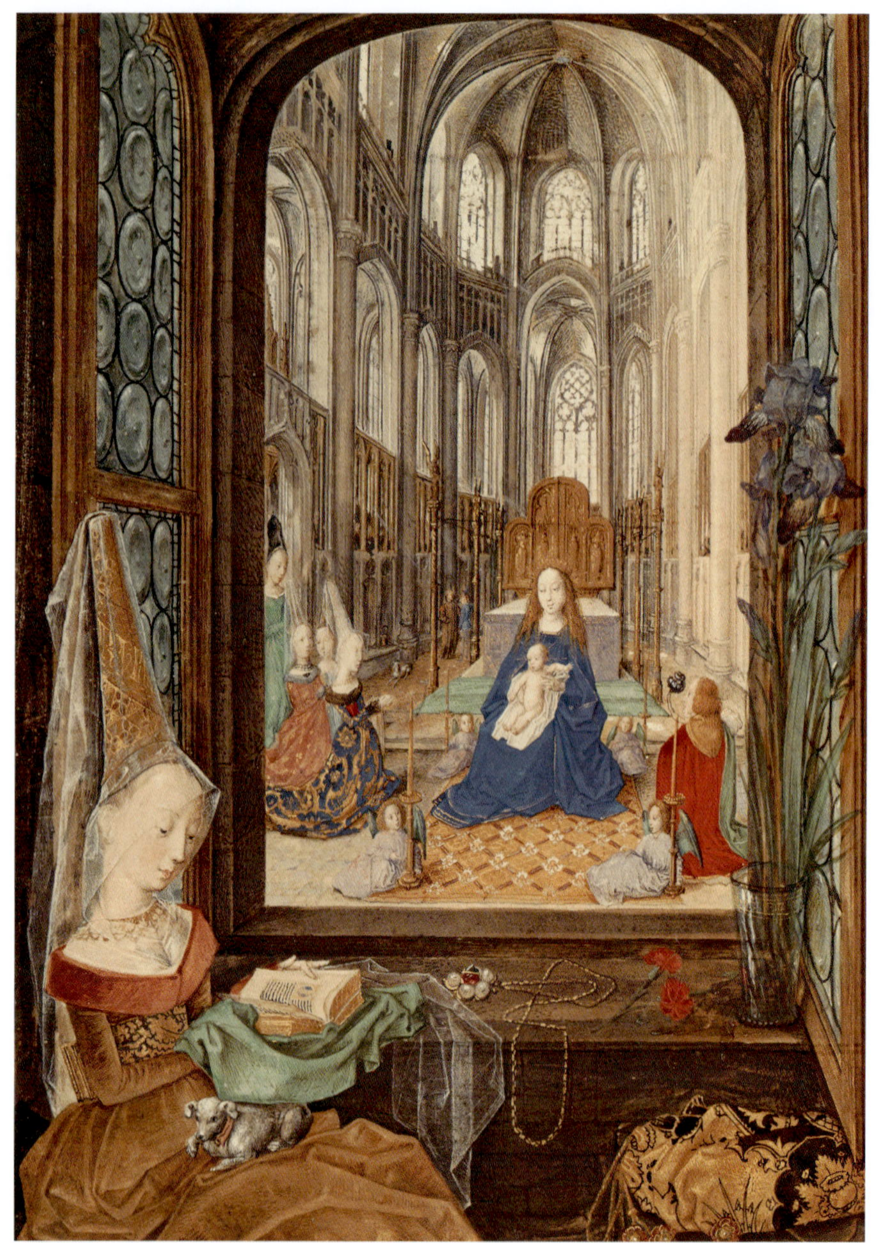

Master of the Hours of Mary of Burgundy

The devotions of a huntress

Window miniature, 1470/1480
22 x 16 cm, Vienna, Österreichische Nationalbibliothek

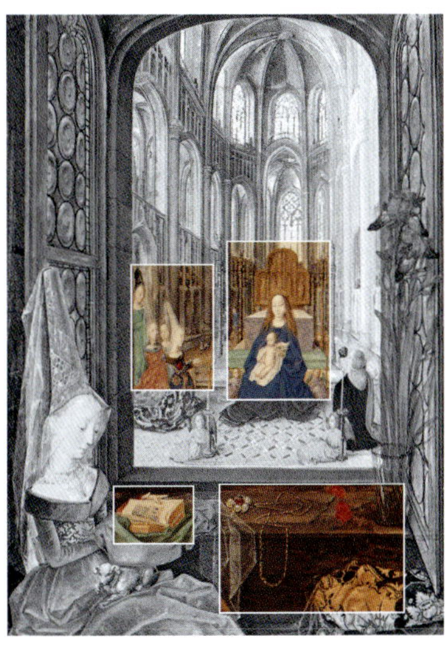

In the Hours of Mary of Burgundy, medieval book painting reached a last, masterly high point.

This miniature was created at the end of the Middle Ages. The tallest buildings in those days were Gothic cathedrals, and the most important of all painted figures were saints. The miniaturist celebrates both – with church windows and columns soaring up to the heights and with the Virgin Mary, the very foremost amongst all the heavenly beings to whom people prayed for succour.

And succour was what the two women – the one in front of the window and the one kneeling before the Virgin inside the church – both needed. The one reading is Margaret of York, sister of the king of England and wife of Duke Charles the Bold of Burgundy. The one kneeling is Charles's daughter from his first marriage, Mary.

Burgundy, today known to many simply as a wine growing region of France, was at that time a power-ful empire in the middle of Europe, extending from the North Sea to the borders of Switzerland. Alsace and Luxemburg belonged to it, as did the coastal regions from Friesland down to Flanders. Made up of many individual parts, the duchy owed its pros-perity to the flourishing industries of its towns and cities, in particular the cloth trade, and to its com-mercially advantageous geographical location. Traffic to and from England passed via its ports and the North-South maritime routes between Novgorod and Spain relied on its Netherlandish points of transhipment. Over a period of some hundred years, three Burgundian dukes – descended from the junior branch of the French royal family – had built up their empire through inheritance, marriage, purchase and conquest, but it remained a patchwork and it lacked a king. The fourth, Charles the Bold, craved the crown. But he wanted too much, was more foolhardy than bold and embarked on military campaigns he could not win. In 1477 he was defeated and slain and his empire once again fell apart.

The Book of Hours created for his daughter Mary, and from which this miniature is taken, was pro-duced – say art historians – in Flanders between 1470

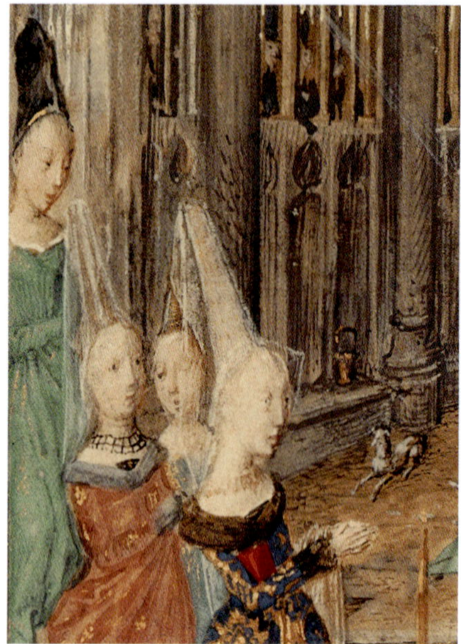

The wealthiest heiress of her day

Mary of Burgundy was born in 1457 in Brussels. Her grandfather had relocated the court from its native Burgundy to the Netherlands. According to one chronicler, Mary's baptism was celebrated at court "with great magnificence, even though she was only a girl". Mary remained the sole heiress. Since, in Burgundy, the female line was entitled to inherit, Mary's legitimacy as duchess was never questioned. Her mother died early on and in 1468 Charles married Margaret of York, who was only eleven years older than Mary. The two became friends.

We have a description of Mary as an adult formulated by her later husband, Maximilian, from the house of Habsburg. Mary was "small and snow-white of body, with brown hair, a small nose… her mouth is a little too high, but chaste and red". So says *Der Weisskunig* (*The White King*), an autobiography by Maximilian, written in 1505 in the form of a chivalric romance but nevertheless full of realistic details. The miniature cannot entirely confirm Maximilian's description: Mary's hair is tucked out of sight beneath her hat, and her nose is long rather than short, but her looks are also shared by all the other women on this sheet. They all have an oval face, the same small mouth, a long nose and eyes that are almost black. As such they corresponded to the Late Gothic ideal of beauty, which demanded elongated and sweeping lines – hence the neck free of hair, the straight bridge of the nose, the shaven forehead. The pointed hat extended the silhouette upwards, the train downwards. It took practice to wear this fashion, with its extravagant headgear and heavy length of fabric behind, with the desired elegance.

Charles the Bold had selected his two wives on the basis of political calculation, and for his daughter, too, he sought a husband who would fulfil his plans for a great Burgundian empire. There was no shortage of candidates. Mary was the wealthiest heiress of her day. The King of Aragon wanted her for his son Ferdinand when she was only five, and the King of France, Louis XI, offered his two-year-old son. The Duke of Lorraine, whose lands would fill the gap in the Burgundian empire, also stood on the list of suitors, as did Galeazzo Sforza, the Duke of Milan, Philibert of Savoy and many others. Louis XI – Burgundy's most bitter opponent, despite being a relative and godfather to Mary – later renewed the offer of his now seven-year-old son, to which Mary's governess, Madame Hallewyn – here probably in the

and 1480. Since the execution of such manuscripts was the work of several years, it might have been commenced before the catastrophe and finished after it. It had probably been commissioned for Mary by her stepmother, Margaret of York, as a wedding present, albeit at a point in time when the bridegroom had not yet been fixed. The distinguished gentleman in the red cloak on the right of the Virgin might be taken for the groom, but would a noble lord swing the incense burner with such vigour?

Mary had no brothers; it was she who would inherit, and hence the choice of the right husband carried an extraordinary significance for the Burgundian empire and for Margaret. The latter is reading a Book of Hours (like the one that she commissioned) seated in front of a window, whose tall panes, with their bull's-eye glazing, are opened onto the choir of a cathedral. This view through the window from one interior into another was a new invention. The two spaces belong to different realities. The foreground is "real", the background imagined; it exists only inside the reader's head. Inspired by her devout reading, the donor sees the cathedral scene in her mind's eye, a celestial apparition within an earthly building, a beautiful fantasy.

black hat standing behind her charge – replied: "It is not a child that you need, but a man to give you children!" This man would be Archduke Maximilian, son of Emperor Friedrich III and himself later emperor.

In his *Der Weisskunig*, Maximilian later provided an admiring description not only of his wife but also of her great passions, riding and hunting. Mary was "a consummate huntress with falcons and dogs". Her favourite falcon was always nearby and spent the night in her bedchamber on its perch near the fireplace. Her dog, too, was not a lapdog like that of her stepmother, but a first-class hunter. "She has a white greyhound … it usually sleeps beside us every night." The dog can also be seen in the cathedral – as close to his mistress as possible but at a distance deemed appropriate in a hallowed place.

Items on the windowsill point to the wedding
The objects lying on the windowsill provide another clue that the Book of Hours was intended as a wedding present for Mary. Pearls were symbols of virginal innocence, a veil referred to virtue and modesty, while red carnations were considered love tokens. When the eighteen-year-old Maximilian came to Ghent and met his twenty-year-old bride for the first time, her stepmother whispered to him that Mary had hidden a flower about her and he was to look for it. Maximilian hesitated, but the Bishop of Trier commanded him to open his bride's bodice; Maximilian obeyed and found a carnation, upon which the chronicler remarked: "He kissed the flower and the altar from which he had taken it."

Jewellery, expensive fabrics and silver tableware were shown off to guests at feasts, and princes took pieces on military campaigns in order to demonstrate their might and to pay the troops. At his first defeat in Grandson in 1476, Charles the Bold lost his baggage train to the Swiss; it included 400 chests of gold and silver fabrics, 100 chests of coats embroidered with gold thread, and a tent lined with velvet and trimmed with pearls.

After Charles's death in 1477, Burgundy was plunged into chaos. French troops invaded the realm and Netherlandish cities rebelled, demanding more privileges and attempting to foist a Flemish husband upon Mary. But she wanted Maximilian "and none other on this earth". Her father had decided upon Maximilian shortly before his death and Mary had a portrait of him. In the opinion of Burgundian chroniclers, he was the "model and living example of all the handsome princes in the world", possessed of "stature and limbs of noble measure" and "shoulder length golden hair in the German fashion". When the imperial delegation arrived in Ghent, Mary said yes without pause for thought. Just two days later the marriage was celebrated *per procurationem*, "by agency": the Habsburg envoy climbed onto the marital bed in silver armour and lay down beside Mary, separated from her only by an unsheathed sword.

In comparison to the luxury-loving Burgundians, the emperor's son was poor. Despite the fact that he was anxiously awaited in Ghent, he spent nearly three months travelling across Germany, so that he could borrow money from the Fuggers in Augsburg and from the wealthy city of Cologne in order to equip himself and his retinue in keeping with his rank. At last the marriage was celebrated – with the usual magnificence, despite the catastrophic political situation – and was soon followed by the birth of a longed-for son. The couple did not spend a great deal of time in each other's company, however: Maximilian was mainly away, endeavouring to keep the rebellious cities in check and to defend Mary's lands from incursions from outside. Only in winter was he home with his family. They danced, went ice skating and rode out hunting together.

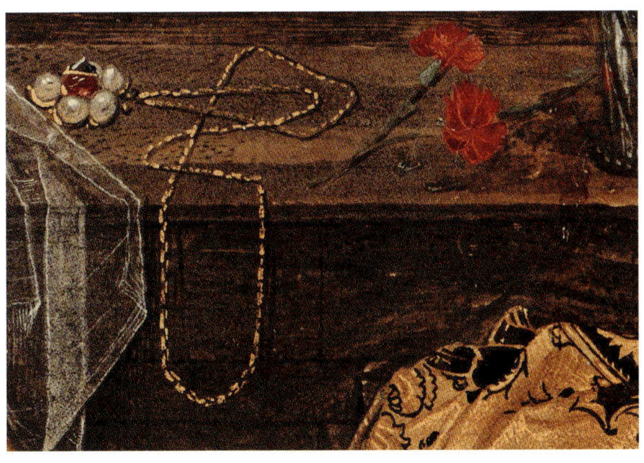

During a falcon hunt five years after their wedding, Mary's horse fell and crushed its rider beneath it. Mary died. "The young king mourned greatly over the death of his wife", Maximilian later wrote in his autobiography, "for they loved each other dearly, of which much could be written."

Our Lady wears blue

The miniaturist gives the Queen of Heaven a fashionably high forehead and clothes her in robes of radiant blue. In earlier centuries the Virgin was always sombrely dressed, usually in black or purple, signifying her presentiment of Christ's death and her own mourning. In the 12th century, as the cult of the Virgin grew, these darker colours evolved into a brighter blue and the grieving Mother of Christ became a Madonna of Mercy whose protection extended to humankind. Mary of Burgundy made a pilgrimage to her shrine at the basilica of Hal, near Brussels, in 1476.

Black was also the official colour worn at the court of Burgundy. The father of Charles the Bold had introduced it as a sign of mourning for the murder of his own father, and from then on black was deemed an appropriate colour for court ceremonies

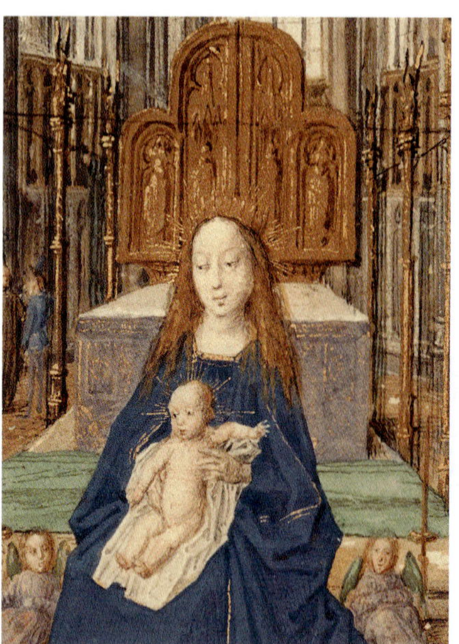

and for the representation of a hierarchical order. After Mary's son, Philip the Handsome, married the heiress to the Spanish throne, Burgundian black also travelled to Madrid. From there it would govern the fashions worn by the ruling classes of Europe for hundreds of years.

Life at court was structured not only by the rules of etiquette but also by the cult of chivalry. Tournaments were no longer fought to the death but were recreated and celebrated in literature; to battle for ladies of noble birth, for honour and glory, remained an ideal. In the real wars of the day, however, knights were being increasingly supplanted by pikesmen. Charles the Bold refused to accept this. In the battle against the confederates, he and his heavily armoured mounted knights faced foot soldiers in tight formation with long lances that lifted riders out of the saddle. Charles, the bold knight, considered it a point of honour to fight alongside his troops in the field. He was slain near Nancy in 1477. His body was only found days after the battle, stripped of clothes and armour, naked in the ice of a frozen pond.

The Swiss mercenaries commanded by the Duke of Lorraine, who defeated Charles at Nancy, were paid by Louis XI. Unlike Charles, however, the French king did not risk his own life in battle. He remained in his palaces, sitting there, as it was said, "like a spider" spinning an ever widening web. He was the first modern ruler and fought with money, diplomacy and economic measures. He forbade his subjects to buy wine from Burgundy or to supply it with grain; his navy impeded its fishing vessels and merchant ships and thus hindered its vital trade with England. Louis' blockade weakened the Burgundian economy; the rural population went hungry and the cities grew poor. Immediately after Charles's death, Louis' troops were able to reconquer the heartland of Burgundy almost without resistance. The king also made a Marian pilgrimage. Mary had asked the Virgin for help; Louis thanked her for his victory.

Prayer books were precious objects

Mary's Book of Hours ranks amongst the masterpieces of the late Middle Ages. Even as it was being created, the first books were being printed. Gutenberg's invention marked the beginning of the end of handwritten and illuminated manuscripts. Such works were costly and precious objects. Their writing in an elaborate script and their decoration

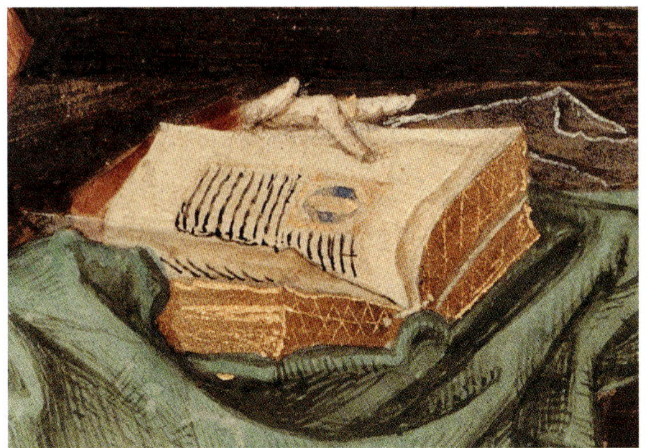

with coloured initials, border figures and full-page miniatures took years and involved several specialists. These latter did not sign their works, and unless their names fortuitously surface in court accounts, they remain anonymous. Thus, while some calligraphers and miniaturists working in Flanders around 1470 are known by name, such as Joos van Gent and Nicolaus Spierinc, in other cases art historians have to make do with designations such as the "Master of the Hours of Mary of Burgundy".

By contrast, the individuals who commissioned or were presented with such books are generally known to us and their portraits often included inside. The dukes of Burgundy were great collectors of manuscripts, which they took with them along with their gold tableware and tapestries when they moved back and forth between their palaces in Ghent, Bruges and Brussels. They owned a "Book of the Hunt", for example, a "Chronicle of the Crusaders", a "Boccaccio", and of course a number of Books of Hours, collections of prayers and devotional texts for private use.

The *Hours of Mary of Burgundy* comprises 189 folios. By way of recreation for the eye and mind during the long offices, it contains twenty full-page miniatures, including our window scene, sixteen smaller miniatures, decorative initials – of the kind visible on the page open in front of the lady reading in the foreground – and ornamental borders of flowers, tendrils and fantastical figures. The opening pages are written in gold and silver on black parchment, the remainder on the usual pale parchment. It is possible that the book was originally created

in a particularly lavish format for the Duke, but was subsequently redesigned by Margaret as a bridal gift for Mary. Not only the veil and the necklace point towards a female recipient, but also an alteration in the Latin text. The scribe has turned an "unfortunate sinner" in the masculine case into an *infelix peccatrix* in the feminine. It remains unclear whether the Book of Hours arose before or after Charles's death, before or after Mary's marriage. The two ladies depicted are not yet (or are no longer) dressed in mourning clothes. The double heraldic shields pre-painted in gold elsewhere in the book are empty, so that it may be assumed that the bridegroom had not yet been finalized. The approximate dating lies between 1470 and 1480. A striking aspect of the window miniature is its preference for the colour green, as found in the cloth on which the Book of Hours is resting, the altar carpet and the angel's wings. Perhaps it was one of Mary's favourite colours, the colour of resurgence and hope – hope of a better future.

Mary's descendants would found the first great European empire of the Early Modern era: her son Philip the Handsome married Joanna of Castile and thereby took the Hapsburgs to Spain. Her grandson Charles V and great grandson Philip II ruled over a kingdom "in which the sun never set". Philip II had his bedchamber in the Escorial arranged in such a way that he could look from his bed through a window into the chapel and onto the altar.

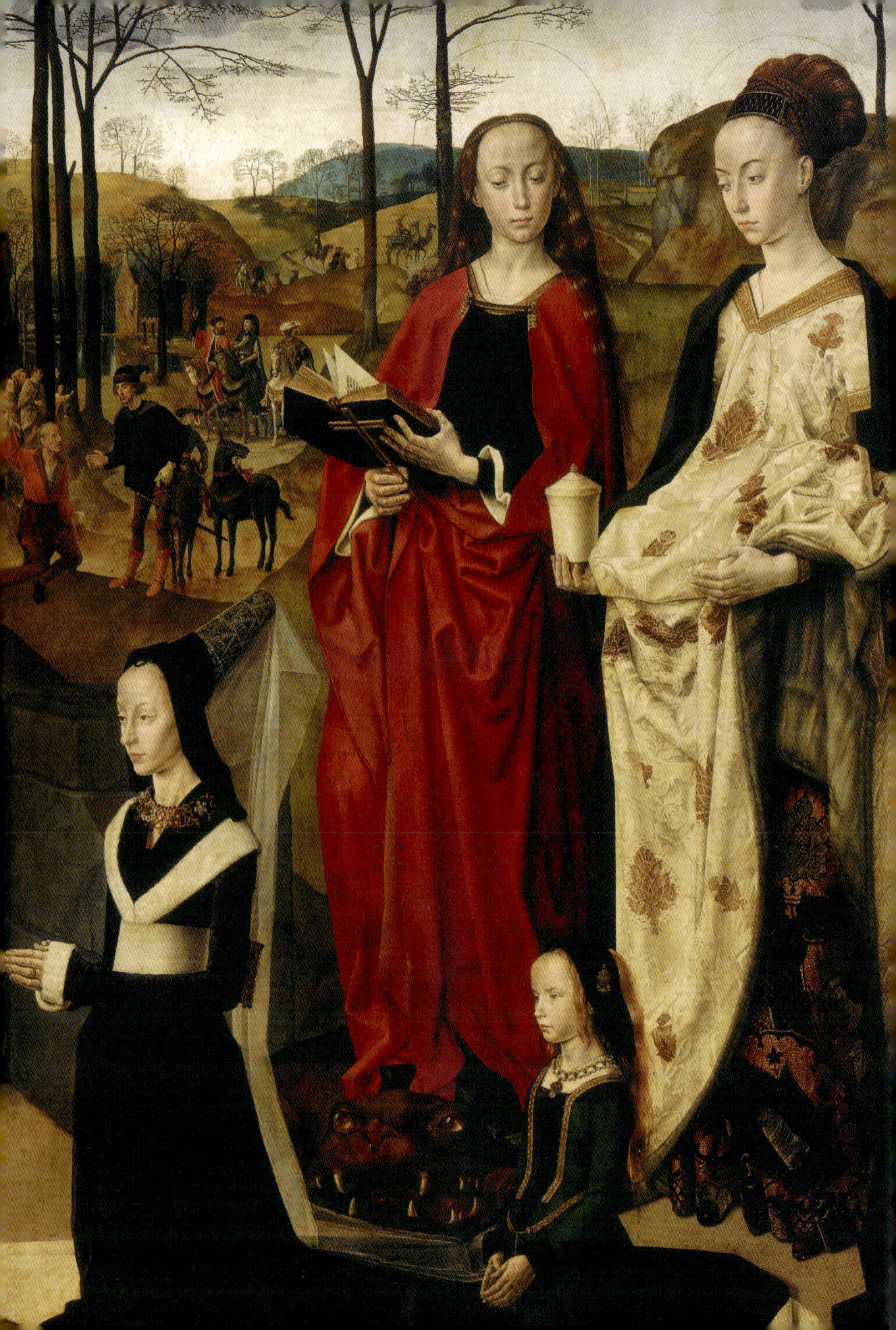

Hugo van der Goes (*c.* 1440 – 1482)

An empire collapses; the painter retreats

The Portinari Altar, c. 1475
600 x 250 cm, Florence, Galleria degli Uffizi

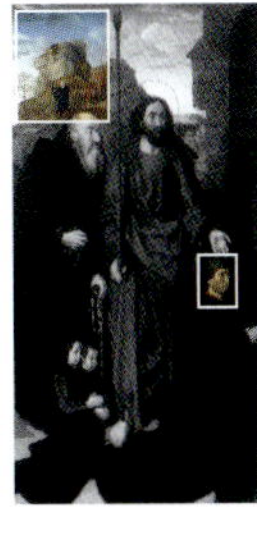
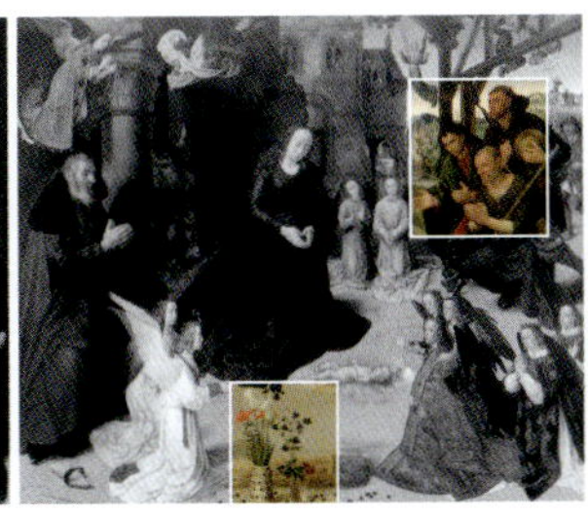
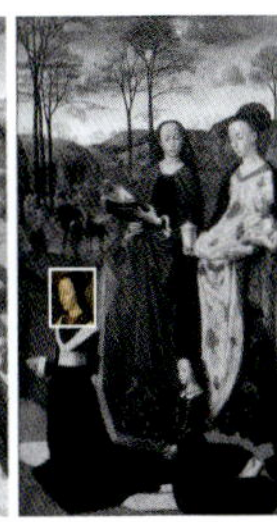

This altar, today part of the collection of the Uffizi in Florence, measures 6 metres wide and 2.5 metres high. It was painted in Ghent, taken to Pisa via Sicily on a merchant ship, from there transported by barge up the Arno to the gates of Florence, and then carried to the church of San Egidio by sixteen men. It reached its destination on 28 May 1483.

Its safe arrival was by no means a foregone conclusion. Ten years earlier, a Florentine banker had attempted to send a *Last Judgement* by the artist Hans Memling back to his native city from Flanders, but the ship was seized by a Hanseatic freebooter and Memling's painting landed in Danzig, where it still remains today.

The church of San Egidio belonged to the Santa Maria Nuova hospital, which was founded in 1288 by the merchant Folco Portinari. The altar by the Flemish artist Hugo van der Goes was donated by one of Folco's descendants, Tommaso Portinari. Tommaso was manager of the Bruges branch of the Medici bank, and was also a councillor at the court of Charles the Bold, Duke of Burgundy.

Van der Goes portrays Tommaso Portinari on the left wing of the altar, and his wife Maria on the right. Their three children – Margherita, Antonio and Pigello – are kneeling behind them. The family are protected by their name saints, who tower over them: St Margaret has her foot on the dragon which,

according to legend, once swallowed her; Mary Magdalene bears the jar containing the ointment with which she annointed Christ's feet; St Thomas has beside him, as his attribute, the lance with which he was killed; and St Antony Abbot, the father of the monastic order, is identified by his bell and rosary. The youngest son has no patron saint of his own; he was probably born after the contents and layout of the altar had already been decided.

In portraying the patron saints on a much larger scale than the donor family, van der Goes was following a well documented medieval tradition, whereby size served as a symbolic indication of importance.

He also obeyed medieval convention in another way, namely by ignoring time and space and bringing together, within one painting, episodes which occurred at different times and in different places. Thus we see not only the actual Nativity, but Mary and Joseph on their way to Bethlehem prior to Christ's birth. On the other hand, van der Goes executed many of the details with an extraordinary degree of realism and drew upon his knowledge of centralized perspective, as evidenced by the buildings in the background.

The Portinari Altar is a work full of contradictions and tensions. In Florence, where medieval tradition had long been overridden by the Renaissance and

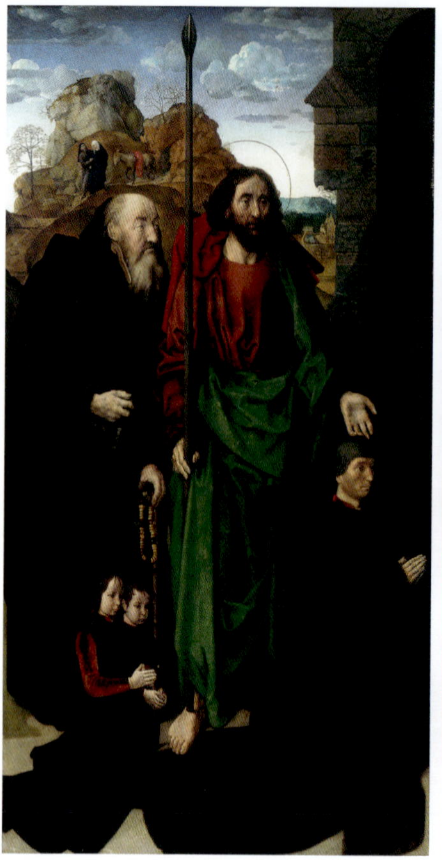

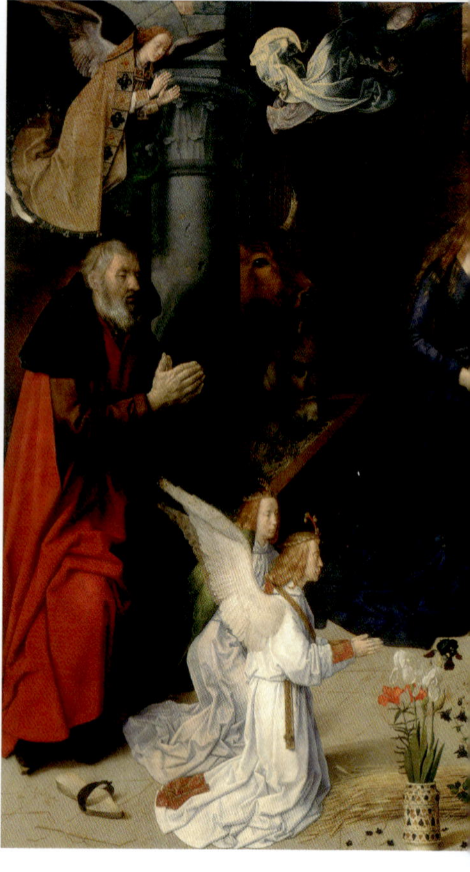

where saints and gods had been brought back down to a human scale, it must have attracted great attention. It came from another world.

An endangered genius

Hugo van der Goes shows an inhospitable, northern December landscape, in which the trees spread their bare boughs against a grey sky. A rocky outcrop towers threateningly over the mountainous path which the pregnant Mary, supported by Joseph, must tread, as they make their way to Bethlehem for the census. The stony path points to the suffering which lies ahead for the Virgin and which she already knows she will have to bear.

In the central panel of the altar, an austere Madonna gazes down at the Christ child with an expression which is almost that of a Pietà. The baby is lying not swaddled in a manger full of hay, but naked on the ground, unprotected in a stable open to all four winds. Nor are the angels singing "Exultate jubilate"; rather, they are looking with stern and serious faces at a sinful world. There is little in this altarpiece to indicate that, with the birth of the Saviour, they have a joyful message to proclaim.

One explanation for the gloomy atmosphere hanging over this holy Nativity may lie in 15th-century events: at the time the altar was painted, the powerful Burgundian empire, of which the

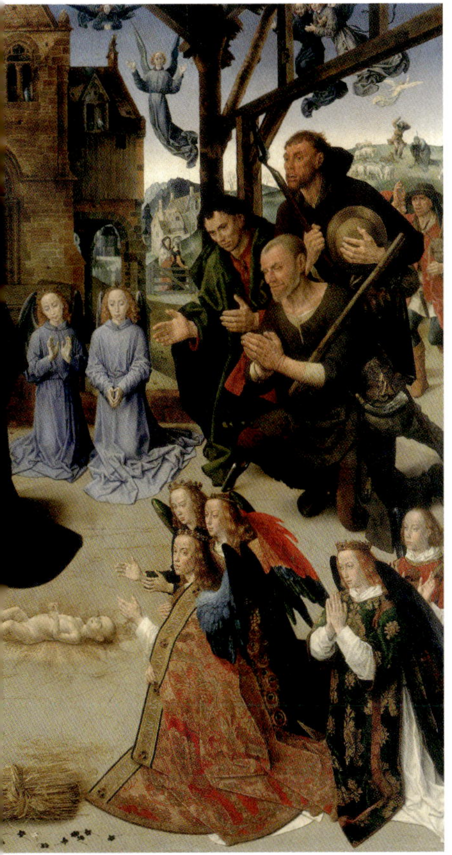

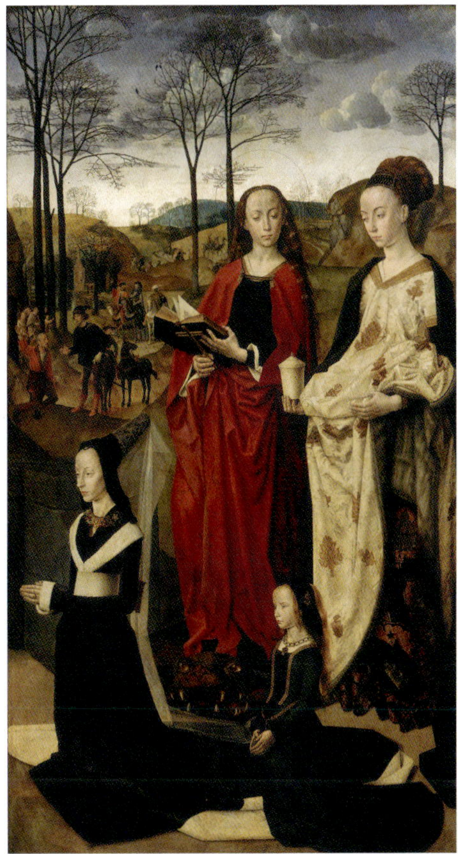

Netherlands was a part, was starting to disintegrate. There may have been more personal factors in play, too: the painter suffered from depression, at least in his latter years. This we know from the detailed records kept by Brother Gaspar Ofhuys, master of the sick in the monastery to which the painter withdrew in 1478.

Van der Goes was born around 1440 in Ghent. Little is known about the early years of his life. In 1467 he was accepted as a master into the painters' guild of Ghent. In 1468 he worked in Bruges – probably alongside Hans Memling and Petrus Christus – on the decorations for the marriage of Duke Charles the Bold. The great masters of

Flemish painting, the van Eyck brothers and Rogier van der Weyden, were by now already dead.

When, in 1480, a charter described van der Goes as "the most outstanding living Flemish master", the Portinari Altar was already finished. It must have been shortly after completing this work that he entered the so-called Red Monastery near Brussels as a *frater conversus*, a rank between canon and lay brother. He embraced poverty, chastity and obedience and continued to paint. His known œuvre comprises some 40 works.

According to Gaspar Ofhuys, "one night, Brother Hugo was seized by a strange sickness of the imagination. He began to wail incessantly that

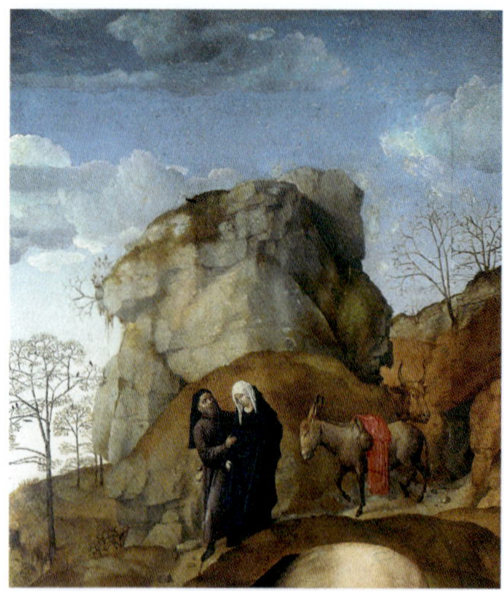

he was damned and condemned to eternal damnation. He would even have inflicted a hurt upon himself, had not those around him forcibly prevented him from doing so." The painter's attacks expressed themselves in religious delusions in line with the beliefs of his day and his environment.

In retrospect, Hugo van der Goes appears as one of the first of a new breed of artist. In the Middle Ages, a painter was simply viewed as a craftsman who carried out the wishes of his clients, be they from the sacred or the secular sphere. He thus worked within clear and narrow bounds. In 1482, by contrast, the Florentine author Marsilio Ficino described the artist for the first time as an endangered melancholic genius, in turn inspired or cast down by Saturn. Creative zeal was followed by crippling despair; 1482 was the year in which van der Goes died.

The donor was an ambitious but luckless banker

The date of the altar can be deduced with some certainty from the ages of the Portinari children: the three portrayed by the artist were born between 1471 and 1474, and a fourth was born in 1476. The work was thus probably painted around 1475/76. The donor at that time stood at the pinnacle of his career – and shortly before its sudden end.

Tommaso Portinari was the representative in Bruges of what was then the biggest banking and trading house in Europe. Around 1470, in addition to their headquarters in Florence, the Medici maintained seven subsidiary offices (in Venice, Milan, Rome, Bruges, Avignon, Lyons and London). Bruges was important because it was here that trade was conducted with the Hanseatic cities of northern Europe.

Born in 1428, Tommaso Portinari had entered the service of the Medici at the age of seventeen. He rose through the ranks and in 1462 became head of the Bruges branch and simultaneously a partner in the Medici empire: he put up two-fifteenths of the business capital and received a quarter of the profits. Each time his contract was renewed, this extremely shrewd businessman negotiated more favourable terms for himself.

His independence grew following the death of Piero de' Medici, the experienced head of the family concern who had profound distrust of Portinari. The running of the bank passed to Lorenzo de' Medici (later called Lorenzo the Magnificent), who was just 21 years old, and who was more interested in large-scale politics than in business.

Tommaso Portinari was granted an increasingly free hand. Although, in 1471, a fixed limit was still imposed on the amounts he could lend to the Duke of Burgundy, two years later this was dropped. Everything was left to his own judgement. A dangerous development, for the banker loved risky

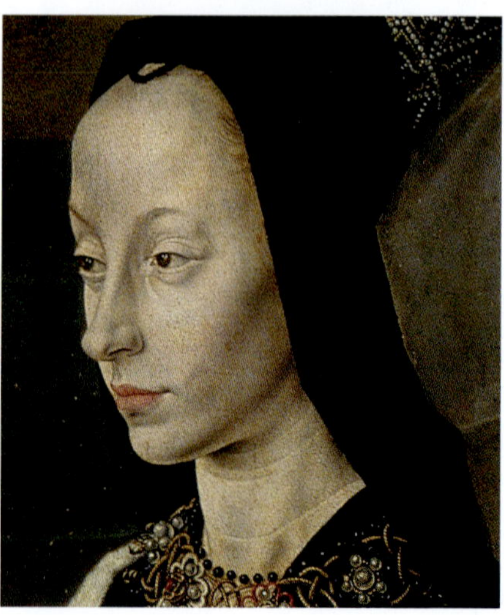

speculation: around 1475 he invested large sums in a voyage of discovery mounted by the Portuguese, which set sail for the African coast and which ended up making an overall loss. Only two decades later, a similar expedition led to the discovery of America. Tommaso, meanwhile, continued to back the wrong horses: he miscalculated with some long-term wool contracts, and was lured again and again into granting massive loans to the Duke of Burgundy.

Bruges at that time belonged to Burgundy, a loose knit empire extending from the Swiss border to the shores of the North Sea. Duke Charles the Bold, its ruler since 1467, needed money to fund his magnificent court and countless wars. Tommaso provided it, "in order" – as Lorenzo de' Medici subsequently accused him – "to court the Duke's favour and make himself important", whereby he "did not care whether it was at our expense." Like many others, the Florentine Portinari was bewitched by the charismatic Duke and dazzled by the aristocratic glamour of his court. He enjoyed cultivating an appropriately ostentatious image and persuaded the Medici to buy one of the most splendid houses in Bruges as the bank's offices.

In the altarpiece, Tommaso's wife Maria is wearing the austere costume of the Burgundian court, with a gold embroidered pointed hat. The daughter of a good Florentine family, in 1470 – aged just fifteen – she was sent to Bruges to marry Tommaso, 42 years her elder. Just a few years later she appears in this painting looking somewhat careworn, exhausted by childbearing and a strenuous life alongside her agile husband.

The shepherds, realistically portrayed, represent the people

The code of conduct at the Burgundian court forbade uncontrolled gestures and the expression of personal feelings. The figures in this altar are

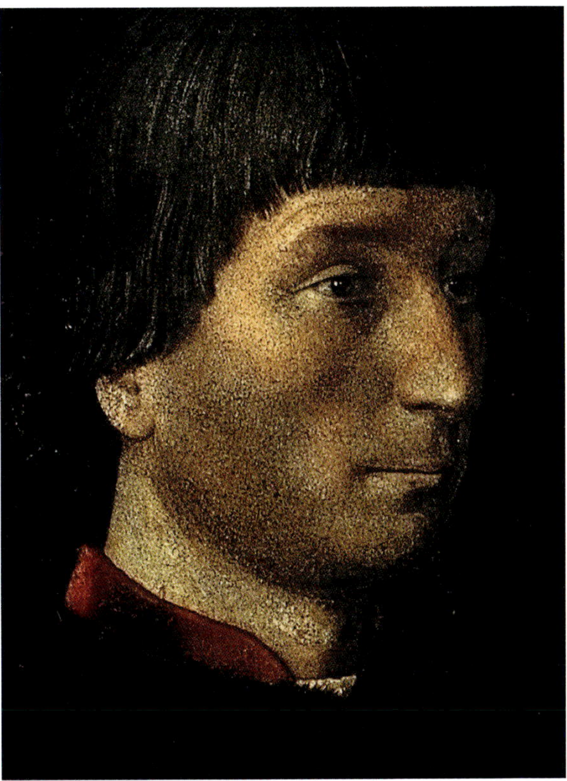

portrayed accordingly, with one exception: the shepherds, who represent the "discourteous" people outside the court. In the background, one raises his clenched fist with a shout, while in the foreground, another throws open his arms. They make no attempt to conceal their curiosity. Large in size and realistically portrayed, they are an unruly bunch thrusting their way into the stable.

Never before had the shepherds been granted such a dominating role in a Nativity scene. Whether coincidentally or not, they call to mind the historical role assumed around this time by the shepherds and peasants of other lands.

Only shortly after this altarpiece was executed, the Swiss Confederation conquered the army of Charles the Bold and thereby destroyed the powerful duchy of Burgundy. The confrontation was sparked by the Duke's attempts to annex the region, which lay in between the individual parts of his empire. As a result, the neighbouring states were effectively forced to unite against him. France gave the orders, while the Confederates (in return for a great deal of money) did the dirty work. In true medieval fashion, Charles fought with heavily armoured knights; the Swiss shepherds and peasants came on foot. They were thus more mobile than their opponents, and they knew the terrain. In 1476 they launched a surprise attack on Charles near Grandson, and plundered his train and treasures near Murten. On 5 January 1477 Charles fell at Nancy.

After his death, France reclaimed parts of Burgundy for itself. Elsewhere in the empire, unrest broke out. Charles' daughter Maria and her husband Archduke Maximilian of Austria inherited a tattered Burgundy saddled with debt. It had lasted just a hundred years, but had seen a late flowering of medieval courtly culture.

The financial losses incurred by the Medici were enormous, and the consequences for Portinari catastrophic. Italian banks had already been ruined by loans to rulers in the past; the Peruzzi and the Bardi banking houses, for example, had lent "sums worth a kingdom" to Edward III (1312–1377). Lorenzo de' Medici disassociated himself from Portinari and forced him to continue the running of the Bruges branch, with its low profits and huge debts, alone. Tommaso spent the rest of his life recovering loans and avoiding his creditors. He lived partly in Bruges, partly in Florence – always half on the run. In 1501 he died in the hospital to which, years earlier, he had donated the altar. His son renounced his inheritance, afraid that his father's debts would outweigh his assets.

The hidden meanings are the sweetest

Standing in the centre foreground, as if placed in front of a built altar, are two vases of flowers – carnations, aquilegia, lilies and violets. Normally they would never bloom in December; these bunches of flowers on the day of Christ's birth are a miracle.

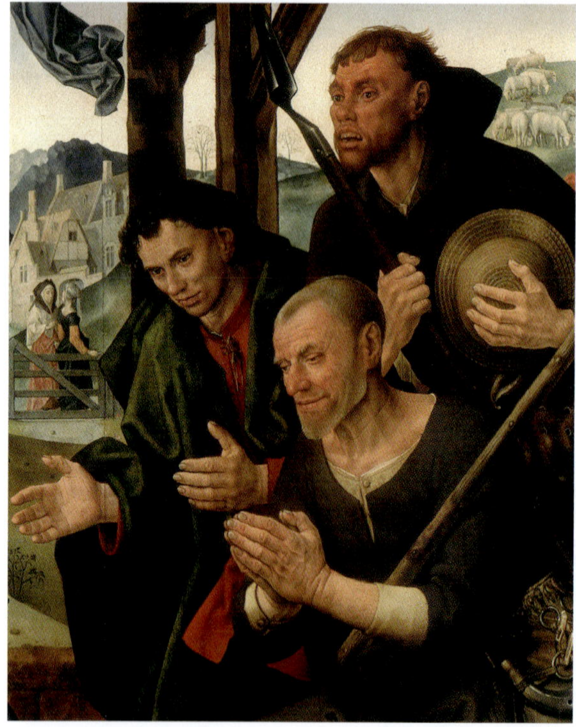

The altar is full of symbolic and biblical references. The harp above the door of the palace in the background signals that this is the home of the line of David, to which Joseph belongs: King David once played the harp to King Saul, who was tormented by an evil spirit, and calmed him. The sheaf of wheat is a reference to Bethlehem, whose name means "house of bread", and also to the body of Christ, the "bread of life". The parallels between the body of the child lying on the ground and that of the wheatsheaf correspond to the belief that the one will transform itself into the other. The painter has thus already incorporated in his Nativity references to the death of Christ, and to Mass and Communion.

According to St Augustine, "the hidden meanings are the sweetest", and in the 15th century the masters of Netherlandish painting took his words to heart, filling their paintings with religious allusions and symbols. After van der Goes, however, these became rare. The need for a Christian superstructure in art was displaced by a Renaissance interest in reality.

In granting the two vases of flowers their central position in the foreground, the painter also accorded them a central significance. In the 15th-century language of symbols, violets stood for humility, modesty, and submission to God's will. Carnations were known in Flanders as *nagelbloem* – "nail flowers"; thus the three carnations recall the nails with which Christ was hammered to the cross. The orange lilies represent the blood of Christ, and the white and blue irises the suffering and purity of the Virgin Mary. St Bridget of Sweden (born 1303) wrote of the Virgin: "For she felt the sharp edge of this sword in her heart just as often as she foresaw the wounds and sufferings of her son in her mind …"

The aquilegia also point to the suffering ahead; they were associated with melancholy and their dark blue was the colour of mourning. Mary is dressed in a dark blue robe, a further indication that this altar is announcing not the glad tidings of Christ's birth, but his future Passion.

It was painted as Charles the Bold was heading for ruin, as his duchy was collapsing. Perhaps something of the contemporary atmosphere of doom and gloom made its way into the altarpiece. Van der Goes was a subject of the Duke and his career was closely bound up with the House of Burgundy. He had documented its marriages, funerals and festive processions, and Charles's death, the collapse of his empire and the uprisings which broke out in Ghent must have affected him. These events may also have been the reason why the shipment of the altarpiece to Florence was delayed – and why the painter withdrew to the seclusion of a monastery.

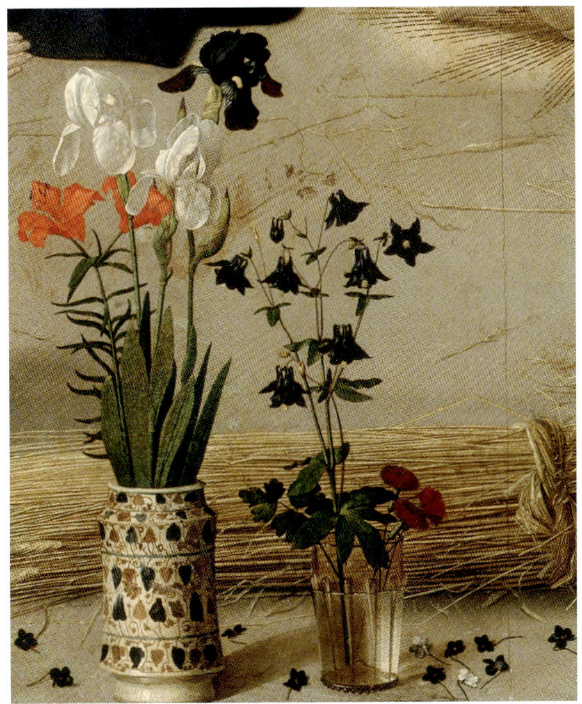

The depressive van der Goes was probably also affected by the intellectual contradictions of his day, and in particular by the conflict between medieval restraint and the more liberal ideas of the Renaissance. Although he never visited Italy, he must have seen works by Renaissance masters in the houses of Florentine merchants in Bruges. Tension is certainly evident in his Portinari Altar. While its subject and symbolism still adhere fully to medieval Christian tradition, its use of perspective and the realism of its shepherds point to the Renaissance. The way in which van der Goes portrayed the shepherds exerted its own influence in Italy, as can be seen in works from 1485 by the Florentine master Ghirlandaio – evidence of a reciprocal artistic exchange between Flanders and Florence.

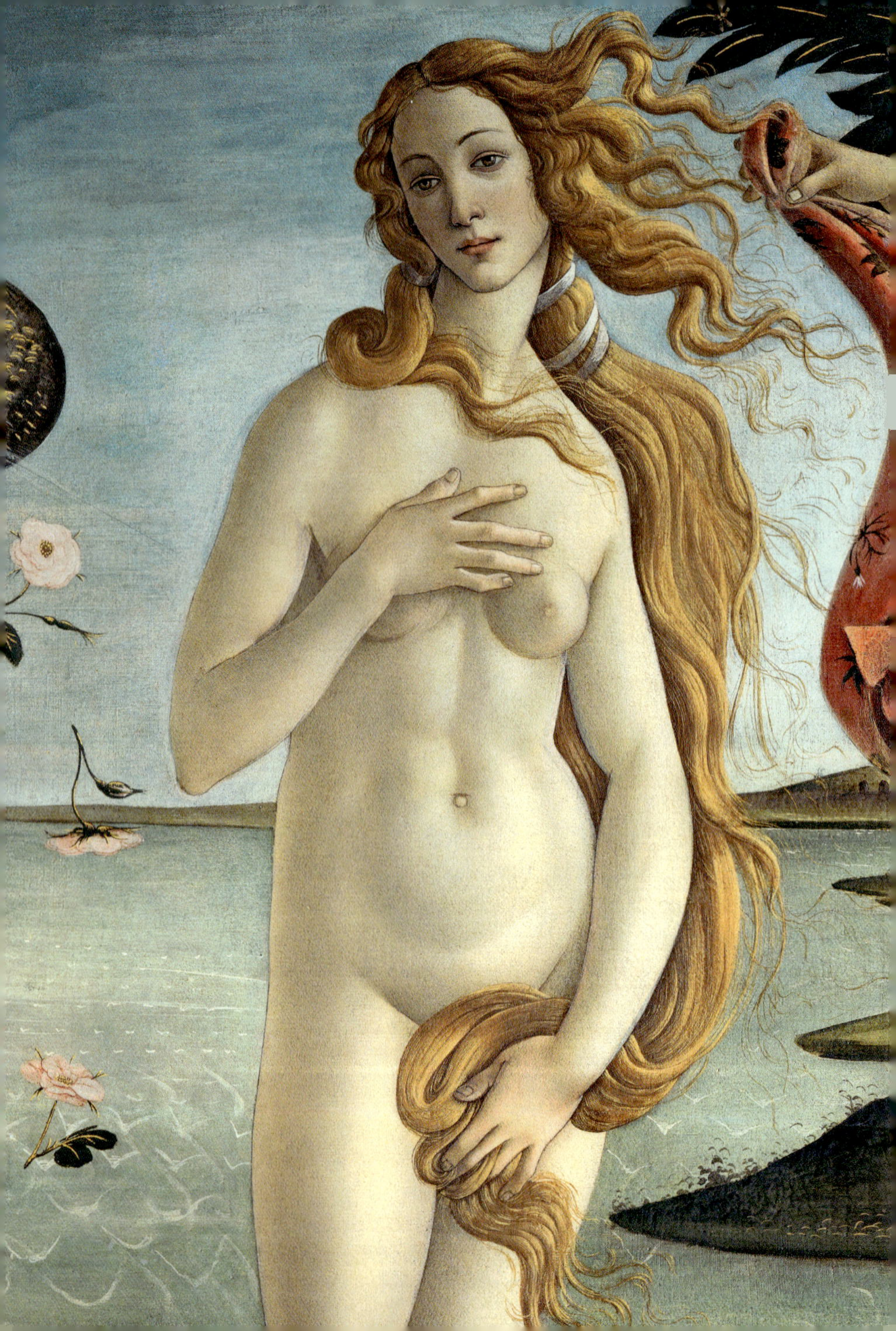

Sandro Botticelli (1445–1510)
(real name Alessandro di Mariano Filipepi)

Fairest daughter of heaven and waves

The Birth of Venus, c. 1486
184 x 285.5 cm, Florence, Galleria degli Uffizi

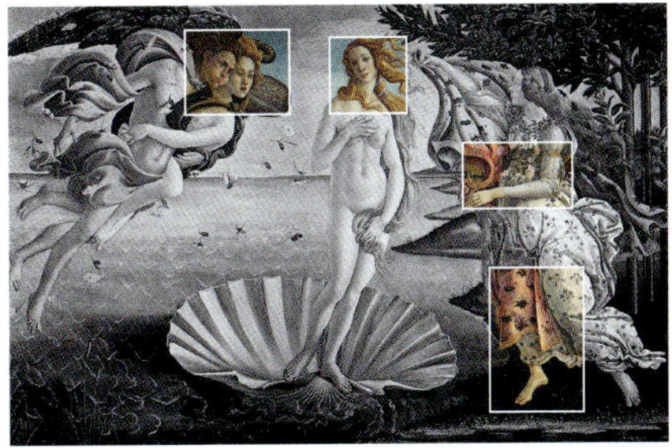

It had been a thousand years since anyone in Europe had seen the like of it: an almost life-sized nude, the representation of a naked woman, a picture of perfect corporeal grace – Aphrodite, the Greek goddess of beauty and love, whom the Romans called Venus, reborn in Renaissance Florence. Arisen from the waves, borne on a breath of wind, she approaches the shore on a shell.

This pagan scene was painted around 1486 by the Florentine Sandro Botticelli, a devout Christian, whose studio concentrated largely on satisfying the enormous demands of the public for devotional pictures: saints, gentle-faced Virgins and the Holy Child. Practically all art had a religious content at the time. It has been calculated that only thirteen per cent of art works had secular themes, the majority of them portraits.

At the peak of his career, Botticelli, the renowned painter of Virgins, decided to turn his hand to something new: four large-scale "mythologies" based on the pagan tradition of Classical myths and legends. One of them was the *Birth of Venus*.

The first male nude of the Renaissance, a young bronze *David*, had been modelled from life in 1430 by the Florentine sculptor Donatello. The fact that the *Birth of Venus* did not appear until over fifty years later is a testimony to the lasting effect of the Christian taboo against the portrayal of the naked female body. Previously, the only female nudes to dare appear in works of art had been Eves with snakes and apples; punished for their sins, they had quickly been expelled from paradise, stooping under the burden of their shame.

Unlike these heavily stylized, Gothic figures of Eve, Botticelli's Venus is patently the product of anatomical studies, as well as the artist's adherence to Classical models. The influence of Greek Classical sculpture is visible in the way the weight of the goddess rests on one leg, in the attractive curve of her hip, in her chaste gesture. The Renaissance artist has drawn her proportions in accordance with a canon of harmony and ideal beauty developed by artists such as Polyclitus and Praxiteles. This included the measurement of an equal distance between the breasts, between the navel and breasts, and between navel and crotch. The canon helped form countless nudes, from Classical Greek statues to figures on late Roman tombs. However, it later fell into disrepute

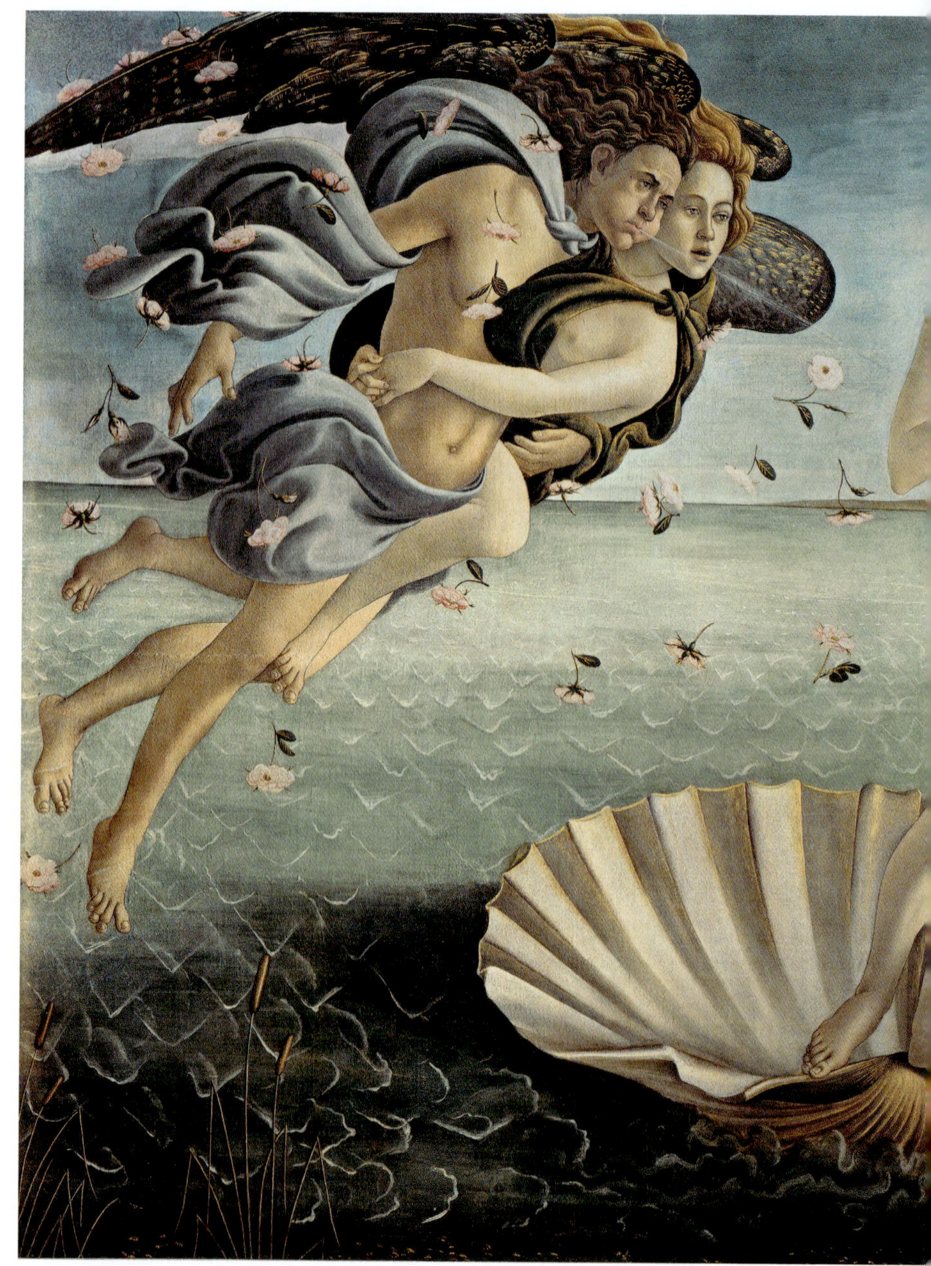

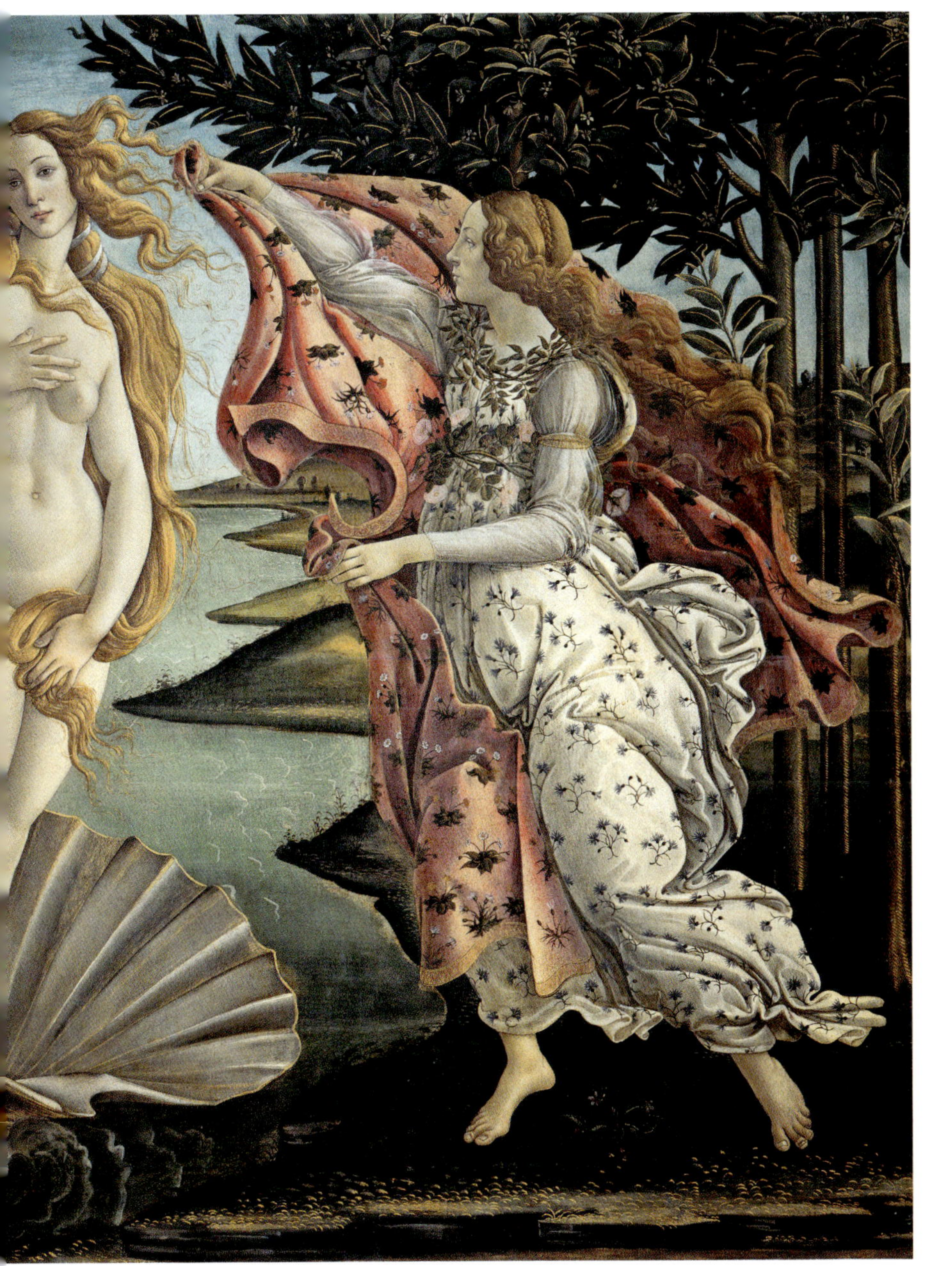

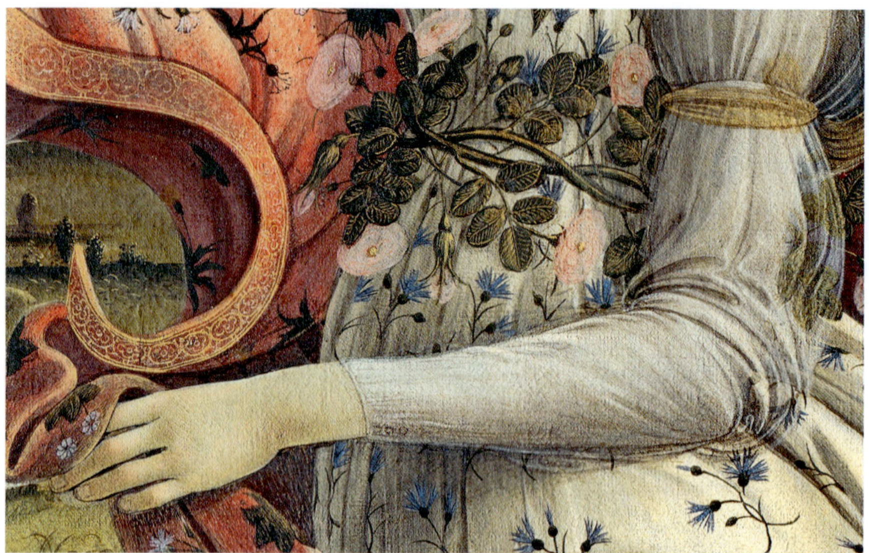

and, eventually, oblivion, where it remained until its rediscovery by the Renaissance. It has influenced our taste ever since.

Botticelli's goddess of beauty is one of the great stars of the Uffizi, Florence. Only with difficulty can she be protected against the fervour of her admirers. The situation has become worse since restoration of the work was concluded in the spring of 1987. A layer of varnish, added some time after the work was completed and darkened to a yellowish-brown patina with age, was removed from the 184-by-285.5-centimetre canvas. The heavens, waves and deities now shine out boldly and brightly in their original tempera.

Decorative blossom for a cool villa

Where the goddess of love lingers, roses fall from the sky. In the place where her foot first alighted on land – according to the Greek poet Anacreon (who lived from 580 until after 495 BC) – sprang the very first rose bush. There are pale red roses, too, wound around the waist of the girl waiting to receive Venus on the shore. Perhaps she is one of the three Graces, thought in Classical antiquity to belong to the entourage of the goddess, or one of the three Horae, the seasons. The anemones at her feet and her cornflower-bespangled dress suggest she is the Hora

of spring – the time of the year when Venus restored love and beauty to the earth after a hard winter.

The *Birth of Venus* could almost be called *Primavera*, or *Spring*, the title of Botticelli's other great "mythology" in the Uffizi. Here, too, a (clothed) Venus holds court in a garden, surrounded by gods of the wind, flower-girls and semi nude Graces.

The painter and art biographer Giorgio Vasari mentions the paintings for the first time in 1550, when they hung together at Castello, a country villa near Florence belonging to Cosimo I de' Medici. Vasari, who was Duke Cosimo's architect, describes one as "The birth of Venus, and the skies and winds who lead her to the Earth, escorted by the gods of love; the other, Venus crowned by the Graces with flowers, announces the advent of Spring."

Art historians have generally assumed that Botticelli painted the works for the owner of this villa. In 1486 the owner was Lorenzo di Pierfrancesco de' Medici, also known as "Lorenzo the Younger" to distinguish him from his cousin Lorenzo the Magnificent, the uncrowned king of the Republic of Florence. However, while a recently discovered inventory has verified the younger Lorenzo's owner-ship of *Primavera*, there is no trace in the inventory of the *Birth of Venus*. It is therefore not known who commissioned it.

A link has naturally been sought between the painting and the two most famous Medici of all, Lorenzo the Magnificent and his brother Giuliano. The splendour, extolled by the poets, of their pageants and banquets has never ceased to fire the popular imagination. The *Birth* thus came to be seen as an act of homage to Simonetta Vespucci, the wife of a Florentine merchant. She had been the "Queen of Beauty" at a tournament organised by Giuliano in 1475, a fact which led various commentators to conclude that the nature of their relationship had been romantic; and since Simonetta was born at Porto Venere (Port Venus) on the Ligurian coast, Botticelli's goddess was said to bear her features. Both died shortly after the pageant: Giuliano stabbed by his political enemies, and Simonetta of consumption, adding a tragic note to the popular appeal of this account of events. Unfortunately, however, there is no real evidence to support the story.

Nor has it ever been explained how the painting later entered the possession of the Medici family. It is quite probable that it was intended for a country house outside Florence. The owners of these cool villas, bankers recuperating from business, noise and epidemics, preferred frescos and canvases with light hearted themes to religious panel paintings. Botticelli probably painted the goddess for one of his Florentine contemporaries, many of whom were capable of combining an understanding of money and politics with a refined sensibility for the arts. His patron may even have been able to appreciate Anacreon in the Greek original.

Relatives: Venus and Mary

Aphrodite, or Venus, was held in high regard by the Greeks and Romans. With the triumph of Christianity she fell into disgrace. During the Middle Ages she was seen as the incarnation of sinful lust and depravity.

The distrust in which she was held until well into the 14th century is documented by the Florentine sculptor Lorenzo Ghiberti (1378–1455). He wrote of an antique statue of Venus, a work "of great perfection", found in the neighbouring town of Siena. The citizens showed great reverence for the statue, placing it on the town well. But when the town was afflicted by war, the mood changed dramatically. "Since idolatry is forbidden by our faith," warned one public speaker, "there can surely be no doubt who has caused our misfortunes." On 7 November 1357 the councillors decided to "smash" the statue of Venus "to pieces" and to "bury its fragments within the precincts of Florence in the hope that they would bring similar misfortune upon the heads of their enemies". The same Ghiberti was lucky enough to witness the rediscovery of a second Venus, which came to light in Florence "while they were digging under the Bunelleschi Villa". However, this statue did not suffer the fate of its Sienese cousin, for the religious climate in Florence had now changed. Tired of the conventions propagated during the Middle Ages, the Florentines sought new models. They found them in Classical antiquity: the movement which came to be known as the Renaissance had begun.

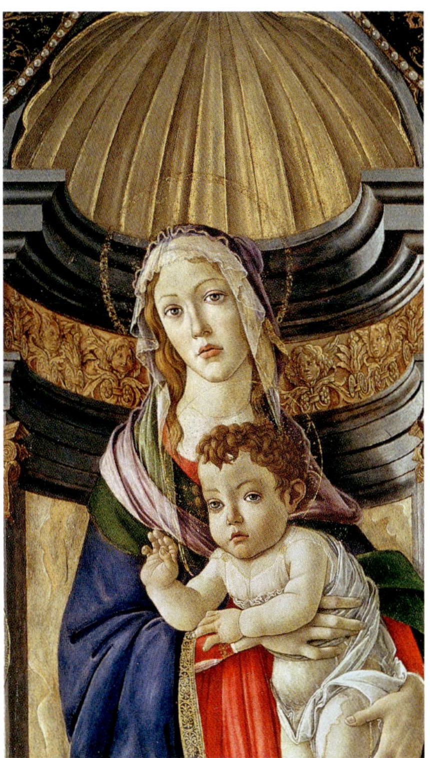

Comparative illustration:
Sandro Botticelli, St Barnabas Altar, c. 1487,
268 x 280 cm, Florence, Galleria degli Uffizi

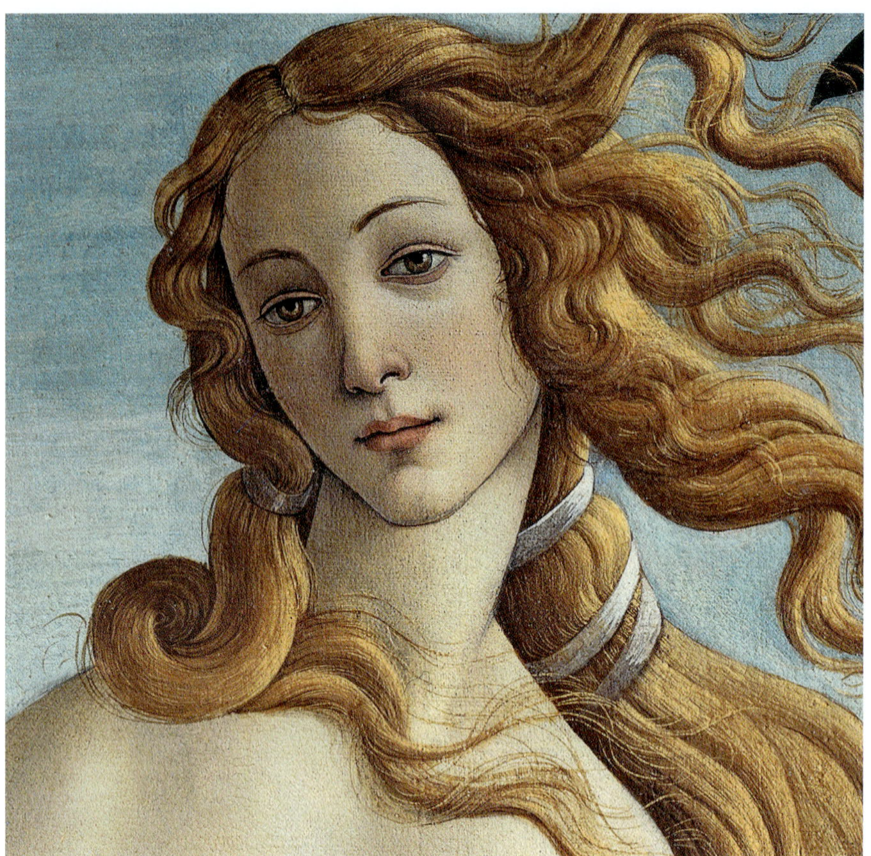

It is not known what inspired Botticelli, one of the second generation of Renaissance artists, to paint the *Birth of Venus*. He was undoubtedly acquainted with the Medicis' collection of antique gems with their Roman depictions of nereids and sea goddesses. It was also at this time that translations by Florentine humanists appeared in printed editions in Botticelli's native town. The *Homeric Hymns*, for example, were published in 1488: "Aphrodite, beautiful, chaste, of her shall I sing … who holds sway over the sea washed embattlements of Cyprus, where the moist breath of Zephyrus gently bore her … to be greeted by the Horae with golden diadem and joy …"

In his *Theogeny*, written in the 8th century before Christ, Hesiod tells of Aphrodite Anadyomene –

i.e. "rising out of the waters". During the battle of the gods, Cronos defeats and castrates his father Uranus, the heaven; his seed flows into the sea, the union of water and heaven producing the goddess of love. The secret of her birth was considered a sacred mystery and was linked to a cult, whose symbols appear in Botticelli's painting. Thus the purple gown, held ready for the goddess on the shore, has not only an aesthetic, but also a ritual function. Its first appearance was on early Grecian urns, where it symbolized the border between two regions: both newly born babies and the dead were wrapped in cloth.

During the Middle Ages, the traditional attributes of Venus – her roses, for example – were passed on to another dominant figure, whose role was utterly opposed: the Christian Virgin Mary. This is also true of her shell. In connection with the pagan goddess, the seashell, like water, represented fertility. Its resemblance to the female genital organs made it a symbol of sensuous pleasure and sexuality. But as the dome above the Virgin's head in Botticelli's St Barnabas altarpiece, it can only symbolize virginity: it was thought that various kinds of mollusc were fertilized by the dew. The ambivalence of the symbols suggests that the dominant mythical female figures of Classical antiquity and the Middle Ages overlap. In any case, Botticelli evidently had no compunction about using the same model for both.

Zephyrus makes their robes flutter

Homer's story of Venus refers to the chubby cheeked god of the wind. His name was Zephyrus, the Wind of the West, on whose breath spring came to the land. The Roman poet Ovid tells of his companion Chloris, whose white legs and arms are clasped around Zephyrus' brown body: after he had raped her, the West Wind made her his wife, turning her into Flora, the goddess of flowers.

Where did the Florentine craftsman and tanner's son Botticelli receive his education in mythology? He was described in childhood as a sickly boy who spent much of his time reading. But could an apprenticeship to a goldsmith, and later to a painter, really leave him as well versed in Ovid and Homer as some of Florence's richer merchants? It seems unlikely, given the size of the library which belonged to the Maiano brothers. These artists came from the same town, the same generation and the same class background as Botticelli. According to an inventory compiled in 1498 they possessed a mere 29 books, half of them religious. The only Classical texts were a biography of Alexander and an edition of Livy's works. The scope of Botticelli's library was probably comparable.

"Required to execute a history painting," the Renaissance architect and art historian Leon

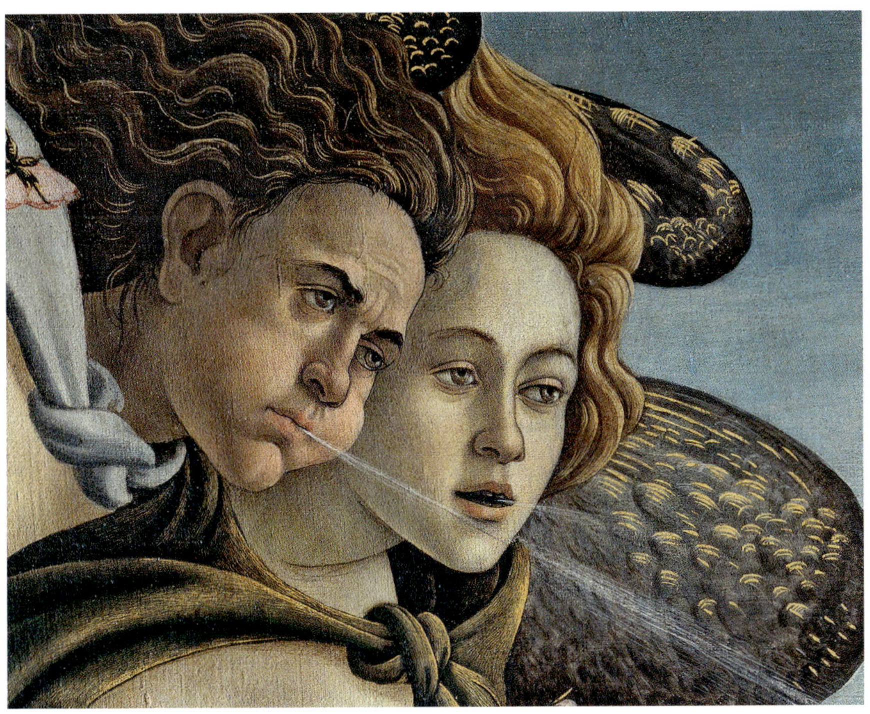

Battista Alberti (1404–1472) recommended "asking friends for advice." Through his neighbour, Giorgio Antonio Vespucci, Botticelli was well connected with the intellectual elite of Florence: scholars who, under the aegis of the ruling Medici, had set about rediscovering Classical antiquity.

Botticelli occasionally collaborated with the humanist and poet Angelo Poliziano (1454–1494). For example, he decorated a jousting banner for Giuliano de' Medici with allegorical motifs devised by the scholar. In a poem written in honour of the same tournament, Poliziano describes a *Birth of Venus* not unlike that by Botticelli. Possibly, the painter's "mythologies" benefitted from Poliziano's expert advice.

However, Botticelli's adviser could just as easily have been the philosopher Marsilio Ficino (1433–1499). Ficino's lifework was an attempt to reconcile Classical philosphy with Christianity (even humanists attended daily mass!): a new doctrine sprung from the union of pagan ideas with medieval theology. "Celestial Venus", as opposed to the pagan earthbound goddess, was given a highly positive role in Ficino's system: she stood for humanity, charity and love, and her beauty led mortals to heaven.

Even if Poliziano or Ficino did not advise the artist directly, their society must have made the ancient divinities acceptable in his eyes, ensuring that a devout Florentine painter in 1486 could portray a naked Venus in good conscience, without having to fear that his work would be "smashed to pieces and buried".

Cornflowers of lapis lazuli blue

Because we take pleasure "at the sight of flowing garments," the theorist Alberti advised painters to show the face of Zephyrus blowing down through the clouds and "robes fluttering gracefully in the breeze". Botticelli followed his advice. In his *Birth of Venus* everything is in motion: the waves, the branches of orange trees in the background, the roses floating to earth, the robes of the different figures. It was also true of the figures' hair: Alberti had demanded that hair be shown "in flowing curls which appear to form rings, or to surge like flames into the sky, or to be intertwined like snakes".

The representation of movement as an expression of life and natural energy in rediscovered Roman statues and reliefs greatly impressed the artists of the Renaissance. They considered it important to take up the idea in their own work. In 1434, Alberti wrote a "modern" aesthetics based on Classical principles, entitled *On Painting*. Although unpublished until the following century, it was already known in Florence much earlier, probably becoming Botticelli's theoretical bible. Cennino Cennini's *The Craftsman's Handbook* had appeared in 1400 and would certainly have been used in Botticelli's studio. It explained how to crush lapis lazuli to extract blue colouring for the cornflowers on the Hora's robe, for example, or how to apply extremely thin gold leaf to Venus' purple gown. However, Botticelli was an innovative craftsman in his own right. His *Birth* is not painted conventionally on poplar. Unlike *Primavera* it is not a panel painting at all, but the first large-scale Tuscan work to be painted on canvas.

Although Botticelli still painted with tempera (Cennini advised using eggs from town hens, since country eggs made the colours too bright), he added extremely little fat to the pigment, achieving exceptional results. His canvas has remained firm and elastic ever since, the paint itself showing very few cracks. Removing a layer of oily varnish that had been added to the painting after its completion, restorers discovered that Botticelli had applied his own, very unusual protective layer of pure egg-white. It was this, together with the "lean" tempera, which made the painting resemble a fresco, making it suitable for a country residence. Indeed, the fact that she was hung in a villa outside Florence may have saved this Venus from oblivion, for it soon seemed as though all the efforts of humanists to rehabilitate the goddess had been overtaken by history. The defeat of the Medici led to the monk Savonarola's strictly enforced Florentine theocracy from 1494 and 1498. On the night before carnival, Shrove Tuesday 1497, he ordered make-up, jewellery and false hairpieces of all kinds, as well as "lascivious paintings", to be burned on a "bonfire of vanities". Botticelli is said to have become a follower of this fanatic monk. True or not, he certainly stopped painting pagan mythologies and naked women.

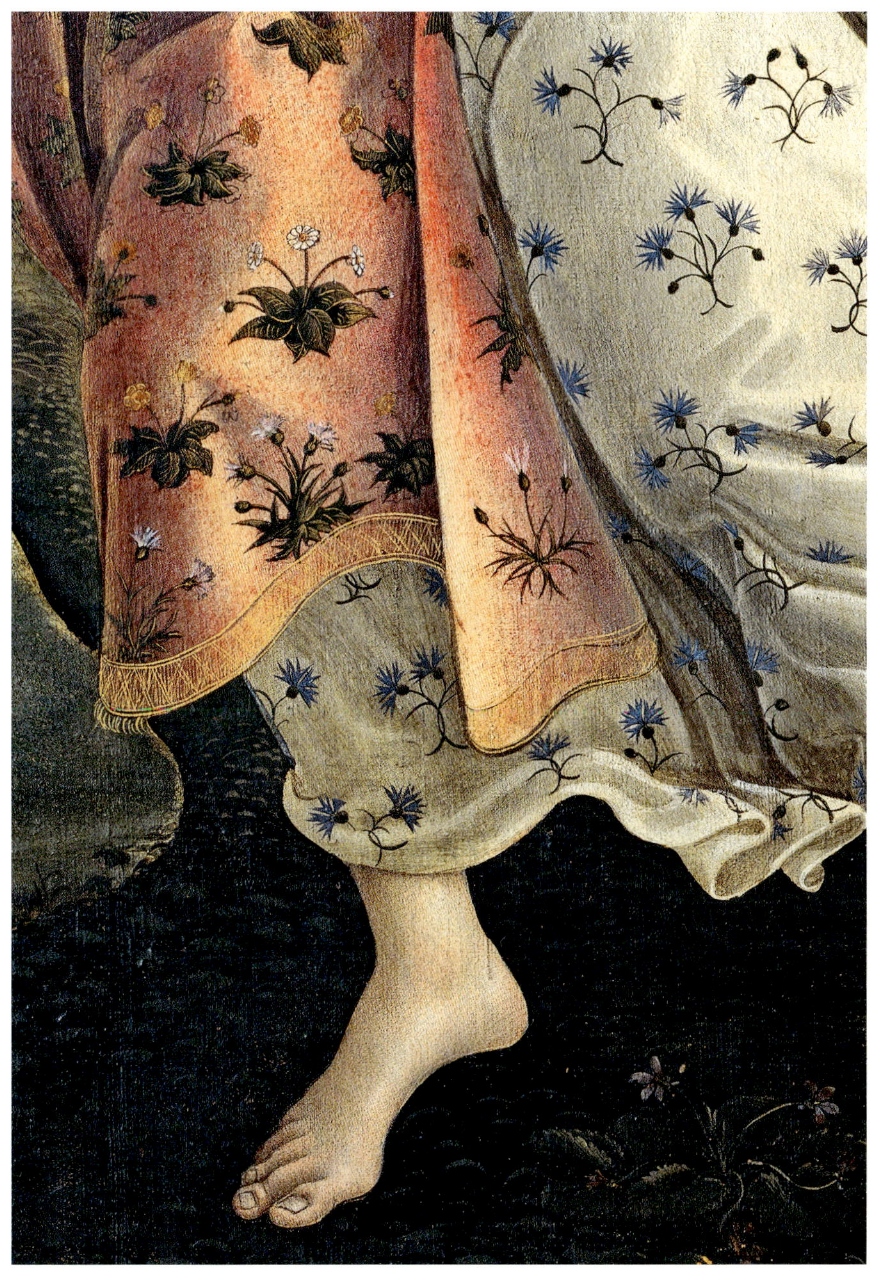

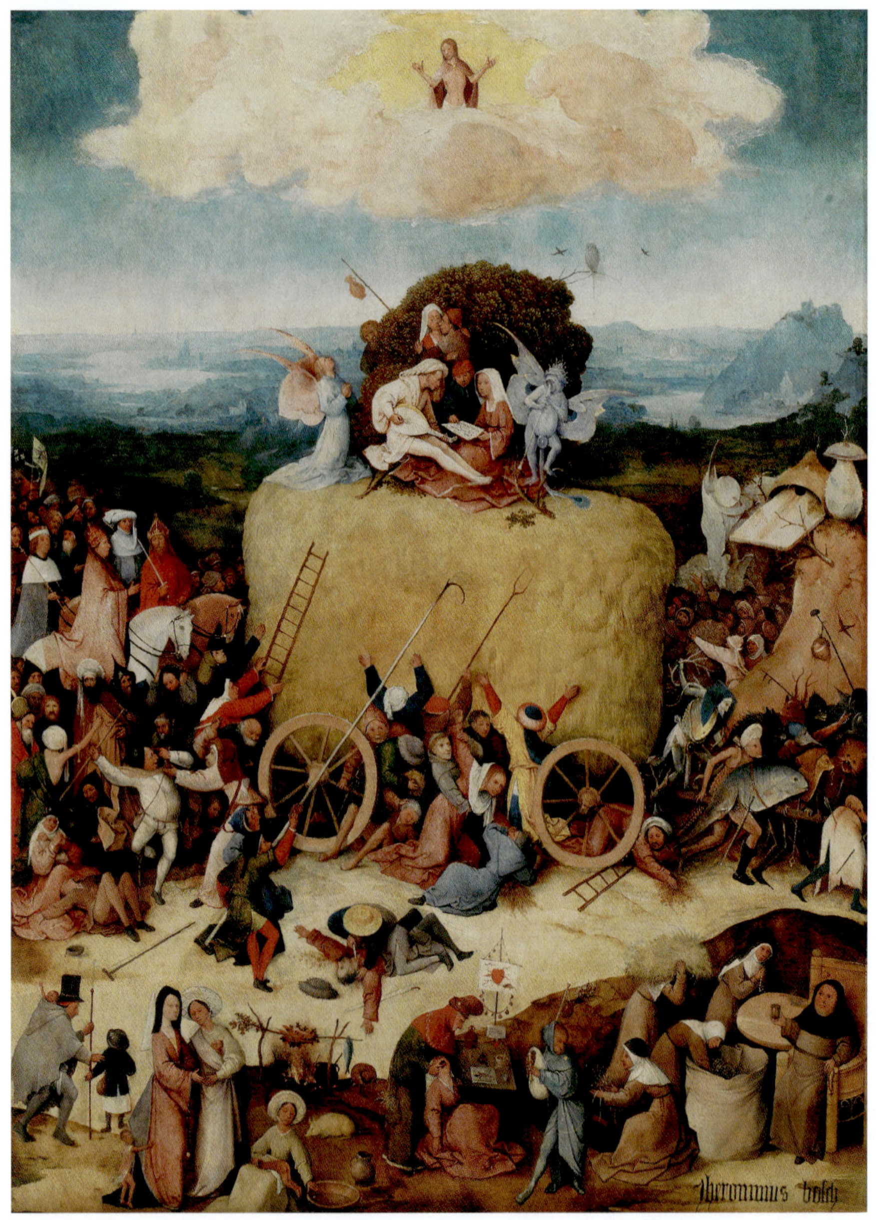

Hieronymus Bosch (1450–1516)
(real name Hieronymus van Aken)

A cart trundles towards damnation

The Haywain, between 1485 and 1490
135 x 100 cm, Madrid, Museo Nacional del Prado

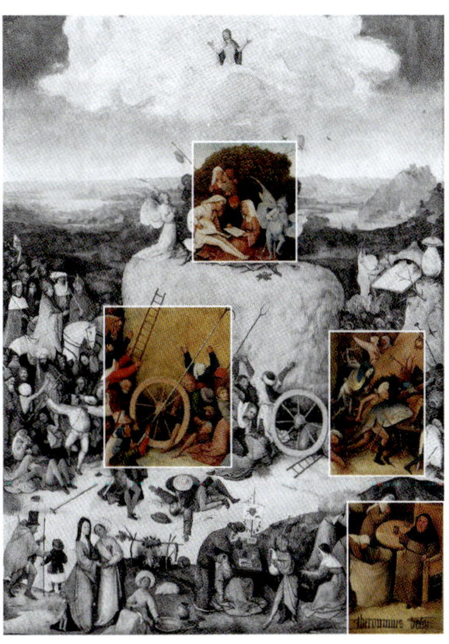

At first sight an alienating picture – overcrowded with objects and figures, bearing little relation to one another. In the middle is a cart laden with hay, with a bush somehow growing on top. In front of the bush, three people are making music; standing beside them – and painted with equal realism – are an angel and a devil. Riding behind the wagon are an emperor, a king and a pope – as if high-ranking rulers had ever provided a ceremonial escort for dried grass! The haywain is accompanied by men and women who, rather than trying to prop up the heavy load, are in fact trying to pull hay off it. They fight, and some of them fall under the wheels.

The wagon is being pulled by strange creatures – demons from the underworld. One of them is not quite a fish and not quite a man,

but has something of both. Behind them, people are streaming out of a mound of earth with a wooden door. There is another contradiction, too, between the wasteland in the foreground and the rich landscape in the upper half of the picture, presented so beautifully and clearly as if to make up for the chaos in front.

The panel, which measures 135 by 100 centimetres, forms the centre of a triptych. The left wing portrays Paradise, and the right wing a sort of Hell. The haywain and its crowd of followers are moving away from the meadows of innocence and towards the place of punishment for all sin. Never before, as far as is known, had a haywain formed the central focus of a painting. Together with its wings, the work resembles an altar. But at the point where

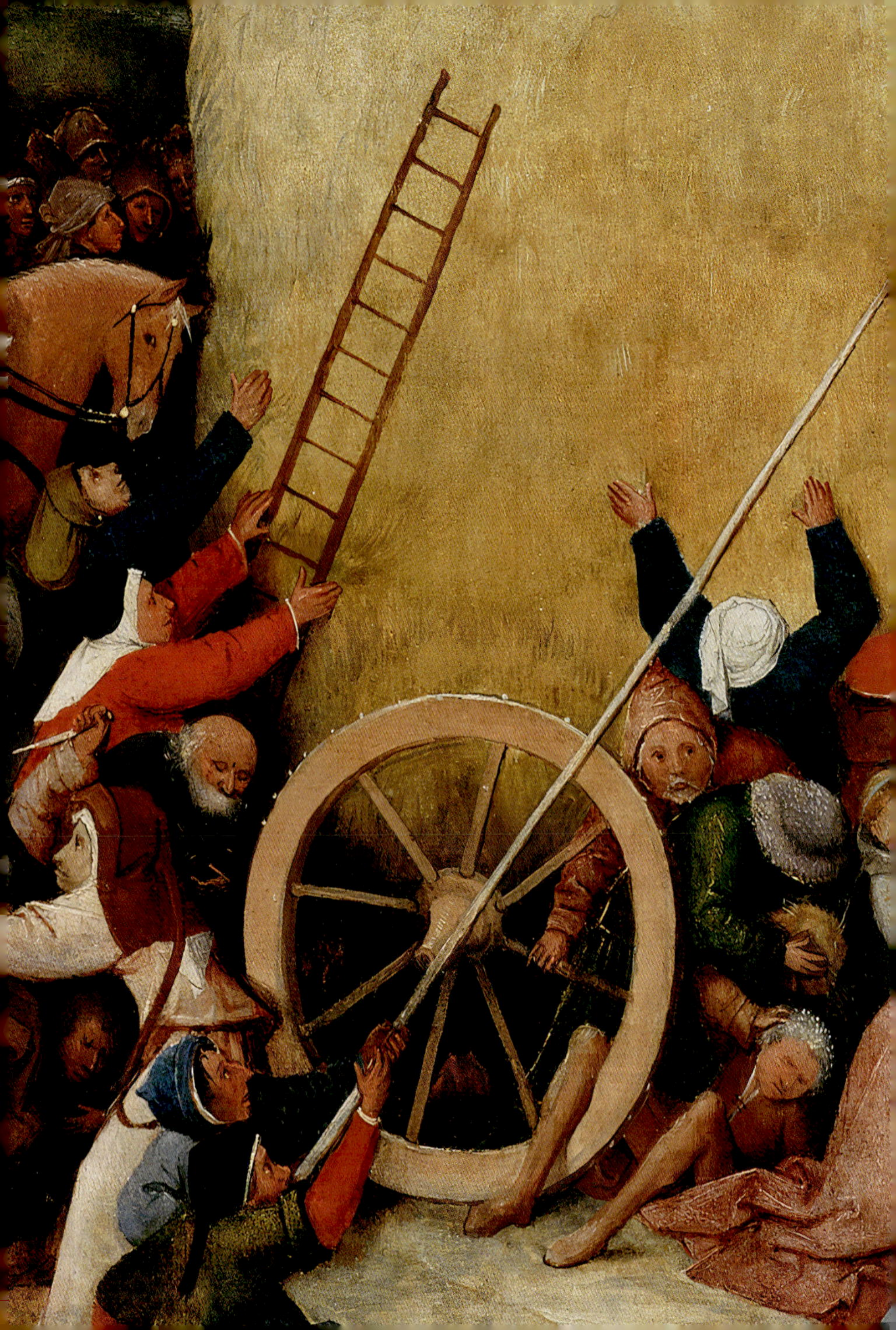

Christ would normally be seen on the Cross, Bosch paints his farm cart, disproportionately large in relation to the surface area of the panel.

The work is undated, but leading Bosch experts place it between 1485 and 1490. In all probability, it was painted in s'Hertogenbosch, the artist's birthplace, from which he derived his name. Born around 1450 into a family called van Aken, he died there in 1516. S'Hertogenbosch was at that time a prosperous town of some 25,000 inhabitants, albeit without its own university or bishop's palace. Its citizens wove linen, forged weapons, and traded, chiefly in agricultural products. Both then and over the following centuries, some 90 per cent of the population worked on estates and in the fields. Bosch's painting thus stemmed from a time when a laden haywain would have been a familiar sight to the viewer, who would also have appreciated the value of hay as winter fodder.

The rise in s'Hertogenbosch's fortunes was accompanied, as in other Dutch towns, by social strife. Since the height of the Middle Ages, all skilled trade activities had been regulated by guilds. Now, however, employers introduced new production processes and based their operations on what would later be termed early capitalist methods. Those who were successful made more profit than traditional masters of a craft, and they amassed large fortunes at the expense of real workers.

The acquisition of wealth was a topical subject in Bosch's day. The ruler of the Netherlandish provinces – the Hapsburg Archduke and later Emperor Maximilian – supported the new production methods, since he profited from the greater volume of taxes they yielded. His banner, with the double-headed eagle, can be seen behind the group of rulers on the left-hand edge of the picture.

Another highly topical subject was the decaying state of the Catholic Church. Bosch painted this picture of everyone trying to grab a handful of hay 30 years before Luther nailed his Protestant theses to the church door at Wittenberg. One of the chief reasons for Luther's anger at the Church was its secularization. The Pope behaved no differently to the princes. Material gain came before spiritual leadership.

The situation was similar in the churches and monasteries, which ranked amongst the biggest landowners. Many of the clergy and those living in monasteries considered their own well-being more important than the leading of a pious life.

The annals of the day are full of scandals; the faithful felt themselves abandoned, and by the end of the Middle Ages there was a widespread sense of scepticism and pessimism. Symptomatic of this mood is Bosch's figure of Christ, pushed away to the upper edge of the picture and displaying his stigmata in a seemingly helpless fashion.

The decline of the Church, therefore, and the abolition of the guild system, together with religious and social uncertainty and a new wealth, characterized the society in which Bosch painted his *Haywain*.

The world is a haystack

Carts on which something was symbolically represented would have been familiar to the 15th-century viewer from festival processions, such as those staged during the annual Shrovetide carnival or to honour a ruler. It is not merely the load carried by the haywain which is important here, however, but also the fact that it is moving forward. The people of the Middle Ages thought and felt in eschatological terms: according to Christian teaching, humankind was heading for an ultimate destination – the resurrection of the dead, the Last Judgement, and eternal life for the blessed. On the Day of Judgement, each person would have to answer for his actions before the throne of God. Each person was heading inexorably, along with everyone else, towards that day of divine reckoning – including those who had lost sight of that fact in the hustle and bustle of earthly existence. The haywain is rolling along. This motif of forward movement is also behind Bosch's *Ship of Fools*, in which religious and secular representatives of society are shown passing the time on board in frivolous pursuits. They pay no attention to the course they are sailing, and instead of landing in the harbour of salvation, they are shipwrecked off the coast of Fool's Land and are unable to stand before God at the Last Judgement.

The cart is laden with hay to a height which – from a realistic point of view – is impracticable. According to a Netherlandish proverb: "The world is a haystack, and everyone takes from it as much as they can grab." Although the proverb is only first recorded in the 19th century, it may be older. This is supported by the text of a Netherlandish song chronicled around 1470: God has piled up all good things like a haystack for the benefit of humankind; a fool

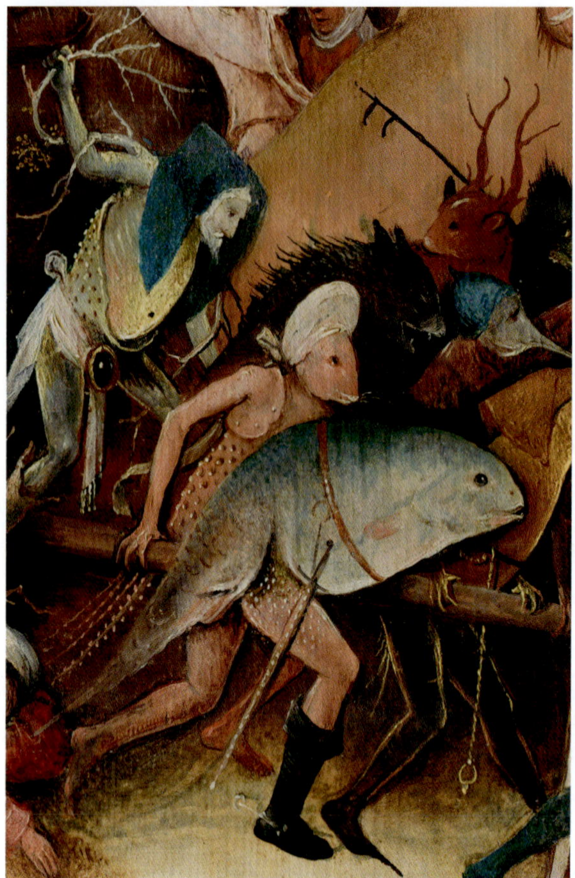

withered." Isaiah 40: "... people are like the grass that dies away ... The grass withers ... but the word of our God stands forever." And in his first letter to the Corinthians, Paul writes of the value of worldly possessions: "... gold, silver, jewels, wood, hay, or straw ... Everyone's work will be put through the fire to see whether or not it keeps its value."

With the hay on his cart, Bosch makes reference to ephemerality and greed. The thought or the sense of the transience of all things, of the unworthiness of humankind and of the approaching apocalypse was particularly widespread within the resigned atmosphere of the late Middle Ages. On the other hand, the introduction of early capitalist forms of industry made it possible for individuals to amass wealth on a scale unimaginable in the days of the old guild system. Bankers such as the Fuggers could decide the outcome of wars with their purses.

When the protector of this early capitalist economic order, Archduke Maximilian, visited s'Hertogenbosch in 1481, the platform erected for him collapsed. This, it was said, was the revenge wreaked by craftsmen who supported the old guild system. In Bruges in 1488 Maximilian was even held hostage by guild leaders. At times, the conflict between those who supported his rule, and with it the new order and the chance to get rich, and those who did not, came close to civil war.

is one who wants to have the whole haystack entirely for himself. Many of the figures in Bosch's painting are caught up in frenzied activity, trying to grab at the hay; only the rulers, accompanying the hay as if it were their rightful property, are calm.

The symbolic meaning of hay would have been familiar to Bosch's contemporaries who, from the Bible, would recognise this reference to the ephemeral nature of all things. Psalm 37: "Don't worry about the wicked ... For like grass, they soon fade away." Psalm 90: "For you, a thousand years are as yesterday! ... You sweep people away ... like grass that springs up in the morning. In the morning it blooms and flourishes, but by evening it is dry and

Opposed to God's order

In the left-hand wing of the triptych, Bosch portrays not just Paradise, but also the fall of the angels, as described in Revelations: "Satan ... was thrown down to the earth with all his angels." Bosch shows the rebel angels as small, insect-like creatures, often with a tail, tumbling out of the clouds and disappearing into the earth. They reappear in the central panel as the demons pulling the haywain.

Revelations describes Satan as "the one deceiving the whole world". With the help of the hay, Satan's helpers are enticing the vain, greedy, warring inhabitants of Bosch's painting towards Hell. As always in his pictures, these demons are a mixture of human, animal and plant. One is a hooded man with branches growing out of his back; another is a fish with human arms and legs, and the face of a mouse.

It may well be that Bosch was here indulging his own distinctive, fantastical imagination. But there may equally well be a theoretical explanation for such figures: whereas God had separated the genera, the bodies of Bosch's crossbreeds are clearly opposed to God's order.

For the majority of people in the Middle Ages, the devil and his helpers were real beings, as clearly emerges from the guidelines issued to help worshippers examine their conscience prior to confession, and from people's life stories and tales of mystical experiences. In the 13th century, for example, the abbot of Schöntal monastery reported that the world was full of evil spirits, who surged around every person like water around a drowning man. The abbot blamed these invisible beings for every indisposition, be it toothache, loss of appetite or a hangover after drinking. It was even they who caused every sort of involuntary noise, whether laughing, sneezing or sighing, for that was how they communicated amongst themselves. In 1487, around the time that this painting was executed, a Carthusian monk wrote that he had stumbled in his cell one night, and a ghost had caused him to fall. Was it the devil, he asked, or was it some poor soul from purgatory who wanted to make his presence known?

There are many records in which it is claimed that people felt themselves pushed or punched by ghosts, without them actually seeing anything. As to the abbot in the 13th century, such spirits were real, but invisible. If they showed themselves, it was usually as animals. To one Eustochia Calafato, who died in 1485, they appeared "now in the shape of dogs, now in that of bears, now in that of pigs". In particular, they often came as unpleasant types of small animals and insects. Goethe adopted this idea into his *Faust*, in which Mephistopheles is the "lord of the rats and mice, the flies, frogs, bugs, lice …"

To nuns, monks and priests sworn to chastity they often appeared as the opposite sex, although of course they also came as deformed creatures with heads as large as cauldrons, crowned with horns. Hybrid figures were nevertheless the exception; they are sooner found as roof decorations or gargoyles on Gothic cathedrals than in written records. It seems they were never experienced at first hand in the

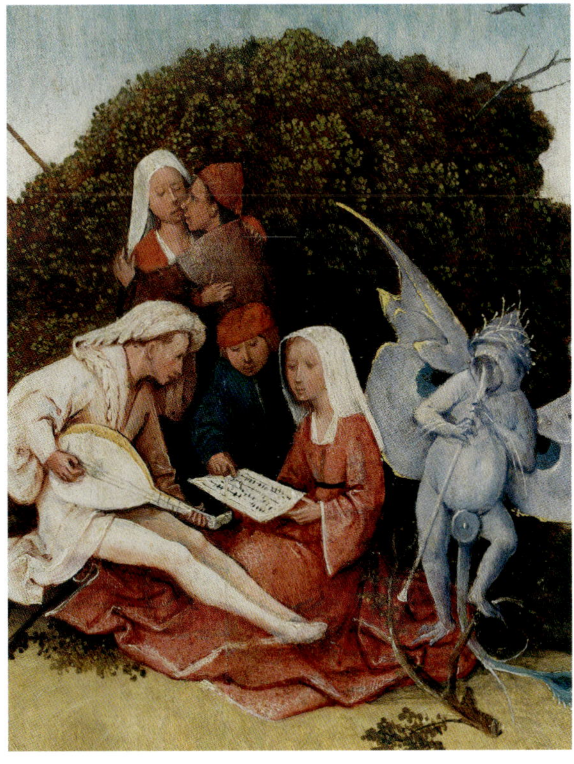

shapes which Bosch created so skilfully and with such variety. His fantasies in paint were richer than those visited in person by apparitions from Hell.

Jarring notes in a musical idyll

Bosch's painting speaks, as we have said, of ephemerality and greed. Along the lower edge of the picture, he arranges people who clearly illustrate deception and theft, inspired by greed. The man standing on the left wears a tall black hat, identifying him as a travelling magician. He has a child in his cape, perhaps stolen. Next to him, a gypsy is reading another woman's palm, while her child tampers with the woman's dress. Further right, a quack doctor is tormenting a female patient. A nun is making up to a devil playing the bagpipes (a symbol of the male sex organ), while other nuns are stuffing hay into a sack at the table of a fat monk with a glass in his hand; they are swindling their church and breaking their vows. Beside the haywain above them, meanwhile, there is murder and death. Only on top of the haywain does Bosch seem to have included something of an idyll, in the group of three figures peacefully making music together: a richly dressed lutenist, a young woman and a young man.

Half concealed in the bush, however, is a couple kissing, watched by an observer behind the bush. Is there a symbolism in this arrangement – in front those communicating chastely through music, behind those whose methods are more physical, and at the back the spy, the voyeur? For all the speculation, the scene remains an enigma. Only the significance of the peripheral figures is clear: the blue demon interrupts the love songs with the blast of his trumpet nose, while the angel looks beseechingly up to Christ. The angel is the only figure in this painting who is aware of the existence of Christ.

Caught between angel and devil, man must make up his mind. According to the teachings of the Church, humankind was by no means helpless against the devil, but Satan's power was great and there were many who made pacts with him. In Goethe, such pacts were written in blood on paper or vellum. In the Middle Ages, they were sealed with the sexual act. "Not without great sorrow," declared Innocent VIII in a papal bull of 1484, had he learned that "in some parts of Upper Germany … very many people of both sexes, deserting the Catholic faith, [had] entered into carnal union with the devil." Those who joined themselves with the devil were

witches and sorcerers, and in the same bull the Pope ordered that they be hunted out and destroyed. This became the particular task of the Dominicans, whereby two members of the order, Heinrich Institoris and Jakob Sprenger, were especially industrious. It was they who wrote the *Malleus maleficarum* (Witches' Hammer), an instruction manual on inquisitions and sermons. The three volume work was first published in 1487 and quickly went into further editions. Sprenger was a prior in Cologne, the capital of the Dominican province to which s'Hertogenbosch also belonged. When Maximilian visited s'Hertogenbosch, he stayed with the Dominicans; sacred and secular power were thus closely linked – just as, in Bosch's painting, the pope, emperor and king follow close together behind the haywain.

The belief in witches, devils and demons, clearly already widespread, was furthered still by the Church. The latter was weak; many of the faithful were turning to sects or anti-Rome movements. By way of warning and as a means of countering desertion, such people were accused of being possessed by demons or in league with the devil.

Erasmus of Rotterdam, the great humanist, condemned the fear of witches incited by the Church. "The pact with the devil", he declared, was itself an "invention of the masters of the inquisition".

A topical message for today

There are two versions of *The Haywain*. One hangs in the Escorial, the other – reproduced here – in the Prado. Whether both are by Bosch, or just one, or whether both are perhaps copies of a lost original, and whether the artist himself put his signature on the panel or someone else – the fact that these questions remain unanswered does not detract from the quality of the painting. One of the two panels, like other paintings by Bosch, was purchased just a hundred years after its completion by Philip II, the Spanish Habsburg king, and taken to El Escorial, his monasterial seat of government.

The years that gave rise to the *Haywain* also saw the completion in Florence of a painting of a very different nature, Botticelli's *Birth of Venus*. Botticelli celebrated – for the first time since Classical antiquity – the beauty of the female body, and with it prized the dignity and strength of humankind per se. He stylized the figure of Venus as a masterpiece of Creation. It is an optimistic work, an early testament to a new epoch, the Renaissance. Botticelli's Venus makes it clear that Bosch, his northern contemporary, was very much a painter of the resigned, pessimistic closing years of the Middle Ages.

There are no written documents, however, indicating to what extent Bosch shared the general mood, or whether he actually believed in demons himself. Did he feel hunted, threatened? Was painting his means of exorcising himself of nightmarish visions? Or of distancing himself from the Church through derisive cariatures? Both opinions can be found in the relevant literature. Bosch's work is open to interpretation. We do not know whether his relationship with the Catholic Church was close or distant. According to records, he was a member of the well-regarded confraternity of Our Blessed Lady, but that alone does not say a great deal. He received one commission from Philip the Fair, son of Maximilian, but little is known about his other patrons. What is certain is that he didn't have to live from his painting; he had married into a wealthy family.

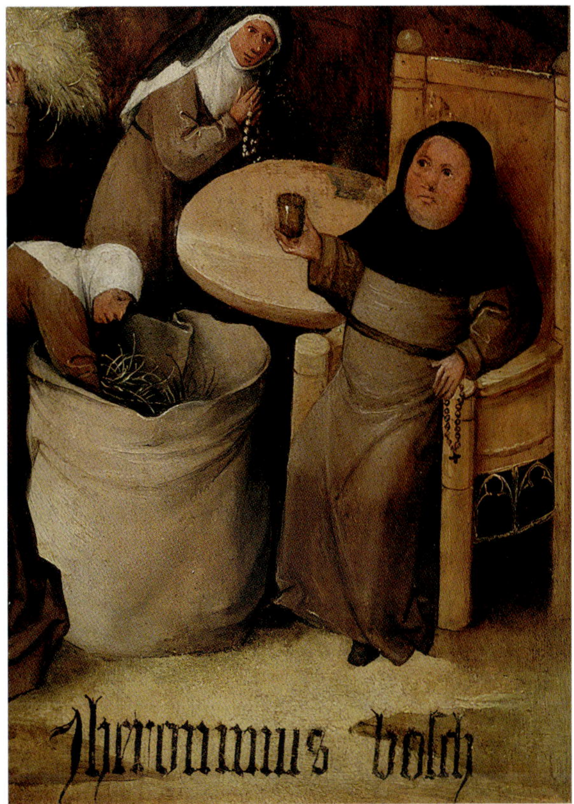

While greed is given pride of place amongst the sins portrayed in this triptych, gluttony also features. It is demonstrated by the stout monk with a glass in one hand and his rosary in the other. The arguments against over-eating today are based on considerations of health, not morality, and we perceive the battle for wealth, too, as a legitimate one. We have internalized liberal and capitalist ideas to such an extent that we are barely able to recognize the pious message contained in this picture: a warning against worldly possessions. It is a warning which runs through the history of Christianity right from the beginning. The fat belly in the monk's habit demonstrates the reason why: someone who drinks wine and has hay gathered for him does not pray; his love of worldly goods reduces his love of God.

For social and economic reasons, this devout warning was particularly apt in Bosch's day. In a strange way, it remains equally appropriate today – not with regard to personal possessions, but to our treatment of Nature.

Not unlike the figures in this painting grabbing the hay, people today are trying – both in cooperation and in rivalry – to seize and exploit the riches of nature for themselves. And like the haywain, one might say, they are thereby heading blindly towards the abyss, the destruction of their world. The crowded foreground in Bosch's painting is already desolate and empty, without water or vegetation. The beautiful background bears witness to what is being lost.

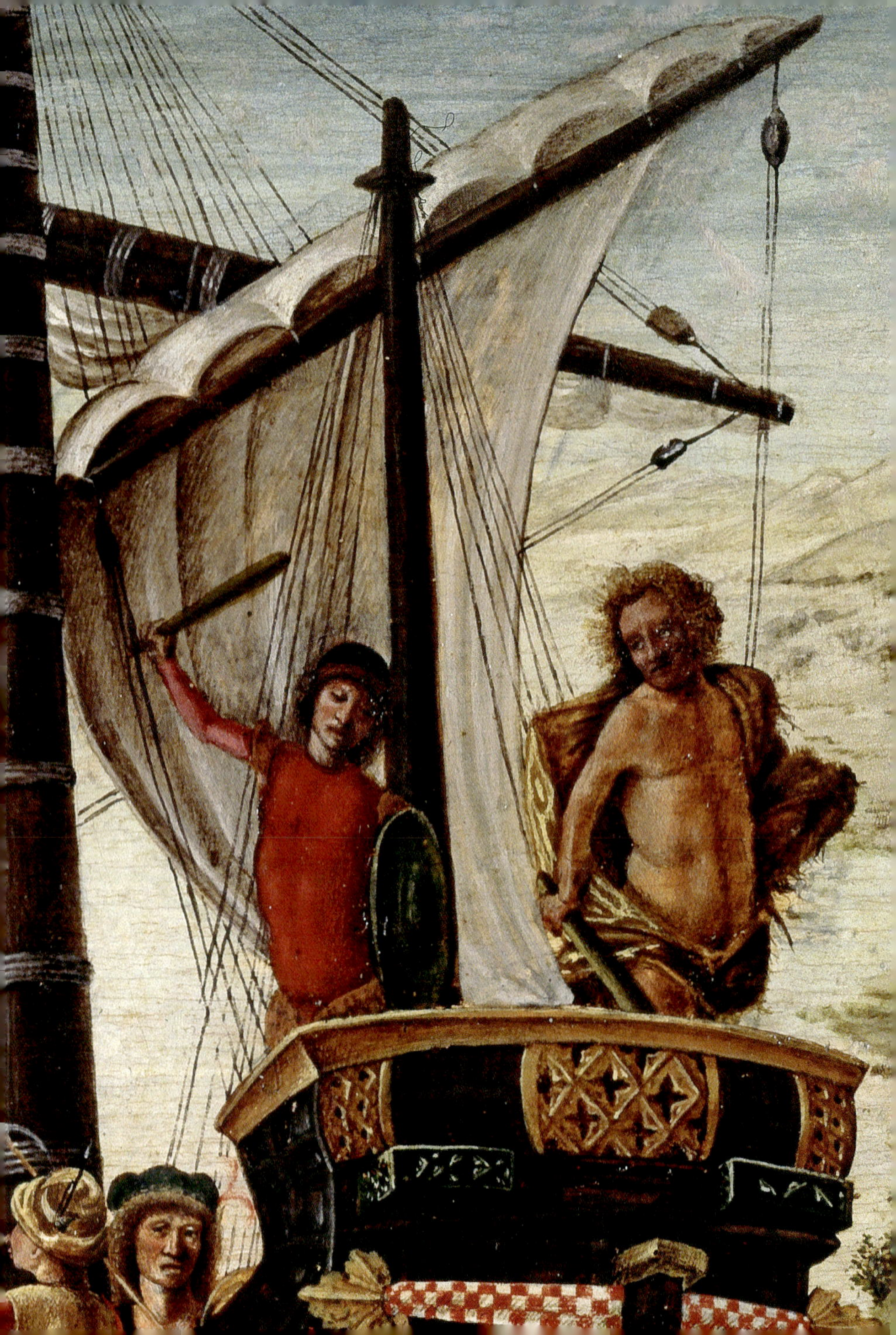

Ercole de' Roberti (*c.* 1450–1496)

Lorenzo Costa (1460–1535)

Jason sails for unknown shores

The Ship of the Argonauts, c. 1480/1490
46 x 53 cm, Padua, Musei Civici

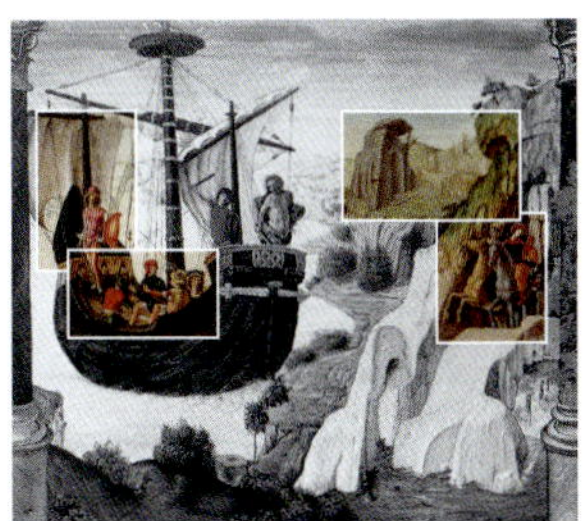

The sails are billowing in the breeze, the ship casts off, and the crew gaze back. On shore, bizarre rock formations tower up. The dark mass of the vessel seems to be hovering over the milky-white waters of the sea. It is almost a surreal landscape, a strange mixture of the fantastic and the real.

This type of ship was common in the 15th century, and was used for cargo transport. But the golden embellishments on the forecastle and stern suggest that this vessel is not putting to sea for a trading voyage. This is an adventurous expedition, and her crew are important people. The athletically built man at the stern, stripped to the waist with a lion's fell over his shoulder and a club in his fist, has the attributes of Heracles, the hero of Greek myth who had superhuman powers. Beside him, wielding a club, is Hylas, his arms bearer and darling, and in the fore of the ship stands Jason, the captain.

What we see in the ship are some of the 50 heroes assembled, according to myth, by the son of King Aeson to undertake the first ever long-distance sea voyage and fetch the Golden Fleece, a ram's fleece guarded by a dragon at Colchis on the Black Sea. For this enterprise, Jason built the largest ship ever seen, the *Argo*. From the ship, the members of the expedition took their name, Argonauts.

They set sail from the Greek port of Iolcus, were embroiled in adventures, demonstrated their mettle, and enjoyed themselves. In Thrace they rid a blind seer of the fearful harpies plaguing him; on Lemnos they bestowed their favours on the women, whose husbands were dead. At length in Colchis Jason

succeeded in seizing the fleece with the help of Medea, daughter of King Aeëtes and an adept in magical charms. She had fallen in love with Jason; he married her and took her back to Greece, but their union ended in tragedy when Medea, abandoned, took fearful revenge and murdered their children.

The first part of the story is one of the oldest adventure yarns in world literature and was retold by many writers, among them Valerius Flaccus, a Roman author of the 1st century AD. In 1474 his *Argonautica* was printed in Bologna and thus made available to a wide public, so the subject had currency when this painting was made in nearby Ferrara between 1480 and 1490. It now hangs in Padua, is neither signed nor dated, and poses numerous problems for art historians.

Measuring 46 by 53 centimetres and painted on oak rather than the usual poplar, the painting will once have adorned the front of a chest, together with other panels. Five more pictures showing episodes from the myth of the Argonauts are in museums and private collections in Paris, Madrid, London and Florence. They were probably attached to two matching chests, each bearing three panel paintings. Subsequently they were owned by the Roman collector Vincenzo Giustiniani. His 1638 inventory notes: "They are believed to be from the hand of Ercole da Ferrara."

Ercole de' Roberti was active in Bologna at the time the panels were painted, as was Lorenzo Costa, who probably helped him with the work. Both painters were from Ferrara.

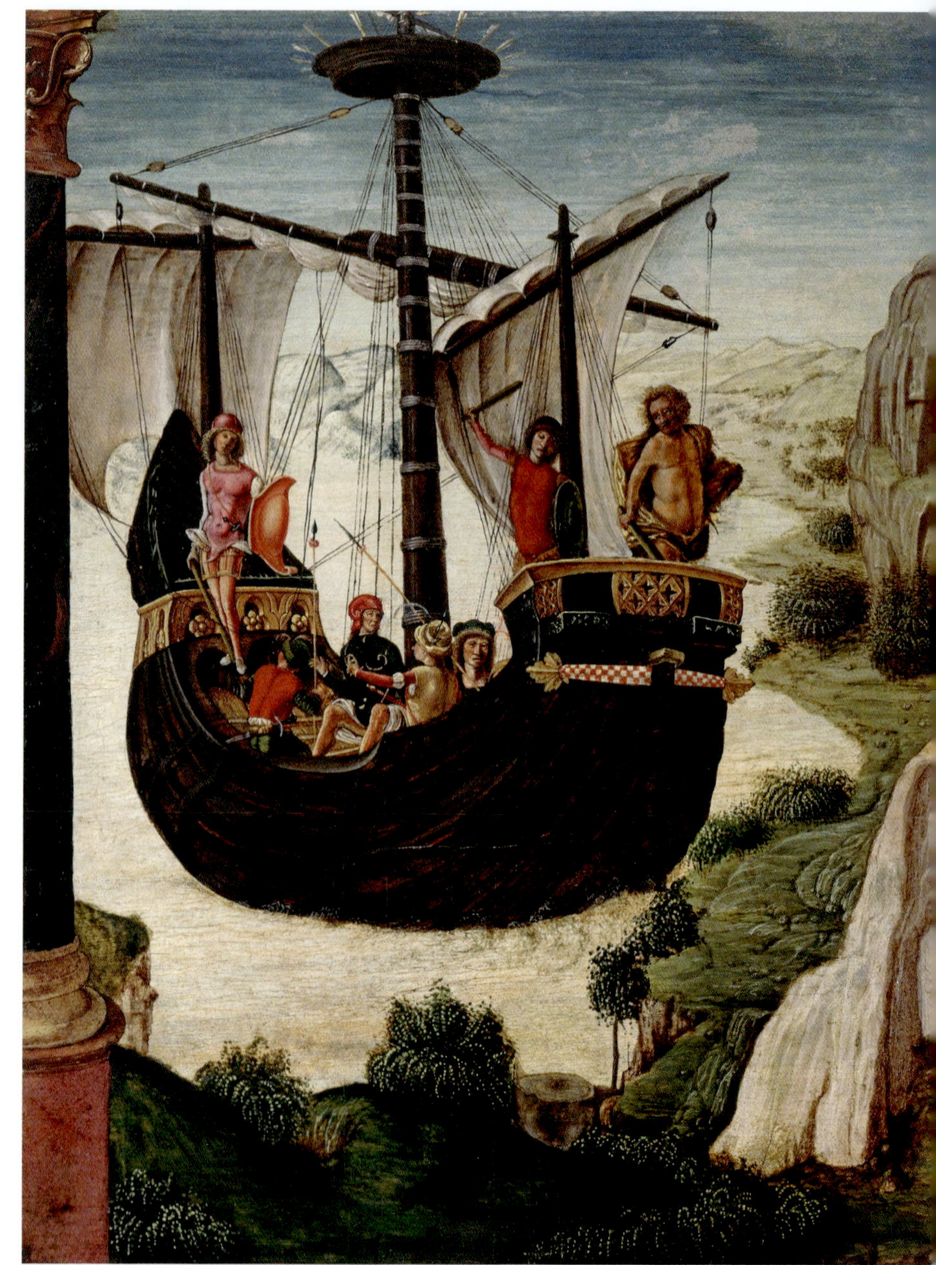

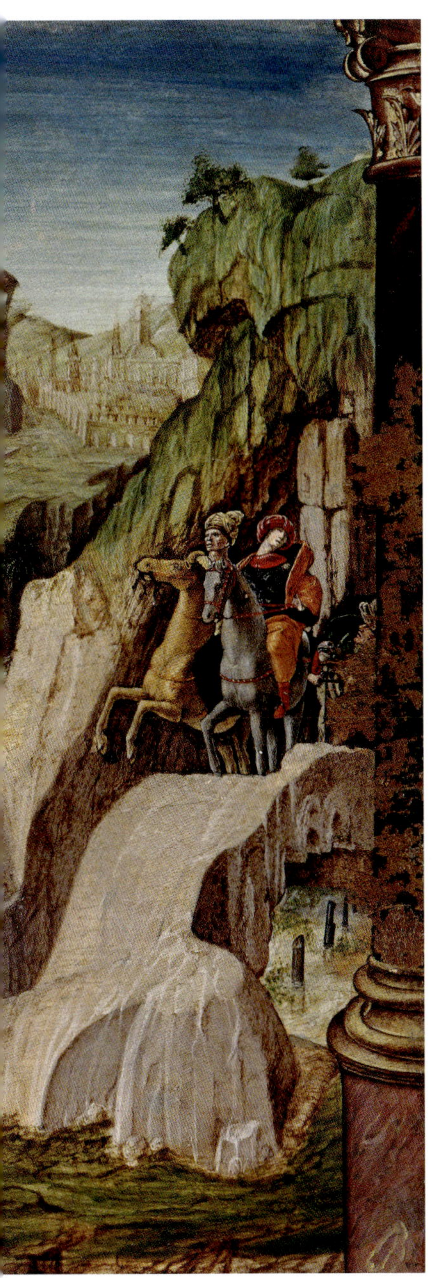

"Vela" was the war-cry of the Estes
It is unclear which artist did which panels – the weaker ones were possibly done by an assistant. Nor do we know for which bride the chests were made.

Bridal chests were a must in Italy when a young woman married: one or more, depending on her property. In these chests, the bride's dowry was ceremonially carried from the house of her parents to that of the bridegroom, where they were assigned a place in the bedroom, beside the bed. Originally plain wooden chests, in the 15th century they were adorned with family coats of arms and colourful pictures, ever more splendidly; during the Renaissance, the decorative motifs chosen would often come from Greek or Roman mythology. Artists who were normally occupied mainly with painting saints and rulers could indulge their imaginations with a little unaccustomed licence in painting these heathen tales of love.

As well as mythical love affairs, the subjects depicted on these chests were frequently steadfast women such as the Romans Lucretia and Portia, whom brides were recommended to take as examples. Other popular themes were the rape of the Sabine women or Jason and the Argonauts returning with Medea. If the unhappy fate of Medea might be read as an ill omen for a marriage, that consideration evidently played no part in the choice of motif.

Doubtless the chests adorned with Argonaut scenes were made for a bride from the highest social circles. On that the experts are agreed; but the identity of the family who commissioned them is disputed. On two of the less skilfully painted panels, the remains of a coat of arms can be made out, with a lily and two stars. These might signify the Guidotti family of Bologna, which had two lilies and six stars in its device. In 1486 a son of the family married an illegitimate daughter of the Bentivoglio family, the Signori or masters of Bologna. Their wedding may have been the occasion for which the chests were ordered.

However, the dominant position of the ship on the two loveliest Argonaut panels, in the Padua and Madrid collections, may turn our thoughts to another and more famous family, the dynasty of the Estes. The dukes of Ferrara likewise had a lily in their coat of arms, and also married off their two daughters, Isabella and Beatrice, in the years 1490 and 1491. Ships were the *impresa* of the family;

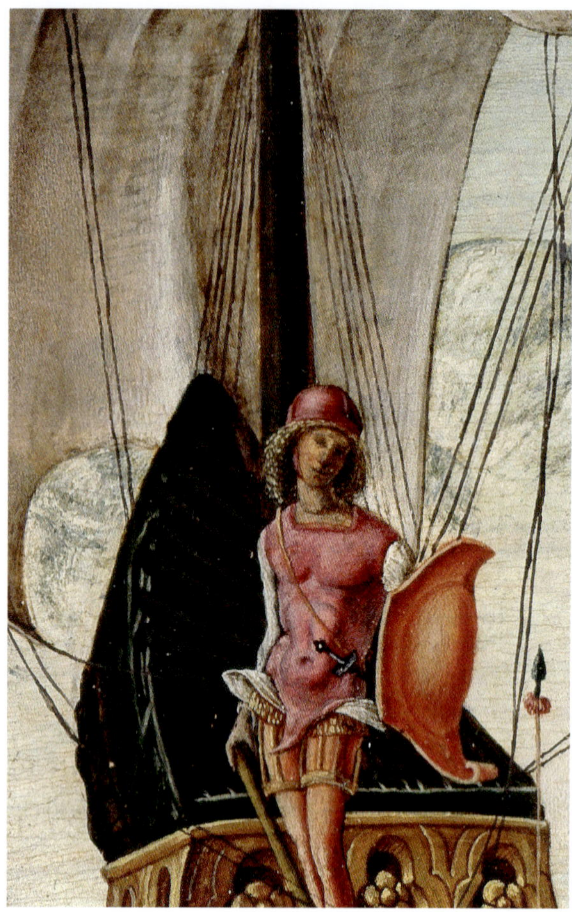

An early example of urban planning

For the Este family, Heracles was an important symbolic figure. There were statues of Heracles in their palaces, and frescos on their walls told of his heroic deeds. The Estes traced their own descent from the ancient superman, claiming ancestry in ancient mythological times – though the fact of the matter was that the Estes had held the ducal title only since 1471, as a fief granted by the Pope. The Estes were absolute rulers, or despots, and if they acquitted themselves with distinction over several generations it was not through any elected kinship with club-wielding heroes. They made shrewd use of the city's strategic position in the Po River delta, developing its port and thus controlling the major waterway into the plains of Lombardy. Customs duties levied on trade goods were a principal source of revenue for the dynasty, and if the sails engraved on their ducats were billowing in the wind we may take it as one more reminder of how important the maritime sector was for Ferrara.

The people of the city enjoyed a modest degree of prosperity. Their rulers had flood barriers built to protect Ferrara from the waters of the Po. The Estes also kept war at bay, playing off the larger powers of Milan, Venice, Florence and Rome against each other and pursuing a risky policy of routinely changing sides, now leading the armies of the one party as *condottieri*, now of the other.

The dynasty and state were served by an efficient civil service. Indeed, Ferrara was the envy of all of turbulent Italy for its order and stability. In 1442, following a visit to the city, the Renaissance architect Leon Battista Alberti wrote: "It was there that I grasped what good fortune it is to live in a state where nothing troubles one's peace of mind,

an *impresa* was not an official heraldic device but a symbolic image which great families in Italy liked to use for decorative purposes and also to express a key quality. The Estes' *impresa* featured ships sailing before a strong wind. It appeared time and again on their frescoes, paintings, and even coins: the gold ducats of Leonello d'Este, who reigned from 1441 to 1450, have the head of the ruler on the obverse, and on the reverse two men in a ship, the sails of which have filled with the wind. And when Leonello d'Este's men went into battle, their war-cry was "Vela", meaning "sail".

beneath the rule of the best of fathers, who respects law and custom."

The Estes were adept at using their prosperity to good ends. As early as 1391, Alberto I founded a university. His work was continued by Niccolò III, and by the latter's three sons, Leonello, Borso and Ercole, who reigned in succession. They brought humanists to the city and prosecuted so many building projects that "the din of the masons' hammers could be heard far and wide". Thus by their efforts a small and marshy place "where only frogs and mosquitoes dwell" was transformed in the course of the 15th century into a centre of courtly culture and style that irradiated all Italy.

Duke Ercole I, who reigned from 1471 to 1505, gave the name that was at once his own and that of the Greek hero to his favourite project. He designated as the *addizione ercolea* a residential extension which tripled the area of the prosperous city. The duke's project was an early and successful example of well thought out urban planning: within just ten years, wide straight streets and some twenty palaces and a dozen churches had come into being, to designs by architect Biagio Rossetti.

These new buildings and streets, known also as the *terra nuova* or new land, were the result of an immense effort. It may be that the city we can make out in the distance in the Argonauts panel is an allusion to this development. The picture was painted at a time when the planning of the *terra nuova* and its funding from taxes and levies were in everyone's thoughts, one way or another.

On 11 February 1490, Ercole's eldest daughter Isabella (1474–1539) married Francesco Gonzaga, the earl of nearby Mantua. The nuptial ceremonies were arranged by that very Ercole de' Roberti to whom the Giustiniani inventory ascribed the Argonauts chests.

Ferrara's painters did Renaissance subjects in a Gothic style

From letters we know that, in the year before the wedding, the painter Ercole de' Roberti was sent to Venice to procure the finest, costliest pigments, such as ultramarine and gold. Eleven thousand gold platelets are reputed to have been used in adorning Isabella's dowry. This included the marital bed, a golden boat, a triumphal carriage, and thirteen bridal chests – everything made to the designs and under the supervision of Ercole de' Roberti. He had begun back in 1483, as soon as the betrothal of Isabella (then aged nine) was announced, possibly with the help of Lorenzo Costa in Bologna; both Ferrara born artists were decorating churches and palaces in that city.

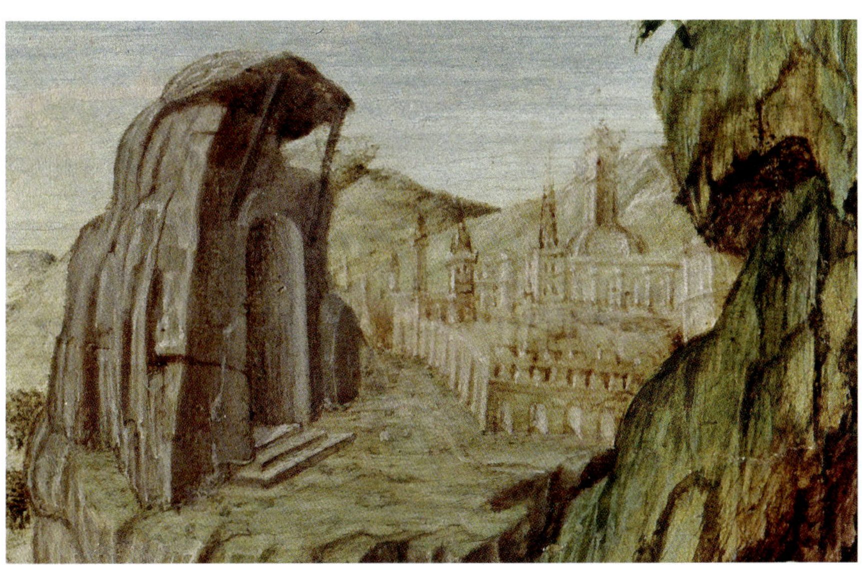

As painter to the court of Este, and master of the nuptials, de' Roberti escorted Isabella to Mantua, but made a premature return, weak and exhausted. A year after the wedding, he petitioned the duke in all humble submission for the payment due to him. In fact it was to be another four years before he received it.

For painters the situation in Ferrara was particularly delicate, because there was hardly anyone but the duke who might commission work, in contrast to Venice, Florence or Rome, where many families were forever competing to hire the best artists. Ferrara's painters were often obliged to earn their living elsewhere – in Bologna, for instance. The teachers of de' Roberti and Costa had done this; they were Cosimo Tura (*c.* 1430–95) and Francesco del Cossa (*c.* 1435–*c.* 1477), the founders of the Ferrarese school.

These artists had developed an elite style for their courtly clientele which differed from the Renaissance style of their fellow Italian artists in the major centres. Art history refers to it as "humanist Gothic". The great breakthroughs of the modern era – such as the discovery of mathematically exact perspective, the realistic representation of the human body – were of limited interest to the artists of Ferrara.

The Ship of the Argonauts is a case in point. The artist gives us little indication of precisely how the crewmen are sitting in the vessel; the elegantly elongated figures of Jason and Hylas are decoratively placed, rather than standing squarely on the boards of a tossing ship. Of more importance to them than capturing reality was the element of the fantastic, as seen in the weightless, hovering appearance of the vessel, or a landscape in which cliff and city gate, Nature and man-made architecture, seem to meld.

Thus the painters at the court of Este interpreted in this "Gothic" style the new subject matter that Renaissance humanists borrowed from antiquity; the style and the theme were in fascinating and highly idiosyncratic contrast. If the art of Ferrara is not well known today, it is because of the fate of the Estes.

The main line became extinct, and in 1598 the Estes had to quit Ferrara. The fief returned to Rome, and Pope Clement VIII systematically destroyed everything that recalled the erstwhile rulers. He had churches and palaces demolished, or let them fall down, and with them the great numbers of large-scale frescos that had been a chief part of Ferrara's art disappeared for ever. The Estes are said to have possessed more frescos, in terms of area covered, than any other rulers. All that remains to attest to the splendour of the Estes are a few partially ruined astrological scenes of the months, painted in the Palazzo di Schifanoia by Tura and Cossa.

The Este art collection was also carted away and sold off. Today, pictures from the Ferrarese school are scattered in 125 cities and some 300 collections around the entire world. In Ferrara, though, scarcely any remain.

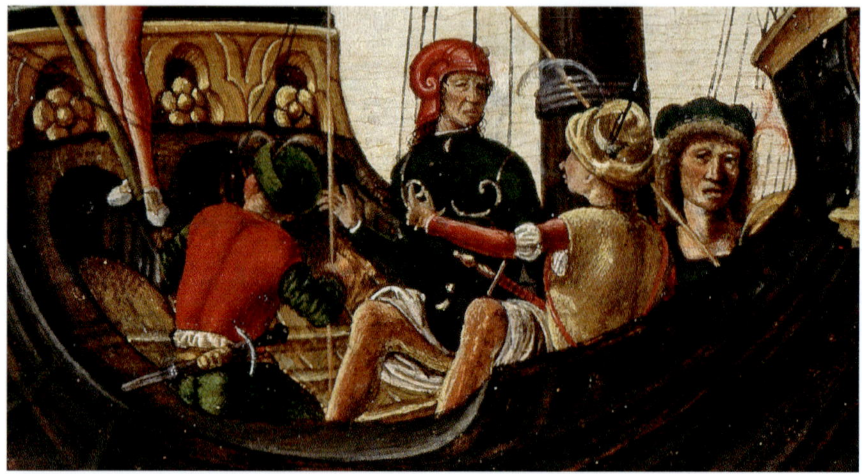

A taste for games of chance and adventure

The life and style of the Estes can be glimpsed in two famous works of literature. From 1472 to 1494 an Italian count at their court, Matteo Boiardo, wrote the lively *ottava rima* narrative poem *Orlando Innamorato*; and in the early 16th century, the poet and diplomat Ludovico Ariosto wrote his great continuation of it, *Orlando Furioso*. Writing in Italian rather than Latin, these poets told of damsels and knights, feats of arms, love, valour and adventure, taking their personae from the legends that had accrued around Charlemagne and King Arthur. Their heroes, knights errant, were purportedly crusading against the heathen Saracens, but in reality they were chiefly interested in acquitting themselves courageously in duels and saving beautiful damsels from dragons or evil sorcerers before making a conquest of them in an idyllic setting.

That at least was what the nostalgic taste of the aristocratic audience demanded, those who listened to the poets "with delight and good cheer" at the court of Ferrara, as Boiardo tells us. At a time when firearms were beginning to decide the outcome of battles, the Estes still saw themselves as knights. In their youth, all of the dukes learnt the arts of war, which were considered essential in a feudal lord, and they were greatly in demand as highly paid *condottieri* leading the armies of Naples, or Florence, or Milan.

In times of peace they jousted at tournaments or went hunting or embarked on long journeys on the pretext of making pilgrimages. In a letter to Isabella d'Este, Baldassare Castiglione wrote of "that accursed vagabond streak that some ancestor of the house of Este bequeathed to all his descendants". Isabella's grandfather Niccolò III and a number of companions had made it as far as Jerusalem in 1413.

That vagabond streak, a taste for risk and for venturing upon the unknown, is apparent (in the symbolic idiom of the age) in another figure associated with the Argonauts. Light of foot like Jason and Hylas, she is seen in other panels standing below billowing sails. She is Dame Fortune, blown hither and thither at the whim of the winds. She is a sister to Ventura – what may come but is not to be foreseen – and of Adventura.

For a *gioco di ventura*, a game of chance, Duke Ercole once neglected the affairs of government for weeks on end, we are told. He was on the River Po, on a pleasure boat, playing cards with a wealthy

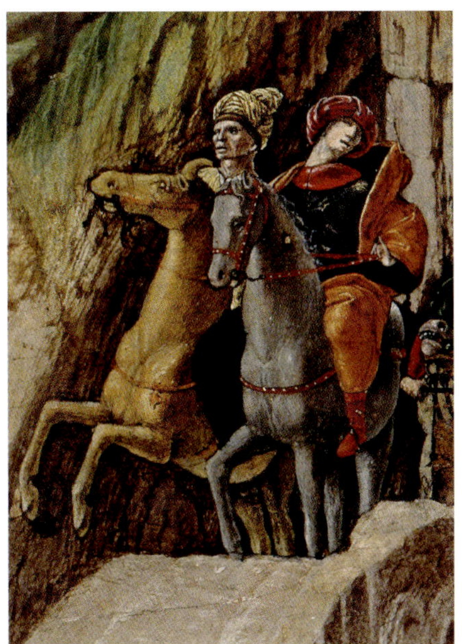

Jew by the name of Abraham, who allowed him to win large sums. Perhaps that pleasure boat of the Estes had the red-and-white chessboard pattern on it which has so puzzled scholars of heraldic devices when confronted with the ship of the Argonauts. Red and white was the strip of the Este jockeys at horse races, where large sums were staked; the colours may have been associated with all of their riskier ventures.

Ercole's daughter Isabella chose as her *impresa* another symbol of Ventura, a bundle of lottery tickets, for she too was a dedicated gambler. The motif of the Argonauts on a bridal chest, standing for pluck and venturesomeness, would have been apt for this strong woman.

Much later, around the year 1512, she ordered a painting from Lorenzo Costa, to adorn her private apartments. Costa was now the successor of the great Andrea Mantegna as court painter in Mantua. He was given a programme to observe, according to which the subject was to be the coronation of Isabella by divine love. In the background of this work, which is now in the Louvre, the ship of the Argonauts appears once again. But this time she is in port, and her sails are furled.

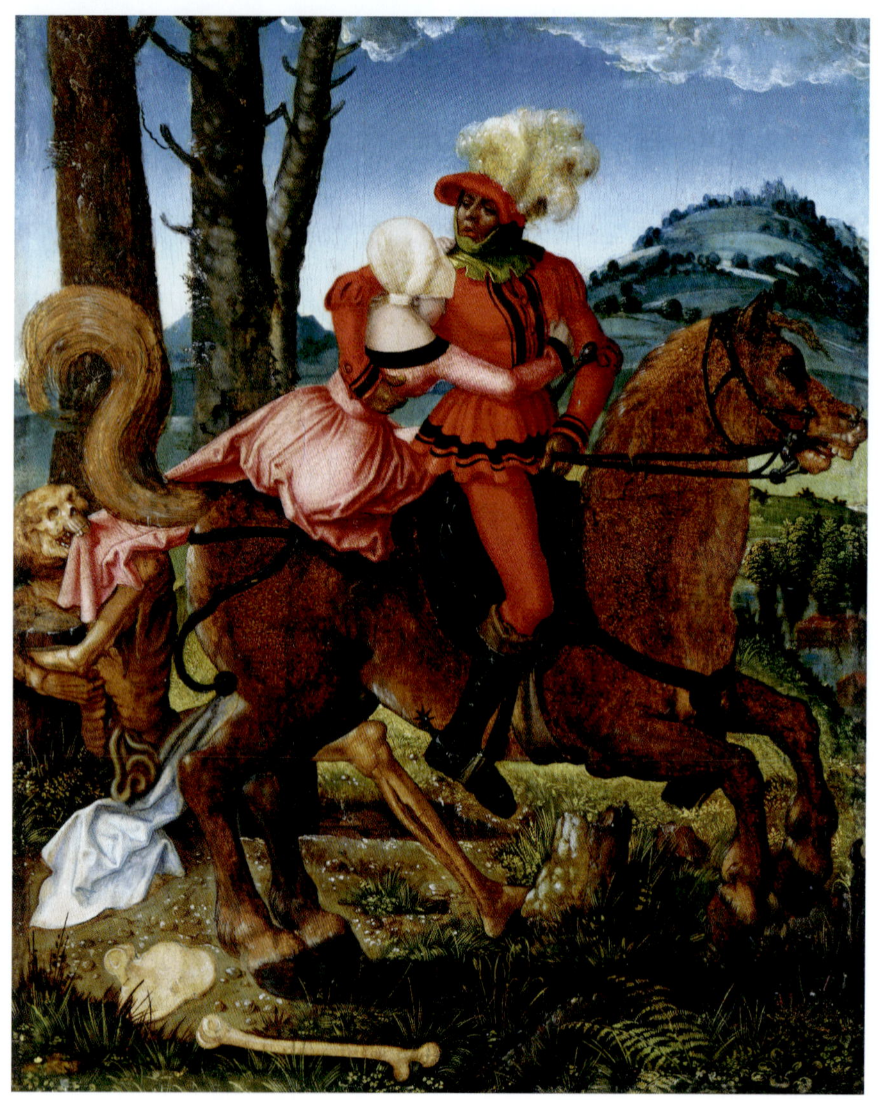

Hans Baldung Grien (1484 or 1485–1545)

Death terrifies the lovers

The Knight, the Maiden and Death, before 1503
35 x 30 cm, Paris, Musée du Louvre

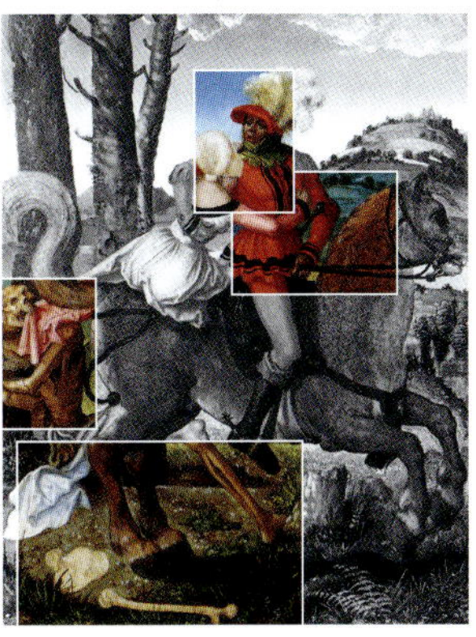

Rarely has the German-speaking world boasted so many important artists as around 1500 – Albrecht Altdorfer, Lucas Cranach, Matthias Grünewald, Hans Holbein and Nildaus Manuel Deutsch were all to be found there, as well as Tilman Riemenschneider, who carved scenes in wood, and above all Albrecht Dürer, the most influential of them all. In 1503 Hans Baldung was taken on by Dürer as a journeyman and for unknown reasons acquired the additional surname of Grien while in his workshop. Baldung was born in 1484 or 1485 in Schwäbisch Gmünd and trained under a master whose name we do not know. When he set up the lime panel for this picture on his easel, he was seventeen or eighteen years old and had not yet joined Dürer's Nuremberg workshop.

One aspect of Dürer's art that must have particularly interested Baldung was his composition of landscape. In this picture, Baldung, too, begins in the foreground with grass, ferns and flat ground, introduces a hollow on the right with trees and houses and works his way upwards in the background with a dome-shaped mountain top and buildings that are too far away to be clearly made out. This is no longer the flat backdrop typical of the Middle Ages: Baldung has composed a three-dimensional painting.

In terms of palette, the upper half of the picture is dominated by blue and red. Alongside black and white, these are the two colours most heavily laden with symbolism and association. Blue is the colour of fidelity, the heavens, infinity and – since the Romantic era – yearning; in former times it was the colour of the aristocracy ("blue blood") and today it is the preferred colour of international peace organizations. From the 12th century onwards the Virgin's robes were also blue. Baldung gives the clouds and landscape a bluish shimmer along with the sky. Red, on the other hand, is the colour of passion and danger, of love, fire and blood. For a long time red signalled a high social rank, as only members of the nobility were entitled to wear red clothes or shoes.

In the top half of the picture, these two dominant colours conjure a stimulating and positive mood, both on their own and through their powerful contrast. It is no coincidence that many nations have blue and red in their flags, often in combination with white. Baldung, too, introduces white in the bonnet, the plume of feathers and the atmosphere above the mountains. This upper section of the picture, down to the horse's tail and reins, gladdens the eye and heart of the viewer simply by the colours it employs. All the more so because these colours seem fittingly to express what the man and woman on their charging horse are feeling: the thrill of happiness and danger, a supremely heightened sense of being alive.

The lower half of the picture is quite different. Death is stepping in as if he were a highwayman. Brown and black are the dominant colours here; even the green grass seems sombre. In contrast to the upper part of the picture, outlines can no longer be made out clearly; one might think the artist had lost his clarity of vision. There is something odd about the horse – the play of light and shadow on and around its body makes no sense – and it is left up to the viewer to work out which bits belong to the skeleton; we shall hunt for its second leg in vain. Baldung has composed a two-part painting and signalled, solely via the means of colour and drawing, that he has here brought together two things that could not be more antithetical: love and death.

The dead have no soul

In Baldung's day, the idea of skeletons that could walk and talk just like living people was already well established. Such skeletons were documented in literature and art from the 13th century onwards, first of all in a legend that originated in France. Three young noblemen go out hunting one day and encounter three dead bodies. The first is relatively well preserved, the second half decayed, and the third no more than a skeleton. They are standing or lying in coffins, clad in what remains of their shrouds. The first of the young men exclaims at their dreadful appearance, the second proclaims that the dead are a mirror that is being held up in front of them, while the third describes out loud their worm eaten mouths, missing noses and vacant eye sockets. Each of the three dead delivers a stern reply carrying a moral message: one day the young people will look just as hideous as the dead themselves; life can come to a very abrupt end; and a good Christian must be ready at all times to justify himself before God.

Today it is difficult to imagine the shock that this tale of the Three Living and the Three Dead

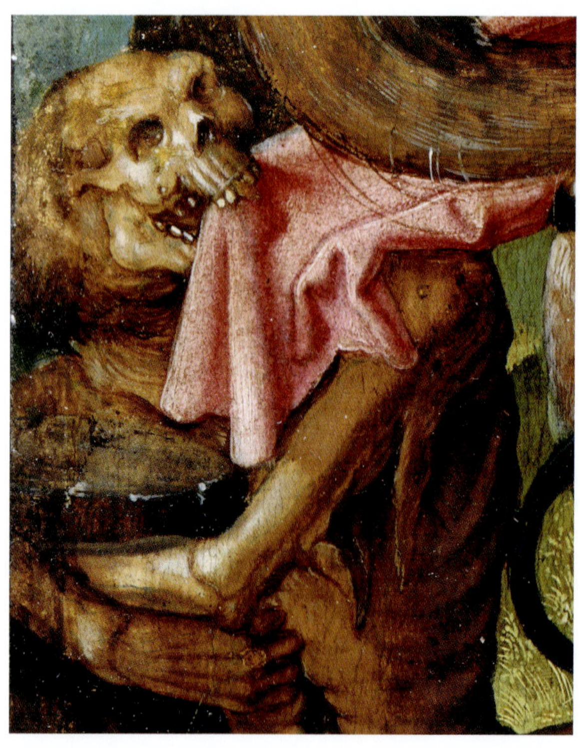

must have caused amongst its original audiences. What was so frightening was less the skeleton, which had been a common motif since Greek and Roman times – as evidenced by sarcophagi, for example. It was more the fact that, in some mysterious way, skeletons should be able to live without a soul. This was a new concept in the late Middle Ages. In the 13th century, the legend was illustrated on one of the walls of the Camposanto in Pisa, and it was also to be seen in Metz, Melfi (Foggia) and Überlingen. In the sphere of art, this acquaintance with the undead inspired the subject of the Dance of Death, with the three young aristocrats transformed into representatives of all social classes, from king to beggar. Each class was led in procession by a skeleton, usually to the musical accompaniment of a skeleton playing a guitar. Dance of Death cycles appeared as frescos in France, Italy and Germany, and as series of woodcuts – such as those by Dürer and Holbein – that were

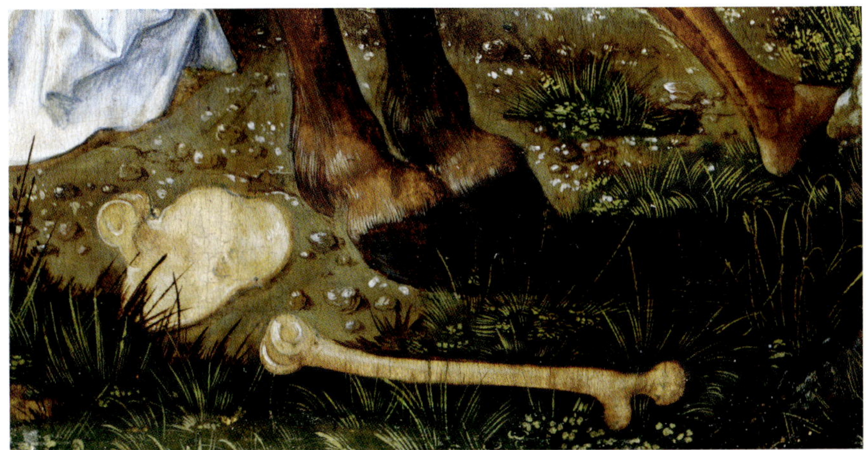

sold at markets and by itinerant preachers. Although they had no place within Church dogma, they were a useful means of priestly admonishment. And the idea that high and low were equal in the face of death may have comforted many a viewer.

These fantastical Dance of Death cycles subsequently inspired individual pictures such as those painted or issued as woodcuts by Baldung. He portrays his undead not as a bare boned skeleton or a withered and shrivelled corpse, however. Although the skull is fleshless and bare, apart from a few wisps of hair on the back, the body is still in a state of decomposition: the leg and upper body have burst open and intestines are spilling out of the stomach. Details such as these were not Baldung's invention or the products of his private necrophile imagination. On the contrary: over 100 years before Baldung, princes and dukes were commissioning two-storey funerary monuments in which they appeared on top as an idealized figure lying in full regalia, and underneath as a decaying corpse in a winding sheet. Such tombs were an aristocratic admonition that God has granted us our body, like our social rank, only for a time, a drastic *memento mori* – "Remember you must die".

Mortal remains

In the Middle Ages as in the Early Modern era, dying was a familiar process and mortal remains were more visible than today. Cremation did not exist, and although every Christian wanted to be buried in the graveyard, there were limits as to how many they could hold. The ruling elite had their tombs beside or inside the church; the common man, however, went into a mass grave. This was emptied and the remains placed in the ossuary as the need arose, which was extremely often during the regular outbreaks of epidemics. The plague that swept Europe from 1347 to 1352 carried off about a quarter of the population. Villages were left deserted and the dead were no longer properly buried under the ground; the smell of rotting flesh was part of daily life. It is no coincidence that the miracles recorded in the lives of the saints should include instances of the body remaining incorruptible after death or of the corpse – like that of St Elizabeth – giving off a wonderful scent.

Baldung earned the major part of his income from commissions for altarpieces, religious paintings and portraits. When it came to his personal interests, he pursued these almost exclusively in woodcuts and drawings, in other words in works that required little expenditure in terms of time and materials. The vast majority are devoted to Death, who is sidling up to a person, usually a woman. Thus he grasps one young female nude by the hair, while she folds her hands resignedly. He approaches another luscious beauty from behind and places a macabre kiss on her cheek, as if he were her lover. A third maiden is accompanied by a little girl and an old woman as representatives of the Three Ages of Woman, while a shabby looking Death holds the hourglass over their heads. Elsewhere Death stands beside a *landsknecht*, both the same height and slim build, two old comrades, and Death merely fingers the soldier's cloak – a peaceful reconciliation. But Baldung's chief interest lay in the unblemished, white bodies of women with their gentle curves in contrast to the angular, brown, eviscerated figure of Death. Indeed, the presence of putrefaction and decay only serves to heighten the erotic appeal of these female bodies. The same can be said of Baldung's witches. Like the subject of Death and beautiful women, witches form a separate complex in his œuvre – with their flying hair, wild gestures and wanton looks.

His witches were sold at markets and fairs in the form of woodcut reproductions and just like Baldung's skeletons were used by preachers as warning propaganda: witches go to Hell and those who succumb to them likewise. There would be no place for them in the churchyard. For good Christians, one of the most important goals in life was to earn acceptance into the world beyond, and around 1500 no genre of literature was more popular than treatises on the *ars moriendi*, the "art of dying". These writings offered instruction on how to attain a good death and thereby secure one's salvation. The invention of the printing press enabled such books, which were written in Latin for the clergy and in German for the laypeople, to reach a wide audience in a short time. They exhorted their readers to live a virtuous life, and carried repeated warnings about sudden, unexpected death, and about dying without a priest at one's side.

The clothes make the man

The knight's trousers consist of two detached legs that were fastened individually to the shirt. The skirt had to cover the buttocks and usually descended as far as the thigh. Black stripes sewn onto red cloth are found in several paintings from this epoch and indicate merchants or officers, in today's terms members of the upper middle classes. If the rider belonged to one of the ruling families, his skirt would be trimmed with fur and the folds of a white silk shirt would spill through the slit elbows. Had our rider been a *landsknecht*, on the other hand, he would be dressed in a more dandyish manner. The woman on his horse is wearing a bonnet and must therefore be married. The viewer must decide for himself whether the rider is embracing his own wife or that of another, i.e. whether Baldung is showing us adultery or legal love.

The young painter had difficulties with the horse. The neck is too thick at the top, the head too small. The nature of its movement is also unclear. If the horse were galloping, its two hind legs would not be standing one beside the other. If it were taking off on a jump, the front half of its body would be reaching forward. It is most likely that Baldung wanted to show a "flying start", of the kind that can be observed at races. Whatever the case, the horse is not well done and some experts interpret this to mean that the work cannot be by Baldung, even less so as he later developed into an equine specialist.

Although horses make only rare appearances in his paintings, they form a group all of their own in his drawings and woodcuts, like his witches

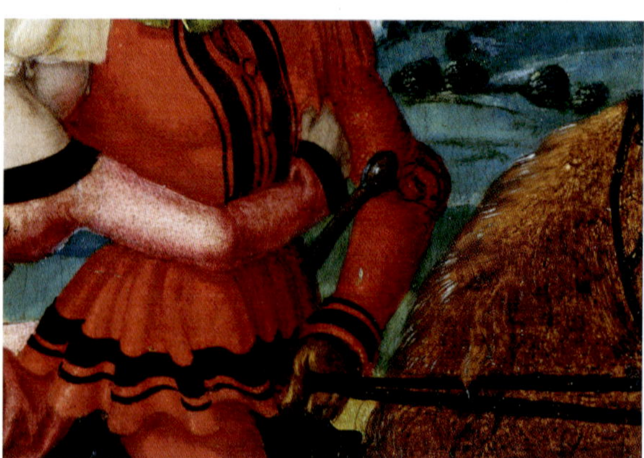

and Deaths. For all artists north of the Alps around 1500, horses presented a new and challenging subject. Like so much else during this period, it had arrived from Italy, where artists studying the natural world had also discovered the horse: of all the animals, man's most important partner. These artists studied the movements of the horse and the play of its muscles and expressed these in ideal forms in the antique manner. Dürer brought the noble steed to the North and set his own standards. Baldung must have painted the present nag before the master was able to look over his shoulder. He later distanced himself from Dürer and his Italian forerunners in a number of horse paintings. At least four of his woodcuts are filled right into the corners with fighting stallions. Without saddle or bridle, they bite and strike each other. The images of horses issuing from Italy and those created by Dürer testify to man's dominion over Nature. By contrast, Baldung tells – as in his witches – of utterly untamed instinct.

Memento mori – memento vivere

The two lovers are clinging to one another as the skeleton seeks to tear them apart. With this image Baldung takes up an old, indeed ancient theme of Western art, namely that of a love that ends in death. In antiquity it was personified by couples such as Pyramus and Thisbe, Hero and Leander, in Norse mythology by Siegfried and Brunhilde, in German medieval courtly romance by Tristan and Isolde, while William Shakespeare brought Romeo and Juliet onto the scene. Officially, at least, it is their external circumstances that spell the lovers' ruin. But when their tragic fate has the capacity to stir human emotions over millennia, there must be more at stake. The knowledge, for example, that ecstatic passion is not viable in the long term. Or the recognition that however well people may rule Nature, there are two forces before which they are defenceless: love and death.

Someone looking for this Western theme in the fine arts will have quite a job. The myths and legends were naturally reproduced – but an original creation? There are many examples of women placing a dagger to their breast, and naked maidens being reminded of life's transience by Death with an hourglass in his hand, for there were periods in which Death heightened the appeal of physical beauty. But there are no pairs of lovers being torn apart, no images of passion – not even in Pieter Bruegel the Elder's *Triumph of Death* (1562), in which entire cartloads of skeletons advance on the living. Right in the bottom corner, two lovers are playing music together, accompanied by a skeleton on a sort of lute; the impression is nevertheless one of harmony and concord rather than of a tragic end.

It is always dangerous to claim that a motif is new, but until proven otherwise it would appear in this case to be true: the young Baldung has invented something. No one before him had painted love and death so dramatically together and at the same

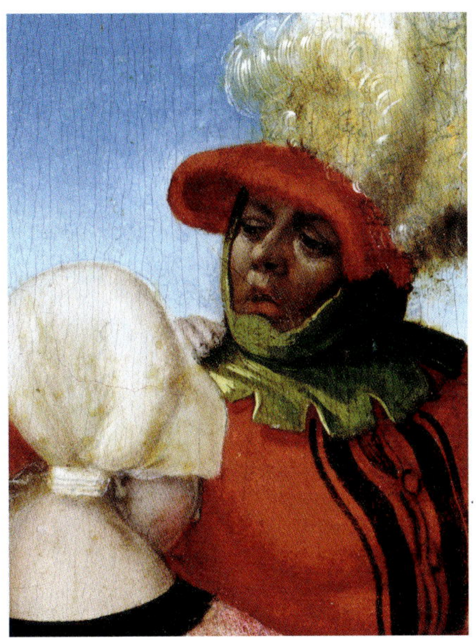

time pitted against each other. It was an invention born of the spirit or the mood of the day. From an intellectual point of view, the late Middle Ages stood under the dictate of the Church, which insisted that the earth was a vale of sorrows and that men and women were sinners whose only hope for redemption lay in the world beyond. The people of the Renaissance, on the other hand, discovered the beauty of the earth and celebrated the life of this world. They countered the *memento mori*, the "Remember you must die", with a *memento vivere*, "Remember you are alive". Translated into Baldung's picture: Death is no longer all-powerful but must give it his absolute all, must exert himself to the point of making himself look ridiculous, if he is to drag the woman from the horse. Whether he manages, whether he succeeds in his attack on love and passion, is left open. The composition has its flaws; Baldung's ambitions evidently exceeded his abilities at this early stage of his career. What inspired him to take up this subject is unknown. It is conceivable that the seventeen- or eighteen-year-old had personally encountered for the first time the forces to which, in his witches, horses and erotic beauties, he would later lend such convincing artistic form.

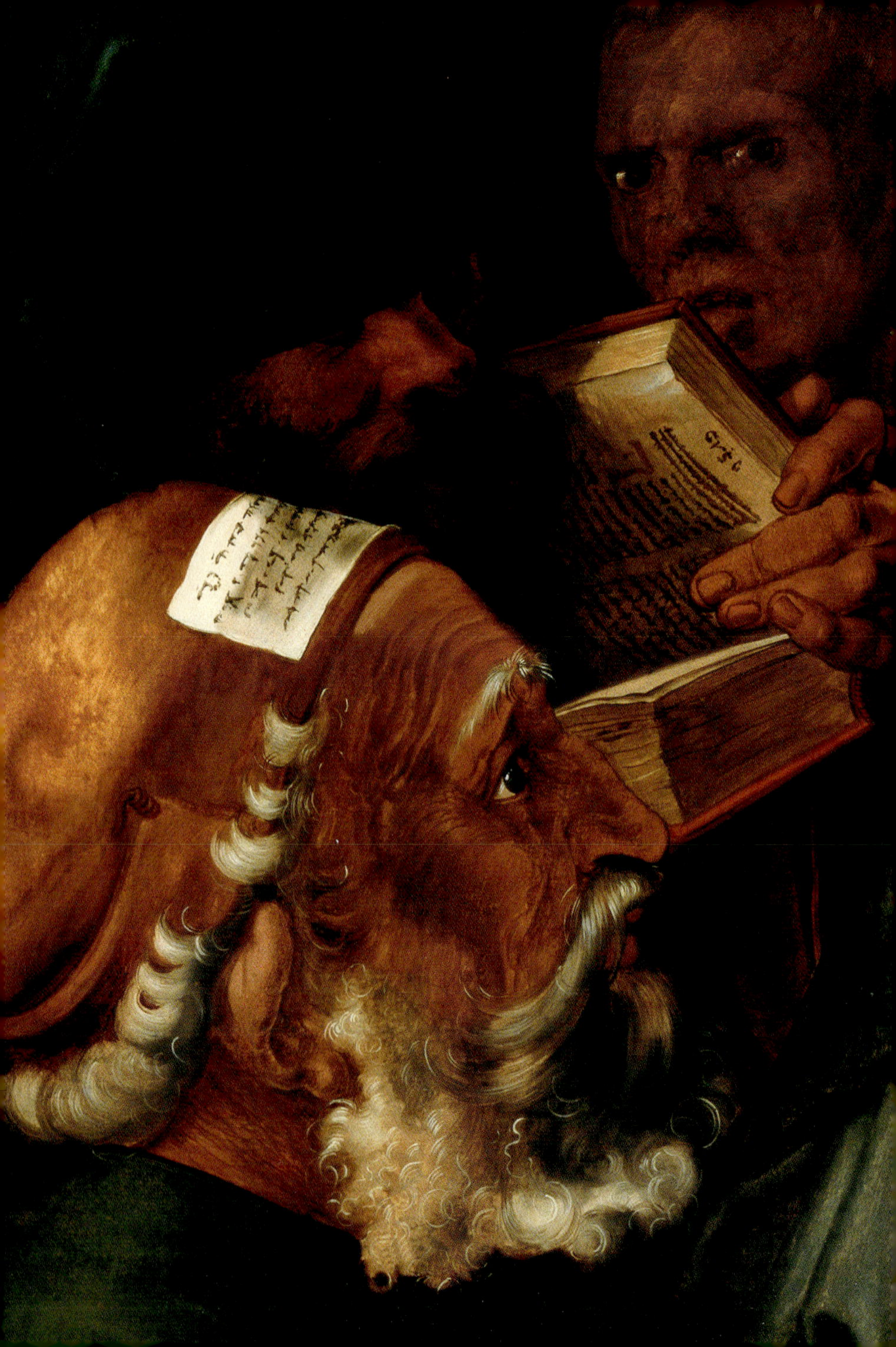

Albrecht Dürer (1471–1528)

God's truth and people's confusion

Christ among the Doctors, 1506
63.4 x 80.3 cm, Madrid, Museo Thyssen-Bornemisza

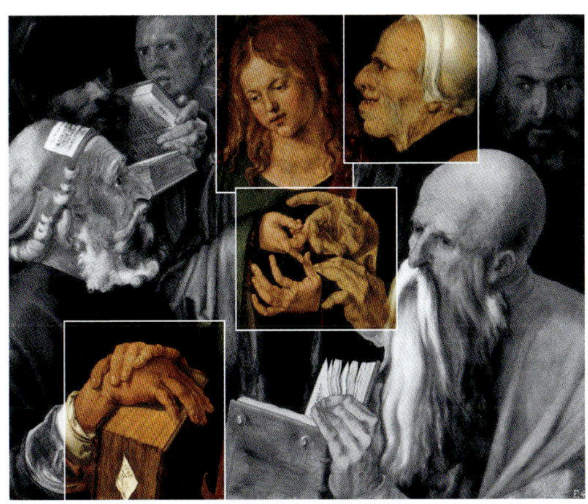

A few years ago the German magazine *art* asked its readers to name their favourite pictures, and among the top results – unsurprisingly – were several by Albrecht Dürer. His *Praying Hands*, *Hare* and *Apostles* are all treasured images in German homes. They are works of artistic mastery with motifs that are comprehensible at first sight. Whether animals or plants, whether a woman's devoutly folded pair of hands or venerable men, they all inspire confidence in the world to which they belong. They make the viewer feel safe and secure.

This is not the case with the twelve-year-old Jesus portrayed in *Christ among the Doctors*. Had *art* inquired after Dürer's least popular works, this small-format painting would have been amongst them: a picture that looks as if it has been cropped along the top and bottom, whose figures sit or stand uncomfortably close together, with a knot of fingers in the centre that looks as if it has a life of its own. We do not know what occasioned the painting or who ordered it. Perhaps it was not commissioned. It was painted in 1506 in Venice. Beneath his monogram, Dürer noted that it was the work of five days – *opus qinque dierum* – a sensationally short period of time. It is probably the picture that Dürer describes in a letter to his Nuremberg friend Freund Willibald Pirckheimer as a panel "unlike any other I have done until now".

Boy, girl or angel?

The story of the twelve-year-old Jesus is
found in the Gospel of Luke, Chapter 2.
Joseph and Mary had left Nazareth and
gone to Jerusalem with their son and other
devout citizens to celebrate the feast of
Passover. After they had started upon the
journey home, they noticed that Jesus was
missing. Mary and Joseph went back to
Jerusalem and spent three days looking for
him. They eventually found him "in the
temple, sitting in the midst of the teachers, both listening to them and asking
them questions. And all who heard him
were astonished at his understanding and
answers." Mary was upset: "Son, why have
you done this to us? Look, your father and
I have sought you anxiously." Jesus replied.
"Why did you seek me? Did you not know
that I must be about my Father's business?"
His parents did not understand what he
meant, but Mary "kept all these things in
her heart".

Dürer had already depicted this scene
on two earlier occasions: in 1496 as one of
the episodes on an altarpiece devoted to the
Seven Sorrows of the Virgin, and in 1503 as a
woodcut. In both cases the scene unfolds in
a spacious interior, with religious scholars
either gesticulating excitedly or looking
bored; some are even asleep. The parents are
entering from the side. Jesus is seated on a
raised chair or – in the woodcut – behind
a desk; Dürer portrays him as a teacher,
distanced from the priests. None of this
is shown in the painting that took five
days. It is impossible to tell who is
sitting and who is standing; there is no
distance between the teachers and indeed
no indication of spatial setting. Dürer
compresses; he paints a close-up view and
includes the contrast of young and old that
was missing in the earlier pictures.

Any viewers unfamiliar with the motif,
however, would be unable to tell if the
childlike person with the gentle face and
the locks tumbling over the shoulders is
meant to represent an angel, a boy or
a girl. Dürer paints the twelve-year-old as
sexually neutral. This may be justified in

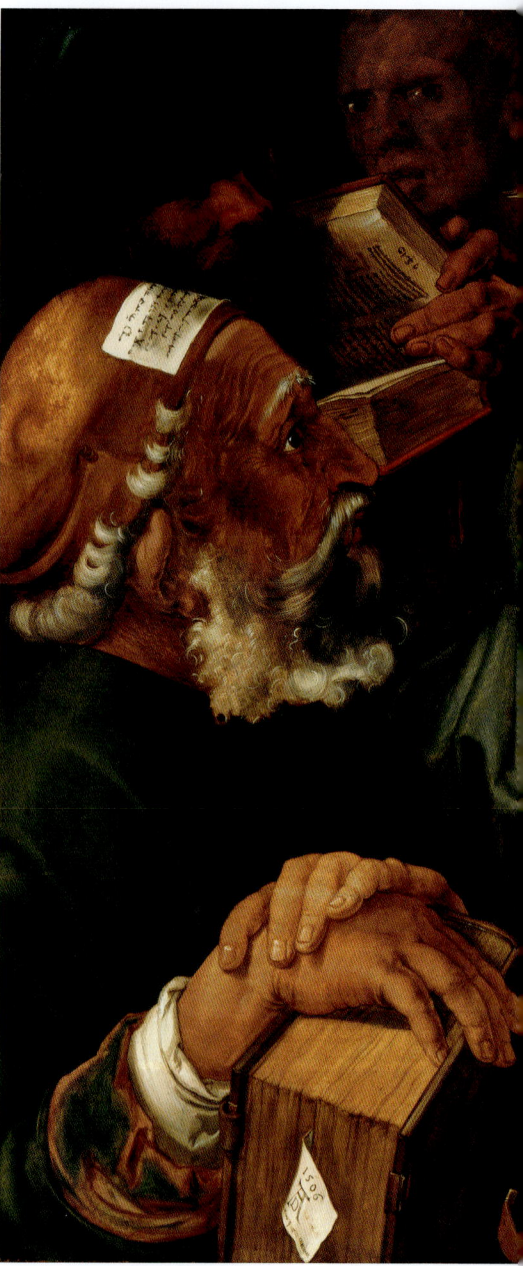

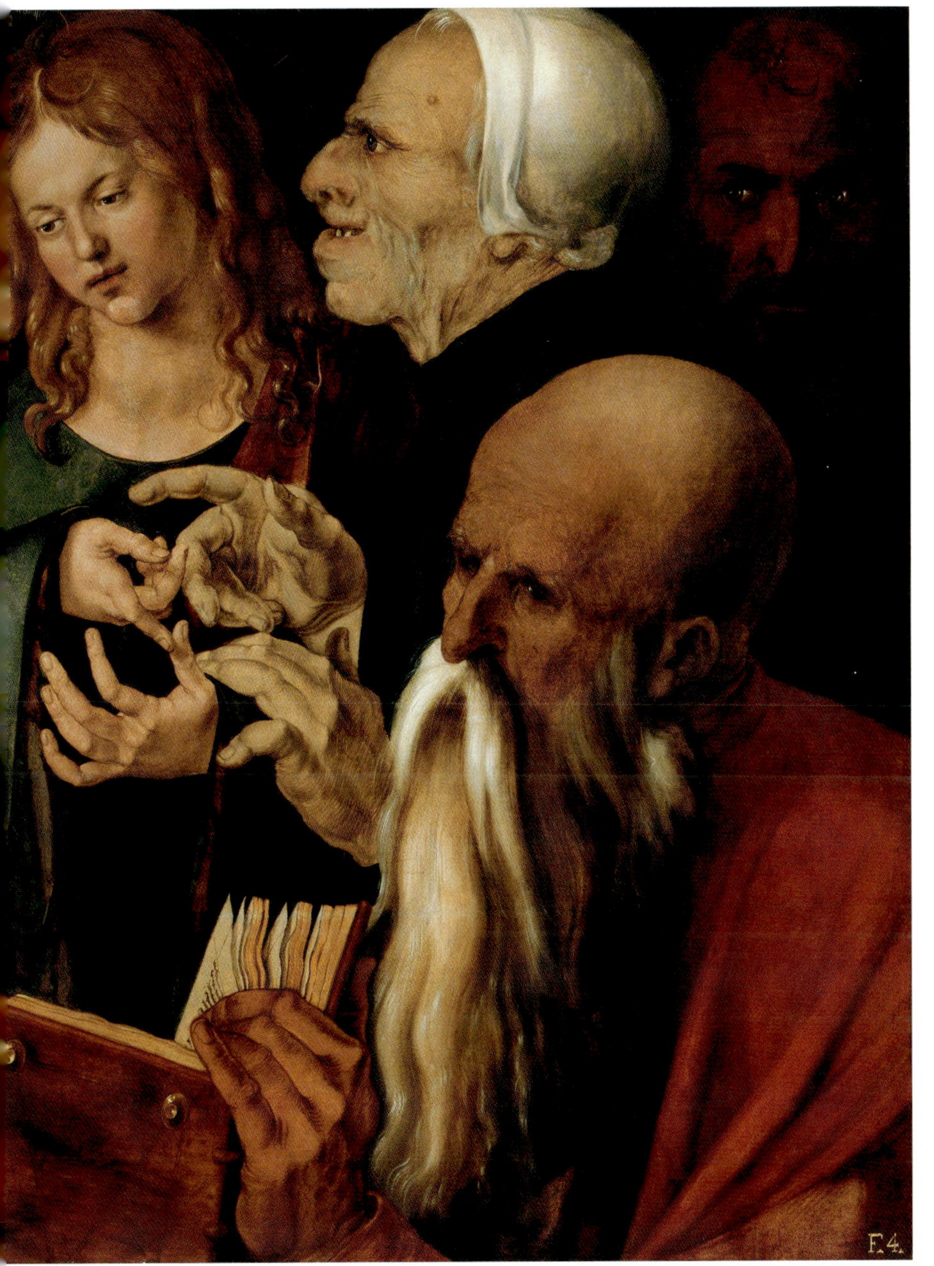

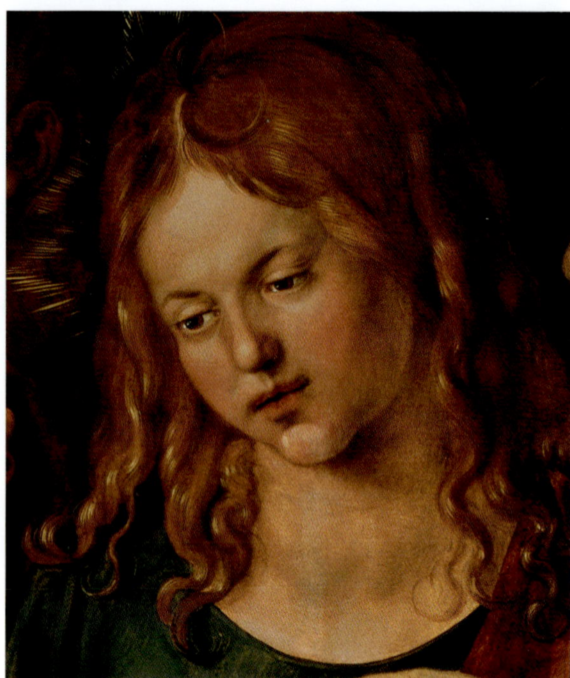

Feast of the Rose Garlands, a large-format altarpiece that he produced in Venice for its German merchant community. Within this heavily populated painting, with its emperor, pope, laypeople, clergy and angels, this detail fails to stand out. In the case of the twelve-year-old in the temple, Dürer appears to have had the supernatural Son of God in mind, in contrast to the earthly realism of the old men with their wrinkles and bald pates, warts and crooked noses.

Was Dürer anti-Semitic?

Beside the sweet, smooth face of the child, Dürer places the repulsively ugly head of an old man wearing a fixed gaze and with a mouth that looks as if it is about to snap. The man does not keep the distance usual in conversation but appears dangerously close. Two of the heads that Dürer leaves in the background also have a menacing air. The whites of their eyes gleam in the darkness and they are looking askance – both common indicators of furtive lurking. Together, the three heads show that Jesus is surrounded by enemies. None is this is found in Luke. The Evangelist simply describes the occasion on which Jesus revealed for the first time that he was more than a son of man. Dürer interprets the scene in the light of Christ's end and bears in mind his scourging, mocking and death on the Cross.

That the Jews had "murdered our Lord" and remained a menace to all Christians was an opinion that had been widespread since the Middle Ages, a phantasmagoria regularly flickering with stereotypical horror scenes. Jews, it was said, desecrated consecrated Hosts, killed Christian children in secret rituals and poisoned wells. Mendicant monks who wandered through the countryside fed simple minds with fears that were intended to drive them into church, but hatred of the Jews was to be found amongst the educated, too. Nicholas of Cusa (1401–1464), a cardinal and a much admired thinker,

terms of developmental psychology, but Dürer thereby touches upon a theological and artistic dispute surrounding the thesis that the Son of God truly became human and was thus truly a man.

Around 1500, i.e. in the period before the Reformation, the need to see Jesus as a person, as a fellow human being, was evidently particularly strong. This may have been a reaction to Rome's increasing – and increasingly lavish – emphasis upon the glorification of Christ and the Church itself. In art, a trend towards an earthly Jesus becomes visible in two motifs. Firstly in treatments of the Virgin and Child in which the boy's sex is not concealed, but in which on the contrary the Virgin points to the tiny penis with her finger. And secondly in Crucifixions in which Christ is portrayed as brutally murdered and physically suffering. The Counter-Reformation would then once again idealize the crucified figure of Christ and prudishly conceal his genitalia.

For Dürer, Christ's dual nature was evidently no problem. He painted the naked Infant on the Virgin's lap on several occasions, including in the

demanded that Jews should wear a piece of coloured cloth on their outer garments so that Christians knew to avoid them. In 1519 the great humanist Erasmus of Rotterdam (1466/69–1536) wrote that every Christian "despises … this type of people". In 1543 Luther published a pamphlet bearing the title "On the Jews and their Lies"; it was later much cited by the National Socialists, who also used motifs by Dürer in their propaganda literature.

This raises the question of whether Dürer was himself an anti-Semite. Answer: there is no evidence that he was. He lived in a society, however, in which hatred of the Jews belonged to the emotions and thought patterns handed down from one generation to the next. He also lived in Nuremberg, a city that in 1349 had burnt to death over 500 Jews. This took place during the great plague that was claiming the lives of large swathes of Europe's population. As the cause of the epidemic was unknown, in many places the Jews were held to be responsible.

In the year 1499, when Dürer was 28, the people of Nuremberg once again got rid of their Jews, this time by expulsion. In a bureaucratically stitched up procedure, some 200 people were forced to abandon their homes. Since the law stated that all Jews were under the protection of the emperor, their houses passed to him, with no compensation being paid. The citizens of Nuremberg proceeded to buy them from the emperor for a lump sum. Among the official reasons for expelling the Jewish population were "usurious practices", i.e. lending money on interest. Since the New Testament forbade the charging of interest, the privilege of money-lending had fallen to the Jews. In the 15th century, however, money was circulating on an ever larger scale, not least due to the growth in long-distance trade, and Christians wanted their share of the profits. The city of Nuremberg granted them permission to open "exchange banks". The expulsion of the Jews was thus also, if not solely, an economic measure. As a member of the city council, Willibald Pirckheimer – the friend of the artist – played a part.

Almost all the larger cities and territories expelled their Jews in the 15th century, not just in Germany but also in France, England and Spain. Many of the displaced settled in northern Italy and later in Poland and Lithuania. Italian merchants exploited their international connections, their doctors enjoyed a good reputation, and Italian intellectuals appreciated their language skills. Antique texts that had been translated into Arabic were translated into Hebrew and from there into Latin, and thus made accessible to the humanists. In 1516, ten years after this picture was painted, the Jews of Venice were awarded their own residential quarter, the Ghetto – in order better to keep tabs on them and also to make anti-Semitic attacks more difficult.

The painter's signature

Over the last hundred years, our means of communication have multiplied: first the telephone, then the radio, then television, and now faxes, portable

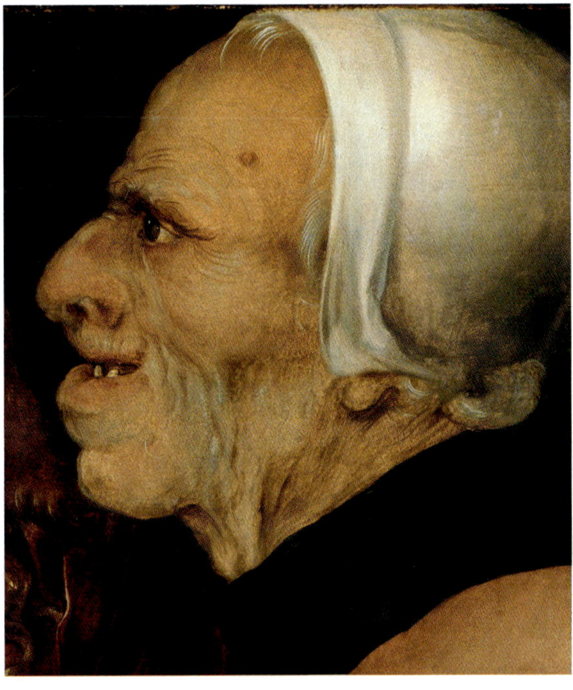

phones, emails and text messages. In Dürer's lifetime just one new medium made its appearance: book printing with movable type. Up till then, books had been written and copied by hand and were beyond the means of ordinary people. As a result of Johann Gutenberg's invention, what had been an elite medium became the first mass medium – a change similarly profound, it is to be imagined, to that which we are experiencing today. Its implications for religious instruction, in particular, were enormous: the Bible, previously found only in the hands of the clergy, now reached those of the literate laity, and thus a growing proportion of the congregation could study the scriptures for themselves. The fact that Dürer trains his spotlight in this picture not only on heads and hands, but also on books, indicates the heightened attention they now commanded.

But there are two other reasons for the book motif, both related to particular features of Judaism. With the destruction of Jerusalem by Nebuchadnezzar in 587 BC, the Jews lost their home and state. Dispersed, they preserved their identity and cohesion through their common faith in the God of the Old Testament and in the laws proclaimed by Moses. God and laws were documented with the aid of writings, whether in the form of a book or in the Torah scroll. These sacred texts replaced the state; they travelled with their owners and gave rise to the notions that the Jews possessed a "portable state" and formed a "People of the Book". In order to convert them to the Christian religion,

so it was claimed, it was first necessary to burn their books. Emperor Maximilian I (1459–1519) commissioned a survey amongst universities and scholars as to "whether one should take from the Jews all their books and get rid of them and burn them". In the Christian view, the Jews adhered far too rigidly to their books, so rigidly that they lost sight of the essentials. St Paul the Apostle targets this fixation upon strict observance of the law in his second letter to the Colossians, when he advises his readers not to let anyone "condemn you for what you eat or drink, or for not celebrating certain holy days or new moon ceremonies or Sabbaths" (Col. 2:16). For these rules were only "shadows of things to come", namely Christ himself. "Because they seek the truth in the external letter", wrote the Cistercian abbot Joachim of Fiore in the 12th century, they do not recognize Christ. The episode with the twelve-year-old Jesus in the temple was regularly cited as proof of this blindness – the Jewish teachers had failed to see that the Messiah prophesied in the Old Testament was standing before them.

Just how much the letter of the law obstructed their vision is here made visible in the written piece of paper that the artist has stuck on the old man's cap. Like the pages of the books, the note is illegible; Dürer has not here copied Hebrew texts. The motif is not of his own invention; it is described in Hartmann Schedel's *Chronicle of the World*, a printed book that aimed to describe and illustrate every part of the world and every epoch, and upon which Dürer probably worked during his apprenticeship in Nuremberg. Jews are regularly mentioned within the *Chronicle*'s pages as wearing "a little piece of parchment on their forehead" on which were written the Ten Commandments "as a reminder of the Law".

Dürer was among the Renaissance painters who lent power of expression to the hands
There can surely be no painting before this one whose centre is composed of four hands. They stand out particularly clearly against the dark background and appear to form a self-contained entity, although they are of differing sizes. The pallid, fleshy fingers of the old man seem to want to push the delicate fingers of the twelve-year-old to one side or to attack them like the pincers of a crab. It is to the younger and apparently weaker figure, however, that the artist assigns the exact centre of the panel, which lies at the

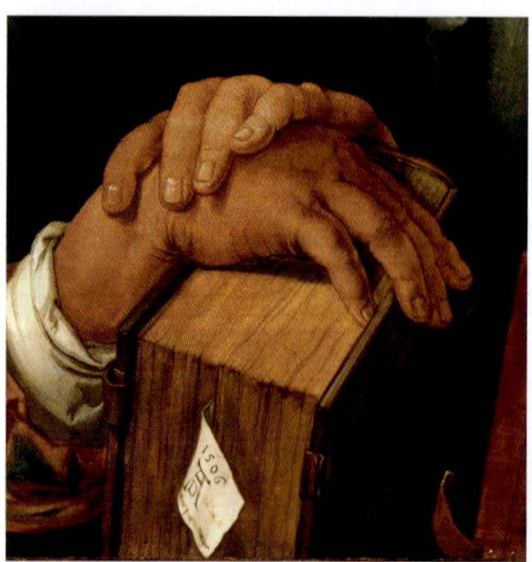

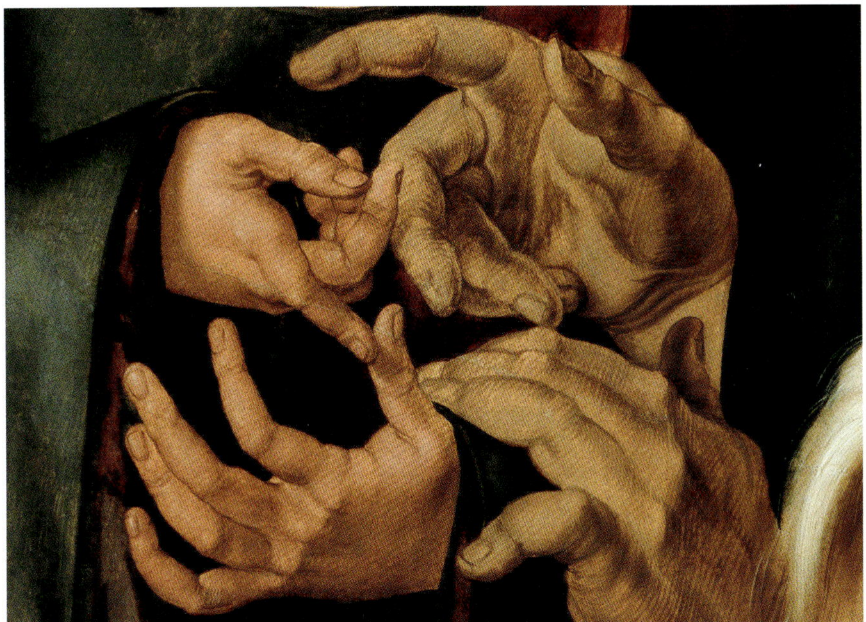

point where Jesus's index finger touches the thumb of his left hand.

Painting is an art form without words, so artists have always used hands and arms to lend their figures a voice. They adhere to traditional stereotypes: the raised index finger demands attention, hands held in front of the face express grief, arms raised to the sides signify triumph or blessing. Jesus's gesture of counting on his fingers signals that this is a debate. Before Dürer's day, such gestures and hands were reproduced in a schematic manner. Dürer gives them a "face", paints them with portrait like accuracy. He was one of the Renaissance artists who discovered the independent expressiveness of the hands. His drawing of *The Praying Hands* is a particularly popular example.

The hands in the present painting are surrounded by a ring of heads and books. Underlying this arrangement is the mathematical figure of a circle and its centre. A mathematical figure can also be sensed within Dürer's *Feast of the Rose Garlands*, namely an isosceles triangle or pyramid, whose pinnacle lies in the crown being lowered onto the Virgin's head by two angels, and whose base is

formed by the spreading cloaks of the emperor and pope. Albrecht Dürer signed this large altarpiece (today housed in the National Gallery in Prague) with the note that he had worked on it for five months. On the picture of the temple he wrote that it had taken him five days.

By telling us how long each work has taken, it is as if Dürer were presenting us with two pendants – one the painstakingly executed masterpiece, the other a rapid stroke of genius. Several critics consider the rush job to be unpolished, unsuccessful, a work that can be passed over. If we examine the two Venetian paintings together, however, they appear as the recto and verso of the same Western past: on one side, Dürer celebrates the unity of Christianity in the most exquisite colours, while on the other he deploys a gloomy and disharmonious palette to illustrate the discord, the conflict that has run through our history since the birth of Christ and as a result of the birth of Christ – a subject that no art lover would commission. Dürer painted it, so it would seem, for himself.

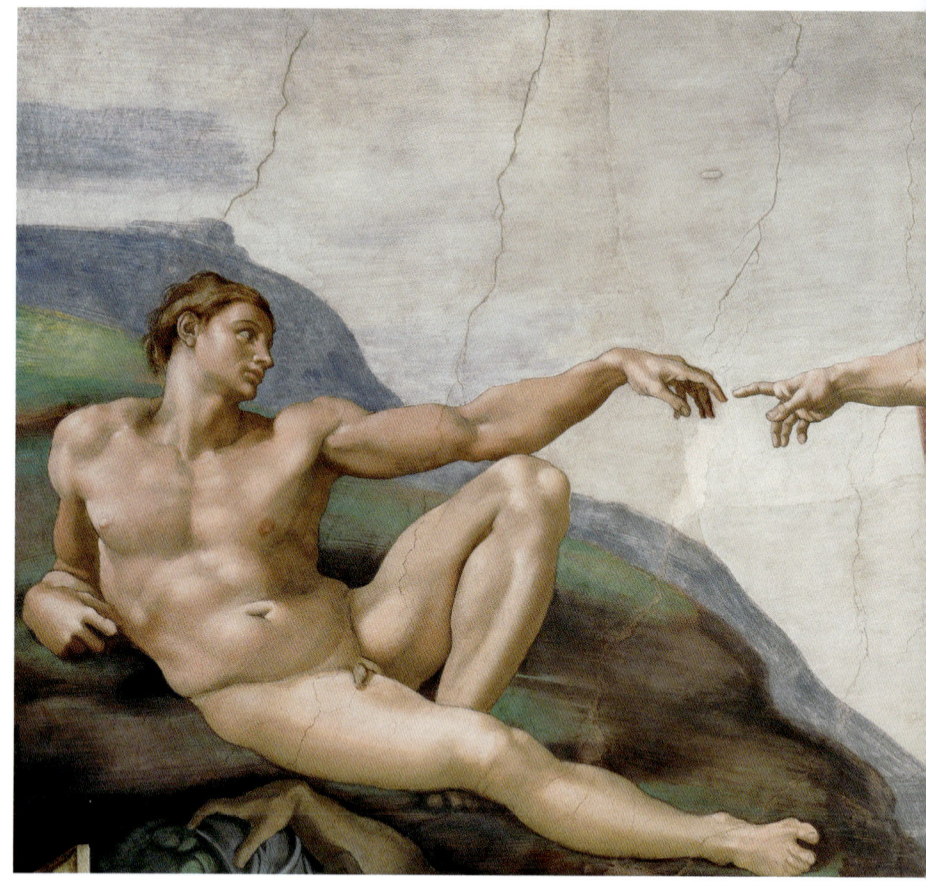

Michelangelo Buonarotti (1475–1564)

God touches man

The Creation of Adam, 1508/1512
Rome, Sistine Chapel

Even those who have never been to Rome and have never read a book on art know the two almost touching hands. The motif has left the enclave of art and entered – at least in Europe – the general cultural domain. It today belongs in our mental library of images, whose archives include not only the Eiffel Tower and Niagara Falls but also the moon landing and the mushroom cloud, and even Asterix and Donald Duck.

It is not the only motif to have escaped the confines of the world of art. Others include Dürer's praying hands, Delacroix' Marianne storming the barricades, the *Mona Lisa* and the drawing of the man inscribed within a circle, the latter both by

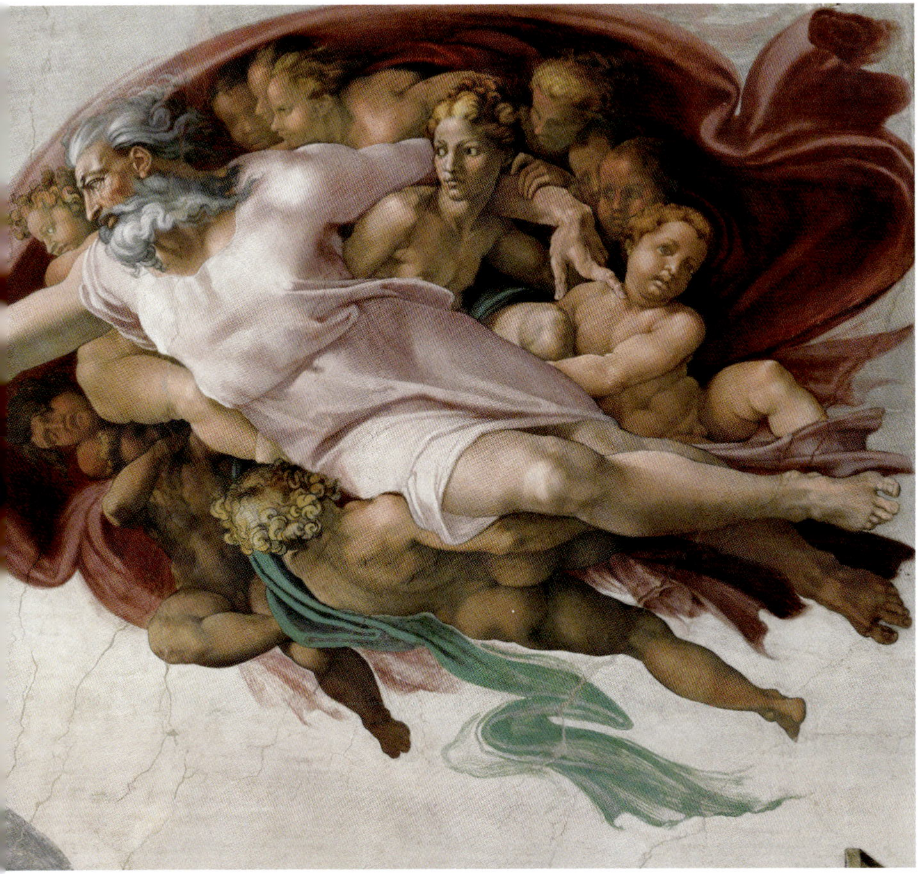

Leonardo da Vinci. Even if statistical proof from across Europe is lacking, there is evidence for the popularity of these individual motifs in the world of marketing. Art motifs are frequently employed in advertising to lend a product a favourable aura, bathe it in gentle irony or simply to exploit the pleasure of recognition in the viewer. Just three examples: "Motivate thy neighbour as thyself" exhorts a magazine for top executives and has sparks flying between the fingertips painted by Michelangelo. A mobile phone company illustrates its slogan "Connecting People" with two hands reaching for each other against a blue sky. On the posters for Steven Spielberg's box-office hit *E. T.*,

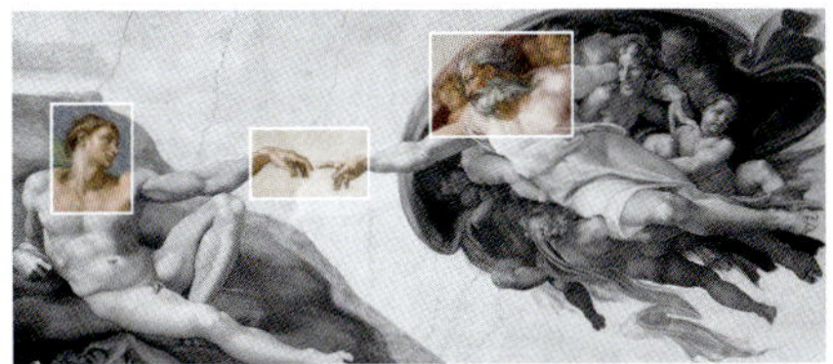

the elongated finger of the alien descending from above touches the outstretched index finger of a human child's hand.

Art lovers sometimes take the view that advertising not merely abuses an original but is actually harmful to it. There is no evidence for this, however. Michelangelo's *Creation of Adam*, at least, has so far proved more powerful than any imitation, a statement supported by advertising strategies themselves – for would they continue to use the motif if it left their target audience indifferent? The question remains as to why this is; why should these hands continue to move us, almost 500 years after they were painted?

A perfect Adam

Michelangelo's Adam is a product of the Renaissance. He arose out of a consciousness utterly different to that of the Middle Ages. Put simply: in the Middle Ages, people saw themselves as miserable sinners in an earthy vale of sorrows. Adam and Eve had disobeyed God and the burden of their guilt was passed on to all their descendants, with salvation only possible in the life to come. Artists accordingly tended to portray Heaven in bright splendour and the people below it as relatively small and wretched. With the start of the Renaissance, i.e. from around 1400 onwards, another image of humankind began to emerge: instead of the man and woman driven out of Paradise in disgrace,

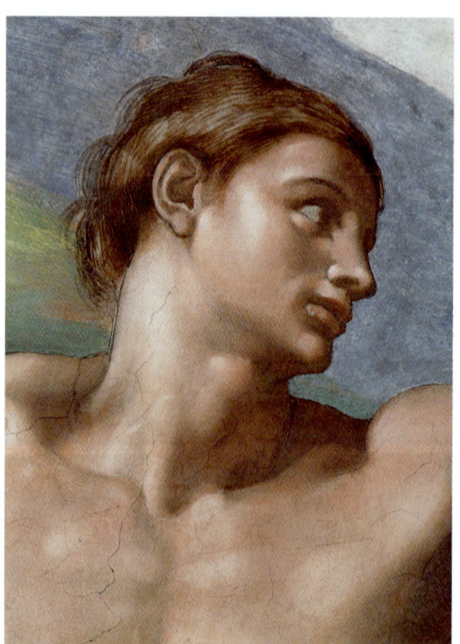

painters depicted Adam and Eve as God had originally created them – beautiful and perfect and in the image of God. As it is written in Genesis (1:27): "So God created man in His own image; in the image of God He created him."

This paradigm shift was accompanied and reinforced by the rediscovery of antiquity, that pre-Christian era which celebrated the sovereign individual and in which a noble character went hand in hand with a beautiful body. In Michelangelo's day, they sought to marry antique and Christian thought. In 1486 Pico della Mirandola – a 23-year-old prodigy of rhetoric and learning – declared, very much in the antique spirit, that man was the crown of creation and "the most fortunate of all creatures and the most worthy of admiration". For as Mirandola devoutly explained, God had placed bounds upon all his other creations; man alone was free. He could descend "into the lower forms of life, the beasts" or ascend "into the higher forms, the divine". He was almost as free as God himself – in every individual lived "divinity clothed in flesh".

Just as the picture of man held by intellectuals changed, so did that held by artists. Even before Michelangelo's day, painters had already learned how to represent their surroundings in three-dimensional perspective. They could convey a sense of distance and model objects with the aid of light and shadow. They made people big and discovered the characteristic features of the human body, with its bone structure, muscles, proportions and the changing pallor of the skin.

In the pictorial world of the Middle Ages, the human figure resembled a pictogram, more of a symbol than a likeness. Michelangelo, by contrast, fills his bodies with muscles and sinews of exaggerated definition. Adam, this first man, still wearing a dreamy look and only just beginning to stir himself, already has athletic shoulders. Nor has Michelangelo forgotten his genitals, any more than in the many other male nudes in his monumental Christian fresco.

And he shows him handsome, as noble and handsome as God. This latter is floating not high above him, moreover, but at almost the same height. The Creator is near his image: he exudes the air of a solicitous father and not the angry God of the Old Testament, who pronounced humankind guilty from the moment of birth and was ready, on several occasions, to see it destroyed.

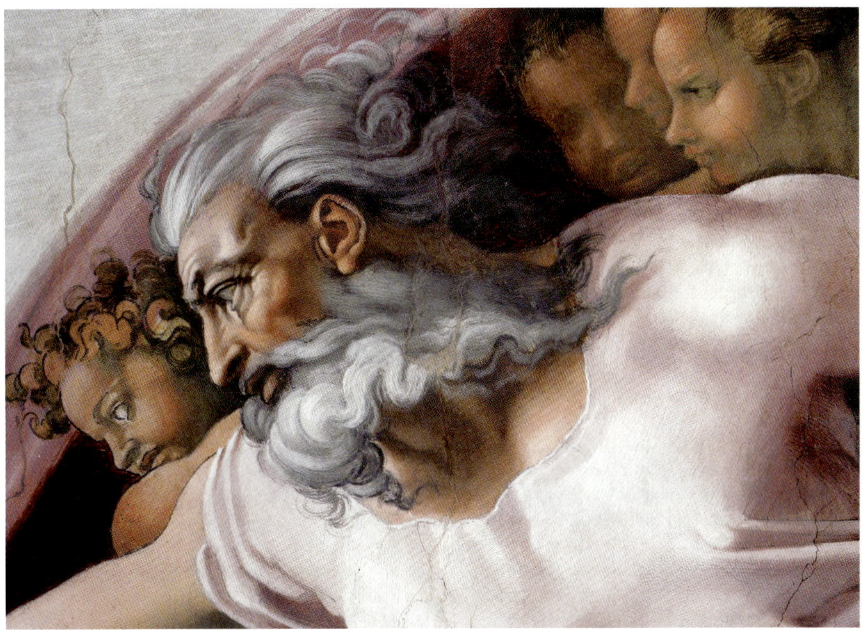

God has a face

According to the Bible, God lies beyond all powers of human imagination. The Christians wanted to see him, however, and visualized him as a venerable old man with a beard. As long as artists were still depicting the figures – and in particular the celestial beings – in their paintings in a symbolic manner, the contradiction between a god who is infinite and beyond imagination and his confinement within human form was probably not so obvious. This changed with the Renaissance, and the new attitude is particularly clear in Michelangelo's *Creation of Adam*, for the painter gives the "invisible" not just a body but also a visage. In committing himself thus, he draws upon earlier models from Classical antiquity, for example Zeus – and also upon himself, as portraits would appear to suggest.

Michelangelo was not alone in this. Albrecht Dürer, too, had stylized himself as Christ in a self-portrait executed a few years earlier, in 1500. If everyone is "divinity clothed in flesh", then an artist may also render that visible in his own person.

Michelangelo has rendered the head and body of God in the same amount of detail as the figure of Adam and thus given God and man the same material substance. The difference lies in their age and movement. In contrast to Adam, who is still, God is approaching at great speed from the cosmos. His beard and hair are swept backwards by the airstream and the cloth in which he is arriving with his companions seems aerodynamically shaped. Perhaps the artist thereby wished to suggest a divine omnipresence. But this sense of movement also calls to mind the ever active Zeus, hurling thunderbolts and moving effortlessly between Olympus and the world of men, and who had become popular with the resurgence of interest in the authors of antiquity.

With the *Creation of Adam* Michelangelo produced an image of celestial harmony, while the land in which he lived was being torn apart by power struggles. Italy's minor states pitched their armies against each other, and Pope Julius II was almost always involved, ever anxious to strengthen the power of the Papal States: a cunning despot who used artists – as he did his troops – to win prestige for the Vatican (and himself).

In 1505 he summoned Michelangelo to Rome so that the latter could design him a splendid tomb.

In 1506 his priority shifted to the construction of the new St Peter's and Michelangelo was given no more money. Furious, the artist returned to his native Florence. Julius ordered him to come back but the artist refused. The Florentine government, anxious to avoid a war with the Pope on Michelangelo's account, asked him to go. Instead of resuming work on the tomb, Michelangelo had to make a bronze statue of Julius in Bologna, where the Pope was now stationed with his army. Michelangelo refused – casting in bronze was not his metier – but was obliged to concede. By 1508 he was back in Rome, hoping to work on the tomb, but was charged instead with painting the ceiling of the Sistine Chapel. His initial response was again to say no, for he saw himself as a sculptor whose material was marble, not paint. But he had to.

Michelangelo found a gesture to symbolize the transmission of divine power from God to Adam – the touch of their fingertips

Adam, so it written in Genesis, was formed from the dust of the ground, and God "breathed into his nostrils the breath of life". In other words, there were two phases. Churches in the Middle Ages almost always showed the first phase: God as an old man, bent over the lying or already seated Adam, sometimes still with his hand on his creation. The second phase, i.e. the breathing in of the divine breath, was visually conveyed by a small winged figure or by golden rays, but disappeared from the biblical catalogue of motifs with the Renaissance. Why? Perhaps because this divine act was hard to align with the more "realistic" outlook of the new art, and perhaps too because blowing into the nose was perceived as indecorous. Michelangelo discovered or employed a new formula for this existential act, also known as "inspiration".

Michelangelo visualized much that was new in terms of form and colour on the ceiling of the Sistine Chapel, but reinvented none of the traditional scenes from the Old Testament as radically and impressively as this one. Instead of the invisible breath, the tips of the fingers, the moment before they touch those of Adam. A touch of an entirely unfamiliar kind: on the one hand – so it seems – full of shyness and tenderness, and on the other hand performed as if on a fly past by someone who cannot be grasped.

The fact that this picture, or rather this detail of a picture, has become so extraordinarily popular is not because Michelangelo used a new formula 500 years ago, however. Nor is it because his figures recline and hover with such convincing naturalism, or because their colours and shapes are so particularly pleasing. More than in many of his other works, Michelangelo here succeeds in triggering something within the viewer that fundamentally has nothing more to do with art. He raises questions that normal adults have long since ticked off, reminds us of needs that we prefer to deny: such as the question

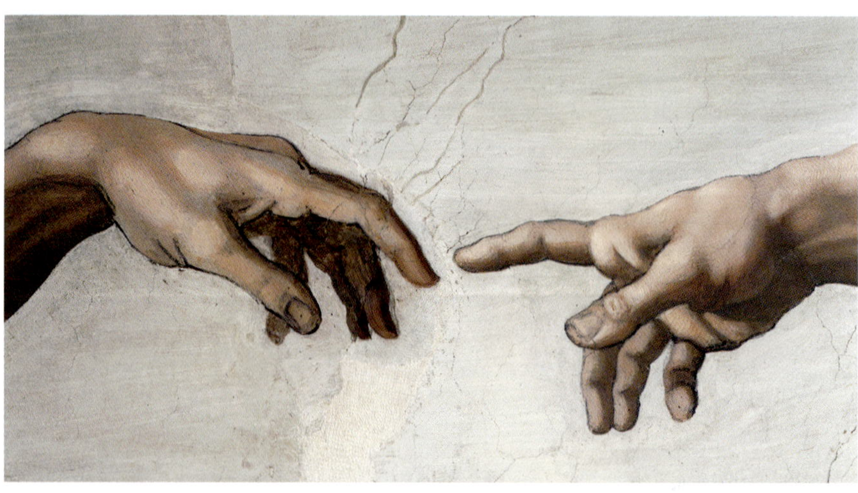

of where people come from, how they were made, whether a higher power indeed had a hand in their creation and created a perfect Adam at a stroke, or whether we really have to accept a much less glamorous descent from an ape like being.

Amongst the needs stirred up by Michelangelo's motif might be the need for guidance, for an earthly counsellor in this confusing world or for a paternal hand reaching down from above. Or it could be the desire for an end to separation: one of the distressing experiences of puberty is that each person lives for himself, enclosed in his skin and in his body, and that like a monad he is able to register others but ultimately cannot become one with them. Michelangelo sees both: Adam alone in an empty world and God in his cosmic cloak enfolding manifold beings. The touch of his finger promises salvation: you are not alone.

In this regard the mobile phone manufacturer with its company slogan "Connecting People" and the two hands reaching out to clasp each other has made a clever choice. And the distributors of the film *E. T.*, whose posters show the finger of a being from outer space touching that of a human child *à la* Michelangelo, were also well aware of the motif's effect. Today, it is true, it has little to do with the Bible and nothing to do with the religiosity of the Renaissance. But Michelangelo lent visual form to something like an archetype and an ideal, one that continues to exert an influence far beyond its own epoch and in entirely different spheres of life than the papal chapel.

"My brush, above my face continually"
The Sistine Chapel, named after Pope Sixtus IV, is the church for the senior members of the Vatican and the place where they assemble, for example to elect a new pope. It was completed in 1481, but before long cracks appeared in the masonry and it had to be restored and the ceiling repainted. Julius II wanted the Twelve Apostles, but for Michelangelo that was too few. Even under duress, he wanted to deliver a work that would surpass anything comparable. He continued to argue with the Pope until the latter said: "Do what you like!"

Michelangelo had just turned 30; his *David* was already standing in Florence. Inside the chapel, he had scaffolding erected, made sketches, transferred their outlines onto large "cartoons", hoisted them up to the ceiling and marked the lines onto the

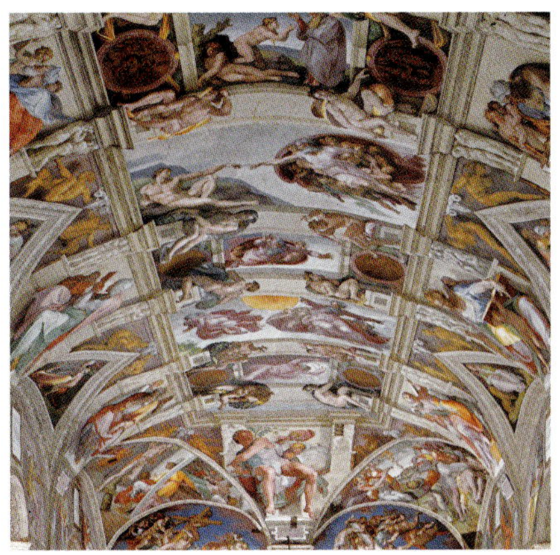

plaster by pricking holes through the paper. The plaster was freshly applied beforehand as the fresco technique requires a damp ground. Michelangelo worked for four years – with only brief interruptions – standing with his head bent backwards: "My beard toward heaven, I feel the back of my brain / Upon my neck … My brush, above my face continually, / Makes it a splendid floor by dripping down." The ceiling itself is a barrel vault; Michelangelo painted down as far as the windows – over 1,000 square metres of plaster. To his assistants he entrusted only minor details. He felt lonely: "I have no friends of any kind and don't want any."

A work fanatic, a lone wolf. The extent to which he conceived his monumental ceiling painting without theological assistance remains to be established. Its themes range from the Creation of the World via the Expulsion from Paradise all the way to Noah, the forefather of the new race of men. The scenes from the Old Testament are surrounded by a wealth of figures: the ancestors of Christ, prophets, antique sibyls and, again and again, nameless nudes to fill in the gaps. Three decades later (1541) – again under pressure from the Pope – Michelangelo would paint the *Last Judgement* on the altar wall. To the prehistory of Christianity he thereby added its end.

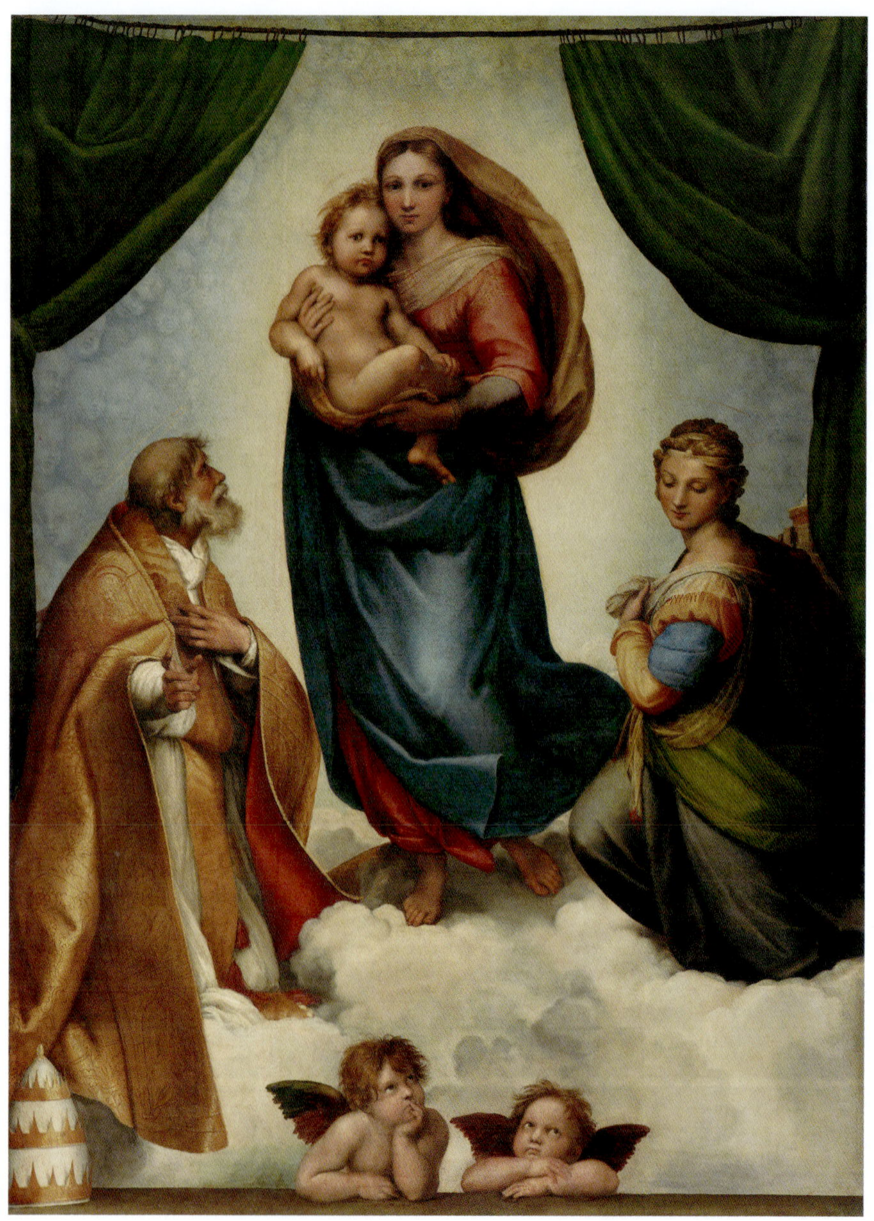

Raphael (1483–1520)
(Raffael Santi)

When the Virgin came to Dresden

The Sistine Madonna, 1512/1513
269.5 x 201 cm, Dresden, Gemäldegalerie Alte Meister

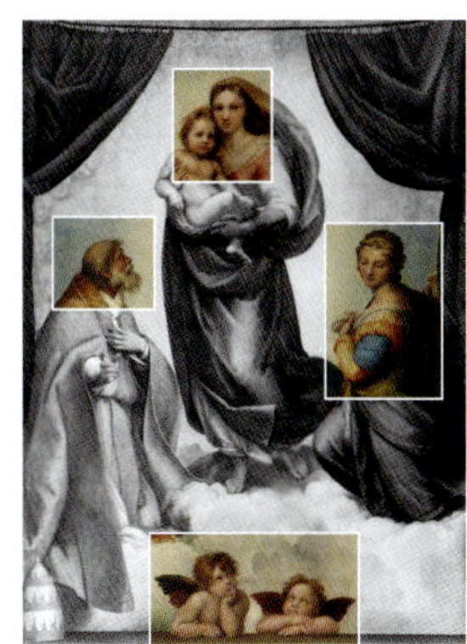

On 1 March 1754 Raphael's Madonna was unpacked in Dresden. She had come from Piacenza, where she had hung on the high altar of the monastery church of San Sisto for almost 250 years. The monks needed money and it took two years to agree terms, but once they were finally settled in January 1754, things moved very fast. That meant crossing the Alps in the heart of winter on "fiendish" narrow roads. The Italian painter Carlo Cesare Giovannini, who was accompanying the painting on its journey, wrote in a letter: "The fog is thick and the rain is getting worse and worse."

Raphael's altarpiece nevertheless reached Dresden without suffering any great damage and was presented to Augustus II in the palace audience chamber. Giovannini noted that "the painting pleased His Majesty extremely". Whether this was first and foremost on account of the fame of its artist remains open. Whatever the case, Augustus III already owned "certain small pictures by Raphael", although Giovannini doubted their authenticity.

In Dresden, building up an art collection was part of building up an image of wealth and power. Between them, Augustus the Strong and his son Augustus III are supposed to have bought over 4,000 works of art. By comparison with Prussia, for example, Saxony had plenty of money: mineral resources of silver and ore had seduced the Electors into buying themselves the title of King of Poland. This elevated rank demanded a collection of art that could compete with the treasures to be found in Vienna or Paris.

As a connoisseur and an Italian, Giovannini found the collection dubious – "many beautiful things are glued together with varnish and patches".

But although he found everything pitiable, "for the sake of prudence and Christian charity it is better to say nothing". Perhaps Giovannini was also angered by the fact that the masterpiece he had brought to Dresden was not treated with the anticipated respect. The leading court official, Carl Heinrich von Heinecken, considered the Infant Jesus to be no more than "a common child", one who "worse still was pulling a sullen face while Raphael was working on the design". Raphael's painting, called the *Sistine Madonna* after its San Sisto origins, was hung in a poor spot and not even granted an engraving in the 1757 catalogue of the collection. At that time, Dresden's favourite picture was Correggio's *Nativity*, painted some ten years after the *Sistine Madonna*. Both paintings show the Virgin and Child, but Correggio offers a highly dramatic scene dominated by chiaroscuro effects. The main protagonists are bathed in brilliant light while the figures around the sides disappear, with much gesticulation, into the darkness. In Raphael's picture, by contrast, we can see right into the corners; the chief figures are firmly outlined and harmoniously distributed across the canvas and the artist exercises restraint in his palette and gestures. There is no harsh lighting and barely a shadow is cast, as if Raphael wished to proclaim that there can indeed be no darkness in Heaven.

Correggio versus Raphael – in Dresden, it was a dispute between two camps. Over the years, connoisseurs came to favour the *Sistine Madonna*, partly under the influence of Johann Joachim Winckelmann (1717–1768), who was at that time librarian at a court near Dresden. He demanded that all new works should be measured against the yardstick of Classical art and

formulated the now famous concepts of "noble simplicity" and "quiet grandeur". He admired Raphael's
Madonna for her inner tranquillity and for the "still-
ness that the ancients allowed to prevail in the images
of their deities." But this was only one of the reasons
why Raphael's painting grew ever more popular.

The murdered pope

Kneeling on either side of the Virgin are St Sixtus
and St Barbara, the two 3rd-century martyrs to whom
the monastery church in Piacenza was dedicated.
Whereas the life of St Barbara is detailed in various
accounts, there is little information about St Sixtus
other than that he was elected pope in 257 and the
following year was murdered while celebrating mass
in the catacombs of Rome. There were no known
portraits of either saint and Raphael had a free hand.
He gave Sixtus a somewhat shaggy monk's tonsure,
a beard of the kind sported by Pope Julius II and a
profile that also resembled that of the Pope. Julius II
had commissioned the *Sistine Madonna*.

The award of the commission is not documented
and nor is the picture dated or signed, but the missing facts can be deduced from the circumstances.
Raffaello Santi, born in 1483 in Urbino, spent the
years 1508 to 1511 carrying out the decoration of
Julius II's private library, today known as the Stanza
della Segnatura. He then moved on to an audience
chamber, today the Stanza d'Eliodoro, upon which
he worked until Julius's death in 1513. Raphael was a
sort of papal court painter, but although this meant
that Julius II was able to call upon his services, it did
not prevent the artist from accepting commissions
from other patrons.

Like all Renaissance popes, Julius II spent vast
sums on art and architecture, whose magnificence
was to advance the fame of the Church as well as
serve the purposes of religious edification. Martin
Luther, as a devout Augustinian monk in Rome
in 1510/11, was repulsed by this worldly ostentation.
Seven years later he would launch the Reformation
with his theses on the church door in Wittenberg.

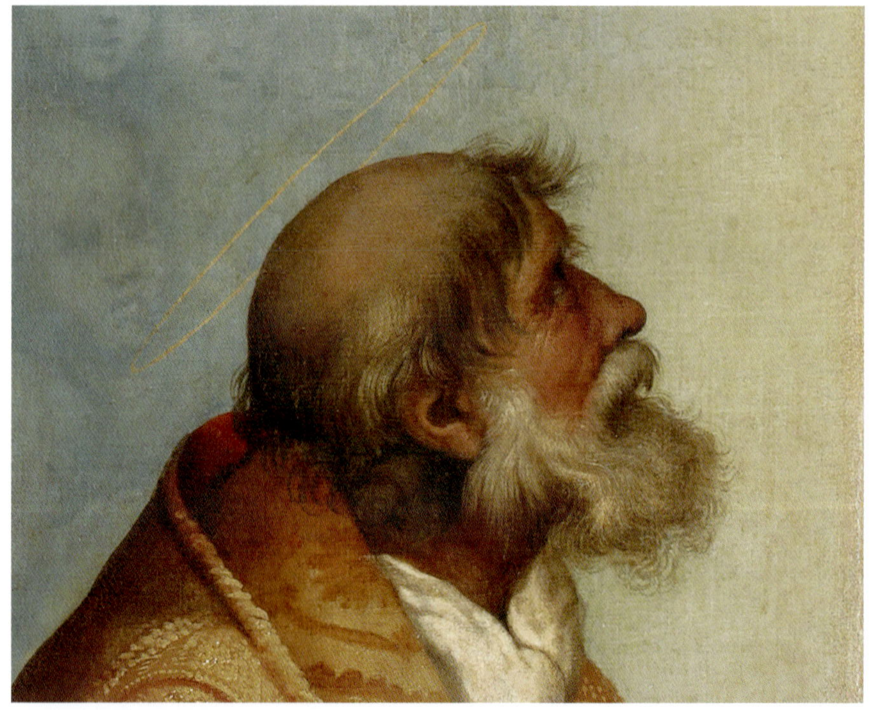

Even more important to the Pope than to enhance his public image with grandiose works of art, however, was to hold on to and expand his Papal States, for territorial holdings meant power and tax revenues. Italian cities and princedoms fought each another almost without interruption, sought protection from more powerful neighbours and forged or broke pacts. Through their changing alliances, they sought above all to prevent one of their number – Venice or Milan, for example – from becoming too powerful. The methods were crude, as was the language: if Julius II wanted to turn Venice "back into a fishing village", as he declared in 1509, the Venetians were equally keen to demote the Holy Father "to a lowly parson".

An ideal of female virtue
In those days Italy was a theatre of war and in 1512 came Julius's year of crisis. In April his army suffered a devastating defeat at the hands of the French and Milanese. His counsellors advised him to flee Rome. Julius stayed. Swiss mercenaries came to his aid. His opponents had lost their generals and were leaderless, and Julius, only just still on his feet, remained the overall victor. Amongst the cities that were thereby won for the Papal States were Parma and Piacenza. It was upon this occasion, it can be confidently concluded, that Julius commissioned the altarpiece from Raphael. He had already been a patron of the church of San Sisto while still a cardinal. Raphael has patterned Sixtus's cape, or pluvial, with oak leaves and adorned the top of the tiara – the papal crown – in the lower left-hand corner with an acorn. The acorn formed part of Julius II's family coat of arms. The monks were to be left in no doubt as to whom they owed their picture.

Sixtus's hair and beard are unkempt and his skin is ruddy: the saint looks like a man who spends more time sitting on a horse than kneeling at the altar. Raphael depicts Barbara, on the other hand, as an ideal of feminine breeding and beauty – her gaze lowered, her hands folded chastely over her breast, her skin flawless, her hair carefully dressed. According to legend, Barbara was beautiful and virtuous, and when her heathen father had to go away, he took the precaution of locking her up in a tower with two windows. Barbara converted to Christianity and had a third window made in the tower as a symbol of the Holy Trinity. Her martyrdom commenced with the return of her enraged father, and when none of his

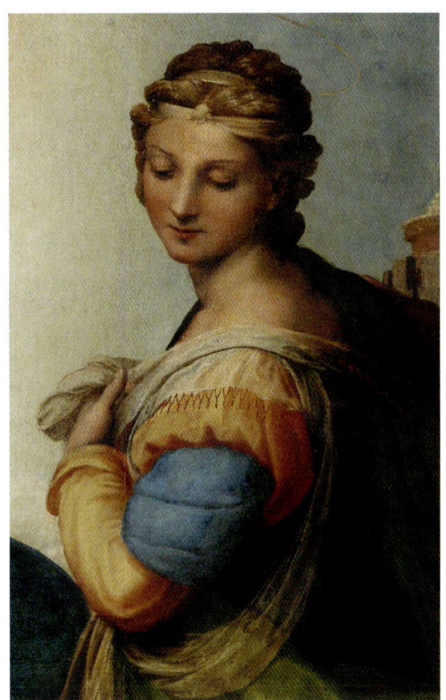

tortures could make her recant her faith, her father beheaded her himself. The tower is her attribute – Raphael squeezes in a glimpse of it between her back and the curtain.

Why is there a curtain in the picture? The commentators are not agreed. They point out that curtains were frequently used to fill corners in pictures. Also that works of art in churches were sometimes hidden from the eyes of the faithful behind a curtain, and Raphael's celestial vision, too, was probably not accessible to everyone at all times. Heavy drapes were frequently used to create a dignified setting in portraits. The curtain in the *Sistine Madonna* is not demonstratively opulent, however, and its attachment by rings to the pole running across the top of the picture gives an impression of shabbiness rather than supernatural perfection. At a later date the top of the canvas was folded over, as a result of which the curtain-pole was lost to sight. It was only rediscovered in 1827 while the picture was being restored and it became apparent that it possessed one if not two functions. In formal terms it marks the upper limit of the composition and provides a counterpart to the ledge along the bottom. From a spatial point of view, the pole and ledge introduce distance into the picture. The painter and viewer are not with the saints in Heaven but inhabit a world in which curtains hang, poles bend and hats need somewhere to be put down.

Two angels go it alone

Like the curtain above, the winged children are regularly perceived as foreign bodies. "The two angels, on the other hand, are done in such a way" that it was "impossible" they could be the work of Raphael, declared Heinecken, who was director of the Dresden royal collection in 1769. Paint analyses have demonstrated that these chubby cheeked children with their uncombed hair were added at a later stage but may have been executed by Raphael all the same. Some commentators claim that the two have hastened ahead of the Virgin and that the finger in front of the lips is calling for respectful silence. It is possible to take a different view: their propped chins sooner suggest that the two angels are bored and perhaps, too, a little fed up with all this holy fuss.

From a theological point of view, angels are divine messengers through whom God renders himself visible to human eyes. In medieval art they frequently appear as powerful beings who have to call out "Fear not!" when they fly down to the shepherds in the fields by night. Something of their mysterious essence can be divined when we register the heads of the heavenly host suggested behind a veil of mist in the upper part of the picture. The plump corporeality of the two children is far from all theology and equally far from the Bible. The two stem instead from the Renaissance and from the rediscovered art of Classical antiquity; they belong amongst the newly revived figures of Ancient Greece – the gods and goddesses, satyrs and nymphs. They are winged genii, also known as putti (from the Italian *putto*, boy). Cupid, the companion of Venus, was the most popular of them all. Raphael included putti in at least two other of his some two dozen Madonna paintings, in both cases making them clearly male.

The *Sistine Madonna* is a variation upon a familiar motif, in which Raphael's inclusion of two extras can be explained on formal grounds. The six figures form a rhombus. The point at the top demanded a pendant at the bottom and hence the two heads of Virgin and Child were counterbalanced by the two genii. The central vertical axis ends between the children's heads, and only becomes visible in the narrow strip of cloud. This bright section of canvas must have been important to the painter, otherwise there seems no reason for him to have made one wing of the left-hand putto invisible.

Thanks to the new reproduction techniques of the 19th century, Raphael's painting became famous. Its celebrity was overshadowed, however, by that of the two supposed angels. Resourceful entrepreneurs extracted them from the canvas, disengaged them from the ledge and embedded them in clouds. As such they adorned poetry albums, decorated walls as framed pictures in their own right, and served as

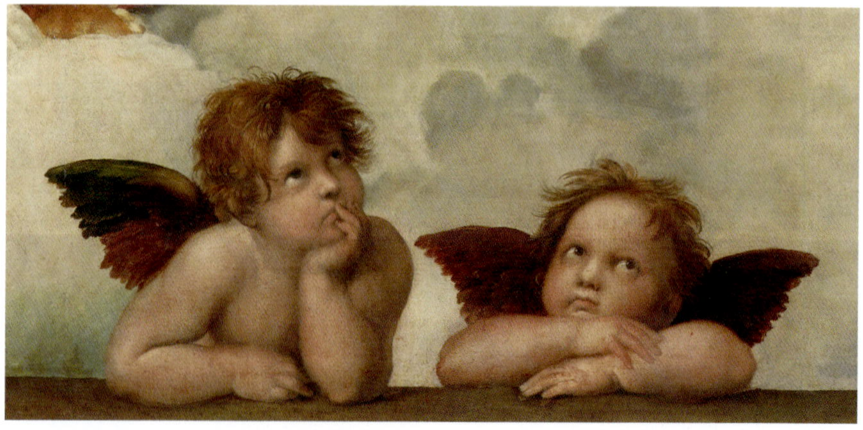

embroidery patterns with which girls and women created their own Raphael on cushions and towels. Over the course of the decades, the two boys were smartened up: their tousled hair assumed well-set waves and the male children became good girls.

The end before their eyes

In Raphael's many treatments of the Virgin and Child, Mary looks solicitously down at her son, who perhaps raises an arm up towards her. At times she holds him close, as in the present painting, where his forehead is resting against her cheek. Most unusual about the Piacenza picture are the expressions on their faces, where we find neither maternal happiness nor the Infant turning towards the Virgin. The seriousness in the Virgin's eyes has supplanted all trace of tenderness. The Child's eyes and pupils are wide, as if frightened, while the pulled down corners of the mouth and the pursed lips signify defiance and resistance. Much has been written about the expressions on these two faces, the most convincing interpretation being that both Child and mother are seeing the future, Christ's brutal end on the cross. It is possible that a *Crucifixion* hung directly opposite the altarpiece on an internal wall, and that it is towards this – and not, as is usually assumed, towards the congregation – that Sixtus is pointing with his right hand.

The nuances of their expressions can only be seen by those standing close up to the picture. Seen from a distance, a floating female figure is holding a child in her arms. Mother and child form an integrated whole, silhouetted and fused within clear outlines. This intimacy stood in marked contrast to the reality of family life, both in the 16th century, when the painting was executed, and in the middle of the 18th century when it reached Dresden. Newborns were viewed as foreign bodies and were disposed of as quickly as possible by giving them to a wet nurse. The wealthy brought these women into their own homes, whereas the middle classes sent their children away to the country. It was important that the mother should be able to resume her place in society or in the world of work as soon as possible. Contact between parents and offspring was little; both death and birth rates were high. In his *Lives of the Artists*, published in 1568, Giorgio Vasari writes that Raphael was suckled by his own mother – a detail that he mentions in the case of no other artist. It must have been something highly unusual.

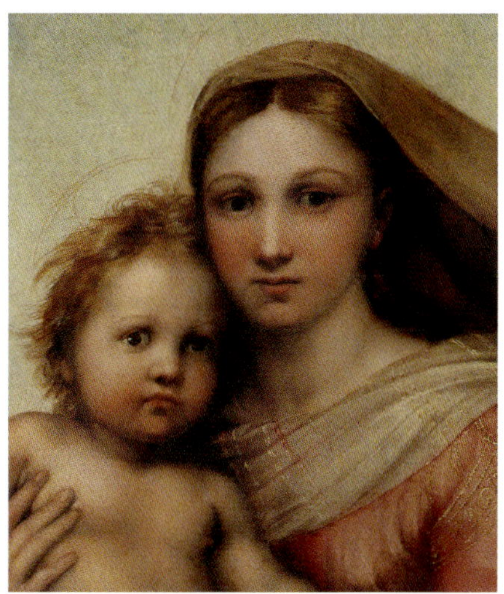

Attitudes towards children started to change in the second half of the 18th century, beginning in France. Jean-Jacques Rousseau (1712–1778) polemicized against civilization and demanded a return to Nature, and French representatives of the Enlightenment called for more personal freedom and sentiment, which would affect family life. When the *Sistine Madonna* arrived in Dresden, such ideas had yet to make themselves felt, but with the subsequent, gradual shift came a change in the way the Italian painting was viewed. Its fame profited not only from the rise of Classicism, but also from the new role of the mother in the life of her children. And also, as psychotherapists have taught us, from the old, secret desire felt by many adults for a maternal figure of protection and guidance – a desire by no means always rooted in religion. Goethe visited the *Sistine Madonna* in Dresden and perhaps had her in mind as he completed *Faust*. The closing lines speak not of the celestial Virgin, but run: "Woman, eternal, / beckons us on."

At the turn of the 20th century, when too much harmony was considered suspicious, when Expressionists and Cubists were distorting the visible world, the fame of Raphael's *Sistine Madonna* suffered, at least within avant-garde circles. The painting survived the Second World War in a railway tunnel and in 1945 was taken to Moscow, before being returned to Dresden in 1955. Today it numbers amongst the most prized icons of European culture.

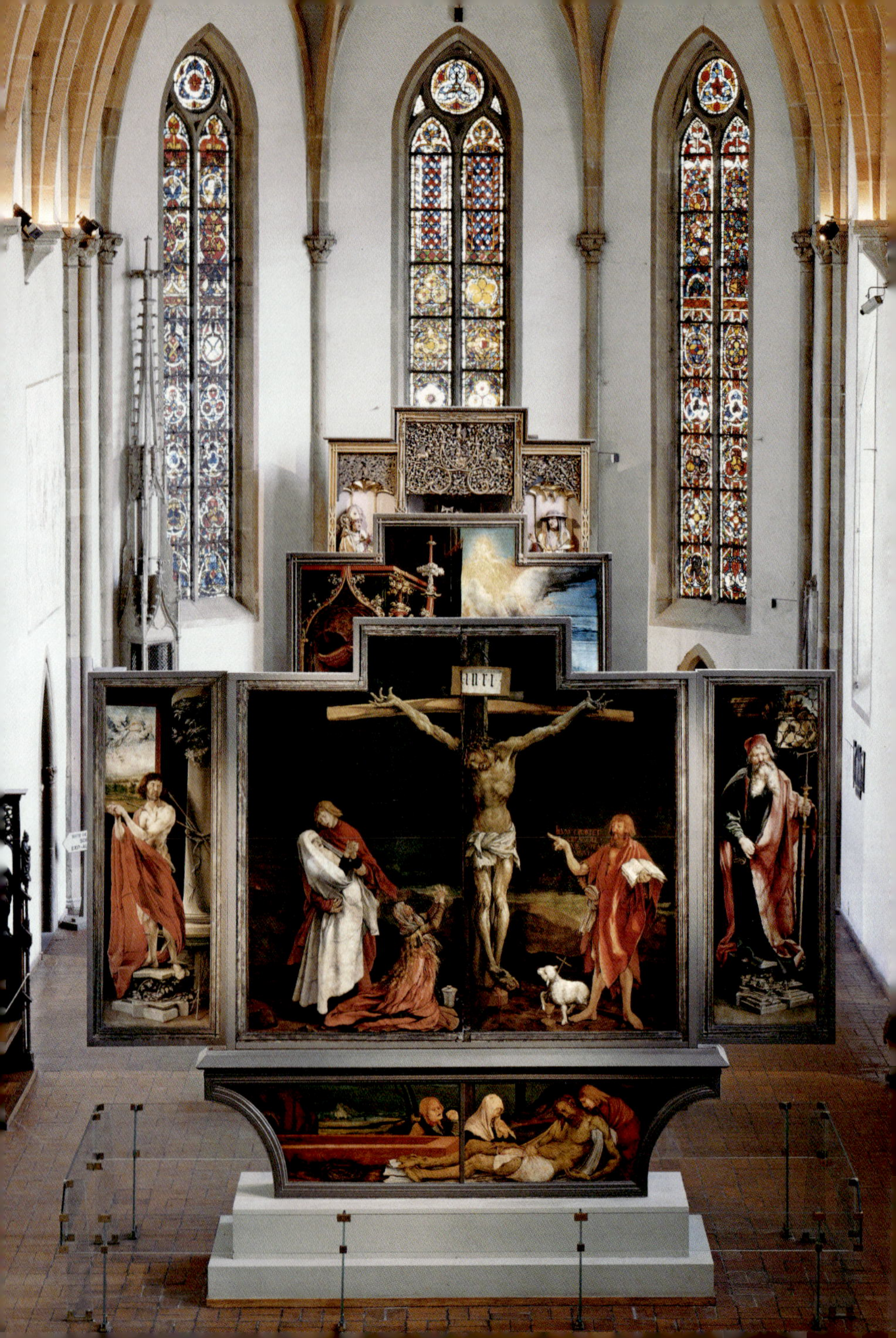

Matthias Grünewald (1460/1480–1528/1532)

With angels and devils through the church year

The Isenheim Altar, 1512–1516
269 x 307 cm, Colmar, Musée d'Unterlinden

There are certain places in Europe that are worth a detour for the sake of a single work of art. Bayeux in Normandy is one: it is home to the 70-metre-long tapestry embroidered with the story of William the Conqueror's victory over the English in 1066. Another is Frankenhausen in the German state of Thuringia, where Werner Tübke's 1987 panorama *Early Bourgeois Revolution in Germany* has its own museum. Another is Colmar for the Isenheim Altar.

The Unterlinden Museum in Colmar houses a number of important art works, but none that has imprinted itself so deeply upon our cultural consciousness as Matthias Grünewald's altarpiece. It was executed between 1512 and 1516 for the Antonite monastery in Isenheim, which lay in the Vosges Mountains, away from the major trade routes of the day. There the panels remained for almost 300 years. When the Church's property was transferred to state ownership during the French Revolution, commissaries were instructed to draw up inventories of all items of value. In 1794 two such commissaries, a lawyer and a painter, arranged for the panels to be taken to Colmar for safekeeping. The altar table that stood behind the panels was lost, as was the original frame, a soaring wooden structure elaborately carved with figures and turrets that is supposed to have doubled the height of the altarpiece.

What was left is termed by art historians a polyptych, a winged altarpiece consisting of a set of hinged and folding panels. Behind the exterior view presented by the panels in the "closed" position lay an interior view, revealed when the wings were opened. Polyptychs are a rarity, probably because their construction of heavy wooden wings mounted one behind the other proved too fragile. The Isenheim Altar offers three views: the first (exterior) view shows the Crucifixion in the centre, the second (middle) view the Nativity and the third (interior) view St Anthony. The second and third views were only opened on liturgical feast days and for most of the year the Crucifixion side was all that could be seen; its colours have consequently suffered the most.

To get from the first to the second view, the two panels making up the central Crucifixion field were folded outwards. The join between these two panels runs vertically left of the Cross; the hinges were positioned on the side wings. With the two front halves open, the second view was revealed: the Nativity and Concert of Angels between the Annunciation and the Resurrection. The gloomy death scene was thus followed by figures of light embodying glad tidings.

In order to understand this altarpiece, the viewer needs to know about its construction. It is like an enormous picture book of which only two pages are open at once. In order to show all the panels at the same time, especially those that are painted on both sides, the altarpiece had to be dismantled.

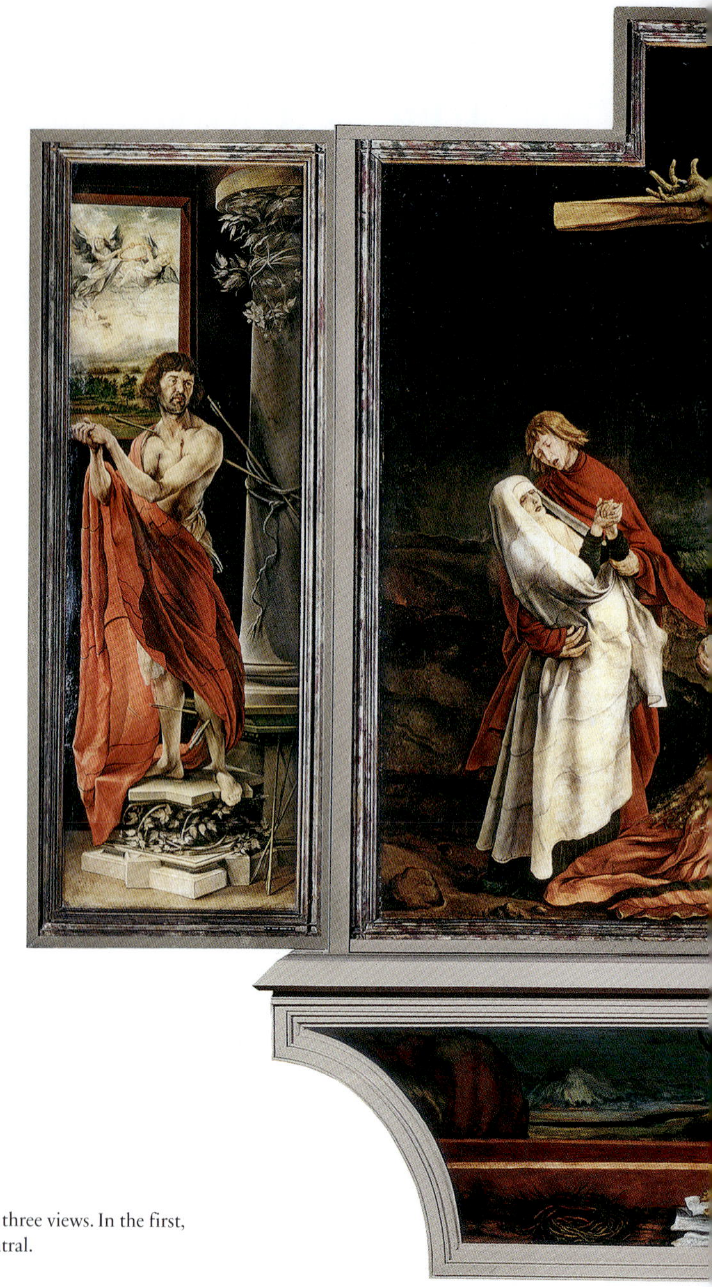

The Isenheim Altar offers three views. In the first,
Christ's Crucifixion is central.

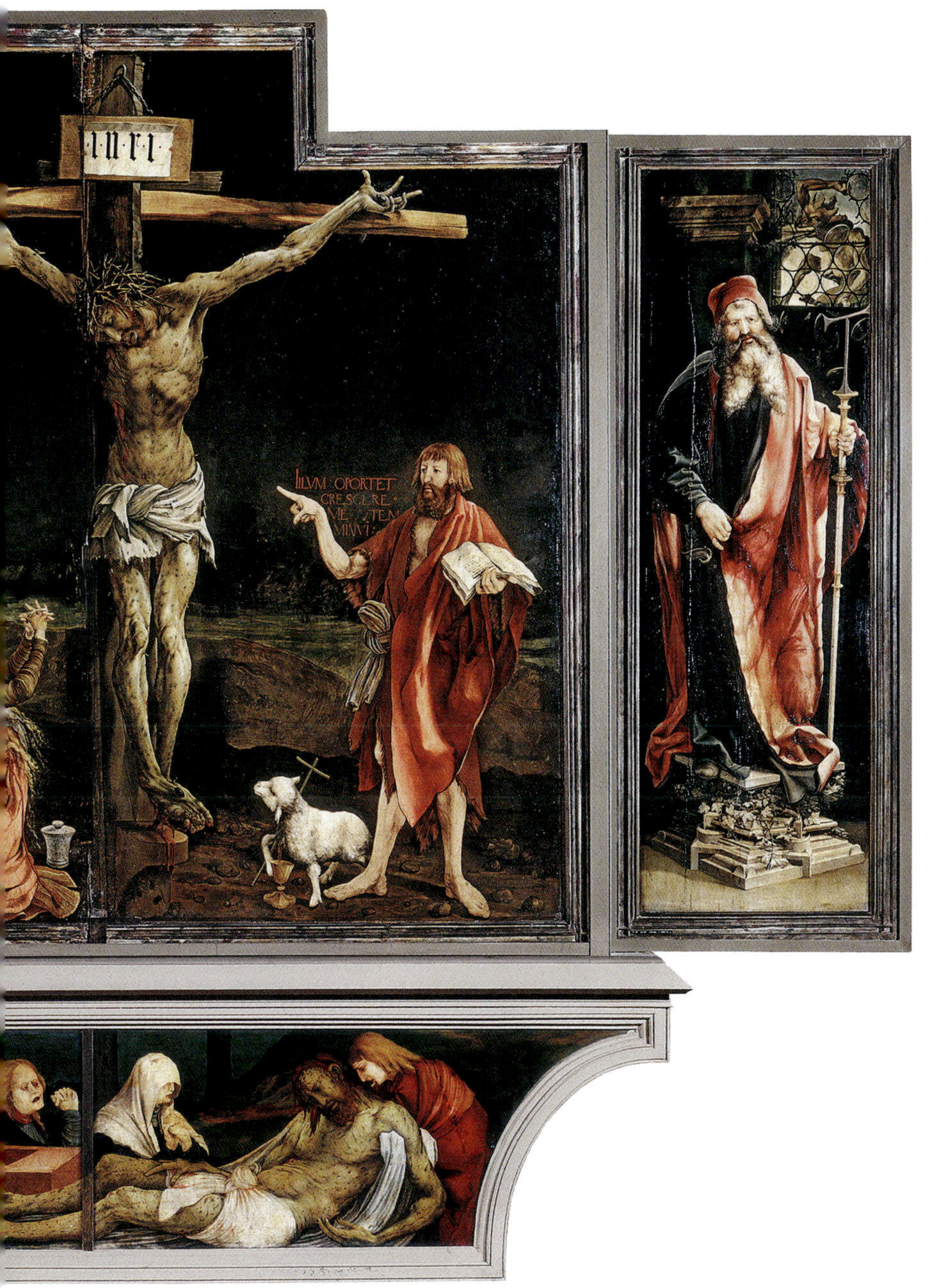
ILLVM OPORTET
CRESCERE
ME AVTEM
MINVI

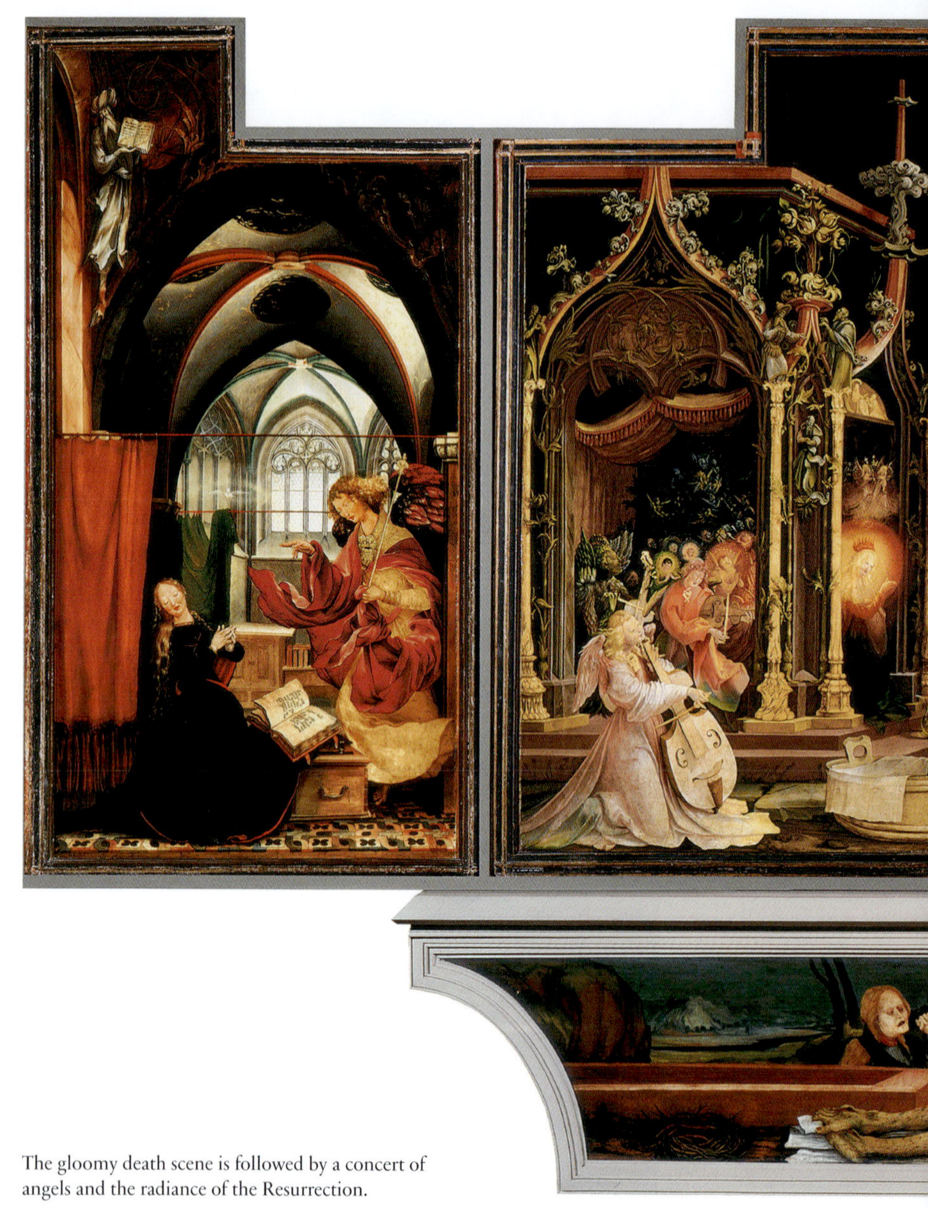

The gloomy death scene is followed by a concert of
angels and the radiance of the Resurrection.

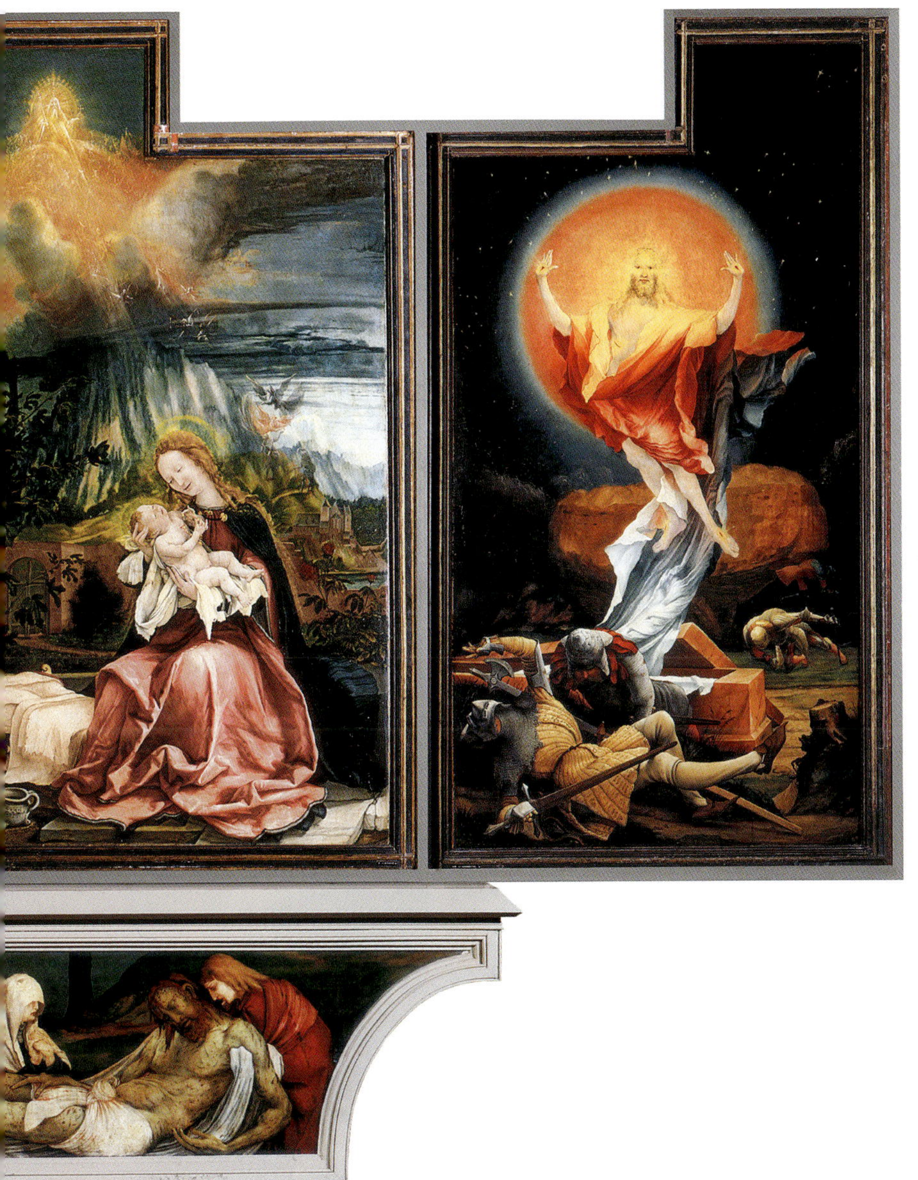

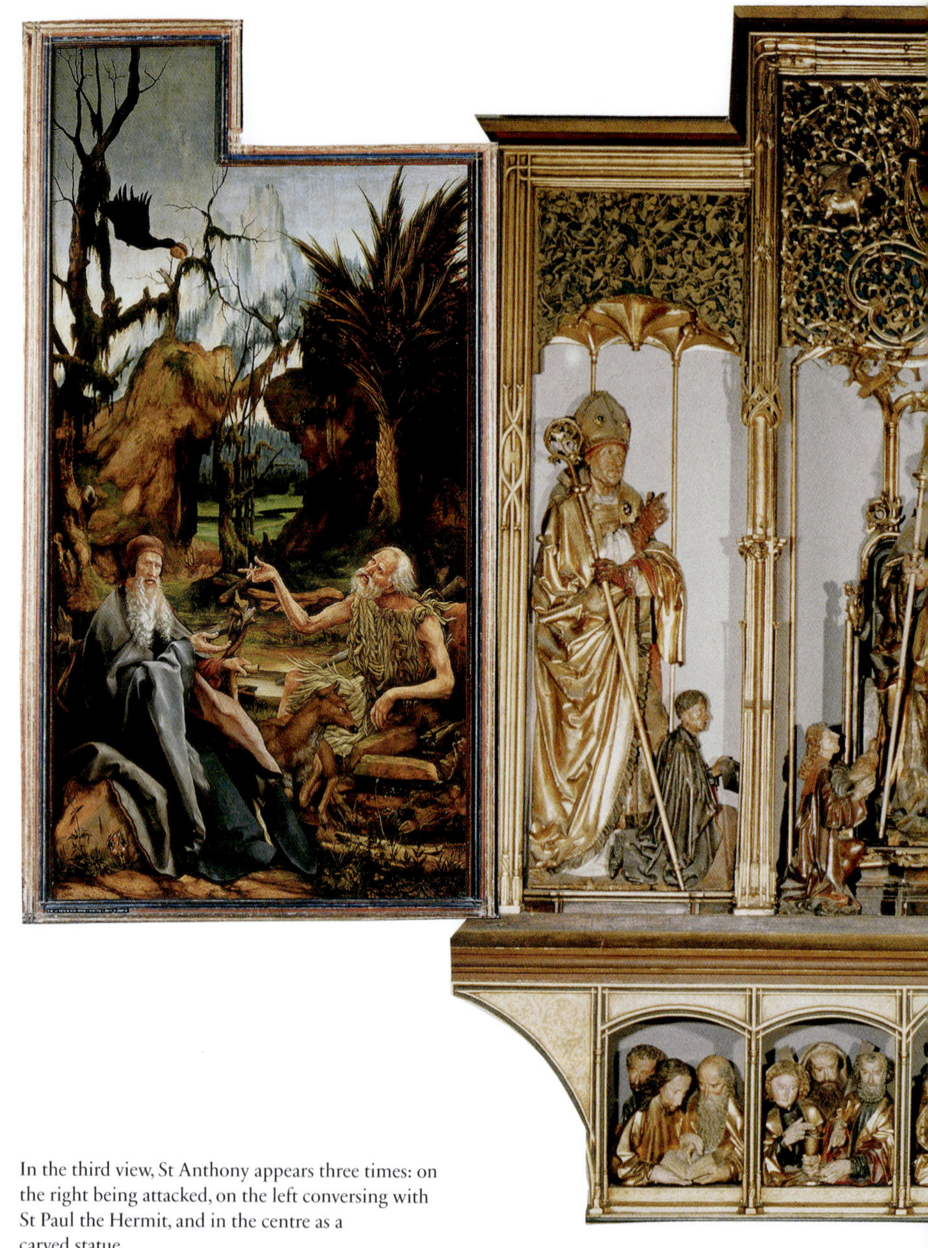

In the third view, St Anthony appears three times: on
the right being attacked, on the left conversing with
St Paul the Hermit, and in the centre as a
carved statue.

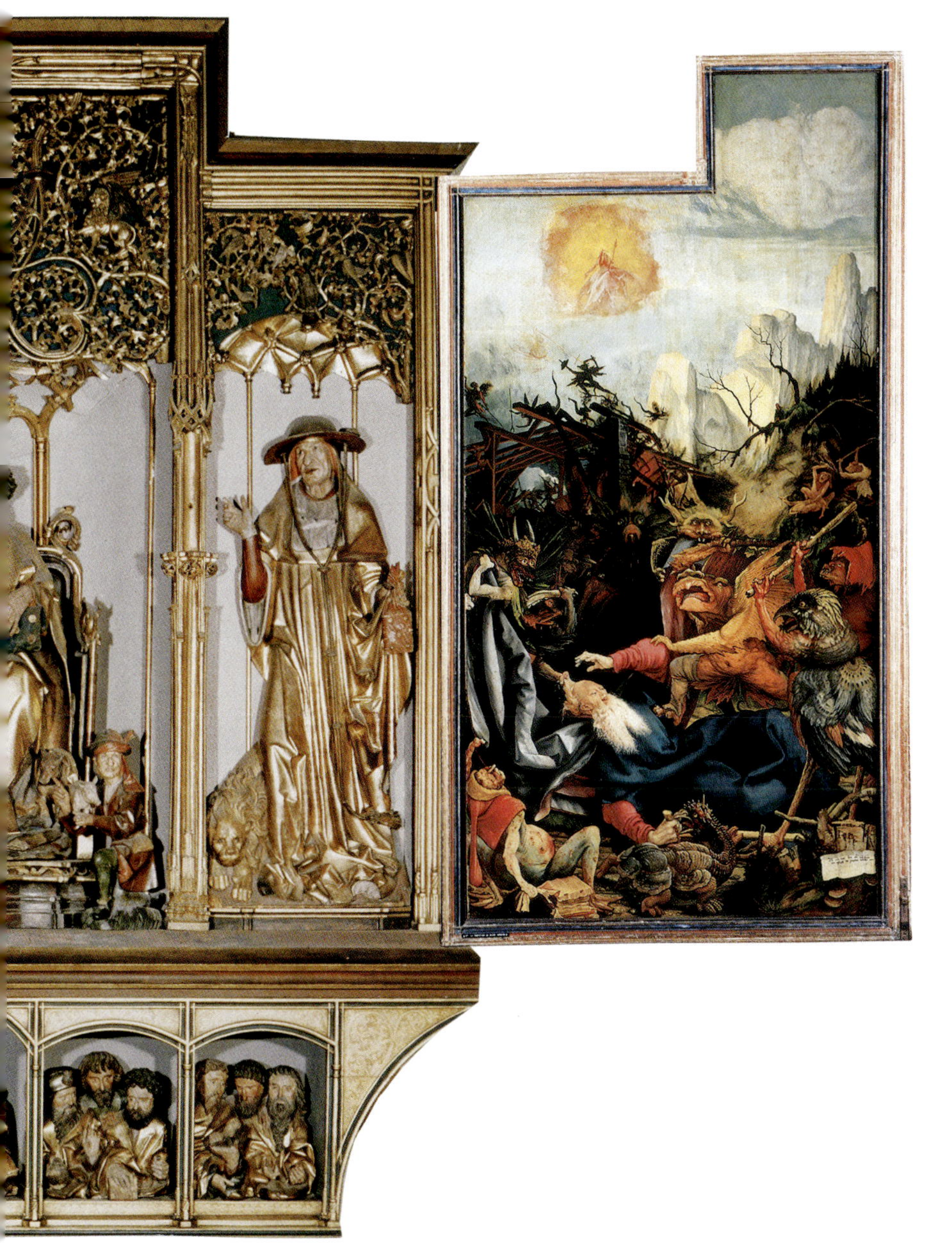

When the dismantling took place is unclear. The panels are on display in the choir of a former nunnery, today the Unterlinden Museum.

Torture and reconciliation

Grünewald's Crucifixion shows the aftermath of torture and ranks amongst the most brutal works in the history of art. The body hangs with all its weight from the nails piercing the two palms. The skin is lacerated and pierced by countless thorns; the head lolls sideways, and blood trickles down from the chest wound inflicted by the lance. The artist paints a man who has been tortured to death and arouses in the viewer – whether a believer or not – contradictory feelings ranging from sympathy to revulsion.

The soldiers who commonly feature in Crucifixion scenes are omitted by Grünewald, who restricts himself to Christ, two women and two men: the Virgin Mary, the mother of Christ, seems to be sinking backwards in a dead faint, while Mary Magdalene stretches her arms upwards in an ecstatic fashion. John the disciple supports the Virgin, while on the other side of the Cross John the Baptist points to the dead Christ and cites from the Gospel of St John: "He must increase, but I must decrease." The quotation is written in Latin above his arm. The fact that the Baptist had died years earlier is

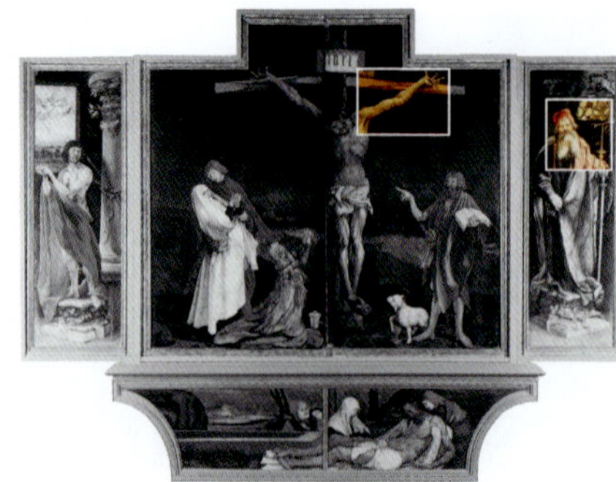

immaterial; what is significant is his objective, lecturing pose. He holds the book, points to the body and demonstrates that the Crucifixion is not about emotions but about something entirely different. It is about the significance of Christ in the history of salvation.

When Adam and Eve ate from the Tree of Knowledge, they transgressed God's commandment and were expelled from Paradise. By sending down his only son to earth and allowing him to be scourged, tortured and killed, God created a new covenant: not a return to Paradise, but the possibility of reconciliation between God and man. For devout

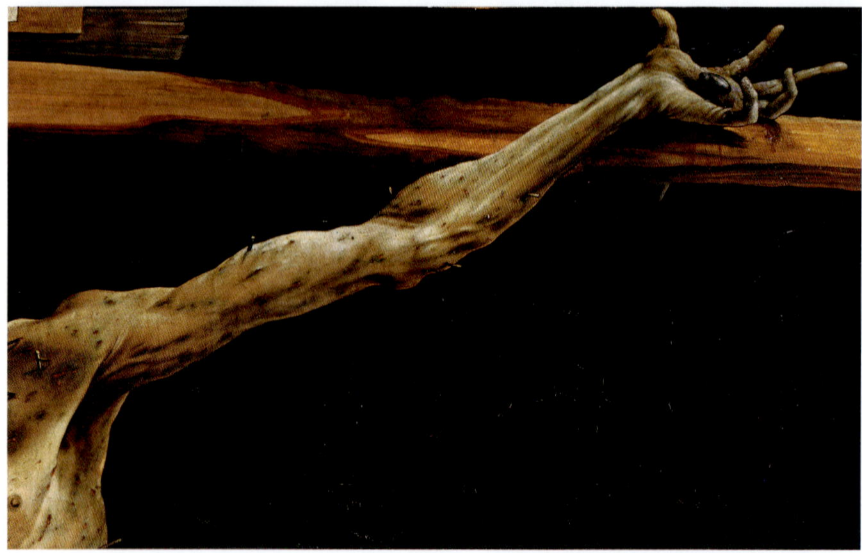

Christians, this reconciliation is a religious truth, one that has changed the world. Grünewald renders this change visible – or to phrase it more cautiously, he designs a scenario that conveys a hint of this change.

What we see is a corpse covered in wounds in a formally harmonious composition. While it is true that Christ's body hangs not along the central vertical axis, but beside it (so that his body is not dissected by the gap between the panels), this shift is compensated by the colour masses. The arms extend upwards at the same angle and in the same length, and form an equilateral triangle with the transom. The same is true of the gleaming heads of the nails in the hands and feet. Grünewald paints the background almost black, as if all light were extinguished with Christ's death, and the splayed fingers signal extreme agony, yet behind the cruelty appear geometric figures of an alternative, eternally beautiful world. The torment arouses a sense of horror, the manner of painting offers consolation. It is these silent contradictions that fix the work in our memory.

Saints to cure the plague and St Anthony's fire
This pivotal event in the history of Salvation, the Crucifixion, is bounded in Grünewald's altarpiece by the Entombment underneath, the transom overhead and by two saints on the side panels. These two saints seem to belong to another world. One might think they were the work of an artist from a different epoch altogether. The person who painted the Crucifixion was still indebted to the Middle Ages: the background has yet to acquire spatial depth and perspective is still lacking. The size of the figures bears no relation to reality but reflects their religious significance. Thus Christ is larger than the Baptist, the Baptist larger than the women. St John the Baptist's overly long index finger directs our attention to what is solely important from a the-ological point of view. The person who painted the two saints, on the other hand, seems to be exploring the way of seeing and the formal vocabulary of the Renaissance.

On the left stands St Sebastian, on the right St Anthony. Sebastian is pierced right through by arrows, yet he stands there as if nothing had happened. No gesture of despair, no face distorted by pain. On the contrary, his body conveys a sense of freedom from injury. Like an antique statue,

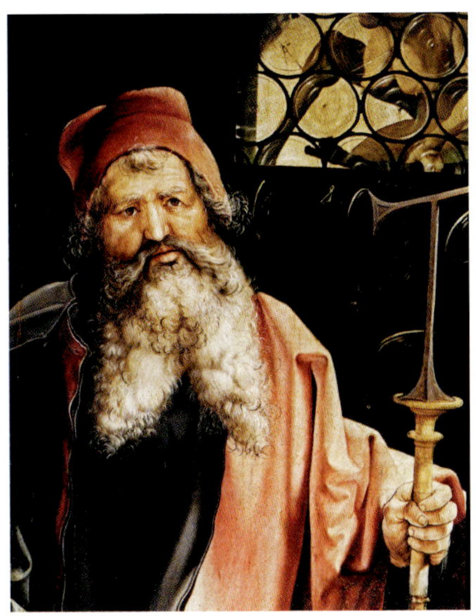

he poses with relaxed elegance on a plinth, his "non-weight-bearing" leg resting lightly on its marble edge. One might say that his faith absolves him of all physical suffering. Or that, in the spirit of the Renaissance, the artist is in search of the ideal human figure.

In the case St Anthony, the question is not one of physical beauty but rather of wisdom and com-passion. His double beard is a traditional sign of dignity; God the Father was always portrayed with a double beard. His slightly inclined head indicates someone who does not wish to dominate but to serve. The female demon who is attempting to break through the bull's-eyes glazing in the window shows that the world around him is full of dangers.

The staff in the bishop's left hand terminates in a Tau cross, a sacred symbol in the shape of a large T found in many ancient cultures. The name repre-sents the last letter in the Hebrew alphabet. In the Christian sphere it surfaces in the 4th century as the "heraldic device" of a community of soldier monks who combated heresy in Ethiopia and Egypt. In Europe in 1095 the confraternity became the Order of St Anthony, dedicated to caring for the sick and providing lodging for pilgrims – hence the Antonite monastery in Isenheim in the Alsace, on the pilgrim-age route to Santiago de Compostela.

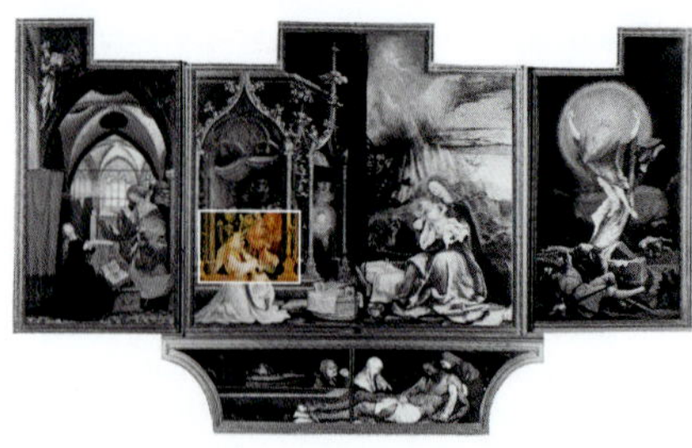

The lay brothers were mendicant monks; the preceptors in charge of the monasteries had to belong to the nobility. The man whom Grünewald painted as St Anthony is usually identified as Guido Guersi. We know almost nothing about him or about what he looked like, but he is thought to have commissioned the altarpiece. Guersi died in 1516 and it was probably this event that prompted Grünewald to bring work on the mammoth project to a final conclusion.

The Antonites in Isenheim cared in particular for patients suffering from what was called St Anthony's fire, a form of poisoning by the ergot fungus that was widespread in the 15th and 16th century. Medicine in those days was unable to offer a cure and the sick had only their faith, their hope of help from the saint who stood before them in life size. On the other wing stood St Sebastian. He was associated with Isenheim not at the organizational level but as the patron saint of plague victims. The plague had decimated vast swathes of the population. The fact that it was spread by rat fleas was still unknown; people believed in invisible plague arrows and in Sebastian, himself pierced with arrows, as the saint to whom the sick could pray for succour.

Music in praise of the Holy Family

If the Crucifixion in the central field of the first, exterior view of the altarpiece is dominated by black, the second view that lies behind it is animated by bright colours from one wing to the other. These announce the glad tidings of the impending Nativity, show a happy Virgin Mary with her Child, and present Christ at his Resurrection within an aureole of almost dazzling radiance. There is no crib, there is no Joseph, but instead a fantastically ornate pavilion within which countless angels are singing and making music.

It is impossible to determine whether this deviation from traditional iconography was the invention of the artist or an adviser. The aim must have been to give new heart to Isenheim's sick and suffering patients, to offer them – after the death on the Cross – images whose colours and figures awaken the hope of a better future. Most people, especially those in rural areas, could neither read nor write, and the monks preaching to them had only limited learning. The population was dependent upon pictures in churches and monasteries. They held power – including through their colours.

Perhaps the artist's advisers included one who knew more about angels than others. Angels were no Christian invention; as hybrid creatures who were part human and part beast, they proclaimed and carried out the Divine Will for the Assyrians and Sumerians, too. In Grünewald's day there was disagreement over the question of their sex. The Christian and pre-Christian heavenly hosts were all considered to be male, like God himself. Around 1500, however, both sexes became acceptable. Michelangelo liked his angels male, but Dürer and Titian painted them as young girls. Grünewald shows some with masculine features, others with a more feminine air. Striking amongst the present group is the green feathered figure: in colour symbolism, green was the colour of Paradise and hence of eternal life.

Just as the angels have their roots in pre biblical sources, so too do the sounds attributed to them, the music of the spheres. This is confirmed by written sources: the Egyptian god Thot had already "harmonized the singing voices of the celestial revolutions", while for Plato, a siren singing a specific note stood on each of the eight revolving heavenly spheres. These otherworldly harmonies cannot be heard by the living, however, who have to content themselves

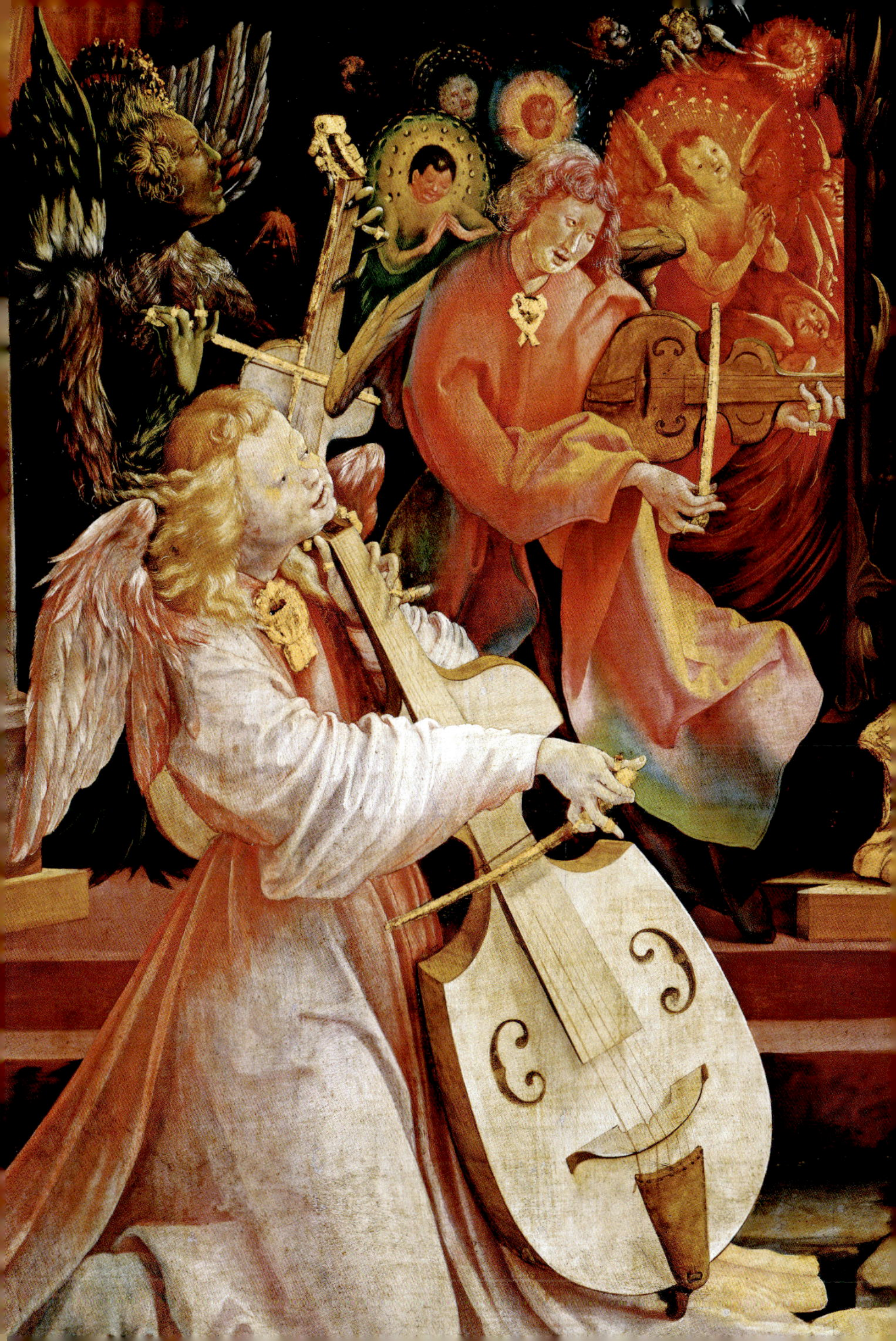

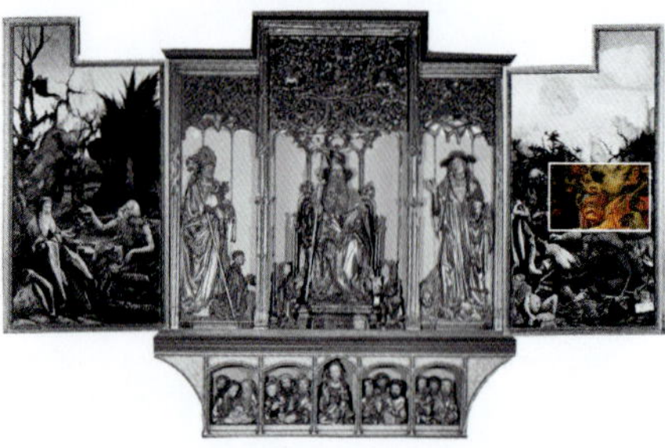

with a substitute – music. Painted angelic musicians are also a substitute, for the sounds of the spheres are difficult to record in a picture.

The power of demonic eyes

When the altarpiece is opened up to reveal its third view, we are confronted by a ferocious group of thugs on the right-hand wing. Grünewald's angels all look very alike, but each of his demons has its own hideous face and fearful body, assembled from human and animal parts. Documents such as court records and accounts of confessions bear witness to the fact that people experienced devils and demons as real. A certain Francesca of Rome, who died in 1440, saw a dragon "with its jaws gaping and its tongue out"; it wore "on its head, as a type of crown, something in the manner of the antlers of a stag with many ends, and from all the ends it spewed out terrible fire."

In Grünewald's wing panel, the mob is attacking St Anthony, who was born around AD 250 and lived to the age of 105. According to his biographer, the devil appeared to St Anthony one night accompanied by "a crowd of demons" who "tore at him so savagely" that Anthony was left lying "prostrated by the pain of his wounds". Unable to stand or even to speak, he prayed for – and received – divine assistance where he lay.

Grünewald fills the beasts' eyes with particular menace, for they were considered to possess a satanic power. This belief was rooted in antique ideas according to which eyes emit rays. If the eyes belong to demons, "a change for the worse takes place in the body of the person they meet, caused by the eyes of the one looking… Their gaze is poisonous and harmful, most of all for children."

These words are taken from the *Malleus Malefi-carum*, the "Hammer of Witches" printed in 1487 and written by Dominicans, whose Order had been charged by the Pope to expose all heretics, and in particular witches and devils.

St Anthony appears no fewer than three times in the third view: on the right as the victim of an attack, on the left in peaceful conversation with St Paul the Hermit, and in the middle as a carved and gilded wooden statue. This last was executed, like the other sculptures making up the altarpiece, by one Nikolaus of Haguenau.

We know almost nothing about the man we call Matthias Grünewald, but whose original name was probably Mathis Neithart, or indeed about what he looked like. Unlike his contemporary Albrecht Dürer, the notion of publicizing himself was foreign to him; in this respect he was still a product of the Middle Ages. He died in 1528 in Halle, where he had regularly worked. He had lost his position as court painter in 1525/6 after taking part in the Peasants' War and displaying open sympathy for the Reformation. He probably painted the present altarpiece in Halle or Aschaffenburg. Documentary proof that he accompanied the monumental work to Isenheim and oversaw its installation has yet to be uncovered.

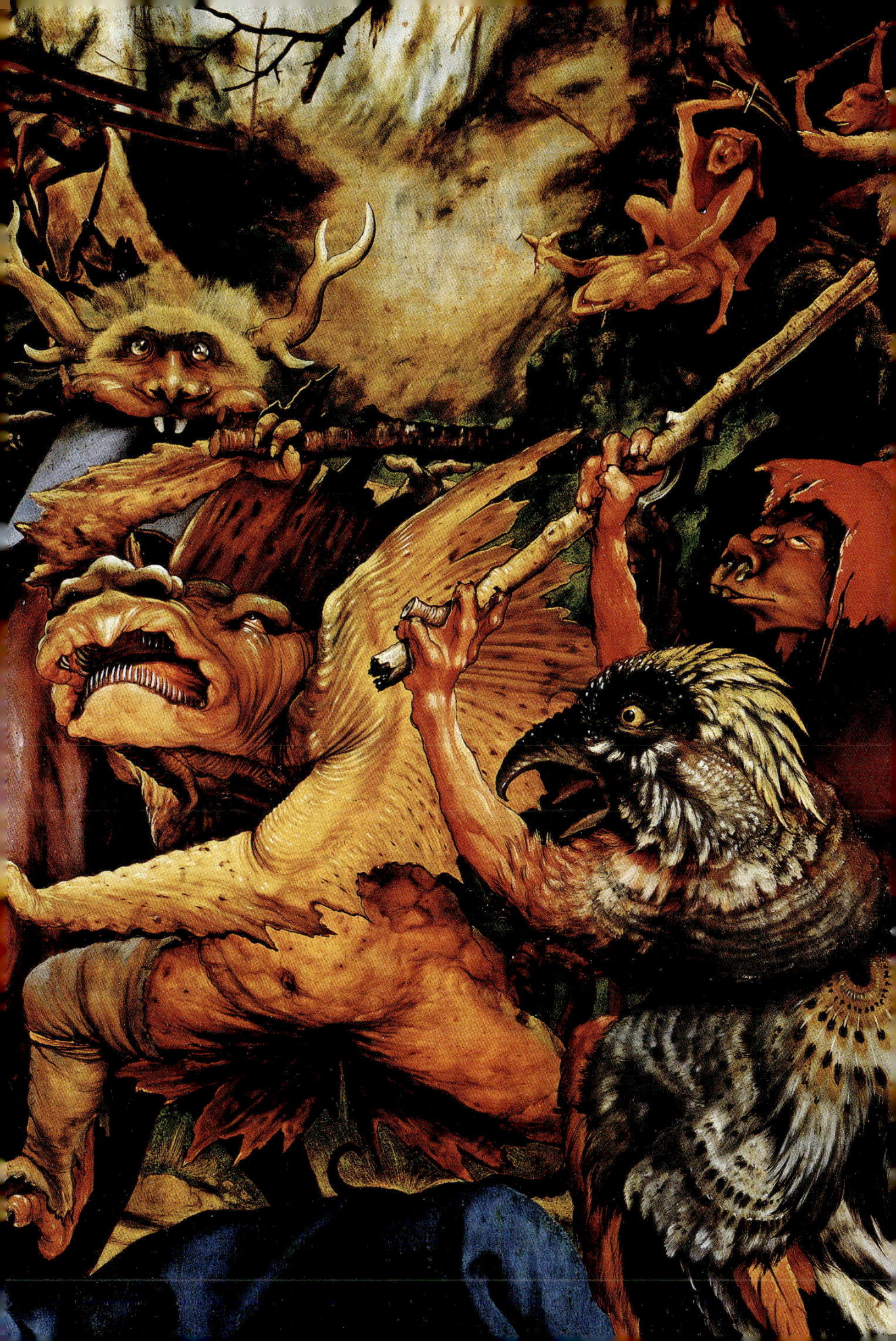

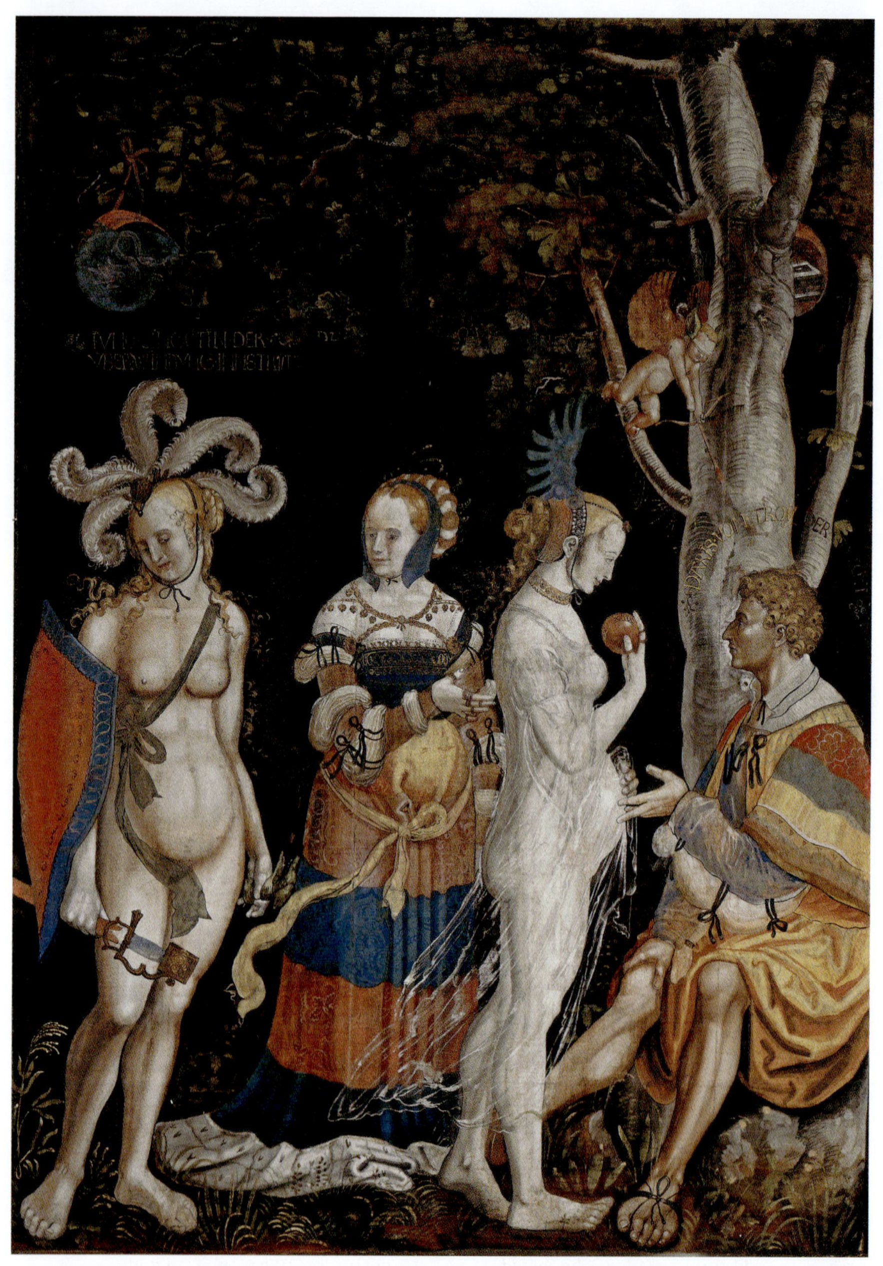

Niklaus Manuel Deutsch (*c.* 1484–1530)

The goddess with the mercenary's hat

The Judgement of Paris, 1516/1528
223 x 160 cm, Basle, Kunstmuseum Basel

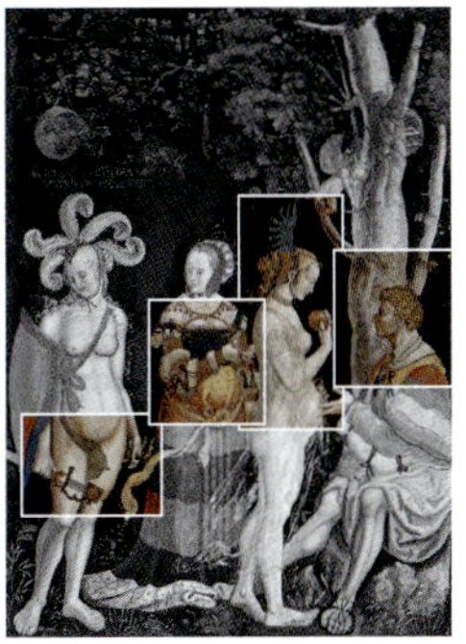

Against a dark background suggestive of night, a curious company has assembled beneath the leafy boughs of a tree. A young man is staring deep into the eyes of a beautiful, transparently clad woman, while two other ladies, one naked, the other sumptuously dressed, stand beside them like extras with their eyes averted.

The figures are identified by inscriptions within the painting. The words PARIS VON TROY DER TORECHT (Paris of Troy, the foolish) are written in gold and silver lettering over the head of the man. The lady equipped with shield and sword is identified as IUNO EIN GÖTTIN DER ÜBERWINDUNG INN STRITS (Juno, the goddess of victory in battle). The woman in the transparent dress is named as Venus – the words FENUS FENUS can be read in gold on her crested bonnet. Around the circumference of the ball in her hand it is also possible to make out the words EN DIESER OP, probably the beginning and end of the German phrase DIESER OPFEL DER SCHÖNSTEN, meaning "This apple for the fairest".

It is clearly a reference to the golden apple marked "For the Fairest" which, in the world of Greek mythology, the goddess of Discord threw onto the table during an Olympian banquet. When three of the goddesses argued over who should have it, the king of the gods announced that the final decision should be made by the fairest of all men. That was Paris, son of the king of Troy, whom the goddesses found tending his father's flocks. Each goddess attempted to win the young man's favour: one offered him fame, the second power and riches, while the goddess of love promised that the fairest woman in the world should be his. It was to Venus that Paris awarded the apple, and with her help he won Helen, wife of the king of Sparta. Paris abducted her, so the legend goes, and thereby unleashed the war between the Greeks and the Trojans that would form the subject of Homer's *Iliad*.

While the artist demonstrates his familiarity with mythology, he has muddled up his inscriptions. The goddess he describes as Juno, wife of Jupiter, is in fact the warlike Minerva, clearly identified by her weapons. Juno herself is the one standing in the middle, richly dressed. The artist naturally calls the goddesses by their Latin names rather than their Greek ones, for at the time this undated painting was executed, probably between 1516 and 1528, Greek antiquity was still in the process of being rediscovered by humanist scholars. Niklaus Manuel was not a Greek expert, and his two trips to Italy were not made for the purposes of study.

The artist probably derived his knowledge of Greek myth from a medieval novel, in which the legend had taken on a moralizing slant. Paris was reproached for choosing not the positive virtues of fame and power, but the pleasures of physical love, which in the Christian Middle Ages was considered sinful. Manuel, too, describes Paris as "foolish" in his inscription, and the painting can thus be considered a warning. This provided the painting with an excuse for its portrayal of naked women and also made it acceptable to the stern city councillors for whom it was probably executed.

The two coats of arms hanging in the tree, a bluish swan and a square white well belonged to the family of a certain Bendicht Brunner, a member of the small ruling class which at that time held sway in Berne. It was here that Manuel was born in c. 1484, in the narrow confines of a medieval city of some 5,000 inhabitants, which lay off the main trade routes. Together with twelve other towns, the "noble Republic of Berne" formed the smallest of the Swiss confederations.

Taking up arms for king, emperor and pope

In the early 16th century, war was the confederates' chief occupation. According to the German human- ist Jakob Wimpheling, they were "obstreperous, sullen and arrogant wild men" … "taught from their youth onwards to take up arms and go to war." For the majority of Swiss, there was little else for them to do – their limited land provided neither jobs nor sufficient food, so mercenaries became the Alpine region's biggest export.

Niklaus Manuel twice left his wife and children to travel to Italy, around 1516 and in 1522, as a merce- nary soldier in the French army. He was skilled in the use of the long, narrow sword for "one and a half hands" which Minerva here holds so casually by its blade. Made in Milan, this magnificent weapon with its richly worked gold handle was one which Swiss mercenaries liked to take home with them. More common in Berne was the so-called "Swiss sword": Niklaus Manuel liked to sign his works with the symbol of this simple dagger, which for a long time formed a sort of Swiss national sym- bol, on a par with the Confederation Cross. That a nation should make a weapon its emblem says much about its self-image.

The Swiss earned their military reputation at the end of the 15th century, when the "cowherds" unex- pectedly succeeded in crushing the knights of Bur- gundy. The services of the "invincible giants" were subsequently sought by the main European powers. In Manuel's day, Italy was the battlefield of Europe. It was here, for 50 years, that the French kings, the emperors and the popes fought each other in constantly changing alliances. Thanks to their geo- graphical position, the Confederates could descend upon Italy, France or Germany with 30,000 men within two weeks; as long as the king of France had them as allies, he could manage without his own army in Italy.

The Confederate cantons hired out their troops for a healthy fee. Individual mer- cenaries often set off on their own initiative too, to sell their services. You could count on the Swiss as long as you paid them regularly; if the money didn't materialize, they would simply pack up and go home or seek compensation some other way. Manuel came away with a hand injury from the plundering of Novara: when the money they had been promised for conquering the city failed to appear, the angry Confederates burned it down and killed anyone who stood in their way. Manuel was also present at Bicocca when the Swiss, contrary to orders,

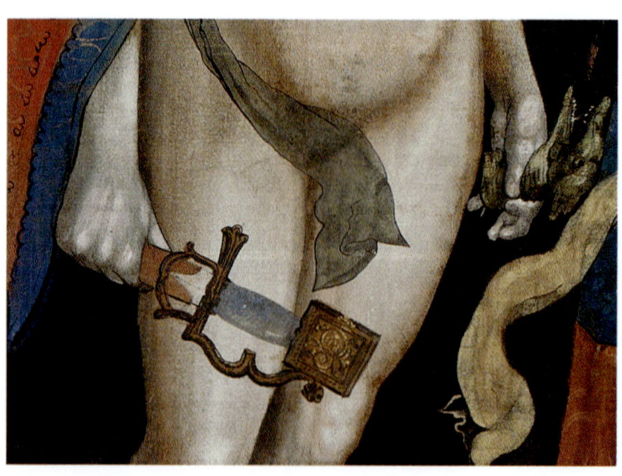

attacked an enemy in a superior position. They had embraced the ideals of the Burgundian knights and considered waiting or playing tactical games to be dishonourable. "We want at them!" they bellowed – and suffered a crushing defeat. Shortly afterwards Manuel composed a satirical song in which he mocked the victors for being so cowardly as to dig themselves entrenchments.

The Confederates refused to wear helmets or armour; they attached importance to agility and elegance on the battlefield. Thus the goddess of war in the present painting does not wear traditional armour, but instead the extravagant plumed toque sported by the boldest Confederate mercenaries.

Lady Venus and the power of women

While the goddess of war exposes her tanned naked body unclad, Venus heightens the shapeliness of her body with a transparent shift. With her small, firm breasts above a rounded belly, whose curves promise fertility (but by no means necessarily imply pregnancy), she thereby falls fully in line with Gothic ideals of beauty in the Middle Ages. The pale, frosty white colour of Venus' skin testifies to her gentility and idleness, but may also be interpreted as a reference to her devilish, wicked nature. Venus the medieval woman knows how to ensnare men, how to cast a spell over them like Parsifal or make a "fool" of them like Paris. The beginning of the 16th century saw a particular spate of warnings regarding the sinful, sensual charms of women. In countless satires and pamphlets, the goddess of Love and the ruinous "power of women" which she represented were attacked with such vehemence that one can only assume that Manuel's contemporaries were particularly susceptible to her arts of seduction.

Venus dominates the picture and the scene; Paris is fascinated by her. The artist probably felt the same way. The attractive naked female body remained one of his favourite subjects. In a number of drawings he furnishes his ladies with "lassos" with which to capture their lovers. In one of these lassos the artist symbolically places his own monogram and dagger: he too is a captive. Women in his paintings almost always appear armed, somehow connected with war, danger and death.

Swiss mercenaries setting off for Lombardy were spurred on not only by the promise of rich rewards and military action, but also by the hope of an amorous affair with a camp follower or an Italian beauty.

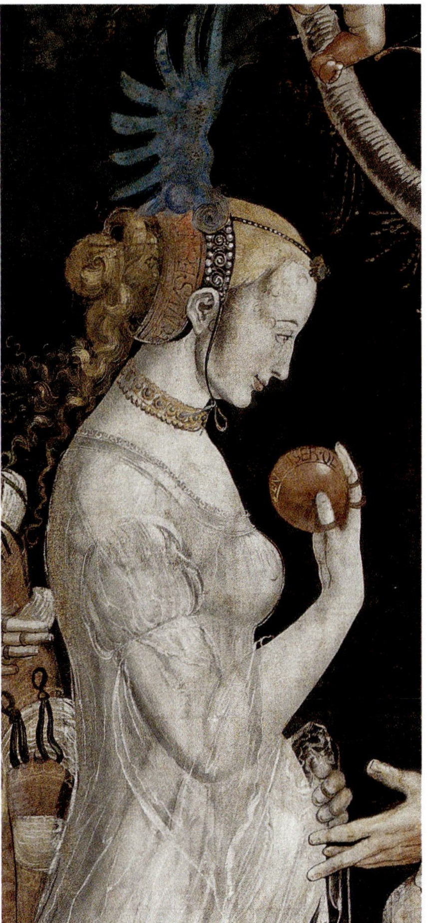

That service under Lady Venus was not without its own dangers emerged when the first mercenaries returned from Italy in 1495. The Bernese authorities found themselves obliged to open a "pox house" in which to isolate the many soldiers suffering from syphilis – victims of the perilous power of women.

Mercenaries set the trend

Wealth is what Juno offered Paris the shepherd, and wealth is stamped all over her appearance. This both corresponds to her status as Jupiter's wife – the bonnet concealing her hair indicates that she is married – and at the same time reflects fashion trends in Niklaus Manuel's day. Her dress, in several shades of sumptuous velvet, ends in an ermine train. The sleeves, a particularly important element of her costume, are slit in four places to reveal a pleated white lining, bunched up to create the popular puffed effect. The sleeve sections are connected at the shoulder and elbow only by decorative black ribbons laced through eyelets. This made it possible to mix and match the various sleeve sections in the latest colours and thereby give the appearance of owning a larger wardrobe than was perhaps the case. The broad sleeves of Paris's shirt are also slit, puffed and laced; at the start of the 16th century, men's fashions were if possible even richer and more splendid than women's. This trend seems to have been set by a piece of male, soldierly inspiration. After their victory over the Burgundians in 1476, a rich booty of velvet and silk fell into the hands of the Confederates. They cut up their plunder, so the story goes, into pieces and embroidered them onto their shabby clothes. Instead of armour, they wore thick quilting to protect themselves against injury and the cold. To give mobility, they slit this quilting at the knee, elbow and shoulder, lined the "holes" with the expensive fabrics and thereby invented their colourful "slashed" style of dress. The German mercenaries liked it so much that they adopted it too. "One must let them have one pleasure in their wretched and miserable lives",

felt Emperor Maximilian I, and gave permission for his foot soldiers to wear such costumes, even though they contravened the official dress code.

Thanks to their high military standing, the Swiss cowherds from the back woods were soon dictating the style of dress worn by men and women of every class in large parts of Europe. Their extravagantly provocative mercenary fashions caused preachers everywhere to fulminate against the devilish impropriety of their slits and puffs. Within the Confederation itself, there were those who bemoaned the loss of "the old Helvetic modesty and simplicity". The Bernese chronicler Anshelm condemned the ostentatious dress worn by certain ladies, including the wife of military commander Albrecht von Stein, who wore an "underskirt of silver and shoes of gold" and more jewellery "than has ever been seen in Berne before". Perhaps Manuel was thinking of her when he painted Juno with her gold necklaces, brooches and numerous rings.

Albrecht von Stein, under whose banner the artist fought twice in Italy, drew a fat pension from the French king even between campaigns; he was a so-called "crown-eater". Many others in Berne were similarly in the secret pay of foreign powers: influential members of the military, councillors, mercenary agents and recruiting officers. Even the authorities accepted money without a scruple: around 1623, French subsidies accounted for a third of Berne's entire income.

Ordinary soldiers had the chance of making more money in short campaigns than in years of working in the fields or in a workshop. Vast quantities of money suddenly came into circulation in a society that had previously been predominantly agricultural. Prices and standards of living rose; everyone was tempted to spend more than they earned, especially on clothes. Envy, dissatisfaction, venality and corruption were the consequences. "This people," observed an advisor to Charles V, "has got so used to the income that buys it idleness, inebriation and luxury, that it can no longer do without foreign money."

A social climber goes into politics
Manuel took full advantage of the restructuring taking place in Bernese society, brought about by the mercenaries and their new found wealth. He rose from being the son of a "foreigner" – his father appears to have been a spice seller in Piedmont –

to being a member of the small ruling class, previously strictly closed to outsiders.

Nothing reliable is known about Manuel's early years or his artistic training. It is possible that he studied under a Bernese glass painter. By 1509, however, he had done well enough to marry into a respectable middle-class family, and shortly afterwards he bought a house in the street today called Gerechtigkeitsgasse. His workshop executed altarpieces for churches and monasteries. One of Manuel's most important works, a monumental *Dance of Death* on the wall of a Franciscan monastery, has long since been destroyed, and is known to us only through a later copy. The head of Paris, with its bold profile and golden curls, reappears in the copy as a portrait of the artist, who paints himself at work at the end of the macabre roundelay. Death awaits him just as it does the other citizens of Berne in the painting, but in his case the skeleton is kneeling humbly at the feet of the clearly very self-confident artist. Like Paris, he is dressed as a magnificent mercenary.

A letter that Manuel wrote from Italy in 1522, applying for a job in the Bernese administration, indicates that he must have been dissatisfied with his position both as a painter and a mercenary. "I am a young journeyman and have many small children … whom I would like to educate properly but which as an artist I cannot afford to do …" Soon afterwards Manuel was appointed bailiff of Erlach and spent over five years managing estates not far from the city of Berne, in a position which not only absolved him of material cares, but also prepared him for more senior positions in government. He probably stopped painting at this point, although he continued to draw. His only known journeyman, Elysius Walter, also changed horses and became a sexton.

As well as being eager to rise up through the social ranks, Manuel had another reason for wanting to give up his job as an artist. In 1517 Luther had nailed his theses to the door of the palace chapel in Wittenberg. With the advent of the Reformation, artists in northern Europe lost their main employer, the Church. Many Swiss, their confidence shaken by their military defeat at Pavia, embraced the new Protestant teachings. Too many of them had experienced at first hand the Catholic priesthood and its lust for earthly possessions: Albrecht von Stein had swapped his own grey stallion for a general indulgence for himself and 500 of his men.

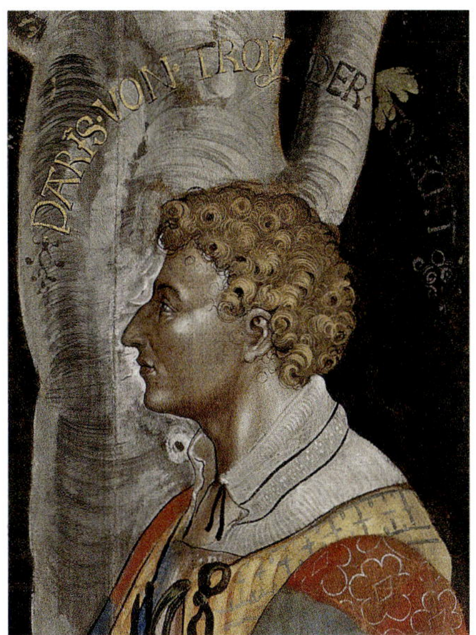

"The Indulgence Seller" was the title of a pamphlet with which Manuel threw himself into the religious debate that would soon divide Berne. The politically very active bailiff of Erlach penned several polemical sketches and essays and thereby played a major role in ensuring that the Reformation triumphed in Berne in 1528. As a member of the executive, from now on – until his death in 1530 – he was directly responsible for a series of strict decrees that put an immediate end to a chaotic, dissolute era.

The churches were cleansed of their "idolatrous images" (some of them painted by Manuel himself). The secularization of Church assets restored the city to financial health and enabled it to "do without foreign money". Serving as a mercenary was forbidden, as was the costume that went with it. The slits in clothes had to be sewn up; gambling, drinking, dancing and whoring were all banned. The power of Lady Venus was crushed. With the active assistance of the artist who had celebrated her beauty in his paintings, the goddess was driven out of Berne.

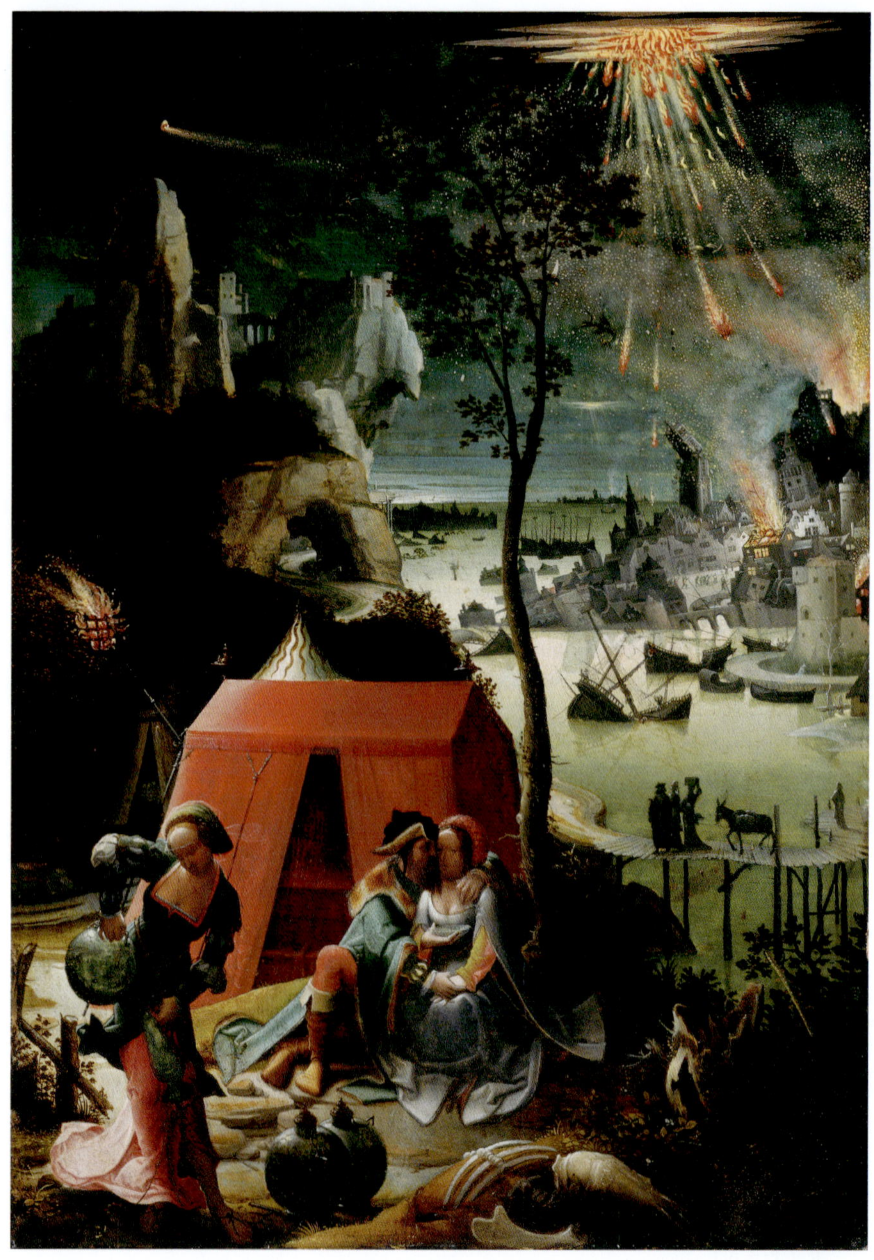

Unknown Netherlandish Master

Sodom burns, while those who have escaped celebrate

Lot and his Daughters, c. 1530
58 x 34 cm, Paris, Musée du Louvre

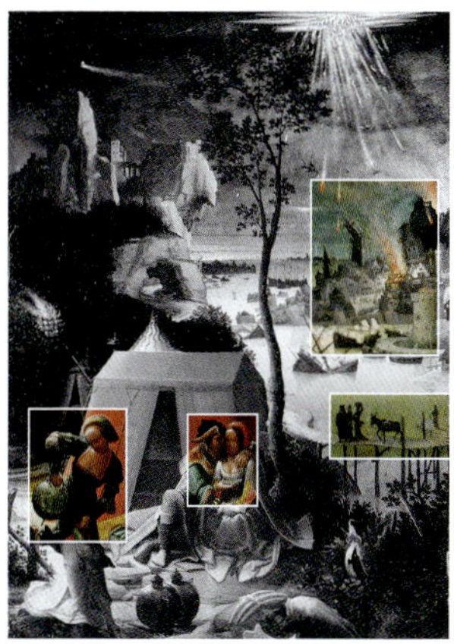

In the foreground women and wine, in the background the end of the world – two scenes composed within triangular fields of the same size which meet at the diagonal running from top left to bottom right and which are held together by the pallid half light. A clearly constructed painting which tells a dark, chaotic tale.

The story of Lot is related in chapters 18 and 19 of Genesis, the first book of the Old Testament, which tells of the creation of the world and the subsequent direction of God's wrath towards humankind. Having expelled Adam and Eve from Paradise after they disobey him, the depravity of their descendants leads God to destroy all but two of them in the Flood. When the people of Babylonia challenge him by building the Tower of Babel, his punishment is to confuse them by giving them many languages and scattering them across the earth. When he hears of the sinful lives of the inhabitants of Sodom and Gomorrah, he decides to destroy the two cities.

Abraham's nephew, Lot, had settled in Sodom and so Abraham started negotiating with God: "Suppose you find fifty innocent people there within the city – will you still destroy it, and not spare it for their sakes?" God replied: "If I find fifty innocent people in Sodom, I will spare the entire city for their sake." Abraham spoke again: "Suppose there are only forty five? … only forty?" He eventually managed to get the number down to ten innocent people. God sent two angels to Sodom, dressed as ordinary men. These are the events leading up to the present scene.

The angels met Lot, who invited them to have dinner and spend the night at his home. All the men of the city of Sodom, godless and immoral, banded together and surrounded Lot's house, demanding that he yield up his two guests. "Bring them out so we can have sex with them." They wanted to homosexually abuse the supposedly defenceless strangers. Lot, the pious, virtuous patriarch, offered the Sodomites his two virgin daughters in place of the strangers: "Do with them as you wish, but leave these men alone, for they are under my protection."

The Sodomites were not interested in the young women; they wanted the strangers. They attacked Lot and tried to break down the door into the house. The two angels pulled Lot inside and revealed their

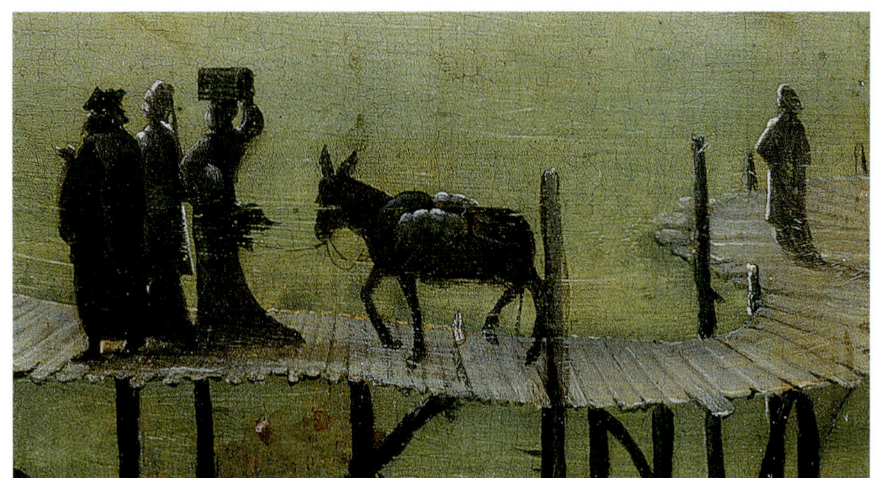

power by blinding the men of Sodom. They then told Lot of God's intention to destroy the city and urged him to leave with his family immediately. "At dawn the next morning, the angels became insistent … When Lot still hesitated, the angels seized his hand and the hands of his wife and two daughters and rushed them to safety outside the city." There they warned him: "Run for your lives! Do not stop anywhere in the valley. And don't look back!" As Lot hurried to safety, God "rained down fire and burning sulphur from the heavens on Sodom and Gomorrah. He utterly destroyed them … But Lot's wife looked back as she was following along behind him, and she became a pillar of salt."

The artist shows Lot and his daughters, safely removed from Sodom, in front of some luxurious tents. The Bible describes them differently, namely as refugees living in a cave in the mountain. Nor are the faces of the three etched with worry and despair, as might be expected after losing one's wife and mother, home, city and possessions. Lot's daughters believed that the whole of the rest of humanity had been destroyed. So the older daughter said to her sister: "There isn't a man anywhere … for us to marry. And our father will soon be too old to have children. Come, let's get him drunk with wine, and then we will sleep with him. That way we will preserve our line through our father." So that is what they did, the eldest daughter the first night, and the youngest the second, and on both occasions Lot "was unaware of her lying down or getting up again". Nothing of this incestuous story can be seen in the present painting. The destruction of Sodom, on the other hand, is portrayed in dramatic detail – the fire falling from the sky and the city going down in flames. The fact that the father was prepared to prostitute his daughters, and that his daughters are now trying to dupe the pious old man – these were things the viewer was expected to know. The artist transforms the misery of the refugees into a conventional love idyll. Conventional, too, insofar as it is the man who is taking the initiative, and not one of the daughters.

Sodom was also called Rome

The artist portrays Lot and his daughters twice within his composition, large in the foreground, and small and shadowy in the background, where they can be seen crossing a narrow raised walkway. One on the daughters carries a piece of luggage on her head, and a laden donkey follows behind. They do not appear to be afraid of falling off (otherwise they would be walking in single file), nor do they seem to fear catching sight of the disaster by mistake. The mother, who was turned into a pillar of salt for casting a forbidden look back, is standing on the winding walkway at the right-hand edge of the picture. The three survivors seem to be strolling along at an unhurried pace, as if on their way to a picnic, which they then consume in the foreground.

Every epoch has taken from the monstrous story of Lot and his family what seemed relevant to its own time. For the peoples of the Old Testament, for example, it was the law of hospitality. As nomads, they lived in a semi-desert; there were no inns, and travellers were dependent upon the help of local inhabitants. These viewed strangers with scepticism, but the law commanded that they gave them food and shelter. Lot, who was even willing to offer his daughters to the Sodomites to be raped so that the strangers in his house should escape injury, thereby upholds this vitally important law.

Prostituting one's own daughters was scandalous, however, as was committing incest, and these two elements posed a challenge for everyone who subsequently tried to interpret the story. One of the earliest, the Jewish philosopher Philo of Alexandria, who died in *c*. AD 50, solved the problem by simply denying that the story was an actual historical event.

Martin Luther took a very different view. Luther exerted a decisive influence upon northern European thinking in the 16th century – the century in which this painting arose. For the father of the Reformation, the story of Lot's family was a real one, and he made many allowances for the behaviour of its members. Why had Lot's wife looked back? "She succumbed to human weakness and temptation, because she could hear such a terrible noise and thunderstorm behind her." Was it possible for a father to sleep with his daughters and know nothing about it? Lot would know about it, granted Luther the psychologist, but he would forget, because "a heart that has been so terribly shocked and overtaken by such a dreadful fate loses all sense of itself." As he explained: "We see the same thing on a much more minor scale in melancholic, depressed people and lovers, who say and do many things that they quickly forget." With his sympathetic commentaries, Luther

wanted to distance himself from the sorts of monk who had no idea what real life was like. He was also, of course, pointing a warning finger at Rome. Just as God had destroyed Sodom and four other cities, Luther argued, he would also destroy the church of the papists if they did not change their ways. For while the Pope "sits on high, he thinks he has the power to do whatever he pleases, and will endure no criticism or punishment, just as the Sodomites did here. Where neither advice nor assistance is accepted, it must of necessity follow that one will ultimately go to wrack and ruin."

Experts date the painting to around 1530 or earlier. The artist, a contemporary of Luther, is unknown. He probably lived in Leiden in the Netherlands, i.e. in an area which during the Reformation liberated itself from Spanish hegemony, and where Luther's writings were widely read.

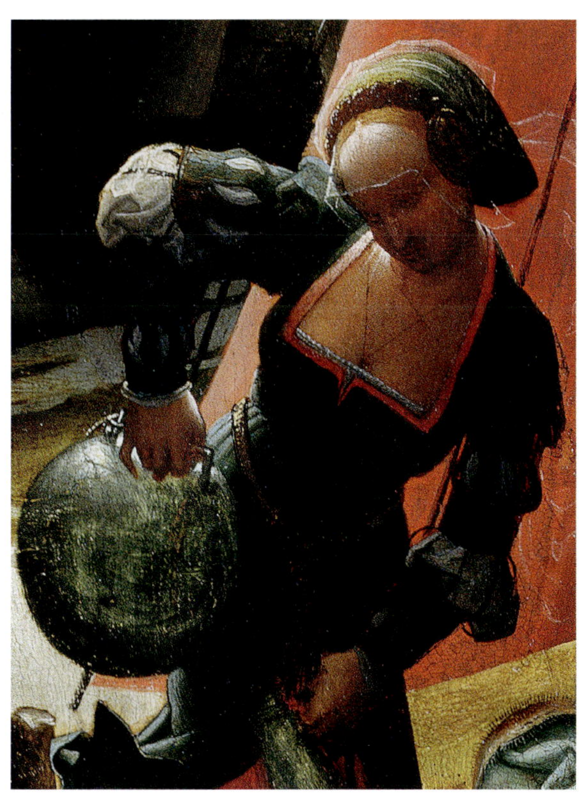

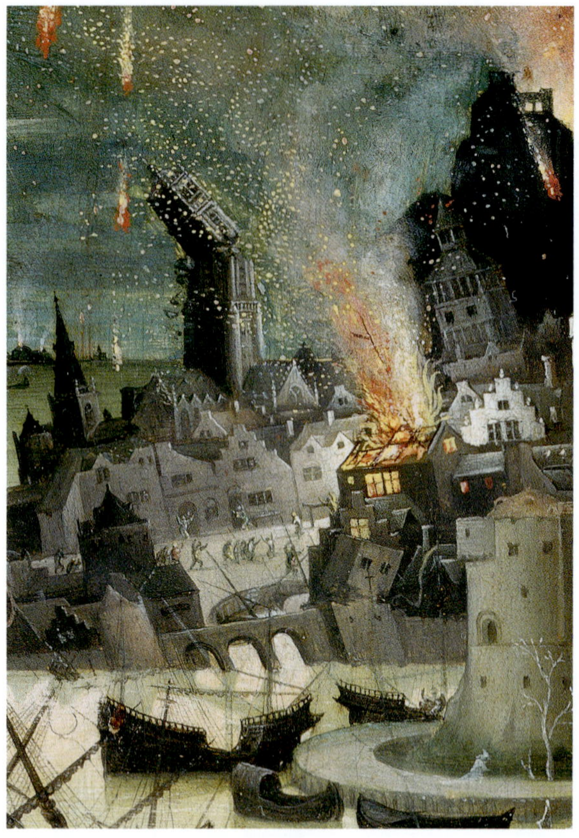

It cannot have been Lot's servants, for they and his herds of cattle were all destroyed along with the Sodomites. After all, Lot's daughters justified their seduction of their father with the argument that he was the only man left on earth.

Both the painting and the Old Testament account leave questions unanswered. One thing that is clear is the role played by alcohol – and long would be the list of Christian preachers who would cite the story of Lot in their campaign against excessive drinking. One such was John Calvin, a contemporary of Luther and the present unknown master. As a reformer in Geneva, he used the threat of severe punishments to coerce his fellow citizens into leading a godly life. He even presumed to declare that God had made Lot's story known so that we should "abhor drunkenness". For it was "true that God demonstrates every day through grave punishments how much this vice displeases him".

Just as Luther barbed his commentaries with criticism of Rome, the monasteries and monks, so Calvin used his own writings to crusade against drinkers. Those who drank too much, he warned, would invoke "the wrath of God". While there is a sense of Lutheran tolerance about the camp in the foreground, the fiery background is Calvinistically harsh.

The story of Lot remained popular over the centuries not because of its drunkenness, however, but because of its incest. Amorous relationships between family members are found as far back as Greek mythology, and today it is not only psychoanalysts who suspect that such Ancient legends give expression to forbidden and repressed desires. The story of Oedipus, who unwittingly murdered his father and married his mother, is the best known of all.

Another story handed down both orally and in writing since antiquity is that of the King of Tyre.

The present master is unlikely to have known them. Although Luther had nailed his 95 theses to the door of Wittenberg palace chapel in 1517, at the time this picture was painted, his commentaries on the Bible were not yet written or distributed. It is certain, however, that during the Netherlands' 80-year war against Spain and Catholicism, people looking at the collapse of Sodom would have associated it with the "depraved" city of Rome.

Drinkers invoke the wrath of God

The big round wine jars are heavy, and it is astonishing how the artist succeeds in showing the strenuous act of decanting them as a graceful movement. Three such jars can be seen. Who carried them and the tents all the way up here?

He loved his daughter, forced her into his bed, and kept suitors at bay with a riddle that they had to solve. If they failed, they were beheaded. If they succeeded, they were also killed, because the solution betrayed his forbidden relationship with his daughter. The Ancient legends explore various incestuous combinations; thus father loves daughter, son loves mother, brother and sister love each other. But it is rare to find a daughter seeking sexual union with her father.

Psychoanalysts are familiar with daughters who are so jealously attached to their fathers that they wish their mother dead or far away, so that they can take her place. But in neither the psychiatric nor the forensic literature does there seem to be a known case of a daughter actually turning her incestuous desires into reality.

Except in the shape of the defence put forward by an accused father. For feminist writers argue that the story of Lot – like the entire Bible – is written from a male perspective. It is deliberately designed to defend a pious man and preserve his reputation untarnished. In fact, however, Lot – so the accusation goes – was the active party. One might see the rigid, passive position of the daughter being embraced by Lot in the present picture as supporting this thesis. The graceful way in which the other daughter is decanting the wine shows that the frozen attitude of her sister cannot be blamed on any lack of artistic skill on the part of the painter.

Houses collapse, boats sink – the world is sliding towards destruction

Geologists believe they can date the destruction of Sodom and its neighbouring cities to the year 4350 BC. At that time, a severe earthquake shook the region around the Dead Sea. Hydrocarbons forced up out of the depths ignited and sulphur dioxides produced acid rain. The people, animals and plants had no chance. Thick black clouds made the deadly catastrophe visible for miles around.

For the Bible, the fire came not out of the earth but from the skies; the artist visualizes it as a volley of blazing darts streaking downwards. No less unnerving than the bombardment from above is the tilt of the buildings and the main square: like a slowly capsizing platform, the city is sinking leftwards as if about to slide into the sea. The church tower is already collapsing, perhaps as the spire of St Peter's in Leiden had done during a fire in 1512.

Ships, too, are breaking up and sinking. Fire is raining down on the city lying on the distant horizon, while another in front of the cliff on the left remains unscathed, as does the tower on the right-hand edge of the picture. The surface of the water, meanwhile, remains smooth and untroubled. This abrupt juxtaposition of catastrophe and calm – a juxtaposition demonstrated not just by the two main scenes, but also within the vision of destruction itself – heightens the viewer's sense of the uncanny and unfathomable nature of these events.

The Bible makes no mention of a sea or any other expanse of water; it has been added here by the painter. Since artists in those days had no hesitation in relocating distant events to the present, and since ports were emerging as the leading economic centres in the netherlands, such embellishment of the biblical narrative seems quite natural. In 1497, however, Dürer too turned Sodom into a port. Because he had just been to Venice? Whatever the case, artistic considerations would also have played a role: the search for effects, for powerful visual contrasts – such as those offered by fire and water.

Fire and water are joined in this painting by the contrast between the flat plain and the mountainous landscape. Also disconcerting is the single tree growing the full height of the picture. The water, the towering rocks, the tree as a structural device, and beyond them all a sweeping view into the distance – these were all components of what might be termed "universal landscapes", artificial constructs which combine a range of different elements which in real life do not belong together. This genre of painting was developed by the Netherlandish artist Joachim Patenier (c. 1480–1524); similar landscapes provide the backdrop to the visions of Patenier's contemporary, Hieronymus Bosch (c. 1450–1516).

Patenier kept to the surface, to what could be seen in the landscape. In the work of Hieronymus Bosch, and later Pieter Bruegel the Elder (after 1525–69), the ground opens up, hellfire blazes upwards and a yawning mouth provides a gateway to the underworld. Just as Sodom is in danger from above, in the pictorial fantasies of Bosch, Bruegel and their followers, the world is threatened from below.

For the majority of people at the start of the 16th century, the earth was not just solid ground on which to build houses and in which to sow corn, but was permanently at risk from the powers of Hell or divine Judgement. The eschatological gloom that had hung over the end of 1400s lingered into the new century. "Since the world is on the decline", wrote Luther, "our own day, as the blasphemers, the papists never stop fuming, will be followed by the end, that is, by the Last Judgement."

The catastrophe recedes into the background
The painting, which measures 58 by 34 centimetres, was acquired by the Louvre in Paris in 1900. Over the years, many art historians have turned detective in their desire to uncover the identity of its artist. The majority come down in favour of Lucas van Leyden (*c.* 1494–1533), who is famed primarily for his engravings. If not Lucas himself, then an artist in his circle, others have suggested. Others again consider the landscape to be by Patenier, the figures to be by Lucas. Yet others attribute the preliminary drawing to Lucas, the final execution to a pupil. According to the latest research, the artist is unknown, but probably worked in Leiden and perhaps also in Antwerp.

A question mark also hangs over the painting's date. The earliest it has been dated to is 1504. Next comes 1512, the year in which the tower of St Peter's church in Leiden collapsed – but is that reason enough? The latest date proposed is 1530. It thus probably arose in the 1510s or 1520s – at the beginning of a period in which the fate of Lot and the destruction of Sodom became extraordinarily popular in art. Between 1500 and 1600, an American art historian has calculated, the Old Testament story of Lot was painted at least 210 times. Before and after this century, on the other hand, the motif appears much more infrequently.

Why was this subject so popular from 1500 onwards? Several developments coincided. Firstly, people were generally more familiar with the Bible. In around 1450 Johannes Gutenberg had invented printing with movable type, and in the wake of the Reformation the Bible was translated into the vernacular languages of northern Europe. For the first time, its text could be read by the laity. Many people lived their entire lives afraid that the world was about to end, and were particularly drawn to descriptions of God's wrath. Others again were attracted by the shockingly risqué element of this chapter from the Holy Book.

Accompanying this increased familiarity with the Bible was the fusion of the story of Lot with two thoroughly secular pictorial motifs highly popular during this era. First, the motif of the "unequal couple", also known as the "wiles of women". Pictures of this type show an older man and beside him a young woman who is making up to him or allowing him to fondle her. The man has money or a purse in his hand. The message: women sell their sexuality, and old men obtain sexual gratification only with the help of money.

The motif of the unequal couple was joined somewhat later by that of the *conversation galante*. Such pictures showed persons of both sexes engaged in flirtatious conversation, more or less advanced along the path to intimacy. If we screen out the catastrophe taking place in the background of the present painting, what remains is a picnic in the hills; servants have put up the tents and poured out the wine and have even lit a fire in an iron brazier in anticipation of falling evening temperatures. In Lot paintings from the second half of the 16th century onwards, the catastrophe recedes increasingly into the distance; what remain are the delights of love, sex and tenderness.

Particularly large numbers of Sodom and Lot compositions issued from the Netherlands, perhaps because so many artists lived and worked there, and because popular demand for works of art was greater there than anywhere else. Perhaps, too, because nowhere else in Europe were people and their needs viewed with so little prejudice. It is possible that even incest fantasies were admitted with less embarrassment.

It is for other reasons, however, that this painting continues to fascinate us today. It recalls the imagery of our dreams; figures, objects, events seem to emerge out of the darkness of the subconscious. Rocks, fire, the solitary tree, the smooth surface of the water assemble themselves in a way that is only seen in dreams. The viewer senses something threatening at the same time as sensing tender intimacy, and he suspects that both may be connected – but how remains a mystery.

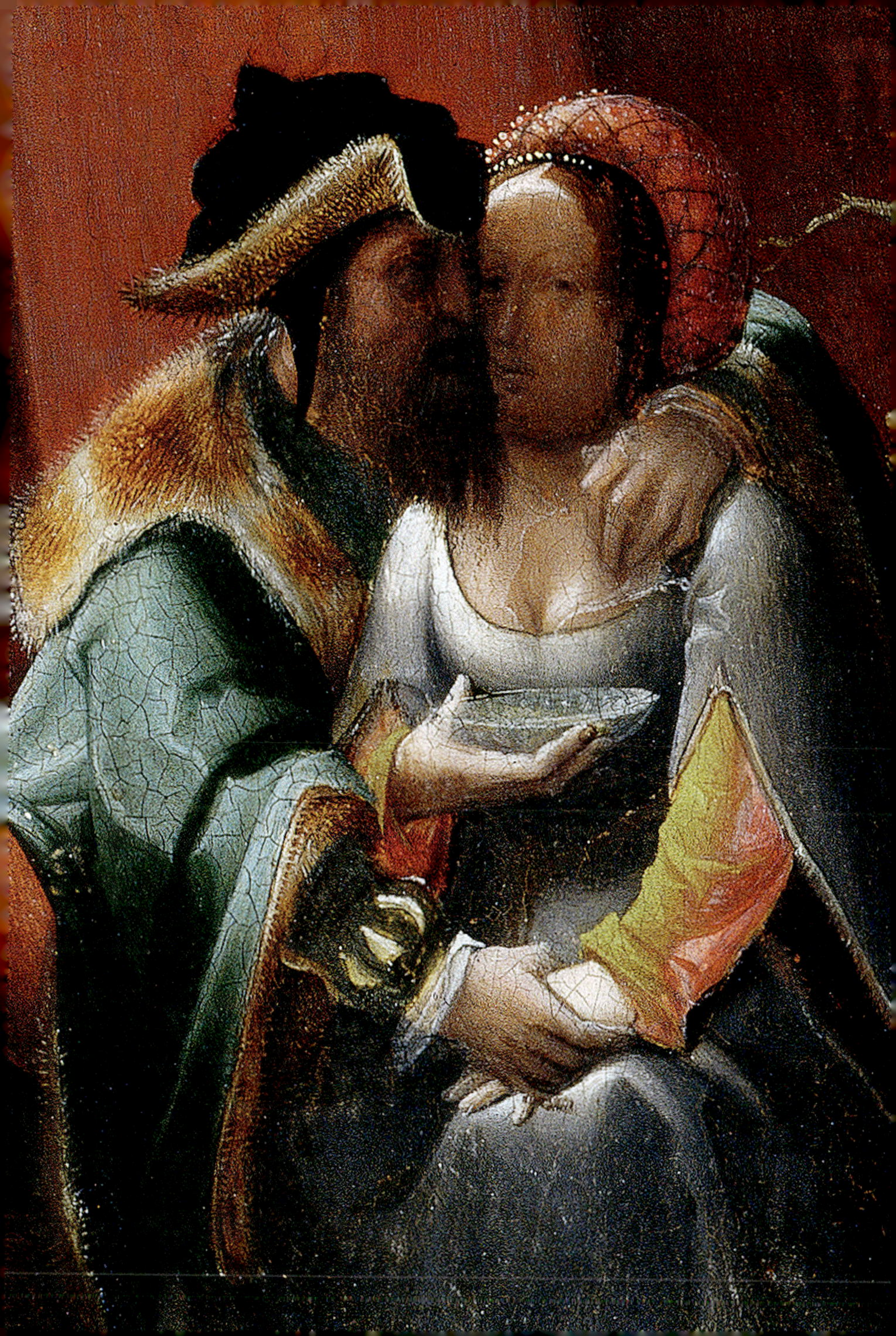

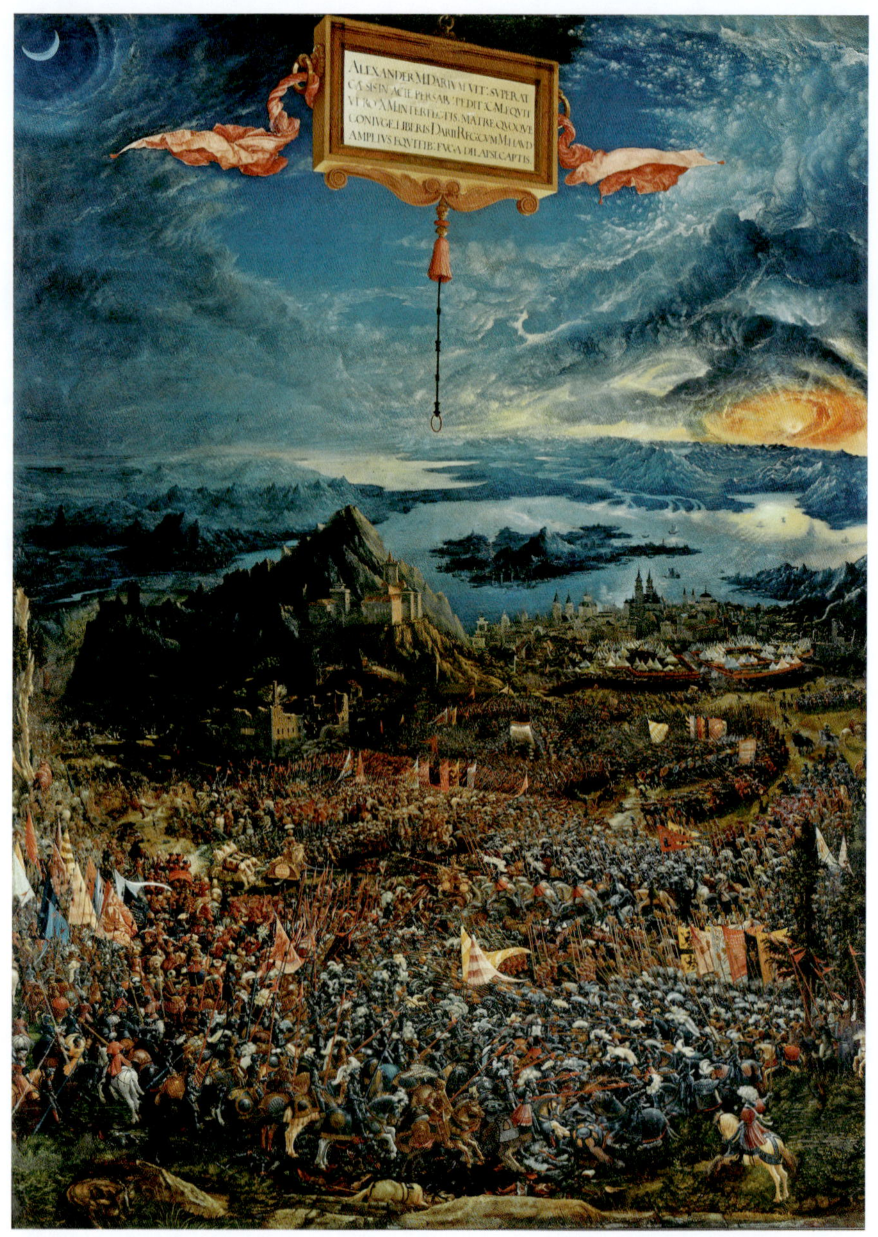

Albrecht Altdorfer (*c.* 1480–1538)

The battle to end all battles

The Battle of Issus, 1529
158.4 x 120.3 cm, Munich, Alte Pinakothek

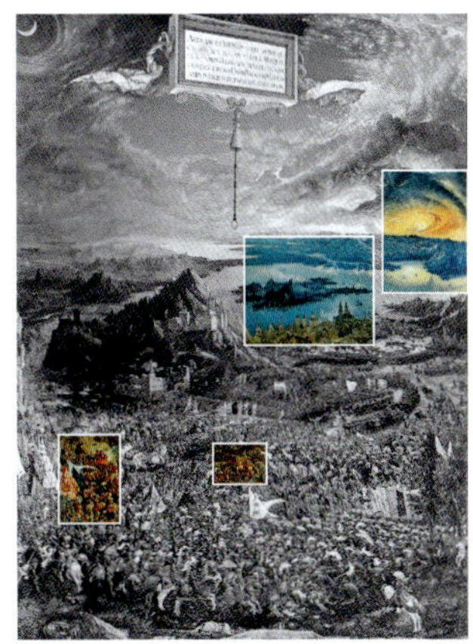

The Wittelsbach Duke Wilhelm IV was hardly one of the more important rulers of his day. He governed Bavaria from 1508 to 1550, during the Reformation, but his strategy of shifting alliances with the powerful Habsburgs, French king and Protestant rulers brought him little advantage; he even made a vain attempt to become German king. On the other hand, he did achieve two things with lasting effect: he ensured that Bavaria remained a Catholic land, and he commissioned one of the most important German paintings, Albrecht Altdorfer's *The Battle of Issus*.

The painter and architect Altdorfer lived in Regensburg, approximately 60 miles north of the ducal residence in Munich. Though situated in the middle of Bavaria, Regensburg was a Free Imperial Town, whose allegiances alternated between the Emperor in Vienna and the Wittelsbach dukes. The same might be said for the Regensburg citizen Altdorfer. Altdorfer executed some 200 works for Emperor Maximilian, most of them miniatures and woodcuts, but he created his masterpiece for Duke Wilhelm in Munich.

Altdorfer must have been almost 50 when he received the commission to paint *The Battle of Issus*. His exact age cannot be established, since his date of birth is unknown. It is thought to have been *c.* 1480. However, documentary evidence does reveal that Altdorfer quickly rose to wealth and prestige. In 1513 he bought a house "with a tower and farmstead". In 1517 he became a member of the Outer Town Council, in 1526 a member of the Inner Council, and on 18 September 1528 he was elected Mayor.

However, Altdorfer declined this high office. His reason for doing so is mentioned in the annals of the Regensburg Council: "He much desires to execute a special work in Bavaria for my Serene Highness and gracious Lord, Duke Wilhelm." This "work" was *The Battle of Issus*.

As an artist and member of the town council, Altdorfer became involved in the conflicts of his age. He announced the town's expulsion of its Jewish inhabitants, making a quick sketch of the synagogue before it was destroyed. His connections to the imperial court were such that, when Regensburg fell into disgrace with the Emperor, Altdorfer was entrusted with the mission of apologizing. When the Turkish army threatened Vienna, he was given the task of fortifying the Regensburg defences.

As a member of the town council, Altdorfer had to interrogate Anabaptists and sit in a committee to appoint a Protestant minister. In his will, he declared that he had no desire for "spiritual accessories", which probably meant that he rejected the administration of last rites, or the holding of a mass. By the time of his death in 1538, he was probably no longer a practising Catholic.

The schism within the Church and the military threat that sprang from the non-Christian Orient were the two main factors determining life at the time. Insecurity and fear were widespread. It is against this background that we must consider the genesis of the present painting.

The artist shows an event from the distant past, a battle fought near Issus in 333 BC. This he sets

against a panorama of sky and landscape; the battle
in Asia Minor thus assumes the aura of a natural
disaster, or a scene from some cosmic Armageddon.
In fact, the battle was seen at the time as a turning
point in world history: the Greek Occident had
defeated the Persian Orient.

The contemporary significance of the subject was
obvious, and the tablet proclaiming victory at the
top of the painting assumed a special significance
in the face of the Turkish threat. The tablet appears
to descend from the vault of the heavens, and bears
a message in Latin: "The defeat of Darius by Alexander the Great, following the deaths of 100,000
Persian foot soldiers and more than 10,000 Persian
horsemen. King Darius' mother, wife and children
were taken prisoner, together with about 1,000
fleeing horse soldiers."

Women on the battlefield

Altdorfer provides details of military strengths and
losses not only on the large tablet, but also on banners and flags. The painting was probably intended
to serve several purposes, one being to keep alive

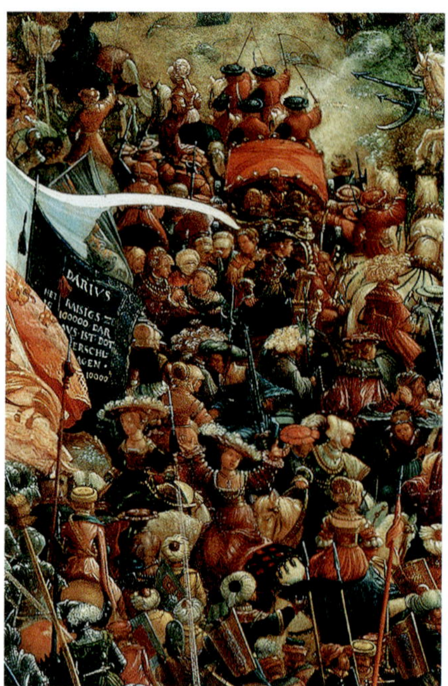

Alexander's strategic fame, which derived from the
Macedonian's defeat of an army many times larger
than his own. According to figures cited in the
painting itself, Darius commanded 300,000 foot
soldiers, while Alexander led only 32,000; the Persian
king had a cavalry of 100,000, his opponent a mere
4,000. One of the great general's admirers was
Napoleon, who, in 1800, had Altdorfer's painting
brought to Paris and hung in his bathroom.

As an artist, however, Altdorfer evidently felt little
obligation to illustrate the details he cited. There is
nothing in the painting to suggest the numerical
superiority of Darius' army; nor has the artist followed historical accounts of strategic deployment.
On top of this, he has clothed the figures in the dress
of his own time. The cavalry wear heavy armour;
some of Persians are shown in turbans of the kind
Turks were known to wear. The women in feathered
toques look like German courtly ladies, dressed for
a hunting party.

That Altdorfer painted women at all on a battlefield must probably be attributed to his passion
for invention. The 16th century became increasingly
preoccupied with Western civilization, but this was
not necessarily accompanied by an interest in historic
truth. Investigative research into the past had not
yet begun; archaeology was a subject of the future.

One of Altdorfer's sources was probably
Hartmann Schedel's "World Chronicle". Most of
the artist's statistics are identical to those given by
Schedel. The book had appeared in Nuremberg
in 1493, 35 years before Altdorfer commenced work
on *The Battle of Issus*. Another source may have been
an account written by Q. Curtius Rufus, a document
probably dating from the 1st century. However,
neither work makes mention of women entering
the fray – one of Altdorfer's inventions.

A highly dramatic scene involving women is
indeed related in Curtius's account, only this takes
place in a camp. According to Curtius, Darius'
mother and wife, taken prisoner in their tents, suddenly began to wail: "The reason for this shocking
scene was that Darius' mother and wife had broken
into loud and woeful lamentations for the king,
whom they thought killed. For a captive eunuch …
recognizing Darius' tunic … which he had cast off
for fear that his clothing would betray him, in the
hands of the soldier who had found it, and imagining the garment to be taken from the king's dead
body, had brought false news of his death."

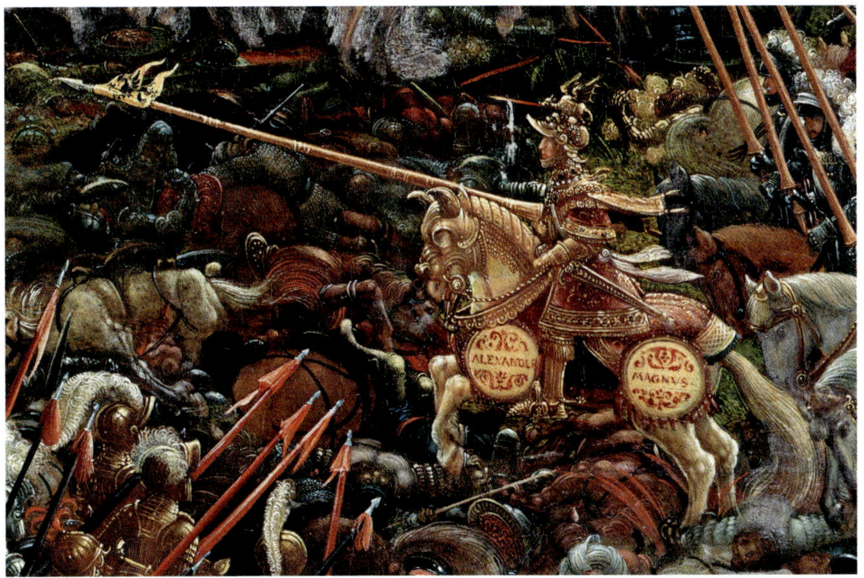

Heroes replace saints

Darius escaped with his life at the battle of Issus.
He was certainly not pursued by Alexander to
within a length of the latter's lance, as Altdorfer's
painting suggests. At least, there is no mention
of this in either historical account. The artist was
faithful to historical truth only when it suited him,
when historical facts were compatible with the
demands of his composition.

It is not known what Altorfer's patron wished
the painting to show: admiration for Alexander's
strategic prowess, the parallel with the Turkish
threat, or – since he was himself such an enthusiastic
participant in tournaments – a celebration of chivalry? All that can be said for sure is that Altdorfer's
painting reflected one of the chief preoccupations
of his age: the reappraisal of Classical antiquity was
a characteristic feature of the Renaissance. During
the Middle Ages, saints had grown in significance
over the legendary figures of Ancient Greece and
Rome, and more value was attached to relics of
Christian martyrs than to antique manuscripts.
However, a change soon began to make itself felt
in quattrocento Italy, spreading north across the
Alps during the century that followed. The saints
began to lose their exemplary status. Of course, this

process was linked to the decadence of the Roman
Catholic Church. Reappraisal of antiquity and the
decline of the Church went hand in hand.

Wilhelm IV commissioned not only *The Battle of
Issus*, but a whole series of heroic scenes: Hannibal
defeating the Romans at Cannae, Caesar besieging
Alesia, the captive Mucius Scaevola burning his hand
to demonstrate to his adversaries the bravery
of the young men of Rome; eight paintings (of
which Altendorfer painted only one) in an identical, upright format. There is also a second series in
horizontal format – possibly commissioned for the
Duchess – showing seven famous women, many
of them Old Testament figures: Susanna bathing,
before defending herself against the advances of two
elders who slander her and condemn her to death;
Judith cutting off the head of Holofernes, the enemy
of her people; and Helen, Troy's ruin.

All of these men and women had distinguished
themselves in some way or other. The interest they
aroused during the 16th century was not only a sign
of the period's rediscovery of antiquity; it was also
the mark of a new sense of self. During the Renaissance people no longer saw themselves solely as
members of a social group, as the citizens of a town,
or as sinners before God in whose eyes all were

equal. They had become aware of the unique qualities that distinguished one person from another.
Unlike the Middle Ages, the Renaissance celebrated
the individual. Altdorfer may have painted row after
row of apparently identical warriors, but the spectators themselves would identify with Alexander and
Darius, figures who had names, whose significance
was indicated by the cord which hung down from
the tablet above them.

Painting in the age of discovery

Schedel's *World Chronicle* was a seminal work,
treasured not only for its comprehensive survey
of the historical knowledge of the age, but for
its detailed approach to geography. The book
contained illustrations of the more important
figures of the Bible and Classical antiquity (naturally wearing 16th-century dress); it also showed
the famous woodcut *vedutas* of towns executed in
Nuremberg after the sketches of travellers.

The *World Chronicle* thus not only reflected
contemporary interest in the history of civilization
"from the beginning of the world unto our own
time", but also a widespread curiosity about geography. In this sense, it is a typical product of the age
of discovery, an epoch marked by Columbus reaching America, Magellan sailing around the world,
and attempts by cartographers to find the appropriate visual form in which to present distant parts
of the world. Altdorfer attempted something similar. His *Battle of Issus* is set against the imposing
panorama of the Eastern Mediterranean.

The inspiration for this was probably provided
by a map in Schedel's chronicle. In the detail below,
Cyprus is shown as a disproportionately large island,
with the Red Sea above it to the left. Above right is
the Nile delta, identified by its eight arms and by the
lakes thought to be its source. The mountain range
beside the Nile has no equivalent in reality, but is
featured in Schedel's map.

The town situated on the near Mediterranean
shore is probably not intended to be Issus. Issus
was an unimportant town in Altdorfer's day, and is
not mentioned in Schedel's book. According to the
Chronicle, the battle took place in 333 BC near the
town of Tarsus. This, by contrast, was a name to
conjure with, associated in many readers' minds with
a school of philosophy which, in Roman times,
had been as famous as the schools of Athens and
Alexandria. First and foremost, however, Tarsus
was known as the birthplace of the Apostle Paul, a
place of significance in Church history. Perhaps this
explains why Altdorfer – anachronistically – embellished the townscape with church towers.

For in spite of the Renaissance, the prevalent
geographical and historical pictures of the world
c. 1500 were still dominated by Church doctrine.
This, too, is reflected in Schedel's book. The acts of
God in creating the world are there presented as no
less factual than the number of soldiers who took
part in the Battle of Issus. Because God created the
world in six days and rested on the seventh, Schedel
divided the entire history of mankind into seven
"ages": "Now, seven is a perfect number, seven days
there are to a week, seven stars
that never sink ..." According to
Schedel's calculations, the human
race *c.* 1500 had reached the seventh, and final, "age". The end
of the world was nigh.

The end of the world is nigh

Many of Schedel's and Altdorfer's
contemporaries were tormented
by the fear that the world was
coming to an end. Even Luther
believed it. One of Luther's
commensals reported: "The
following day he again spoke
much of the Day of Judgement
and of the end of the world, for
he has been troubled by many

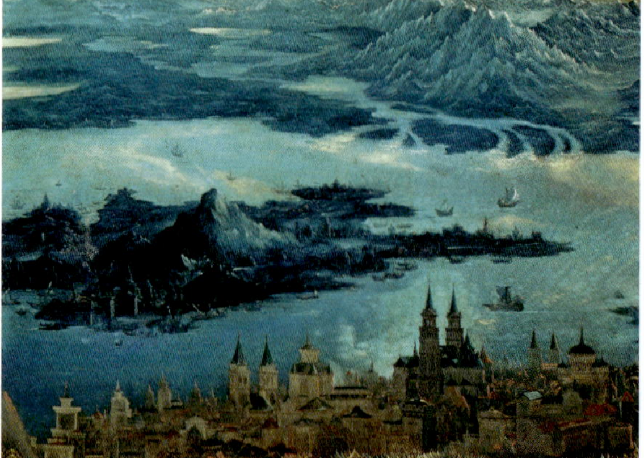

terrible dreams of the Last Judgement this half year past …" On another occasion Luther complained: "Dear Lord, how this world is reduced … It is drawing to a close." Or: "When I slept this afternoon I dreamt the Day of Judgement came on the day of Paul's conversion."

Dreams, premonitions and prophecies of the end of the world were fed not only by calculations based on the "seven days" premise, as in Schedel's work. Calculations of an entirely different order, those of the prophet Daniel, seemed to point in the same direction. He had predicted that four kingdoms would come and go, before the coming of the kingdom of the Lord. The four kingdoms were thought to be Babylon, Persia, Greece and Rome. This was problematic, however, for the Roman Empire had long since passed away. A route out of the quandary was found by propounding that Rome still existed – in the form of the papacy. By Luther's time, however, the papacy was so much gone to seed that it really did seem on its last legs. According to Luther: "Daniel saw the world as a series of kingdoms, those of the Babylonians, Persians, Greeks and Romans. These have passed away. The papacy may have preserved the Roman Empire, but that was its parting cup; now that, too, is gone into decline."

This comment, along with other examples of Luther's "table talk", was recorded in 1532, four years after Altdorfer began work on his painting. Altdorfer was undoubtedly aware of the eschatalogical preoccupations of his contemporaries. As a member of the leading body of the town in which he lived, he was forced constantly to deal with questions relating to the Church.

If we take for granted that Altdorfer knew of these things, and that he, too, sensed what it was to live at the end of time, then the sky over the Battle of Issus assumes a new meaning. In the original work, the sky was bigger; the painting was reduced in size at a later date when strips were cut from all four sides, with the largest section removed from the top. The moon, too, originally stood further from the corner of the painting. Even in its present size, however, the sky covers more than a third of the painting's surface. With its sharply contrasting lights and darks, dynamic congregation of clouds and sun reflected in the sea, it suggests the occurrence of an extraordinary event.

The exact nature of this event was expounded by Daniel: the second of the kingdoms anticipated

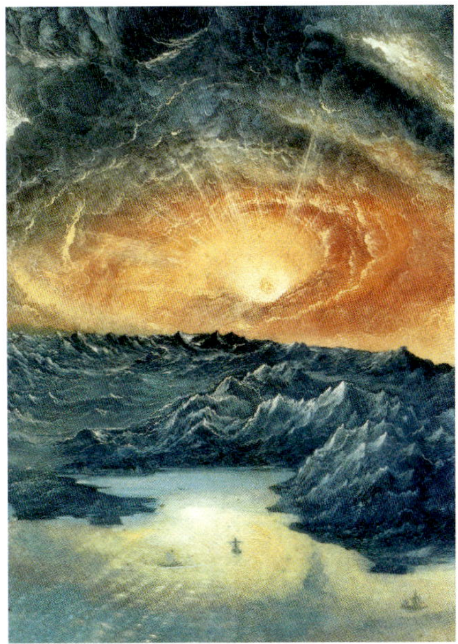

by God and prophesied by Daniel cedes, near Issus, to the third, as the Greeks defeat the Persians. However, the change of power is, at the same time, a stage further on the world clock, a step closer to the impending end of the world. Viewed in this way, *The Battle of Issus* had a direct bearing upon the present.

It is thought that Wilhelm IV wanted the painting to celebrate the grandeur of the individual. He wanted a Renaissance painting. What he got was a work whose view of the world was dominated in equal parts by new ideas and medieval tradition: even the cleverest and boldest of individuals cannot decide the course of world history – that is the province of God alone.

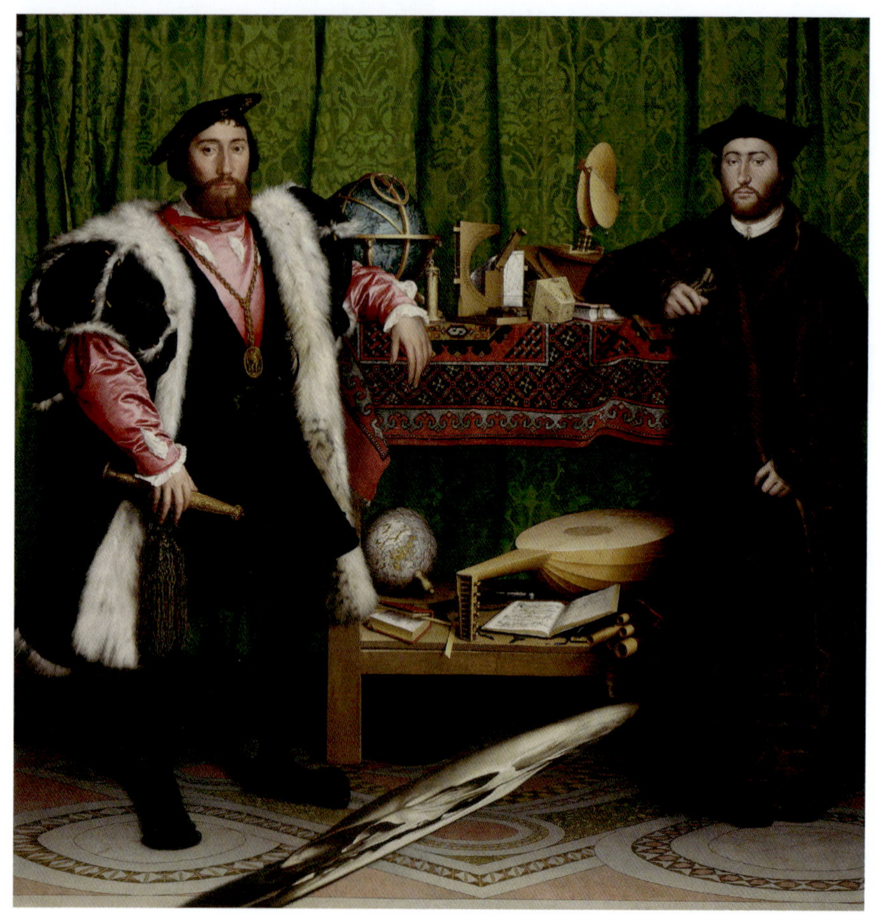

Hans Holbein the Younger (1497/1498–1543)

Careers in the king's service

The Ambassadors, 1533
207 x 209 cm, London, The National Gallery

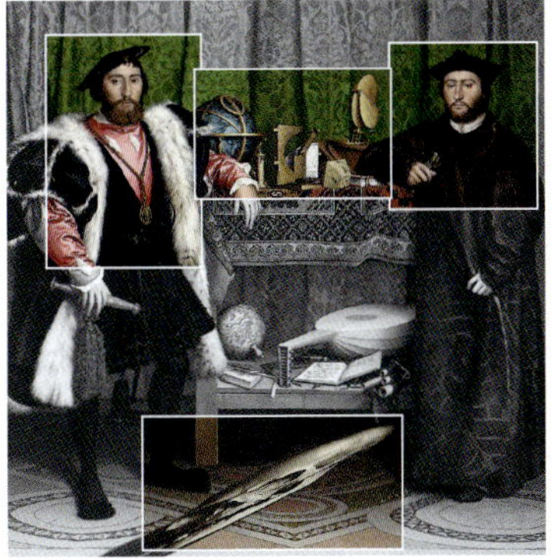

A young French bishop visits a young French diplomat in England. They were friends, and the artist shows us some of the interests they shared: music, mathematics, astronomy. Death, too, is concealed in the painting. The double portrait is in The National Gallery, London.

An official portrait: two men whose bearing, respectability and earnest mien make them look about 40 years old. But they were both much younger; the man on the left was 29, the man on the right 25. Life expectancy in the 16th century was shorter than today; people tended to enter important posts at an earlier age. One of the men is already a bishop, the other is French ambassador to the English court.

The churchman, himself occasionally entrusted with ambassadorial duties by the French king, is visiting his friend, the diplomat. The two represent different sectors within the diplomatic corps, named after their styles of dress: *l'homme de robe courte* and *l'homme de robe longue*. Men of the short robe were worldly ambassadors; those with long robes were clergymen.

To be sent on a diplomatic mission by the king was an honour, but seldom a pleasure in the 16th century. Above all, it was expensive. The king granted fiefs, benefices and allowances to both clergy and nobility. In return, they were obliged to perform services, a duty extending to the disposal of their incomes. They were expected to pay for their stay in foreign lands out of their own pocket. Once there, they were generally treated with due politeness, but also with suspicion. Diplomats were thought to combine their official duties with spying. In 1482, for example, it was strictly forbidden for Venetians to talk of public affairs to foreign diplomats; and one Swiss ambassador reported from London in 1653 that a member of parliament who spoke to a foreign ambassador risked losing his seat. Certainly, it was one of the ambassador's main tasks to collect as much accurate information as possible about the country he was visiting. Newspapers did not exist at the time.

Contemporary manuals and memoirs give us some idea of the abilities expected of a diplomat. First of all, he should cut an appropriately representative figure, wearing clothes that were fine enough, and expensive enough, to be worthy of his master. He should be eloquent, have an excellent knowledge of Latin (the *lingua franca* of the day), and be educated to converse with scientists and artists. His manner should be urbane, charming, never too curious; he must be able to retain full composure while listening to the worst of news, and be skilled in slowing down or speeding up negotiations whenever necessary. His private life should be impeccable, precluding even the slightest hint of a scandal. His wife must stay at home, of course; after all, she might gossip. It was considered of the utmost importance to retain an able cook; good food is often a ticket to the best information.

The 16th century was the cradle of modern diplomacy. Previously, the affairs of European states in the Holy Roman Empire had been regulated centrally by the Emperor. This system had lost much of its authority. Instead, bilateral agreements had grown in significance, and with them the art of diplomacy. However, permanent embassies remained an exception; diplomatic missions lasted only a few weeks or months. It was not yet essential, as it later became, for foreign policy to direct its energy toward establishing relationships of mutual trust over long periods. Short-term success was more important. If a contract no longer served a country's interests, it was broken. These were times of great insecurity. The balance of power changed from month to month. There was one means alone of securing an alliance of real duration – marriage.

The changing structure of alliances in the 16th century is reflected in its record of engagements and their dissolution, its history of marriages and their annulment. As a young man, the English king

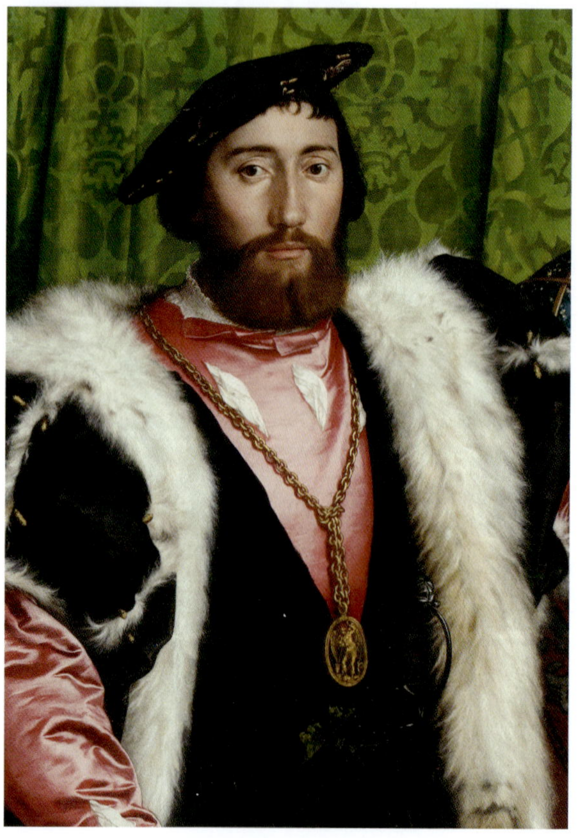

Henry VIII had married Catherine of Aragon. She was an aunt of the powerful Spanish king, Charles V. Henry and Catherine had a daughter, Mary, who herself became engaged to Charles V of Spain. However, while Mary was still a child, Charles V dissolved his engagement to her, for he wished to marry Isabella, the Infanta of Portugal, a match which would directly increase his wealth and sphere of influence. Henry, meanwhile, in whose opinion Charles V was becoming altogether too powerful, sought to ally himself by marriage with France. Before remarrying he needed the pope to declare his marriage to Catherine null and void. But the pope had been dominated by Charles V since 1527. He was therefore unable to annul Henry's marriage. The matter was made even more complicated by the Privy Council, who wished to see the English noblewoman Anne Boleyn, rather than a French princess, on the throne of England.

It was against this background, in the spring of 1533, that a French ambassador was sent to London. While there, the diplomat had his

portrait painted in the company
of his friend. Hans Holbein documents the execution of the painting on English soil by means of
the mosaic on which his subjects
are standing; the design is that
of the mosaic laid by Italian
craftsmen in the sanctuary floor
at Westminster Abbey. Today, the
floor is heavily worn and covered
by a large carpet. Only at the
carpet's edge is it possible to see
the original ornamental work.

Nobleman on a delicate mission
The French ambassador is Jean
de Dinteville. Born in 1504, he
resided at Polisy in Champagne.
As a manorial lord, he had the
right of jurisdiction; he was also
King's Proxy at the provincial
capital of Troyes, an office held
by his father before him. Jean de
Dinteville did not belong to one
of the great noble families of the
land, nor was he one of the great
historical figures of his time.
He was, however, an archetypal

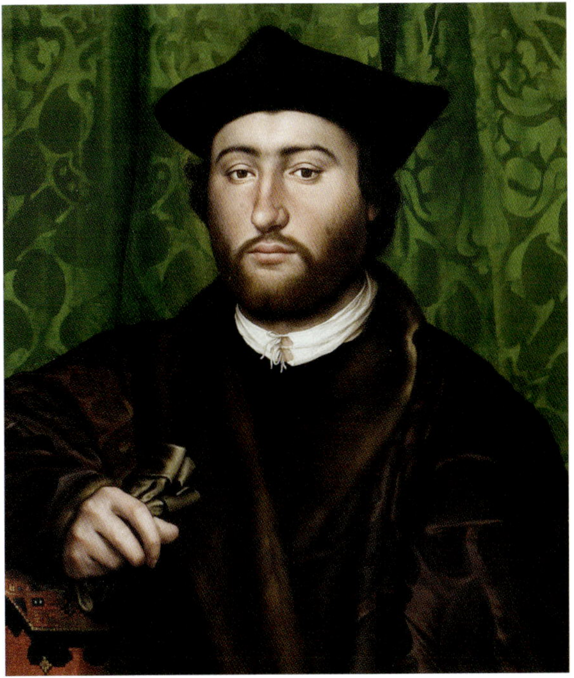

Renaissance nobleman: a humanist with an interest
in music, painting and the sciences. He was active
in the king's service, and dependent on the king's
goodwill. His greatest gift to posterity was his decision to have himself portrayed with his friend by
Hans Holbein.

The artist portrays the nobleman with the Order
of St Michael hung on a long golden chain around
his neck. This was the French equivalent to the
Spanish Order of the Golden Fleece or the English
Order of the Garter. The 16th-century royal orders
had nothing to do with the orders of the late Middle Ages, brotherhoods dedicated to a way of life
combining monastic and chivalric ideals. Instead,
they were a means of endorsing the allegiance of a
loyal subject, awarded to capable men in the hope of
ensuring their devoted service to the throne. Their
prestige derived partly from their limited membership. There were only 100 holders of the Order
of St Michael at any one time.

Francis I, the French king, had sent Jean de
Dinteville to London for the first time in 1531.

In the spring of 1533, he was sent to London again,
for in the meantime, the alliance between the two
countries had become even more confused. Henry
VIII had secretly married the pregnant Anne Boleyn
in January, though the pope had not yet annulled
his previous marriage. Francis I offered to use his
influence in the Catholic Church on Henry's behalf.
A meeting was arranged between Clement VII and
Francis I; but Henry procrastinated. He had the
Archbishop of Canterbury declare his old marriage
null and void, thereby encroaching upon papal
rights. He obstructed negotiations between the
French king and the pope. On 23 May 1533, Dinteville informed his master by letter that he had asked
Henry VIII "if it should please him to make a secret"
of the archbishop's decision, "so that our Holy Father
is not informed of this matter before Your Majesty
speaks to him of it. He replied that it was impossible
to make a secret of this, and that it must be made
public even before the coronation."

Anne Boleyn was crowned at Westminster Abbey
on 21 June. High honours were conferred upon

the French ambassador during the festivities that followed. In the meantime, however, the subject of negotiations between Dinteville's sovereign, Francis I, and the pope had changed: the French king now sought to marry his son to the pope's niece. His aim was to win over Milan. Henry's interests were forgotten. There was therefore little left for Dinteville to do in London. He left on 18 November 1533.

Dinteville was present in London not only for Anne Boleyn's coronation, but also for her execution. He was entrusted with three further diplomatic missions to England, before his family fell into disgrace. Apparently, his three brothers had plotted against Francis I. Jean de Dinteville died, aged 51, at Polisy. Before his death, he conducted renovations at his castle, employing – like the English kings and Francis I – Italian craftsmen to execute the work. A tiled floor in the Italian style exists at Polisy to this day. Holbein's painting hung at the castle for many years. Today it is in London's National Gallery.

A pious man fears for the Church

Unlike his worldly friend, the bishop does not hold an ornamental dagger in his right hand, but a pair of gloves. His arm rests on a book, on whose fore-edge part of a sentence may be deciphered: aetatis suae 25. If we add the word anno, the sentence, rendered into English, reads: "in the 25th year of his life". Dinteville's age, incidently, is written on his dagger. Facts like this helped identify the figures. The bishop was Georges de Selve.

As can be expected from a representative portrait of this kind, the subjects' faces are almost expressionless. Without their different styles of beards, the two friends might even look quite similar. Their eyes, on the other hand, are distinctive. Those of the bishop are smaller, with their pupils more heavily shadowed by the lids. Accordingly, the bishop does not appear to concentrate quite so intently on his immediate surroundings as the worldly ambassador. A similar distinction may be made in respect of their dress and bearing. Dinteville's puffed up fur makes his shoulders twice as wide as those of his friend. The diplomat wears his fur coat wide open; the clergyman is holding his coat so that it completely covers his body. The life of one is more outward going, the other's more introspective. Their different personalities allow Holbein to characterise two castes: *robe longue, robe courte*. Georges de

Selve's father, president of the Parlement de Paris, had been rewarded for his many services to the crown by the bestowal of a bishop's fief upon his son. Georges, then aged twenty, was made Bishop of Lavaur in the southwest of France. Although the minimum age for this office was 25, a dispensation from the pope rendered exceptions possible. These were frequent enough. Bishops who were too young for office received an income and title, while their clerical duties were performed by priests.

Even after Georges de Selve was permitted to take up ecclesiastical office, he spent most of his time outside his diocese. In the autumn of 1533, following a private visit to London, the French king sent him as an ambassador to Venice; later, he was entrusted with a mission to the pope in Rome, and then to Charles V in Madrid. In 1540 de Selve requested to be relieved of his offices for reasons of health. In April of the following year he died, aged 33.

Georges de Selve's writings bear testimony to his piousness. He saw the solution to the problems of his time, including those of a worldly nature, in a total regeneration of religious life. He criticized not only the condition of the Church, but also the selfish machinations of kings and princes. De Selve evidently had some sympathy for Luther's endeavours as a reformer; he nevertheless opposed the division of the Church. In all probability, De Selve was France's delegate at the Diet of Speyer in 1529, holding a great speech there in favour of confessional reunification.

Holbein refers to the notion of reunification by means of a hymnal lying open on the lower shelf. The book is neither French nor English, but the German Johann Walther's *Book of Hymns*, printed at Wittenberg in 1524. The book lies open at two of Luther's hymns: "Kom Heiliger Geyst Herregott" and "Mensch wiltu leben seliglich". The first is a German translation of "Veni Creator Spiritus", the second points to the importance of the Ten Commandments. In content and tradition both are good "catholic" texts, emphasizing the common ground between the new Lutheran and old Roman Catholic standpoints.

Central role of mathematics

The figures portrayed in 16th-century double portraits are usually shown close together. Not so Dinteville and De Selve. Holbein sets them as far apart as possible, placing them right at the edges of

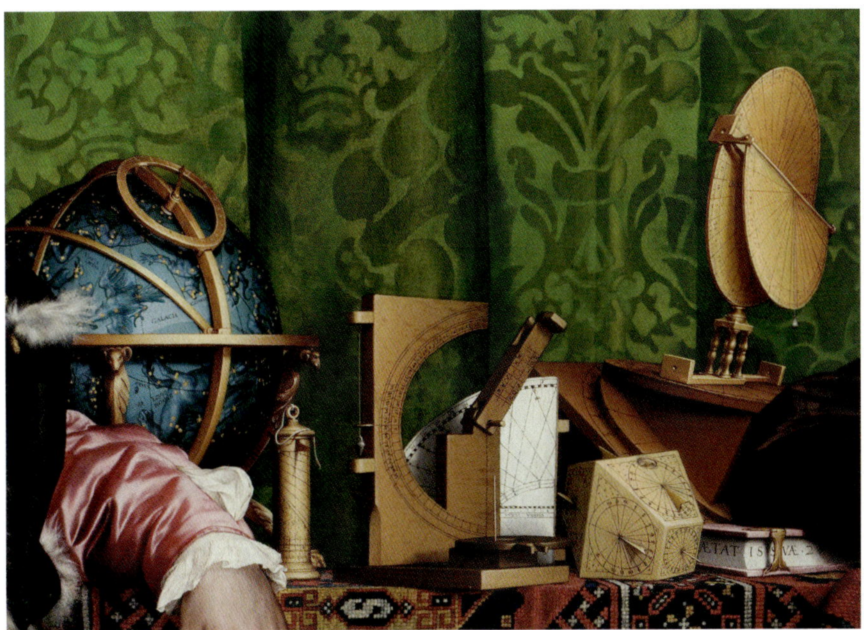

the painting. Between them, a plain, two storeyed cupboard displays a large number of books and instruments. It is almost as if Holbein wished to indicate that the bachelors' friendship was based on a common interest in natural science.

All of the instruments are linked in some way or another to applied mathematics. On the left there is a celestial globe; next to it, a cylindrical sundial, or shepherd's timekeeper. There are several sundials on the faces of the polyhedron; these were used for travel. Then there are two different types of quadrant, and on the lower shelf a small, portable globe, a level, and a compass lying under the neck of a lute. Music, too, was considered a mathematical art at the time. The tubes probably contained maps.

It might seem strange to us today that a display of instruments of measurement should be considered fitting attributes for a diplomat and a churchman, but it would not have seemed so at the time. Both men had been to university, where mathematics had become one of the most important academic disciplines of the Renaissance. This contrasted with the Middle Ages, when a religious explanation of the world had been considered more appropriate

than the study of natural sciences, and mathematics had consequently fallen into neglect. However, as times changed, scientists began to search once again for laws of mathematics and physics which would make it possible to explain how the world functioned. Even painters occupied themselves with the study of mathematics. In his *Instructions for Measurements taken with the Level and Compass*, Holbein's compatriot Albrecht Dürer had celebrated geometry as the true foundation of all painting. Perhaps the inclusion of these two instruments in Holbein's painting was a reference to the older artist's work.

The level is inserted between the leaves of a book, which, like the *Hymnal*, has been identified: *A sound instruction in all calculation for merchants, in three volumes, including useful rules and questions*. This was a textbook on the principles of calculation in business, written by Peter Apian, a university teacher at Ingolstadt, and printed in 1527. Apian begins with the fundamental operations of arithmetic and guides his reader via a series of steps to the extraction of square roots. With the aid of practical examples, he shows how silver value equivalents

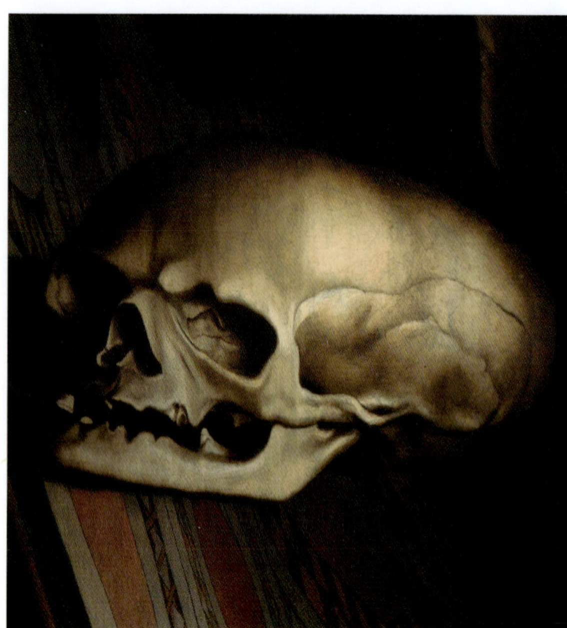

Death concealed in a puzzle

Everything in Holbein's painting, whether persons or things, is represented more or less realistically, with one exception: the skull suspended above the floor. At first glance it is hardly identifiable. It is only recognizable as a skull when seen from the right or left edge of the painting, and only when it is viewed through a lens which alters its proportions altogether does the image become quite distinct.

Anamorphoses, or distorted images of this kind, were a well-known trick at the time. They were usually applied to portrait drawings, and were achieved by means of a ruler and length gauge, that is by the use of mathematical instruments. First, the artist would draw the contours of a normal portrait, over which he would then draw a grid of lines. On a second sheet of paper he would distort the grid, squashing it flat in one direction, and exending it in the other. He then transferred the portrait to the dimensions of the corresponding grid squares – a mathematical picture puzzle.

There is yet another skull in the painting: a very small one set in the brooch on Dinteville's beret. The double appearance of the skull cannot be put down to chance; Holbein's painting is too well thought out, its effect too precisely calculated. Their meaning may become clearer if we consult two paintings by Fra Vincenzo dalle Vacche, painted around 1520 for a church in Padua.

The paintings do not contain anamorphoses, nor do they even contain figures; however, like Holbein's painting they show a number of different objects on shelves. One of the paintings, entitled *The Vanity of the Worldly Power of the Church and Laity*, shows a bishop's staff, a crown, an hourglass and a skull. The objects shown in the other painting, entitled *The Vanity of Science*, are a celestial globe, a sextant, a mathematical textbook, a sheet of music and a viola with a broken string. Holbein's lute also has a broken string. His own arrangement of instruments seems deliberately to combine the effect

can be converted into gold value, or how to convert currencies. Then come the "useful questions", which are not much different from those used in schools to this day: "A messenger leaves Leipzig and takes 18 days to reach Venice; another messenger leaves Venice at exactly the same hour and takes 24 days to reach Leipzig. The question is: how many days pass before they meet?"

The globe behind Apian's book has been attributed to Johannes Schöner of Nuremberg. Holbein himself came from Augsburg, and it may be supposed that the objects from southern Germany which are exhibited in the painting were introduced by the artist rather than the patron. However, Holbein has altered Schöner's globe to suit Dinteville's wishes. This is evident from a comparison of the names on the painted version with those on the original. They both have about 100 names in common, but there are also 20 names which appear on Holbein's copy only. These names all have some bearing on the lives of Dinteville and the members of his family: Burgundy, Avern, or Polisy, for example.

of the two Italian paintings. The common theme is vanity, or *vanitas*.

The notion of *vanitas* had wider connotations at the time than it does today. It meant blindness towards the most important things in life; also, the futility of human endeavour. A vain person forgets all too easily that he must die. A vain person believes that science can give him knowledge of the world. In a pamphlet in Latin in 1529, shortly before Hans Holbein executed his painting, the German writer Cornelius Agrippa complained of the "uncertainty and vanity of all art and science". Art and science, he continued, "are nothing but the laws and imaginings of human beings"; the truth, on the other hand, is "so great and free that it cannot be grasped by the musings of science, but by faith alone …"

We must conclude that Holbein's painting is not merely a double portrait. At first glance, its subject seems entirely worldly, entirely temporal: the official portrait of two young men surrounded by instruments of scientific and mathematical research. Even the composition of the painting, with its emphasis on powerful horizontals and verticals, seems arranged according to mathematical principles. Only the anamorphosis, apparently floating diagonally through the picture, contradicts this regime of calculated rectangularity, giving the work an aura of contemplation and suggesting the presence of some hidden commentary on human affairs. After comparing the painting with Agrippa's text, or with paintings like those by Vincenzo dalle Vacche, one might conclude that its message was the vanity of art, science and high rank. In order to make such a statement, however, Holbein need not have disguised the skull. He therefore seems to be saying that study of the arts and sciences need not be vain at all. On the contrary, it may lead us to a deeper, more comprehensive appreciation of the world. Indeed, it is sometimes only by scientific means that we can make visible the presence of death behind phenomena, behind the pleasing appearance of things. That, after all, is what the painting achieves.

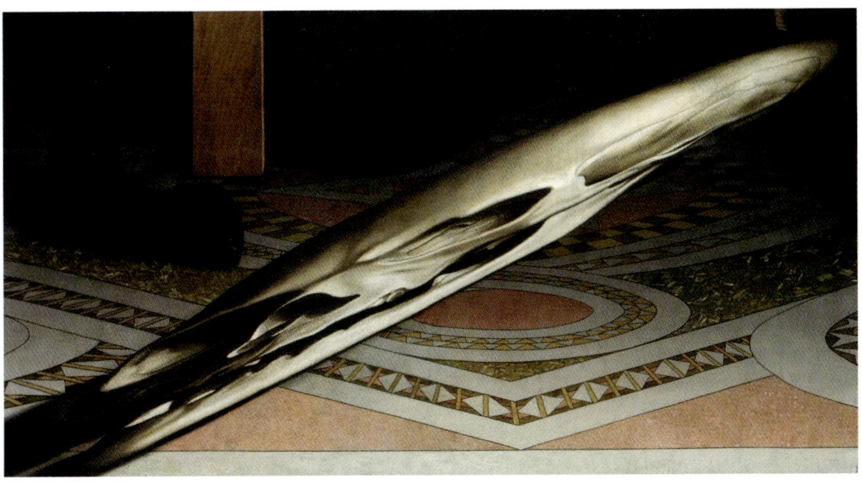

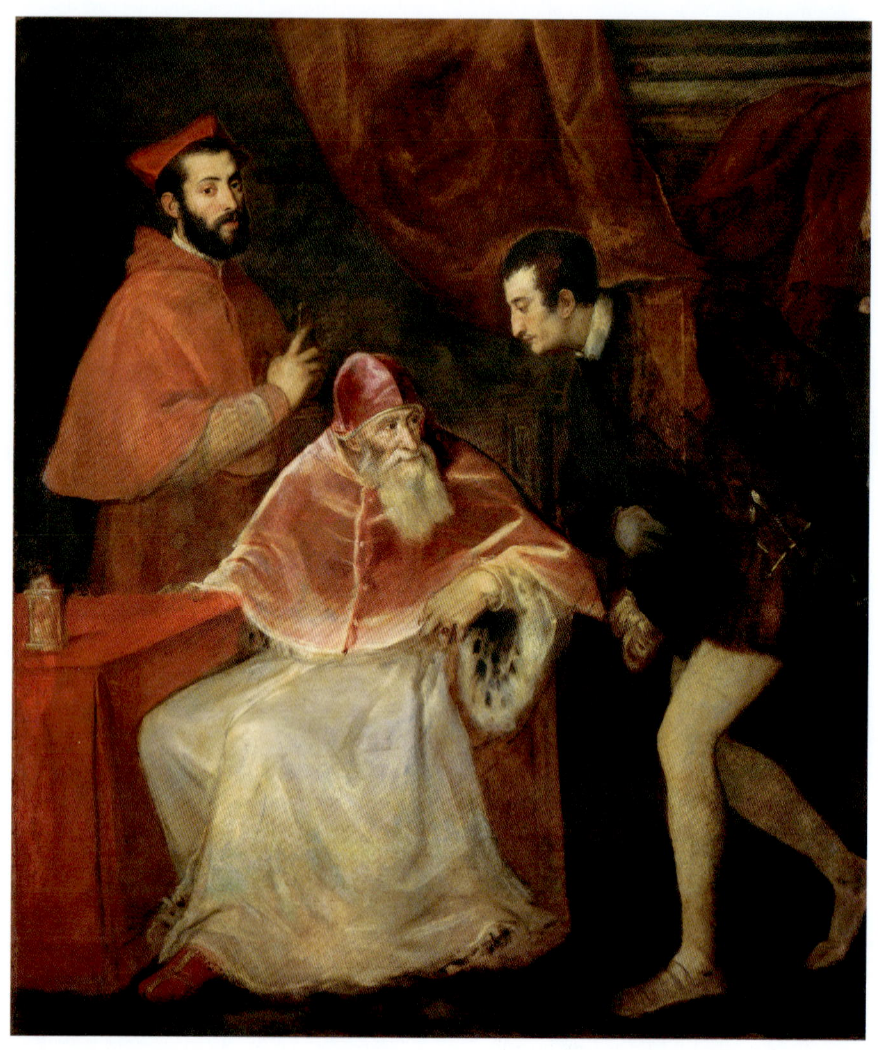

Titian (1488/1490–1576)
(real name Tiziano Vecellio)

In the end the artist, too, was cheated

Pope Paul III and his Grandsons, 1545
200 x 173 cm, Naples, Museo Nazionale di Capodimonte

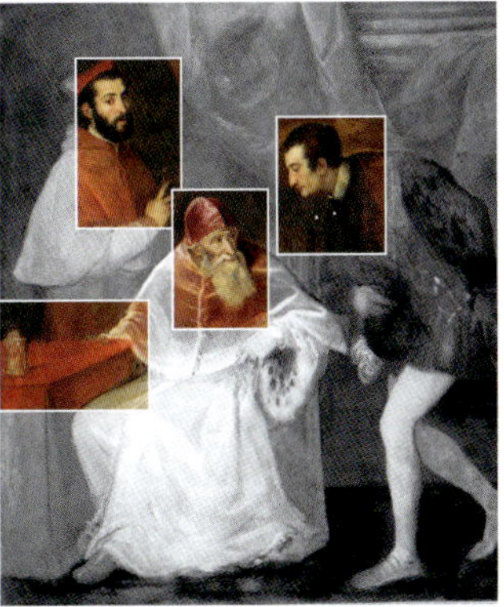

When Titian left Venice in the autumn of 1544 to travel to Rome, he was around 55 years old. It was only with reluctance that he said goodbye to his home, his workshop and Venice itself, whose lagoon made it well protected against attack.

Tiziano Vecellio (born between 1488 and 1490, died 1576) was at that time regarded not only as the most famous painter in Venice, but also as the most outstanding portraitist in southern Europe. Princes in particular valued his ability to ennoble individual characteristics with ceremonial dignity. Charles V, Holy Roman Emperor, preferred Titian above all other artists when it came to having his portrait painted. He made the artist a count and a member of the imperial court, and promised him an annual pension – even if it usually wasn't paid.

The long standing dispute over who held the highest rank in Europe – the Holy Roman Emperor or the Pope – also extended at times to the issue of who had the best artist in his employ. Charles had already been painted by Titian when Paul III, a member of the Farnese family, ascended the papal throne in 1534.

The Farnese naturally wanted to engage the artist's services for themselves. They knew Titian didn't like travelling; on the other hand, it was beneath their rank to visit him in his Venice studio. So they established preliminary contact with him via a child: they sent the Pope's grandson, twelve-year-old Ranuccio Farnese, who was studying in nearby Padua. His portrait today hangs in the National Gallery of Art in Washington.

That was in 1542. The contact had been engineered by Cardinal Alessandro Farnese, who appears standing behind the papal throne in *Pope Paul III and his Grandsons*. He asked Titian if he would like to move to Rome and enter the full-time service of the Pope. The artist declined. In 1543 the cardinal invited him to Bologna, where Paul III was meeting Emperor Charles V. It was here that Titian executed his first portrait of the Pope. This was followed by an invitation to come to Rome at least for a few months. The Venetian agreed.

Two factors prompted Titian to accept. Firstly, although already an old man by the standards of his day, he had never been to Rome or the far south and had thus never seen Italy's Classical architecture, ruins, mosaics and sculptures with his own eyes. He was a Renaissance artist who had not had

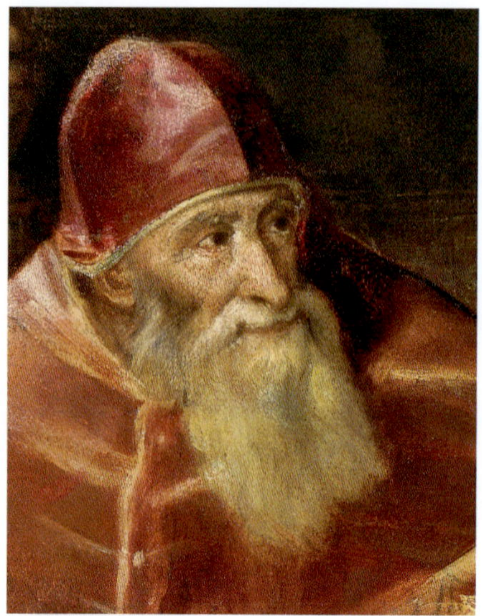

the obligatory exposure to antiquity. He had been offered several invitations to work in Rome, but had never accepted – perhaps because he was afraid that the works of the great masters would throw his own ideas on art into disarray. Now, however, he felt secure enough in himself. He is said to have spent his first few weeks doing nothing but gazing in wonder at the remains of Rome's Classical culture.

The second factor prompting Titian's trip to Rome was his paternal desire to help his own family. His son Pomponio had embarked on a career in the Church and was hoping to be offered a living at a monastery or church. Titian thought of the prosperous abbey of San Pietro in Colle, which bordered on some land he owned. Cardinal Farnese gave him reason to be hopeful; in Bologna, he implied that the matter had already been decided in Titian's favour.

A year later, in March 1544, Titian made enquiries on the subject but received no answer. Cardinal Alessandro Farnese was clearly aware how much the artist wanted St Peter's in Colle for his son – and used this as a sort of covert blackmail. In September 1544 the Venetian nuncio informed the cardinal in Rome that because of the benefice the artist was now prepared "to paint Your Honour's highly illustrious household in its entirety, right down to the cats."

The country which Titian crossed in autumn 1544 was fragmented and unstable, and consisted of cities and duchies which, although for the most part formally independent, in practice could only exist in alliance with a foreign power – in other words, with France or the emperor, resident in Spain. Armies of mercenaries were constantly marching through Italy; the Duke of Urbino, whom Titian visited along the way, even decided to supply the artist with a bodyguard for the last stage of his journey.

In Rome, Cardinal Farnese received the artist with great ceremony and had an apartment made ready for him in the Vatican palace.

Frail and full of energy

In order to hold his own against Spain and France and their Italian allies, the spiritual head of the Catholic Church needed soldiers, money and good connections. Without them, the Pope risked being steamrollered, even on religious issues, by his powerful international neighbours. Pious monks were thus considered unsuitable for such high office – the leader of the Papal States needed to be a man with experience of diplomacy and war and someone happy to use their cunning and power.

Paul III had no scruples on that score, as his own career reveals. He came from the lower aristocracy, from a family with no useful contacts within the Curia, but he had a very attractive sister. He sent her off "to have an affair with the Pope", as Martin Luther described it, "and was made a cardinal in return".

As a cardinal, Paul III also kept a concubine, with whom he fathered three sons and a daughter. This prompted Luther, in far off Wittenberg, to accuse him of being an "epicurean swine". In Rome, however, such behaviour was considered justified because it ensured the preservation of the family line. The latter's perpetuation – or even simply the plan to found a dynasty of rulers – provided a legitimate excuse for breaking the rule of chastity. Since his elder brother had only produced a sickly son who died young, the later Pope was obliged to make provision for the future. There is no evidence that he did so unwillingly.

There is also little evidence that he applied any of the Church's precepts to himself. For men such as him, a religious career meant first and foremost the opportunity to profit from the income of the Church. The Vatican possessed countless pastorates, abbeys, land holdings, woodlands, villages, towns, bishoprics and offices. They all brought in money and were awarded as sinecures to senior members of the clergy. As a cardinal, the later Paul III owned several bishoprics, even though he had not taken the higher orders necessary to be a bishop. So he appointed someone to represent him, paid this deputy a percentage of the takings and thereby put him in a position of dependency. Dependants strengthened one's influence and power.

When the Farnese Pope had himself painted by Titian with two of his grandsons, he was 77 years old and in a tricky situation. North of the Alps, Protestantism was growing and Germany's Lutheran princes had combined their military forces into the Schmalkaldic League. Charles V needed to fight the League and imperiously demanded financial support from Paul. At the same time, however, Charles called for the convocation of an ecclesiastical council which would agree reforms and not least remedy the deplorable state of affairs which Paul had unscrupulously exploited for his own benefit.

Quite what sort of man we are looking at in the present portrait Titian makes it difficult for us to tell. On the one hand, he shows us a shrunken old man whose shoulders are barely able to support his head upright, whose flesh is melting from his face and whose beard is unkempt. Yet on the other hand, the Pope seems full of dynamism: the fact that his body and head are pointing in different directions creates a sense of tension and movement. While his bent back and head jutting forward imply frailty, they also call to mind someone who is getting ready to pounce. The pontiff's eyes are wide open and full of energy, unlike those of most elderly people. This ambiguity, this blending of two aspects of the same person, lends Titian's pope an unsettling air.

How to stake a visible claim

Paul's son Pier Luigi produced four sons, the two eldest of whom – Alessandro and Ottavio – are included in the present portrait. They were called "nepots", an expression which meant both nephew and grandson, and which thus elegantly veiled the fact that the Pope was getting his picture painted with blood descendants he was not supposed to have.

Alessandro was appointed a cardinal at the age of fourteen. That was in 1534, directly after his grandfather's election as Pope. For the majority of Curia members, there was nothing improper about this:

at the end of the day, a Pope needed as many votes as he could get in the college of cardinals. Paul also wanted to be able to pass on the benefices that he had assembled over the previous years to a member of his own family. Protection of one's family, expansion of one's power and possessions – these were absolute priorities, not just amongst the Farnese, and not just in Italy. The Pope put his grandson Alessandro in the way of some thirty bishoprics.

Alessandro Farnese felt himself no more obliged to model his behaviour on the teachings of the Church than his grandfather. On several occasions he came close to giving back his cardinal's hat. He kept a mistress (and possibly several), fathered a daughter and, in his early years as papal ambassador to the French court, danced so elegantly that Queen Catherine de' Medici could still remember it 30 years later. He used the money that flowed so copiously his way to extend the Palazzo Farnese in Rome and fill it with antique treasures and contemporary works of art.

An X-ray of the canvas has revealed that Alessandro was originally positioned further to the left. It was probably he himself who persuaded

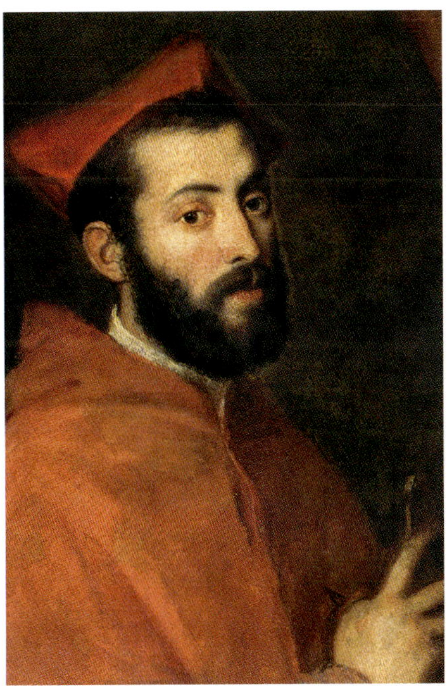

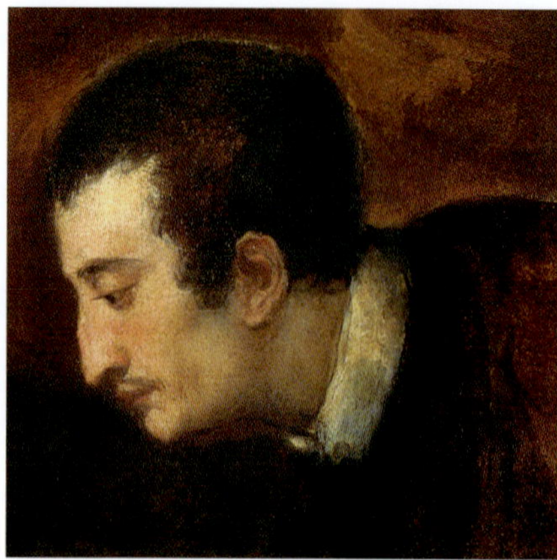

Titian to move him closer to the Pope and portray him grasping the knob on the back of Paul's chair with his right hand – as a sign that he was laying claim to the papal succession. His claim failed: he attended seven conclaves but was not elected. The Counter-Reformation demanded a different sort of person to the type represented by Alessandro, his grandfather and the earlier Renaissance popes from the houses of Borgia and Medici.

Alessandro is the only one of the three figures in the painting who is looking out at the artist – and like the figure of the Pope, the look he casts is difficult to judge. Is he staring intently at the man behind the easel, or gazing more generally out into space? Does Titian portray him as impassive, as the English art historian Harold E. Wethey believes? Or is the young cardinal looking to see whether the elderly man at the easel will swallow a Farnese's vague promises? It was Alessandro, after all, who lured Titian to Rome with the prospect of a living for his son, and the artist establishes with him, so it seems, fleeting, meaningful yet expressionless eye contact.

No upright grandson

Titian portrays Ottavio Farnese, the 21-year-old grandson, paying reverence to the Pope in the prescribed fashion. Persons approaching the Pope had to bow three times and then kiss the papal foot. Paul's red shoe can be seen at the bottom edge of the painting and signals how low the young man in his secular dress will have to stoop.

Ottavio had a lump on his nose, and the X-ray of the painting shows that Titian had not overlooked this feature. In the finished work, the bridge of Ottavio's nose is impressively straight, almost as sharp as a knife – an improvement common in portraits, but which lends the face a smoothness which, together with the lowered eyelids, rounded back and bent knees, seems somehow suspicious. Titian was a master of body language, and in Ottavio's smoothness and the snaking pose of his body the artist portrays – without disparaging caricature – a person who is not "upright".

Nor did the young man have much incentive to behave in a straight and upright fashion. Paul III deployed his grandsons like pawns in a political game; he used Ottavio to create a family alliance with Spain, marrying him at the age of fourteen to a daughter of Charles V. In 1545 the emperor needed money from the Pope for his campaign against the Protestants. The Pope gave it, but demanded in return the rights to the imperial cities of Parma and Piacenza, with which he wanted to establish a duchy for his family. He sweetened the deal by promising that Charles's son-in-law Ottavio would become duke and his own daughter duchess.

Thus far the interests of Paul III were identical to those of his grandson. The situation was complicated, however, by two members of the family who do not appear in the painting. One was Ottavio's father, Pier Luigi. He demanded the new duchy for himself. The Pope said yes, the emperor no: he let it be known that he would tolerate his son-in-law as duke, but on no account the latter's father. Ottavio's prospects of a dukedom were thus directly threatened by his own father. He plotted secretly with the emperor against his father and grandfather.

The second member of the family to question Ottavio's right to the new duchy was a younger brother. The Pope had been planning for several years to marry him to a French princess, for he wanted a family alliance not just with the emperor, but also with France, the second major power in Europe.

In order to make the marriage proposal more attractive, the Pope decided to promise the new duchy not to Ottavio, but to the future son-in-law of the French king. The split newly emerging between Paul III and the emperor made a change of allegiance necessary. Ottavio thus saw himself cheated of his future both by his father and his brother, and beyond them by the Pope. If Titian paints him as someone whose devotion masks only anger and hatred, he is simply portraying the situation as it really was. Two years later, Ottavio finally succeeded in becoming duke – after his father was murdered by one of the emperor's henchmen.

The wrangling over the duchy took place in the first half of 1545. Titian stayed in the Vatican palace until the end of May and must therefore have been well informed about what was going on. He must have been aware, too, that the cardinal was jealous of his younger brothers: as the first born, the new dukedom should have been awarded to him. Only with difficulty was Paul able to restrain him from taking action himself; he mollified his grandson by assuring him that, once Pope, he would have far more power than some duke of Parma and Piacenza.

The Pope's hand is missing

Strictly speaking, the Pope's hand should be visible on the far edge of the table, but Titian has not painted it. Nor did he sketch it in prior to painting; he seems to have worked for the most part directly with the brush. Michelangelo (1475–1564), who dominated the art scene in Rome, criticized the lack of *disegno*, or design based on drawing, in the Venetian's work, but praised his colouring. In *Pope Paul III and his Grandsons* this is centred – as so often in Titian – on red, which the artist explores in all its variety and in dramatic nuances.

The Pope's right hand is not the only thing missing; other parts of the canvas, too, have been primed but then taken no further. The painting is unfinished, and why work on it should have been abandoned has been the subject of much speculation. There is no evidence of any quarrel between the artist and one of his subjects. A letter that Titian later wrote to the cardinal rules out any suggestion of an open disagreement.

It would be quite understandable if Titian felt let down, distrustful and full of resentment towards the Farnese, for the anticipated benefice for his son never materialized. Although, in Rome, he received his board, lodging and an honorary citizenship, as far as we know he was not paid a fee. Nor was he paid for the other paintings he executed for the Farnese during the same period. It all went towards the bill for the abbey, so to speak, for which he would have to wait a while longer.

The Italian historian Roberto Zapperi has looked closely at all the conceivable reasons why Titian should have stopped work on the portrait, and concludes that the likeliest explanation is the shift in political allegiances which took place even as the painting was in progress. When the canvas was begun in December 1544, Spain was the Pope's preferred ally; when it was abandoned in May 1545, the ally was now France. Since large-format portraits (the present work measures 200 by 173 centimetres) also served as types of official statement, Titian's work was politically no longer opportune. And so the picture vanished unframed into the Farnese cellars in Rome. Over a hundred years would pass before it was honoured with a place on the wall.

Today it hangs in the Museo Nazionale di Capodimonte in Naples and is revered as a masterpiece of a portrait which both venerates and questions its dignitaries, as a masterpiece of colour, psychology, eye and body language. Deceit and hypocrisy were considered important qualities and were highly prized by Paul III. Titian had the ability to make them transparent: in the tranquil assembly of *Pope Paul III and his Grandsons* he conceals hints of the secret war of emotions and interests. He also points to the transience of hopes and dreams – the ink bottle that stood on the table has been replaced by an hourglass.

Vain, too, were Titian's own hopes. He never got the living he had expected to earn with this painting. Instead, his son was fobbed off with a small parish – a humiliating reward for Titian's hard work in Rome and a sign of autocratic arrogance. Another quality captured for posterity by Titian's brush.

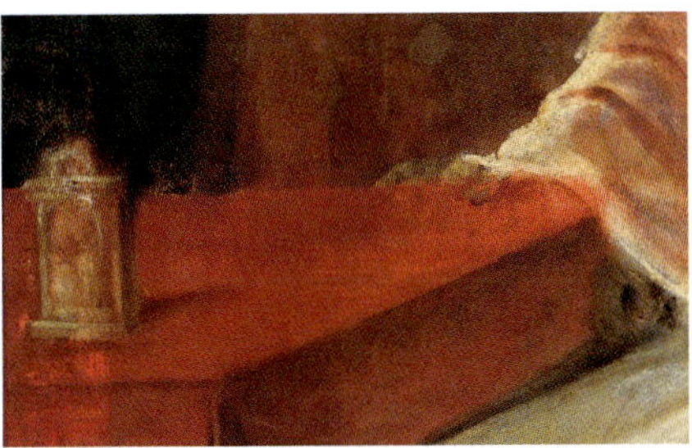

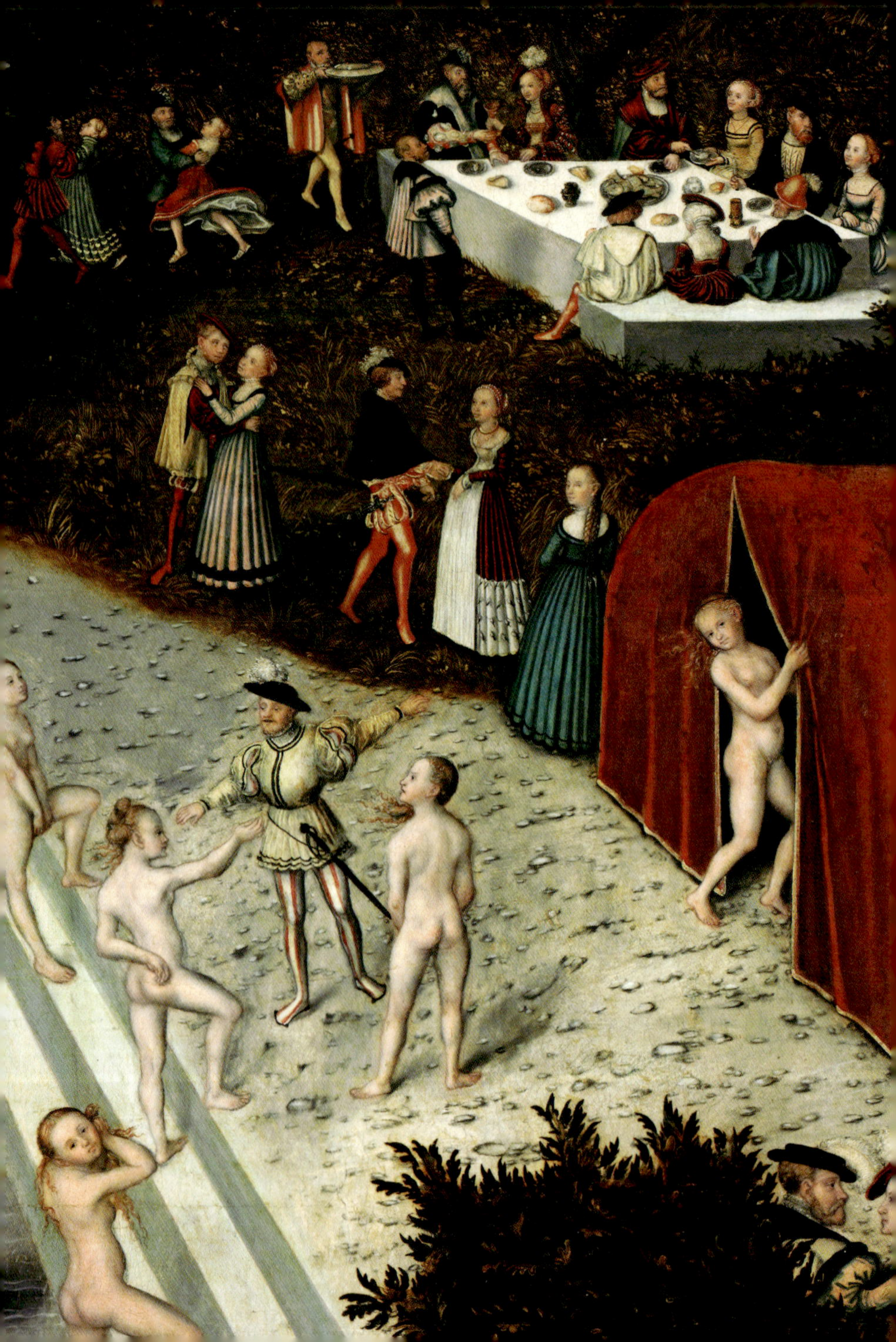

Lucas Cranach the Elder (1472–1553)

The miracle in the water

The Fountain of Youth, 1546
121 x 184 cm, Berlin, Staatliche Museen zu Berlin,
Gemäldegalerie

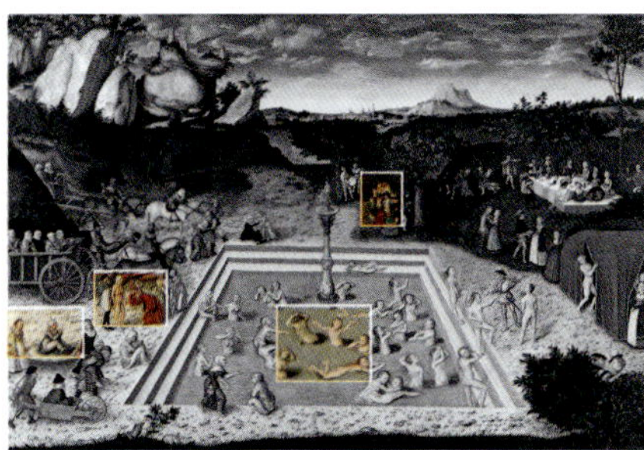

In 1578, a professor of medicine describing the
Swiss town of Baden and its curative waters noted:
"The open air pool, also known as the *Bürgerbad*
[public pool], lies beneath the clear skies." The pool
"is 30 feet long and 24 feet wide, so that over a hundred people can bathe in it at once." It was lined
with stone slabs "and contains a number of seats".

Not everything in Cranach's painting of the
legendary fountain of youth is thus invented. Such
pools existed and were open to the general public.
The professor continued: "In this pool everyone,
both locals and visitors, can bathe for free … On
Saturdays, in particular, the people come from
the town and the countryside in their masses, and
women and men seek to enjoy themselves and
improve their looks."

It was forbidden to carry weapons in the vicinity
of baths. When Cranach portrays the men in the
right-hand half of the picture with swords, he is
departing from contemporary convention. The fact
that only women are shown bathing in the pool is
another departure from 16th-century reality;
normally, both men and women sat in the pool,
occasionally separated by a wooden partition. Ladies
did not bathe entirely naked, but wore shifts that
were bound beneath the bosom and covered at least
the lower half of their bodies.

Therapeutic spas seem to have been popular
throughout the Middle Ages; civic and church
records occasionally mention the fact that such

and such a number of days were granted for a
trip to a spa. Poor citizens were awarded travel
allowances from the public purse. As for the rich:
in 1534 Count Palatine Philip travelled to Gastein
with 60 horses, stayed seven weeks and returned
home cured; in 1584 Elector August of Saxony set
off with 225 horses in order to bathe in the waters
of Schwalbach, which he had carried to a nearby
palace for him.

Such journeys were not always made on health
grounds alone. In Lucerne in 1566, a number of
canons "asked the Council for permission to go to
Baden with their wives to take the waters, something which was refused on account of the scandal".
The fact that they asked, however, suggests that such
pleasurable excursions with ladies were nothing out
of the ordinary.

Wealthier visitors to Baden did not use the
open air pool but went to guesthouses with indoor
baths. "Some of them visit three or four such baths
daily, and spend the large part of the day there
singing, drinking and – after their bath – dancing."
The indoor pools were surrounded by galleries from
which people could look down on the water below.
"Nothing can be more delightful to the eye or the
ear than when budding maidens or those fully blos-
somed into young women open their mouths to
sing, with the most beautiful open faces, like goddesses in their figures and conduct, their garments
floating on the water and each a different Venus."

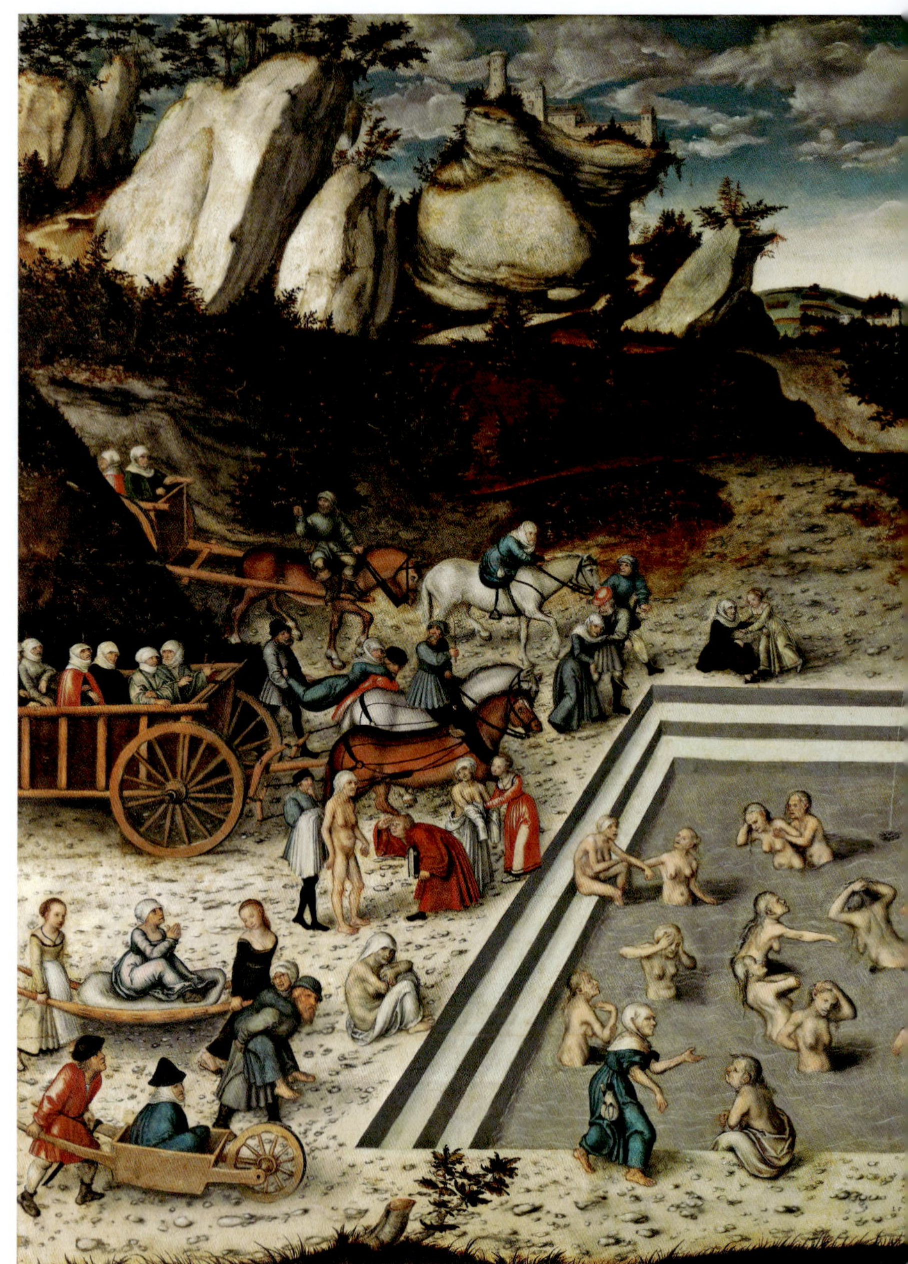

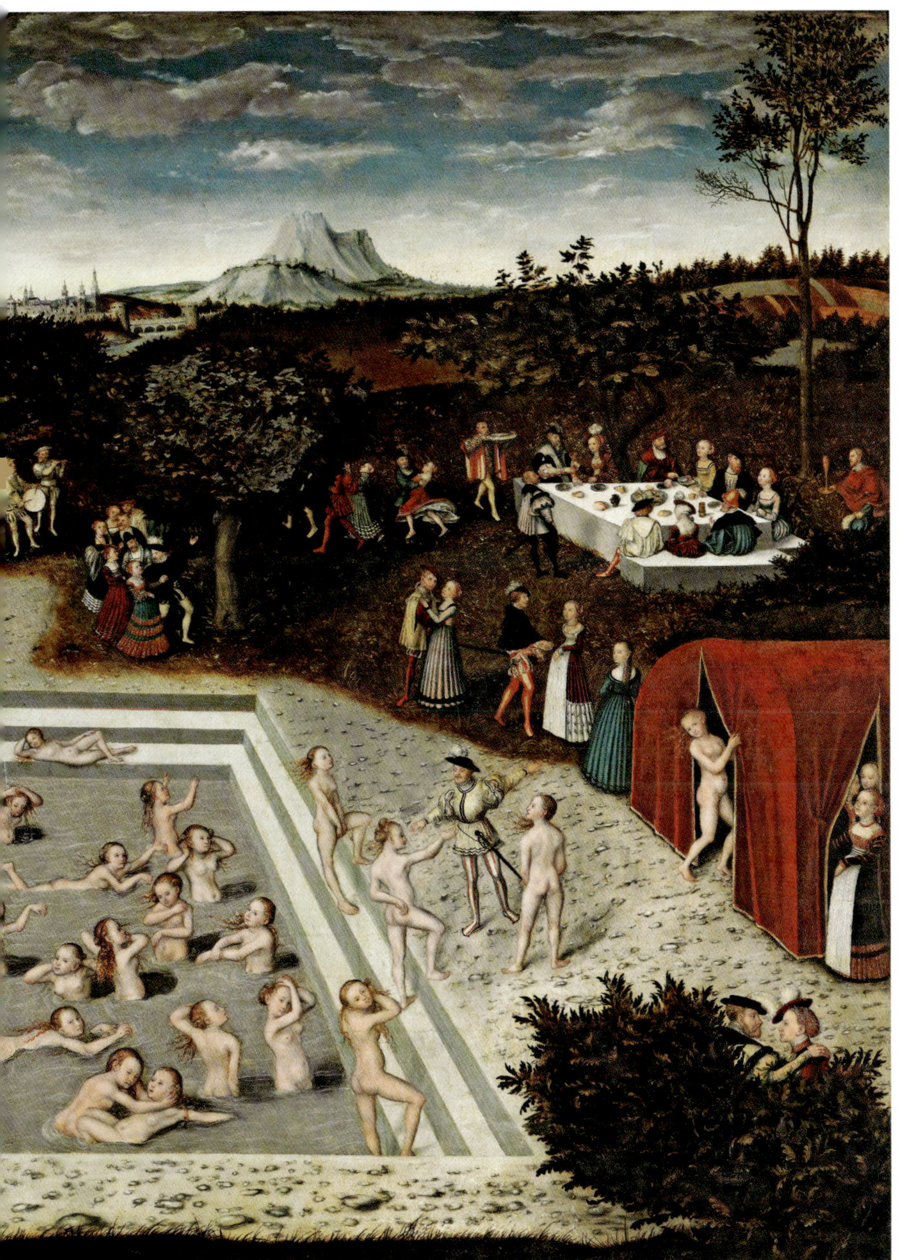

This enthusiastic description comes from a papal secretary who visited Baden in 1417 while attending the nearby Council of Constance. His references to dance and music were confirmed in 1573 by the doctor to Pope Sixtus V, who added that these were normal practice in all German baths. In the case of the dancers and musicians in the right-hand half of the present composition, Cranach is thus adhering to the reality of his day.

Praying and bathing

News sheets that have survived from the 16th century frequently relate to sightings of unexplained phenomena, such as calves with five legs, fishes with human faces, a hand coming out of the clouds, and fire in the heavens with streaks as long as a lance, first white, then blood red – "a sign from God sent to warn us and make us lead better lives".

Just as much in Cranach's mythical scene is actually taken from real life, this belief in miracles was also – however paradoxical it may seem – normal for the time. People took for granted the fact that extraterrestrial forces might directly intervene in earthly affairs at any time, be they sent from God or the devil. Luther really "saw" Beelzebub when he threw his inkpot. The distinction between the natural sciences and religion with which we are familiar today was not yet clear. Science was still in its infancy. This is particularly clear in the sphere of medicine. Anatomical studies of corpses were still rare, and medical treatment continued to be based on the classical theory of the four humours. If you fell ill, it was because these humours were out of harmony, and so you were bled. It is understandable that patients should trust God rather than medicine, and that they should hope for a miracle from Heaven sooner than a cure by their doctors – the elderly woman unable to walk is praying as she is carried to the water.

The mineral spas were amongst those who benefited from the primitive state of medicine. In 1568 one Martin Rulandus wrote: "Since no medicine has been discovered or invented up till now to preserve the health", there remained "only water and baths". He pronounced drinking mineral water and bathing in spas as a cure all, albeit with a shrewd proviso: "if you do it correctly". The beneficial effects, if they made themselves felt, were naturally ascribed to God. This emerges from many documents, including the testimonial which three men took with them to the Luthernbad baths near Willisau in 1583. This confirms that they have by no means left their wives and children to come and have a good time, but solely to be able to "enjoy this divine gift".

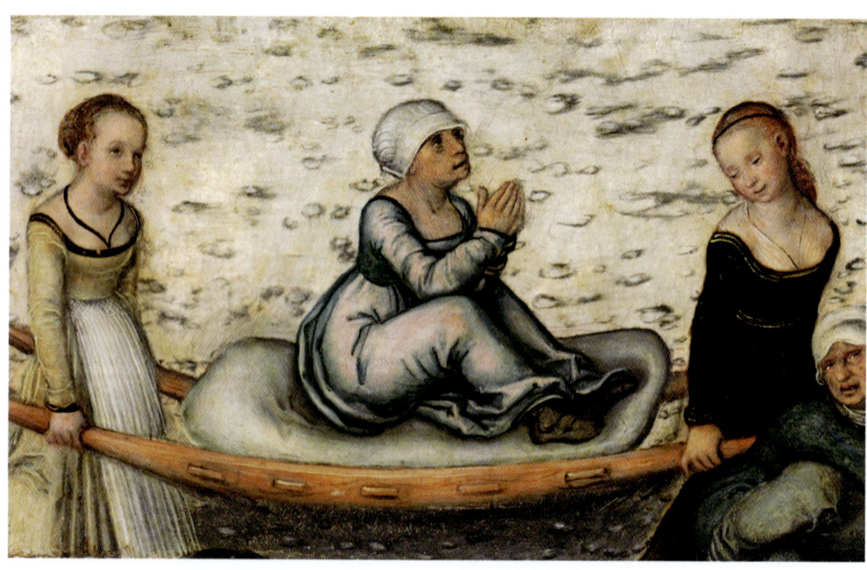

In the 16th century, a spa in the county of Spiegelberg (present day Bad Pyrmont) acquired an almost sensational reputation for its miraculous properties. In its waters, "Almighty God generously displayed his charity and goodness to the people every day". Around 10,000 people are supposed to have descended upon the spa in the space of four weeks; all the neighbouring villages were full to overflowing with invalids and the sick. The next year, however, almost no one came. The spa had lost its alleged power, as it had done 300 years earlier. In both cases it was God who had personally withdrawn his blessing from the waters, in order to punish certain people. The first time it was the Count, because he had charged money for the use of the spring. The second time it was the visitors, because they had fornicated openly in its waters.

Those who are healthy feel young

The waters of Spiegelberg-Pyrmont were supposed to heal stab wounds, gaping cuts and shot wounds, eye and ear complaints, all types of rash, and sprained or stiff arms and legs. Anyone who regains the use of their limbs and sense organs and comes away with a clear skin is going to feel not just healthy but usually rejuvenated, too. Every health spa is at the same time a little bit of a fountain of youth.

The existence of a spring that could really restore aged bathers to their youth, which could really turn fragile elderly people into vigorously dancing and flirting young men and women, was probably something that few people even in the 16th century thought likely, for all their belief in miracles. Even in those days, the fountain of youth belonged to the world of myth and legend: Jupiter is supposed to have turned the nymph Juventa into a spring that rejuvenated all those who bathed in it. In Norse mythology, one of the springs near the great ash tree Yggdrasil had the power to restore people to youth and beauty. In the medieval Wolfdietrich epic, the coarse Else is transformed by water into a lovely young woman. The motif appears again and again, indicating just how widespread was the desire to renew oneself through baptism in water, to undo things that had happened or to start life over again as a young person with the experience of old age.

It was a dream also dreamed by the German poet Hans Sachs, a contemporary of Cranach, who naturally turned it into verse. As he slept, it seemed

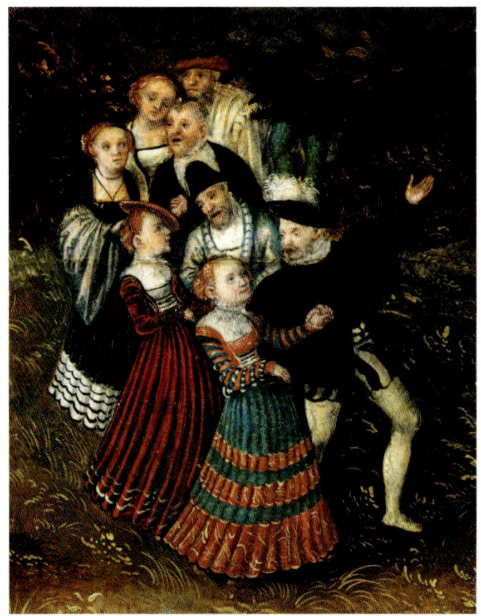

to him that he came to a large pool "of brightly polished marble". There were many people around him, coming "from every country far and near, in litters, sleighs and carts". They were "wrinkled, toothless and bald, trembling and itching all over". But after an hour "they leapt out of the round pool, beautiful, shapely, fresh, young and healthy, light-hearted and cheerful, as if they were twenty years old".

Hans Sachs was 62 when he composed the poem about his fountain of youth dream; Lucas Cranach was 74 when he painted his fountain of youth picture – if it was indeed he who painted it, and not his son, Lucas the Younger. It is a question that has yet to be resolved. Nor is it important. Most of Cranach's paintings are workshop productions on which his sons and assistants were also involved to a greater or lesser degree. Copies of his most popular compositions were regularly turned out to meet demand. Cranach saw himself as an artisan, as the head of a manufacturing team. Only at the start of his career did he initial his own works; later he used the workshop emblem of a winged snake.

The Fountain of Youth also bears the snake emblem, but as far as we know was only painted once. The decorative Venus and Cupid motif on the splashing fountain, however, left the workshop some thirty times in only slight variations. Lucretia holds her dagger to her attractive bosom no fewer than 35 times in Cranach's oeuvre. Cranach's workshop supplied the pictures that people wanted. Alongside impressively splendid paintings for churches and palaces, it produced pictures for private apartments: devotional scenes for the ladies, transparently clad young women representing Lucretia, Venus, nymphs or graces for the gentlemen. *The Fountain of Youth,* with its large numbers of young women lolling naked in the water, must also have been produced for a male client. In its style, the painting corresponds to the gently satirical poem by Hans Sachs. The only question that remains open is at whom its satire is directed: the women with their desire for youth, or the men with their desire for young women?

Young is beautiful and old is ugly
The small scene with the man in the red coat contains more than just gentle satire. He is bending down in front of an old woman with not a stitch on her body and ogling her sagging flesh. Whether he is intended to be a doctor or a clerk compiling an official register of miracles, what he is doing seems shameless, at least to us today.

In the 16th century, however, people had different ideas about what was embarrassing and what not. They lived closer together and knew each other more intimately. But even in those days, the aged body did not number amongst the usual subjects of painting. Although the Renaissance is celebrated as the era in which the human body was rediscovered, it was only the young body in its physical prime. The elderly remained covered up.

Young bodies were not simply discovered, however, they were also strongly idealized at the same time. The pattern this followed is clearly illustrated in Cranach's picture. The feminine ideal of beauty included a swollen belly and gently curving lines throughout. Bones were unsightly and were left out. Backbone, collarbone, hipbones, knees – like the rest of the body, they were all enveloped in a soft mass of flesh hiding any sharp edges. Some of Cranach's young women give the impression of being as boneless as mermaids. Accompanying these soft curves are long flowing locks, which Cranach portrayed as golden in all of his rejuvenated young women, in line with the ideal of his day. Just as edges and corners were avoided, so too were all sexual

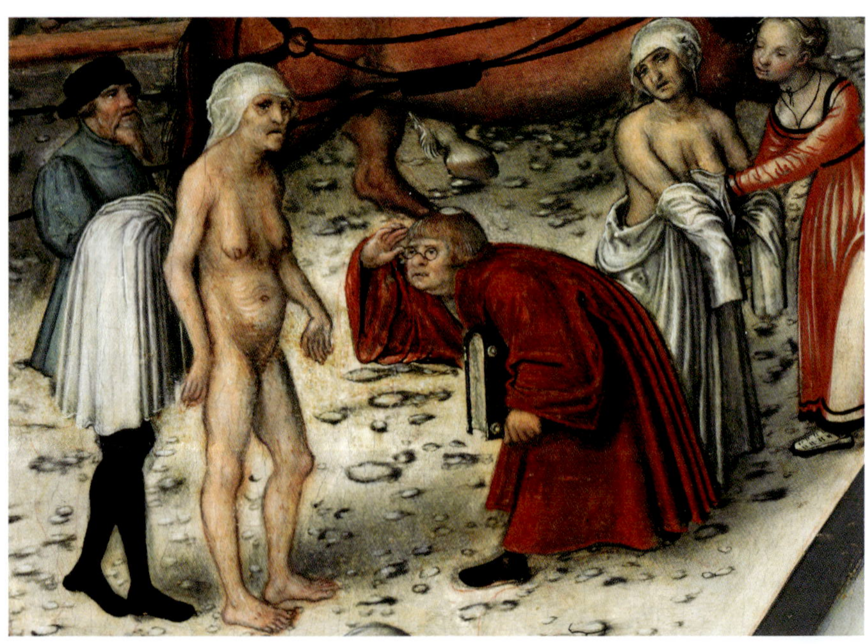

characteristics. It is true that the painters of the Renaissance vied with each other when it came to portraying a beautiful bosom; indeed, they virtually established a standardized bust – not too small, not too full, and always high. But the nipples and their areolae were only hinted at, and pubic hair was usually omitted. Nipples and pubic hair together provide the most important colour accents in the adult female body, however. They signal that it does not want to be appreciated solely as an aesthetic object. Leave them out, and the body is desexualized and at the same time translated into a prepubescent state; it appears childlike, innocent, an impression which the gay splashing about in Cranach's painting only serves to reinforce.

The bodies of the elderly women do not fit into the Renaissance ideal of beauty. Other painters confirm this insofar as they show naked old women, if at all, only as witches or – in the case of Dürer – as the personification of miserliness. The situation remains little changed today. It is true that, in the last hundred years, a few artists have portrayed the bodies of elderly people in a slightly kinder light than was the case almost 500 years ago. But the taste of the public in general – as evidenced above all by advertising – continues to uphold the cult of youth dating back to the Renaissance and antiquity.

The myth and the reality

Cranach's fountain of youth differs from those of other artists of his day insofar as only women are bathing in it. The men on the right clearly don't need to: they are all in their prime, smartly dressed and waiting simply for the next naked young woman to climb out of the water, get dressed and allow herself to be wooed. Wishful male superiority? A product of age-old male fantasy?

Not entirely. In the 16th century, this fairytale was not just about lust and its satisfaction, but about solving a practical problem. Young women were necessary to ensure progeny. An heir was vital, be it to run the farm, take over the workshop or beg for alms. In an era in which there was no state pension for the elderly, women of childbearing age had to provide the only form of security available – offspring.

This cost far more of them their lives than is the case today. They died in childbirth or, weakened by repeated pregnancies, were carried off by one of the many epidemics. In the population aged between

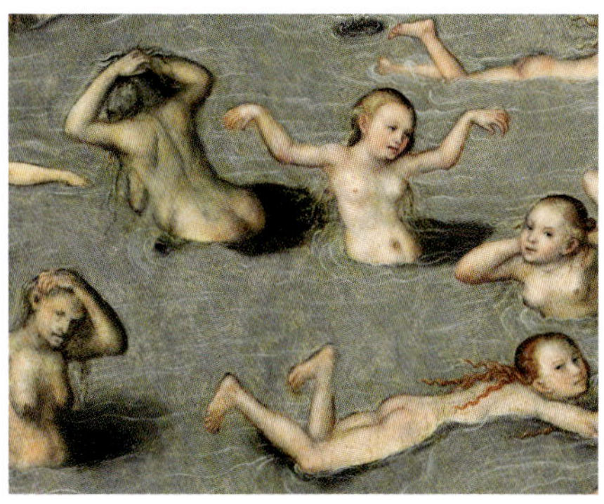

40 and 60, there were only two women for every three men. One man in three thus remained a widower or unmarried, unless he married a young woman in his advancing years. Seen in this light, the idea of rejuvenating some of the remaining elderly women and thereby boosting the numbers of the next generation of young women made logical sense.

The high mortality rate among women and the economical situation very often led to marriages between partners of very different ages. A widower with children couldn't carry on without a new wife; a farmer's widow could not manage her farm without a strong man. An apprentice would marry his master's widow and thereby inherit both his wife and his position. These marriages between young and old were a frequent target of satire. Hans Sachs wrote a poem about them in *Altweiber-Roßmarkt* (*Old Women's Horse Fair*) and Lucas Cranach painted the motif of the "unequal couple" some twenty times.

There is no trace of such mockery in *The Fountain of Youth*, however. The young women are met not by toothless old men, but by dignified gentlemen who to some extent suit them in age – a miracle probably attributable less to the God of the Bible than to the pagan deities Venus and Cupid, who stand and watch on top of the fountain near the centre of the painting.

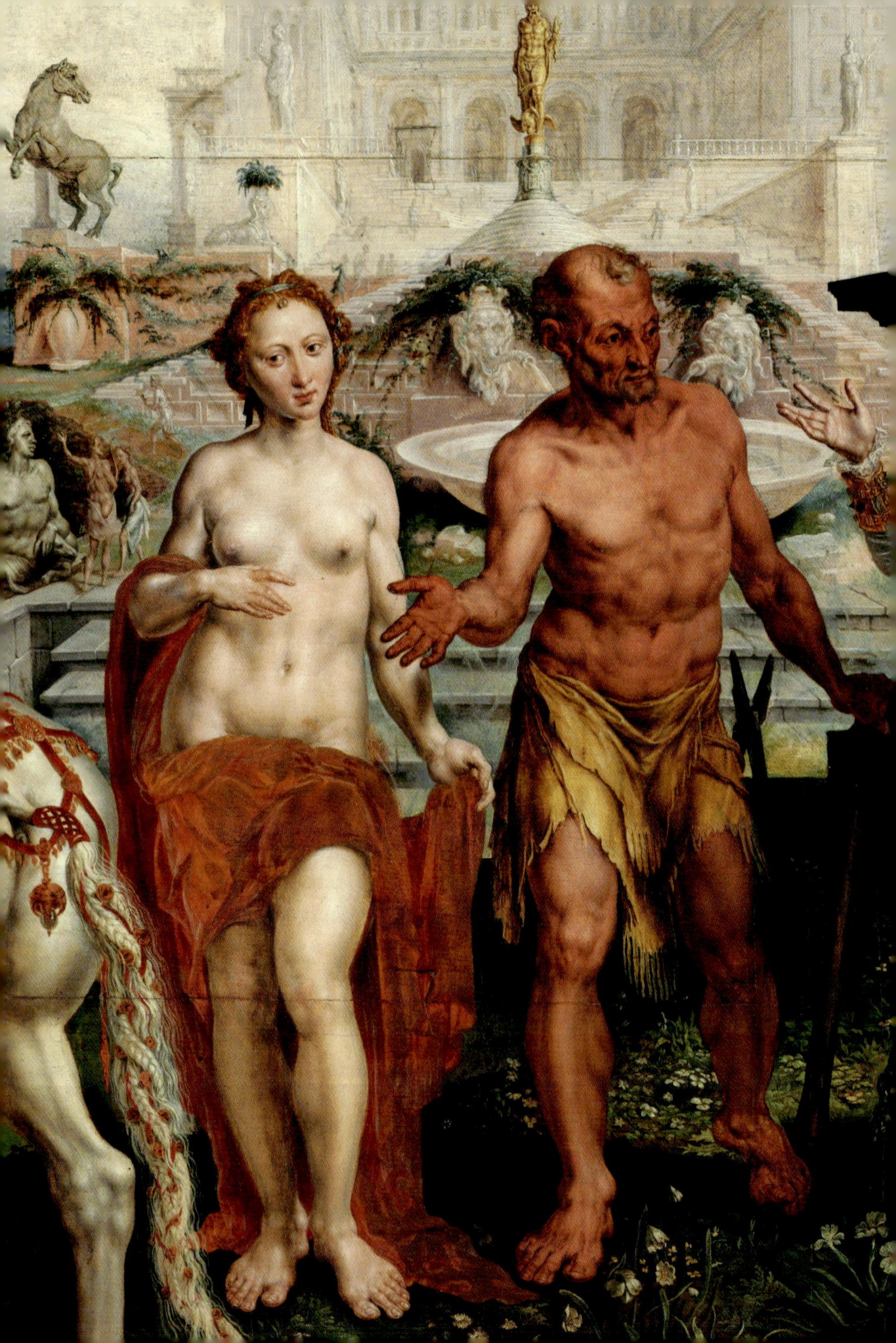

Maerten van Heemskerck (1498–1574)

A critic who spares not even the gods

Momus Criticizes the Works of the Gods, c. 1561
120 x 174 cm, Berlin, Staatliche Museen zu Berlin,
Gemäldegalerie

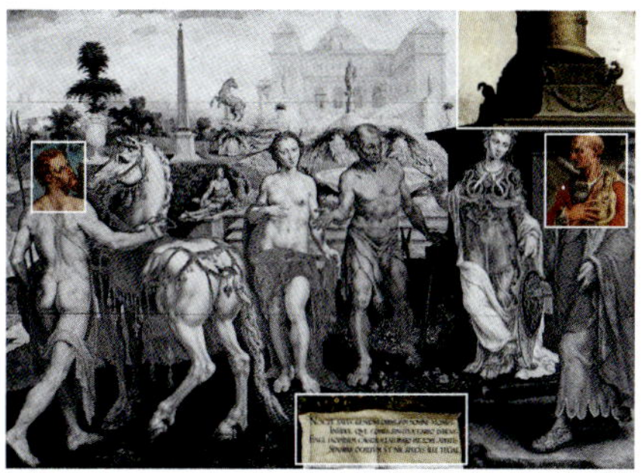

The people of antiquity and their gods loved competition. In the grounds of the Temple of Zeus in Olympia, the Greeks battled for sporting honours; on Mount Ida three goddesses asked Paris to judge which of them was the most beautiful. Less well-known is the competition between Pallas Athena, Poseidon and Hephaestus, not over physical prowess or beauty but over creative ability. Each was to construct or fashion an object – not all the same, so that these might be easily compared, but entirely according to his or her own divine fancy.

As arbiter they appointed Momus, a god known for his critical opinions. The Netherlandish artist Heemskerck paints Momus pronouncing his final judgement: standing on the left is Poseidon, recognizable by his trident and the shells that he has hung along the harness of the horse that he has created. In the centre, Hephaestus – his skin ruddy from the fire of his forge – gestures towards the woman that he has fashioned. Beside him on the right is Athena, the goddess of peace and wisdom, identified by her lance and her shield with the head of the Gorgon: she has designed the palace in the background.

All three are looking in the direction of Momus, who is arriving from the right.

The painter has permitted himself a few departures from the traditional version of events: Poseidon is in fact supposed to have fashioned not a horse but an ox, and Hephaestus a man, not a woman. But Heemskerck probably wanted a second female figure in his composition, and he was also a keen horse painter.

The final verdict must have surprised everyone. Momus declared of the ox that its horns ought to be below its eyes, not on its head, so that the beast could be more accurate in its aim; he lamented the lack of wheels underneath the palace that would be required should its inhabitants wish to relocate the building in order to get away from unpleasant neighbours. And he would have liked a grille window in the human figure's breast, so that everyone could see whether the person was lying or telling the truth. So no winner! What Momus meant by his criticism – to make fun of the gods with their childish whims or to invite them to improve the world – is a question that remains open.

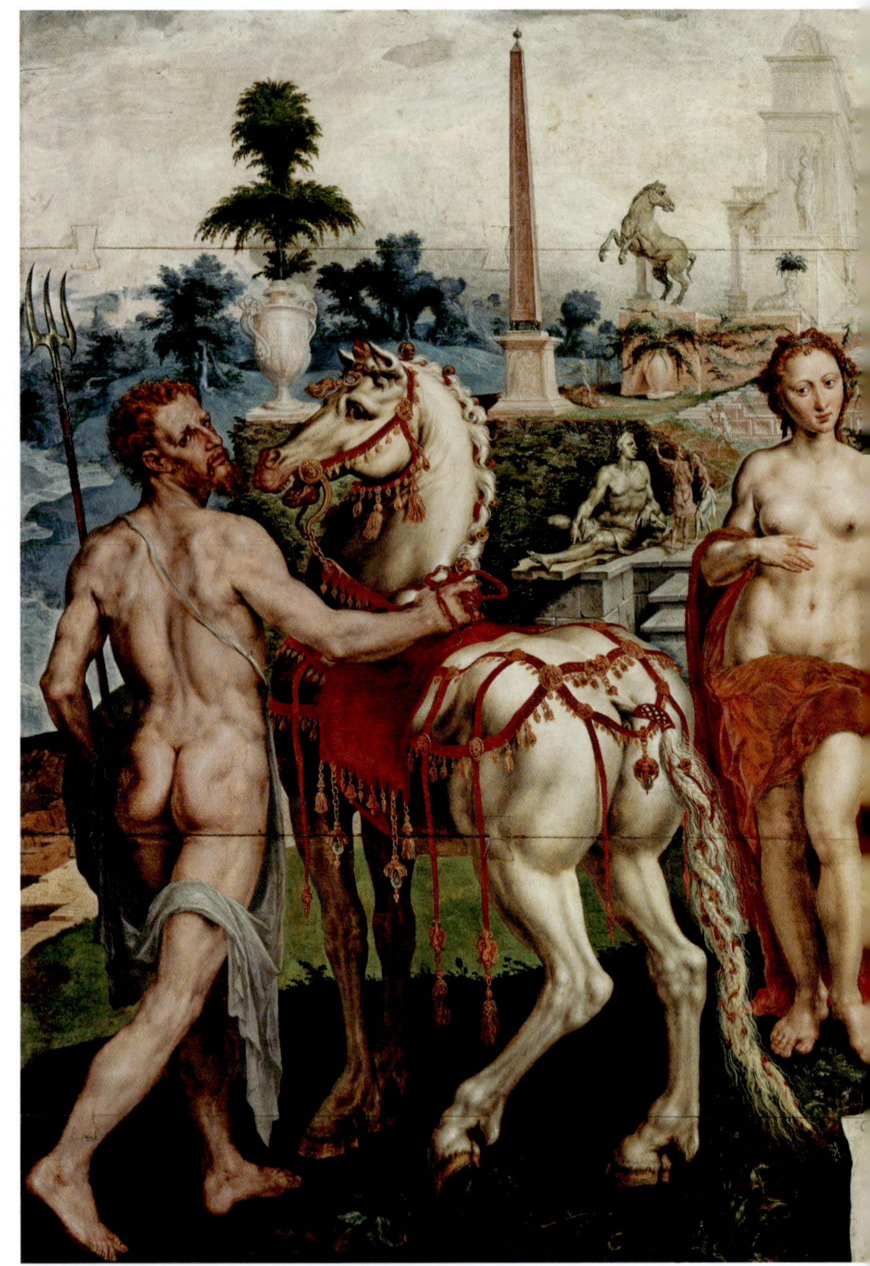

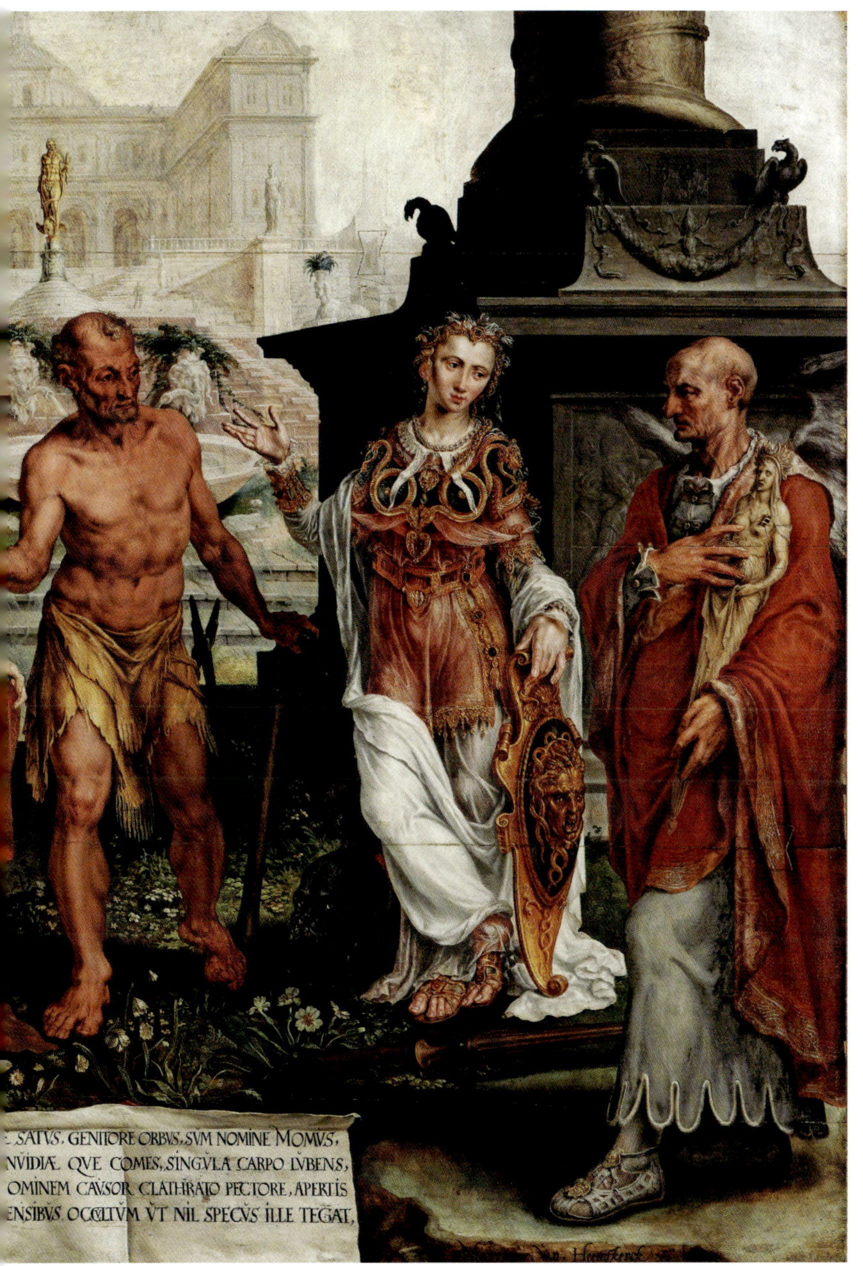
SATVS, GENITORE ORBVS, SVM NOMINE MOMVS,
NVIDIÆ QVE COMES, SINGVLA CARPO LVBENS,
OMINEM CAVSOR CLATHRATO PECTORE, APERTIS
ENSIBVS OCCVLTVM VT NIL SPECVS ILLE TEGAT,

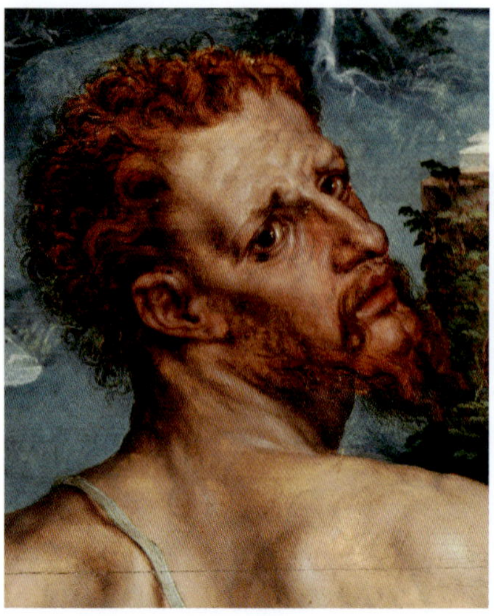

The artist plays Poseidon

The artist gave his own features to the face of Poseidon and thereby discreetly indicated that he, the son of a farmer, felt thoroughly at home in the world of the Greek gods. Born in 1498 in the Netherlandish village of Heemskerck, he was apprenticed at a young age to an artist in Haarlem, only to fetched back by his father, who probably needed his help on the farm. In order to show how unsuited he was to a life of agricultural labour, the son spilled a pail of milk. His father chased after him, ready to give him a hiding, but Maerten fled to Delft, which lay not too far away.

He trained under various masters and had his first successes with portraits and religious subjects. Portraits for the aristocracy and the rising middle classes, paintings for churches and monasteries – that was how artists earned their living in those days. Like the majority of his colleagues, he made his way to Rome, where a new form of art was being born. He copied the Italian painters of the Renaissance and studied the way in which they represented people in their pictures, how they rendered bone and sinew visible beneath the surface of the skin. Then he sketched the sculptures and ruins of Ancient Rome and built up a library of images that he would draw upon in later works. A selection from his extensive collection appears behind the main

figures in the present painting: the magnificent marble vase near Poseidon's head, the obelisk, the large horse rearing up on its back legs, the statue of Jupiter in front of the palace, the sphinxes beside the steps, the elephant headed figures behind the basin of the fountain, and the reclining statue with the Janus head. These or something similar can all be found in Rome even today.

The art and life of Maerten van Heemskerck were described by his younger compatriot Carel van Mander (1548–1606), who pronounced Heemskerck to be "very good at portraying the nude". He was to be reproached, on the other hand, for a "dryness in the figures that clings to us Netherlandish [artists]". Van Mander does not mention the *Momus* painting but may have had it in mind. This alleged "dryness" rests in the fact that the painter does not use light and shade. He renounces this usual vehicle of contrast and dramatization and relocates his gods from the sunny South to a rather dismal North. Van Mander was the first artist biographer north of the Alps and he included in his *Lives*, so it seems, everything that he was told. Back in the North, he tells us, Heemskerck married "a beautiful young girl" who died in childbirth eighteen months later. For a "second wife he took an old maid" who was neither beautiful nor clever, but rich. According to van Mander, the artist lived in constant fear "of being reduced to penury in his old age", which is why he frequently negotiated the payment of an annuity rather than the usual flat fee.

For the last 22 years of his life Heemskerck was a warden of St Bavo's, the biggest church in Haarlem. He died in 1574. The painter himself made sure of his posthumous fame: he bequeathed one of his properties to a foundation that provided a dowry for orphan girls who got married beside his grave. A certain amount continued to be paid out right up to 1787.

A Roman column in the garden of the gods

The column rising from the plinth on the right is one that the painter saw in Rome. It is Emperor Trajan's victory column – recognizable by the frieze, carved in bas relief, which ascends in a spiral around the column and which glorifies Trajan's victory over the Dacians. The column was built in AD 113. Heemskerck uses it to document the year in which he completed his painting: 1561. He has signed the panel at the bottom, on the stone slab on which Momus is standing.

Trajan's column undoubtedly numbers amongst Rome's most impressive monuments, but it bears no obvious relationship with the anecdote from Greek myth. Its inclusion makes sense, however, when the plinth is taken as a colour mass that provides a counterweight to the blue landscape behind Poseidon's head. Artists in those days employed bluish hues in their landscapes to convey the illusion of distance. In Heemskerck's painting, however, the blue-grey zone commences in the middle ground and is confined to one quarter of the left-hand side. An arbitrary decision, it would seem – but it was part of his method: Heemskerck paints a spatial collage made up of three sharply delineated zones, one dark, another in blue-grey and a third in diffuse yellow.

Viewed in its historical context, it might be read as a protest. The artists of the Renaissance had conquered space a hundred years earlier; they had succeeded in integrating human figures into a three-dimensional world in a visually convincing manner. Heemskerck was now destroying the ideals he had adopted in Rome.

He was not alone in doing so. Art historians group the various forms taken by this protest under the heading of "Mannerism". It arose not simply out of a surfeit of old forms. The 16th-century world picture had changed, for example the idea of the Earth as the centre of the cosmos. It is true that the Catholic hierarchy still clung to this thesis, but the counter thesis, according to which the cosmos was centred on the Sun, was quietly finding acceptance. Thus humankind on Earth was no longer motionless at the centre but revolved around the Sun. This new understanding rocked the existing consciousness and cut the ground, as it were, from under people's feet. The much vaunted spatial depth of Renaissance art, with its all ordering linear perspective, was devalued and cast into question by these findings.

The roof of the Catholic Church under which all Western Europeans had previously been united also collapsed during this period, in the century of the Reformation. A multitude of confessions sprang up which demanded a choice from the faithful, provoked conflicts and led to war and devastation. This was particularly true in the case of the Netherlands: first came the Lutherans, then the Anabaptists and finally the Calvinists. The Netherlands belonged to the Catholic Hapsburgs, however, who resided in Madrid. For Philip II, the reigning king in 1561, all non-Catholics were heretics and bad subjects. In order to keep a closer eye on them, he took steps to have great numbers of bishops installed and inquisition tribunals set up.

Heemskerck lived in Haarlem. In 1561, the year in which he painted his Momus scene from pagan antiquity, the city was given its own bishop for the first time in its history. In 1572 his successor was expelled by the people of Haarlem, in retribution for which the city was besieged by Philip's troops. Following its capitulation, 2,000 citizens are said to have been executed by the Spanish.

"Born of the night, I am called Momus"

The sheet of paper or parchment looks as if it has been slipped into the picture from below. Lines of text were common in engravings but somewhat rarer in paintings. The sheet reinforces the impression of a collage: the unnatural colours of the landscape are joined by the medium of the word and the impression of a stage.

The words are placed in the mouth of the main character: "Born of the night, I am called Momus. As the companion of jealousy, I love to criticize everything right down to the last detail. I argue that man should be created with a grille in his chest so that, for those whose eyes and ears are open, this cavity conceals nothing hidden." Actors liked to

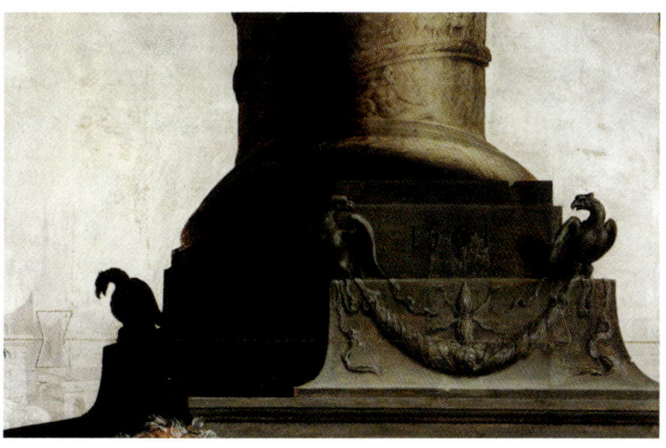

introduce themselves in this or a similar manner, and the arrangement of the main characters is also reminiscent of a stage performance: they stand side by side in a row, as if presenting themselves to an imaginary audience.

Over the course of history, painters and theatre artists have frequently cribbed from each other, served as sources of mutual inspiration and ultimately joined forces in stage productions. Theatre played an outstanding role in the 16th century, in a similar fashion to book printing. Both became leading communications media and reached a public whose intellectual nourishment had previously been handed down first and foremost from the pulpit. Now those who were interested were able to broaden their minds by reading and were introduced, through the comedies and tragedies of antique dramatists, to a picture of man that was virtually irreconcilable with that in the religious mystery plays of the Middle Ages. The book and the stage altered their consciousness in a similar way to television, computer and internet in our own day.

In the Netherlands, plays were put on by the grammar schools, which staged works in Latin as part of their students' education, and by chambers of rhetoric. These latter were civic associations independent of the Church and dedicated to language, philosophy and the sciences. In Haarlem, a prosperous city with some 18,000 inhabitants, there were two chambers of rhetoric. Perhaps the artist was a member. According to van Mander, Heemskerck's wedding celebrations included the performance of a comedy by the Rhetoricians. Whether they ever staged a play about Momus is unknown, but that tells us nothing, since in those days scripts were rarely preserved.

The popularity and importance of stage productions in the chambers of rhetoric is reflected in the lavish drama competitions that were held across the country. In the year in which Heemskerck painted his *Momus* and included the "monologue" in his picture, one such festival was held in Antwerp. It went on for a whole week and opened with a ceremonial parade involving some 2,000 participants and attendants, the majority in triumphal chariots with symbolic figures. This was followed by a succession of church services, banquets and fools' plays, and culminated in the actual competition. All the chambers of rhetoric had to perform a piece whose theme had been announced in advance. In 1561 the subject was: "What most awakens people to art" – in other words, after the entertainment and ceremony came a philosophical discourse delivered with the visual aid of theatrical figures.

Among the most popular of these dramatis personae were the gods and heroes of antiquity. Already familiar to the audience, they could be introduced in just a few lines. The Momus material would have suited itself well to a play about the point and pointlessness of criticism – a highly contemporary and explosive topic at a time when criticism signified first and foremost criticism of the Catholic Church. At this, however, the line was drawn. The authorities issued a warning to the Rhetoricians before their Antwerp meeting: any texts that "directly or indirectly insulted the Catholic religion or ecclesiastical persons" were forbidden.

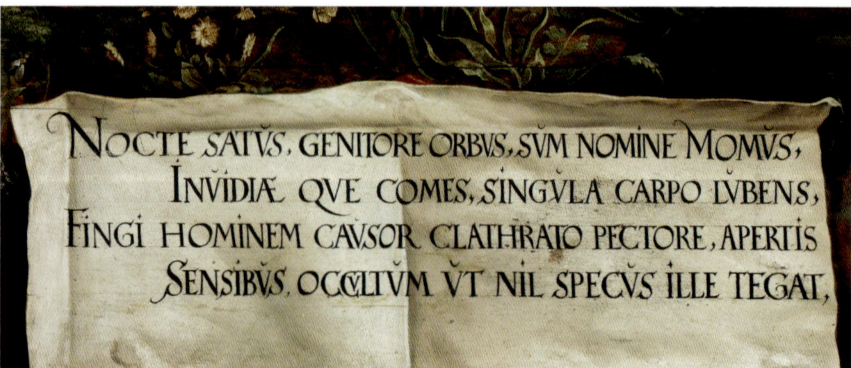

The fate of a critic

In another Momus episode, Aphrodite delighted the gods with her dancing. Everyone was happy – only Momus had a bad word to say. Her sandals, he complained, had squeaked. He was then "thrown out of Heaven and flung down to Earth, because his wisdom annoyed the gods and marred their happiness". Thus wrote Erasmus of Rotterdam (1469–1536), the great Netherlandish humanist.

On the one hand wise, on the other an irritant. This contradiction also emerges from the introductory lines in the painting, which associate criticism with jealousy and thereby defame it, but at the same time make a positive suggestion for improving human relations – a greater degree of openness. And so that the viewer can see what Momus wants, Heemskerck places in his arms a statue whose chest contains a barred but nevertheless open window.

Erasmus spoke in Momus's defence because circumstances had forced him into the position of a critic. The target of his attacks was first and foremost the Catholic Church – the pomp and ceremony of religious services, the worldliness of its monks and priests and their efforts to keep the faithful uneducated and dependent. At first Erasmus supported Luther in his efforts to reform the Church, but then they fell out. Luther wrote angrily that Erasmus was a "Momus, a real Momus, for he ridicules everything, the whole of religion and even Christ".

The accusation of ridicule is probably a reference to *In Praise of Folly*, a book that is still amusing to read even today in which Erasmus praises to the skies everything that he in fact wishes to castigate. It was an indirect assault in an epoch in which direct criticism could prove life-threatening. A disguised attack is also contained in his collection of adages compiled from classical literature, published in 1500. Through it, Erasmus offered a broader public an introduction to humanistic learning, to a world in which thoughts were directed not primarily towards Heaven but towards a dignified, peaceful life amongst men. Erasmus was still a leading light even in Heemskerck's day. The artist may have known Erasmus's face from engravings, and a certain similarity with the head of Momus is evident. Of Momus, the feared critic, Erasmus wrote: "No mortal will take the outcast into his home, even less so the princes in their palaces, for there all hearts are ruled by flattery…" Heemskerck remained faithful, at least outwardly, to the Catholic Church. He was a member of the board of St Bavo's

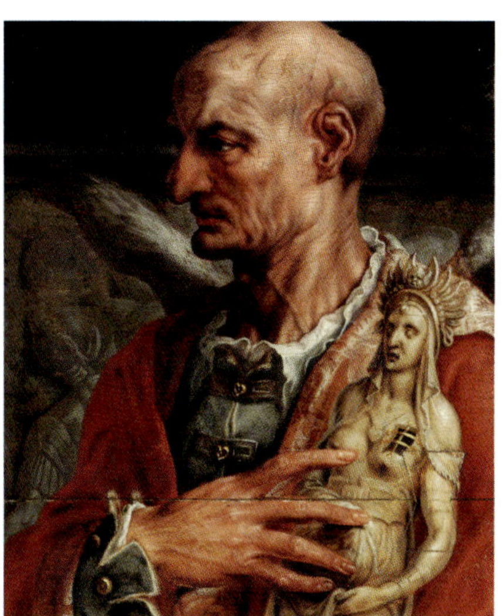

right up to his death in 1574. But he also painted subjects from antiquity, counted several humanists amongst his friends and had a comedy performed by the rhetoricians at his wedding. Since the industrious van Mander makes no mention of the *Momus* painting, it probably hung away from public view in the home of a humanist in or outside Haarlem.

This Olympian competition has evidently never been painted since. The god Momus undoubtedly numbers amongst the more eccentric inhabitants of Olympus; only at this particular juncture in history, from Erasmus to Heemskerck, did he serve as an example of the perilous situation of an overly critical mind.

Perhaps Maerten van Heemskerck's Momus has a completely different role here: not as a critic of religious and political circumstances but as an artist who wishes to put down the achievements of the Renaissance. A number of details point in this direction: the statues dotted around the background might be viewed as a derisive allusion to earlier forerunners.

And instead of spatial depth constructed with the means of perspective, Heemskerck paints colour zones. In none of his other paintings does he go so far in his alienation of space. Momus as Mannerist? Entirely plausible. The fact that art was a subject of intensive debate in the year that this picture was painted is demonstrated by the large theatre festival held in Antwerp.

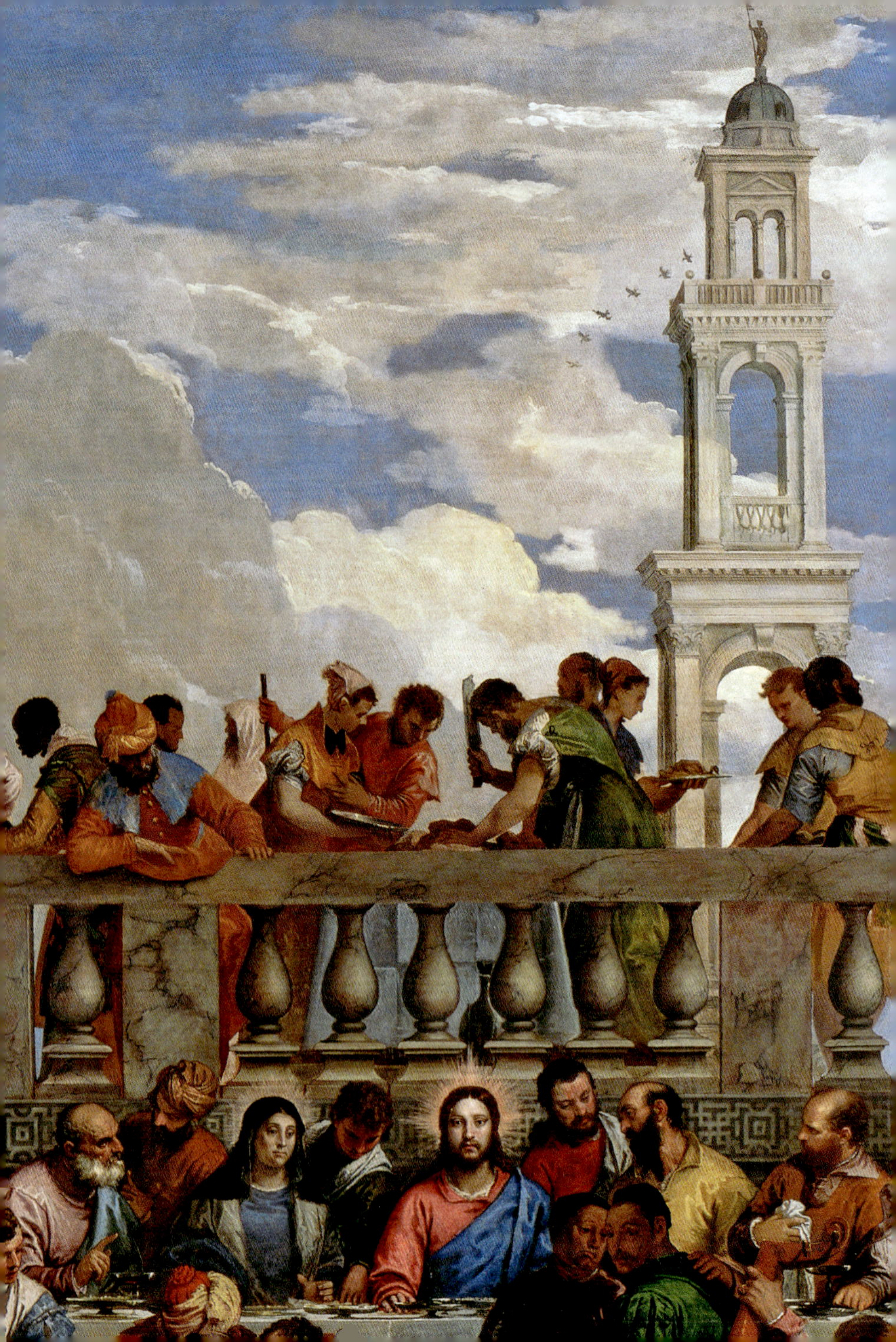

Paolo Veronese (1528–1588)
(real name Paolo Caliari)

The Lord sits at the table of lords

The Marriage at Cana, 1562/1563
669 x 990 cm, Paris, Musée du Louvre

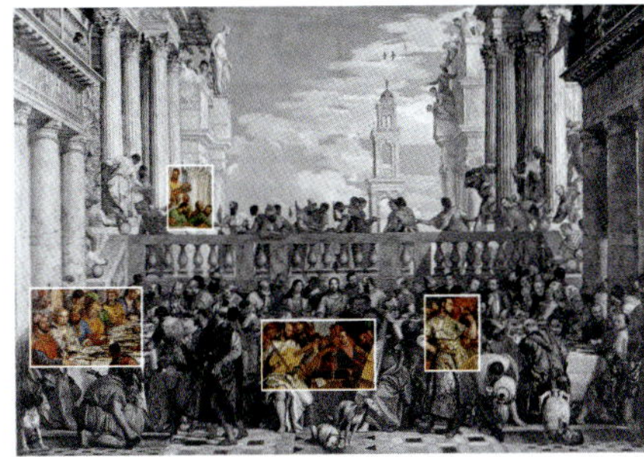

Despite rules forbidding them to raise their eyes from the plate while eating, the Benedictine monks at the monastery of S. Giorgio Maggiore decorated their refectory walls with the painting of a sumptuous feast. Their excuse was that the work illustrated a miracle: Christ's turning of water into wine at the marriage in Cana of Galilee. Napoleon had the painting removed to Paris, where it now hangs in the Louvre.

At 6.69 by 9.90 metres, this is one of the largest works ever to be painted on canvas. The contract concluded between the monks of the Venetian monastery of San Giorgio Maggiore and the painter Veronese (1528–1588) on 6 June 1562 specified "a painting as wide and as high as the wall" for the end wall of their new refectory.

During the 16th century, while the rich Venetians built one splendid Renaissance palace after another, the Benedictine monks of Venice added a new dining hall (refectorium), cloister, library and church, thereby greatly embellishing their island opposite St Mark's. Since many were the younger sons of the lagoon-Republic's ruling families, they had access to wealth and could therefore afford building works on this scale.

The refectory of the Benedictine monastery made its architect Andrea Palladio (1508–1580) famous. Palladio took his inspiration from antique temples, and his cleverly calculated proportions imparted a rare sense of harmony to the large, simply decorated hall. The background of *The Marriage at Cana* is strongly reminiscent of Palladio's architectural style. Veronese draws the spectator's eye through to palaces, a campanile and balconies – in other words into an ideal Renaissance townscape, set against a bright and cloudy sky.

The open square with the marriage feast in progress is framed on either side by columns in antique style. Servants scurry back and forth on a gallery, while the guests sit around the banquet table in the foreground.

Christ presides at the centre of the painting, surrounded by his mother and disciples, while some of Veronese's patrons, the Bendictines of San Giorgio, sit at the right. These elderly gentlemen with their rich robes and well fed faces do not seem at all disinclined to partake in the feast of life. Nor does it seem beyond the bounds of credibility that they took great pleasure in Veronese's portrayal of the feast during their own mealtimes – despite the strict rule

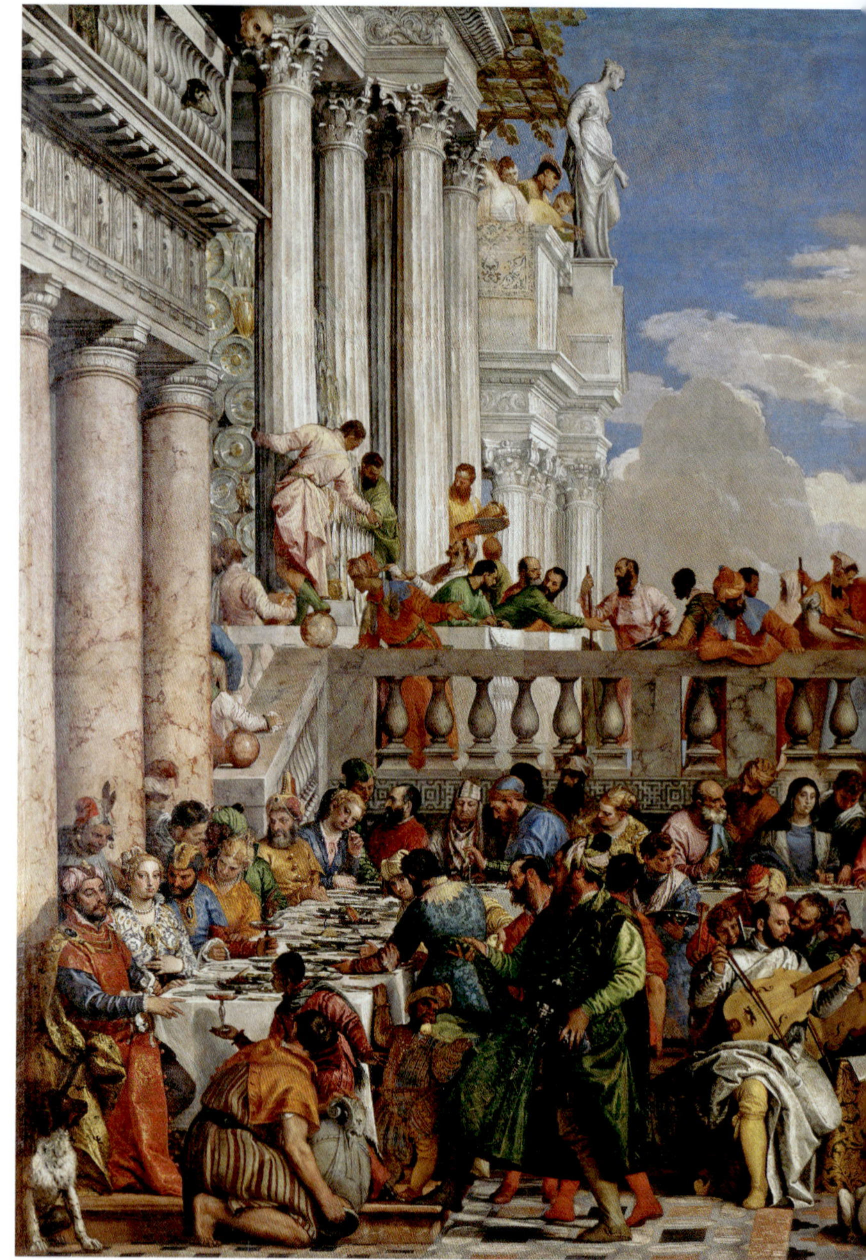

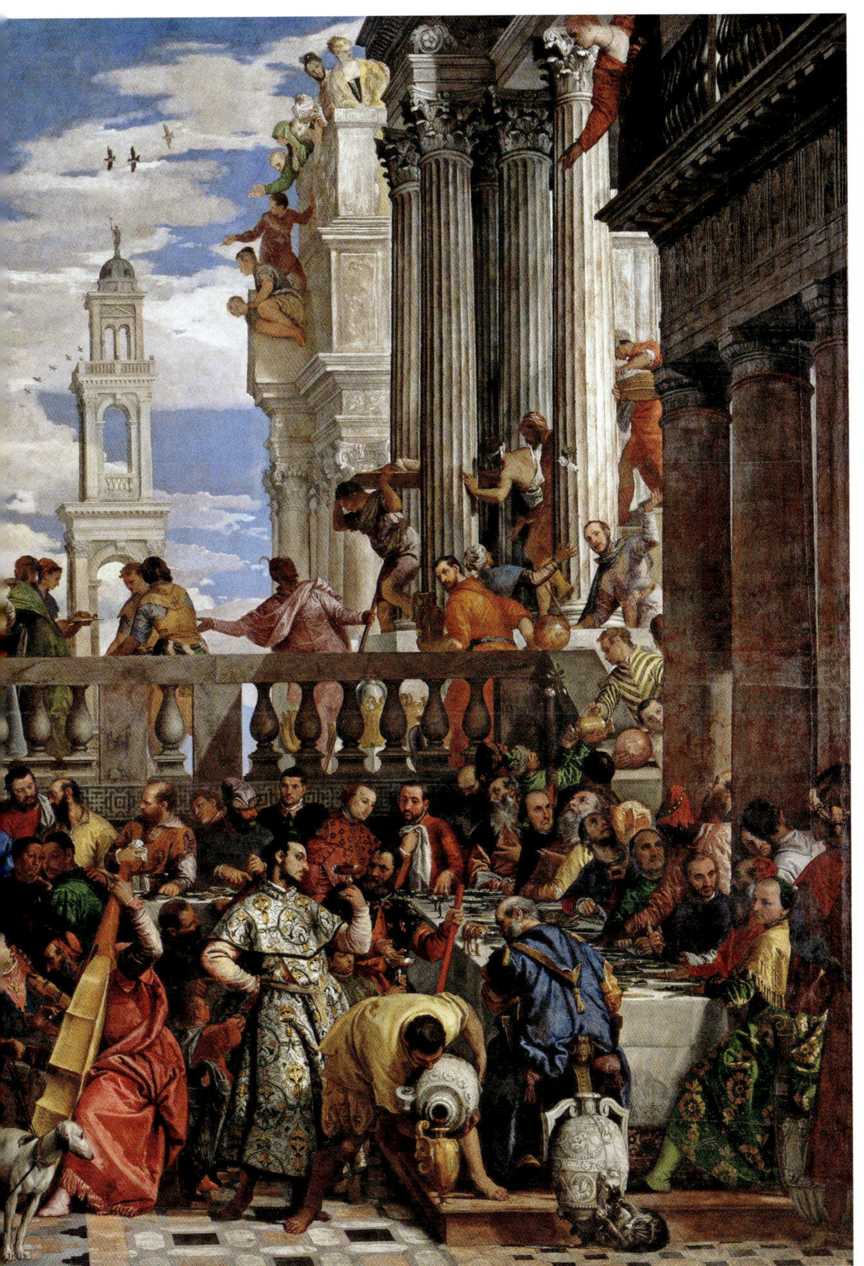

which forbade Benedictine monks to raise their eyes from the plate while eating.

Enough wine, but hardly any water
Large-scale canvases like *The Marriage at Cana* were only possible as the collective work of a studio. According to Veronese's sketches, his brother Benedetto Caliari, a nephew, and a host of nameless assistants and apprentices all worked in his *bottega* at the time.

Benedetto was responsible for the execution of architectonic aspects of the painting, and occasionally sat as model. His striking face with its characteristic Roman nose appears in many of Veronese's paintings. Here, Benedetto is portrayed as a Master of Ceremonies, raising a glass of wine to his expert eye.

This glass is the site of a biblical miracle – the changing of water into wine (John 2:1): "This beginning of miracles did Jesus … and manifested forth his glory" at "a marriage in Cana of Galilee". There was no wine left, and "Jesus saith unto them, Fill the waterpots with water … Draw out now, and bear unto the governor of the feast … When the ruler of the feast had tasted the water that was made wine," he was astonished, asking the bridegroom why he had "kept the good wine until now".

Veronese's richly clothed majordomo does not seem to be asking any questions, however, but to be examining the colour and taste of a wine, an everyday event for a Venetian connoisseur. Consumption of wine in the city in the lagoon was considerable, partly because of the shortage of drinking-water. The Venetian historian Marino Sanudo, writing in 1533, mentions this paradox: "Venice in the water has no water." Although the senate occasionally looked at plans to bring water to Venice by aqueduct, the inhabitants had to make do with rainwater. Collected in a large number of marble cisterns distributed around the town, the water is reputed to have left an unpleasantly muddy, or sandy, aftertaste, so that the Venetians tended to prefer wine.

The biblical miracle of the changing of water into wine does not appear to have found many admirers among the guests of Veronese's *Marriage*. Instead, they seem fully preoccupied with food, music and each other. Certainly, Christ's figure is the focal point of both the banquet and the painting. The cruciate halo shines around his head, while the activity on the gallery immediately above his head is presumably intended to be ambivalent: servants are butchering meat, though they might equally be slaughtering a sacrificial lamb.

Nonetheless, the significance of the miracle goes unrecognized in the hubbub of the feast, and Jesus is only one of well over 100 figures. Worldly things seem to have displaced the spiritual dimension; the guests are more interested in present enjoyment than in the afterlife. This was hardly an unusual state of affairs in Venice at the time, and one that was frequently described. The Venetians were trying to "turn the world into a pleasure garden," wrote the German pilgrim Felix Faber after visiting Venice in 1480: "The Turks and other infidels who see these gleaming palaces say the Christians who built them cannot esteem the afterlife, nor can they expect to gain very much from it."

Exotic splendour of the banquet
Goblets and bowls of finest glass, gold and silver sparkle on the damask tablecloth. The ambassador of the Republic of St Mark to the Imperial City of Augsburg in 1510 expressed his astonishment that even the rulers of the Empire ate from earthenware

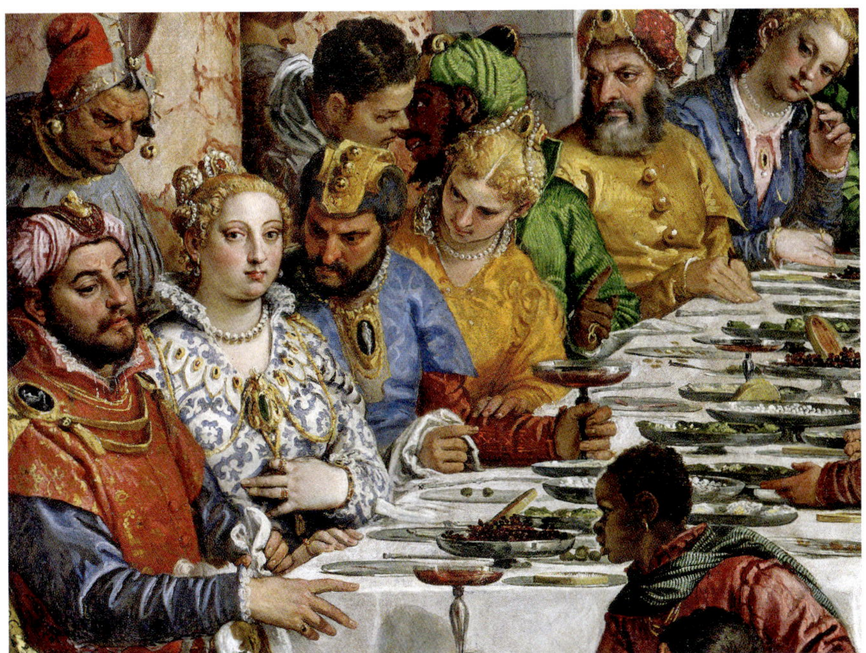

dishes, whereas gold and silver dishes had been in widespread use in his own home town for some time. Even the toothpicks – a lady in the painting is shown raising one to her mouth – are said to have been made of gold. The guests at one noteworthy banquet, held in 1574 in honour of Henry III, were amazed and delighted when their Venetian hosts presented them with some highly inventive, and very costly decor: cutlery, crockery and tablecloths of pure spun sugar.

The government of the city, whose preferred tone was generally inclined to discretion and understatement, used state functions and feasts as a means of demonstrating that Venice was still the richest and most luxurious city on earth. The more dubious Venice's role as a great power, the greater the need for such demonstrations became.

The patricians gathered around the festive table in the painting evidently still conceived of themselves as rulers of the waves. Almost all of them wear robes of rich and exotic materials. Their services to the Republic will have taken most of them to posts in the Levant as diplomats or colonial administrators.

The Venetian Empire itself had included Istria and Dalmatia, and had extended to Constantinople. At its zenith in the beginning of the 15th century, it had held sway over the Adriatic and Aegean, over Crete and Cyprus. Eventually, however, it began to disintegrate. Bit by bit was lost to the Turks. At the same time, the discovery of a sea route to India in about 1500 broke the Venetian trade monopoly on pepper and spices. By then, the Venetians were no longer in a position to redress such political and economic setbacks. Instead of pumping more and more money into adventurous trading expeditions, as they had done in the past, they preferred the security of investment in property on the Italian mainland, leaving trade on the high seas to up-and-coming cities like Antwerp and Amsterdam. A Venetian visitor, Tommaso Contarini, saw "neither luxury nor pomp" in these cities, neither silver nor silk robes, noting that "these were unknown in our own town at the time of our forebears."

Shortly before Veronese painted his *Marriage at Cana*, an especially sumptuous feast had been held to celebrate the coronation of the Venetian dogaressa

Zilia Priuli on 19 September 1557. Following nine heads of state who were all bachelors, Doge Lorenzo Priuli had at last set a woman beside him on the throne. His reputation for meanness had made him particularly concerned on this occasion to display his magnificence. Perhaps the memory of the feast is reflected in Veronese's painting. According to one contemporary chronicler, nothing like it had been seen for over a hundred years.

Veronese brings on the servants

The kitchens and other rooms where food was prepared were generally situated in a separate building or cellars, far from the banqueting hall, or at least out of sight of guests and spectators. Kitchens and those who worked in them therefore rarely appeared in paintings.

Veronese broke with this convention. He painted a third level between the guests seated around the table in the foreground and the spectators looking down at the feast from their balconies in the background: a gallery, joined to the dining area by two staircases at either end, stretches across the entire painting. This is the site of bustling activity:

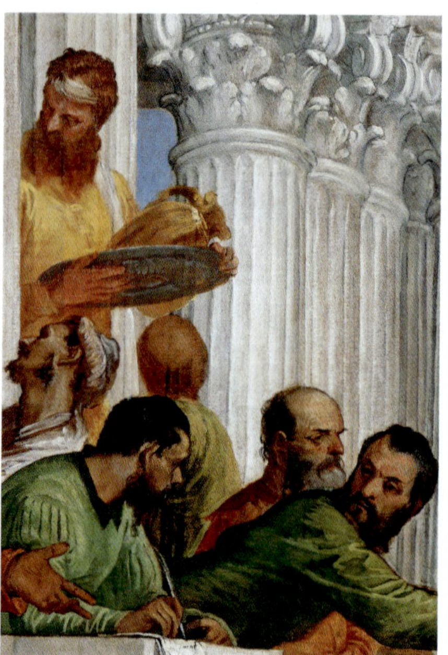

several porters are carrying a roasted ox. A black boy waits on the left with a tray for the roast which a bearded man is holding out between the columns. Those not carrying food or passing it on seem equally busy making sure that everything happens according to plan.

The Venetians ate an astonishing amount at their feasts. No fewer than 90 different foods would be served to 100 guests at a banquet lasting about four hours. The artist's unconventional look at the trivial world of servants was not to everyone's taste, however. Some years later in 1573, when Veronese had again painted a large-scale picture for the refectory wall of a Venetian monastery, he was summoned before the Inquisition. He was accused of having crowded a biblical scene, *The Last Supper*, with vulgar and irreverent figures such as servants, common mercenaries and even dogs. "If there is room in a painting, I decorate it as I see fit," Veronese answered. "I painted a cook, thinking to myself that he would probably have come out to have some fun and see what was going on." Veronese was aquitted, but instructed to change the title of the painting. The Inquisition demanded it be altered to *A Feast in the House of Levi*.

In *The Marriage at Cana*, too, the servants have come out to have some fun and are seen taking part in the general hubbub on the servant's gallery, taking time off to watch the festive goings on over the balustrade. Their exotic dress and dark faces under turbans and feather caps identify them as the natives of Venice's traditional trading partners. Saracen, Tartar and Circassian slaves served in almost every household in Venice. In Veronese's day, slaves were readily available at the public auctions held in the Rialto market.

Attempts by Holy Roman emperors, popes, patriarchs and doges to forbid the slave trade in Venice had always ended in failure. It was simply too lucrative. Countless female slaves worked in Venice as wet nurses and maids. Without their labour, and without the enormous sums of money gained by trafficking slaves, the Venetians' very pleasant, very lavish lifestyle would not have been possible.

Painters play for the guests

It is said that Veronese portrayed many of the famous figures of his time, including Francis I of France (died 1547), among the roughly 150 guests depicted in *The Marriage at Cana*. However, we do not owe this notion to the testimony of his contemporaries, but to art historians of the 16th and 17th centuries. Equally unproven, though more enticing, is the art theorist A. H. Zanetti's contention in 1771 that the little orchestra in the middle of the painting was composed of the most wellknown painters in Venice. "Titian is playing the double bass," he wrote, describing the man on the right dressed in red. "Paolo portrayed himself as the figure in the white robe with the cello," he went on, and, of the

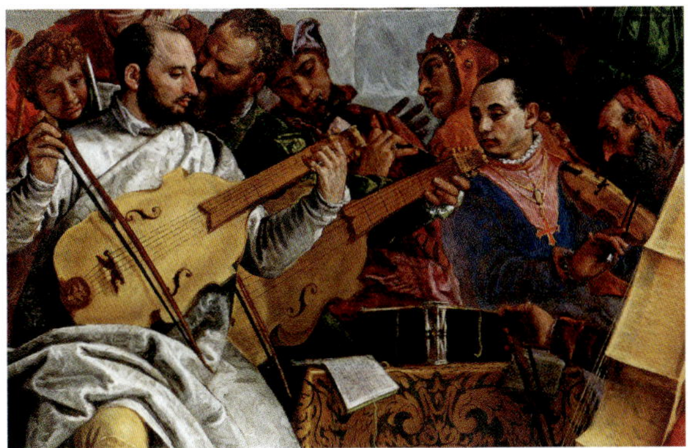

musician sitting next to him: "It is correct to suppose that this is Jacopo Tintoretto."

If this is true – and comparisons with other portraits appear to corroborate the claim – then the unchallenged masters of 16th-century Venetian painting, the three great colourists, were gathered here to make music. All three received major state commissions and worked hard to decorate Venice's churches and government buildings with their paintings. Paolo Caliari was the youngest of the three, born in 1528 at Verona, the reason for his nickname Veronese. His first success at the city on the lagoon had come when he was commissioned to decorate St Mark's library. Already an old man in 1557, Titian is said to have rewarded the artist by hanging a gold chain around his neck.

Tintoretto (1518–1594) was an eccentric who, during his lifetime, did not achieve such great public recognition as Titian (c. 1477–1576), who was knighted and celebrated as a "divino", one of the divine.

Perhaps the painters met at Titian's house. He possessed an organ, bartered from an organ builder in return for the latter's portrait. Music was played there just as it was everywhere in Venice in the 16th century. Even in 1506, Dürer had written of the city-state that he had heard people playing violins so sweetly there that the players themselves had been moved to tears.

It is quite possible that the music played at Veronese's feast would have been by Andrea Gabrieli, the organist at St Mark's and leading composer of his time. His melodies were heard at the time in the salons, theatres and on public squares. Gabrieli's studies in the field of harmony must have fascinated

painters and sculptors, too: "Just as vocal proportions are harmonious to the ear," explained the learned monk Francesco Giorgi in 1525, "so physical proportions are harmonious to the eye. Such harmonies provide the greatest of pleasure without anyone knowing why, except for One who understands the causal connections between all things."

The search for these "causal connections", and for perfect harmonies of tone, proportion and colour, was taken up by composers, architects and painters alike. As a result, 16th-century Venice entered a period of unparalleled flowering of music and the arts, at a time when the city was long past its political and economic heyday. This was made possible by the continued wealth of the city, together with the artistic sensibility of its ruling class. Unwilling to risk adventurous journeys on the high seas or to engage in pioneering trading expeditions as they once had, the patricians of the Republic of St Mark had become a class of highly educated, hedonistic humanists who were fond of spending large sums of money on the arts. The Benedictine monks of San Giorgio, who had their refectory built by Palladio and painted by Paolo Veronese, and who wished to eat to the accompaniment at least of painted music, are themselves an excellent example.

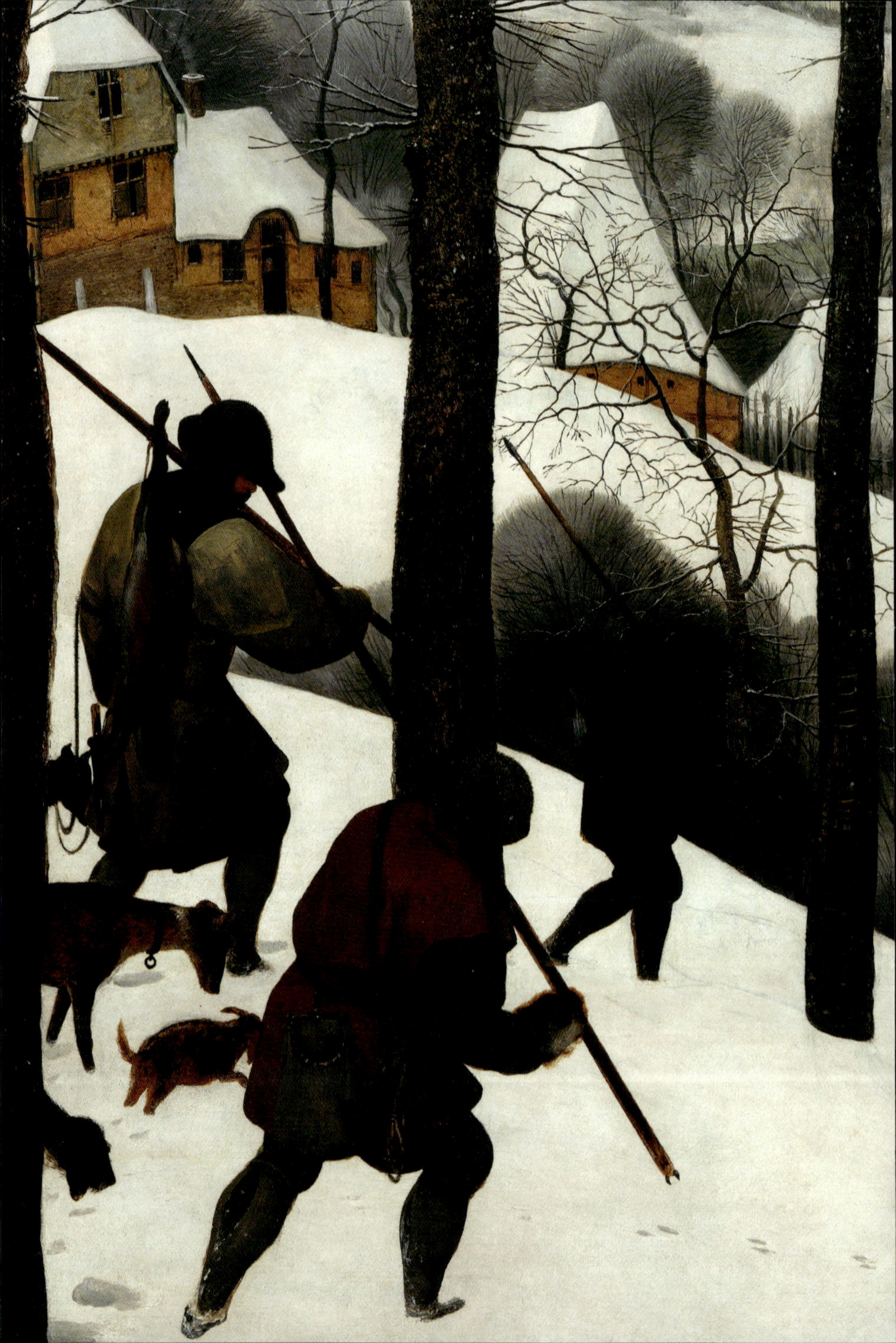

Pieter Bruegel the Elder (*c.* 1525/1530–1569)

Five o'clock in the afternoon on a December day

Hunters in the Snow, 1565
117 x 162 cm, Vienna, Kunsthistorisches Museum

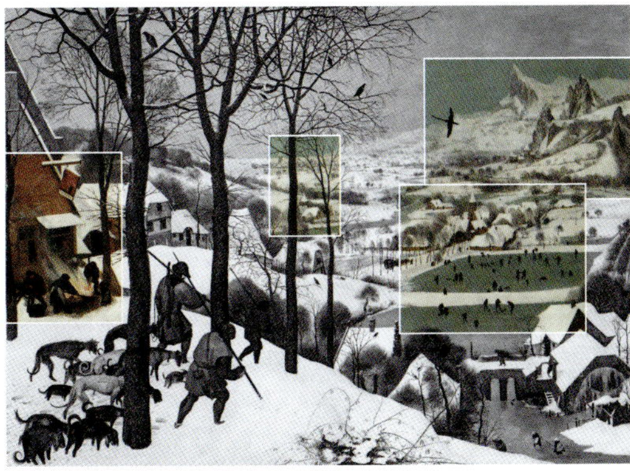

Nowadays we see landscapes in images every day, whether we like it or not, be it in milk adverts showing fields of cows or in satellite photos. We are used to it and often don't even give such landscapes a second glance. It is hard for us to imagine that there were once people whose knowledge of Nature on a grander scale was limited only to what they had seen in the original, at first hand; who had never stood before a reproduction of a landscape, but only ever within the countryside in which they lived and worked, like the hunters and the figures wrapped up against the cold enjoying themselves on the ice.

Painting had remained almost exclusively a figural art right up to Bruegel's day. Its subjects were biblical characters, antique gods and heroes. In the Renaissance, Italian artists celebrated the human body and dominated European painting with their cult of beauty. Landscape remained in the background, deemed insignificant and unworthy of treatment as a subject in its own right. In the

patronizing opinion of Bruegel's contemporary, Michelangelo (1475–1564), "women will like it".

The painted landscape spread in the North and was there granted its own means of representation. This new technique was developed before Bruegel, chiefly by the Netherlandish artist Joachim Patinier (*c.* 1480–1524). How is a painter to transfer sweeping landscapes onto panel or canvas? By choosing an elevated point of view, by portraying the panorama from the top of a hill as in the present painting, where the hunters are about to descend a steep slope down to the flat plain. Distance is conveyed in the traditional manner by reducing the scale of the figures, trees and houses. Patinier further introduced a progression of colours that suggests growing distance: darker shades – mostly earthy browns – for the foreground, green for the middle ground and pale blue for the background. Five landscapes showing different seasons of the year survive from Bruegel's hand, and it is clear that he has orientated himself towards Patinier's example. But in this snow

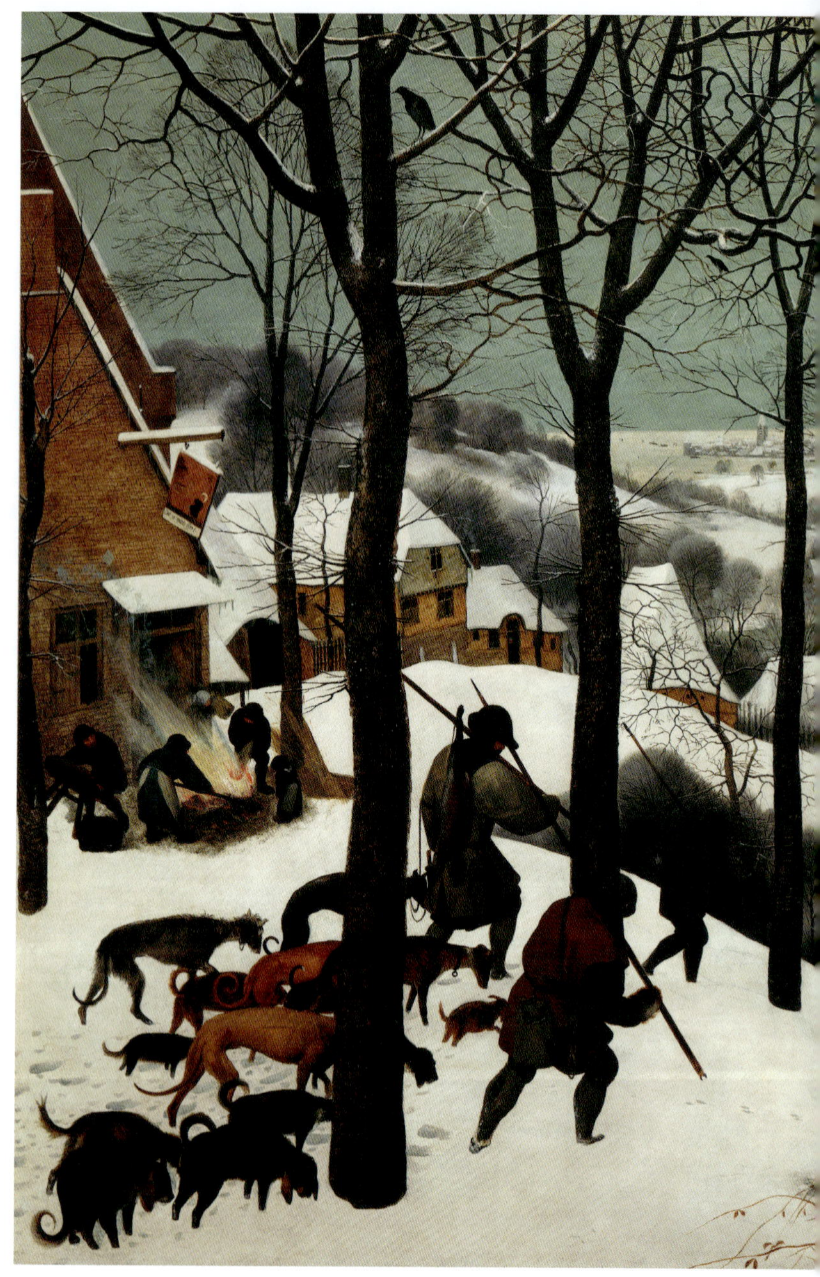

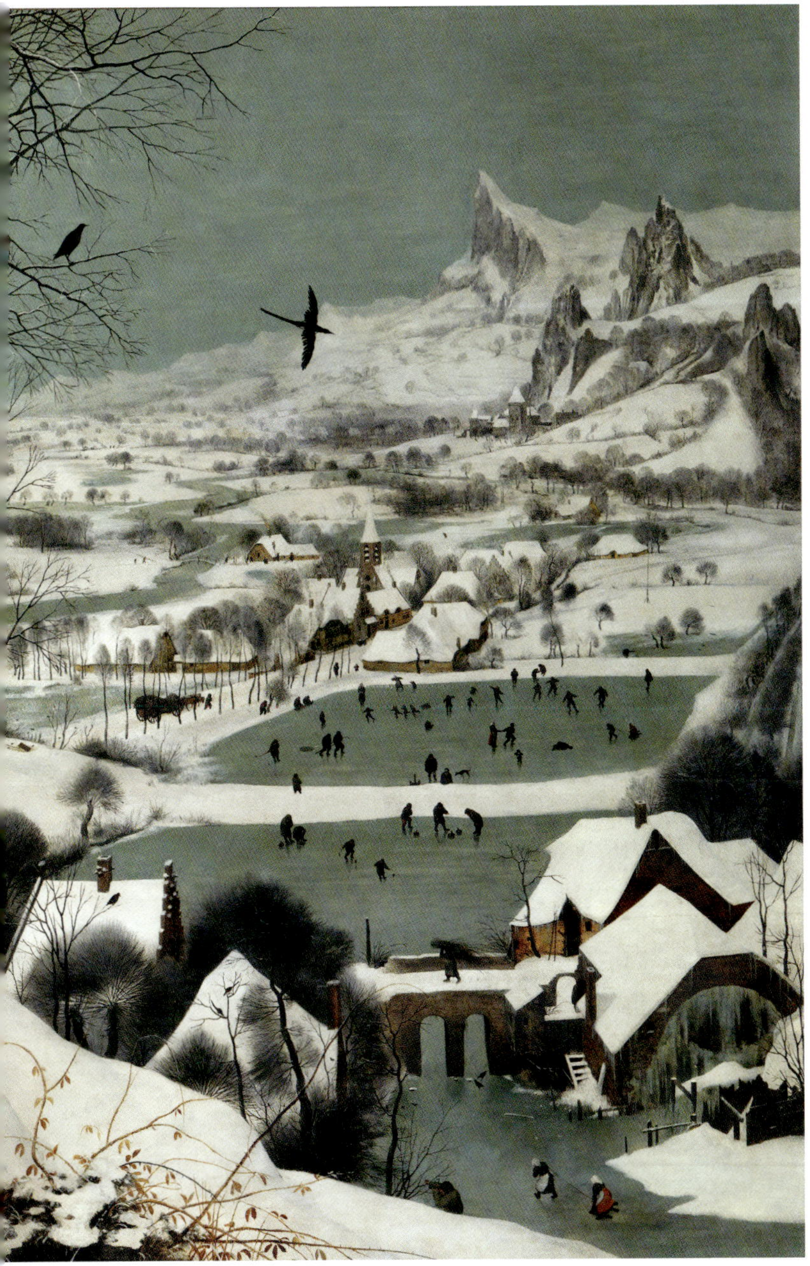

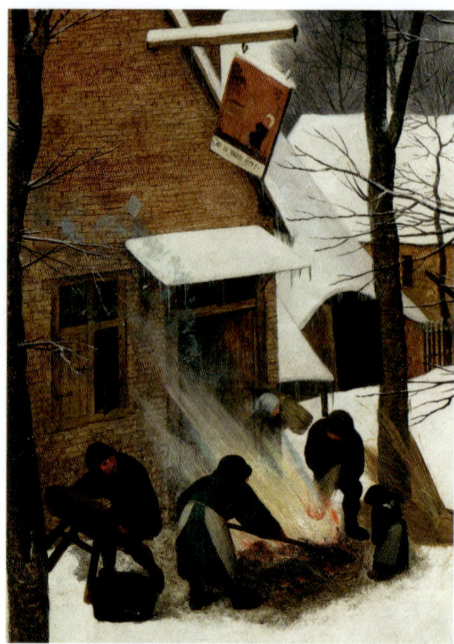

covered landscape without sunlight or shadows, he had to find his own solutions – no one before him had portrayed the colours of winter in such an impressive manner.

Inns were houses of ill-repute

The depiction in art of the various seasons of the year was not new; it was to be found, for example, in what are known as Books of Hours. These books of prayers for wealthy members of the laity included twelve miniatures illustrating the calendar months, as a means of rendering visible to the devout reader the transience of life. The individual months were characterized by activities typical of their time of year: servants chopping wood in February, crops being harvested in summer, hunting in autumn and slaughtering in December. Bruegel does it differently. His picture is dominated not by people but by the colours of the season. His snowy land-scape probably depicts December or the beginning of winter. Why the people have lit a fire in front of the house is not immediately apparent: perhaps they are roasting grain, or more likely singeing the bristles off a butchered pig. Swine foraged for their food in the woods; if the ground was frozen and

buried beneath snow, they went under the knife. The sign over the door shows that this is an inn; the fact that it is hanging crooked implies a run-down establishment. Inns in general had a bad reputation since they were frequented by rovers and provided a bed for wandering pedlars and itinerant students. In a stable society, in a village where eve-rybody knew everybody else, strangers were always viewed with suspicion.

Our picture contains a second building of possibly dubious renown, namely the watermill on the right. Millers were reputed to cheat their customers: when weighing out grain and flour they had plenty of opportunities to do so. But mills were also sometimes used as brothels. The authorities speak of "mill prostitution", and a decree issued in 1573 by the Braunschweig police expressly forbad the committing of adultery in municipal mills. It is perhaps no coincidence that both inn and watermill should be relegated to the edges of Bruegel's composition.

Flour was the most important foodstuff. After a poor harvest and a hard winter, in spring the prices rose so high that families with no reserves had to go begging. In 1557 famine and mutiny threatened, whereupon Amsterdam – Europe's most impor-tant point of grain transhipment – proceeded to impound rye and wheat from Danzig that was supposed to be shipped on to Spain. In exceptional cases domestic peace was worth more than the inter-national trade that had made the city rich.

The weary hunters with their spears and pack of a dozen hounds are coming home with just one fox, slung over the shoulder of the man on the left. They were probably only allowed to go after small game; large game belonged to the forest owners, old established aristocracy or well-to-do merchants in the city. Haunches of venison were not served on villagers' tables; their only opportunity to taste the lives of the rich was as beaters in battue hunts. They were permitted to trap birds, which provided a welcome addition to their monotonous diet, and Bruegel depicts bird catching in several of his paintings. In *Hunters in the Snow*, the black birds call to mind the winter hunger felt by man and beast. But the painter also employs them to aesthetic ends: whether flying or perched in the branches, they reinforce within the viewer the sense of airiness and space that is so characteristic of this painting.

Winter sports in the 16th century

In winter, village sport took place on the ice. It must have been more fun and games than serious training, and was enjoyed, too, by girls and women, recognizable by their headscarves and aprons. Ice skates were still fairly primitive: they consisted of wooden planks about two feet long, mounted on a blade of iron or alternatively on runner shaped pieces of wood or animal bones. Evidently these were not safe enough for skaters to perform the elegant movements that later became typical of the sport. But Bruegel shows heavy pieces of wood with handles for curling, and in other winter pictures he paints children's skates cobbled together out of wood and sometimes out of the jaw bones of horses or cattle.

Society lived outdoors much more than today. Its meeting places were the markets and the wells, and until nightfall in winter – at least for its younger members – the frozen ice, which was swept clean right to the edges. There was not much to do inside the home, where usually only one room was heated by a fireplace or stove. The windows were small and the illumination provided by oil lamps or tallow lights was poor. Only the rich could afford the brighter-burning candles that were made from beeswax. Everyone lived by necessity cheek by jowl, with no room for privacy, and not knowing what it was, people probably felt no urgent need for it. Bruegel's *Hunters in the Snow*, with its wan light beneath overcast skies, is probably set in the late afternoon, perhaps around five o'clock, but people in those days did not wear watches. Even without them, the hunters knew when it was time to head for home and shortly the skaters, too, will no doubt disappear into their houses and the village will lie in darkness. Bruegel has captured in his picture not just a season of the year but also a specific time of day.

Any of the young ice skaters who wished to make their fortune had to leave their parental village. The fastest way to earn money was in the field of

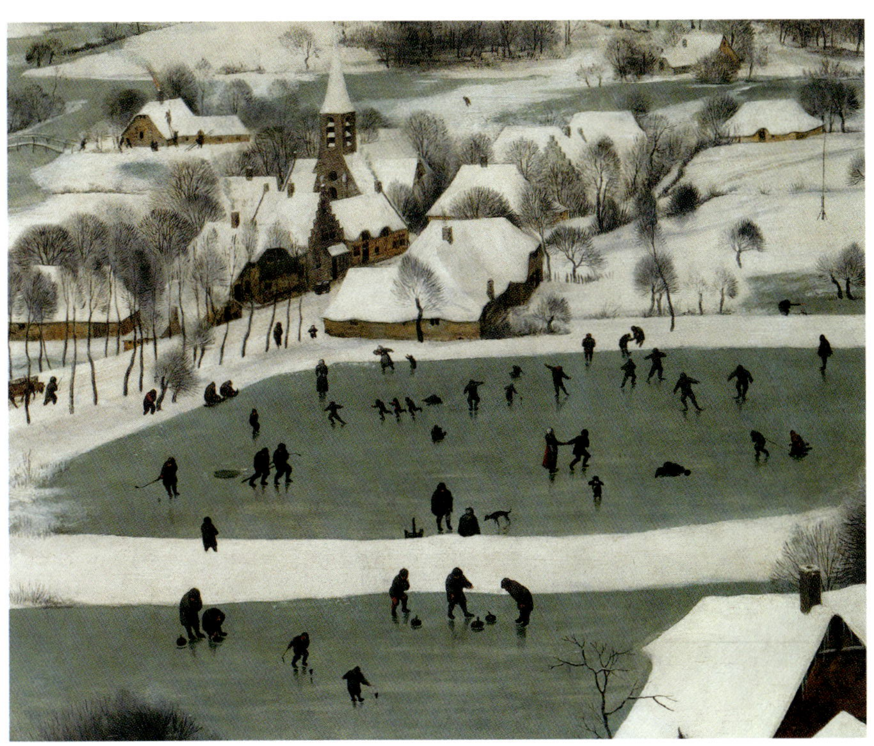

commerce, which meant going to the major ports, Amsterdam and Antwerp, where to rise up the career ladder you had to be able to read, write and add up.

Which everyone in Flanders could do, as one Italian visitor, Ludovico Guicciardini, remarked in astonished admiration. But this was an exaggeration: the rural areas had neither school buildings nor trained teachers. Lessons were held on the marketplace or in a stable and children would attend for about two years – and even then, only if they were not needed in the fields or at home. A small number of boys, funded by the Church or a generous patron, would then go on to attend the Latin schools in the towns.

Churches, churches everywhere

Wherever his paintings contain a cluster of houses, Bruegel invariably also includes a church. He does not forget to give his church towers the louvre openings that allowed the bells to be heard from afar. The clocks found on church towers in the towns and cities are absent in Bruegel's pictures, probably in line with rural reality. Churches not only served religion but were also the only buildings within which the village inhabitants could assemble all year round. They were not normally

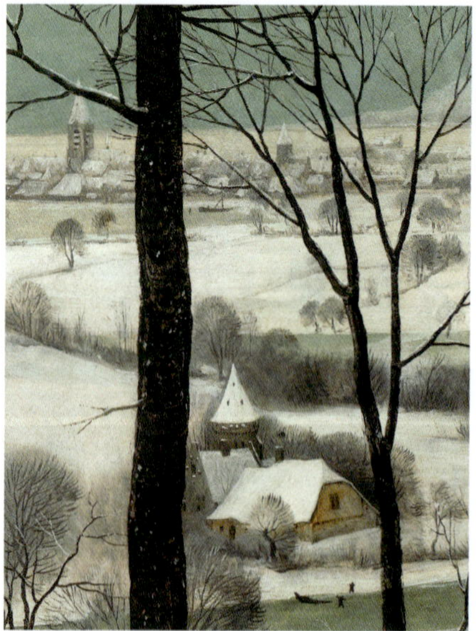

filled with rows of pews; instead, the congregation stood or brought their own chairs. As well as a place of worship, a church also had a social function. In Bruegel's day, the Church indirectly contributed to the fact that ever more people wanted to read. Amongst Catholics, the Latin Bible was reserved for priests. The two reformists, on the other hand, Luther and Calvin, demanded that the laity should be given access to the Christian scriptures. The teachings of Calvin, in particular, were widely embraced in the Netherlands and led to bloody confrontations with the Habsburg rulers with their seat in Madrid – first with Charles V, then Philip II, both staunch Catholics. They had inherited the Netherlandish provinces and for them the established church was the Church of Rome. Anyone who left or opposed it became a heretic and an enemy of state.

During the later years of Bruegel's life, Philip endeavoured to place ever greater restrictions on the liberties of his distant Netherlandish subjects. Edicts against heretics and the founding of new bishoprics were designed to strengthen the Catholic Church, while financial pressure was increased by the imposition of new levies. The Netherlandish provinces were the richest in the vast Spanish empire, and the rulers in Madrid were always short of cash. Money and religion – the combination led to civic unrest. Count Egmont, a member of the Netherlandish council of state, journeyed to Madrid to ask for tolerance. Philip's reply: "I would rather sacrifice 100,000 lives than cease the persecution of heresy."

He said this in 1565, the year in which Bruegel painted his snow-covered landscape with the hunters returning home. Although not in this picture, the artist makes allusion to the Spanish threat in other paintings, ones taking biblical motifs and transposing them, as was the norm, into the Netherlandish present. An example is his *Census at Bethlehem*: near the spot where those who have been counted are clustered to pay their tax, there hangs a shield with the Habsburg double eagle. Another is *The Massacre of the Innocents*: a bloodbath on the village square watched by a troop of Spanish riders led by a man dressed in black with a long beard, the distinguishing trait of the Duke of Alba. Both paintings are dated to 1566. In 1567 Alba arrived in person and instituted a reign of terror under which several thousand Netherlandish citizens lost their lives. In 1568 he also ordered the execution of

Count Egmont. Bruegel died in 1569, the year in which Netherlandish resistance erupted into open rebellion. Before his death the painter is supposed to have instructed his wife to burn a number of his drawings because their captions "were too caustic and steeped in derision". According to Karel van Mander, Bruegel's first biographer, he took this step "either because he regretted them or because he feared that they might cause his wife some unpleasantness".

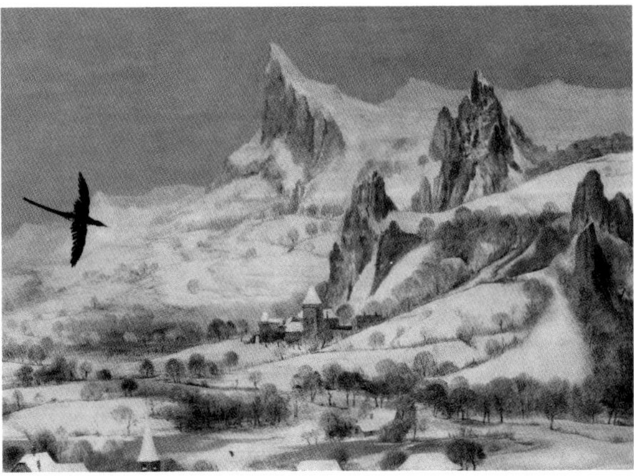

Bruegel "swallowed mountains and rocks and spat them out as paintings"

We know neither precisely when nor where Bruegel was born, and details of his life are equally scant. He was married and had two sons, who as painters were nicknamed "Hell Bruegel" and "Velvet Bruegel". In 1552 he travelled to Italy, as evidenced by sketches and paintings. Van Mander writes that during his crossing of the Alps, Bruegel "swallowed mountains and rocks and spat them out as paintings".

These consumed and regurgitated rocks include the ones in the top right-hand corner of our picture. Bruegel combines them with a typically Netherlandish low-lying plain crossed by waterways. He has not portrayed a real landscape but creates his own out of various elements: the rise in the foreground, from where he can look out across the countryside, and the rocky cliffs soaring menacingly in the right-hand background. With the trees that rise the full height of the panel, he establishes a structure perpendicular to the horizontal lines of the landscape. He employs just three colours: the white of the snow, the pallid green of the sky and ice, and the black of the trees and people. Tiny variations ensure that the colours do not appear flat. An artificial space, in other words, carefully engineered in a reduced palette – an artificial space that seems as natural as if we were seeing it for real.

Each of Bruegel's five paintings of the seasons has its own colours, its own lighting, its own mood. This was something new. His figures, too, were different, at least when measured against European standards. There are no naked female beauties, no glorious warriors or shining saints. Bruegel does not paint aristocrats and popes but peasants from the country, men and women who are working or eating or dancing or skating on the ice. Usually solidly built and almost always shabbily dressed, they stand at the opposite end of the scale to the idealized figures of the Renaissance. In Bruegel's hands, they seem real. This was how he saw people; his image of humankind recalls the story of Creation and the fashioning of man from a lump of clay into which God breathed life. While his contemporaries celebrated this divine inspiration, Bruegel shows the clay in God's hand.

By the same token, he attaches no importance to individuality. Even the hunters returning home are denied faces. The artist shows us not what distinguishes them as individuals, but only what they have in common. The same is true of the skaters: they possess no more character than the birds in the air. Bruegel's people are hungry just as the animals are; they are related to everything that lives and moves. They are not the masters of Nature, but an integral part of the natural landscape to which Bruegel has opened our eyes.

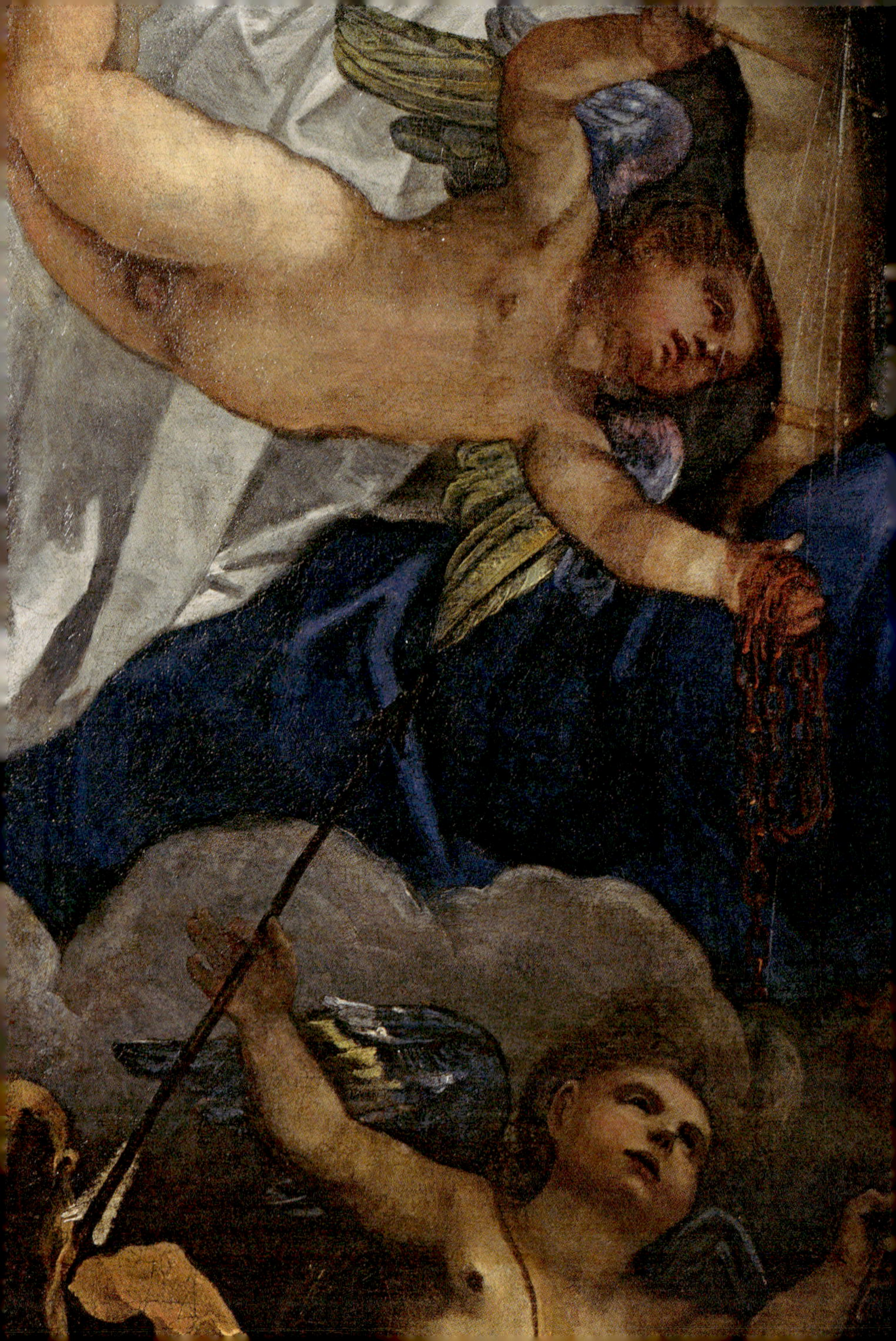

Tintoretto (1518–1594)
(real name Jacopo Robusti)

Aspirations to immortality

The Origin of the Milky Way, c. 1580
148 x 165 cm, London, The National Gallery

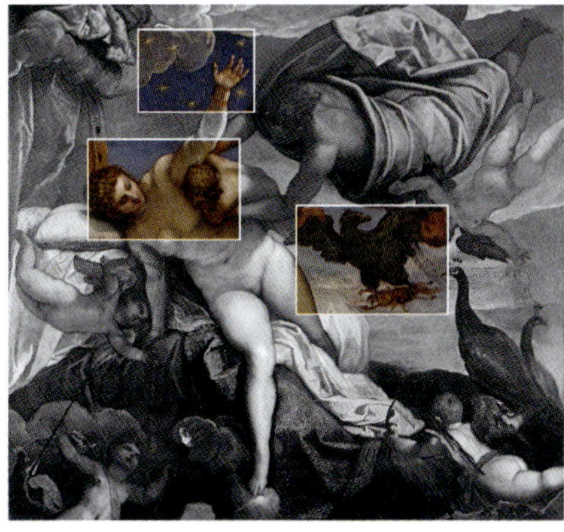

Jupiter, father of the gods, is known to have loved a number of mortal women. One of these was Alcmene, with whom he begot Hercules. Taking advantage of his wife Juno's slumber, he held the baby boy to her breast, thus letting him drink the milk of immortality. The goddess started up in surprise, sprinkling milk into the firmament. The drops of milk immediately turned into stars. This explanation for the origin of the Milky Way was given in the 1st century BC by Gaius Julius Hygienus, librarian to Caesar Augustus. Here, the Venetian Jacopo Robusti, known as Tintoretto, an artist of highly refined dramatic sensibility, has painted the climax of the story, the moment of surprise. Lying on her heavenly bed of clouds, nude Juno starts up from sleep. A skilfully foreshortened Jupiter sweeps down towards her, baby on his arm. Putti and birds surround the two main figures.

Tintoretto's work normally shows angels or saints. He earned his reputation in Venice as a specialist in Christian miracles, rendering spectacular episodes from the Bible in large format. Erotic scenes from pagan mythology rarely feature in his paintings. Tintoretto was swamped with official commissions

when – between 1578 and 1580 – he painted the (undated) *Milky Way*. Although he could not have met the great public demand for his work without the help of his busy studio, it has been established, not only that the *Milky Way* is from Tintoretto's hand, but that he actually painted it twice.

When the London National Gallery restored the 148 by 165 centimetre oil painting in 1972, X-rays revealed that a first version of the work had been carefully painted over. The original was a treatment of the same subject but executed in a much less sophisticated manner, in the "rapid and resolute" style so characteristic of Tintoretto's work. Art historians have suggested that the potential owner of the *Milky Way* changed before work on the painting reached completion. The new owner was not just anybody, but a personage entitled to demand the highest standards: Emperor Rudolf II, who had decided to go about establishing a new collection of art.

The painting is not mentioned in an (unreliable) inventory of the collection, compiled during the emperor's lifetime. However, an Italian pamphlet, dated 1648, mentions that Tintoretto executed "four

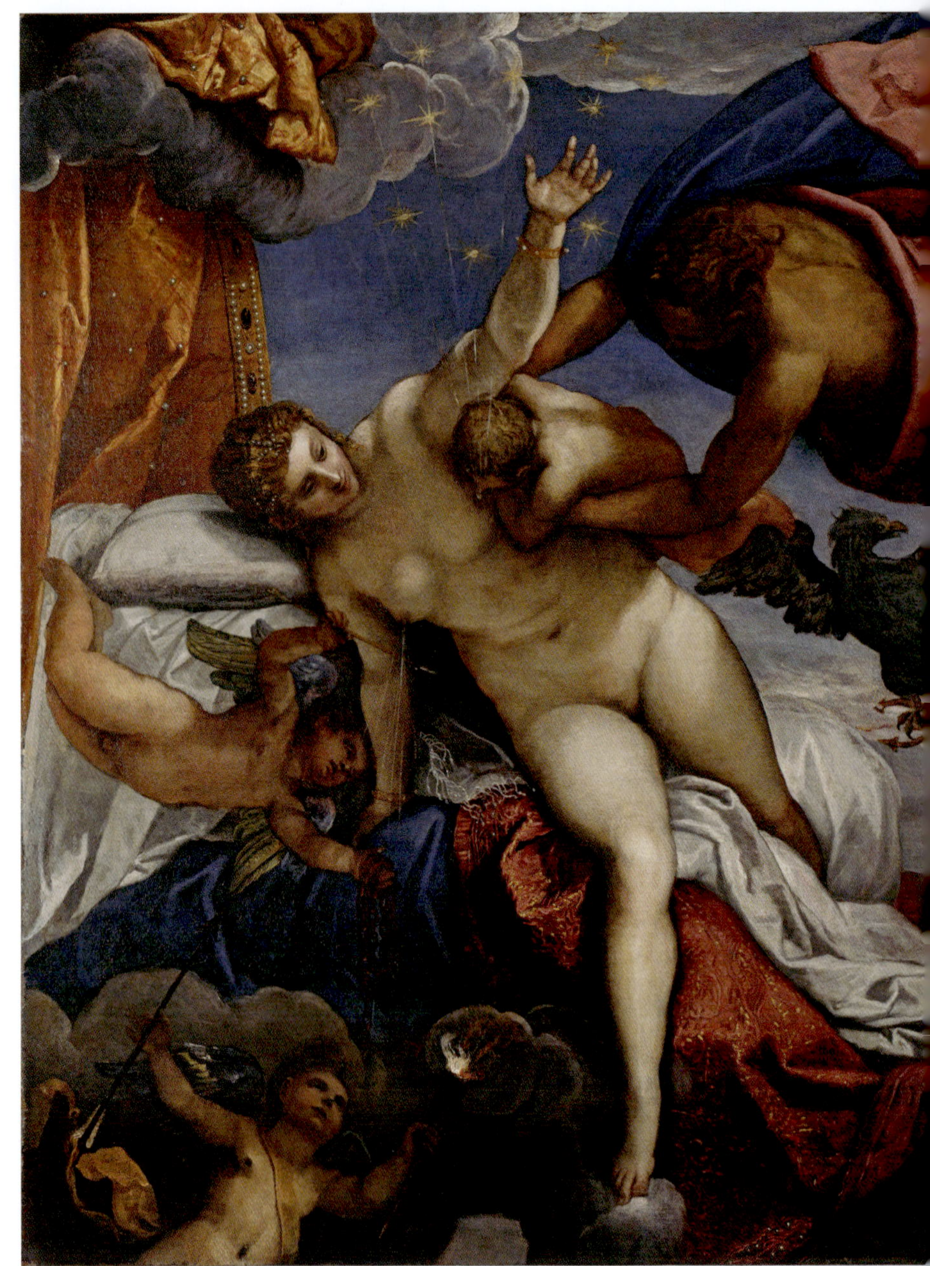

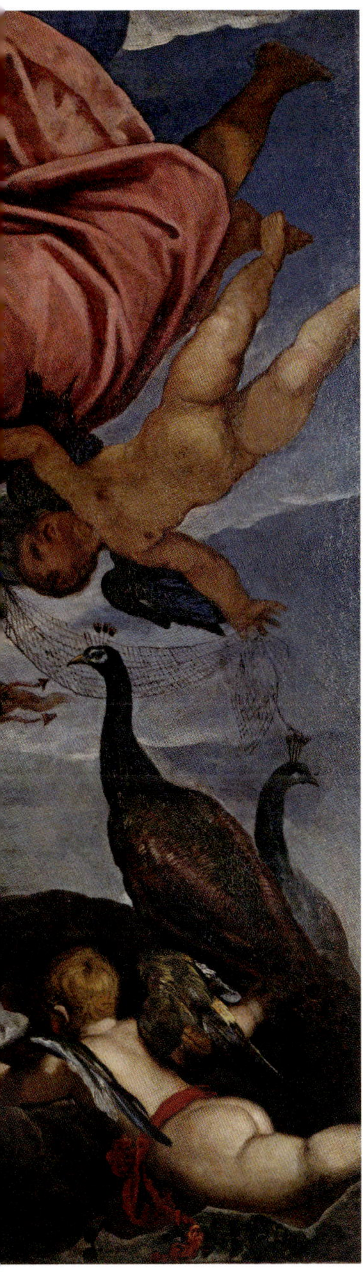

paintings of fables" for the emperor, among them "Jupiter holding a little Bacchus to Juno's breast".

If we assume that the writer has mistaken Hercules for Bacchus, then the *Milky Way* probably hung in the Imperial Palace at Prague – although not for very long. For in 1648, shortly before the end of the Thirty Years' War, Prague was taken by the Swedes, whose soldiers looted Rudolf's collection of paintings, taking many away with them when they left Bohemia. In the confusion, about a third of the *Milky Way* canvas was lost.

An ambitious doctor

The original appearance of Tintoretto's painting can be ascertained from a sketch, now kept in the Kupferstichkabinett at Berlin, executed in Prague by the imperial court painter Jakob Hoefnagel. In the sketch, there is a second female nude below the Olympian scene, probably Jupiter's mistress Alcmene. She is lying among long stalked lilies, which, according to a later version of the legend, are supposed to have sprung from drops of Juno's milk which fell to Earth.

This version of the Milky Way legend was published in Venice in a Byzantine tract on botany in 1538, several decades before Tintoretto started work. It was perhaps here that he found the extravagant, and extremely rare iconography of his painting. In any case, there was one person known to the painter who was certainly acquainted with the theme: a medal struck in 1562 in honour of Doctor Tomaso Rangone showed Hercules at Juno's breast, as well as stars and lilies. As documented in a series of receipts, this Venetian doctor commissioned, and paid for, a series of paintings from Tintoretto in honour of St Mark.

Born at Ravenna as Tomaso Gianotti, he had managed to rise from a poor background, take a doctor's degree and, probably through adoption, acquire the respected Venetian family name Rangone. Perhaps it was due to the reputation of the Milky Way legend as mythology's first example of an adoption, albeit an involuntary one, that Rangone chose it as a motif for his medal and coat of arms.

Juno sent two snakes to kill her "adopted" infant, but Hercules, by then already immortal, strangled them. Doctor Rangone also offered his patients a first step to immortality, selling them expensive "magic potions" which, so he promised, would help them live to at least 120 years old. He became immensely rich in the process. Besides medicine, he had studied physics and astronomy, and, clever charlatan that he was, operated a successful business, exploiting the widespread inability of his customers to distinguish between science and magic.

In order to ensure his own survival, however, Rangone put his trust in art. A spirited patron of the arts, he succeeded in having his bust mounted between a celestial sphere and a globe on a Venetian church façade for which he had donated the money, despite the fact that this form of immortality was officially reserved for nobles and persons born in Venice. Rangone also appears several times in Tintoretto's sequence of paintings on the life of St Mark. Here, he is shown as a life sized figure with a central role in the depicted events – much to the displeasure of the public, who demanded that Tintoretto remove the Rangone portraits. However, his striking head has remained a characteristic feature of the paintings

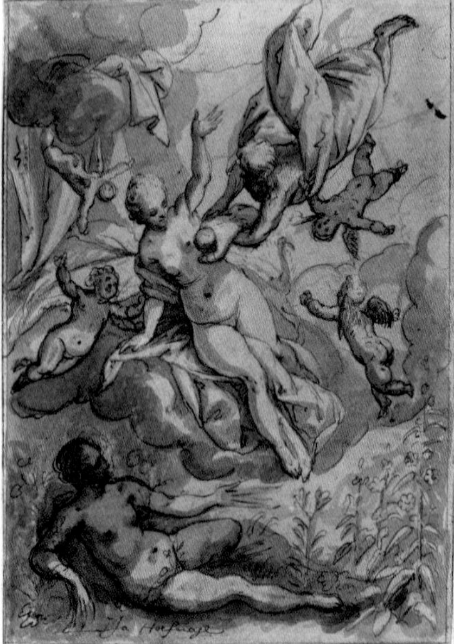

Comparative illustration:
Jakob Hoefnagel, *Origin of the Milky Way*, sketch after Tintoretto, c. 1620, Berlin, Staatliche Museen zu Berlin, Kupferstichkabinett

to this day. The doctor, vain as he may have been, has achieved his aim!

It was for Rangone that Tintoretto probably painted the first, "rapid" version of the *Milky Way*. When the doctor died in 1577, the artist found a new buyer: Emperor Rudolf II, who had been crowned in 1576. However different the Venetian charlatan and the Habsburg emperor may have been in background and social standing, they did have one thing in common: both of them used alchemy, astrology and art in their attempts to fulfil their aspirations to immortality.

Art for the sovereign

The Hercules legend was exactly suited to Emperor Rudolf's taste, for the ancient hero was already part of the Habsburg family tradition. At the beginning of the 16th century, Rudolf's predecessor Maximilian I had had himself celebrated as "Hercules Germanicus". A demigod who had strangled the Nemean lion, exterminated the many headed hydra and cleaned out the stables of Augeas provided the ideal model for any temporal ruler. Rudolf, too, liked to have himself portrayed wearing a lion's skin and carrying a club, both attributes of Hercules. This was an indication of the emperor's political aims, showing him committed to following the example of his ancient model by protecting his subjects and securing peace and order in the Empire.

However, Rudolf II found it exceedingly hard to keep his promise. Born in 1552 as the son of Maximilian II, crowned Emperor of the Holy Roman Empire at the age of 24, he inherited an empire that was deeply divided, and threatened by the Turks from without. Ruling was made difficult for him by religious conflicts, regional disputes and Habsburg family feuds. During his lifetime, however, he managed to maintain an unstable balance of power. It was not until after his death that the Thirty Years' War broke out.

The vigorous man of action chosen by the ruler to symbolize his power was not in the least like Rudolf as a person. In 1583, he gave up Vienna and retreated to Prague. As a depressive "eccentric in the imperial palace", he did his best to ward off the demands made on him by a chaotic environment. He relaxed from the unpleasant business of ruling by collecting precious objects and works of art.

"Whoever wishes to see something new," wrote Karel van Mander, a contemporary biographer of

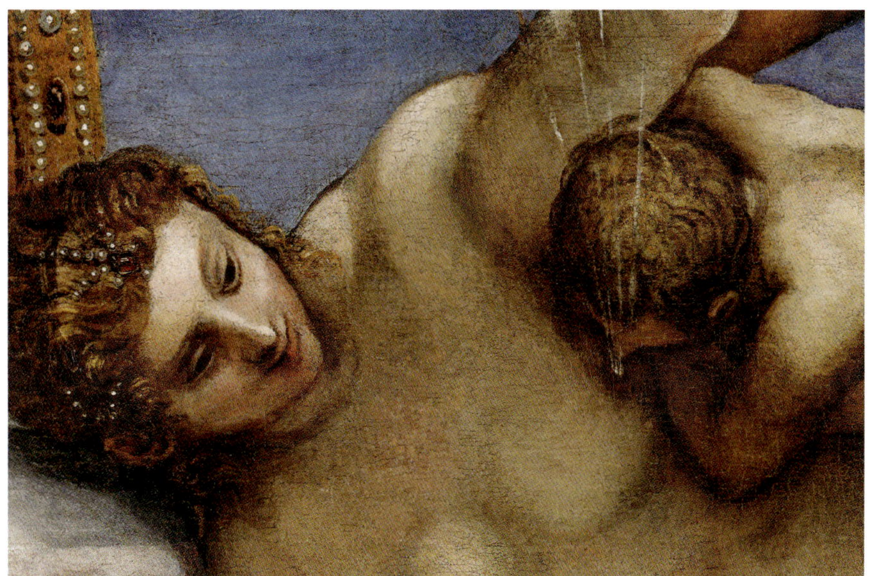

artists, "must seek an opportunity to visit Prague and the greatest living admirer of the art of painting, the Holy Roman Emperor Rudolf II, in his imperial residence."

Tintoretto's completion of the *Milky Way* and Rangone's death in the 1670s were concurrent with Rudolf's decision to collect paintings in earnest. He was especially interested in works by Dürer. Following a extensive correspondence with the town council of Nuremberg, he was able to purchase Dürer's *All Saints' Altarpiece* in 1585. Rudolf also had a penchant for the Venetian colourists and, over a number of years, bought many works by Titian and Tintoretto. Several works were officially presented to the emperor as gifts by the Venetian Republic; others he bought through his ambassador, or under the guidance of official advisers such as the Mantuan Ottavio Strada, official "antiquary" to the imperial collection.

Ottavio Strada himself sat for Tintoretto in Venice in 1569. It is quite possible that he bought the *Milky Way* for his master ten years later, together with three other works showing the amorous adventures of Hercules. After all, it was not only the subject of these paintings that was suited to Rudolf's taste, but also their erotic qualities; although he steadfastly refused

to marry and provide an heir for his throne, Rudolf was much given to "visual enjoyment".

Fascination of the enigma

A work of art was not only there to provide sensuous or aesthetic pleasure, however. To please the emperor it needed an aura of mystery, a hidden meaning which only the initiate could decipher. An elitist predilection for coded messages and arcane reference in art and literature was not unusual at the time. But it was cultivated particularly intensively by the imperial court at Prague, where the emperor, according to one of his contemporaries, "despised common life and loved only what was extraordinary and marvellous".

In the course of his duties, the "antiquary" Octavio Strada evidently advised the artists in some detail concerning their choice of subject and development of various artistic projects for the emperor. The imperial preference was for "mythologies" which, like the *Milky Way*, intimated to the spectator that the cosmos and human psyche were interrelated at some deep and hidden level.

At first glance, Tintoretto's painting seems easy enough to read; its different elements are derived from a relatively well-known repertoire. Two of the putti playfully circling around the Olympian figures carry erotic symbols: Cupid's bow and arrow and the flaming torch of passion (of Jupiter for Alcmene). The other two bear the chains of marriage (between Jupiter and Juno) and the net of illusion (whose powers so often came to Jupiter's aid). Juno's traditional pair of peacocks are seen at her feet.

Jupiter's eagle accompanies the king of the gods, a figure with whom the Habsburgs were no less inclined to identify than with Hercules, and whose bird they had long included in their coat of arms.

The creature held in the talons of Jupiter's eagle provides some grounds for speculation, however. Are its arrow-shaped extremities intended to suggest an embodiment of lightening, Jupiter's traditional weapon? Or does it represent a crab? Cancer was the sign of the zodiac under which Emperor Rudolf had been born on 18 July 1552. The arrangement of figures would seem to confirm this thesis: Cancer comes between Aquarius, represented in the painting by the putto with the net, and Sagittarius, whose incarnation here is the putto with the bow.

It is possible that Tintoretto has integrated into the painting's iconography details of a horoscope cast for Rudolf II by the famous French astrologer Nostradamus. It is said to have been none too favourable – a veritable disaster for a sovereign whose belief in the influence of the stars on human fate was no less powerful than that of his subjects. He was, for example, quite unable to make a decision without consulting his astrologers, and persons seeking his audience had first to be vetted by having their horoscope cast. In the hope of escaping his ruinous destiny and influencing by magic a reality he could not change, the emperor later decided to move his date of birth so that it fell under the more favourable influence of Taurus, a sign under which the Roman Caesar Augustus was thought to have been born. However, the ruse does not seem to have helped Rudolf much. Lonely, stripped of his power, he died in 1612 in his castle at Prague.

Reaching out to the universe

Rudolf was a devotee of yet another occult science: alchemy. He would spend nights on end in his laboratory, bent over a glass flask in which mysterious substances bubbled over a fire. This met with disapproval in a report sent to Florence by the Tuscan ambassador: the emperor, he wrote, "neglects his duties of state in order to spend time in the laboratories of alchemists and the studios of artists." The ruler, like so many of his contemporaries, was searching for the "philosopher's stone", which not only was a means of transforming base metal into gold, but could make its owner immortal.

Tintoretto's painting, in which everything circles around the subject of immortality, can be interpreted as a study in alchemy. It contains, for example, a number of symbols reminiscent of the vivid language of the "cognoscenti": the *prima materia* which they attempted, in long and difficult operations, to transmute, had first to be bathed in a mysterious substance called "Virgin's milk", also known as *succus lunariae* or "moon juice". In the

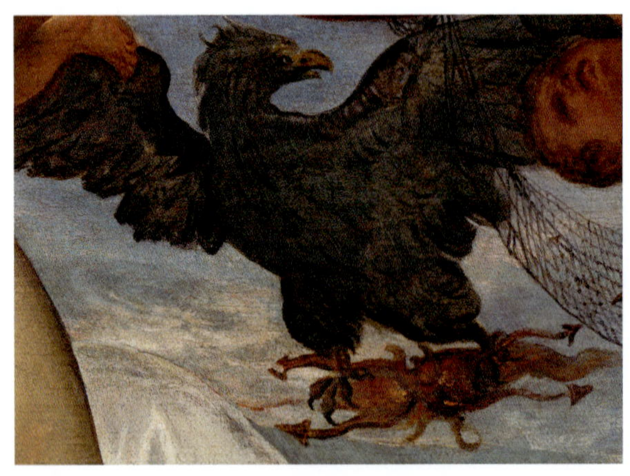

course of this process, the more earthy part of the prime material, the "toad", was united with the ethereal element, the "eagle". The arrows held by the putti were symbols of the alchemist's knowledge; they frequently decorate Rudolf's portraits and emblems. The *Milky Way* is so full of references to alchemy that one is inclined to suspect that those in Venice who referred to Tintoretto, the painter of so many devotional works, as a "necromancer", or sorcerer, did so with some justification.

The original patron of the work, Doctor Rangone, would

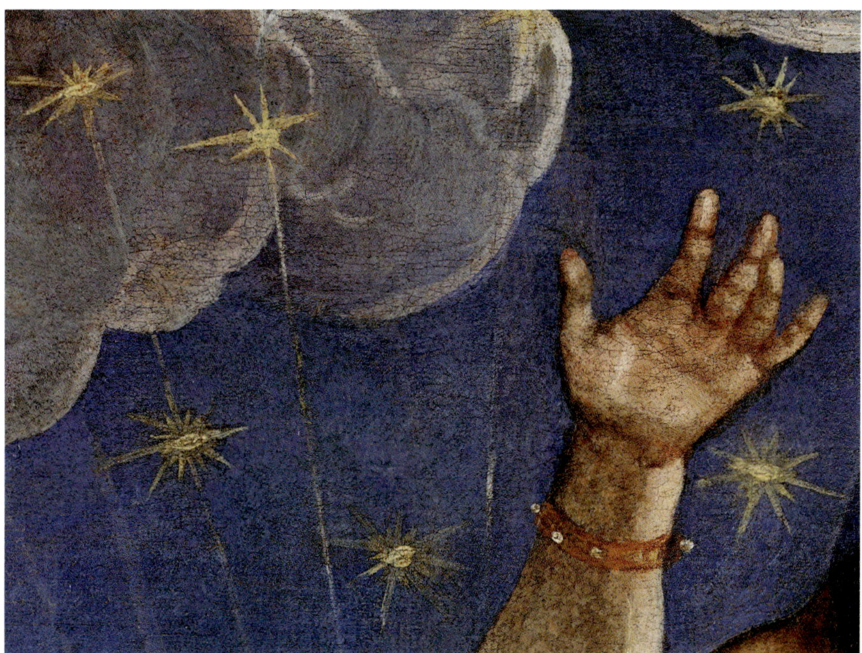

naturally be acquainted with alchemy, too, as would most of the imperial physicians. Scientists and charlatans of different kinds made their way to Prague in large numbers at that time. Once there, they were safe from persecution by a Church that was determined to prevent the questioning of received dogma. The emperor's protection allowed them to explore Nature and investigate its causal sequences. Most of them were searching for the *harmonia mundi*, the correspondence between the human microcosm and divine macrocosm, or universe, with its stars and planets. They did so partly by occult means – and prepared the way for modern science.

Two mathematicians, both court astronomers to Rudolf, were largely responsible for the "disenchantment of the universe". The first, the Dane Tycho Brahe, had magic potions sold under his name, but he also set up an observatory near Prague and determined the position of 777 stars. His successor, the German Johannes Kepler, who cast horoscopes and wrote a "Warning to the opponents of astrology", made an important discovery in 1605: "The heavenly machine is more like a clock than a divine being."

This turned the traditional view of the universe on its head. It was in Prague, too, that Kepler evolved a theory of the astronomical telescope, an instrument which would, at last, enable scientists to explore the distant Milky Way. Hitherto, all explanation of this heavenly body had been limited to the type of conjecture made by the ancient Greeks, or it had taken the form of a mythological account of its origins.

Rudolf II's patronage of the sciences and arts won him everlasting fame. "The imperial star shines" was a hopeful motto thought up for him by Ottavio Strada: *Astrum fulget Caesareum*.

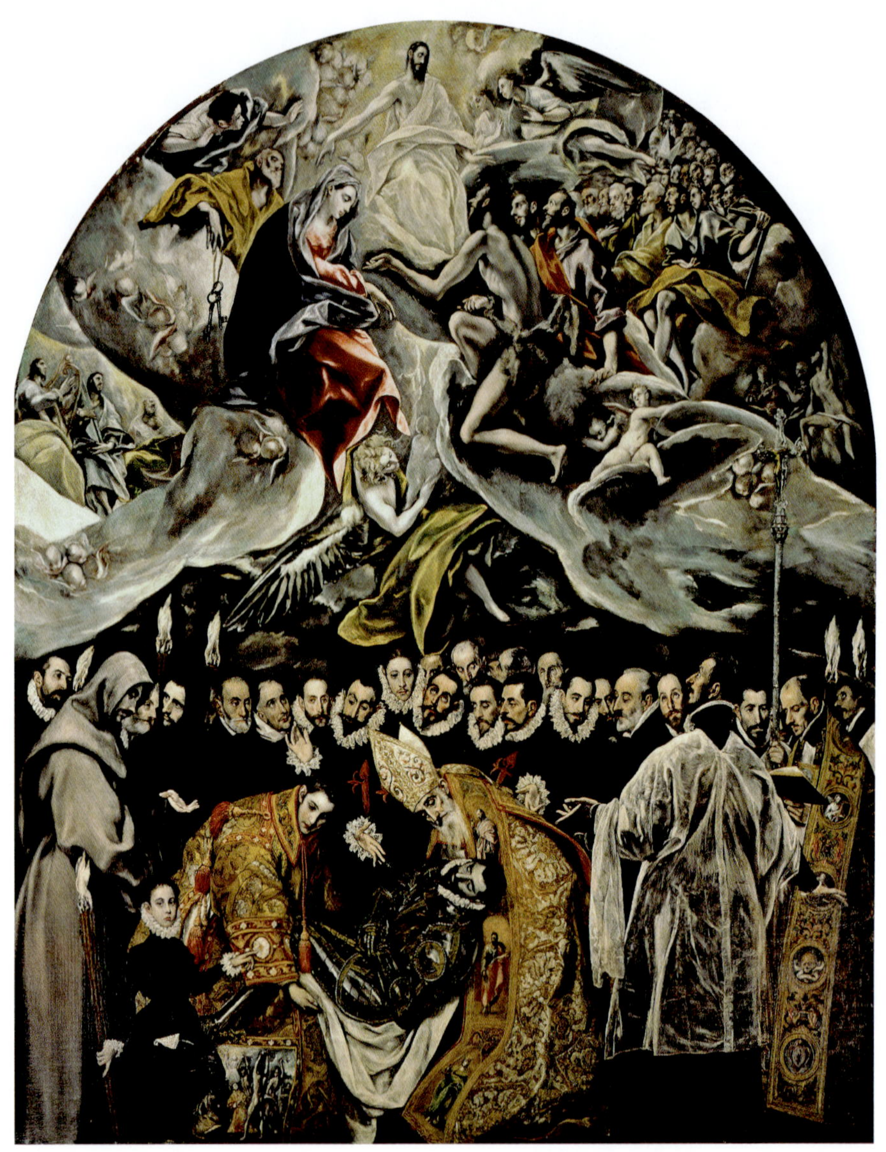

El Greco (1541–1614)
(real name Domenikos Theotokopulos)

Two saints bury the munificent donor

The Burial of the Count of Orgaz, 1586
480 x 360 cm, Toledo, Santo Tomé

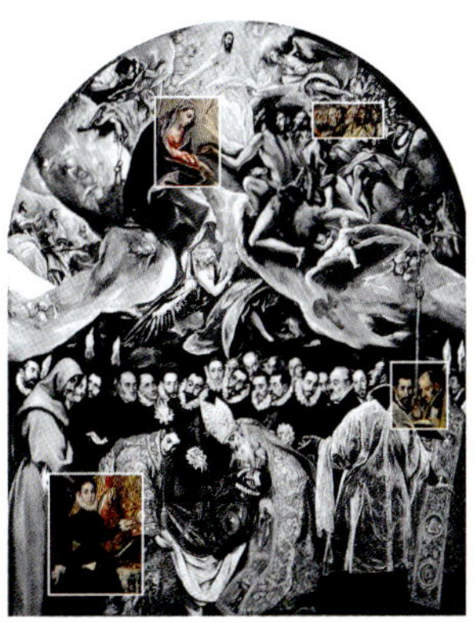

The canvas, 4.8 metres high and 3.6 metres wide, covers the entire wall of a chapel, reaching from the arch of the ceiling almost to the ground. The figures are life sized, painted in 1586 for the Santo Tomé church in Toledo by the Cretan artist Domenikos Theotokopulos, known in Spain as El Greco, the Greek.

El Greco's painting shows a miracle, said to have occurred in the Santo Tomé church at the burial of Don Gonzalo Ruiz in 1312. According to legend, St Stephan and St Augustine appeared and laid the mortal remains of Gonzalo Ruiz in the grave.

Ruiz, erstwhile Chancellor of Castile and governor of Orgaz, was a man of great wealth and influence, whose benificence had been especially apparent towards institutions of the Church. Through his good offices, the Augustinian Order acquired a developable site within the Toledo town walls. He gave financial support to the construction of a monastery, too, and to the building of the church of Santo Tomé. He even made provision that the town of Orgaz should, after his death, make an annual donation to both church and monastery of two lambs, sixteen chickens, two skins of wine, two loads of firewoood and 800 coins. According to the testimony of the saints who attended his funeral, their presence there conferred high distinction upon one who had "served his God and saints".

On vanishing, they are said to have left a divine fragrance on the air.

El Greco made no attempt to clothe his figures in medieval dress. Social or political change was little understood at the time, and attention to detail of this kind would, in any case, have conflicted with his patron's wishes: the painting was not intended to recall an historical event, but to encourage contemporary spectators to follow the worthy example it honoured.

Emphasis on the contemporary relevance of the subject probably contributed to the artist's realistic rendering of many details in the lower, more worldly half of the painting: ruffs, lace cuffs, the transparent supplice. Furthermore, the Toledans would have recognized, among the gentlemen in black, several of their best known citizens.

El Greco gives to the two returned saints the appearance of ordinary persons (showing them without the nimbus which typically invested such figures). He portrays Augustine, the great church father, as a venerable greybeard in a bishop's mitre, while Stephan, reputed to be the first Christian martyr, appears as a young man. A further painting is inset in his mantle: the lapidation of St Stephan. Stephan was the patron saint of the monastery to which Gonzalo Ruiz had given his support. The robe of the priest standing at the right edge

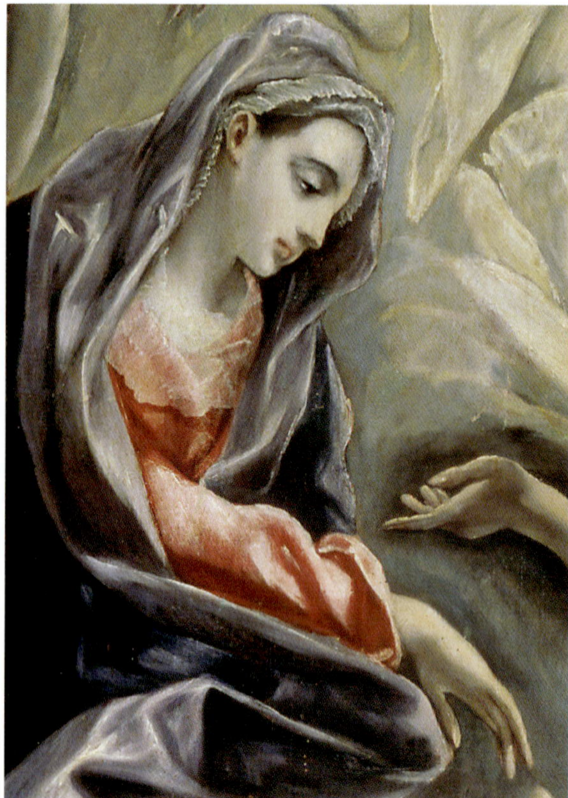

at the church of Santo Tomé. The artist's vision conflated past and present, simultaneously showing the miracle and its incorporation into ecclesiastical doctrine.

El Greco's Heaven comes in muted tones; only the Virgin Mary is somewhat brighter in colour. The figure behind her is Peter with his keys; further down are the Old Testament "saints": King David with his harp, Moses and the stone tablets of the decalogue, Noah and his ark. John the Baptist kneels opposite Mary, while Jesus Christ is enthroned on high. El Greco depicts the soul of the dead Gonzalo Ruiz as the transparent figure of a child borne up in the arms of an angel. The soul's progress appears obstructed, however, or restricted to a narrow strait between two converging clouds.

This might seem surprising, given the high distinction conferred upon the pious man at the burial of his mortal remains. An inconsistency perhaps? In fact, the artist had good reason not to take for granted the soul's unimpeded progress to Heaven. The reason lay in the political predicament of the Church at the close of 16th century.

of the painting carries a series of emblems referring to St Thomas, patron saint of the church and also of architects, whose attribute was usually a builder's square.

It seems the artist chose the theme of the miracle in order to deliver a lesson in hagiology. This may explain why, confronted with such an extraordinary event, the figures maintain their composure: not one is shown throwing up his hands in fright, or sinking in a state of shock to his knees. On the contrary, the monks on the left are engaged in discussion, while others calmly point to the event, as if illustrating a tenet of doctrine.

Indeed, to 16th-century Toledans that was exactly what the painting meant. The legend was part of general religious knowledge, related and reinterpreted each year in a service held on St Stephan's day

Fighting for the Holy Virgin

El Greco painted in the century of the Reformation. Protestant thought had found few followers on the Iberian peninsula, but the Netherlands, where it had spread very quickly, and where Spaniards and Netherlandish mercenaries fought each other over towns, ports and the true faith, was part of the Spanish empire.

News from their northern province filled pious Spanish souls with terror: church statues of saints had been cast down from their pedestals, paintings of the Virgin pierced by lances – satanic forces were at work. That the events had less to do with the revival of the Church than with the work of the Devil was confirmed by reports of iconoclasts tearing the saints to shreds and leaving the demons at their feet intact.

It was the demotion of their most highly venerated Virgin Mary that disturbed the Spaniards most. Luther, so it was reported, had said Mary was no holier than any other Christian believer, while yet another Reformer had said that if Mary had been a purse full of gold before Christ's birth, she was an empty purse afterwards, and that anybody who prayed to the Virgin was committing blasphemy by exalting a woman to the rank of a god.

The great respect commanded by the Holy Virgin south of the Pyrenees stood in peculiar contrast to the disregard shown to women in Spanish society. Their status was far below that of women in Italy, Germany or France. One explanation may lie in the fact that large tracts of Spain, including Toledo itself, had been under Moorish rule for many centuries. The Moors thought of women as base creatures who, easily tempted, required constant surveillance, Although there were famous nuns in Spain, the mistress of a king, by contrast with her French peer, had no influence whatsoever. Women had no place in the public sphere, as El Greco's painting so ably demonstrates: Mary is the only large-scale female figure among countless men in Heaven and on earth.

In the 16th and 17th centuries the Virgin Mary was the most significant religious and cultural figure in Spanish life: many works by Lope de Vega and Calderón are dedicated to her.

The militant adoration of the Virgin climaxed in the dispute surrounding her Immaculate Conception. This did not, as might be imagined, refer to the begetting of Jesus Christ, but to Mary's own procreation. Her mother was said to have conceived her either without male contribution, or, if a man's presence at the event were conceded, without original sin, for the man was merely God's instrument. Although the pope did not raise the Immaculate Conception to a dogma until the 19th century, it had been tantamount to a dogma in Spain long before. In 1618 Spanish universities were put under obligation to teach and actively defend the Immaculate Conception.

From a Spanish point of view, however, the Protestants had not only debased the Holy Virgin, they had also got rid of the saints, who were tremendously important to the Catholic faith. To say that El Greco underlines the integral function of the saints in this painting would be an understatement. Together with the Virgin, it is they who intercede with the distant, enthroned figure of Christ on behalf of the souls of the dead; only through their supplication can the barrier of clouds dissolve and the soul find its way to paradise unhindered. The painting's theological intervention demonstrates the rupture of the vital dynamic suggested in the

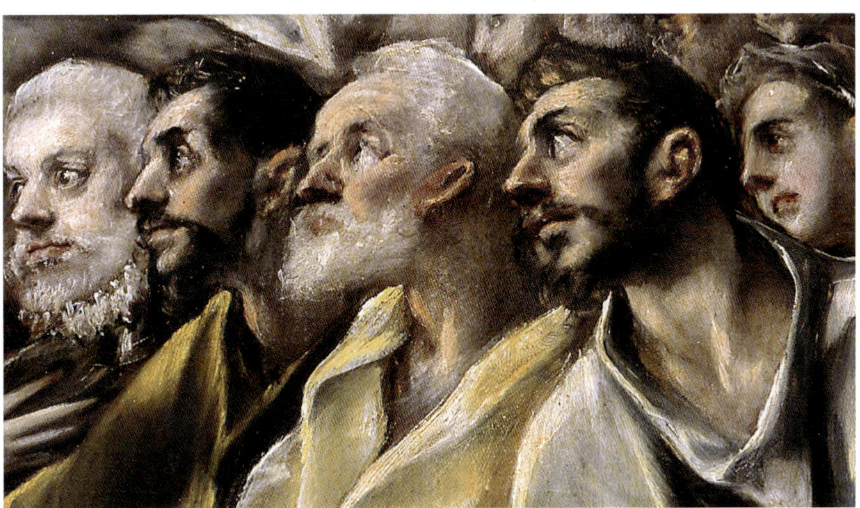

brightly lit undersides of the clouds: the upward surge through the vortex of light to Jesus Christ is obstructed. Since the Reformation had degraded the Virgin and the saints, it was now the task of the Counter-Reformation to effectively demonstrate their significance.

A king among saints

The painting also contains a portrait of Philip II of Spain, who, in 1586, was still on the throne. He is shown sitting among the saints who, gathered behind John, are interceding for the soul of Ruiz. Philip's empire was the largest of all European states. It not only included the Netherlands and Naples with southern Italy, but colonies in Central and South America, some of which were literally borderless. This was the empire on which – in the words of the well-known dictum – the sun never set.

Of course, his life was as remote from his many subjects as any god. Furthermore, the court etiquette he had inherited from his father ensured that court and government officials kept their distance. Only a small elite was ever admitted to his presence, and anybody who handed something to him in person was obliged to do so on his knees. However, there was one important element of his father's etiquette which, characteristically, Philip altered: priests were no longer obliged to genuflect before him. He gave to the ambassadors of the kingdom of God, though appointed by himself, a status far greater than that accorded to the representatives of worldly affairs.

This was altogether typical of Philip's rule. He set greater store by defending his faith than his empire. No personal loss could hurt him more deeply, he wrote upon receiving news of the Netherlandish iconoclasts, than the slightest insult or disrespect to the Lord and his effigies. Even "the ruin" of all his lands could not hinder him from "doing what a Christian and God fearing sovereign must do in the service of God and in testimony to his Catholic faith and the power and honour of the Apostolic See."

Philip II had a powerful instrument at his disposal: the Inquisition. In other countries the authorities who condemned apostates, unbelievers and witches were purely clerical; afterwards, offenders were handed over to the state authorities, who would then enforce the penalty. In Spain even the trial was subordinate to the throne. The king appointed the Grand Inquisitor, and the persecution of non-Catholics served interests of state. For over 700 years the Moors, finally defeated in 1492, had ruled over almost the whole Iberian peninsula. Only families who converted from Islam to Christianity were permitted to remain in Spain. The same applied to Jews. They, too, suffered enforced baptism.

Though hundreds of thousands of Jews and Muslims had left the country, or were in the process of doing so, Philip still saw Catholic Spain threatened by unbelievers who merely paid lip service to Christ, or by heretics secretly plotting insurrection. The Inquisition acted as a secret

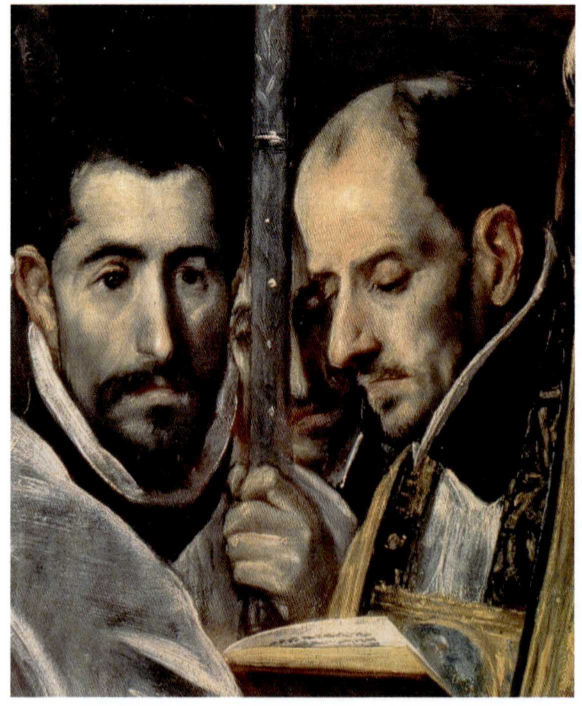

police force, defending the status quo and transferring to the state the wealth and property of those it condemned.

Combined religious and racial persecution was one of the chief factors leading to the decline of the Spanish empire. The Jews had been specialists in foreign trade and finance; the country's best physicians were Jews, and they constituted the cream of its university teachers. It was thanks to Jewish scholars and translators that forgotten manuscripts by antique philosophers were translated from Arabic into Latin, thus becoming available to Christian theologians.

For their part, the Muslims had farmed vast areas of the country, and the success of agriculture depended on Moorish irrigation systems. Now that they were gone, the fields were bare, the villages depopulated, and the businesses of the merchants collapsed. For Philip, however, as for the clergy, the Spanish grandees and a large section of the Spanish population, this was less important than defending the faith.

Yet Philip's unrealistic religious zeal was not the only factor that earned him a place among the saints in Heaven in El Greco's painting. Other artists, too, for example Dürer in his All Saints' Altarpiece of 1511, gave a place in Heaven to their most prominent contemporaries. In so doing, they enjoyed the support of St Augustine's "City of God", in which the domains of Heaven and earth were interwoven, providing theological justification for the depiction of mortals as the inhabitants of Heaven.

Monument to a priest

The priest portrayed reading is Andrés Núñez, who, at the time in question, was responsible for the parish of Santo Tomé. It is to him that we owe the existence of this painting. Commissioning El Greco to execute the work was the final act in a campaign Núñez had conducted for decades in an attempt to bring just renown to Gonzalo Ruiz and – lest it be forgot – himself.

His first undertaking of this kind had been the attempt to move Gonzalo's grave. The pious Castilian chancellor had chosen an inconspicuous corner of the church of Santo Tomé as the resting place of his earthly remains – apparently a sign of his modesty. Núñez wanted his bones moved to a more auspicious place, but his superiors rejected the request, for "the hands of sinners" should not touch the body of one who had been "touched by the hands of saints".

Consequently, Núñez decided to build a chapel with a high dome over the immured coffin. Soon after this demonstrative deed in memory of the lord of Orgaz (it was his descendants who received the title of count), the citizens of Orgaz decided to annul the 250-year-old legacy of two lambs, sixteen chickens, two skins of wine, two loads of firewood and 800 coins. Núñez instituted legal proceedings, winning the case in 1569. In order to record his triumph he had a Latin text mounted above the grave, recounting the legend and referring to the rebuttal of the town of Orgaz through "the vigorous efforts of Andrés Núñez".

The smart priest thus created a monument to himself. After applying to the archbishopric in 1584, he was granted permission to commission a painting of the miracle of the interment. El Greco was commissioned in 1586 and delivered the painting in the same year. Whatever the work may owe to the personal ambition of a priest, it has to be said that propagation of the miracle of the burial was also fully in keeping with Counter-Reformation church policy. It was seen as important not only to exalt the Virgin and saints, but to defend the need for charitable donations and the worship of relics. According to Catholic belief, the route to Heaven was paved with "good deeds", a view rejected by Reformers, for whom faith and divine mercy were all that counted. The Reformers also vehemently opposed the veneration of relics, a cult of considerable significance in Catholic countries. It was at this time, too, that Gaspar de Quiroga, appointed archbishop in 1577, brought the bones of St Leocadia and St Ildefonso to Toledo, thereby greatly adding to the status of its cathedral. Santo Tomé's painting of the burial extolled the piety of charitable donations, at the same time defending the worship of relics. For had not two saints touched, and thereby honoured, the mortal frame? Was it not therefore correct to infer that all Christians should honour the mortal remains of the pious, the saints and the martyrs?

The painting's gigantic format complied with Counter-Reformation propaganda in yet another sense: its stunning visual impact. The Protestants, by contrast, wished to see their churches purified of all ornamentation. Places of worship were to be free of graven images, or at least not crowded with visual distractions from God's word. But the

Catholics thought otherwise: since the church was God's house, why not use every means possible to decorate it in His honour? The exuberant splendour of Baroque churches was, not least, a reaction against the plain churches of the Reformation.

Reality as a stage set

The boy pointing so meaningfully at the saint was El Greco's son; his year of birth, 1578, can be deciphered on his handkerchief. When his father painted the miracle, he was eight years old. The contract was concluded on 18 March. El Greco finished the work, whose value was estimated by two experts at 1,200 ducats, by Christmas. Since the price was too steep for the parish council of Santo Tomé, it appointed two experts of its own, only to find that they arrived at a value of 1,600 ducats. It was not until July 1588 that the parties agreed – on the lower sum.

El Greco was dogged by financial problems almost all his life. He was not a prince among painters, like Titian, in whose Venice studio he had trained. "The Greek" was born in 1541 on Crete, which, at that time, was under Venetian rule. He learned icon painting, left for Venice where he became a master of spatial representation and architectonic perspective, then moved to Rome. When Pius V, disturbed by the nudity of some of the figures in Michelangelo's *Last Judgement*, wanted some of the frescos in the Sistine Chapel painted over, El Greco is reputed to have offered to paint an equally good, but more decent, work if the original were destroyed.

It is not known when, or why, El Greco settled in Spain. It is possible he felt ill at ease with the Italian artists' exaltation of corporeal and architectural beauty; perhaps he hoped his celebrations of the after life would find greater recognition in Spain. Spanish cardinals, resident in Rome, are likely to have spoken of the Escorial, Philip II's palatial monastery, and El Greco may have hoped to find work there. Instead he settled in the old religious capital of Toledo, the seat of the archbishop. In 1579 the king commissioned a painting from him – the only order he received from that source. Philip apparently disliked the Greek's paintings.

Spiritually they had much in common. For both, the afterlife was more important than this life. Philip longed to rule from the Escorial in the company of monks, and to be able to see an altar even from his bed. This view meant more to him than his empire: his Armada was defeated in 1588; in 1598, the year of his death, financial pressures forced him to give up his war against France, and the northern provinces of the Netherlands were already as good as lost.

El Greco's whole life's work, and this painting in particular, bears witness to his belief that the kingdom of Heaven was more important and more real than the world in which we live. Though he is painstakingly exact in his detailed rendering of the lower, worldly half of the painting, the realistic heads and dress have the effect of drawing the burial scene into the foreground, while the isocephalic arrangement of onlookers' heads gives the appearance of the top of a stage set. It is only here, behind this dividing line, that the true life begins. Only the upper half is dynamic, vital through and through, an effect achieved with the help of lighting and a use of depth and line that draws the eye upward.

It remains to be said that not all Spaniards ceded to the uncritical renunciation of reality. The writer Miguel de Cervantes, for example, a contemporary of El Greco and Philip II, took a different point of view. Though he did not attack the religious zeal of his compatriots, his character Don Quixote, a chivalrous and deluded idealist, illustrates the dangers that may befall a person who inhabits a world of fantasy rather than facts, someone who, in pursuit of ideals, loses sight of the ground beneath his feet.

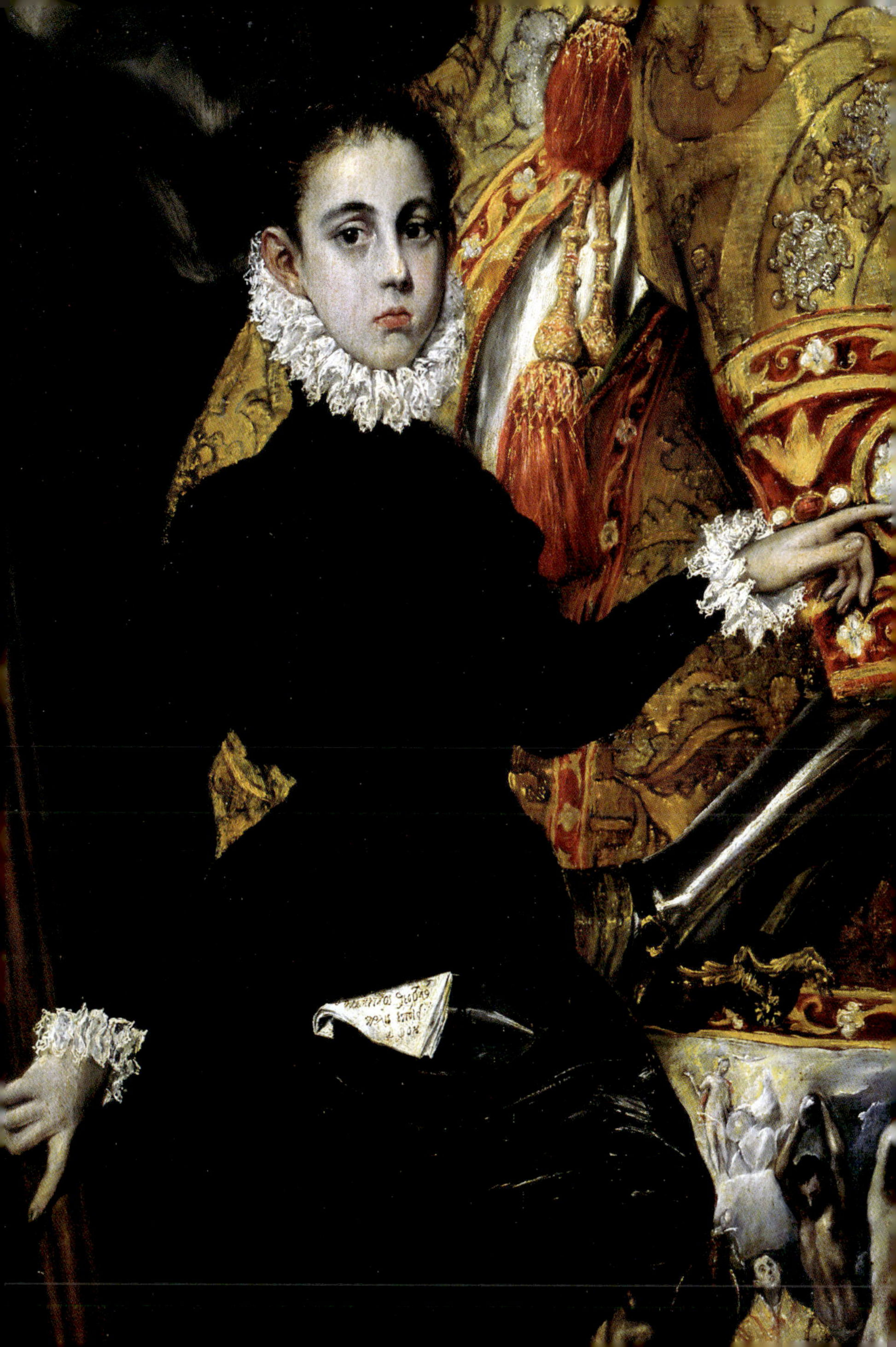

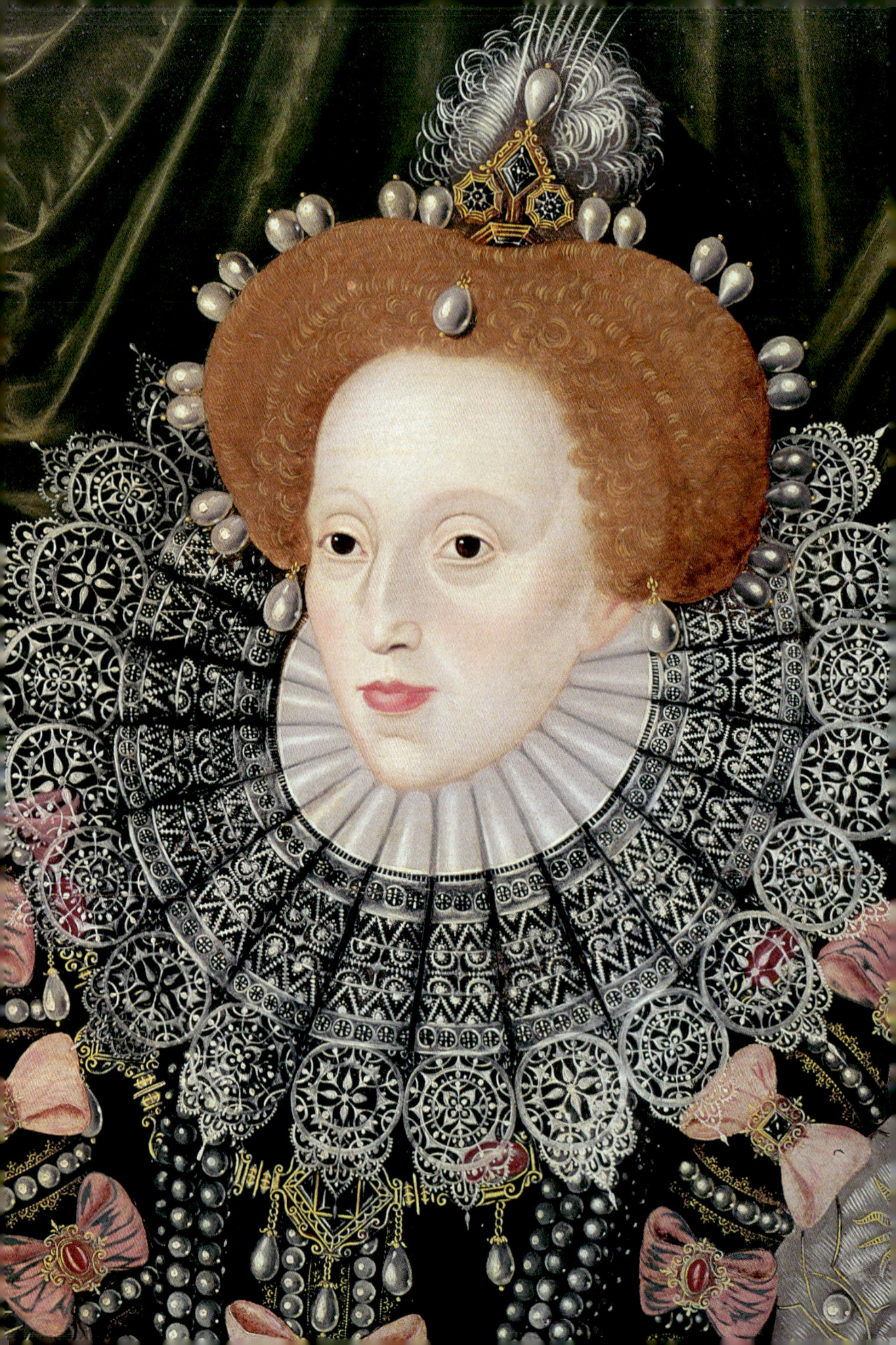

George Gower (1540–1596)

A woman thwarts Spain's pride

Armada Portrait of Elizabeth I, c. 1590
105 x 133 cm, Bedfordshire, Woburn Abbey

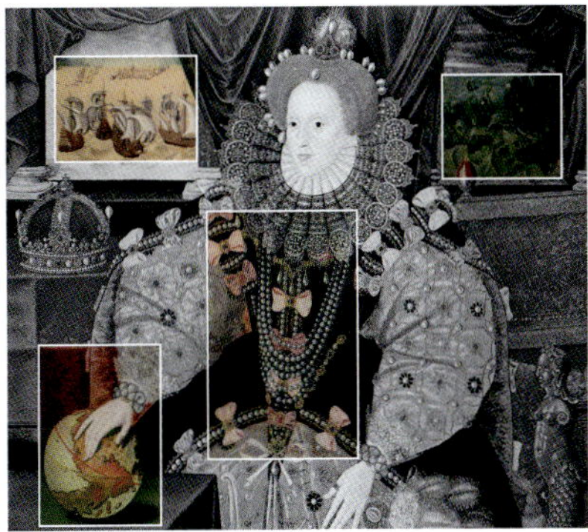

In his portrait of Elizabeth I, executed around 1590, the English artist George Gower presents his queen as a self-confident sovereign. He also pays tribute to her greatest triumph: the decisive defeat which Her Majesty's navy had inflicted upon the vast Spanish fleet in the English Channel just a few years earlier, in 1588. The sinking of the Armada marked the beginning of England's rise to major international power. Gower's portrait today belongs to Woburn Abbey.

She was painted many times and had many of her portraits subsequently destroyed; it seems she felt the pictures did not show her to enough advantage. Her red hair needed to shine, proper justice had to be done to her famous pale complexion, and no shadow was to be allowed to darken her face.

When Elizabeth I sat for the present portrait, with its two background views of the sea and ships, she was about 56 years old. Her hair was false and her face plastered with a thick layer of white makeup. But the fiction of youth and beauty had to be maintained, in art as at court. The ageing queen kept young suitors and had been negotiating marriage with a French prince for decades. She enjoyed having many admirers, but had absolutely no intention of wedding any of them. At the mere

age of eight she is supposed to have announced: "I will never get married!" She had good reason to make up her mind so early: that same year her stepmother was beheaded, while her own mother, Anne Boleyn, had already been executed. The cruelty displayed by her father, Henry VIII, towards his wives may thus have shaped her attitude towards marriage; it is more probable, however, that her own thirst for power left no room for a husband to reign at her side.

Portraits of this extraordinary woman were fashioned not simply to flatter her vanity, however, but also for reasons of state. Like her carefully stage managed public appearances, these pictures were also part of a propaganda programme which had no call for realism. Thus the two scenes visible through the windows at the back took place neither at the same time nor in the same place: weeks lay between the first appearance of the Spanish Armada and its eventual defeat off the coast of England.

The painting nevertheless makes sense as a glittering tribute to its sitter – it shows the most glorious event in the reign of Elizabeth I, a reign that lasted over 40 years. It was painted by George Gower (1540–1596), Serjeant Painter and one of the artists who for many years had the privilege of painting the queen.

A battle over trade and trifles

The traditional insignia of power – orb and sceptre – are missing from this picture. Instead of a sceptre, the queen holds an ornate fan of ostrich plumes in her left hand, while her right hand rests on a globe. Just as the traditional Roman orb represented the whole world, so the globe offered a modern 16th-century version of the old symbol.

In those days, globes existed only in small numbers. The first had been constructed in Nuremberg barely 100 years earlier. George Gower has not taken pains to reproduce one of the English models exactly; he was evidently more interested in the queen's hand lying on the globe, which demonstrates in impressive fashion Elizabeth's hegemony beyond the bounds of her small island kingdom.

It was no coincidence that Gower's painted globe should also show ships, for in those days world domination meant sovereignty of the seas. When Elizabeth came to the throne in 1558, the major political and naval powers were still Spain and Portugal, both nations of explorers. In 1580 Philip II of Spain annexed neighbouring Portugal, and from then onwards, declared, "all the Americas, known and unknown" belonged to him.

Elizabeth vied with him on this score. Her subject, Francis Drake, became one the first people to sail round the world and thereby proved that the Spaniards were not the only ones capable of such a pioneering feat. Drake and other English freebooters captured Spanish galleons and diminished the profits which Philip hoped to reap from his American colonies. A small scale war ensued. Although Elizabeth had not officially taken up arms against the number one world power, she permitted her subjects to lay Spanish gold and silver at her feet.

She needed the money, because when she took up office she had inherited a mountain of debts. According to a report by the Venetian ambassador, when Elizabeth paid back the last of the money owing,

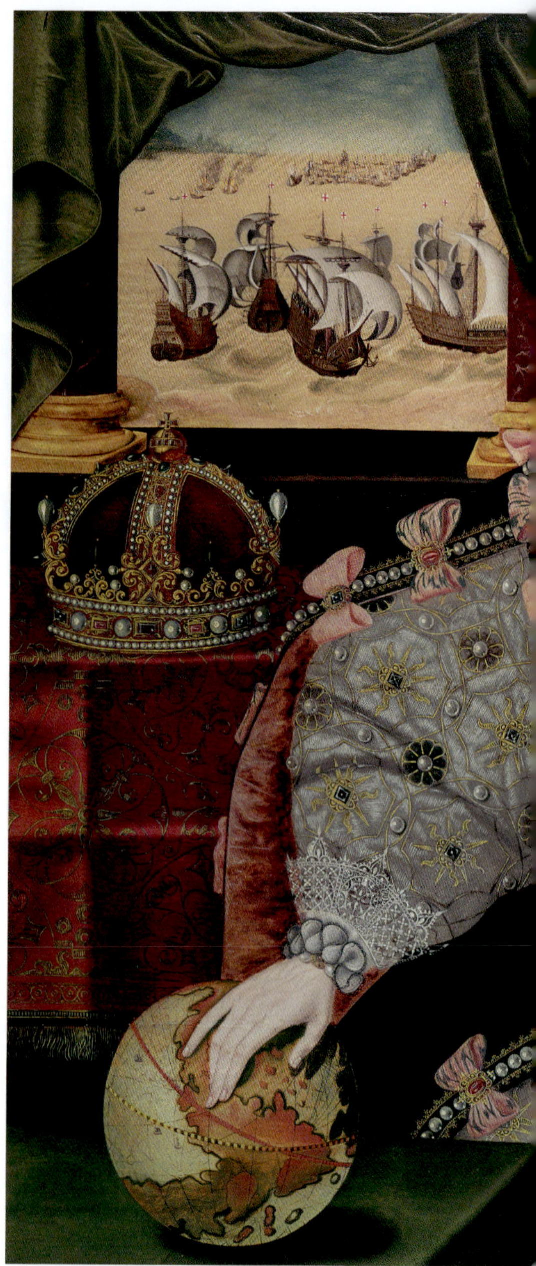

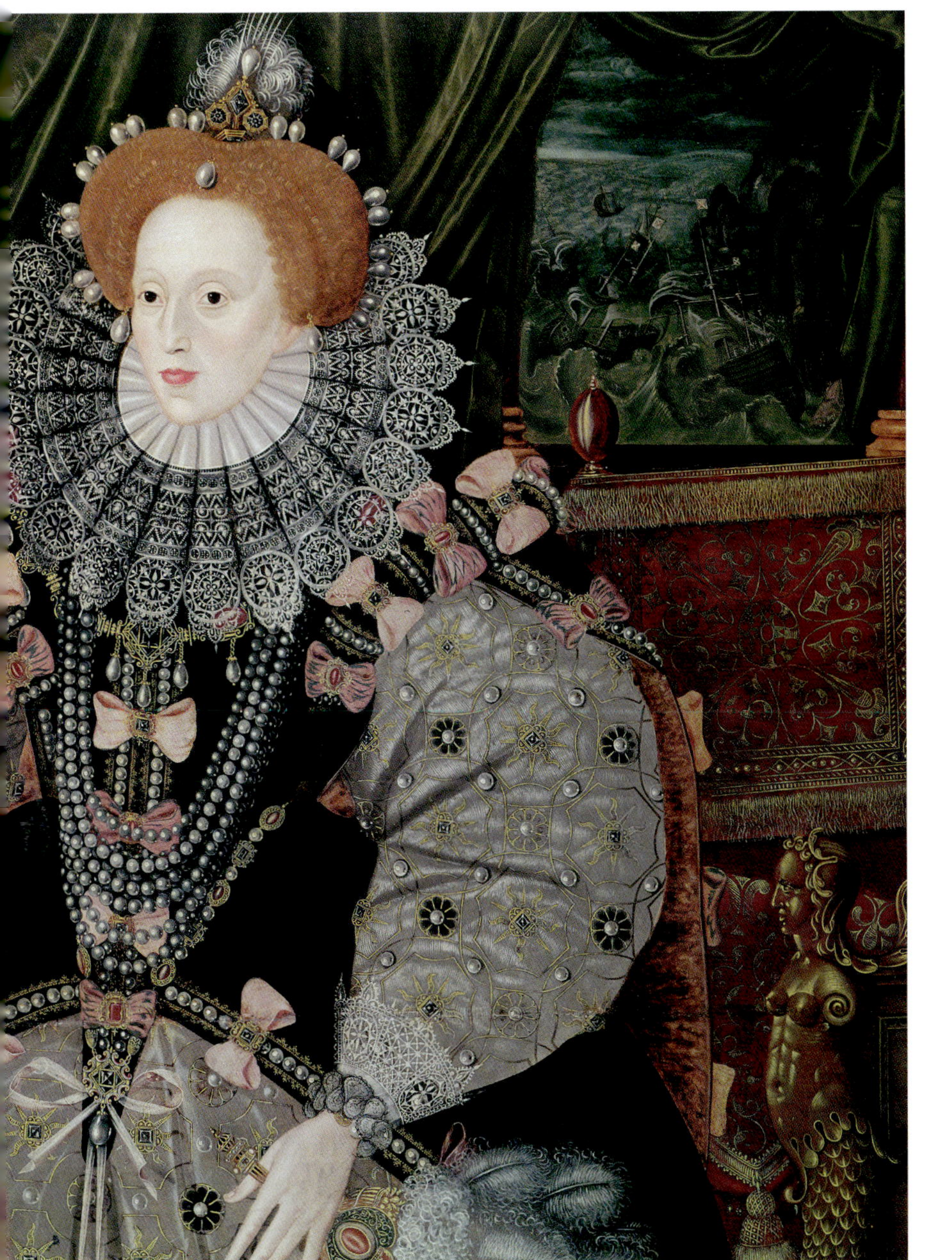

she was "hailed by the people as if she were a second Messiah". But the English buccaneers embarked on their perilous voyages not just in search of booty. Philip had a monopoly on trade outside Europe, something which Elizabeth was not prepared to accept. In this she had the backing of the English merchants. The new merchant classes wanted their own slice of the international market, and Elizabeth rightly hoped that they would bring prosperity to her impoverished country.

There was yet another factor, too, in the increasingly bitter conflict with Spain. Philip II was an ardent, fanatical Catholic; Elizabeth, on the other hand, like the majority of her subjects, was a Protestant. Philip appointed himself the battlefield champion of his Church – Elizabeth had no other choice but to fight for her own.

It was a fight she did not want. As far as she was concerned, it was pointless to shed blood for one or the other variation of the faith. Her father, Henry VIII, had renounced Catholicism because he wanted to divorce the first of his many wives and pocket the possessions of the Church. His daughter, "Bloody Mary", had attempted to turn back the tide of the Reformation by torturing people and burning them at the stake. She was followed onto the throne by

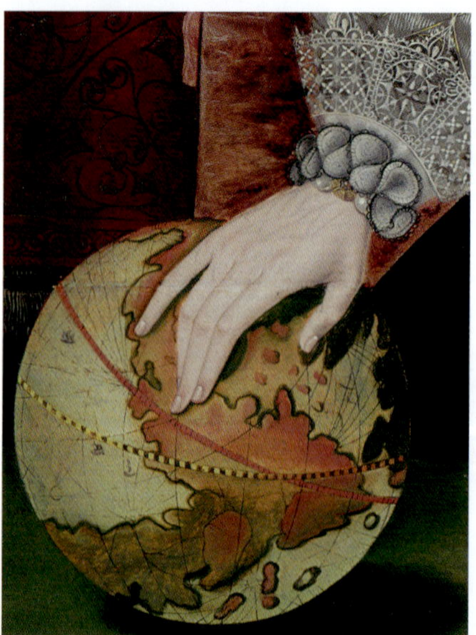

Elizabeth, who had thus experienced her father's abuse of religion and her sister's religious fanaticism, and who represented instead – even if she couldn't always act upon it – the law of tolerance: "There is only one Christ Jesus and one faith; the rest is a dispute about trifles."

The trick with the fireships

The view through the left-hand window shows the Spanish Armada in the background, as tight knit as a floating fortress. They possessed more majesty than the English fleet, according to a contemporary report, but advanced only slowly even in full sail, because their hefty superstructures made the ships heavy. They approached in a crescent formation, the two cusps of the crescent at least seven miles apart.

The Armada comprised exactly 130 ships with 30,656 men on board, including over 100 priests and monks. The voyage to England had the character of a Crusade; it was mounted against heretics. The Armada was planned as a transport fleet which would sail to Calais, pick up another 40,000 soldiers from the Spanish Netherlands, and then cross the Channel. Once on land, matters would be settled by force.

The English did not succeed in stopping the floating army on its way to Calais despite the fact that they used a new tactic. The English ships were lower and faster than the Spanish "sea elephants", and although their cannons did not fire the heavy shot of their opponents, their range was longer. They therefore attempted to manoeuvre themselves close to the Spanish one behind another in a line, so that they could let off their broadsides while themselves remaining out of firing range.

To appreciate just how new this English style of warfare was, it is necessary to go back seventeen years to the last great naval battle, which took place off Lepanto in the Mediterranean in 1571 and which was fought against the Turks by the Venetians and Spanish. In this confrontation, both sides used rowing galleys to board the enemies' ships and overpower their crews. Rowing galleys were not suitable for the rough seas of the Atlantic, however, and the Spaniards had to leave them behind. Boarding nevertheless remained their chief strategy, and they despised the English for not wanting to approach.

In the same view through the window, a number of the English ships are visible in the foreground, recognizable by their traditional St George's flag

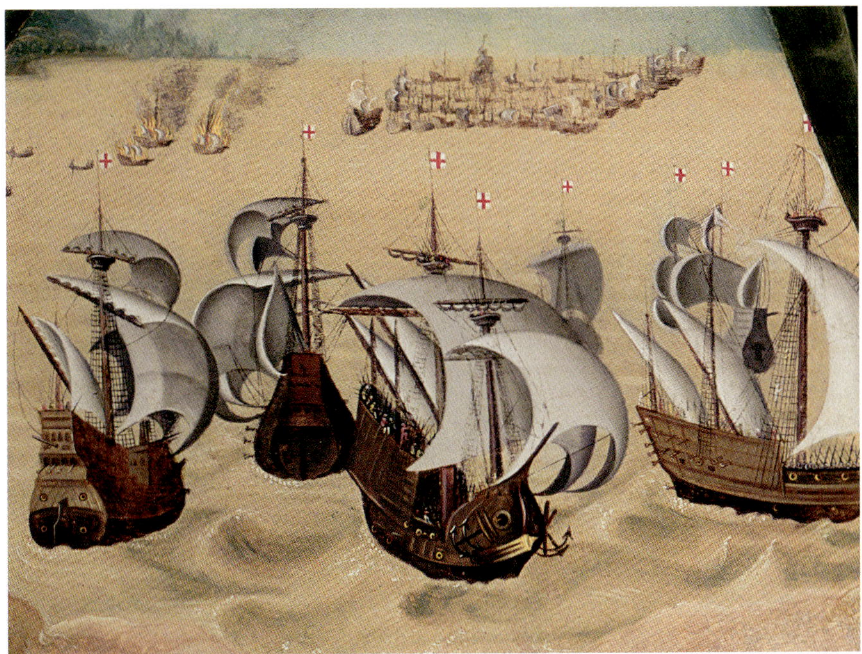

with its red cross on a white ground. The English fleet was headed by Lord Howard of Effingham, who was intelligent enough to call upon the nautical experience of the former buccaneer Drake. As Sir Francis, ennobled by the queen, he held the position of vice admiral.

Gower shows the famous encounter off Calais. The English had so far failed to halt the Spaniards, and Elizabeth did not possess a standing army; the troops she had hastily rallied together were not nearly so well trained as those of Philip. The danger of England becoming a Catholic province of Spain was great. On 29 July 1588 the English set fire to several of their own ships and let them drift across to the Spanish Armada. The ships burnt out without causing any damage – but their psychological effect was enormous. The Spaniards, sailing so close together, feared nothing more than fire, and they also suspected that the English ships were concealing explosive powder kegs. Panic swept through the fleet, and the ships wildy broke forma-tion and fled individually. A trick had blown the floating fortress apart.

Spain's Armada sinks amidst the waves

The ships seen here foundering in the waves bear the Spanish national ensign, the diagonal cross of St Andrew. Following the initial dispersal of the Armada on 29 July, the decisive naval battle took place off Gravelines. For the first time, the Spaniards emerged as clearly inferior: they lost eleven ships and counted 600 dead and 800 wounded. According to contemporary reports, when one holed Spanish ship capsized, streams of blood could be seen flowing into the sea.

The English only suffered 60 fatalities. They owed their light losses not just to their speedy ships and long range artillery, but also to the miserable Spanish command. As in most countries in those days, it was the tradition in both England and Spain to appoint a high-ranking noble to the position of supreme command. Philip II had chosen a gran-dee who was prone to sea sickness and who had previously only fought on land. Nor did he have a Francis Drake as his vice admiral. The second in command in the Spanish fleet had no reputation and no authority.

The battle off Gravelines left the Spanish demoralized. They had considered the Armada invincible and were not prepared for defeat. To avoid being shot apart by the English any further, they had to escape, and took advantage of a strong breeze which carried them north.

The Armada could no longer fulfil its instructions to transport an invasion force to England. Spanish pride, however, and a fear of Philip, meant it could not admit to failure. While the ships held their course northwards, the fleet's commanders decided to return to the English Channel "as soon as conditions permit". They all knew that would not be straightaway. Silently, the captains prepared themselves for the long and perilous voyage home, one which would take them over 1,500 miles around England, Scotland and Ireland.

The captains were instructed to sail far from the coast. But when their water and food supplies ran out, they had to seek the land, and many ran aground on rocks and sandbanks. Many ships were already damaged even before they started the journey north. These problems were compounded, too, by navigational errors made by sailors who were unfamiliar with the North Sea and the North Atlantic. Altogether, the Armada lost another 59 ships on its voyage home. Only some 10,000 of over 30,000 soldiers and sailors eventually made it back to Spain.

The Armada was ultimately defeated not by the English, but by the forces of Nature. The English expressed it differently. While not wanting to appear triumphalist, they did not want to attribute the victory to Nature either; they announced instead that "this time Christ showed himself to be a Protestant."

A virgin as queen of the seas

The English could have won the day outright had their queen not been so thrifty. Her fleet only had water and provisions for two days, and the gunpowder ran out early. Under these conditions, it would have been impossible to pursue the fleeing Spaniards. In vain, Elizabeth's advisers tried to persuade her that war could only be waged successfully

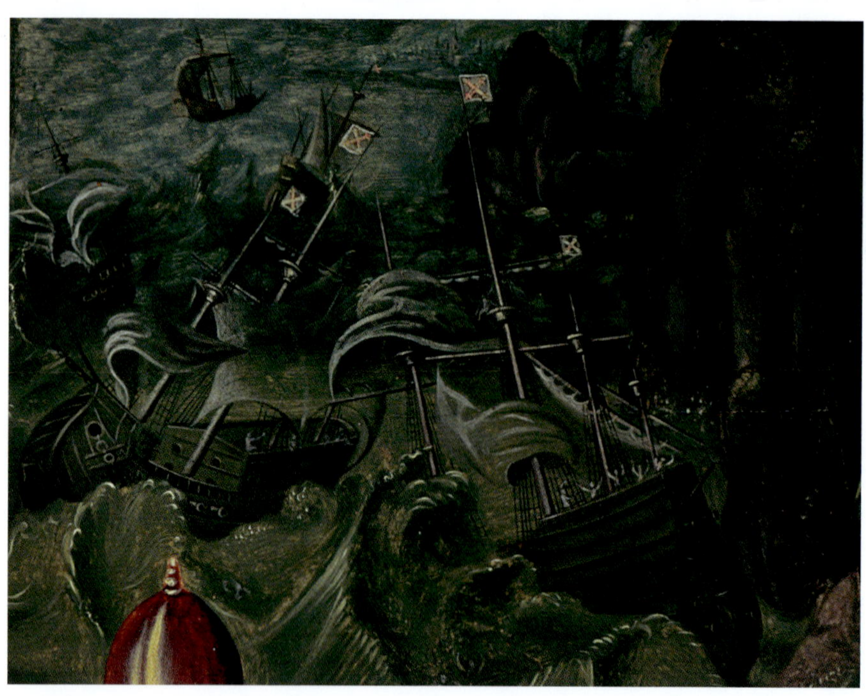

if sufficient means were made available, and in particular if the ships had adequate provisions.

Barely had the immediate danger of an invasion passed than the queen ordered the English fleet to disband. Unlike Philip, Elizabeth possessed almost no ships of her own; those leased from merchants and buccaneers were given back, and the soldiers and sailors dismissed. There was no money with which to pay them off.

More men died of poverty, hunger and typhoid after the war, it is said, than fell in the battle against the Spaniards. No wonder many of the English considered their queen not just thrifty, but mean.

Faced with the magnificent outfits in which she had herself painted, and which she also donned for her public appearances, the tight rein which Elizabeth exercised over her spending seems something of a contradiction. But the lavish dresses and expensive jewellery cost her little: she had them given to her. On 1 January every year she graciously accepted clothes and jewels from her admirers and courtiers. After his circumnavigation of the globe, Francis Drake presented her with a crown of gold and precious stones which he had plundered from the Spanish. Elizabeth acquired the six strings of pearls which she is wearing in this picture from her sister Mary Stuart, at a price well below their true value.

The many bows, lace trimmings, pearls and diamonds adorning Elizabeth's dress were not merely the attributes of a vain queen, however. They also helped to lend Elizabeth the individual a symbolic stature. The various precious stones carried their own meaning. Pearls, for example – especially predominant in the present Armada portrait – come from the sea: they testify to the fact that, following the defeat of the Spaniards, Elizabeth has become the "queen of the seas". Pearls were also viewed as symbols of virginity. Like the diamonds and topaz on her dress, they are a declaration of purity. What the real state of affairs was, and how far Elizabeth actually went with her lovers, is another question, one often asked at her court and much loved by her biographers. But as the representative of her island, as a symbolic figure, she was emphatically a virgin.

For in order to assert themselves against Spain, the English urgently required a highly stylized, almost mystical figurehead. What was at stake was not money or ships, but religion. Philip had the

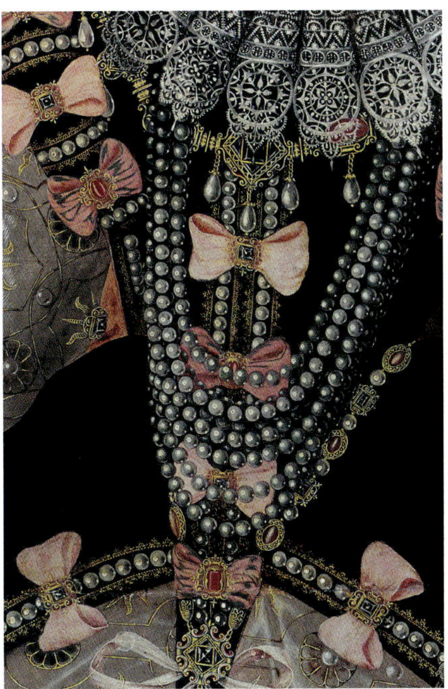

entire ideological power apparatus of Rome behind him. Elizabeth possessed nothing comparable. She had to appear both as England's regent and the head of its Church. If the others were fighting for the Virgin Mary, the English could at least fight for their Virgin Queen.

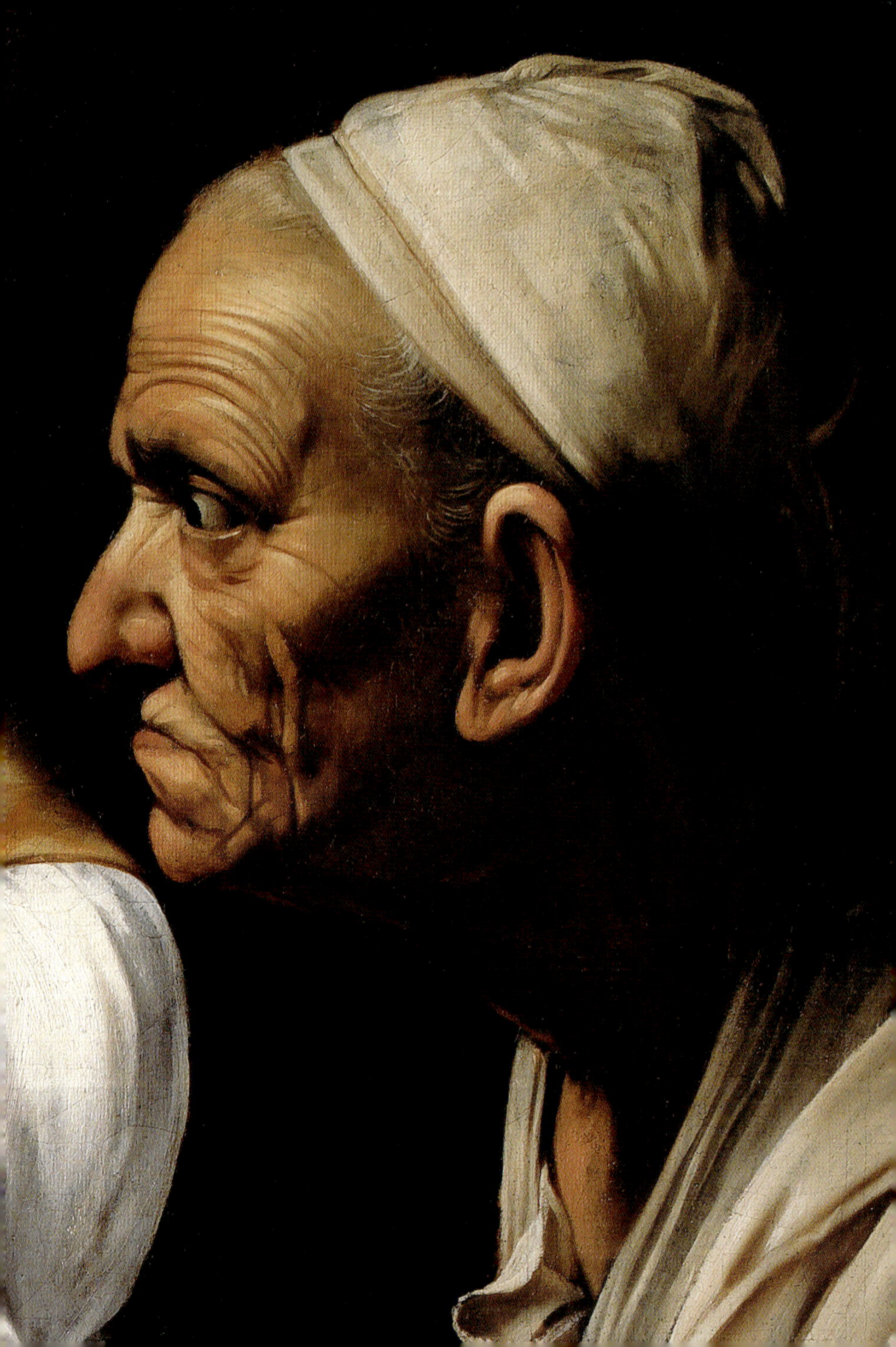

Caravaggio (1571–1610)
(real name Michelangelo Merisi)

Tyrannicide by tender hand

Judith and Holofernes, c. 1599
145 x 195 cm, Rome, Galleria Nazionale d'Arte Antica

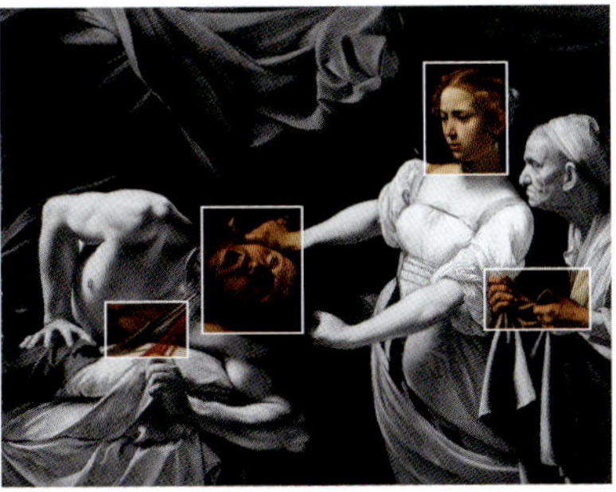

The lovely Jewish widow Judith, who beheaded an Assyrian leader because he had threatened the lives of her people, was held up as a shining example by religious fanatics. Caravaggio's subject was highly topical at the time of the Counter-Reformation. Today, the painting is in the Roman Galleria Nazionale d'Arte Antica.

"Now when Holofernes was stretched out on his bed, and was drunk and asleep … Judith stood weeping at his bedside and said in her heart, O Lord, God of Israel, give me strength and look in this hour upon the work of my hands … She … took his sword … and held him fast by the hair of his head and prayed again … Then she struck his neck twice with all her might and smote off his head … Soon afterward she went out and gave Holofernes' head to her maid, who placed it in her food bag."

This account is taken from the Book of Judith. It recounts an incident in the history of the Jews, but since the original manuscript is lost and the text itself is difficult to date, the Book of Judith is considered apocryphal (not accepted as canonical) by Jews and Protestants. It was, however, included in St Jerome's Latin translation of the Scriptures,

the Vulgate. Caravaggio's painting of the scene, executed in 1599, follows the biblical version, except that the maid does not wait outside but is painted alongside her mistress – her wrinkled skin offering the artist a welcome contrast to the peachy skin of his heroine.

The "very comely" and rich widow Judith, "of whom nobody could say ill", had put off her mourning clothes, dressed herself in her finest garments and entered the enemy camp in order to rescue her people. The Assyrian army, led by Holofernes, stood in arms before the city of Bethulia. The Jews had lost heart, were on the point of giving up, and yet this woman set out on her own to seduce the enemy. After her bloody deed, the enemy soldiers fled in panic; Israel was saved and Judith returned "unsullied by sin" from the libertine's tent.

"Thou art the glory of Jerusalem, thou art the great boast of Israel, thou art the great pride of our nation." Such were the high priest's words of praise for the heroine. "Exalted thou art in the eyes of the Lord for ever and ever! And all the people said Amen."

This episode has featured in the work of many artists throughout the centuries, many of whom have been less attracted by the political and religious

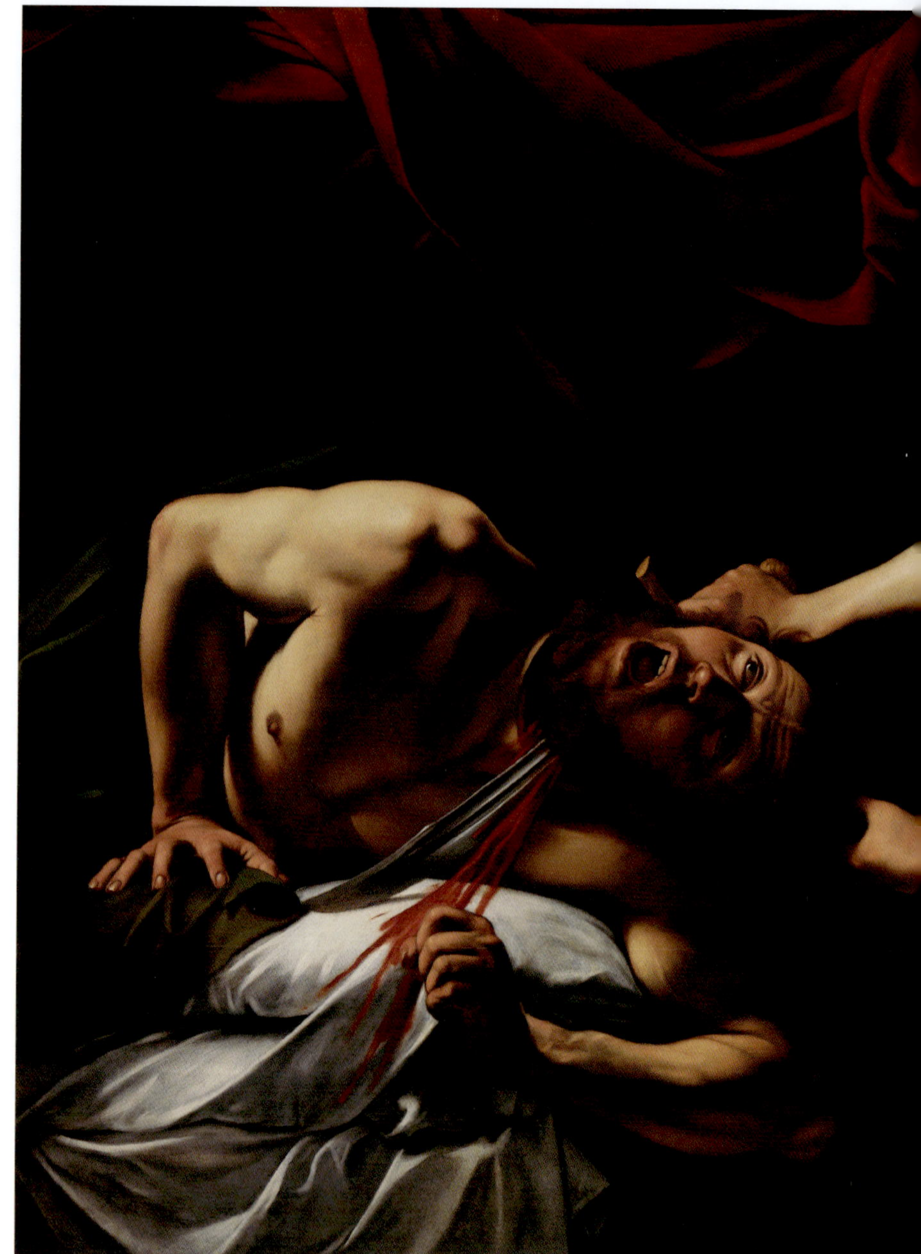

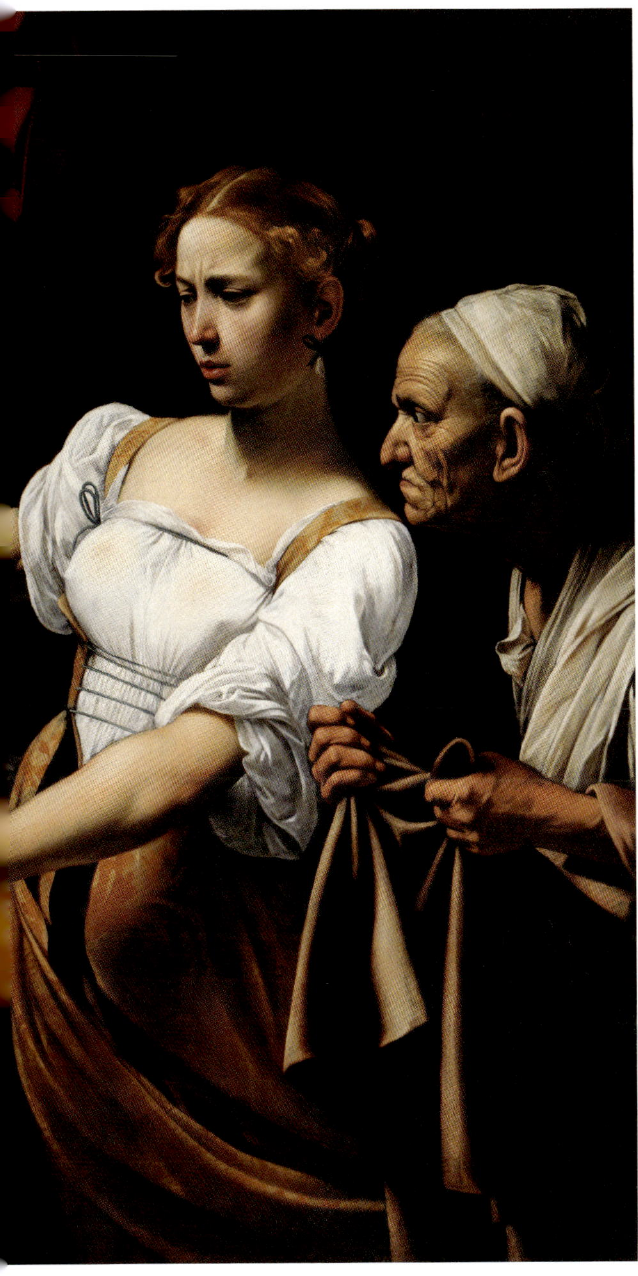

implications of the tyrannicide than by the violent eroticism which lends the biblical murder story its great narrative tension.

A blow against the Protestants
Holofernes had to die because he had attempted to force the Jews to worship the Assyrian king Nebuchadnezzar instead of Jehova. He was a gentile, and Judith's fatal blow was dealt for the greater glory of her – only true – God. This made her deed highly topical when Caravaggio painted the picture in Rome at the end of the 16th century.

The struggle to repress heresy by whatever means possible, including fire and the sword, was the central preoccupation in the capital of the Papal States. It was the time of the Counter-Reformation. The Catholic Church was attempting to recover those dominions that it had lost during the first half of the 16th century. England and Sweden, and parts of the Netherlands, France and Germany, had followed Luther, Calvin or Zwingli. They no longer accepted the authority of the Pope and refused to pay taxes to Rome.

It had taken some time before the Catholic Church and loyalist states (Spain, Italy, Poland and the heartlands of the Habsburg Empire) were capable of taking up the counter offensive. The Council of Trent had met repeatedly between 1545 and 1563 before finally reaching a consensus on reforms: the removal of the worst forms of abuse leading to the schism, and the establishment of strict rules of faith. The assembled representatives of the Church thus succeeded in laying down the foundations of spiritual renewal, while turning the Church itself into a force to be reckoned with. The hierarchy was tightened up, the Pope's authority strengthened and the organization of the Church in Rome was centralized. Several religious orders grew in power and influence, particularly the Jesuits, who, as defenders of the faith, were organized along military lines and set to work to convert the heretics – or exterminate them.

The most spectacular example of the persecution of heretics was the St Bartholomew Massacre of thousands of Huguenots on 23/24 August 1572. But at a time when the faith of monarchs automatically determined that of their subjects, it seemed a far more practical business to strike a blow against the Protestant rulers themselves. Thus Pope Gregory XIII publically denounced Elizabeth I of England as "the cause of so much damage to the Catholic faith and of the loss of millions of souls"; he could see "no doubt, but that he who dispatches her from this world with the holy intention of serving God commits no sin, but is deserving of reward".

At the dawning of the age of absolutism and the divine right of kings, the authority of the royal sovereign was officially unquestionable; if a monarch left the one true faith, however, he was declared a usurper and an outlaw. This was Catholic doctrine in 1600; proclaimed from the pulpit and broadcast by countless pamphlets, it encouraged all kinds of fanatics and madmen who heard voices and thought they were heeding the call of God to take up daggers and firearms.

While Elizabeth I managed to escape countless assassination attempts, finally dying in her bed in 1603, William I of Orange, Stadtholder of Holland, Zealand and Utrecht, was shot in 1584, and Henry IV of France, who had survived a dozen attempts on his life and had even returned to the bosom of the Church in 1593, was stabbed to death by a religious fanatic. Judith was held up as a shining example by many fanatics: in contemporary pamphlets calling for the murder of heretics, Judith was celebrated as a paragon of virtue.

A chaste heroine
Judith's features betray neither triumph nor passion, but determination and disgust. She slays the defenceless man without using force, keeping as great a distance as possible between her victim and herself. Nor does this demure heroine appear in a magnificent Baroque gown, like the Judith painted by Christofano Allori just a few years later, but in the best clothes of a woman of the people. Perhaps

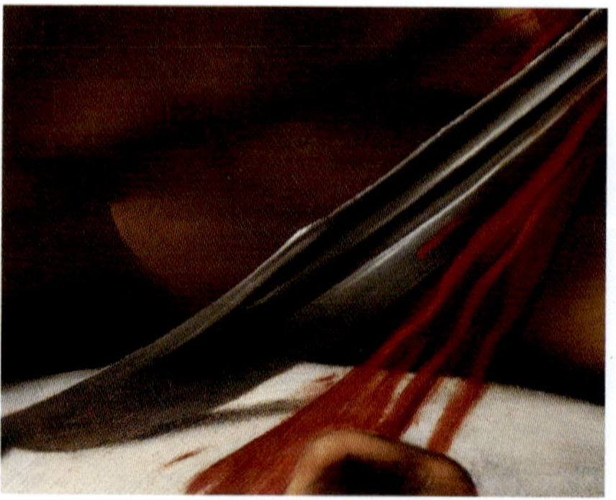

Caravaggio's model was a woman called Lena who is thought to have been his mistress and, according to a police report of 1605, was usually found "loitering at the Piazza Navona", which was tantamount to saying that she worked as a prostitute.

Travellers to Rome around 1600 generally found the large number of prostitutes worthy of comment: there were many unmarried men among the masses of pilgrims and Church servants who came to the Catholic capital. There were more than a million visitors to the Eternal City during the Holy Year of 1600. The innkeepers and tailors also did a good trade, the latter providing sumptuous robes for ecclesiastical dignitaries. Otherwise, there was no trade or industry in Rome; the majority of the city's inhabitants lived in poverty and were dependent on the charity of the Church.

It was at this time, too, that Rome, following its destruction by mercenaries in 1527, was being rebuilt – despite the greatly reduced income of the See – to the magnificent city we know today. The building boom was a product of the Counter-Reformation: it was intended that the capital city of the the Catholic faith should shine out for all to see and that its spiritual hegemony in the world be reflected in its material glory. It was hoped that the magnificence of Roman architecture would impress the uneducated masses and reinforce their piety.

Pope Sixtus V (1521–1590) commissioned the construction of magnificent avenues, had viaducts built and had the huge dome of St Peter's finally completed. Clement VIII (1536–1605) and his cardinals commissioned as many palaces, churches and chapels as they could, attracting architects, masons, sculptors and fresco painters to Rome from all over Italy.

One of these was Michelangelo Merisi, born in 1571 in the Lombardic village of Caravaggio, near Bergamo, a village whose name he later adopted as his own. Arriving in the papal city at the beginning of the 1590s, his life had initially been all but easy. A Sicilian art dealer had employed him to produce "three heads every day", and given him only salad at mealtimes. But his talent was discovered in 1596 by Cardinal Francesco Maria del Monte (1549–1626), who offered the painter food, wine, pocket money and lodgings at his palace. Caravaggio painted for him in return: semi-nude boys making music, Bacchus with a sensuous mouth, adorned with flowers, gentle angelic figures. Such works appealed to the cardinal, who loved the company of young men.

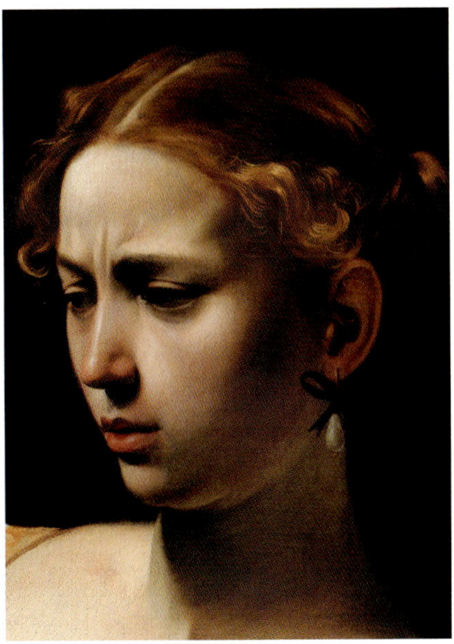

It was not long before Caravaggio's fame spread abroad. On receiving his first noteworthy commission in 1598/99, the decoration of a chapel, Caravaggio left the homosexual milieu of the cardinal's palace, where he is thought to have lived with another painter.

It was at this time that he painted Judith, his first erotically attractive female figure, although in fact she is modestly dressed – Caravaggio never painted a female nude. Perhaps it was the image of Judith as both a devout heroine and, at the same time, a corrupter of men which so appealed to the artist. Like Delilah, who took Samson's male potency when she shaved off his locks, Judith appears, in the struggle of the sexes, as the incarnation of the male fear of ultimate vulnerability to a woman.

Fascinated by decapitation

Most artists painting this theme have shown Judith after the deed, holding up the head of the dead Holofernes in her hand. By contrast, Caravaggio has painted the precise moment in which he is beheaded: the victim is still alive, his head only half severed from his body. His eyes have not yet grown dim in death, but are staring out of his head,

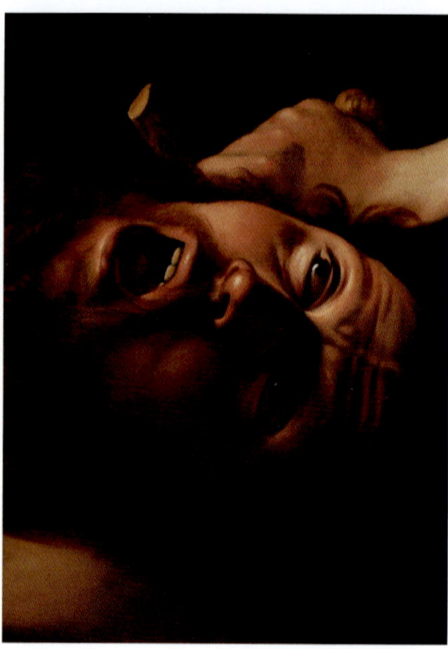

full of mortal fear, and his mouth is wrenched open in a scream. Caravaggio sought to capture the moment of shock and horror, an effect also loved by his English contemporary William Shakespeare. The latter's plays *Macbeth* and *King Lear*, with their bloody murders and scenes of torture, were performed for the first time in 1606.

It was not only on canvas or on the stage that such brutal scenes took place, however; artists were confronted with violence of this kind every day, whether in Elizabethan England or in Rome during the Counter-Reformation. There were said to be more severed heads nailed to the Ponte S. Angelo over the Tiber than melons on the stalls of Roman markets. The "Avvisi", a kind of handwritten newspaper, reported in 1583: "The Papal States are in chaos … The countryside is in the hands of bandits … who murder … rob the couriers, lay waste to towns and houses." These bandits were political outcasts from everywhere in Italy, peasants ruined by papal taxes and bad harvests, monks fleeing from their monasteries and other social misfits. It was reported that the Papal States were imperilled from time to time by as many as 27,000 brigands. In Rome they performed the function of armed

bodyguards; known as *bravi*, the "daring", they accompanied any citizen or visitor who could afford their services, always ready to defeat their employer's enemies, or to engage in street battle with the papal police, the *sbirri*.

"Practically no day passes," the Venetian ambassador to Rome reported in 1595, "without our seeing the heads [of dead bandits] they have brought into the city, or of the men they behead at the Castel Sant' Angelo in groups of 4, 6, 10, 20 and sometimes even 30 at a time. It has been calculated that over 5,000 persons have died a violent death in the Papal State since the death of Sixtus V (1590), whether condemned to death, or murdered by bandits."

Decapitation – a form of execution reserved for criminal members of the aristocracy – was generally linked to a number of macabre rituals. The severed heads were publically exhibited at the Castel Sant'Angelo, displayed on a black cloth between two burning torches. When the 22-year-old Beatrice Cenci was found guilty of patricide and beheaded in 1599, Caravaggio may have attended the execution. A contemporary textbook on art advised painters to accompany the condemned to the scaffold in order to observe their twitching eyelids and rolling eyes. It was at this time that Caravaggio was working on *Judith*.

Decapitation must have fascinated the artist. In 1603 he painted the *Sacrifice of Isaac* by Abraham; his *Beheading of St John the Baptist*, painted in 1608 and now in Valetta Cathedral, Malta, bears Caravaggio's sole extant signature. The words "F Michel A" can still be read on the badly damaged painting; they are written in the paint he had used for the blood dripping to the ground from the martyr's neck. The head of the Baptist in Salome's hands reappears in a work executed in 1610, while another, later painting shows a young David holding up Goliath's head. Contemporary spectators noticed the similarity in looks between Goliath and Caravaggio himself, who was said to be "dark skinned, with grave eyes and thick black eyebrows and hair".

Holofernes' screaming, suffering face may also have been a self-portrait, letting Caravaggio act out a masochistic fantasy of himself as the victim of brutal violence.

Undaunted by reality

Caravaggio, whose fame had grown quickly, was patronized by Monsignori and cardinals. He found it difficult to adapt his work to their taste, however.

In decorating churches he frequently departed from the conventions laid down by the Council of Trent, which had stipulated that while paintings of the Scriptures were to be used to educate the ignorant masses, the artwork itself must remain dignified and aloof. Caravaggio's work offended against this "decorum" by showing saints with dirty feet and a drowned Virgin Mary whose corpse had swollen in the water.

At the same time, his style broke with the Renaissance ideal of beauty. His vision and aesthetic were novel and realistic, and his works, treasured by a small circle of supporters who paid high prices for them, shocked many of his contemporaries. Instead of copying conventional models, Caravaggio painted directly from life. In so doing, he suppressed neither the furrows and lines on a face nor the wrinkles produced by a life of toil on the hands of an old woman. "Too natural," was all the artist Annibale Carracci could say about his contemporary's painting of Judith.

It was here that Caravaggio first used a device that was to become characteristic of his work: figures, accentuated by artificial, almost subterranean lighting effects, standing out against a dark, nocturnal background.

The fact that darkness and violence were themes to which the artist continually returned may possibly derive from his character. Various incidents show Caravaggio to have been rowdy and a thug. On 28 May 1606, he mortally wounded a certain Ranuccio Tomassoni in a brawl over a wager on a tennis match. This was by no means his first brush with the law, however, as the numerous demands for sentences recorded in the Roman archives show. On one occasion, the painter threw a plate of artichokes at an impolite waiter at the Osteria del Moro; on another, he insulted a policeman who had asked to see his licence to carry a weapon.

Caravaggio led the adventurous life of a Roman *bravo*. Although he delivered his paintings on time, his biographers say that he rarely stuck it out at work for very long before setting out with his gang of toughs, attending one tennis

match after the other, "always ready to fight a duel or engage in a brawl". The sword he carried at his side on these occasions is said to have been conspicuous for its size.

Swords, daggers and knives may be seen in almost all Caravaggio's paintings. Like blood and decapitation, they constitute a kind of sadistic leitmotiv in his work. In the artist's everyday life, they were not only the means of self-assertion, but also status symbols. The offence taken by Caravaggio at the policeman's demand to see his licence to carry such a weapon is explicable: wearing a sword was considered a nobleman's privilege, and, despite the torn and dirty clothes he usually wore, it was as a nobleman that Caravaggio wished to be seen. He was a social climber, and his aggression was most likely a means of compensating for a social inferiority complex.

Parallel to the refusal of several of his best works on grounds of theological incorrectness and the consequent reduction in the number of his official commissions, Caravaggio's aggressive behaviour increased, climaxing in the murder of 1606, which forced him to flee Rome. He spent the rest of his life tormented by a persecution complex, driven from one place to another, leaving behind him a trail of masterpieces that were to have a lasting influence on 17th-century European art. He died, a lonely man, in exile in 1610 – "as miserably as he lived", as one contemporary noted.

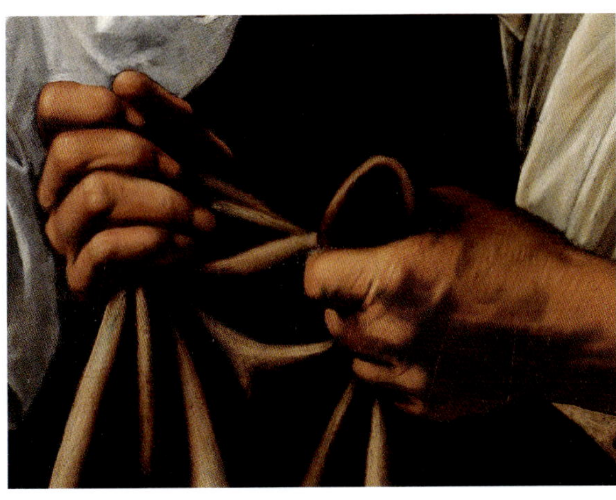

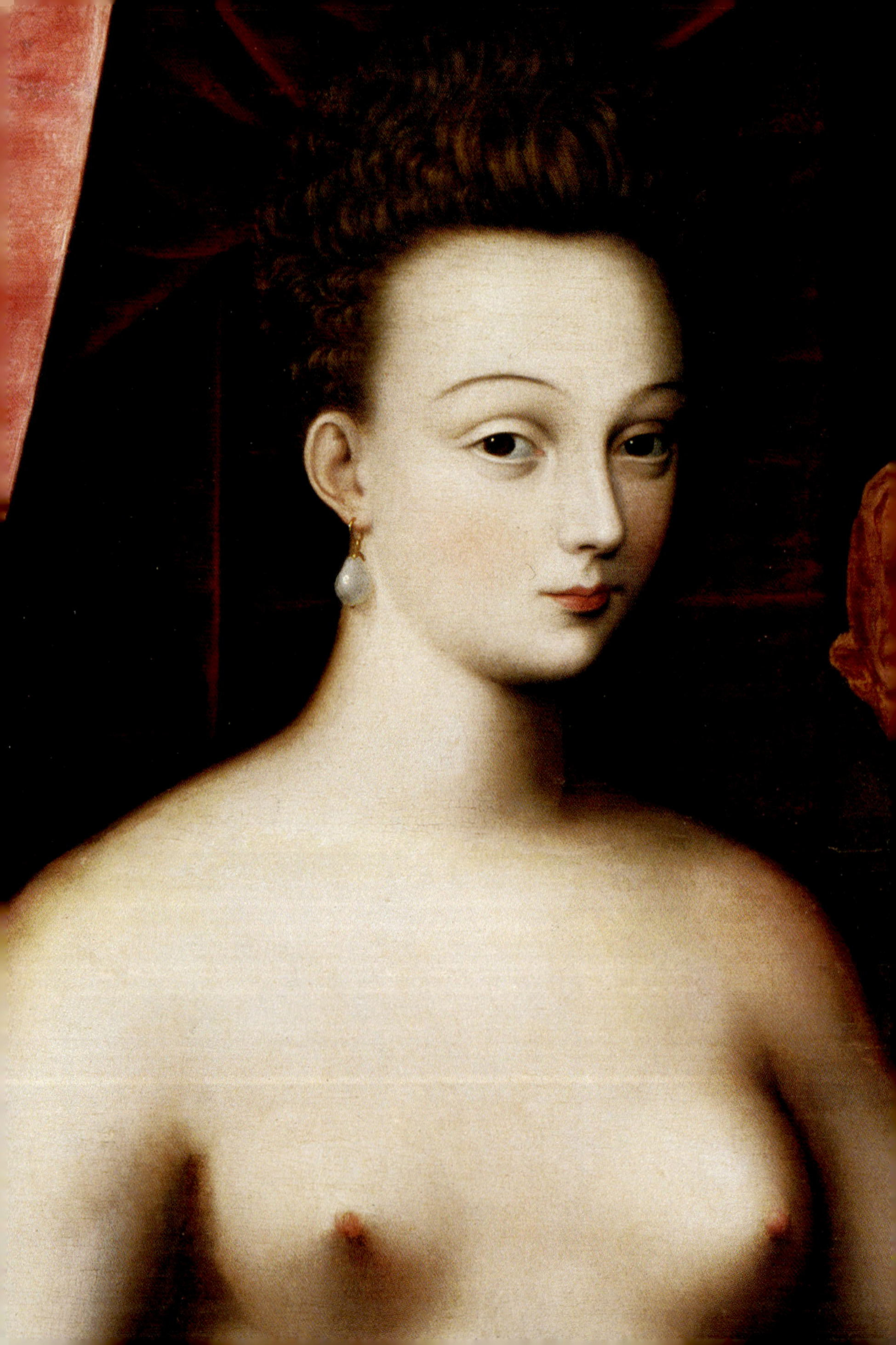

School of Fontainebleau

Two cool beauties in the tub

Gabrielle d'Estrées and one of her sisters, c. 1600
96 x 125 cm, Paris, Musée du Louvre

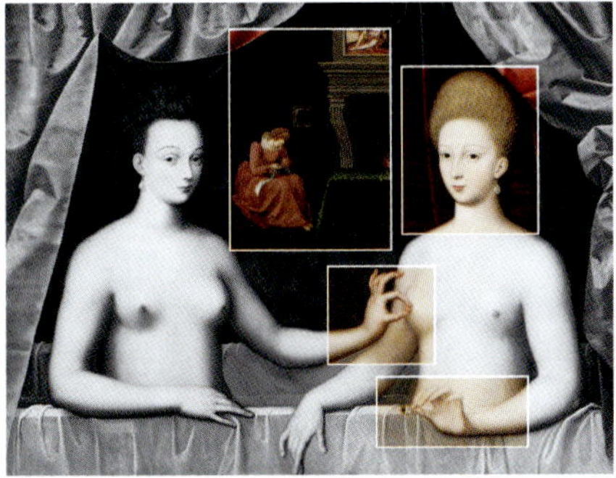

Two naked ladies disport themselves in a bathtub. They are protected from the cold of the marble by a light, shiny cloth draped over the edge of the tub. Heavy red silk drapes hang down from an invisible baldachin, gathered up at the front and half drawn closed at the back, to screen off draughts.

At the time when this picture was painted, very few people in France took a bath. In the 16th and 17th centuries the general condition of every class of people was incredible filthiness. The baths and steam houses that were so numerous in the Middle Ages had long been shut down, at the urging of the watchdogs of the Reformation and Counter-Reformation, who condemned places where men and women bathed and met socially for amusement. Syphilis, in all probability brought from America in 1493, had transformed bath houses into dangerous places of contagion. Before long doctors were approving the trend away from bathing, and even warning against it: one's hands might be washed, wrote medical scientist Jean de Renou, but the feet should only rarely be in contact with water and the head, if possible, never.

Evidently the last thing the two ladies in our picture would dream of is to bring their heads, and their beautifully styled hair, into contact with this dangerous element. They are made up and wearing pearls, and are most assuredly not taking a bath as a means of cleansing themselves but for beauty purposes. Quite likely the tub is filled not with water but with wine or milk, which since antiquity had been considered a means of perpetuating youth. In 1610 a Hungarian lady, Countess Bathory, went even further for her beauty's sake and bathed in the blood of slaughtered virgins.

Magical powers were often ascribed not only to blood but to other fluids too. Bathing, indeed, was generally seen in superstitious terms. Astrologers advised that baths should be taken only when the moon was waning and the stars were "hot". At St John's Eve, water was said to wash away threatening evils. St Walburga's Eve (the "Walpurgisnacht" of witching fame) was thought especially auspicious for all kinds of bathing magic. Witches prepared for their sabbath by taking a bath; they heated the tub with rotting firewood and burnt herbs that had a deadening effect – according to the records of witch trials, at least. Since the clergy condemned not only witchcraft but also bathing, the two transgressions were often linked. The devil was said to copulate

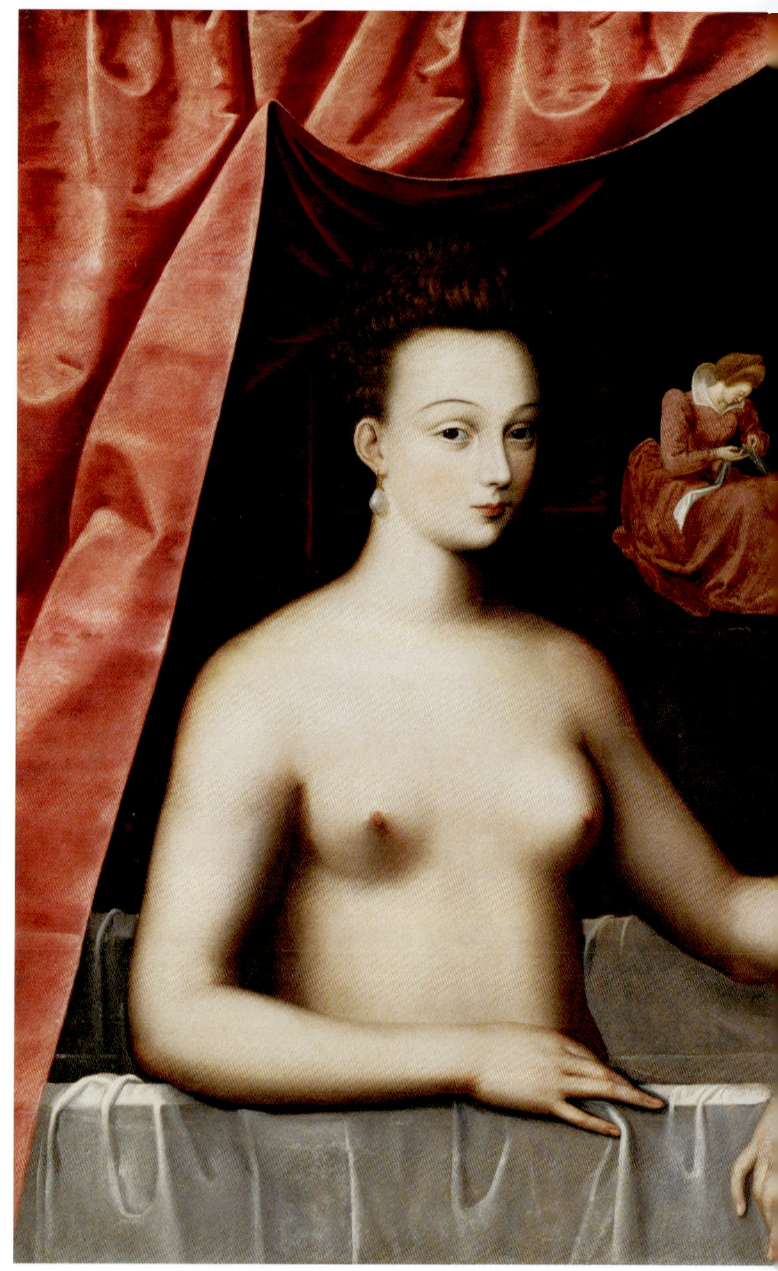

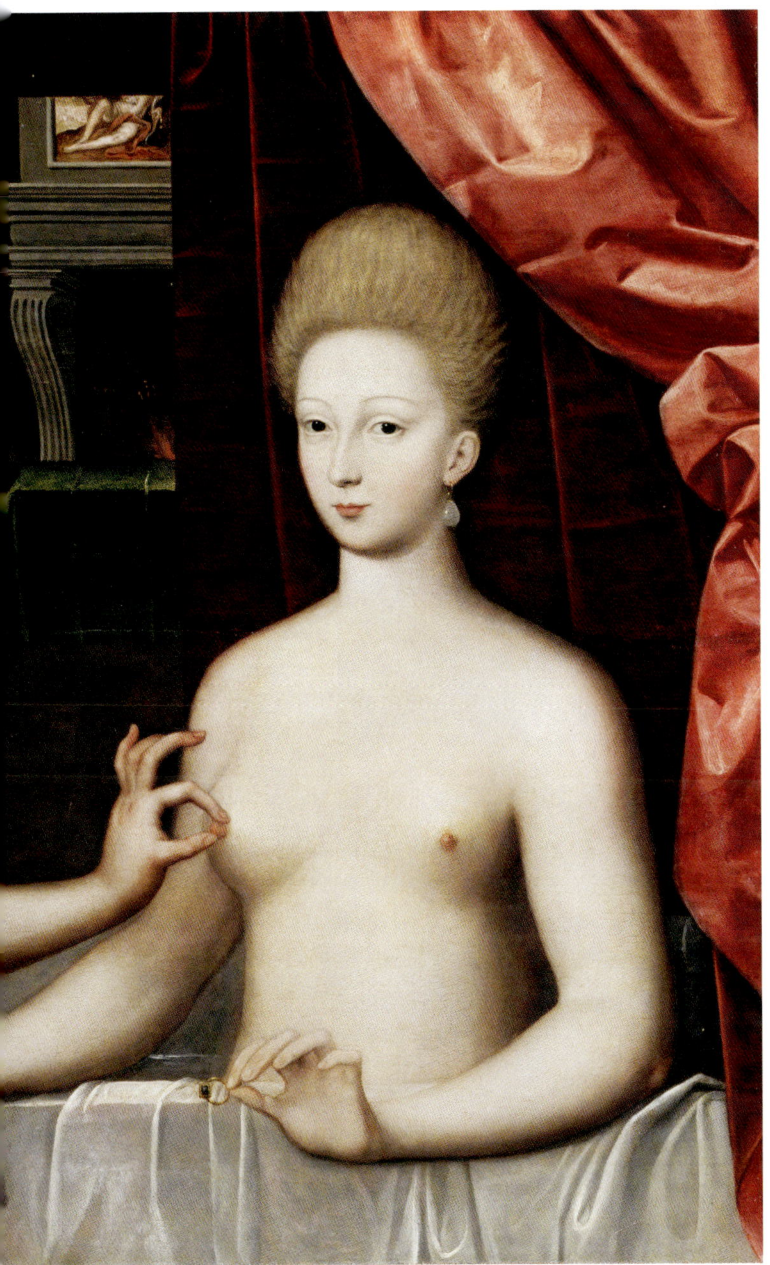

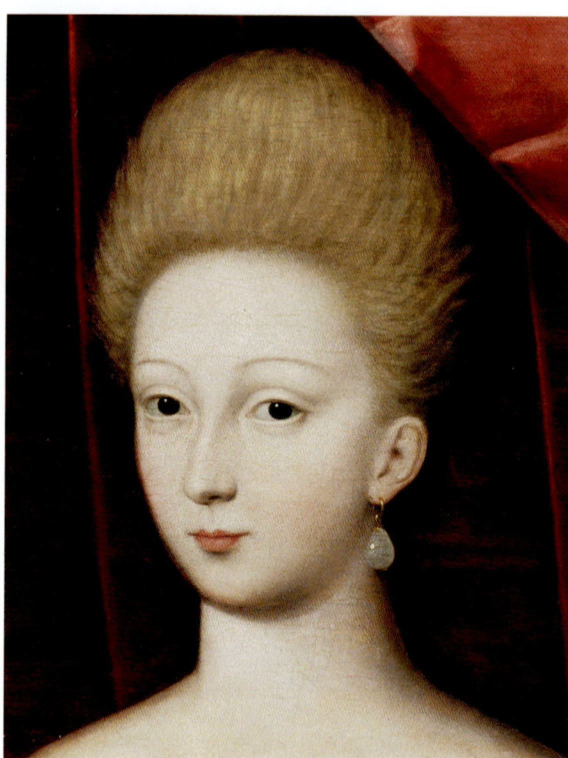

hung the finest paintings in his possession, such as Leonardo da Vinci's *Mona Lisa*. Here too there doubtless hung a large number of pictures such as this one of two beauties in the tub. Only a few have survived. Many were over-painted with "decorous veils", and most the Queen Mother Anne of Austria had burnt in 1676, as inde-cent and "the work of the devil".

We do not know who painted our picture; it is unsigned. And we can only guess when it was painted. The hairstyles of the two ladies in the tub were fashion-able between 1594 and 1598. The inscription on a later copy of the work alleges that the blonde woman on the right was Gabrielle d'Estrées, one of the most beauti-ful and most hated women of her century, the favourite of a king. Indeed, she very nearly became queen herself.

Born in 1573, Gabrielle was fif-teen when she arrived at the court of the last Valois king, Henri III. The court was a hotbed of scandal, and before long she was reported to have had various affairs, one with the handsome M. de Bellegarde. Henri III was assassinated in the course of the religious wars that divided France into two armed camps for decades, and his legitimate heir and successor, Henri IV, first had to conquer his own realm – for he was a Prot-estant, and his Catholic subjects did not recognize him. M. de Bellegarde was the master of the royal stables and fought alongside the monarch. During a pause in the fighting, he was so incautious as to tell Henri of his beautiful lover, Gabrielle d'Estrées. And on 7 November 1590 Bellegarde introduced the two.

The prettiest of the seven deadly sins

Gabrielle d'Estrées must have approximated pretty exactly to the feminine ideal of her age: long-limbed, blonde and pale of complexion. Her face "was as smooth and translucent as a pearl, with all its delicacy and lustre". This was not written by some flattering courtier but by a woman who had reason

with witches in the bathtub, and he would show them the faces of their future husbands reflected in the water.

But at the time when this picture was painted, people associated not only magic, the fear of conta-gious disease, and ecclesiastical damnation with bath-ing. From Italy, the rest of Europe derived the ideas and visual code of the Renaissance, and with them the numerous unclothed goddesses of antiquity. In France they came into fashion, and court beauties had themselves painted rising from the waves or bathing in springs, feeling close to the heathen dei-ties in the process and profiting from their prestige. Painters from Florence and Bologna decorated the rooms in the palace of Fontainebleau ("beautiful fountain") with goddesses and nymphs. The archi-tects devised a suite of *appartements des bains* which included resting rooms, changing rooms and marble baths. It was here that King François I (1494–1547)

to be critical of Gabrielle: Mademoiselle de Guise, a rival for the king's favour. She continued: "Though she wore a dress of white silk, it seemed black compared with the snow of her skin."

Of course this pallor was assisted artificially. Thick white make-up was applied not only to the face but also to the shoulders and bosom. The mouth and nipples were rouged. At the court of the cultivated Valois kings, the immediate predecessors of Henri IV, the arts of make-up had evolved to the utmost degree of sophistication, for both sexes. The ladies at least continued to practise these arts under the new and distinctly ill-groomed "masculine" king. They continued to pluck their eyebrows and draw in a fine line in their stead; if they did not wear wigs, they coloured their hair with white lead and powders. To achieve the popular blonde, they bleached their hair with acrid tinctures and then exposed it to the sun for several days, taking care all the while that the sunlight did not fall upon their white skin. Parts of the body that were not covered by clothing were protected with gloves or face masks of silk or velvet when out riding or even walking. Ladies exposed their skin only within thick walls or behind silken drapes.

Gabrielle's diminutive blonde head seems relatively small on an over long neck and a sturdily built body, and her finely waved hair, taken up in a severe coiffure, reinforces this impression. It is a head designed to surmount a broad starched ruff or a high stiff lace collar. There was no room for long hair or tumbling curls in this type of head. At that time, the costume of the Spanish court was worn in France too – stiff and unnatural clothing, a product of the Counter-Reformation's hostility to the body. Women's bodies were forced into straight, tube-like iron corsets and a stiff, padded, wide skirt. It was as if the bosom, waist and hips did not exist. Even on Gabrielle's naked body we can detect the evidence of this fashion, for it is a body without curves, and even liberated from its corset it remains straight and smooth. In addition

to their clothing, the ladies generally wore so much and such heavy jewellery that they had to proceed at a measured pace, "as if they were reliquaries". Only when out hunting did the provocative Gabrielle, who preferred to ride in a man's saddle, occasionally display a leg – encased in a green silk stocking.

On her mother's side, Gabrielle d'Estrées was of a family which the chronicler Tallemant des Réaux described with palpable relish as "the richest in spirited ladies that France has ever seen. There are at least 25 or 26 of them, nuns and married ladies alike, all of whom delight in sexual congress." Among the married ladies was Gabrielle's mother, who ran away with a lover when the children were small. One of the nuns was Gabrielle's sister, the abbess of Maubuisson, who was eventually obliged to leave her convent after bearing twelve children by different fathers.

Another sister is probably seen here with Gabrielle in the bathtub: Julienne d'Estrées, Duchess of Villars. She did not balk at sitting bare breasted below the pulpit when a Capuchin monk she fancied was preaching. The God fearing man was forced to flee the confessional and indeed the city, so persistent were her passionate advances. No wonder Julienne, the abbess, Gabrielle, three further daughters, and the one son of M. d'Estrées were widely known collectively as "the seven deadly sins".

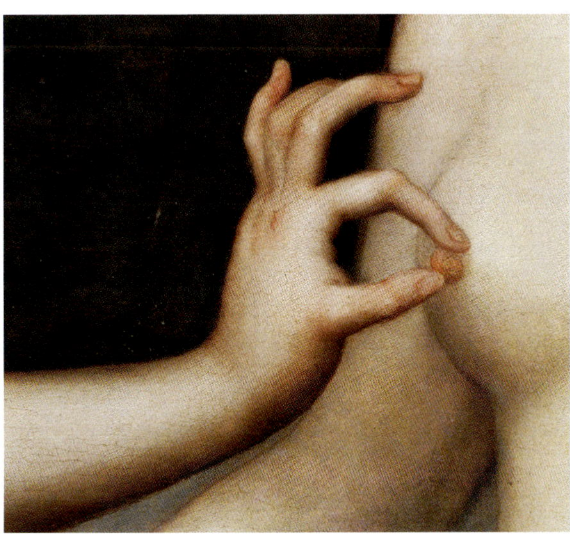

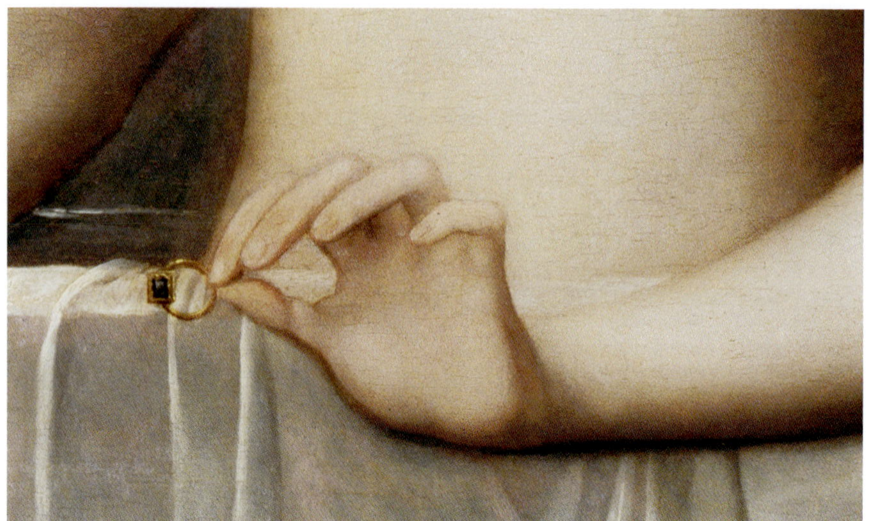

Eloquent hands

Sitting in the bathtub, the Duchess of Villars is tweaking one of her sister's rouged nipples with her fingertips. It is a gesture guaranteed to monopolize our attention.

The face and hands alone were not concealed by court costume, which meant that around 1600 they were of especial importance. Convention dictated that the subjects' faces be innocent of all expression, and as long as their impassive gaze is fixed on nothingness, as in our picture, it is only the hand movements that tell us these wax dummies are in fact creatures of flesh and blood. Only from their gestures can we infer what feelings, what hopes and fears, lie within them.

Juliette de Villars' gesture, a tender and highly intimate one, might imply that the sisters had a lesbian relationship. Not for nothing had they come of age at the court of the decadent Henri III, who liked to be seen wearing women's clothing. For a certainty, nothing human was unfamiliar to "the seven deadly sins". But the gesture not only suggests a lesbian tie, a notion that lends the painting a thrilling aura of the taboo: to contemporaries it could also suggest something else entirely – that Gabrielle d'Estrées was pregnant.

Today we would look to the belly for the first sign of pregnancy, but a rounded belly was in any case an essential feature of feminine beauty in the medieval and Renaissance view of things. Even virgins delighted to have rounded bellies. For this reason, numerous paintings showing the biblical Mary and Elizabeth in pregnancy have them extending their hands to each other's bodies, perhaps to feel the heartbeat or movements of the child within. The gesture was the painters' code to signal pregnancy; the artist who painted the present picture rang a charming change on it.

Gabrielle d'Estrées expected a child by Henri IV on four occasions; in 1594 she bore him a son, César, and subsequently another son and then a daughter. In 1599 she was pregnant once again, and precisely this fertility endeared her to the king. His queen, Margaret of Valois, from whom he had long been living in separation, had borne him no children, so that he and his realm still lacked an heir. He had fathered bastards, and had recognized them as his children, but with none of the pomp and ceremony that now accompanied the birth of Gabrielle's children. For the first time in his life, the king found everything he prized in women united in one, Gabrielle: in addition to her fertility, her "beauty of form, modest demeanour, gentleness of nature and spirit".

At first, Gabrielle was apparently not especially attracted to the king, and preferred the master of the stables. But she was bartered for substantial material advantages for the Estrées, and sent to the king's bed. Report had it that at times Bellegarde would still be departing hastily by the window of Gabrielle's bedchamber when the king came in at the door. Fearing the two might still wed, the king married Gabrielle off to an impotent and obedient courtier.

In time, Gabrielle began to enjoy her life as the king's recognized concubine. She savoured the king's triumphal progress, which was the more successful after his conversion to Catholicism. When Paris was finally conquered, she entered the city at the king's side. She accumulated titles and gold; others could not approach her without kissing the hem of her robe; more and more she enjoyed the status of a rightful queen. But she did not reside in the Louvre with Henri. She lay there in the bed of queens for only a single night, could not sleep, and next morning fled the ghosts of the dead Valois, moving instead to a nearby city residence. Gabrielle did not care for Paris, and even followed the king into the field, for, as a courtier named de l'Estoile reports, "She was tormented more by her conscience than anyone, and did not feel safe in Paris whenever the king left the city."

A stain on the honour of France

The ring that Gabrielle d'Estrées is holding over the rim of the tub was placed on her finger by the king on 2 March 1599. It was the investiture ring, with which France was ceremonially entrusted to Henri IV at his coronation. He gave it to Gabrielle when she was pregnant as an engagement ring: Henri meant her to be his lawful wife and queen. It was an outrageous notion. Moreover, he wanted to marry her within a few weeks, on the first Sunday after Easter. Gabrielle publicly declared her confidence that now only God or the death of the king could come between her and her happiness.

In 1599, Henri had achieved his aims. He was at the peak of his power. For eighteen years he had led the Protestant forces in the civil war, and then in a further five years of fighting, as designated king of France, he had conquered his realm by the sword. At long last he sat securely on his throne. The country had been pacified, and was at peace at home and abroad. Now Henri wanted to found a dynasty, with the woman who had already borne his heir and who had stood by him in the years when he was mocked as "a general without funds and a king without a

throne". He had long since informed his horrified ministers of his intention; Gabrielle's marriage was annulled, and the dissolution of his own was being pursued in Rome.

"The redoubtable sovereign was on the point of committing the grossest stupidity that anyone can, and nonetheless he was resolved," writes Tallemant des Réaux, and most contemporaries fully shared this conviction.

Everyone was opposed to the marriage, which the Pope described as "a stain on the honour of France". The French nobles were outraged at the prospect of one day having to accept as king the bastard César, the fruit of a twofold adultery (both Henri and Gabrielle being married to other partners at the time of his birth). The French people hated and despised the king's mistress, the "queen of filth", for her extravagant gowns, her expensive jewellery (with which she even "outshone the torches"), her parties, and her lavish lifestyle, which contrasted so starkly with the king's own simplicity and the wretchedness of the country. Almost 50 years of civil war, sieges and epidemics had left their mark. "The king is a decent man," one poor Seine fisherman told Henri, not recognizing him in his hunting outfit, "but he keeps a dreadful whore who is ruining us all."

At this the king merely laughed; the objections of the Pope, his ministers, and the nobles, he brushed aside. He ordered preparations to be made for the wedding. The bridal gown had already been sewn. On 5 April, Henri sent Gabrielle, now extremely pregnant, back to Paris alone to spend Easter there. His beloved accepted the hospitality of a wealthy Italian banker named Zamet, who was famed for the cuisine at his table and who helped cook personally for distinguished guests. Gabrielle was taken with pains; on 8 April she gave orders to be removed to her aunt's house, and there, the following day, gave birth to a stillborn child. Her condition deteriorated and she began a fearful struggle with death; neither doctor nor priest attended upon her, and everyone deserted the dying favourite. On 9 April, the king was informed that she had died, to prevent him from hastening to her. In fact Gabrielle d'Estrées died on 10 April, "a revolting and terrible death, her eyes rolling, her neck contorted and bent back upon itself". When doctors finally went to her, they declared "this was the hand of God" – not daring to say "the hand of the devil" aloud.

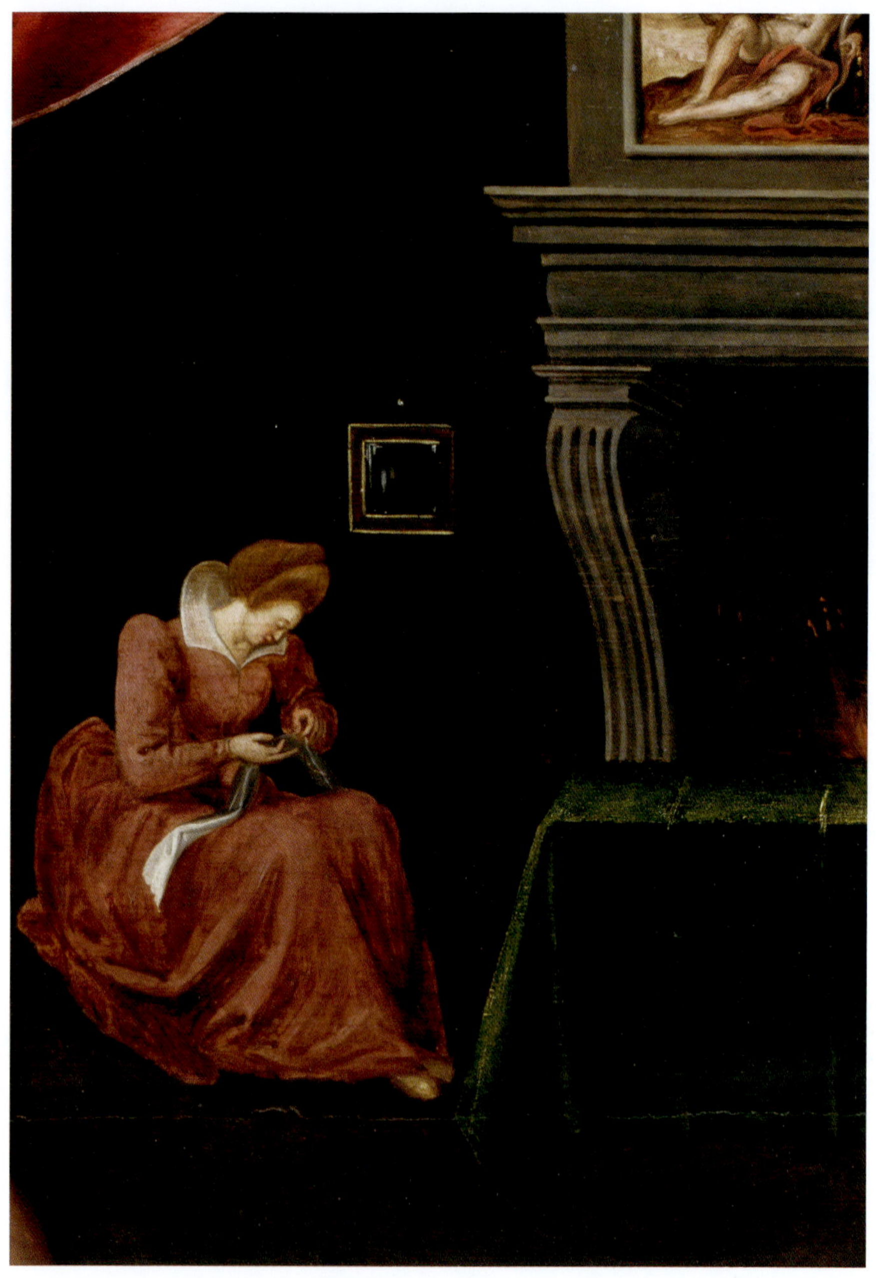

There are more things between Heaven and earth
The official version given out by the French court was that Gabrielle d'Estrées died of complications in her pregnancy, but no one believed the story at the time. Tallemant des Réaux, for example, assumed Zamet had poisoned her, and thus "had done Henri a great service". The king might have ended the religious wars that had so long cleft France into two warring parties, but there were still countless religious fanatics in the country. To them, killing an enemy of the "true" religion (which invariably means one's own) was not only legitimate but also pleasing to God. There was no end to the attempts on the king's life, and his mistress, his counsellor "in the hours of the day and of the night", was detested by Catholics and Protestants alike. Rather too many people had an interest in getting Gabrielle d'Estrées out of the way.

Others inclined to a different explanation of her death. They saw in it the direct intervention of higher powers. As they generally did in times of war, catastrophe and woe, people tended to blame whatever went wrong on the evil one and his helpers. Never since the darkest Middle Ages had belief in witches and sorcerers been so widespread. Like Shakespeare's *Hamlet* (the play was first performed in 1600), Gabrielle's contemporaries were convinced that there were more things between Heaven and earth than were dreamt of in their philosophy. More powerfully even than religious zeal, superstition governed their thinking, and led them to suspect the worst even where we would see only a prosaic everyday scene – as in the background of our picture.

Between the curtains we see a woman, possibly a wet-nurse, sewing at a table by the fireplace. To the superstitious eye, though, the scene looks very different. The heavy silk, the red of royal purple or shed blood, hangs over the bathtub and reveals the dark room to the rear. The fire of life is a mere flicker in the hearth, and a Fate or witch is unpicking the thread of Gabrielle's life. Beside her is a coffin, covered with green velvet, Gabrielle's favourite colour. All we can see of the picture on the wall is the bare nether parts of a man, an allusion to the immoral conduct of Gabrielle with the king. The mirror is dark; it reflects no life. This is a symbol of death, a prop associated with witches and devils.

"All witchcraft is borne of the lust of the flesh, which is insatiable in women," declares a 1489 treatise on witches, the *Hexenhammer*, a handbook used by persecutors everywhere. Among the seventeen tell-tale signs by which a witch may be recognized, were "distorted features" and "rolling eyes and a revolting manner". Rumours were rife following the report of Gabrielle's appearance on her death bed. The devil, people said, had probably taken her. Everyone knew that the evil one liked to enter into beautiful women, or seal a contract with them. People remembered poor Louise de Budos, to whom the devil had evidently promised that he would make her the lady of some great man, for she was unexpectedly taken to wife by the Constable de Montmorency. But one evening when she was holding court, a guest in mourning was announced who did not wish to join the others. Louise burst into tears and bade farewell to the ladies present. Shortly after she was found dead in the ante room. There was no trace of the man in black.

Henri IV was surely one of the very few men of his time who was free of all religious zeal and superstition. In his lifetime, political circumstances had obliged him to convert more than once; in any case he was a sceptic by nature. In that same month of April 1599, because he realized the part superstitious fears had played in Gabrielle's death – no one had dared go near this woman "possessed" – the king ordered an immediate stop to the persecution of witches. But the word was that there were more than one hundred thousand warlocks and witches in France at the time; one of their number had only recently confessed as much under torture. Even a sceptical king could not save them all. In the years that followed, the pyres kept on being ignited, and in 1609 in Bordeaux one particular judge condemned 80 witches to the flames in a single session.

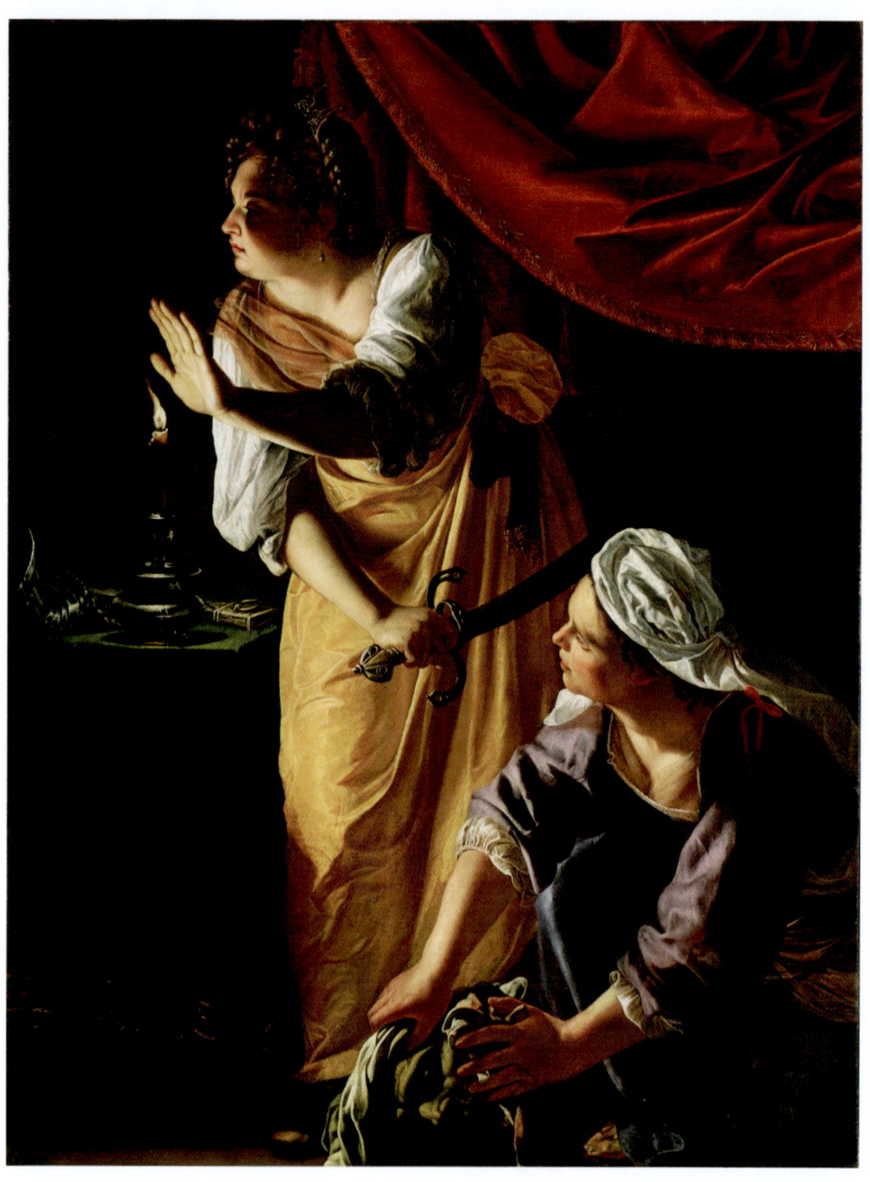

Artemisia Gentileschi (1593–1652)

Murder in the artistic style of the day

Judith and her Maid, 1625/1627
182 x 142 cm, Detroit Institute of Arts

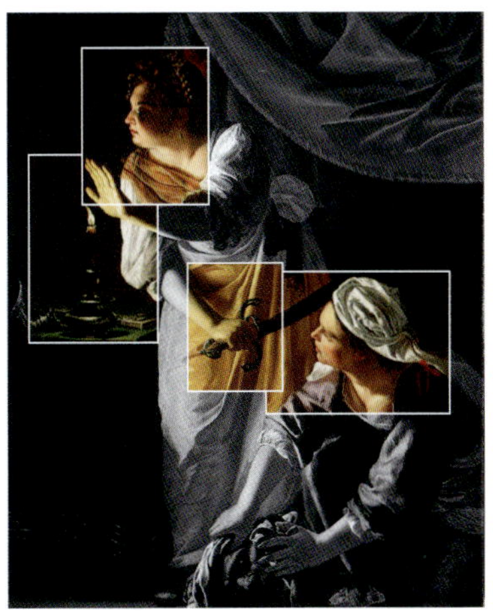

The story of Judith and Holofernes was a favourite subject of Baroque art, but only Artemisia Gentileschi could lend the scene such tension.

It is the moment immediately after the deed: the two women have paused and are listening intently to a noise. Danger looms. They are behind enemy lines in the middle of an army encampment, in the tent of the Assyrian general, Holofernes. They have killed him; his severed head is still lying on the ground, stuffed halfway into a bag. They want to escape with their trophy and are ready to defend themselves with the dead warrior's weapon. Their life-size figures bear down upon us and force the viewer to feel their emotions: fear and resolve.

The two women in the flickering candlelight against a background of nocturnal darkness are called Judith and Abra, and their story is told in the Bible. When the Jewish city of Bethulia was besieged by the Assyrian general Holofernes, its inhabitants abandoned hope and prepared to surrender. Just one woman – the "exceedingly beautiful" young widow, Judith, "of whom no one spoke an ill word" – took courage. She laid aside her mourning clothes, put on her finery and set off for the enemy camp in order to seduce the general. She dined with the lecherous Holofernes in his tent,

where the soldier proceeded to get drunk and eventually fall asleep. Praying through her tears, Judith then "loosed his sword … took him by the hair of his head … and she struck twice upon his neck, and cut off his head". She then gave Holofernes' head to her maid "and bade her put it into her sack". The two women managed to escape; Judith returned to Bethulia and the Assyrian soldiers fled in panic. The city was saved and Judith was celebrated as a heroine in a hymn of praise: "Her sandals ravished his eyes, her beauty made his soul her captive, with a sword she cut off his head."

This episode from the history of the people of Israel has no basis in fact: neither a city of Bethulia nor an Assyrian general by the name of Holofernes are known. The original text is lost and hence for Jews and Protestants is considered apocryphal – that is, not part of the biblical canon. But St Jerome included the Book of Judith in his Latin translation of the Bible, the Vulgate, and in the course of the Counter-Reformation that followed the Council of Trent in the middle of the 16th century, Judith's gruesome deed became a popular subject, standing as it did for the triumph of Good over Evil, of Catholicism over heresy. The figure of Judith served as an ideal symbol for a militant Catholic Church that was reacting to the defection of

Protestant countries and was demanding the eradication of heresy, if necessary with fire and sword.

Following Renaissance painters such as Botticelli and Michelangelo, many Baroque artists also portrayed Judith. In around 1599 Michelangelo Merisi da Caravaggio caused a scandal with a realistic murder scene. One of Caravaggio's drinking companions on Roman nights was the painter Orazio Gentileschi (1563–1639). Admired for his angels swathed in magnificent silks, his work is today known only to art specialists. But he had a gifted daughter, Artemisia, to whom he gave lessons. Her painting of *Judith and her Maid* of 1625/1627, which today hangs in Detroit, is considered her masterpiece. She treated the subject of Judith at least seven times over the course of her life, approaching her theme – so her feminist biographers argue – from a decidedly female point of view.

The candle is an homage to Caravaggio

On a table covered by a dark green velvet cloth lie the general's gauntlet and the scabbard of his sabre: a still life. The contrast between the hard, gleaming metal and the soft velvety fabric is a tribute to the artist's solid technique, taught to her by her father

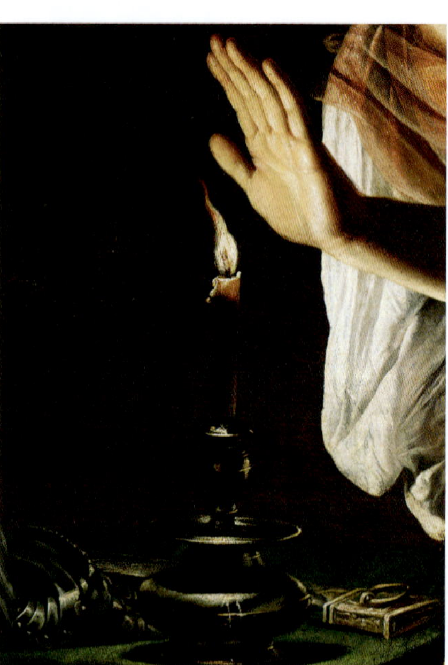

Orazio. He had learned it from Caravaggio, who broke with the cult of beauty and the idealism of the Renaissance, picked his models off the streets and painted realistic saints with dirty feet in dramatic lighting. Artemisia, who was born in Rome in 1593, can barely have known Caravaggio, who had to flee the Papal States in 1606 after killing a man and who himself died four years later. In her picture of Judith, nevertheless, the candle lighting up the night time darkness inside Holofernes' tent shines in homage to the master of chiaroscuro.

That Artemisia was not prepared to content herself with still life and portraiture – two minor genres that were considered just about within the capacity of women artists – is demonstrated by her first signed work, *Susanna and the Elders*, 1610, which is a history painting. Just two years later Orazio wrote to the Grand Duchess of Tuscany that his daughter was now so accomplished "that I may make so bold as to say that there is none today to match her". The widower guarded his daughter closely and to protect her from leering eyes only permitted her to go out for some fresh air at daybreak. Yet in 1611, wishing Artemisia to receive instruction in perspective painting, he seems to have had no qualms about inviting a colleague, the landscape painter Agostino Tassi, to come and live with them, despite the rumours of robbery, incest, sodomy and even the murder of his wife that clung to Tassi's name. Cutting the commanding figure of a gentleman, he whispered in his female pupil's ear: *Non tanto depingere!* – "Don't paint so much!" What happened next was the subject of conflicting statements in the trial that followed. The girl described her brutal rape in vivid terms, but subsequently consented to sexual relations with him, probably on the strength of a promise of marriage. Only when Tassi refused to honour this pledge did Orazio lose his patience and in 1612 accused him of "the deflowering and violation" of his daughter. Tassi denied everything and described the girl as a whore who was known throughout the city. But the court believed Artemisia. Tassi was banished but within a short time was back in Rome.

Just one day after Tassi's sentencing in November 1612, Artemisia was wedded to one Pierantonio Stiattesi and shortly afterwards moved with him to Florence. Through this marriage, the honour of her father, at least, was restored – and it seems that this was the main consideration. In the society

of her age, Artemisia needed
to be married if she was even
to contemplate working as an
artist. Shortly after the trial she
produced her first painting of
Judith's decapitation of Holofernes: realistic, dripping with
blood, gruesome and in a large
format. Under the application
of thumbscrews (the records
survive), Artemisia stated: "When
I found myself free, I took a
knife and went for Agostino with
it." A woman's revenge on her
torturer with painterly means?
But her good reputation was
destroyed, and for centuries she
was rumoured to have been
"wanton" and "of loose morals".

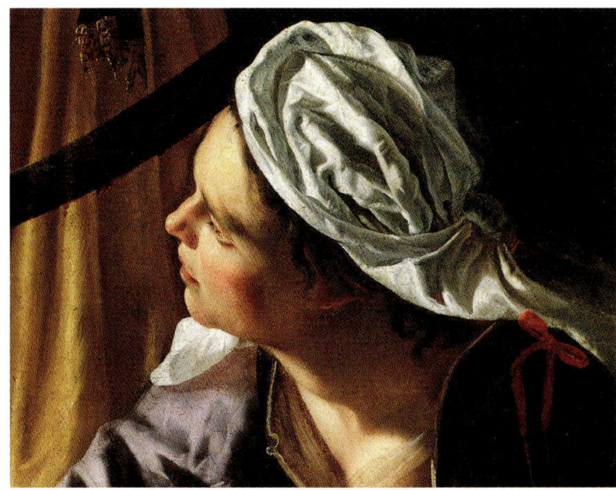

The headscarf identifies the maid

By around 1625 Artemisia was once again living
in Rome, as a mother bringing up her children
single handedly, as the head of a household and as
an artist. In Florence, alongside the births of four
children and the worry of her husband's debts, she
had achieved professional success with her *Caravaggisti* style, which was still novel in Tuscany, and had
become the first woman ever to be made a member
of the highly regarded Accademia del Disegno,
within which the best Florentine artists were assembled. Information relating to her second Rome
period, during which she produced the present
Judith and her Maid, is sparse: the Santa Maria del
Popolo parish register indicates that from 1621 until
1626 Artemisia lived in the via del Corso, together
with a daughter, her husband and a maid. This last
was called Dianora Turca; in 1625, according to the
magistrate's records, she filed a suit against Artemisia for unpaid wages. Perhaps the
artist used her as a model. Whereas most artists
portray Judith's maid as an ugly old woman, whose
weather beaten face allows her mistress's beauty
to shine all the more brightly, Artemisia's Abra is
young, with fair skin, and only her white linen
headscarf indicates her lowly status.

In 1622 "Pierantonio Stiattesi, *Pittore* [artist]"
set upon a group of Spaniards who had serenaded
his wife and the police had to be called. From 1623
he no longer lived in the family household and

Artemisia lost all touch with him. "Can you give
me any news of my husband, dead or alive?" she
enquired in a later letter. From this point on
she appears to have lived alone with her daughter
without a husband. Whether she had other partners
in her life is unknown, but she earned her livelihood alone. Her contemporary Giulio Mancini
tells us that a good painter might earn three to
six ducats a day, whereas a tailor made barely
one-fifth of a ducat.

Artemisia was awarded no official commissions
in her native Rome, however. Because she was a
woman? Or because realistic Caravaggism went out
of fashion in 1620s Rome and was superseded by a
more pleasing style? In Naples, on the other hand,
which stood under Spanish rule, dramatic realism
in painting was still in demand. In 1627 Artemisia
received the sum of 147 ducats for a large-format
Hercules and Omphale for King Philip IV's palace in
Madrid, where her painting was to hang as the equal
of works by Rubens and van Dyck. The artist consequently moved to Naples and remained there, with
just a short interruption, until her death in 1652.

Her customers were predominantly aristocrats
and wealthy men who wanted to expand their art
collections with pictures of powerful women,
whether murderesses or seductive nudes. Titillating
subjects, all the more so when they were painted by
a woman, so that the heroines on the canvas and the
female artist with scandal still attached to her name
flowed into one.

Sword and dagger were everyday wear
Paradoxically, the biblical Judith, prized as "the glory of Jerusalem", "the joy of Israel" and the honour of her people, had also acquired a scandalous reputation. When Florence decided in 1504 to replace Donatello's statue of the heroine in front of the Palazzo Vecchio with Michelangelo's *David*, it was because Judith was thought to bring bad luck: "It is not seemly that a woman should be killing a man…" Her statue was shut away; a woman with a weapon remained a monstrosity. Artemisia Gentileschi's œuvre features several such well armed heroines, and she even signed her most brutal beheading of Holofernes on the naked blade of the sword. In our picture, too, Judith's hand is still gripping the handle of the weapon whose owner she has just used it to kill, an Oriental curved sabre as appropriate to the biblical scene.

Armed gentlemen were an everyday sight in the alleyways of Rome. Sword and dagger, originally the privilege of nobility, were a standard part of male dress and everyone carried at least a knife. Even the decapitated heads of criminals were not an unfamiliar sight in that violent epoch; they were left to putrefy outside the gates of Castel Sant'Angelo as

a general deterrent. In the belligerent age of the Counter-Reformation, even the churches were decorated with the images of martyrs running with blood. In 1622 Pope Gregory XV had founded the Congregation for the Propagation of the Faith, since when preachers speaking from their pulpits had incited the fanatics in all countries to kill the heretics in their midst. The St Bartholomew's Day massacre in Paris, which lay 50 years in the past, was etched on people's memories. Stage blood flowed copiously inside the theatres, too, and Catholic audiences applauded numerous dramatizations of the story of Judith, such as the play by Federico della Valle written around 1600. Artemisia might have seen it: her depiction of Judith and her maid recalls one of the key scenes. Even in schools, Jesuit pupils reenacted the murder of Holofernes – even if it usually took place off stage. In our picture, too, the body of the lustful general is discreetly tucked away at the bottom of the canvas. The destruction of the enemy was a favourite theme of the epoch: the dark skinned, black haired Assyrian embodied the heathen and the barbarian, called to mind the very present threat posed by the Turks and stood in general for the "other" and for evil.

And yet – for male artists Holofernes was a fellow man with whom they felt solidarity. In contrast to the youthful David, for example, whose defeat of the giant Goliath assured him general esteem, Judith was suspect. For the positive heroine, even though she had returned to Bethulia "without pollution of sin" and effectively symbolized the Church, virtue and civilization, had nevertheless seduced the libertine with her feminine charms and by taking up his weapon had assumed the role of the man and assured his downfall and death.

She thereby found herself bracketed together with Salome and Delilah, the Bible's infamous *femmes fatales*, who were perceived as a threat to the whole of the male sex. Her story is in truth not a parable of edifying piety but an erotically charged and therefore particularly tasty scandal. Artemisia Gentileschi's contemporaries may have judged her conduct to have resembled that of Judith; both became outsiders who did not conform to the standard role of women in a patriarchal society.

"Artemisia gold", the artist's trademark
There is little of the erotic seductress about Artemisia's powerful Judith. It is true that she has

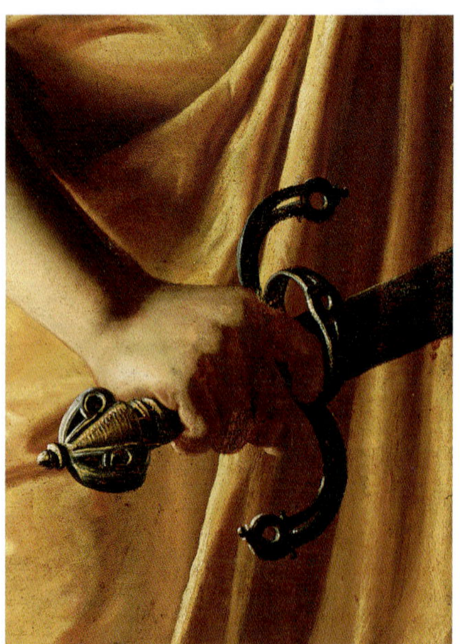

twisted her hair into ringlets and adorned herself
with a diadem and earrings, but unlike other of
Artemisia's heroines she does not show a plunging
neckline or wear a see through dress that emphasizes
the curves of her body. She is attired not in an Old
Testament fashion but in clothes that the artist might
have worn. Their gleaming yellow silk was one of
the artist's trademarks, known as "Artemisia gold".

An unflattering, implausible shadow – the candle
is not correctly positioned to explain it – falls across
Judith's face. This belongs not to a tender, youthful
beauty but to an experienced woman in her mid
thirties, a female type that appears in many of the
artist's early pictures. An almost imperceptible detail
reveals the heroine's true nature: protruding beneath
the hem of her dress are not the sandals mentioned
in the Jewish song of praise, but a sturdy pair of
shoes suitable for fleeing through the enemy camp!
Artemisia's Judith stands with both feet on the
ground, not a lascivious seductress but a woman of
action. This is probably how the artist best liked to
see herself. Not without good reason: she had
emancipated herself from her father and her husband, fed herself by the fruits of her own labours
and conquered the male domain of history painting.
Her self-confidence is evident in her self-portrait, in
one of her works, as the Allegory of Painting and in
her declaration to a customer: "I will show what a
woman can do. You will find the courage of Caesar
in the soul of a woman!"

The American Mary Garrard compares Judith
and her maid with two "guerrilla warriors func-
tioning heroically in an alien territory", who with
feminine solidarity are asserting themselves in a
patriarchal society. Garrard is one of the feminists
to whom Artemisia owes her rediscovery after
languishing in oblivion for almost 300 years. Along
with the works of the other *Caravaggisti*, her pictures fell victim to changing tastes in art and were
spurned, overpainted and even destroyed. With the
emergence in the 20th century of a new sensibility
vis-à-vis the Baroque, feminist art historians proclaimed Artemisia a forerunner, a "great painter of
the war between the sexes" (Germaine Greer). They
praised her particular "female outlook", which they
traced back to her traumatic experience of rape, and
celebrated the artist's independent spirit. By reading her biography in this way, however, they simply
swapped one stereotype for another, the promiscu-
ous woman with loose morals for an early feminist.

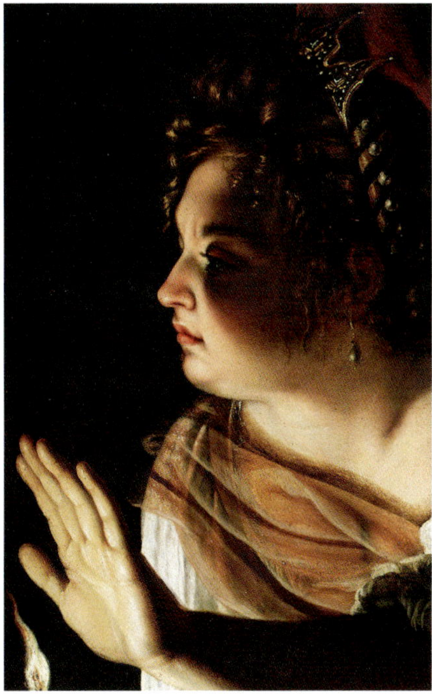

Little is known about Artemisia's real personality. Her statements during the court case and in
letters to clients reveal almost nothing. In her choice
of subjects and her painting style, the artist was
ultimately dependent upon the tastes of wealthy
men. Once Caravaggism became *passé* in Naples,
Artemisia's heroines, too, became more graceful and
pleasing – at least from what we can judge. Amongst
those of her paintings documented in invoices and
letters, only some 60 are currently known, whereas
108 remain missing. But new works are continually
coming to light, hidden behind incorrect attribu-
tions. They include a growing number that do not
fit the feminist mould: instead of strong heroines,
they show women dominated by men and no less
than nineteen female nudes, including a reclining
Venus. In 1916 the art critic Roberto Longhi praised
Artemisia as the "only woman in Italy who ever
knew what painting is, and colour", and in whose
work there was no trace of "female *peinture*". She
remains an artist to be discovered.

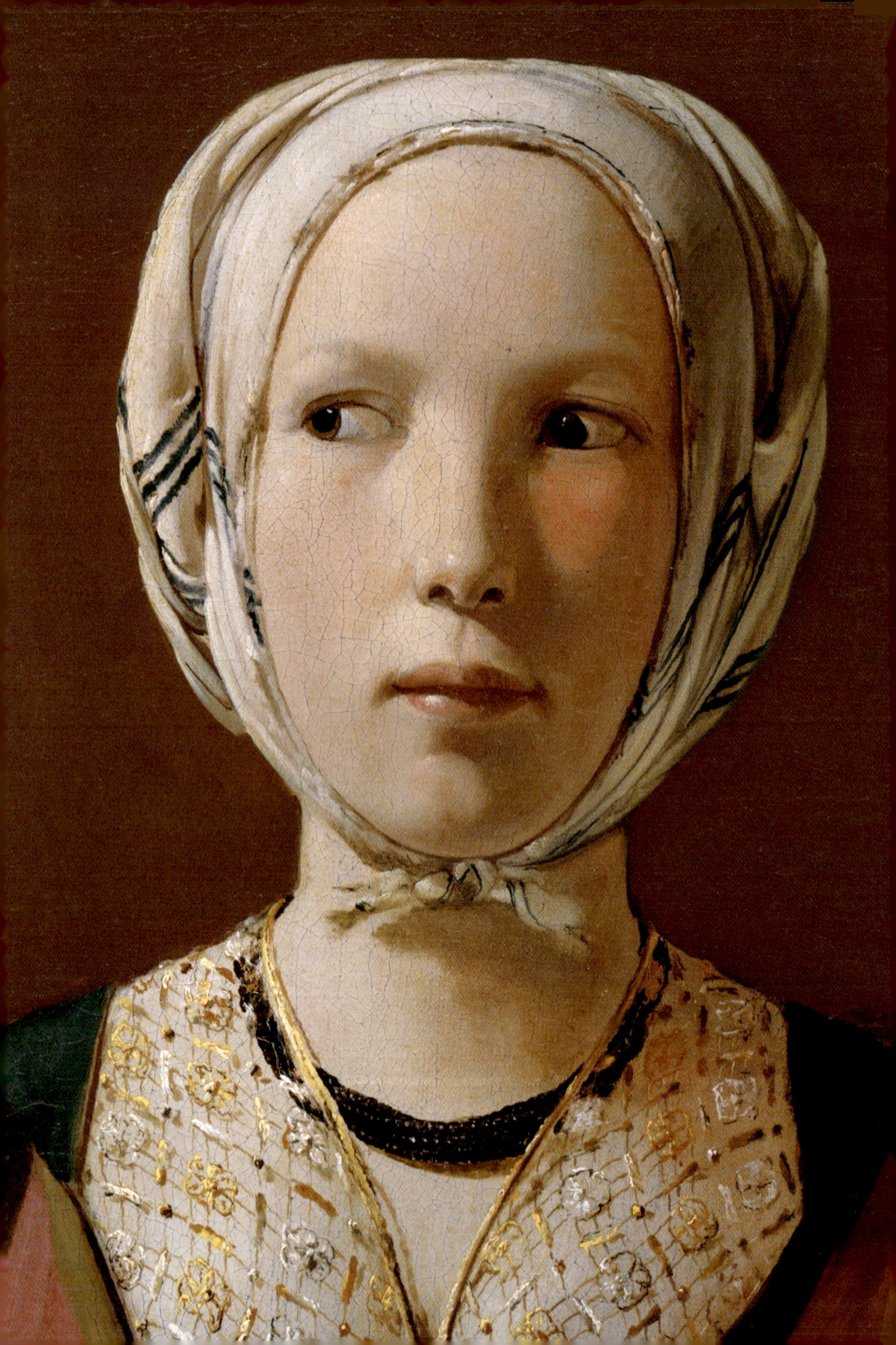

Georges de La Tour (1593–1652)

Double-dealing hands and eyes

The Fortune Teller, after 1630
102 x 123 cm, New York, The Metropolitan Museum of Art,
Rogers Fund, 1960

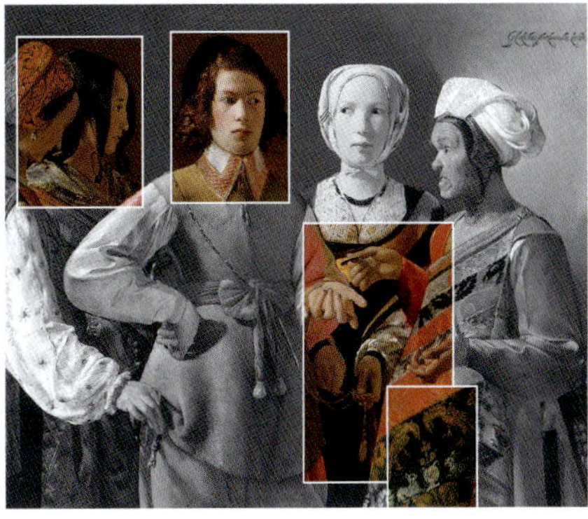

A French masterpiece was once secretly smuggled out of France. In 1960 the New York Metropolitan Museum bought *The Fortune Teller*, a work attributed to Georges de La Tour (1593–1652), for an unknown but "very high sum of money". When the affair became publicly known, critics raised their voices in the French press against this sordid victory of the dollar, complaining of irretrievable loss to the "national heritage". The Minister of Culture, André Malraux, attempted to explain to parliament how the Louvre had let the opportunity to acquire such a treasure slip by unnoticed. It was never fully explained how a licence to export the painting had been acquired in the first place; the head of the Louvre Old Masters department at the time remained silent.

Hardly anyone had seen the painting before 1960, and the story of its discovery is mysterious. In 1942, so the story goes, a monograph on the works of La Tour entered the hands of a French prisoner-of-war. The reproductions in the book reminded him of an old painting which hung at his uncle's castle. When the war was over, he had the painting examined by a priest who had an expert understanding of art. The latter, concluding that the painting was a genuine La Tour, informed the Louvre. Secret negotiations were then conducted to arrange for the purchase of the work. However, the art dealer Georges Wildenstein outbid the Louvre, finally buying *The Fortune Teller* in 1949 for 7.5 million francs. The painting then remained in his possession for the next ten years, accessible only to a small number of experts. In 1960, the Metropolitan Museum presented its sensational acquisition to the public for the first time.

It portrays a 17th-century picaresque scene: four sly thieves in the act of robbing a young man. The latter's attention is fully occupied by an old woman who is about to tell his fortune by reading his palm. He is thus unaware that he is the victim of a plot: while one girl is removing his purse from his pocket, her accomplice's hand is already held out to spirit it away; at the same time, a pale skinned beauty is cutting a gold medal from the chain around his neck. The protagonists are turned to face the spectator

like actors on a stage; indeed, it is quite possible that the artist borrowed the scene from a
play. According to experts at the Metropolitan
Museum, the oil painting is in "excellent condition". The sweeping calligraphy of the signature
"G. de La Tour Fecit Luneuilla Lothar" in the
top right of the painting proves it to be the
original work of the artist, who spent most
of his life in the small Lotharingian town of
Luneville. The details of his life are obscure.
At the beginning of the 20th century only his
name and two paintings were known. In the
meantime, however, several dates and various
other facts have been found in archives, and in
1972, at the first major La Tour exhibition at
Paris, 30 paintings were attributed to his hand.
The Fortune Teller is one of the few spectacular
"daylit paintings" of an artist whose reputation,
until the 1930s, rested entirely on his execution
of candle-lit "nocturnal scenes".

In spite of his military-style doublet, the
richly dressed young man has rather a babyish
face. He is probably still a student at one of the
colleges visited by wealthy, upper-class boys
until – at the age of fifteen – they were introduced to the world of adults. Contact with the
adult world must have started for many of them
at an early age, however, for "before they even
reach Aristotle's lessons on restraint," according
to the essayist Michel de Montaigne, "a hundred
schoolboys already have syphilis."

There would certainly be no shortage of
places to contract such diseases – inns, hostelries
and brothels – within even a short distance of
the college gates. La Tour has not defined where
the scene in his painting is taking place; perhaps
the old woman will not be content with her fortune telling, but will attempt to prostitute one
of her young accomplices to the young man.
Their dark skin, black hair and richly coloured
Oriental dress show the old woman and two
girls on the left to be so-called "gypsies", a term
common at that time but no longer used today.

La Tour's contemporary, the Lorraine artist
Jacques Callot, portrayed them in similar fashion in some of his etchings. Callot is reported to
have accompanied an itinerant group as far as
Rome after running away from home at the age
of twelve. He was discovered there by merchants
from Nancy and sent home to his parents.

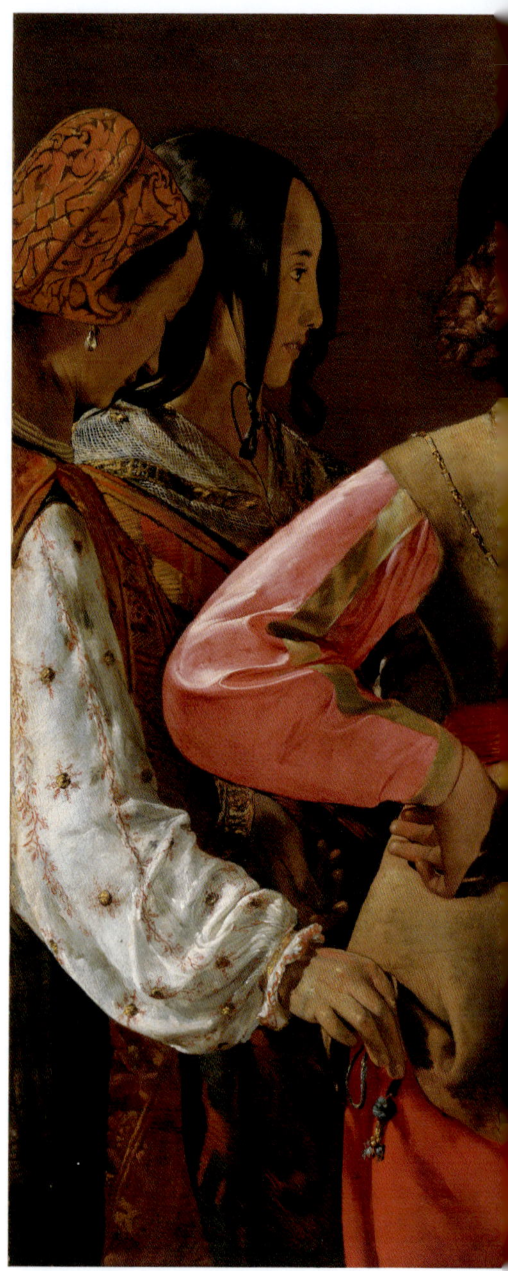

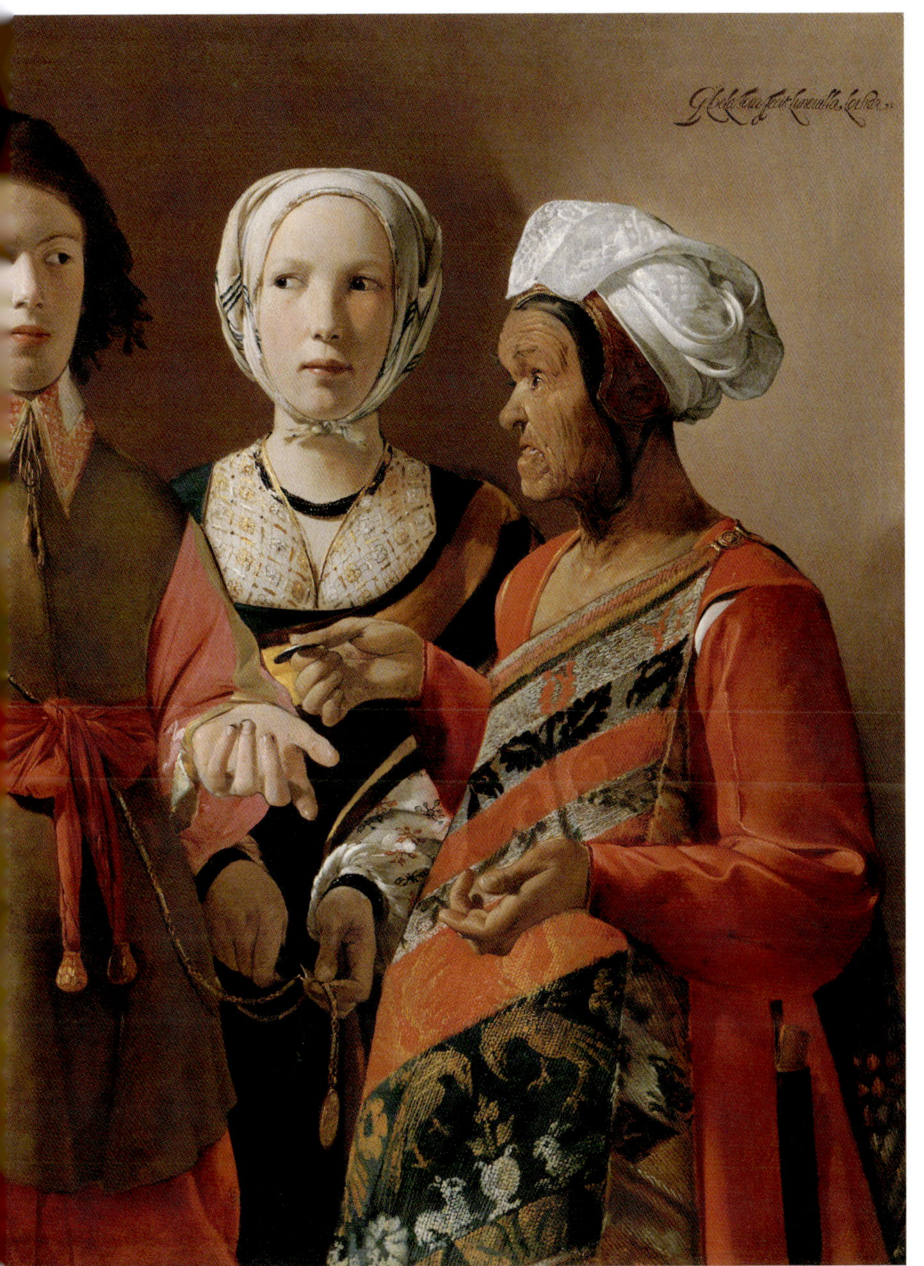

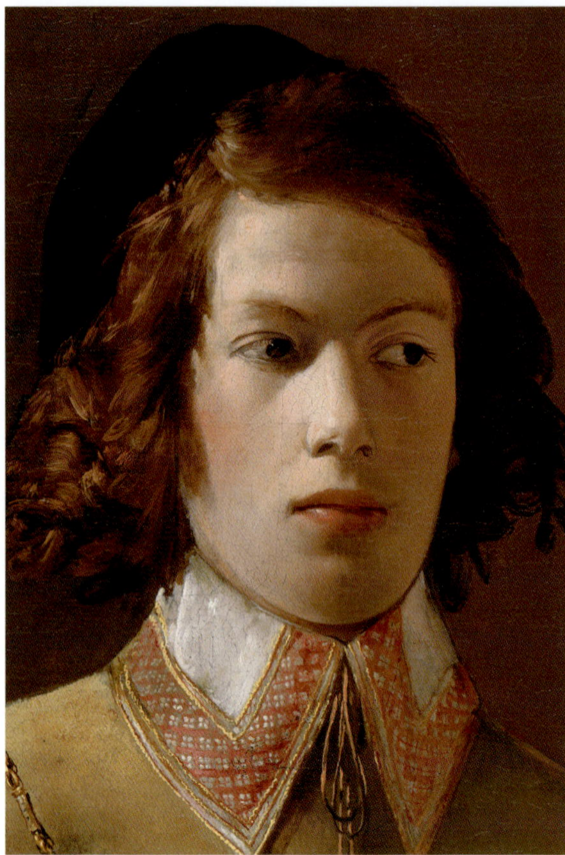

in conjunction with warnings against "vice".

La Tour's message appears to have been more serious than that of many of his contemporaries; he refrained from painting gay scenes of "dissolute" life. The faces of victim and thieves are less cheerful than concentrated. Fortune telling and robbery were dangerous businesses. If caught, the youth could theoretically expect to be excommunicated – although he would be more likely in reality to be given a good hiding by one of his teachers. Watch thieves usually had both ears cut off in the 17th century; they were tortured with red-hot pincers and branded, or even hung, drawn and quartered. Social outsiders were publically whipped and banished without trial for the slightest offence.

In this painting, whose protagonists form a close group and yet are nonetheless isolated from one another, the Lorraine artist, like his contemporary, the scientist and philosopher Blaise Pascal, appears to be warning the spectator against the dangers of an evil world: a world full of greed, selfishness and traps.

The other two great "daylit" paintings attributed to La Tour show comparable scenes. In the paintings *Card-sharper with the Ace of Clubs*, and *Card-sharper with the Ace of Diamonds* a young victim is about to lose the pieces of gold piled up before him to a cunning card-sharper and his lovely accomplice. Perhaps all three pictures illustrate episodes from the biblical parable of the prodigal son who "took his journey into a far country and there wasted his substance with riotous living".

This story from the Gospel of St Luke was a favourite among the painters of the 16th and 17th centuries, since it allowed them to portray popular, low mannered scenes with drinkers and brothels. Such subjects were only tolerated by the Church

A palm crossed with gold

A gold coin twinkles in the old woman's deeply lined hand. It is both the reward for her work and an essential part of the ritual of fortune telling. Before looking into the future, she must cross the soft, white hand that the youth so trustingly holds out to her with the gold coin.

The custom is described by Preciosa, the so-called "little gypsy girl" (*La Gitanilla*) from Cervantes' eponymous short story, published in 1613 in his *Novelas Ejemplares* ("Exemplary Novels"). "All crosses are good," she explains, "… but silver or gold crosses are the best, and crossing the palm of the hand with a copper coin, you must know, reduces good fortune, at least, the good fortune I foretell."

The fortune teller naturally retains the coin she has used – and gets to keep it for herself, whereas everything else that she earns, begs or steals must be shared with all, in line with the unwritten laws of her people. The youth's purse, for example, and the medallion cut from its chain by the deft fingers of the pale young woman. In performing the latter, the pale beauty observes her victim from the corners of her eyes. Movement in the painting is restricted to fingers, or to eyes, whose lines of vision cross, or appear to avoid meeting.

Tension in the painting derives from its inherent contrasts: pretended calm and concealed activity; innocence and cunning; the girls' youthful vigour and the weathered features of the old woman. It is this tension – including its erotic aspect – which appears to have interested the artist most; neither the rich materials, the elaborate clothing nor the gleam of gold in the diffuse light can distract from it. In his later "nocturnal" works, La Tour dispensed with such decorative trimmings and reduced his saints almost to their abstract corporeal mass, lit by the glow of a single candle.

Recent expert opinion has placed the origin of the undated *Fortune Teller*, as well as that of the two *Card-sharpers*, between 1630 and 1639 – a time when the Thirty Years' War had broken out in the border country of Lorraine, bringing with it pestilence and famine. Luneville, the small town where La Tour spent most of his life, was besieged, plundered and pillaged on several occasions. The painter himself is said to have profited from these times, making a fortune in grain speculation and rising to the station of a land-owning squire. Thus gold coins played as important a role in his real life as they did in his paintings.

An ostracized people
Because they made their own laws and did not feel bound to Christianity, a sedentary way of life or property, the basic values of Western societies, itinerant peoples were discriminated against and ostracized as "vagabonds and crooks" wherever they went in Europe, where they had first made their appearance in the 15th century.

Court records document the presence of people described as "Egyptians and Saracens" in the Duchy of Lorraine, and testify to torture, banishment and execution as punishments for robbery, blasphemy and witchcraft. They travelled through the transit region of Lorraine, where their caravans would have passed those of the armies fighting the the Thirty Years' War. Callot's etchings record both their hardships and the more romantic, colourful aspect of their lives. La Tour, who had become a rich landowner, would probably have viewed them with distrust; the court records at Luneville also betray that he would flog anyone with his own hands who trespassed on his property.

In younger years, the artist – like Callot – may have accompanied a travelling group some of the way to Italy, where he possibly underwent part of his training. At least one detail in the painting bears testimony to his knowledge of their customs and traditions: the hair of unmarried women and girls was worn loose, while that of married women was tucked under a bonnet, or into a scarf knotted at the nape; a scarf knotted under the chin, however, like the one worn by the beauty at the centre of the painting, was a sign that a woman was neither a virgin nor married. Perhaps she worked for the bawd on the right.

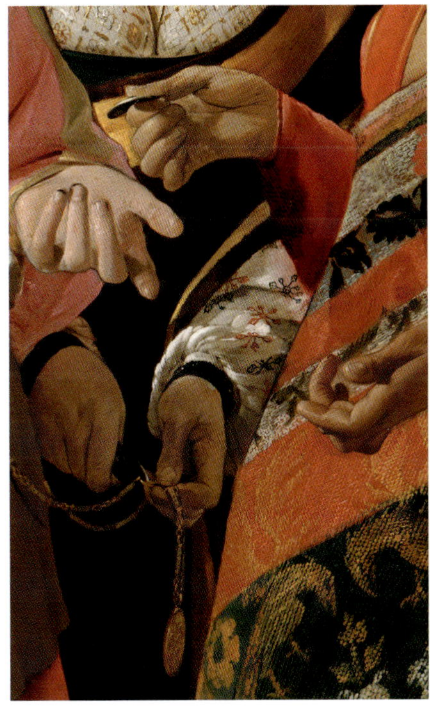

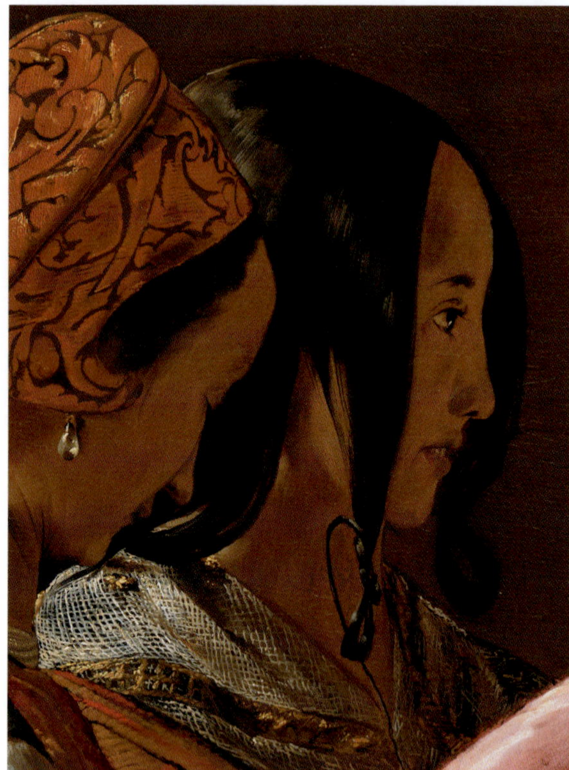

Pale skinned female members of these ethnic groups were considered particularly attractive, since they were closer to contemporary ideals of beauty than their dark skinned, black haired sisters. In novels and comedies, they usually turned out – as in Cervantes' Preciosa – to be daughters of Christian families who had been abducted in infancy. It is possible that La Tour's figures are acting out a play with a similar storyline on the stage, which would also explain their unusual richness of clothing for travelling people.

The costumes they are wearing are products of the imagination, entirely inconsistent with expert opinion on 17th-century Lotharingian fashion. Leather doublets of the type worn by the youth in the painting, for example, were always tied at the front. In rendering the old woman's shawl with its Oriental design, the painter, usually at pains to reproduce textiles in meticulous detail, has been astonishingly lax: the weft of the folded back inside of the fabric runs in a different direction from that of the outside. The shawl itself is conspicuously similar to a carpet lying at the Virgin's feet in the Netherlandish Joos van Cleve's 16th-century work *Virgin and Child*, even down to distortions of perspective. It was these discoveries at the end of the 1960s that began to puzzle the English art historian Christopher Wright. His suspicions increased when he found the French swear word MERDE (shit) woven into the scarf worn by the second girl from the left.

An ingenious forgery?

In the La Tour monograph published by Benedict Nicolson and Christopher Wright in 1974, *The Fortune Teller* was listed among works known to be from the painter's hand. Ten years later – Nicolson had died in the meantime – Wright revised his opinion that the work had been painted in the 17th century and claimed that the painting exhibited in the Metropolitan Museum was the work of a 20th-century forger who had been intelligent enough to use an old canvas and mix his paints with the help of old recipes.

Why this change of mind? In a book entitled *The Art of the Forger*, published in 1984, Wright described how pressure was brought to bear on him as a young academic to suppress his doubts as to the authenticity of the painting. Finally, he had submitted to the reputation of international experts and to pressure from the powerful authority in matters of art of Sir Anthony Blunt; Blunt, frequently consulted by the art dealer Wildenstein, was later exposed as a Soviet spy.

The authenticity of *The Fortune Teller* had originally been proved in 1972 at the Paris La Tour exhibition by comparing it with the other two "daylit" paintings, the two versions of the *Card-sharper*.

These two paintings had been discovered in the 1920s; having remained since then in private collections, they could now be examined for the first time because one of them had just been purchased by the Louvre. According to Wright's later opinion, this had been a case of several forgeries confirming each others' authenticity. He nevertheless kept silent. In his book in 1984 Wright attributes several of the other "daylit" paintings to an unknown master, while calling the authenticity of the two *Card-Sharpers* and *The Fortune Teller* into question.

Wright's hypothesis was that all three may have been the work of a French restorer called Delobre who had worked for Wildenstein in the USA; according to Wright, the first two were probably painted at the beginning of the 20th century, the third during the 1940s. Delobre died in 1954. In Wright's opinion, the forged *Fortune Teller* replaced an older painting with a similar theme which had hung in the castle and could be traced back as far as 1879. The painting was of inferior quality, so the Louvre had not bid especially aggressively for it at its auction. It had therefore been easy enough to obtain a licence to export such a work.

It is entirely understandable, according to Wright, that experts and museum directors should not be swayed in their opinion of the authenticity of a painting they have helped "discover" themselves, or whose purchase they have advised, or for which they have had to pay millions. Not one of them acknowledged the bizarre detail brought to light by Wright: the French swear word *merde*. Could it have been a forger's joke? In 1982 the Metropolitan Museum made it known that this "later addition" – in whose existence nobody but Wright had previously shown any interest at all – had been removed during cleaning of the canvas.

The museum still stands by its version of the work's authenticity. However, there is a certain piquancy in the proximity of Wright's hypothesis of the painting as a forgery to the shady double dealing shown in *The Fortune Teller* itself: we evidently live in a world of lies and deception in which not only immature youths, but also museum directors can be fleeced by cunning rascals.

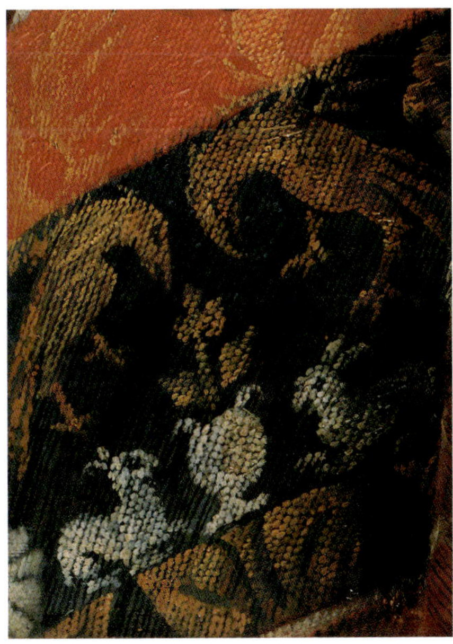

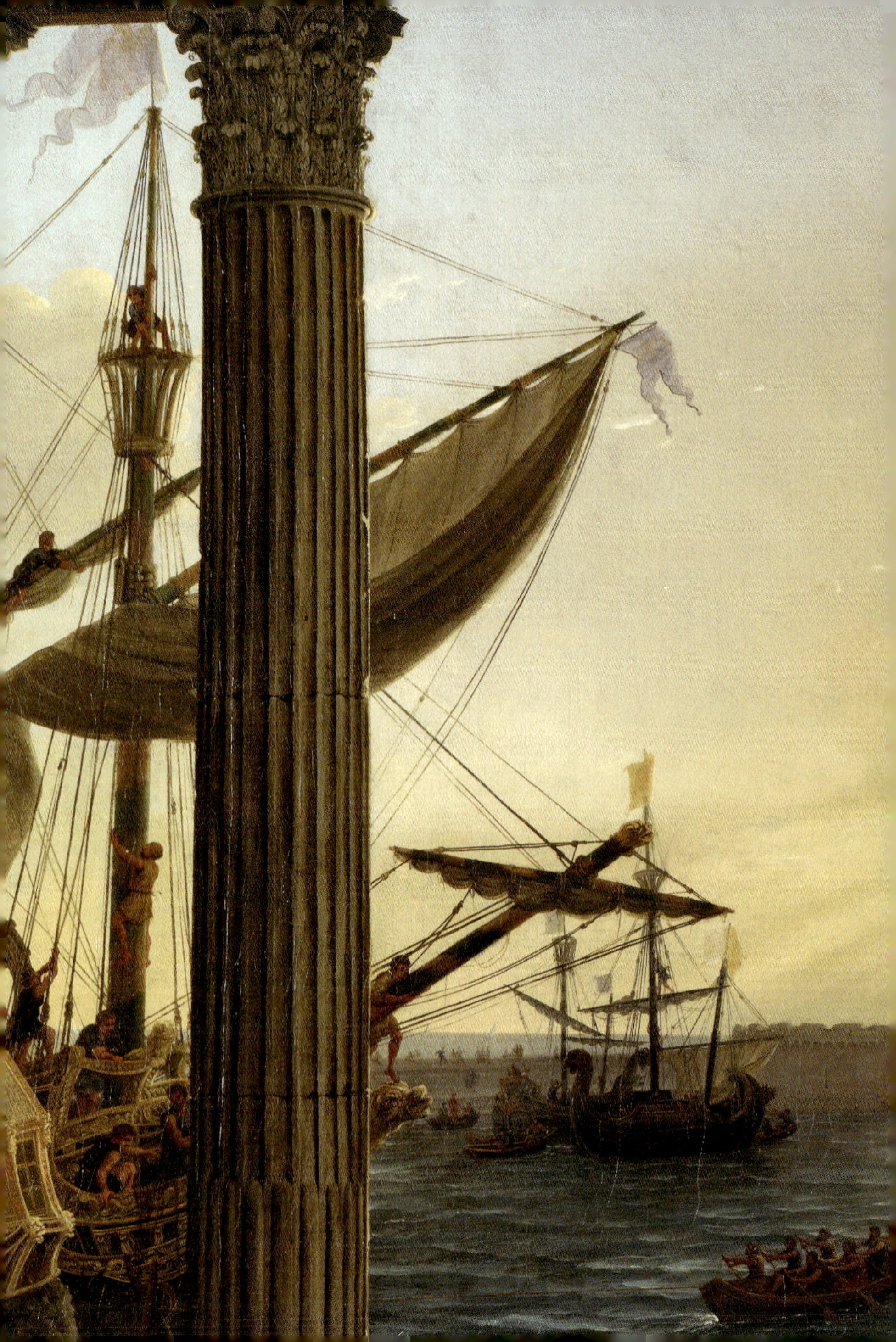

Claude Lorrain (1604–1682)

The dream of a safe harbour in stormy times

Seaport with the Embarkation of the Queen of Sheba, 1648
148 x 193 cm, London, The National Gallery

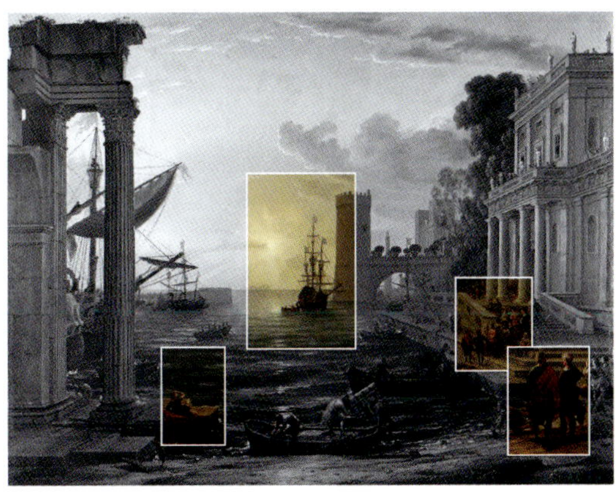

Columns in the Corinthian style, an imposing white palazzo with a portico and a flight of outdoor steps, a lighthouse and a harbour mole – these were the set pieces out of which Claude Lorrain composed his harbour views of the 1630s and 1640s. A number of three-masted sailing boats lie at anchor between them. The horizon is always low and the dominant impression is one of water, sky and cascading sunlight.

Such scenes were the invention of the artist and had started out as no more than simple bays with fishing boats. Over the course of the years, however, Claude expanded them into splendid seaports which he made the setting for major events and state occasions, populated by noble figures from

mythology, the legends of the saints and the Bible. The *Embarkation of the Queen of Sheba* of 1648 was the last of these compositions and is considered the high point of Claude's some 50 sea pieces. From now on he would concentrate upon bucolic landscapes filled with Classical ruins and peopled by shepherds and nymphs beneath tall trees. Claude Lorrain worked extremely slowly, but Rome's cardinals and princes were willing – in a city home to artists from all over Europe, vying with each other for commissions – to wait a long time for his pictures. These they liked to order in pairs – a light filled seascape accompanied by a pastoral idyll – even though the genre of landscape painting at that time ranked low down in the hierarchy of art.

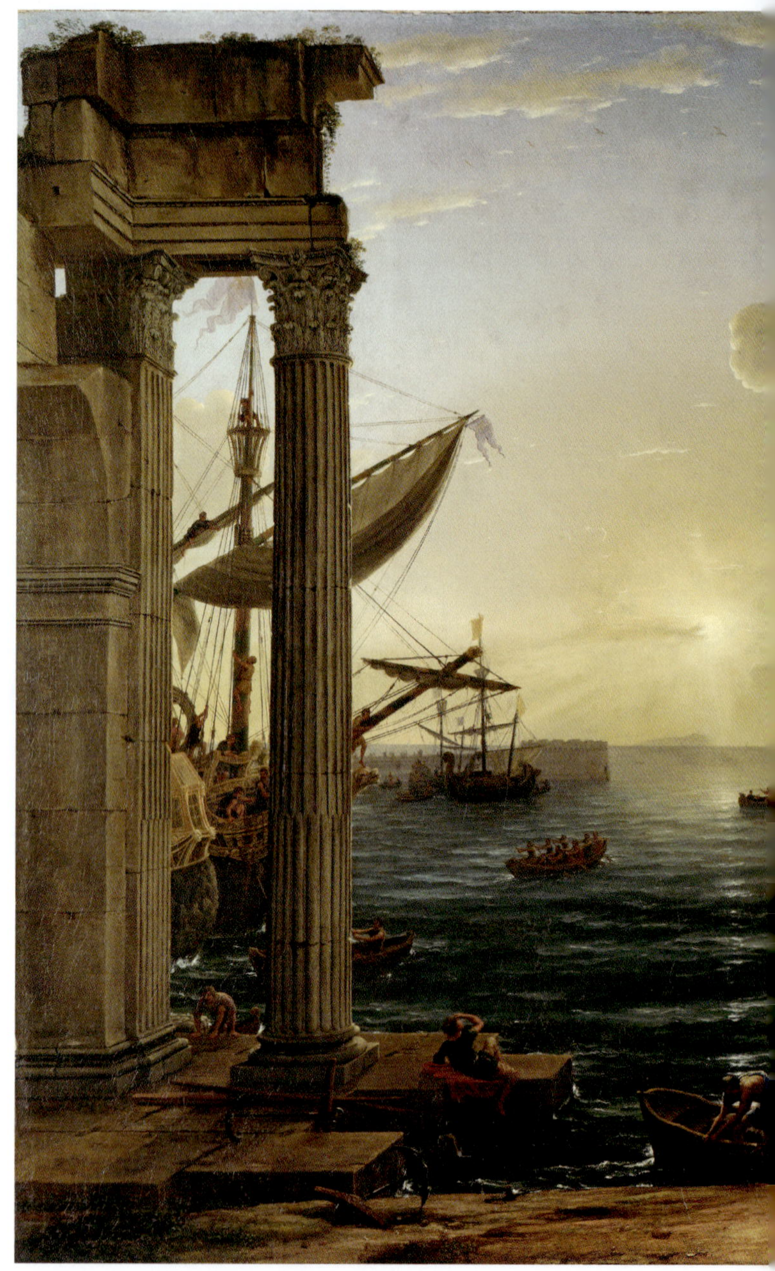

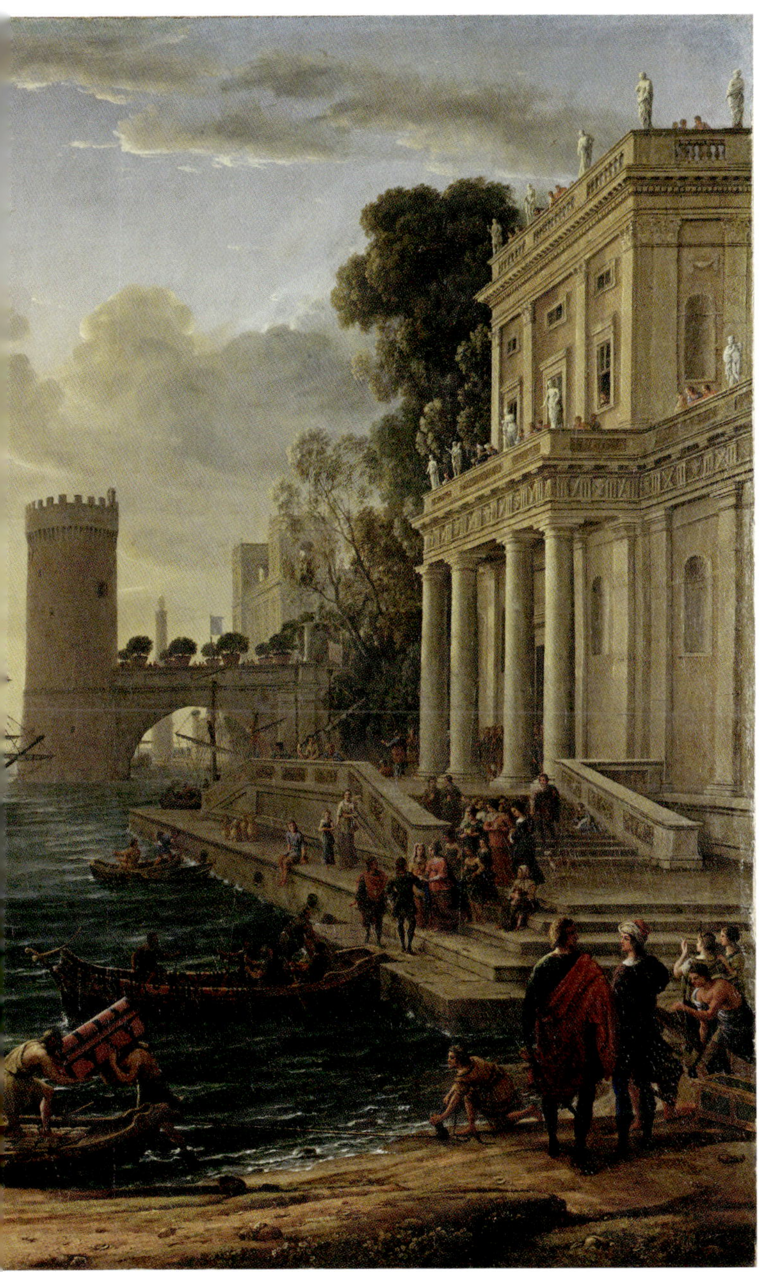

Two aristocratic patrons

The *Embarkation of the Queen of Sheba* must originally have been commissioned by Prince Camillo Pamphilj (1622–1665) in 1647. The painter noted the prince's name on the back of a preliminary drawing, but later crossed it out and replaced it by another. Claude's list of patrons reads like a guided tour through the upheavals of political life in Italy and Europe. Constant change was also on the agenda in the capital of Christianity, which along with pilgrims attracted hordes of tourists, diplomats and émigrés and where each new pope immediately filled the most important posts with his favourites and family members. Giambattista Pamphilj, who in 1644 became Pope Innocent X, had just one nephew to help cement his dynastic power base: Camillo. This latter is said to have been interested chiefly in horses, although he also awarded a commission to the architect Gianlorenzo Bernini. His uncle was uncertain in which position his nephew could be most useful to him; having first of all appointed him commander in chief of the armies of the Papal States, he shortly afterwards changed his mind and made him a cardinal instead. Camillo was unhappy with this and in 1647 got married –

throwing in his cardinal's hat, for which the vexed Pope banished him from Rome for several years. Camillo was thus no longer able to take delivery of the picture he had commissioned.

Claude finished the painting and wrote on it the title of its new buyer. Below left, chiselled into a block of stone beside the signature of the artist, is the inscription: FAICT POVR SON ALTESSE LE DVC DE BVILLON A ROMAE ("Made for his Highness the Duke of Bouillon in Rome, 1648"). This was Frédéric-Maurice de la Tour d'Auvergne (1605–1652), scion of a famous French Hugenot family. Prior to his arrival in Rome, he had fought as a general for and against his country, been involved in two conspiracies against the powerful minister Richelieu, been sentenced to death and pardoned. He fled to Italy and from 1644 to 1647 (following his conversion to Catholicism) commanded the papal troops. By the time the Duke acquired the *Embarkation of the Queen of Sheba* and its pendant, the *Marriage of Isaac and Rebekah*, he had already left the Papal States. He became reconciled with his king, reconverted, fathered twelve children and as far as we know purchased no other works of art apart from the two pictures by Claude.

Rises and falls were typical of the biographies of Baroque individuals such as Pamphilj and Bouillon. It is possible that they are represented by the two men on the right-hand edge of the painting, identified as aristocrats by their rapiers, and since both briefly commanded the papal fleet, they would not be out of place in a seaport.

A pale queen with black serving maids

Were it not for the words LA REINE DE SABA VA TROVVER SALOMON ("The Queen of Sheba goes to find Solomon") chiselled in stone beneath the steps on the right, it would be almost impossible to guess what is taking place in the distance and almost on the very edge of the composition. "Now when the Queen of Sheba heard of the fame of Solomon concerning the name of the Lord, she came to test him with hard questions," according to the Old Testament Book of Kings. "She came to Jerusalem with a very great retinue, with camels that bore spices, very much gold, and precious stones" (I Kings 10:1–3).

The Bible is brief and does not even give the queen's name, thereby leaving all the more scope for the imagination. The Queen of Sheba became a myth and countless legends sprang up around her person, some of them identifying her country, for example, as Yemen or Ethiopia. According to Ethiopian Christians, she had a son by Solomon who subsequently ruled Ethiopia and introduced Jewish customs there. In the 12th century she appeared on an altar in Klosterneuburg as a black beauty; Claude paints her with a pale face but shows her accompanied by her two female train bearers of exotic appearance. It is very probable that the artist from the Lorraine was also familiar with the bizarre legend according to which the Queen of Sheba walked on the hairy, webbed feet of a goose. She was popular in France as Queen Pédauque (from the Italian *piede d'òca*, goose feet) and was portrayed in this manner in stone carvings on the portals of Dijon and Nevers cathedrals. She is also mentioned in the Koran: "Your face has the beauty of the most beautiful" Solomon said to the Queen of Sheba, "but this beauty is not matched by your feet!" In Claude Lorrain's picture this flaw cannot be made out.

As is the case with St Ursula and St Paula Romana in two other *Embarkation* pictures by Claude, the queen is only distinguished from the figures around her by her crown. Artists such as Piero della Francesca, Paolo Veronese and Raphael had all set the scene within a palace, where the Queen of Sheba is shown meeting Solomon or paying homage to him – a subject interpreted as prefiguring the Adoration of the Magi before the Infant Christ. Her embarkation for Solomon's kingdom is not mentioned in the Bible. The spices, gold and precious stones that she took with her must be contained, in Claude's picture, within the chests being loaded into the boats. A galleon can be made out between the columns on the left and more three masters lie in the background.

The name of Sheba had been associated since ages past with fabulous treasures, the fairytale Orient and the allure of far away places, and in Claude Lorrain's day it had taken on a new reality. At the start of the 17th century the Dutch and English had founded East India and West India trading companies, corporations which were listed on the stock exchange and enjoyed state privileges. Their galleons imported luxury goods from the Orient to Europe.

Dutch artists during this period became the first to depict maritime scenes in their painting – chiefly naval battles or cogs tossed about in stormy seas, usually victorious in their own battle against the elements. All of them were examples of the courage

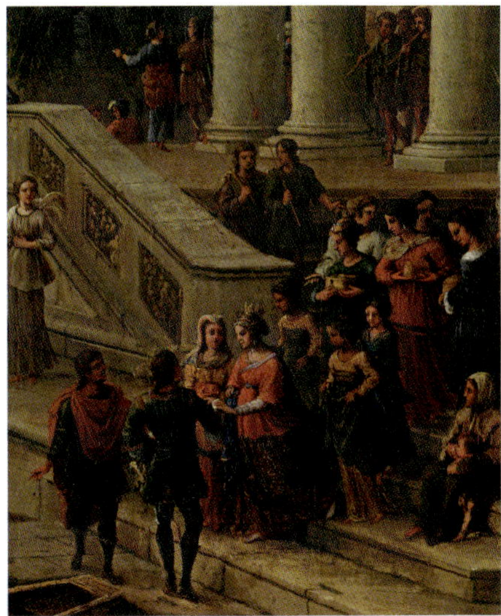

and strength of the mariners and of their valour in the face of the trials and tribulations of Fate.

Claude took over this successful northern genre of the "sea piece", but left out of his works the terrors of the sea with its tempests, broken masts, leaking hulls and shipwrecks. Of his many ships, barely one has hoisted its sails. The other three masters rendered by the artist in such painstaking detail lie at anchor in a safe harbour, their sails furled. The painter is said to have endured "numerous and terrible storms" on a sea voyage that he made in around 1627, when he travelled from his native Lorraine via Marseilles to Italy. In Claude's seaport pictures, the high-ranking personages may be planning to embark on a journey but are still all on land. No one actually sets off. The artist himself spent almost his whole life firmly settled in voluntary exile in Rome.

Sparkling waves and a rising sun
All the figures in the foreground seem to be busy with tasks or immersed in conversation, with just one exception – the young man who is leaning back, semi recumbent, on his cloak. With one hand shielding his eyes, he is gazing out into the distance. Playing the part of the viewer, he lies there in the early morning and enjoys the sparkling waves and the rising sun.

The artist's own youth had been very different. Born Claude Gelée, he became known as Le Lorrain in Rome after his Lorraine origins. He was born in 1604 or 1605 (and not 1600, as was long assumed) into impoverished circumstances and at the age of twelve or thirteen was sent to Italy as a pastry cook, like many of his compatriots. Several hundred of them, so Sandrart informs us, were employed in the kitchens of Rome in those days.

The boy entered the service of the artist Agostino Tassi, who decorated Roman palaces with illusionistic landscapes and architecture. Since Claude "carried out his cooking and household duties very willingly", writes Sandrart, "cleaned everything, ground the colours ready for painting and rinsed the palette and brushes", he rose to the position of apprentice and assistant. It was to Tassi that the novice owed his first introductions to Roman society.

In the middle of the 17th century, Baroque Rome was still a good place for artists. Despite the economic crisis, construction was booming and the many palaces, churches and chapels needed decorating. Wealthy tourists from far and wide bought panel paintings to take home as souvenirs.

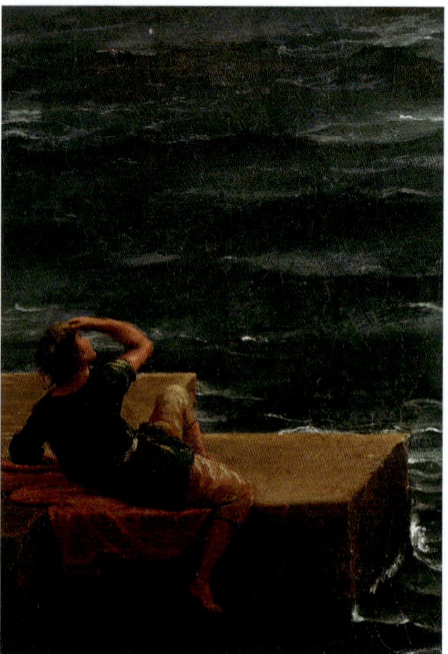

Claude consequently spent his time not staring dreamily at the water or the Campagna Romana countryside but making endless sketches of his surroundings (he bequeathed over 1,300 masterly drawings to posterity) and collecting motifs for his oil paintings. These he conceived in the fashionable pastoral genre: effectively a landscape populated by shepherds and occasionally also by fishermen. The artist thereby idealized his setting and, using selected elements of reality which he assembled into a harmonious whole, composed a better and more beautiful world.

When Claude was 30 years old, "cardinals and finally princes of all kinds began to visit his studio", records his Italian biographer Filippo Baldinucci (1624–1696), "and from that point on it was for ever denied all those who were not great princes or clerics to commission pictures from him or to procure them other than through the agencies of these latter for a high price or with much trouble and a great deal of patience". An agent warned Cardinal Leopold de' Medici against Claude: "But what is worse is that he will have to be paid very generously because he only fixes a price for people of lower standing."

Praised by Baldinucci as a "friend of good morals", Claude led a modest existence and worked in a studio in the vicinity of Santa Maria del Popolo. In the evening he occasionally drank a glass of wine with his French colleague Nicolas Poussin (1594–1665), another voluntary émigré. Both appreciated the particular atmosphere of the Eternal City. "This air fills me with something great and generous that I had not felt before," enthused another visitor to Rome, the French author Guez de Balzac, in 1620. "If I dream for two hours on the banks of the Tiber, I become as wise as if I had studied for eight days".

Ultramarine lends depth to the water
Claude recorded details of his some 250 paintings in what he called his *Liber Veritatis* or "book of truth", the earliest catalogue raisonée compiled by a painter himself. He probably created the book as a means of exposing pictures that were in fact copies by imitators. He worked without assistants and, in a protracted process, built up his paintings out of numerous semi-transparent layers through which he created water surfaces of iridescent colour and hues. Reflections of sunlight infuse the waves with

movement and expensive ultramarine lends the water an impression of depth. Claude's works were and are exquisite collector's items but are also particularly sensitive to environmental influences and poor handling.

For his contemporaries, the painter's love of order and geometry made him modern. The ship's rigging is a case in point, as is the pictorial composition with its emphasis upon the horizon line, the sun standing exactly halfway up the canvas and the built architecture extending the same distance into the picture on both sides. At a time when Rome was still dominated by the flourishing forms of the Baroque style, Le Lorrain rendered visible a new taste in art, a taste that twenty years later would hallmark the gardens of Versailles palace, where meadows, streams and marshland would become straight paths, *rond points* and pools of water contained within stone borders. Versailles demonstrated that Nature could be tamed, that the instinctive and the unpredictable could be subjugated to rational laws. Just like the French royal gardens, Claude's sea pieces also convey a sense of order and security. For men with stormy fortunes like his clients Pamphilj and Bouillon, he offers a welcome illusion of calm in a safe harbour.

But geometry and symmetry do not alone explain why pictures such as the *Embarkation of the Queen of Sheba* fascinate us even today. There is something more: Claude's framework of mathematical stability carries us into the far away distance. The glittering, dazzling sun creates a pull; its silvery reflections open up a path that leads beyond the horizon into the realm of the boundless – just as the water, too, appears infinite and the ever rising sun conveys a sense of unending time. And just as the Queen of Sheba, as a mythical figure, represents immeasurable wealth in an unknown, far away land. Claude's art lies in his ability to convey security and order and at the same time to dissolve them.

His pictures thereby fell into what in the 17th century was considered a lowly genre, one rated inferior to portraiture and in particular inferior to history painting, whose heroic scenes carried an edifying moral. Landscape, so it was held, lacked great invention; it was more imitation than original creation, something for the eye, not the mind. This is not true of Claude's landscapes and sea pieces. They probably bore little resemblance to the ports

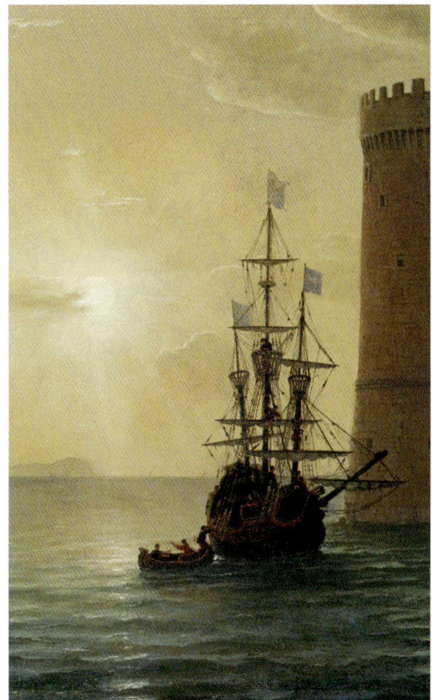

of Naples and Marseilles, both of which the painter knew. His paintings are not souvenirs of his travels, nor can they be made to serve a moralizing purpose. Rather, they transform those who contemplate them into philosophers and dreamers.

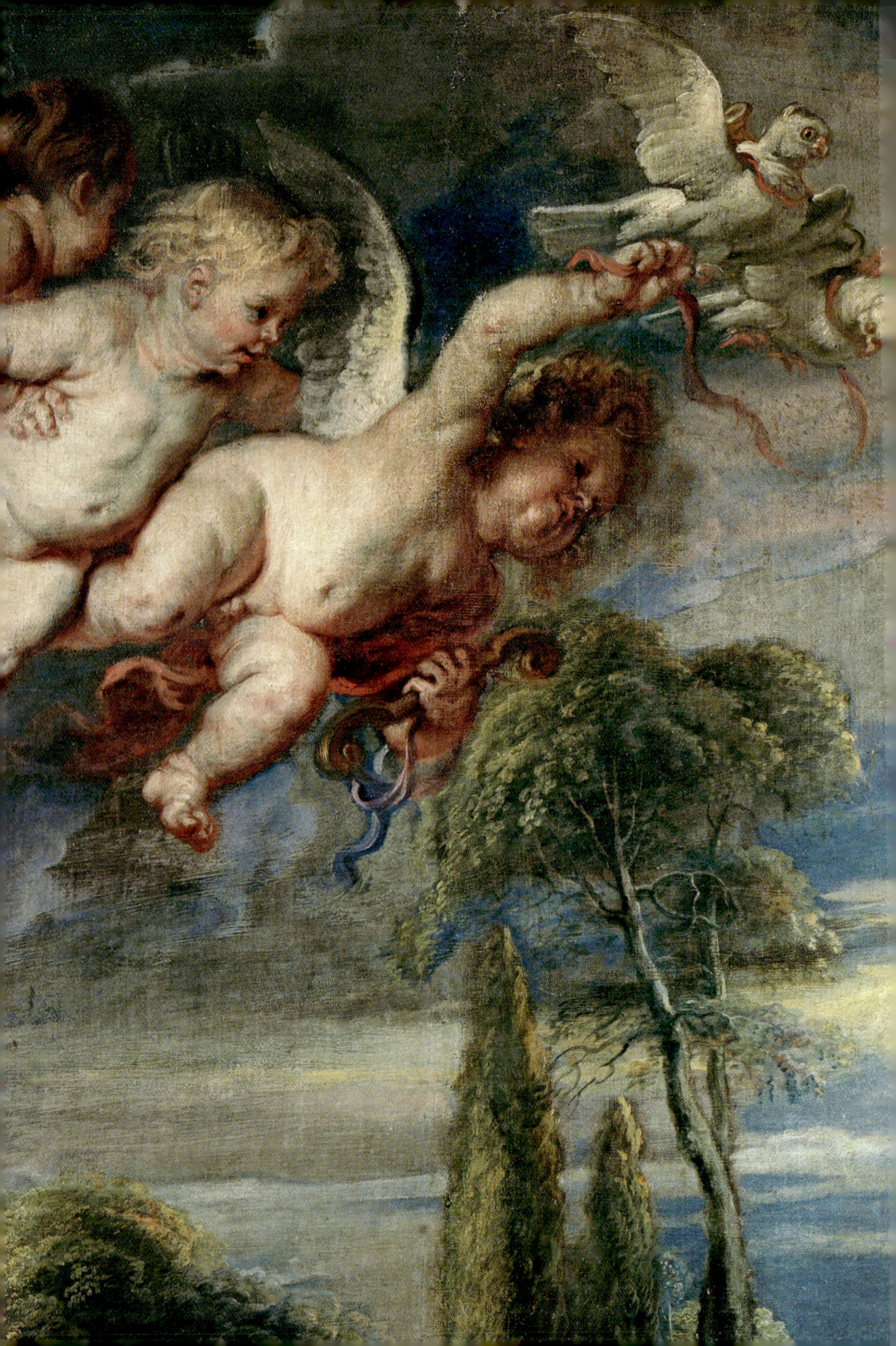

Peter Paul Rubens (1577–1640)

Grateful for the gift of sensuous pleasure

The Love Garden, c. 1632/1634
198 x 283 cm, Madrid, Museo Nacional del Prado

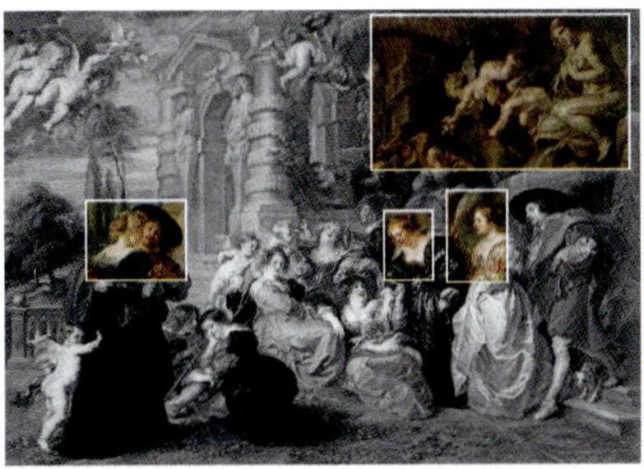

A painting that overflows with the joys of love: the widowed artist had married a sixteen-year-old. Rejuvenated, he filled an entire canvas with images of himself and his wife. Cherubs and Classical architecture make their happiness timeless. The intimate work is in the Prado, Madrid.

Peter Paul Rubens married his second wife in 1630. He was a 53-year-old widower, his wife a mere sixteen-year-old. Although the age difference would have been considered more than unusual even in those days, it was hardly a matter to worry Rubens: he was a man in his prime, a respected, wealthy gentleman, a painter at the height of his fame and fortune.

The painting, now in the Prado at Madrid and known as *The Love Garden*, was executed shortly after the wedding. Experts have dated it to between 1632 and 1634. Unlike most of his work, it was not done for a wealthy patron, but for himself. Nor was his own intervention restricted to the initial sketch and finishing touches, as was the case with so many of the paintings that left his busy studio, including those executed during the same period for the Banqueting House in London.

In spite of its great size – 198 by 283 centimetres – it is an unusually private painting. It expresses the feelings of a man who is already advanced in years and has regained a happiness thought for ever lost.

"I have regained a life of contemplative tranquillity," he wrote to a friend, adding: "How gladly we accept this gift of sensuous pleasure! And how gratefully!"

The painting tells of the pleasures of wealth and good company, of sensuous joy and love of life. The gentleman on the left, his arm placed tenderly around his blonde companion, is trying to persuade her to lay aside her reserves; a magnificently dressed couple descends from the staircase on the right, while the ladies in the centre of the painting listen to a lute player.

The swords are a sign that the gentlemen belong to the nobility or at least to the upper bourgeoisie, while the ladies in their finery reveal as much shoulder and bosom as permitted, or rather demanded, by the latest French fashions. The only nude figures in the painting are its many cherubs: winged, mythological creatures. Here they are shown strewing flowers, caressing the splendidly dressed, politely chatting figures or giving them an encouraging little shove – to help them, in various ways, to enjoy "this gift of sensuous pleasure", which is, after all, what they are there for.

Comparison of the female heads reveals that all of them have the same straight noses, very round and slightly protruding eyes and fair hair. They all resemble the artist's new wife, so that several art historians think that Rubens may have painted her in the company of her sisters. However, the men, all of whom

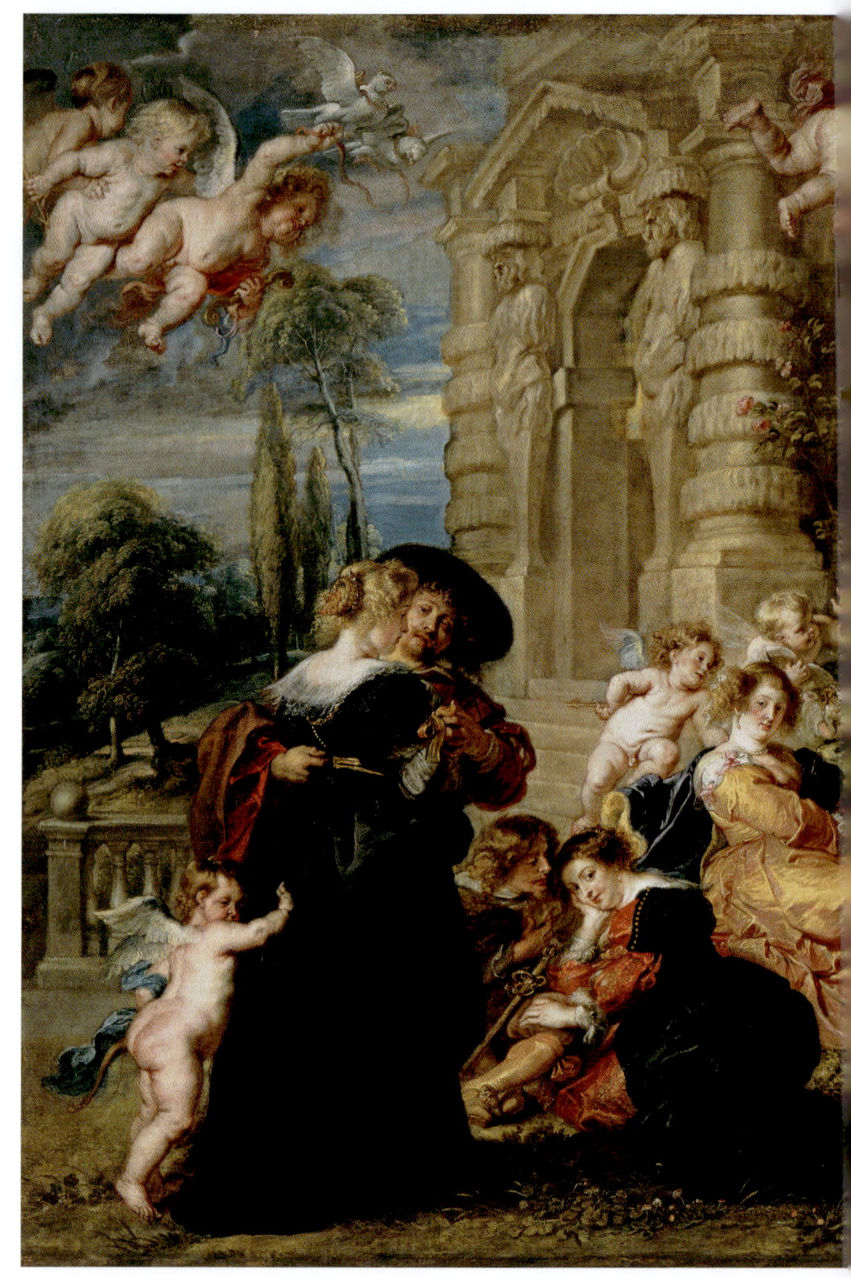

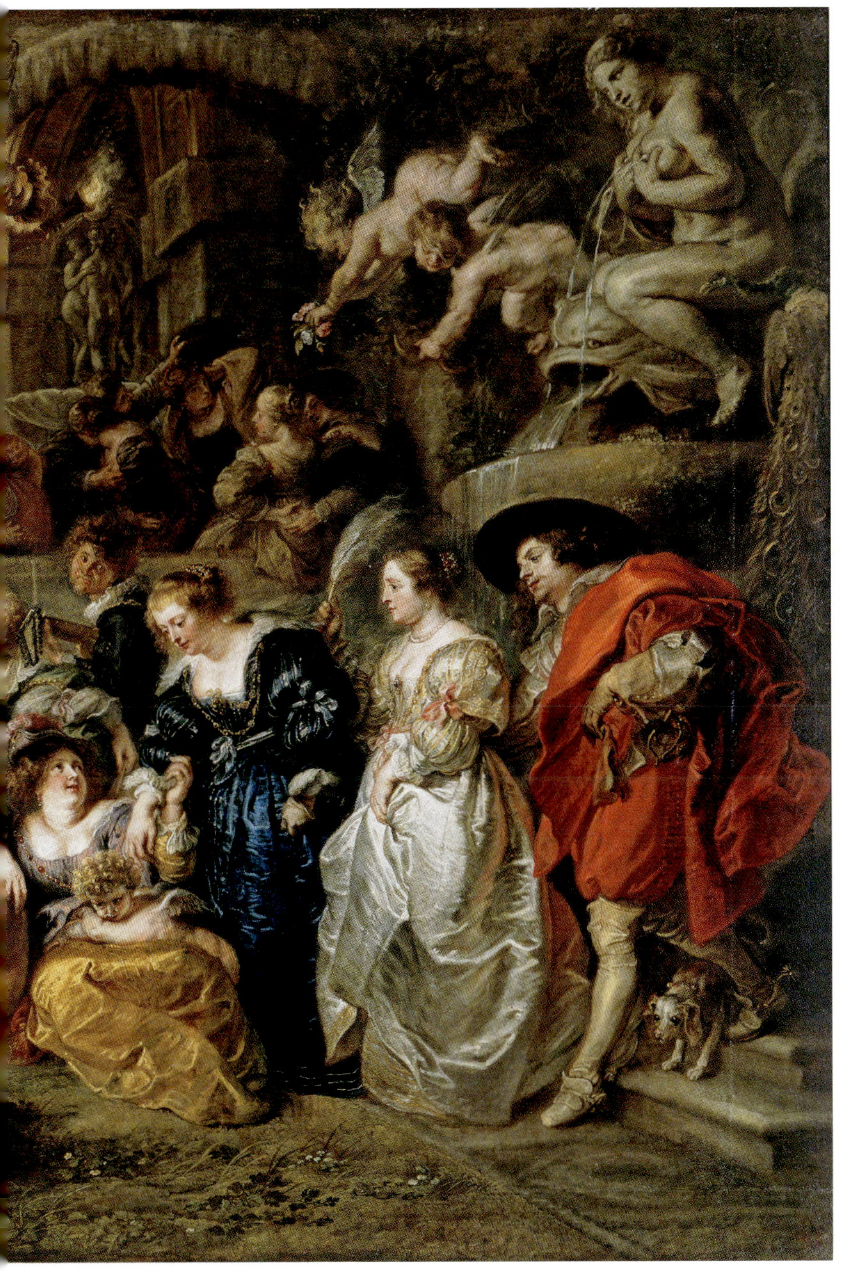

wear moustaches and beards, are also similar in looks. They resemble the artist himself. In painting the picture he probably was thinking of his wife and himself. On the other hand, a self-portrait painted not long afterwards shows that Rubens already looked much older at the time. He has rejuvenated for the *Love Garden*, adapting his age to that of his young wife, or showing himself as his new marriage made him feel.

The artist as a nobleman

Shortly before his wedding, Rubens had been knighted by Charles I. The English king had given him as a present the sword, set with diamonds, which he had sed for the ceremony. Rubens was now permitted to call himself Sir Peter.

He was probably knighted less for his artistic than for his diplomatic services. But it was his art which had provided him with a significant diplomatic advantage: unrestrained access to European royalty. While other emissaries had to haunt the antechambers and seek a path between hostile intrigues, Rubens gained admittance without effort. Easy access would have brought him relatively little advantage, however, were he not also a man of discretion, charm and considerable persuasive powers. The German painter and art historian Joachim von Sandrart had this to say of him: "He … was polite and extremely friendly to everyone, a welcome and much loved guest wherever he went."

Rubens undertook most of his secret diplomatic missions in the service of the Spanish vicereine of the southern Netherlands. It was here, in the seaport of Antwerp, that Rubens lived. The vicereine also recommended him to the Spanish king in Madrid, who sent him to London in 1629 to find out whether the old hostilities between Spain and England could be laid aside. A peace treaty was concluded, and Rubens wrote: "I can honestly declare that my travels in Spain and England have been crowned with the greatest possible fortune. Matters of great import have been settled to the full satisfaction of my lord, indeed to the satisfaction even of the opposing party."

Rubens was sent by the Spanish vicereine on several occasions to carry out secret missions in the northern Netherlands, the so-called States General. These provinces had gained independence from Spain in 1579, since when there had been war between the two parts of the Netherlands, interrupted only by highly unstable periods of truce. The Netherlands formed a subsidiary theatre of the larger European conflict: the Catholic Habsburgs in Vienna and Madrid versus the Protestant states and France.

Rubens succeeded in enlisting England for the Catholic cause, but he was unable to do anything to promote lasting peace or the reunification of the Netherlands. It was the fact that he felt unable to achieve anything for his own country that finally prompted him to give up diplomacy following his triumphant mission to London. After the death in 1633 of the vicereine, whom he had greatly admired, he declined further missions abroad. He wanted to paint.

Majestic proportions

Rubens had begun to find courtly life quite "repulsive": "In that labyrinth, beleaguered day and night by bothersome crowds of people … under obligation to attend … without cease." His Spanish contemporary, the painter Diego Velázquez, decided otherwise, accepting offices at the Spanish court, shutting himself away in the corridors of the royal administration, rarely, in later years, returning to his work at the easel.

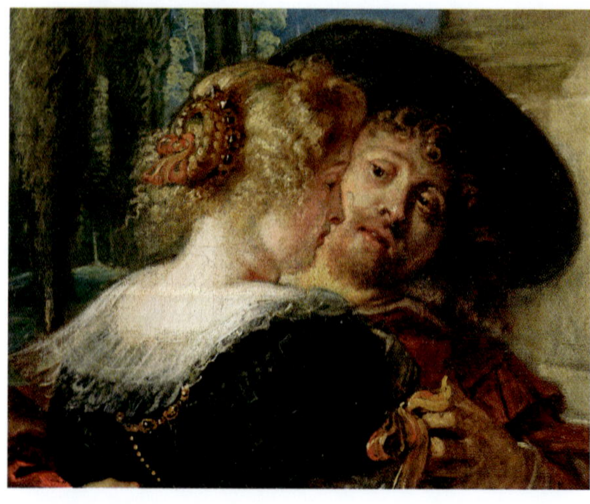

It was not easy for Rubens to leave. He had to force himself to "sever the golden knot of ambition," as he wrote. The freshly knighted widower rejected advice to marry into a noble family: "I feared that notorious quality of the aristocracy, their self-conceit, especially so in someone of the opposite sex, and thus I am more attracted to a woman who does not blush when she sees me lift the tool of my trade."

He did not reveal in this letter to a friend that his young wife Hélène Fourment was considered a beauty, indeed as "one of the most beautiful women here", according to the newly appointed Spanish viceroy.

Unlike today, the ideal female body in Rubens's day had an ample layer of fat beneath the skin. Visible or indeed palpable bones were considered inappropriate; opulent curves were much in demand, as was a plump neck and a large bosom. Furthermore, a beautiful woman was required to have "a majestic deportment, fine proportions, a luscious head of thick ash blonde curls ... and sweet white hands". Thus the description in a book printed in 1655 and entitled *Le Mérite des Dames*.

Rubens had been painting this type for decades. Even the facial features in this painting are found in his previous work: perhaps one of Hélène's elder sisters had sat for him, or perhaps the artist simply found this the most comely of female forms. Some art historians have maintained that in painting the *Love Garden*, Rubens illustrated a process: Hélène's progress from a young girl and bride to a wife and mother.

According to this hypothesis, the hesitant girl on the left is invited by a careful lover and cherub's encouraging push to lay aside all reservation and sit down on the grass. The next scene shows her doing exactly that, with her hand on her lover's knee and her dreamy gaze staring out of the picture, as if looking into the painter's eyes. Finally, the scene on the far right shows her as the confident wife, stepping majestically down from a staircase on the arm of her husband. The three women seated at the centre of the painting would then represent different kinds of love: ecstatic love, companionship, motherly love. The figure of maternal love with a cherub on her lap is drawing the young woman down to her. This interpretation is supported by the suggestive objects brought by the little Cupids. Accompanied by turtledoves, the symbol of conjugal love, they hold up the torch of Hymen, the god of marriage, strew bridal

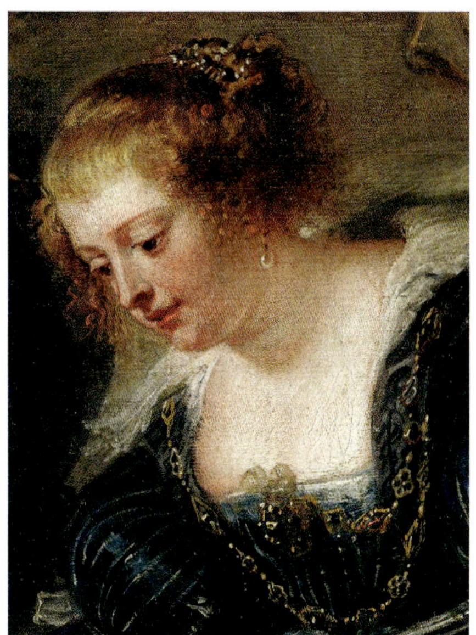

bouquets and bear the yoke of matrimony. The peacock at the far right of the canvas is an attribute of Juno, the patroness of marriage.

The artist's second marriage was as happy as his first. "In your arms, damsel, he shall grow young again," it said in a poem for his wedding, for she would not let him him suffer "the perilous burdens of ageing". He was to father five children in the ten years left to him, the last born after his death. Hélène became a rich widow; she also married again.

Venus rules the garden

Having "severed the golden knot of ambition", Rubens retired from the public stage. The theme of the painting suggests he had followed the advice of his mentor Justus Lipsius, Professor of Philosophy at the University of Leuven. Lipsius extolled life on the land and the cultivation of gardens. Only far from the golden fetters of court life was it possible to live happily and do as one wished.

Rubens, of course, had a garden of his own; in 1635 he even bought an estate with a small castle. His garden was in the grounds of his house at Antwerp, an imposing building to which he added an extension, built in the style of the late Renaissance and containing his studio.

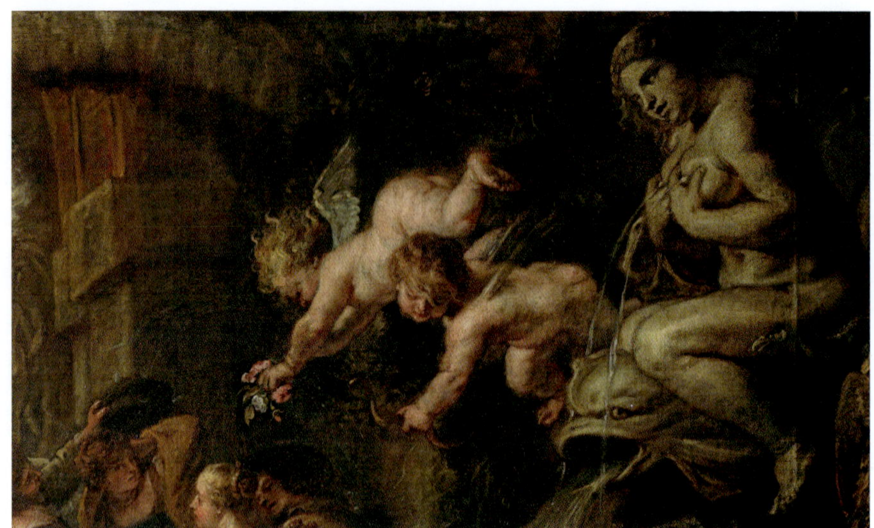

In order to connect his studio with the main house, Rubens built a portico; it had three passageways and was supported by massive columns, similar to those in the painting. A balustrade decorated with stone balls, like the one just visible on the left, divided the domestic area from the garden.

Gardens were important in the 17th century, partly because they were considered status symbols. They were divided into four categories.

The common people, if they had one at all, had a vegetable garden in which they might also cultivate medicinal herbs. Besides containing a vegetable patch, the garden of a somewhat more prosperous family would be for walking and contemplation.

A nobleman, or a wealthy burgher like Rubens, would have a landscaped garden with grottos, arbours and summerhouses; the parklands of princes and kings would further contain artificial lakes and smaller castles. The most luxurious example of the latter was to be the later palace at Versailles.

The fact that the artist has restricted meadows and trees to a relatively small section of the canvas is entirely in keeping with contemporary views of Nature. There was little demand for wildness at the time. Hedges and flowerbeds were designed to accord with a perfectly calculated, geometrical scheme.

Only domesticated Nature was considered beautiful or inviting, so gardens contained as many wells, balustrades, statues and artificial grottos as possible. A garden was seen as a kind of open air salon.

According to Justus Lipsius, this provided the ideal background against which a sophisticated gentleman might stroll and, whether alone or in conversation with a friend, draw lofty distinctions between the important and less important things in life. In upper-class society it was fairly common for ladies and gentlemen to conduct their rendezvous in the "park", where they could promenade, picnic, listen to serenades or participate in pastoral plays.

Gardens and love went hand in hand in the 17th century. There were practical reasons for this. Palaces and large houses offered little opportunity for intimacy; too many people lived in them; there was a constant toing and froing of servants, and most of the rooms served as passages to adjoining rooms. It was far easier for lovers to share their intimacies in little groves, behind hedges, or in the seclusion of a grotto.

Besides such practical considerations, the idea of the Garden of Love, or pleasance, has a place in cultural tradition and can be traced back to notions of paradise where human beings could live together in happiness, surrounded by a permanently clement, natural world. Each era had its own version of the paradisial Garden of Love: in the 16th century it became the evil garden of lust, whereas in Rubens's circle, the Garden of Love probably symbolized the harmony of physical and spiritual love.

The artist has included the figure of Venus on a well in the top right corner of painting. Water is sprinkling from the breasts of the goddess, a sign of fertility. She is riding a dolphin, the incarnation of playful and tireless pleasure in love. The shell on the portico is an attribute of Venus, and the many cherubs, brothers of Cupid, could be her sons: indeed, "Venus' court of pleasure" was another title given to the painting.

Women take command

The painting's title, *The Love Garden*, probably dates from the eighteenth century. During the artist's lifetime, works of this kind were usually referred to in a mixture of Flemish and French as *conversatie à la mode*.

Conversatie was conversational discourse, and it was *à la mode* since discourse of this kind between men and women, the easy interchange of thoughts and opinions accompanied by flights of flirtatious wit, was considered a particularly worthwhile pursuit.

The new fashion of conversation had originated in Paris as a reaction against the rude, military tone that had dominated the court of Henry IV. Thus it was women who decided the new rules and determined what was to be considered appropriate behaviour in society.

The importance attached to elegant, witty conversation can be deducted from the countless references to individual manners found in contemporary letters and memoirs. Rubens was frequently praised for the "infinite sweetness of his conversation".

But the new vogue of conversation was not the only fashion to change. For almost a hundred years the ceremonial black of Spanish conventional decorum had dominated women's fashion at the majority of European courts. They were forced to wear stiff, uncomfortable dresses which veiled from sight all but the hands and face and hid away their necks behind a broad, stiff ruff. Over twenty years had passed since Rubens had painted his first wife, dressed in the Spanish manner, "in a bower of honeysuckle". In *The Love Garden* he presents his second wife, Hélène, in soft, flowing robes which reveal her neck, nape and bosom, and evidently please her husband.

Like the new style of conversation, the latest clothes fashions also came from Paris, both attesting to a view of female roles that departed radically from the behaviour traditionally expected in Spain. Spanish women were locked up at home, their reading restricted to religious literature. They remained uneducated and were closely protected. French women, by contrast, had a certain freedom of movement, and were using it to gain a dominant position in society. One of the women in the painting by Rubens has the air of conducting social affairs with her peacock feather.

The liberated, confident behaviour of women in Brussels and Antwerp must have greatly irritated the Spanish in the Netherlands, as well as leading to occasional misunderstandings, as may be illustrated by a letter written to Madrid by the new Spanish viceroy: "They are so free and easy, and this allows us much opportunity. But their careless manner of intercourse is reserved solely for society; at home they are difficult, and nothing can be got out of them."

The influence of French fashion was a reflection of the growing political power of France. Spain was still a world power, but a weak and disorganized one. France would determine the styles and politics of the future. Thus even a very private painting betrays something of the changing balance of political power in the era of its origin.

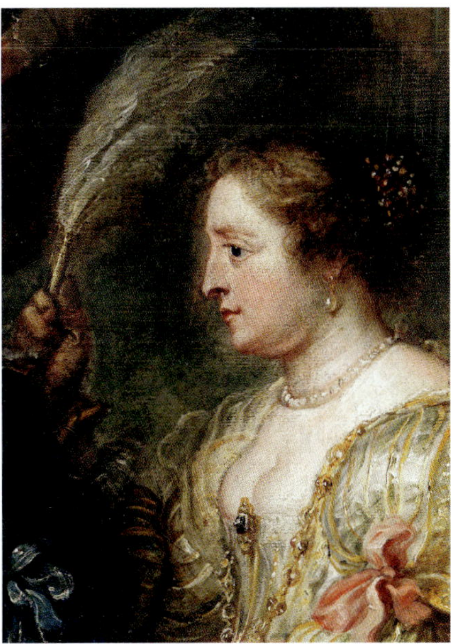

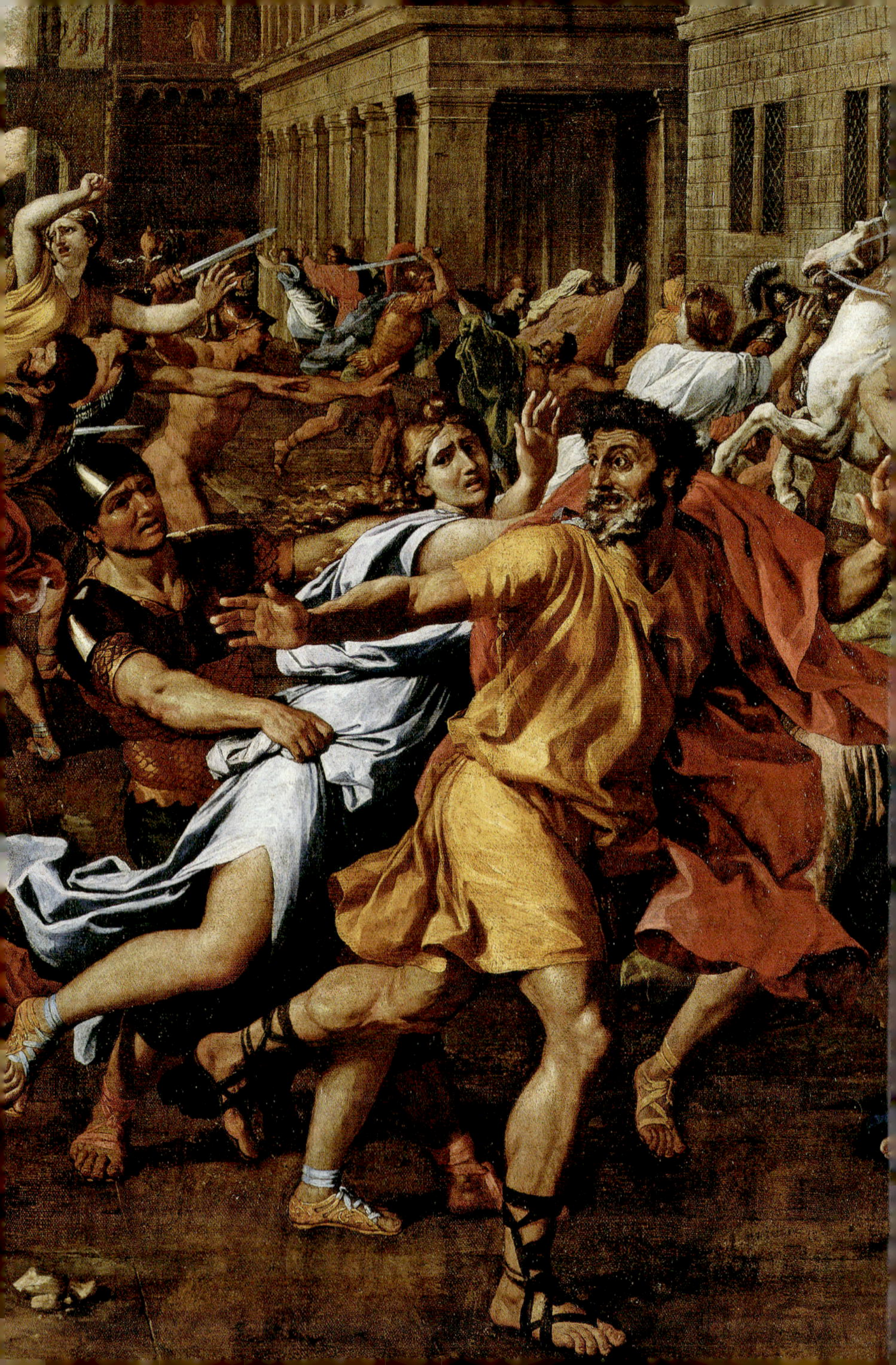

Nicolas Poussin (1594–1665)

A Frenchman in Rome

The Rape of the Sabine Women, 1637/1639
159 x 206 cm, Paris, Musée du Louvre

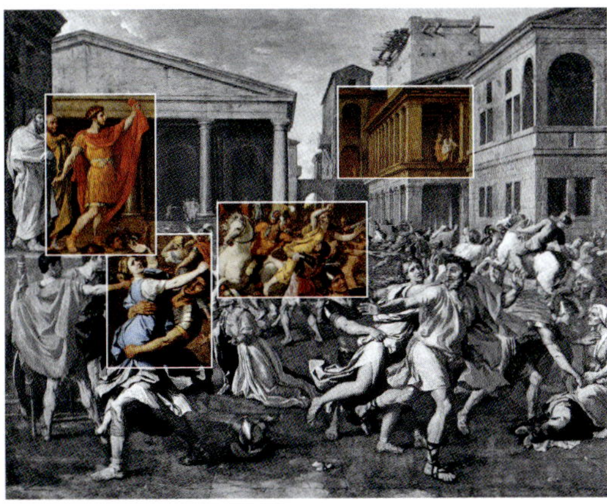

Tumult on a square in Rome. A turbulent and chaotic crowd, with austere buildings all about. Thus the French painter Nicolas Poussin saw the rape of the Sabine women.

The story of the rape is part of the foundation myth of Rome. The fledgeling settlement apparently attracted homeless and often criminal men in search of a refuge. This new rough and ready society lacked women. Romulus, the leader, proposed to obtain some; according to the Greek writer Plutarch, he spread the rumour that he had found the altar of a deity buried in the ground, and took the occasion to throw a magnificent sacrificial feast. Among the guests who came were the Sabines, a people who lived nearby. At a sign from Romulus, the Romans drew their swords and, emitting loud cries, made for the Sabine daughters and carried them off, leaving the rest of the tribe to disperse unmolested. In other words, no blood was shed; nor is any to be seen in Poussin's picture.

Plutarch considered that this breach of the rules of hospitality was justified by the need to provide a population if Rome was to have a future. Brutal though the act was, it served a higher purpose. Something similar appears to have been in the artist's mind: the chaos on his canvas in fact masks a meticulously conceived order.

The ideal ancient hero

Romulus, in crown and armour, is standing at a raised vantage above the confusion. The sign agreed for the abduction, according to Plutarch, was that Romulus would stand up, unfold his purple robe, and then wrap it about him once more. Poussin thus painted the gesture that started the enterprise, with the attack of the Romans and the first frightened responses of the Sabines.

This city founder must have been an uncivilized, violent man. According to the legend, he was raised by wolves, and killed his twin brother, Remus, in the struggle for power. He obtained his women by wiles or brute force. But Poussin has depicted him as the noble and beautiful are customarily portrayed. Romulus does not have both feet firmly planted on the ground, as a man giving orders normally does, but is resting his weight on one leg, in the ancient manner, while the other is gracefully relaxed and his hip is back turned. His arms, too, are in a harmonious balance, the one outstretched before him, the other behind. Poussin has given him a grace that recalls a dancer.

The artist was not after psychological plausibility. He wanted to reveal an inner truth, an ideal: the beauty of man. Beauty always included nobility of character. Poussin was one of many artists who saw this ideal as being embodied in the artworks of antiquity, and they were best studied in Rome.

It was not easy for Poussin to get there. He was from Normandy, a poor rural region, and had to save up for a long time before he could venture the journey to Rome. His first attempt was abandoned for lack of money. In 1624 he finally made it.

In Rome, visitors had to have letters of recommendation. Poussin had one addressed to Francesco Barberini, the nephew of the Pope. Although Barberini left the city shortly after the artist's arrival, he passed him on to the Marchese Vincenzo Giustiniani, a wealthy banker from Genoa. Giustiniani gave Poussin permission to study his own collection of ancient artworks, a privilege of real importance for a young painter, for the better of the movable ancient artworks were almost all in private hands. Giustiniani also collected paintings. From Poussin he bought a *Massacre of the Innocents* and an *Assumption of the Virgin*.

Of still greater importance for Poussin was Cassiano dal Pozzo, a senior official at the papal court and a friend of the astronomer Galileo Galilei. Dal Pozzo was a well informed collector of archaeological

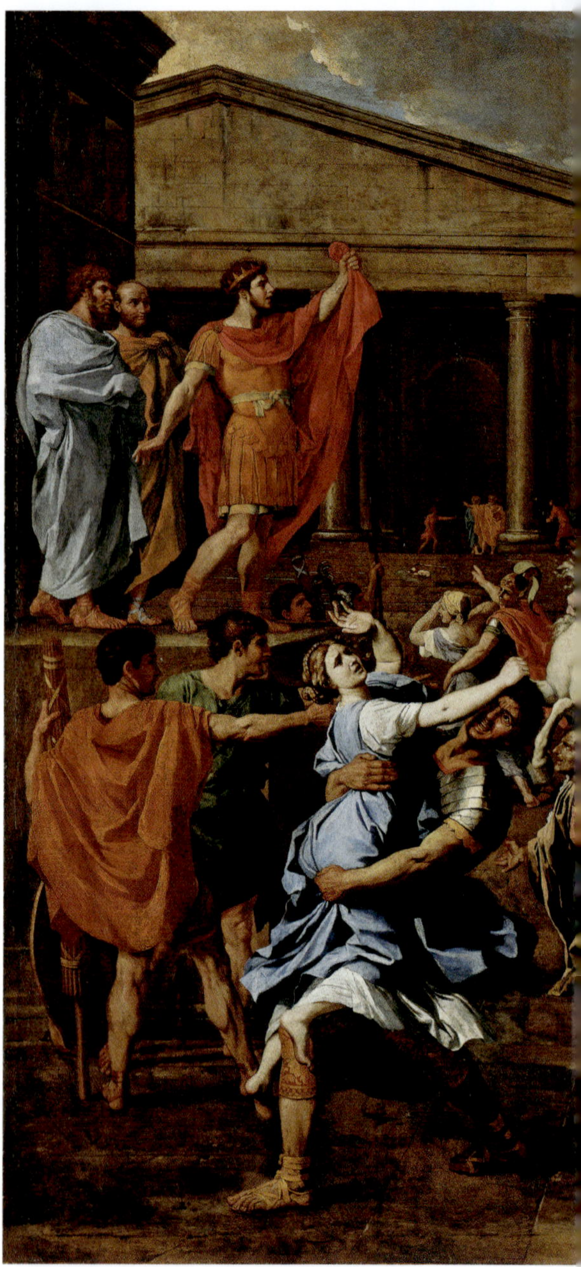

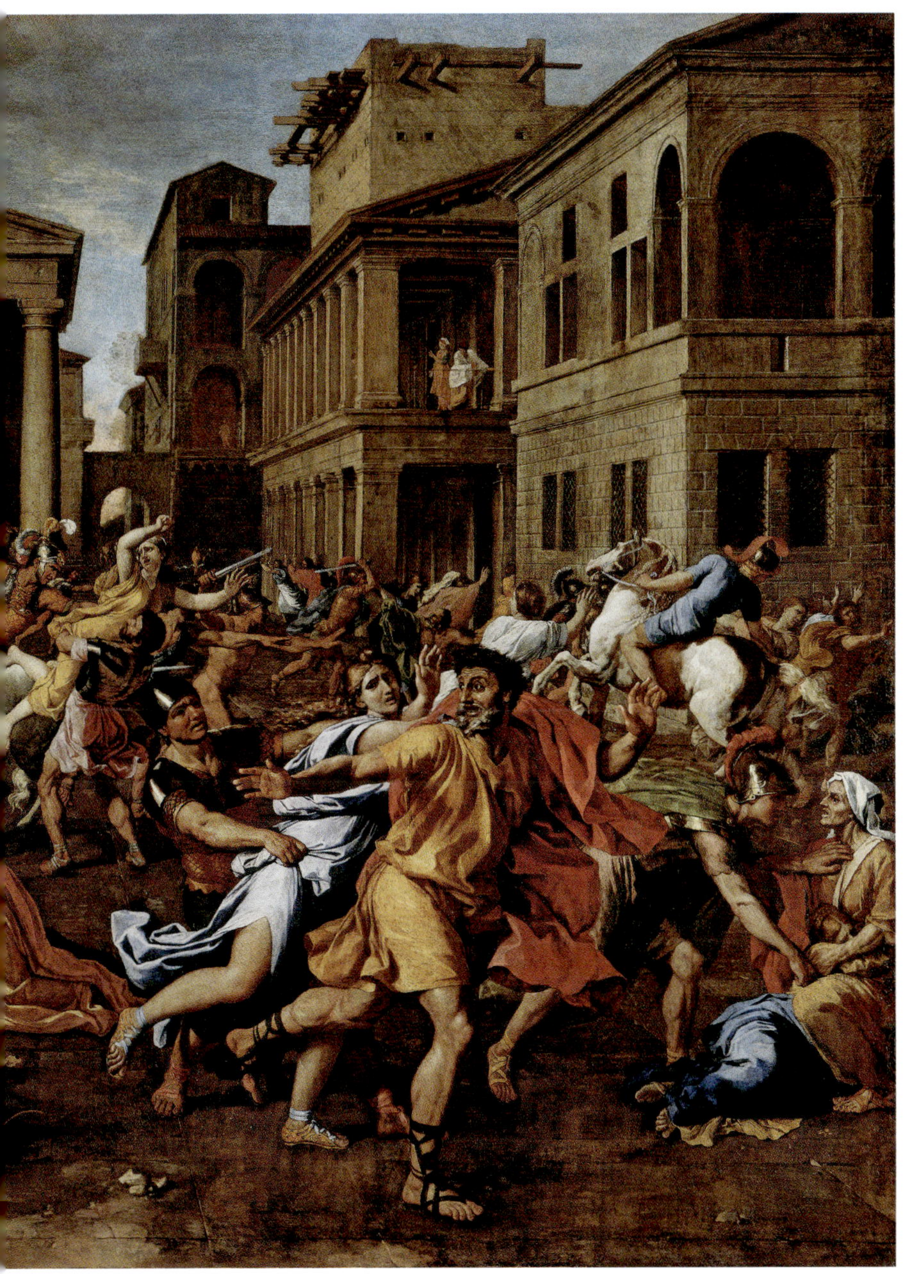

remains and old manuscripts. Poussin, who had probably attended a Jesuit school and unlike many other painters knew Latin, was able to extend his own education in the humanities through dal Pozzo. The collector became widely celebrated for his "paper museum": he had had drawings made of some 1,500 ancient ruins, busts, and medals, and had had the leaves bound into books – an iconographic collection of outstanding quality.

For Poussin, the paper museum possessed a twofold significance: by drawing copies, the young man was able to earn a living, and at the same time he was helped in his all important quest for ideal forms. Behind his Romulus we can detect the

Apollo Belvedere or perhaps an Augustus Caesar. In the decades that lay ahead, dal Pozzo was to be one of Poussin's most important clients; he bought some 50 paintings from him, a quarter of the artist's total output.

Rome, the marketplace of the world

In Poussin's day, Rome was effectively the centre of Europe. With a population of 100,000 it was one of the few large cities, and as the seat of the papacy it was the spiritual and intellectual centre of the Catholic world. Hardly any other city can have had so many diplomats in it, or attracted so many visitors – artists, pilgrims, travellers. Rome was "the

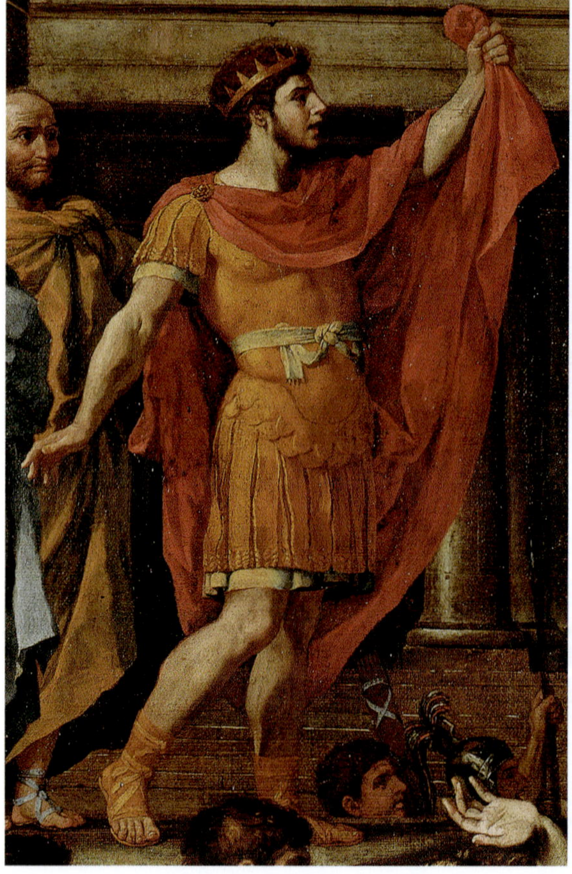

marketplace of the world", wrote Pietro Contarini, the Venetian ambassador, in 1623. For its "ancient remains and also its modern sights", it was "as much home to those from elsewhere as to its own citizens".

The financial means came from elsewhere, too. Church revenues poured in to the Vatican from many another state; and Pope Urban VIII, with his family and his protégés, spent it uninhibitedly. They endowed churches and chapels, built palaces, collected art, and had their apartments decorated with frescoes. Poussin's *Rape of the Sabine Women*, painted between 1637 and 1639, was purchased by Aloisio Onodei, subsequently appointed cardinal by the Pope and also commander-in-chief of the papal army. After a military campaign ended in defeat, however, he was obliged to sell the picture, and in 1685 it passed to Louis XIV in Paris, where it now remains, in the Louvre. A second version is in the Metropolitan Museum in New York.

The remnants of scaffolding on the tower at the upper edge of the picture are not so much a reference to the building that was proceeding apace in Baroque

Rome as to the founding of the city by Romulus. The architecture of Poussin's own age held little interest for him. His eye was on the ancient edifices, which he reconstructed in his paintings. At the left he has an ancient Roman temple in the background, and at the right the frontages of residences or palaces that recall Roman buildings, though they also have an air of stage sets. Since the 16th century, theatre set designers had been fond of using a perspective view along building façades to suggest spatial depth. Poussin does the same – he draws in our gaze, past pillared arcades and walls to trees and some distance beyond the city precincts.

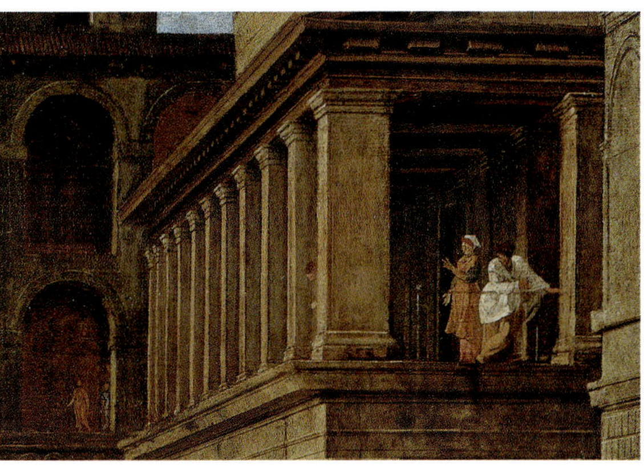

The "modern sights" Contarini referred to were Rome's Baroque buildings. They were not conceived in terms of straight lines and right angled structures; quite the opposite. Architects such as Gianlorenzo Bernini (1598–1680), Pope Urban's favourite in the field, made walls look as if they were made of sweeping folds of fabric; their windows and gables were rounded. Instead of contained order they aimed for dynamic movement; they sought to liberate masonry from the limitations imposed by static materials. Many of the buildings in Poussin's paintings have the effect of a protest against Baroque excesses.

Other artists adored the new style and flocked to Rome to admire it. Their prospects of work were good: all the newly built churches and palaces had to be decorated with altarpieces, frescos, ceiling paintings and statues, and all the ancient remains had to be drawn or painted. Demand for art being so great, the artists had no need to work for one master only. They now had greater freedom. There were no guilds either, which (as in Paris) would have regulated the work of painters and imposed limits.

Poussin must have had an especially strong desire for his own freedom and independence. He never stayed for long with any of the French masters from whom he learnt his craft, and in Rome, too, he preferred not to take up residence in the palace of his patron. Rather, he made his own way, as an artist without means, living with fellow artists in a part of the city that was full of the artistic, around the Piazza del Popolo.

Grand gestures, ambitious ideas

With people of various nations living together, conflict was unavoidable. Fights and the need to escape were very much part of Poussin's experience. "Nicolas came with two of his compatriots", reports biographer Giovanni Battista Passeri, "and encountered a number of soldiers who drew their swords. He defended himself with his portfolio of drawings. … One slash of a sword very nearly cost him the middle and index finger of his right hand." Poussin fled, and in future chose clothing that did not instantly identify him as a Frenchman.

In the painting, the turbulent crowd consists of individual groupings. In the left foreground, a Roman is picking up a Sabine woman and losing his helmet in the process. The woman is tearing at her abductor's hair with one hand. She might use the other to scratch his face or gouge his eye, but instead she is raising her arm and hand in an imploring gesture. Poussin was not so much interested in the realistic options as in art: these two figures are borrowed from a relief done by Giambologna in 1583.

A hand raised over the head, if possible with the palm upward, was part of the Classical repertoire of gestures and signified an appeal or lament, despair, a cry for help. It is always a gesture made by the weaker at the mercy of the stronger. In this painting, it is assigned almost stereotypically to all the Sabine women. Indeed, gestures and attitudes play a dominant part in the composition: the graceful pose of Romulus, the backward-flung arm of the man fleeing in the right foreground, the hands of the kneeling old woman raised in supplication, the muscular grip in which the strong arms of the Romans seize their prey.

Physical gestures are the painter's way of telling us what is happening, and we are supposed to grasp the action right away. On the other hand, Poussin took little interest in faces, individualized features, and expressions. Only three heads of the young Sabine women are done with closer attention; they are turned towards us and were painted after one and the same model, a blonde woman with her hair parted in the centre and dark brows that met in the middle. The profile of Romulus is lacking in all expression. The facial expression of the Sabine woman looking back, in the right foreground, was taken from a theatre mask. Poussin took his bearings from ancient statuary, in which the individual was made to conform to an ideal. And he was opposed

to Caravaggio (1571–1610), whose figures, painted with brutal realism, were widely imitated.

Poussin took his subjects from the Bible, from history, and from ancient mythology. They are large themes, but the pictures are in fairly modest formats, at least by Baroque standards. *The Rape of the Sabine Women* measures 159 by 206 centimetres, a humble size compared with the frescos then covering walls and ceilings, and considering the number of figures that crowd the canvas. Restricting himself to medium and small formats was part of Poussin's programme. He wanted to place every brush stroke personally, and, even when a successful artist, he did not employ a whole workshop of assistants and apprentices, as fellow painters did in order to cope with large-format commissions. His view was that a painter's work could contribute to the education of mankind. His ethical ambition demanded that he be as near perfect as possible.

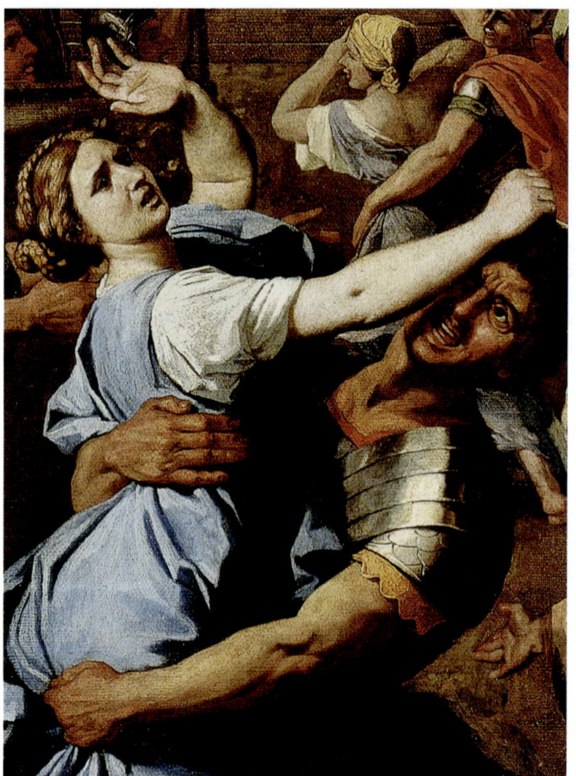

A description of his meticulous manner of painting has come down to us from the German artist Joachim von Sandrart (1606–88). On a board, Poussin would position "a tableau of bare wax figures made for the purpose of illustrating the action". These bare figurines "he would clothe in wet papyrus or subtle taffeta, as he wished them". In this way the artist built a stage on which he could rehearse his foreshortenings, the overlap of one figure over another, the effects of light, and above all the harmony of the overall impression.

The higher order within chaos

X-ray examination of the painting has revealed lines drawn on in the planning of the composition. The meeting point, from which they radiate like a star burst, is the head of the mounted Roman in the plumed helmet. This point is right beside the vertical centre axis. In the upper half of the painting, that axis is unmistakable since it coincides with the wall to the right of the temple, running

down between the plumes and
a woman's raised arm. The horizontal centre axis is marked by
the dais Romulus is standing on.
Both axes are visible at only one
point in the painting; elsewhere
they are out of sight, obscured
by figures and so forth, since
otherwise the composition could
appear sterile in its too rigorous
proportions. Still, Poussin is after
balance. Thus to either side of the
Sabine woman with upraised arm
in the centre, there is another,
one on the left, one on the right.
There is a white horse on the left,
and another on the right. To balance the group of three on the left

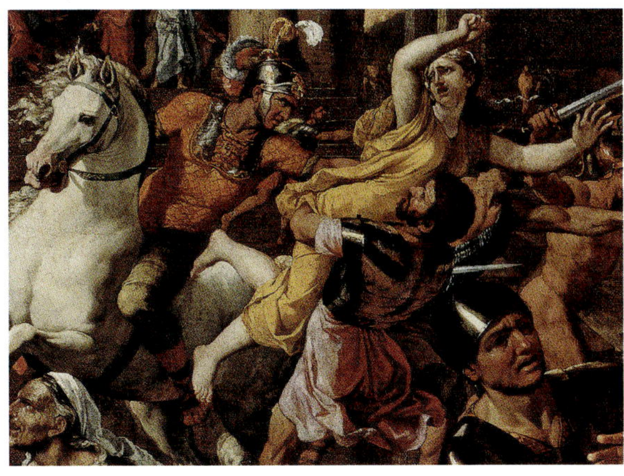

that includes Romulus there is a twosome on the
right, up on the gallery – much smaller, but then the
placid temple façade on the left is offset on the right
by a dynamic perspective.

All of this accords with ideas of symmetry and
balance handed down from antiquity. If these were
not obeyed, so the received wisdom insisted, a work
of art could not be considered beautiful.

In 1640, Nicolas Poussin made a return journey
to Paris. Louis XIII had badgered him to do so, leaving the artist no alternative. Poussin was needed.
After long years of civil war, stability had returned to
France; the economy was reviving; the country was
bidding fair to become the major power on the Continent. But an art apt to this new status was lacking.
Poussin was to supply it. Honours were heaped upon
him, and he was appointed painter in ordinary to
the king, with instructions to superintend the decoration of the great gallery in the Louvre, to design
majestic fireplaces and decorative stairwells, and to
supervise the labours of countless assistants. In short,
his task involved all those things he had spent his
life avoiding. Poussin stuck it for two years, then fled
back to Rome.

There he resumed work on his own, living modestly in the Via Paolina. The small house was full of
Classical busts. Poussin had no servants; his wife, the
daughter of a French chef, looked after him. Social
climbing did not feature among his ambitions. In
this he was unlike many of his contemporaries:
Rembrandt in Amsterdam sought a secure foothold
among the upper middle classes, Diego Velázquez

in Madrid aspired through his art to a more exalted
position in the court hierarchy, Peter Paul Rubens
in Antwerp led the life of a veritable prince of art.
But Poussin was true to the ideals of antiquity in
the conduct of his life, leading it in a modest, ascetic
manner, in the service of a higher task. In a self-portrait, he presents himself to us with a cloak wrapped
about his shoulder like a toga.

Until his death he remained in Rome – and
nonetheless he rose to be seen as the foremost
painter of France. There, the impassioned excess of
the Baroque was not in demand. The rational vein
of an artist able to bring harmony and order to
chaos was more to French taste. Today, Poussin is
regarded as a founding father of French classicism,
albeit also as a precursor of academic painting, that
manner that was to elevate the dry imitation of
ancient art into a lofty goal – and drive countless
artists all over Europe to distraction.

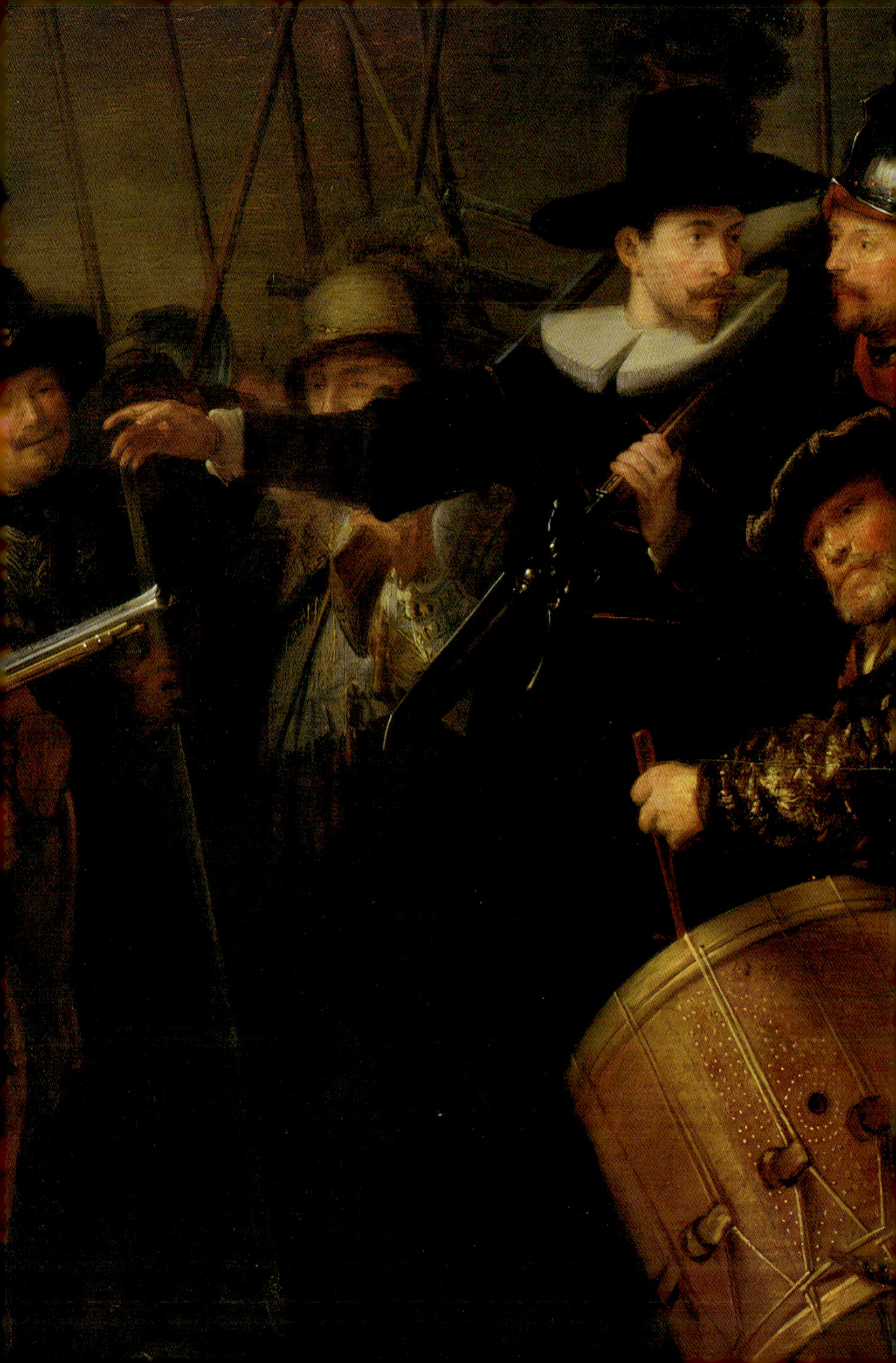

Rembrandt (1606–1669)
(real name Rembrandt Harmensz. van Rijn)

Parading for Amsterdam

The Night Watch, 1642
359 x 438 cm, Amsterdam, Rijksmuseum

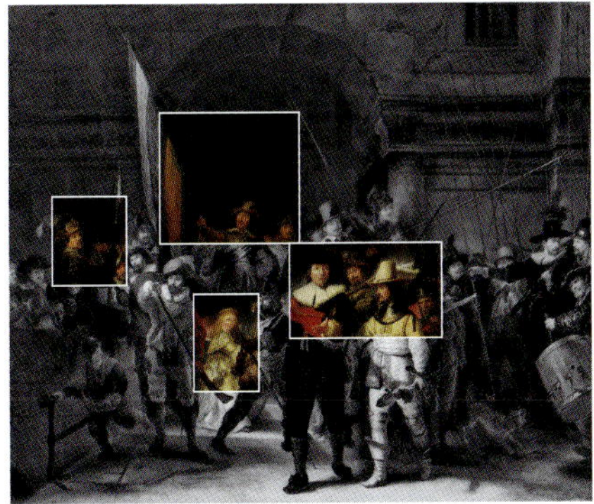

The Night Watch, like the *Mona Lisa*, is one of the most popular works in all of Western culture. Such works are like stars that leave everything in their vicinity looking pale. And yet what is special about them is fully evident only when we understand the context and the age in which they were created, and, rather than being awestruck by them as works of genius, bear in mind the time and society in which the artist worked. In the case of *The Night Watch*, this means asking what else was being painted, or not being painted, in Amsterdam around 1642.

Pictures for churches were not being painted, for example. The Calvinists had stripped houses of worship of all images in 1566, believing that the way to God should not be obstructed. Thus the most important source of commissions for artworks since the Middle Ages had dried up, and religious subjects were no longer much in demand.

Nor were pictures of rulers being painted. There were the Princes of Orange, true, who had commanded the forces of the northern Netherlands against the Spanish, and aspired to establish a hereditary monarchy. But they led the lives of burghers rather than of kings. In Madrid at this period, the portrait of King Philip IV was painted time and again by his court painter, Velázquez, and in Paris the royal widow Maria de' Medici was glorified by Rubens in a sequence of immense paintings. But Rubens came from Brussels, in the southern part of the Netherlands, which had remained loyal to Spain and to Catholicism. In the northern part, in Holland and especially in the city of Amsterdam, this cult of monarchs was frowned upon. It ran counter to the worldview of the burghers.

The absence of a wealthy and powerful royal house was felt not only in art but in the very

appearance of Amsterdam itself: there were no
great palaces, no equestrian statues, and sculptors
received but few commissions for tombstones.
The streets and canals of the city were lined with
burghers' houses topped by storage lofts and
pulleys. It was these narrow houses, built wall-to-
wall against each other, rather than the few large
and free standing buildings, that constituted
the architectural charm of the city, and still do
to this day.

In addition to ecclesiastical art and pictures
of rulers, battle scenes were also almost entirely
absent from the painters' repertoire, despite
the fact that the Netherlands were at war. The
occasion for this war had been the iconoclastic
looting and burning of the churches and
monasteries by anti-Catholic mobs. From
Madrid, the Spanish rulers of the Netherlands
responded by despatching the Duke of Alba;
and it was against his reign of terror that the
Dutch rose, in part, in 1568. In 1579 the northern
provinces united; and in 1648, under the Treaty
of Westphalia, they were recognized as an independent state.

In other words, when Rembrandt painted
these finely garbed militiamen his country was
still fighting for its independence. Indeed, the
struggle to throw off the Spanish yoke lasted a
full eighty years. Nevertheless, there are scarcely
any scenes of siege, defence, or victory, no counterpart to the *Surrender of Breda*, which Velázquez painted for the Spanish king. Evidently the
subject held little interest for painters. And presumably the burghers of the cities, who had the
money to commission art, had no interest either.

Paintings of naval battles were all the more
popular, though; and, even if they were not
generally painted by artists of the first rank, the
demand was great. The land forces were mainly
hired mercenaries, on both sides, and the conflict
was a protracted war of attrition rather than one
of decisive battles; the Dutch navy, on the other
hand, was as large as the French and English combined, according to contemporary sources. The
Dutch were successful in their naval campaigns
against the Spanish, and established colonies in
the West Indies and South America. This was a
sector of daring, expansion and triumph; while
the Netherlands were still struggling for their
independence on land, they were simultaneously

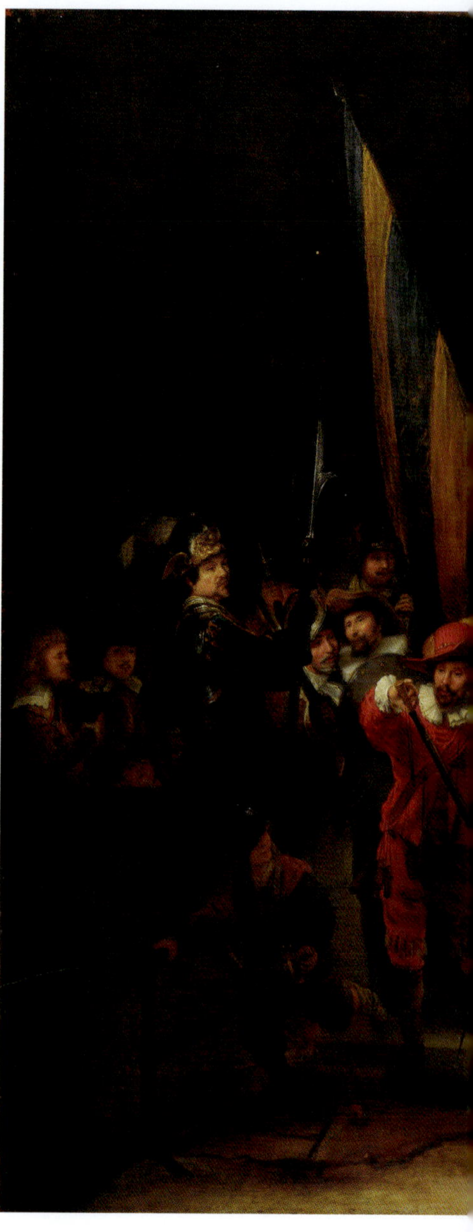

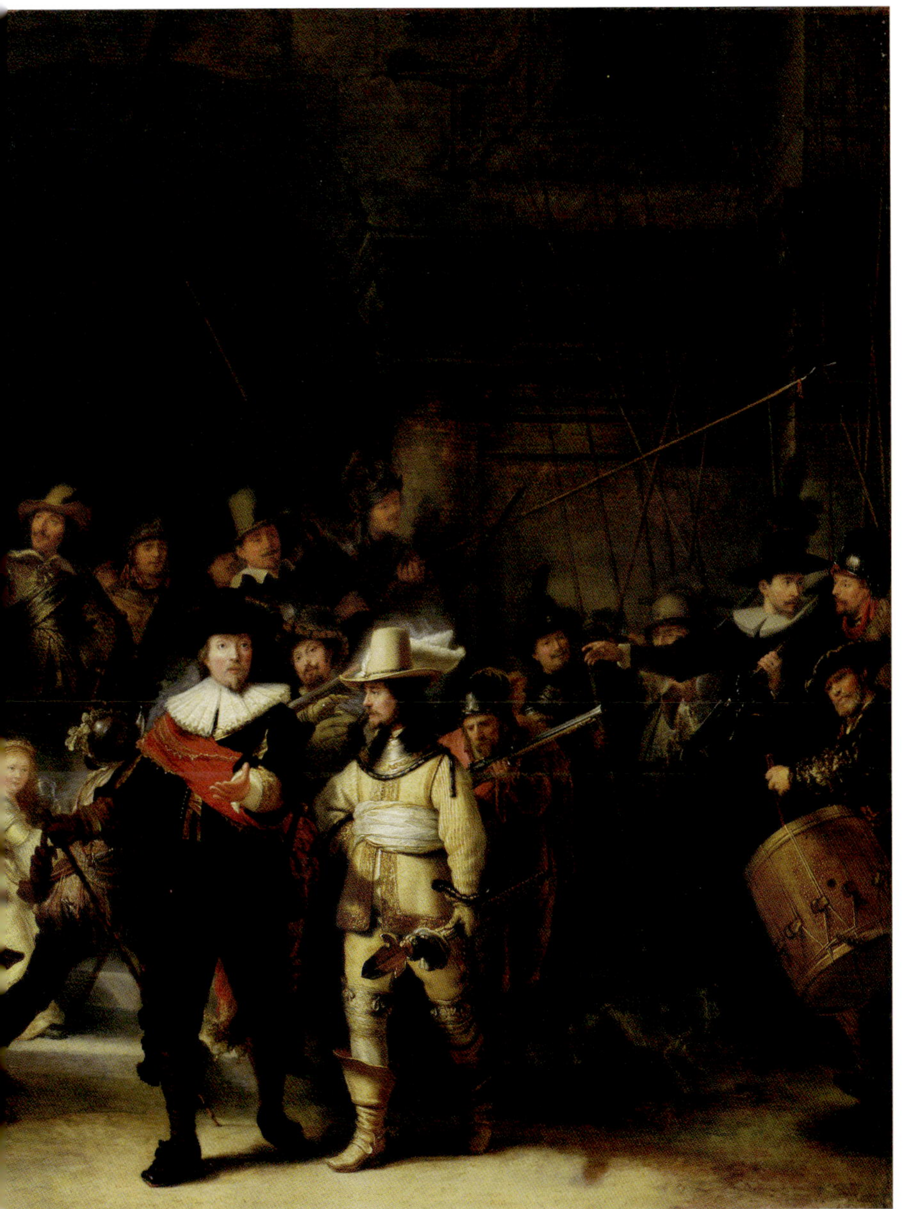

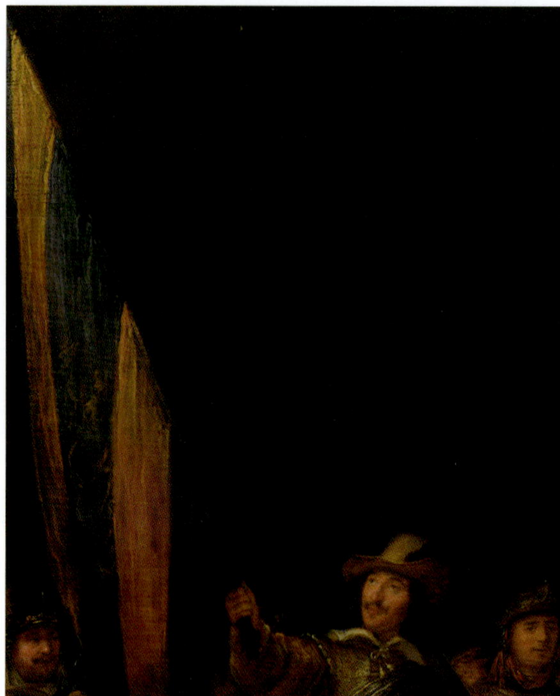

In *The Night Watch*, Rembrandt too painted members of one of these militias. According to a contemporary memo, Rembrandt has portrayed the moment when the captain gives his adjutant the order to start the company marching.

The rise of a city

Many an expert has tried to identify the precise place in Amsterdam where these militiamen assembled to begin their march. But in vain. The tall buildings with the archway, and the wall to the left on which the man in the golden helmet is sitting, did not exist, or at least not next to each other; Rembrandt put together the backdrop for his scene to suit himself.

The city is represented by the three crosses on the flag, which are on the Amsterdam coat of arms. The flag bearing this emblem is not held aloft with any symbolic insistence, but it is plainly visible. Amsterdam at that date was one of the largest cities in the world, and its population was growing rapidly. In 1585 it had numbered 35,000; in 1631, when Rembrandt moved to the city, it must have been 115,000; and in 1642, when he painted *The Night Watch*, the city was nearing the 150,000 mark. In just a few decades the population had increased fivefold, and the city walls had to be moved further out more than once. These were boom times for Amsterdam, such as we associate in more recent times with the cities of America's western expansion.

rising to become the foremost economic power in Europe. More Dutchmen are said to have died at sea, or during conquests driven by economic motives, than in battles on land.

In addition to naval battles there were three other kinds of picture that enjoyed popularity: genre paintings that paid small-format homage to everyday life and domestic labour; individual or family portraits, a continuance of the ruling classes' customs by the middle class of burghers; and group portraits, usually showing the boards of merchant guilds or members of militia companies.

Like genre painting, the group portrait is a Dutch speciality. Nowhere else were so many group portraits painted. Fifty paintings showing companies of militiamen alone are in Amsterdam to this day. Some are a full twelve square metres in size. They reflect the self-confidence of the middle classes and the pride of the new republic, and exemplify the Dutch alternative to the monarchic forms of rule in the countries all around the Netherlands.

Amsterdam's sensational rise in Rembrandt's lifetime had a number of causes. The most important was that it was very favourably situated for trade. The mariners of Amsterdam sailed not only to far flung destinations overseas but to northern parts as well, bringing timber and grain from Poland and Scandinavia. Antwerp, the close rival, had the same advantages of location but was part of the Spanish ruled, Catholic southern part of the Netherlands, and ruined by the financial demands of the Spanish king and the dictatorship of the Duke of Alba. Antwerp's undoing was the making of Amsterdam: merchants transferred their businesses from the one city to the other, bringing their trading connections with them, and often their money. It was not only economic reasons that prompted them and many others to make the move. In the Spanish sphere of influence, only the Catholic church was approved. The reform movement that had been spreading right across northern and central Europe was suppressed there; Calvinists, Lutherans, and Anabaptists were obliged to flee elsewhere if they wished to practise their faiths openly. The same applied to Spanish Jews: those who declined to convert had first emigrated to Portugal and then, when that country became Spanish by marriage, many of them sailed north to the Netherlands. In Amsterdam they constituted an important and wealthy community. It was Spain's religious and power politics that inadvertently helped Amsterdam become the foremost trading metropolis in Europe.

Another key factor in that rise was the oft-praised and equally often doubted tolerance of the Dutch. Calvinism was effectively the state religion, but other churches were tolerated. Apart from the iconoclastic phase, religious fanaticism won little ground. The persecution of witches shows this clearly: the last execution took place in 1595, whereas in other countries it did not end for another 100 or 150 years. On the other hand, while various forms of Christian faith were allowed, atheism was not. When the great Jewish philosopher Baruch Spinoza doubted the god of the Jews and Christians, he was expelled from Amsterdam. The situation in terms of political leadership was similar: oligarchy, not democracy. The lord mayor of Amsterdam was admittedly elected, but those entitled to vote were a small number of wealthy burghers. Still, compared with the ever increasing absolutism of rule and mounting religious dictatorship in other neighbouring states, the provinces of the Netherlands constituted an island of relative liberty and tolerance. Business people, and artists and artisans, too, were attracted there. Rembrandt, who was born in the small town of Leiden, the son of a miller, transferred his workshop to Amsterdam at the age of 25.

How to make a career

The captain of this militia company was named Frans Banning Cocq. Arm outstretched, he is pointing the way for the company. He is wearing the broad lace ruff then common in Holland, a red sash, and at his left side a sword. Like the standard bearer and drummer, he is not in fact holding a weapon. In his right hand he has a long staff, a symbol of his military rank, and a glove, a sign of his social standing.

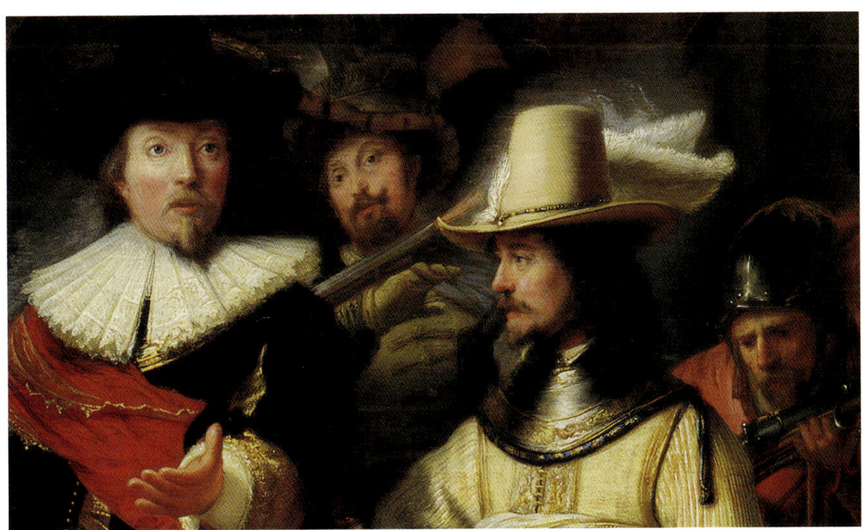

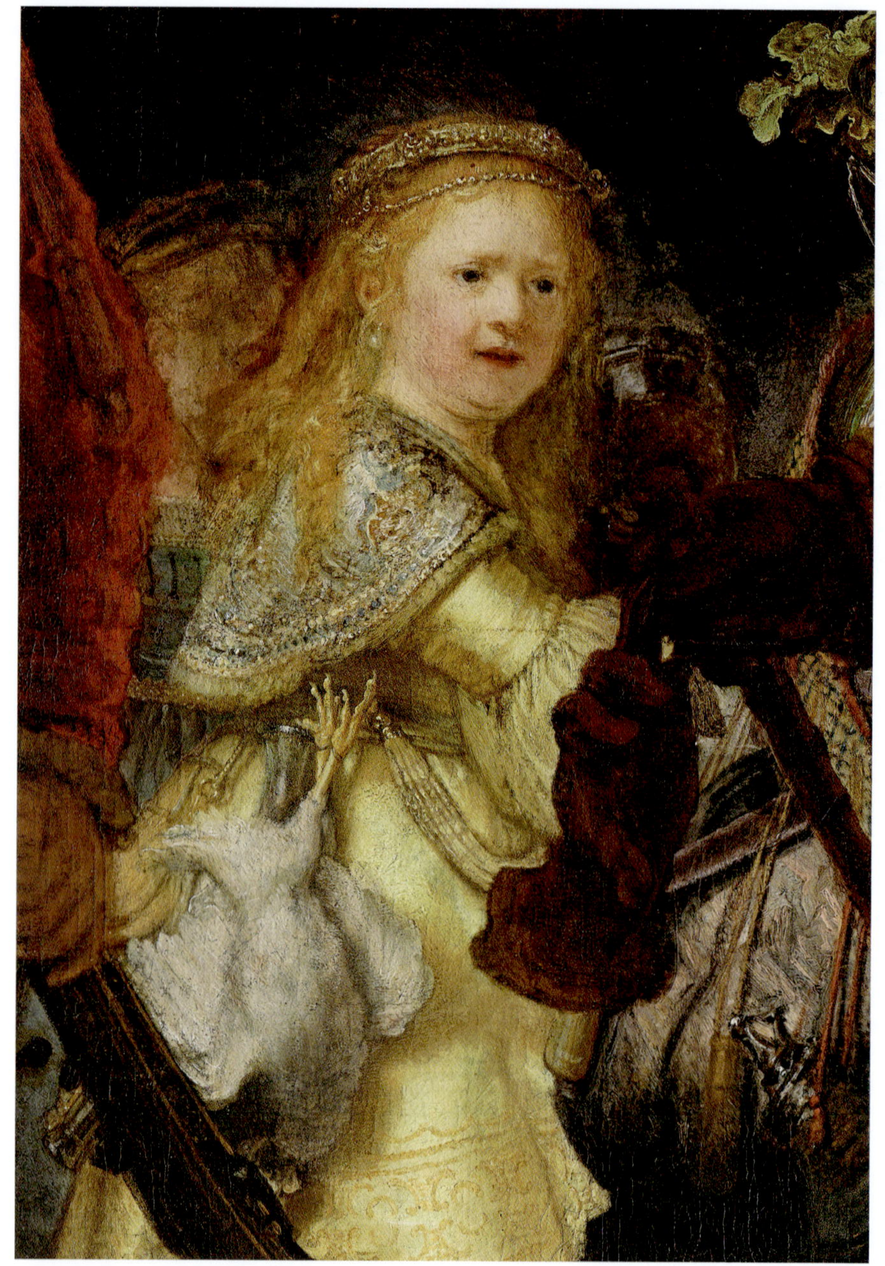

Of course the captain is not actually leading his men into action. Amsterdam was not attacked during this time, and the men in this painting never in fact had to defend their city. Nor is he leading them out to do the rounds of a watch; for that, they are too finely dressed. In Rembrandt's presentation, they look more than anything as if they are going to some festivities or to provide a guard of honour such as escorted the French Queen Mother Maria de' Medici when she entered the city in 1638. According to one contemporary report, "some of the guard had dressed up as they felt appropriate and were clad in armour head to foot". But helmets, shields, and armour were no longer usual with forces that did battle: firearms were by now highly developed, and armour no longer afforded sufficient protection. All that remains of medieval armour here is the plate collar, which was occasionally worn as a symbol of an officer's standing.

The captain was the son of immigrant parents. His father was said to be from Bremen, who, as the story had it, went begging from door to door in Amsterdam. He found employment in an apothecary's, subsequently established his own, married a Miss Banning, and – perhaps because the name enjoyed a certain reputation in Amsterdam – their son, Frans, later adopted that name as a middle name. Frans Banning Cocq, born in 1605 (the year before Rembrandt), studied law, took a doctorate, and married above his own station, wedding the daughter of the mayor. At the age of 25 (the same age as Rembrandt was when he moved to Amsterdam) Cocq inherited the fortune of his affluent father-in-law, and thenceforth every position in the community was his for the asking. Towards the end of his life (he lived to be 50) he himself served more than one term as one of the city's mayors. His career well illustrates the opportunities open to outsiders in a city growing so rapidly, provided they were able and hardworking, married advantageously, and possessed a fortune.

Anyone familiar with Rembrandt's predilection for strong contrasts and extreme effects of light and dark might well suspect that the artist costumed the two central figures so differently for aesthetic reasons. But this cannot be the case. These were both men of high standing, and members of the group who commissioned the painting. Their clothing expresses an attitude, at least in the captain's case. Black was the colour of the conservatives of firm burgher conviction, of councillors and great merchants, and in Amsterdam black was furthermore associated with a republican, Calvinist position. It is surely no coincidence that it is the newcomer bent on a career in the city's hierarchy who is wearing the black garb of the conservative.

The fashion in light colours arose early in the 17th century at the French court. The Princes of Orange, who did not abandon their monarchic aspirations in the Netherlands, adopted this French fashion to distinguish themselves from the Spanish and possibly also from the dark-clad citizens of "their own" provinces. Thus if a burgher dressed in light coloured clothes, he was seen as of the Prince's party, or simply opposed to the clique of burghers who ruled the cities and provinces. He might of course merely be expressing *joie de vivre* in his choice of colours; for the Netherlands, this was the Golden Age, and the people of Amsterdam fared particularly well.

The girl with the chicken

Judging by her size, the female figure is a girl; judging by her face, a woman. This figure bathed in light, and the second female figure adumbrated behind her, have attracted a good deal of speculation. Some say Rembrandt intended her as a goddess of victory. Others maintain this was his wife Saskia, who in reality then lay dying. But there is a realistic reason to introduce a girl into the picture, as we see if we consider pictures of militia exercises. There are always children present, boys tricked out in finery like their fathers, girls with baskets on their arms, apparently playing the sutler. Rembrandt's girl is in fact carrying a chicken at her belt, as a sutler woman might, and the painting also features a boy with a powder horn in the left foreground.

The claws of the chicken are particularly carefully rendered. These were an old emblem of civic guards. Three militia guilds emerged in Amsterdam in the late Middle Ages: the oldest was that of the archers, then came the crossbow marksmen, and the most recent, established after the introduction of firearms, were the Kloveniers. The word came from *kloven*, the butt of a gun, and that word was cognate with *klauw* or claw; the emblem of the guild consisted of a gun and a claw.

In other words, these men of the civic guard in *The Night Watch* were members of the Kloveniers guild. But by 1642 the heyday of the militia guilds

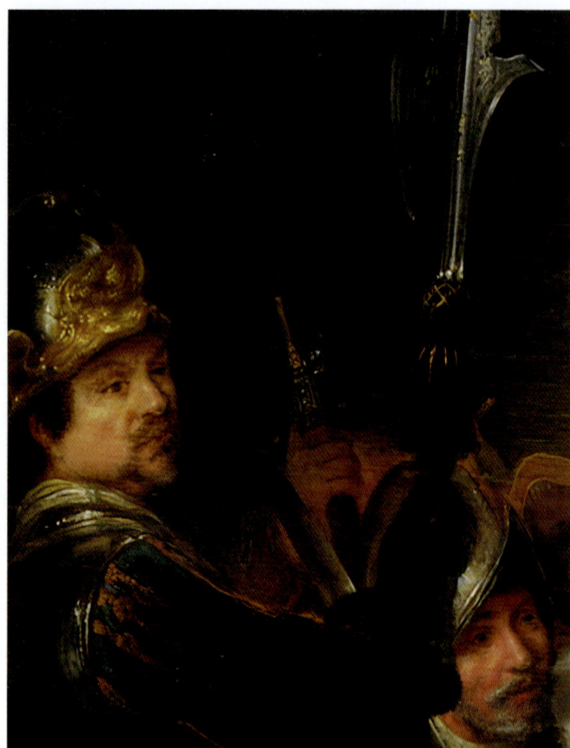

At least, that was the official version. Within the companies, groupings of the rich emerged once again. And this can be seen on the group portraits of militia companies. Thus there were some 120 men in Frans Banning Cocq's company, but only nineteen of them are shown in the painting. The rest, half seen or merely adumbrated, Rembrandt deploys as part of the scenery, as it were. Of the nineteen, one – the drummer – was not in fact a member of the company; he was a city employee and assuredly made no payment for his inclusion. The others, depending on where they were positioned, paid up to 100 guilders each to be included, and the captain and lieutenant no doubt paid more than that. Their names were all recorded on the oval panel in the entry.

The painting was commissioned for the extended festivities hall of the Kloveniers guild. Seven pictures were commissioned for the hall, and Rembrandt got only one of these jobs. Some of those depicted are reported by his pupil Samuel van Hoogstraten to have been dissatisfied because he "was more interested in the overall conception than in the individual portraits he had been asked to paint". The response can be understood if the other guild paintings are taken as the standard. They present the men standing or sitting close together as in any group photograph, their heads given equally precise attention. What Rembrandt painted was a moment of action, of setting out on a march; he placed his highlights "capriciously"; and he included persons who had not paid, such as the girl with the chicken.

From group portrait to national treasure
For the first 200 years after it was painted, *The Night Watch* was not rated especially highly. Partly this was because the militias declined after the Treaty of Westphalia in 1648; Holland's independence as a sovereign state was recognized internationally, the

was long over. In the 16th century they had had political and military power, and for that reason had been prohibited by the Spanish in 1572. When the northern provinces united against the Spanish, it was the members of these outlawed militias who occupied the Amsterdam town hall in 1578 and deposed the vacillating councillors.

After this, the civic guards were reconstituted with all due ceremony, but in a different form. The burgher associations of old were no longer enough. The threat from without called for a greater defence capability. In every one of the Amsterdam districts (by 1640 there were twenty) a company of guards was established. Every company numbered some 120 men. These district companies, while each was grouped under one of the traditional guilds, were no longer the exclusive preserve of the wealthy, but instead socially mixed and municipally organized units with officers assigned by the city council.

guilds formed for defence were no longer active, and these group portraits were not required any more. It was not many years after *The Night Watch* till the very last pictures of this kind were commissioned.

But lack of interest was not the only reason. Aesthetic tastes were changing, too. Those who loved the light colours and delicate, fluid shapes of Rococo art, or the strict symmetry and clear outlines of Classicism, had little time for a painter like Rembrandt. In 1715 his picture was re-hung in a hall of a military court and cut down because the wall space was too small. A broad strip was trimmed off at the top, and another, not so wide, at the bottom; together, about 30 centimetres were taken off. Previously the captain was stepping forward within the composition; now his foot was touching the edge of the picture. At the right, the drummer was cropped, and at the left two militiamen (who had paid) behind the broad shoulders of the man in the golden helmet were removed. From contemporary copies we can see exactly what was removed. The man in the golden helmet, holding a pikestaff, was moved to the very edge of the painting, where he is a strong marker at the left margin, while the captain is now precisely on the centre axis: to a Classical sense of composition, the trimming of the picture was a definite improvement.

It was not only the format and composition that changed; the colours underwent change, too. In 1785, presumably with reference to the girl and the lieutenant, one viewer observed that "the picture is steeped in bright sunshine". Some decades later the title *Night Watch* was first used. The gradual darkening was caused by ageing of the varnish, though restoration may have assisted the process. In the 19th century, picture restorers felt that Old Masters should be dark, and when working on old paintings they often applied a yellowish-brown varnish to give them the tonal finish desired by galleries. *The Night Watch* was not alone in being affected by this preference. The painting became popular in its dark incarnation, in the first half of the 19th century. Again, as in the process by which it was forgotten, this was due to a conjunction of aesthetic and political reasons. The Romantics rediscovered the work, being fond of night and of all that was darkly intuitive, and indifferent to the bright and balanced world of Classicism. Their idea of the artist included a struggle against society, wherever possible one that ended in failure. This seemed to be the fact

of Rembrandt's own life: he enjoyed little recognition, went bankrupt, and spent a lonely old age.

In political terms, after the northern and southern provinces had been reunited under Napoleon, a revolution in Brussels in 1830 led to their final partition as Holland and Belgium. This partition reinforced the need for national identity. The Dutch sought it by harking back to their Golden Age, those decades that saw the political birth of their nation and were also so very fertile an era in the arts. *The Night Watch* attested to both artistic mastery and a political stance that emphasized burgher values, and moreover, not unimportantly, it was of an impressive size.

So it was that in 1885 the painting was moved to a room in the new Rijksmuseum building, where it came into its own as the principal work in the collection and indeed of Dutch art, and was revered as a national treasure. Clearly the extraordinary respect in which the Dutch hold this painting has spread to art lovers throughout the world.

To establish a cult around a painting can provoke aggression, as was shown in 1975 when an unemployed teacher deliberately damaged the picture. The subsequent restoration was performed excellently, so that the painting is probably closer to its original state now than it was a hundred or two hundred years ago.

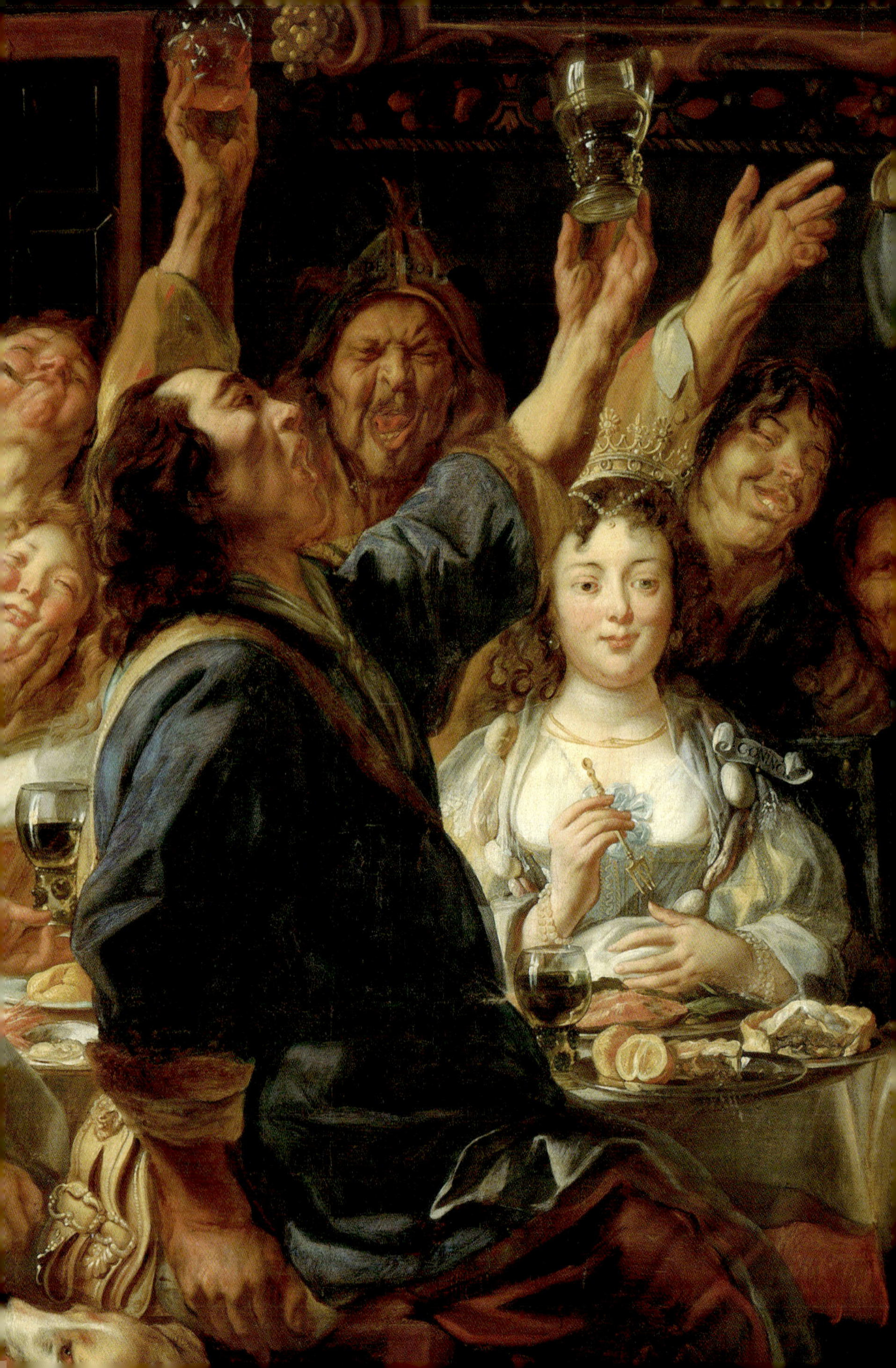
CONINC

Jacob Jordaens (1593–1678)

Tho' our wealthy days be done, here's to a life of luxury

The King Drinks, 1640/1645
242 x 300 cm, Vienna, Kunsthistorisches Museum

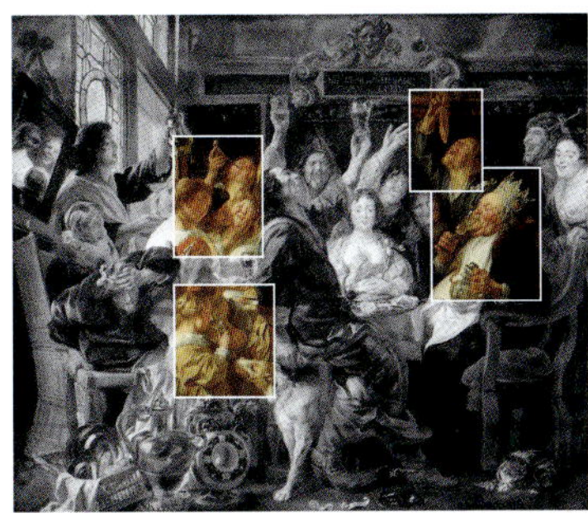

"The King drinks!" was a toast pronounced by the assembled company when an old man wearing a crown raised his cup to his lips – whereupon everyone drained their glasses. Such was the custom at the Twelfth Night feast in many Catholic countries of Europe. The 6th of January is still widely celebrated today, if not with the roistering gusto exhibited by the revellers in the painting. Some are shown yelling at the tops of their voices, others gesticulate wildly; one is depicted in the act of vomiting. It seems that none of the company takes umbrage at a proverb fixed to the wall at the back: *Nil similius insano quam ebrius*, or "Nothing resembles the mad-man more than a drunkard".

Light at the window suggests a daytime scene. Feasts of this kind would last from noon until midnight, the revellers keeping themselves amused between courses with songs and games. The Twelfth Night Feast, also called the "Feast of the Bean King", was an occasion to which relatives, special friends and servants were invited. Children would also partake and, like the blonde girl in the foreground, were sometimes allowed a sip from the wineglass. Cats and dogs completed the scene.

Jacob Jordaens (1593–1678) probably used his family and servants as models for this scene, setting it in his own house in Hoogstraat, Antwerp. The picture was executed between 1640 and 1645. Business was good; the artist was highly successful, and paintings of this kind sold particularly well. Twelfth Night festivities had provided the subject for six of his paintings. He devoted a similar number of canvases to yet another company at table. These were entitled: "As the old cock crows, the young cock learns". Both sets of paintings celebrated values that were greatly cherished by his clientele: the family, prosperity, pleasure. Coarse detail, such as the drinker vomiting, was not considered inappropriate here. Other works depict children waiting for adults to clean their bottoms.

An imposing format was important to buyers; this work, now at the Kunsthistorisches Museum in Vienna, measures 242 by 300 centimetres. A large number of figures was also important. Most of Jordaens' commissions came from the wealthy bourgeoisie of the southern Netherlands, a region roughly equivalent to today's Belgium. At that time, it was part of the Spanish Empire. Both the southern and northern provinces had attempted to gain independence from Spanish rule; following a protracted struggle, the north alone had been successful. As a result, the northern provinces flourished, while trade in the south stagnated. Jordaens' patrons had lost much of their business and were forced to draw on the amassed wealth of fatter years. This may explain

their predilection for the artist's portrayal
of them as folk whose zest for life appeared
quite unbroken.

Ownership of this painting eluded them,
however. Instead, it was acquired by a Habsburg: Leopold Wilhelm, the Spanish viceroy
at Brussels. In 1656, he left for Vienna, taking
the painting with him.

A mediocre painter – but a great boozer

The popular figure of the old man wearing
a golden, pasteboard crown is no stranger to
Jordaens' work. He is Jordaens' father-in-law,
Adam van Noort, a member of Jordaens' household until his death at the age of 80. Although
a mediocre painter, Van Noort became one of
Antwerp's more wealthy citizens. His status in
the history of art, however, is based solely on
the reputation of his two famous pupils: Peter
Paul Rubens and Jacob Jordaens.

The old man's crown distinguishes him
as the King of the Feast. It was customary in
Antwerp to determine the king and queen
of the feast and members of their court by
drawing lots. Lots, called *billets de roi*, were
hawked on the streets on the days before
6 January. Two such tickets, inscribed "Sanger"
(minstrel) and "Hofmester" (Controller of
the Royal Household), are seen on the floor
between the dog and the cat, while others are
worn by the guests: the man with the fish is
the Carver; the *billet* pinned to the hat of the
vomiting drinker identifies him as a *medezijner*
(doctor of medicine). The drawing of lots
does not appear to have decided the "cast" of
Jordaens' paintings, however; the oldest man is
always the king, and the most beautiful woman
is always queen.

In some parts, a bean or coin was hidden in
a cake; whoever found it was king, and would
choose his own entourage. The painting, like so
many other depictions of the same theme – by
Jan Steen for example – is also known as "The
Feast of the Bean King". Pieces of Twelfth Cake
were cut not only for the guests, as the 16th-
century German preacher and chronicler
Sebastian Franck observed: "To honour God,"
he wrote, pieces were kept for Jesus, the Virgin
Mary and the Magi. As soon as lots had been
drawn, the new king was lifted into the air

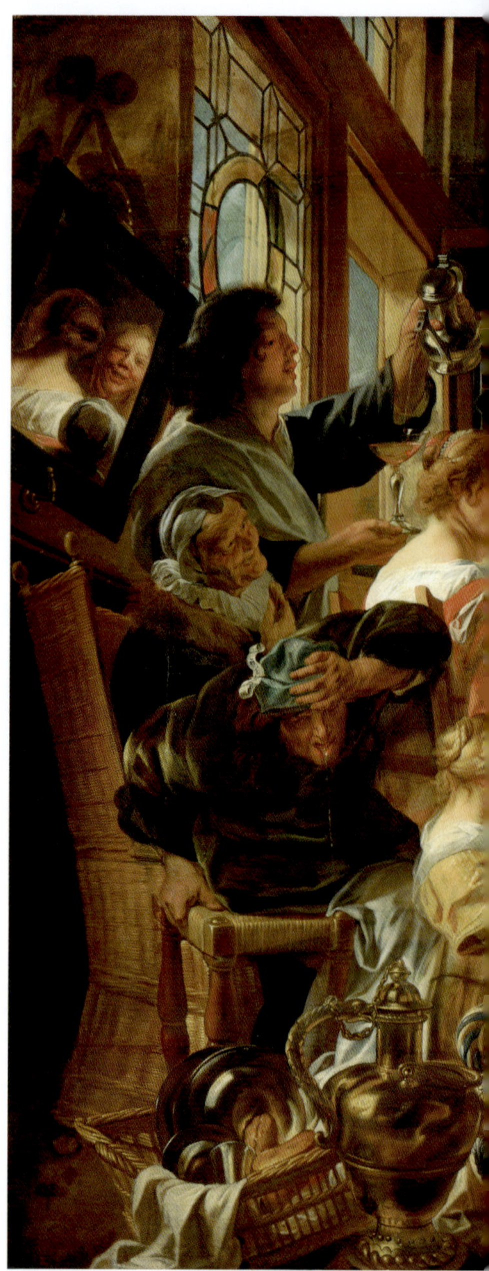

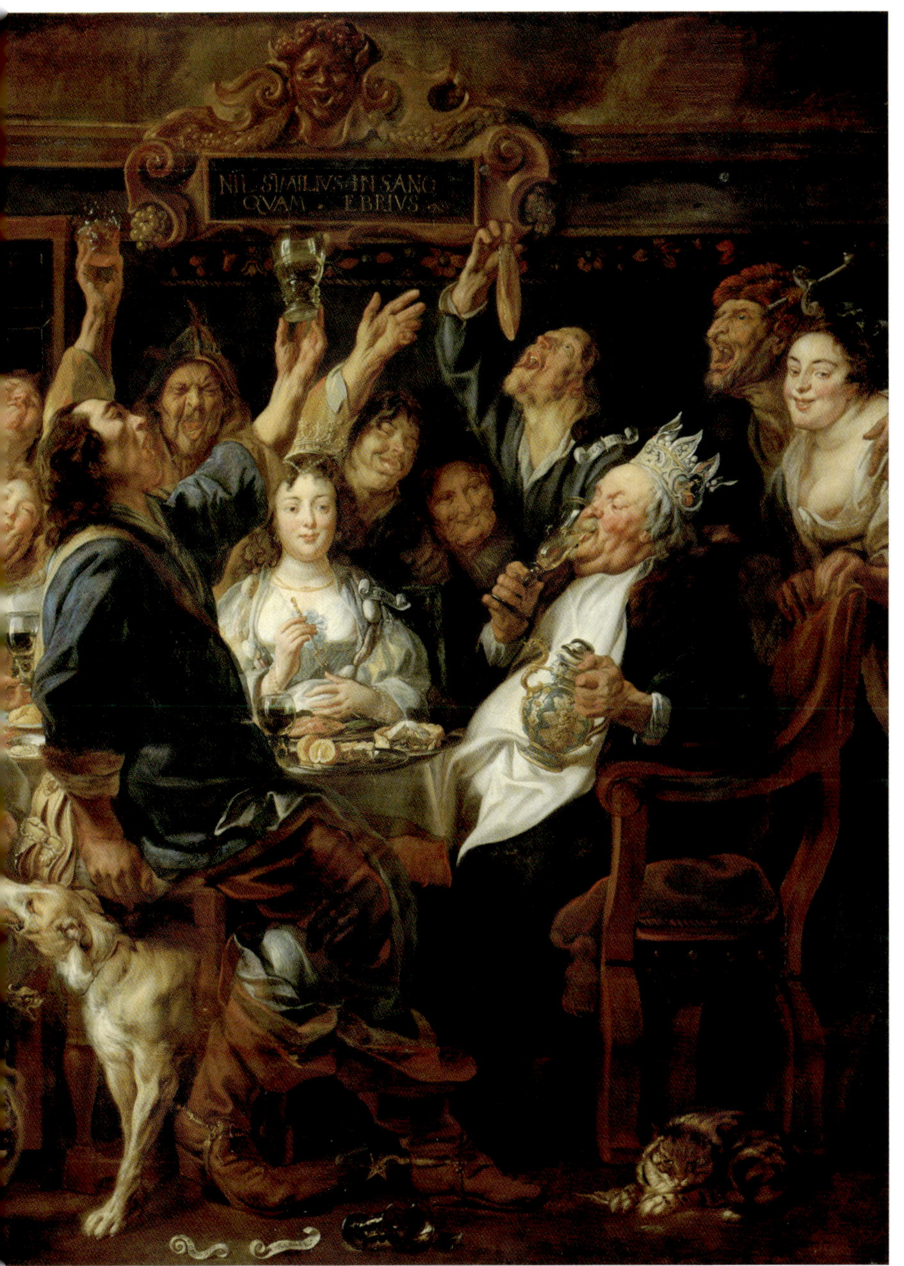
NIL SIMILIVS INSANO
QVAM . EBRIVS

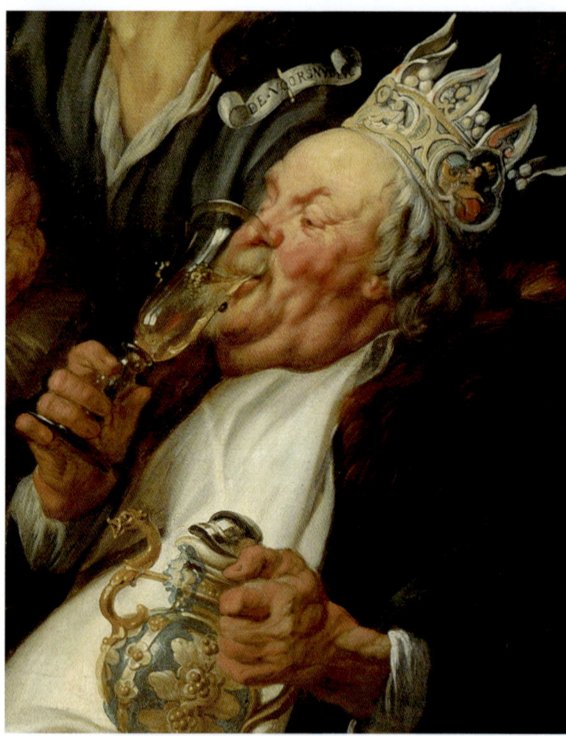

6 January, but a spiritual birth. The day was reserved for the festival of the Epiphany, the day of baptism and manifestation of Christ's glory. Christ had manifested himself to the Gentiles in the person of the wise men of the East. Popular belief saw the Magi not only as expert astrologers who had followed a star to Bethlehem, but also as scientists and magicians. They thus had practically become auxiliary saints with the power to ward off evil, guard against fire, sickness and bad weather, or, since they had come so far themselves, give protection to travellers. Their names, Caspar, Melchior and Balthasar, were sometimes invoked in blessings.

In the 9th century, the three wise men, now promoted to the status of kings, were adopted by the Christian liturgy. From the 11th century on, their day was marked by carol singing and entertainments. The tradition of sumptuous feasting can be traced back as far as the 14th century: it was customary, following the service at Epiphany, for the deans of churches in the north of France to invite their chapter to a banquet at which they would preside as King of the Feast. Groaning tables were greeted as a presage of good fortune in the new year; leftover food met with disapproval.

three times, to the applause of the assembled company. According to Franck, the king then went solemnly about the house chalking crosses on floorboards and beams to ward off evil spirits and ill luck. Ritual ceremonies of this kind were held throughout the Catholic countries of Europe; in some places, the tradition remains unbroken to this day.

The 6th of January had always been a significant date in the Christian calendar. The birth of Christ had originally been celebrated on this day. After a long dispute between various communities in the Christian world, the date had been brought forward to 25 December. The new Christmas was evidently intended to displace popular pagan festivals which had taken place on that day: the rites of the Egyptian goddess Isis, for example, or the Nativity of the "Sol Invictus", the Unconquered Sun, celebrated throughout the Roman Empire.

From now on, Christian believers no longer celebrated the corporeal Nativity of Christ on

Occasions for revelry

Sumptuous banquets lasting several days at a time were also held on other occasions. These were expensive for the host and, since they frequently ended in excessive drinking and brawling, a thorn in the side of the authorities. The government did what they could to contain such dissipation, but even the "Decree against excessive behaviour at weddings and excursions for the purpose of banqueting" from 1613 was no more effective than previous decrees. The Guild of St Luke at Antwerp, a professional association of painters, had been founded to provide mutual assistance in time of sickness and distress.

During the 17th century, however, the Guild
was much given to the organization of festivities.
Practically its entire income was spent on an annual
banquet held on St Luke's Day. It is therefore hardly
surprising that Jordaens attempted – in vain – to
decline his election to the post of Dean of the Guild
in 1621. He presumably felt that he would be unable
to foot the enormous bill for expenses which he
knew his new office would bring. Even death
provided opportunities for revelry. No fewer than
four funeral feasts were held at Antwerp to mark
the occasion of Rubens's death in 1640: one by his
friends and next of kin at the house of the deceased;
another, at the Town Hall, by the members of the
Town Council; a third, for the Romanist Brother-
hood, took place at an inn called "The Marigold";
while the fourth, a feast organized by the Guild
of St Luke, was held at an inn called "The Hart".

Feasting was widespread even in monasteries and
convents. On the occasion of one young lady taking
the veil at the Falcon Convent at Antwerp on 10
February 1664, the convent archives report a celebra-
tory feast attended by nineteen guests who, between
them, ate "twenty half-stivers-worth of white bread, a
boiled leg of mutton, two hams, two pieces of salted
meat, three bowls of rice, three bowls of mutton
stew with vegetables, sausages and dumplings, and
three bowls of plum puree. That was the first course."
This was followed by two equally abundant courses,
the whole feast being repeated on the following
day. Even when festivals like Twelfth Night were
celebrated within the family, at least a dozen substantial dishes would usually be served. The guests in
the painting have already eaten their fill, leaving the
table almost empty, although one of the ladies
is still shown picking at her food with a fork. The
only other visible food consists of a half-eaten pie,
a few pieces of orange and, at the other end of the
table, a few prawns to go with the alcohol, or perhaps to encourage thirst, like the salted herring one
guest is depicted as dangling above his open mouth.

A custom linked with the Twelfth Night feast
was the practice of looking up at the stars through
the chimney. The number of stars counted by the
viewer determined the number of glasses of wine he
was then permitted to drink. The rummers of the
celebrants were probably filled with Rhine wine and
Moselle. "Taking away a Fleming's glass," wrote one
French traveller in the 18th century, "would be like
cutting off the roots by which a tree draws up its sap."

Almost two thirds of Dutch genre paintings depict
drinking scenes in the home or the tavern. Even ceremonial group portraits capture highly respectable
town councillors in the act of raising their glasses.

They live like veritable animals
Cardinal Infante Ferdinand, a predecessor of Leopold
Wilhelm as Viceroy of the Spanish Netherlands,
once visited Antwerp's great fair. Filled with disgust,
he reported what he had seen to his brother King
Philip IV. After the procession, he wrote, "the people
sat down to eat and drink until eventually they were
all drunk. It is apparently impossible to celebrate any
other way here. They live like veritable animals."

For the Spanish, concerned above all with posture and bearing, a drunk was someone utterly lacking in human dignity. "Drunkard" was considered
so violent a term of abuse that its use could provoke
a duel. The example quoted above reveals how
distant were relations between the Spanish and the
Dutch, who had been brought together by a royal
marriage and inheritance. In the 16th century, the
Spanish Habsburgs had inherited the seventeen rich
Netherlandish provinces (today's Belgium, Holland
and Luxemburg) as part of Burgundy. King Philip

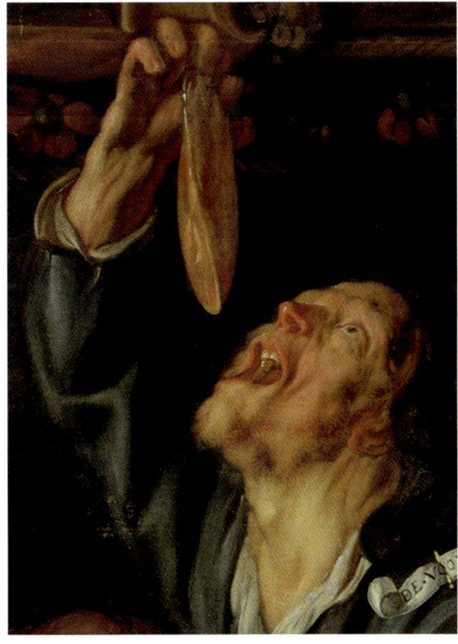

II's policy of centralizing power and his intolerance drove the freedom-loving, partly Protestant Dutch to rebel against their Catholic overlords. After 80 years, the struggle was concluded by the Treaty of Westphalia in 1648: the northern provinces would receive their independence as a Calvinist "Republic of the United Provinces of the Netherlands"; the southern provinces remained under Spanish rule – politically disabled, strictly Catholic and economically feeble. Jordaens painted his Twelfth Night feast during the final phase of the struggle, between 1640 and 1645. The fighting had all but ceased, especially as far as the southern provinces were concerned. Spain, with its incompetent burocracy, chronic lack of money and demoralized army, had relinquished its former military power. Even if it had managed to hold on to the southern provinces, Spain proved incapable of defending the strategically important Scheldt estuary. A blockade imposed by the northern provinces cut Antwerp off from the North Sea trade routes to which it owed its affluence.

An Englishman travelling in the southern provinces described the "devastated countryside, demoralized inhabitants … an impoverished nobility and degenerate merchant class … towns destroyed … general poverty". This was written some time before Jordaens painted his picture. In the meantime, Antwerp had largely been rebuilt and the causes of the more acute misery eliminated. A century earlier, the town had been one of the richest trading centres of the world; now it had lost half its inhabitants. The English and Italian banks had fled. In 1648, the Municipal Library moved into the empty Stock Exchange.

The cultivation of entrepreneurial skills was practically taboo in a country where aristocratic pedigree and land ownership were all that counted. The sons of once-prosperous merchants now gave up their fathers' business and set about purchasing titles and estates. Strict censorship by the Catholic Church inhibited art and cultural development; French became the dominant language, replacing the indigenous Flemish tongue, which was now thought fit only for "the tavern and the kitchen". At the same time, this had the effect of robbing the people of pride in their national independence and past achievements. All that was left was retreat into the privacy of their own homes, where they could hold feasts, and talk, sing, yell and swear in Flemish as much as they liked.

Bourgeois domestic scenes

The chubby faced blonde drinking from a wine glass with such abandon turns up repeatedly in the artist's work. She was probably one of his daughters. Jordaens would frequently use the same motif over and over again. He did this more often than other artists, finding it hard to paint from the imagination. Moreover, the constant stream of commissions for altarpieces, pagan

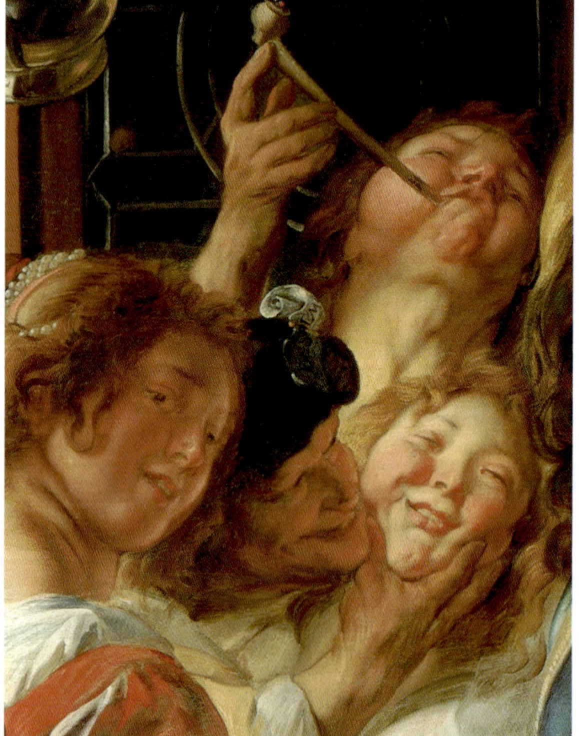

mythology and bourgeois domestic scenes during the second half of his life left him little time to invent new scenes.

Rubens, sixteen years Jordaens' senior, had spent decades of his life supplying wealthy patrons throughout Europe with the Christian genre pieces and mythological themes favoured during the age of absolutism and the Counter-Reformation. Like Jordaens, Rubens lived in Antwerp, and both artists had shared the same master. Jordaens occasionally assisted at Rubens' studio, for even a tireless genius like Rubens was only capable of meeting the great demand for his work with the aid of a workshop run almost along factory lines.

In 1637/38, Rubens was commissioned to paint a series of 56 allegorical paintings for the King of Spain over a period of fifteen months. To meet this demand, a team of otherwise independent artists had to work under Rubens' direction. One member of this team was Jacob Jordaens, who was considered a competent, minor painter. One year later, in 1639, the English court considered giving a particularly large commission to Jordaens instead of Rubens. Jordaens, after all, did not charge as much.

Rubens died in 1640, a year before the other great Flemish painter of the period, Anthony van Dyck. Their deaths made Jordaens the pre-eminent artist of the southern Netherlands. As a result, he was able to take on more pupils. His wealth and reputation quickly grew, although his fame would never match that of Rubens. Jordaens lacked Rubens' international clientele, and his work was less sought after in aristocratic circles. Unlike Rubens, he had never left Flanders; nor did he share Rubens' experience of diplomacy or life at court. Whereas Rubens had risen to the ranks of the aristocracy, Jordaens remained an ordinary citizen. His best customers were affluent townsfolk. Finally, unlike Rubens, he did not receive commissions from the most important churches in the land. The powerful, aristocratically-minded Jesuits, for example, had never sought his services.

At about this time, a new and highly idiosyncratic bourgeois art was emerging in the northern provinces, which had emancipated themselves from their Spanish, aristocratic overlords. Instead of the usual portraits of rulers, artists there were painting groups; and instead of mythological scenes, quotidian scenes from the limited world of the tranquil bourgeois interior were now considered worthy of art. Artists such as Gerard Terborch and Pieter de Hooch, and

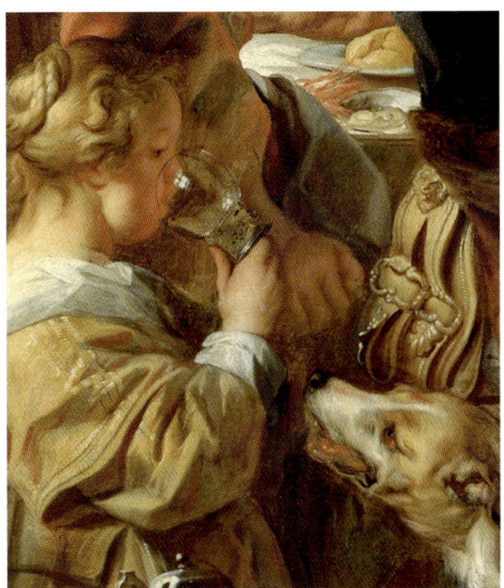

later also Vermeer, painted small, unpretentious scenes from everyday life with very few figures. These artists formed the avant-garde in a Europe otherwise dominated by grandiose Baroque display.

Although executed under Spanish rule, Jordaens' images of boozing and gluttony also depict everyday scenes in bourgeois interiors. But Jordaens' works have nothing of the plain candour demonstrated by his northern contemporaries. Instead, he favoured the lavish Baroque style so ably and peerlessly promoted by Rubens. However, Rubens had never intended his style to be applied to crude, everyday reality. On the contrary, he had chosen to paint fantasy worlds in which the fortunes of rulers were directed by the gods. His drunkards appeared in the guise of Sileni, frolicking in the company of Bacchantes.

The Baroque pathos of the style contrasts with the painting's somewhat banal subject. Jacob Jordaens has painted a small world in a grand manner. The sweeping gestures seem too large for the narrow interior, and the mirth on some of the faces has a static, almost masklike quality. This contradiction reflects something of a dilemma in the southern provinces, whose citizens would have liked to live in the grand style they had enjoyed in the old days. Only those days were over. The economic centres now lay to the north. The citizens of the south had grown poorer. Their feelings of impotence and fear are hidden behind an emphatic display of *joie de vivre*.

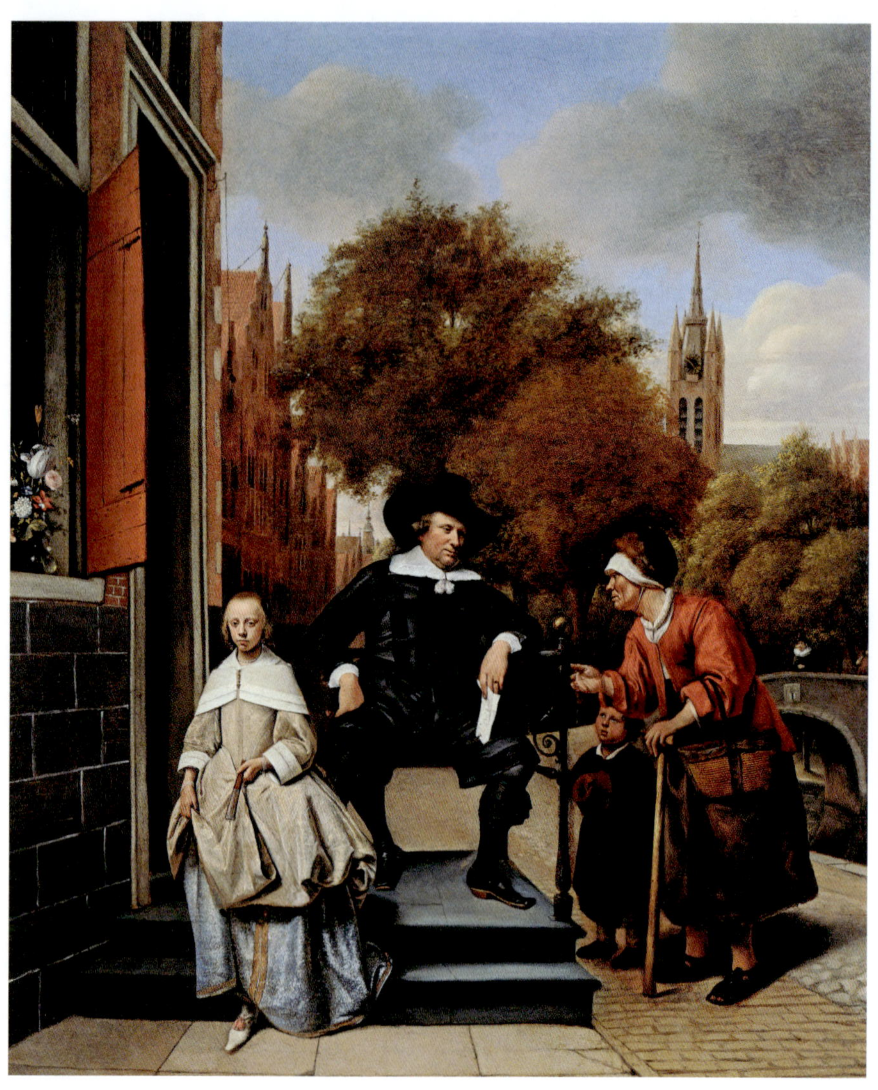

Jan Steen (1626–1679)

A rich man sitting in the street

The Burgher of Delft and his Daughter, 1655
82.5 x 68.6 cm, Amsterdam, Rijksmuseum

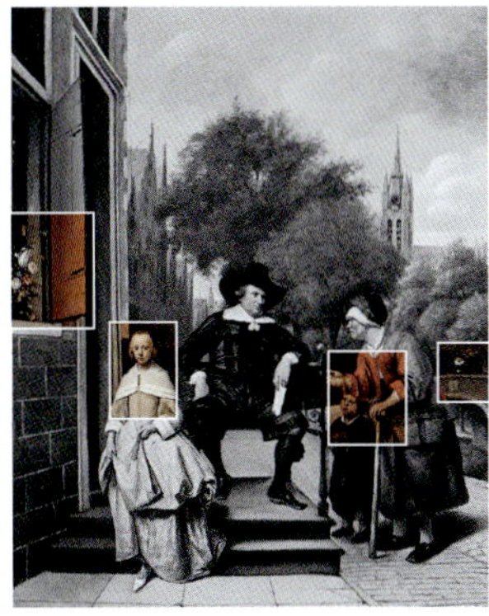

A man is sitting in the street. Or rather, he is sitting on the stepped threshold of his house, and thus at a place at once public and private. Not only this raised entry before his front door but also the paved area in front of the house is on his own land. Beside the paved strip is the brick public footway, on which an old woman and a boy are standing. Further to the right is the cobbled street intended for horses, carriages, wagons, and so forth.

This raised threshold, with a railing and a seat, known as a *stoep*, was often found in the Netherlands, and probably served as a place to hold conversations. Of course one might talk to passers-by from the window, where the flowers are, but it was easier without an intervening wall and on the same level. Furthermore, the seat conferred a certain dignity and placed the owner of the property on show. For someone who held public office, conversations held here could be of importance. For a long time, historians identified the man in this painting as the lord mayor of Delft, but for this there is no evidence. All we know of him is what we see. One of the things we know is that the location where he had himself portrayed is the west bank of the canal known as Oude Delft. In the background is the Oude Kerk,

and to the left the twin gables of the Delflands Huis. Maps of the town show that residences on the canal-side were very narrow, and built close against each other, and extended a long way back from the street. Behind the houses were equally narrow gardens, running as far as the next canal.

Jan Steen (1626–79) painted this unknown man in 1655. At that time the town of Delft had a population of about 25,000 and was in the provinces of the Netherlands, which had thrown off Spanish rule after a protracted struggle. The Treaty of Westphalia (1648) had recognized Dutch independence. What remained contentious, however, was the form of the government. During the wars of liberation, the Dutch had made the Princes of Orange their stadtholder, but in times of peace they were too powerful for the people's liking, and in 1651 the office of stadtholder was rescinded. Henceforth, it was the patrician burghers who ruled. The man we see sitting with such self-assurance had been living for seven years in a newly sovereign state. And for four years it had not been ruled by the House of Orange but by men of his own class. The artist has portrayed him on an afternoon in late summer; by the church clock it is ten to five.

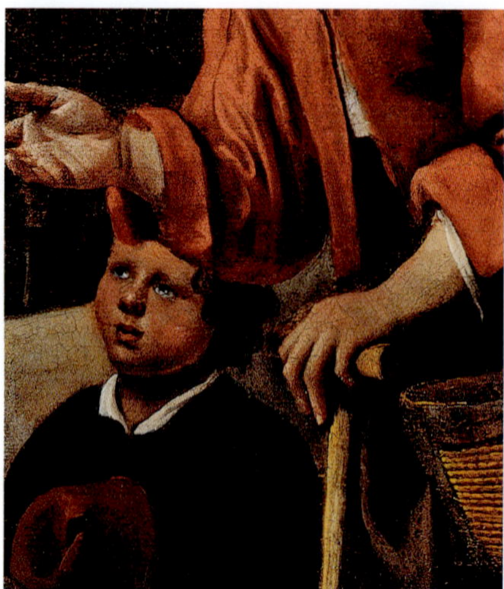

The registration of the poor

Steen's painting, now in a private collection, was made in the heyday of bourgeois culture in the Netherlands. One of the pillars of that culture was its strong civic sense. The government in The Hague was responsible for foreign policy and defence only; all other matters were for the provinces or cities to decide. The indigent lay in the jurisdiction of the cities, as did the administration of justice. There was no written penal code, and every town decided these matters at its own discretion, though invariably with rigour. Guilty parties were beheaded or hanged, drowned or burnt alive; a hand was amputated; if the offence was less serious, the guilty party's shoulder was branded with a red-hot iron. Executions were always held in public, as an entertainment but also a deterrent. Begging was subject to penalties.

A clear distinction was made between the poor of a municipality and beggars from without. The municipal poor were registered and had a licence permitting them to beg for alms. Their numbers included the sick, orphans, and old people unable to work, such as the woman in the painting, supporting herself on her stick and holding out a beseeching hand. The scrap of paper the affluent burgher is holding may be her licence. Steen does not portray this man as one who would spontaneously open his purse, or call back his daughter

to fetch bread from the house and put it in the old woman's basket. This man is thinking it over, holding the licence in his hand as he ponders what is to be done. Such deliberation was considered a civic virtue and duty, since un reflecting charity might benefit frauds, especially those from elsewhere.

Every town was on its guard against itinerant tramps. They were strangers in the tightly woven fabric of a town and thus were invariably met with suspicion; they had no fixed abode to which a magistrate might have sent them back. They might be discharged mercenaries, landless peasants, workers from industries that had gone out of business, travelling people, or criminals fleeing justice. Since they could not always be turned away at the city gates, they would be given a permit to stay for a limited time, perhaps three days, perhaps a month, and if at the end of this period they had not found work they had to leave the city, or the municipal officers would set their dogs on them.

The magistrates and burghers took an entirely different attitude to the poor of their own municipality. They provided them with food and shelter (in former Catholic monasteries, for instance). Thus where the Sint Agatha Klooster had been (the tower can be seen over the shoulder of the seated burgher), the Oude Vrouwen Charitaathuis, an almshouse for old women, was built. It may be that this old woman lived there, or that the seated burgher held honorary office there.

Despite the much vaunted Dutch civic sense, provision for the needy was repeatedly the subject of municipal dispute. Before independence from Spain, charity had been the province of the Catholic church. In 1572, the Delft council expropriated the church there, and took over all its charitable duties. The strongest religious institution in the sequel was the Reformed (Calvinist) Church. It attempted to define social responsibilities as its own domain, while at the same time lending support to the House of Orange, which had just been ousted from power by the government representing the burghers.

So if a man chose to be painted in 1655, in a place outside the church, pondering an act of charity, this might be interpreted as a statement: against the House of Orange, against a church that arrogated social responsibilities to itself, and for the rule of the burgher.

A daughter dressed in the court style
The burgher is sitting at his ease. His left arm is resting on the railing, his right is on his thigh. Both are supporting him and thus easing his upright posture; but they also tell us something about the man. He has not the palm but the back of his hand on his thigh, which has the effect of bringing the elbow forward and so making the sitter appear broader, of more substance. The left, relaxed arm sends a message of potential goodwill and concern; the right signals that this is not a man to be trifled with.

Jan Steen was among those Netherlandish painters who discovered everyday life, and, with it, everyday gestures. He became a master of body language. In his paintings, even legs and feet talk. With his knees apart, this man again seems more substantial, while the position of his feet seems to be asserting his ownership of this plot. The right foot, below the angled elbow, is somewhat withdrawn, which may be either playful or suggestive of readiness to leap to attack or defence. It is not the posture of a scholar who spends his time at a writing desk; it is far more that of a mounted military commander.

The impression made by his daughter is quite different. She is holding the hand with the fan in front of her, and with her other hand she is raising her overskirts in the manner she has presumably been taught by her dancing instructor that is appropriate when descending steps. At the time, good (i.e. courtly) deportment required that the feet be kept close together and the arms flush along the sides, without any ostentatious or extravagant posturing.

Requirements such as these were laid down in etiquette books. Erasmus of Rotterdam, in his treatise on education published in 1532, explicitly disapproves of placing the hands square against the sides whilst sitting or standing; such a position might be permissible in a man of arms, but in others would be undignified. In *Il Galateo* (1558), Giovanni della Casa likens those who strut about with their hands against their sides to peacocks. And in 1644 John Bulwer declared the posture expressive of pride and boastfulness, and unbecoming in a gentleman.

This burgher of Delft was evidently no more troubled by such considerations than many of his contemporaries were. If pictures are to be believed, this attitude of self-confidence was highly popular. It can be seen in the groom in wedding scenes, and in many group portraits, such as Rembrandt's

The Night Watch of 1642, in which both the showily clad lieutenant and the standard bearer have an arm against their sides, lending to a peaceable scene of departure an air of swagger and aggression.

What the writers of etiquette books spurned was acceptable to Dutchmen; indeed, they may have adopted behaviour unacceptable in court circles as a form of provocation. Or they may have intended to demonstrate their own strength: the burghers' new self-esteem established its own repertoire of gestures. But as the century wore on, it was abandoned again, and the well-to-do took their bearings from aristocratic circles once more: the prim and proper daughter is showing her splay legged father how those of her generation propose to conduct themselves.

Looking back to the past
Jan Steen liked to tell stories in his paintings: of brawls in taverns, of Twelfth Night festivities, of weddings and family outings. There is always something happening between his personae, and the father and daughter in this double portrait are no exception. The story emerges from the presence of the impoverished woman and the boy. The father is pondering what he will do; his daughter seems

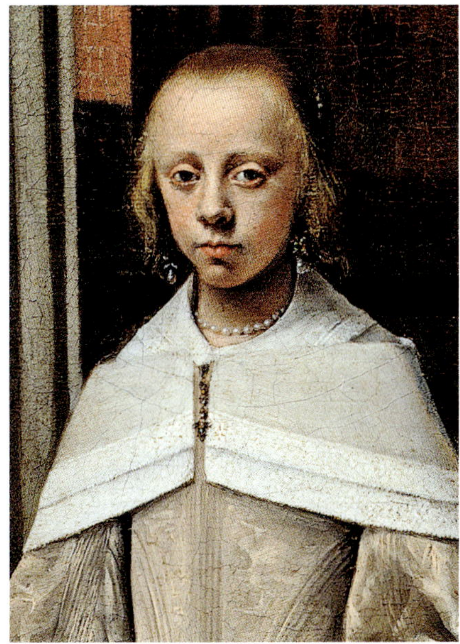

indifferent, self-absorbed, in a world that is all about costly garments and descending steps with style.

On the bridge in the background Steen has placed two men. One, whom we can barely see, is probably a farmer, carrying a sack to the nearby market. The other is a burgher dressed in the fashion of yester-year: his hat is taller than was usual in 1655, he is wearing a stiff ruff rather than the soft collar of the principal character in the foreground, and the cut of his beard is no longer much seen. This elderly gentleman is watching the scene in the foreground. With his black and white attire, he looks like some remote double of the foreground burgher; the quality of the gaze suggests some relationship. The artist offers no explanation, but with the gentleman on the bridge he has introduced the past into his painting, a brief look back in a picture that takes pride in the present.

Some years earlier, the bridge over the Oude Delft had been a flat, wooden construction. The arched stone bridge betokens progress and prosperity. The arms are those of the city of Delft. The Delflands Huis, the twin gabled building seen to the left, was the seat of the office of public works, transport and waterways. This was one of the most important of public authorities, for flat Holland was criss crossed by a network of rivers and canals, and they consti-tuted a major pillar of its prosperity. Neither France

nor England had anything approaching so good a system of waterways, and Germany, Spain, and Italy lagged far behind. Canal transport was slower than road transport, but a horse could move 50 times the load by water. Travellers preferred gliding down the waters in the comfort of their cabins to bumpy coach rides on unsurfaced roads. All the towns of the Netherlands were linked to the seaports by the waterways, and goods arriving at the coast could thus easily be moved inland.

The Netherlands not only had the best canal system, they also had the largest of all European fleets. Their most powerful rival was England. A naval war between the two countries, from 1652 to 1654, ended in disaster for Delft: in 1654 the powder depot exploded, destroying a large por-tion of the city. This was the year before Jan Steen painted his burgher.

Steen himself experienced hardship during the war. Hostilities crippled trade, much reducing the chances that ships bound for America, Asia or the Baltic would make the return voyage safely. There could be no more thought of processing Eng-lish wool. The demand for faïence ware, a speciality of the Delft porcelain manufactories, fell. And so, too, of course, did the demand for art. Steen had moved to Delft because his father had taken a lease on a brewery for him there. The artist could not support a family on paintings, and he had learnt the brewer's trade in his youth. Like the burgher's house, the brewery was on Oude Delft, though on the opposite bank. Steen was unable to make a success of beer in Delft.

From there he moved with his family to Leiden, later to Warmond, thence to Haarlem, and then back again to the city of his birth, Leiden, where he opened an inn. What he observed there, the revelling over-consumption of beer and tobacco, the brawls, the card playing, is all to be seen in his paintings. To what extent he himself participated is a moot point. The fact that Steen's paintings are to be found in museums all around Europe demonstrates that he was a prolific artist; and yet he left his widow only an inn up to the hilt in debt when he died in 1679 at the age of 53.

Flowers in memory of the dead

Painters generally positioned what was of impor-tance in the centre of a picture. Details on the edges were not expected to excite undue attention.

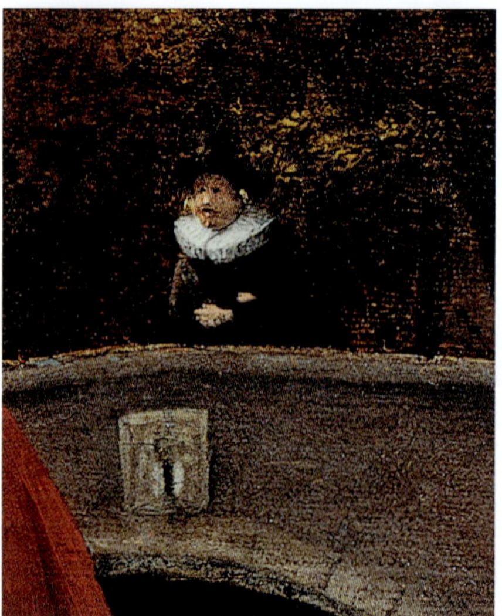

Steen, however, broke this age old rule with his flowers. They are more colourful than any other part of the composition, and they are so detailed and so carefully nuanced that we might be standing right before them and not (as the structure of the work implies) a few metres away.

The flowers are isolated. They are like a picture within the picture, like a still life. This type of painting enjoyed great popularity in 17th-century Holland, and indeed the very term came into being at this period: *still-leven*. The motionless subjects of such paintings tended to be food and kitchen utensils on a table top, dead game birds and animals or a skull beside books, or, frequently, flowers in a vase. These pictures were notable for their relish of limited scope, and the closeness with which they scrutinized everyday items.

Steen places his vase on the window ledge and, in doing so, draws our thoughts toward the interior of the house. Well-to-do burghers felt that a presentable and indeed impressive interior, with carved chairs and tables, ornate mantelpieces, and floral decoration, was of great importance.

But perhaps the flowers are intended to point us not only to the interior but also to the person who must once have been there, the burgher's wife, now presumably deceased. The floral still life invariably prompted thoughts not just of beauty but also of transience. This miniature masterpiece on the edge of the painting may be a kind of memento mori, in remembrance of the dead. It is visible only to us as we look at the painting. It is discreetly screened by the window shutter from the family members in the painting, who live entirely in the present.

The dominant flower in the bouquet is one that enjoyed extraordinary popularity in the Netherlands at that time. In the 16th century an Austrian legate was the first to bring tulip bulbs back from Constantinople to Vienna, and in the 17th century tulips spread throughout Europe. In the Netherlands a tulip mania ensued, aggravated by profiteering and botanical experimentation. The potential for creating hybrid strains seemed unlimited, and new varieties of tulip were dealt on the stock exchange (using painted images of the tulips) and resulted in wild speculation. In 1637 the Dutch tulip market crashed, and with it the financial well-being of many a small investor. Thus the tulip already had a famous, or

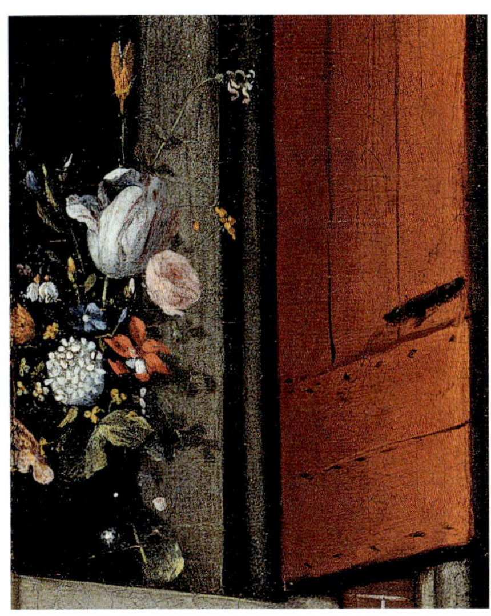

notorious, history by the time Steen included it in his Delft bouquet.

If we take a careful look at the burgher of Delft's home, we realize that his house, with its window of flowers, does not fit in with the perspective alignment of this receding line of buildings. It is more to the fore, and seen more from the side. This is an error by the artist. But only by committing it could Steen satisfy the requirements that either he or the burgher from whom he had his commission had set: to place the head of the sitter in the middle of the composition, to leave the sitter squarely on his *stoep*, and still to present a panoramic view of the town.

We see clearly the special qualities of Steen's painting if we compare it with works by, say, his contemporary Rembrandt (1609–69). Rembrandt liked to shroud his sitters in a dark, mystical aura. Instead of that aura, Steen prefers a profusion of concrete details. Through them he gives us a character portrait of the burgher and also of his city, showing the individual as a member of the society in which he lives and works.

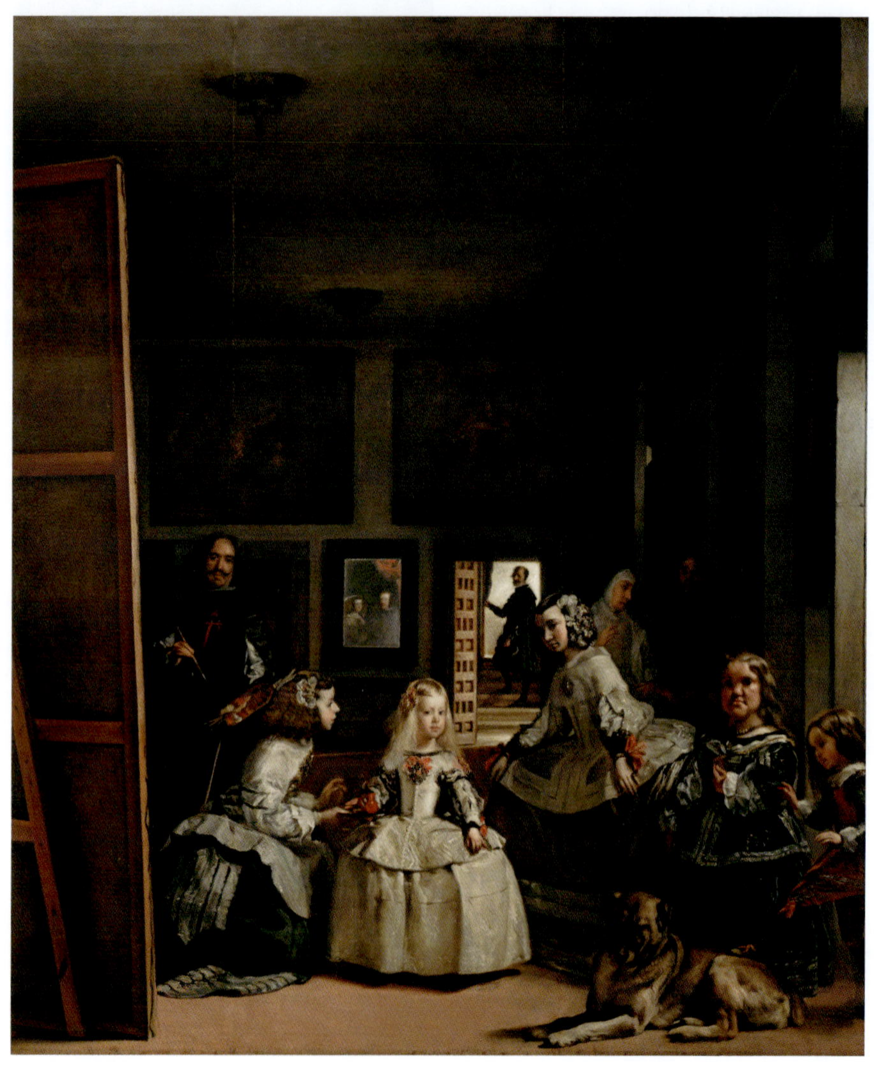

Diego de Silva y Velázquez (1599–1660)

The end of the Habsburgs in Madrid

Velázquez and the Royal Family (Las Meninas), 1656
318 x 276 cm, Madrid, Museo del Prado

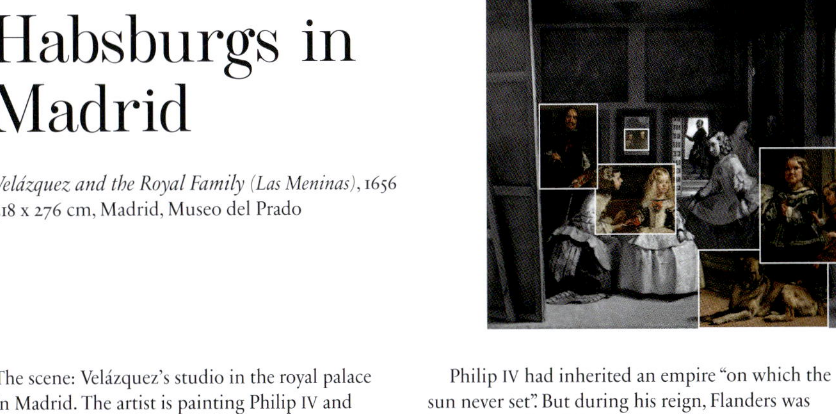

The scene: Velázquez's studio in the royal palace in Madrid. The artist is painting Philip IV and his queen, Mariana; the royal couple can be seen indirectly, reflected in the mirror at the rear. At the centre of the picture stands the five-year-old Infanta, Princess Margarita, who appears to have just come in with her maids of honour (*las meninas*) and other attendants. The light, and doubtless the gaze of her parents, are on the girl. Velázquez conveys an impression of family happiness, of wealth, and of a hopeful future, personified in the little princess.

The picture was painted in 1656. At that date the king was 51, and in poor health; he had ruined Spain politically and economically; in reality the court's coffers were empty, in winter there was no firewood to warm the palace, and the fish served up on golden platters came stinking to the royal table.

The Habsburgs had been on the throne of Spain for five generations, and time and again they intermarried. The degeneration that resulted was most apparent in Philip IV, in his almost morbid weakness of will. Politically he was at the mercy of his first ministers, and in private life at that of his sensual desires. He is said to have fathered 32 illegitimate children, and had more mistresses than Louis XIV of France. Being a pious man, he felt that adultery was a sin. He wrote prolix, emphatic letters to a nun, confessing his sins and swearing to mend his ways; broke his word; swore his oath anew, and broke it again; and besought the nun to do penance on his behalf, with all the other nuns in her convent.

Philip IV had inherited an empire "on which the sun never set". But during his reign, Flanders was lost; Portugal and Catalonia cut their ties with Madrid; French armies ravished the country; and the routes to the colonies that produced silver were threatened by the growth of England's power at sea. Under Charles I (of Spain, simultaneously Holy Roman Emperor Charles V) and Philip II, his great-grandfather and grandfather respectively, the vast Spanish empire had already become impossible to defend militarily, but it had come through, thanks to a combination of political skill, personal dedication, and the aura of Spanish power. Now all of that was gone. The reign of Philip IV proved one long chain of disasters.

Together with the empire, Philip had inherited the Spanish commitment to fight for a Catholic Europe – under Habsburg leadership. The Habsburg emperor in Vienna had abandoned that goal following the Thirty Years' War, recognizing that a Catholic monopoly on power was untenable. Philip IV never fully grasped this insight. He bled his country for the sake of a superannuated idea, disregarding the new realities. The older he grew, the more often he withdrew to El Escorial, the palatial mausoleum where the tombs of his great ancestors were. For hours he would pray, taking refuge in religious mysticism. To bear so great a burden of personal failure as Philip IV must exhaust or defeat the powers of any man.

An unhappy couple

There is no other Velázquez painting in which the king and queen appear together. This is the only one; and here, though united, they are unclear, mere apparitions. The fact was that they had little in common. Princess Mariana was thirteen when she was sent from Vienna to Madrid to marry Philip. Then, she was a ruddy-cheeked, naïve girl who loved a good laugh, according to descriptions. One anecdote tells that, in one of the towns her procession passed through, local artisans wished to make her a gift of a hundred pairs of stockings. The Spanish lord chamberlain spurned the offer in outrage, declaring: "A Spanish queen does not have legs!" Where upon Mariana is said to have asked whether her legs were to be cut off in Madrid.

She did not lose her legs, but she lost very nearly everything else that makes the life of a young girl worth living. Corsetted into the strict ceremonials of life at court, she had nothing to do but make a majestic impression and, more important, bear an heir. Boredom, loneliness, homesickness, and illness in consequence of her never-ending pregnancies, transformed the lively girl into "that wilful, mulish German". Philip gave her his attention for only a brief period. He was 30 years her senior, and her uncle. He had married the daughter of the emperor in Austria in order to consolidate the alliance between Madrid and Vienna – in vain. By 1656,

the date of the painting, when the royal marriage was seven years old, hopes for an heir to the throne had still not been satisfied. Apart from the Infanta, Princess Margarita, Mariana bore an annual succession of stillborn babies. Subsequently she did give birth to two sons, who died in early infancy, and to a semi-retarded boy who in due course succeeded Philip IV on the throne of Spain, and put a miserable end to Habsburg rule in that country.

A well-bred Infanta

When this picture was painted, then, Margarita was the royal couple's only child. The fact that she was there at all, and enjoyed good health, encouraged hopes of a male heir to the throne. The periodic ebb and flow of that hope should be borne in mind if we are to understand the light upon the girl properly. Unusually in one of her age, the five-year-old is taking a jug while not so much as looking at the maid of honour. In this we can see the first fruits of a royal upbringing that emphasized self-control and awareness of one's station. Like most of the others in the picture, the Infanta is looking at the king and queen, whom we must imagine seated in front of the painting, as it were. Margarita is showing them how well she can already stand motionless, with a majestic manner. No doubt she already knows that a Spanish king or queen never laughs in public. This was something her mother had to be told, on the journey to Madrid. Her father was supposedly only ever seen to smile in public twice in his entire life.

The maids of honour (to either side of the Infanta) were chosen from the first families of the nobility. The one on the left is kneeling not in affection but because protocol requires her to. One had to kneel when proffering anything to a member of the royal family, and only very few were permitted to do so at all. Possibly it was the duty of the maid of honour on the right, who is dropping the hint of a curtsey, to fetch the jug: everything involved more than one person. When the queen ate, her food was passed down a succession of ladies-in-waiting of rising rank, the last kneeling as

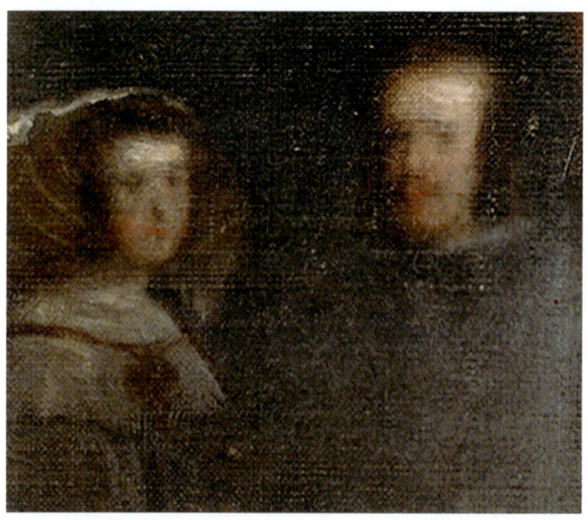

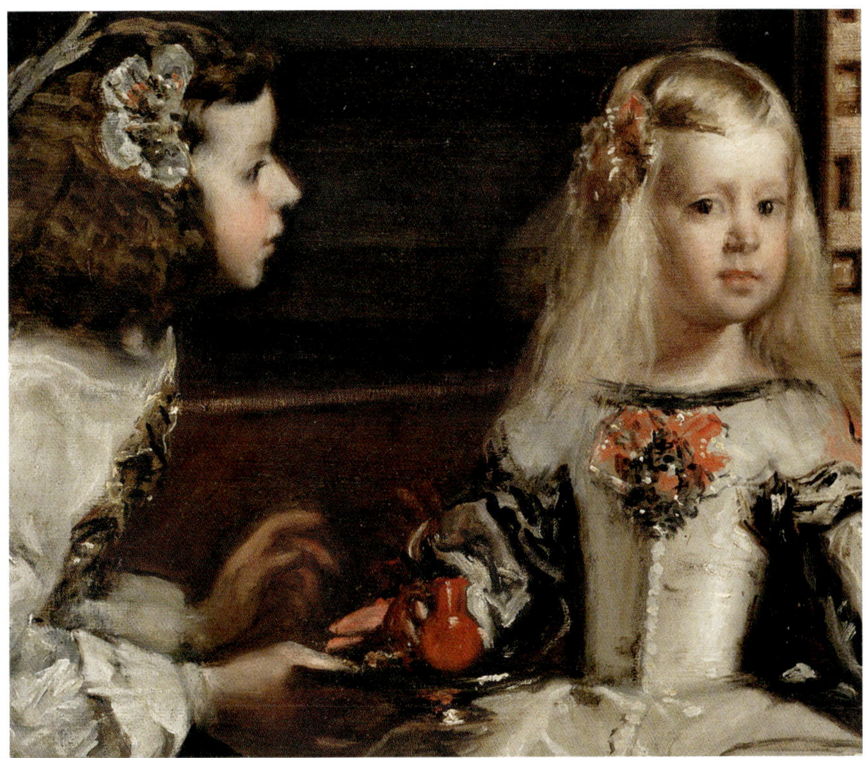

she proffered it to the queen. No other European court of the period was so riddled with protocol and ceremonials. The protocol even increased as the realm declined: when everything is going under, you cling to etiquette.

Living by rules could be literally lethal, as a story told of Philip's father, Philip III, shows. He was sitting in his study, near a coal-burning stove. The coal was giving off too much heat, too much "vapour". But the noble equerry whose office it was to tend the stove was nowhere to be found. No one else dared attend to the problem. That night, the king fell ill, and died within a few days.

The dog and the "monster"

So that the rigid protocol and everlasting tedium of the palace might be a little more bearable, court jesters and dwarfs were part of the household. No other court in Europe had as many as the Spanish.

Maria-Bárbola, the female dwarf, was from Germany; the young male dwarf at the far right, Nicolas de Pertusato, was from Italy. Both were members of the royal household. They had fool's licence, leading lives outside the court hierarchy, kept much as animals were. It is no coincidence that they are shown standing by the dog. Nor is it coincidence that Velázquez has allowed only one character in the picture a spontaneous gesture – the young dwarf is teasing the dog with his foot.

Dwarfs were numbered among the "monsters" kept at a court, along with those suffering from water on the brain, physical deformities, or mental deficiencies. Maria-Bárbola, with her old woman's head on a childish body, was by no means the worst specimen. These people were dubbed "the vermin of the palace". Others, of normal stature, felt superior and attractive in the presence of the dwarfs; the "vermin" raised their self-esteem. The Infanta and

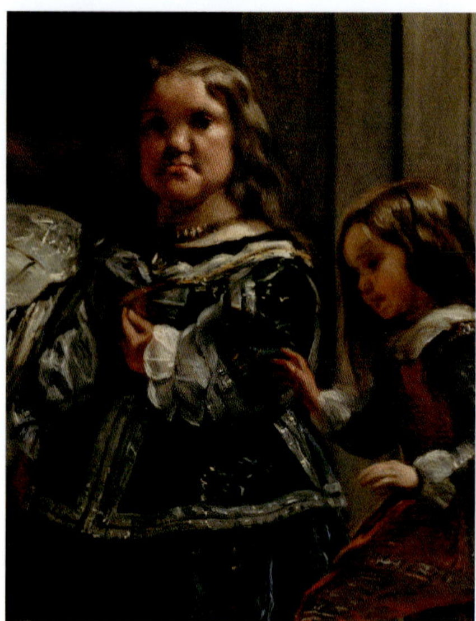

her maids of honour are all the more appealing in the presence of Maria-Bárbola.

The end of a painter

Velázquez is wearing on his chest the Cross of the Order of Santiago; but in 1656 he was not yet a member of the order. He was not inducted into it until three years later. First, a lengthy process had to establish the "purity" of his blood (no Jews or Moors were admitted); an exception had to be made because the details of his aristocratic ancestry were incomplete, an involved business; and more than a hundred witnesses had to confirm that he had never painted for money, but only for the delight of the king. Some other hand added the Santiago Cross at a later date.

It seems that membership of this exalted order, and thus climbing the human pyramid at the top of which stood the king, mattered at least as much to Velázquez as art. There are various pointers to this suspicion. The most telling is this: four years before painting *Las Meninas*, after having spent years performing largely honorific

duties at court, which allowed him time to paint, he applied for the position of marshal of the royal household. He was an experienced courtier and knew what this would entail. The position would be high in the hierarchy, but he would be responsible for an oppressive burden of paltry tasks. Velázquez had to see to the king's bed linen, the straw palliasses of the guards, and the reed matting that covered the floors in winter; he had to procure firewood and coal; he had to superintend cleaning staff; at public banquets he had to hold the king's seat. A note in the 1657 archives reads: "Diego Velázquez, marshal of the royal household, reports that he is owed his salary for one year, a sum of 60,000 reals. The palace sweepers and other servants dependent upon his office have ceased to work, and, what is worse, there is not a single real to pay for firewood for His Majesty's chambers."

Even more exhausting than his duties in the palace were the tasks Velázquez had to perform when the court undertook its many journeys, to summer palaces, to theatres of war, or (in 1660) to the French border, where Philip gave his daughter from his first marriage to Louis XIV, to be his bride. In July 1660 Velázquez wrote: "I have returned to Madrid, worn out by journeying all night and working all day." A month later he was dead. In the last years of his life he scarcely painted anything at all.

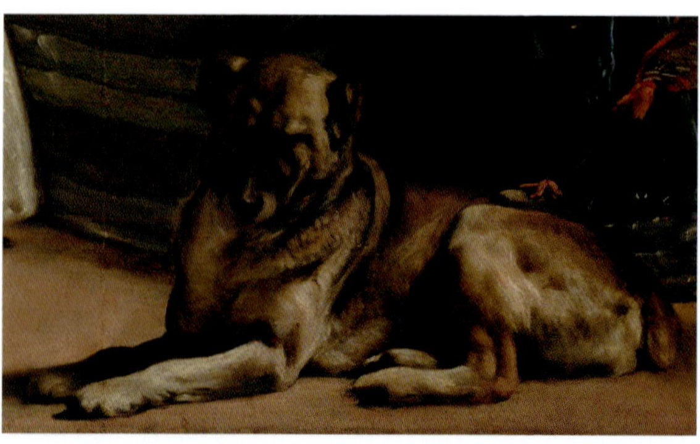

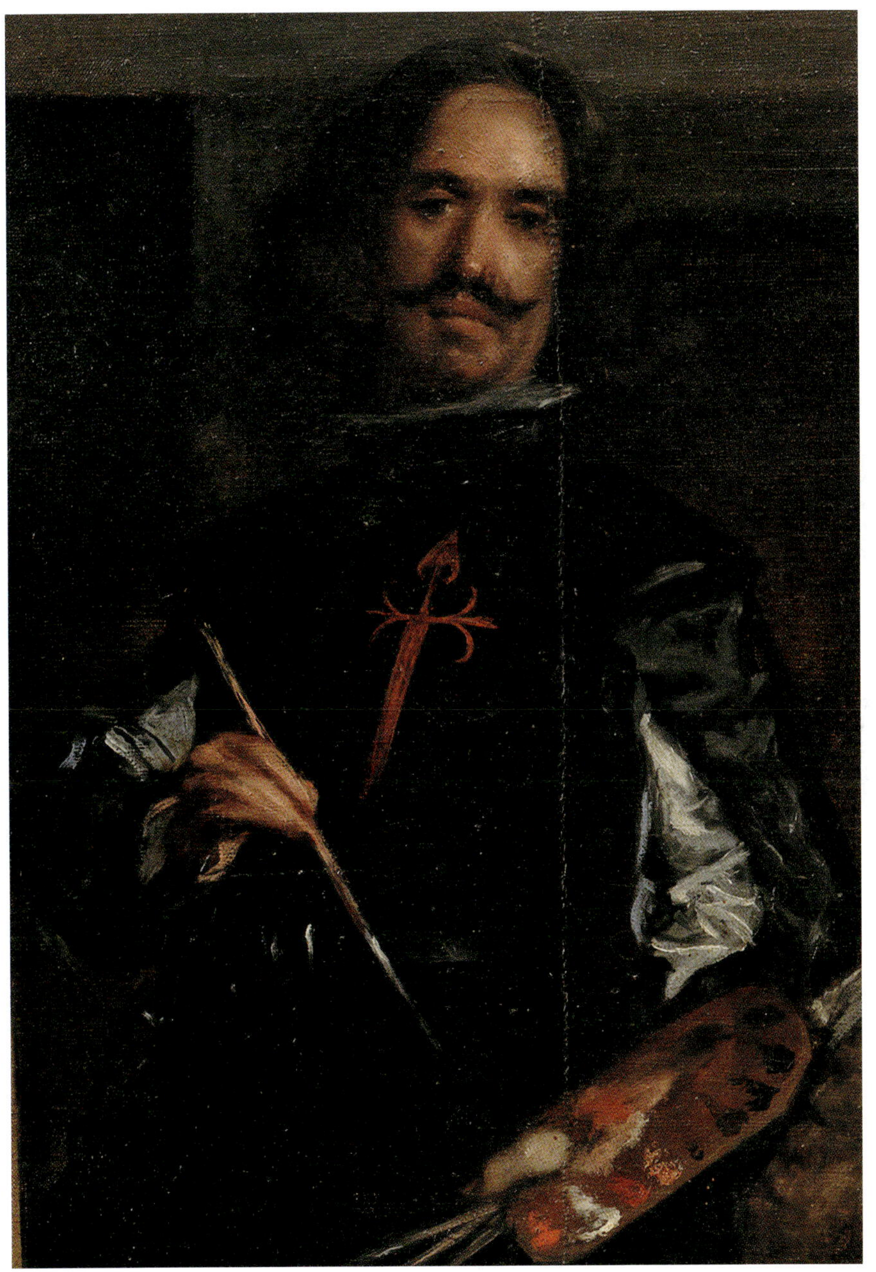

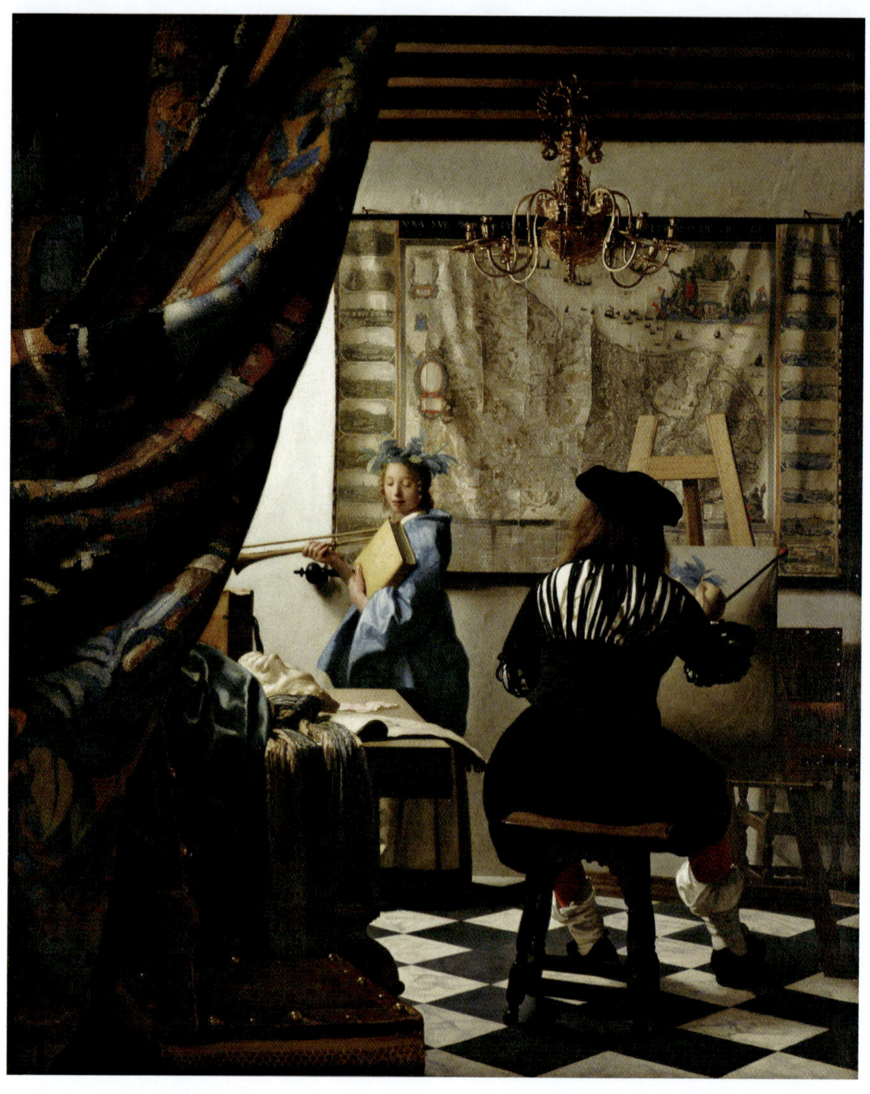

Johannes Vermeer (1632–1675)

The untold story

The Art of Painting, 1665/1666
120 x 100 cm, Vienna, Kunsthistorisches Museum

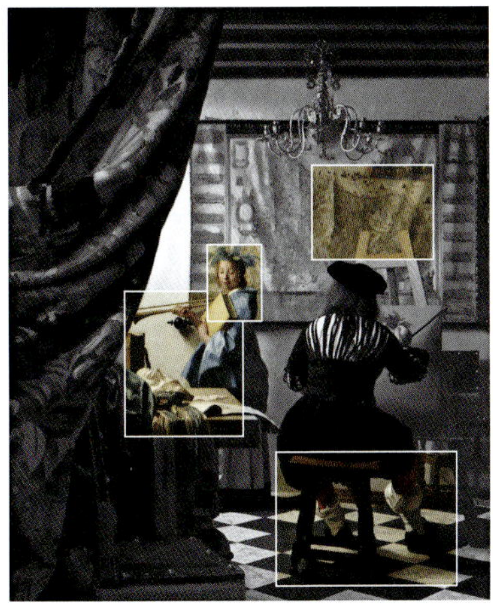

When we think of Baroque painting, we imagine splendour and exuberance, extravagant gestures and major events unfolding between Heaven and Hell, love and death. The artists of the Renaissance had imposed order on the visible world; the painters of the Baroque era sought life and found it in movement –princes were now portrayed on horses holding a levade with their forelegs tucked in, while Christ on the Cross was given a loincloth that billowed to one side.

The Baroque era lasted from approximately 1580 to 1750 and Johannes Vermeer's *Art of Painting*, produced around 1665, falls right in the middle, chronologically speaking. In terms of content, however, it does not belong. No wind blows into the room through the invisible window and the young woman is standing still; the only movement is in the fingers of the artist. All ostentatious splendour is lacking. Vermeer was not alone in practising this sort of anti Baroque style in the Netherlands: like him, many of his colleagues painted scenes from the daily lives of ordinary people. They paid homage to a society that had previously not been seen in art – or if so, then only so as to provide a lowly foil against which the upper classes would appear even more genteel. The Netherlandish painters depicted peasants bringing in the harvest, women at market, families ice skating, men in the inn. The list of their names runs from Pieter Bruegel the Elder right up to Jan Steen, who like Johannes Vermeer lived in Delft for many years. Their pictures exude a love of life as it is, painted without pretentiousness, and a love, too, of the reality that surrounded them and which they captured with the same fidelity and lack of pretentiousness.

The Netherlands trod a separate path, one that can be traced back to their particular political situation. They had been fighting against their overlords, the kings of Spain, for almost 80 years, during which time they had flooded parts of their own country in order to drive out the Spanish troops and paid massive ransoms to prevent their cities from being plundered. In Delft a powder magazine had exploded and destroyed an entire district of the city. In 1648 the Netherlandish provinces were officially divided under the terms of the Peace of Westphalia: those in the south remained under Spanish rule, while those in the north became the Netherlands, present day Holland. These northern provinces also included Delft.

For the artists in the north, this victory meant the loss of their traditional patrons, the Catholic Church and the Spanish-Burgundian aristocracy. The few remaining nobles had little money and their agents were viewed with suspicion in the newly founded republic. The middle-classes wanted government for themselves, and it would not have been opportune for members of the aristocracy to pose for self-congratulatory portraits. The Church found itself in a similar situation. The war with Spain had also been a war against the Catholic Church and its claim to autocracy. For Rome, art was an instrument of propaganda: the magnificence of its pictures was intended to illustrate the might of the Church. Christian worship in the North was dominated by Calvinism, with its focus upon the biblical scriptures. Anything that might distract from the proclamation of the Word was removed from the interiors of churches and in some places destroyed in outbreaks of violence. The only type of religious paintings left for artists were small-format devotional images for domestic use.

The artists sought a new clientele and found it in mayors, merchants, artisans who had grown prosperous and farmers. And just like the nobility before them, these new customers also wanted pictures that showed people of their own class, in rooms just like the ones they lived in. Life between middle-class walls: this was what Vermeer painted.

Maps as mural decoration

The light is falling from the left, where there must be a window. But it is not visible. The only indication that there is a world outside the walls of this room is the map. It hangs on the wall like a painting or a mirror. Maps were displayed as part of the interior décor in the Netherlands, as can be seen in the works of Vermeer and his contemporaries. They also appear in domestic inventories of the period. It can be deduced from sales catalogues that many maps were produced in two versions – one for practical use and one for decoration. The decorative map painted here by Vermeer also survives in a functional version which includes neither the twenty cityscapes illustrated in the two side margins nor the strips of text above and below. These additions form a sort of frame and give the map – which is made up of a number of single sheets pasted together – the semblance of a painting. The wooden rods along the top and bottom gave it stability. Such wall maps lent their owner the aura of a man who was interested in worldly things (and not just in what the Church had to say, be it from a Catholic or a Calvinist perspective). Those who studied maps were aware that knowledge of the world was constantly expanding: many regions, especially those inland areas far from the coast, were still just blank spaces. The Earth was believed to be a perfect sphere; its flattening at the poles was calculated by a scientist barely a decade after this picture was painted.

Vermeer's map still shows North on the right – and not at the top as would later become the convention – and the Netherlands prior to its political division. The ships drawn on the sea served to remind the viewer that the Netherlands

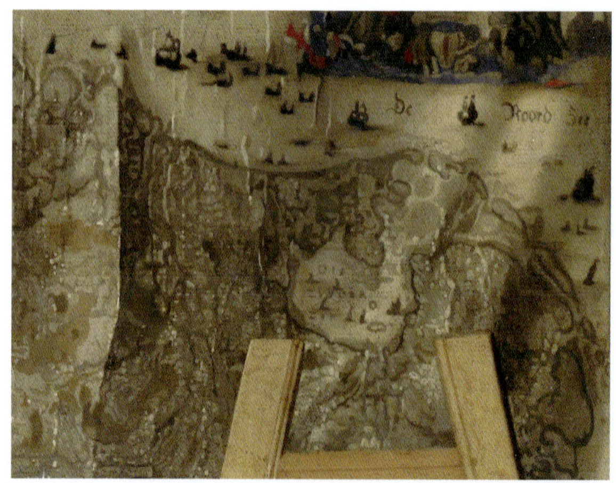

possessed the largest fleet of all the countries of Europe. In 1602 Dutch merchants had founded the United East Indies Company, which set up trading posts on Ceylon and Java and from there established links with China and Japan. Its ships brought back spices, tea and tobacco to Europe and much-envied wealth to the Netherlands.

In 1665 the English diarist Samuel Pepys inspected the hold of a captured Dutch ship, where he saw "the greatest wealth lie in confusion that a man can see in the world. Pepper scattered through every chink, you trod upon it; and in cloves and

nutmegs I walked above the knees: whole rooms
full. And silk in bales…" Shares were traded on
the stock exchange, allowing artisans and peasants
to participate in the profits and risks. There were
few emigrants, however. The Dutch had difficulty
cementing their colonial empire (in the way the
French and English were able to) since people who
emigrate are normally those who see no future at
home. For the citizens of the Netherlands, this did
not apply: they had their new republic, and relative
prosperity came to them.

The attributes of History

Johannes Vermeer was born in Delft in 1632 and died
there in 1675. As far as we know, he never left the
Netherlands. He lived a sedentary life. He painted
three or four pictures per year, but what he earned
from them was not enough to feed his wife and
fifteen children (even if four of them died young)
and for most of the time he was dependent upon the
help of his extended family. When he died, the works
left in the house were auctioned in order to satisfy
his creditors. Before an inventory could be drawn up,
his widow quickly took *The Art of Painting*, which
was still in the house, over to her mother's.

He was an at-home husband and a parlour
painter. Of the some 30 surviving pictures that are
attributed to him, around two thirds show private
interiors occupied by solitary female figures. One is
reading a letter, another trying on a necklace, a third
playing the guitar, a fourth opening the window, but
without the viewer being able to see outside. Vermeer also painted women out in the courtyard and
two or three views of his native Delft. One of these
(today in the Mauritshuis, The Hague) is considered
by many Vermeer connoisseurs to be one of his most
beautiful paintings. He could do the outside world
too, but the interior view was what he loved.

On rare occasions a man is also in the scene, for
example taking a glass of wine, as a music teacher or
in the present case as a painter. The young woman
whose laurel wreath he is capturing on his canvas is
posing as a Classical Muse. Since Vermeer's widow
titled the work *The Art of Painting*, she must represent the Muse of Painting, but in antiquity none
such existed. The Greeks and Romans considered
painting to be a craft, not an art. The artists of the
17th century took a different view. They invented a
new allegorical figure, whom Vermeer portrays as
Clio, the Muse of History, probably because history

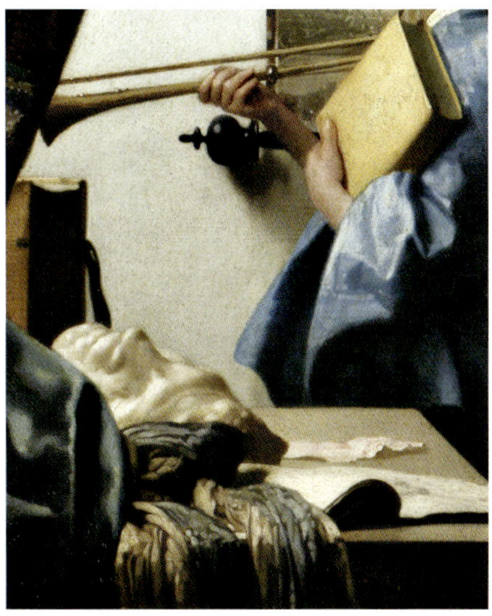

painting was considered the highest category of
art. The folio volume held in her arm and the one
on the table represent the writing of history, while
the trumpet announces heroic deeds and the laurel
wreath stands for fame. The plaster cast on the table
may be a reference to the past.

By far the largest object in this room is the curtain. Starting from the bottom left-hand corner, it
rises upwards, preventing us from seeing the full
length of the trumpet and covering almost half the
picture at the top. We use curtains today to protect
ourselves from the cold outside and from people
looking in, but in Vermeer's day rooms were heated
individually and curtains were hung over interior
doors to keep out cold draughts from other parts
of the house. They were part of the furnishings.
Vermeer painted this particular curtain, with its
floral motifs, on several occasions. It probably hung
in front of his studio. He thereby followed other
Baroque masters, who used heavy drapes to provide
their figures with a distinguished setting or simply
as a decorative means of filling an upper corner
of the canvas.

In Vermeer's painting, the curtain is not an ornamental accessory but part of the pictorial construction. Together with the chair in the foreground, it
forms an area of shadow. Only via the contrast provided by this area of shadow is the artist able to lend

luminosity to the weak light passing through the invisible window. The curtain's black edge focuses the viewer's attention upon everything that is to be seen further right, whereby contrast is not the only compositional factor at play. Unlike most other Baroque paintings, the curtain hangs not behind the figures but in front of them. It has been pulled back beyond the left-hand edge of the picture and we cannot see what is holding it in place. But it is gathered in such great folds that, even if we fail to realize it at first sight, we involuntarily take into account the curtain coming undone and falling, and thereby shielding not only the trumpet, books and table from our sight, but also the model dressed half in blue. The studio appears peaceful, but our view into it seems endangered.

Silence reigns in Vermeer's painting

Vermeer shows a painter at work. This was a common motif in the 17th century and testified to a heightened sense of self-esteem. In the past, painters who wished to celebrate their own craft or their own art invoked the figure of St Luke. According to legend, St Luke received an apparition from the Virgin Mary, who sat while he painted her portrait.

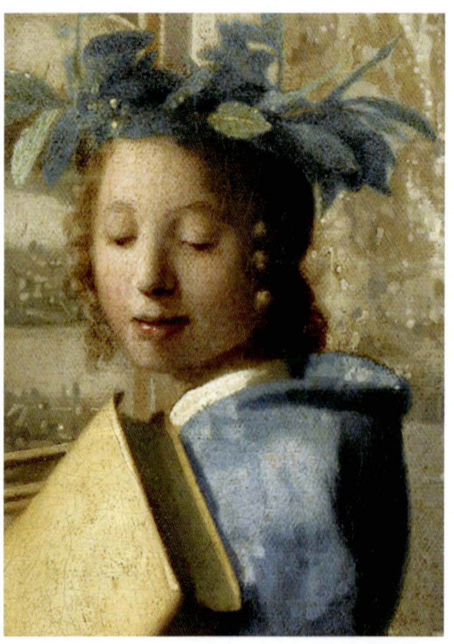

This led to him being chosen in the Middle Ages as the patron saint of painters and related professions. Delft, too, had its own Guild of St Luke, of which Vermeer was twice the head. In 1661 the guild moved into new premises and it is not impossible that Vermeer conceived his *Art of Painting* for these new rooms. But this is speculation. Vermeer does not take up the Christian tradition but paints a sort of Clio, or more specifically, a young girl who is posing as a Classical Muse. He remains in the real world and amongst the individuals whom he most liked to paint and who almost solely fill his pictorial world – women aged between about fifteen and 35, in other words always of childbearing age. His preferences were not purely artistic: his wife bore him fifteen children. But he paints no female nudes. He paints no old women and no old men, and even children appear only as incidental staffage figures. He was not interested in the variety of the forms of human existence. Class differences are limited to the occasional inclusion in his paintings of a serving girl.

Just as his interiors always appear clean and tidy, so his women, too, are always neatly dressed. Anything that does not fit the orderly bourgeois world, he leaves out. On just one occasion, as far as we know, as a 24-year-old, did he paint a cheerful prostitute with a man placing his hand on her bosom, whereby the bosom is covered. After this, nothing similar recurs in his work. Men and women in Vermeer's painting do not touch. Their hands occasionally stray close, for example when a music teacher passes his female guitar pupil a sheet of paper or when a cavalier extends his hand beneath that of a woman holding a glass of wine, but without actually touching her. Skin contact is avoided.

Everything in Vermeer is discreet and simple. The grandiose and heroic are absent, as is the disreputable. There is no indication of loud noise coming in through the window or out of the kitchen. We hear strains of music, and occasionally of conversation, but no more. For the most part, silence reigns. All movement remains barely discernible. In the case of the painter, for example, it can be detected in the fingers of the hand resting on the maulstick; in the girl, with her lowered eyelids. As a Muse who proclaims fame she should be looking triumphantly outwards, but Vermeer paints her as a real woman or as a girl not yet full grown. Perhaps she is supposed to be reading the pages of the book lying on the table in front of her. Maybe Vermeer

has portrayed the action of blink-
ing that moistens the eyeball.
Nor can we rule out the possibility that she does not wish to
return the painter's gaze. Vermeer
provides no further information.

The painter's legs

The human likenesses of art history are usually painted in such a
way that the viewer knows immediately what he is to think of the
sitter. Portraits of kings exude
dignity and power, portraits of the
bourgeoisie success and prosperity. Mary Magdalene grieves, while
lovers exude happiness. Vermeer
leaves us guessing; he veils his

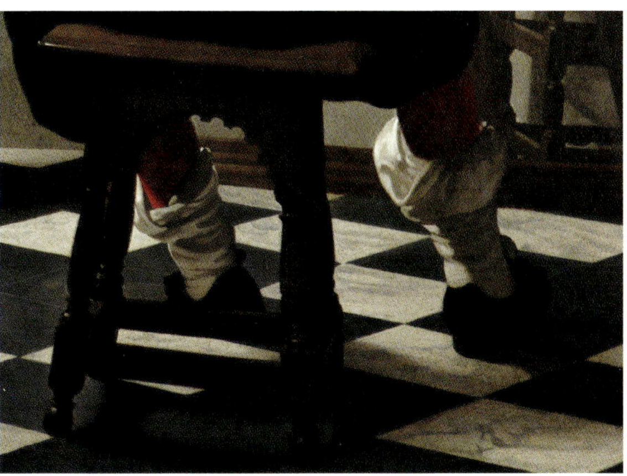

figures with discretion; it could be said that he
leaves this girl's beautiful face in peace. But she
is not alone. Of the painter we see a pair of broad
shoulders, the back of a full head of hair turned to
the left and a hand holding a slender brush. Whether
the doublet with its slashed back was still worn in
Vermeer's day or whether the painter was "historicizing" remains a matter of dispute.

Only his legs invite us to attempt to characterize the man. They are planted wide apart, which
could indicate a commanding manner, but from
the stockings that have slipped down his calves,
we might conclude that not all is in order. Do we
interpret the painter as a threat to the young thing
in the blue shawl? On the other hand, if you are sitting on a seat without arms or backrest, you have to
spread your legs in order to remain steady. That is
a working position, not an arrogant pose. And the
over-stockings bunched around the calves are not a
sign of negligence but were the height of fashion in
the Holland of the day. For a number of years they
were worn exactly as they are painted here and represented a cloth version of top boots – the civilian
equivalent of military footwear.

The painter's face remains hidden. But he is
physically very present, and where two people are
together, some sort of emotional relationship arises.
In this case it might consist of boredom on the one
hand and purely objective interest on the other. Or
it could be about power and opposition, secret
attack and mute supplication, flirtation and dalli-
ance. What is passing to and fro between these two,

without touch, without words, without musical
accompaniment, forms the real subject of this
painting – unpainted and untold. The setting
conveys a convincing impression of depth and of
fidelity to detail, and the map with its cracks and
undulations is nothing less than a showpiece of realistic painting. This cannot be said of all parts of the
painting, however. The left leg of the easel is missing, for example. It ought to rest on the stone tiled
floor somewhere near the painter's left stocking.
Clio's position is also entirely unclear: how has she
squeezed herself between the table and the wall?
If the floor tiles leave her no room, they nevertheless convey far greater spatial depth than the beams
below the ceiling.

Vermeer was a realist only where it mattered
to him. His interiors provide a setting that is sooner
imaginary. He designed them like self-contained
theatres inside which his protagonists, protected from
the outside world, act out their roles. And occasionally he paints his curtains as if they are about to drop
and thus divide us, too, from the stage. The audience,
the sympathetic viewer, might indeed think that
the real adventures of this world are perhaps sooner
to be found between familiar walls than on the
shores of distant oceans.

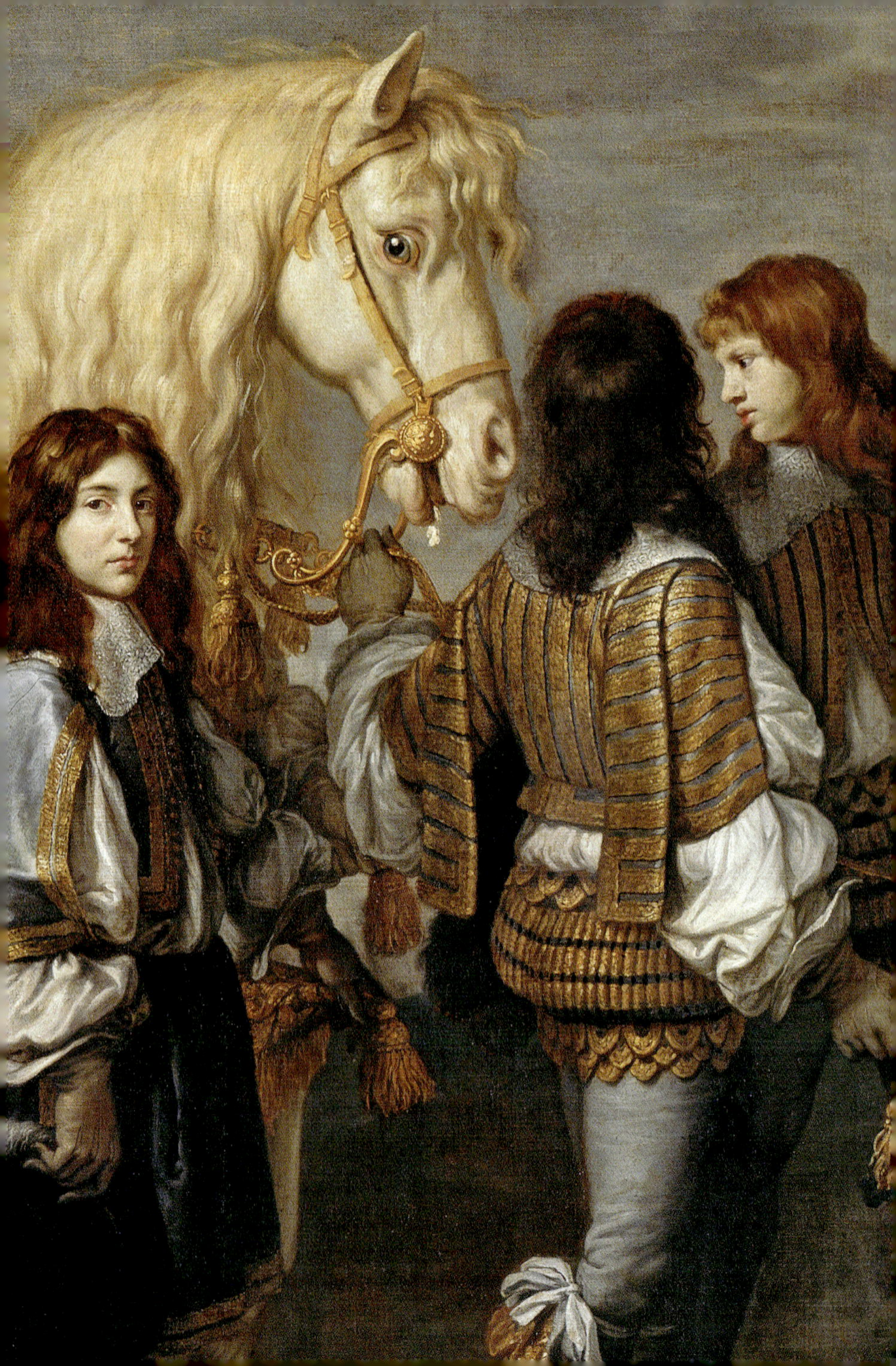

Charles Le Brun (1619–1690)

A careerist bathes in the Sun King's radiance

The Chancellor Séguier, after 1660
295 x 357 cm, Paris, Musée du Louvre

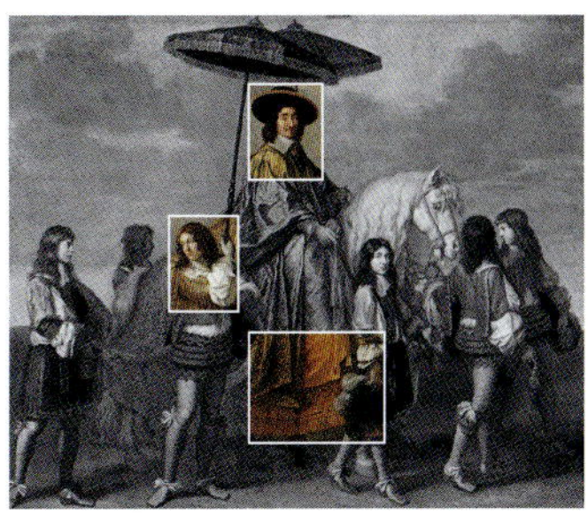

The aged Chancellor, shown on horseback with an entourage of young, fleet footed pages, cuts a dignified figure. In stiff robes of gold brocade, Pierre Séguier, Duke of Villemor, has all the makings of an idol or a Chinese mandarin. In fact, his swagger was the official pose of the Lord Chief Justice of France and head of that country's civil service in the mid-17th century; above all else, the grandeur of the portrait by Charles Le Brun (1619–1690) shows how Séguier wished the world to see him. The painting, measuring 2.95 by 3.57 metres, hangs in the Louvre, Paris.

Two violet silk parasols sway above Séguier's head. Conspicuous insignia of his rank, these also provided welcome protection against the scorching sun under whose burning heat Paris sweltered on that 26 August 1660. Indeed, so great was the heat, according to one contemporary chronicler, that the Chancellor, contrary to official protocol, was obliged to allow his entourage to don their hats now and then. The representatives of the state chancellory were participating in a procession that moved gradually through a Paris decorated with triumphal arches and obelisks, while at His Majesty Louis XIV's side, his newly-wed wife Maria Theresia celebrated her entry to the capital.

The 21-year-old French monarch and the daughter of Philip IV, King of Spain, had been married shortly before in a town at the border. The purpose of the match was to seal the peace between the two states. France had emerged victorious from the struggle for European hegemony which had marred relations between the two countries for almost 30 years, but it had emerged almost as exhausted as the vanquished Spain.

Before Louis XIV came of age, the nobility and parliament had endeavoured to augment their respective power at the cost of the monarchy, plunging the country into civil war in the process. France was bankrupt; there was a depression; the population had been decimated by invading armies, famine and epidemics were rampant. It was time for a change.

The orderly procession was intended as a sign to the cheering Parisians that a new epoch of peace and glory had dawned. It was led by the retinue of His Eminence, the all-powerful minister, Cardinal Mazarin, who had arranged the peace treaty and wedding. Next came the royal household and then the royal stables. Following them, in fourth place, came the representatives of the chancellory. Besides Séguier himself, counsellors, treasurers and secretaries, as well as those at the bottom of the hierarchy, the beadles and court ushers, all took part in the procession. Their appearance is captured in an ironic description of the event by Jean de la Fontaine, written in rhyming verse: "The sires of Council a splendid sight, in their midst was the Chancellor, a pillar of might, dressed from his head to his toe in brocade, while his retinue made the splendid parade …"

The parade was an impressive testimony to the power of a healthy monarchy. It was one of the first great manifestations of this kind to take place under the auspices of the young king. Louis XIV soon proved a master of the art of using pomp and circumstance for propagandistic purposes, in the service of absolutism as well as his own fame.

From burgher to duke

The Chancellor takes obvious pleasure in his appearance on this occasion. According to the anecdotal "Histories" of the writer and worst gossip of the 17th century Tallemant des Réaux, he was "greedy for glory", avaricious, and "driven by such extraordinary vanity that he was incapable of raising his hat to another person." Nobody attached quite so much importance as he did to "external appearances …, and he could hardly walk two feet without calling for his lackeys and an armed guard." Like most of his contemporaries, Tallemant was not particulary fond of the Chancellor.

Séguier, who held his exalted office for 37 years and exercised power ruthlessly, was one of the most hated men in France. In 1648, while civil war raged in Paris, he was obliged to hide from the people, who "wanted to tear him to pieces", in the lavatory of a private house until troops came to his rescue. The Marquise de Sévigné, famed for her correspondence, likened the Chancellor to the spiteful figure of Tartuffe, the hero of a comedy by Molière, first performed in 1664. It was not until 1672 when Séguier, with due composure, died the edifying death of "a great man" that the lady felt bound to remember his more positive qualities: piety, wit, a talent for oratory, and a remarkably good memory.

Séguier was undoubtedly an unusually gifted lawyer and administrator, abilities which rendered his services indispensible to two prime ministers in succession. As their "most loyal lackey", as Tallemant contemptuously put it, "a man who could swallow anything", he served

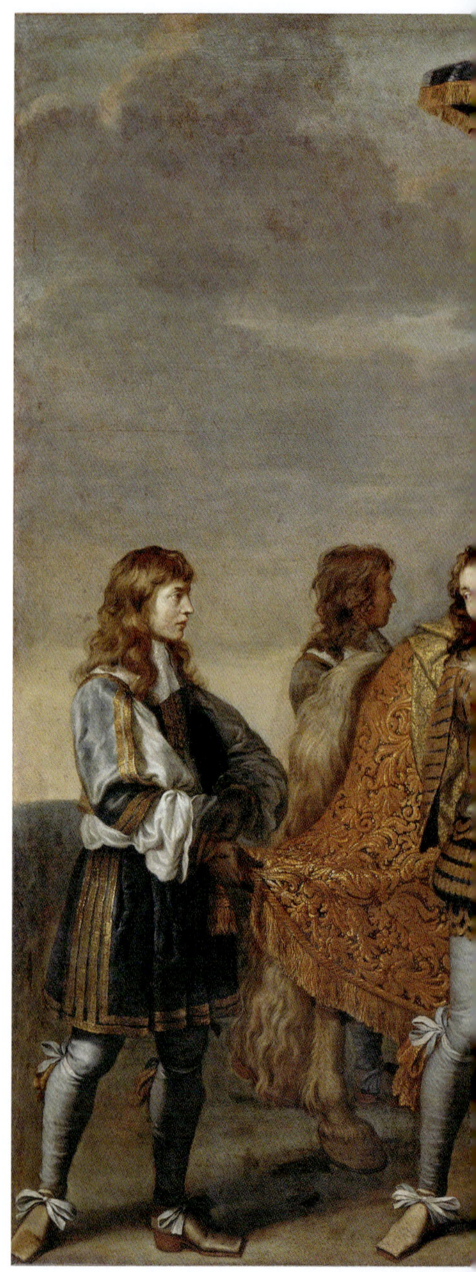

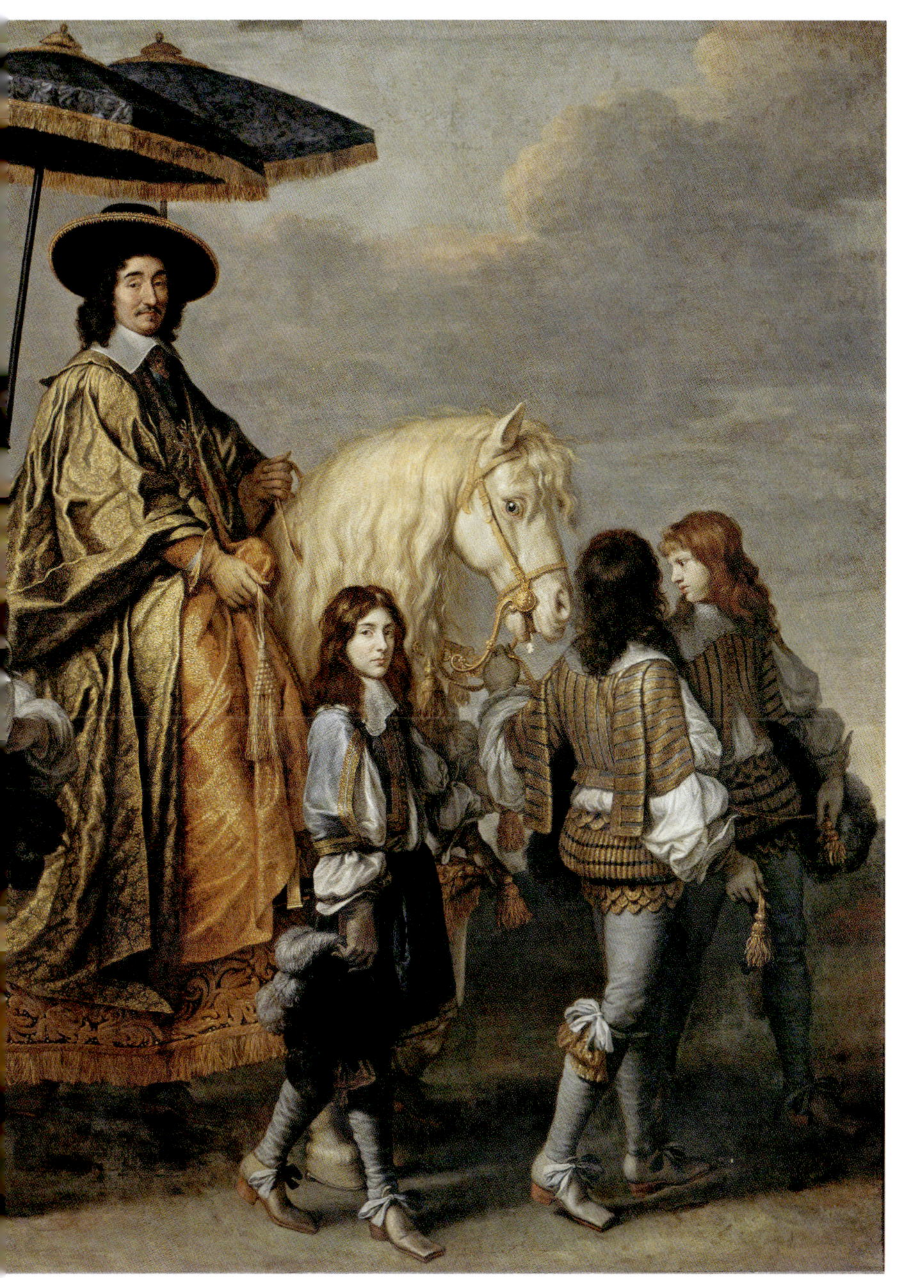

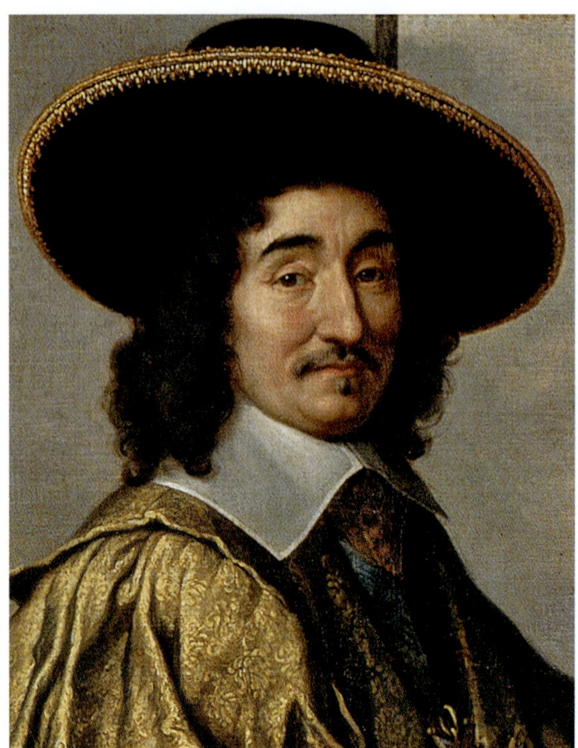

Cardinals Richelieu and Mazarin, who ruled France under Louis XIII and during Louis XIV's youth.

Like many 17th-century politicians, the Chancellor was from a bourgeois background. His family came from Parisian merchant stock and had slowly climbed their way up the administrative ladder by marrying into the right circles and using their money to buy profitable public positions. It was quite normal at the time for public offices to be bought and sold; such posts were seen as a form of capital investment, offering their owners both income and independence: civil servants could be neither transferred nor dismissed.

The Séguiers supported each other wherever they could. In 1612 one of his relations lent Pierre, born in 1588 and made an orphan early in life, 56,000 livres for the purchase of his first public office. He became Counsellor of Justice to the Parisian parliament. Then, using the dowry of his wife, the

daughter of a wealthy army treasurer, who brought 80,000 livres into their marriage, he purchased the office of President of the Parliament for the bargain sum of 120,000 livres. This allowed the career-minded public servant to recommend himself to Cardinal Richelieu by steering various political trials in an opportune direction. Having caught the minister's attention, Séguier rose through the ranks rapidly.

In 1634 Séguier's daughter was married to Richelieu's nephew. To be connected with the house of such a powerful man brought advantage and honour, but it also meant the ambitious burgher was obliged to provide a dowry of 500,000 livres, an enormous sum of money. In the following year he was made Chancellor – a non purchasable office – and remained so until his death. He survived, practically without damage to position or person, both the transition into Mazarin's service following Richelieu's death in 1642, and the confusion of the civil wars. In 1650 he was made Duke of Villemor. By his death in 1672 Pierre Séguier had amassed a fortune of over four million livres.

But the apotheosis of Séguier's career had come in 1639/40 when Richelieu, investing him with the power of a viceroy, sent him to Normandy at the head of a punitive force whose task was to subdue the revolt of the so-called *nu-pieds* – poverty stricken rebels who went barefoot – against the war tax. Suppressing the uprising with unprecedented ruthlessness, the Chancellor entered the conquered town of Rouen in triumph, surrounded by his generals and saluted by cannon. This time he was not part of another's entourage, but the most celebrated figure present.

The seal of state on a magnificent steed
Entering Paris with the royal couple, Chancellor Séguier was preceded by a magnificent steed sporting a feather headdress and decked with a

lilac silk shabraque. The horse was unmounted and carried a gold-plated casket containing the French seal of state, the instrument of Séguier's power. Four *chauffe-cires* (wax warmers) held silk cords to steady the casket. Their work, heating the wax and applying the seal, could apparently be done only by illiterate nobles. This was thought to prevent abuse of their office.

Drawn in ink and red chalk, the scene is one of fourteen drawings in Stockholm which show the entire chancellory department of the procession. They include a portrayal of Séguier's immediate group that is identical to the group in Le Brun's painting. The drawing mentions by name several of the counsellors and secretaries in the Chancellor's company. The same names are recorded in lists of chancellory employees.

The drawings probably formed part of a project commissioned by the Chancellor and carried out by one of Le Brun's collaborators. A display of chancellory personnel with its dignitaries dressed in the pomp of office must have been a welcome prospect to Séguier, with all his concern for external appearances. Whether the sketches were intended as preliminary studies for a series of prints or oil paintings is unknown. Only the Séguier group found its way onto canvas.

It was the Chancellor's solemn duty to preside over the application of the seal – given such lavish pride of place in the drawing – to royal correspondence, decrees and documents. Without the seal, sentences, pardons and elevations to noble rank remained null and void.

If necessary, the Chancellor could refuse to apply the seal. He was answerable only to the king, who had appointed him for life. He combined the functions of a viceroy and Chief Justice, and as head of the civil service he also had executive powers. However, his main function was as the king's official spokesman.

"I have come to bestow my good will upon the parliament. The Chancellor will tell you everything else." Thus Louis XIV's dignified utterance on the occasion of his first political appearance in 1643, following the death of his father. He was four years old.

Séguier, together with the queen mother and Mazarin, held a seat in the regency council. He occasionally took a personal interest in the infant king's upbringing. "My Lord the Chancellor was here", writes one courtier in his memoirs of 1651, "to see the king at his studies. He was highly satisfied and exhorted the king to continue."

Ten years later, Séguier's condescension towards the king would have been considered quite inappropriate. The day after Mazarin's death, the king, though previously so submissive, threw off the shackles of patronage. On 10 March 1661 at seven o'clock in the morning, according to one report, he called for his ministers and addressed the Chancellor in a tone worthy of a man who was "Lord over himself and all the universe": "My Lords, I have asked you to assemble here to let you know that … the time has now come for me to govern my own affairs. You shall come to my aid with your council should I require it … I demand of you, indeed I order you, Lord Chancellor, to put my seal on nothing, and to do nothing in my name, until we have spoken of the same, but to act solely at my command."

The old Chancellor continued to serve the young king for several years before his death. On his deathbed, he asked his confessor to convey his undiminished loyalty to Louis XIV and had his seal returned to the king: it was Séguier's last official act.

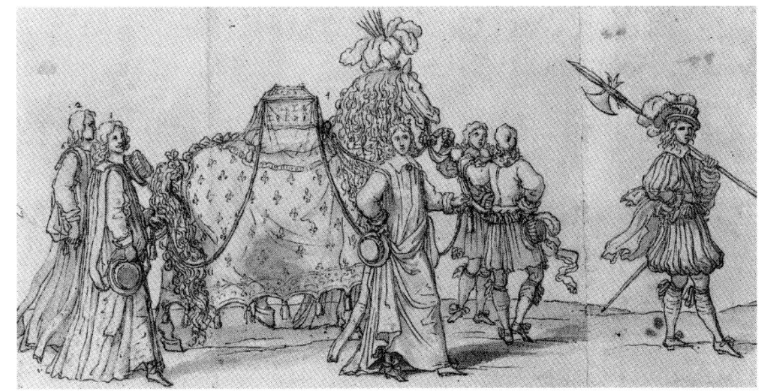

Comparative illustration:
François Chauveau or Charles Le Brun. From the cycle: *Chancellor Séguier at the Entry of Louis XIV into Paris*, after 1660
Stockholm, Statens Konstmuseer

Artist with a parasol

The elegantly poised figure in shining white linen holding the parasol is said to be Le Brun's self-portrait. Showing himself in the Chancellor's company was realistic enough; the son of a Parisian sculptor, he had enjoyed Séguier's patronage since his childhood. The arts and sciences not only fell under Seguier's official brief, he was also a patron of the arts in his own right – hoping, no doubt, to "have his praises sung", griped Tallemant.

The Chancellor had become acquainted with the talented young lad in 1631 or 1634, at an early stage in the latter's career. He provided lodgings for him at his town palace, where he had also set aside a number of stipends for writers. He sent Le Brun to study under well-known masters and was soon able to show his work at court: a drawing, executed in 1638, celebrating Louis XIV's birth, and an allegory dedicated to Cardinal Richelieu. For his patron, the young artist painted mostly altarpieces and portraits. In 1642 Séguier sent him to Rome, equipped with letters of recommendation, expenses and a commission to make copies of Raphael's works.

Three years later, defying the orders of his patron, Le Brun returned to France. He had shown signs of insubordination before, during the years of his apprenticeship in Paris. However, once back in Paris he remained obedient, gradually adapting his personality to the dictates of an era in love with order, in which artists were required to show discipline and good manners.

Le Brun led an exemplary life. He was pious and diligent, showing little sign of passion, and none of vice. Women (other than his wife) had no place in his life or work, to which he dedicated himself assiduously. His career was favoured by the timely death of two important painters and rivals: Simon Vouet (1590–1649) and Eustache Le Sueur (1617–1655). As soon as the Sun King climbed the throne, they left the stage to Le Brun without a struggle.

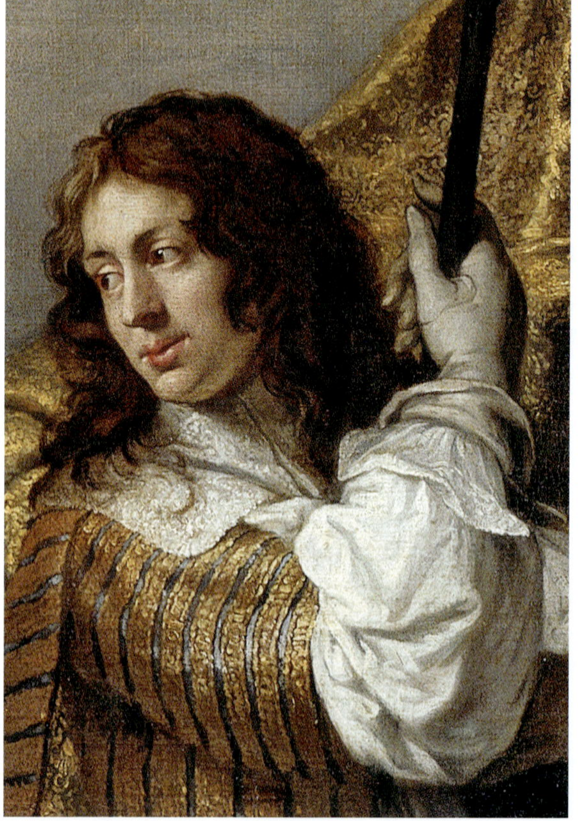

Le Brun had caught the monarch's attention through his work on the palace of the Minister of Finance, Fouquet, at Vaux. The artist was responsible for the entire decorations there, from frescos to fountains in the park and displays of fireworks on festive occasions. Louis ordered the artist to paint a scene for him from the life of Alexander the Great. Le Brun executed the large heroic work to the full satisfaction of the monarch, painting it in front of his very eyes. From that time onwards he enjoyed the king's favour and worked to spread his sovereign's fame.

However, Le Brun did not forget Séguier, his first patron. Though the exact date of his

portrait of Séguier entering Paris
is unknown, Le Brun designed,
following the Chancellor's death
in 1672, the decorations for a
church in which Parisian artists
held a memorial mass in the
Chancellor's honour. Madame de
Sévigné was present, and reported
as follows: "The mausoleum was
as high as the dome itself, decorated with a thousand candles and
several statues made up to honour
the man … with the insignia of
his high rank … the judge's cap,
ducal coronet and order … They
really were the most beautiful
decorations imaginable."

If Pierre Séguier really did
attach so much importance to having "his praises
sung", then he could not have done better than invest
in Charles Le Brun.

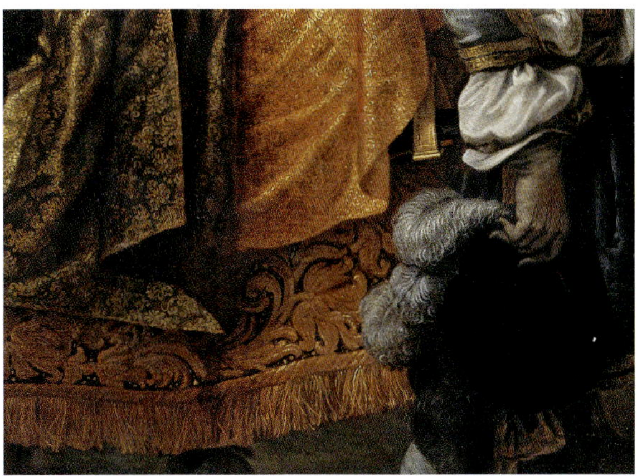

Fashion as royal propaganda

To "lend distinction to the highest ranking courtiers",
according to the philospher Voltaire (1694–1778),
Louis XIV personally designed "a blue doublet,
embroidered with gold and silver. To be invited to
wear this piece of clothing was considered a great
honour, an occasion for pride, and it was as highly
coveted as an order on a chain."

Elements of fashion such as patterns and colours, especially gold, assumed a special value under
the influence of the young monarch. To help
establish his absolute authority as the Sun King,
he subordinated all style, form and design, as well
as politics and etiquette, to the interests of his
personal propaganda.

Le Brun soon emerged as the dominant figure
among the group of artists employed by the king.
He brought discipline to the art world, turning
the Academy of Fine Art, previously little more
than a loose association of artists, into a tightly
knit state organization. The Academy assumed a
monopoly over the teaching of art; it awarded stipends, prizes and state commissions, imposing strict
stylistic orthodoxy. Art, shown to be reducible to a
universally applicable set of precepts, was required
to subject itself to a doctrine of clarity and ration-
ality explicit in the rules of French Classicism.
For twenty years, Le Brun, the chancellor of the
Academy, kept a dictatorial eye over the strict observance of these rules.

Le Brun was also responsible for the mass-
production of artworks and artefacts. Under his
direction, 50 painters and 700 craftsmen worked
at the Royal Gobelin Factory, which opened in
1663. Here, not only tapestries, but frescos, wood
panelling, furniture, vases, locks and coaches were
made to Le Brun's design. Produced to the highest
standards and showing excellent taste, these
artefacts were intended for Versailles and for export.
Le Brun was the arbiter of taste in all matters of art,
design and cultural management; he created
Louis XIV's official court style, which, like the
French language and French fashions, quickly
spread to the rest of Europe.

All this left Le Brun with little time for his own
painting. His great masterpiece, the decoration
of Versailles – he also influenced the architecture of
the palace and gardens – proved ephemeral. He was
forced to stand by and watch as furniture and vases
of silver and gold which he had designed were
melted down to provide funds for Louis' wars. The
unique synthesis of art and design that was Versailles
may have existed to perfection only at such moments
when, paying homage to the "Roi Soleil", courtiers
perambulated in the galleries to the music of
Jean-Baptiste Lully. Le Brun, who had devoted his
life to his sovereign's fame, was permitted, upon
his elevation to the nobility, to include Louis XIV's
personal emblem in his coat of arms: a resplendent,
golden sun.

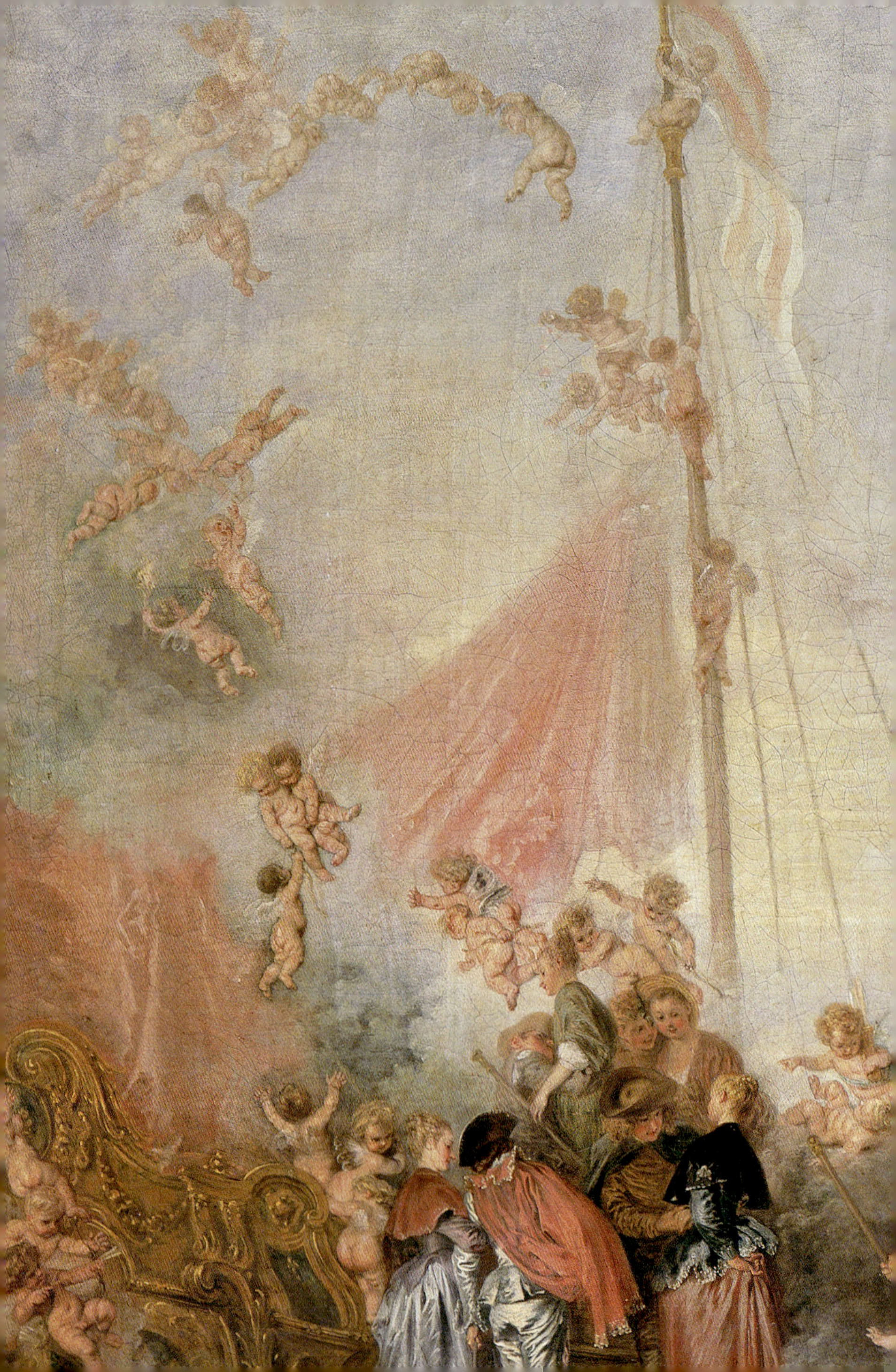

Antoine Watteau (1684–1721)

Flirting on the shores of the island of Venus

Pilgrimage to Cythera, c. 1719
129 x 194 cm, Berlin, Schloss Charlottenburg,
Stiftung Preußische Schlösser und Gärten, Berlin-Brandenburg

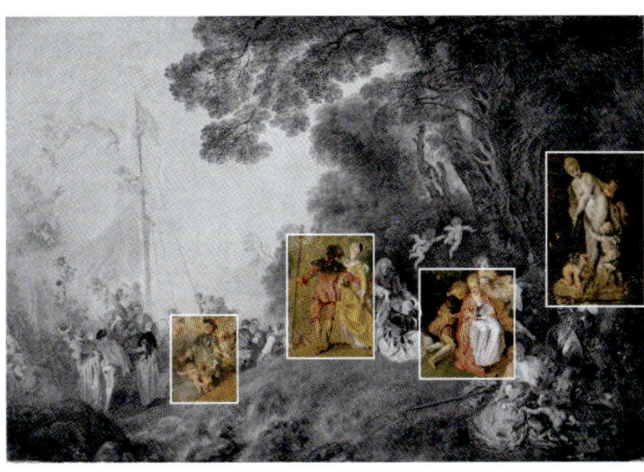

This painting was bought by King Frederick II of Prussia. He was one of those hard-working men who were especially captivated by Watteau's fantasies of a carefree life of ease, dedicated solely to the delights of love.

In 1983 and 1984, an offertory box stood in front of one of the most popular paintings in Berlin. The city's residents were invited to make a donation to ensure that Antoine Watteau's *Pilgrimage to Cythera* would stay in Charlottenburg palace. The work was namely only on loan from its owner, Prince Louis Ferdinand of Prussia, who now wished to sell it for a price of DM 15 million. To try to prevent the precious painting from going abroad, Bonn and Berlin each pledged DM 5 million – if the remaining third could be raised from private donations. The citizens of Berlin dug deep into their pockets, and thus paid a second time for a painting originally bought by the Prussian king Frederick II – with the thalers collected in taxes from the citizens of Prussia.

The much-loved work tells a charming tale of the pleasurable aspects of love. Gentlemen toss roses into ladies' laps, whisper sweet nothings into their ears, and accompany them to a boat. Watteau paints a ballet of seduction and the willingness to be seduced. Surrounded by putti, the magnificent barque is sailing for Cythera – an island south of the Peloponnese, and one of the places where, according to ancient legend, Venus is supposed to have stepped onto land after she had sprung from the foam.

Watteau painted the embarkation for Cythera at least three times. The first, somewhat stilted version is dated 1710 and hangs in the Städel Institute in Frankfurt. The present Berlin picture was executed in 1718 or 1719 for a private client. It is a slight variation upon a second version, which Watteau submitted as his presentation piece to the Royal Academy of Arts in Paris, of which he became a member in 1717. This Academy version now hangs in the Louvre.

The age of feasts of courtship
On the document testifying to Watteau's acceptance into the Academy, the title *L'embarquement pour Cythère* is crossed out and replaced by *La fête galante*. Over the preceding years, the *fête galante* (feast of

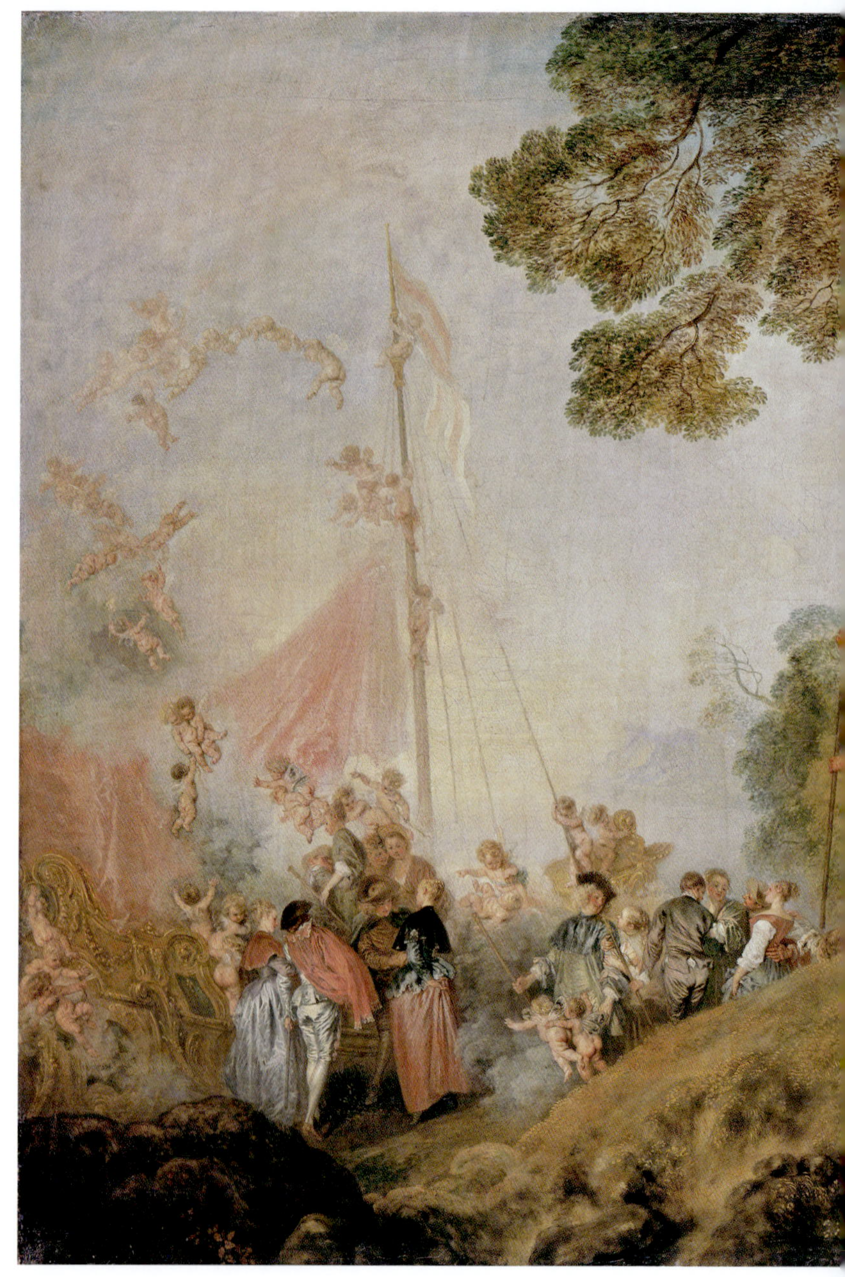

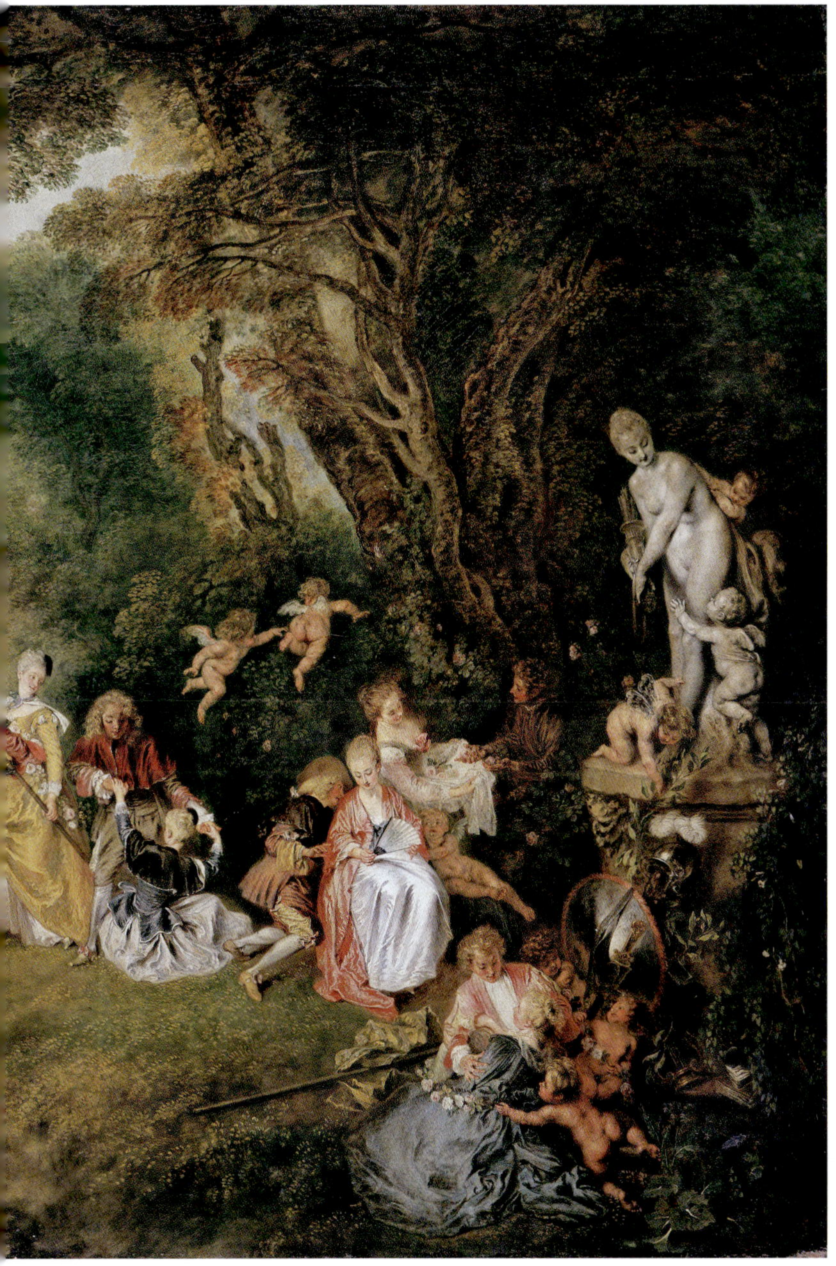

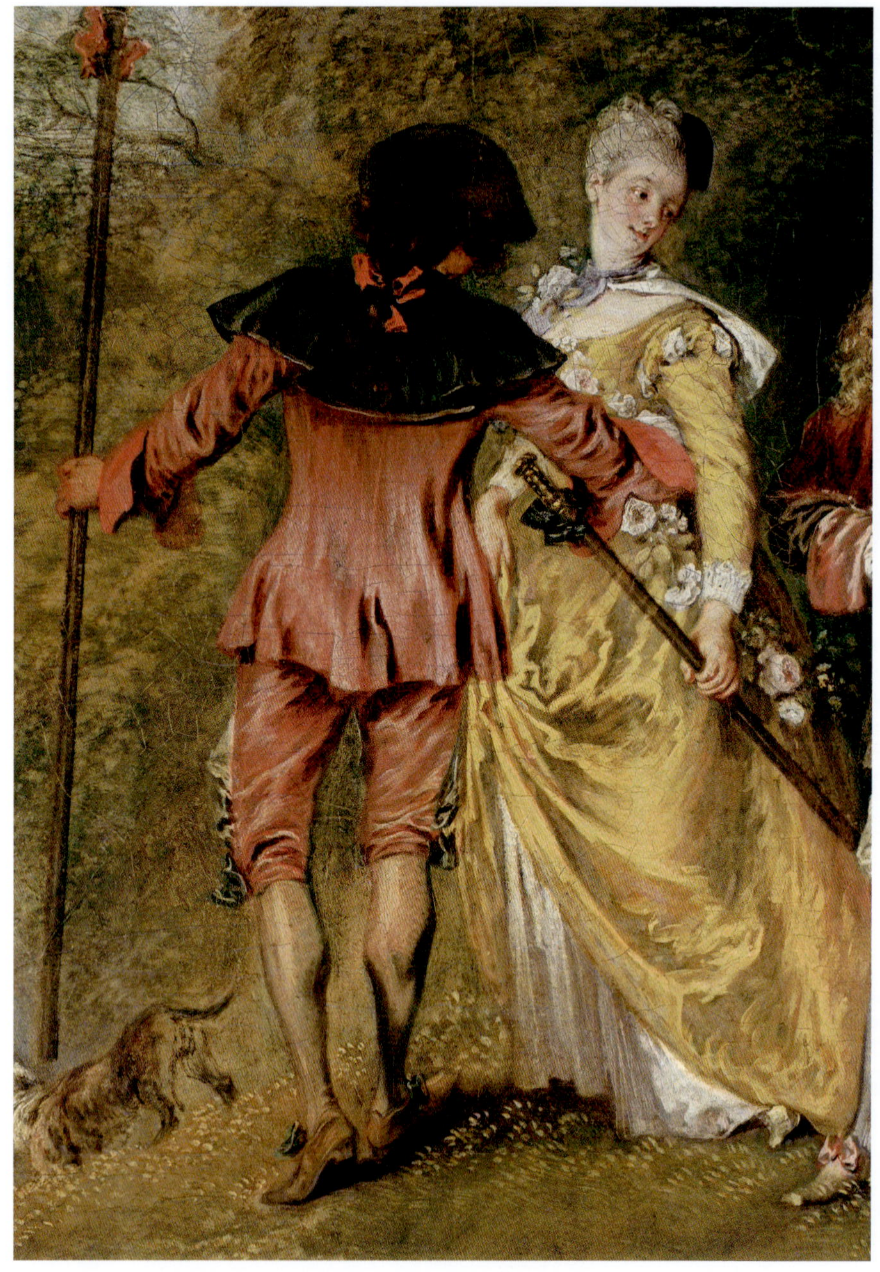

courtship) had become a genre in its own right, like history painting and still life. It was a genre which Watteau himself had invented and with which he had made his name. He had already produced over 50 "feast of courtship" paintings, most of them employing a small format, unlike the Paris and Berlin *Cythera* canvases. They all depict handsome young men and women who are chatting, dancing, flirting and making music. They are mostly dressed in a rustic style or in the costumes of the Italian *Commedia dell'arte*. In the present painting they are carrying long pilgrim's staffs, for they are making a pilgrimage to a sanctuary of love.

These pictures are all set in cultivated parkland, from which all the cares of daily life seem excluded. This was far removed from the surroundings in which Watteau grew up: he was born in 1684 in Valenciennes, a long way from Paris, and his father was a roofer. Determined to be an artist, the young Watteau arrived in Paris without money or belongings in 1702. He found a job with a theatre painter and then with a man who decorated the walls of houses with ornamental designs and figures. Watteau not only learned his craft, but also learned how to tap into the fantasies and longings of theatre goers and well-to-do Parisians – the tastes of a new age.

These were the years following the death of Louis XIV, who had reigned as the Sun King for 72 years, who had cultivated in Versailles an artistic style dedicated to showy self-glorification, and who during his latter years had ruined the country with expensive – and unsuccessful – wars. When he died in 1715, the French breathed a sigh of relief.

Philip II, Duke of Orléans, took over as regent on behalf of the five-year-old heir to the throne, and moved the seat of government from Versailles to the much livelier Paris. His time in office, the Régence, lasted from 1715 to 1723, years which corresponded with Watteau's chief period of activity.

The epoch brought the arts a new breed of customer: hard-working members of the middle classes who made their fortunes in trade and industry. After a period of stagnation, the economy boomed; the new regent brought peace, and the country's wealth was no longer swallowed up by the military. As money started to circulate more freely, so the rigid class society became more permeable. The newly rich middle classes copied the lifestyle of the aristocracy, built themselves splendid houses and

furnished them with luxury goods and art – including small-format oil paintings such as those executed by Watteau: fantasies of a carefree life of ease.

Ease and intimacy also flourished in the theatre, and what Watteau was to painting, the dramatist Pierre Carlet de Chamblain de Marivaux (1688–1763) was to the stage. His first comedy, performed in 1720, was entitled *Arlequin poli par l'Amour*. It tells the story of the young, greedy, butterfingered Harlequin, who is "polished" – in other words, civilized – by Love and taught gallantry, the "nobility of spirit and manners".

The idea that love should inspire attentive, sparkling exchanges between the sexes finds its echo in Watteau's *Pilgrimage to Cythera*. The painter shows nothing of the pleasures of the senses, and permits no more than fleeting or delicate contact between his figures.

The lightness of being

The bodies of the young people are carefully clad in the latest fashions – only Venus and the swarm of pink putti are shown naked. They embody sensual love; Watteau thus employs figures from mythology to indicate the ultimate goal of gallantry and flirting.

It is odd that the painter should include Venus in the scene, considering that the boat is supposedly waiting to depart for her island. He places her statue in the shade of the trees, like a goddess of nature. Are we perhaps already on the island of Cythera, with the pilgrims preparing to return home? While this much debated question is probably as old as the painting itself, whether we are at Point A or Point B is not important here. What matters is the closing of the distance between the couples. Watteau documents this process in several stages: some couples are arm in arm, while in other cases the gallant has placed his arm around his beloved's waist or his head in her lap. There are intimate whisperings, exchanges of flowers, and everywhere the industrious putti are pushing and pulling. Watteau's paintings celebrate the journey between men and women and the desire to embark upon it. In love, according to a Parisian opera of 1705, "the pleasures of the voyage are almost worth as much as those of the port".

Like the repetition with which Watteau executed these studies of courtship, the faces of his figures all look very much the same. All appear smooth powdered; personalized traits are rare. The painter

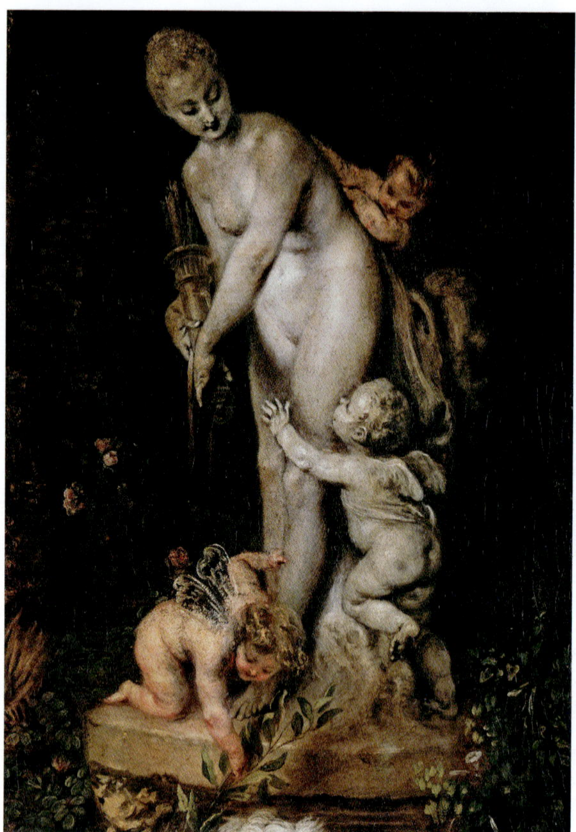

enjoyment of love amidst a company of willing followers.

Almost every French writer of the 18th century commented on this fleeting form of love – whether praising it in the aria that places the joys of the voyage above those of the port; whether summarizing it more objectively in the formula *"On se plaît, on se prend, … on se quitte"* (one takes one's pleasure, one takes each other, one leaves each other); whether dismissing it sarcastically in the words: "Love … is simply the exchange of two fancies and the contact of two skins"; or whether with a leaning towards paradox, as for example when Marivaux describes love as "a sickness of the soul which makes the body healthy".

Neither Watteau nor Marivaux tackled the serious social or philosophical issues of the day, for which both were taken correspondingly to task. Voltaire, the great thinker of the Enlightenment, said of Marivaux what he might equally have said of Watteau – namely that he had spent his life "in weighing trifles on scales made of cobwebs". The criticism, which was meant unkindly, describes the entire culture of the Régence, that brief, happy entr'acte in the history of France.

is concerned not with individuals but with a collective fantasy of the lightness of love, and the lightness, too, of being.

The same can be said of Marivaux, Watteau's literary counterpart. Both, painter and writer, consciously distanced themselves from the high tragedies of the Louis XIV era, in which the only type of love considered worthy of artistic treatment was the grand passion which led to catastrophe.

Every epoch had its own image of love – in the second half of the 18th century, for example, it was inconceivable without tears, extravagant effusions and confessions delivered amidst heartrending sobs. Between the tragic pathos of the past and the emotional wallowings of the future, however, Watteau painted a Venus who celebrates the carefree

Education through love

A quite different picture of love is painted by the letters of the highly moralistic Liselotte of the Palatinate. Unhappily married to Philip I of Orleans, the brother of Louis XIV, she lived at the court of the Sun King and was horrified by the "atrocities that go on here. I am amazed that the whole of France does not go down like Sodom and Gomorrah." Of her son, the regent, she wrote: "as for my son and his mistresses, they are hustled in and out without the least gallantry." She makes no mention of "nobility of spirit and manners" or the joys of the voyage sung on the stage.

The Régence was probably no more liberal on matters of sex, however, than the strict regime of Louis XIV and the bigoted companion of his old age, Madame de Maintenon. It was simply that under Louis, libertinism was not the court style. The regent, on the other hand, publicly embraced it. The fact that the finer details of gallantry thereby tended to be skipped over only meant that these were trumpeted all the louder on stage and in art. Gallantry also dictated an important part of women's education. Girls from the aristocracy and the well-to-do bourgeoisie only learned the bare essentials of writing and arithmetic, but made up for this by honing the agility of their bodies and minds. They knew how to dance, how to play and sing, how to use a fan and how to discuss pictures

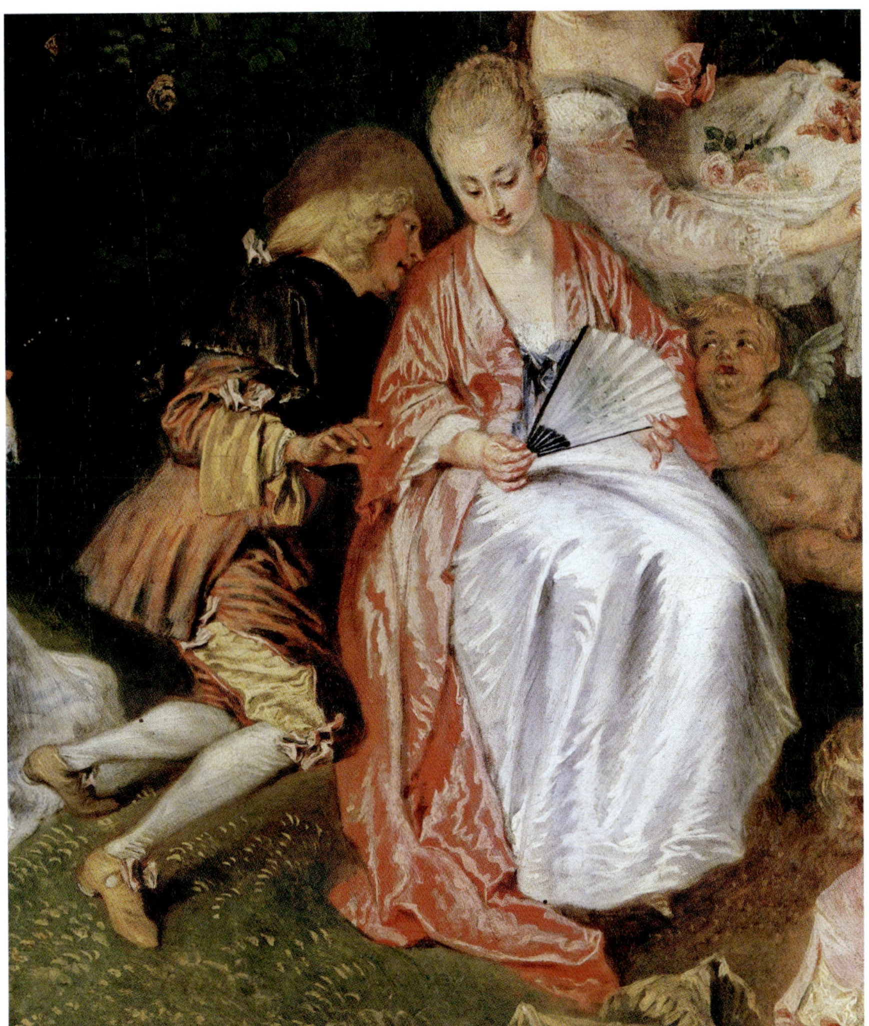

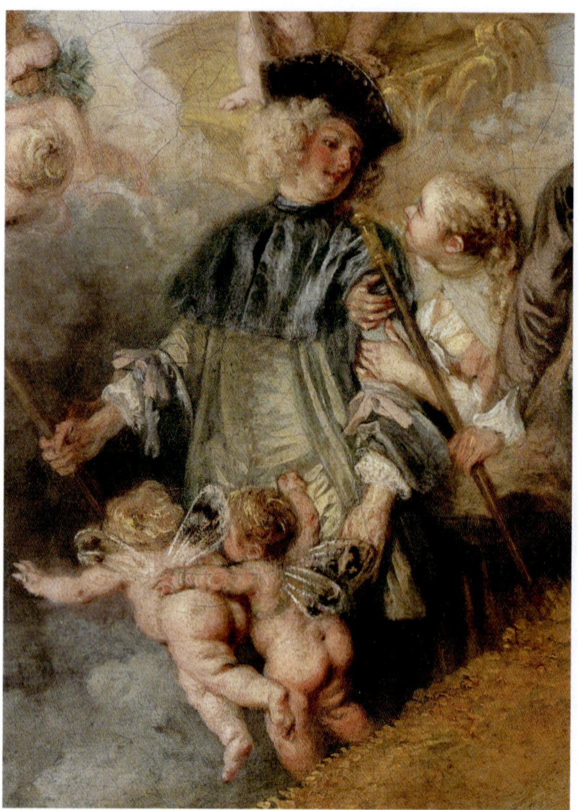

only needed to tell a lady she was pretty three times: the first time she thanked you, the second time she believed you, and the third time she rewarded you.

Alongside the woman who educates a man through love, there are others who play the less ideal roles of accomplice and, ultimately, victim. "To love one's wife", reported Liselotte of the Palatinate, "has gone quite out of fashion". In his comedy about the harlequin who is "polished" by love, Marivaux observes: "When a woman is faithful, she is admired; but there are modest women who are not vain enough to want to be admired … less glory and more pleasure, that's the spirit!"

In the wake of the general relaxation in the moral code, perhaps the odd husband even allowed his wife the freedom to take a lover – but he naturally retained the power to put her inside a nunnery for the rest of her life on grounds of adultery.

Watteau was praised not simply for his new, delicate palette, which anticipates the innovations of the Rococo, and for his rich nuances of body language, which can be studied so clearly in this picture. He was equally admired by his contemporaries for his representation of Nature. Even his park landscapes testify to the spirit of the Régence: forgotten are the geometrical paths, flower beds and hedges of the Sun King's gardens at Versailles. Watteau's parks are "raw and uncombed", but at the same time embellished with artificial elements, such as statues, grottoes and little temples. The mossy ground offers a soft cushion; there is neither wind nor rain, and few signs of the seasons. These are salons held within unspoilt, friendly Nature, an ideal setting for escapist feasts.

Whether Watteau himself ever took part in a *fête galante* is not known for sure. It is possible, but not certain, that he received occasional invitations to attend such feasts from an immensely wealthy financier called Crozat.

and books. It was the ladies who set the gallant tone in the salons and at feasts, but it was also their task to divert any overly instinctual drives displayed by their admirers into more intellectual areas – in other words, to "polish" the rougher characters. Watteau makes the success of their efforts patently clear in the bended knees, tender glances and delicate gait of his young men.

The sphere of women was entirely restricted to the home and the salon. They could only exert an influence on the world outside these walls through men. Women had no serious responsibilities or opportunities for development: boredom was thus a widespread malady amongst the ladies of the upper classes in the 18th century. And the more bored they were, they more receptive they were to compliments and seduction. It was unkindly said that you

A world of make believe for hard-working men

Crozat, who collected older works of art, employed the young artist to decorate the walls of his city palace, where he also provided him with accommodation for a while. During this period, Crozat might have invited Watteau to his country house 20 kilometres from Paris, where his Parisian friends met to indulge in what they called "outdoor pleasures".

It is unlikely that the roofer's son from the provinces would have felt at ease in such company. He is invariably described as difficult by his contemporaries. He was "always dissatisfied with himself, and with those around him", as well as being restless, moody, impatient and shy, and "of a cold and awkward character".

Even his success became a burden to him. He hid himself away from the wealthy collectors who were now taking an interest in his work, repeatedly changed his lodgings and wanted only, as a friend noted, "to live a quiet life". In this voluntary seclusion, he devoted himself entirely to his work. He died in 1721 aged 36 – it is presumed from the effects of lead poisoning. He used lead to mix his paints.

Watteau probably painted the Berlin version of the *Pilgrimage to Cythera* for the collector Jean de Jullienne; the painting was certainly in the latter's collection in 1733, when he had an engraving made of it. Like Crozat, Jullienne was a typical representative of the up-and-coming bourgeoisie: the son of a cloth merchant, he made his fortune as a manufacturer of textile dyes. He rose to become the director of a dyeworks and in 1736 was elevated to the nobility.

Jullienne was amongst Watteau's first customers and owned at least 40 of his works. But if he thus put money into the painter, he also made good money out of him: in the 1730s he had copper engravings made of a whole series of Watteau paintings, bound them into books and sold them. By popularizing Watteau's works in this way, he increased the value of the originals, which he was then able to sell for a hefty profit.

Jullienne was undoubtedly a wealthy man, but he worked hard for his money. An obituary states that he rose at 5 o'clock in the morning every day, even in winter – in an age when it sufficed to appear at noon in order to make a fortune. He must have had little time for lover's idlenesses of the kind portrayed by Watteau.

The same was true of the Prussian king Frederick II, who purchased the *Pilgrimage to Cythera* between 1752 and 1765. The same period saw the Seven Years' War and several defeats for Prussia, carrying Frederick to the brink of suicide and his country to the edge of ruin.

These were catastrophic years – and one might ask what it was the king saw in a Cythera painting at such a time? Perhaps it was the memory of his years as crown prince in Rheinsberg Castle near Neuruppin, where he lived from 1736 until his accession to the throne in 1740. A clue lies in a letter he wrote to his married sister in Bayreuth, describing his life at Rheinsberg: "We pass our time with trifles and give no thought to the things which make life disagreeable."

Frederick was never much of a one for women and flirting, but the carefree existence he describes was clearly something he prized. And indeed, it was while at Rheinsberg that he bought his first Watteau. He later went on to own fourteen genuine Watteaus, together with numerous forgeries and paintings by Watteau imitators. It was surely Watteau's celebration of a paradisaical, unattainably carefree life that exerted such a fascination on both king and hard-working citizens alike.

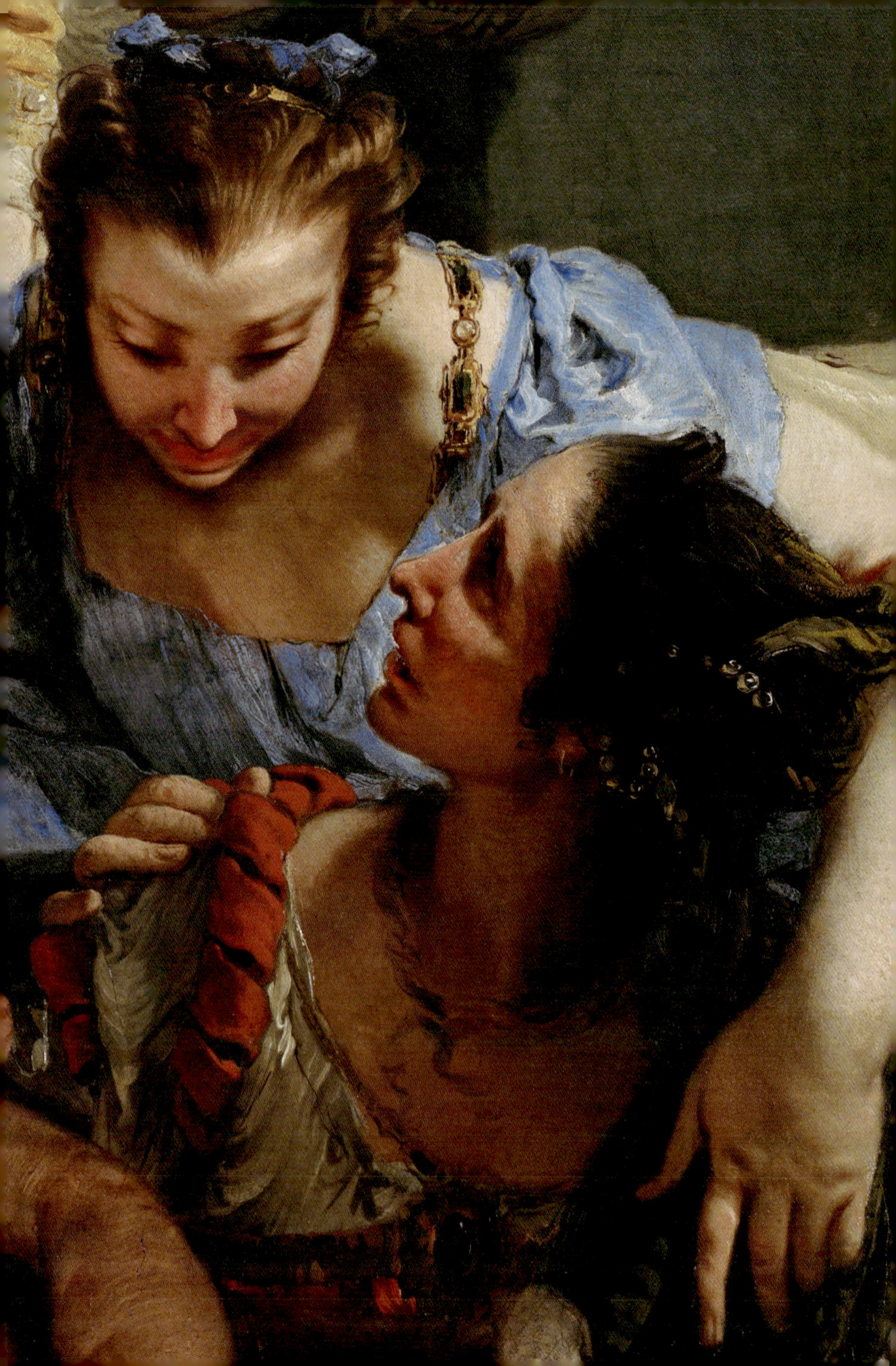

Giambattista Tiepolo (1696–1770)

Pharaoh's Venetian daughter

The Finding of Moses, c. 1738
202 x 342 cm, Edinburgh, Scottish National Gallery

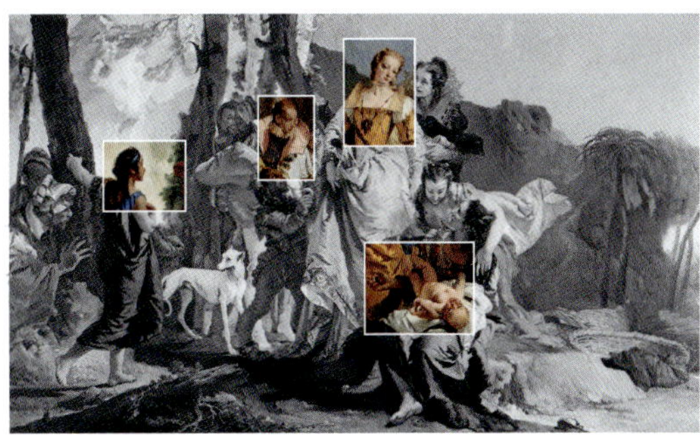

In 1996, numerous exhibitions in Europe and America marked the 300th anniversary of the birth of the Venetian artist Giambattista Tiepolo. Yet 150 years ago there was almost no interest in his paintings – they were forgotten. Today their sumptuous palette and serene elegance captivate the viewer just as they did the artist's own contemporaries.

One woman stands taller than all the rest. She is wearing a splendid dress cut in the European style – but she represents an Egyptian, the daughter of a pharaoh. The child in the maid's lap is Moses. Giambattista Tiepolo painted the scene between 1736 and 1740 in Venice, and his contemporaries, thoroughly familiar with their Bibles, naturally knew that the daughter of Pharaoh was standing beside the Nile, and that the baby boy had just been carried to the shore in the basket visible on the right.

Moses was hidden in the basket by his mother, because Pharaoh had ordered that all Jewish boys were to be killed. He felt threatened by the Israelites originally received into Egypt as guests, and in these semi-mythical times, murdering male infants was almost a conventional way of securing one's own rule. Cheops, for example, who built the tallest of all the pyramids of Egypt, is supposed to have attempted to murder triplets named as his successors. The biblical king Herod later ordered the massacre of all the young boys in Bethlehem, in order to kill Jesus, the prophesied "king of the Jews".

The Pharaoh's daughter felt a compassion not shared by her father, but thereby brought misfortune upon her own people. For it was Moses who, at his God's command, would lead the Israelites out of Egypt. The cautious Pharaoh did not want to let them go, and attempted instead to crush them through forced labour. By way of divine punishment, the God of the Jews inflicted a succession of ten plagues upon Egypt, the last of them being death for Egypt's firstborn sons – "from the oldest son of Pharaoh" onwards. This final scourge persuaded the ruler to give in and let the Israelites go. Moses' time in Egypt was thus characterized by brutality, struggle and catastrophe – quite unlike

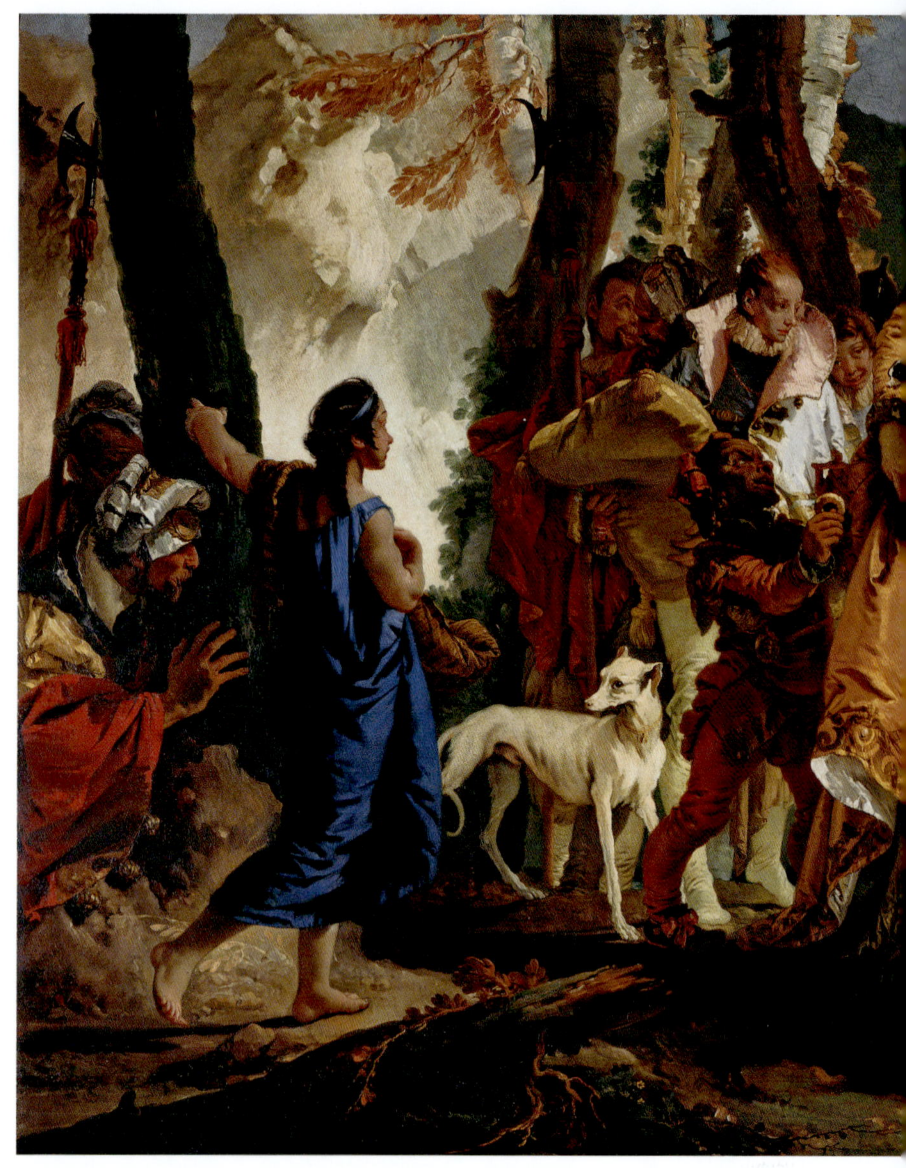

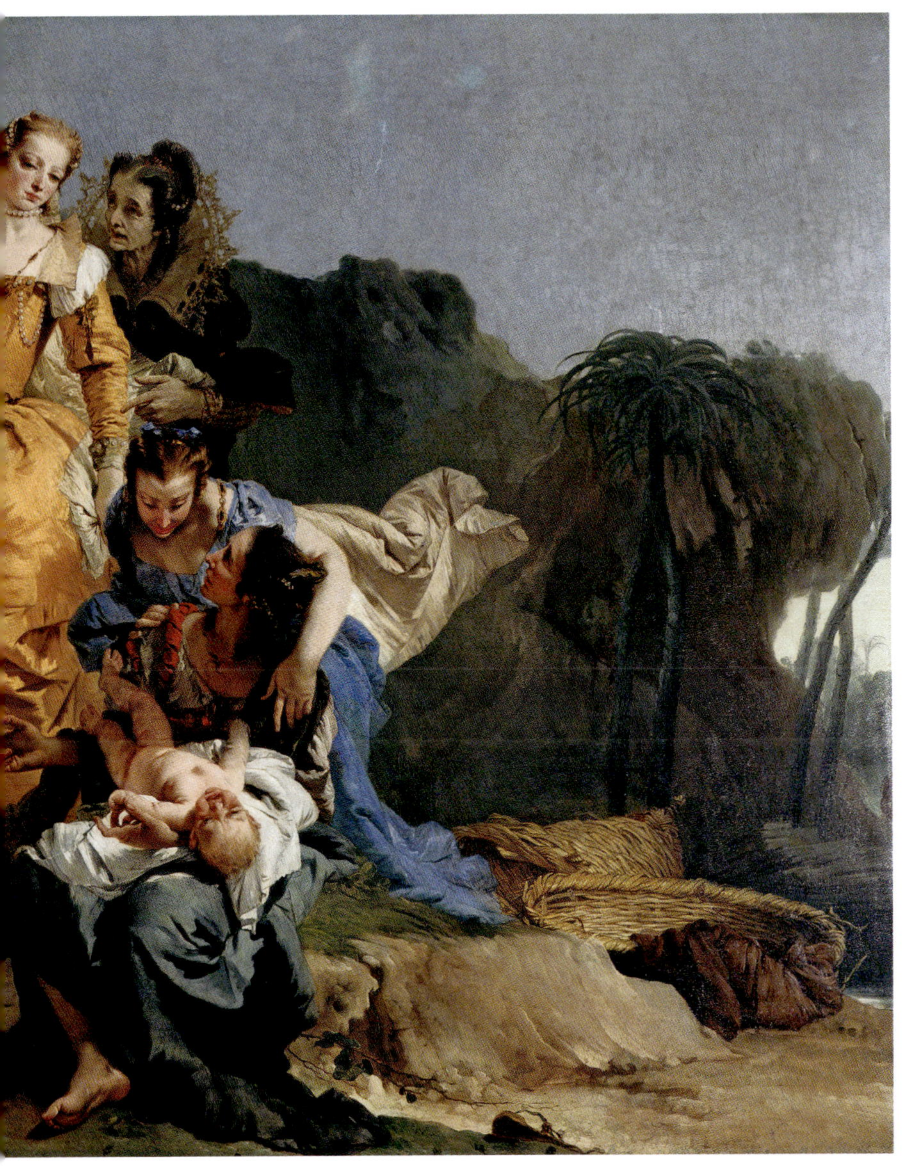

the painting by Tiepolo, with its handsome figures and sumptuous palette.

Miriam against a bright background

The young woman in the blue shift, who only has one foot on the ground and has clearly just arrived on the scene, is most probably Miriam. She is Moses' elder sister and has followed the progress of the basket along the Nile. She approaches the Egyptian princess and offers to find a Hebrew nurse for the baby. And thus Moses is reunited with his mother.

Moses was popular in Venice. There must have been few other cities in which the Old Testament prophet and leader had his own church: San Moisè. A few decades before this picture was painted, the church was given the overladen façade which it still presents today. It was famed for its high altar of coloured rock, piled up into a mountain crowned by Moses and a pharaoh.

It must be the same pharaoh who – worn down by the ten plagues – first let the Israelites go and then pursued them with his army; the pharaoh who saw the waters of the Red Sea part for the Israelites, only to feel them close again over his own head and those of his soldiers, drowning them all. It was with a painting of this subject that Tiepolo made his first appearance in an exhibition. That was in 1717, in his native city of Venice, and the artist was 21 years old.

When he painted *The Finding of Moses*, he was around 40 and a famous man. He drew his inspiration from another important work in the Venetian tradition of Moses pictures, namely a painting of the same scene by Paolo Veronese (1528–1588). In Tiepolo's day it hung in a Venetian palazzo; in 1747 it was sold to Dresden, where it can be seen today in the Gemäldegalerie Alte Meister.

Tiepolo held Veronese in the highest regard, and regularly incorporated the figures and motifs of his Renaissance predecessor into his own works – as evidenced here by the dwarf, the greyhound, and the dress worn by the Egyptian princess, which in the 18th century had long since fallen out of fashion.

The background of Veronese's *Finding of Moses* reveals an Italian city with a river and a bridge; in Tiepolo's version, the figures are simply set against trees and rocks. What Tiepolo meant by the dazzlingly bright background behind Miriam's profile is unclear. The burning bush from which Jehovah first spoke to Moses? The pillar of fire into which Jehovah turned himself at night in order to show the Israelites which way to go? The answer is probably neither; this luminous area is simply one that the artist, out of sheer delight in colour and colour contrasts, wanted to see at this point in his composition.

Dressed like a Venetian

For whom Tiepolo painted *The Finding of Moses* is not known for certain. The picture is said to have hung in the Palazzo Barbarigo delle Giglie, not far from the church of San Moisè. A few years later, in 1744/45, Tiepolo would decorate this same palazzo with frescos and pictures, illustrating subjects such as "Virtue and Noblemindedness conquer Ignorance". In one of these pictures, the Barbarigo coat of arms is combined with that of another patrician family, the Sagredos: Pietro Barbarigo married Caterina Sagredo.

There are a number of indications that Tiepolo's *Finding of Moses* may have been executed on the occasion of this marriage – as a homage to the beauty and "noblemindedness" of the bride. For one, the Venetian princess bears a certain resemblance to a portrait of Caterina Sagredo by Rosalba Carriera (1675–1757), which today hangs in Dresden and which appeared at about the

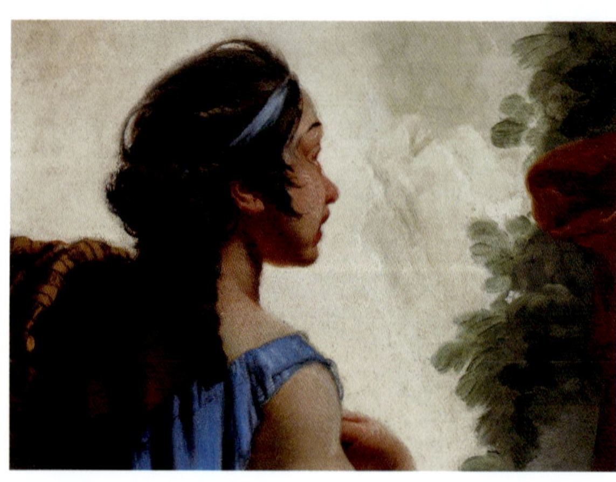

same time as Tiepolo's painting. But as in most of his large history paintings, Tiepolo avoids any overly individual characterization of his figures; instead, he adheres to the general Venetian ideal of beauty, namely a pale skin and fair, strawberry blonde hair.

Whatever the case, Tiepolo – like Veronese – painted a married woman. This is indicated by her pearl necklace, which in Venice only married women could wear. As part of the wedding ceremony, it was presented to the bride by her mother-in-law in the presence of numerous guests, prior to the religious rites. The necklace had to be worn for a whole year, and families who did not own such a valuable piece of jewellery could hire it for this length of time. Tiepolo's princess wears her string of pearls wound once around her neck and then falling generously into two loops, which are scooped up and hooked into her bodice.

Unlike his great model Veronese, Tiepolo includes a page with a large cushion. He clothes the boy in a dark doublet and a short, pale cape with a wide collar, exactly as would have been worn at patrician weddings. The page – called a *ballerino* – led the bride by the hand when she presented herself to her parents-in-law at the entrance to her father's palazzo. At this point in the ceremony, she was required to kneel. To make it more comfortable for her, the page would place a large velvet cushion on the ground in front of her.

The little information we have about Caterina Sagredo Barbarigo is conflicting. A book of sonnets praises her politeness and intelligence; the nobility and humanity of her character, it seems, made one forget the distance which separated her from others. These are the same standard formulae that Tiepolo illustrated on the walls of the palace. Quite different were the sentiments which Caterina Sagredo Barbarigo expressed in a letter to the Abbé de Bernis, the French ambassador: he could rest assured,

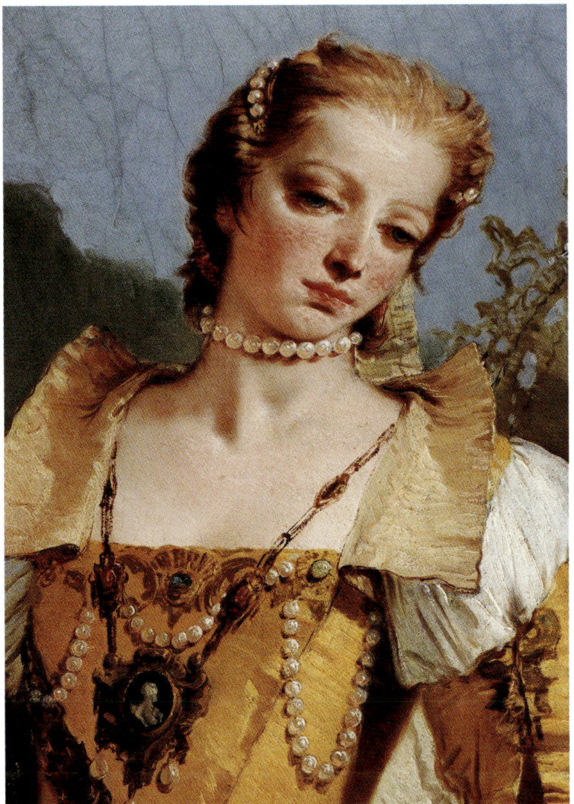

she promised, that she "would be always constant and never faithful" to him. Just a witty, meaningless phrase?

Like many patrician women, Caterina ran her own casino, a sort of pavilion where she received guests after the theatre, and where they could chat, flirt and gamble, often for high sums. In 1747 her casino was shut for a while by the authorities. This would happen when the hostess displayed a "too liberal, free and easy manner", as it was formulated by the state inquisition – "reprehensible in any woman, intolerable in patrician ladies".

A realistic baby in an idealized company

Moses was a foundling. The fact that he was rescued so quickly from his basket on the Nile was, in the eyes of the faithful, an act of divine providence.

The fact that he was reunited with his mother similarly distinguishes him from many other foundlings, whose chances of survival in Tiepolo's day were slim.

In Venice, unwanted newborns were left outside the doors of those charitable institutions who took care of the sick and "abandoned". These *Ospizi di Carità* did what they could for such children. But "the money spent by the hospitals doesn't bring any returns", wrote the Frenchman Claude-Humbert de Chamousset in 1756 – many of the children simply grew up to be beggars, while "most die before reaching an age when one might be able to get some use out of them".

Society in the 18th century had a pronouncedly negative – to us, highly disconcerting – attitude towards children. Something of this can be seen in the pose adopted by the Pharaoh's daughter: she keeps her distance, clasps her dog tenderly to her side and leaves the crying baby to the care of the maid. Things were not much different in real life: in courts and in cities, families who could afford to do so, including even merchants and craftsmen, placed their offspring in the care of a wet nurse on the very day they were born, straight after having

them baptized. To breastfeed your own child, it was thought, harmed your beauty and your marriage.

Only the very wealthy took the nurse into their own houses; the rest sought a wet nurse in the market and packed their children off the country for several years. The French statesman Charles-Maurice de Talleyrand, born in 1754, recalls in his memoirs how his aristocratic mother never asked after him once, and only learned of the accident that had crippled him when he was brought back to the family home at the age of four.

This indifference towards small children only began to disappear after the French philosopher Jean-Jacques Rousseau published his *Emile*. This treatise, which called for better education, became a European bestseller. Amongst other things, it advocated that mothers should nurse their own children and should treat them from the start as individuals in their own right and as full members of the family. It would nevertheless be a long time before these ideas were put into practice.

There were many reasons behind the high rate of infant mortality in the 18th century, including inadequate standards of hygiene and the fact that there were no paediatricians. The decisive factor,

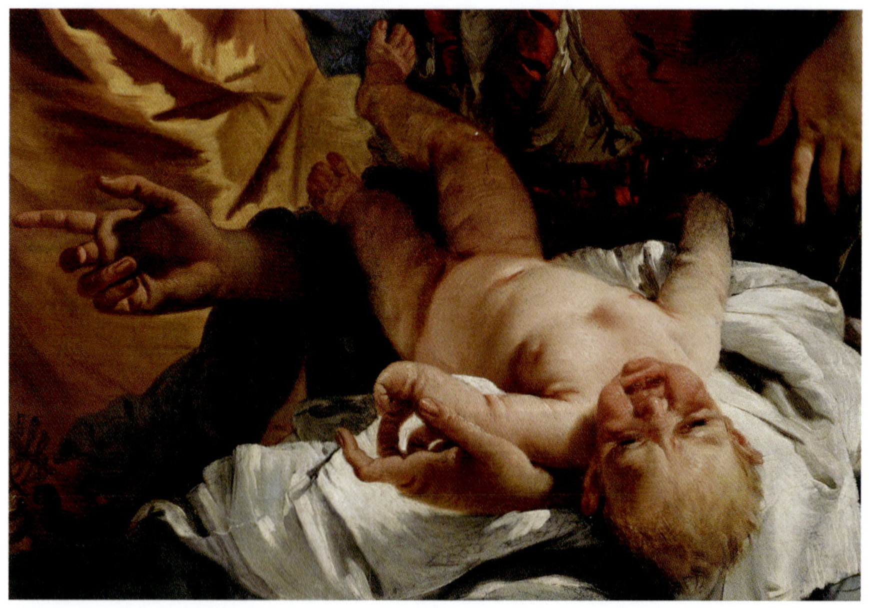

however, was parents' relative lack of interest. This
also explained the high numbers of children who
were abandoned or exposed, and half of whom
– according to one French statistic – died within
their first month of life.

Beauty married to irony

When Tiepolo's youngest son was born in 1736,
the painter may have already been thinking about
the child Moses. He certainly knew what crying
babies looked like. The page, meanwhile, looks like
the artist's eldest son, Giandomenico, born in 1727.
He too became a highly talented painter, who
collaborated with his father on the decorations
for the archbishop's palace in Würzburg, and later
accompanied him to Spain, where Giambattista
Tiepolo died in 1770.

While the son naturally adhered to the style of
his father, he also liked to portray his fellow humans
as slightly ridiculous creatures. He thereby picked
up on a tendency only hinted at by his father – for
example, in the contrast between the Pharaoh's
daughter and the bawling child.

Veronese, whose earlier version of *The Finding
of Moses* provided Tiepolo with an important source
of inspiration, portrayed Moses as an infant bravely
refusing to cry. Other artists showed him swaddled
up to the neck – the child as a civilized being.
Tiepolo, on the other hand, paints him in his
natural state, his face bright red and swollen from
crying. And he emphasizes the princess's aloofness
in the face of this uncivilized creature. Is there not
a trace of irony in this contrast? Is the artist perhaps
poking hidden fun at supposedly "nobleminded"
attitudes? Why else should he have portrayed the
child with such realism, quite in contrast to his
normal practice?

Giambattista Tiepolo was no realist – he celebrated
the beauty of the world. And since that beauty
seemed all the more magnificent the further back
in the past it lay, the subjects he painted were drawn
almost exclusively from the Old and New Testaments,
antique myth and Roman, Venetian and Spanish
history. And he liked to dress his women as Veronese
had done, 200 years before his time.

But tastes in art changed; with the advent of the
Enlightenment, mythology and religion were supplanted by a new interest in the natural sciences and
the real world. Venetian painters such as Antonio
Canal and Bernardo Bellotto adapted themselves to

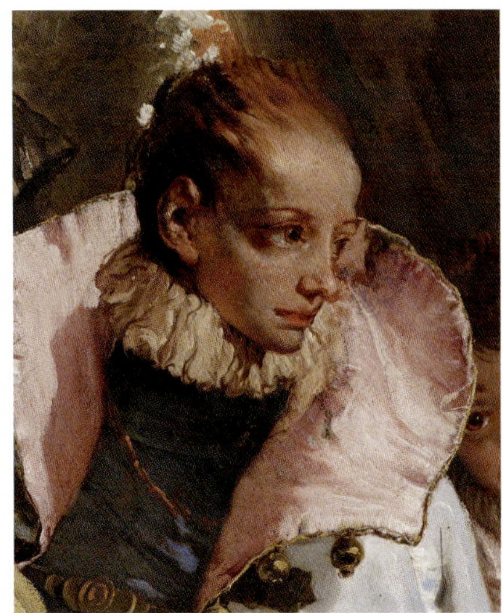

the new situation, executing cityscapes with a seem
ingly mathematical precision. Similar requests were
made to Tiepolo, too: the art agent Francesco Alga-
rotti tried to persuade the painter at least to cement
his mythical scenes within a recognizable historical
architecture. It would have been easy, for example,
for Tiepolo to localize *The Finding of Moses* in Egypt,
just by introducing a pyramid. He didn't want to.

Tiepolo's art was held in low regard right up to
the end of the 19th century. This was perhaps
the reason, why someone felt able to cut his Moses
painting in two. The section reproduced here
measures 202 by 342 centimetres, and hangs in the
National Gallery of Scotland in Edinburgh. The
section missing from the right-hand side measures
202 by 132 centimetres, and is housed in a private
collection in Turin. It shows a halberdier, who is
looking not at the women, but at his dog.

Today Tiepolo's art is once again accessible to
us, and his imagination, his palette and his serene
elegance are a source of renewed delight. In 1996,
numerous exhibitions of his work marked the
300th anniversary of his birth.

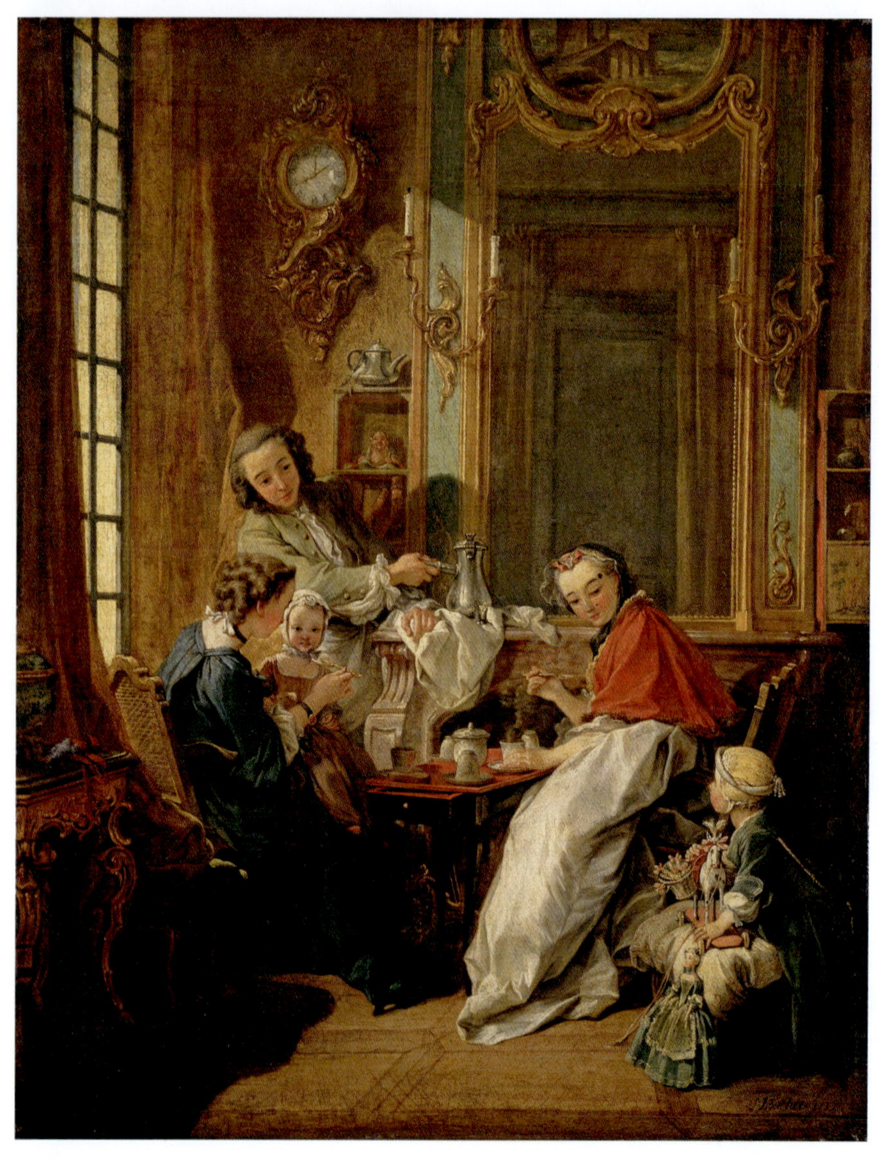

François Boucher (1703–1770)

The birth of the nuclear family

The Breakfast, 1739
81.5 x 65.5 cm, Paris, Musée du Louvre

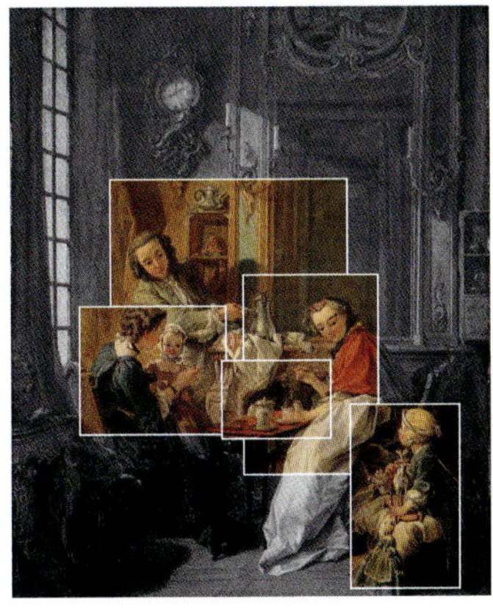

To today's viewer, this breakfasting scene has the air of a family idyll, harmless and a little conventional. To the artist's contemporaries, however, what Boucher was showing – chinaware, a large window, a small fireplace, rocaille decoration, breakfast, hot drinks, adults attending to children – was highly modern. For viewers in the 18th century, the painting reflected a new style of everyday living and also a new attitude towards life.

It was executed in Paris in 1739; the date can be read in the bottom right-hand corner, next to the signature. It was a period of prosperity in France. Louis XV (1710–1774) had so far waged no wars; good harvests had at last followed decades of catastrophic weather; commerce and industry were expanding. The lower classes had enough to eat, and in the higher echelons of society, amongst the aristocracy and industrious bourgeoisie, fortunes were being made. The family seen breakfasting here are members of one such wealthy bourgeois household.

They might even be members of Boucher's own family. In 1739 his wife, Marie-Jeanne, was in her mid twenties. She was famed for her beauty and often served as Boucher's model. Their two children, Elisabeth-Victoire and Juste-Nathan, were four and three years old, more or less the same age as the children in the picture. The room is one that Boucher painted several times and it may well have formed part of his own apartment. The artist was 36 years old and already earning an excellent income.

Boucher, the son of a craftsman, learned the rudiments of painting under second rate artists, but honed his skills by studying the works of Rubens and his compatriot Antoine Watteau. He executed copper engravings of Watteau's works for a wealthy bourgeois by the name of Julienne. Painting in the gracefully ornate style of his day, he produced designs for tapestries, furnishings, theatrical decorations, and porcelain services. For his wealthy clients, he also decorated areas above fireplaces and mirrors. The lower half of such a wall painting can be seen at the top of *The Breakfast*.

The landscape above the mirror and the mirror itself are linked by a motif that recurs throughout the Rococo era and the Louis XV style: the scallop shell. Just as Venus can be seen stepping out of such a shell in many of Boucher's paintings, so his contemporaries, too, rose from chairs decorated with scallop motifs. The same scallops decorated their mirrors, and the gold and silver ornaments on the walls of their apartments were similarly reminiscent of shells and waves.

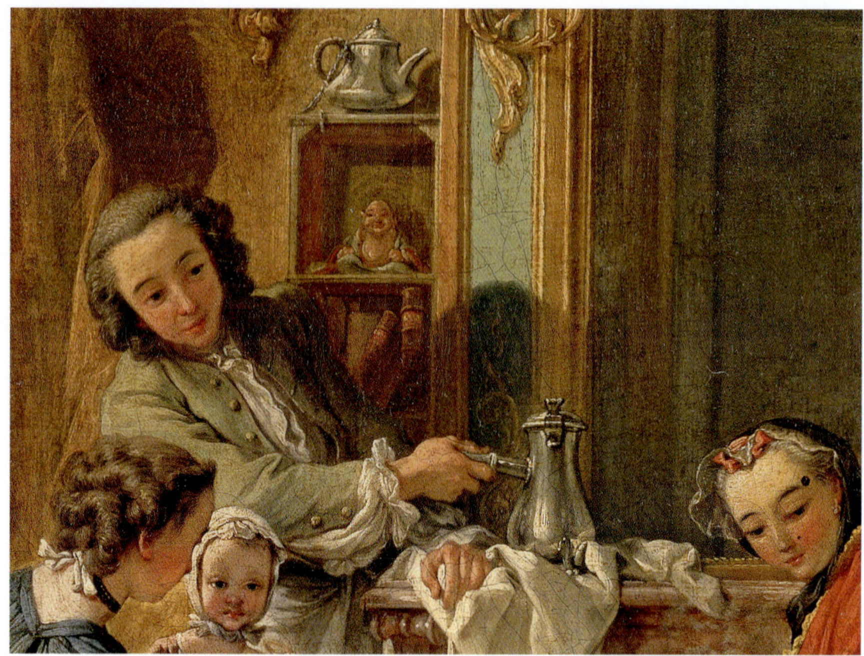

Apartments were changing during this era.
In 1728, an architect by the name of Patte wrote:
"The art of living comfortably and by oneself was
previously unknown."

"Comfortably and by oneself" – these were new
ideas. Up till then, the nobility and upper middle classes had lived in large households with an
emphasis upon public display. There now emerged a
new desire for privacy, for a certain intimacy. Rooms
became smaller, ceilings lower. So that the new
rooms would not feel too cramped, large mirrors
were installed, and since glass was becoming
cheaper, windows were made bigger. Rooms became
lighter. They also became warmer. Newly designed
small fireplaces heated more efficiently than the
huge fireplaces of old. In the past, it had been
necessary in winter to don an extra layer of clothing
when you came indoors; now you could take
something off. Dressing gowns and house coats
were no longer lined with fur as frequently as before;
cold splendour was being replaced by cosiness.
Even Louis XV abandoned the vast halls of Versailles
palace and withdrew, as far as court etiquette

permitted, into the *petits appartements* of the entresol,
with their smaller rooms and lower ceilings.

Rooms not only became smaller, but were laid out
differently. Previously, each room had opened directly
onto the next; to reach the one at the end, therefore,
you had to pass through all the others. Now houses
were given corridors. No more through traffic. An
opportunity to shut yourself away, to be "by yourself".

The introduction of the corridor was accompanied by the emergence of new types of room. In the
past, all rooms served multiple functions. Depending
on the size of the apartment and the prosperity of
its occupant, the same room might serve as kitchen
and dining room, bedroom and drawing room. The
aristocracy and wealthy bourgeoisie now began to
indulge in a separate kitchen and a designated dining room. Visitors were no longer welcomed beside
the bed. The salon arose, and between the salon and
the bedroom, the boudoir. The name comes from
bouder (to pout or sulk); it was the place where you
could go and sulk.

In later eras the boudoir acquired a dubious
reputation. In literature and the fine arts, it has come

down to us above all as the setting for amorous encounters. Vast numbers of politely termed *galant* engravings – "through the keyhole" pictures of varying degrees of artistic subtlety – served to reinforce its erotic associations. The demand for such pictures almost completely obscured the other, equally if not more important aspect of the boudoir, namely as somewhere to be together with one's family, undisturbed; the boudoir as the setting for the new, growing sense of family, as a place where parents could pay loving attention to their children.

The boudoir arose simultaneously with the discovery of privacy, with the growing appreciation of domestic intimacy. These developments were probably in turn a reflection of the greater importance starting to be attached to the emotions in the 18th century. This was the era in which the nuclear family was born. The family was now seen as a "valuable emotional unit". Boucher's *The Breakfast* is one of the first artistic records of this development.

Breakfast is a French invention

The young man in the green frock coat was long thought to be the artist, François Boucher himself, serving breakfast to his family in person. Even King Louis XV is known to have warmed and poured out his own coffee when living in his *petits appartements*. It was all part of the new lifestyle. But the man in green seems much younger than a 36-year-old; moreover, he is wearing a white apron. (This apron is even more evident in a preliminary study for the painting.) He is thus more likely to be a servant. He has just brought the pot, wrapped in the white cloth now lying on the mantelpiece, from the kitchen, or – more probable still – from across the road. For in the first half of the 18th century, the fashionable drinks of tea, coffee and chocolate were for the most part brewed and served in public houses. The young man with the apron is probably a *garçon limonadier* (a "lemonade boy"). He would have worked for the guild of lemonade and liqueur sellers, who towards the end of the 17th century also began serving hot chocolate and coffee in silver pots.

The idea of supplying the Parisians with hot drinks in their own homes was nothing out of the ordinary. All day long, traders selling herbal teas plied the streets; a shout would bring them hurrying to your front door. Cold and hot water was similarly carried up to people's apartments. In the early morning, the streets of the city filled with the cries of bakers' boys from the suburbs selling their rye rolls, country girls touting fresh eggs, and milkmaids announcing their arrival. Boucher made their familiar cries the subject of a series of engravings. From nine o'clock in the morning the streets were thronged with bustling waiters delivering breakfasts to people in their own apartments.

Breakfast is a French invention of the 18th century. Louis XV was the first king to have bread or a roll in the morning with a hot drink. His royal predecessors had started the day with dinner at around ten o'clock. Over the course of the decades, this large, hot meal moved closer and closer to midday and eventually became lunch. Louis XIV ate his dinner at one o'clock, but did not have breakfast. This was something only introduced by his descendants.

It was because of the new hot drinks that breakfasting became so popular. Not everyone liked them, however. Liselotte of the Palatinate, married to the Duke of Orléans, wrote from Paris: "I rarely take breakfast … Tea to me tastes of hay and manure, coffee of soot and lupins, and chocolate is too sweet for me. What I would really like to eat would be … a good beer soup. That wouldn't give me a stomach ache."

Coffee, tea, or chocolate?

Some critics claim that the drink being consumed in this painting is coffee, but this is not true. It is hot chocolate, thick and sweet – a beverage for children, ladies and the aristocracy.

The drink can be identified from the pot that the young man has unwrapped from the cloth. It is not a pear-shaped coffeepot, nor is it a teapot like the round bellied one standing on the top shelf above the Chinese figurine. The silver or pewter pot on the mantelpiece has the traditional slender shape of a chocolate pot with a straight handle. The spout is short and wide, so that the thick chocolate can be poured out with greater ease. It was usually whisked to a froth before serving.

In the 18th century, chocolate was made from cocoa, sugar, cinnamon and vanilla. It was sold in tablets and enjoyed as a drink, dissolved in hot water or hot milk. It was very different to the drink we call cocoa today. Since the 19th century, cocoa beans have had the large part of their oil extracted, making them less nutritious but easier to digest.

Yet it was precisely its high nutritional value that originally made chocolate so popular. It was first

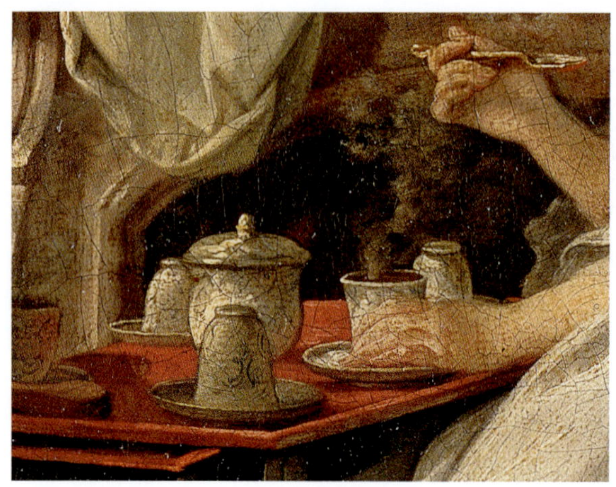

coffee at the street corner in the morning were largely members of the working populace.

A few hours later, the Boucher family would drink "aristocratic" chocolate, not labour-fuelling coffee, in their comfortable boudoir. This may also be seen as an indication of the artist's ability to embrace the habits of his clients. That he was career minded is evidenced by the addresses at which he lived. As he grew more successful, so he moved to ever "better" areas of Paris. Finally, in 1752, he moved into an apartment in the royal Louvre palace, even though it would be 1764 before he was appointed Painter to the King.

imported from South America into Spain in the 16th century. During the lengthy and in those days very strict periods of religious fasting, the Church permitted the consumption of fluids. With the help of the sweet, nutritious drink, these fasts were easier to endure. When a Spanish princess, Anna of Austria, became Queen of France in 1615, she introduced chocolate to the French court. Its success was enormous: within a short space of time, chocolate had become the favourite drink of the French and subsequently the European aristocracy, and thereby a public status symbol.

It was usually enjoyed in bed or, as in Boucher's painting, in the boudoir, as a sweet upbeat, so to speak, to a day of leisure. Madame de Pompadour, the long-term mistress of Louis XV, is said to have sought help for her frigidity from hot chocolate: she added three times as much vanilla and a pinch of ambergris so as to boost her flagging libido.

Clergymen, on the other hand, who were required to live in celibacy, were recommended coffee, considered to be an anti-erotic and sobering drink. It came into fashion in Europe following the siege of Vienna by the Turks in 1683. It was drunk in particular in Protestant regions, and in 1732 the choir master and organist Johann Sebastian Bach even composed a cantata in its praise. Coffee was seen as a general panacea, which supposedly strengthened the liver and gallbladder, cleansed the blood, calmed the stomach, and increased one's energy. In the Paris of the 18th century, the people downing a cup of hot

Porcelain: Meissen was just 30 years old

Together with the raw ingredients for the new drinks, the merchant ships arriving from distant parts also brought chinaware to go with them: coffee cups from Arabia and tea cups from China, fancy vases and pot-bellied deities, such as the ones in Boucher's boudoir. The elegant, fragile cups and saucers on his table appear to be decorated with a Chinese motif. They have no handles and are therefore hot to the touch; the ladies use spoons. Slender and graceful, such porcelain fitted well with a lifestyle in which form and elegance played an important role. Such china allowed the taking of hot drinks to become a formal social occasion, and not just something to be done alone and "by oneself".

The French upper classes were at that time searching for new and sophisticated tableware appropriate to their status. In the past, the rich had eaten from plates of silver and gold. In 1709, however, Louis XIV had made them melt down all their magnificent dinner services as a way of getting money to fund his wars. Since then the wealthy had used French faïence pottery. Very few people in the years around 1739 could afford a service made of delicate porcelain. It was expensive because it had to be imported either from China or, more recently, Saxony. In 1708 the alchemist Johann Böttger and the naturalist Tschirnhausen unravelled the Chinese secret of porcelain manufacture and began producing "white gold" in Meissen.

Experiments were conducted in France, too. There were attempts in several cities to make porcelain, but one vital ingredient – kaolin, which gives china its hardness – was still lacking. It was eventually discovered near Limoges in 1768. Up till then, manufacturers had confined themselves to bone china, the production of which increased when Madame de Pompadour, the royal favourite, started to take an interest in it.

Madame de Pompadour turned her attention to fragile plates and cups not for economic reasons but as a means of rescuing her Louis from boredom. That was her chief occupation. She sang and danced for him on a stage in the palace, and took the opportunity to remind him that his forebear Henri IV had overseen the setting up of the Gobelin tapestry workshops. So Louis XV financed the founding of the Royal Porcelain Factory, first in Vincennes, then in Sèvres, not far from Madame de Pompadour's *château de plaisance*. And the favourite in turn engaged her favourite painter, Boucher. He designed patterns and motifs and thereby also helped shape the tastes of his day.

The hairdresser comes after breakfast

The lady sitting on the right is still in her negligée. She will get fully dressed and made up only after she has finished breakfast. She is wearing a red make-up cape. The hairdresser will arrive later to comb and powder her hair, which is still hidden beneath her lace bonnet. In the mornings, one contemporary recorded, the horde of *garçons limonadiers* in the street was joined by a swarm of hairdressers, on their way to make their wealthy clients presentable for the day. Beneath her make-up cape, the lady in the painting has not yet donned her skirt and stiff corset, but is still wearing a morning gown. This gown is a status symbol: it shows that the lady does not have to work. The author Nicolas Restif de la Bretonne informs us in one of his novels that the daughter of a peasant who has become rich may be granted the form of address "Demoiselle" only if she wears such a morning gown at home.

Prosperous bourgeois wives did not lead a life purely of leisure, however. Even the daughters of the aristocracy learned how to run a household in the convents in which they were educated from the age of seven to sixteen. Later on, after all, they would have to manage their own staff. A middle-class wife had to keep a close eye on her stocks of table linen,

bed linen and clothing, a major task in itself. These stocks formed the pride of the household, represented a considerable amount of money, and – since laundry was washed at most twice a year – were extensive.

Boucher's wife did even more. She sat as a model for her husband, in this painting probably in two poses, to the right and left of the table. She also painted miniatures based on her husband's paintings and engraved them in copper; two engravings bearing her signature appear in a volume with those of her husband. Madame Boucher attained a certain independence and thereby differed from most other women of her century. Women could rise to prominence only as artists, shopkeepers, and mistresses. The most famous example in Boucher's day was Mademoiselle Poisson, in other words a young lady named Miss Fish. She became the favourite of Louis XV, who presented her with the earldom of Pompadour and thereby a finer-sounding name.

Nevertheless, a number of intelligent, rich, and socially adept women rose to positions of indirect influence via their salons. They operated through the men they manipulated. *En France, tout se fait*

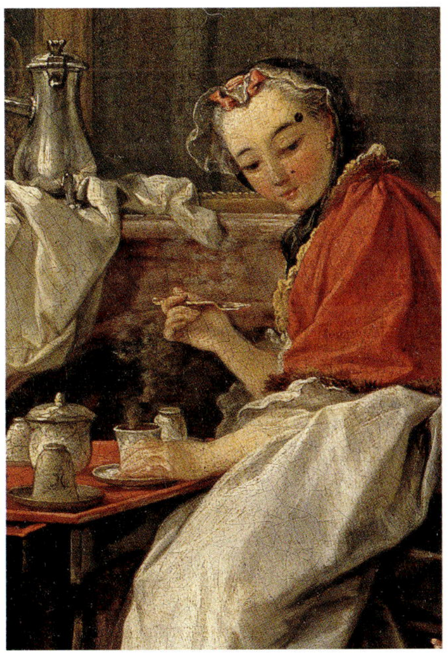

par les femmes, it was said – everything was done by women. "They have got the upper hand over French men to such an extent … that the latter cannot think or feel except through them." While these words may seem exaggerated, in one sphere France's women may have influenced not only their salon guests but also broad sections of the public – namely in the validation of human emotion. Literary works testify to this shift in attitude: tears flow, even men sob. In 1731 Abbé Prévost published *Manon Lescaut*, a novel whose protagonists live only for love and passion.

This revalorization of feeling changed family life, the relationships between the spouses, and the attitude of parents towards their children. Each woman in this painting is turning towards a child. This was by no means commonplace in 1739.

Children had yet to become people
It is astonishing that the children in this picture are even allowed into the boudoir with their mother.

Three- and four-year-olds were usually either still living with their wet nurses in the country or were cared for in the family home by domestic servants. At the age of seven, the children of France's aristocrats and upper middle classes were sent away from home once again, the girls to convents, the boys to Jesuit boarding schools. The loving attention being paid to the children in this painting was highly unusual for 1739.

Small children were not thought of as people. They were considered to be closer to animals and at the mercy of the devil. Only a harsh education, it was thought, could turn them into human beings and good Christians. It was permanently feared that they would "revert back into utterly godless creatures". As soon as they started to walk, they were given reins of the kind that can be made out on the back of the right-hand child in the present picture. Such reins were not to stop children from running away, but to prevent them from "crawling around on the

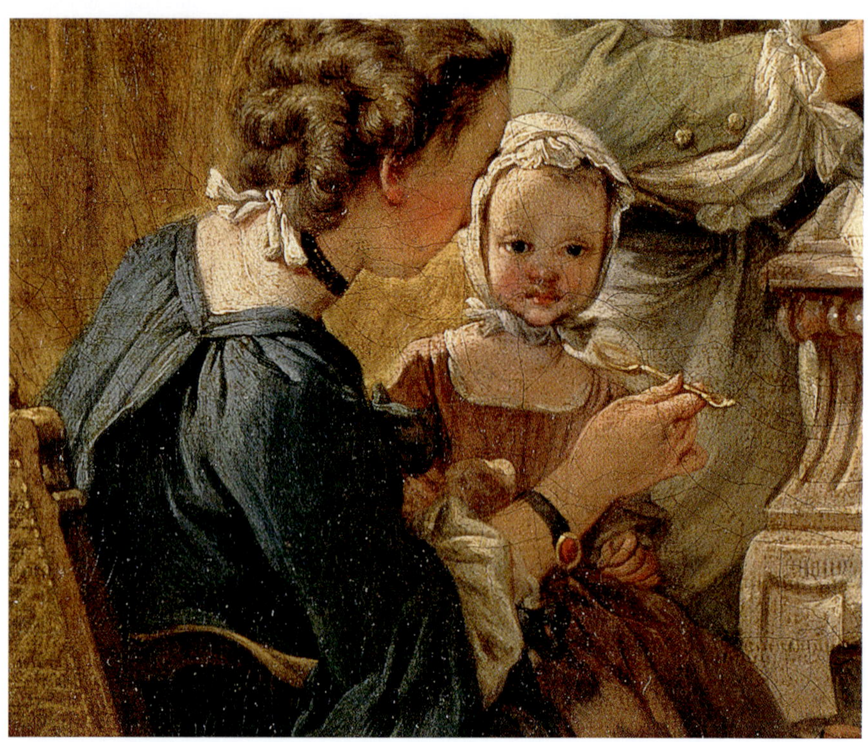

ground like animals". Everything animal-like was to
be quickly and thoroughly eradicated.

Only a modern mother fed her child herself
Parents who could afford it kept their children
at a distance. They gave them to a wet nurse in
the country. To breastfeed your own child was
considered "swinish".

Only rich families with a great deal of space
brought the wet nurse into their own homes. Most
parents sent their new-born infants away for several
years. They placed their children through agents.
For the rural population, nursing children was an
important form of self-employment. A police survey of 1780 reveals how widespread the profession
remained. According to the police figures, 21,000
children were born in Paris every year. Of these,
some 700 were nursed by their own mothers. These
were the children of the very poor. Another 700 were
looked after by a wet nurse in the parental home.
These were the children of the very rich. Seventeen
thousand, however, were sent away to the country
by their parents. That represents 80 per cent. The
remaining 2,600 were abandoned at birth.

To this depressing picture can be added statistics
from the city of Rouen: every third child given by
its parents to a wet nurse never returned, and of the
children nursed at home, one in five died. This high
rate of infant mortality may have been one of the
reasons why parents rejected or avoided emotional
bonding with their new-born children, as form of
self-protection, of avoiding pain. It was probably a
vicious circle: for ideological reasons, parents took
little interest in their offspring; their neglect led to
increased infant mortality; this high rate of mortality
only served to encourage parental neglect as a form
of self-defence.

The turnaround in this situation is generally
dated to 1762, the year in which Jean-Jacques
Rousseau published *Emile*, an essay on the education
of children. Rousseau argued that mothers should
breastfeed their children and that children should be
allowed to develop freely in the care of their parents.
He thereby gave voice to a trend that had been present beneath the surface for many years. In Boucher's
painting, executed more than twenty years earlier,
it is already apparent.

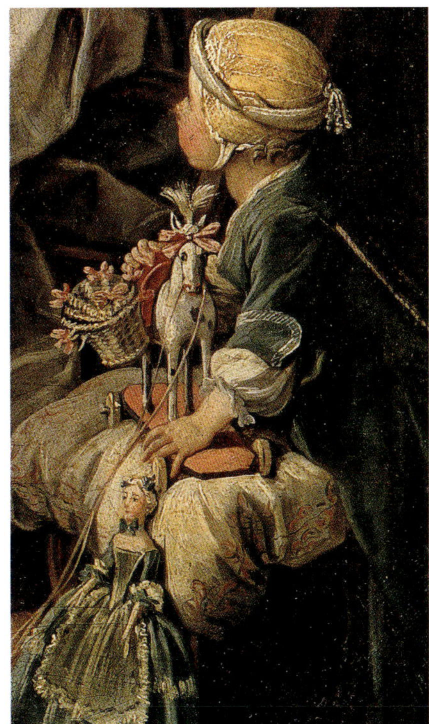

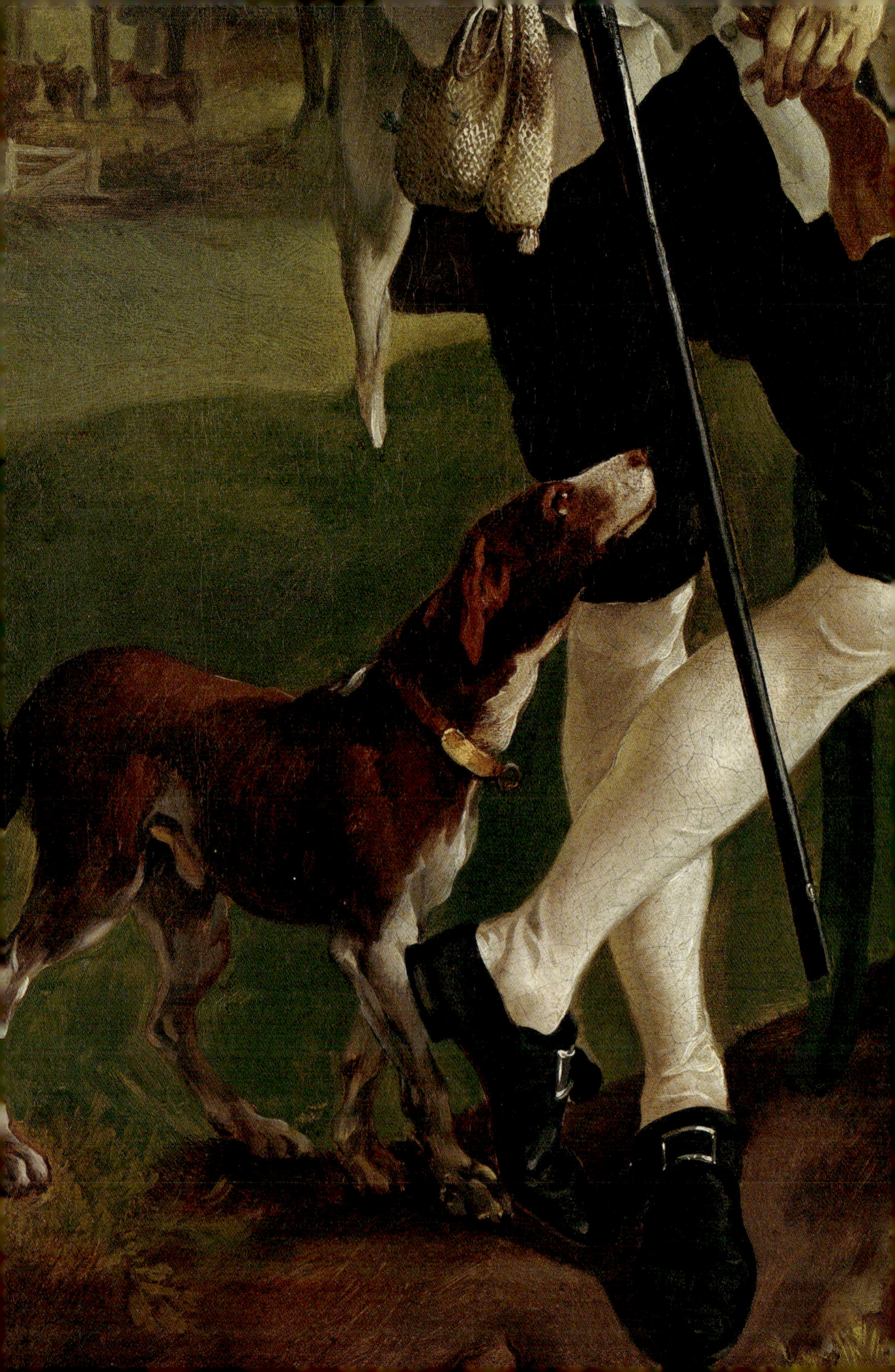

Thomas Gainsborough (1727–1788)

The proper combination of activity and leisure

Mr and Mrs Andrews, 1749
70 x 119 cm, London, The National Gallery

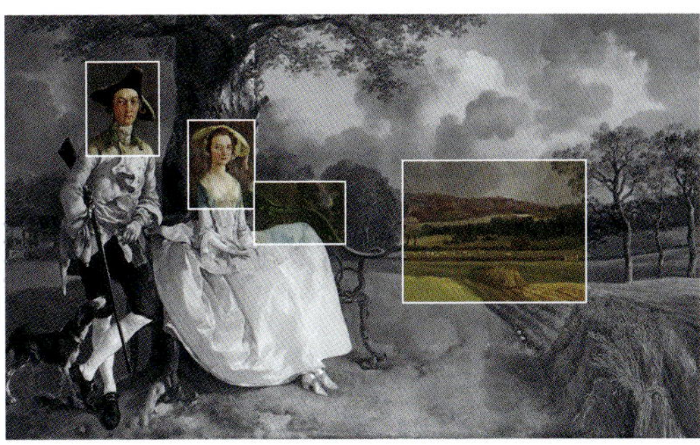

*A young couple, their cool gaze fixed on the specta-
tor, poses before a broad country prospect. They are
newly married. The woods, meadows and fields
belong to their estate. Various details of the painting
characterize their marriage, or comment on the state
of contemporary agriculture. The work is in The
National Gallery, London.*

A young couple, Mr and Mrs Robert Andrews, pose
before the trunk of a mighty oak. The depiction
of Auberies, their estate, with its fields, meadows
and trees, takes up more space than the double
portrait itself. No English painter before Thomas
Gainsborough had chosen to allocate space in this
way; nor did Gainsborough himself ever return to
this pattern. Is it the experiment of a young artist?
Or did the division of space correspond to his
patron's wishes?

The identity of the couple has been passed down
by the Andrews family, in whose estate the work
remained for over 200 years. An entry in the parish
register of the small Suffolk town of Sudbury records
that Robert Andrews married Frances Mary Carter
there on 10 November 1748. He was 22 years of age,

his bride sixteen. Also newly wedded, albeit one year
younger than the bridegroom he was to paint, was
Thomas Gainsborough himself. In a London chapel
notorious for its secret weddings, he had taken the
pregnant Margaret Burr to be his lawful wedded wife.

After a number of years spent in apprenticeship
in London, he then returned to his native town of
Sudbury. He probably painted the portrait only a few
months after his patrons' marriage, in the late summer of 1749. The corn is cut, and the sheaves stand
ready bound in the field.

Ripe ears of corn are a fitting fertility symbol for
a wedding portrait. Gainsborough's realistic landscape holds a number of other symbolic references
to the couple's consummate marriage and hope of
issue: a little tree grows between two larger ones
on the right; the man's casually lowered shotgun
and the bird in his wife's lap may also be seen as
discreet erotic allusions. The bird, no more than a
suggested outline against a lighter patch of colour,
is possibly the victim of a certain nonchalance –
towards finishing paintings that bored him, for
instance – to which the artist was occasionally
prone. "Painting and punctuality," he wrote to one

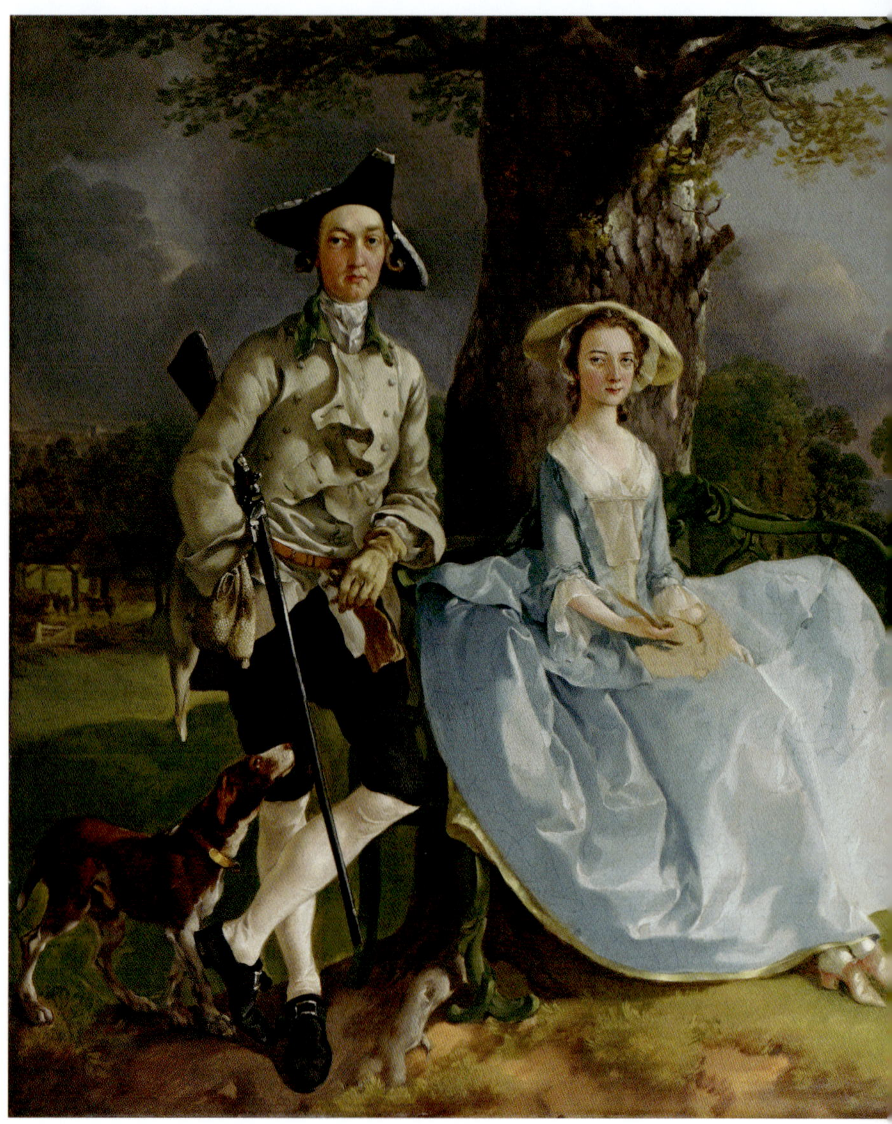

patron, "mix like oil and vinegar," and "genius and regularity are utter enemies."

Garden bench with a Rococo flourish
The church spire of St Peter's, Sudbury, a market town about two miles from Auberies, can be seen peeping out from behind the trees in the background. The Andrews had been married in the somewhat finer All Saints' Church. Sudbury had three churches, a reminder of more affluent times

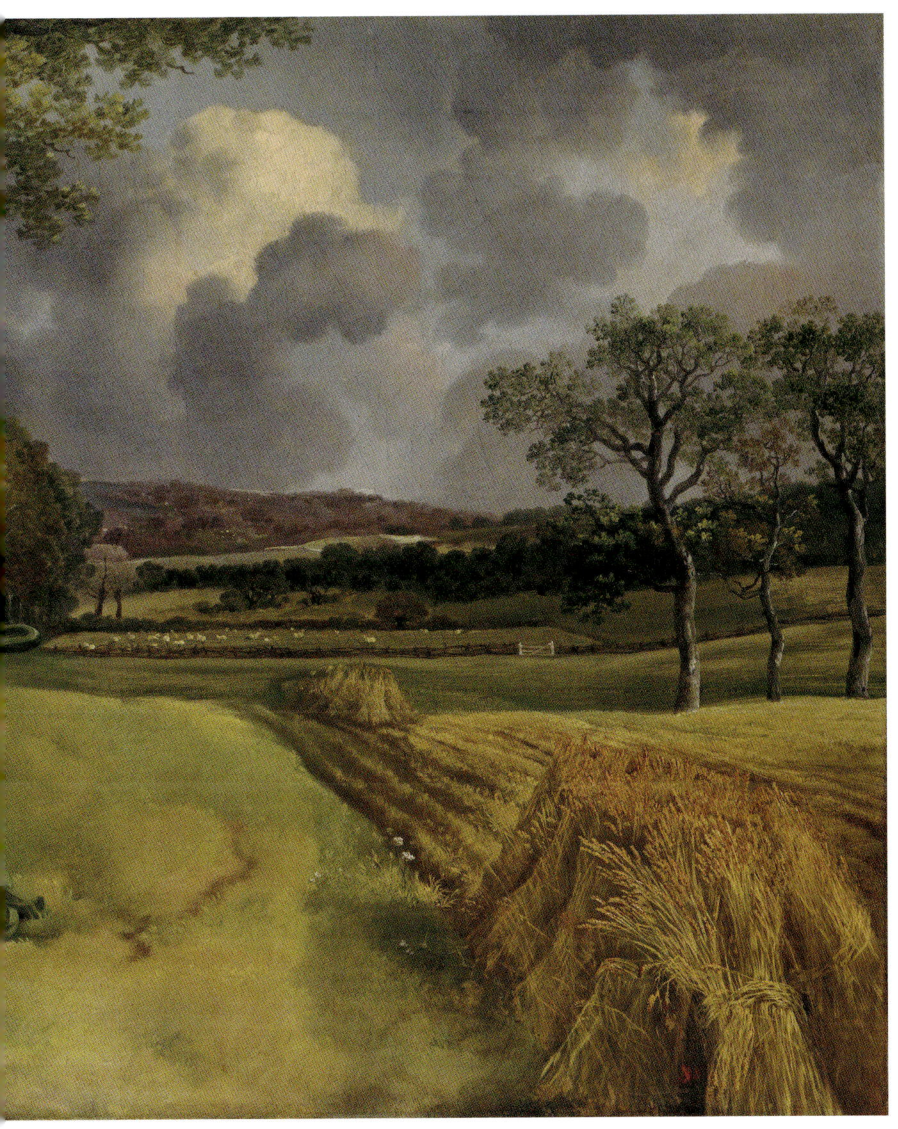

in which there was a flourishing textile industry.
The bride's grandfather had made his fortune in the
drapery business. He had invested his money in real
estate, eventually becoming one of the region's
largest landowners. His family were thus spared the

consequences of the decline of the textiles industry.
Its ruin was brought about by political instability
towards the end of the 17th century, and wars at
the beginning of the 18th. The latter had led to an
increased tax burden, the destruction of the home

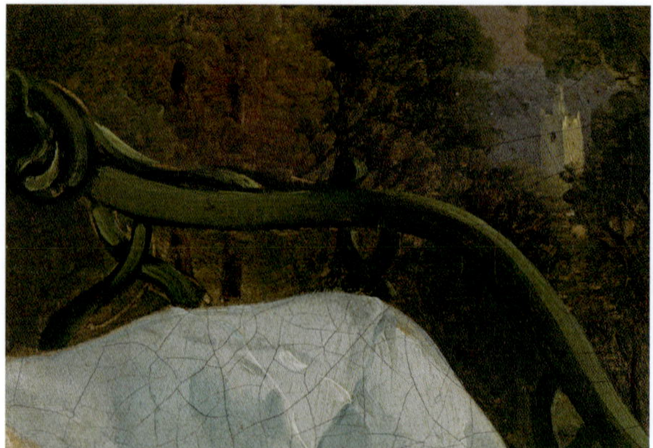

In 18th-century England, representative likenesses were the order of the day. Returning to his native Sudbury with his young wife in 1748, Gainsborough could probably reckon on a number of sitters among the wealthy squires of the region. Perhaps the Andrews portrait, with its unusually generous accommodation of the surrounding countryside, was intended to give potential patrons a demonstration of his skills in realistic landscape painting. To judge from the portraits he executed in the years that followed – in which his sitters were shown against a neutral background, or in conventional Rococo garden settings – his innovative proposal was taken up neither by the Suffolk gentry, nor by the members of society whose celebrated portraitist he later became.

Upwardly mobile

"There is not such a set of Enemies to a real artist" as the "damn Gentlemen", stated Gainsborough, railing against a class he was forced to portray all his life. "They have but one part worth looking at," he went on, "and that is their purse." It is as a member of this species that Mr Robert Andrews, leaning casually on the garden bench with his legs crossed and his blasé expression, presents himself here. His ease of attitude, pale coat and pure white, fashionably bound neckerchief suggest, together with his shooting gear, a gentleman's proper combination of activity and leisure. His feet rest on the roots of an oak, a tree which traditionally symbolized stability and continuity, and sometimes even eternity.

Andrews poses as a member of the landed gentry, the freeholding class of squires and recent peerage, who not only owned most of the country, but had parliament in their hands, too. Without their consent, George II could neither impose taxes nor raise an army. "In my eye," as one contemporary statesman wrote of this class, "you are the great oaks that shade a country, and perpetuate your benefits from generation to generation."

The landed gentry is thought to have numbered some 8,000 to 20,000 families (estimates vary considerably). The majority of these families owned estates

market and a sharp fall in all foreign trade. The writer Daniel Defoe, who passed through Sudbury in 1724, described the town as poor and highly populated. The poor, according to Defoe, were on the point of devouring the rich – at least in number.

The modest clothier's business run at Sudbury by Thomas Gainsborough's father was declared bankrupt in 1733. He was evidently not quite as astute in such matters as the Carters. The painter, born in 1727, and one of eight children, may well have inherited his father's lackadaisical attitude to property. More than earning money, he preferred to pick up his viola da gamba and walk out to a pretty village where he could paint landscapes.

By the age of thirteen, Gainsborough was already so skilled at drawing from the life that his family sent him, possibly with the support of a patron, to study in London. Under the designer and decorative artist Hubert-François Gravelot he learned the fashionable French Rococo style, which, in England too, had replaced the pompous solidity of the Baroque. Its influence can be seen in the elegant curves of Mrs Andrews' garden bench. It was in London, too, that Gainsborough became acquainted with the realism of Dutch landscape painting. Gainsborough made several essays in this genre himself. However, landscapes were not in demand at the time. They were extremely badly paid and considered little more than decorative space fillers, to be hung over doors or above fireplaces.

Gainsborough was therefore forced to earn his living with portraits – "face painting" as he called it – which he enjoyed far less than landscapes.

large enough to bring them an annual income of some 1,000 to 3,000 pounds, allowing them to lead a life of leisure or enter politics. Of course, even larger estates were owned by the small elite of peers and lords of ancient aristocratic lineage.

The franchise was based entirely on land ownership at the time. The great mass of the population, who owned no land at all, nevertheless enjoyed equality before the law, by contrast with their cousins on the continent. The shrewdest businessmen among them were also able to purchase land. It is probable that the Andrews family came to wealth and rank in this way. Robert is not as blue-blooded as he might appear. His father was apparently an artisan, a silversmith, in London. It is known that the young Gainsborough, during his stay in London, was put up by a silversmith. Perhaps Mr Andrews senior was his unsuspecting patron.

Old bankbooks reveal Robert Andrews' father to have lent money at very high interest rates. There were many large landowners among his debtors. In 1743 he lent the substantial sum of 30,000 pounds to Frederick, Prince of Wales, and was later appointed "remembrances" (debt collector) to his household. He ran a successful business from his house in Grosvenor Square, buying ships and trading with the colonies. He was one of a new generation of merchants and factory founders who paved the way for the Industrial Revolution. They had made England the world's leading trading nation and would soon hold the political reins in their hands: capital and factories had become more important than land.

In 1749, however, such days were still far off. Mr Andrews gave his son Robert, who was born in 1726, a gentleman's education at Oxford and, with the profits of usurious business deals, bought him an estate and a squire's daughter as a bride, thereby ensuring his son's entry to the upper classes. Robert, by all

accounts, became a worthy member of his new class. Although he did not enter politics, and despite a long life (he died at the age of 79), his occupations are unlikely to have left him much time for rural recreation. With the death of his father in 1763, he took over the family financial empire. He did everything within his power to increase the family fortune and, if eight offspring are anything to judge by, to strengthen the family tree: a field of endeavour so suggestively symbolized by Gainsborough's ancient oak.

A good match

Feelings had little sway in the matter of marriage between two wealthy families. The bride was often promised at a very tender age and, like Frances Mary Carter, married off at the age of fifteen or sixteen. She was little more than a pawn in a business deal, in which each party was concerned to increase its wealth, property or influence by means of the most

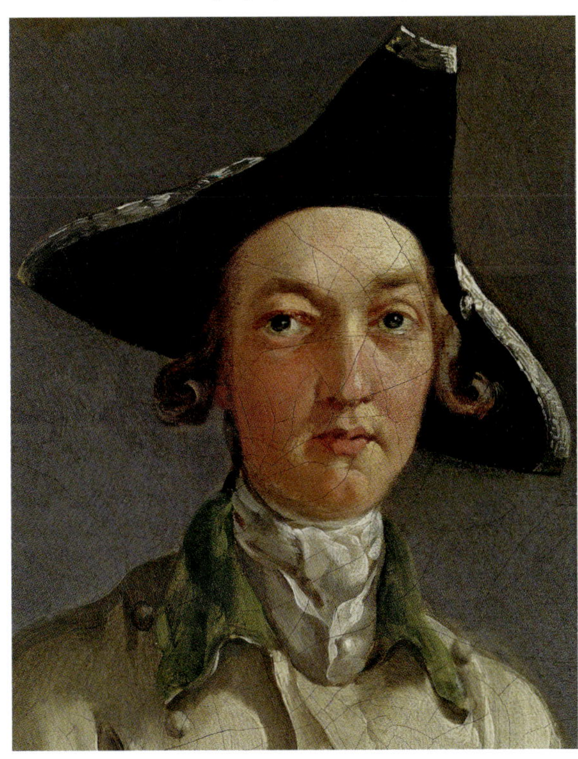

advantageous match. Family lawyers would haggle for weeks over marriage contracts, thinking up endlessly sophisticated clauses to insure family fortunes against every conceivable danger. It was imperative that the wealth accumulated with such great care should be passed on undiminished for the benefit of generations to come.

As a final ditch against incompetent or reckless heirs, family trusts were set up which left successive heads of the family no more than usufructuary rights on the property they inherited. Moreover, the precaution was frequently taken of determining the younger sons' inheritance and daughters' dowries in advance, indeed before they were born, lest these prove an undue strain on family resources. The sum designated for the lady of the manor's private expenses, as well as her widow's allowance, were also the object of negotiation. For "the only hope that keeps up a wife's spirits", according to the cynical Mr Peachum, a character in John Gay's popular

Beggar's Opera, is "the comfortable estate of widowhood", while losing her husband "is the whole Scheme and Intention of all Marriage Articles".

Frances Carter was undoubtedly an excellent match. The estate of Auberies, upon which Gainsborough has painted the couple, was probably part of her dowry. Auberies bordered on Ballingdon, her father's estate. According to a description of 1769, Auberies consisted of "a modern regular and uniform building of bricks … situated upon an eminence … commanding a most delightful prospect … with gardens … and several ponds". Gainsborough's painting includes none of these features. The Andrews may have had their mansion built later, of course, possibly even on the spot where their garden bench stood.

It may be assumed that the bridegroom will have gone to some expense in furnishing both his country seat and town house on Grosvenor Square. Unlike the established landed aristocracy,

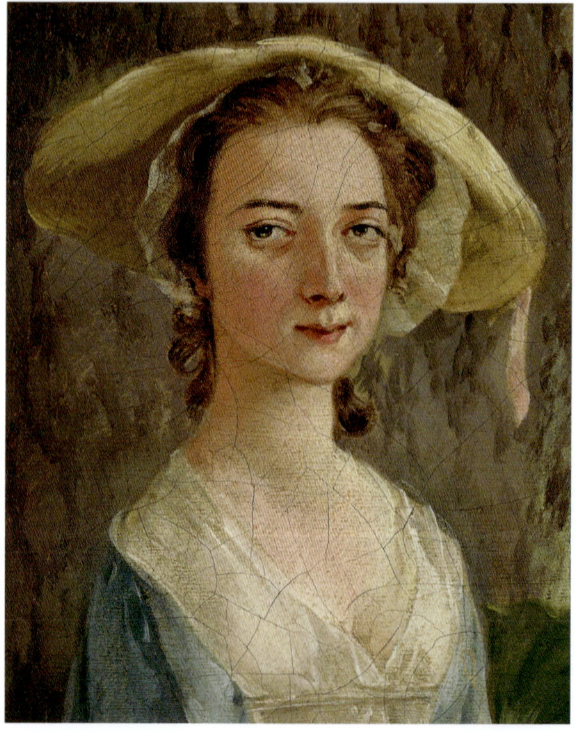

merchants and gentry attached great value to comfort and spared no extravagance in acquiring it. The material for Frances Carter's fashionable dress is much more likely to have come from London or Paris than from her family's local cloth mill. Its full blue silk over hooped, pale-yellow petticoats hardly has room on the Rococo bench. Unlike most of his contemporaries, Gainsborough did not employ a drapery painter. He devoted no less attention to the iridescence of shot silk than to the play of colours in a cloudy sky.

If we are prepared to accept the views of an artist who strove to go beyond mere likeness in revealing his sitter's character, then Frances Carter must have made a fitting companion for her businesslike husband. She died in 1780, 26 years before him. The cool gaze and tight lips of this young woman suggest that the accumulation and retention of property may have come quite naturally to her. In this, at least, the couple will have been compatible – unlike Gainsborough and his wife.

As an illegitimate, unowned child of the Duke of Beaufort, Margaret brought a lifelong annuity of 200 pounds to her marriage. This provided the couple with a modest security, but Margaret's pettiness and greed were a cramp on Gainsborough's Bohemian lifestyle. She kept a tight control over his income, making sure he painted portraits and driving away his merrier and more distracting friends. The painter seems to have submitted calmly: "She was never much formed to humour my happiness."

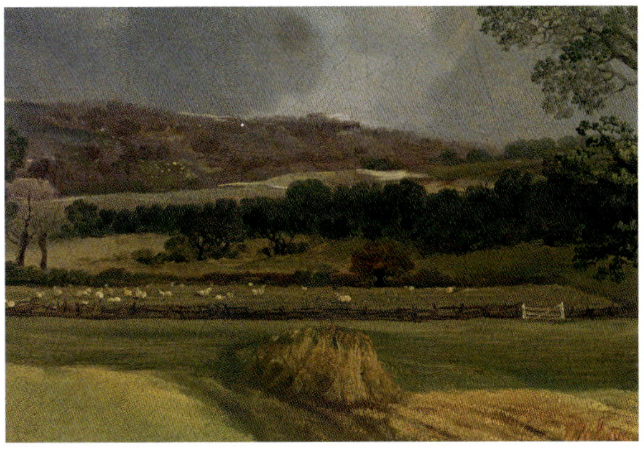

Illusion of a pastoral idyll

The view from the garden bench gives the appearance of a boundless idyll – not unlike the ideal parkland proposed by the most famous 18th-century landscape gardeners. It even includes an occasional cluster of trees: aesthetically indispensable for the interruption of vistas that would otherwise seem too wide, or too symmetrical. However, functionality in all its forms was considered inappropriate in one of the new English parks. Corn fields and herds of sheep, not to mention the byre just visible in the background on the left, would be quite out of place. Gainsborough, it must be concluded, has not painted Mr and Mrs Andrews in a park, but on a farm.

The inconspicuous wooden pen enclosing grazing land for sheep would have been equally unlikely to feature in a parkland scene. It is rather a testimony to the Agrarian Revolution, which changed England some 50 years before the Industrial Revolution by doubling agricultural produce. Enclosure, the fencing in of previously open land, had been a precondition of more intensive cultivation. For centuries, the old patriarchal feudal system had guaranteed access to the open fields. This meant that large areas of common land had provided a more or less subsistence holding. Any villager had the right to put his cow or geese to pasture on common land after the harvest. The right proved a fetter on the rationalization and intensification of farm cultivation, and therefore had to be reversed. A new type of highly effective farming began in the middle of the 18th century when the more progressive landowners began to combine strips of land to create larger fields (in Nottinghamshire, for example, where 322 narrow strips were joined to form 23 pastures). They ploughed up land that had previously been infertile or forest, and they had the fields fenced in, thus preventing the villagers putting their own cattle to graze – much to the disadvantage of the rural poor, who were ruined by the loss of their rights.

As far as the landowners were concerned, however, the "enclosures" proved one of the most profitable investments of the 18th century. Among the agricultural pioneers of the time were men like Mr Andrews, merchants who had recently bought themselves into land. Used to investing capital for profit, they were also more open to innovation than were the longer established, landed gentry.

It is therefore not beyond the bounds of possibility that the young London financier, proud of his "model farm", asked for a generous depiction of it in his wedding portrait, or at least reacted warmly to the artist's suggestion of the idea. Even in commissioning the portrait from Gainsborough, a mere beginner after all, Andrews proved his acumen for highly profitable investment in "future markets". For the gentleman at the foot of the durable oak undoubtedly contributed to the welfare of his descendants, who sold the painting for 130,000 pounds at Sotheby's in 1960.

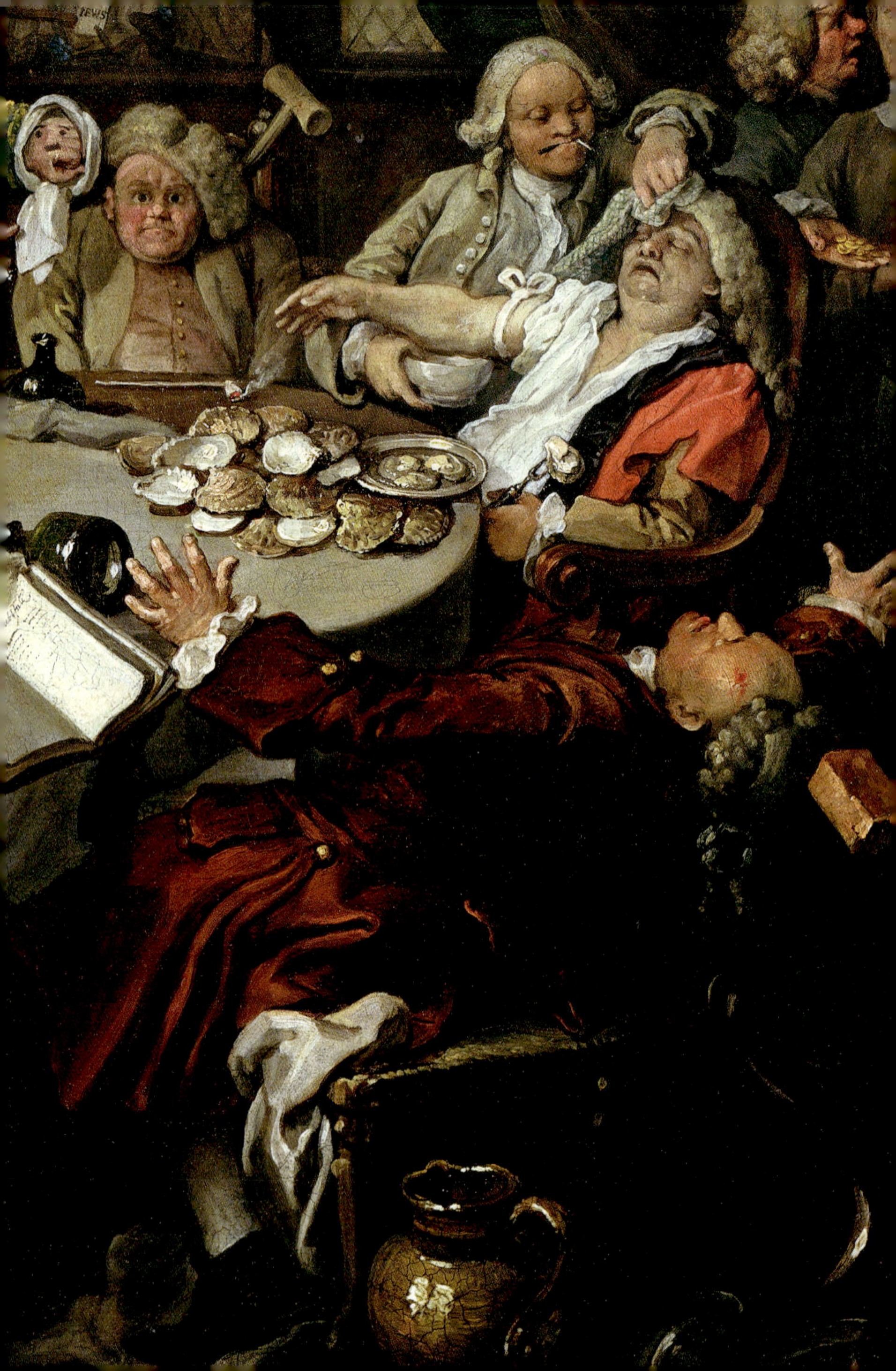

William Hogarth (1697–1764)

Politics as a dirty business

An Election Entertainment, 1754/1755
102 x 127 cm, London,
Sir John Soane's Museum

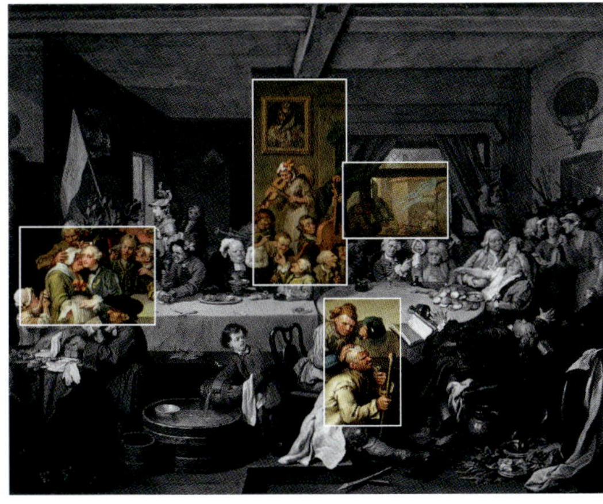

Democracy was still in its infancy when Hogarth executed this painting. After the English parliament had succeeded in restricting the rights of the monarch, elections to the House of Commons became increasingly important. The candidates fought with every means at their disposal – including bribery, intimidation and fraud. Hogarth's biting satire on these chaotic conditions today hangs in Sir John Soane's Museum in London.

When William Hogarth painted *An Election Entertainment* in 1754/55, the English throne was occupied by a German monarch. King George II did not like his kingdom; in his view, "there wasn't an English baker who could make sweetmeats, an English musician who could play, [or] English coachman who could drive … English entertainments were worthless, whereas in Hanover all these things were performed with the greatest accomplishment." George's low regard for English entertainments was not simply a reflection of his poor knowledge of the language. Like his father George I, with whom the

House of Hanover came to the island's throne in 1714, George never felt at home in England. His "foreign rule" helped accelerate a process with consequences that are still with us today: the restriction of the monarch's rights by parliament and thus the development of modern democracy.

Hogarth painted his picture, therefore, when our present form of government was still in its infancy. It is not a very flattering image. The first of a series of four paintings about a parliamentary election, it shows a dinner in a tavern. The representatives of the host party are sitting on the left. Opposite them at the other end of the table, a local dignitary is slumped in his chair: he has eaten too much and is being bled. Demonstrators are throwing stones through the window, and in the front left-hand corner, election gifts are being laid out.

The other three pictures in the cycle also portray chaotic proceedings in a down-at-heel society. The fact that something new was nevertheless taking place seems to escape Hogarth's eyes. Or at least, he does not show it.

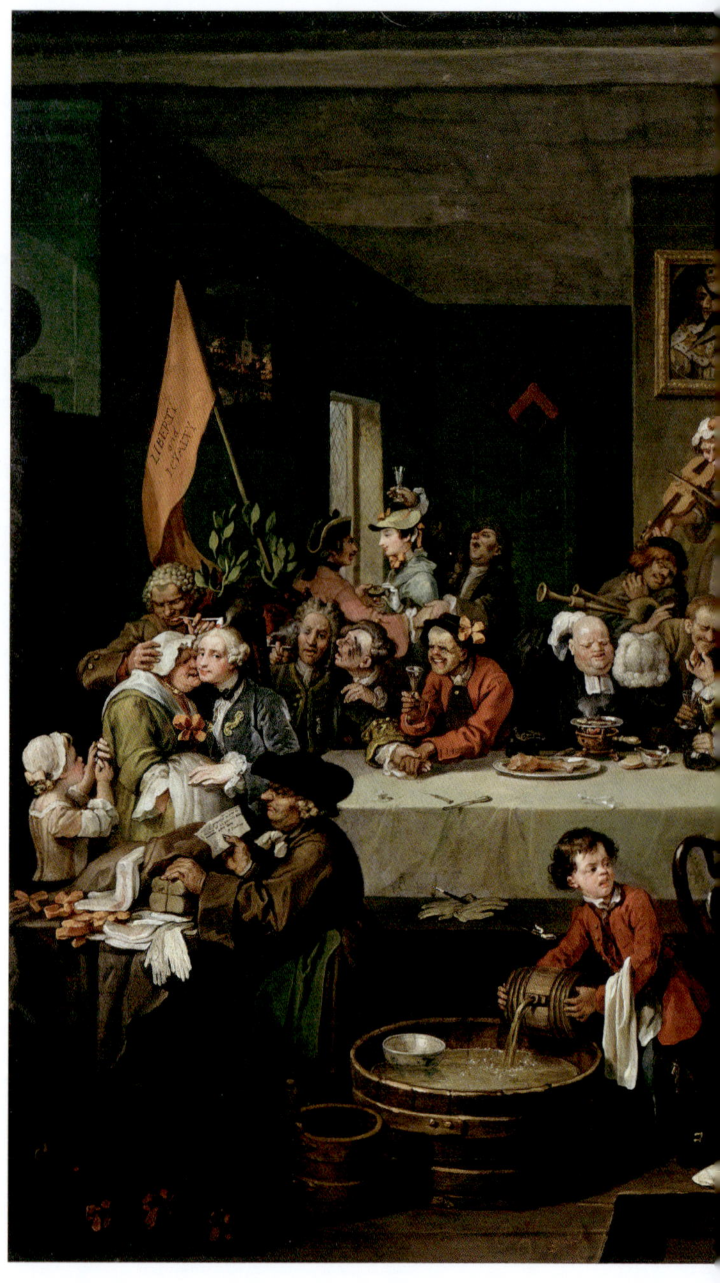

LIBERTY
AND
LOYALTY

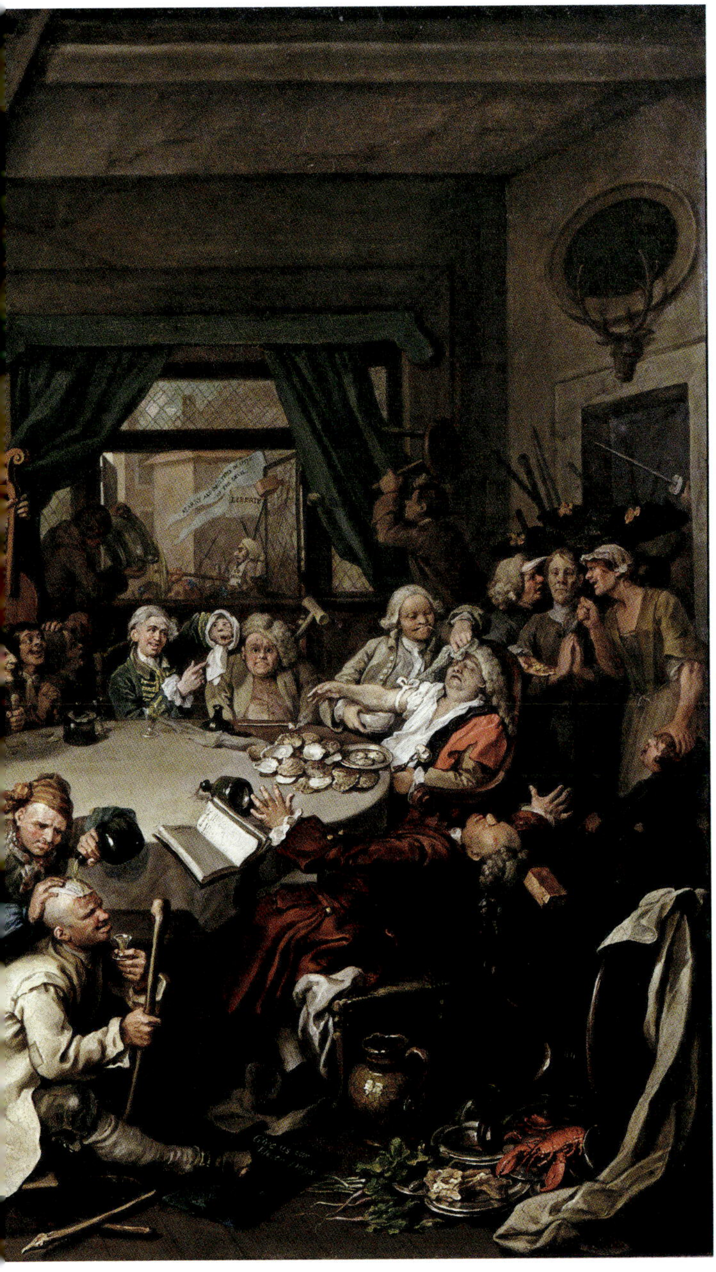

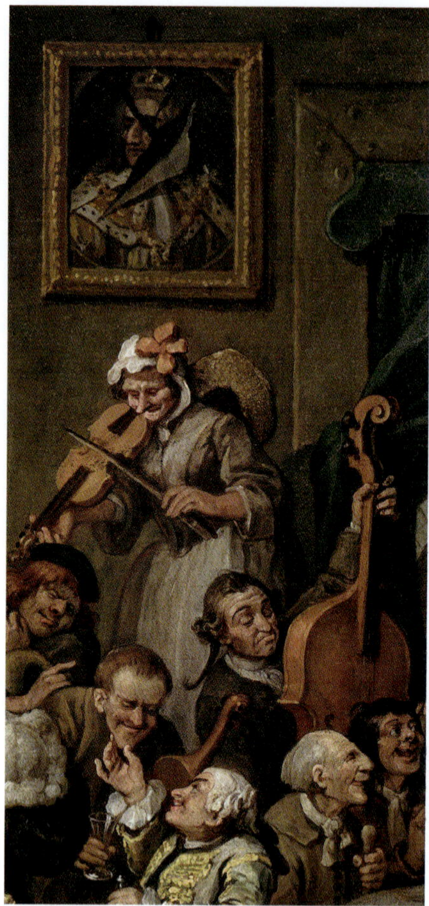

his predecessor, James II. A member of the House of Orange, William was also the governor of the Netherlands and the son-in-law of the deposed king. He came to the throne in 1689, 65 years before the election painted by Hogarth.

With William's appointment, however, the British made it clear to their foreign monarch that from now on the king was there for the people, and not the other way around. William had to approve the famous Bill of Rights. This guaranteed electoral freedom and freedom of speech in parliament. It was no longer forbidden to criticize the Crown, and members of parliament were no longer chosen by the monarch, but elected by the voters. Without the approval of parliament, moreover, the king was no longer allowed to maintain an army in peacetime, and thus lost his instrument of power.

William and his successors regularly tried to get round the Bill of Rights; one such attempt had probably infuriated the visitors to the tavern so much that they slashed the King's portrait.

In those days, only a small proportion of the population in England were actually allowed to vote. In 1754 it was fewer than 16,000 people – naturally all of them men. As a rule, to be eligible as a voter, it was necessary to own land. Even a modest farmer could vote if he lived on his own land, whereas a tenant farmer could not. Merchants and manufacturers similarly were denied suffrage. Parliament was dominated by the landed gentry.

To get into the House of Commons, you had to suffer

The two smartly dressed gentlemen seen here on the right and in the middle are the hosts and the victims of the dinner. The one seated further back is being pestered by a pushy man with a smoking pipe, while the younger man in front endures the unpleasant embrace of a fat old woman. Someone is deliberately trying to singe his wig – a common prank in those days. Perhaps the young girl on the left is even slipping the ring off his finger. From beneath raised eyebrows, he looks out at the viewer with an ironic, long suffering expression: if you want to be elected, you have to suffer, you have to smile even at malicious tricks.

Whether the two men are actually candidates themselves, or are simply canvassing for votes, is unclear: well paid agents often had to do all the real work in election campaigns. From their yellow

The scuffle for power

Even in those days, music was all part of electioneering. The man playing the bagpipes is scratching his neck, for of course he is a Scot, and according to English prejudice all Scots had the itch. The violin is being played by Fiddling Nan, a popular figure in Oxfordshire. It was the 1754 Oxfordshire parliamentary elections which provided Hogarth, a Londoner, with the starting point for his political satire.

Above the small orchestra hangs a badly damaged portrait of William III. Like the Hanoverians, he too had been fetched in from abroad. He was offered the crown after the English had driven out ribbons (and the flag behind them), however, we know that their money and their feelings are being sacrificed on behalf of the Whigs, whose party motto was "Liberty and Loyalty".

Elections to the House of Commons in London were held every seven years – or at least they were supposed to be. In Oxfordshire, however, it was over 40 years since the last ballot. In another district, there were only three elections in the whole of the 18th century. Instead, the landed gentry frequently decided amongst themselves who should represent their region. The rules of democracy may have been written down, but they were not yet being exercised.

In London, seats in parliament were occasionally offered openly for sale. Their buyers were mostly unemployed younger sons of large aristocratic families. In a letter of 1767, Lord Chesterfield described how he approached a dealer and offered him £2,500 for a "safe seat". The dealer merely laughed in his face and told him that you couldn't buy a borough for that price any more. Over the course of the century, prices for a seat in the House of Commons rose to £5,000.

Elections were expensive at the best of times. In 1754 a candidate in Eastbury spent £3,400 on canvassing, but probably didn't pay the electoral deputy enough: the latter declared fifteen votes cast in his favour invalid and pronounced the rival candidate the winner. The sorts of things a candidate had to pay for were listed in a satirical article: ribbons for suits and hats, cudgels and bottles of brandy, coach rides, perjurers, coffee house gossips, demolition of houses, incitement of unrest, legal costs.

Just as the candidates bought their voters, once inside the House of Commons they could count on having their own vote bought. They were not paid a regular salary. But as Robert Walpole, for many years the British prime minister, once said: "Every man in the House of Commons has his price." Members of parliament whom he invited to dinner would sometimes find, tucked under their serviette, remittances of £500. Walpole was particularly delighted with one of his ballot victories because it had only cost him £900. Bribes were a generally accepted political tool. In the words of one member of parliament: "I have heard many speeches in the House of Commons which have changed my views, but none that have influenced my vote."

Every coal man a politician
The man sitting on the floor with the cudgel in his hand, and the one rinsing out the wound on his

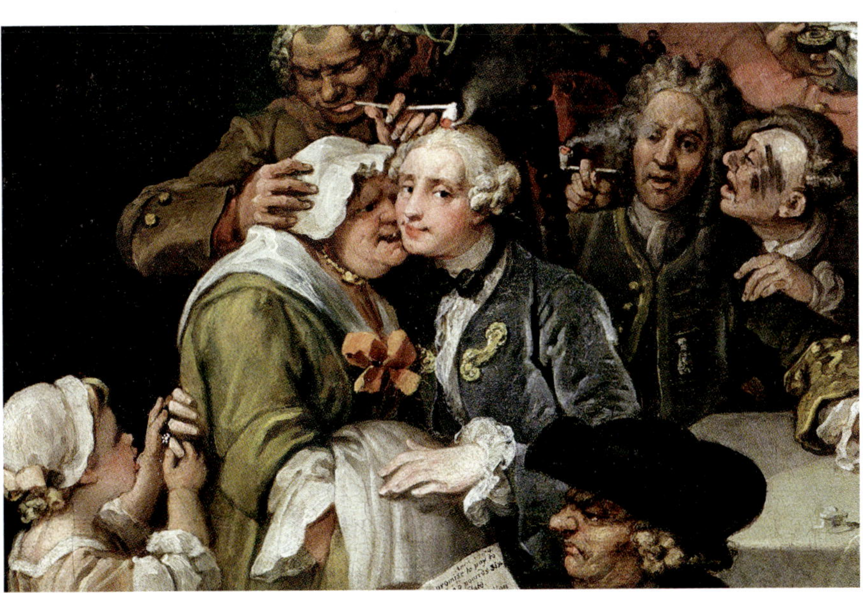

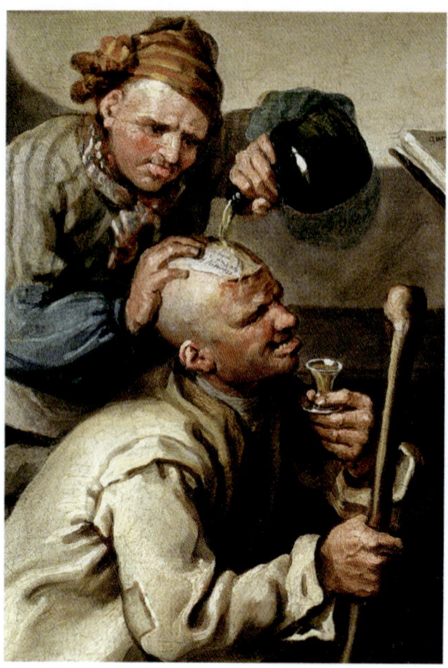

head with gin, the alcohol of the poor, had no vote: they belonged to the proletariat. Their services were nevertheless required in the election campaign. Even in Oxfordshire in 1754, votes were not only secured with money, but also with intimidation and force. And for that, a strong pair of arms was always useful. On this occasion the Tories won, but the Whigs contested the result on the grounds that it was obtained with threats and bribery. And since the Whigs held the majority in the House of Commons, they won their appeal in Oxfordshire too.

The proletariat grew steadily over the 18th century – thanks to improvements in sanitation and increasing agricultural output, and as a consequence of burgeoning industrialization. More and more people left the countryside for the city, swelling the numbers of those looking for work and thereby suppressing wages. A fourteen- to sixteen-hour working day, six days a week, became the norm. Both the exploited and the unemployed vented their dissatisfaction in large-scale fights – especially at election time. In 1790 the opposing parties in Leicester thought they had found an ideal solution: they would bypass all the militant electioneering

and simply share out the seats amicably amongst themselves. Upon learning of this decision, the disappointed mob stormed the town hall and stock exchange and plundered the homes of the wealthy.

The mobilization of the unemployed or underpaid population in the election campaign had its positive sides, too. Many of them took a real interest in the issues, discussed parliamentary decisions and took sides. According to a letter written in London: "Here every coal man is a politician and airs his views in public with the importance of a man who knows he is serving the common weal." Public pressure on parliament was so strong that it became impossible for House of Commons debates to remain confidential. As from 1771, the newspapers were allowed to carry reports on Commons business, thereby enabling the activities of parliament to be generally monitored.

Quite clearly, interest in politics in 18th-century England was much more widespread than in the countries on the European continent. This is apparent in art as well. Witness Hogarth, who is regarded as the founder of a distinctive English school of painting – and whose first works in that school were satirical portrayals of English society. Witness too, for example, a man such as the librettist John Gay, who wrote *The Beggar's Opera* in 1728. Bertolt Brecht made it famous in our own century as *The Threepenny Opera*. But while it was nothing unusual to put beggars on the stage in Brecht's day, 200 years ago it was entirely unprecedented and ran counter to every convention. And Gay not only made raga muffins into heroes, but showed their lives to be no more immoral than those of their masters: corruption was rampant throughout all the classes.

Literary and art historians are fond of insisting that the works of Gay and Hogarth arose as a reaction to Italian art, as a deliberately coarse reply to glorifying opera and flawless painting. That would be only half the truth, however. Gay's opera and Hogarth's pictures reflect more than just the artistic situation of their day; they also mirror their social surroundings. It is hard to imagine them being created in any other country than chaotic, early democratic England.

The dispute surrounding the new marriage laws
Outside the tavern window, the Tory supporters are mounting a demonstration. They are throwing

stones into the room and in return are being showered with water, or perhaps even urine. The election campaign in Oxfordshire in 1754 was a fierce one – and left dead and many wounded in its wake. While Hogarth hasn't actually painted bubbles coming out of people's mouths, he has nevertheless incorporated a considerable amount of text, which he uses to pinpoint the hottest issues of the day. The Tories, for example, are protesting against a bill which will allow Jews to be naturalized. "No Jews" are the words written on the chest of an effigy being carried past the window.

Even more topical is the Tory text being waved on a banner: "Marry and multiply in spite of the devil" – "and in spite of Lord Hardwicke's law", as contemporaries added. This new law stated that in future, marriages would only be valid if they were concluded with the publication of the banns, a licence, parental permission if necessary and an official ceremony conducted by a lawful member of the clergy.

Before that, it had been much simpler. It sufficed for a man and a woman to declare in front of witnesses that they wished to be married, to exchange rings and to consummate their marriage. From a legal point of view, that was all that was required. The Church attempted to step in by forbidding marriages of this kind, but with no success. It even forbade its

priests to bless couples who wished to get married, but again to no avail. There were plenty of clergymen without a permanent appointment, and the cheapest of all were the ones in the debtors' prison. They would marry you for just a few shillings.

The result was a profusion of secret marriages, concluded against the wishes of parents or in violation of promises of marriage already given. Hogarth, too, had eloped with his future wife and married her in secret. There were often no written records of such ceremonies, which meant that any later claims to an inheritance could not be settled. Bigamy was hard to prove. The English novels of Hogarth's day were full of elopements, adultery, and illegitimate children fighting for their rights. They reflected the realities of life within the aristocracy as within every other class of society. The majority of the opponents to the new law were conservative Tories. They argued that it represented an inadmissible incursion into the personal freedom of the individual.

Both marriage practices and political practices testified to the chaotic situation reigning in English society of the 18th century. It was a time of upheaval, of laborious reorientation. Upon one point, however, the majority were essentially agreed: it no longer wanted the dictatorial order represented by Frederick II in Prussia, for example, or Maria Theresia in Austria.

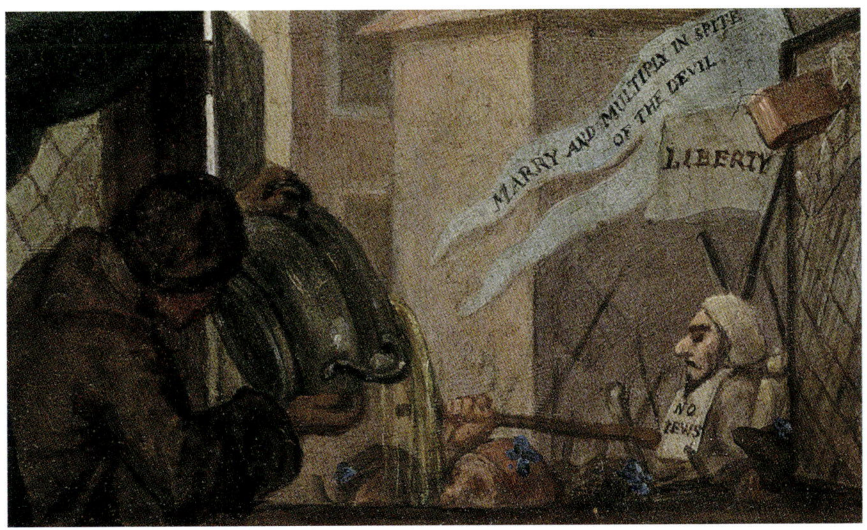

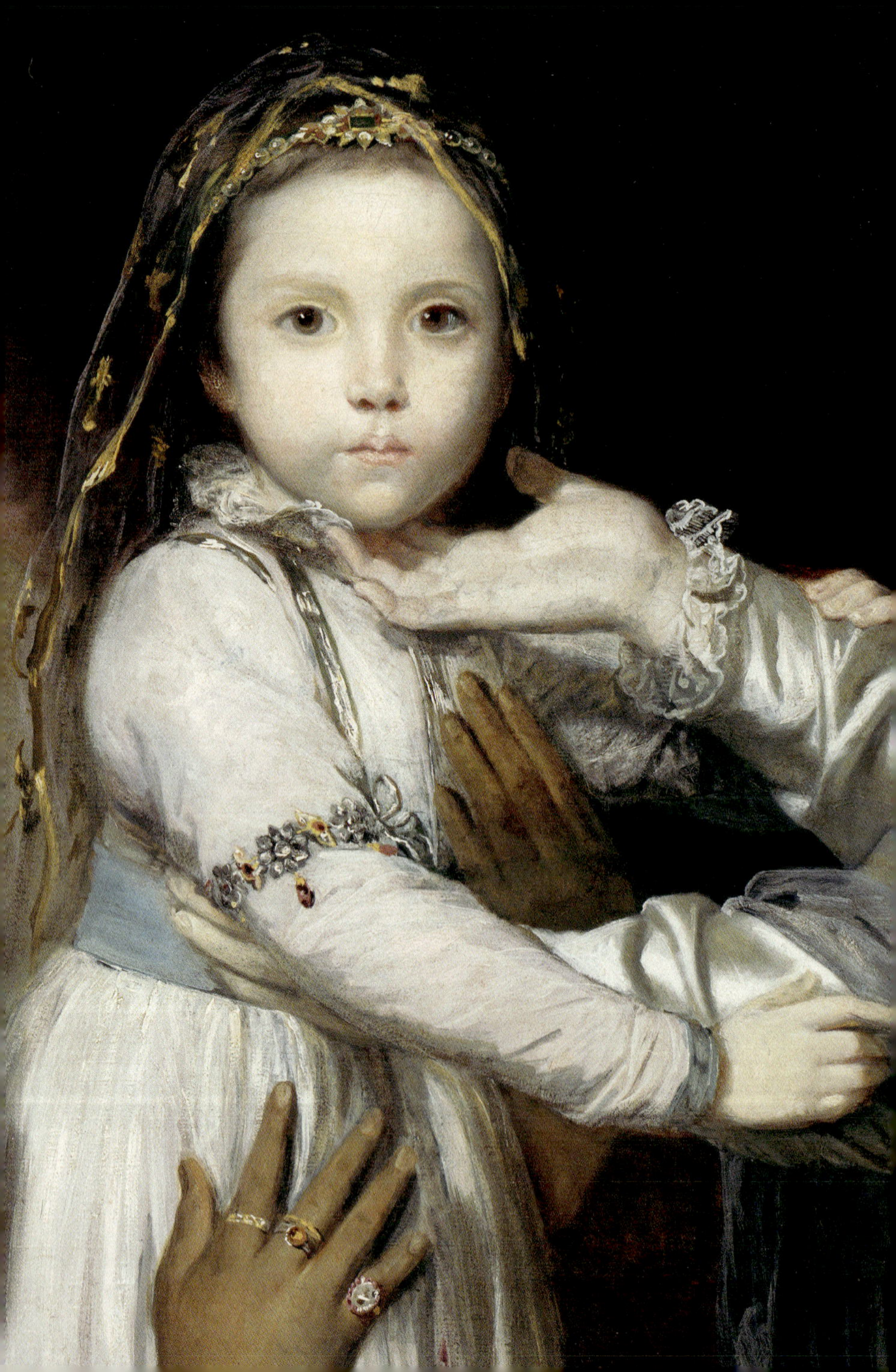

Sir Joshua Reynolds (1723–1792)

Those with no prospects in England go to India

George Clive with his Family and an Indian Maidservant, c. 1765
140 x 171 cm, Berlin, Staatliche Museen zu Berlin,
Gemäldegalerie

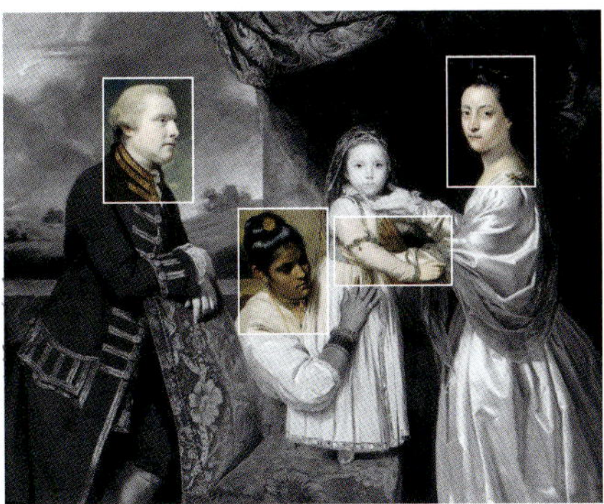

Two adults, one child – and a maidservant. Sir Joshua Reynolds (1723–1792) was the portraitist of the British upper classes. With his carefully balanced compositions he created an impression of order and tradition. Heavy drapes provided a sumptuous backdrop to the individuals in front.

It was uncommon to include domestic servants in family portraits, and the nursemaid's lowly position is given visible expression in the fact that, while the parents and child are standing, she is the only one kneeling. The man is looking at his wife and child, the child and wife are looking out at the viewer; only the maidservant must lower her eyes. Had she been a white woman, it is highly unlikely that she would have been pictured with her employers, but she is Indian. She is wearing Indian jewellery, and not only her own manner of dress, but also that of the pale little girl – silk, bangle, veil – indicate that far off India played a role in the life of this family.

For the 1700s were not only the century of the Enlightenment, of nascent industrialization, of the French Revolution, but also the century of advancing globalization. The Europeans were establishing new trading stations and military outposts all over the world, and were fighting each other over their newly claimed territories. England was thereby more successful than other countries. Its king, George III, was simultaneously Elector of Hanover, but his island subjects had few commercial interests on the European mainland. They saw their future on the seas, and invested in the building of merchant vessels that if necessary could also be deployed as warships.

Sea captains and merchants made their fortunes and began to change the rigid structure of English society. The old-established families of the land owning aristocracy were now joined by those who returned from overseas as wealthy men.

The Clives were amongst the colonial profiteers who had risen in society. The Indian servant in their family portrait serves as a sort of emblem of this.

Not a slave, but family property
Overseas trade was no longer a matter of shipping gold from Mexico or spices from Asia back to

Europe, as the Venetian Republic and Spain
had done in the past. The 18th century saw
the establishment of worldwide trading
networks. The most famous example was
the triangle between Europe, Africa and
the Caribbean: the British sailed out to
West Africa in ships laden with arms and
used the proceeds to buy slaves who they
then transported to the Caribbean,
where they loaded up with tobacco and
sugar for England.

At the time this picture was painted,
the English crown was still uninterested
in India. The landowners who dominated
parliament cared little about acquiring
overseas territories. The vision of a global
empire was still indistinct. Government
involvement went only as far as regulating
trade with India. In 1600, Queen Elizabeth
I had granted a monopoly to the East India
Company, making it the only company
permitted commercial dealings with and
within the distant continent.

In order to defend its foreign trading
posts and friendly Indian princes, the
London based East India Company – a
public corporation – maintained its own
army. This army extended its protection
over an ever-larger area and at the same
time exerted an increasing influence upon
internal Asiatic trade. Not until 1773, almost
a decade after the present portrait was
painted, would the East India Company,
by now playing an almost governmental
role in India, be brought under the control
of the Crown.

The young, dark skinned woman was not
a slave, but belonged to that class of Indians
who were treated almost like property by
their own princes and by British merchants.
Europeans saw India as a land of adventure
and a place to make one's fortune. The
journey by sea took six months, but once
there the British could become vastly rich
in a very short space of time. They were
able to cultivate a lifestyle they could never
have afforded in London: a domestic staff
of one hundred was considered nothing
unusual, and would include someone to
carry the hookah, a hairdresser, a wig maker

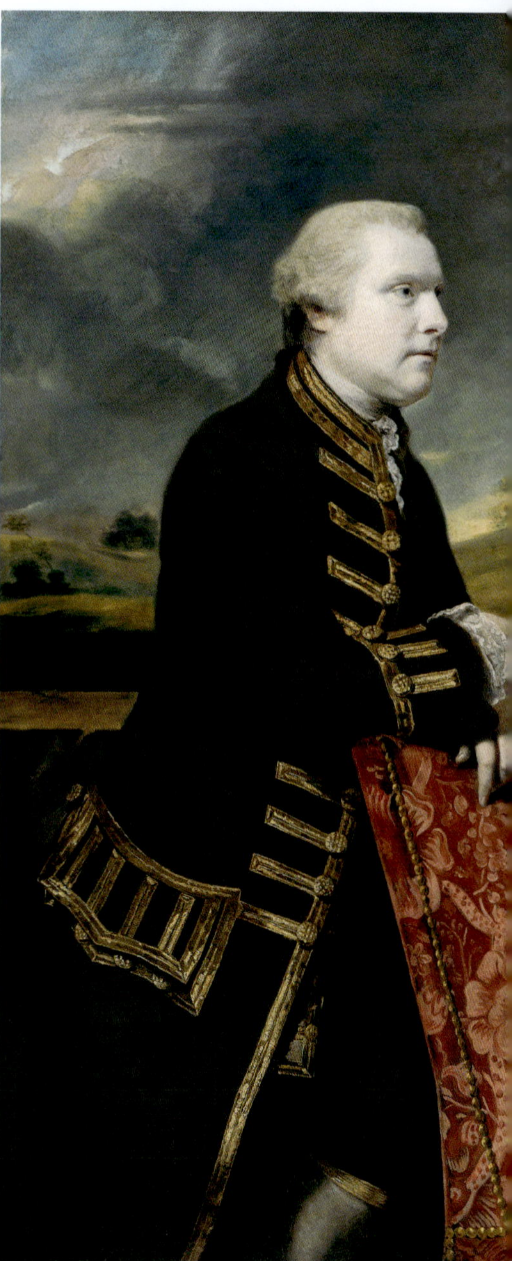

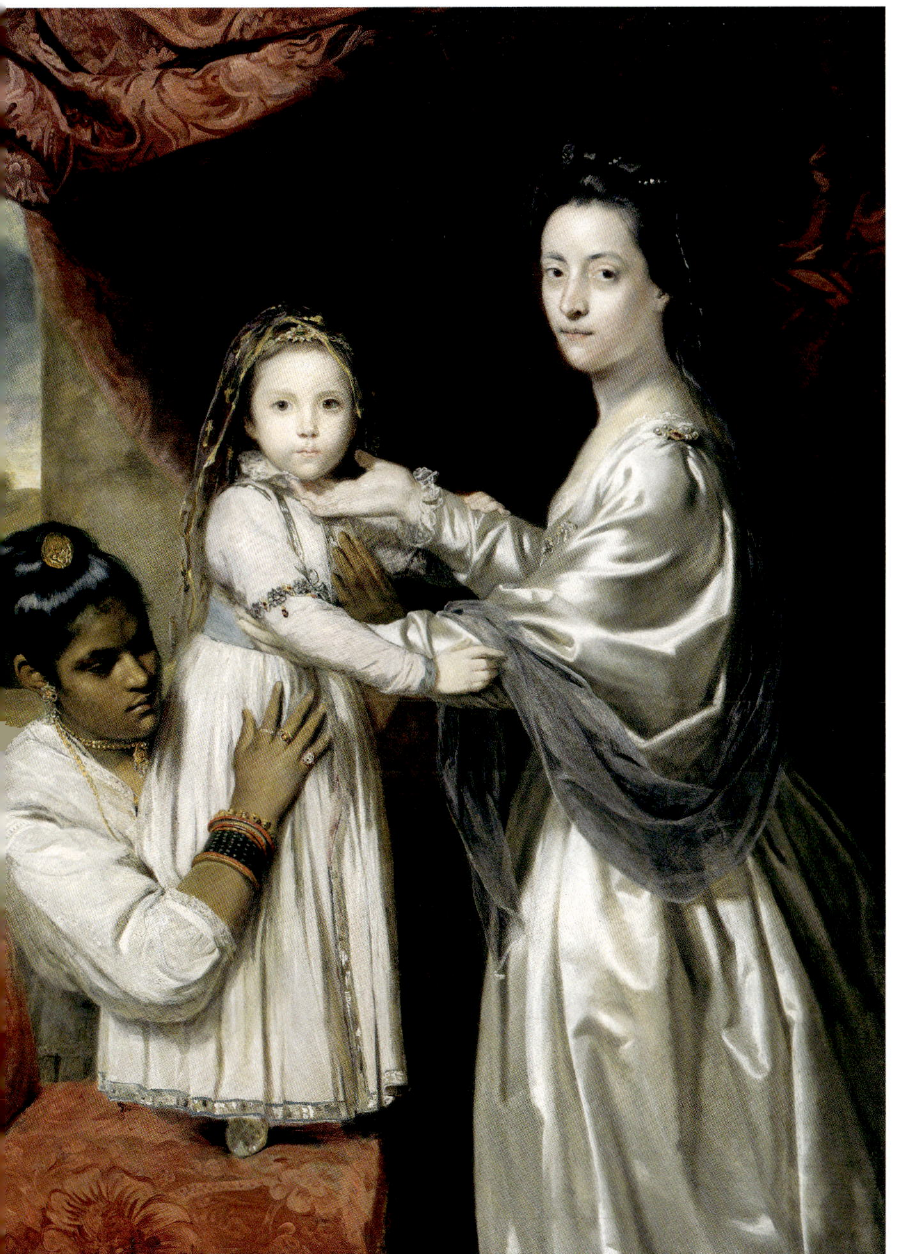

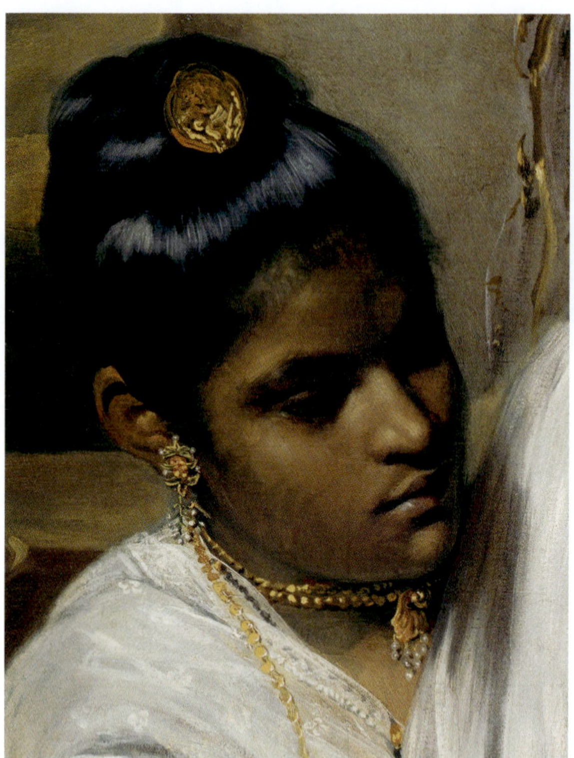

unscrupulous buck, set sail for Indian shores. This emerges from the diary of the Scottish author James Boswell. As a young man, he sought a commission as an officer in London. He had no luck, and became despairing. In a diary entry of 26 December 1762, he records reviewing in his head "a multitude of wild schemes" – including even the idea of "enlisting for five years as a soldier in India".

A pastor's son makes good

Reynolds kept a sitter book in which he noted down all the people who sat for him for their portraits. In 1764/65 the name "Mrs Clive" is mentioned several times. This confirms the assumption that the present painting must have been executed in the mid-1760s. When it later went under the hammer in 1817, the auctioneer no longer knew who it portrayed, and called it "Family Group with Black Maidservant".

In 1835 an art dealer claimed it portrayed the family of Robert Clive, the most famous of all English trade pioneers in India. In the 1970s the picture was purchased by the Staatliche Gemäldesammlung in Berlin and subjected to fresh scrutiny. On the basis of comparisons with other portraits and information gleaned about the family members, it is now thought to show not Robert Clive, but his nephew George Clive, who also spent time in India. But in the words of the former director of the Berlin museum, Henning Bock, "we can probably never be absolutely sure".

Both George and Robert Clive were typical of those who were obliged to seek their fortunes outside England. Robert is said to have been a difficult boy; he went from one school to the next until finally, at the age of eighteen, he was packed off to India by his father, a lawyer with a small country estate. He worked as a clerk for the East India Company in Madras, where according to the *New Encyclopædia Britannica* he "was moody and quarrelsome, attempted suicide, and once fought a duel". At the age of

and a group of litter bearers. Not that any of this was possible on the fixed salaries paid by the East India Company alone. The money came from other sources. Financial bribes discreetly tendered by local princes and other traders soon added up and led the company's servants to act in their own interests rather than those of their employer. "Corruption, Licentiousness and a want of Principle seem to have possessed the Minds of all Civil Servants," wrote Robert Clive of the situation in Calcutta; "by frequent bad examples", the English had grown greedy and prodigal "beyond Conception".

The reason for the situation lay not just in the opportunities that India offered for corruption, but also in the type of ex-patriots who made it their home. Those of good standing in British society remained on their native soil; only those who saw no future for themselves in London, those unable to find a useful role, those happy to make an

25 he volunteered to go to the military assistance of an Indian prince allied with the English East India Company, who was under siege from another Indian prince allied with the rival French East India Company. With 200 European and 300 Indian soldiers, Clive led a diversionary attack. His tactics were successful, and he went on to pocket a fortune. Two years later he returned to England.

He arrived back in 1753. He didn't stay in London for long; by 1755 he was rounding the Cape of Good Hope on his way back to the East Indies. He had been commissioned by the English East India Company to expel the French competition once and for all. Clive won back Calcutta and was made governor of Bengal. He instated a new Indian ruler, who gratefully presented Clive with an estate that brought him in £30,000 a year, together with £234,000 in cash. When the facts of these "gifts" were later uncovered, they sparked angry attacks against him.

In 1760 Clive returned to England. Four years later, the East India Company engaged his services once again. He was sent back to Calcutta to reestablish political order and in particular to stamp out the corruption endemic among the company's servants. For this he earned himself both plaudits and enemies. After his return, he was obliged to defend himself in parliament against accusations of corruption. In 1774 he killed himself.

The *New Encyclopædia Britannica* describes him as a man of "melancholic temperament" on whose health India had by now taken its toll. "Clive's talents were outstanding," it concludes, "his character no more unscrupulous than that of many men of his day, and his work marked the real beginning of the British Empire in India."

Like Robert, George Clive also came from a middle-class family of little means. His father was a rural pastor and a headmaster. It would seem that George failed to find a career in England, for at the age of 30 he departed for India. Five years later he returned – he, too, as a wealthy man. He built himself a large house near London, procured a seat in parliament through his cousin's connections, and from there championed the latter's interests in far away India. In 1779 he died, with little more being known about him.

A dignified portrait in timeless dress

In 1764 George Clive's wife gave birth to a daughter. The little girl's age in this portrait can thus be reckoned in months rather than years – no wonder she has to be held up by her mother and her maid. She would be too young for the well-proportioned figure that Reynolds gives her here, and she would most certainly have been incapable of such an elegant stance, in which she offers us a glimpse of a dainty foot beneath her dress. Children's hands at that age are also chubbier, and the fingers are normally curled rather than straight.

Hands were in any case never Reynolds' strong point. At times it appears as if he left them right to the end, as can be seen in the case of the maid-servant. Her right hand, with its rings and bracelets, is portrayed with close attention to detail, whereas her left hand, supporting the little girl under her arm, remains ill-defined, and its fingers considerably longer than those of the hand on the front of the dress. In fact, this left hand was probably executed not by Reynolds, but by a member of his workshop. Reynolds himself usually sketched in the overall composition, painted the heads and those details he considered important, and then left the rest to his pupils or a fabrics expert.

Reynolds was considered an artist who not only captured a particularly accurate likeness of his sitters, but who also surrounded them with a discreet

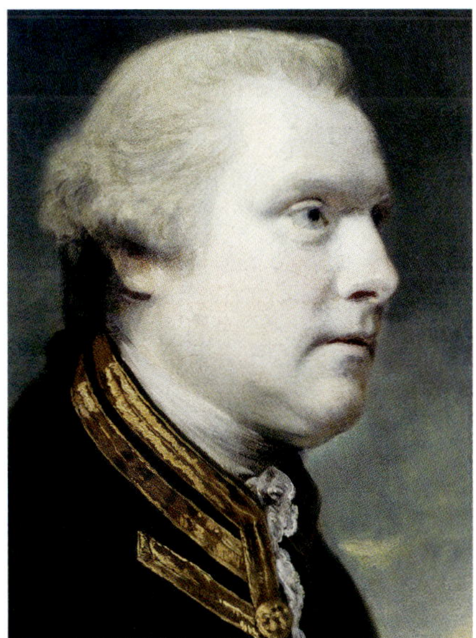

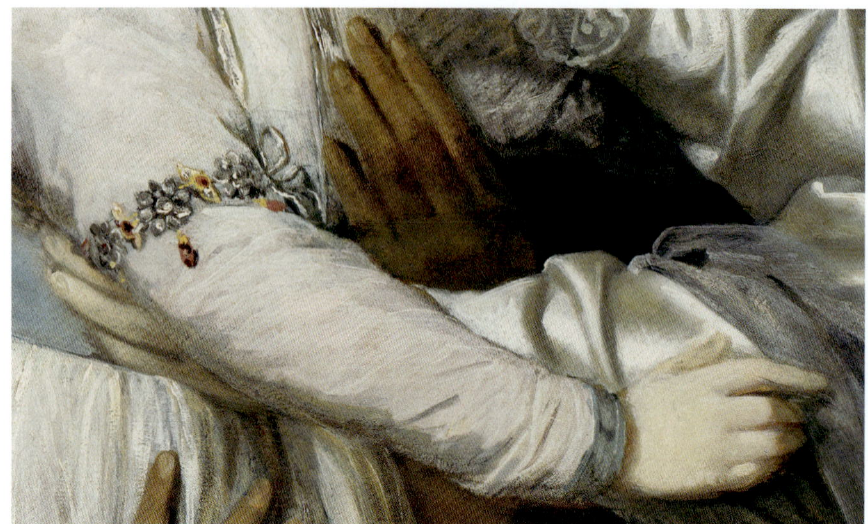

aura. "He … who in his practice of portrait painting wishes to dignify his subject," he declared in his seventh *Discourse on Art*, delivered to the Royal Academy in 1776, "will not paint her in modern dress, the familiarity of which alone is sufficient to destroy all dignity." This is also true of Mrs Clive. Her dress, with its silk scarf fastened to the shoulder and looped over her arm, bears no relation to the fashions of the day, but is intended to capture "the general air of the antique". Such references to antiquity are even more emphatic in other paintings by Reynolds. Thus he portrayed a Mrs Hartley as a nymph, for example, and a Mrs Patrick as Juno.

Part of the artistic intention of a family portrait was to illustrate the importance of the individuals within it and their relationship to one another. In most cases, the standing husband towers above his seated wife and is thus symbolically portrayed as the head of the family. In the portrait of the Clives, this is different: husband and wife are both standing, probably for compositional symmetry. The child is positioned somewhat lower, and the maidservant lowest of all, in line with her social rank. The head of the Indian maid, however, is located at the centre of the composition, and thus in an important place. An X-ray has revealed that it is made up of two sections of canvas sewn together. It is likely that the original plan was to paint just the mother, child,

and servant, and that the decision to incorporate the husband came later. None of this can be seen on the painting's surface. The maidservant only found herself in the centre of the composition when the second canvas was added. To avoid overemphasis upon her head, Reynolds – as the X-ray also reveals – extended the wall in the background further leftwards, painting over the bright clouds in the original background.

A striking feature of the present portrait is the close juxtaposition of the three female figures. It may have been dictated by the format of the original composition. But it also fell in line with 18th-century convention: only when the only child was a boy was he shown at his father's side, for the son would inherit the title and family estate. The bloodline was continued through the men, not the women.

A face posing questions

Reynolds' remarkable facility for characterizing the people in his portraits is evident in the head of the young mother. Her eyes look out at the viewer from a face that is half turned towards her daughter. Reynolds thereby creates an impression of movement. Mrs Clive's expression appears reserved, perhaps timid, and her lips seem somewhat pursed. She is supporting her daughter with both hands, but – in contrast to the maidservant – at a slight distance, as if she is obliged to remember her role as wife and lady of the house as well as mother. It is a face that provokes questions and which thereby testifies to the skill of the artist.

There were some 2,000 portraitists working in London in Reynolds' day, and judging their works was a social pastime. "Temple and I breakfasted with Captain Blair," noted James Boswell in his diary entry of 20 June 1763, "after which we went and saw Reynolds' portraits, which pleased us much. I then went with Erskine and had some games at billiards."

Portraiture, the only genre of art to be fashionable in England, was practised in the 18th century by a number of outstanding masters. Reynolds and Thomas Gainsborough (1727–1788) are the best known. Before them, England had strangely failed to produce any great artists. It had brought forth extraordinary talents in literature, theatre, and music, but not in painting and sculpture. The gap was filled by foreigners. Hans Holbein, Anthony van Dyck, and numerous Italians worked in England; agents in Venice, Florence and Rome, acting on behalf of English collectors, bought works, which then disappeared into castles and mansions.

This situation changed in Reynolds' lifetime, not least as a result of his own efforts. Like the Clives, he came from modest circumstances. He was born in 1723 as the seventh of eleven children. His father was a headmaster. Like the Clives, Reynolds first had to earn his fortune. In 1760 he took a large house in Leicester Fields, a smart area of London, where he could receive clients from the ruling classes in suitable surroundings. He lived there like a prince of painters, even if – most unaristocratically – he was always working. The king appointed him the first president of the newly founded Royal Academy of Arts, through which he was able to raise standards of training and organize public exhibitions of the work of British artists. He himself was a great buyer of paintings,

and his private collection is supposed to have been the largest of its day in England. In 1792, following his death, Christie's auction house put up over 400 pictures for sale, including Rembrandt's *Susanna and the Elders*, a painting that, like the portrait of the Clive family, today hangs in Berlin's Staatliche Gemäldesammlung.

If portraiture would awaken the urge amongst Reynolds' compatriots to establish a British school of painting, its own popularity was founded on factors unrelated to art. Portraits were a statement of social success. They had a utility value, especially for families who had amassed a rapid fortune through trade and foreign postings. Like aristocrats whose wealth accrued from the family estates, they could afford to be painted by expensive artists, in portraits that elevated them to a class into which they were not born.

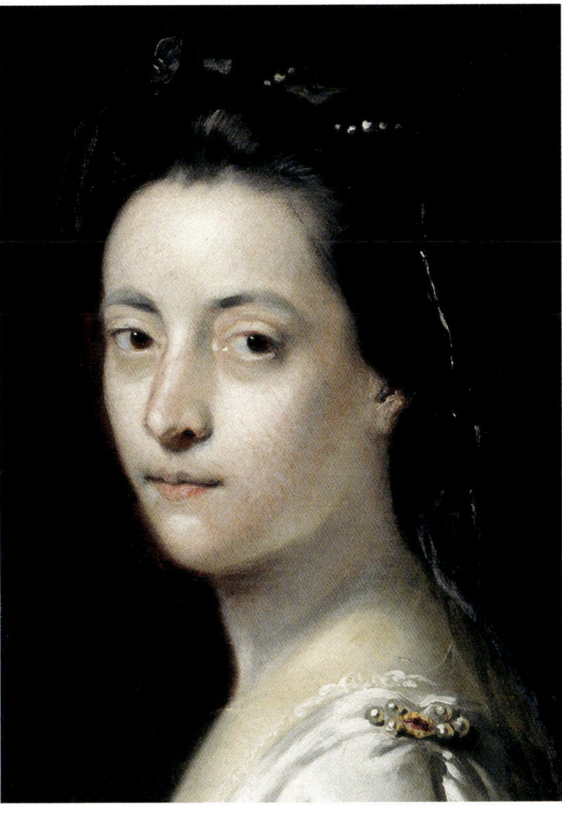

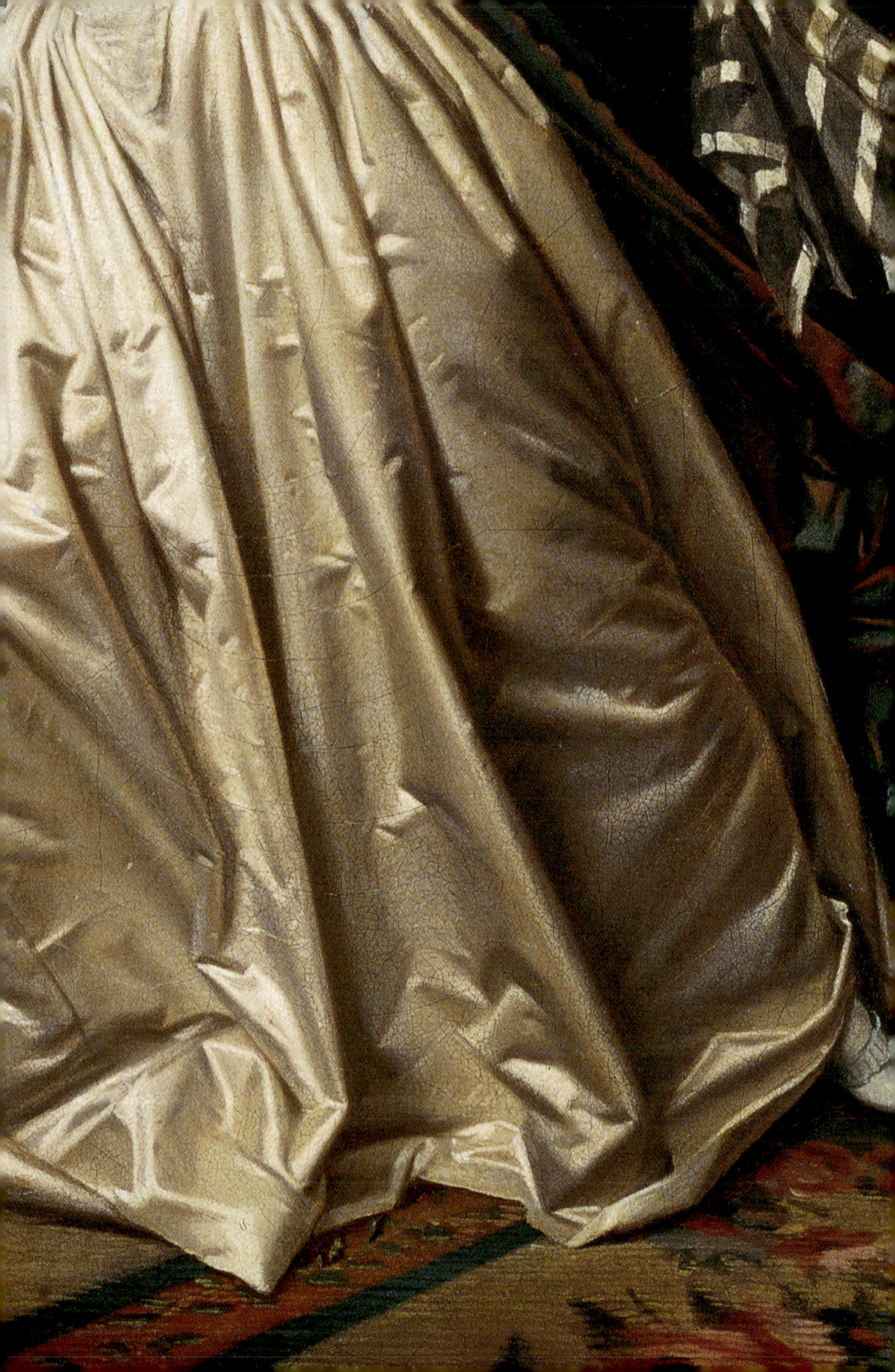

Jean-Honoré Fragonard (1732–1806)

A kiss in revolutionary times

The Stolen Kiss, 1787
45 x 55 cm, St Petersburg,
The State Hermitage Museum

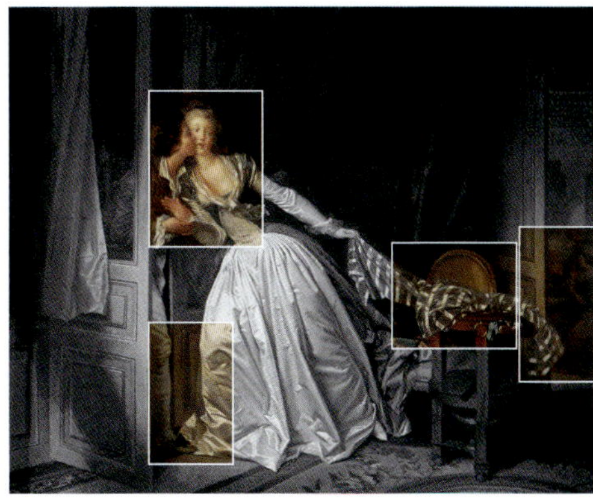

Jean-Honoré Fragonard's art was sought after by his contemporaries far beyond the borders of France, both by the general public and by the rich and powerful. His pictures of scantily clad girls on soft cushions and of pairs of lovers in charming landscapes – images full of *joie de vivre* and eroticism – corresponded to Rococo taste. The many engravings after Fragonard's œuvre, produced and sold in Paris shortly after the originals were finished, helped make *The Stolen Kiss* popular in France, even though it is more discreet than earlier works.

A young lady has left the salon in order to fetch a shawl from an adjoining anteroom, where the youth has caught her by surprise – or where, perhaps, she expected to find him. He plants a fleeting kiss upon her cheek, to which she puts up little resistance. We may suspect that a bedroom lies behind the glazed door, but the door to the salon on the right has been left open: the girl is under supervision.

Some art historians find this innocent scene – despite the typical sophistication of the composition and lighting – so untypical of the frivolous Fragonard that they hesitate over its attribution. The artist has neither signed nor dated the painting, but because the sale of the engraving was publicly advertised under his name in 1788, it can be assumed that he painted the original himself around 1787. Shortly afterwards, on 14 July 1789, the people of Paris stormed the Bastille. *The Stolen Kiss* was thus painted on the eve of the French Revolution, and if we look more closely at its private idyll, we may discover portents of this radical change.

The elders are seated in the salon

The door standing ajar on the right offers a glimpse into a salon. Two ladies are playing cards and a gentleman is looking over their shoulders. He wears a braid wig – like powdered hair, a fashion from an epoch that was drawing to a close, the *Ancien Régime*. It is a salon to which Fragonard could have belonged. As a member of the Academy of Fine Arts, he was at that time living and working with his family in an apartment in the Louvre palace, which the French court had long since exchanged for Versailles.

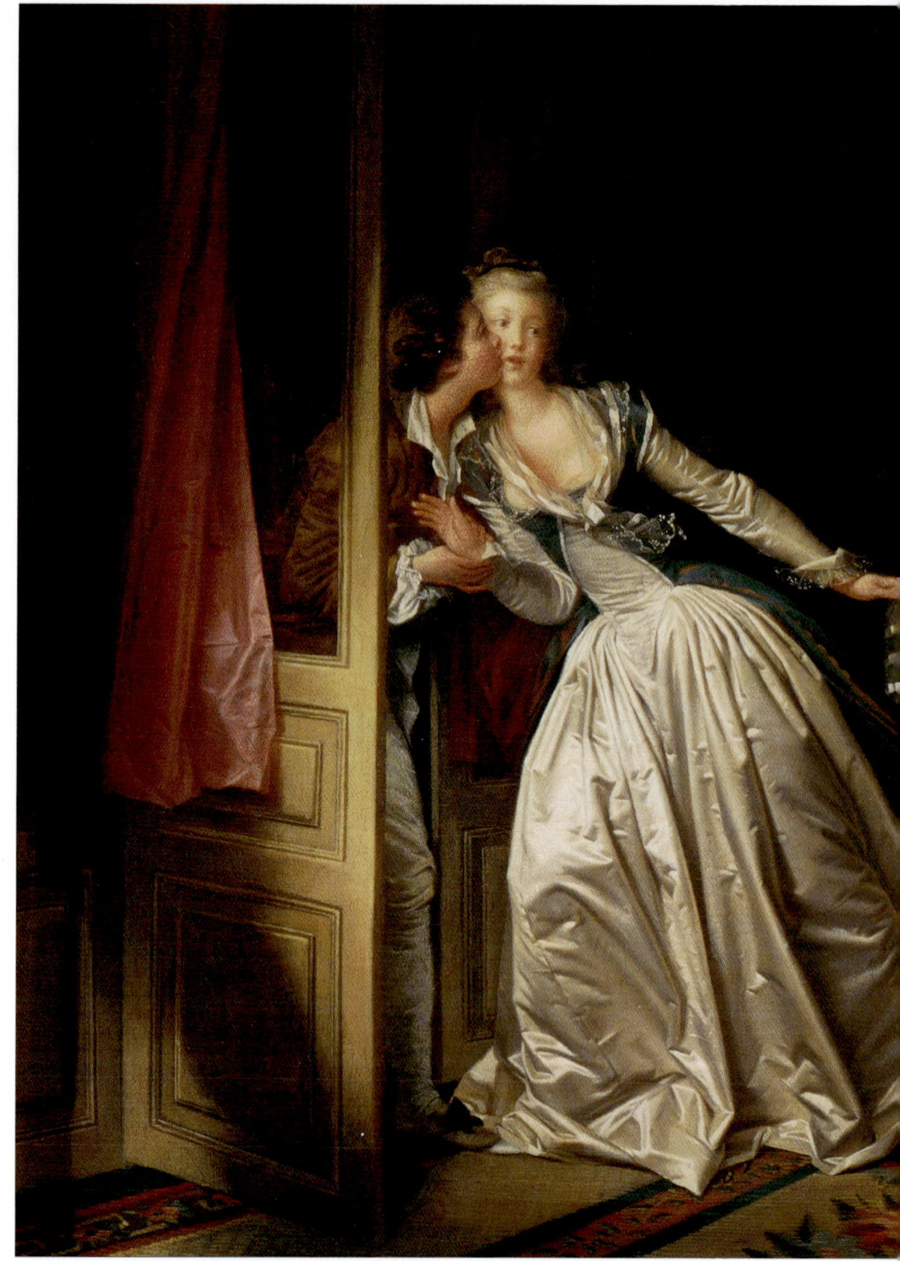

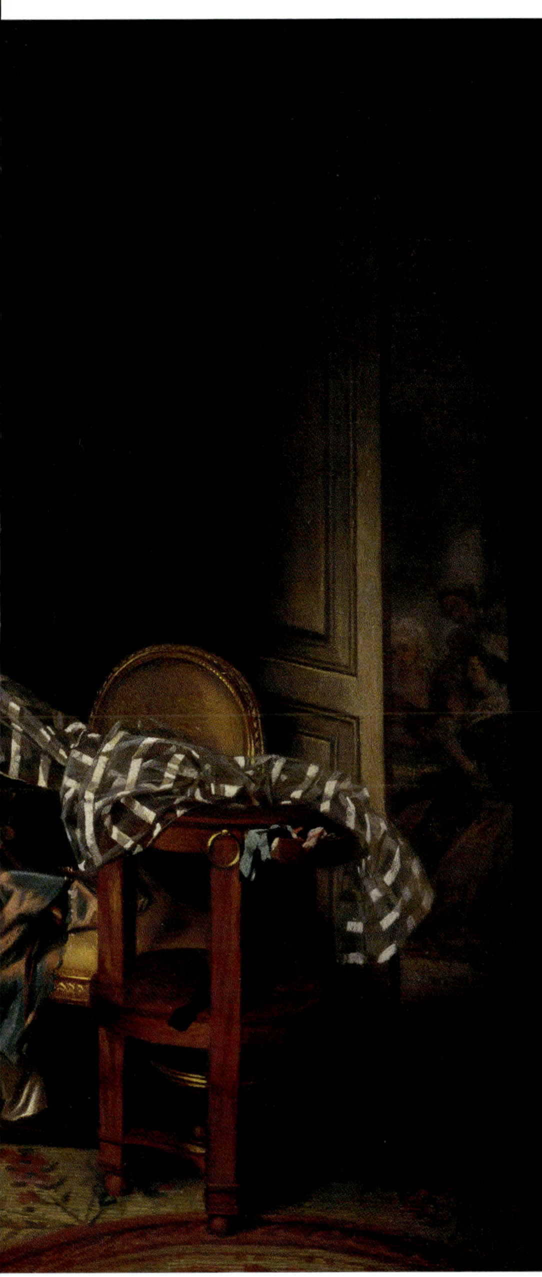

Such quarters were fitting for a successful man.

Fragonard came from a lower middle-class family. Born in 1732 as the son of a glove maker in Grasse, in the Provence region of France, he grew up in Paris and trained under François Boucher (1703–1770) and Jean-Baptiste-Siméon Chardin (1699–1779). After the obligatory trip to Rome, he caused a stir in Paris in 1761 with a number of large-format history paintings. With these, an official career leading to royal painter or Academy director appeared to lie before him, but he turned his back on it, probably out of dread of the obligations it carried. He was considered difficult; he wished to remain independent and fluctuated between decoration paintings and genre scenes, between the biblical *Adoration of the Shepherds* (*c.* 1775) and goddesses surrounded by cupids, between humble washerwomen and poetic landscapes. The customers who bought his over 450 works were private collectors – they paid better and faster than the court. Success came in 1767 with *The Swing* (or *Happy Accidents of the Swing*, as it was originally titled) for Baron de Saint-Julien, the idea for which was outlined by the Baron himself. The painting was to show the nobleman's mistress high in the air on a swing that was being pushed by a bishop, while the Baron himself watched her from an advantageous position below. Fragonard's vivacious composition was received with pleasure: he had succeeded in capturing on canvas a sunny, cheerful world, what was called *douceur de vivre*, the lightness of being. He painted the wishful dreams of a decadent society, and collectors scrambled to acquire titillating titles such as *The Chemise Removed* (*c.* 1770) and *Futile Resistance* (*c.* 1775).

The artist himself, after a few youthful years of travel, lived a fairly

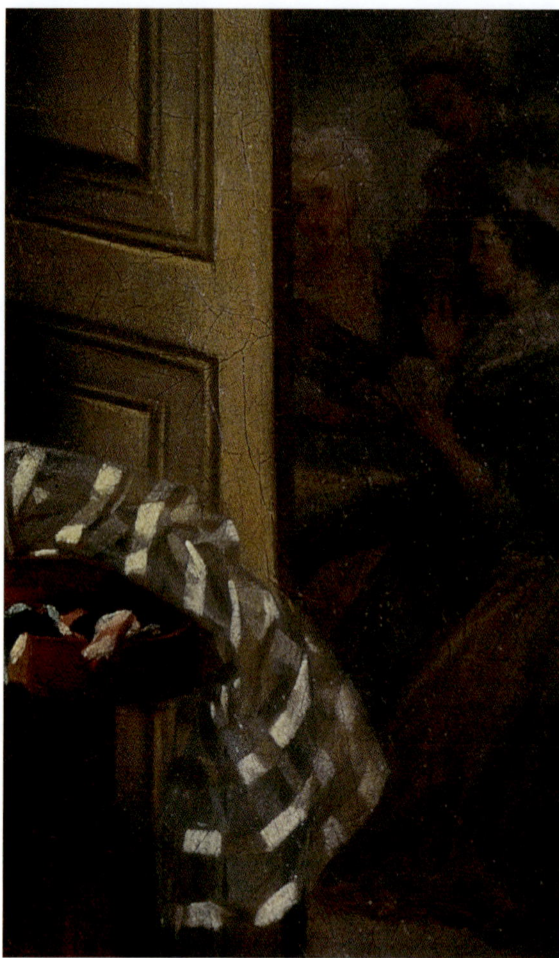

It would not be long before the salons were replaced by political clubs, in which Danton and Robespierre exhorted their listeners to overthrow the monarchy and ultimately to drive peaceable citizens like the Fragonards from their luxury apartments.

A chaste kiss on the cheek

The youth and the girl wear their hair unpowdered – a sign of the new era. Their freshness and innocence are what give this picture much of its charm. On this occasion probably nothing more passes between them than a chaste kiss on the cheek, and the young man has probably hesitated a long time before finding the courage to attempt it, like the Romantic hero of *The Sorrows of Young Werther*, the novel published in 1774 that brought Goethe European fame. The young Werther speaks rapturously of the lips of his adored Lotte, "o'er which celestial spirits hover", but vows that he shall never presume to kiss them. In order to prevent anything more, the aristocracy used to cloister its daughters in convents, where they were educated until being married off to a man whom their parents had selected solely on the basis of the family's interests.

Under the influence of the Enlightenment and Jean-Jacques Rousseau, however, a change of mentality began to appear amongst the bourgeoisie. Rousseau was the guru of the young generation. With his novel *The New Eloise* (published in 1761), he moved all sentimental, day dreaming readers to floods of tears and encouraged them to aspire towards happiness and fairness as part of a virtuous life.

Fragonard's daughter Rosalie, who was about eighteen years old at the time, may have served here as her father's model. She poses in a dress of shimmering white silk – plain, in the latest English fashion, but of a sumptuousness that the daughter

bourgeois existence. Colleagues and their wives gathered in his salon to play cards and talk. Philosophers and writers cultivated the art of conversation – "that refined pleasure belonging only to a highly civilized society" – in the salons of Paris right up to the 1760s. By the 1780s, however, most French were discussing not literature and philosophy but politics. The enlightened middle classes were concerned about the state deficit and about hoped-for reforms of the entrenched class system, which reserved all privileges for the aristocracy.

of an artist probably did not wear every day. Rosalie died just a year later, in 1788, and we do not know how she felt or thought or whether she had read Rousseau. What we do have is the correspondence of a slightly older woman of her own class, the daughter of a well-known Parisian engraver.

This Manon Phlipon, born in 1754, attended convent school only briefly. An avid reader, she proceeded to devour everything that the lending libraries had to offer. Under Rousseau's influence she vowed: "I will only ever give myself to a man with whom I can communicate and share my feelings as well as my ideas." She rejected all the grocers and tradesmen whom her parents proposed as marriage candidates. But for a girl of no means from a bourgeois background, there were few means of escaping a dull existence other than taking a rich older "protector". In the end, the attractive and intelligent Manon resignedly accepted Monsieur Roland, an administrative officer twenty years her senior, and resolved to make him a virtuous wife.

Barely had she granted him his first kiss than the date of their wedding was set: "I know what virtue is! I have vowed in my heart to follow it always." Manon had read not only Rousseau but also Plutarch and had been inspired by the latter's examples of heroic self-denial and steadfastness. Robespierre and many of his generation had studied the Greek moralists and preached antique values against the profligacy of their rulers. The cult of virtue reached its high point during the Revolution. But the philosopher Denis Diderot had already demanded a new morality in the arts, one that would "uplift the soul of the peoples". Even the new King Louis XVI followed this dictate: shortly after ascending to the throne, he banned all representations of the nude from the grand Salon in Versailles palace.

A give-away detail

When Fragonard painted *The Stolen Kiss*, the artist was already out of fashion. Although engravings of his works were still selling well, in 1774 Madame Dubarry, the mistress of Louis XV, rejected a set of paintings commissioned from the artist two years earlier to decorate one of her small palaces and substituted them with works in the strict Neoclassical style. The 1780s were marked by a triumphant return not just to Plutarch but also to Classical antiquity: the excavations at Herculaneum and Pompeii had caught the public imagination and a young painter, Jacques-Louis David, was exhibiting scenes from the lives of Roman heroes to great acclaim – in 1784 the *Oath of the Horatii*, for example, and in 1789 a *Brutus*.

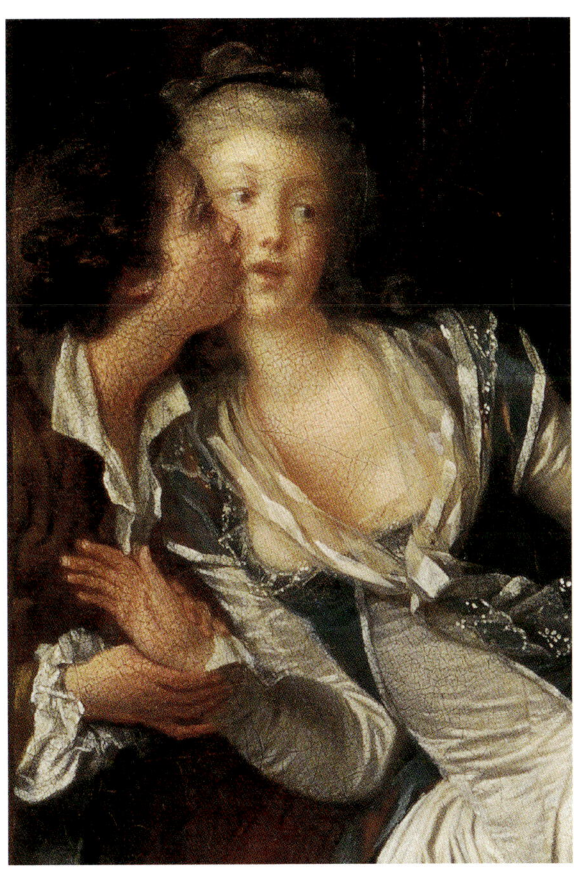

This was entirely in the spirit of Diderot, who as long ago as 1765 had demanded paintings for "people of great taste, of austere, antique taste".

Rococo frivolity was no longer in demand. Fragonard, at the age of 55 an old man for his day, tried to adapt to the market. Although he may not have painted the heroes of Classical antiquity, he took up subjects from Greek and Roman mythology and around 1785 composed an austere *Fountain of Love* set in a gloomy park – a work between Classicism and Romanticism. Another style lay closer to his heart, however. A new bourgeois breed of collectors – officials and freshly ennobled bankers – developed a penchant for paintings from the Golden Age of 17th-century Dutch and Flemish art, domestic scenes by Gabriel Metsu and Pieter de Hooch. Fragonard was familiar with these artists; he had copied Peter Paul Rubens and Jacob Jordaens during his time in Italy, and it is possible that he later even made a trip to the Netherlands. Now, therefore, he painted idyllic interiors inhabited

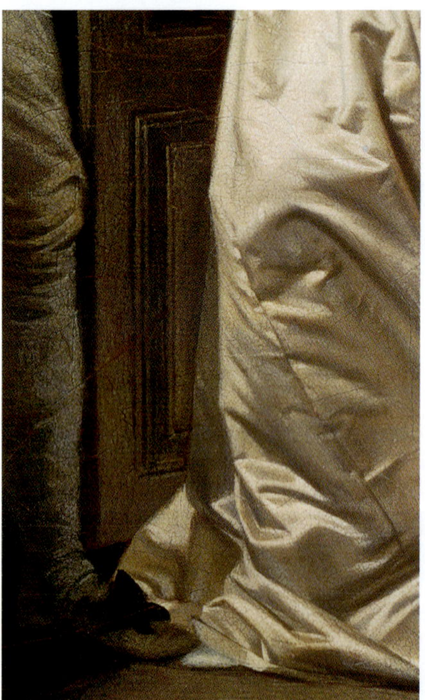

by beautiful people: pictures like *The Stolen Kiss*. There is nevertheless one detail in this chaste picture that betrays the old, "gallant" Fragonard: the youth has pinned the hem of the girl's dress beneath his foot so that she cannot run away. This discreet allusion is far removed, however, from the directness with which Fragonard had portrayed desire and lust a few years earlier, for example in his masterpiece *The Bolt* (see opposite).

As the models for his domestic scenes, the artist used members of his own family: his wife, their two children and his sister-in-law Marguerite Gerard, who came to live with them in 1775, when she was fourteen years old. Not only did Fragonard paint this girl, but he made her his pupil and taught her to make engravings from his drawings. The artist is said to have fallen in love with the assistant 29 years his junior, becoming (according to his friends) "a young man in an old skin". Marguerite later became a sought-after artist. To what extent she contributed to *The Stolen Kiss* remains a matter of dispute. She appears to have been responsible for the furniture and clothing, but in her own works the figures remain stiff and the colours cold. At all events, the virtuoso composition, the sweeping sense of movement, the sophisticated lighting and the palette demonstrate the hand of the older master.

Stripes as a sign of the Revolution

It is no coincidence that, around 1787, the gauzy shawl spilling so casually over the sides of the mahogany table should have a striped pattern: such straight and unfussy lines suited the aesthetic of Classicism, just like the solid little table itself. The Louis XVI chair also satisfied the new demand for simple, practical furniture. The only remnant of the Rococo is the carpet with its rose motif. Revolutionary France was hallmarked by stripes. For hundreds of years they were associated with convict's clothing and with outcasts. But when the English colonies in America declared their independence in 1776 and chose a flag with a striped pattern, this latter became a symbol of liberty for all England's enemies. In 1790 the Republic was proclaimed in Paris and the striped Tricolour hoisted aloft. The revolutionary "patriots" also wore stripes; Robespierre's vertically striped tailcoat became his trademark.

When Fragonard painted *The Stolen Kiss*, people were still hoping for reform. "We believed that the

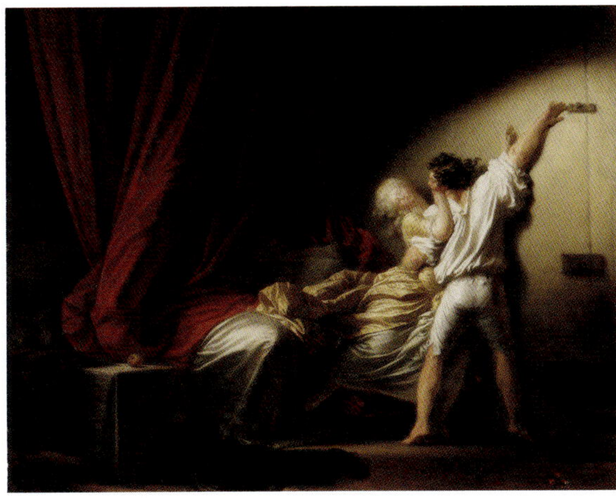

Comparative illustration:
Jean-Honoré Fragonard
The Bolt, c. 1778
Paris, Musée du Louvre

Revolution would end the degrading misery of this unfortunate class, which has so often distressed us," Manon Phlipon later wrote in her memoirs; "we greeted it with a storm of enthusiasm." As Madame Roland, she became the behind the scenes leader of the Girondists, the moderate Revolutionary faction, and in 1793 mounted the scaffold with the composure of a Plutarchian heroine. Many others thought as she did: on 7 September 1789 the wives and daughters of Paris's artists took their jewellery to the National Constituent Assembly in Versailles, in order to present it to the nation. The Revolution also changed Fragonard's life, but while his former clients emigrated or were pursued, imprisoned and guillotined, he survived unscathed the bloody events unfolding around him: in 1792 the September Massacres, the abolition of the monarchy and the proclamation of the Republic, and the following year the execution of the king, the fall of the Girondists, the Jacobin Reign of Terror and the reaction to it.

Fragonard must have been a *citoyen* above suspicion. His patriotism, his competence and the good word of David, court painter to the Revolution, secured him a post in the new arts administra-tion. He was involved in the founding of the Louvre and from 1797 until 1800 supervized the transport of the art works being seized by French troops all over Europe and shipped back to Paris. Under Napoleon, however, new men took charge of the art world. Fragonard lost his offices, his pension and his apartment. He died lonely and forgotten in 1806, having painted virtually nothing for almost twenty years. *The Stolen Kiss* must have been one of his last works.

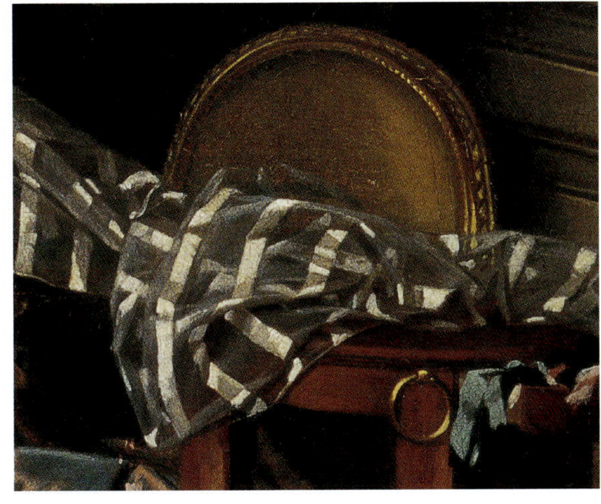

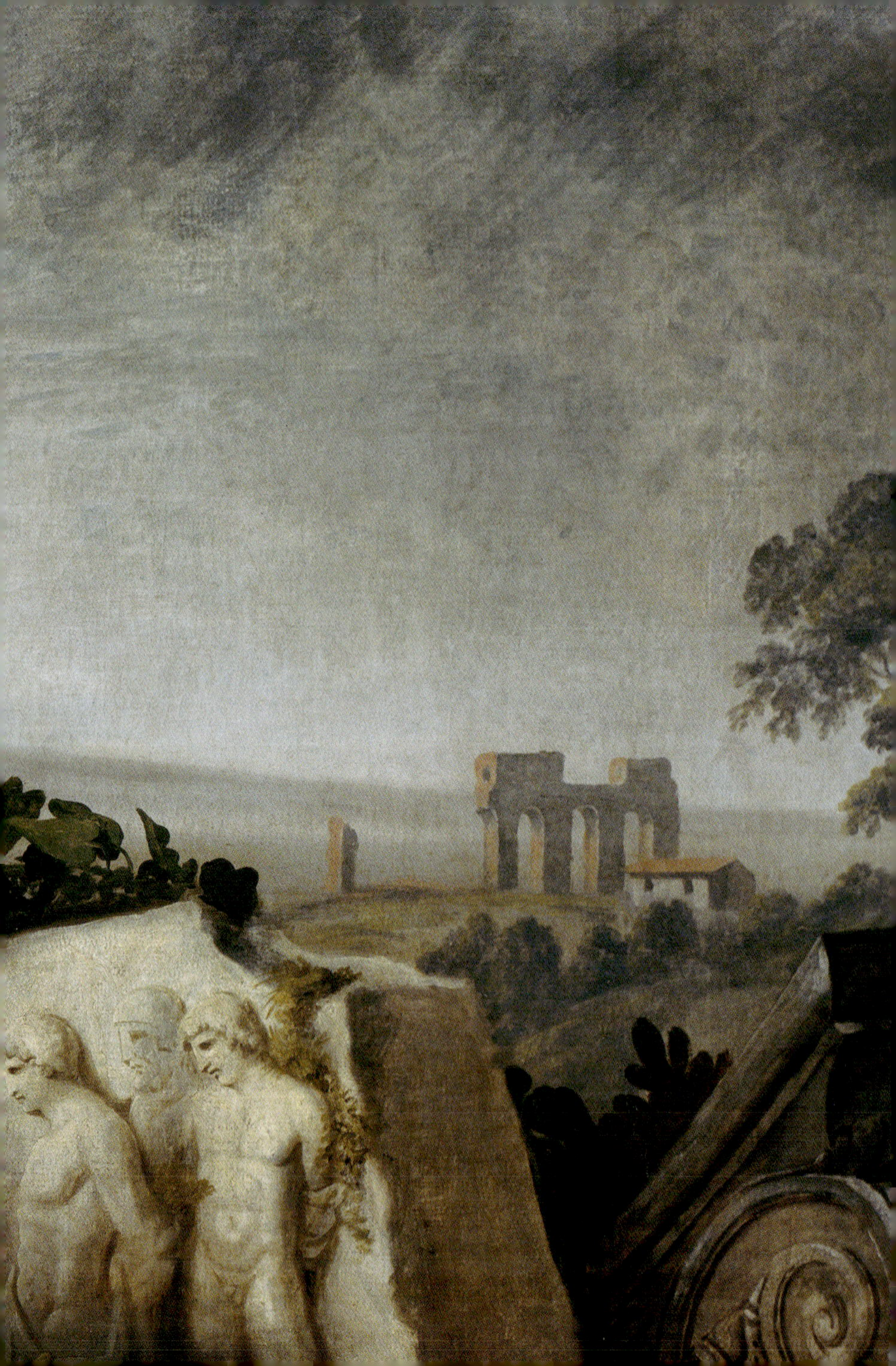

Johann Heinrich Wilhelm Tischbein (1751–1821)

A German icon

Goethe in the Roman Campagna, 1786/1787
164 x 206 cm, Frankfurt, Städel Museum

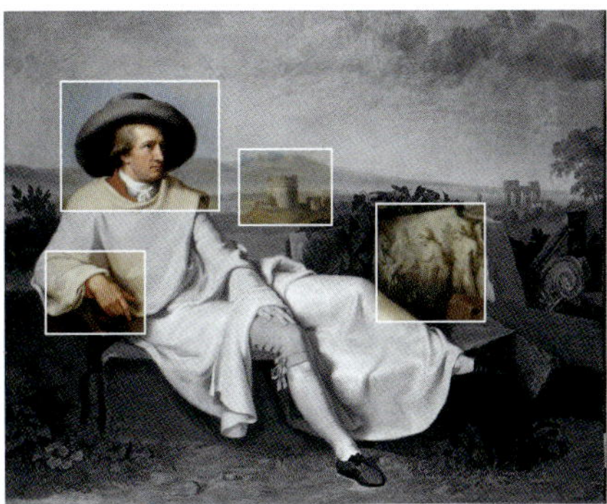

Towards the end of October 1786, soon after Johann Wolfgang Goethe's arrival in Rome, Johann Heinrich Wilhelm Tischbein began his portrait of the poet. The painting is one of the most popular in Germany. Hardly a schoolchild would fail to recognize it, a fact which makes it particularly well loved by advertisers. *Goethe in the Roman Campagna* is as familiar as a trademark, as sacred as an icon. The work has come to symbolize Germany's Classical humanist ideal: German *geist*.

The painter admired Goethe – and it shows. He gives the poet a broad-rimmed hat, which has something of the appearance of a dark halo, enlarging the poet's head and showing his profile to advantage. The poet's facial features are idealized; his mantle is a timeless gown; his eyes are focused on infinity. This is no normal man with both feet planted firmly on the ground. Only one foot touches the earth, and his supine position makes him appear to float. He is evidently not of this world.

The painting was sold by a private collector to the Städelsches Kunstinstitut, Frankfurt, in 1887, when the Goethe cult was at its height. The citizens of a newly formed German Empire sought shining paragons among the generations of past Germans. Goethe and Schiller thus attained a national status far beyond their significance as writers. A distinction was drawn between the drab, low level of politics and economics and the higher life of the mind, of art, of culture. A vaguely floating Goethe, whose walking tour through Italy has not soiled his shoes, fitted into the picture perfectly.

Were it not for this painting, the artist's name would be known only to a handful of art historians. During the 18th century, however, the Tischbeins were a widely-known family of painters, working in Hamburg, Lubeck, Haina, Hanau and Kassel. Various uncles and cousins worked as portraitists, directors of art galleries and court painters. Johann Heinrich Wilhelm, born in 1751, received a stipend from the academy of art at Kassel to enable him to travel to

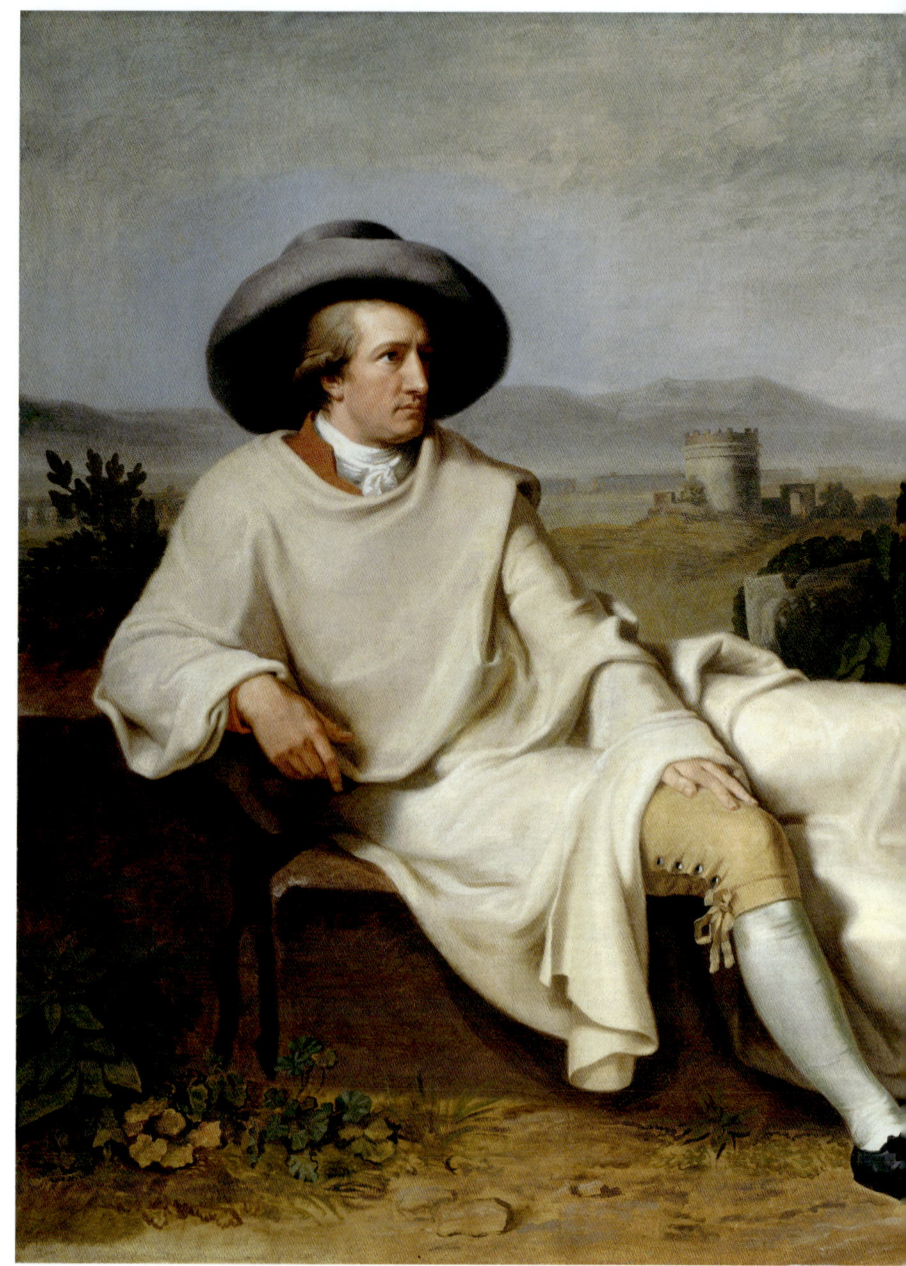

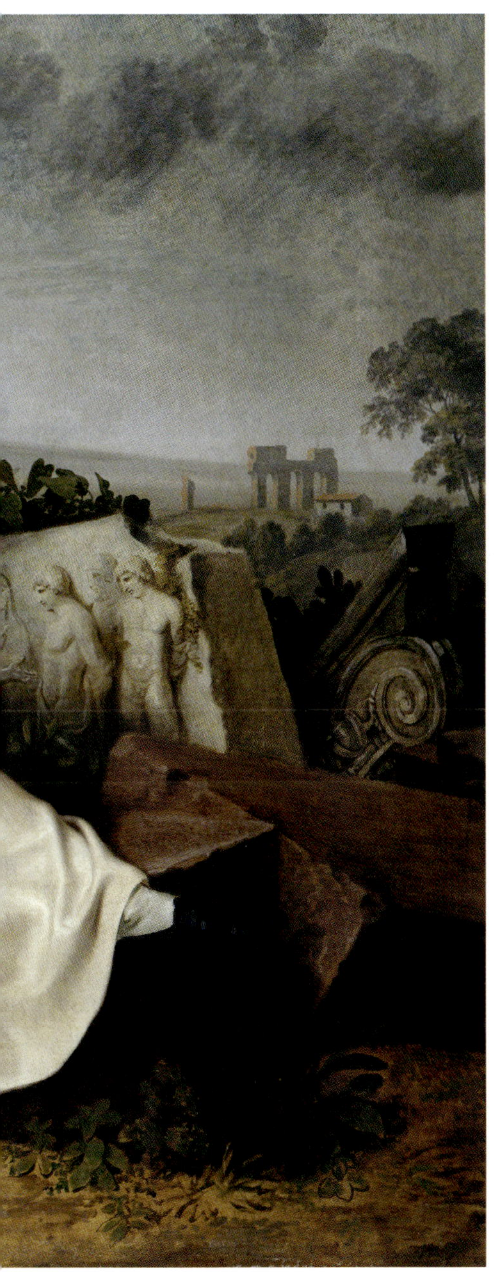

Rome, where he wanted to study the Old Masters. When his funds were exhausted, he travelled to Zurich, where friends provided contact with Goethe. Tischbein then sent letters and sketches to Weimar, and Goethe used his good offices with Duke Ernst of Gotha to procure a second Rome-stipend for Tischbein. Thus contact between the two was established. Then Goethe, poet and supporter of artists in distress, himself came to Rome: "… I'm here, and have sent for Tischbein," he wrote in his journal. Some time later, in a letter back to Weimar, he wrote: "We are so well suited that it is as if we have always lived together." It was during this period of close friendship that the portrait was executed, although Goethe never saw it completed. Divergent interests drew the two men apart, and Tischbein makes no mention of the work in his memoirs. The memory of it must have harboured unpleasant associations.

My eyes are receiving the most unbelievable education

Goethe had left for Italy in secret. He had not asked the Duke of Weimar, whom he served as a minister, for a holiday, nor had he taken leave of his friend, Charlotte von Stein. Goethe, at the age of 37, had simply packed his bags and fled. There are a number of explanations for this total breach of decorum and injury to his oath of allegiance. Firstly, he was making no progress in his career as a writer. Early success with *Werther* and *Götz von Berlichingen* had made him the Germans' favourite author, at least among the younger generation. But since coming to live and work at Weimar, he had had no comparable success. *Torquato Tasso*, *Faust* and *Egmont* were either unfinished, or had not progressed beyond the planning stage. Neither Werther's sensitivity, nor Götz's lack of it, were particularly interesting to him any more. He was stuck.

Then there were relationship problems. Frau von Stein had taught him how to behave properly when he had first arrived at the court of Weimar; she had shown him that there were orders of precedence and all kinds of unwritten rules – at court and in love. Goethe wrote to her almost every day, but recent

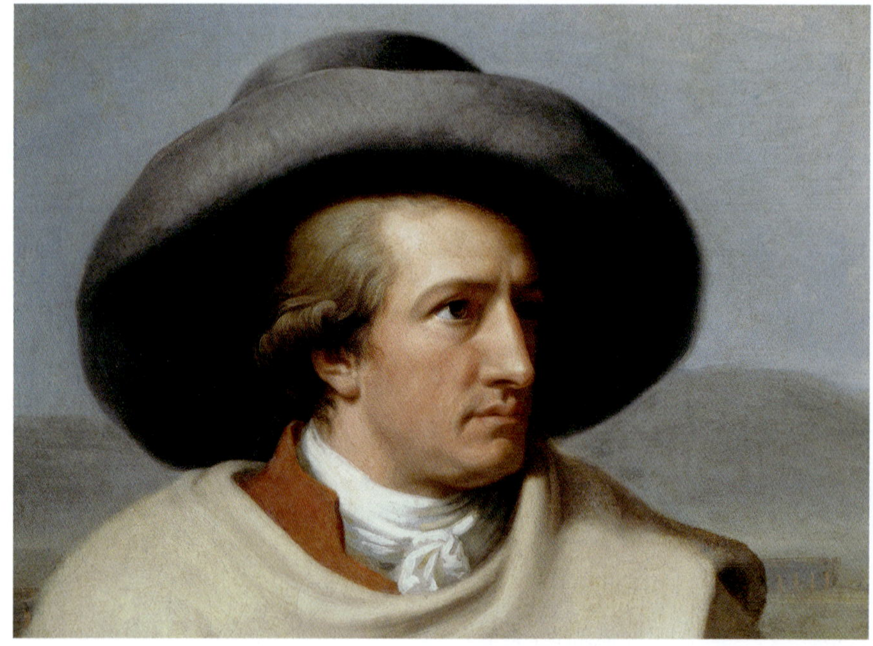

research has shown that these notes were destined not for her but the Duchess. Was Frau von Stein simply a go between? A passionate love seems to have developed between Goethe and the Duchess, and when this became impossible to conceal, Goethe fled to Italy.

The portrait betrays none of Goethe's restlessness or sense of crisis. Goethe appears in full command of his faculties, a prince of poets. What Tischbein actually knew of Goethe's state of mind at the time is not known. Like the other German painters living in Rome, he will have known that Goethe, the famous poet and Weimar minister, wished to remain incognito. He took refuge in Tischbein's rooms under the name of Filippo Miller, *pittore*. When eventually it became impossible for him to maintain the credibility of his pseudonym, he nonetheless declined invitations from aristocratic society.

Goethe makes little reference to his private problems in his book of memoirs, *Italian Journey*, which was compiled almost 30 years later from his letters and notes of the period. He describes the twenty months he spent in Italy as an educational journey. Education, in the Goethean sense, does not mean adding to one's knowledge, but adding to one's abilities; it is a form of work on one's own person, the transformation of the self.

The faculty which interested Goethe most was that of seeing: "I have again seen outstanding works of art here, and have felt my mind clear and move in new directions," he wrote. "My eyes are receiving the most unbelievable education, and I shall work, lest my hand lag behind them."

He spent much time drawing, asking Tischbein and other painters to correct his work. He probably hoped his talent would grow beyond that of a mere dilettante. Tischbein has painted him as a man of vision, a man captured in the act of looking. His large hat was fashionable at the time among the German artists in Rome.

Iphigenia recognizes Orestes

Anybody who is acquainted with today's Rome will find it hard to imagine that Goethe should have travelled there, of all places, to find himself. If his wish was to escape the crippling narrowness of the

Weimar court, he could easily have travelled to Paris, Vienna or London, or, indeed, have hidden himself away on some country estate. But he wanted Rome. Venice had managed to hold his attention for all of two weeks, Florence for only three hours: "The desire to get on to Rome was so great, and continued to grow so quickly, that I simply could not stay any longer …" He called this desire to reach Rome "a kind of illness". The only remedy was "the sight and presence of the place". And then: "I am here at last, and quiet, and it seems I shall have peace for the rest of my life."

Goethe was not the only one who sought a cure at Rome. During his first journey to the city in 1779, Tischbein had expressed himself similarly: "The further we travelled," he wrote in his memoirs, "the more I returned to my self and the greater was the thought that I was to see the beautiful land of Italy, where vitality and the highest spiritual values dwelled among the people, and more than anything, it was the thought of beautiful Rome itself, the greatest city in the world!"

Rome distinguished itself from Venice or Florence by its Classical monuments. Travellers went there in search of an Ancient Roman and Greek sense of humanity; with its help, they hoped to recover their own strength and form their opinions. Tischbein, already an expert on Rome, took the new arrival to see all the wells, portals and columns. He knew which collections held the most beautiful statues.

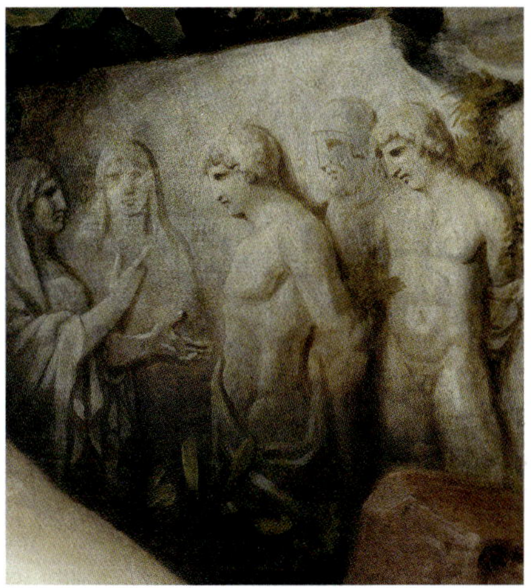

Goethe purchased plaster casts of the heads of the gods and goddesses and took them back with him when he returned to the north. He also travelled to Sicily, but did not visit Greece, which was under Turkish occupation.

Enthusiasm for Classical antiquity was partly a reaction to the more recent styles in art: the ecstatic exuberance of the Baroque, and a Rococo tendency to belittle things by turning them into a harmless source of frivolity. Although there were wonderful examples of work from both periods at Venice, Goethe took no notice of them. He was searching for "noble simplicity and serene grandeur" – words the archaeologist Johann Joachim Winckelmann (1717–1768) had chosen to characterize the essential quality of Classical Greek art.

Goethe's *Iphigenia* bears testimony to this search. Begun in Weimar, set to verse in Italy and finished at Rome, it is a play about a priestess who releases her brother from the curse of matricide and pursuit by the Furies. On 6 January 1787 Goethe wrote: "Yesterday, I found it very uplifting to place the cast of a colossal head of Juno in my room. The original is at the Villa Ludovisi. She was my first love in Rome, and now I possess her … But I feel I have earned the company of such noble society in future, too, for I am able to report that my *Iphigenia* is finished at last …"

In the evening, Goethe read the new work out loud and was moved by Tischbein's reactions: "His strange, original views on the piece and manner of explaining to me the state of mind in which I wrote it have shocked me … There are no words for the depth of human feelings he has sensed behind the hero's mask." Goethe was worried. Had Tischbein discovered the extent to which Goethe's own feelings were expressed in the play? Tischbein wrote: "In the evenings you read us your *Ephigini*. It is the only time a reading has entered me so deeply, and I ofttimes hear it still in my mind and thoughts surge that I should like to describe."

Tischbein has left a monument to this reading in his portrait of Goethe: Iphigenia recognizing her brother Orestes. At the same time, the relief is intended to symbolize Greek art, just as Roman art is symbolized by the ruined capital beside it. Egyptian culture was originally suggested by hieroglyphs on the block of stone to the left, but Tischbein removed these from the final version. Perhaps he found the effect, a kind of visual catalogue of ancient cultures, too academic.

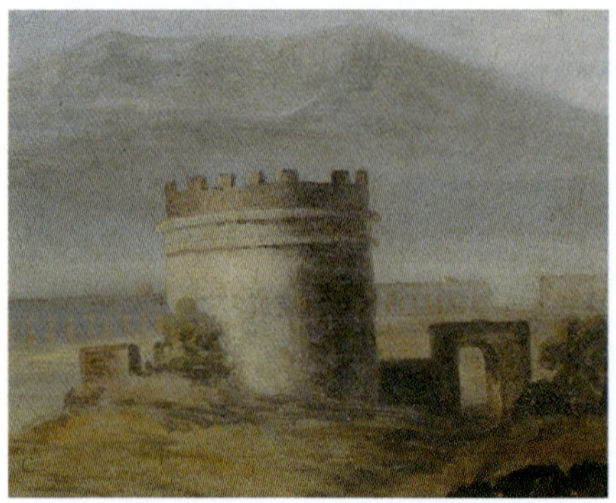

Life-sized

Tischbein, too, had turned away from Rococo style and the demands made of artists by the courts. "Portraits of powdered hair and rouged cheeks which cannot be painted from life because the sitters are too artificial …" had become anathema to him.

He found inspiration not only in Ancient Rome, but also in Zurich. It was there, in the literary circle around the famous history professor Johann Jakob Bodmer (1698–1783), that first attempts to formulate a national consciousness were made. Bodmer demanded that the "deeds of noble and great German men be presented to the nation as sacred in the works of poets and painters; for this will form the character of the people, awakening and nourishing in them a love of the fatherland …"

"These were the paintings I felt I wanted to paint," recalled Tischbein, "paintings which had a strong effect on the minds of Germans, patriotic themes" or "persons … worthy of being held up as an example in a painting …"

Goethe, though hardly a German patriotic theme, was "sacred" to Tischbein. He painted him life sized; the portrait is 206 centimetres wide and 164 centimetres high. "A fine picture," Goethe noted on 29 December 1786, "only it is much too large for our northern dwellings." The poet never saw the finished work, but wrote of a bust, taken by the sculptor Alexander Trippel, that it had been "executed in a pleasing and noble style, and I have nothing against perpetuating the idea that I should once have looked like this". He would probably have thought in much the same way about Tischbein's ennobling portrait.

Tischbein not only paints him in large format, he also portrays him large in relation to his surroundings of ruins in a Roman landscape. The very objects of Goethe's journey to Italy are here reduced to the status of appurtenances, mere decorations. Goethe's gaze is not one of admiration for these ruins, but is focused beyond them in "profound thought on the ephemerality of all things", as one traveller wrote in the *Teutscher Merkur* in 1788, adding that "the terrible thought of transience" seems "to float in his very face".

Comparing these words of veneration with Goethe's own diaries of the period, or with his *Italian Journey*, it is evident that the fugitive poet in fact spent relatively little time thinking about the ephemeral nature of things. He was much too interested in other things, much too involved in thoughts about his own development and ability to see things, about his changing personality and the regeneration of his creative powers. On returning home, his wish was to "let my friends find something in me to please them". He was taking himself back to Weimar as a present, or work of art.

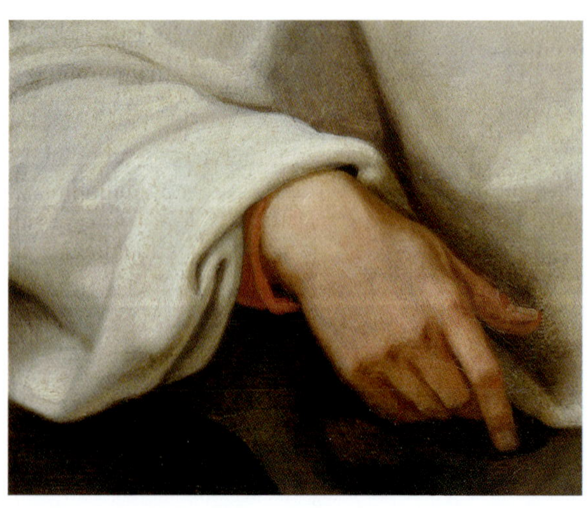

Repressed, forgotten

When Goethe arrived in Rome, he and Tischbein immediately became the best of friends. To Goethe, it felt as if he had always lived with his new companion. They lived in adjoining rooms, often eating together. Tischbein's drawing of his friend leaning out of a window bears testimony to their relationship.

But harmony between them did not last. After three months in Rome, they travelled to Naples, where their ways parted. Goethe wanted to go on to Sicily, while Tischbein, financially less secure than the minister from Weimar, remained in Naples in the hope of a position as director of the academy of art. That, at least, was the outward reason for their separation. The inward reason, however, was that they could not stand each other's company for any length of time. Critically, Goethe noted that Tischbein's mind was "jostled by a thousand different thoughts, and occupied by about a hundred persons", adding: "He is unable to share in another person's life because he feels so restricted in his own endeavours."

These comments reveal something about the writer, too. Goethe did not like the painter to spend so much time with other people; he wanted Tischbein's full attention. At the same time, he gives a fitting description of Tischbein's weakness of character. He was too indecisive, and not radical enough in pursuing his talents.

His talents lay in exact observation, and in his rapid grasp of a subject. A casual Goethe leaning out of the window, seen from behind – Tischbein's masterdrawing immediately puts us in the picture. In his paintings, however, Tischbein did not attempt to capture momentary, or natural attitudes; what he wanted on canvas – and what the times demanded – were grand, and highly significant poses. These constantly eluded him, however. His historical and mythological themes seem crude and dull. Their beautifully drawn lines and meaningful gestures are empty. Only his Goethe portrait has retained its appeal; whether due to its quality as a painting, or simply to familiarity, is hard to say.

Unlike Goethe, Tischbein does not criticize his companion in his memoirs. He writes only of their trip to Naples, not of their meeting in Rome. The painting is not mentioned at all. The only explanation for this is that Tischbein himself wished to forget it. Goethe – whether on canvas or in real life – was probably too large a figure for him. Goethe took himself seriously; his great gift lay in giving full

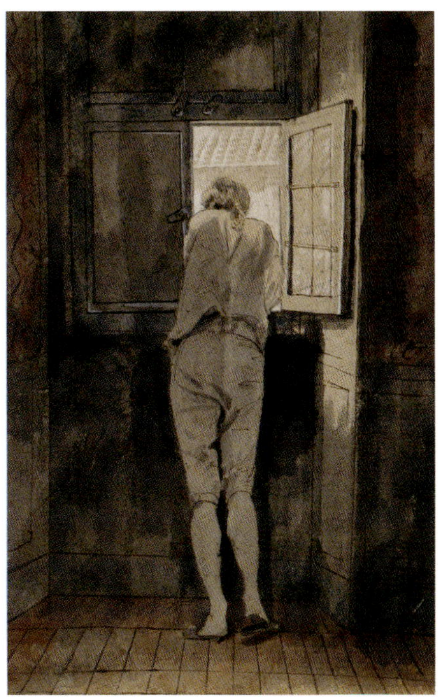

Comparative illustration:
Johann Heinrich Wilhelm Tischbein
Goethe at the window of the apartment on the Via del Corso in Rome, 1787
41.5 x 26.6 cm
Frankfurt, Freies Deutsches Hochstift,
Frankfurter Goethe-Museum

rein to his genius, in pursuing his personal interests and abilities to their utmost. This had always eluded Tischbein. Instead he remained subaltern to the dictates of fashion, a product of his time.

While living with Goethe, Tischbein must have found this difference between them depressing. He would presumably have felt hurt, had he known that it was for his portrait of Goethe, more than for any other work, that the Germans would remember him.

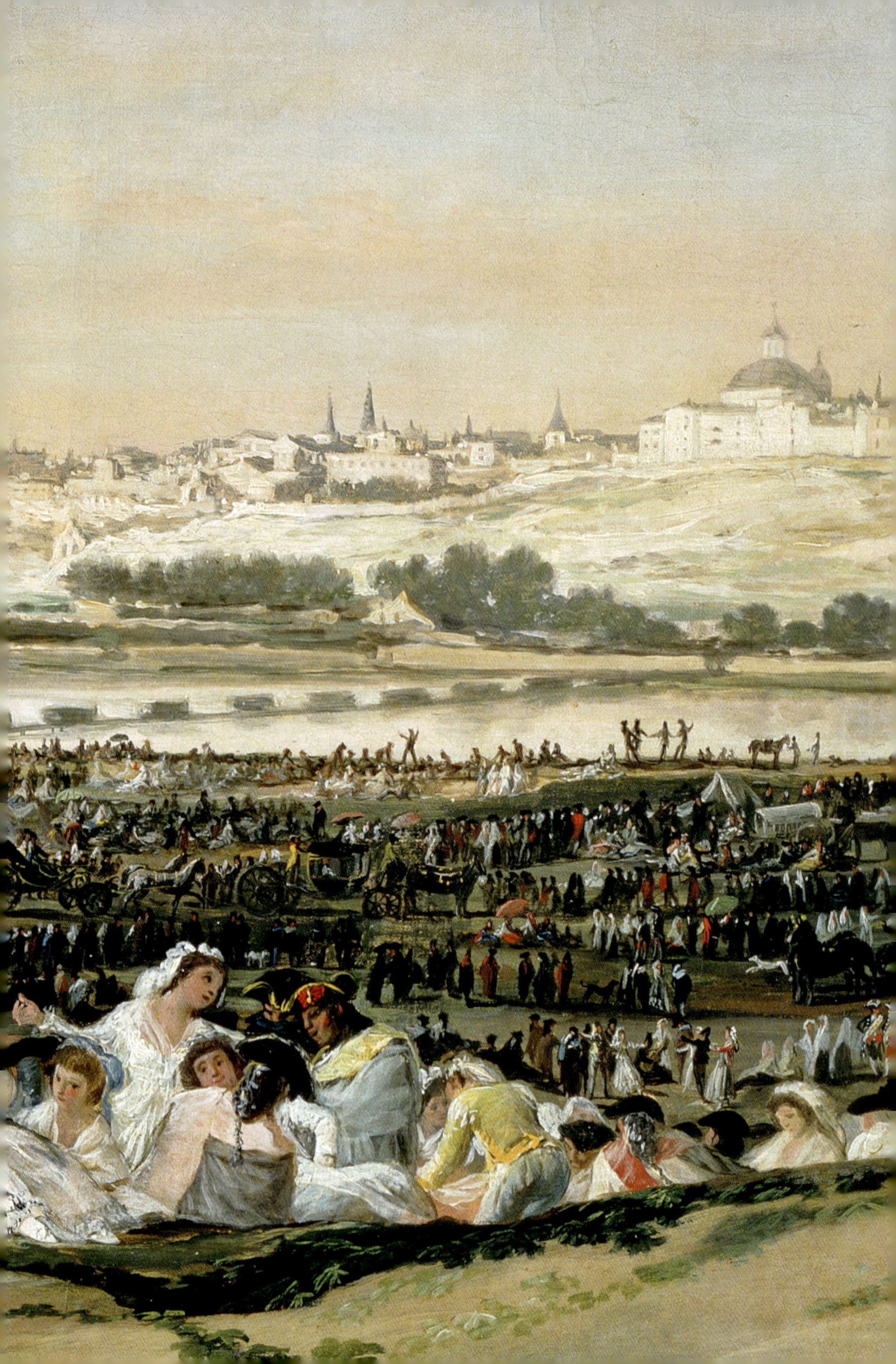

Francisco de Goya (1746–1828)

(real name Francisco José de Goya y Lucientes)

The sunny and the sombre side of a festival

The Meadow of St Isidore, 1788
44 x 94 cm, Madrid, Museo Nacional del Prado

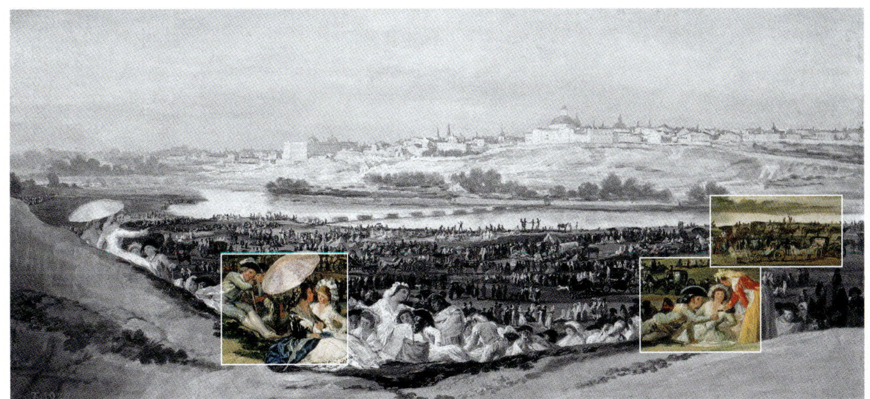

The people of Madrid are in a large meadow. As on 15 May every year, they are celebrating the feast of St Isidore, patron saint of their city. In the morning, after Mass in the main church, they walked in procession behind priests and brass musicians across the river and up the hill to the saint's hermitage. There the faithful attended High Mass, drank from the miracle-working spring and called upon Isidore to answer their prayers. In the afternoon they streamed down to the fields along the banks of the Manzanares River, where they are now eating, drinking and dancing while enjoying a panoramic view of the municipality of Madrid.

Visible in the distance are the Segovia bridge on the left and, further right, two works of architecture that were new when the artist recorded this scene: the massive complex of the royal palace, built after the old palace, the Alcázar, burned down on New Year's Eve 1734, followed by the domed Basilica of San Francisco el Grande, completed in 1785, for which Francisco de Goya (1746–1828) painted an altarpiece.

All of these are still visible from the hermitage even today – just as the feast of St Isidore is still celebrated on 15 May in the meadows beside the river. Nowadays, those in attendance include politicians, who use the occasion to deliver electioneering speeches and to proclaim what it is they prayed for after drinking from St Isidore's holy spring – a safe city and the victory of their own party in the next elections being amongst their requests. As in Goya's day, it all ends with a grand firework display, the traditional sign to head for home.

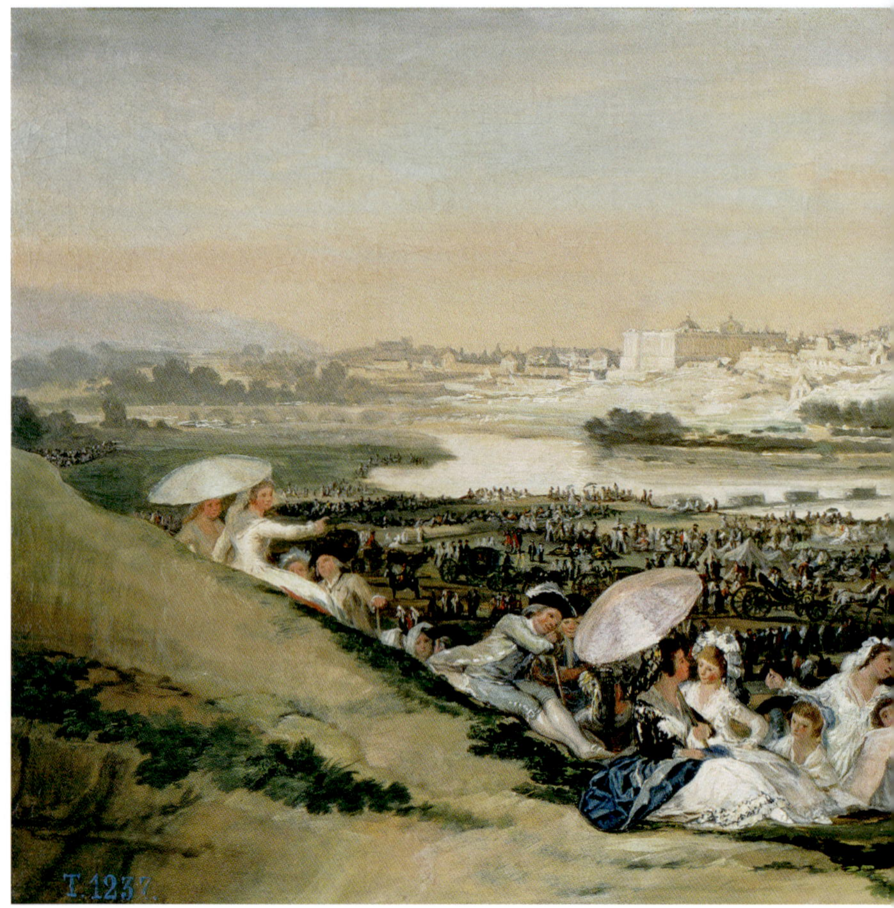

Maja and *majo*

The colourfully clad woman on the right is serving red wine or perhaps the popular liqueur by the delightful name of "Perfecto Amor". She comes from the lower-class districts of Madrid and earns her money as a street vendor, market trader or maid-servant. She is dressed as a *maja*, whose costume included a short, close fitting jacket decorated with tassels and buttons, a bonnet with ribbons or a lace mantilla on her head, and her long hair worn in a net. A true *maja* had to have a ready supply of cheeky jokes, keep male suitors at bay with her mockery and be *salada*, salty, in her character and appearance.

Her male counterpart, the *majo*, also wore his uncut hair in a net, together with sideboards. He thereby distinguished himself from men of the wealthier classes, who wore wigs. In contrast to these, too, he accentuated his shoulders with epaulettes and wore a *capa*, a broad cloak behind which it was easy to conceal one's identity. When the *capa* was banned by one of Spain's ministers in the 1760s, there was a public uprising. The *majos* did not want to be deprived of their costume.

In 1788, when Goya painted the public festivities to mark the feast of St Isidore, *maja* dress was also donned by ladies of high society on occasions such as

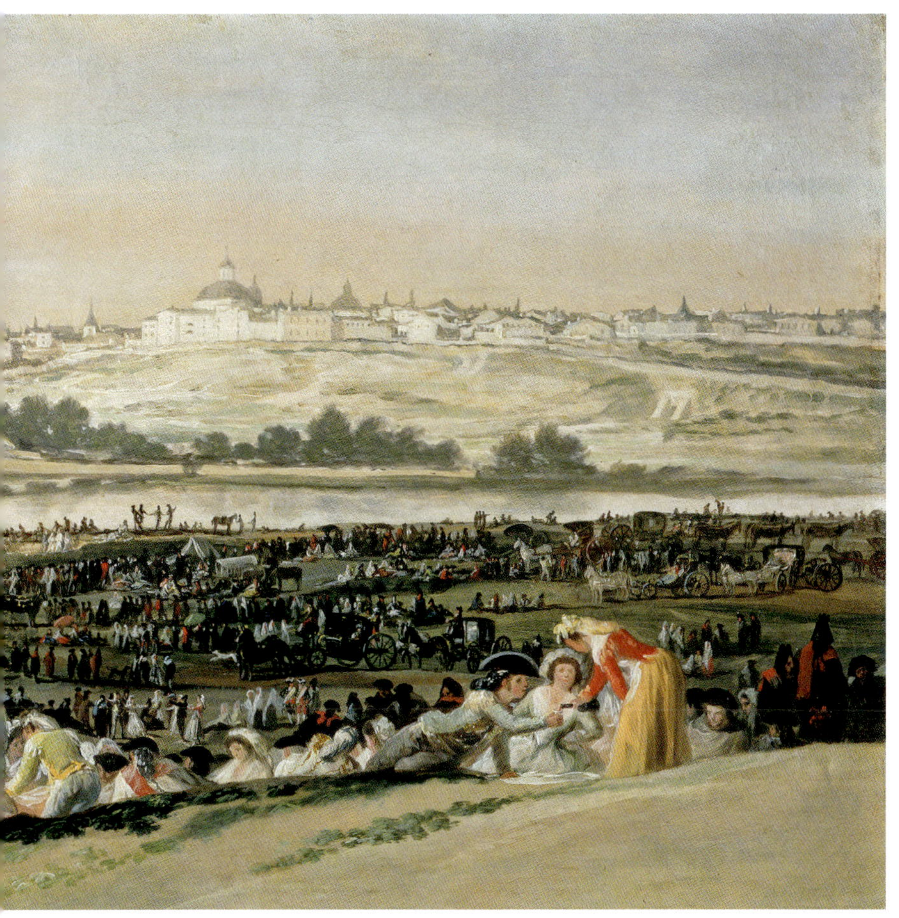

masked balls, bullfights, or when sitting for portraits. No doubt to some extent a playful whim of fashion, it was also a mark of support for Spain and all things Spanish – and hence of opposition to everything French. Since 1700 Spain had been ruled by kings from the French house of Bourbon, who sought to modernize the backward, impoverished country along French lines. This included efforts to combat the excessive power of the Church and cautiously to propagate the ideas of the Enlightenment: physics instead of mysticism, reason instead of superstition.

The imitation of the *maja* style of dress by the upper classes was considered a profession of faith in Catholic Spanish tradition. More than that, however, it expressed a yearning for a life of greater freedom in natural surroundings.

In Rococo France women dressed up as shepherdesses, while in England the Romantics stylized the Scottish Highlander in his tartan kilt as their ideal. American culture had the romantic figure of the cowboy who lived away from cities in the country.

In Spain, liberation from the constraints of society was identified with the *majo* and *maja*, and Goya contributed much to their popularization with his œuvre.

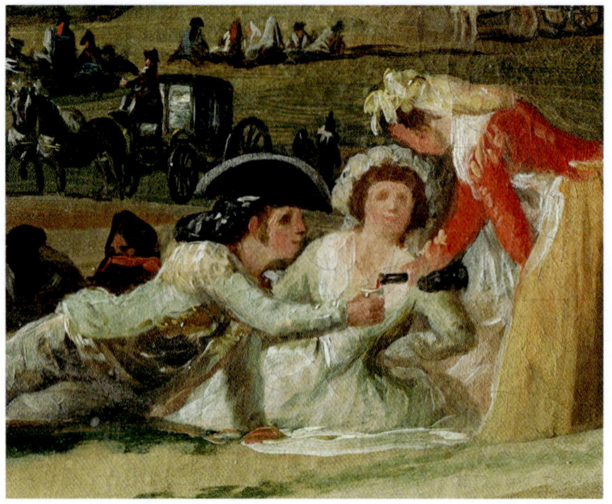

Carriages as status symbols

He was limping, Goya wrote to a friend in summer
1786, after turning over in a *birlocho*, an open-topped
horse-drawn carriage with four wheels and no doors.
The accident had happened during a test drive: "the
owner and I were driving very grandly at a dignified
pace", but "once outside Madrid we broke into a furious gallop…". The seller asked Goya if he would like
to learn how to do a "Neapolitan turn". Goya handed
him the reins and immediately found himself "turning somersaults in the air" along with the horse and
carriage. The letter is bursting with pride in his new
conveyance. The artist bore the title of "Painter to
the the King" and earned a good income, but was
still able to view himself with a touch of self-irony
on occasions.

Carriages were a status symbol: those who owned
one no longer belonged to the class of *gente de la
pie* – people who went on foot. Goya was 40 when
he purchased the carriage. A difficult path lay behind
him: the son of a gilder of no means, he had grown
up in Saragossa, in the provinces. He tried twice
to be allowed to study and exhibit at the Royal
Academy of Art in Madrid. Only in 1775, after he had
married the sister of an established painter, did he
obtain work in Madrid as a tapestry designer. It was
not a very highly regarded or lucrative job, but
it allowed him to gain a foothold in the capital.

He worked for the Santa Bárbara tapestry factory,
which had been founded by the Bourbon king

Philip V to boost the local industry and economy. Wall coverings
were needed to protect against the
cold in the Escorial and the Pardo,
two royal residences outside
Madrid, where the court spent
part of the autumn and winter.
Tapestries traditionally portrayed
mythological motifs or heroic
historical events – but this would
now change. Goya and other
young artists were to illustrate
scenes from present-day Spain.
A first set of wall hangings was to
show hunting scenes and a second
"popular diversions".

Goya proceeded to design
scenes of *majas* and *majos* in
Andalusia, of boys climbing trees,
and of high-ranking ladies and
gentlemen dressed in French and Spanish fashions
playing blind man's bluff in a sunny landscape. It
was a charming, carefree, erotically playful world
that the royal family brought into its gloomy,
clammy palaces. And as far as the popular diversions
were concerned, it was also a world in which the
members of the court could not take part. They lived
in a straitjacket of strict etiquette.

The artists were required to produce preliminary
designs which, if approved by the court, they then
worked up into "cartoons". These were canvases on
the same scale as the final tapestry, in each case several
metres in height and width. The weavers proceeded
on the basis of these cartoons, endeavouring with
their threads to come as close as possible to the original in colour and form. The tapestry was the goal –
the cartoons disappeared into the cellar and the
preliminary designs remained in the hands of the
artist. One such design is *The Meadow of St Isidore*, a
plein air panorama sketched with rapid brush strokes
that anticipates the works of the Impressionists, who
would follow a hundred years later.

Goya's design was never woven. Amongst the
reasons for this may have been its complexity and
its wealth of small detail. It would have been impossible, for example, to weave the number of carriages
that Goya has assembled in this picture. After he
worked for Santa Bárbara for over ten years, Goya
would know this. But by that time it was no longer
of any concern to him. Designing tapestries had

by that stage become a burdensome task that he considered somewhat beneath him, and he strove to extricate himself from it. In this respect the gaily complicated Impressionistic work also contains a pinch of protest.

A world for young princesses

He could afford a little protest, for he was doing well: his work was in demand and all too many wanted him to paint their portrait. But when, as he wrote, he was "commanded from above", he had to deliver. Two weeks after the feast of St Isidore in 1788, he was feeling the time pressure, "because the things are so difficult", as he complained to a friend. "I can find neither sleep nor rest until I have finished with it." And: "you cannot call the life that I lead a life."

The tapestry illustrating *The Meadow of St Isidore* was destined for the bedroom of two young princesses. It was to be bright and cheerful and contain lots of female figures, but no erotic allusions. Amongst the women whom Goya has here characterized in more detail, only a few issued from the lower-class districts: poverty and eroticism were no subjects for princesses. The ladies with parasols belong to the upper and middle classes; their clothing is not as colourful as the *maja* who is serving wine, and they use their parasols to protect their pale complexions – another feature of their class. But they also use them to shield themselves from the eyes of others. Like the fan and the mantilla, the transparent scarf worn over

the head and shoulders, the parasol was a popular accessory in the game with the opposite sex. In Goya's painting, it looks as if the two young ladies beneath the parasol wish to keep the gentleman with the walking stick seated behind them at a little distance from themselves. He, too, is a man of rank. He wears his hair beneath a wig, not in a net like a *majo*, and he does not have sideboards or emphasize his shoulders with epaulettes.

Clothes were an indication of the class to which their wearer belonged, and the adoption of a style of dress to which one was not entitled and the confusion this sowed was a popular theme of comedies – including the light-hearted entr'actes commonly performed in Madrid during the intervals of tragedies. Their most important author, Ramón de la Cruz (1731–1794), wrote a piece that takes place during the feast of St Isidore and in which people from every class are assembled in the meadow: gentlemen in search of conquests, dull witted peasants, *majos* looking for a fight and flirtatious *majas*. Along come a lady's maid and a manservant: they are supposed to be guarding the house but don't want to miss the fun beside the Manzanares River. Naturally they run into their employers, who are dressed as a *majo* and *maja*, leading to confusion, concealment and finally reconciliation. The theatre audience knew that incidents of this sort were a regular occurrence on the banks of the Manzanares on the feast day of St Isidore.

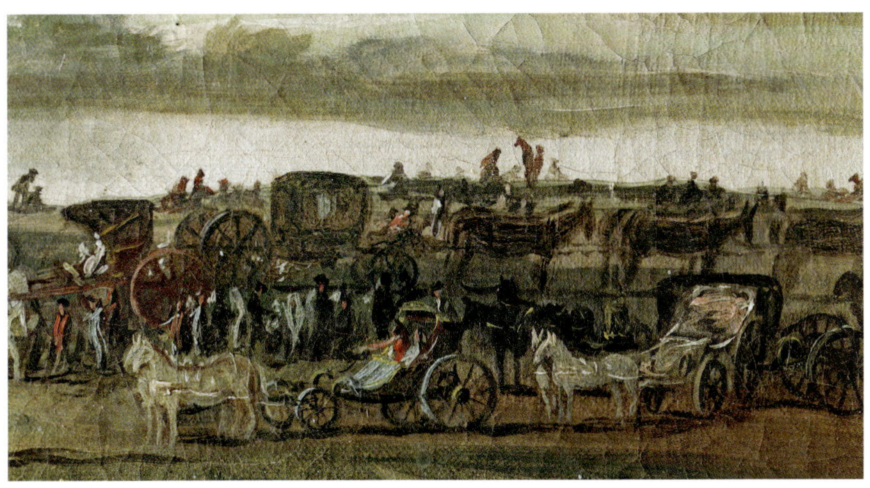

For Goya, the depiction of a large crowd of people and the landscape format that was required posed certain problems. On the one hand, he had to portray individuals and make it possible to see what they were doing and who was talking to whom. On the other hand, he had to ensure that the overall composition did not disintegrate into small groups. His solution was to position clearly characterized individuals at the top of the slope in the foreground, and handle the mass of people dancing or seated lower down in a more anonymous manner. He employs the river and the panoramic view of the city as pictorial elements whose lighter colours provide a soothing foil to the dark confusion below. Corresponding to this bright section at the top of the picture is the triangulated stretch of meadow at the bottom. In itself, this flattish area of ground says nothing. From a formal point of view, however, it is like a shallow bowl whose sides curve upwards, protectively cupping the main scene. These two luminous zones above and below the mass of people lend the picture its calmly harmonious atmosphere.

Were we to cast an eye over Goya's 1,800 paintings, etchings and sketches, we would see that architecture held little interest for him and cityscapes none at all. If he included them here, it was in order to fulfil the commission. He adapted himself to requirements, but he always prefered painting figures to buildings. In the many lively, cheerful country scenes that he designed for the tapestry factory, he was obeying the wishes of others, but the creative inspiration that he brought to them shows that they fascinated him nonetheless. They fit in with his own attitude to life, with the delight he took in carriages and driving fast and probably also in women.

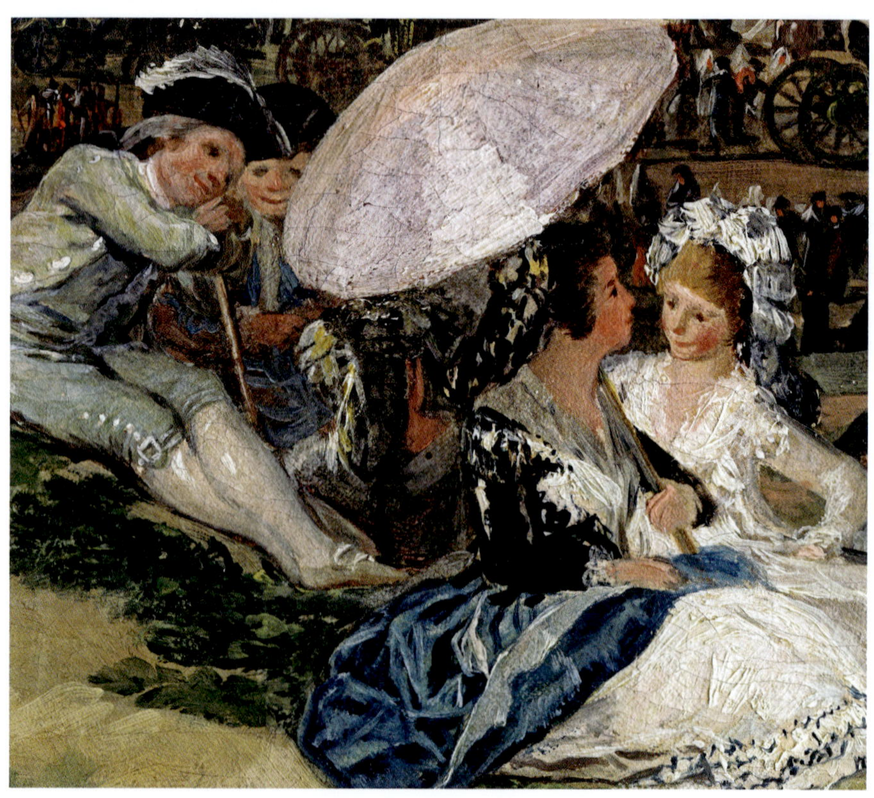

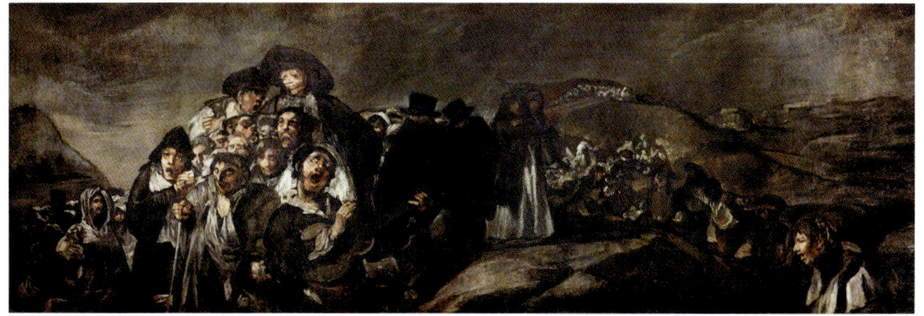

How the elderly Goya saw the world

Over 30 years later he would once again paint people outside the city on the feast day of St Isidore. Not for princesses, not as the design for a tapestry, but as a fresco on one of the walls of his own home. Thirty years – that meant the French Revolution, the rise and fall of Napoleon, the occupation of Spain, the horrific guerrilla war and afterwards a young Bourbon on the throne, one who thwarted all attempts to embrace progress and modernization. The Inquisition regained its old power and hauled in Goya, no friend of the Church, to defend himself. He felt himself watched, in danger, left Madrid and bought a house on the other side of the river – in roughly the location that would have allowed him to see the cheerful afternoon gathering on St Isidore's meadow.

His house, a single storey building, was situated amidst large grounds and quickly became known as the Casa del Sordo, the "house of the deaf man". He had lost his hearing in 1792 and it is probable that he withdrew from the city because of his inability to take part in communication, because he felt excluded. The court no longer called upon his services.

Over these 30 years, Goya's picture of humankind had changed. The mostly young men and women who had enjoyed life in each other's company had turned into a society that lied, tortured and murdered, into people who felt themselves persecuted by the weird figures of their imagination. In two series of etchings, *Los Caprichos* and *The Disasters of War*, Goya visualized a world full of horror and without redemption – two series he did not publish or immediately withdrew because they did not fall in line with the ideas of the king and Church.

Inside his own house, he threw caution to the winds. He covered the walls of two whole rooms with frescos that have become famous as his "black

Comparative illustration:
Francisco de Goya,
Pilgrimage to St Isidore's Hermitage, 1819–1823
139 x 436 cm, Madrid, Museo Nacional
del Prado

paintings". Later removed from the wall, they today hang in the Prado. Almost without exception, they are pictures of fear. Saturn, a shaggy monster, devours the bloody corpse of one of his sons; witch like creatures fly ominously over the countryside; two men try to beat each other with cudgels, both standing up to their knees in sand so that neither can escape. And then the pilgrims making their way up to St Isidore's holy spring on a dark morning.

What a contrast to the princesses' cartoon! There is no formal bowl to contain or restrain the throng of people; on the contrary, the pilgrims in the foreground form a human tower that sways threateningly towards the viewer. The day painting presents the world openly; by night it becomes mysterious and unsettling. What makes the pilgrims most menacing of all are their expressions: gaping mouths, gaping eyes, black throats and whites of eyes. Such facial features had been avoided by painters since the Renaissance, but Goya employed them again and again – in particular the open mouth. It offers a glimpse into the body's interior, into a region of ourselves in which we barely differ from animals and beyond the reach of all conscious efforts at self-mastery, individuality and rational behaviour. Goya incorporates it into his vision. He sees man both as a civilized citizen on a friendly afternoon and as a nocturnal monster. The fact that he saw both and could lend pictorial expression to both lies at the heart of his genius.

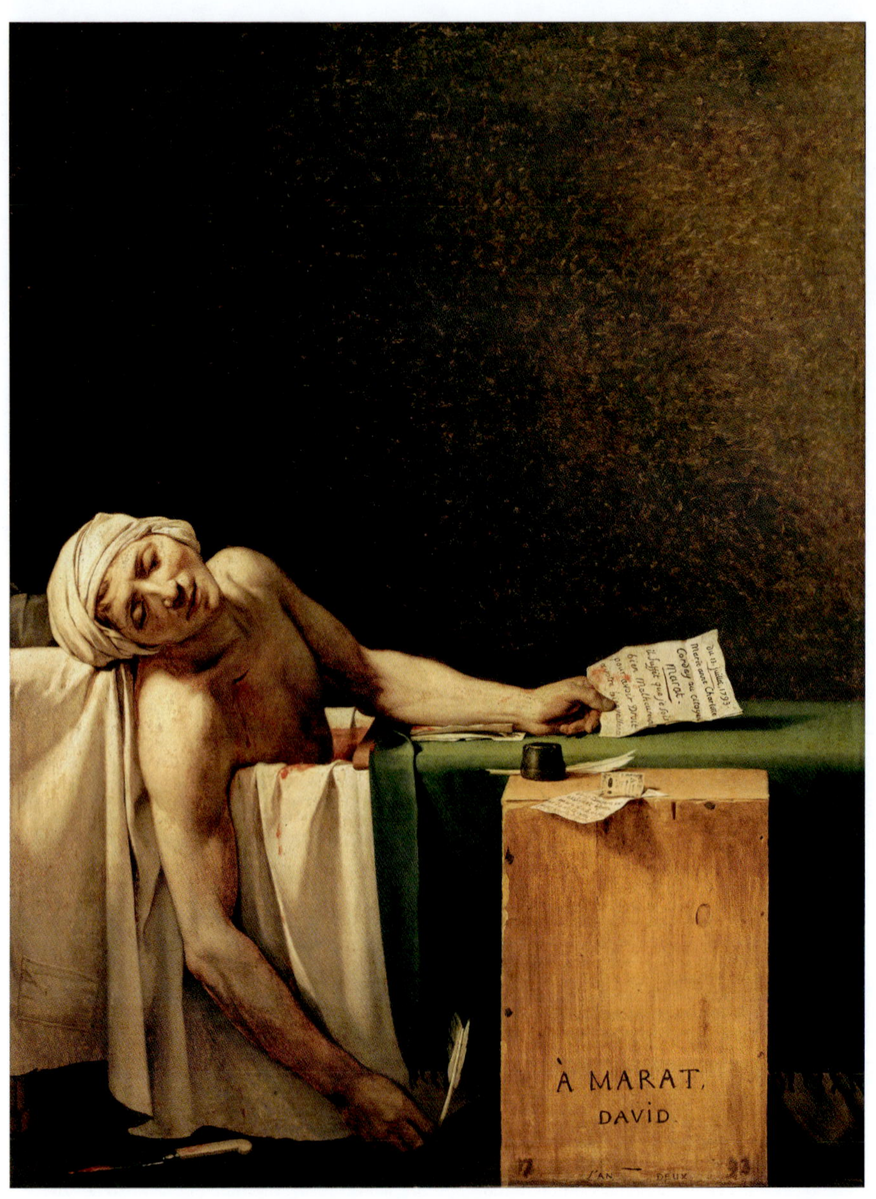

Jacques-Louis David (1748–1825)

The holy revolutionary

The Death of Marat, 1793
165 x 128 cm, Brussels, Musées royaux des Beaux-Arts de Belgique

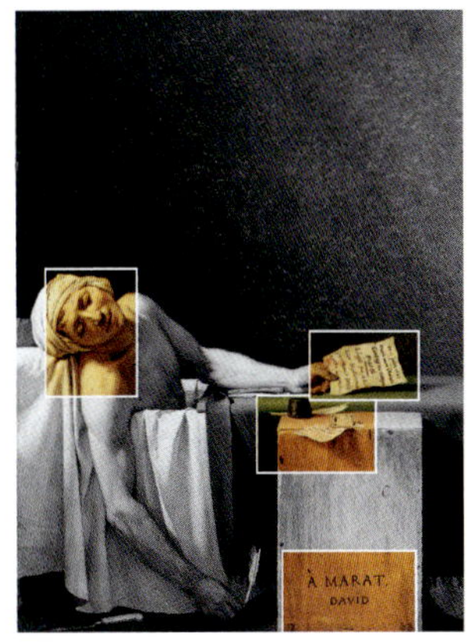

In 1793, a young aristocratic woman stabbed the Parisian journalist Jean-Paul Marat in his bath: the French Revolution had its martyr. The painter Jacques-Louis David was officially commissioned to turn the murder into propaganda. His canvas, painted in a suitably "grand" manner, was completed in the same year, and can be seen today in the Musées Royaux des Beaux-Arts, Brussels.

The writer Nicolas Restif de la Bretonne was strolling through the streets of Paris when he heard a shopkeeper talking to his neighbour: "She was about to flee. She was stopped at the door. He's dead." Soon, the whole town was buzzing with the news, and wherever he went, whether on the street or in cafes, the novelist heard "a hundred mouths talking of the terrible misfortune" that had befallen revolutionary Paris. A girl from the provinces, Charlotte Corday, had murdered the Deputy Marat in his bath, where he had retired to relieve his skin trouble and to correct the galley proofs of his newspaper. It was the evening of 13 July 1793.

Jean-Paul Marat was one of the most popular revolutionaries. The poor, whose rights he defended in his newspaper *L'Ami du Peuple* (*The Friend of the People*), worshipped him. The royalists hated him, but in this they were not alone. The moderate supporters of the Revolution opposed him for his leading part in the "September massacre" of captured opponents of the Revolution. Naturally, he had

also voted for the king's execution in January 1793. Jacques-Louis David had done no less.

David was not only a painter; he was the director of the Fête de la Revolution. The festival was a massive spectacle, conducted in the interests of political propaganda. Its organizers based their plans on the example of Roman Catholic ceremonies, providing magnificent displays, like those which had been put on to honour Renaissance princes.

Now that the princes had been deposed and beheaded, the churches closed and the priests driven away, the valuable experience they had accumulated in the field of propaganda and indoctrination was put to new use. David turned Marat's funeral into a particularly ostentatious campaign.

Naked from the waist up, his body was laid out in state in a former church so that anybody who wished could see the fatal wound. In front of the pedestal was placed his bath, the wooden crate that had served him as a table, and, on it, his inkpot and quill. The objects were displayed like holy relics. During the funeral procession, which ended at the Panthéon, a cannon resounded at five minute intervals. The staging of the funeral turned Charlotte Corday's victim into a martyr: a saint of the revolution.

David's festival displays are history, but many of his paintings have stood the test of time. His style was influenced not only by the Renaissance, but also by Classical antiquity. He had come to love Classical

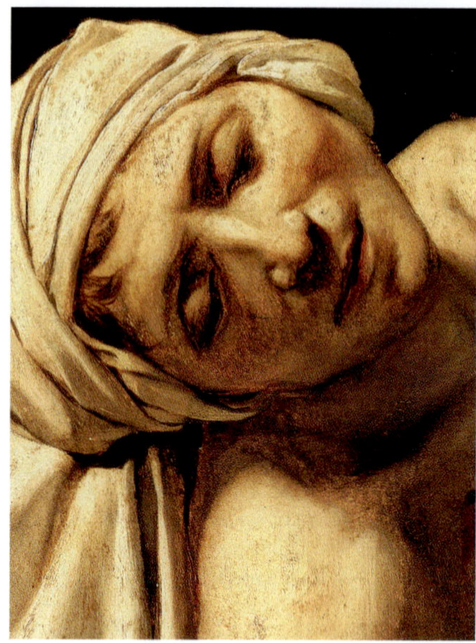

themes long before the Revolution. In 1784 he had painted *The Oath of the Horatii*, followed in 1789 by *Brutus and his Dead Sons*. Both works tell of the triumph of patriotism over individual happiness and family love.

Classical antiquity was *à la mode*, even in clothes fashions, but David's approach was more unremitting and he used Classical themes more convincingly than his contemporaries. He was a master of the *grand gout*, as the "grand manner" of the day was called. He preferred large formats and grand gestures, leaving everything superfluous aside. Simple lines dominate; the structure is monumental. His works may be viewed from a distance, a quality also necessary for the success of a public spectacle.

Having tested his style on Classical themes, David turned his hand in 1793 to the depiction of a topical event: the death of Marat. He succeeded in turning a murder whose manner was far from "grand" – having taken place in a bathtub – into a painting of extraordinary political effect and artistic merit.

The sublime features of heroism

The French revolutionary Jean-Paul Marat was born in 1743 in the domain of Neuchâtel, which, at the time, was a Prussian enclave in Switzerland.

His mother was Swiss; his father, a former monk, hailed from Sardinia. His son must have inherited his father's desire to preach, to instruct, to direct.

Young Marat studied medicine and physics, writing a treatise on the spectral colours. Goethe later attested to his "insight and accuracy". However, his scientific work did not bring him the recognition which – in his opinion – he deserved. He remained poor. Feeling underrated, he saw himself as the object of unfair discrimination by envious colleagues. He also ruined his health by overworking.

The loner's radical ideas were undoubtedly a constant barrier to recognition. In 1774, fifteen years before the Revolution, he published, in England, a tract entitled *The Chains of Slavery*, purporting to disclose "royalty's most unscrupulous attacks on the people". In 1789, during the first year of the Revolution, he founded the paper *L'Ami du Peuple* in Paris. Unlike most revolutionaries of the period, his ideas had been firmly established from the outset. It was against the background of these ideas that he judged all future events. As the self-appointed censor of political affairs, his intention was to use *L'Ami du Peuple* to "keep the National Assembly under surveillance, to disclose its errors, to guide it unceasingly back to the correct principles, to establish and defend the rights of citizens and to supervize the decisions of the authorities".

Initially, the Revolution was a bourgeois affair, a revolt against the king's financial sovereignty. The people stormed the Bastille, which brought them little benefit. "What use is it to us," wrote Marat, "that we have broken the aristocracy of the nobles, if that is replaced by the aristocracy of the rich?"

He fought not only against the royalists, but also against bourgeois revolutionaries and profiteers, making enemies on all sides. As a result, his paper was repeatedly banned and Marat hounded by the authorities. He fled, returned, hid in cellars. In 1791, the King himself was forced to flee; the supporters of a constitutional monarchy were done for. Marat became a Deputy at the National Convention. He saw terror as a legitimate revolutionary weapon: society must "be purged of its corrupt limbs!" he wrote. "Five or six hundred cut-off heads would have guaranteed … freedom and happiness … A false humanity … will cost the lives of thousands." Marat warned that bourgeois forces would triumph, and he was proved right. He wrote that only a dictatorship could help to overcome the crisis of the Revolution, and Napoleon's rule confirmed his prediction. It was his violent death which turned this controversial revolutionary into a national hero. David painted him with a gentle face; nothing in his features betrays the zealous demagogue. The painter wanted to portray the "sublime features of heroism and virtue", as he put it in conjunction with another painting, an artistic apotheosis of the first martyr of the Revolution, Lepelletier: "I shall have fulfilled my task if one day my work moves a … father to say: Look, my children, this was the first of your representatives to die for your freedom; see his features, how serene they are! That is because a person who dies for his fatherland is beyond all reproach."

Accessories as holy relics

A speaker at the National Convention calls upon David to paint Marat's portrait: "David, where are you now? Have you not passed down to posterity the image of Lepelletier dying for the fatherland? Now you have another painting to do!" Whereupon David answers: "Aussi le ferai-je!" The French words somehow contain more pathos than their English equivalent: "I'll do that too!"

David had visited Marat on the eve of his murder. He describes the wooden crate beside his bath. On it, he says, were ink and paper, "and his hand, stretching out from the bath, was writing his last thoughts for the welfare of the people … I thought it might be interesting to show him in the position in which I saw him last."

Marat was a sick man when he was murdered; he may even have been mortally ill. He had been unable to go to the Convention for weeks and had written very little for the newspaper. He had a constant fever and was tortured by a fearful rash. He sought to relieve his itching skin in water. He went back and forth between his bathtub and his bed, wound cloths soaked in vinegar around his head, took only fluid nourishment and drank inordinate amounts of black coffee.

It was David's task to portray this human wreck in a manner that aroused admiration. He removed all sign of skin disease and placed Marat's body in an

imaginary space. In real life, the bathtub had stood before a papered wall with painted columns. Not so in David's painting. His largely dark background – taking up almost half the canvas – not only points to the frugality of Marat's ascetic way of life, but suggests that the space in which his figure is placed may be eternity itself. Its effect is reminiscent of the gold ground of medieval paintings.

The letter and banknote in front of the inkpot were probably the artist's invention. The letter reads: "Give this banknote to the mother of five whose husband died defending the fatherland." At the trial which followed the murder an exact inventory of the objects found in the bathroom was read out, but the letter and banknote were not among them. David used them to portray Marat as a friend of the people. Marat's newspaper wrote that he had spent much of his time "hearing the complaints of numerous misfortunates and giving weight to their demands by petitioning on their behalf". The benefactor's own poverty – a wooden crate instead of a table, or the mended patch of cloth at the bottom left of the picture – emphasized his magnaminity.

David has painted Marat's body in a pose whose effect is particularly resonant: his limp arm hanging down, head lolling to one side and body half-leaning to face the spectator, supported under one shoulder, the white cloths – this pose had been used for centuries to portray Christ's Descent from the Cross. Here, David was exploiting images that were stored in the public memory. He may also have responded to a widespread need for objects of religious veneration. His Man of Sorrows was Marat.

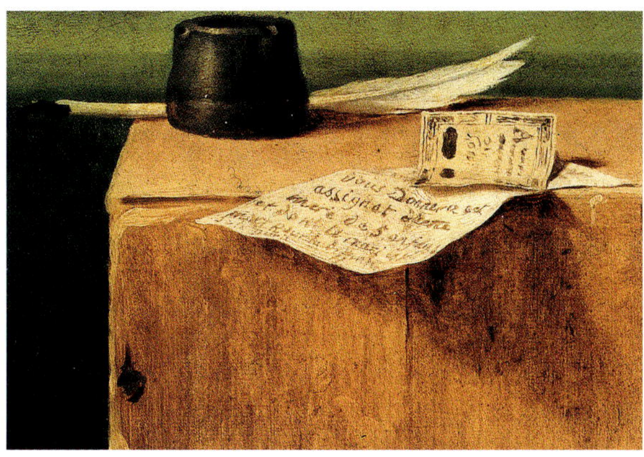

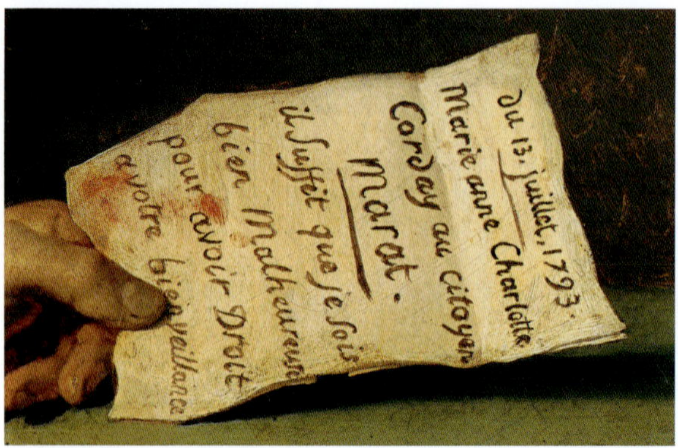

She bought the knife that morning

As one might expect, some contemporary pictures include the figure of the murderess. David's subject was not the drama of the murder, however; it was the awed hush that followed it. He painted an icon, in which feud, disorder and passion had no place.

The only signs of the murderess in the painting are the knife on the floor and the letter in Marat's hand. It reads: "13 July 1793. Marie Anne Charlotte Corday to the citizen Marat. It is enough that I feel unhappy for me to have a right to your goodness." Marat never received the letter, but Charlotte Corday had a similar note in her possession when she was arrested. The real letter did not include the word "goodness", however. Again, David has added it to underline Marat's philanthropism.

The murderess was 24 years of age at the time, and no less eccentric than Marat. Her full name was Marie-Anne Charlotte de Corday D'Armont. Her family were of impoverished aristocratic stock, but she had been brought up in a wealthy convent. She had become engaged to a man of noble, and equally impoverished, background. While he had joined the royalist cause, she supported the bourgeois revolutionaries. Her fiancé wanted to emigrate; Charlotte refused. Patriotism may not have been her only motive, but it was certainly one of them. Following the Roman example, she declared the fatherland more important than personal happiness.

She might have found like minded revolutionaries among the Parisian aristocracy, but in her native town of Caen there was nobody. She was ostracized and soon became estranged from her family. It was only when her father and an uncle who was a priest were forced to go into hiding, and when her fiancé and his brother were executed, that she turned against the increasingly bloody upheavals, deriding the "false demagogues … who drape themselves in the togas of people's advocates" to "establish tyranny and usurp the Republic".

She meant men like Marat who held the majority in the Convention and persecuted the moderates. Several moderate Deputies had fled to Caen, where they organized an uprising. However, when they called for volunteers to fight against the Convention, only seven men turned up. Charlotte Corday had made up her mind: "Surely we have not survived these four years of affliction only to allow a man like Marat to rule over France!" she exclaimed. "Too long have agitators and scoundrels been permitted to confuse personal ambition with the welfare of the people!"

She kept her decision secret. Buying herself a pair of good shoes, she took the mail coach to Paris on 9 July 1793, where she stayed the night at the Hôtel de la Providence. Her plan was to stab Marat to death at the Convention – hoping she would then be killed immediately by his supporters, thus maintaining her anonymity and avoiding any trouble for her family. She was disappointed to hear that Marat's illness had prevented him from appearing at the Convention for some time.

On the morning of Saturday, 13 July, she bought a knife; but she was turned away at Marat's door. She tried again that evening. Marat heard her voice and demanded that the unknown supplicant be admitted. She told him she had come from Caen. Marat then asked her about the Deputies who had fled there. Charlotte asked: "What do you intend to do with them?" Marat replied: "I shall have them all guillotined in Paris." According to Charlotte's later testimony, these words had sealed his fate.

Full of grand gestures, but no guts

Charlotte Corday was arrested immediately. Four days later, during the morning session, she was brought before a judge. That same evening she mounted the scaffold.

She had been "a Republican long before the Revolution," she explained to the tribunal, adding that she had killed Marat "because he embodies the crimes that are devastating the country". As for herself, she had "never lacked energy". "What do you mean by energy?" the presiding judge had asked. Energy, she answered, was a quality demonstrated by persons who were "capable of setting aside their personal happiness and laying down their lives for their country".

Thus she went to her death, as "sublime" a heroine as any admired in Ancient Rome. Insisting on a right to curiosity, she pushed away the executioner who wished to spare her the sight of the guillotine. She laid her head under the blade herself. It was not long before she, too, was hailed as a martyr – by moderates who abhorred the Terror and defended the citizen's right to property. The royalists also championed her, generously overlooking the fact that she had been a convinced Republican.

David had acquired Marat's death mask for the portrait, and had Marat's bath, ink pot and the knife brought to his studio.

He wrote a modest sounding dedication on the wooden crate in Roman style: "For Marat, David". At the same time, he painted his own name in letters that were not much smaller than the name of the dead hero. He dated the painting "Year Two", after the new revolutionary calender.

In October 1793, the painting was exhibited at his studio and in the courtyard of the Louvre. In November, he handed it over to the National Convention along with its pendant, the portrait of Lepelletier. "My colleagues, I offer you the homage of my paint brushes!"

The Convention had both works hung in the assembly chamber and – a demonstration of their blind faith in the future – passed a decree which prohibited future legislative bodies from removing the paintings.

By June the following year the moderates had taken power, sending Robespierre and about a hundred of his supporters to the scaffold. Sensing an imminent reverse in his fortunes, Robespierre had cried out in the Convention: "It remains for me to take hemlock!", an allusion to the death of Socrates. David, in a gesture as grand and noble as any ever seen in Rome, answered: "If you drink hemlock, then I shall drink with you!" When Robespierre was removed from power in a tumultuous session the following day, however, David stayed at home. He did not reappear until well after the radical revolutionaries had been executed and the authorities had grown weary of the guillotine.

Five years later, in 1799, the artist declared himself willing to complete an earlier, unfinished revolutionary work, painting over the real historical figures and replacing them with new ones "who have come to the fore in the meantime and will therefore be of far greater interest to future generations". No sign here of those celebrated Roman virtues! David had become a master in the art of adapting to new circumstances; it was not long before he was celebrating the new dictator, Emperor Napoleon. With the fall of Napoleon in 1814, however, David decided to go into exile. He took the Marat painting – removed from the Convention in 1795 – with him to Brussels. The portrait of Lepelletier entered the estate of his daughter, who, having meanwhile become a fanatical royalist, did away with it. It has not been seen since.

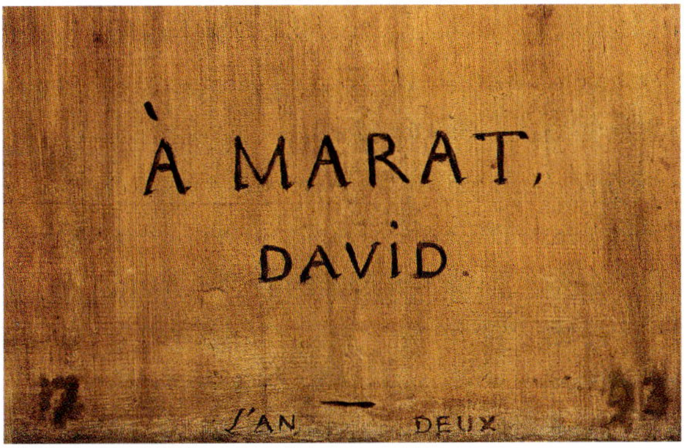

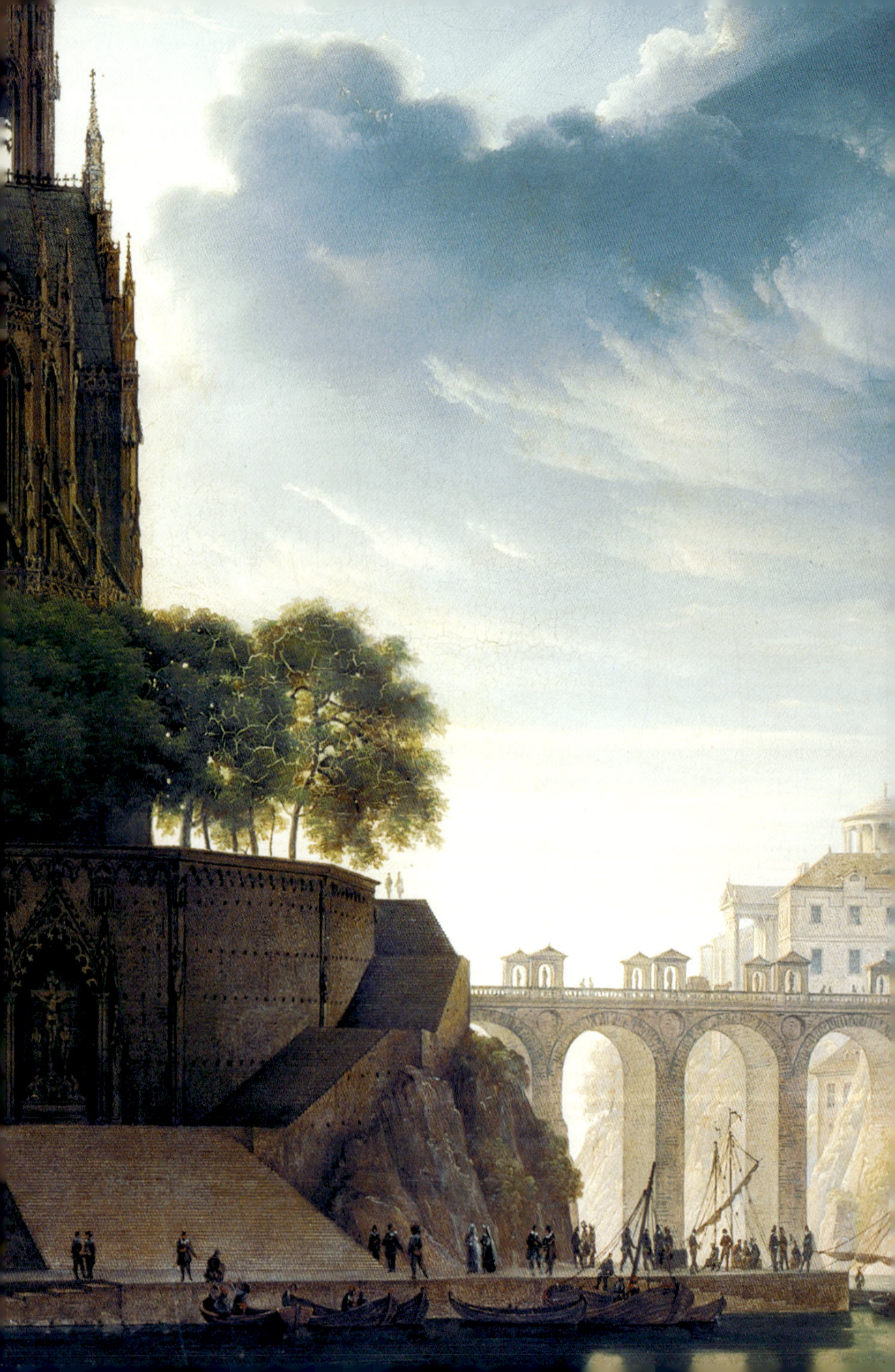

Karl Friedrich Schinkel (1781–1841)

Fantasy of an unemployed architect

Cathedral Overlooking a City, 1813
94 x 126 cm, Munich, Neue Pinakothek

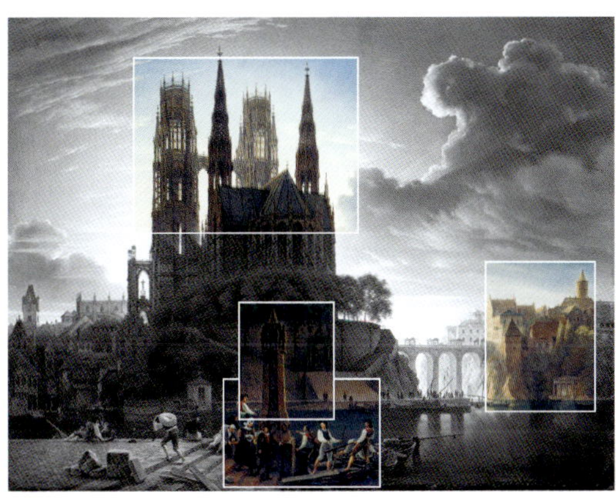

Karl Friedrich Schinkel first showed his painting of a vast medieval cathedral rising beside the sea in 1814, at the Academy exhibition in Berlin. The work later hung in the Berlin palace of the Hohenzollern family. It then passed to the Berlin National Gallery, which loaned it to a large exhibition on the Romantics in the Munich Glaspalast. There, on 6 June 1931, it was burned to ashes, together with some 3,000 other works, including nine by Caspar David Friedrich. The fire at the Munich Glaspalast was one of the greatest disasters in the history of German art exhibitions.

A second version, which Schinkel had kept for himself, fell victim to the Second World War. After Schinkel's death in 1841, it passed to the Schinkel Museum in Berlin, and later to the imperial chancellery, where it was probably destroyed in the fighting of 1945. The painting was allegedly known simply as "Schinkel 1913".

Two copies have survived. One belongs to the Nationalgalerie in Berlin, the other to the Neue Pinakothek in Munich. The Munich version shown here (94 by 126 centimetres) is so good that it was long thought to be another original by Schinkel. It is probably the work of Eduard Biermann, however. It is thanks to the copyists that this important composition, highly characteristic of the 19th century, can still be admired today. The original was executed in 1813, a critical juncture in European history – the year of the German wars of liberation against Napoleon and the defeat of the French emperor at the Battle of Leipzig.

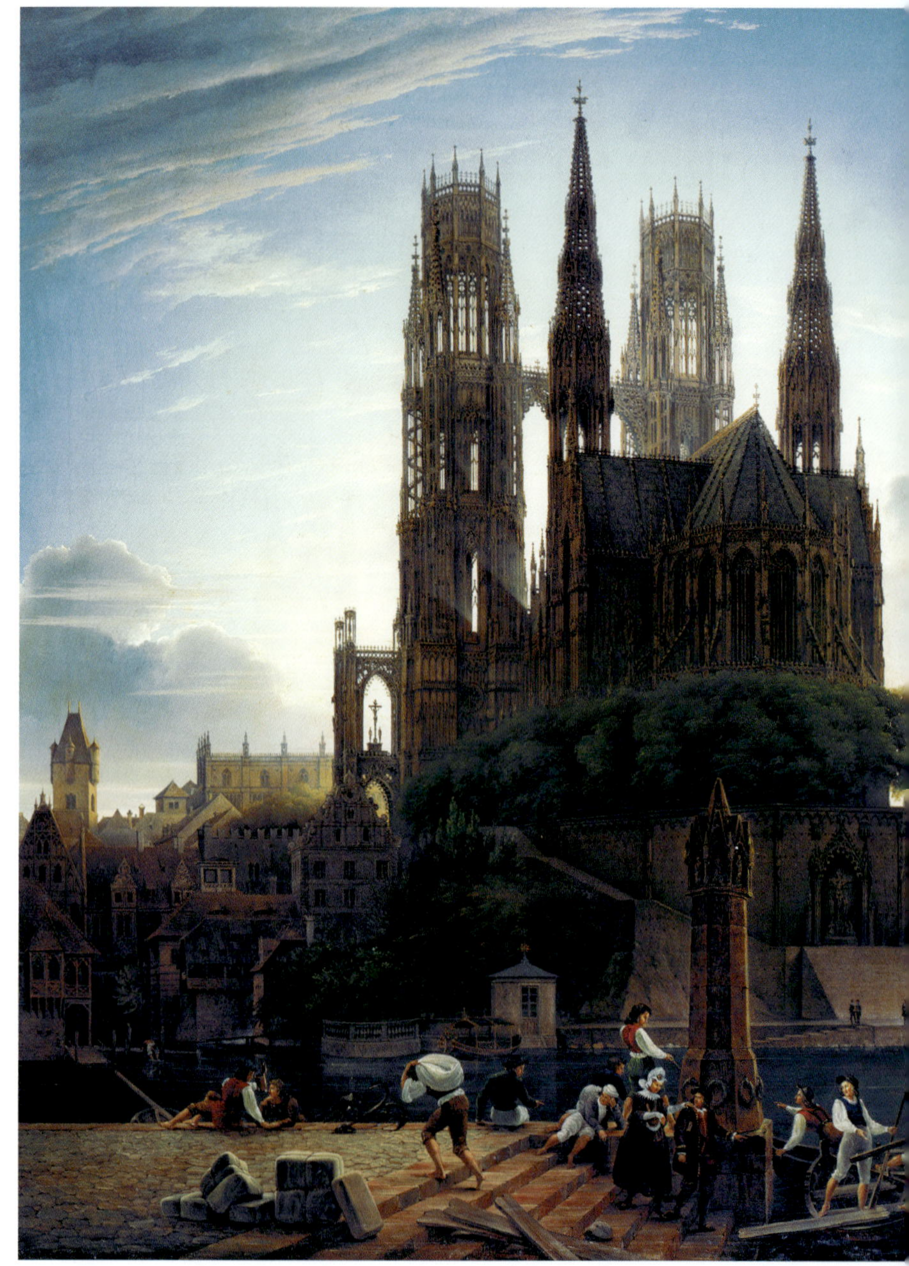

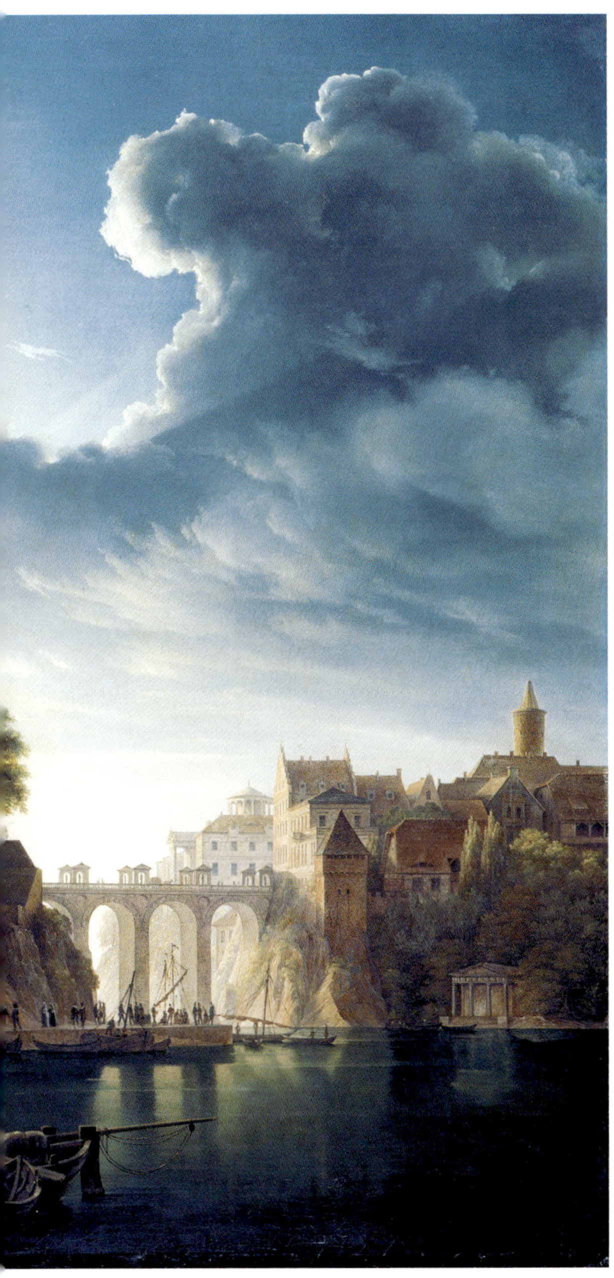

Schinkel paints because he can't build

Beside the flight of steps, in the shadow of the cathedral, stands a sculptural Crucifixion group and by the harbour wall in the foreground a memorial column that cannot be more specifically identified. Monuments played a major role in Schinkel's life. He designed a good number of them, even if not all went on to be built. For him, this painting too possessed the character of a memorial or monument. It was intended to symbolize a large, unified Germany.

But the reality was still quite the opposite: Germany was occupied by French troops, the nobility dependent upon Napoleon's mercy, the population divided into the friends and foes of the powerful Corsican. In 1806 the French had defeated the Prussian army at Jena and Auerstedt; the Prussian king had fled to East Prussia and Napoleon had marched into Berlin. He had ordered the goddess Victory and her quadriga to be taken down from the top of the Brandenburg Gate and shipped off to Paris – a dispiriting act of despotism.

More humiliating still were the demands for reparations that proceeded to ruin the country. The salaries of civil servants were not paid, landlords whose houses were used as quarters for the French troops lost their rents, and artisans waited in vain for commissions. In 1808 the publisher Friedrich Nicolai wrote that "in these desperately sad times since November 1806 I have lost half my fortune". During this same period, Wilhelm von Humboldt noted: "Berlin has become a village. There are hardly any carriages … at dinners and suppers, tallow is burnt" – instead of the usual candles.

Karl Friedrich Schinkel grew up in these years of deprivation. He was born in 1781 in Neuruppin, studied architecture in Berlin, and spent the years 1803–05 in Italy. When he returned home, the prospects of getting work as an architect seemed slim. There was no money to spare for houses, churches or palaces. Schinkel became a painter for the annual Christmas market. He produced dioramas, full-size representations that, flanked by mock columns and viewed from a distance, were dramatically lit and frequently brought to life with music and mechanical figures. He also painted a circular panorama of Palermo, which was 4.50 metres high and 27 metres long, and which could be viewed in a round wooden building. Schinkel was thereby working to entertain a large public. Illusion was in demand. The Berliners wanted to be shown an exotic location or an event from recent history. Over Christmas 1812 they were given the burning of Moscow, with which Napoleon's fall from power had begun three months earlier.

In 1813 Germany once again became a battlefield. Over 100,000 would fall at Leipzig in October alone. August had already seen a fierce skirmish at Grossbeeren, near Berlin. The Prussians were victorious, and the Berliners travelled out to the field of battle. They saw a "chaos of people, soldiers, corpses, dead horses". Many had taken food with them, and "at five o'clock everyone ate, surrounded by bodies", according to a banker by the name of Müller. The road to Berlin was full "of carts carrying nothing but wounded – a sad sight".

Gothic against Napoleon

Schinkel's *Cathedral Overlooking a City*, in which the setting sun and low vantage point combine to lend the cathedral a monumental grandeur, also dates to 1813. It was a year full of chaos, bloodshed and political volatility. Only when virtually forced to by his army and subjects did Friedrich Wilhelm III, Prussia's king, openly challenge the Corsican. He also created a new military decoration, not of gold or silver, but – as appropriate to wartime and because it was intended for the troops – of iron. He made a preliminary sketch of his "Iron Cross" and instructed Schinkel, who was

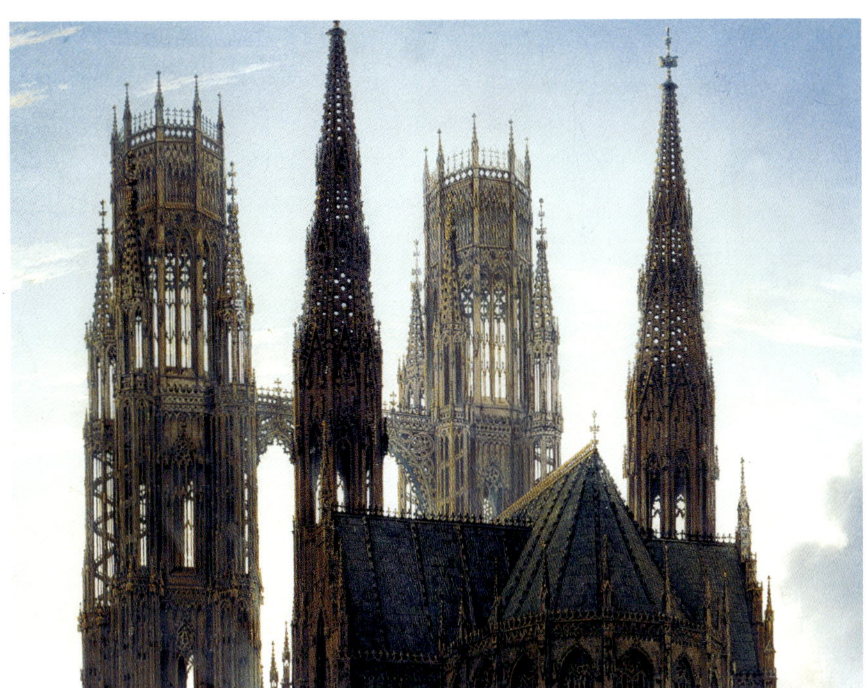

by now privy architectural adviser in the Department of Public Works, to produce the final design.

In March 1814 the armies allied against Napoleon marched into Paris, and Schinkel was given another commission by his king – a national cathedral that was to be erected in thanksgiving for the liberation of Prussia. The domed building with relatively low towers that he conceived in response to this request bears little resemblance to the cathedral in the present painting. What Schinkel the artist imagines soaring into the heights, Schinkel the architect kept firmly on the ground. The only Gothic features he retained were the pointed arches. Gothic, neverthe-less, was what the king's commemorative cathedral was meant to be. It was considered the most quintes-sentially German of all architectural styles.

This misconception can be traced not least to Johann Wolfgang von Goethe. As a young man he was enraptured by Strasbourg cathedral, and in 1772 – without ever having seen the cathedrals of Milan, Reims or Chartres – he rather ignorantly pronounced the Gothic style a "German architecture,

for the Italians can boast none of their own, and even less so the French".

Goethe's enthusiasm for the Gothic style chimed in with the growing tendency to eulogize Germany's past. Young poets celebrated the bold knight Götz von Berlichingen, the Grimm brothers collected old folk tales, and Dürer's Nuremberg became a symbol of peaceful civic coexistence. Everything about the old days seemed better than the present: no par-ticularism, no despotism either at home or abroad. Gothic was thereby chosen as the stylistic code for such retrospection; it was declared the "stirring style of medieval German architecture", which would produce the "power for the future". Thus wrote Schinkel about his cathedral project for the king. He was just one of many during this period who painted Gothic cathedrals or, like Caspar David Friedrich (1774–1840), Gothic ruins.

Schinkel would never build a national cathedral to commemorate the wars of liberation – probably because the public purse was empty. In its place, however, he erected a Gothic memorial on a hill

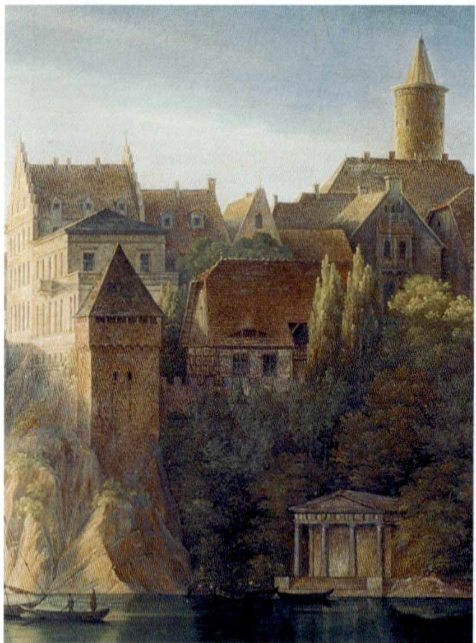

to issue from below, from the people. The architectural language of Classicism, on the other hand, spoke of order, harmony, and reason. These virtues came not from below, but from a lofty intellectual tradition, and were especially popular with rulers. For you can rule only if you can have order and control.

Love for the one did not preclude love for the other, but the older Schinkel got, the more he tended towards the classical idiom. Goethe, too, distanced himself in his later years from his youthful admiration of Strasbourg cathedral. Schinkel visited him several times in Weimar. At their last meeting, in 1826, Goethe spoke of the "character of the pointed arch in architecture as no doubt sometimes useful but lacking in beauty …"

What Goethe called beauty, Schinkel understood as calm. For him, an impression of calm was the supreme goal of architecture; no ornamentation, just clarity and harmony. "The calmest is the building which [combines] columns and architrave … The pointed arch, because it renders visible the conflicting forces, contains profound restlessness."

The word "calm" had a history in Prussia, albeit not in Schinkel's sense. After the Prussian defeat at Jena, announcements posted on the city walls informed the Berlin populace that "The King has lost a battle. Calm is now the first duty of all citizens." Later, even after Prussia and its allies had won their decisive victory over the French, the king continued to insist emphatically upon calm. Any desire for greater civil rights or national unity – causes that had also been fought for – was forcefully repressed. Like all German princes, Friedrich Wilhelm was afraid of losing his power.

Whether Schinkel publicly took sides is unknown. Similarly unknown is whether a fear of revolution and chaos perhaps reinforced his personal need for calm and straight lines. Quite apart from his own artistic preferences, however, it is clear that as a Prussian civil servant he was not in a position to do anything but what his monarch and other patrons demanded, namely design buildings in the Classical style.

in Berlin. It stands there still. In reference to the cross on top of the monument, the hill and the suburb that grew up around it were later renamed Kreuzberg (Cross Hill).

Schinkel's path to Classicism

In 1815 Schinkel was commissioned to design a building to house the royal guard on Berlin's prestigious avenue, Unter den Linden. The resulting Neue Wache (New Guard House), which remains one of Schinkel's best loved buildings, was furnished on its front façade with a Classical portico employing ten columns and surmounted by a low-pitched triangular gable. Schinkel had employed such a gable, albeit supported on just four columns, in the very first building he ever designed, a garden temple in Potsdam. It can be seen in the present painting, too, in the small temple that appears beneath the city and which is almost identical in its proportions to the Potsdam temple.

Gothic pointed arches on the one hand, classical porticos on the other, the curve versus the straight line – these were not just questions of artistic taste, but of political conviction. The Gothic style was associated with everything German, as well as with originality and emotion. Gothic art was considered

The architect of Berlin

In paintings by Caspar David Friedrich, Schinkel's slightly older contemporary, the sea frequently appears as something mysterious, as a diffuse mass cloaked in mist or as a surface containing enormous ice floes crushing a sailing ship. Schinkel's painting is quite different. His sea is smooth. Its surface conceals nothing, and within the composition it provides a horizontal base for the soaring spires above. The people in this painting play no more than walk-on parts. They add interest to the foreground, probably rather like the mechanical figures that stood in front of Schinkel's Christmas dioramas. Supposed to convey the impression of happy Germans in a happy epoch, they are light-footed and graceful in their poses. But their diminutive size and muted palette mean they are easily overlooked, as indeed is the intention – all eyes are drawn to the cathedral.

The cityscape that Schinkel paints here was part of a genre that had grown rapidly in popularity since the previous century. Its origins lay in the souvenir pictures painted for tourists by artists such as Francesco Guardi (1712–1793), who recorded the buildings and squares of Venice. These were followed by much grander paintings, such as those executed by Bernardo Bellotto (1720–1780), for example, and intended for emperors and kings who wanted views of their magnificent capitals to hang on their walls. Both Guardi and Bellotto thereby recorded what was before their eyes. The Romantics, on the other hand, painted architecture in order to render visible something that had nothing to do with a real building. They were interested not in the pointed arch

as such, but in what lay behind it. The height and the light-flooded mass of Schinkel's cathedral were understood as symbolic values.

As soon as Schinkel was able to build, in other words from 1816 onwards, he put painting aside. He had enough to do: promoted to privy councillor, inspection trips took him to all the Prussian provinces, and also to Cologne, where for more than twenty years he would be involved in the construction of the cathedral. He designed furniture, staircases, interiors, and – drawing on his experience at the Christmas market – over 100 stage sets.

The main focus of his energies remained Berlin, however. After the Neue Wache and Friedrichswerdersche church, he went on to build the Schauspielhaus theatre and concert hall in the Gendarmenmarkt, the Schlossbrücke, the Altes Museum in the Lustgarten and the Bauakademie school of architecture. No other architect shaped the face of the city so profoundly as Karl Friedrich Schinkel. Most of these buildings are Classical in style and imbued with a sober harmony. If we compare them with the imaginary, Romantic architecture of his painted cathedrals, we can recognize something of the two faces of Prussia during these years.

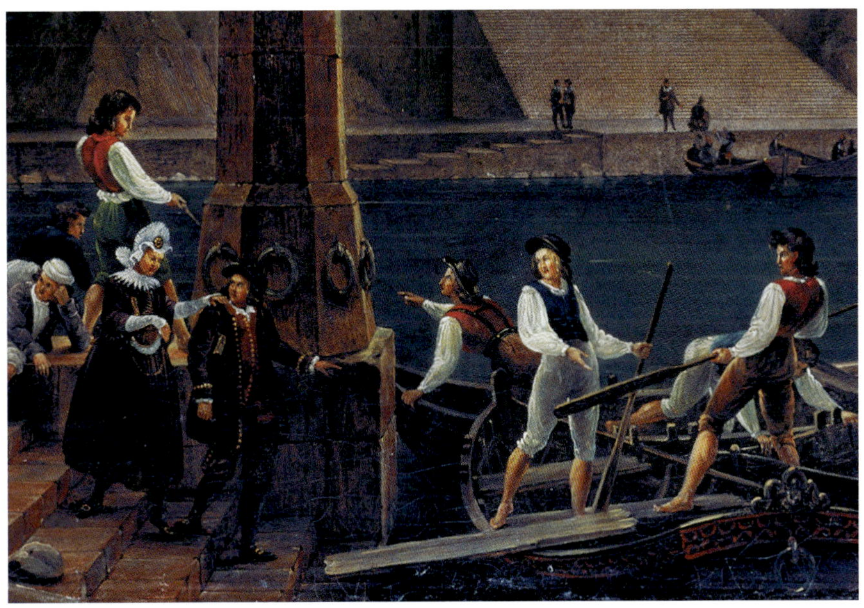

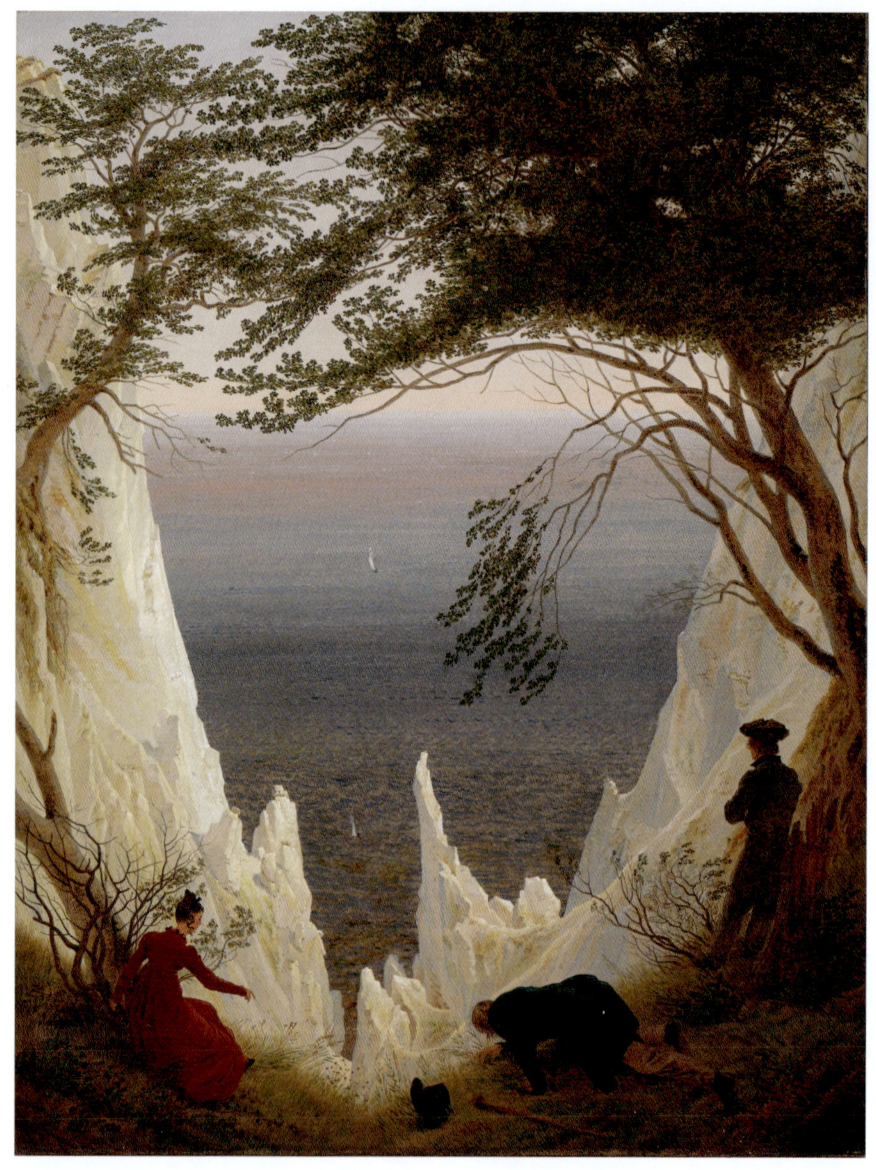

Caspar David Friedrich (1774–1840)

A view to infinity

Chalk Cliffs on Rügen, c. 1818
90 x 70 cm, Winterthur, Museum Oskar Reinhart

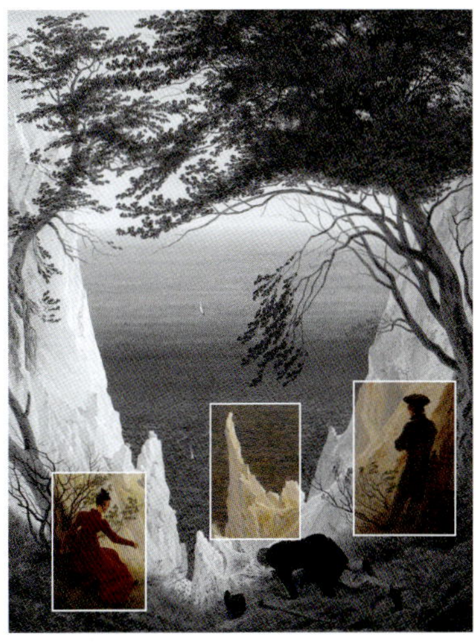

The boundless ocean, figures at the edge of a precipice, old-fashioned clothing, huge chalk cliffs as witnesses of the distant past – the painting by the Romantic C. D. Friedrich is evidently more than a view of a North German landscape. It belongs to the Stiftung Oskar Reinhart, Winterthur (Switzerland).

Caspar David Friedrich was born in 1774 at Greifswald on the Baltic coast. Across the bay lay the island of Rügen, where Friedrich liked to go walking. When he married in 1818 – by then he lived in Dresden – he showed his wife not only his native town, but also the island. His painting, set in the chalk cliffs there, was probably executed shortly after his honeymoon. It is not dated.

Friedrich frequently made drawings on Rügen, basing several of his later paintings on the sketches. His written references to the island (which was not yet linked to the mainland) are few and far between. However, an account of a walking tour on the island was made by Friedrich's friend, the doctor and art critic Carl Gustav Carus. The two men had become acquainted in Dresden, and it was presumably Friedrich's enthusiasm for Rügen that inspired

Carus's trip to the Baltic coast. His visit fell in 1818, when Friedrich married and may also have painted his *Chalk Cliffs*.

"To put over to Rügen across the broad Greifswalder Bodden, we hired a little yacht," recalled Carus, "and I first set sail under a fine morning sky on 14th August." The island was entirely unprepared for tourism: "Instead of a well-appointed hotel to welcome the island's guests, there was nothing among the scattered blocks of granite but a fisherman's smoky cabin, where new arrivals could satisfy their most urgent needs."

The reader will learn little from Carus about the people who lived on Rügen, about their work or way of life. The features he describes are those which also interested Friedrich: "I came across an ancient oak right in the middle of the island. It was almost completely withered; its monstrous, grey branches stretched up worn and shining into the blue sky …" Carus walks to Cape Arkona, "the most northerly point on German soil". He visits a place "where peculiar, old rune stones enclose an ancient burial mound, or some kind of sacred hill". The withered oak tree, Cape Arkona, megalithic barrows – these

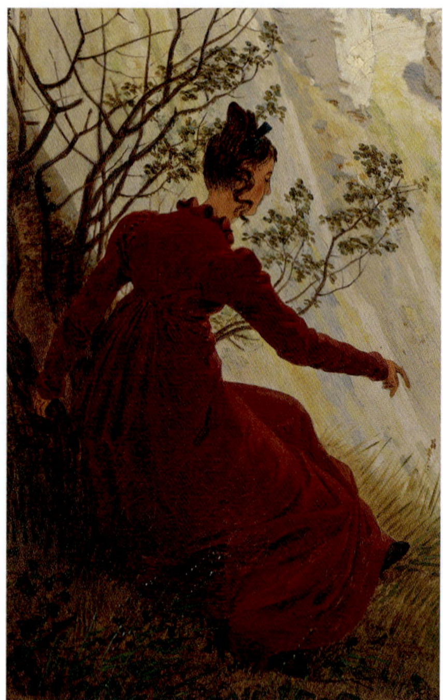

were legacies of the past, symbols of a national history, and Friedrich returned to them again and again in his drawings and paintings.

However, by far the most moving spectacle for Carus was the view from the top of the cliffs that made Friedrich famous and turned tourism on the island into a mass industry: "Towards evening we took the forest path, listening to the distant roar of the waves mingling with the rustle of the wind in the leaves around us. All of a sudden, the forest ended and we were standing at the top of the sheer chalk cliffs at King's Seat, where the long, drooping branches of young red beeches swayed over the foaming surf far below, and the blue-grey mirror of the Baltic stretched out in a broad sweep to the barely perceptible line of the horizon …"

At the seaside in a high-necked dress
At the time, swimming and sailing were not yet thought of as holiday pursuits. Visitors were drawn to the watering places which had begun to spring up along the German coast, just as they were to the spas

of the interior, solely on account of the healing powers attributed to water. Indeed, once there, they were more likely to bathe in a tub than in the sea.

The Mecklenburg court had made a start on the Baltic coast in 1793, near Doberan, the later Heiligendamm. Travemünde followed six years later, with a casino added in 1822. Like the famous spas at Karlsbad and Baden-Baden, the new seaside health resorts wished to offer their guests an attractive social life.

While Friedrich was painting his seascape, upper class families were discovering the pleasures of the seaside. In the interests of modesty, the English had invented the bathing machine: "The bather mounts a two wheeled vehicle, a carriage, upon which is a small wooden hut … Attached to the back is a kind of tent." The description is from an essay, entitled "Why does Germany have no large, public, seaside resort?" written by the Göttingen philosopher Georg Christoph Lichtenberg in 1793. To enable ladies to bathe in such tents, English seaside resorts offered special "loosely-fitting suits", which, "although they float on the surface, allow their wearers the security of feeling fully dressed". Ironically, Lichtenberg adds that this "security" will "be ever sacred to the innocent, whether on the ocean or submerged in total darkness".

Traditionally, Christian doctrine decried the body as the adversary of the spirit; the female body, especially, was thought to be the devil's instrument of temptation. Hostility towards the body was particulary pronounced in 18th- and 19th-century bourgeois culture. Washing the body was avoided; in pietistical circles, it was considered immoral for women to see even their own bodies naked. Friedrich was prudish, too, at least in his pictures. He was interested in Nature, not in the naturalness of the body. Like the woman in the painting, almost all his figures are fully dressed. Only their necks, heads and hands are visible.

The woman's long, loose dress, with its high waist girded just below the breast, was a development of the Empire gown. This had become fashionable in France at the time of the Revolution, at least in the upper classes. It was worn sleeveless, had a low neckline, and was generally made of transparent materials.

In adapting the dress for the German bourgoisie, however, everything free or transparent was removed. The style has more in common with Gothic than Empire style. This may be the reason why Friedrich painted this type of dress so frequently; the Gothic, after all, was supposed to be a German style. The pseudo-Gothic dress thus serves as a reminder of German history.

Fashion as a pledge of loyalty

The man wearing a beret and leaning against a tree is also dressed in "old German" style. The so-called "national costume" was, in itself, a pledge of loyalty. Its origin lay in the wars of liberation against Napoleon. It was a pledge against foreign dictatorship, against the despotism of German princes, for a unified Germany and for human rights.

It had been middle-class burghers, not the princes, who had mobilized an army against the French occupation. The self-confidence this had generated now sought official recognition. Once the French had been expelled, however, the German princes attempted to reestablish absolutist structures of power. In 1819, their ministers passed a series of repressive laws: censorship of the press, prosecution of all "demagogues", banning of radical students' associations, prohibition of the "old German" costume.

The costume had been propagated by another of Rügen's native sons, Ernst Moritz Arndt, born on the island in 1769. In 1814, one year after the war of liberation ended, he wrote an essay entitled "Of Manners, Fashions and Costumes". Although he had few suggestions to make on the subject of women's clothing, Arndt insisted that a man's proper dress was a frock coat buttoned to the neck and a wide shirt collar. Hair could be worn long and was to be covered with a velvet beret. From about 1815 onwards, the majority of men in Friedrich's paintings appear in this, or similar, dress.

In memoirs recalling his youth, Arndt also described what he wanted to abolish: "All that rigmarole with periwigs, that whole foppish way of dandified dressing with its jesuitical, arabesqued, Frenchified squiggles and twirls – a style which survived from Louis XIV to the French Revolution." Arndt had suffered under this style of dress: "It often took the best part of an hour until your queues were starched up and your toupet and curls were waxed down and you were properly smoothed over with pomade and piled with hairpins and powder."

Arndt's fate was fairly typical for a man of his political persuasion. "The Rhine is Germany's river, not Germany's border," he wrote in defiance of Napoleon. Under the latter's occupation he was

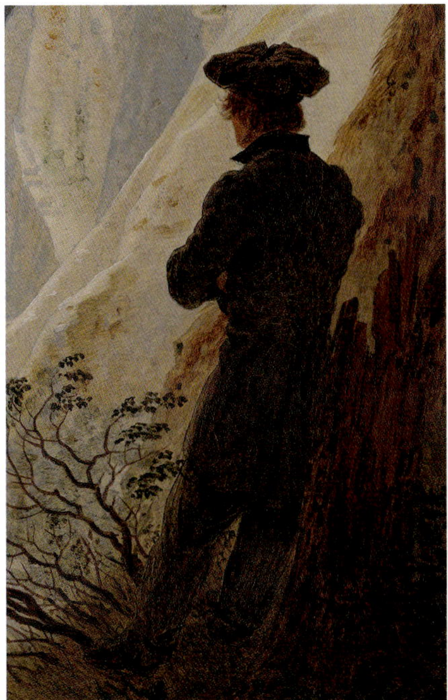

forced to flee to Russia. Following Napoleon's defeat, he was made professor of history at Bonn university, but was dismissed as a "demagogue" two years later: "because I had acted in the spirit and best interests of what I understood to be – and, as it happened, actually were – the spirit and best interests of Prussia."

He was prohibited from returning to his profession for twenty years. The file compiled at the time of his removal from office contained a letter, dated 1814, from Caspar David Friedrich: one of many statements of the painter's political sympathies.

Friedrich wrote that he would like to paint a memorial to Scharnhorst, the Prussian military reformer: "I am not a bit surprised that no memorial has been erected, whether to honour the people and their cause, or to remind us of the noble-minded deeds of individual Germans. As long as we remain the minions of despots and princes, nothing great of that kind will ever happen. Whenever people are denied a voice, they are also prevented from feeling who they are, or from taking pride in their own achievements."

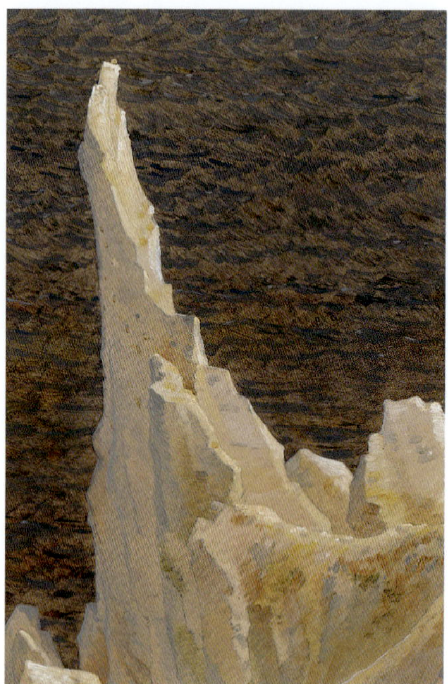

Beyond landscape

A view from chalk cliffs belonged to the category of "landscape paintings", a genre not thought particularly worthy of respect. The importance of a painting was decided less by its quality than by its subject.

In 1802/03, the philosopher Friedrich Wilhelm Schelling reflected on the relative importance of subjects. At the top of his hierarchy was the history painting; at the bottom, the still life. Landscapes came somewhere in between. According to Schelling, landscapes lacked objective meaning: "Only the outer mantle is actually shown; the thing itself, the idea, is without form; it is therefore left up to the spectator what he makes of this flimsy, formless state of being."

Friedrich would never have agreed with Schelling's point of view. His aim was not to show the "mantle", or to reproduce an existing landscape. When Goethe asked him to sketch cloud formations for his scientific studies, Friedrich refused. He did not portray nature *au vif*; he rearranged it. He introduced distance where there was none.

He moved the ruins of Eldena monastery from its setting near Greifswald to the Giant Mountains. He also changed the chalk cliffs until they fitted his idea of them.

Friedrich was not the only painter of his time to use landscapes to express "ideas". In Rome, his German contemporary, Joseph Anton Koch, was painting combinations of very different landscapes, attempting to illustrate different moods and states of mind.

This kind of thing did not interest Friedrich. It is not only his emphasis on things German that springs to mind when one looks for "ideas" in his work; tranquillity and distance are equally important. He avoided stirring movement; wind, storms or battle scenes are not found. The movements of the figures on the chalk cliffs serve to underline the general sense of peace and tranquillity. Conversely, his version of Nature lacks the sequestered, leafy intimacy which Ludwig Richter so often extolled in his landscape idylls. The three ramblers on the chalk cliffs are quite clearly standing on the edge of a dangerous precipice.

Rather than intimacy, it is a sense of great distance which the picture evokes. With its dark foreground, bright middle ground and high horizon, fully framed by the trees and rocks, it is like a window with a view to infinity.

Besides tranquillity and the infinite, there is a third idea which recurs in Friedrich's work: the past. He painted burial mounds, Gothic churches, ruins and churchyards. The chalk cliffs, too, are the legacy of geological events which took place millions of years ago. Men like Friedrich and Arndt found strength in the past; they looked to history for models of a better Germany. At the same time, Friedrich's motives for turning to the past were by no means solely political. He was a religious man. His writings show his belief that God revealed Himself through Nature. He attempted to convey this feeling of divine revelation in his landscapes, returning again and again to notions of tranquillity, eternity and infinity.

The art of contemplation

The identity of the three persons on the cliff edge has given rise to much speculation. The woman may be Caroline Friedrich, with whom the artist visited Rügen in 1818. One of the men might then be Friedrich himself, the other possibly his brother,

Christian, who, with his own wife, accompanied the newlyweds on their tour.

Or was the artist thinking here of his friend Carus? Why is one of the men looking down, while the woman appears to be pointing at something, or waving, as if warning of some danger? Perhaps she has lost her hat: like the men, she would certainly have worn one. Is their gaze into the depths symbolic?

Friedrich himself offered no explanation. What we do know is that the figures are painted more or less from behind, and that this is consistent with the figures in almost all of his paintings. Since individuals are generally recognized by their faces, it is logical to assume that Friedrich's rear views do not portray individuals, indeed that he was not interested in portraying individuals in his landscapes at all. Rather, he was interested in them as vehicles: they are shown in the act of gazing, thus inviting the spectator to do the same. It is not the figures themselves who are significant, but the object of their gaze.

Whether gazing at the moon, a mountain top or the sea's horizon, Friedrich's figures, like the man on the right, are usually shown looking into the distance. Their pose, in so doing, is almost always an expression of inner peace. They are meditative figures, seemingly lost in thought. According to Carl Gustav Carus, it was preferable to visit the island "alone", "entrusting oneself" to Nature. Once "alone", one's "gaze from the mighty chalk cliffs" could "accompany distant sailing ships across the iridescent ocean waves …"

The poet Novalis described the romantic notion of "entrusting oneself" to Nature as a difficult art: "The art of contemplation is hard. Gazing creatively at the world demands austerity, the ability to engage in uninterrupted, serious reflection; the reward will be … only the pleasure of knowledge and growth, of touching the universe at a deeper level." Novalis died in 1801. Friedrich painted his self-portrait in 1810.

Friedrich's crayon drawing does not show the artist in contemporary dress, but in a cowl resembling, more than anything else, a monk's habit. The garment thus gives its wearer the exalted aura of someone who is used to "contemplation". A person who spends his time "touching the universe", or communicating with the Infinite, is no longer in touch with reality – with the social world of normal human beings.

Social reality, for someone of Friedrich's political sympathies, was as oppressive in 1810 as it was later, in 1818. For if, in 1810, Germany was occupied by Napoleon's army, by 1818 the German nobility was firmly back in place. Friedrich did not flee to Russia; nor was he removed from office, like his fellow-Pomeranian Ernst Moritz Arndt. Friedrich fled to the Infinite. The narrowness of the political scene intensified his longing to "touch the universe".

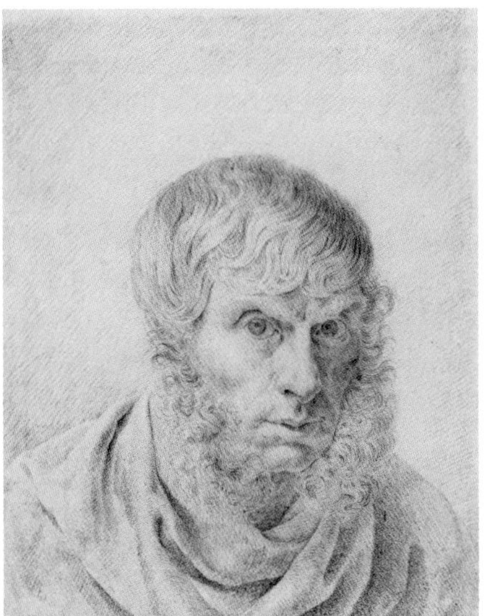

Comparative illustration:
Caspar David Friedrich
Self-portrait at the age of 36, c. 1810
22.8 x 18.2 cm, Berlin, Staatliche Museen zu Berlin, Kupferstichkabinett

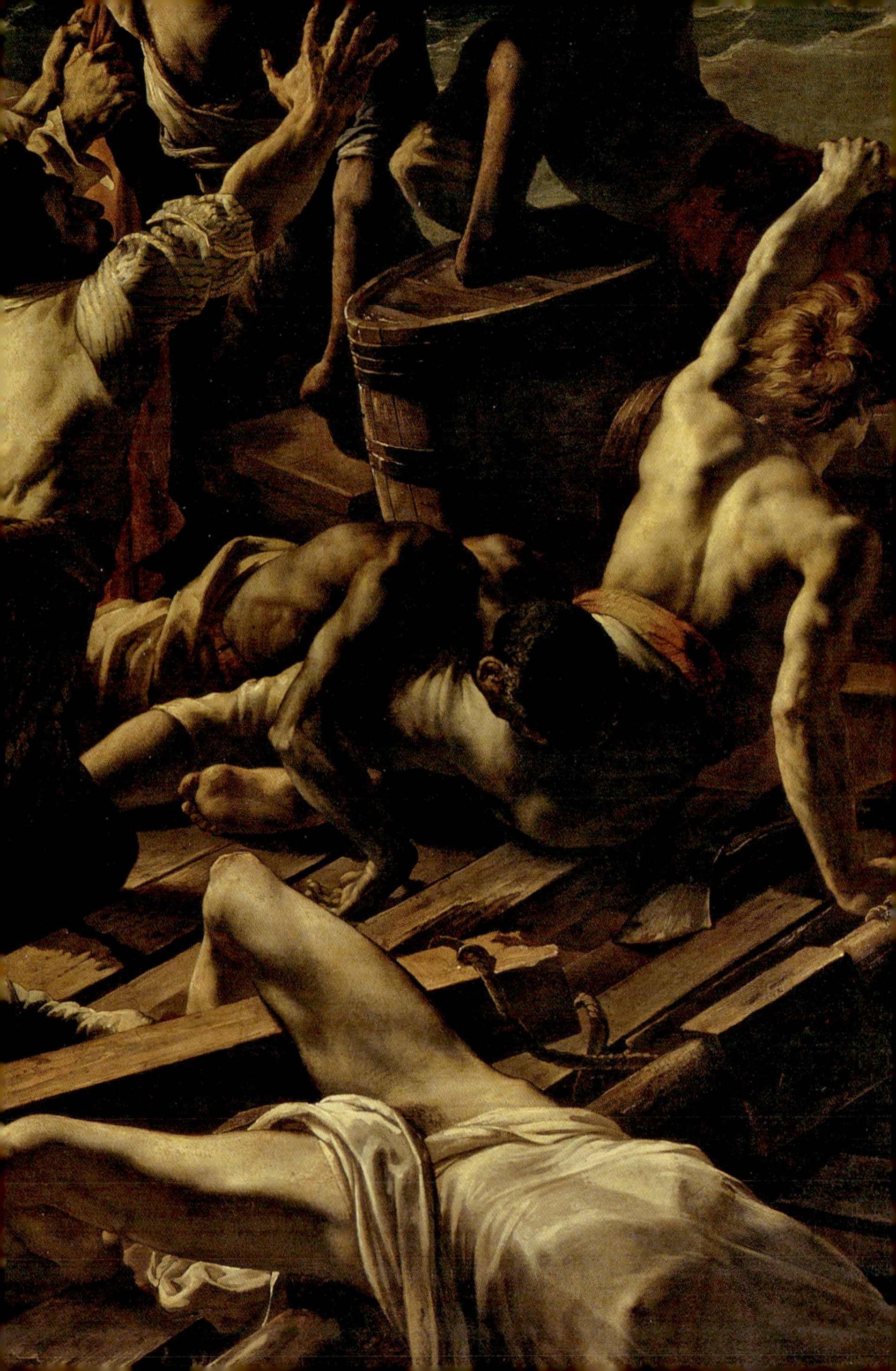

Théodore Géricault (1791–1824)

Dramatic struggle for survival

The Raft of the Medusa, 1819
491 x 716 cm, Paris, Musée du Louvre

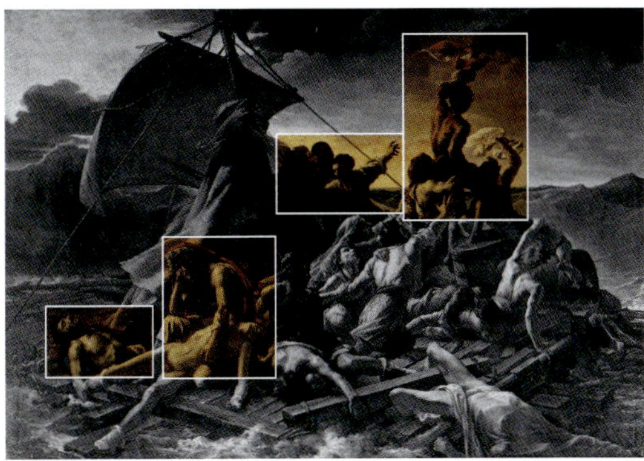

Originally, 27-year-old Théodore Géricault had hoped his "Scene of a Shipwreck", submitted to the Paris Salon of 1819, would merely bring him fame. But it was not long before the monumental canvas, now in the Louvre, became recognized as a powerful testimony to the pathos of suffering humanity.

The press leapt on the story like a hungry animal. The first report of the wreck of the frigate *Medusa* was published in September 1816 by the Parisian *Journal des Débats*. Inquiry into the cause and exact circumstances of the disaster occupied the French newspapers for months to come. A tale of human misfortune – only 15 of the 147 castaways on the raft had survived – snowballed into a political scandal. Government attempts to cover up the full extent of the catastrophe were exposed in the press by the opposition; public outrage led to the dismissal of the minister responsible, together with 200 naval officers.

The disaster and ensuing furore were not forgotten by the time Géricault came to exhibit his painting three years later. The title he had chosen for the work sounded anodyne enough: *Scene of a Shipwreck*. Without it, the painting might not have gained entry to the official Salon of 1819, an exhibition whose function was no less political than artistic. The Bourbons, returned to the throne in 1814, needed a glamorous show to demonstrate France's stability and prosperity under its legitimate ruler.

Inevitably, the artists whose submissions were selected for the exhibition were practically unanimous in the respect they brought to the regime and its closest ally, the Church. Two thirds of the large-scale history paintings – the centre of attention at every Salon – showed scenes from the lives of the saints; the rest paid tribute to previous French monarchs. (Interestingly enough, the majority of these works were by artists who had celebrated Napoleon's victories.) By contrast, Géricault's painting flattered neither crown nor cloth; nor did it have much to contribute to "the nation's honour". On the contrary, it served as a reminder of a scandal which the new regime would rather have forgotten. The picture was a provocation.

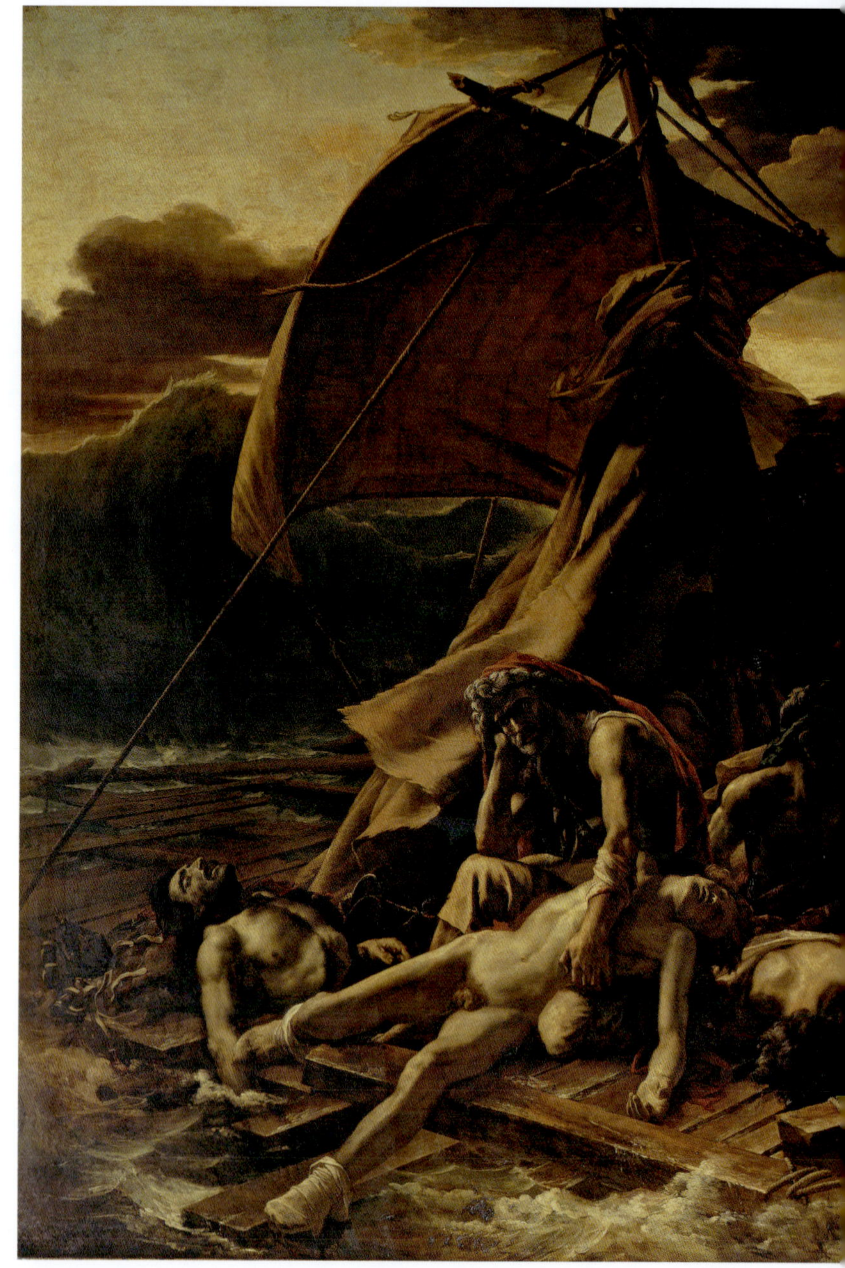

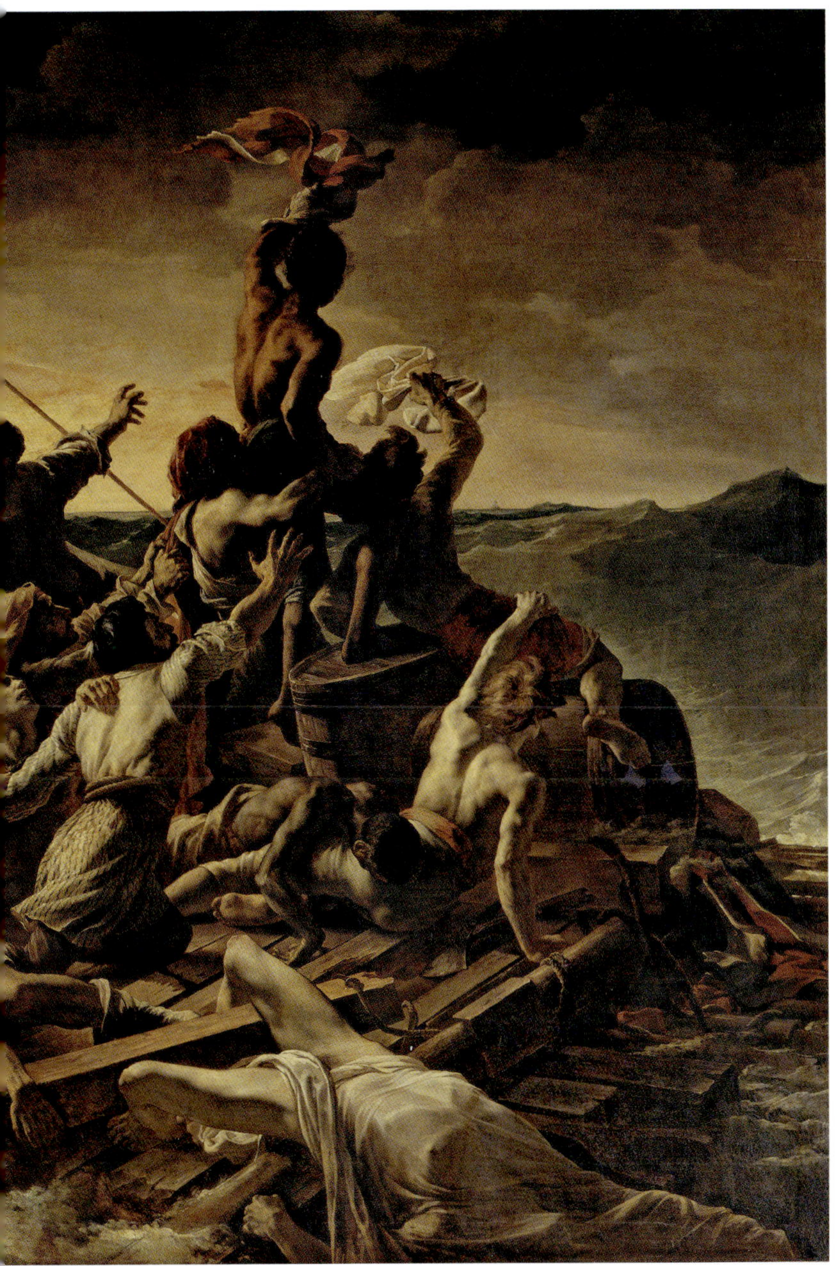

Abandoned to the mercy of the Atlantic

The first report of the wreck of the *Medusa* was published by Henri Savigny, one of the 15 survivors, who had served on the frigate as the ship's surgeon. Géricault portrays him standing to the right of the mast, together with another survivor, the cartographer Alexandre Corréard.

Géricault was personally acquainted with both men and had read the book in which they recounted their experiences of the ordeal. The book was intended as a means of soliciting damages for the victims. Not only had all previous appeals been rejected, but their troublesome petitioning of the authorities had cost them their jobs in the civil service, as well as fines and even a brief spell in prison.

For all its subjectivity, there is no more revealing an account of the events that occurred on the raft. The royal frigate *Medusa* had left its French port on 17 July 1816, bound for Saint-Louis in Senegal. Described as the "swiftest and most modern vessel of her day", her mission was to take possession of the West African colony of Senegal, which England had recently handed back to France. On board was the newly appointed Governor of Senegal, together with his family, civil servants and a marine battalion equipped "for the protection of overseas territories". Corréard was one of 60 scientists whose task was to explore and map the colony. All in all, there were some 400 people on board the frigate – more than usual, and certainly more than the lifeboats could hold.

Instead of obeying orders to sail in convoy with three other ships, the swift *Medusa* hurried on ahead, facing the long journey alone. The ship was under the command of Hugues Du Roy de Chaumareys, who, having fled from Napoleon, had spent the next 25 years of his career, not on the high seas, but visiting emigré salons in Coblenz and London. When the Bourbons took over from Napoleon, they rewarded their loyal subject by making him the captain of a ship: royalist sentiment was evidently more important than nautical prowess or sea-going experience.

En route to Senegal, aristocratic arrogance appears to have prevented the captain of the *Medusa* from heeding his officers' advice. Quarrels arose, and catastrophe finally struck: on 2 July, calm seas and good visibility notwithstanding, navigational error and incompetence left the frigate stranded on the shoals of Arguin off the African coast between the Canaries and Cap Verde – a peril marked on every nautical map.

After several half-hearted attempts to refloat the vessel, the captain and leading officers lost their nerve and ordered the evacuation of the ship. The undue haste with which they did so led to panic, selfishness and brutality. The Governor, captain and officers crowded into six lifeboats, while 147 people, finding no room in the boats, were forced to clamber on board a makeshift raft, constructed out of planks, parts of the mast and rigging. A solemn promise was given that the boats would tow the raft to the nearest land. Two hours later, however, and under circumstances which have never been fully explained, the ropes linking boats and raft were severed. "We could not believe that we were entirely abandoned until the boats were almost out of sight," recalled Savigny, "but our consternation was then extreme."

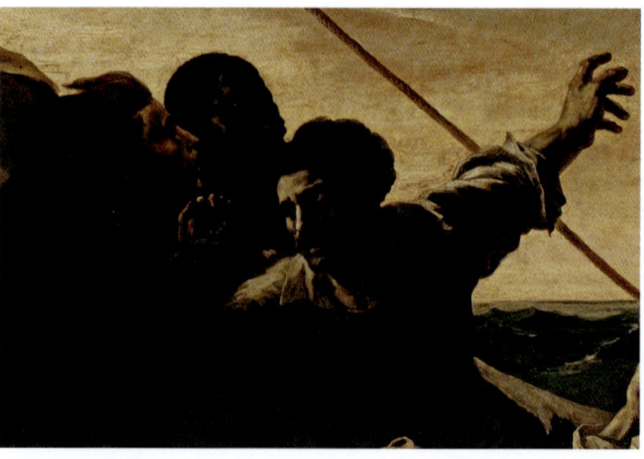

The survival of the fittest

The struggle for survival on board the raft now began in earnest. The 147 castaways had only one case of ship's biscuits between them, and that was consumed on the first day. The water supplies went overboard during the first night; a few barrels of wine were all that was left to drink.

When fighting eventually broke out, it was not over biscuits and wine, but over the safest positions on the raft. A surface area of eight by fifteen metres ought to have left space enough for all, but the edge of the raft was frequently submerged under heavy seas, forcing the men to seek refuge nearer the centre. It was here that the few officers and civil servants who had not found a place in the lifeboats had taken up position, Corréard and Savigny among them. They had weapons, too, whereas the ordinary sailors and soldiers had been disarmed before coming on board. Twenty of these, who attempted to hold out at the edge of the raft, vanished overnight.

On the second night, fighting broke out as the men struggled for survival: "they all crowded towards the centre." The survivors of the ordeal, officers all but one, said there had been a mutiny: men who were drunk or mad with fear had tried to destroy the raft, attacking the officers who intervened. In legitimate self-defence, the latter had killed 65 men.

It is now generally thought that the officers exploited a welcome opportunity to rid themselves of as many rivals for wine and space as possible. After the first week only 28 survivors remained. However, even that was too many: "Out of this number fifteen alone appeared able to exist for some days longer; all the others, covered with large wounds, had wholly lost their reason", Savigny later wrote. "After a long deliberation, we resolved to throw them into the sea."

Savigny, a doctor of medicine, selected the victims himself. Later, he prepared a doctoral thesis on "The Effect of Hunger and Thirst on the Survivors of Shipwrecks", reporting that the survivors of the *Medusa* had supplemented their wine rations with sea water or urine from the fourth day onwards, and that cases of cannibalism had already begun to occur by the third day.

"Those whom death had spared", Savigny recalled, "threw themselves ravenously on the dead bodies with which the raft was covered, cut them up in slices, which some even that instant devoured. A great number of us at first refused to touch the horrible food; but at last, yielding to a want still more pressing than that of humanity, we saw in this frightful repast the only deplorable means of prolonging existence."

It was Savigny himself who suggested cutting the flesh of the dead into strips in order to let it dry in the sun. The sailors who later rescued the survivors

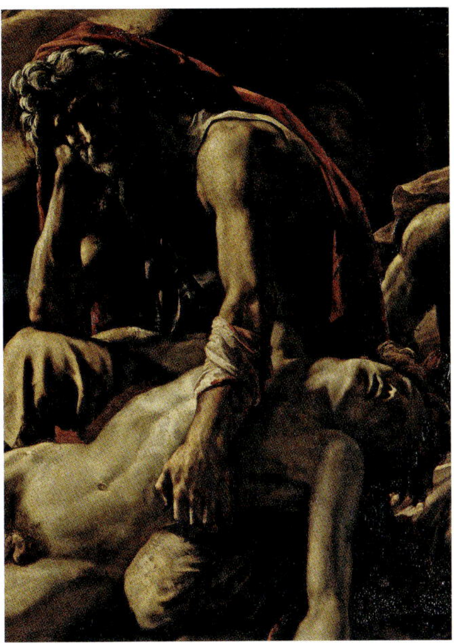

found these shreds of flesh particularly repugnant, at first taking them for drying clothes, or sails. Géricault does not include this detail in his work; there is no sign of cannibalism in the painting. Only in one of his many preliminary studies for the work did Géricault include two naked men eating a dead body. Cannibalism was taboo, and examples of its treatment in Western art are few and far between. However, Géricault does include a cryptic reference to it in the form of the classically paternal gesture of a figure supporting the dead body of a youth. The figure was reminiscent of Count Ugolino, the subject of several well-known contemporary paintings. The legendary Ugolino, accompanied by his sons and grandsons, was imprisoned by his enemies in a tower without food. When the children died, the Count tried to keep himself alive by eating their flesh, as his account in Canto XXXIII of Dante's *Inferno* suggests: "and for two days I called them, after they were dead, then fasting had more power than grief."

Hope on a distant horizon

After thirteen days on board the raft, the remaining survivors of the *Medusa* saw a ship: it was a brig called the *Argus*, which had been sent to search for them. It "was at a very great distance; we could only distinguish the tops of its masts", wrote Savigny. "Fears, however, soon mixed with our hopes; we began to perceive that our raft, having very little elevation above the water, it was impossible to distinguish it at such a distance. We did all we could to make ourselves observed; we piled up our casks, at the top of which we fixed handkerchiefs of different colours …"

Géricault shows the tiny ship on the distant horizon; he paints the barrels and cases on which those waving supported themselves, with a black man at the highest point. The name of the latter was Jean-Charles, probably the only "common man" among the fifteen survivors, the rest being officers, scientists and clerks. Jean-Charles had to obey orders; it had been his job to throw overboard the victims of Savigny's selection. Like four other survivors, he later died on board the *Argus* after eating too much too hastily.

In order to paint the work Géricault went to considerable lengths to research his material thoroughly. He conducted interviews with Corréard and Savigny,

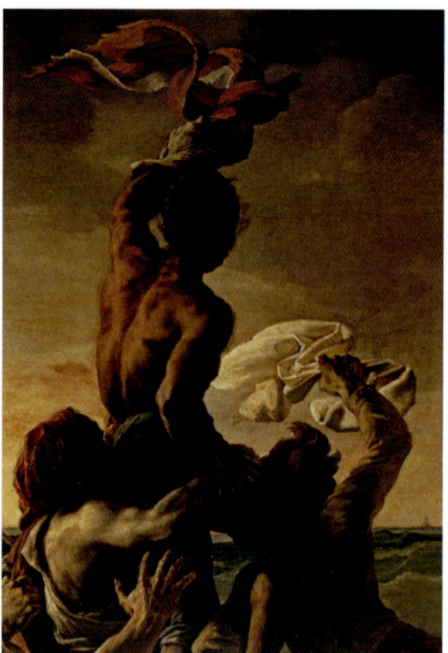

and even had a small model built of the raft. The painting was so large (491 by 716 centimetres) that he was forced to hire a more spacious studio. He found one near a hospital where he was permitted to make sketches of the sick and dying, even taking home dead limbs in order to observe their discolouration in the early stages of putrefaction. He collected all the information he could find for a realistic picture, which he did not paint.

For example, he gives Jean-Charles the back of a muscular, well fed young man; after thirteen days without food, however, the muscles are reduced and bones show through the skin. In Corréard and Savigny's report, the mens' skin was burned red by the sun, their bodies covered with weals and fissures. There is no sign of this in Géricault's painting. Rather than the reddish blue of real corpses, his dead have a certain idealized lividity. Whether dead or alive, the men are all clean shaven and relatively well-kempt, whereas reports of the incident speak of long and tousled hair.

Nor do the weather conditions depicted in Géricault's work reflect those actually recorded on 17 July 1816. The sky was clear and the sea calm, but Géricault shows gathering clouds and towering waves. The effect – a perilous sense of foreboding – would have been difficult to achieve against the background of a calm sea.

Despite the powerful presence exercised by the ocean here, it in fact occupies only a small area of the picture space. Traditionally, maritime scenes devoted large areas of the canvas to the water itself, with persons and ships kept relatively small. Earlier versions of Géricault's painting show similar proportions. As work progressed, however, increasing prominence was given to the raft, so that the spectator of the final version feels practically able to step on board. As the figures grew larger, the water was marginalized and emphasis was given to the pyramidal structure of the composition. It was not realism Géricault sought, but sophisticated grandeur on a monumental scale.

Flight from responsibility

On delivering the finished painting and seeing it for the first time outside his studio, Géricault discovered formal weaknesses. He is reported to have added, working at phenomenal speed, a corpse to the bottom left and bottom right of the canvas, broadening the base of the pyramid of bodies, stabilizing the composition and strengthening the monumental effect of the painting.

Monumentality, both in format and execution, was a stylistic feature of history painting, a highly esteemed genre at the time. The history painting, so it was said, showed whether an artist was truly talented. Its prerequisites were stylistic fluency and thematic concentration on famous or dramatic incidents drawn from national, Christian or antique history. Géricault's work did not fulfil these requirements: the *Medusa* scandal was too contemporary. One of the spectators immediately accused the artist of "slandering the entire Ministry of the Navy with the facial expression of one of the men in the painting."

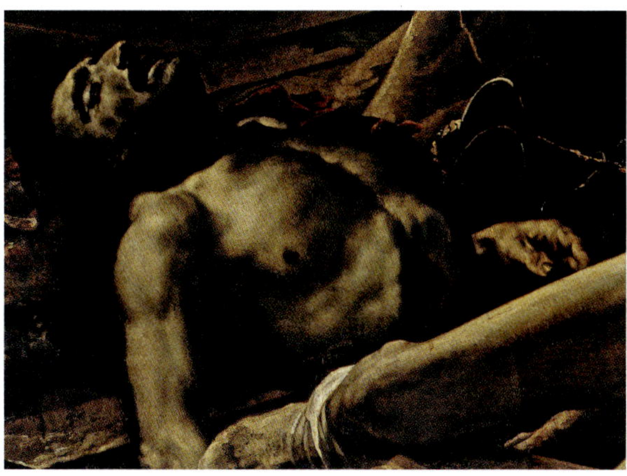

Contrary to Géricault's hopes, the painting was not purchased by the Bourbon king, and the criteria by which the critics judged it were not so much artistic as political. Echoes of its political resonance can be felt even in our own time: 1968 saw the premiere in Hamburg of an oratorio composed by Hans Werner Henze entitled *The Raft of the Medusa*, which the composer deliberately turned into a demonstration with red flags and the appropriate slogans. The police intervened and the affair ended up in court.

It has never been satisfactorily ascertained whether Géricault actually intended his painting to have a political effect by denouncing the corruption of the regime. There is much to suggest that this was not the case. For one thing, the artist seems to have been genuinely surprised that the government did not buy his work. There is also his choice of potential subjects for the painting: Barbary horses being driven through the streets of Rome during Carnival, or a murder scene in provincial France. His real aim was to paint a work on such a grand scale and to such tremendous effect that he would finally – at the age of 27 – achieve the recognition he felt he deserved.

Personal considerations may have been more important than political convictions in determining his choice of subject. He began to paint the raft after a love affair with the young wife of one of his uncles. His mistress was banished to the country, the child she bore him taken from her and given away for adoption, a course of events which the artist did nothing to prevent. So meticulous was his family in hiding the threat to its reputation that the affair only came to light recently, 150 years after the event.

From what is known of this period in Géricault's life it seems he spent much of it in the big studio he had hired, tortured by the thought of his cowardice and guilt. For like the captain of the *Medusa* he had deserted his dependants in their hour of need. He cut himself off from his friends and had his head shaved to prevent himself going out, sentencing himself, as it were, to eighteen months' hard labour. Evidently, however, the long hours he put into the *Shipwreck* were not enough to expiate his sense of guilt and personal failure, for as soon as his masterpiece was finished, he redoubled his efforts to punish and, indeed, destroy himself: he undertook several suicide attempts, and rode everywhere he went at breakneck speed, causing a series of accidents. Eventually, he was badly injured falling from a horse, and died in 1824, at the age of only 32.

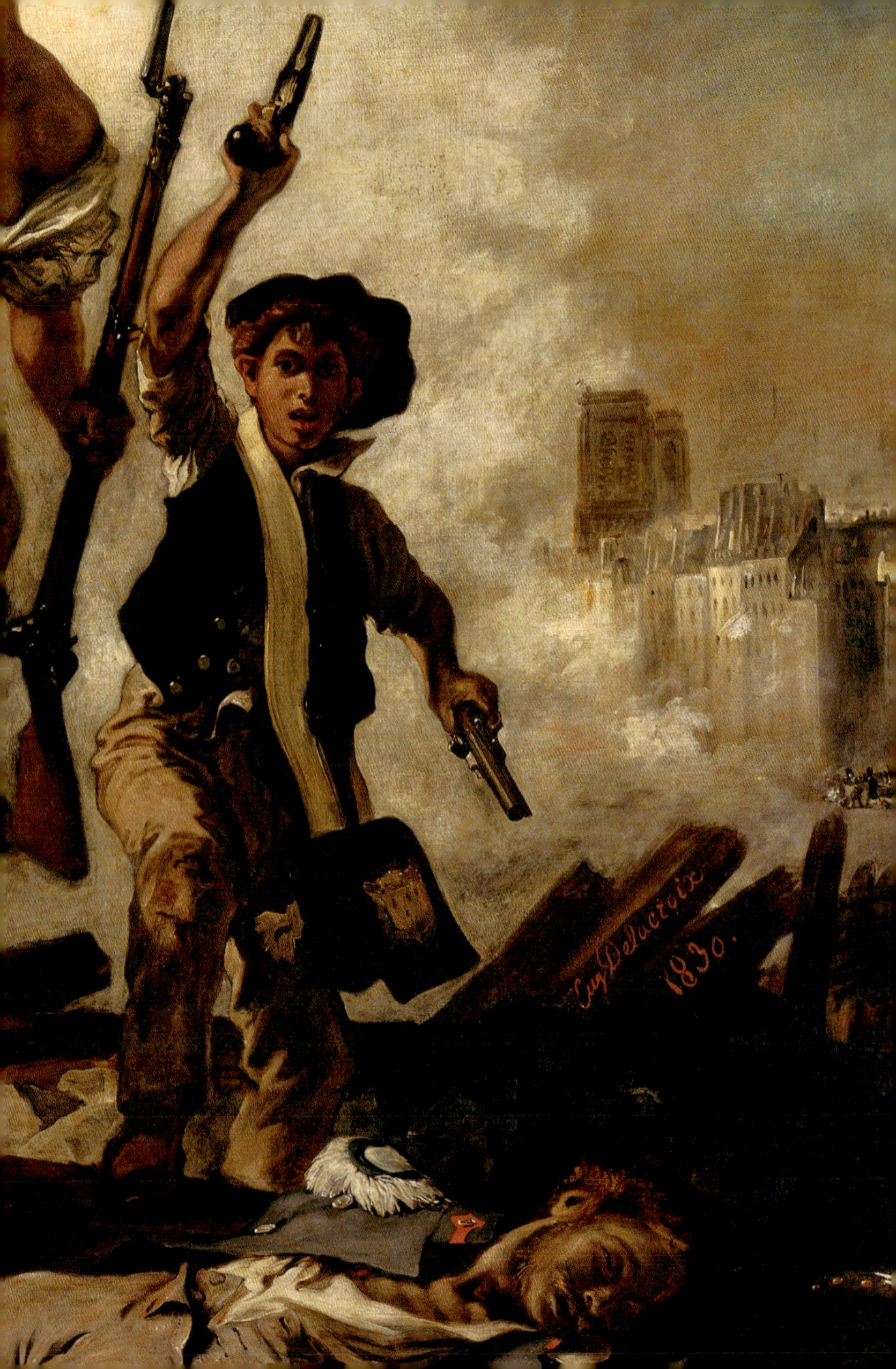

Eugène Delacroix (1798–1863)

A painter on the barricades

Liberty Leading the People, 1830
260 x 325 cm, Paris, Musée du Louvre

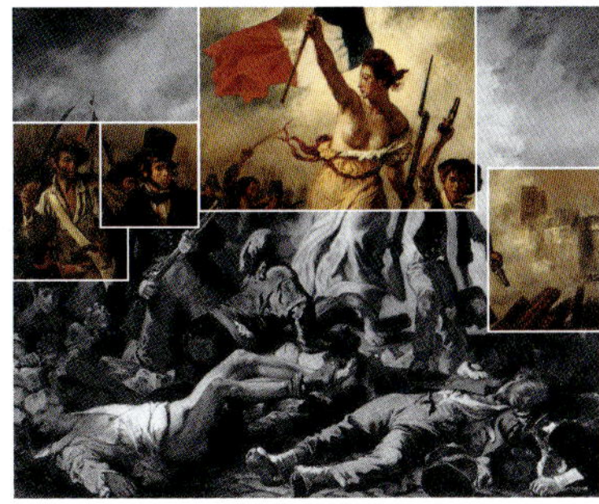

The sun beats down on Paris through a haze of gun smoke; 28 July 1830 was a hot day. At the palace of St Cloud a few kilometres outside Paris, where King Charles X spent the summer months, it was already 35°C in the shade before lunch, announced one of royal pages. There had been fighting in the capital since the day before. The citizens of Paris and the King's troops had formed ranks on opposite sides. Barricades had been erected. Shots had been fired. People had been killed. Early that morning, the senior commander of the royal troops informed the King: "This is no longer a riot. This is a revolution."

Fighting alongside each other on the barricades were men from widely differing backgrounds. The bourgeois, in his top hat, frock coat and neatly tied cravat, has taken up a shotgun. The worker in his cap and open-necked shirt is wielding a sabre. An adolescent street urchin is brandishing a pistol in each hand, and in the background a two cornered hat identifies its wearer as a student of the École Polytechnique. Some 7,000 to 8,000 militant Parisians fought at the barricades that day, women and children amongst them. That seems barely a handful in a city of 800,000 inhabitants. But the insurgents could count on the sympathy and active support of virtually the entire population. They were supplied all over the city with munitions and refreshments, while cobblestones and items of furniture rained down on the heads of the soldiers from the windows above.

The insurgents did not have a leader. In Delacroix's painting, they are headed by Liberty, personified as a Greek goddess. Over the bodies of fallen cuirassiers, she leads her followers to glory, to *gloire*. Thus the three days of 27, 28 and 29 July 1830 went down in history as *les trois glorieuses*. "Holy July days: how beautiful was the sun", wrote Heinrich Heine, the German poet who had made Paris his home, "and how great the people of Paris!"

The Parisians had gone to the barricades in revolt against the policies of a king who wanted to turn back the wheel of time. Charles X came late to power and wanted to be absolute ruler. It was an ambition that had cost his eldest brother, Louis XVI, his head. Only in 1814, after the downfall of Napoleon, had the victorious allied forces restored the Bourbons to the French throne, albeit with instructions to grant their people a parliament and a charter, a form of constitution. Because Charles X considered the newly elected parliament of 1830 too liberal, he resolved to set aside the charter and govern by decree.

The uprising in Paris was directly sparked by three royal decrees published on 26 July. They abolished the civil rights set out in the charter and announced the introduction of censorship of the press, the dissolution of parliament and the implementation of a new electoral system that would ensure the King a compliant popular assembly. The timing seemed favourable: the new parliament had not yet met and everyone of any influence spent the summer months in the country anyway. "Whatever you do", the Prefect of Paris assured the King on 25 July, "Paris will not stir."

When the Parisians nevertheless stirred
with such speed and violence, the King's
generals were taken by surprise. Only some
12,000 soldiers could be mustered at short
notice in the Paris area, and many of these
refused to fire at civilians. Entire units
deserted, and their commander, the Duke of
Ragusa, was unable to quash the uprising. By
the third day the revolutionaries held all the
strategically important points in the city; they
even stormed the Tuileries, the royal palace
that Ragusa had made his headquarters. The
troops were forced to withdraw from Paris
and the King capitulated to the demands of
his people. He could expect no assistance
from any of the other European monarchs,
who had guaranteed the original charter and
were angered by his actions. Charles X was
forced to abdicate in favour of his cousin
Louis-Philippe, Duke of Orleans.

The July Revolution wrought changes in
France: there was no more talk of kings "by
the grace of God". The new monarch had to
swear his allegiance to the constitution and
called himself the "Citizen King". The events
that had brought him to the throne –
a violent popular uprising – made the King
uneasy, however. Hence the new regime was
at pains to cleanse the revolution of its
threatening image and glorify it in ceremonies and with decorations.

Medals were awarded to the "courageous
barricade fighters", and collections were
taken for the orphans and widows of the
insurgents. A column to commemorate the
dead was quickly erected, unveiled with
much pomp and numerous performances of
the *Symphonie funèbre et triomphale* specially
composed for the occasion by Hector Berlioz.
(The monument can still be seen today on
the Place de la Bastille.) Art, too, helped in
the assimilation of the bloody events of the
recent past: over 40 portrayals of the "three
glorious days" filled the Paris Salon of 1831,
Delacroix's canvas amongst them. It was
purchased by the King for 3,000 francs and
earned the artist – like the barricade fighters –
an official decoration.

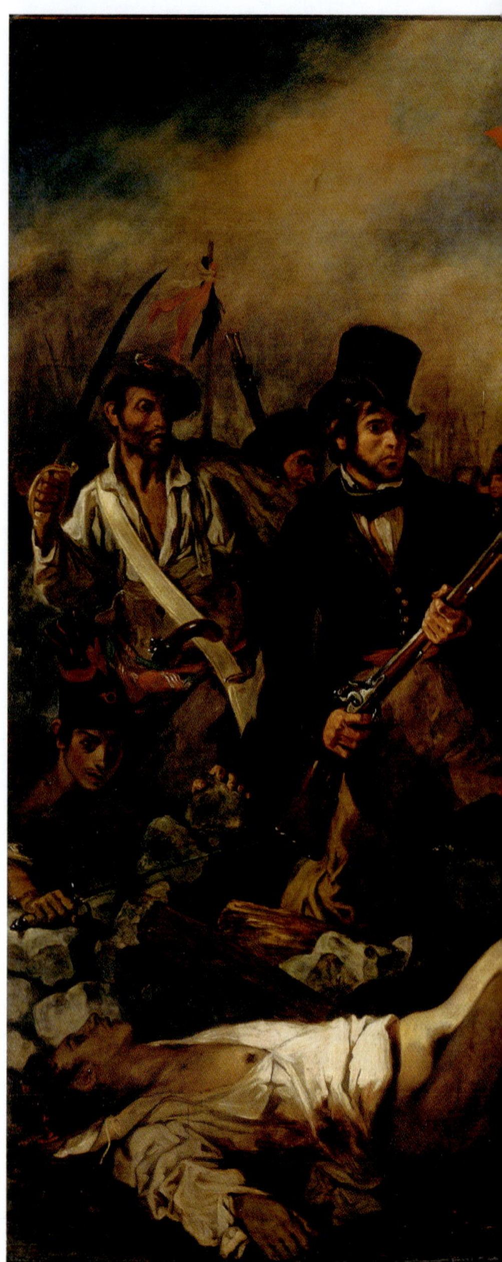

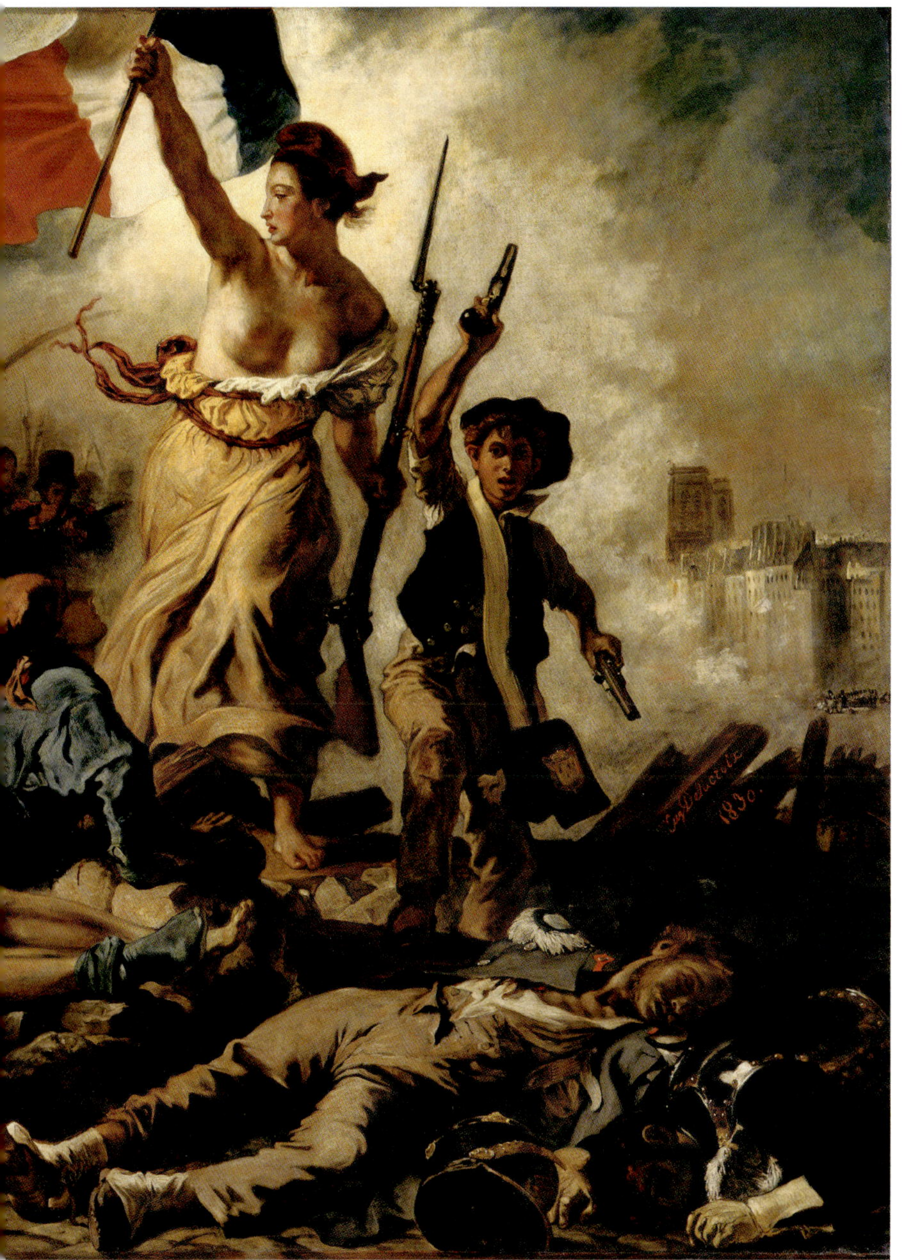

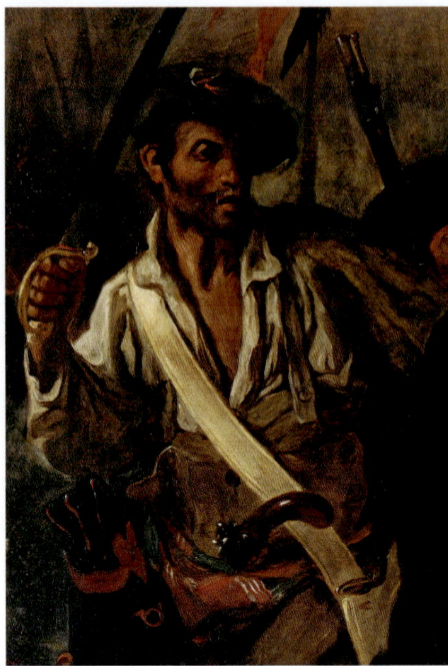

Wielding a sabre for the freedom of the press
His braces are not concealed beneath a jacket and
waistcoat, and his pistol is thrust into the red, white
and blue revolutionary's scarf around his waist. This
insurgent is no bourgeois, but more likely a worker –
perhaps one of the 6,000 printing workers who suddenly found themselves out on the street on the
morning of 27 July because the newspapers were
no longer allowed to go to press. When royal troops
tried to clear the crowds thronging the centre of the
city that same afternoon, it was angry printers, so it
is said, who threw the first stones. The closure of the
print shops was the first consequence of the royal
decree curtailing the freedom of the press. Newspapers, "whatever their content", had to be submitted to
the censors eight days (!) in advance of publication.
They were perceived by the Ministry as "instruments of disorder and sedition"; should they appear
without permission, they were impounded and their
printing presses destroyed. A number of pamphlets
still managed to appear that day. Inflammatory protests against the muzzling of the press were printed
in secret, posted on house walls, read out in public.
They whipped up emotions and created the climate

in which printers armed themselves with cobblestone and soldiers, without command or warning,
opened fire on the crowd.

The Parisians were driven onto the barricades
first and foremost in defence of freedom of the press
and their elected parliament. That workers should
also join their ranks was, for many bourgeois, unexpected and unhoped-for. Why should they fight for
a press that they couldn't read? For a parliament in
which they had no representatives and in whose elections they were not permitted to take part, because
they owned no land? Prior to 1830, no political party
had concerned itself with the rights of the working classes; they were isolated, for strikes, collective
agreements and gatherings of more than twenty
people were all prohibited by law.

Economically, too, the workers were badly off. Of
224,000 Parisian households, 136,000 were officially
classed as "needy". Unemployment was rife, wages
had fallen by 22 per cent over the past five years,
while prices had risen by 66 per cent. Poverty and
hunger have always provided fertile ground for
revolt, and when the first shots rang out, the majority of workers were quick to grasp what the uprising was really about. Old memories of 1789 were
suddenly rekindled: liberty was once more at stake.
"Down with the tyrants!"

The proletariat soon made up the majority of
those fighting. Author and eyewitness Stendhal
wrote: "On 28 July there was just one well dressed
man for every 100 men without stockings or jacket."
That the workers were willing to submit to the
command of the bourgeois on the barricades was
something regularly commented upon. The middle
classes were astonished, too, at the fact that the
workers drank hardly any alcohol and were at
pains to respect the property of others. There were
only a few instances of looting and arson during
the July Revolution.

At the end of the July Revolution, the populace
dispersed back to its suburbs with just as much
discipline as it had fought. The comradeship
between worker and bourgeois that Delacroix
portrays on the barricades quickly evaporated. The
uprising brought benefits only to the land owning
bourgeoisie; apart from medals and glory, the workers gained nothing from it. The price of bread continued to soar, unemployment grew, and four years
later the government of the Citizen King would
open fire on striking workers.

The young Romantics loved a fight

Although Delacroix was resident in Paris during the July Revolution, according to eyewitnesses he took no active part in it. He wrote to his brother: "If I haven't lived for my country, at least I shall paint for it!" It is his eyes that stare out from beneath the fashionable silk top hat of the bourgeois on the barricades. The 32-year-old artist portrays himself as the writer Théophile Gautier (1811–1872) describes him: "his pale complexion, his abundant black hair, his eyes with their feline expression, surmounted by thick brows slightly raised … a physiognomy of strange and exotic beauty, fierce and almost unsettling; one could have taken him for an Indian maharaja." It was often said that he looked like a prince. His real father was probably Prince Talleyrand, his mother's lover. Officially, however, he was the son of Delacroix, an official in the imperial administration, and he was brought up in a bourgeois household.

Alexandre Dumas the Elder (1802–1870) observed that the artist was not particularly enthusiastic about the uprising at first, and that his sympathies were only truly aroused by the sight of the tricolour fluttering from the towers of Notre-Dame. It was the flag for which one of Delacroix's elder brothers had died at the Battle of Friedland under Napoleon. His other elder brother had formerly served as a general. Following the restoration of the Bourbons, he had been demobilized and put on half pay: like many of Napoleon's soldiers, he mourned for the "great" times that lay in the past.

Mourning alongside the old veterans was the entire younger generation, to which Delacroix also belonged – a generation of 20- to 30-year-olds, "conceived between two wars, brought up in schools to the rolling of drums", as the poet Alfred de Musset (1810–1857) described them. They were the discontented *enfants du siècle*. They had spent their childhood hearing about and dreaming of heroic deeds and *grandeur*, and now they felt cheated: under the Bourbons, it was the cautious bankers and bourgeoisie who had the say.

In the years prior to the July Revolution, this frustrated younger generation had tried to fight the battles that had otherwise escaped them by transplanting them to the intellectual and artistic arena. They sought refuge from drab reality in far-off, exotic lands or in a savage, heroic past. They thereby formed part of the Romantic movement that since the beginning of the century had been challenging the rules, authorities and traditions of art. "All power to the imagination", proclaimed the young Romantics. They mocked and provoked their "narrow-minded" enemies, and sometimes even fought them: on 25 January 1830 they staged their first great battle – in the theatre. At the première of *Hernani*, a Romantic drama by Victor Hugo (1802–1885), they set to with fists and sticks against the supporters of the Classical school. The painters, too, took part in the auditorium battle; their own preference for wild, exotic and dramatic scenes imbued with Romantic pathos had been in evidence since the Salon of 1827. Delacroix's own exhibits included *The Death of Sardanapalus* and *Greece Mourning on the Ruins of Missolonghi*.

The Romantic artists called for freedom – freedom in art, freedom in daily life and freedom, too, in politics. On 28 July 1830, however, only a few mounted the barricades themselves. The rest – for a variety of reasons – stayed at home. Even the liberal journalists penned their impassioned calls for resistance against the despotism of the state from the safety of their writing desks. They were no men of action.

But their words were heard by a young generation who, filled with Romantic enthusiasm, rushed out to fight and to die. Of the 1,800 insurgents who fell in the July Revolution, the majority were young men or even boys, such as the urchin brandishing the two pistols in Delacroix's painting. The Romantic author Victor Hugo (who stayed at home on 28 July because

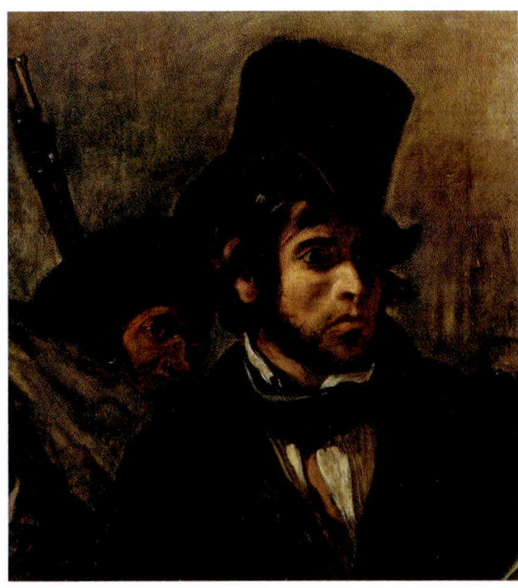

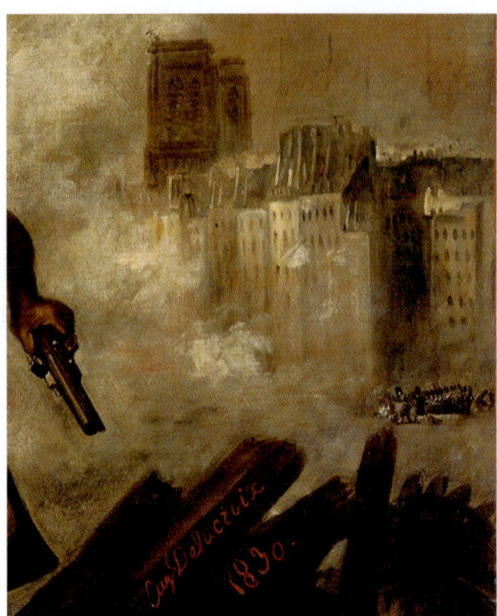

his wife was in labour) created a monument to them in his novel *Les Miserables* of 1862. Gavroche is the lad from the Paris gutter who loves humour and anarchy and who, caught on the wrong side of the barricade, faces the muskets shooting at him with a satirical song on his lips. He dies a hero's death. Perhaps Victor Hugo was inspired by Delacroix's painting, which with its stirring atmosphere and political charge has become a masterpiece of French Romanticism.

Paris invented the barricade

Weapons were in plentiful supply in Paris in 1830. Just three years earlier, after disrespectful shots had rung out during a ceremonial parade in front of the King, the government had decided to dissolve the traditional militia. Incomprehensibly, however, it failed to call in the weapons these troops held. The workers – who were excluded from the militia because they couldn't afford to equip themselves – looted the arsenals and armed themselves with shotguns, revolvers and sabres seized from the museum of historical weaponry. Anyone still left empty handed simply waited for a comrade to fall on the barricade, and then took up their gun.

One of the dead soldiers in the foreground of Delacroix's painting has also been stripped of his shoes, stockings and trousers. The uprising brought not only workers and bourgeois out onto the streets, but also organized gangs of beggars and criminals from the Paris underworld, who appeared at the first exchange of fire.

There were some 4,000 to 6,000 barricades in Paris on 28 July 1830. The word comes from *barriques*, the barrels which, filled with earth, formed their base. Piled on top of them were felled trees, tables, cupboards from nearby houses, the occasional over-turned omnibus and indeed anything else that came to hand. Sandwiched in between were mattresses, intended to absorb the bullets. The whole was nailed together with planks, and a makeshift flight of cobblestone steps was constructed on the defenders' side, so that they could storm over the top in a massed attack as the main figures in Delacroix's painting are doing.

Heinrich Heine marvelled at the speed with which the barricades were erected. "The high bulwarks which German thoroughness would need a whole day to complete", he wrote, "are here improvized in just a few minutes."

The French capital had a tradition of building barricades. Its militant citizens had already blockaded the streets in 1588 and 1648 and battled against the royal troops. On both occasions the then sovereign, first Henry III, then the young Louis XIV, had been hastily forced to leave the city. Louis never forgave the recalcitrant Parisians and later moved to Versailles.

When Heinrich Heine's compatriot Ludwig Börne arrived in Paris in September 1830, he felt the urge to take off his boots, for "one should only tread these sacred cobbles barefoot". He knew the role the hard, rounded sandstone cobbles had played in the July Revolution. They could be dug up quickly, and as well as being an important constituent of the barricades, they were also hurled out of windows onto the heads of many of the King's soldiers. Future governments would learn their lesson and rapidly replace the dangerous stones with gravel and asphalt. They would also tear down the buildings in the historical heart of the city, so as to destroy the winding alleys which offered ideal locations for barricades and which made it impossible for the royal cavalry to attack on horseback. Barricades would neverthe-less continue to be built in Paris – in 1848, in 1872 and most recently in 1968.

Delacroix's barricade stands not in a narrow alleyway in an old part of the city, but on a spacious square, probably the former Place Saint-Antoine (today Place de la Bastille), where the royal prison once loomed and the July Column still rises. In 1830 the square was a wasteland, covered in building rubble. In the background, royal troops are marching past. The alarm bells rang out without interruption and, it is reported, the strains of the *Marseillaise*, the banned hymn of the Revolution, were regularly heard. The crowds cheered and wept when towards three o'clock in the afternoon they saw, for the first time since 1815, the old flag – the tricolour – fluttering from the distant towers of Notre-Dame.

The tricolour stirred every heart

Blue, white and red: the large flag at the centre of the picture billows over the heads of all, fighting, injured and dead. Improvized out of three scraps of cloth tied together, it also flies in the background. The three colours are repeated even in the clothes of the injured man looking up at the goddess Liberty. According to eyewitnesses, on the afternoon of 28 July they suddenly appeared all over Paris.

The tricolour had been created during the Revolution of 1789, when the Paris militia started wearing cockades in the city's two colours of red and blue. Louis XVI was obliged to accept them, but added the royal white before adopting them himself. The revolutionary troops made the tricolour the French national flag, and Napoleon retained it. In 1815 the Bourbons banned it and replaced it with their white flag. In 1830 the tricolour was accompanied by very mixed and at times contradictory emotions: for the young generation and the republicans, the old flag signified the sovereignty of the people and the victory of liberty over tyranny. For the majority of people, it evoked quite simply a patriotic nostalgia, memories of the "great" era in French history, when the tricolour under Napoleon had carried liberty, civilization and France's glory across all of Europe.

The powerfully built woman who is waving the flag is also a relic of the Revolution. The Classically educated patriots adopted the personification of Liberty from the Ancient Romans and used it to adorn their coins

and letterheads. In 1789 statues of Liberty were erected everywhere. (At the end of the 19th century France would even give the United States its Statue of Liberty!)

The red cap on Liberty's head, however, would have shocked most of those who saw it. In 1792 it had served to identify the militant revolutionaries of the Jacobin club, who instituted the Reign of Terror during the 1st Paris commune. Since then the cap had symbolized both Republic and bloodthirsty Terror. The two seemed inseparably linked: you couldn't have one without the other. This was the attitude adopted by politicians, bankers and journalists while others were battling on the barricades. To them, the safest way of ending the civil war was to keep the monarchy, but change the monarch. To the disappointment of the republicans and the young generation of insurgents, it was their solution that won the day. Instead of freedom, reforms and progress, there was order, authority and stability.

The tricolour would remain the national flag, but the canvas in which it here billows would never find its way into the throne room for which it was purchased. It disappeared instead into a gloomy palace corridor, and it was not long before Delacroix was asked to take it away. It was fetched out again briefly during the revolution of 1848, but only went on permanent display in 1855. Since 1874 it has hung in the Louvre. Prior to the introduction of the Euro, its two main figures – Liberty carrying a rifle and the pistol-touting urchin – adorned the 100 franc note of the Fifth French Republic.

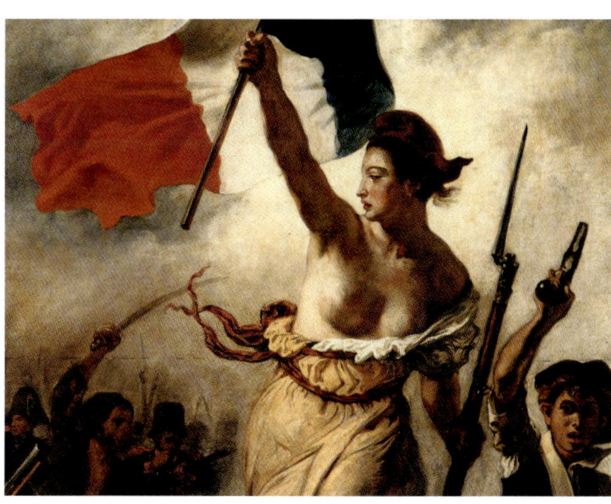

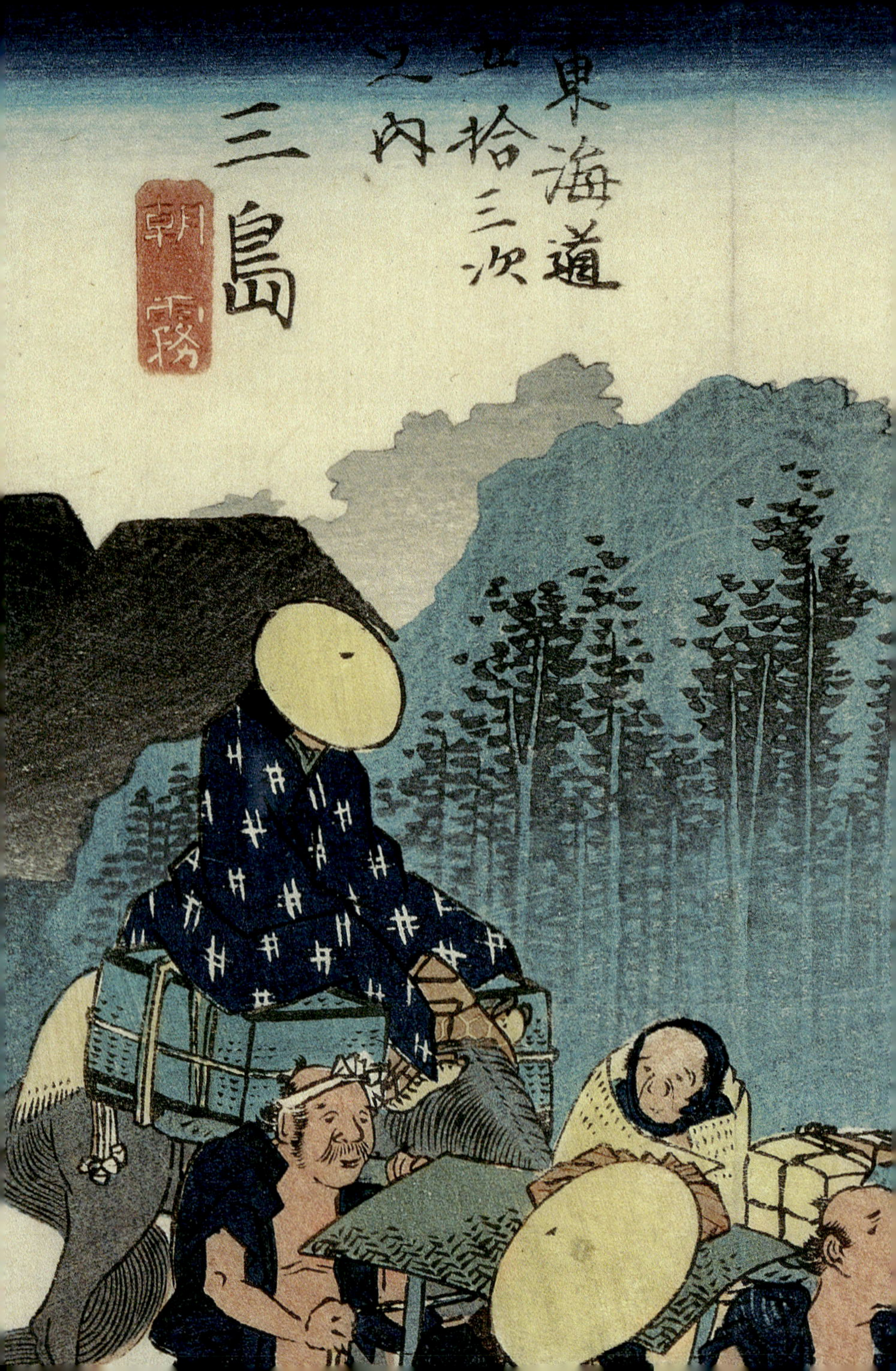
東海道五拾三次之内
三島
朝霧

Ando Hiroshige (1797–1858)

Japanese on their travels

Morning Mist at Mishima, c. 1833
Station number 12 from: *The 53 Stations of the Tokaido Highway*
woodcut, 25 x 38 cm, Staatliche Museen zu Berlin, Museum für
Asiatische Kunst

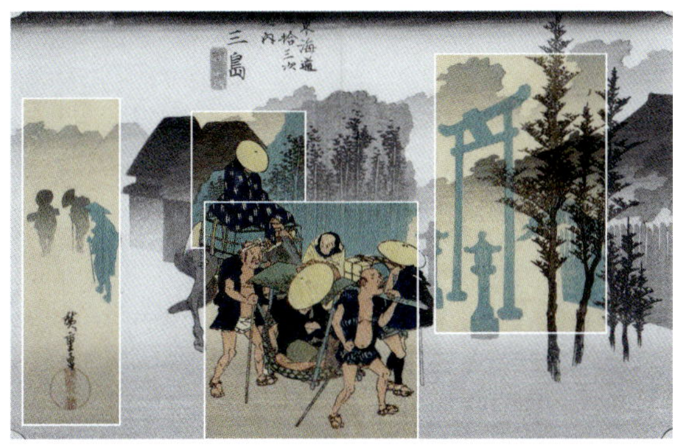

Ando Hiroshige, master of the Japanese woodcut, liked to portray the landscape partially concealed – beneath a blanket of snow, behind a curtain of rain, or palely swathed in mist. In the present print, only the group in the foreground – two travellers, three porters and a man leading a horse – can be clearly seen. Further back, the trees, the gateway, the roofs, and the three other figures are reduced to silhouettes and a single shade of colour. They float in the mist at a distance we cannot define. The woodcut is dominated not by the colours and forms of a specific landscape, but by what conceals them – a misty atmosphere, a diffuse light.

The red seal at the top of the picture reveals its title, *Morning Mist*. The black characters to the right state that the woodcut depicts the town of Mishima and forms part of the series *Fifty-three Stations on the Tokaido Highway*. The Tokaido was a road some 500 kilometres in length. It crossed mountains and rivers and linked the two most important cities in the country, Edo (present-day Tokyo) and Kyoto, the old imperial capital. The emperor's role was by then purely symbolic; real power lay with the shogun, the military dictatorship in Edo.

Hiroshige's *Tokaido* series went on sale from 1833. In those days, colour woodcuts of this kind cost between twelve and sixteen copper coins. Not a lot more than a bowl of noodle soup or a pair of straw sandals. They were particularly popular as souvenirs. In Europe, by contrast, they were accorded the status of high art. In the late 19th century, Japanese prints served as sources of inspiration for Edgar Degas, Claude Monet, Vincent van Gogh, and many other artists. Today, Japanese collectors are buying back such woodcuts for a great deal of money.

The road was strenuous and dangerous
What travelling along the Tokaido was like is described in a picaresque novel by the Japanese writer Ikku Jippensha. His heroes are called Yaji and Kita,

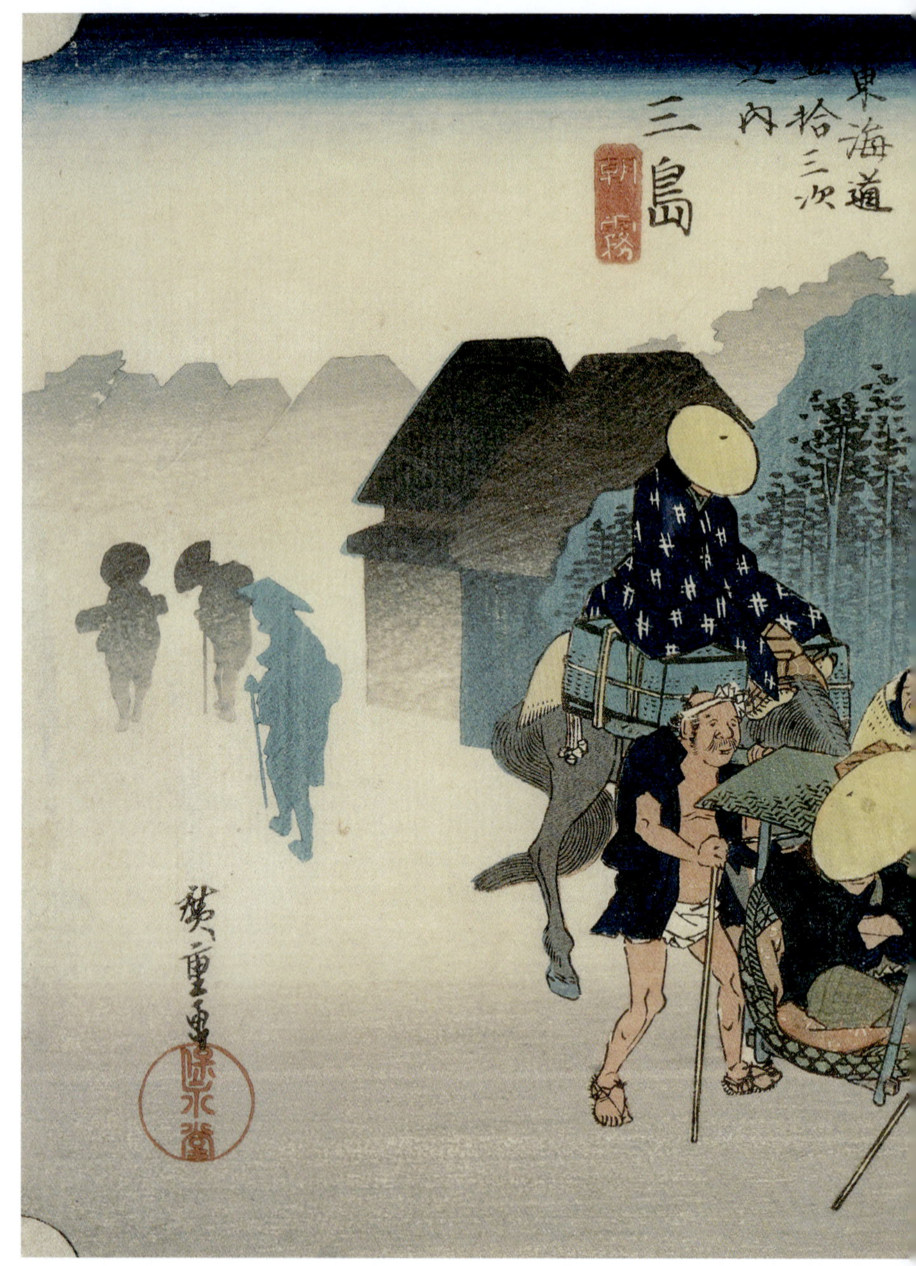

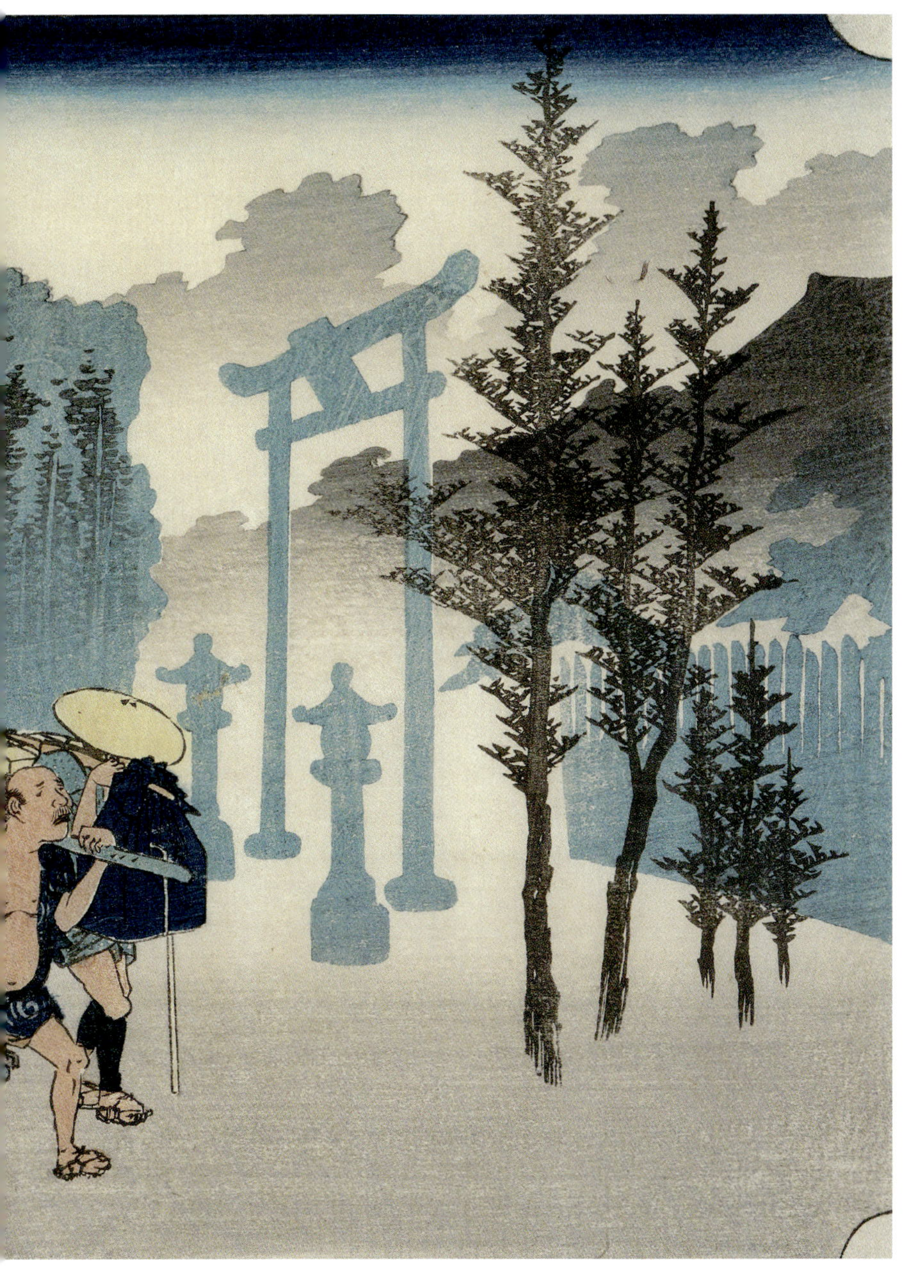

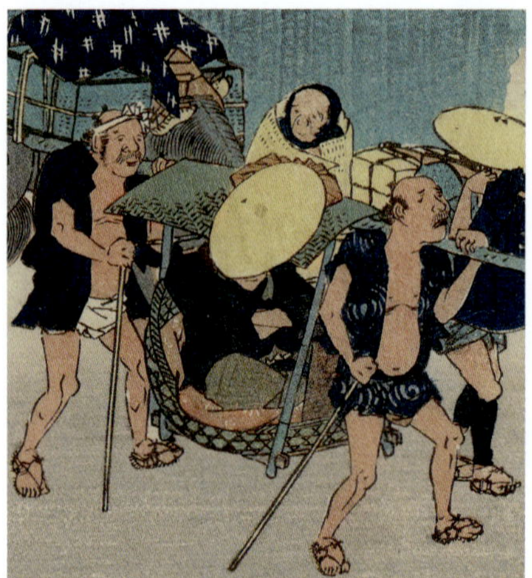

and the two might well have bought a souvenir print to remind themselves later of the adventures, exertions and attractions of their journey, "so that when we become old and bald we shall have something to talk about over the teacups".

The novel was published in instalments, starting in 1802, and its title might be translated as "On Shank's Pony". Journeys were usually made on foot. A fit man could walk up to 40 kilometres a day, and would take between twelve and fourteen days to cover the entire distance between Edo and Kyoto. Travellers furnished themselves with a large straw hat to protect them from the sun and rain, a walking stick for slippery paths, and a protective rain covering made out of rice-straw mats, as worn in the present woodcut by the man leading the horse. Straw sandals were on sale at every station; broken sandals lay scattered along the roadside. Yaji and Kita set particular store by a good salve to massage into sore feet.

The Tokaido road was in many sections a difficult one and unsuitable for carts, but it was possible to hire a horse or litter. The type of litter that Hiroshige portrays is very simple, consisting of a woven basket into which the traveller squeezes with crossed legs and bent head. His hat lies on top of the mat designed to protect him from the rain. The litter is suspended from a pole that sways with the movements of the men carrying it; many travellers made sure they packed something for motion sickness.

All the accidents that typically occurred on such journeys naturally happened to Yaji and Kita, too. Thus the bottom of one of their baskets gave way and they "fell with a great crash onto the ground". That could have brought trouble upon the heads of the porters, for they were responsible for their customers' well-being. In the case of high-ranking individuals, they were liable for their safety with their own lives.

Porters were chiefly peasants from the local vicinity. They travelled only a specific section of the road between two stations, a distance of about eight kilometres. Hiroshige portrays the men, shouldering their heavy load, with little sympathy. Perhaps because he was a town-dweller and had a low regard for impoverished samurai farmers? By contrast, he conceals the face of the person travelling – so that the viewer can identify with him more easily?

From Mishima, which lay some 200 metres above sea level, the road rose up to the Hakone pass at an altitude of a good 1,400 metres. It was a dangerous section. At the top, where no other path crossed, lay a fenced enclosure, one of the many official checkpoints. All travellers had to pass through it. Unless they were princes or samurai, the military aristocracy, they had to remove their hats, kneel down and present themselves and their travel papers for inspection.

Japan was a surveillance state. It had been ruled for more than 200 years by shoguns from the Tokugawa family. They were constantly on their guard against the other feudal lords, against uprisings and against secretly assembled armies.

One of their most effective means of controlling insurgent feudal lords was to compel them to spend part of the year in Edo, under the watchful eye of the shogun. If they returned to the provinces, they had to leave their families behind as hostages. There was thus much toing and froing, especially along the Tokaido. The road was regularly blocked by princes and their large retinues, much to the annoyance of simple travellers like Yaji and Kita, and the many others who bought souvenir prints such as this one. "On some days," wrote one of the few foreigners in Japan some 140 years before this print was published, the Tokaido is "more crowded than the public streets in the biggest cities of Europe".

Pilgrimage and holiday
The Japanese believed Nature was full of deities and spirits, to whom they prayed for protection

and assistance in Shinto shrines. Such shrines also stood along the Tokaido. The gateway to the shrine in Mishima appears in the background of the present woodcut. Before it stand two stone lanterns. On the right-hand edge of the picture is a fence, and above it the silhouette of the roof ridge of the main hall.

Shinto shrines and Buddhist temples were not as deserted as it would seem on this misty morning. They were besieged by pilgrims and beggars, and drew visitors by selling amulets and often, too, by holding theatre performances. Yaji and Kita remember the people selling tooth powder, who lure their customers with elaborate sword games, as well as t he eating places and teahouses, and the almost overwhelming selection of culinary delights. "Ah, the sweet cakes and the fish …!" Their novel resembles a gastronomic guide to the Tokaido.

Mishima, the town, is indicated on the left by just two houses and a few roofs. It actually comprised some 50 lodgings. The better houses offered tea, a hot bath, and a massage by blind masseuses, and the maids were happy to join their guests in bed. That was all part of the service. In the late afternoons, they stood by their front doors in red aprons and white powdered faces, noisily drawing attention to themselves, tugging at the sleeves of arriving travellers. The visitors would certainly have to spend the night somewhere, for only the couriers of the shogun were allowed to travel at night. As we know from Yaji and Kita, your purse and your kimono could sometimes disappear next morning along with your maid.

None of the famous trade and pilgrimage routes in the Western world has ever been recorded in pictures so exhaustively as the Tokaido. Hiroshige alone made it the subject of over 800 woodcuts. The fact that the road was so heavily used is insufficient to explain this prodigious output. More important was the Japanese need to see somewhere different. Since 1603 Japan had been ruled by shoguns of the Tokugawa family, who had pacified the country, which had been ruined by the civil wars fought by roving armies. They had maintained peace and stability in particular by limiting mobility.

For a long time it was virtually impossible for either peasants or town dwellers to travel about. In Hiroshige's lifetime, however, this situation relaxed. The population had become more prosperous, officialdom more open to bribery, more receptive to "fees for sweets". The longing for a change of scenery, pent up for generations, the desire to embark upon

an adventure, to see Japan's famous sights with their own eyes, to broaden their horizons, attracted ever more people onto the road.

This travel boom also boosted the market for souvenir prints. By publishing the woodcuts in large editions, the prices could be kept down, which in turn fuelled increased demand and the production of more and more new prints.

Woodcuts as souvenirs

Kimonos featuring the "water-well pattern" were worn by both sexes. Perhaps the traveller in our picture was a woman. That would only be revealed at the next checkpoint, when he or she took off his or her hat. Even then, you could never be quite sure, for women often disguised themselves as men. It was made particularly difficult for women to travel, since they were expected to stay at home with their families. "Women who go on pilgrimage and drink a lot of tea should be divorced," proclaimed a government edict of 1649.

After confining people to their own locality for more than 200 years, however, the old rules and

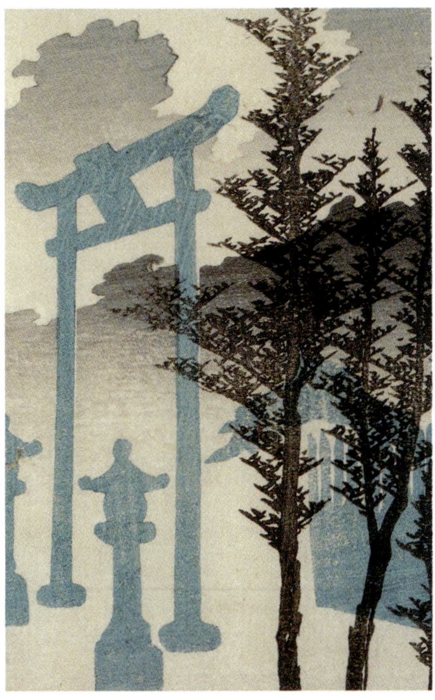

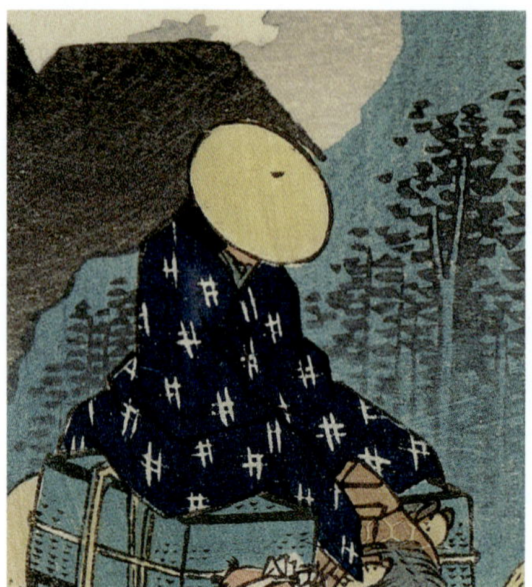

restrictions started to lose their hold. Pilgrimages, for example, could no longer be prevented. Officials, concerned with provisioning the population, sought only to postpone them till after the rice harvest.

In 1830, just a few years before the appearance of the *Tokaido* series, a spontaneous mass pilgrimage of women, children, and maids descended upon Ise, a Shinto shrine very near the Tokaido. It was prompted by the rumour that amulets had rained down from the sky. Over five million people are said to have set off for Ise – a fifth of the population! Another story tells of a noblewoman in northern Japan who, having said she was going on a short pilgrimage, secretly met her son and sister and spent six months travelling round the country with them, visiting all the famous sights – without any sort of travel permit.

The relaxing of travel restrictions was also bound up with the growing amount of money in circulation. The social structure was traditionally based on land ownership, and its currency was the rice ball. This was replaced by coinage. The despised merchant classes increased in prosperity and influence. The samurai, on the other hand, the military class supporting the shogun, were not allowed to engage in commercial activity. They grew poorer and poorer.

The rider between the packages tied up in woven rice matting might be a woman or alternatively a merchant. In front walks a porter. Yaji and Kita went travelling partly for financial reasons – they were running away from their debts. "On the road," so the novel says, "one has no trouble from bill collectors at the end of the month." They take repeated delight in their new freedom to move, and extol its pleasures: "The Edo man can make acquaintance with the Satsuma sweet potato and the flower-like Kyoto woman. You can go as if you were taking part in a picnic, enjoying all the delights of the road. You can sit down in the shadow of the trees and open your little tub of sake. Truly travelling means cleansing the life of care. With your straw sandals and your leggings you can wander wherever you like and enjoy the indescribable pleasures of sea and sky."

This desire to set out and explore the country gave rise to a whole new travel industry, and also a travel culture. Nowhere in Europe in the first half of the 19th century, so the experts claim, could you get a travel guide as good as the ones in Japan. Maps were painted on fans and sightseeing tours offered in the cities. When it came to buying souvenirs to take home, in first place alongside combs and white face powder were woodcuts. They were issued in editions of up to 20,000. Taking charge of their production and distribution was a publisher. It was he who engaged the artists, block cutters and printers and financed the venture. Once the original drawing was passed by the censor, it was transferred onto wood blocks, whereby only the parts that were to be printed were left in relief; everything else was cut away. There was one block per colour. The artist checked the colours, and the printer made sure the blocks were correctly assembled. In the case of large editions, the intensity of the colours inevitably varied. At other times, slight changes to the woodblock meant that prints of the same scene differed. In a number of *Mishima* prints, for example, the viewer can read an advert for a well-known brand of face powder, attached to one of the stone lanterns. In another print, a teahouse presents all its specialities. It was all paid advertising.

In the realm of symbols

The artist, it is reported, travelled the Tokaido himself in 1832, albeit not on foot, but as a member of an official and splendidly equipped mission. Every year the shogun sent the emperor a present of valuable horses, a symbolic gift by those in power to the powerless but revered descendant of the Sun goddess.

Hiroshige, born in 1797, was a member of the military aristocracy. He spent almost his entire life in the shogun's enormous palace, serving as head of the fire brigade for twenty years. It was an important position in a city built of wood and permanently in danger of burning down. Hiroshige was thereby in charge of a great number of tattooed and – like the litter-bearers in this print – mostly scantily clad men.

Hiroshige inherited the post, and with it responsibility for his family, when he was just twelve years old, following the sudden death of his father. At 33 he in turn passed on both the job and the responsibility for the family to a nephew. He could earn more producing original drawings for prints.

He began with the usual portraits of actors and beautiful women. These were followed by *Famous Places in the Eastern Capital*, and in 1833 by the first and most successful *Tokaido* series, from which our print is taken. Altogether, in addition to his 800 views of the Tokaido, he produced some 1,000 views of Edo and 800 of famous places in the provinces. Alongside his somewhat older contemporary Katsushika Hokusai (1760–1849), famous in particular for his *Thirty-six Views of Mount Fuji*, he was the best-known artist of his era.

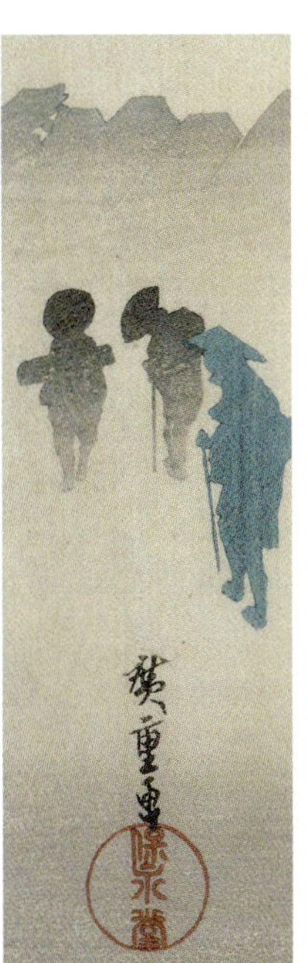

Although his prints were praised as "naturalistic views with landscapes and people", by European standards the majority were not true to nature. The artist omits, condenses, suggests. On the left of the present picture, all we are shown of Mishima, a town of 50 dwellings, are vague outlines. The shrine is reduced to its roof ridge and gateway. The figures walking past in the background are merely silhouettes who take on life only through their movement. Like many Japanese artists, Hiroshige often uses symbols instead of an object itself. He empties the composition and thereby lends force-fulness to the colours and the strokes of his pen. The viewer is invited to fill in the details, both by recalling the actual scene and by using his imagination.

To achieve smooth gradations in shading, the printer used a special technique called *bokashi*. A cloth soaked in ink was dabbed onto the printing block with varying degrees of pressure, so that upon printing a correspondingly large or little amount of ink was transferred to the paper. Hiroshige also made a point of including all the various times of day and seasons of the year in his series. Thus *Morning Mist at Mishima* is followed by an evening scene, and in other prints trees in blossom give way to autumn rain and snow-clad winter landscapes. Leafing through their album of woodcuts over a cup of tea, someone in their latter years would not only be reminded of specific places but invited to meditate upon distance, space and the passage of time.

To Europeans, Hiroshige was a "wonderful Impressionist", as the painter Camille Pissarro described him in 1893. A number of Pissarro's contemporaries, including Édouard Manet, incorporated Hiroshige's prints into their own works by showing them hanging on the walls of their interiors. They were all interested in how the Japanese artist made his pictures so airy, so atmospheric, in how he suspended perspective, let three-dimensional space vanish, in how he avoided the shadows through which an artist models figures and objects, in how his figures float freely on the surface. These were all things that the Impressionists, and later the Cubists, wanted to achieve – to accept a picture as a two-dimensional plane, to get away from the illusion of spatial depth, not to let reality dictate colour.

The fact that Hiroshige drew so many pictures of snow, rain, and mist suggests that these subjects were his particular favourites. But they were also weather conditions that he was experiencing at firsthand. Between 1830 and 1840 Japan was repeatedly struck by catastrophic rainstorms. Failed harvests led to famines that claimed tens of thousands of lives. The situation sparked civil uprisings that would contribute to the end of shogun rule. In 1868 the emperor was restored to power. The country was reformed, industrialized, and covered by a network of railways. The great age of the Tokaido was over. Hiroshige did not live to see these changes, however; he died in 1858 during a cholera epidemic.

His name appears in black characters beneath the three figures in the left-hand background, and below it is the red seal of the publisher, Hoeido.

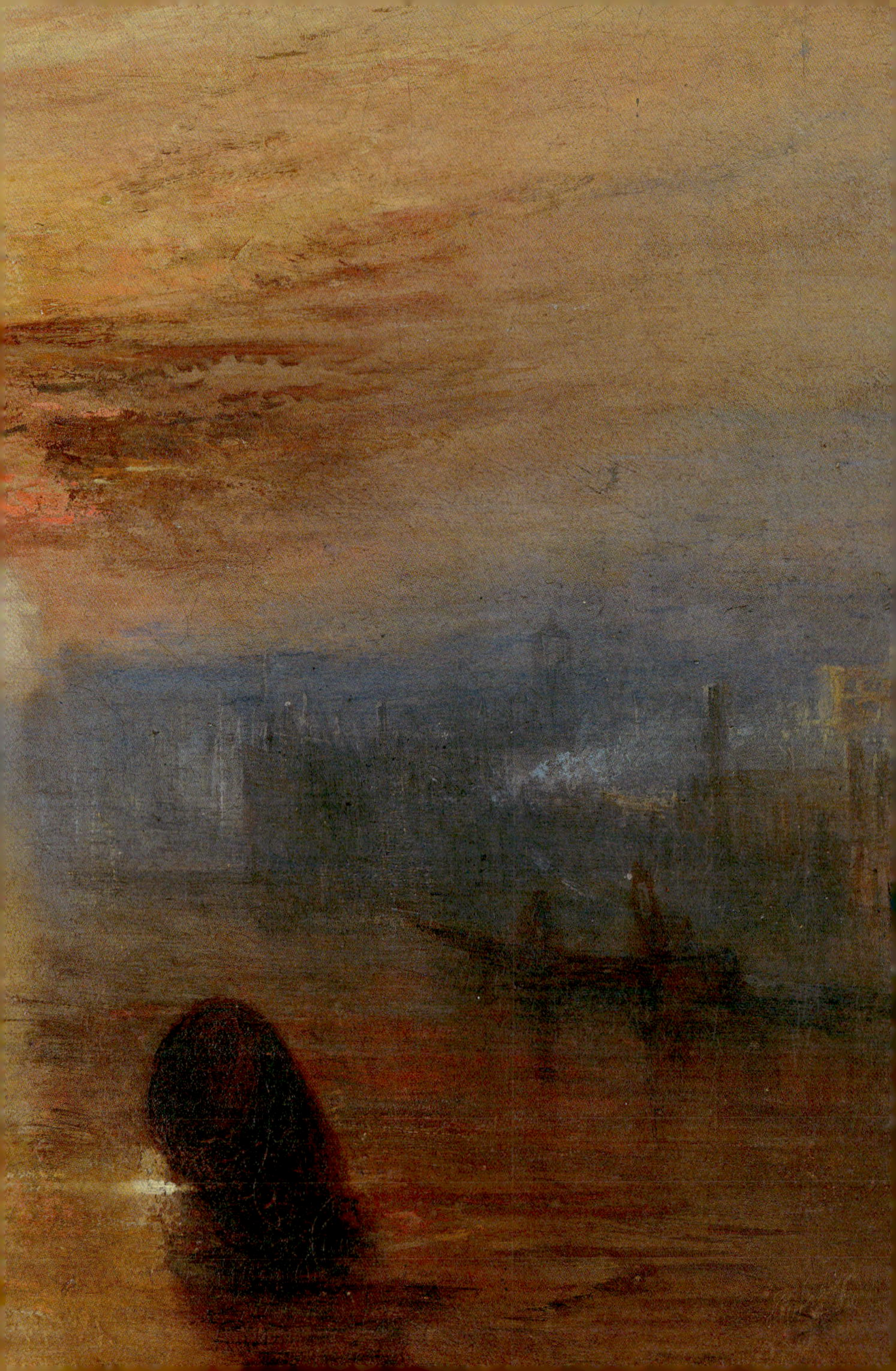

William Turner (1775–1851)

Tragedy on the Thames

The "Fighting Temeraire" tugged to her Last Berth to be broken up, 1838, 1839
91 x 122 cm, London, The National Gallery

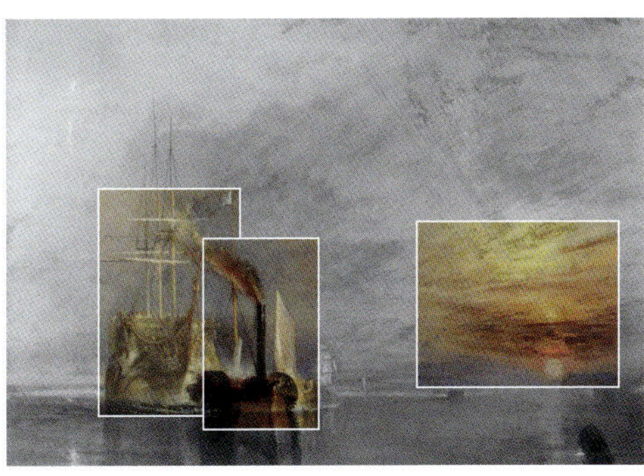

William Turner makes the final voyage of a famous old battleship into a poignant image of the end of an era.

A dark smoking tug in front of a sailing vessel that might almost be a ghost ship, seen against a sky studded with clouds and the setting sun – William Turner's canvas of 1839 is the "Greatest Painting in Britain", according to a poll of the British public conducted by the BBC. The pictures that received the greatest number of votes included works by Jan van Eyck, Vincent van Gogh and David Hockney, but as favourite in first place stood Turner's *Fighting Temeraire*.

It is a reminder of the battle off Cape Trafalgar, where in 1805 the British defeated the combined fleet of the Spanish and French. Admiral Nelson had been mortally wounded during the fighting, but his naval victory cemented Great Britain's rise to world power. The three-master by the name of HMS *Temeraire* had fought commendably at Trafalgar. It is probably for this reason that Turner called the ship gliding peacefully towards the breakers' yard in 1838 the *Fighting Temeraire*, as if she still carried in her hull the great deeds of her past. Eight months after the vessel was scrapped, Turner exhibited the *Fighting Temeraire* at the Royal Academy. Several newspapers immediately proclaimed it the finest of all the works on display. For the young novelist William M. Thackeray (1811–1863), the power of this image of an old sailing ship being towed to the breakers lay above all in the associations that it evoked. These naturally included in first place the bravery of the British crews off Trafalgar. It is possible that the British who voted this their favourite picture in the 21st century were no longer thinking solely of Trafalgar and the subsequent rise of the British Empire. Perhaps the sight of the *Temeraire* making her final journey also reminded them a little, too, of the subsequent decline of Britain's imperial might.

His Majesty's ship

The name has a history. Charles *le téméraire* – Charles the Bold – was one of the dukes of Burgundy. A French warship named after him was captured by the British in 1759 and incorporated into their own fleet. It saw good service and, as in the case of all

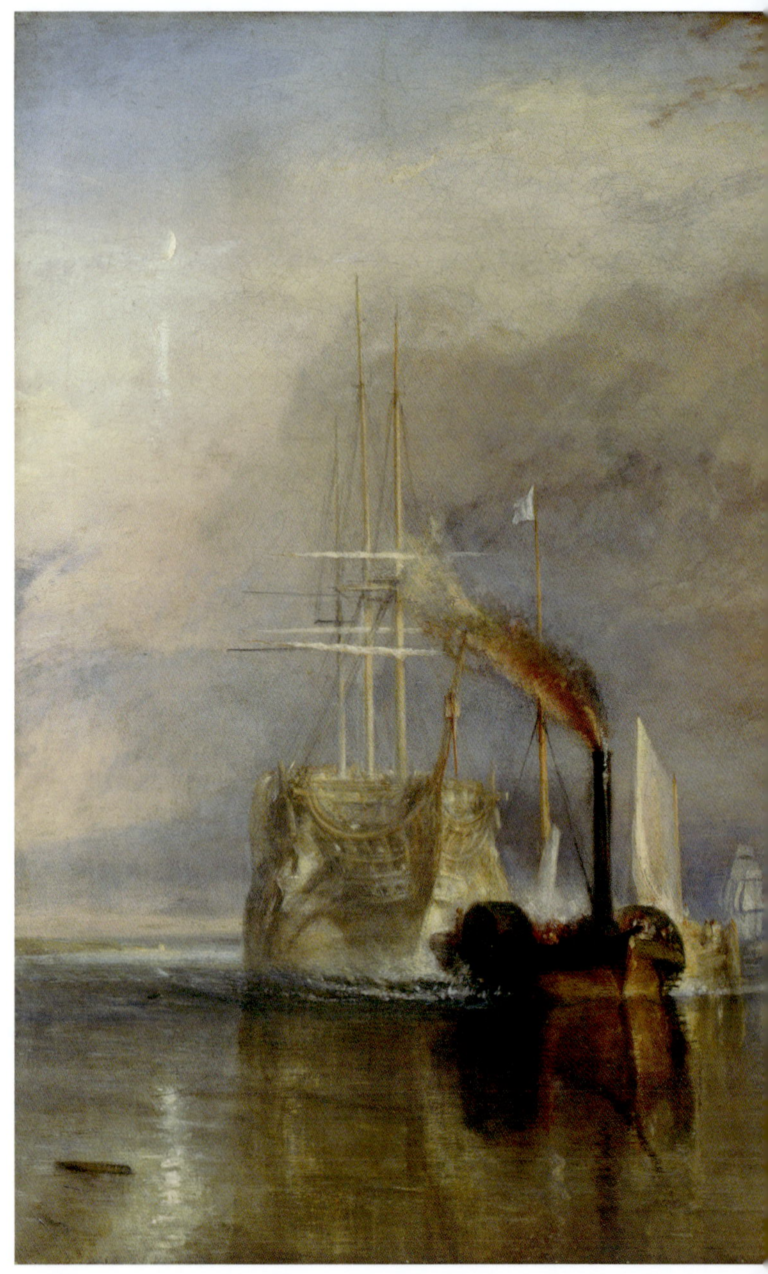

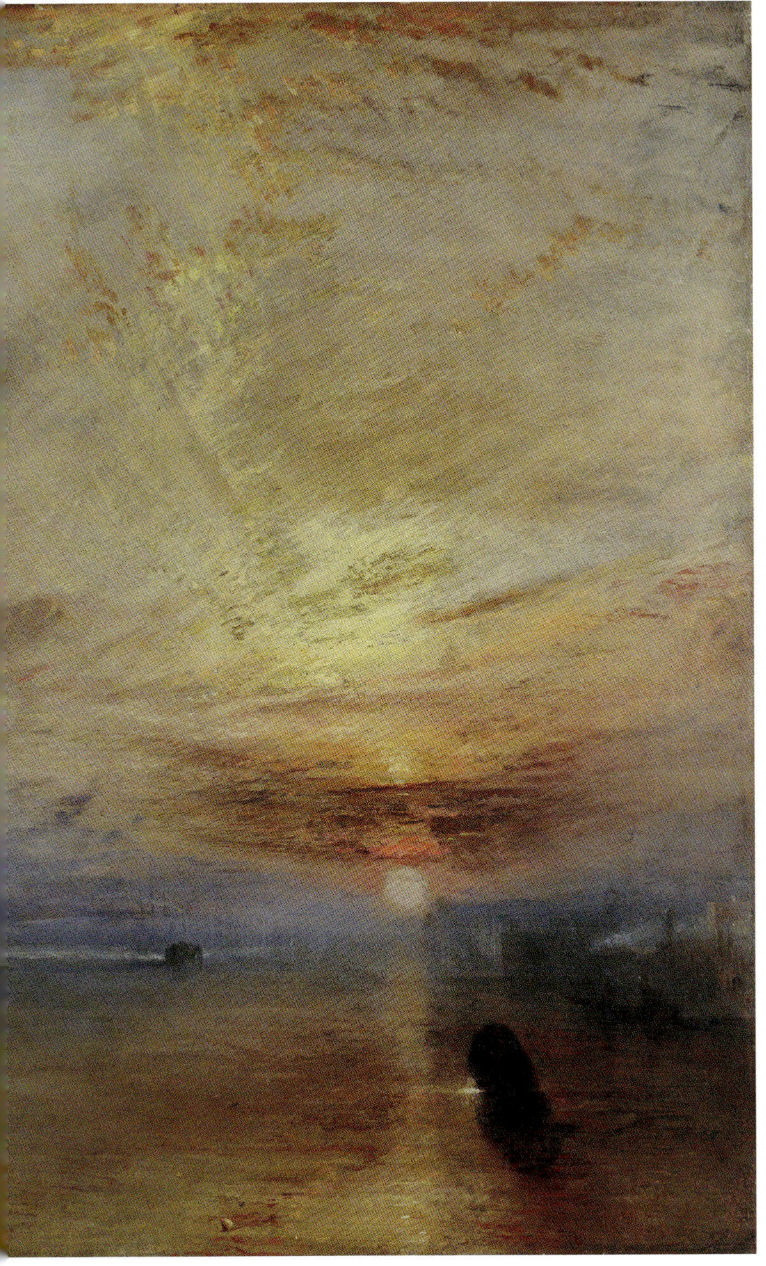

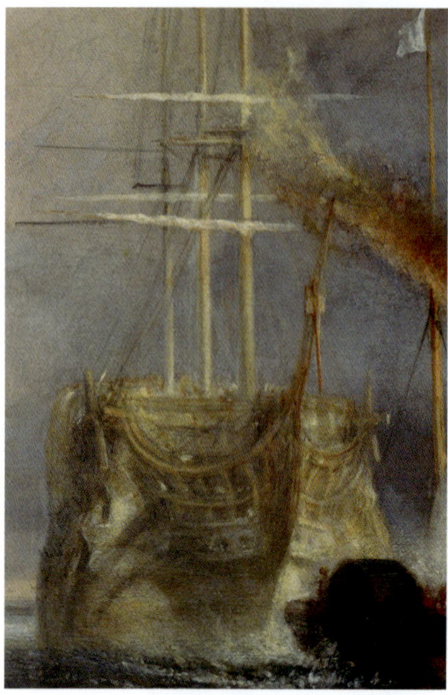

famous vessels, after its final decommission its name was handed on, albeit without the French accents. In 1798 HMS *Temeraire* was launched.

She measured some 195 feet in length and some 51 feet from the keel to the upper deck – a large ship by the standards of the day, with up to 98 cannon on board. Turner has only vaguely indicated the three decks along which they were arranged and the closable gun ports behind which they stood. The three-master was built of sturdy oak like all British warships, which are still celebrated as "hearts of oak" in the official march of the Royal Navy today. The sailors who manned them were said to be no less tough. It is easy to imagine how, as he painted the ship in gleaming gold, Turner might similarly have romanticized the crew who once fought so bravely aboard the *Temeraire*. This consisted of around 750 men, many times more than on a merchant ship of the same size. As well as the large numbers needed to man the guns, the crew also included soldiers whose duty was to defend their own ship and board enemy vessels. Captured ships were treated as prizes whose value was shared out amongst the crew.

Life on board was harsh. Sleeping arrangements consisted of hammocks slung side by side in low-ceilinged cabins; food was rarely fresh. Although women could come aboard when a ship was in harbour, the mariners were not allowed ashore. They lived in prison conditions and their wages were only paid upon their discharge.

Uprisings were brutally crushed, as happened on the *Temeraire*. In December 1801 she lay off Ireland. It had been nine years since some of the sailors had set foot in England and the crew were hoping to return home, but the Admiralty ordered the ship to set sail for the West Indies. The protests that followed were classed as mutiny and fourteen of the leaders were hanged. Some of them were "sent into eternity" from other ships, for the British Admiralty was ever eager to show the entire fleet how disobedience was punished on His Majesty's ships.

The *Temeraire*'s day of glory arrived on 21 October 1805. Together with 26 other British warships under the command of Admiral Horatio Nelson on his flagship *Victory*, she attacked the combined Spanish and French fleet off Cape Trafalgar. During the action, the *Temeraire* "was boarded, by accident or design, by a French ship on one side and a Spaniard on the other; the contest was vigorous, but in the end, the combined ensigns were torn from the poop decks, and the British hoisted in their places." Thus Cuthbert Collingwood, the successor to the fallen Nelson, described events in his report to the Admiralty, proudly observing that this "circumstance […] strongly marks the invincible spirit of British seamen in action, when engaging the enemies of our country". Collingwood congratulated the captain: "I have not words in which I can sufficiently express my admiration." The Admiralty published the reports of the battle, the press printed them and the *Temeraire* was celebrated as a national heroine.

Steam replaces sail

The battle lasted four and a half hours. Forty-seven of the *Temeraire*'s men were killed, 76 wounded, and the two boarded ships were destroyed by the storm that followed, losing the surviving members of the crew their prize money. The *Temeraire* was herself disabled. One of the frigates accompanying the fleet towed her to Gibraltar, where she was provisionally repaired before cautiously making her way back to Great Britain. On the return voyage, her captain noted that the *Victory* sailed past with "her colours half mast, as she had the body of our late Admiral Ld. Nelson on Board".

That was in December 1805; the scene painted by Turner of the *Temeraire* being "tugged to her Last Berth" belongs to the year 1838. The period in between had yielded no fresh opportunities for heroic deeds. In 1812 the bold *Temeraire* was retired as a warship and from then on served variously as a supply vessel to other units, a prison, and a receiving ship for outward-bound crews. While the Admiralty assigned her to menial duties, in British minds her fame lived on and she was celebrated in poems, songs, books and pictures.

Other ships that had taken part in the Battle of Trafalgar were also broken up, not just because of their age but also because they no longer met modern requirements. Steamships were taking over from sailing vessels. Just as the railways were transforming travel overland, so paddle steamers changed traffic around the coasts and along the waterways. They would soon be crossing the English Channel separating Great Britain and France, and the same year that the *Temeraire* was scrapped, a steamship opened the first trans-Atlantic shipping line between Bristol and New York.

A new age had dawned. The most important source of energy was coal, whose smoke hung over factory cities, trailed the waterways and became the hallmark and symbol of industrialization. The black funnel, the dark housing over the two paddlewheels and the smoke belching in front of the elegantly soaring masts – these make Turner's tug look like a sombre proletarian and elevate the contrast between the tug and the golden-gleaming sailing ship into a historical drama, a tragedy of progress, in which the New inexorably clears away the Old. When the *Temeraire* was finally auctioned off to a ship breaker, she was no more than a hull. Her sole value lay in her oak and copper nails. She had already been stripped of her sails, rigging and ropes, and probably also of her masts. What remained was a powerless hulk, incapable of moving by itself. She was towed by two tugs, but the second probably did not suit Turner's vision for his picture and he left it out – although he could also have claimed that it was behind the ship, acting as a brake and helping to steer the *Temeraire* in the right direction.

Hurtling out of focus

During his life Joseph Mallord William Turner (1775–1851) travelled widely, painting landscapes as he went. These were frequently commissioned by publishers, who had the original watercolours engraved and then sold them as series, such as *Picturesque Views in England and Wales*, *The Ports of England*, *The Rivers of England* and indeed also of France and Germany. Most of these landscapes recorded incidental details about the people who inhabited them and the ways in which technology was changing their environment. An extreme example, not intended for the "picturesque" series, is Turner's oil painting of the train hurtling along in pouring rain. The artist was not opposed to technological progress, and here he sought to capture it on canvas.

Both paintings, Turner's *Fighting Temeraire* and his steam train, bear witness not only to progress but also to a new vision. The first decades of Turner's career were governed by objectivity: his landscapes are rendered with topographical exactness and even

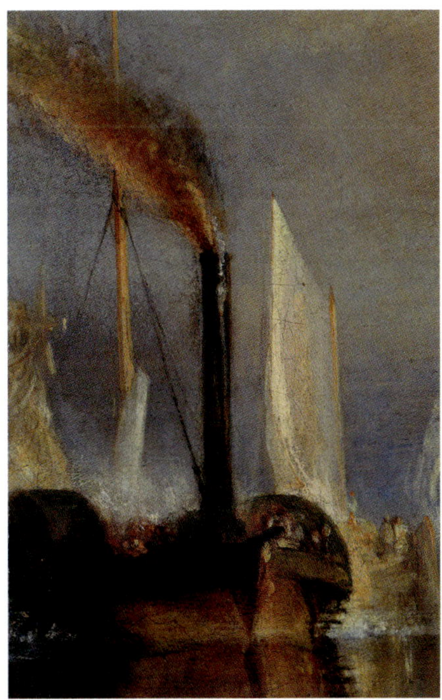

distant details remain recognizable. Over the course of the years, this type of precision with its clear outlines interested him less and less. His subjects became less distinct, their colours blending into the surroundings. The tracks appear softened, the spans of the bridge indistinct, and the fire in the loco-motive remains enigmatic.

The viewer might be able to relate such inexacti-tudes to the speed at which the train is supposedly racing along, or to the impressions registered by the passengers on board. By titling his picture *Rain, Steam and Speed*, Turner identified optical obstacles and offered a practical explanation for his artistic style. As he grew older, he would carry this style to ever greater extremes and demand for his works fell.

Only several generations later was it possible to recognize that Turner had anticipated a new man-ner of painting that would go down in art history as Impressionism. In place of an object rendered in precise outline, he showed what part of the object is actually registered by the eye and what is left out when it is seen through mist and beneath the reflection of the light.

Perhaps he would happily have gone even further. Large areas of his paintings convey the impres-sion that he would have liked to have banished the representational dimension from his work entirely. Meteorological information is virtually absent from his skies; the weather becomes a mere incidental that now serves only – so it seems – as a backdrop

for pictures that are solely about colour. In the 20th century this painting would evolve into abstract art.

Sensing more than one sees

One critic merely saw "soapsuds and whitewash" on Turner's canvases and described the *Fighting Temeraire* as "a great flame-coloured Mexican cactus". His name was Walter Thornbury and he represented those art lovers who were vexed by the absence of objects in clear focus or who liked to complain about "mistakes". Turner's engraver also corrected supposed mistakes. Turner's works only become known to a wider public in the form of black-and-white prints, and the painter normally supervised the creation of reproductions very closely. In the case of the *Fighting Temeraire*, however, he only saw the sheet after its completion – and had a fit of rage. The engraver had altered the tug's funnel and mast. Turner knew very well that tugs in those days had their mast at the front and the funnel behind. In his painting, however, he placed the funnel at the front and made it taller than normal. The engraver did not want to inflict such an "error" upon his nautically-minded customers and so switched the mast and funnel back.

Turner's intention is clear: he wanted to make the tug appear more brutal, and give it a broader beam. The plume of fiery smoke streaming from its funnel obscures part of the venerable ship and already heralds its end. The engraver also added

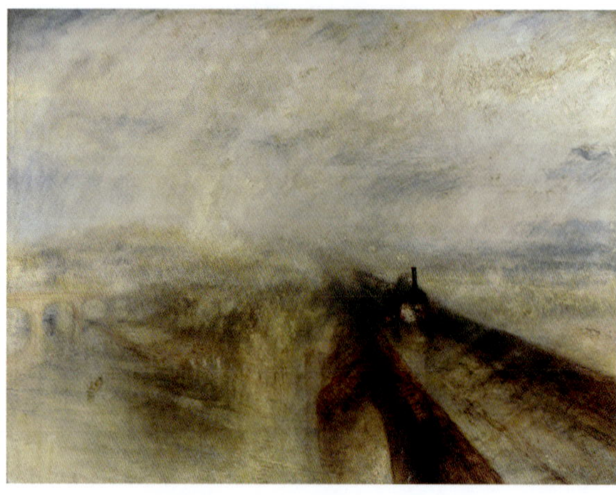

Comparative illustration:
William Turner, *Rain, Steam and Speed – The Great Western Railway*, 1844
London, The National Gallery

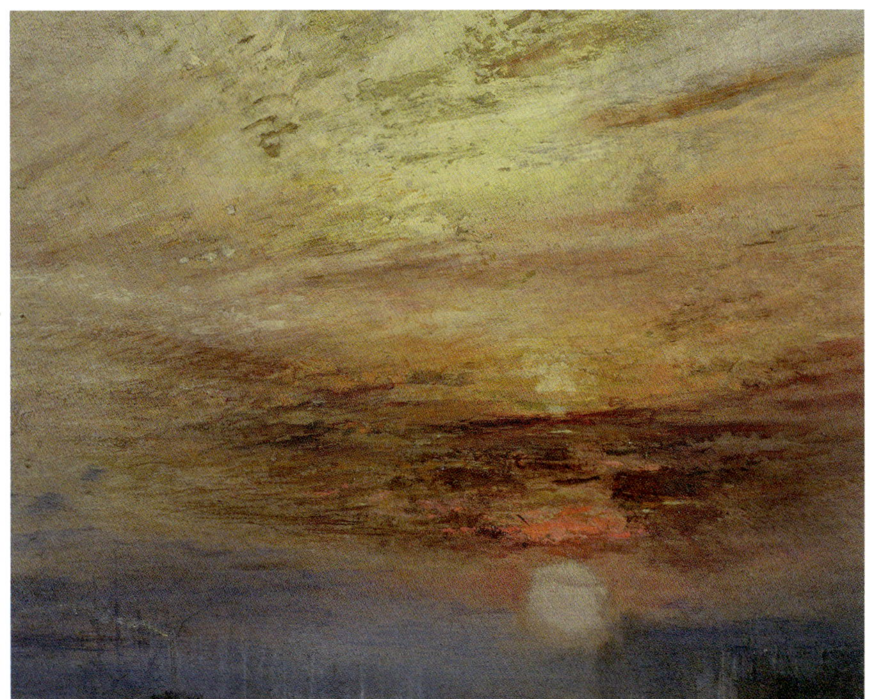

tow ropes. Turner had left them out; in his vision, the ship seems to be heading voluntarily towards its doom. Of course Turner knew that the *Temeraire* had yellow and brown stripes, but with the aid of the setting sun he lends her a golden shimmer and thus shows her in the colour that we associate with the beautiful, the noble, the sacred. He has removed from around her everything ordinary and everyday other than the tug: the buildings on the shore and the handful of other sailing boats on the water are out of focus, while behind the evening clouds the sky conveys a sense of the universe – something that goes far beyond the actual event, which was the subject of a number of articles in the press.

William M. Thackeray, who later became famous with his novel *Vanity Fair*, described the 1839 exhibition at the Royal Academy and praised Turner's painting, proclaiming it "as grand a picture as ever figured on the walls of any academy". In his view, the venerable warship should never have been

allowed to be scrapped; rather, the Admiralty ought to have kept it as a monument. Thackeray saw the *Fighting Temeraire* as a patriotic work. But he also asked if it was not "absurd… to grow politically enthusiastic about a four-foot canvas, representing a ship, a steamer, a river, and a sunset." His simple reply: a great artist "makes you see and think of a great deal more than the objects before you".

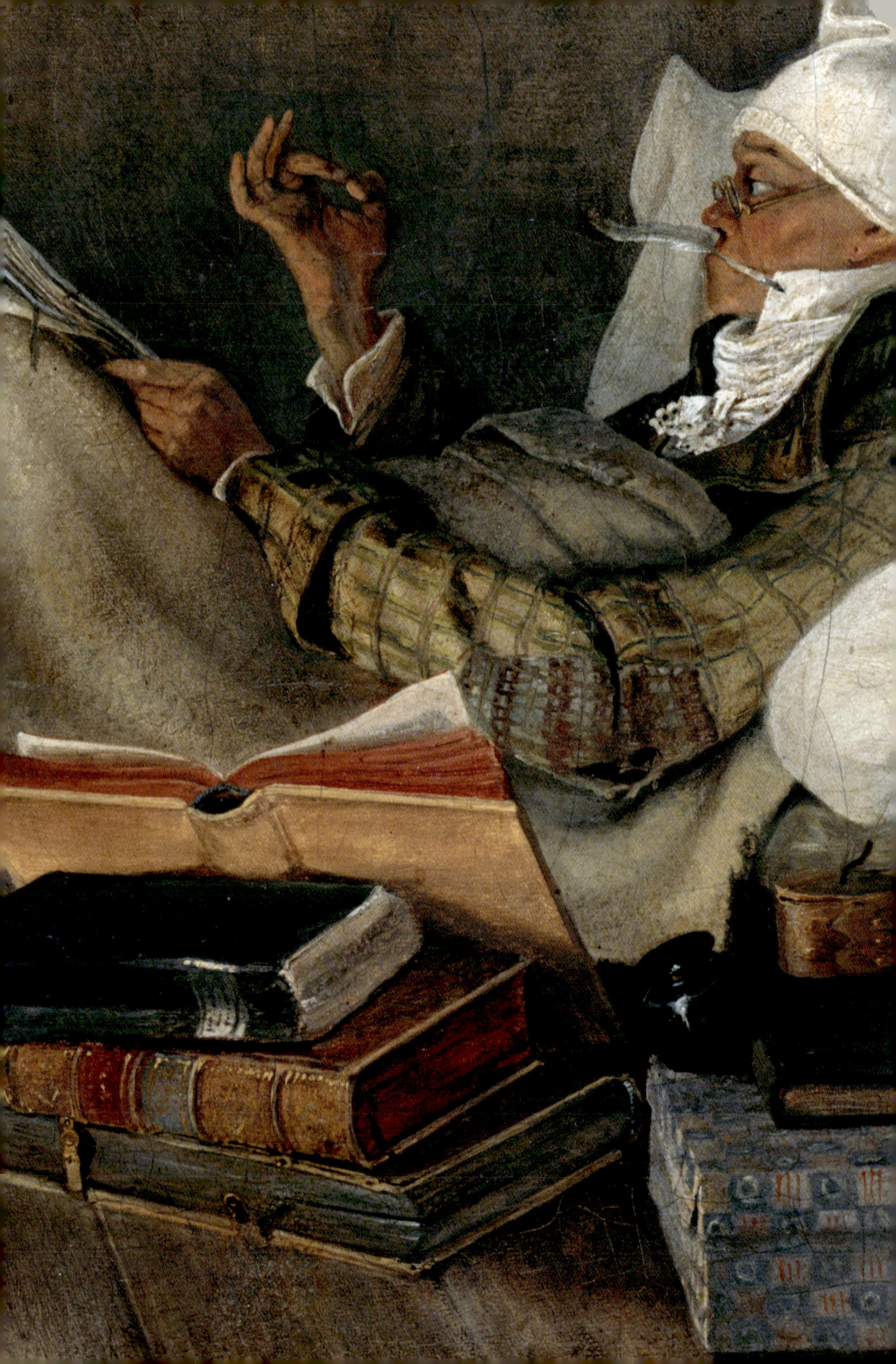

Carl Spitzweg (1808–1885)

The German painting best-loved by Germans

The Poor Poet, 1839
36 x 45 cm, formerly in Berlin, Schloss Charlottenburg, Stiftung Preußische
Schlösser und Gärten, Berlin-Brandenburg

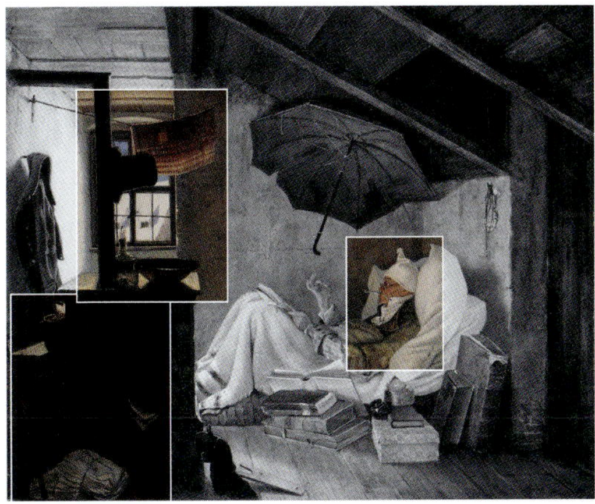

A young man pushes a companion in a wheelchair into Charlottenburg palace in Berlin – in the room housing the pictures by Carl Spitzweg, the pair snip the retaining wires of two paintings with a tool they have kept concealed. The alarm goes off, guards block the path of the intruders, but the thieves escape into the crowd. With them go Spitzweg's *The Love Letter* and *The Poor Poet*. That was on 3 September 1989. The paintings have not been seen since.

The Poor Poet had already been abducted once earlier, in 1976, but on that occasion it was returned after only a few hours. Spitzweg's works are frequently stolen. In autumn 1992, 36 of his pictures appeared in the German Federal Crime Department's list of missing works. Their handy format – *The Poor Poet* measures just 36 by 45 centimetres – makes them relatively easy to steal. But the main motive for their theft is, of course, the

painter's extraordinary popularity in Germany, where a survey of people's favourite paintings revealed *The Poor Poet* in second place, behind Leonardo da Vinci's *Mona Lisa* and in front of Albrecht Dürer's *Hare*.

It was painted by a beginner. Spitzweg was born in Munich in 1808, and at his father's wish he became a pharmacist. In 1833, a few years after his father's death, he gave up his profession with a sigh of relief and devoted himself entirely to painting. This was made possible by an inheritance. In 1837 he sold his first two pictures; in 1839 he painted two (almost identical) versions of *The Poor Poet* at the same time. One was sold to a private client, and the other exhibited first in the Munich Kunstverein, then in Hanover and then Regensburg.

One curiosity that has survived is a sheet of tracing paper which the artist evidently used to copy his own work; the outlines are marked with pinpricks. One version hung until 1989 in Berlin, the other hangs in the Neue Pinakothek in Munich. There is also a third version in a private collection.

No one at the time predicted the painting's future popularity. It was first mentioned in the press in 1840, in a review of the Hanover exhibition carried by the *Morgenblatt für gebildete Leser* (*Morning News for Educated Readers*): "Of the genre paintings … Dielmann's *Children Playing in front of a Saint's Shrine*, S. G. Meyer's *Grandmother with her Grandchildren* etc., then, Flüggen's *Interrupted Marriage Contract*, Spitzweg's *Poet*, Kaltenmoser's *Hat-plaiter* …" Six more works are named, before the lengthy sentence eventually concludes with "… deserve honourable mention."

While none of the other works listed by the reviewer have enjoyed lasting fame, their subjects indicate the context in which *The Poor Poet* was viewed. These were sentimental scenes of artisans, children and family upsets. The reviewer said: "There is a lavish predominance of genre paintings, and within these domestic scenes." *The Poor Poet* as a "domestic scene"?

Above the rooftops of Munich
Spitzweg remained a bachelor. He liked travelling and knew life in a garret from first-hand experience: he would dent his skull, he wrote from cramped quarters in Franconia, if he should awaken suddenly in the night and sit up – "for which reason I always ask for sweet dreams before I go to sleep …"

He liked living up high. In 1833 he moved spinto an apartment on the top storey of a house in Munich's Old Town: "The view is magnificent … all around a vast mountain chain of roofs, studded with chimneys and attic windows like castles and ruins … and the sky so close – it is unrivalled." The young artist's happiness as he looked out over the

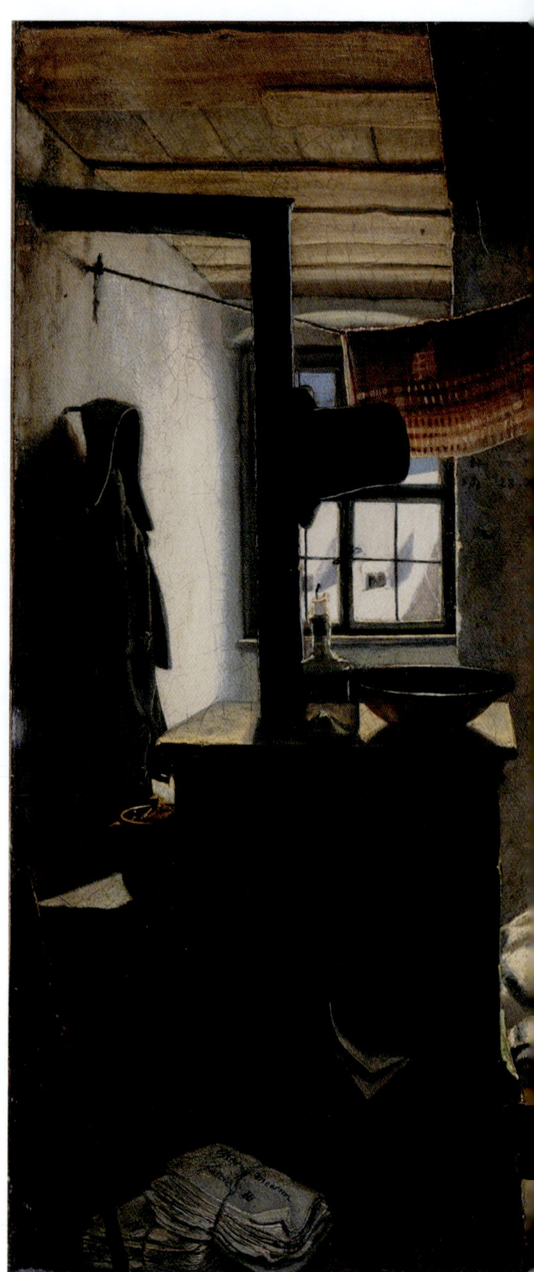

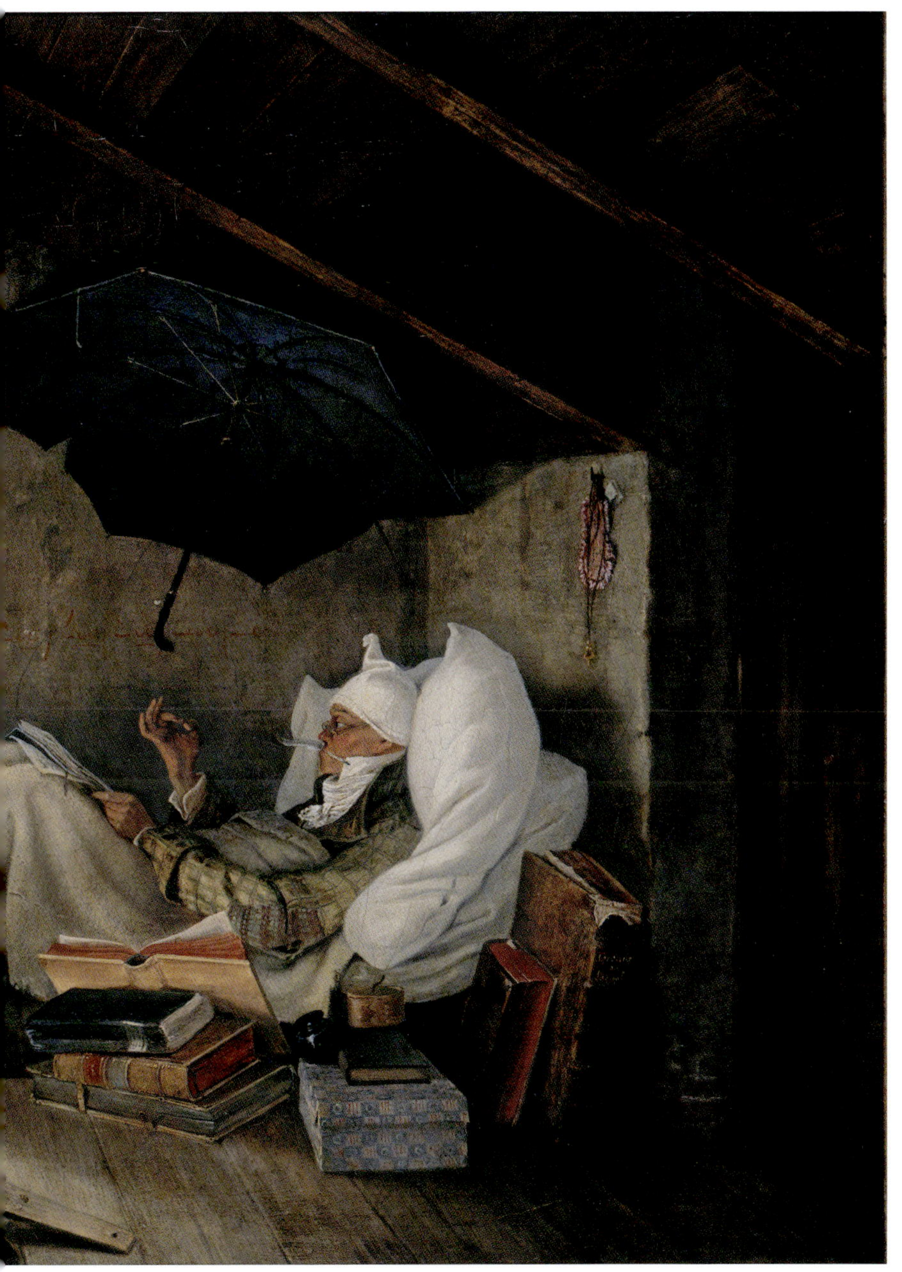

roofscape is captured here in this painting. In front of and below Spitzweg's window lay the city of Munich, with its king, court and almost 100,000 inhabitants. It was a Munich in the throes of change: since coming to power in 1825, King Ludwig I had enlarged the narrow medieval city through the addition of magnificent avenues such as the eponymous Ludwigstrasse, with its Generals' Hall and Victory Arch. He built the Glyptothek sculpture gallery and the Pinakothek art gallery, the court and national theatre, all inspired by the architecture of the Italian Renaissance. Munich was to become a "German Rome", or the "Athens of Germany".

King Ludwig built without consulting his citizens. Like the other princes in the German Federation, after the July Revolution of 1830 he actively suppressed all democratic tendencies. In 1836 he decreed that his officials should use the old term "subjects" instead of "citizens", because "citizens … leads to arrogance". The king determined what was said and written, and also what kind of art could be taught at his Academy. He had been profoundly impressed by Italian culture ever since his trip to Rome, and appointed Peter Cornelius (1783–1867), a German "Italian", as head of his Munich Academy.

Cornelius painted frescos and enormous tableaux depicting mythological and historical scenes. His figures are beautified, polished, powerful, and far removed from the harsher side of everyday life. He had no time for painters who preferred small formats and modest, unheroic subjects. Spitzweg did not even attempt to get into the Academy of Arts. He taught himself within a circle of artist friends.

It is evident from *The Poor Poet* that he started with a great deal of drawing. Everything has a clear outline, and gives the impression of having been coloured in almost as an afterthought. There is as yet no trace of the vibrant palette of his later works. The subject – a poet in poor digs – was not entirely new: the English artist William Hogarth had treated it in 1736, and his compatriot William Turner in 1809. The Italian Tommaso Minardi used the theme a few years later for a self-portrait. A poet's garret was drawn by a Munich artist called Kaspar Braun in 1832, followed in 1842 by the French artist Honoré Daumier, and no doubt by many more since.

The image of the poet living in poverty was evidently widespread – not just in pictures, but also in books and on the stage. In 1812 August von Kotzebue wrote a play entitled *Der arme Poet* (*The Poor Poet*); perhaps Spitzweg's title was borrowed from him. In 1851 Henri Murger's novel *La Bohéme* was published in Paris, and subsequently provided Giacomo Puccini with the story for his opera of the same name. The author opens with a description of an artist's cold room. Table, chair and bed have already found their way onto the fire, and hanging on the wall is a notice to quit issued by the bailiff.

An unprofitable occupation

The view out of the window forms the brightest part of the picture, and the tiled oven beneath it the darkest. While the view of snow-covered rooftops brought the artist pleasure, he uses the tiled stove to show what a sorry state of affairs his figure, the poet, finds himself in. The stove is obviously cold – otherwise the top hat would not be hanging on the flue, the sheaf of papers would not be lying in the oven door, and the poet would probably not be huddled under the bedcovers in his dressing-gown or dress coat.

Cold rooms were something with which everyone was familiar. Ovens and fireplaces only ever kept parts of houses and apartments warm. Every morning the fires had to be lit afresh – if there was

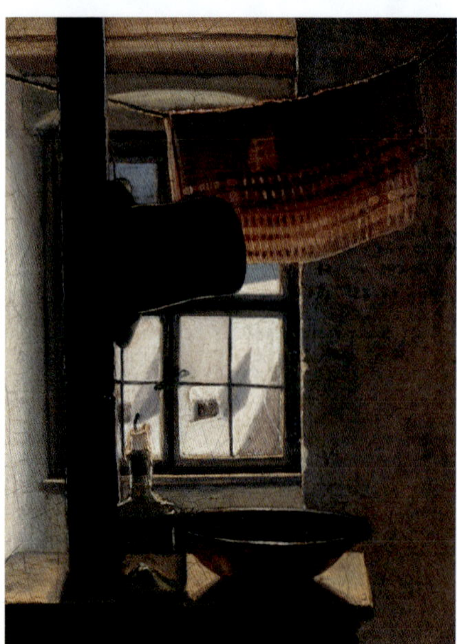

any fuel available. Top of the list of offences against property was not theft of food, but theft of firewood. According to Prussian statistics, four-fifths of all thefts concerned fuel. Spitzweg even has his poet burn his own writings to keep warm. Lying in a bundle in front of the soot-blackened oven door are his "Operum meor. fasc. III" and "IV"; parts I and II of his works have probably already gone up in smoke.

If we take a closer look at the lives of Munich writers in the 1830s, it emerges that the poet's wretched situation is not necessarily a reflection of any lack of talent. You could earn a living in Munich as a painter, but not as a poet. "There are only very few here who live exclusively from their literary earnings," according to a book on Munich life published in 1840 by one Herr Daxenberger. "Journalism is restricted to just a few local papers and these pay almost nothing. Encouragement is lacking. Munich has no literary market like Leipzig or Stuttgart, no literary public like Vienna." Although there were literary circles, Herr Daxenberger continues, the sorts of people whose works they presented were headmasters, members of the royal household and university professors. They were thus almost all employed as civil servants, and indulged in writing merely as a hobby. Just like their king, who dictated the standards in so many areas and who described his own position in verse thus: "Happy! he appointed to a throne; / Steps to ascend he has none, / No one on earth stands above him!"

To earn one's living with poems, stories, novels or travelogues was difficult not just in Munich. Heinrich Heine, who had moved to Paris to escape censorship and repression, lived more from inheritances than from his (many) royalties. Eduard Mörike kept body and soul together for many years as a country parson, and the aristocratic Joseph von Eichendorff – like many of his contemporaries – considered it "ridiculous" to make a "profession" out of "writing poetry".

Spitzweg's poet is thus out of touch with reality because he has taken up poetry instead of securing himself an income as an official – and also because he is composing in such an old-fashioned manner. Heavy literary tomes, such as those on the floor in front of the mattress, were looked down on by the Romantics of his day. Words were to flow freely from one's own experience, from one's own fount of language, and not within the prespecified feet of

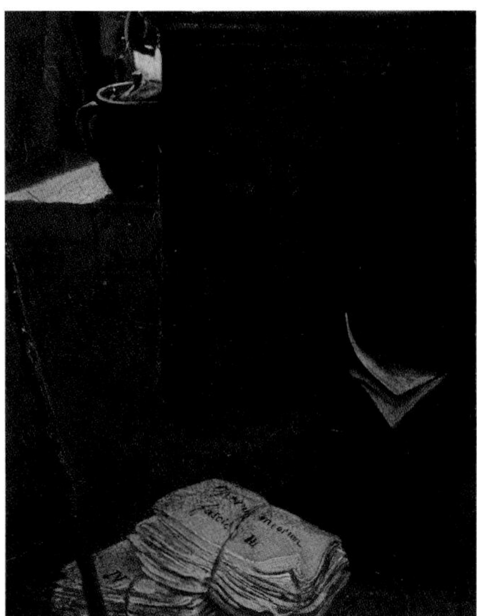

a hexameter, whose rhythms the poet has noted in marks on the wall. He seems to be counting the syllables with his fingers, to make sure they fit the classical metre. Heine makes a similar jibe in *Ata Troll* (1847), where he writes of a young bear who "… scratches himself on the head / like a poet seeking the rhyme / he too scans with his paws."

The cravat makes the man
To protect himself from the cold, the poet is lying in bed dressed in a tattered coat and wearing, like many of his contemporaries, a nightcap. He has tied a cravat around his neck, as if ready to go out. Cravats were one of the most important accessories in a man's wardrobe. They could be tied in an almost inconceivable multitude of ways. The French novelist Honoré de Balzac (1799–1850) even claimed *La cravatte, c'est l'homme* ("The cravat is the man").

He might have said the same thing about walking sticks. These were swung in the left hand, in other words on the side on which a man of class would, prior to the French Revolution, have worn his sword. One manufacturer offered 500 different models. The walking stick, like the cravat, was one of the means by which a man could distinguish himself from others and lend himself a touch of individuality. The poor poet's stick is leaning against the wall

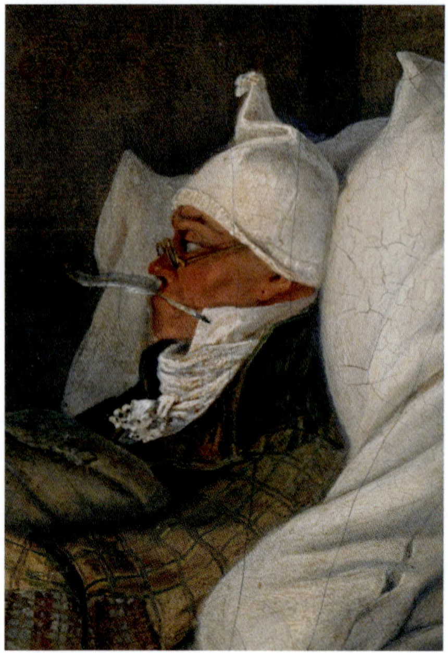

on the left. It is one of the economical, sturdy types, and has a T-shaped head, making it a "Fritz crook", so-called after the Prussian king Frederick II.

The open umbrella over the bed is probably one of Spitzweg's own pictorial inventions; no one, as far as is known, had painted the motif before. The umbrella itself had been around for a while; it had come into fashion in the 18th century. However, it sheltered only those few young gentlemen, who could not afford their own carriages. That changed after the Paris revolution of 1830: Louis Philippe of the House of Bourbon, France's citizen king, used an umbrella as a means of demonstrating his proximity to the people. The pedestrian's practical accessory thus became a symbol of populist political leanings.

The same was true of the top hat. It acquired its cylindrical shape during the French Revolution, when it came to replace the tricorne and the wig. In the 19th century it lost its originally subversive significance and became the standard dress for ordinary, law-abiding, royalist men. Top hat, umbrella, cane, cravat – these all held an immediate significance for contemporary viewers of Spitzweg's picture. Both in

reality and in art, they characterized the individual in terms of class and personality. They rendered differences visible.

Today we view the reclining poet and the characteristic items of his wardrobe from a different, almost opposite angle. For us, he is not the individual who distinguishes himself from others, but the symbolic figure of an entire epoch – the Biedermeier era.

The Biedermeier period, which lasted from 1815 to 1848, was dominated by the restoration of a feudalistic style of government. Constitutionally minded "citizens" were once again to become "subjects". Most citizens reacted to this pressure from above by withdrawing into the private sphere. The term "Biedermeier" today evokes images of large, happy families, pastoral scenes and a sentimental life far removed from all political activity. But just as the epoch only acquired its name after it had ended, so rimmed glasses, top hats, umbrellas and walking sticks only became the symbolic attributes of a private lifestyle over the course of the years. Spitzweg, who painted right up to his death in 1885, played an influential role in transforming the objects of daily life into symbols of the spirit of the age. But that was in the years after *The Poor Poet*. In this painting, only the stocking cap has an added significance. It was an item of clothing worn by "German Michael", a figure who originated in the 16th century and who represented a caricature of the German nation or of the typical German.

A different sort of "typical German"?
Spitzweg's painting is still the subject of minor academic controversy, possibly instigated by the artist himself. At issue is a preparatory drawing on which four words have been hastily scrawled. The last two words can be deciphered as "weg floh" ("away flea"). This suggests that the man in the bed is not scanning syllables, but squashing a flea between his thumb and forefinger.

But has the inscription been correctly deciphered? And even if it has, argues the opposition, perhaps it was not the poet who wanted to be rid of the flea, but the artist who wished to shake off the suspicion of having fleas?

Whatever the case: the contrast between the poet's flights of fancy – the words *ad parnassum* are printed on one of the tomes – and the poverty of his room is already striking enough. The point about the flea would be a nice touch, but not an indispensable one.

The question remains as to why Spitzweg's painting is so popular, and why it seems to be the German painting best-loved by Germans? Surely not simply because it is used to illustrate the Biedermeier era in every school history book? Such books contain other utterly unmemorable pictures.

Perhaps the work is so popular because it comes close to one of our own occasional dreams – of retreating to within our own four walls, of devoting ourselves to books rather than to reality, of escaping from the ugly world outside into a safe, inner world of beauty, cushioned by soft pillows, beneath a sheltering umbrella.

The escapist appeal of *The Poor Poet* is not the only possible explanation for its popularity; a second factor – more national in character – must also be taken into consideration. Since the beginning of the 19th century, at least, the caricature of "German Michael" was generally portrayed in a pointed nightcap. Was the poor poet perceived as a modern-day brother to this "typical German"? Have the Germans taken Spitzweg's poet so much to their hearts because he illustrates the positive side of their formerly negative image – as a man who, in the face of all adversity, "strives ever onwards"?

During these years of repression and revolution, there arose in France, too, a painting in which the French were able to recognize their national characteristics: *Liberty Leading the People*, executed in 1830 by Eugène Delacroix. It is impossible to imagine a more striking contrast to Spitzweg's poetry-composing Michael – a female figure storming over the barricades, an idealized Liberty holding the tricolour in her raised hand and followed by armed citizens, workers and children.

In the sphere of art, one prerequisite of great popularity is often a certain simplicity. Like the *Mona Lisa* and Dürer's *Hare*, Spitzweg's garret can be assimilated at a glance. There is no complicated perspective: room, window, stove and mattress are presented parallel to the pictorial plane. Everything is clearly delineated, and even if the viewer doesn't quite know what the object hanging on the wall on the right is supposed to be, it doesn't disturb the overall effect.

Another condition of popularity: pictures must speak to our feelings. The Mona Lisa's smile exudes a mysterious charm, and we would like to stroke Dürer's hare. In the case of Spitzweg, however, the viewer's feelings are mixed: we are not entirely sure if we are looking at an idyll or a satire. Spitzweg probably had both in mind, and therein lies the true appeal of this painting. As in many of his other pictures, Spitzweg is here caricaturing human weaknesses, but in an affectionate manner. He portrays his heroes in all their eccentricity, but without derision. He accepts and loves people as imperfect as they are. A wise philosophy – albeit entirely unsuitable for revolutions.

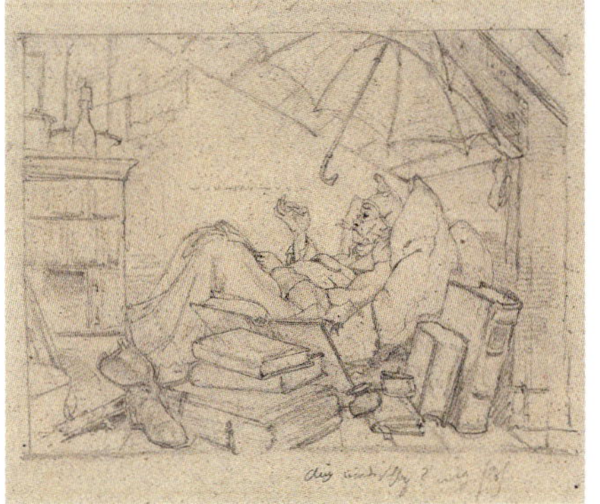

Comparative illustration:
Carl Spitzweg
Sketch for *The Poor Poet,* before 1839
Munich, Staatliche Graphische Sammlung

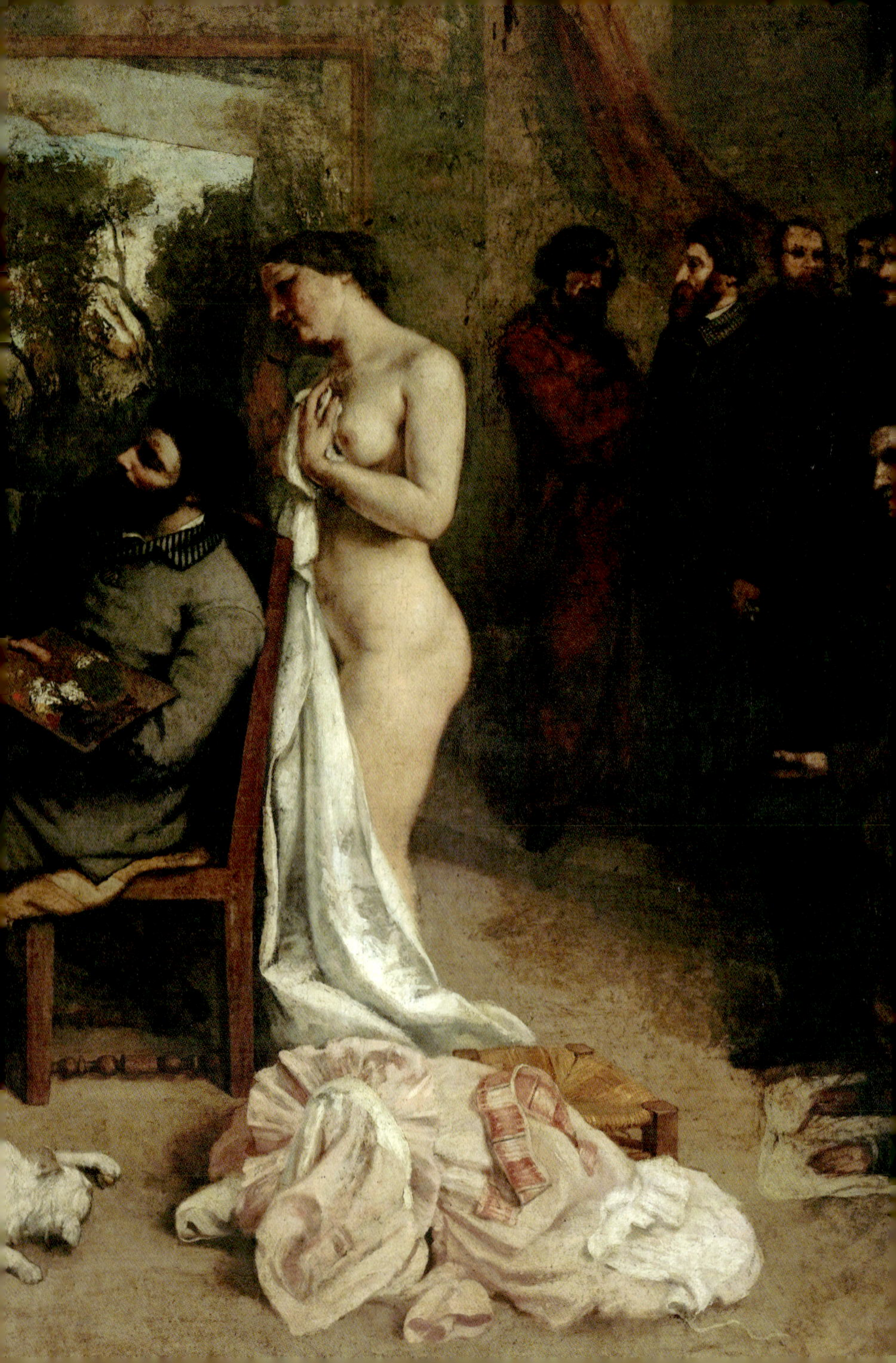

Gustave Courbet (1819–1877)

A studio opens its doors to the world

The Studio, 1855
359 x 598 cm, Paris, Musée d'Orsay

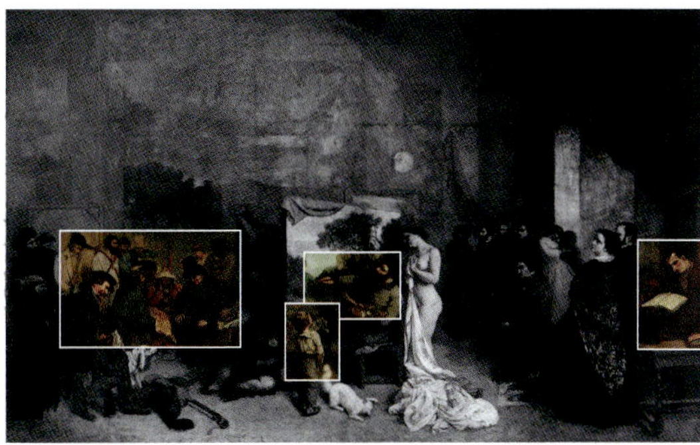

When Courbet started painting in 1840, France was still dominated by Neoclassicism. Right from the start, however, he championed a new, realistic way of seeing. His Studio of 1855 is not simply an attack on ossified academicism, however, but also a statement of the artist's political standpoint.

The brightly lit female nude standing behind the painter is the first of the 30 life-sized figures in Gustave Courbet's *The Studio* to strike the eye. The model draws our attention – quite unlike the second nude, a male figure, who is draped around a stand in the semi-darkness like a martyred saint.

For Courbet's contemporaries – or at least those of them familiar with the artist's thinking – these two nudes were pointers to an underlying agenda. The figure in the semi-darkness is a jointed mannequin of the type used by artists to study poses and proportions, and which for Courbet symbolized Academy tradition and its remoteness from reality. He himself adhered less to tradition than to real life, embodied in the most literal sense in this painting in the figure of the naked woman.

Gustave Courbet considered the world around him more important than the world of art. In his view, an Academy training only served to spoil an artist's eye. What Courbet thought was the right way to go about art is demonstrated by the boy kneeling on the floor to the right of the model and sketching away like mad. It is no coincidence that he has excluded the jointed mannequin from his field of vision.

For Courbet, the world around him also included people who, at that time, were not considered worthy of artistic treatment: labourers, begging veterans, the far from Madonna-like woman nursing her child. These are some of the characters whom Courbet assembles on the left-hand side of his huge canvas, which today hangs in the Musée d'Orsay in Paris. On the right he portrays friends and companions – people directly involved in his work. The atelier itself is only suggested – Courbet has painted less a real room than an imaginary one. It embraces, as the artist noted, "seven years of my artistic life".

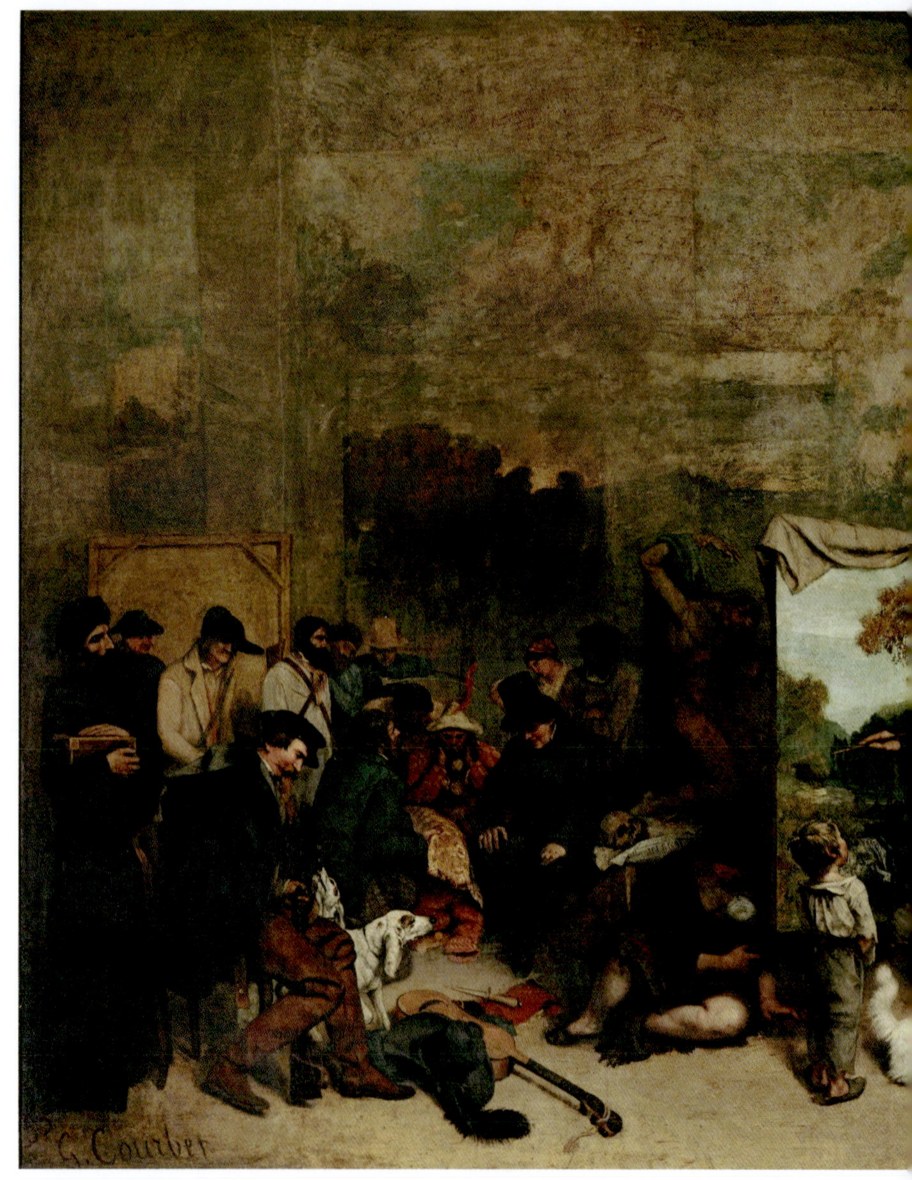

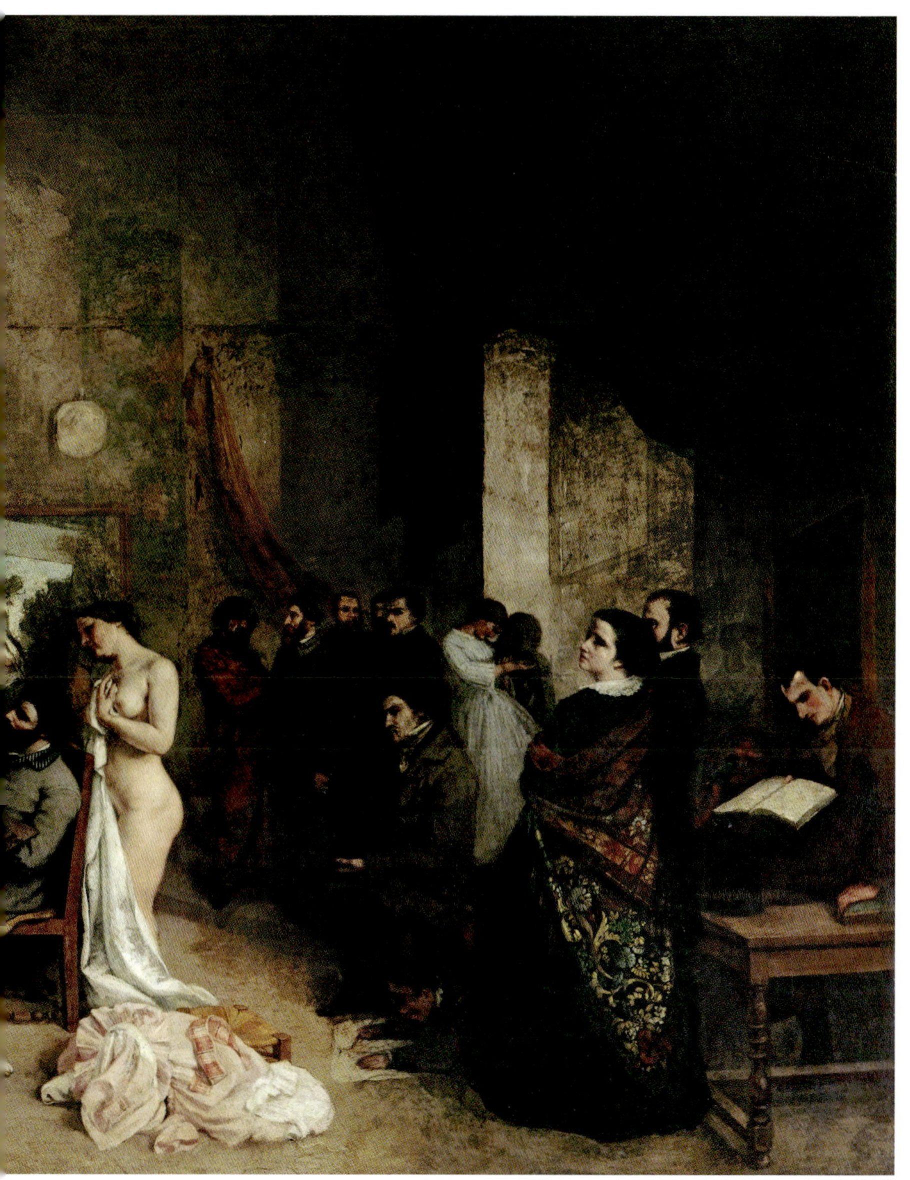

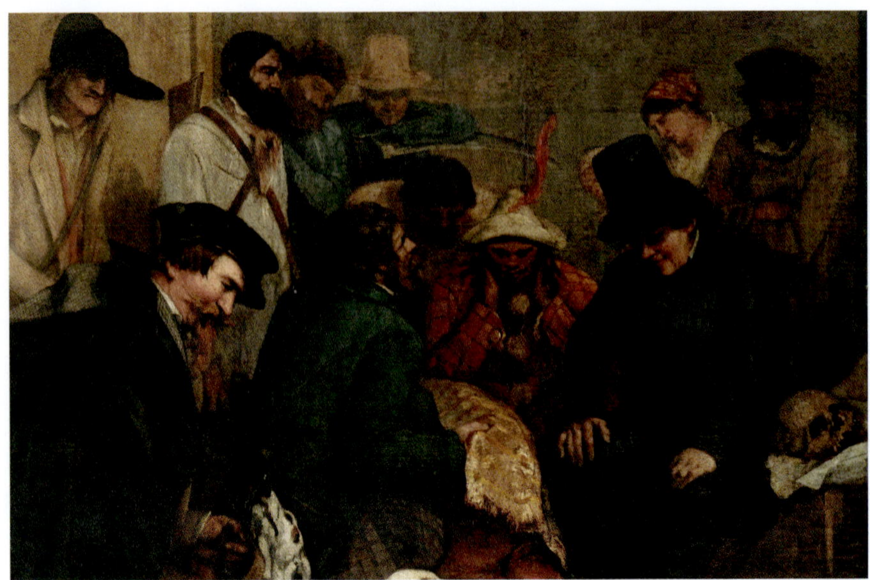

History in a gallery of Courbet's contemporaries
The picture was painted in 1855. Seven years earlier,
France had been profoundly shaken by revolution:
in 1848 Parisians stormed the Palais Royal, forced
King Louis Philippe to abdicate and proclaimed
the Second Republic. Street battles ensued, leaving
10,000 dead. Courbet did not take up arms,
but stood firmly on the side of the revolutionaries and designed a logo for one of their short-lived
newspapers.

He had already been influenced as a youth by
the anti-monarchist and anti-clerical ideas of his
grandfather. Courbet portrays him in this painting
in the top hat and black coat of a gravedigger, and
thereby recalls his earlier painting of 1849/50, *Burial
at Ornans*. "In 1848, he was 83", the artist later wrote.
"One day, while dining, I said to him: 'Grandfather,
we are living in a republic [again]!' 'A republic!' he
replied. 'I warn you, you won't keep it going for long,
and besides, you'll never achieve as much
as we did!'" Courbet commented: "For me, these
words were hurtful; for what is the point of life if
children don't achieve more than their fathers?"

The elderly man on the left, with the pale coat,
wide-brimmed hat and bag slung across his chest, is
a veteran of the French Revolution of 1789. Courbet,
who was born in 1819, would have seen such old
revolutionaries in his youth, and the fact that he
includes him in his personal history gallery bears
witness to the importance he attached to the revolutionary tradition of his country.

The seated man with the dogs is a hunter. (A new
hypothesis has recently been put forward in which
it is suggested that this hunter represents Emperor
Napoleon III; the present authors remained uncon-
vinced, however.) Courbet hunted a great deal
himself and later painted a whole series of hunting
scenes. Between his grandfather and the hunter sits
a draper, peddling his wares. To hawk gold fabrics
to people with little money – Courbet must have
viewed such merchants as tempters and exploiters
of the poor. A similar character appears in Gustave
Flaubert's novel *Madame Bovary*: here, he lures the
luxury-loving heroine into debt and thereby contributes to her downfall. The novel was published in
1857, two years after Courbet executed his painting.

While a fairground juggler dressed in a colourful
costume examines the proffered cloth with interest,
the labourer with his arms folded across his chest
remains utterly unmoved. He wears a peaked cap,
the counterpart to the top hat worn by the bourgeoisie, and represents the new class of the proletariat.

Its members were still defenceless, working up to fourteen hours a day and only earning a pittance. Nor were they permitted to take industrial action: local strikes were quickly crushed.

A number of intellectuals recognized the wretched condition of the working classes, publicized it and called for redress. One such was the writer Pierre Joseph Proudhon (1809–1865). He can be seen standing on the right-hand side of the picture, amongst the group of men in the back-ground, recognizable by his bald forehead and rimmed glasses. It was he who formulated the provocatively militant phrase: "Property is theft".

An assault on good taste

Proudhon rejected *The Studio* because it wasn't political enough for him. It was rejected, too, by middle-class critics, because it didn't correspond to current notions of art. Pictures, it was at that time believed, should create ideals and transfigure the world; they should exalt greatness – great men and great minds – and disregard the commonplace; they should contribute to the moral improvement of humankind through their portrayal of religious subjects and heroic deeds. They might inspire the imagination with exotic scenes and symbolic landscapes, but only within politically safe bounds.

Courbet, the son of a wealthy landowner from the former duchy of Burgundy, brushed all these rules aside. In his *Burial at Ornans*, completed in 1850, for example, we are shown nothing of the pathos of grief or of a metaphysical dimension to death – there are only simple villagers, a dog, bored acolytes and a sullen priest.

This "realistic" painting caused just as much of a scandal as *The Stone Breakers* executed the year before: here, Courbet shows two road labourers in dirty, tattered clothing, examples of an oppressed existence. The two stone breakers were imitated and satirized in the press of the day, and in all these caricatures the size of the wooden clogs worn by one of the two men was grossly exaggerated. The small boy in front of the easel is also wearing clogs, and is not dressed in the bourgeois manner either. Through him Courbet makes reference to *The Stone Breakers*, just as he recalls the *Burial at Ornans* in the figure of the gravedigger.

His contemporaries, however, were struck less by such references than by the situation in the studio itself. Their reactions to the painting were triggered not just by artistic criteria, but also by their bourgeois sense of decorum. One critic was horrified to see "A beggar-child in front of the easel, about eight years old … looking at the naked bather before described." What today appears a harmless sentence, in those days signalled a shocking contravention of the rules. Firstly, it was unacceptable that a lady (such as the one on the right-hand side of the picture) or a child should be exposed to the sight of a naked person in public. And for a lady to see children looking at a naked person was quite unforgivable – in the prudish society of the Second Empire, such a thing was perceived as a provocation. Secondly, in the growing towns and cities of the 19th century, the rich were strictly divided from the poor. The nobility were distanced by their elevated birth, while the bourgeoisie, grown wealthy through trade and industry, demonstrated their separateness by creating their own suburbs. Figures such as the "beggar-child" or, in the words of the same critic, the "coarse, fat, greasy beggar-woman" with the infant at her breast – these were people one didn't want to see, either in real life or on canvas.

The artist painted *The Studio* for the Paris World Exposition of 1855. London had set the trend with its Great Exhibition of 1851, and now the French capital

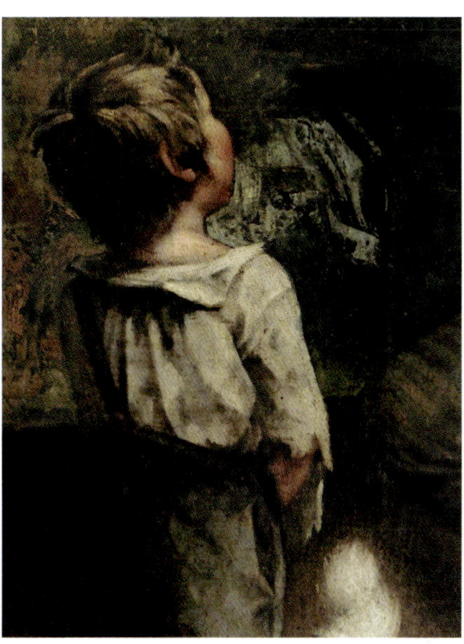

was determined to go one better. Each world exhibition strove to outdo the last. In contrast to London, the Paris exhibition included domestic items for working-class households, designed "to improve the situation of the less well-off", as well as works of art. Courbet submitted fourteen paintings; eleven were accepted. Amongst those refused was *The Studio*.

A salute to the poet of evil

One of the people in Courbet's circle of friends between 1848 and 1855 was Charles Baudelaire (1821–1867). The painter had known the poet since the July Revolution; Baudelaire had been one of the founders of *Le Salut Public*, the radical newspaper for which Courbet designed a logo. At the end of the 1840s, Courbet painted Baudelaire sitting at a table, reading. He copied this portrait for his *Studio*, this time seating Baudelaire on top of the table – probably for no other reason than lack of space.

The writer is lost in his book, paying not the slightest attention to any of the other visitors. Nor is he aware of the painter: gone are the days when they fought side by side for a better future. Baudelaire

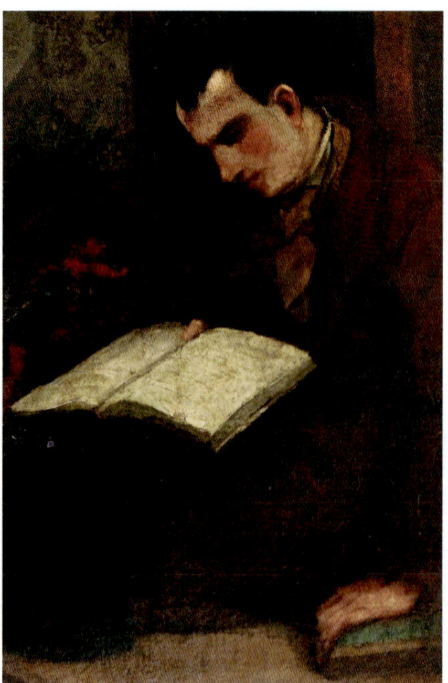

had lost all faith in progress. He scoffed at those "good French people" who thought that "progress … was the power of steam, electricity and gas lighting, miracles unknown to the Romans", and who believed that "these discoveries amply testified to our superiority over the ancients". He also warned against the hope of progress in the arts or social behaviour. Even if a look back over the past seemed to suggest that such progress had indeed been made, "where, I ask you, is the guarantee of progress for tomorrow?" Courbet's question, by contrast, had been: "What is the point of life if children don't achieve more than their fathers?" The two no longer had very much to say to each other.

Baudelaire's words are cited from a article which he wrote on the World Exposition of 1855. The optimism about the future which radiated from such an exhibition was odious to him. He preferred to celebrate the forces of destruction and self-destruction, and was fascinated by the beauty of evil and nothingness. "Under a pale light, life runs, dances and winds without reason," he wrote in his collection of poems *Les Fleurs du Mal* (*The Flowers of Evil*). A first selection of these poems appeared in the same year as the World Exposition, 1855.

Amongst the women with whom Baudelaire fell suicidally in love was the negress Jeanne Duval: "Sorceress with the ebony flank, child of black midnights, more exquisite than opium …" Courbet included her in *The Studio*, looking at herself in the mirror. By the time of the exhibition, however, Baudelaire was in love with another; Courbet was obliged to paint over Duval, whose figure nevertheless still lingers like grafitti on a wall.

Women, as far as we know, played no dominant role in Courbet's own life. Nor does he seem to have experienced Baudelaire's periods of self-destructiveness. He was nevertheless tormented by a desire for recognition which, for all the accolades he received, was never satisfied – or so it would seem, judging by his craving for celebrity, which was probably very hard to put up with. In *The Studio* he places himself centre stage, surrounds himself with an audience designed to reflect his glory, and wields the brush with an almost imperious gesture. He even manages to show himself in profile, an angle of which he was particularly proud, even though – considering the distance at which he is seated from the easel – he should strictly speaking only be visible from the rear.

The fact that he was not to be allowed to show off this of all his paintings to the world's public was a disappointment he could not endure. He applied for permission to mount his own show, for which he erected a small wooden pavilion directly beside the entrance to the main exhibition. The sign on the pavilion read: "Realism. G. Courbet".

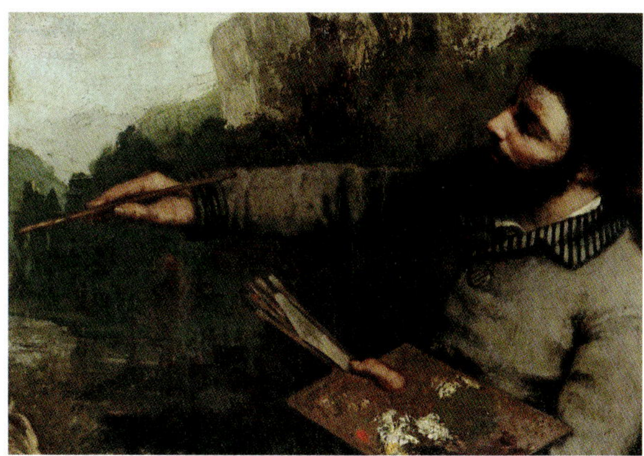

The painter goes into politics

A comparable act of independence had "never been seen in France", the painter wrote proudly of his one-man show. To a certain extent, Courbet was right: no individual artist in Paris had ever before taken the liberty of showing in public works rejected by the official jury. But the counter-exhibition met with little success. Most of the reviews were negative, and few members of the public came to view it. Why should they, indeed? Next door they could see works from several European countries, including a number of pictures by Courbet. Furthermore, he was charging admission. That was not the common practice.

After the exhibition, the enormous canvas was rolled up and returned to Courbet's Paris atelier, the room it depicted. It was only sold after the artist's death, and it was not until 1920 that a small number of art lovers realized that it in fact represented one of the masterpieces of the 19th century. With the aid of a public collection, the picture was acquired for the Louvre.

After *The Studio*, Courbet refrained from painting the types of people whose poverty might offend the sensibilities of the bourgeoisie. But he remained true to his socialist and republican views. This was demonstrated in the calamitous year of 1871, following France's defeat in the Franco-Prussian War. In March the government fled Paris for Versailles. The people rebelled and founded a socialist municipal council, the Commune.

Courbet offered his services and was appointed deputy for the fine arts, in which capacity he organized the protection of museums from the street mobs. He wanted to rededicate the column on Place Vendôme, a symbol of imperial rule, "to the dead rubbish of history", and re-erect it in front of Les Invalides. Instead, it was destroyed.

After government troops had gunned down the Commune and in the process killed 25,000 people in a single week, Courbet was thrown into gaol. He was held responsible for the destruction of the column and was to be made to pay. Government agents forced their way into both his studios and requisitioned furniture and pictures. Courbet fled to Switzerland, where he died in 1877, bitter and destitute.

The artist was not the only person appearing in *The Studio* to suffer persecution. Baudelaire had to appear in court to defend his *Fleurs du Mal* against charges of obscenity. Proudhon was sentenced to imprisonment for his socialist writings. Max Buchon, a childhood friend of Courbet, who is standing to the right of Proudhon in the painting, was forced to emigrate after the 1848 revolution.

The Studio is not simply one of the most important works of art of the 19th century, but also a political document: both the nature of its composition and the biographies of some of the individuals it portrays testify to the battle which Courbet and numerous of his contemporaries waged against the prevailing opinions and ruling forces of their day.

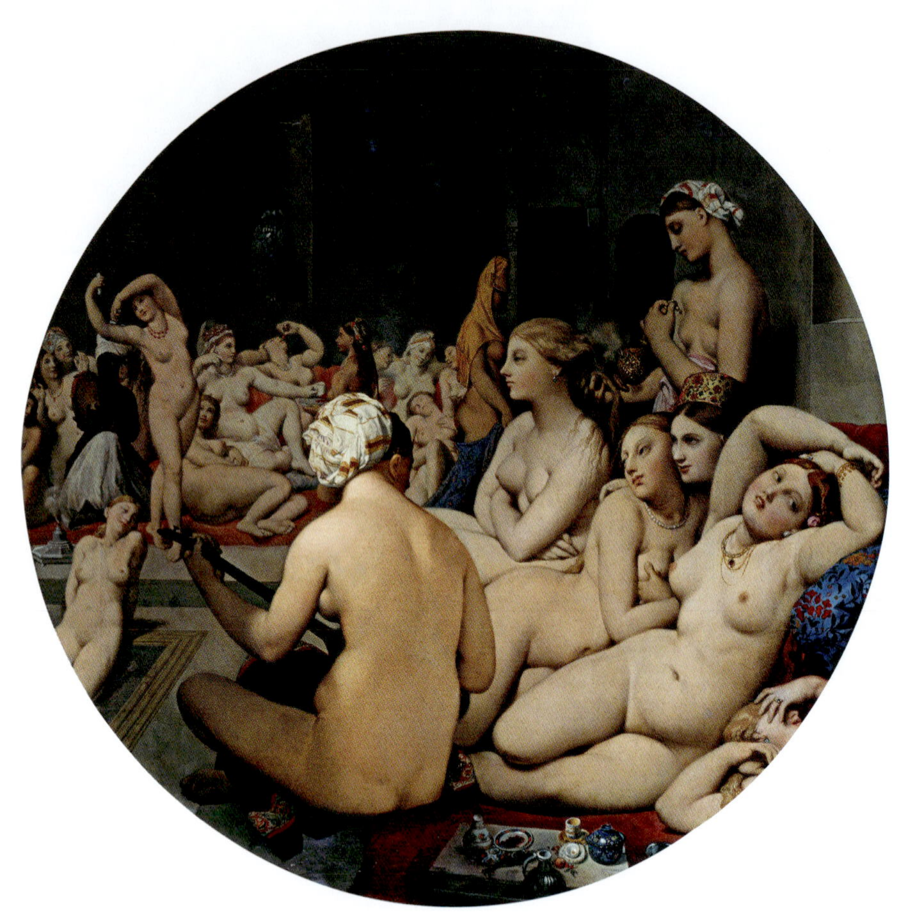

Jean-Auguste-Dominique Ingres (1780–1867)

A fragrance of women and the Orient

The Turkish Bath, 1863
108 cm diameter, Paris, Musée du Louvre

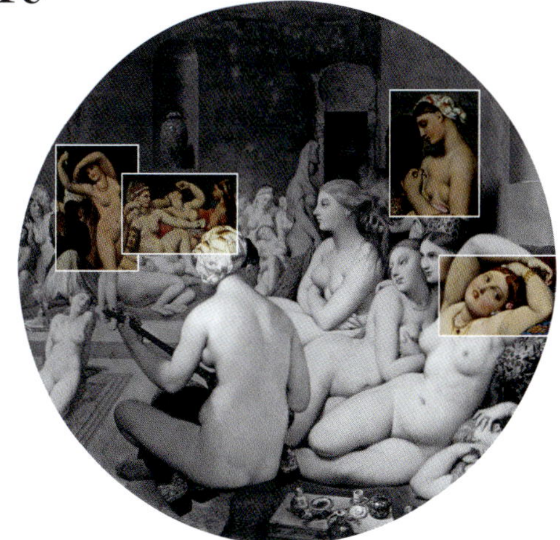

This gathering of nude young women was painted by an old man. AETATIS LXXXII – "at the age of 82" – Jean-Auguste-Dominique Ingres wrote on the painting. And not without pride: for in the last years of his life – he died in 1867 – Ingres reported that he still felt "the burning passions of a 30-year-old man". He spent six hours at his easel every day and his work was much praised by fellow artists and the emperor alike. In 1862, 250 French artists had a medal designed in his honour, while Napoleon III appointed him "Representative of the Arts" to the Senate.

Ingres signed *The Turkish Bath* in 1862, but continued to work on it for at least another year. The painting, 108 centimetres in diameter and containing twenty figures, was the sum of his life's work. He did not need to call a single sitter to his studio, for he was able to fall back on the large collection of sketches and pictures he had made over the years. Thus the painting is a gathering of old friends: "women bathing", "women sitting", "odalisques lying" (white slave women in a harem), and exotic sultanahs. He had returned to these figures again and again, with his pen, with his brush – usually

as single figures lying on a couch, or painted from behind at the edge of a pool. They were a testimony to the painter's lifelong, sensuous response to the female nude.

It is not known exactly when Ingres started work on *The Turkish Bath*, but its figures, decor and atmosphere had certainly interested him half a century before he actually executed the work.

In a notebook that accompanied him to Italy for eighteen years from 1806, there is a passage in his handwriting which includes the following description: "We came to a room full of sofas … Steam entered through pipes, bringing with it a pleasurable warmth and most agreeable fragrance … Here, a group of women were waiting for the sultanah to finish her bath, so that they could dry her beautiful body with towels and massage her with precious oils … Here, the sultanah could enjoy the most voluptuous relaxation." The text, whose source has remained a mystery to this day, carries the title "The Baths at Mohammed's Seraglio".

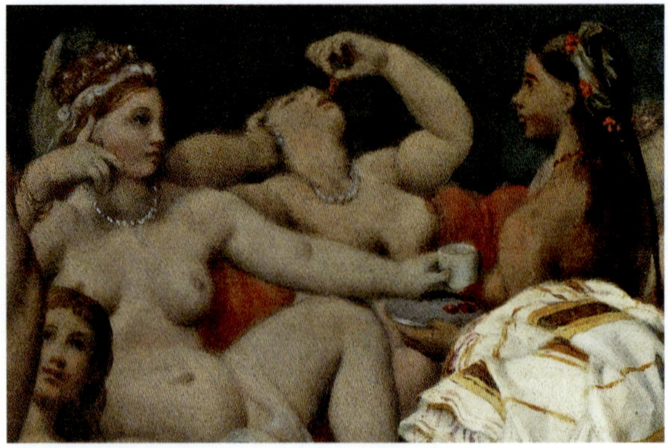

Male fantasies

"I think there were 200 women in all," it says in a "Description of the Women's Baths at Adrianople" from which Ingres made notes some time after 1825. Perhaps he had already started work on *The Turkish Bath*. He found the text in Lady Mary Montagu's *Turkish Letters*. She had accompanied her husband, a diplomat, to Turkey. At the baths, "a women's coffee-house, where the town's latest gossip is exchanged and scandals are invented", she modestly refused to undress. It was only with some trouble that she could be incited even to loosen her corset. Yet the atmosphere of the place was quite free: "Beautiful naked women in all positions … some talking, some at work, others taking coffee or sherbet, many casually reclined, while their slaves (generally attractive girls of seventeen or eighteen) braided their mistresses' hair in the most playful manner."

Lady Montagu's letters were reprinted eight times in France between 1763 and 1857. There was great curiosity about distant lands, with Rococo-style chinoiserie and turquerie already popular in 18th-century art. A military expedition in 1798 intensified public interest: Napoleon's invasion of Egypt. Although it ended in a fiasco, the adventure was fantasy-material for generations of restless adolescents, who, after Napoleon's abdication in 1814, took refuge from the dreary, everyday reality of France in dreams of a beautiful Orient.

The "Egyptian fever" received new sustenance from the Greek uprising against the Ottoman Empire in 1822. The Greek insurgents met with considerable sympathy in Europe. Poets and artists became involved in the struggle: Victor Hugo wrote his *Orientales*; Lord Byron hurried to Greece; and Eugène Delacroix, in 1824, caused a furore with his painting on the Oriental war, *The Massacre at Chios*.

With his paintings of odalisques – white, female harem slaves – Ingres was fully in tune with the times. But while Delacroix at least travelled to Islamic North Africa for his "Oriental" studies, Ingres never got further than Italy. Nor did he support the Greek liberation struggle directly. In fact, his notebooks, in which he describes various painting projects, show that he rarely took inspiration from politics at all, but rather from books. He used exotic elements sparingly in his work: at the most, his odalisques wear head-dresses or scarves with oriental designs. Heavy gold jewellery, carpets or musical instruments merely suggest a setting.

For Ingres, it was only the reclining female body that was important. In the female nude, he sought a degree of sensuousness that he and his contemporaries thought extinct outside the world of the *musulmanes*. Delacroix's visit to an Algerian harem had sent him into raptures: "Moments of fascination, and the strangest bliss … They were my idea of what a woman should be: not flung outward into life, but withdrawn to its very heart, to a place where life could not be more secret, more sensuous, more movingly consummate."

A celebration of Classical beauty

It was customary neither in Lady Montagu's nor Ingres' time to indulge in the pleasures of communal bathing. Parisians usually bathed once a year in the privacy of their bedrooms, possibly in one of the 1,059 bathtubs which 78 different firms delivered, along with hot water, to private homes. Some visited the Chinese or Turkish baths. These were to be found in the Rue du Temple. There was a magnificent half-moon over the entrance and the decor and equipment were "after the Asiatic form and fashion". For 30 sous, customers could have a bath "à la Mahomet" in water freshened with "perfumes of Araby", and with music in the background.

However, while Lady Montagu noted that it was forbidden on pain of death for a man to appear in the women's baths at Adrianople, the Parisian institution seems to have been a regular trysting-place for clandestine lovers: men would dress in women's clothes and creep into the little cubicles where their sweethearts were taking a bath. Even here, bathing was a private affair.

It was only through their knowledge of Classical antiquity that Ingres and his contemporaries were familiar with the notion of the communal bath at all. There had been thermal baths – with steam baths, sweat-rooms, cold-water basins and rooms for resting – everywhere Ancient Greek and Roman culture had spread. All that remained of these baths in Europe were the ruins. In Islamic countries, the baths had been preserved; they were now rediscovered by educated Europeans as a sign that the Classical spirit had survived. Indeed, it was altogether fashionable at the time to draw comparisons between Classical antiquity and the Orient: a new translation of the *Iliad* accompanied Lady Montagu on her travels through the Ottoman Empire, and Delacroix found Algeria "as beautiful as in Homer's time".

Archaeological finds at Pompeii and Herculaneum during the 18th century had brought a new urgency to the study of Classical antiquity, and the "republican" Greeks and Romans were highly fashionable during the French Revolution. Their champion was the painter Jacques-Louis David (1748–1825). The young Ingres had been a pupil in David's studio before spending eighteen years in Italy, where he studied the art of Classical antiquity and the works of Renaissance painters. The latter, in the 15th century, had rediscovered the ancient canon of ideal beauty: "Art should be nothing if not beautiful, nor should its doctrine be anything but beauty,"

exclaimed David, declaring the Italian artist Raphael to be his "God".

An 1827 study for Ingres's work *The Apotheosis of Homer* shows the goddess Victory crowning the Greek poet with a laurel wreath. In *The Turkish Bath*, painted in old age, we recognize the same profile and the same Classical purity of line in the contour of her shoulder. Here she holds a costly vessel containing incense or perfume: an example of the close correlation between the world of Homer and 19th-century Turkey.

As far as Ingres was concerned, line was the "queen", colour her servant. Clarity of form and visual harmony were his precepts. If *The Turkish Bath*, in spite of its many figures, succeeds in avoiding irregularity and unrest, it is because the artist has employed the traditional "golden section",

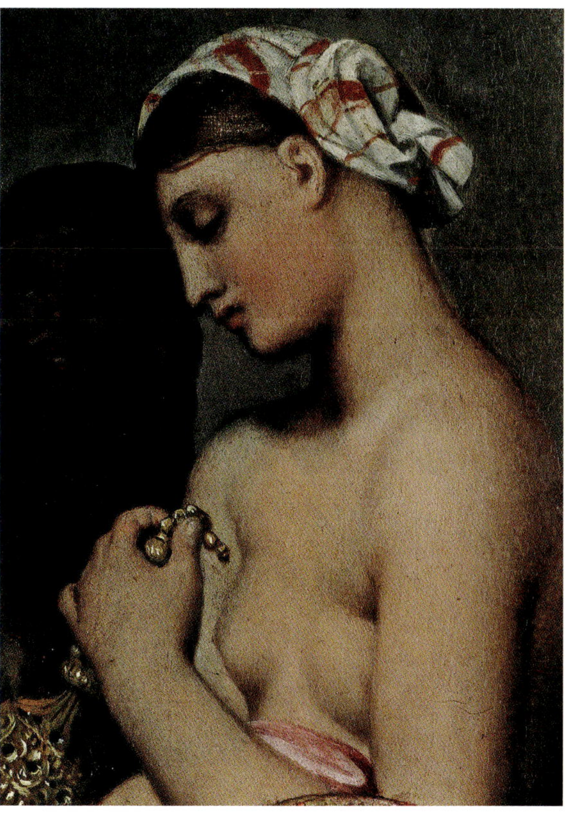

a formula known since antiquity. The painting is geometrically constructed and was originally square. Shortly before its completion, in 1863, Ingres gave it its round form, turning it into a "tondo".

His motifs were often copied

Ingres respected not only the great artists of the past; his own art was sacred, too. On discovering what he thought to be an excessive desire for dancing in the woman whom he had intended to become his second wife, he did not hesitate to dissolve the engagement. He had foreseen a threat to his art, which he placed above all else, including his private life. In order not to make the same mistake again, Ingres thereafter left the choice of his future wife in the hands of good friends, who sent a young relative, Madeleine, to Italy. The ensuing marriage lasted 36 years; his biographers have failed to attribute a single extramarital escapade to the artist. Madeleine was handsome, faithful, an excellent housekeeper and, above all, made sure he had peace to work. When they went walking together in Rome, Madeleine would protect her husband's eyes from the repulsive

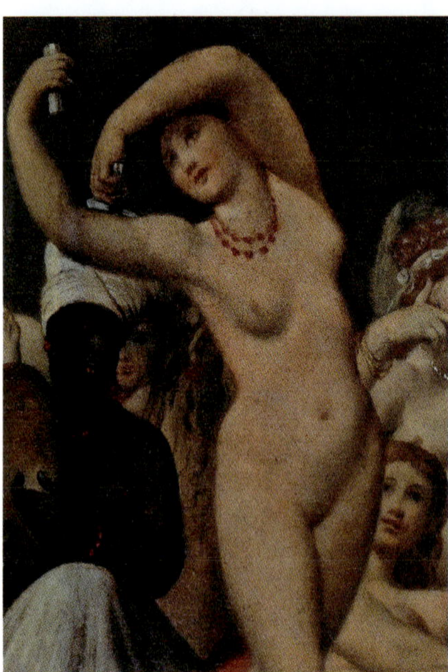

sight of a beggar by covering them with a corner of her shawl.

Ingres left Italy in 1824 and returned to Paris, where his work immediately received great critical acclaim. The timeless, Classical beauty of his paintings was considered a welcome contrast to the work which certain other, younger artists had dared exhibit. In 1819 Théodore Géricault had created a furore with his *Raft of the Medusa*, a passionate indictment of an incompetent government whose negligence was responsible for a shipwreck. Five years later, Delacroix's painting *The Massacre at Chios* showed Turkish atrocities during the struggle for Greek independence, exposing the indifference of the European powers. These were disturbing pictures by angry, politically engaged artists who were not afraid to show disorder, suffering and ugliness in their work.

None of these "Romantic" innovations were found in Ingres's work, however. Beside Delacroix's *Massacre* in the Salon of 1824 hung Ingres's *Vow of Louis* XIII, celebrating religion and the legitimacy of the monarchy. The painting was perfectly suited to the political landscape of the Restoration after Napoleon's downfall. The Parisian establishment welcomed Ingres with open arms, granting him official commissions and electing him to the "Académie des Beaux-Arts", which not only brought him honour, but assured him a substantial pension until the end of his days. Ingres, who had painted a portrait of Napoleon before leaving for Rome, had no trouble adapting to the Bourbons, nor, later, to the Orléanists or Napoleon III. He had no interest in politics.

His commitment to art and painting, on the other hand, was intense. Many pupils described him as a strict teacher. He subjected them to a disciplined regime of copying Old Masters, for "art, if it will survive, must turn to the past". He used material by other artists in his own work, studying pictorial documents in libraries and tracing them to make copies.

The Romantic artist Narcisse Díaz de la Peña accused Ingres of a lack of imagination: "Lock him up in a tower where he has no recourse to engravings and the man will end up at the end of the day with a white canvas. He is incapable of producing anything from his own head." But adopting motifs from other artists did nothing to diminish Ingres's sense of ownership: "My painting belongs to me; it's got my signature scrawled on it."

The painter who loved women

Ingres was held in high esteem as a portraitist by the rich and mighty of the Restoration and Second Empire. No other artist attained such a precise, empathic sense of the dignity of these imposing figures on canvas. The critic Elie Faure once made the derisive remark that Ingres had mastered the art of "weighing the bellies of the bourgeois gentlemen and the bosoms of their wives".

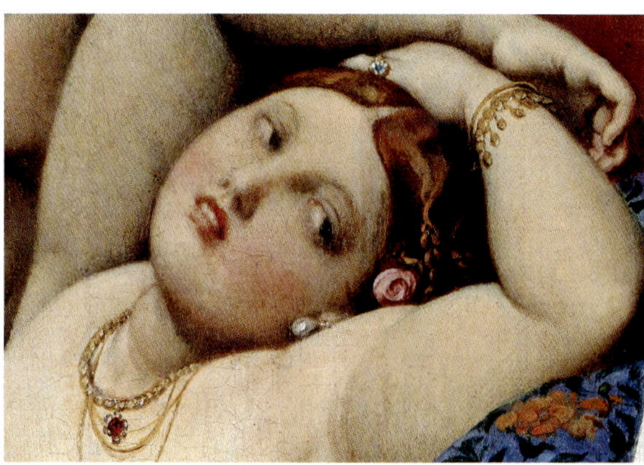

Yet Ingres wished to devote himself only to "great and noble art", considering portraiture an unworthy genre for a man of his talents. It may well have been his predilection for the company of beautiful society ladies which finally swayed him to condescend. "One of the things that distinguish Monsieur Ingres," wrote the poet and art critic Charles Baudelaire, "is his love of women"; or: "Beautiful women of generous build, fully reposed and bursting with health are … his joy."

However, the French doctor Laignel-Lavastine cast doubt on the health of Ingres' favourite models. On the contrary; he diagnosed insufficient function of the thyroid gland. The symptoms: "Thick necks, thyroid with two enlarged, protuberant lobes, the passive gentleness … of a face with full cheeks and thick lips … large, soft, melting eyes that have lost their sparkle … very round, fat arms, shoulders sunk into folds of flesh."

In *The Turkish Bath*, the figure who best fits this description is the odalisque with raised arms, stretched out in the foreground of the painting. Ingres painted her after a sketch he had made of his wife, Madeleine, many years earlier, in 1818. Perhaps she, too, was one of those "submissive creatures" who, according to the doctor, "avoid thinking as much as possible and prefer lying about on sofas".

Since most of the other women in the baths appear to confirm the doctor's impression, one detractor referred to the painting as a "heap of brainless cattle"; another compared it with a "bed of cultivated mushrooms"; while Paul Claudel described it as a "can of maggots". The artist's admirers, meanwhile, probably for the same reasons, described it as the "Ninth symphony of the Eternal Feminine".

Above all, however, the *Turkish Bath*, with its risqué accumulation of nude bodies, was a shock – at least at the time. Its first purchaser, a relation of Napoleon III, was forced to return the work several days later, since his wife had found the painting too "unseemly" to hang in her salon. In 1865, the painting found a second owner; appropriately enough, he was a former Turkish ambassador, Khalil Bey. It then disappeared into the latter's private collection in Paris, and was seen in the ensuing years only by a small circle of friends.

Perhaps it was for this reason that the painting did not cause a scandal like Édouard Manet's *Déjeuner sur l'herbe*, which was rejected by the committee of the official Salon of 1863 and publicly exhibited at the Salon des Refusés instead. In any case, the Oriental scene continued to meet with disapproval. When art patrons in the early years of the 20th century bequeathed *The Turkish Bath* to the Louvre, the museum rejected the offer twice. It was only when the Staatsgemäldesammlungen at Munich took an interest in it that the Louvre finally, in 1911, decided to accept the unpopular work.

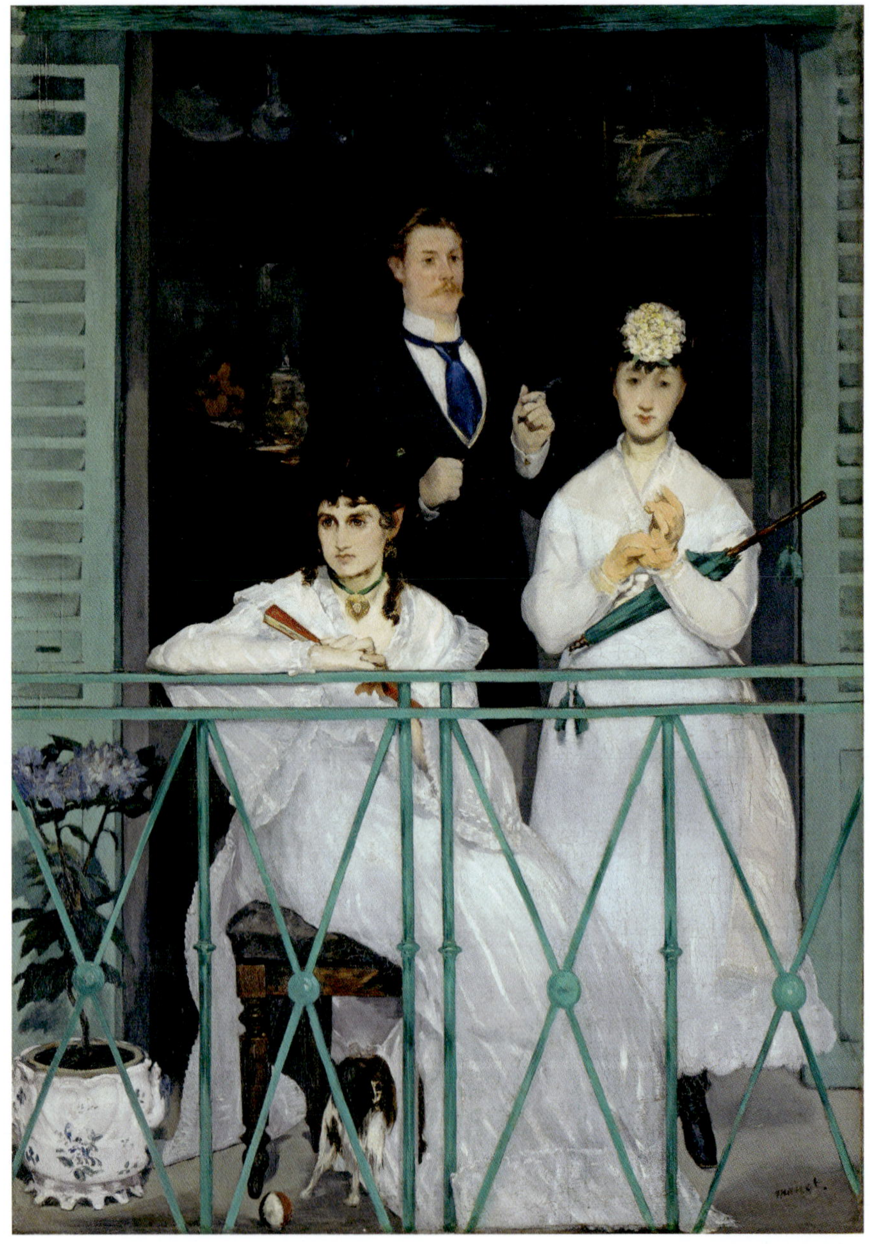

Édouard Manet (1832–1883)

The discreet charm of the bourgeoisie

The Balcony, 1868/1869
169 x 125 cm, Paris, Musée d'Orsay

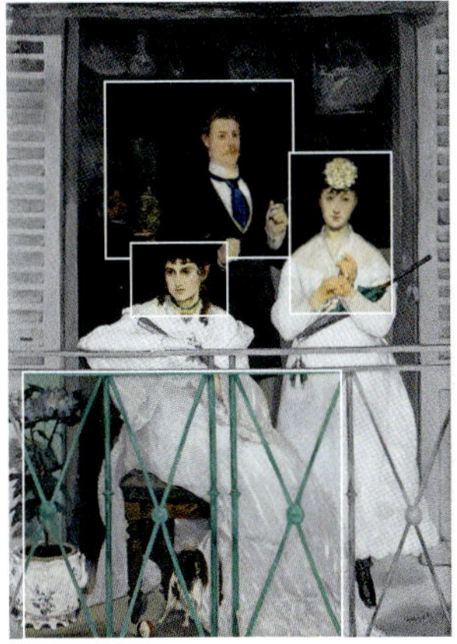

Three young people on a balcony. They were members of the artist's circle of friends: we know their names, and we know that they were all in their twenties. They are sitting and standing half inside the room, half outside it – that much is clear. But what are they doing there?

Francisco de Goya painted a similar balcony scene. He shows his figures leaning in towards each other, touching; we can almost hear them whispering and giggling. Manet might have known Goya's Spanish scene, but his own young Parisians are silent. They appear to take no particular interest in each other, either, as all are gazing in different directions.

Manet's *Balcony* is not instantly transparent and its fascination lies not least in the questions it raises. A viewer from the 20th or 21st century might think the artist wished to demonstrate loneliness within a group, the isolation of the individual. The Belgian Surrealist René Magritte probably saw the picture in this light: in 1950 he painted a variation of Manet's *Balcony* in which the three figures are placed inside coffins, of which the one of the left is shaped to accommodate a seated occupant.

There is nothing to suggest that Manet wanted to convey a silence of such finality. There are undoubtedly more banal reasons for the non-communication between the figures. Manet painted his sitters in the studio, where they posed both as a group and individually. He took a long time over them and the atmosphere may well have been strained. We know from a letter that the artist had made the man standing behind the women pose for him fifteen times and still didn't feel he'd got him right, and that the woman wearing the small hat had been "atrocious" – whether because she was fed up with the many sittings or because she thought the artist hadn't made her pretty enough, is unclear.

Manet's style also raises certain questions. The figures are portrayed in a realistic manner, as are the shutters, the iron railings and the flowerpot. Manet paints the scene as if he were seeing it at eye level. In the Paris of his day, however, balconies were not situated on the ground floor but were found in front of the rooms on the second storey and then usually again on the fourth. By painting as if he is standing at the same height as his subjects, Manet goes against our notions of reality. Similarly unrealistic is the fact that absolutely no light falls into the room leading off the balcony. In portraits, it is true, the background is frequently reduced to a dark, anonymous plane so that the sitter can stand out more clearly. In the case of the present group and the foreground

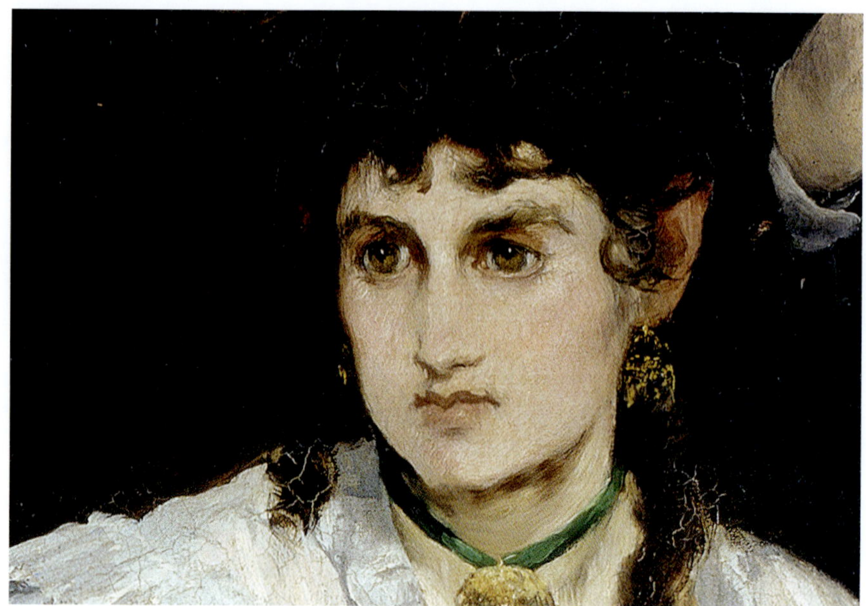

rendered in such clear detail, however, the darkness becomes a contradiction. The floating position into which artist elevates the unsuspecting viewer, and the uneven lighting with which he confronts him, contribute to the effect of this picture. They disconcert, maintain distance, raise questions – less about what the figures are doing on the balcony than about what the painter is doing with them, and why Manet has treated them in such different ways.

The face of an artist

Berthe Morisot was 27 years old when Manet painted her in *The Balcony*. They had met two months earlier in the Louvre, where the young woman was copying a work by Rubens. Improving one's technique and eye by copying Old Masters was common practice in the 19th century, much more so than today and in particular for women, to whom the art academies were closed. This was because their curriculum included painting from life models and well-bred young ladies were only permitted to leave the house in the company of a chaperone.

Berthe came from a well-to-do, liberal family. Her father, a senior government official, had a studio built in the garden of his home for Berthe and her two sisters and engaged tutors for them. The most important of these was Camille Corot, who was one of the first artists to go out into the countryside to paint his landscapes, rather than design them in the studio according to Classical or Romantic precepts. His female pupil also painted landscapes and earned her first appearance in the Salon early on in her career. The Salon was an official exhibition under the patronage of the emperor, held once a year and featuring some 2,500 works selected by elderly gentlemen with conservative tastes. Women artists had to stick to what were considered gender-appropriate subjects, in other words the beauty of nature, children at play, and gentle portraits in limpid colours.

When Berthe Morisot was introduced to Manet, nine years her senior, she had already shown more regularly in the Salon than he. The reason lay with Manet's subjects, which were frequently not Salon-compatible. A case in point was his now famous *Déjeuner sur l'herbe* of 1863, showing a naked woman beside two well-dressed gentlemen in a clearing in a wood. All three are seated on the ground and have breakfasted together. Behind them, a second woman is bathing in a shallow pool. This the official Salon selection panel could not tolerate. What was considered particularly offensive was the fact that the naked woman looks out at the viewer as if the whole scene were perfectly normal. Another example was the *Execution of Emperor Maximilian* in Mexico, a political scandal for which France's emperor, Napoleon III, shared the responsibility. In January 1869, while Manet was working on the three figures on the balcony, he was quietly informed that he was not to submit the *Execution* to the Salon.

Berthe Morisot did not touch upon such subjects. To what extent it was society that forbad her to do so, and to what extent she was uncomfortable with themes outside the female sphere, remain matters of conjecture. She later freed herself stylistically from the stipulations of Salon painting and attached herself to the much-derided Impressionists. When Manet decided to paint three young people on a balcony, the desire to see his work exhibited at the Salon may have played a role. It is a picture that neither offended the emperor nor shocked the moralists, but it was not as cheerfully harmonious as one might have expected and as Goya had made it.

With gloves and parasol

The woman or mademoiselle with the jaunty little flowery hat was called Fanny Claus. She was 22 years old and we know little more about her other than that she played the violin. With a slightly far-away look, she gazes straight ahead, with the absent-minded air of someone who is doing something with their hands without following it with their eyes. Fanny is pulling on or off her gloves, which were worn by ladies of rank whenever they went out.

Her expressionless face shows no signs of life – quite different to that of Berthe Morisot, whose shadowy eyes struck some Salon visitors as those of a *femme fatale*. Her letters reveal that she was unhappy: "Everyone is abandoning me; I feel alone, disillusioned and old." Her sister had got married, given up painting and left Paris. Berthe wrote to her that she should not feel "ungrateful towards fate" even if she now found herself a long way from her friends and family. And she is referring to herself when she reminds her sister that "solitude is sad" and "a woman has an immense need for affection".

It is only possible to speculate about Berthe Morisot's feelings for Manet and his for her. In one of her surviving letters she laments that Manet is having little success at the Salon, a remark that might simply be interpreted as an expression of sympathy for a colleague. The fact that he painted her eleven times, however, undoubtedly testifies to more than a professional interest. And he almost always shows her alone. The presence of other people in the *Balcony* – his first picture of her – may have been for reasons of etiquette. Both came from families of the upper bourgeoisie and a young woman from such circles was not permitted to visit an artist's studio alone. Manet probably brought in the two other figures not – or not only – to realize his artistic vision for this painting but also to overcome initial barriers.

As is clear from his handling of her face, Berthe is the focus of the artist's interest within this group of three. He seats her right at the front, against the balcony railings, in other words as close to the viewer as possible. With her filmy summer dress reaching to her feet, her wide sleeves and delicate frills, she takes up a substantial, carefully painted area of canvas – more than Manet allocates to the young Fanny. From a realistic point of view, the volume of fabric is justified, for balconies were narrow and to sit on a chair you had to turn sideways.

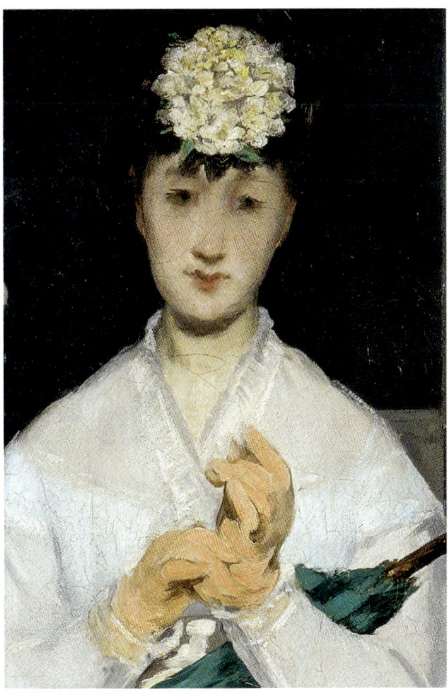

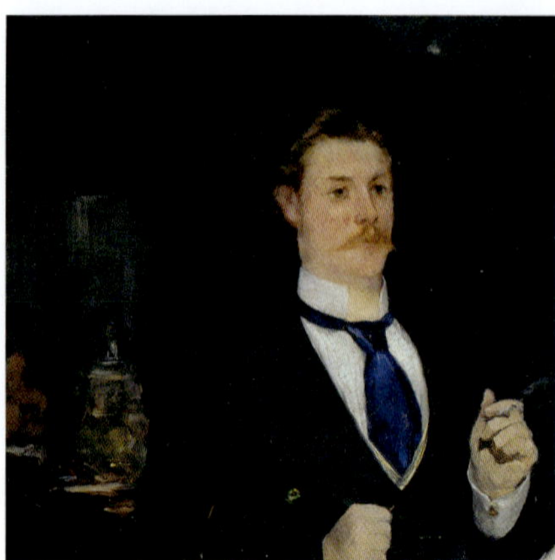

As far as we know, Berthe Morisot never painted a portrait of Édouard Manet. Men were not amongst the subjects she was allowed to paint, and leafing through catalogues of works by other women artists, we can see that this applied to all her female contemporaries. She made one exception. Seven years after she had been introduced to Édouard and sat for the *Balcony*, she married Édouard's brother Eugène. By now aged 33, she was long past the usual marrying age and this was probably one of the epoch's many marriages of convenience. The proximity to Édouard that went hand in hand with this alliance may have played a part in her decision. Berthe painted her husband, albeit not alone but with their daughter. In this case, therefore, it's not a male portrait but a family idyll.

Two men – one visible, one not
Behind the two women is Antoine Guillemet (1842–1918), a well-known landscape painter in his own lifetime but today practically forgotten. He avoided anything in his pictures that might cause offence and was a regular exhibitor at the Salon. Thanks to his good reputation, Guillemet was also in a position to put in a favourable word for others, and it was not least to him that Manet owed one of the coveted medals awarded by the Salon jury.

Standing beside Guillemet is someone else, barely visible in the darkness – a young man with a tall pot on a tray. He is Manet's illegitimate son, here shown serving tea or coffee. He was born in 1852; his mother was a young Dutchwoman named Suzanne

Leenhoff who gave piano lessons in Manet's home. The artist, who was twenty years old when his son was born and came from a wealthy background, rented a small apartment for the mother and later moved in with her. He only married her after his own father had died. Manet painted his son several times but never legitimized him, and the child was passed off as his mother's younger brother. The fact that Manet did not get married while his father was still alive was probably out of consideration for the latter's position in society. He was a senior official in the Ministry of Justice and his wife the daughter of a diplomat, and in their circles marrying a piano teacher was considered beneath one's station.

The artist and his wife remained together right up to his death in 1883. He did not embrace the much-publicized Bohemian lifestyle enjoyed by other Parisians: he was always correctly dressed, avoided the usual artists' cafés and adhered to the rules of well-bred society. This was probably another reason why he did not wish to tarnish his reputation with a child born out of wedlock.

The class to which both Manet and Berthe Morisot belonged, namely the upper bourgeoisie, had grown wealthy in the 19th century through trade and industry. Like every group that forms for the very first time, it had invented for itself a particularly strict set of rules. These governed sexual mores, for example, and meant that Édouard Manet and Berthe Morisot would not have been able to live together as an unmarried couple. Other rules concerned interaction with the lower classes and required statements of personal wealth in the form of a house in the country and a spacious apartment in the city.

The bourgeois system also placed power in the hands of men. It was husbands who disposed of the family fortune, even if it had been the wife who had brought it into the marriage, and it was easier for men to obtain a divorce than for women. A husband's extramarital affair was tolerated, but a wife's easily led to exclusion from better circles. Manet has incorporated this bourgeois notion of male superiority in his portrayal of Antoine Guillemet. Sporting a cravat of striking blue, Guillemet gazes out over the ladies with his shirt front bulging in a simulation of manly strength and with his hands – despite the cigar or cigarette between his fingers – raised like those of a boxer. The artist takes account of the superior status granted to men and at the same time presents it from an ironic distance.

The picture is brought to life not simply by the figures themselves but, even more so, by the artist's different and contradictory attitudes towards them: distance from the man, attraction towards the woman at the front, Fanny somewhere in between, the son more absent than present. These figures who neither converse, nor look at each other nor touch are held together by colour and compositional structure: the unreal black of the room behind, the white of the summer dresses, the green of the shutters and the balcony railings, and finally a splash of blue. With the railing, shutters and the suggestion of a balcony overhead, Manet gives the scene a frame. He thereby fuses the differences and contradictions within the group portrait into a harmonious whole.

Balcony railings in modern Paris

Balconies had existed in Paris in earlier times, but in Manet's day they spread across the façades of all large new buildings. This was Baron Haussmann's doing. Under Georges Eugène Haussmann, Prefect of the Départmente of the Seine from 1853 to 1870, the city on the Seine was modernized: old houses on crooked, narrow streets were torn down and replaced with spacious boulevards and splendid squares. There were several reasons for the redevelopment: sanitation, the influx of people to the capital, the demand amongst the wealthy bourgeoisie for residential housing in the city centre and not least the fact that wider streets would make it easier to crush uprisings such as the one that took place in 1848.

Haussmann insisted that the broad new boulevards should be lined not by detached houses but by buildings whose size and façades recalled the palaces of the aristocracy. Balconies were one of the features he wished to see on their fronts. Like a decorative band, they ran (and still run) from one end of the façade to the other. They were not designed for comfort but nevertheless provided residents with contact with the outside world. In 1867 Larousse's *Grande Dictionnaire Universel du XIX. Siècle* proclaimed: "Today the fair sex is no longer condemned to live shut up indoors; the pleasure of observing passers-by and of being observed by them has become general… the fashion for balconies is everywhere… over a hundred thousand can be counted in Paris." In other words, the green railings were modern and showed that the figures and their dog resided in one of the new, well-to-do parts of town. Although Manet was not an Impressionist in his style, preferring to work in the studio than out of doors and not seeking to capture fleeting phenomena, he nevertheless fulfilled one of Impressionism's demands, namely by painting the present day instead of histories of the past.

Manet was permitted to exhibit his *Balcony* in the Salon but failed to find a buyer for it. He kept the canvas in his studio right up to his death. It was subsequently purchased by Gustave Caillebotte, the Impressionist painter, connoisseur and generous patron. He kept it right up to his death. Caillebotte left his collection – which included works by Degas, Renoir, Monet, Pissaro and Sisley that have since become famous – to the French state, whose committee of experts only accepted half of the bequest. This caused a double scandal: the progressives protested because half had been refused, the conservatives because Impressionist works were entering public collections. Two works by Manet were accepted, *The Balcony* being one of them. In 1894 it passed into the Musée du Luxembourg, the then home of modern art, and in 1929 into the Louvre; today it hangs in the Musée d'Orsay.

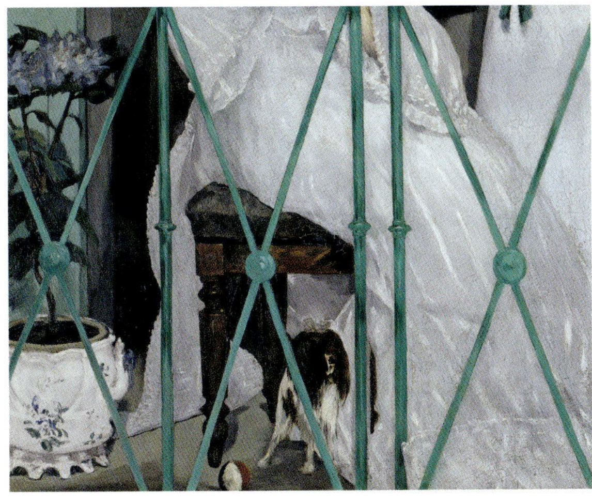

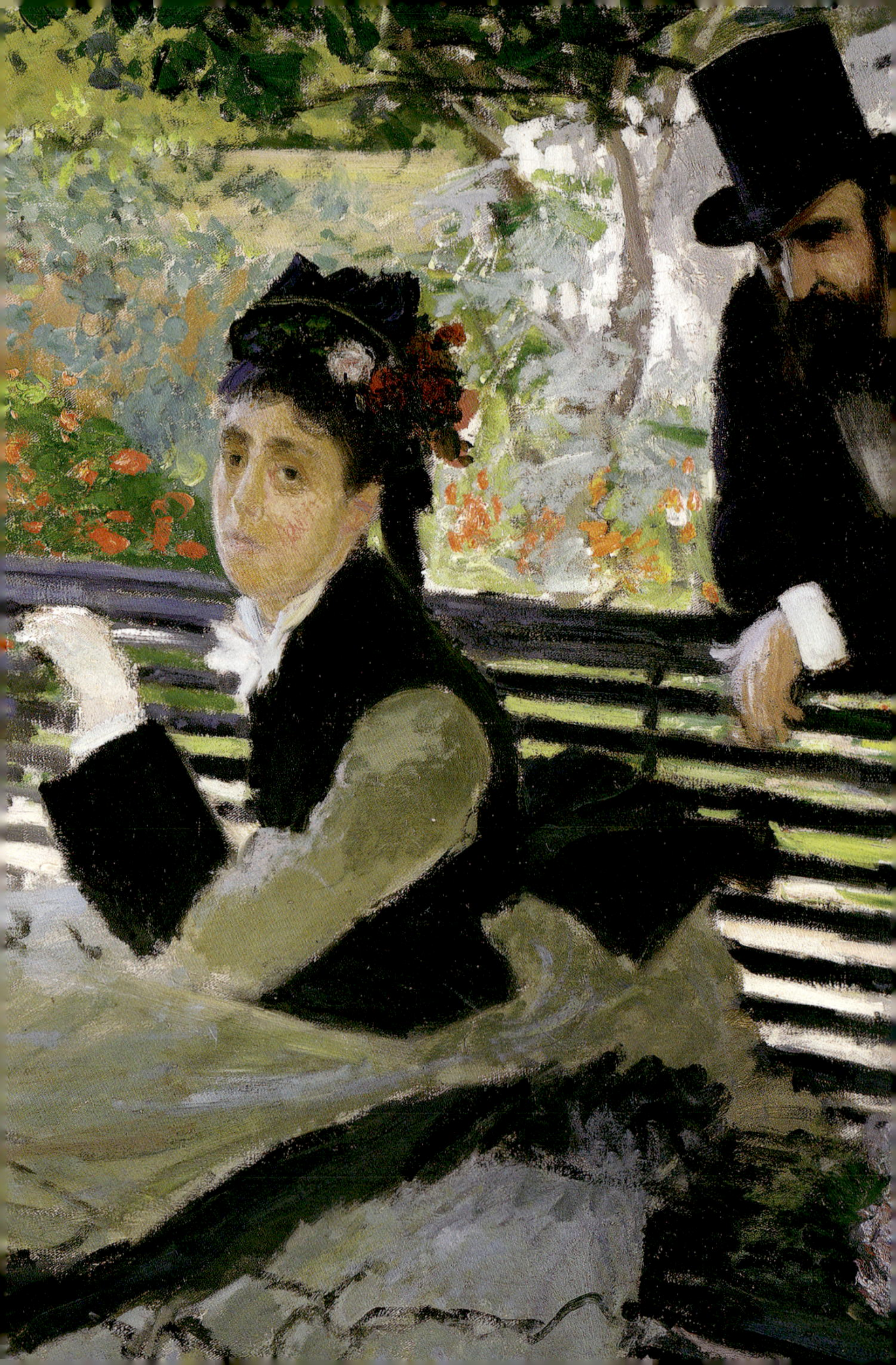

Claude Monet (1840–1926)

Unease in the shade of the trees

Camille Monet on a Garden Bench (The Bench), 1873
60.6 x 80.3 cm, New York, The Metropolitan Museum of Art,
The Walter H. and Leonore Annenberg Collection

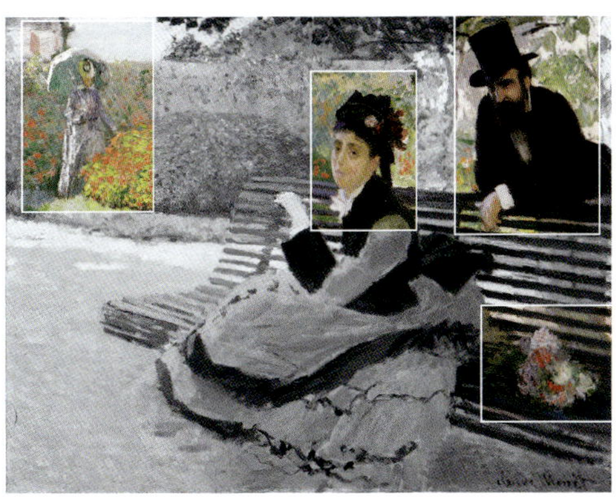

Three figures in a garden, two women, one man.
The woman on the bench can be clearly identified
– she is Camille, the artist's wife and his favourite
model. Leaning slightly forward, she turns towards
the viewer, looking out at us with large, dark
eyes. Beside her lies a bouquet of flowers, perhaps
brought by the gentleman leaning over the back
of the bench.

A horizontal stroke of the brush indicates that
Camille is holding a letter in her white-gloved hand.
Art historians suspect that it may be news of a death
or a letter of condolence. "A piece of bad news
awaited my wife … her father died yesterday," wrote
Monet on 23 September 1873, the period during
which this undated canvas must have been painted.
For Claude Monet, these were enormously prod-
uctive years; again and again he painted the banks
of the Seine, meadows, fields, and the garden we see
here. It lay in rural Argenteuil and belonged to the
house into which Monet moved at the end of 1871
with his young wife and four-year-old son Jean.

The suburb was then a popular destination amongst
Parisians, who came to row and sail on the Seine.
It is familiar to art lovers through the pictures
of Monet, Auguste Renoir, Édouard Manet and
Gustave Caillebotte, all of whom endeavoured to
capture – in *plein air* painting beside the river,
away from their city studios – light, air, and the
reflections on the water. Argenteuil thereby became
one of the chief theatres of the golden era of
Impressionist painting.

Monet painted the garden, and Camille, too,
over and over again. At first sight, these are harmonious, bucolic paintings that speak of elegant
city-dwellers who are enjoying country life in idyllic
nature. Yet there is something disquieting about a
painting like *The Bench*, because the viewer is unable
to fathom the relationships between the figures,
because he senses a story and doesn't know what it is.

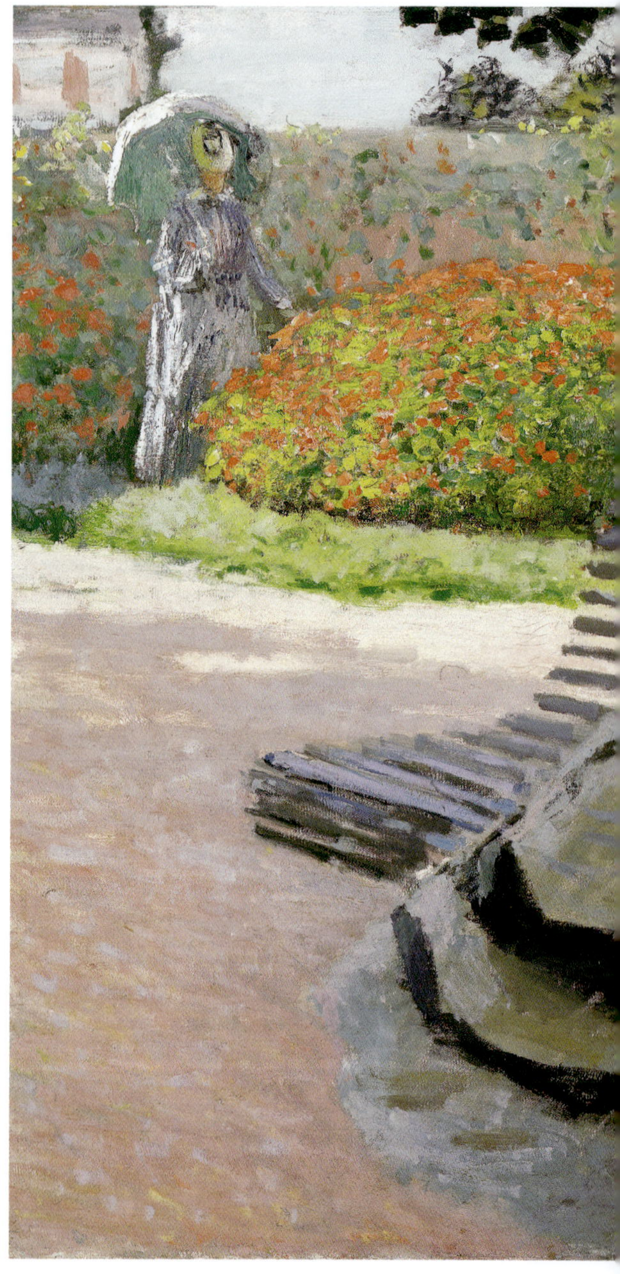

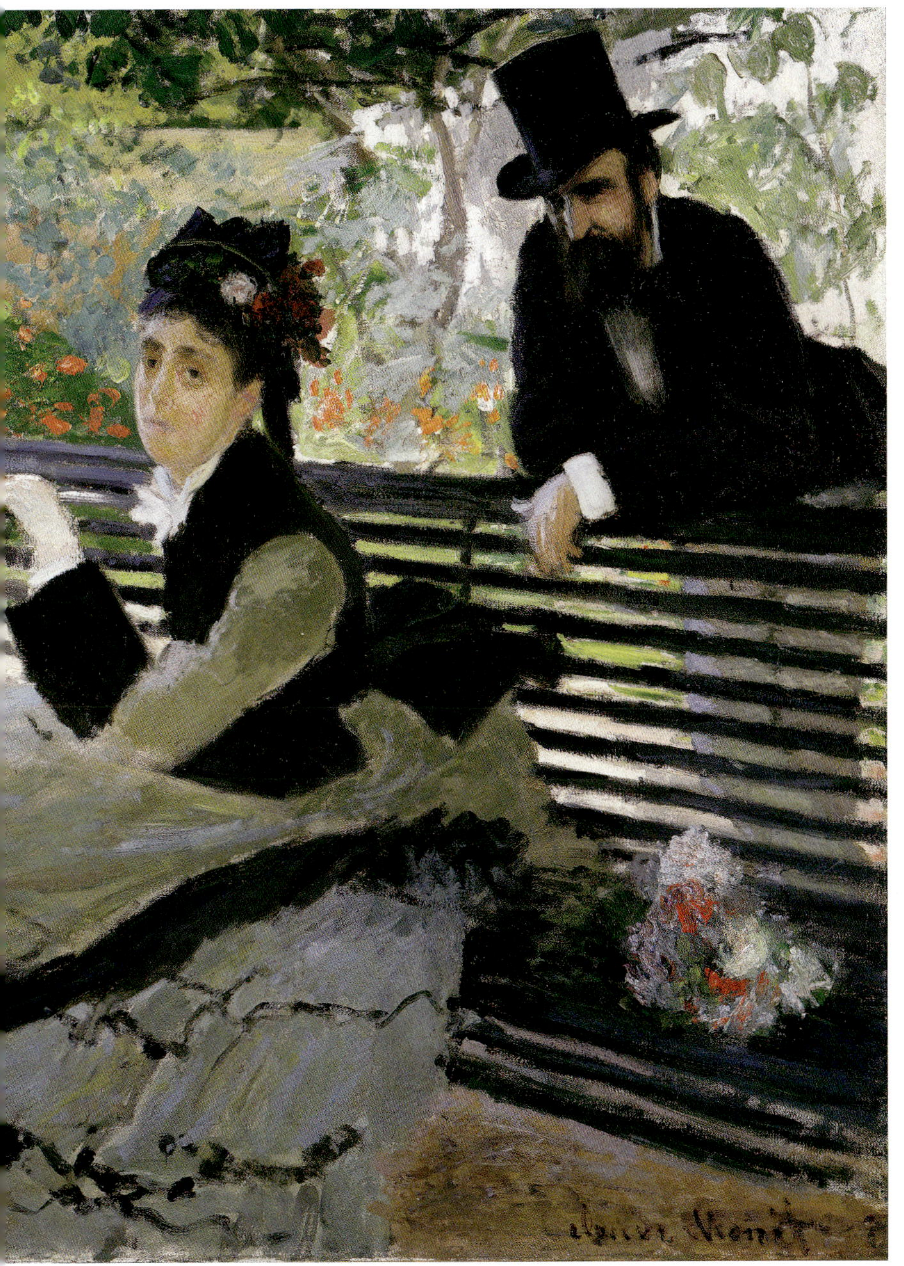

Out of poverty at last

In the background, a woman beneath a parasol is studying the flourishing bed of geraniums. She is standing in such a way, however, that she can also see the other two figures. Above her parasol can be seen a corner of the house that Monet started renting in late 1871. The house and garden were situated in the better part of Argenteuil. Monet paid 1,000 francs a year in rent; by way of comparison, a factory worker took home about 2,500 francs over the same period. Monet was now earning a decent salary, albeit only since recently.

He came from a middle-class but impoverished grocer's family from Le Havre. In 1859 he moved to Paris. He was financially supported by a wealthy aunt, Madame Lecat, who demanded in return a regular lifestyle, hard work, and professional success. If he failed her, she stopped his allowance. The young artist felt ill at ease in the established art academies, and left them in order to experiment with new motifs and techniques in the open air. Only a few of his works were accepted into the official Salons, and for years he led a life that can be romantically described as Bohemian, but which in reality bordered on absolute poverty.

Begging letters to his wealthier friends testify to his state of affairs: Monet had debts and feared the imminent arrival of the bailiffs. The painters Frédéric Bazille and Gustave Caillebotte helped the "starving" artist, and before Renoir – himself hardly rich – left his parents' house to visit Monet, he would stuff his pockets full of bread. Things with Monet, who was by now living with his model Camille, were "pitiful", reported Renoir in 1869: "They don't even eat every day."

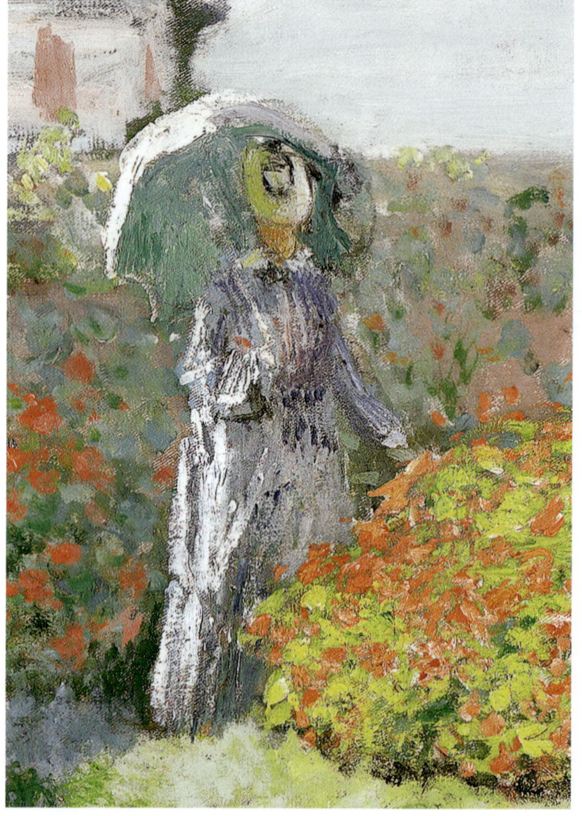

But then Monet met the gallery-owner Paul Durand-Ruel, who became his dealer. By the age of 31, the painter could afford a house and garden in Argenteuil. In 1872 he sold paintings worth a total of 12,100 francs, and in 1873 – the year in which he painted *The Bench* – he earned 24,800 francs, roughly the annual income of a Parisian doctor or lawyer. He was now able to order wine by the case from Bordeaux and hire a cook, nursemaid and gardener. But he remained behind with the rent, didn't pay his laundry bills, and continued to ask his friends for help – old habits. Monet was a man with no head for money. A man, however, who also believed he should live as munificently as his rich aunt, upon whom he had been dependent for so many years.

This is illustrated by Monet's pictures of his garden. If we compare them both with each other and with a painting by Renoir, showing his friend Monet at his easel in the garden, it becomes

clear that the garden in Argenteuil
cannot have looked as park-like
as it appears in *The Bench*. The
flourishing bed of geraniums, if it
existed at all, is a reflection less of
reality than of a life Monet longed
for. The same bed of geraniums is
found in his painting of the gardens of his Aunt Lecat and also
in a picture by Caillebotte of his
family's country estate. It must
have been something of a status
symbol. The fact that Monet
allocates it so much space on the
canvas shows that it was important to him.

No woman of the world

For a long time she was just the
artist's mistress and spurned by
his family as the "unmarried
mother of his bastard son". Now
at last, the 26-year-old Camille
Léonie Doncieux could show
herself in elegant surroundings as
the respectable Madame Monet.
Her pose seems a little strained
and she is dressed more in the
style of the city than the country.
The dark ribbon on her hat, the
black velvet of her bodice, and the
black velvet trim along the hem
of her dress may all be signs of
mourning. All these things were
expensive, elegant and highly
fashionable – as a glance through the pages of the
magazine *La mode illustrée* of 1873 reveals.

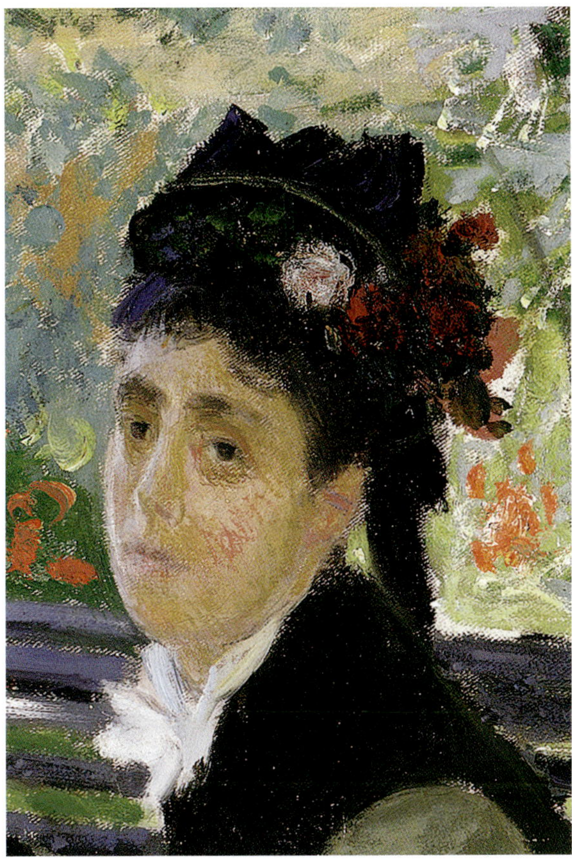

Camille came from a petit-bourgeois background.
In 1865 she started working as a model for Monet.
A very beautiful young woman, she wore an expression of fascinating arrogance on her pale face. But
"when you see Camille walking", noted a middle-
class observer, "the provocative way in which she
stumps along the pavement, you can immediately
tell she is not a woman of the world". She was certainly not treated as one. Although, when Camille
fell pregnant, Monet did not take his father's advice
and immediately break off the relationship, he
nevertheless departed hastily for his aunt's country
estate, in order to reassure her that he had not "gone

astray" and thereby safeguard his monthly cheque.
He left Camille behind in Paris, heavily pregnant
and penniless. He found it difficult to adjust to
the new responsibilities of having a family. He
acknowledged his son, but waited another three
years before marrying Camille in 1870. It was the first
year of the Franco-Prussian War, and as a married
man Monet would not have to do military service.

During their seven years together in Argenteuil,
Monet painted his wife over and over again. Apart
from the fact that she remained his favourite model,
however, no other evidence of his affection or love
for her or his children has survived. Monet condes-
cendingly describes Camille in a letter as a "good
girl" who must be "sensible".

His behaviour was not untypical. Afraid of breaching the conventions of his day and his class, Monet's elder artist colleague, Édouard Manet (1832–1883) went so far as to conceal the existence of his mistress, the piano teacher Suzanne Leenhoff, from his family and friends for thirteen whole years, maintaining her in a small apartment. He married her only after his father's death, but never recognized the son they had together. Suzanne had to refer to him all her life as her "little brother".

Camille, too, showed she could be "sensible", and even accepted the presence of another woman under her own roof. Following the ruin of his patron Ernest Hoschedé, Monet invited him, his wife, and six children to come and live with the Monet family. It was the pious and dutiful Alice Hoschedé who nursed Camille when, after the birth of a second son in 1878, she fell ill with cancer of the uterus and died the following year. In contrast to Camille, Alice was a "woman of the world". She became Monet's influential, respected companion and, after the death of her own husband, the artist's second wife.

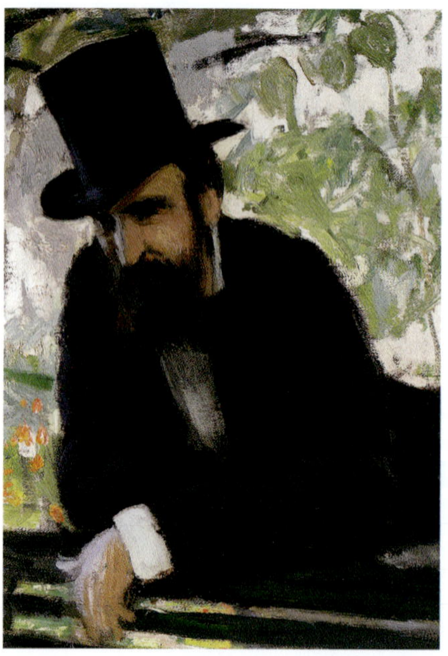

Neighbour or messenger of death?

Three figures in a summer garden, arranged in such a way that the viewer suspects there is a hidden connection between them. The black-bearded, black-coated man leaning over the back of the bench and coming very close to Camille has been interpreted by some as an admirer, by others as Death, or at least one of his messengers. Later, however, Monet remembered the man much more prosaically as a neighbour from Argenteuil.

We meet the same man again in two famous paintings by Édouard Manet. In *Le Déjeuner sur l'herbe*, the picture that caused a scandal in 1863, he is seated on the grass beside a naked female model (cf. *What Great Paintings Say*, Volume III). He is wearing a light suit, appropriate for a country picnic. In *Music in the Tuileries Gardens* of 1862, he is much more formally dressed, in a top hat, as he mingles with the elegant crowd. He bears a close resemblance to the present visitor behind the bench – the same dark beard, the same sideburns, even the same slightly stooped pose.

Manet's very wealthy family had long owned a country house on the other side of the Seine from Argenteuil. Édouard became infected by Monet's enthusiasm for painting out of doors and often went to visit him, bringing his younger brother, Eugène, with him. Documentary evidence compiled by art historians indicates that this latter is the neighbour and supposed messenger of death in the present picture. When Monet painted *The Bench*, Eugène Manet was 40 years old and a year later became engaged to the artist Berthe Morisot. He was very popular for his cheery disposition, and in Monet's portrait of him here, the possibility that he may be smiling behind his dark beard cannot be dismissed.

Eugène also painted, but considered himself to have little talent. His contribution to art took the form of selfless support of his artist friends. He had time to spare, was financially independent, and did not need to practise a profession. Without his ability to mediate between the egocentric personalities involved and to persuade them to reach agreement, the first exhibition of "Independent Artists", staged in 1874, might never have taken place. (It was at this exhibition that Monet would show the picture *Impression, Sunrise* that would give the Impressionists their name.) Even as he was painting *The Bench*, Monet was involved in the arguments surrounding the organization of the exhibition.

Bande à Manet – Manet's gang – the group of artist friends were called. They included Renoir, who only a little while previously had stuffed his pockets full of bread for the starving Monet. They watched each other work, motivated each other. Monet recalled: "Manet, excited by the colours and the light, embarked on a picture in the open air of people beneath the trees. While he was working, Renoir came along. He in turn was captivated by the charm of the moment. He asked me for my palette, a brush, and a canvas, sat down next to Manet and started painting."

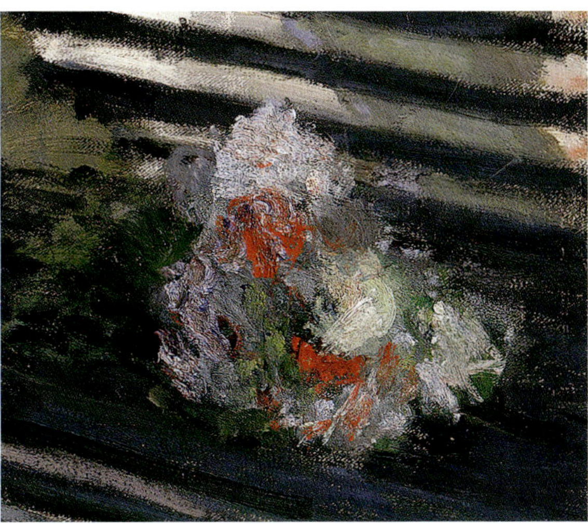

People vanish

Contemporaries upbraided the Impressionists for the speed at which they worked: the bunch of flowers is tossed onto the canvas with a few passing strokes of the brush, using wet paint on wet paint and with no corrections, just an accent of colour catching the eye on the dark bench. Monet wanted to capture the mood of the moment. The bed of geraniums, the woman with the parasol, and the overgrown wall all lie in full sunlight, which brings out the vibrant red of the blooms. In the shade, by contrast, the palette is muted. Monet deploys grey-blue brushstrokes on the gravel path, bench, dress, and even bridge of the nose to characterize areas of broken light.

Capturing the changes in the light at different times of the day and year and in varying weather conditions became Monet's obsession, one which he pursued above all in series of paintings of the same subject, such as the façade of Rouen cathedral and the water lilies in his garden in Giverny.

These series show only buildings, flowers and landscapes; people, if present at all, are reduced to brief brushstrokes. *The Bench* of 1873 marks a watershed in Monet's oeuvre; it is the last painting in which people are the main focus. That same year Monet painted another, larger-scale view of his garden from almost the same angle. Here, however, the people are relegated to the background, leaving just the bench and a table bearing the remains of a meal in the foreground. The painting is entitled *The Luncheon* – but there is no one actually eating.

Monet continued to paint single figures and portraits, but people played no further role in his cityscapes and landscapes. The three figures in his Argenteuil garden are merely – so his later pictures would seem to suggest – means to an end: they provide him with an opportunity to paint variations in light, and specifically the different effects produced by sunlight as it falls either directly or indirectly on skin, clothes, path, flowers and bench.

Monet was well aware that this fixation upon the visual delights of the surface was not without its dangers. "I was once standing at the bedside of one who had passed away who was and shall always remain very dear to me," he later wrote, meaning Camille. "I caught myself watching her tragic temples, almost mechanically searching for the sequence of changing shades that death was imposing upon her rigid face. Blue, yellow, grey, whatever. Such was the state I was in …"

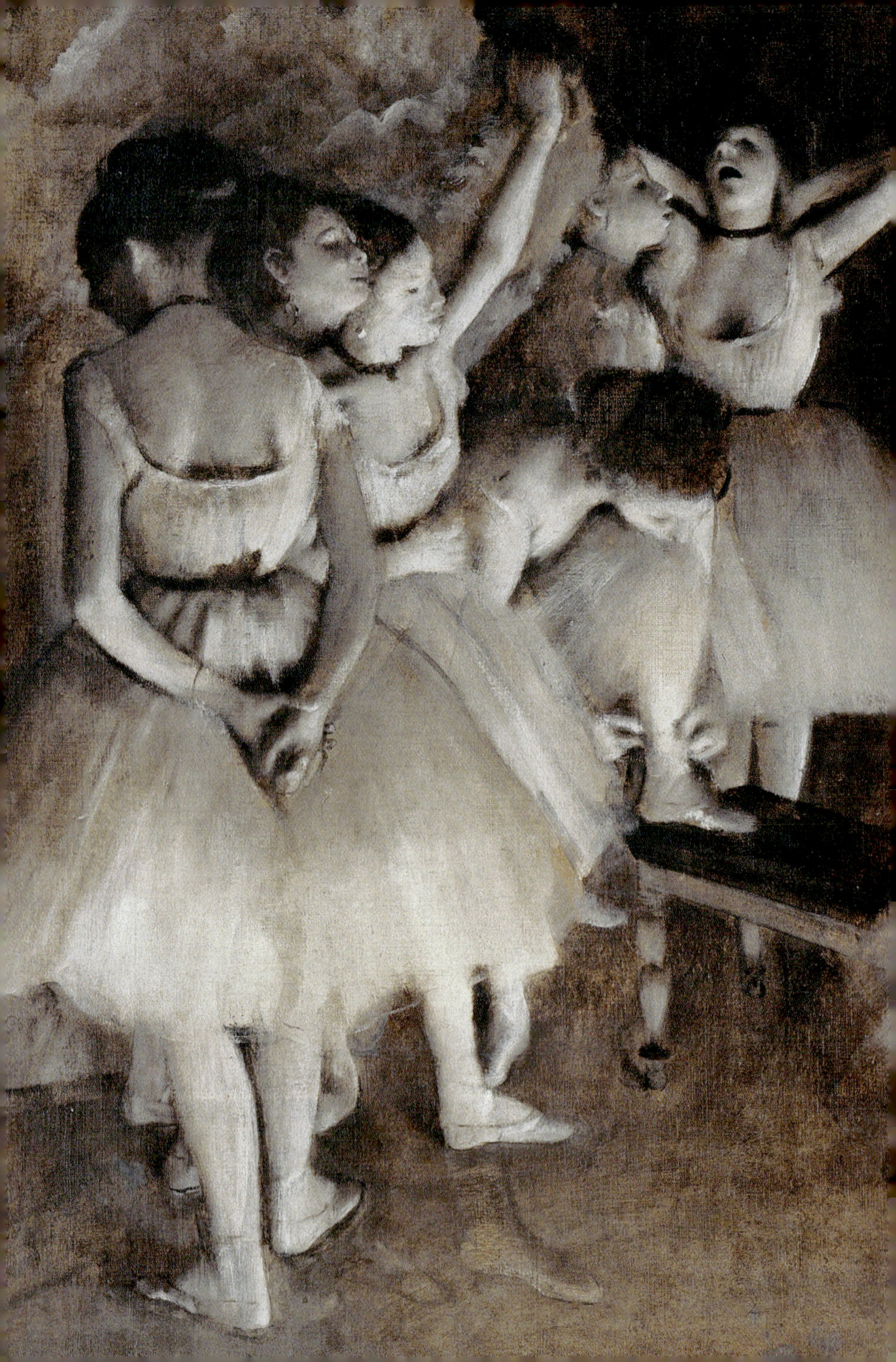

Edgar Degas (1834–1917)

A look behind the scenes

The Rehearsal on the Stage, 1873
65 x 81 cm, Paris, Musée d'Orsay

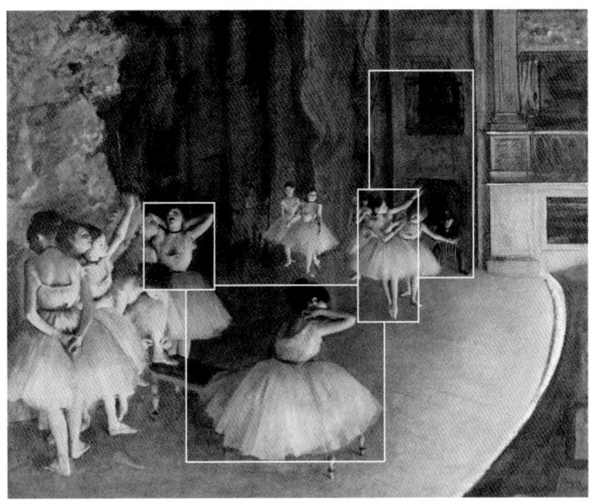

In 1873, when Edgar Degas painted this picture, "tout Paris" revelled in the romance of the ballet. But the elegance and grace of the ballerinas, who appeared to float across the stage, was not its only source of appeal. It was the done thing for a Parisian gentleman of leisure to maintain a "liaison" at the theatre, while dancing offered many girls their only opportunity to escape from poverty. The painting "The Rehearsal on the Stage" is now in the Musée d'Orsay, Paris.

At his death in 1917, the 83-year-old Edgar Degas left behind some 1,200 paintings and sculptures, more than 300 of them depicting ballerinas: at the bar, at their toilet, resting, or rehearsing – witness the present work – on a half-lit stage. It was through Degas that ballet attained its renown as a subject of paint-

ing, though by Degas' time, the stage art itself was in dire need of innovation.

The history of ballet had begun some 300 years earlier in the form of a ceremonial courtly dance whose function was to demonstrate the glory of the sovereign. Only when ballet became professional were the dancers joined by women. During the Romantic era, the female dancers became the centre of attraction, appearing to float across the stage, scorning gravity. The new technique of the toe dance made ballerinas more suited to typical Romantic parts, such as elves, spirits or fairies. Their male partners receded into the background, their main task from now on to support or lift the ballerinas, emphasizing the latters' lightness and grace.

The Romantic ballet was born in the 1830s and 1840s and, in Paris, was the dominant style even

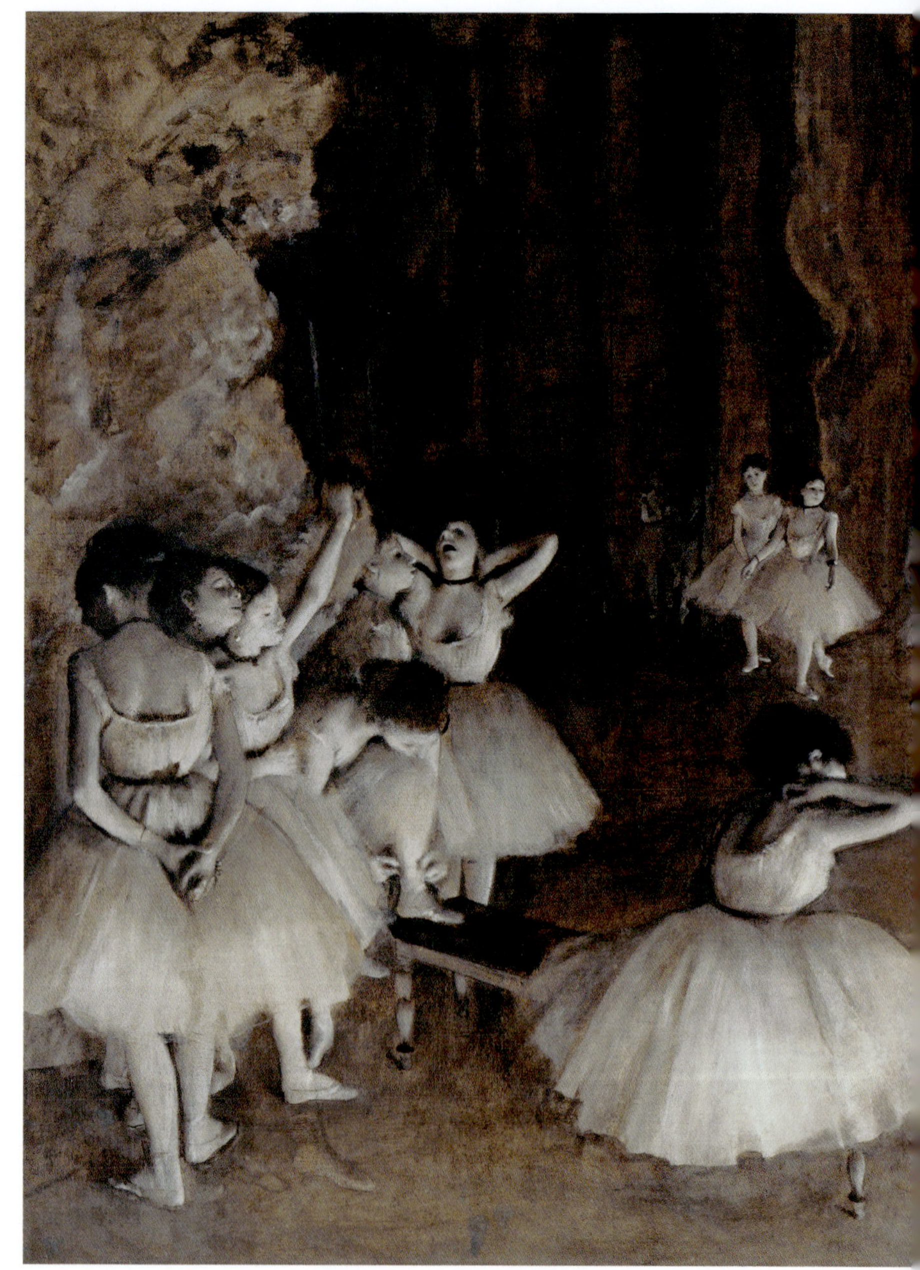

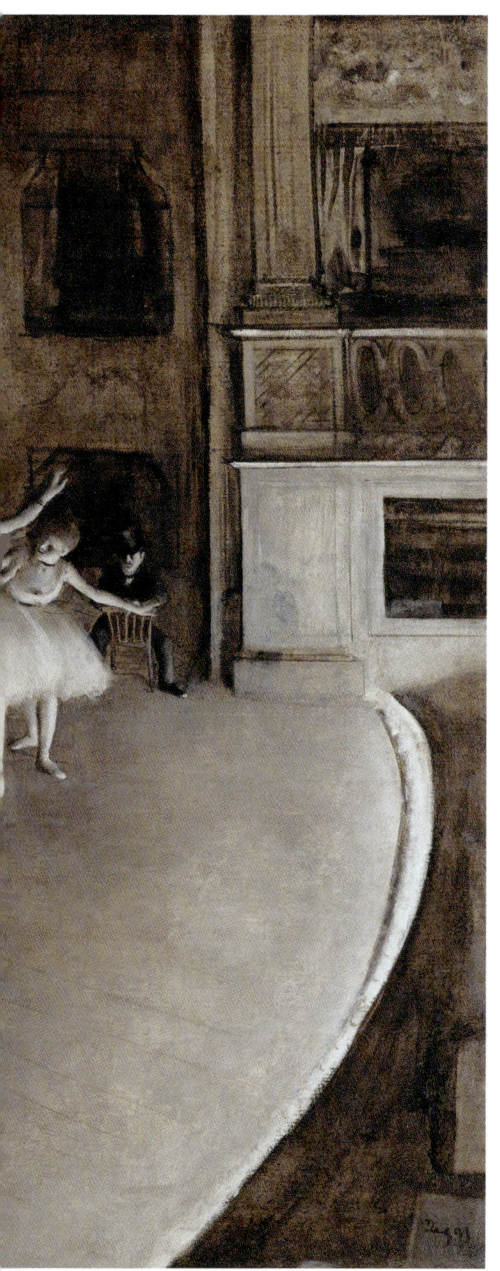

when Degas came to paint the present picture in 1873. In literature and theatre, Romanticism had been largely repudiated by more realistic modes, while in Italy, a choreographer had attempted to convert current events, like the construction of a tunnel through the Alps, into dance. No such development took place in Paris, however, where the theatre-going public stuck largely to what it knew.

Degas's exclusive preference for female dancers conformed to contemporary taste. Eventually, helped by Tchaikovsky's music, ballet was given a new lease of life at St Petersburg; but it was not until the 20th century that male dancers regained some of the recognition they had once enjoyed.

"Long, lascivious legs"

The lightness of the Romantic technique allowed the ballerinas to lay aside all heavy clothing and shoes. Elves floated better without such unnecessary ballast: ballet shoes were now made without their formerly wide soles and heels, and the ballet costume itself was reduced to a sleeveless bodice and flared skirt of white muslin. The skirt billowed when the ballerina alighted, prolonging the illusion of her floating gently to earth. Originally calf-length, it had shortened to the knee by Degas's day.

Ballerinas had begun to reveal more of their bodies, especially their legs, covered only by thin tights. Though this favoured artistic expression, it was also seen as an affront to conventional morality; it was considered indecent in the 19th century for ladies to show their legs. Heinrich Heine cites two English ladies who "were barely able to express their disgust at what met their eyes when the curtain rose and those wonderful, short-skirted ballerinas began a graceful, elaborate movement, stepping out with long, lovely, lascivious legs and, with a sudden bacchanalian leap, falling into the arms of the male dancers who came springing towards them … Their bosoms grew pink with indignation. 'Shocking! For shame, for shame!' they constantly groaned."

Understandably, few male spectators showed signs of outrage. Unlike women and

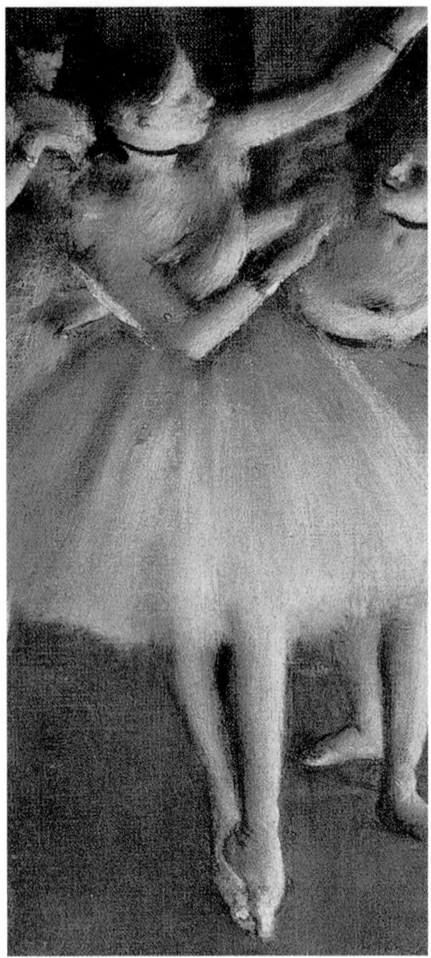

backgrounds, with perhaps a laundress or seamstress as a mother, they were as likely as not to have grown up in a dark, one-room flat overlooking a back yard. The theatre offered one of the few opportunities to escape a life of poverty and misery. With luck, they would be accepted, at the age of eight or nine, into the Opéra dance school, the Académie Royale. They made their first stage appearance at the age of fourteen or fifteen, and retired twenty years later. Though a girl of mediocre talent might never be more than an ordinary dancer in the corps de ballet, earning no more on stage than she would as a seamstress, she nonetheless had a better chance as a ballerina of attracting the attentions of a wealthy gentleman. A girl needed their patronising, self-serving attentions if she were to escape from hunger and that gloomy back room. Apart from anything else, male patronage could be advantageous in determining the outcome of professional rivalry between dancers.

Rear view of a career

The biography of almost every 19th-century Parisian ballerina contains the name of a rich, and more or less powerful patron. One example serves to illustrate many: that of Emma Livry and her mother. Emma's mother, an unsuccessful ballerina at the Paris Opéra, had become the mistress of a baron; Emma was their child. The baron eventually left Emma's mother to marry a princess, and was replaced by a viscount. The viscount was said to have had a whole string of relationships with ballerinas. He "knew all the scandals and intrigues, was informed of all the storms in teacups that constantly shook this small, inward-looking world. He liked to intervene, too, taking sides, hoping to influence matters to further his own interests and, more importantly, those of his mistress."

He exerted his influence to help Emma, the daughter of his mistress. He ensured that her debut in the corps de ballet did not go unnoticed, put in a good word for her with the director of the Opéra, used his good offices in the imperial household, negotiated her contract himself, and even protected her against a series of intrigues designed to delay the premiere. In the end Emma Livry's performance in *La Sylphide* in 1858 was a sensational success; she was sixteen years old at the time. She died at the age of 21, her short skirt set alight by a gas lamp behind the scenes.

girls, men were given more or less free rein to seek gratification for their erotic urges. For them, ballet took on a new meaning, and the pronounced tendency among 19th-century choreographers to bring ballerinas up to the footlights more frequently than their male colleagues surely cannot be ascribed solely to the artistic gain derived from the introduction of the toe dance.

The ladies in the boxes may occasionally have been consoled by the knowledge that their stage rivals were deemed unmarriageable. From low-class

Patronage of ballerinas was a pleasureable diversion for gentlemen of leisure from traditionally affluent backgrounds. Since the latter were disinclined to be punctual, the ballet was not introduced before the second act. The Paris premiere of Richard Wagner's *Tannhäuser*, with ballet included in the first act, was booed out in 1861. Though not the only reason for the flop, premature entry of the dancers was certainly a major contributing factor.

The power of subscribers

The ballerinas in Degas' painting are nameless, like the gentleman sitting on the chair. He may be the director or choreographer, or perhaps the especially privileged friend of one of the girls. The theatre itself is easily identified: the Grand Opéra in the Rue Le Peletier. It was here that Emma Livry's star rose so briefly, and here, too, that Richard Wagner's *Tannhäuser* flopped.

The theatre in the Rue Le Peletier had 1,095 seats; it became the Grand Opéra as a result of an assassination in 1821. The son of the French heir to the throne was attacked near the building in the Rue de Richelieu which had housed the opera hitherto. The injured man was carried into the theatre. Meanwhile, his friends sent for the Archbishop of Paris to administer the last sacrament to the dying man. However, the bishop agreed to enter the building only on condition that it was torn down afterwards. This was done – an impressive demonstration of the Church's power in its struggle against the theatre as an immoral institution.

The narrow boxes vaguely indicated behind the sitting gentleman were a characteristic feature of

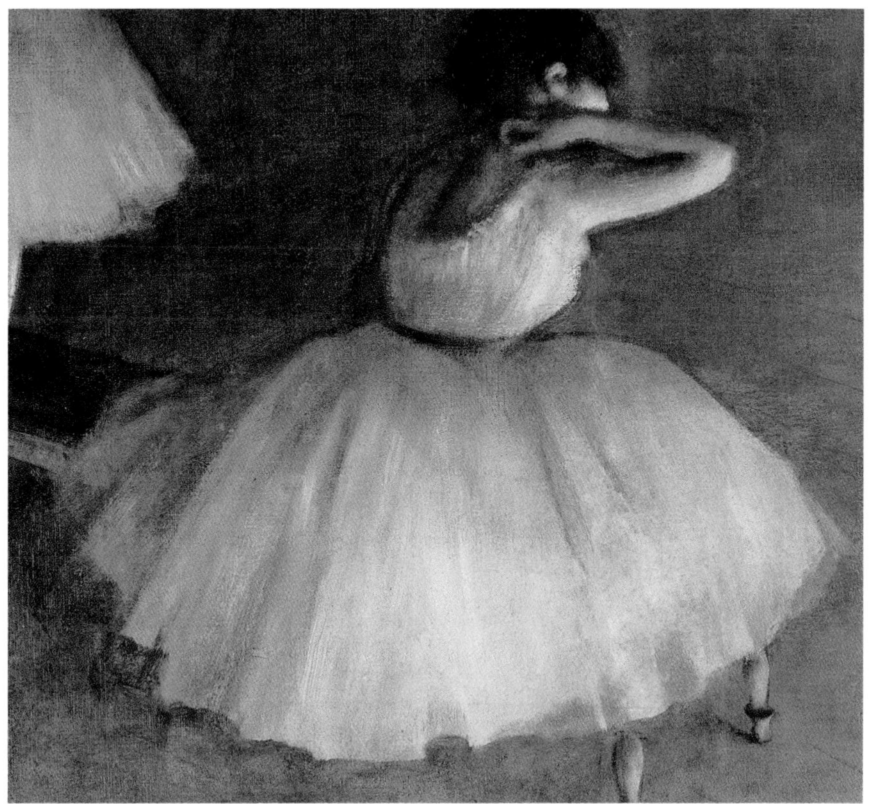

the new Grand Opéra in the Rue Le Peletier. These boxes, built above rather than in front of the stage, were referred to as *baignoires* or *boîtes tiroirs*, in other words as "baths" or "drawers". They were reserved for the director, or for influential subscribers who were more interested in physical proximity than the aesthetic experience.

The power of subscribers had continually grown in the 19th century. The future of a theatre now depended less on the good will of a local ruler than on its ability to sell seats. Subscribers could rent a box, or a seat in the stalls (for men only), which, during the season, they occupied at least once a week. Their interest was in constant need of renewed stimulus, and in their attempt to provide it, theatres would occasionally seek recourse to methods that were less than artistic: in 1831 the Director of the Grand Opéra allowed access to the Foyer de la Danse, the dancers' rehearsal room, to some of his more refined clientele. Degas would often sit there, sketching the scene. It was a large room with a golden frieze below the ceiling and imitation marble columns along the wall, a high mirror and the usual training bars, hardly comparable with those neon-lit, highly functional rooms with mirrors covering all four walls in which today's dancers practise their steps.

The Foyer de la Danse was open during intervals and after the performance, only to the girls' mothers and certain male subscribers. The purpose of this was obvious. The modern equivalent might be the welcome-lounge of a massage parlour.

In October 1873 the theatre in the Rue Le Peletier was destroyed by fire. A new, magnificent building, the Palais Garner, where ballets are still performed today, was opened in January 1875. A competition for the design of the new opera house was held in 1860. Both the text of the announcement and, ultimately, the building itself betrayed the social function of opera at the time: artistic performance seen as the appropriate ambience for the cultivation of social status and gratification of the male libido.

Boxes, according to design recommendations, were to have an adjoining salon whither parties who wished to converse might withdraw. The plans were to include *boites tiroirs* [boxes built above the stage], too, which remained in use until 1917. The building was to have three separate entrances: one for the Emperor, who no longer existed after 1870, one for the subscribers and a third for the public. The broad staircase to the first floor, imitating the stairway at the Rue Le Peletier, had 63 steps. The much cosseted subscribers were not expected to alter their habits. They were provided with a special lounge for intervals, and the Foyer de la Danse was transformed into a palatial hall with chandeliers, stucco and the portraits of famous ballerinas. At the same time, however, the director raised the entry fee; only gentlemen who subscribed three evenings a week were allowed access.

Like looking through a keyhole

Degas made his preliminary sketches in one of the front boxes, executing the painting some time later in his studio. By the time he painted *The Rehearsal*

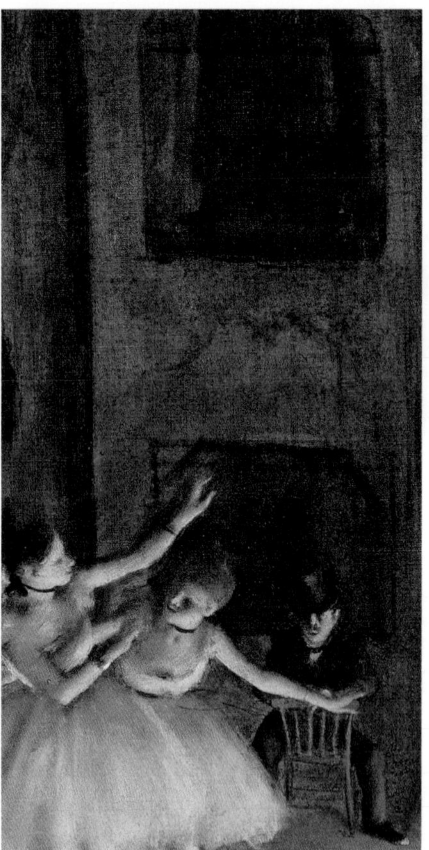

on the Stage, the theatre in Rue Le Peletier had probably burned down. Like all contemporary stages, it was lit by dangerous, open gas flames. The lights were generally situated at the edge of the apron. Degas marks the footlights with a series of bright brushstrokes.

He was almost 40 at the time, but was not one of the ballerinas' lovers. On the contrary, he lived the life of a reclusive ascetic, rarely leaving his studio. He needed to be alone, remaining a bachelor, declaring, on one occasion: "A painter has no private life!"

Besides ballerinas, there were two other subjects he favoured: women at their bath and jockeys at the races. All three have one thing in common: movement. The details printed here make it clear that Degas was less interested in the ballerinas as individual characters than in their movement and gestures. Their faces are usually pale, anonymous. With regard to their gestures, what interested him most was what they did more or less sub-consciously when they were not playing to the public. Degas paintings are full of women combing, washing and dressing themselves – automatically, as it were. "Up until now, the portrayal of nudity has always presupposed exposure to the public eye," he wrote, "but the women in my paintings are simple, good people, thinking of nothing and pre-occupied with nothing but their own bodies"; it was "like looking through a keyhole." On another occasion he referred to them as "animals in the act of washing themselves".

In the *The Rehearsal on the Stage*, too, the girls stand or sit about quite unself-consciously: yawn-ing, scratching, stretching, utterly self-absorbed and attending to their own needs. There was a grace here which fascinated Degas. It was a quality he found in dancers who were resting between scenes, but also – on few and fortunate occasions, and with a differ-ent level of intensity – in those who were actually

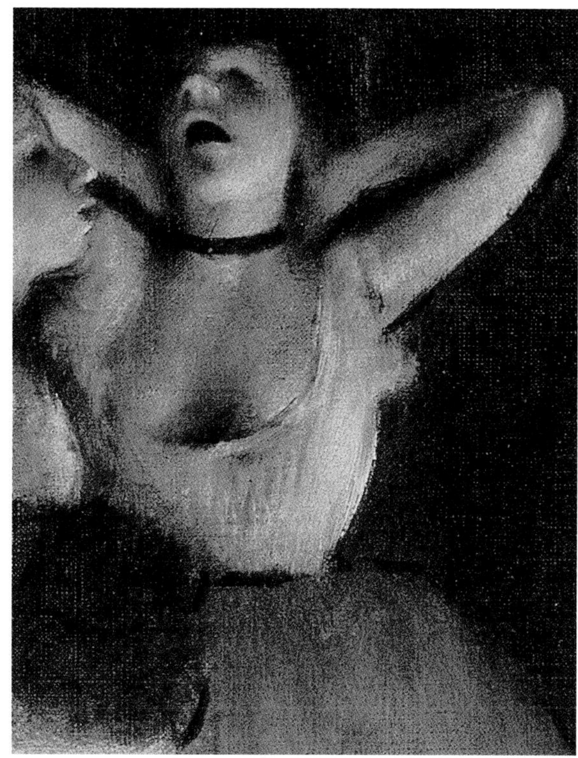

dancing: it was not the natural grace of a woman which interested him then, but a grace she had acquired by dint of artistry, the grace of a ballerina who is entirely engrossed in her art.

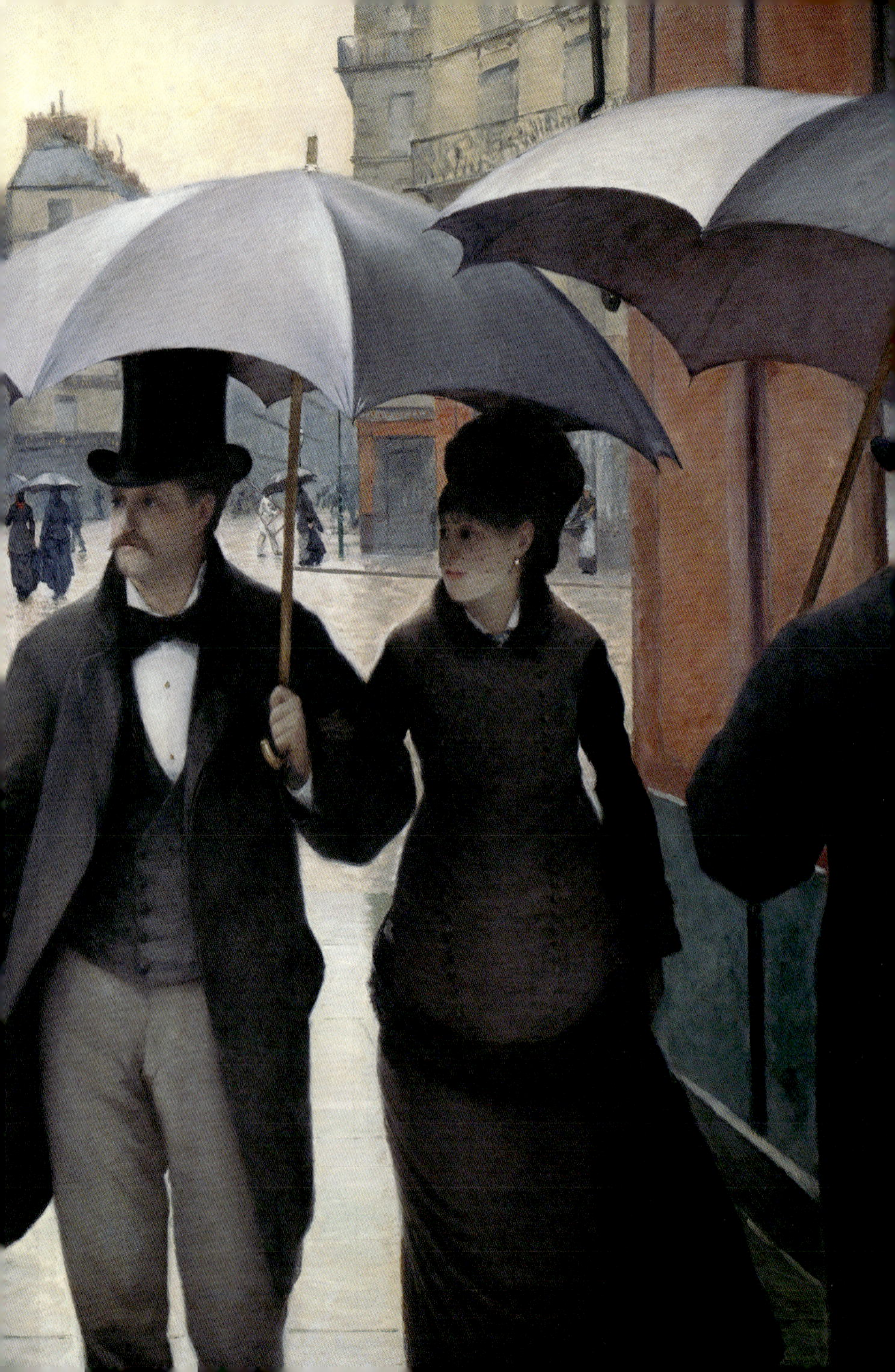

Gustave Caillebotte (1848–1894)

Under the umbrella, loneliness

Paris Street, Rainy Day, 1877
212 x 276 cm, The Art Institute of Chicago,
Charles H. and Mary F. S. Worcester Collection

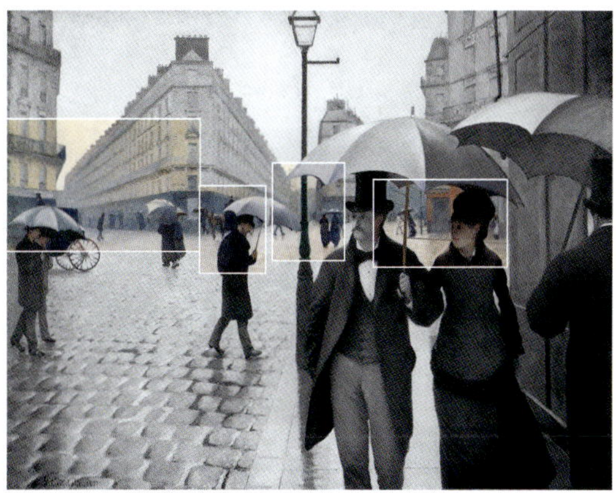

The first retrospective ever devoted to the French painter Gustave Caillebotte was mounted in 1994. By that time he had already been dead for 100 years. The large-scale exhibition, which was subtitled "Urban Impressionist", brought together over 100 portraits, interiors, still lifes, landscapes, and – to particularly impressive effect – large-format cityscapes. It travelled from Paris to Chicago and Los Angeles and introduced the public to an artist who had previously remained virtually unknown in both Europe and America.

Art historians were familiar with Gustave Caillebotte (1848– 1894) at best as an important friend and patron of the Impressionists. He provided the impoverished artists with financial assistance and purchased their pictures at a time when virtually no one else was prepared to do so. The fact that he was himself a painter and exhibited many of his pictures alongside those of the Impressionists became lost along the way. He never sold a single one of his works, because he didn't need to. Unlike his colleagues, he was a wealthy man from a wealthy background.

Even after his death, his paintings remained in the possession of his family. Few of them entered museum collections and they were only very rarely lent out to exhibitions. Nor, in the 20th century, did they enjoy the extraordinary popularity of the other Impressionists, since they were not available as reproductions. Only in the 1950s did the Caillebotte family start to sell his paintings; art historians at last got to see them and organized the first exhibitions in the United States. In 1964 *Paris Street, Rainy Day* was purchased by The Art Institute of Chicago.

The painting portrays a complex intersection in Paris on a wintry afternoon: broad avenues, a spacious view, uniform façades. It is the Paris that

can still be seen today. When
Caillebotte painted it in 1877,
it was new and modern.

A selfless patron

Caillebotte came from a wealthy
family belonging to the *haute
bourgeoisie*, a class to which a
number of people in the present
painting would also have belonged. His father had made his
money supplying beds to the
French army, and he bequeathed
to his widow and four sons several
apartment buildings in Paris and
a country estate. At the age of
26, following his father's death,
Caillebotte already had a considerable fortune.

He had studied law and then
painting under Léon Bonnat,
a highly regarded artist who
remained indebted to the academic tradition. Caillebotte was
unsatisfied by the mythological
and historical themes of academic
art, however, and joined up with
a group of artists who wanted to
get out of their studios and search
out natural, living light and contemporary subjects. They included
Auguste Renoir, Edgar Degas,
Claude Monet, Camille Pissarro
and Alfred Sisley, all somewhat
older than Caillebotte.

Unable or unwilling to exhibit
at the official Salon, they formed a
"society of painters, sculptors, and
engravers" and in 1874 mounted
their own exhibition. It caused a
scandal. The critics were horrified;
borrowing from the title of one
of the works submitted by Monet,
Impression, Sunrise, they coined
the term "Impressionists" to describe the young artists. Although
Caillebotte was not included
in that first exhibition, he was
represented by several works in
the group's second show, staged

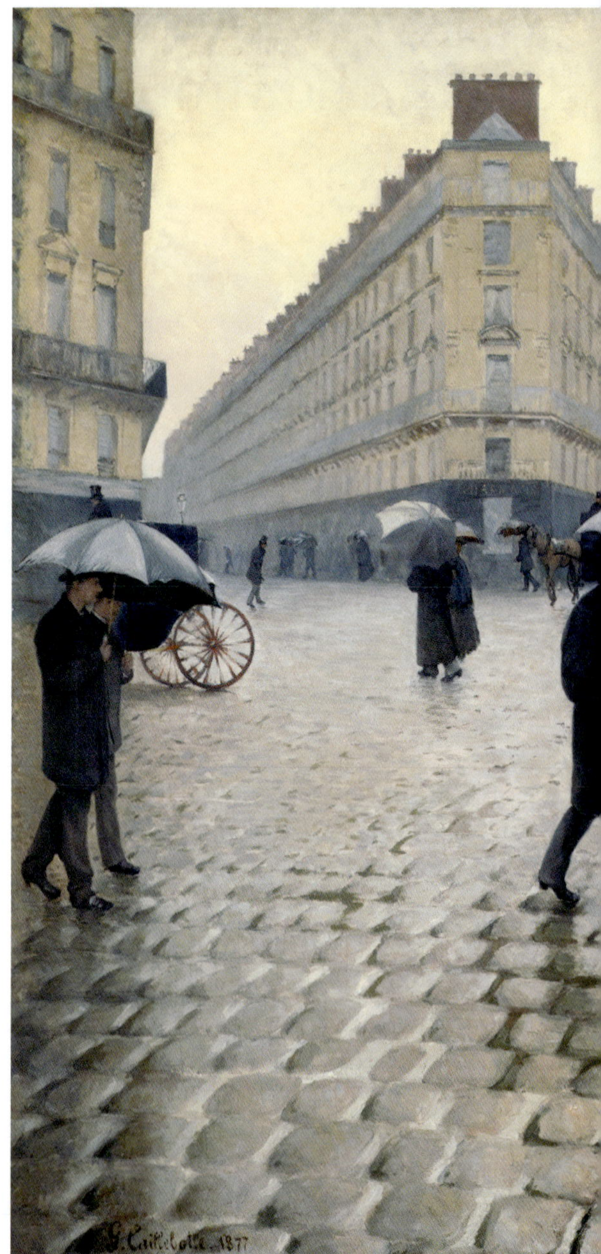

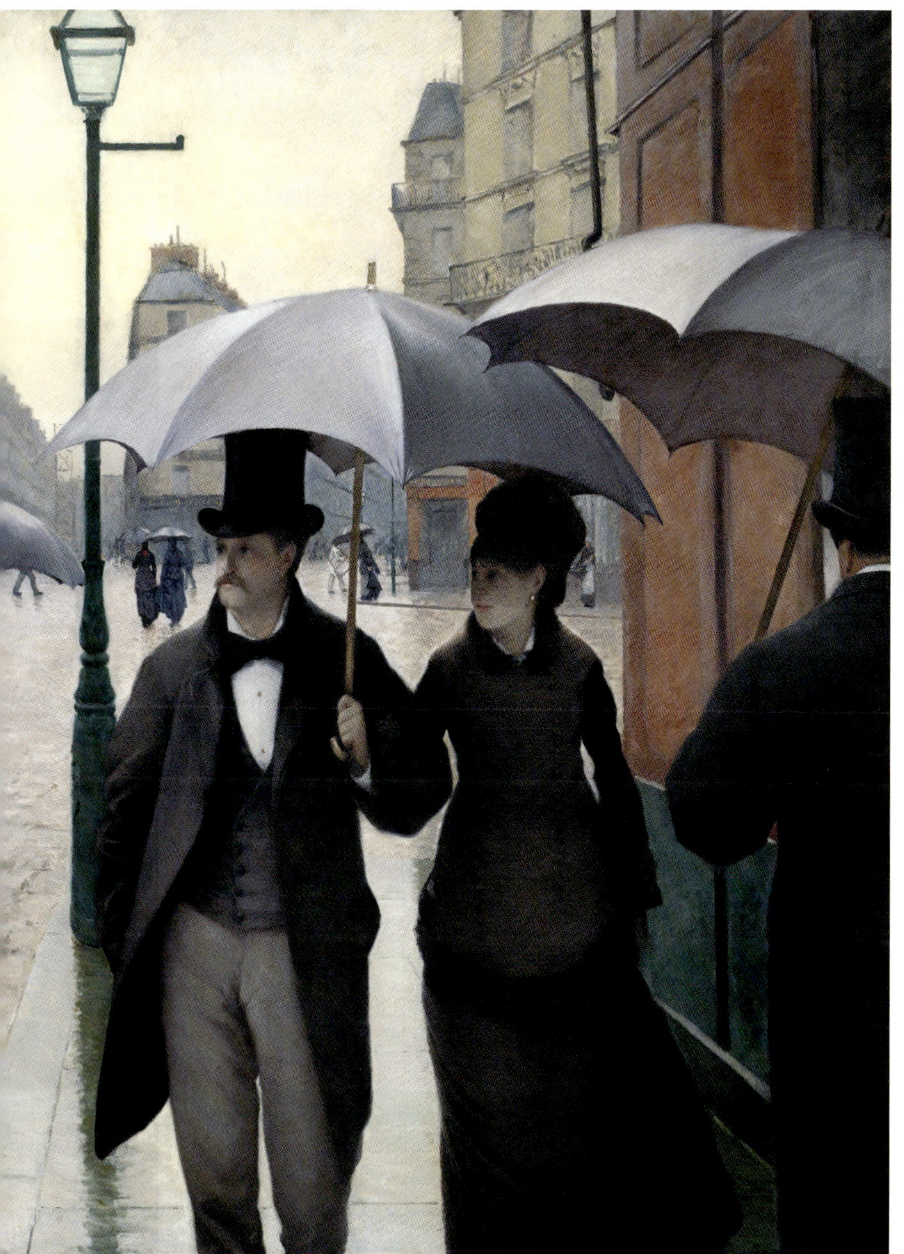

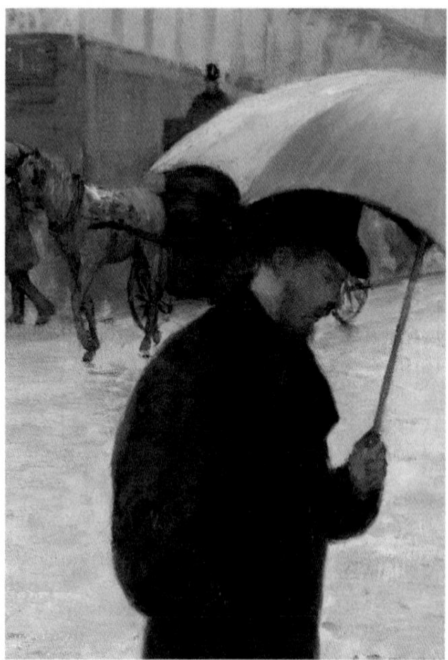

in 1876. At the third show, held in 1877, he again exhibited a number of works, amongst them *Paris Street, Rainy Day*. One of the critics, Georges Rivière, noted approvingly: "An intrepid seeker, on whom we pin well-founded hopes." Three years later, the novelist Joris-Karl Huysmans predicted that "some of his canvases will one day take their place alongside the best."

Huysmans was right, but even so, for nearly a century Caillebotte was thought of simply as an impresario and patron who rented exhibition rooms for the Impressionists, got the picture frames, took care of the advertising, and put up the money. In 1878 he made Pissarro a gift of 750 francs; he paid Monet's removal costs and rent and bought a total of eighteen of his paintings. He admired the colleagues who had turned their backs on tradition – perhaps because he also wanted to free himself from the bourgeois milieu from which he came.

In 1876 his younger brother died suddenly. Gustave subsequently felt prompted to draw up his own will. The terms of this will would make art history, by assuring the Impressionists belated but at long last public recognition. Caillebotte namely

bequeathed his collection to the French nation, albeit with the proviso that it was exhibited "neither in an attic nor in a provincial museum" but in an appropriate setting, and only when the public would accept such painting. That, Caillebotte felt, might take "twenty years or more".

He was not mistaken. It was not until 1897, three years after his death and following heated arguments, that his bequest was officially accepted. For the first time, 40 paintings by the Impressionists were now hung in a national institution, the Musée du Luxembourg.

The bequest included just one painting by Caillebotte himself, *Les Raboteurs de Parquets (The Floor Strippers)*. It was added by Renoir, his executor; modesty had prevented Caillebotte from forcing his own works upon the nation along with those of his admired colleagues.

Urban planner Baron Haussmann loved long lines

Although the title of the painting mentions just one anonymous Paris street, there are in fact several to be seen, all of which can be identified. Running from the foreground into the background is the rue de Turin; coming in from the left and crossing the centre of the composition is the rue de Moscou; and in the background we can also see rue Clapeyron. The intersection is today called the Place de Dublin and lies near the Gare Saint-Lazare.

These streets were laid out during Caillebotte's youth on a hill which lay beyond the old city limits and which had burgeoned into a residential district for the wealthy bourgeoisie. Not far away lay the – similarly newly designed – city centre, with its opera house and spacious boulevards lined with elegant cafés and expensive department stores.

This was all the work of Baron Georges Eugène Haussmann, Prefect of the Département of the Seine from 1853 to 1870. He had been instructed by Napoleon III to tear down the medieval city centre, with its narrow alleys and damp housing, after two cholera epidemics had claimed thousands of lives. No government had previously risked such a step, but Napoleon III wanted progress and better living conditions, and gave Haussmann his orders "to take Old Paris" with the "army" of his officials. The Baron not only took Old Paris, but also conquered new territories to the west of the city and transformed them into residential districts.

Huge loans were taken out to finance the ambitious project. The authoritarian regime gave the Prefect a free hand. Haussmann's department had sole responsibility for all new building, both public and private. From 1850, changes to the law paved the way for expropriation on a massive scale – even bypassing the legal process in the name of the public interest. Buildings were demolished and new ones were built, as property speculation fuelled increases in the price of land for development. The wheels of dispossession, wrote the novelist Émile Zola, turned like "a mighty machine which ploughed through Paris for fifteen years, producing fortunes and bankruptcies".

It was a period during which Caillebotte's father also grew rich. In 1866 he bought a plot of land with building permission "from the City of Paris, represented by Baron Haussmann," for 148,780 francs. When he died, his massive fortune lay largely in apartment buildings in the splendid new districts of Paris.

Although such buildings were the product of private enterprise, they were constructed under the supervision of the authorities and in line with strict regulations giving rise to the homogeneous architecture visible in Caillebotte's picture. Wide streets were to lead in a straight line from one square to another, or from one particularly important building to another, and in each case offer a spectacular view. Haussmann loved perspective and symmetry, and he liked to have streets converge upon a square like the arms of a star, as in the intersection portrayed here.

The new Paris was to consist not of detached houses, but of monumental apartment buildings housing luxury flats and employing uniform ashlar façades. The height of the eaves was stipulated for each district and usually extended to four or five storeys. The first floor and attic storey were required to have balcony railings running the entire length of the façade. Many of the city's squares and avenues continue to owe their aesthetic homogeneity and harmony to Baron Haussmann even today.

Streetlights and cobblestones recall the Commune

Caillebotte is said by his family to have executed the preparatory sketches for his canvas while seated inside a specially glazed "omnibus", a large horse-drawn carriage which protected him from the rain and cold. But "even when working from nature, one has to compose", as Degas said, and thus Caillebotte selects an angle that yields an almost geometrically structured canvas. At the centre of the composition stands a gaslight, its shadow falling towards us across the wet cobbles. Such standardized, industrially manufactured gaslights studded the streets of Haussmann's Paris at regular, rhythmic intervals, and Caillebotte, too, uses it as an ordering element, which serves to divide the composition vertically in two.

The picture is divided horizontally by the street running diagonally across it and by a line which passes through virtually every head, giving rise to a symmetrical cruciform construction that approaches Haussmann's own aesthetic preferences. This geometry is frequently and deliberately obscured, however: through the emphasis upon linear perspective, through the ever smaller figures of the passers-by, the eye is led into the background. The arching curves of the large umbrellas contrast with the verticals of the figures and façades. The man beneath the umbrella on the far right, cut off by the edge of the canvas, conveys the impression that this is merely a snapshot, a casual, momentary view, rather than a composition that has been carefully planned.

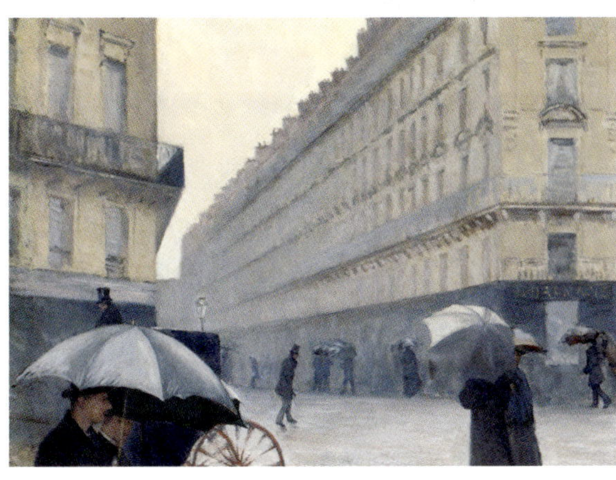

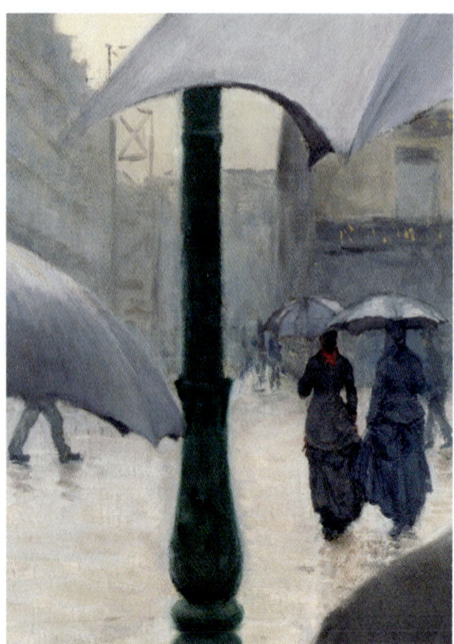

As well as *Paris Street, Rainy Day*, Caillebotte also showed his large-format *Pont de l'Europe* at the exhibition of 1877. In the bright sunshine of a spring or summer morning, workers and members of the bourgeoisie cross a bridge above the tracks of Saint-Lazare station. The views of Paris exhibited by the other Impressionists in the 1877 were similarly cheerful – they celebrated the city as somewhere to stroll, to idle, and to twirl around in popular dance halls.

The mood they captured was not merely confined to art. In the war of 1870/71, France had been defeated by the Germans, and Paris besieged and bombarded. Next the revolutionary Commune had seized power in Paris, set fire to public and private buildings, and finally gone down in a bloodbath. By 1877, however, the reparations to Germany had been paid, the economy was flourishing and the Republican government was getting ready to celebrate France's recovery with the International Exhibition of 1878. In a series of articles, Renoir called upon artists to contribute to the process of democracy and to immerse the city in colour. In a third painting at the 1877 exhibition, Caillebotte portrays decorators in a grey street painting the façades of the buildings with colour.

One of them can be seen with his ladder in the background of *Paris Street*. But this is not a painting of a gay, convivial Paris that is trying to erase its memories of the past. On the contrary, most of the people in the picture seem lonely. They are not out for a stroll, but hurry through empty streets, shielding themselves with their umbrellas not just from the rain but also, so it seems, from other passers-by. And at the sight of the cobbles, which almost entirely dominate one quarter of the canvas, many viewers will have involuntarily thought of the Commune: the revolutionaries had hurled cobblestones from their barricades. They had battled for days on the Place de Clichy, which lay very close to Caillebotte's intersection. "The cobblestone," wrote Victor Hugo, "is the symbol of the people." That same uprising had also started with the streetlights being overturned.

No one looks at anyone else

The pearl in the woman's ear appears as a luminous dot; it is the only one in the painting, and it gleams brighter than the white shirtfront of the man beside her. Yet the person to whom the artist has thus drawn attention also wears a veil, which distances her from the viewer and signals discretion.

The two protagonists walk towards the viewer in almost life size. Their faces are highly individualized and must surely be portraits, although of whom we do not know. On one of his preparatory sketches, the artist jotted down the name of Clotilde – but who was Clotilde?

The man is wearing a frock coat and top hat, the woman a fur-trimmed outfit whose cut and colour combination struck one critic in 1877 "as modern – or should I say, the latest fashion". Even her umbrella, he thought, seemed to have been freshly purchased from one of Paris's new department stores, the Bon-Marché perhaps. It was only three years previously that umbrellas of this kind had actually been invented – by the Englishman Samuel Fox in Sheffield. Caillebotte wanted to be modern like the other Impressionists; he wanted to paint not what was past but what belonged to the present.

Characteristic of this painting and the artist is the fact that both of the main figures are looking to one side – and not at the man coming towards them, who is unable to step out of their way and whose umbrella is already dangerously close to their own. Eye contact is avoided, including with the viewer.

Almost all the people in the painting are hurrying through the streets absorbed in their own thoughts, protected by their umbrellas.

Caillebotte, too, managed to shield his private life so well that few details of it have come down to us. We know that he never married. A census of 1891 records him as the head of a household with three domestic servants, four sailors, and a 28-year-old actress, registered as a "friend", who for reasons unknown called herself Charlotte Berthier but whose real name was Anne Marie Hagen. Renoir painted her.

Caillebotte was at that time living in Petit Genevilliers, a small town on the Seine near Argenteuil, where he dedicated his organizational skills, innovative thinking, and financial resources first to rowing and then yachting. He maintained his own crew, owned his own boatyard, and designed ever faster yachts. For three years he was the best regatta sailor in France. He remained true to painting, however. When he died in 1894 at the age of just 45, he left some 500 pictures, even though he had long since given up exhibiting and had also withdrawn from his former circle of artist friends, no doubt fed up with their bickering. The group had by now disbanded and its individual members were no longer dependent upon his financial support. Caillebotte nevertheless continued to attend their monthly dinners at the Café Riche, and as always paid the bill for everyone.

His famous colleagues Renoir and Monet never, as far as we know, expressed an opinion about their patron's work; it is possible that a man who painted for pleasure remained an amateur in their eyes. Caillebotte's wealth was probably detrimental to his fame: his own works remained unknown long after those whom he supported had become famous. By the time they were discovered, the paintings by his Impressionist friends were already filling the pages of countless art books.

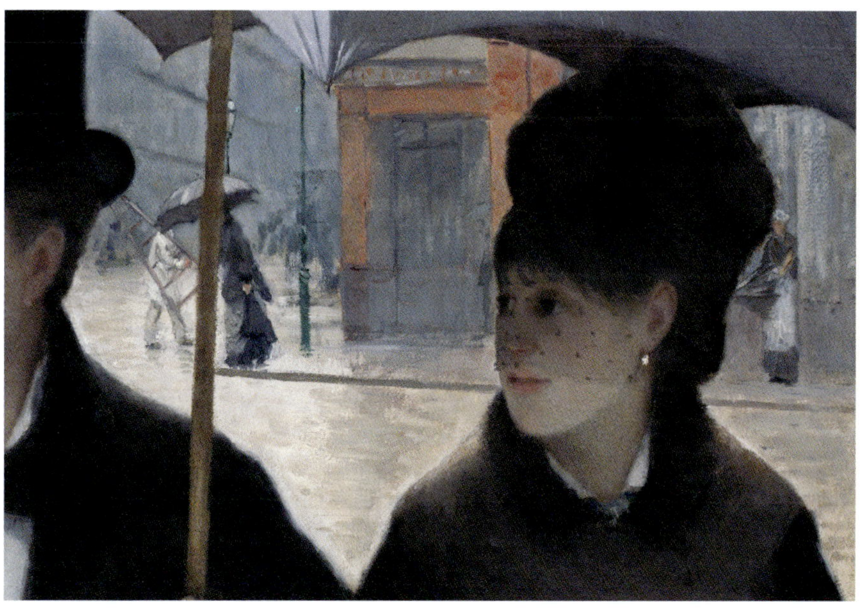

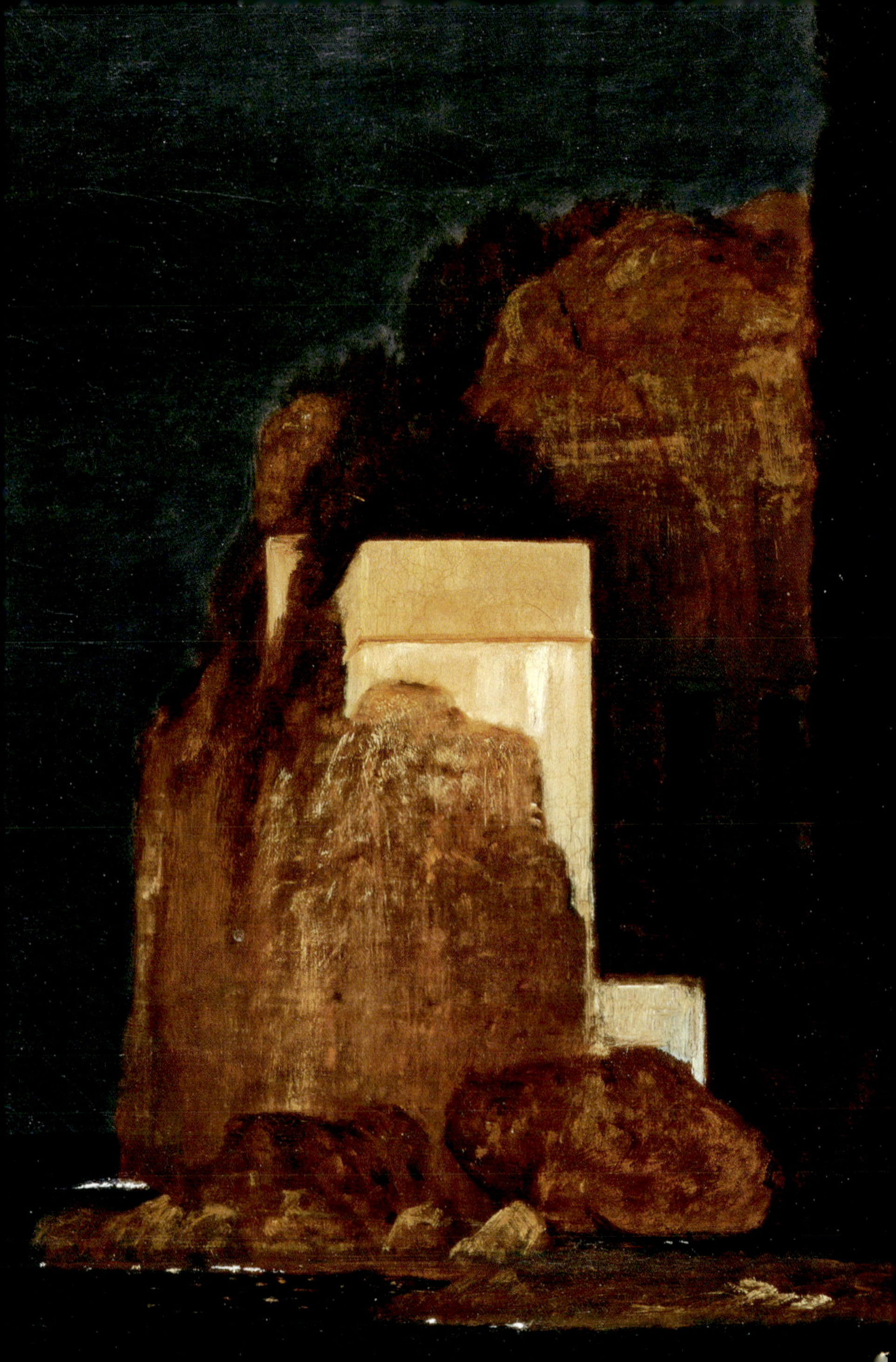

Arnold Böcklin (1827–1901)

A dream of the South and of death

The Isle of the Dead, 1880
111 x 155 cm, Basle, Kunstmuseum Basel,
Depositum Gottfried-Keller-Stiftung

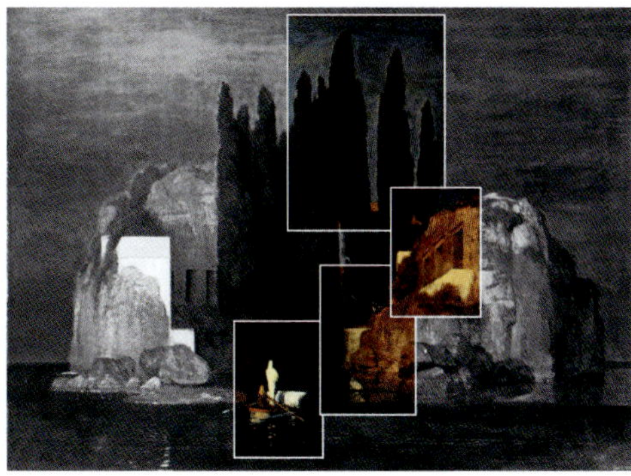

Between 1880 and 1886 Arnold Böcklin painted five versions of *The Isle of the Dead*. Four of them still exist – in Basle, Berlin, Leipzig and New York. The Berlin picture once hung in the German Chancellery: a press photo of November 1940 shows Hitler and Molotov, the Russian foreign minister, standing in front of it. The following year, German troops would invade Russia.

Hitler had purchased "his" *Isle of the Dead* while Chancellor of the German Reich, and it had initially hung in his house in Berchtesgaden. Eleven paintings by Böcklin were also amongst the works of art purchased and requisitioned at Hitler's behest for a mammoth Nazi museum planned for Linz. For Hitler, whose tastes in art had been shaped at the start of the century, when he himself had wanted to become an artist, Böcklin ranked among the great masters. His opinion was shared by many: Arnold Böcklin was at that time one of the most popular artists in the entire German-speaking area.

Proof of this fact can be found in literature. There is scarcely an author between 1890 and 1910 who does not make some reference to Böcklin. Gottfried Keller, Paul Heyse and Hugo von Hofmannsthal dedicated prologues and poems to him, while in his drama *Michael Kramer*, Gerhard Hauptmann even held him up as a shining example: "Always work, work, work … Just look at a life like that, how a man like that works, someone like Böcklin. That way you make something of yourself, you accomplish something."

And what the artist accomplished again and again was *The Isle of the Dead*. Richard Dehmel left a holiday resort because "its similarity with Böcklin's *Isle of the Dead* would not have done me any good in the long term". Detlev von Liliencron and Hermann Hesse owned prints of the painting; as a young bookseller's assistant, Hesse moved to Basle "with Nietzsche's works … and a framed copy of Böcklin's *Isle of the Dead* in the trunk containing my possessions".

Just how far Böcklin's impact extended can be seen in a guide for newly married wives, entitled *In the German Home* and published by one Luise Holle

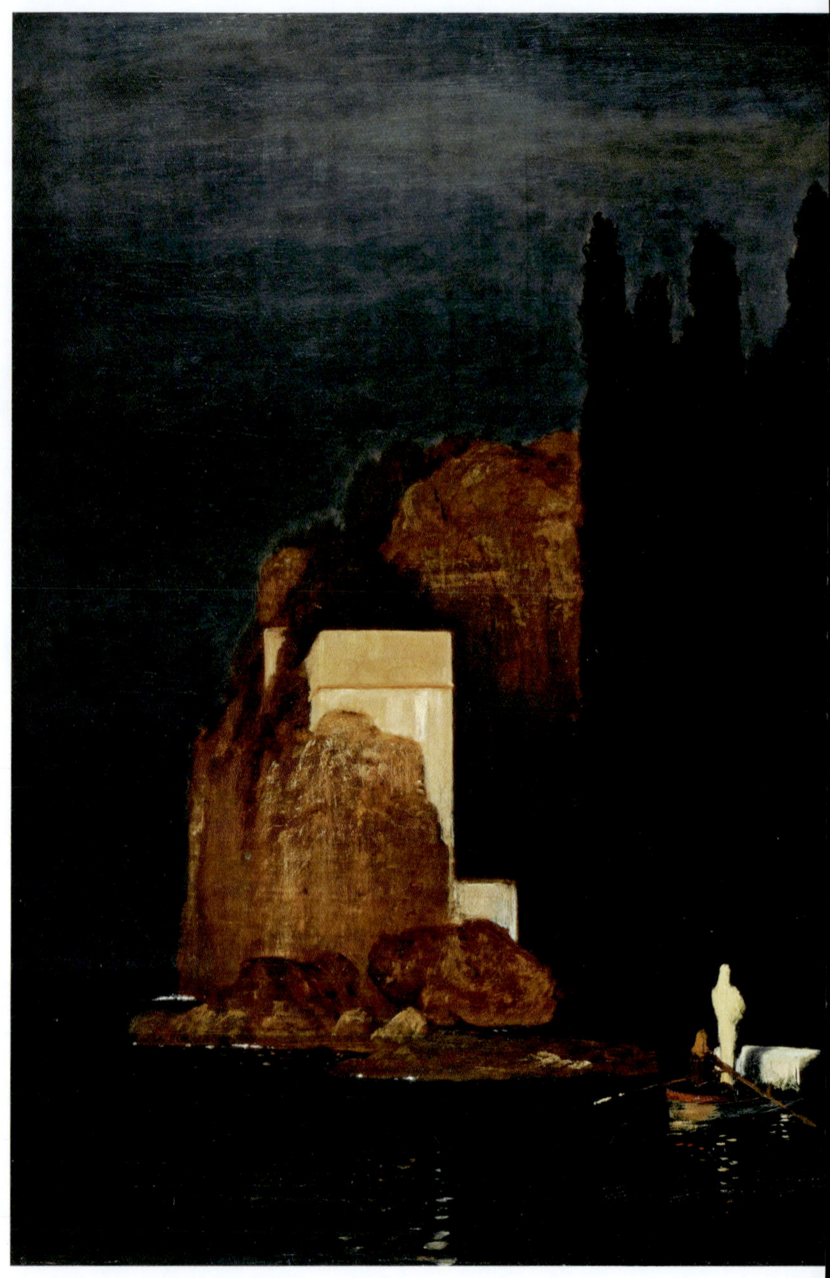

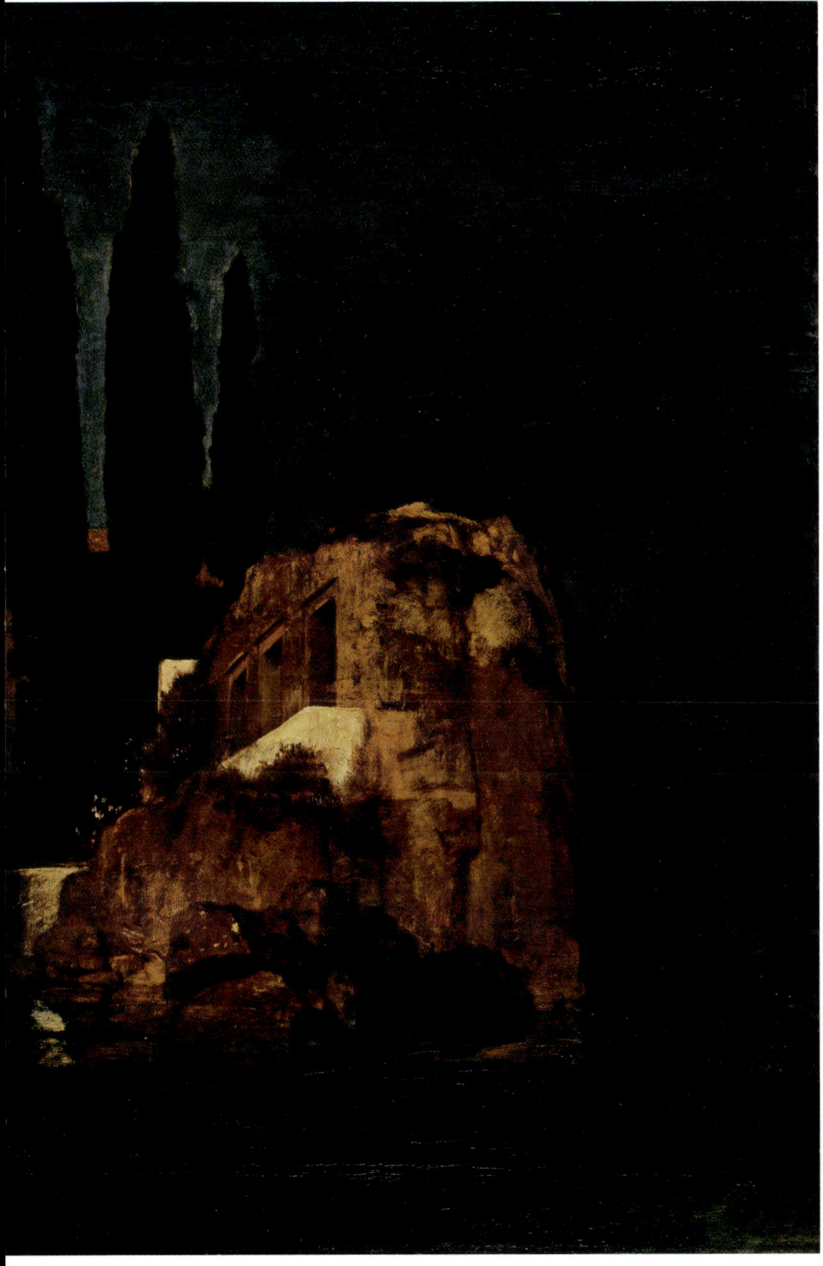

in 1903. It offers pertinent advice on everything from interior furnishings and maternal duties to carnival pranks. "In the living room, the pictures should not be overly animated in either palette or subject, since when looked at every day their effect may prove unsettling," it explains on page 88. Although no specific artists are recommended by name, what it means is clear from one of its illustrations of a model room. There, in a dark frame against the dark wood panelling surrounded by a broad mount, hangs a print of *The Isle of the Dead*.

The popularization of Böcklin's works had been greatly assisted by a new printing technique, heliogravure, which permitted gradations of light and dark previously unobtainable in a print. For the first time, it was possible to create a reproduction, albeit only in black-and-white, good enough for lovers of art to hang on their wall. The Bruckmann publishing house in Munich was one of those quick to exploit this new technology. It signed exclusive contracts with artists and sold their works as prints in large-format portfolios. Menzel, Lenbach, Kaulbach, and Kalckreuth were all Bruckmann artists, as was Böcklin.

When he reached his 70th birthday in 1897, he was at the pinnacle of his fame. Two commemorative exhibitions were mounted in Germany, in Hamburg and Berlin: "In neither city had an exhibition ever attracted such crowds," wrote Alfred Lichtwark, at that time director of the Hamburg Kunsthalle.

Lost in a daydream

This present, first version of *The Isle of the Dead* was painted in 1880. Böcklin, who was born in Basle but who moved many times throughout his life, was at that time living in Florence. He was 53 years old and poor. His works were only just beginning to find acclaim. While Germany was still dominated by history painting, first reports of the Impressionists were arriving from France. Böcklin's mythological landscapes and figures, his sturdily painted fauns, centaurs, and mermaids, fell into neither of these categories, and his circle of admirers was still small. It included one Marie Berna, who was widowed young and who later married a Count Oriola in Büdesheim. She visited Böcklin in Florence and commissioned "a picture for daydreaming over".

The fact that the painting was commissioned by a woman, and that she expressly wanted something to daydream over, may simply be coincidence, but seems symptomatic of the upper middle classes of the day. Their situation is described in the novels of Theodor Fontane, the sharp-eyed observer of Wilhelmine society. His Effi Briest was no particular lover of art, but was taken to the Nationalgalerie in Berlin as a young girl to see Böcklin's *Elysian Fields*. (The work had hung there since 1878.) Effi's fate: marriage at seventeen, affair with an officer, her husband kills her lover in a duel, Effi is cast out by her husband and parents and dies. The novel appeared in 1894.

Fontane's Effi falls for the officer because she is bored as a housewife. She has nothing to do. Her house and children are looked after by domestic staff, and any latent intellectual interests she may have are never awakened. She waits for her husband to come home, plays the piano, goes for walks, and endeavours to lose herself in daydreams. Her parents know "there was nothing she loved more than gentle daydreaming, free from care". Although Effi at times considered her daydreaming a sin, she liked doing

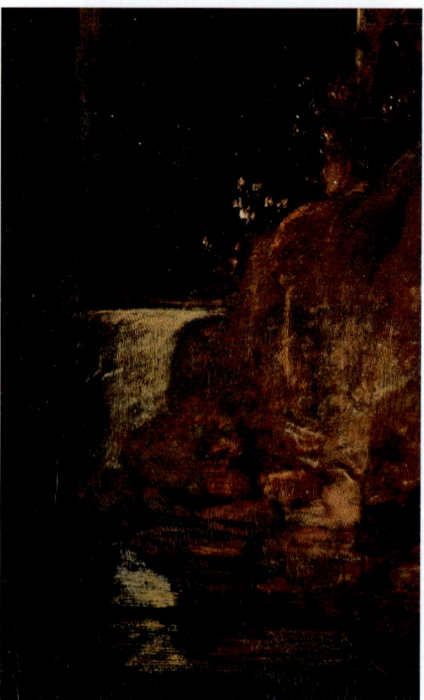

it; what she didn't appreciate was how much she was lured into it by middle-class society, for all but a tiny facet of the real world was closed to her. Political and social affairs were considered unpleasant. Only men were allowed to engage in such things. Nor was it considered proper for a woman of her class to work. Even after Effi has been cast out, she keeps a maid-servant who continues to do everything for her. For women of the upper classes, denied the experience of reality, there remained little other than the world of the imagination, little else but to escape into dreams. Art thereby provided them with a welcome point of departure.

Yearning for the South

The centre of the composition is dominated by towering cypresses, trees that stand in almost every cemetery in southern Europe. They were planted beside temples even in antiquity. Apollo, the god of Light, is said to have turned a youth into a flame-shaped cypress, and gods of the underworld were also connected with the tree. Its symbolic character is ambiguous: evergreen and long-lived, it serves as a symbol both of life and of eternity after death.

The Florentines like to claim that Böcklin took his inspiration from their English cemetery with its long rows of cypresses, while in Montenegro it is said that a small island in the bay of Kotor served as Böcklin's model. The same is alleged of the fortress of Alfonso of Aragon outside Ischia, and Böcklin is certainly known to have visited Ischia in 1879, just a year before he painted the first version of *The Isle of the Dead*. Whatever the case, the motif is typical of southern Europe, and this fact undoubtedly contributed to its extraordinary popularity.

For people in Germany had always dreamed of the South, of the crucible of classical culture, and of the paradise of easier living it seemed to represent. And since the middle of the 19th century, they had been able to experience it for themselves. Up until then, those who had visited Italy were first and foremost young members of the aristocracy on their grand cultural tours of Europe, along with artists and art lovers willing to endure the hardships of travelling lengthy sections on foot and by horse and carriage. Women remained at home. The situation changed only with the advent of the railways.

In the second half of the 19th century, a network of railway track was laid down across the whole of Europe. Luxury hotels sprang up in every major town and city, travel agencies were founded, and a new strata of society started to travel to faraway places. They included Fontane's Effi Briest. Her parents had never seen the South, but on her honeymoon she travelled as far as Capri and Sorrento. And when, at the end of her short life, she fell ill, the doctor declared: "We'll get [her temperature] down again, and then she must go to Switzerland or Menton." Trips to the South had become normal. As a consequence, paintings employing southern motifs began to assume a different function. For more and more people they became souvenirs, enduring mementoes in an age without photography. Pictures incorporating the most characteristic features of Mediterranean islands – cypresses, rocks, and Classical-style gateways – held a particular appeal.

But it was not just this love of the South that made such paintings more popular, but also a new desire for Nature. Industrialization was causing the cities to grow, as people flocked from the countryside to find jobs in the ever-increasing numbers of factories. In 1870 two-thirds of Germans were still living in rural communities, with one-third living in cities. By 1910 that ratio had been reversed.

Unlike in earlier centuries, those living in the cities no longer owned fields and gardens outside the city walls. Not only was the population simply too big, but it was no longer the fashion. The bourgeoisie lived an emphatically urban life in dark rooms behind heavy curtains, constricted by their corsets, stiff collars, and social rules. Nature was only permitted on excursions and in flowerpots and picture frames – at least until the emergence, around the turn of the century, of the Wandervogel ("rolling stone") movement, made up of young middle-class Germans who, clad in light clothing and carrying guitars, set off out of the cities to walk in the fields and woods.

Coffin or urn – a contemporary issue
The subject of burial, however far back in time it may seem in Böcklin's painting, was in fact a current one. It was being discussed in connection with what was then a new word – crematorium. According to an issue of *Westermanns Illustrirten Deutschen Monatsheften* of 1875, "whether to be cremated or buried in the traditional way has, for the past few years, been one of the questions of the day, indeed, apart from politics and the Church, one of the most urgent

questions facing a century transforming itself in every area." Three years later, Germany's first legally approved crematorium opened in Gotha. It was built by Siemens. In 1896 Böcklin's own birthplace of Basle even held a referendum on the issue, in which cremation was approved by the smallest of majorities.

There was a history to the debate surrounding cremation. For the past one hundred years or so, there had been much fear surrounding the vapours given off by decomposing bodies. They were reputed to spread epidemics. Graves became "plague pits of horror", cemeteries "birthplaces of decay". The municipal authorities responded by creating graveyards outside the city boundaries. But the cities grew and swallowed up the cemeteries, and they had to be moved even further away. The new railways made this possible: in London, a special Cemetery station was built next to Waterloo station, providing a direct rail link to Woking cemetery 25 miles away.

In the second half of the 19th century, however, the mood changed. In 1868 it was discussed in Paris whether to create a new cemetery 30 kilometres from the city centre. Here, too, a special "railway for the dead" was proposed. The majority was against it: "The idea that the dead should be transported by the dozen in railway trucks arouses the fury of the general public," a reader wrote to one editor; "they are obviously being treated like mere items of freight."

The Paris authorities rescued themselves from the dilemma by commissioning an investigation, designed to establish whether or not cemeteries were really harmful to the health. The conclusion: no. In the face of deep-rooted and largely irrational prejudices, however, it was hard for this latest finding to gain acceptance. Worries about "plague pits" did not disappear overnight and helped the cause of the crematorium lobby. Urns containing ashes were absolutely safe in terms of hygiene, it was argued, and could be housed in space-saving vaults within the city.

The spectre of industrialization appeared frequently in the burial debate. Some people rejected the prospect of corpses being carried by rail, others were against the idea of the "high-tech" crematorium. To many people, the rapid changes taking place in their cityscape and society seemed incompatible with the concepts of death and eternity. This may have been one of the reasons why those who often "daydreamed" were happy to send their dead far away, to a beautiful landscape, away from the noise and dirt of the factories. For example, to an island somewhere in the South.

Lethe, Styx, and a beautiful death

Böcklin not only locates his island geographically far from his German-Swiss public, but also sets it in a different time. "In the portrayal of his figures, Böcklin is supposed to have drawn upon an old Italian legend, according to which the dead person stepped into the coffin himself," wrote one earlier biographer. The standing figure might also be interpreted as an ancient priest; Böcklin leaves that open. The dark waters, which separate the realm of the living from that of the dead, evoke associations with Lethe, the river of oblivion, and the Styx, across which the dead were rowed by Charon, the ferryman. Böcklin painted him in a different picture. Names and images taken from Greek mythology belonged to the standard repertoire of middle-class conversation.

To portray the transition from life to death as a gentle passage across water also corresponded to the tastes of the day. There is no reference to organ failure, no reference to physical decomposition. Matters relating to the body were simply not discussed in Wilhelmine – or indeed Victorian – society; everything below the waist was taboo. This prudery and dislike of the physical body was carried over onto the dying and the dead. With the growing emphasis upon hygiene, noses had become more sensitive. Smells seemed harder to bear. Although the dying were not yet sent off to hospital, the circle of those present at their end grew smaller. Fontane, too, spares his readers Effi's death. She gives a slight cough, she runs a high temperature, and in the next chapter she already lies beneath the ground.

This revulsion at physical decomposition, at the process of putrefaction, spurred on the introduction of cremation and also gave rise to tomb statuary that would endure through the years. The memorials grew ever more elaborate, ever more emotional: marble angels raise the dead aloft, children embrace their mother, families weep for their father – in stone or metal, the body became eternal. Tomb art thereby served to suppress the aspects of death that no one wanted to think about.

In the 18th century cemeteries were viewed with horror or indifference. In the 19th century they became destinations for visitors, places of meditation. Even for Effi Briest, when she was still alive: "Here everything was in bloom, butterflies fluttered over the graves … It was so quiet and so beautiful." She said: "I like visiting churchyards."

Like the tombstones of his day, Böcklin transfigures the reality of death and decay. He also suggests the idea of life continuing after death. One of his admirers, a Professor Victor Widmann, conveyed this notion in verses written on the occasion of Böcklin's death. "A boat glides towards the Isle of Death / Its approach is watched by spirit eyes / and spirits wait to receive it." The dead are thus not dead at all; they live on as spirits, greeting the artist with singing. "Floating up to the treetop / from the calm harbour, the dark gateway, / a faint song, a majestic choir." At the end of the song there is mention of dreaming. The spirits are thereby speaking not to the viewer of the picture, however, but to Böcklin himself. They call to him: "Dream in your shade's body! / And from now on the world remains outside! / Illuminated by the radiance of your beauty."

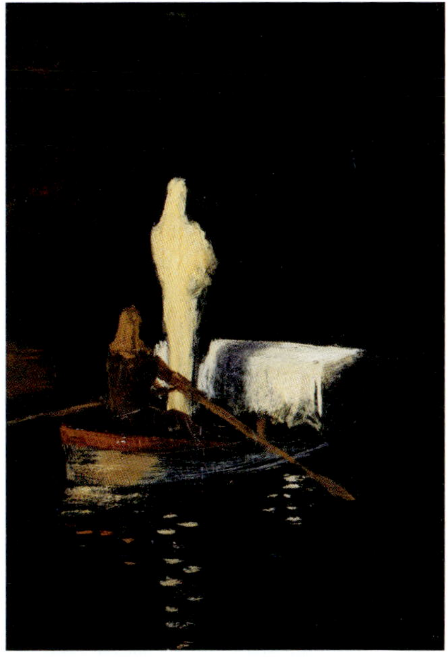

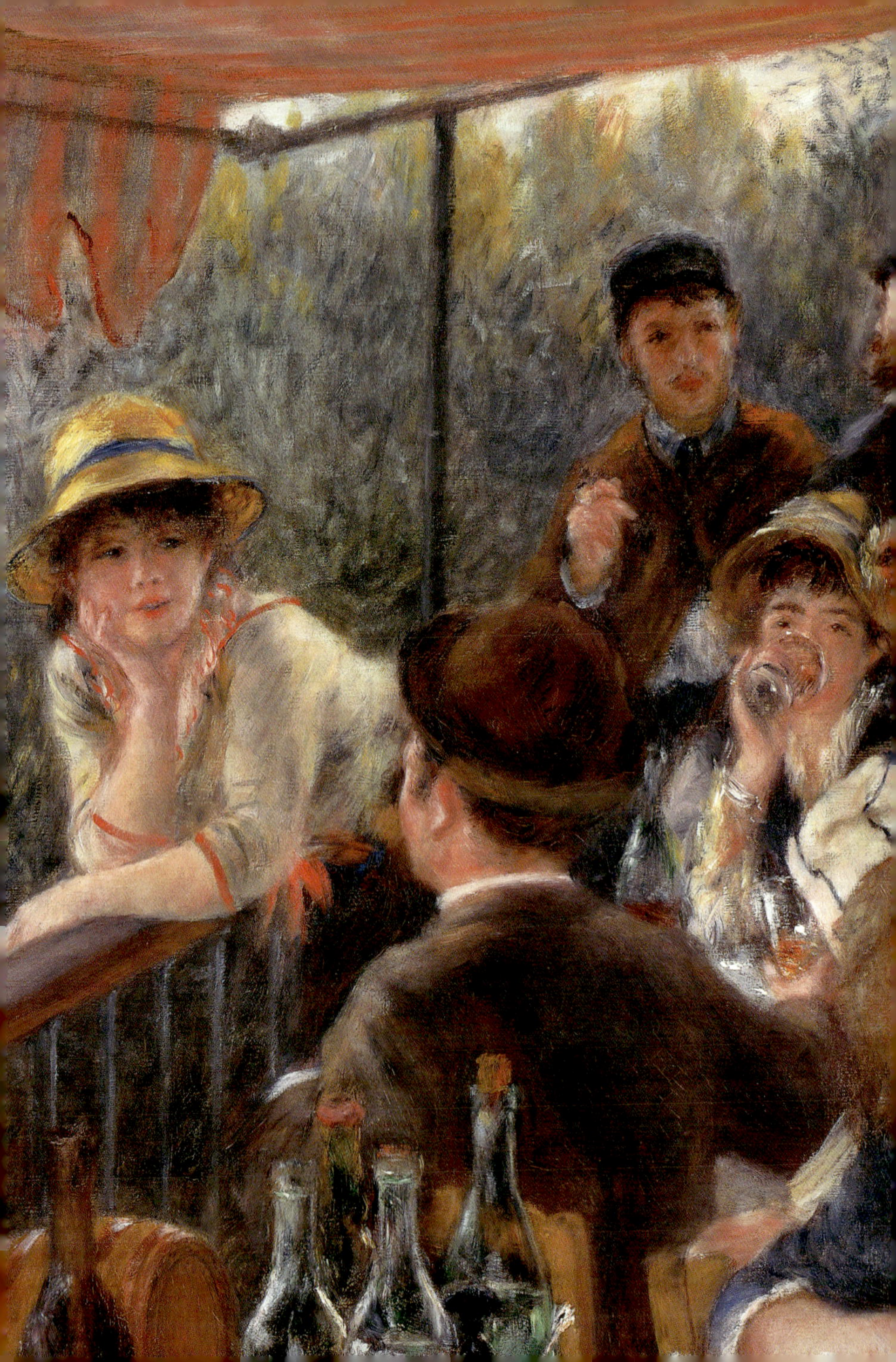

Pierre-Auguste Renoir (1841–1919)

Venue for gentry, bourgeoisie and bohème

The Luncheon of the Boating Party, 1881
129.5 x 172.7 cm, Washington, DC, National Gallery of Art,
The Phillips Collection

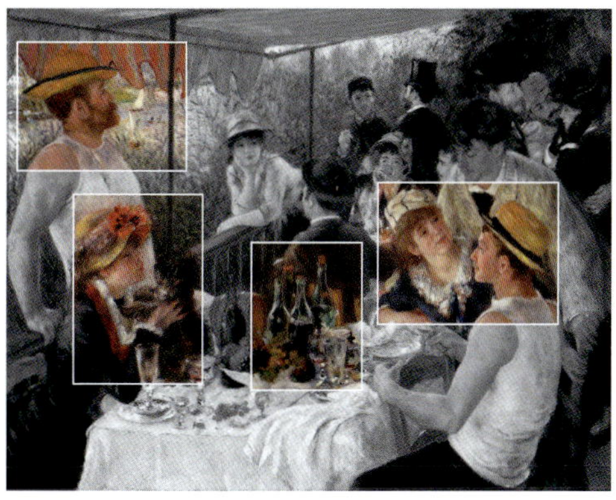

It took Pierre-Auguste Renoir, from his studio in the centre of Paris, a mere twenty minutes by train to reach the open countryside. Every half hour, a train left on the new line to St Germain – a popular technical achievement in an era which could boast of little in the way of public transport. As a consequence, rural Chatou on Sundays was packed with Parisians who, like the artists, longed for fresh air and light. They promenaded along the banks of the Seine, "roamed aimlessly under high poplars", went boating or swam in the river, unperturbed by the many floating carcasses of dead animals.

Thus the account that Renoir gave retrospectively to his son, the film director Jean Renoir, and to the art dealer Ambroise Vollard, both of whom recorded the artist's memoirs in writing. The circumstances under which Renoir painted *The Luncheon of the Boating Party* are therefore widely documented.

According to Renoir, two establishments were especially popular among Sunday trippers. One, situated on an island on the Seine, was called the "Grenouillère", literally the "frog pond". The name was a pun, referring less to croaking amphibians than to the Parisian girls who went there in search of a lover.

The clientele at the "Restaurant Fournaise", on the other hand, consisted largely of "young sporting types in striped singlets", Renoir recalled. "It was a sort of water sports club," a hotel proprietor having "hit on the idea of doing up a wooden shack he owned on the island and serving lemonade there to Sunday-trippers … He was a rowing enthusiast himself and knew all about hiring boats out to Parisians." Monsieur Fournaise appears in the picture in the appropriate outfit, a white cotton singlet stretched over his bulging chest; he is apparently observing the activities of his guests.

Renoir had frequented this establishment since the 1860s, forming an acquaintance with the proprietors and introducing several of his artist friends.

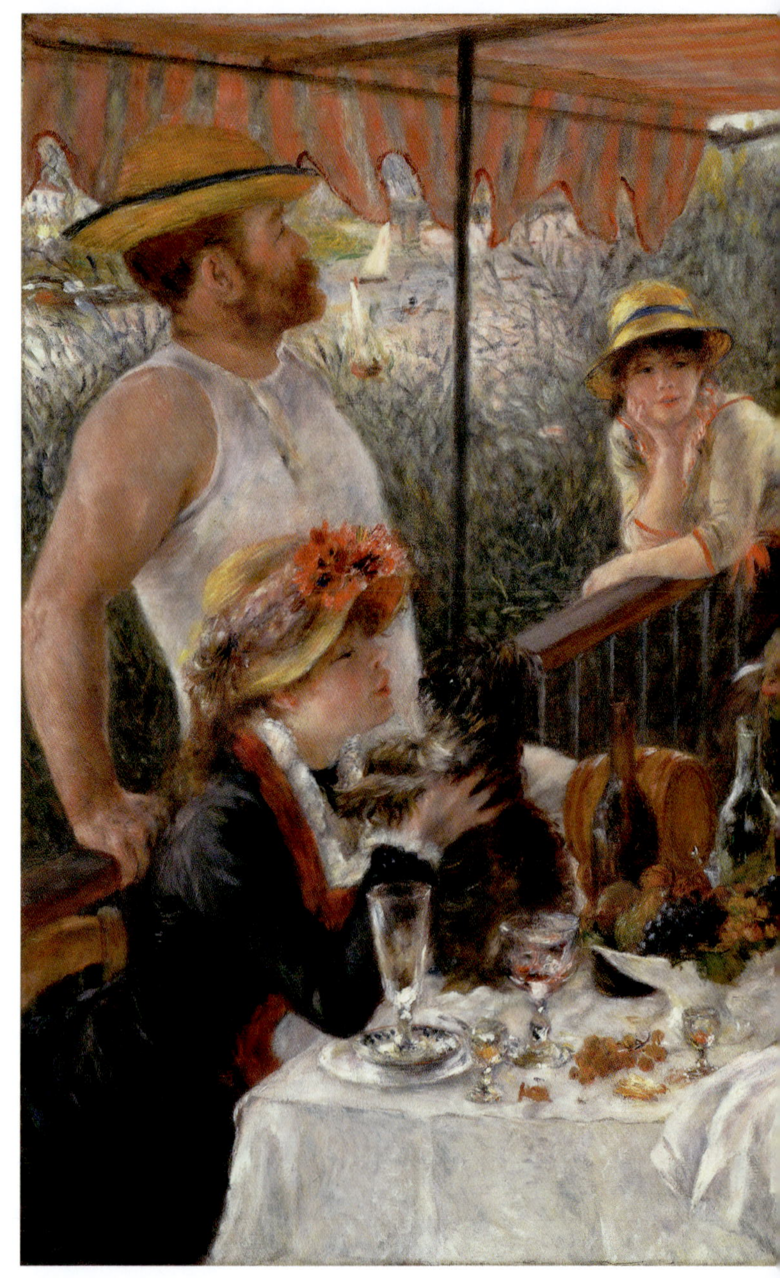

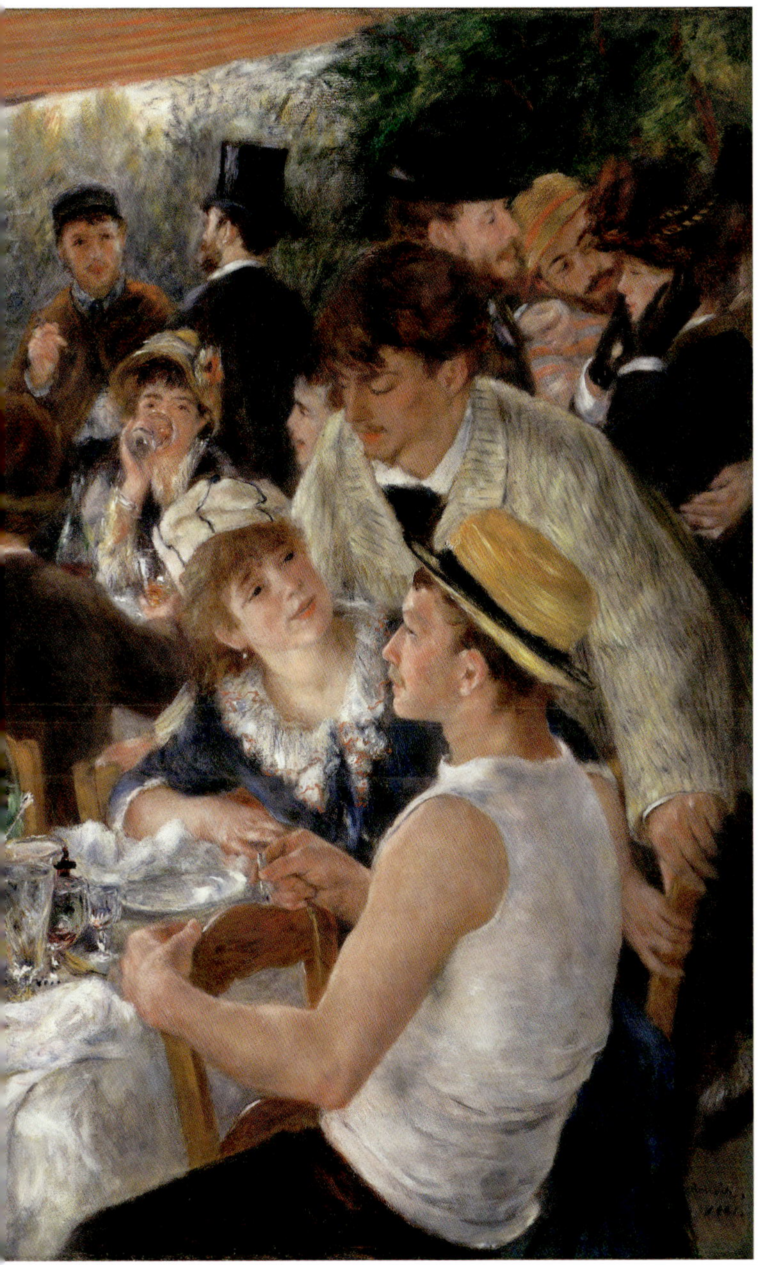

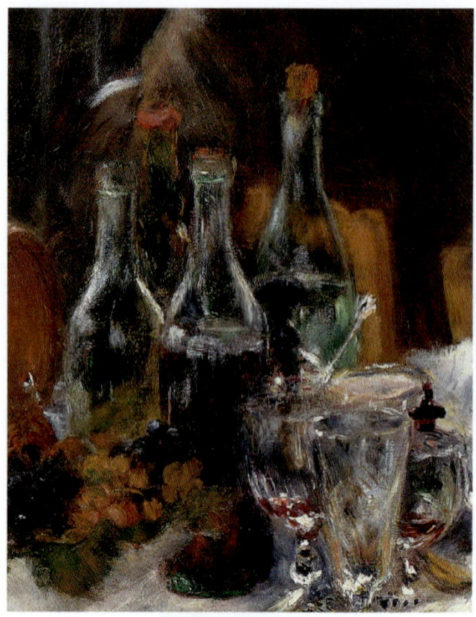

He loved to patronize this "amusing restaurant" where "you could always find a volunteer to play the piano of an evening" – whereupon the tables would be cleared on the terrace outside to make room for dancing.

Here, over the years, Renoir painted a large number of landscapes, as well as portraits of the landlord and his family. In 1880 he decided to embark on a large-scale work, "a picture of boaters, which I've been itching to do for a long time … One must from time to time try things beyond one's strength." The painting is equal in size to another ambitious work begun five years earlier: *Le Moulin de la Galette*. Before completing it at his Paris studio, Renoir had worked on the painting from April to September 1880 on the terrace of the riverside restaurant. It would appear that he enjoyed himself: "The weather is good and I have models", he wrote in a letter. He later looked back on the experience with nostalgia: "We still had life ahead of us; we denied ourselves nothing … Life was a never-ending celebration!"

Paintings to pay the bill

The boaters and their lady-friends, having finished eating, sit back among the debris of the meal, relaxed and sated. In a novel written in 1868, the brothers Edmond and Jules de Goncourt, contemporaries of

Renoir, described the mood after a full meal in the country: "The day was there solely to be enjoyed: the fatigue … the fresh, invigorating air, quivering reflections on the surface of the water, piercing sunlight … that almost animal intoxication with pleasure."

On the white tablecloth, besides crumpled linen napkins, we see a bowl of fruit, a small barrel of brandy, half-full bottles of wine and various glasses: round ones for red wine, tall ones for coffee, smaller ones for "chasers", cognac or liqueurs. In his *A Day in the Country*, published in 1881, Guy de Maupassant includes the menu of a simple riverside restaurant: baked fish, rabbit stew, salad and a sweet. The characters also order a local wine and a bottle of Bordeaux to go with their meal. This was a fairly large repast, costing about one and a half francs per person, a luxury Renoir and his artist friends were unable to afford for many years.

"I don't always have enough to eat," he told the artist Frédéric Bazille in 1869. "I'll write you more some other time, because I'm hungry and I have a plate of turbot with white sauce in front of me. I'm not putting a stamp on this letter. I have only 12 sous in my pocket, and that's for going to Paris, when I need it." In the 1860s and 1870s the works of avant-garde painters who were ridiculed as mere "impressionists" were worth practically nothing. Artists who, unlike Édouard Manet or Paul Cézanne, did not come from wealthy families, had a particularly hard life. Claude Monet had the hardest time of all; with a wife and child to support, he very often had little more than the bread Renoir sometimes brought him after visiting his parents.

The latter, artisans who had retired to the country, may not have been rich, but at least they had bread on their plates and a coop full of rabbits. Renoir, too, would probably have been better off had he stuck to the trade he had originally learned: porcelain painting, a skill which had enabled him to earn a living at the age of fifteen. But at 21 the artist, born in 1841, turned his hand to painting in earnest. He learned "anatomy, perspective, drawing and portraiture" at the studio of a well-known teacher, where he also met other young painters.

These artists would meet at a Parisian café to talk about new forms of perception and revolutionary painting techniques. Meeting at a café was necessary because most of them stayed in such miserable lodgings. (It is thanks to deplorable housing conditions that cafés, restaurants and bars have come to play such a vibrant role in French culture.) For many years Renoir's furniture consisted of no more than "a mattress lying on the floor, a table, chair and chest of drawers … and a stove for the model".

The artist used the stove to make his daily bowl of bean or lentil soup. According to his son, Renoir enjoyed "fresh basic foods", detesting margarine or sauces made with flour. However, he was able to indulge his innate epicurean leanings only by accepting the occasional invitation of some rich patron, or by dining at the "Restaurant Fournaise". Here he was seldom presented with a bill at the end of the meal: "You gave us that landscape," the proprietor would say. "My father insisted his painting was without value: 'I'm warning you, nobody will want it.' 'What does that matter to me if it's beautiful? Anyway, one must hang something on the wall to hide those patches of damp.'"

Sporting and other friends

For much of his career Renoir could not afford to pay the fees of professional models, a single sitting costing as much as ten francs – the price of several meals. However, even when he was much better off, he preferred to paint his family and friends. He was interested in people and their relationships. He was a social being: "I need to feel a bustle going on around me."

According to Renoir, all the social classes met under Fournaise's striped awning. They had two things in common: friendship to the artist and an interest in art or sport. The man in the shiny black top hat, for example, was an art collector called Charles Ephrussi, a banker and owner of the art magazine *Gazette des Beaux-Arts*, in which, in 1880, he devoted a study to the Impressionists.

By contrast, the bowler-hatted man at the centre of the painting was interested only in "horses, women and boats". The former officer and diplomat, Baron Barbier, is reported to have told Renoir: "I don't know anything about art, and even less about your art, but I like helping you." When he

heard of the artist's plans for a boating picture, he offered to take over the organization and provide boats. Aristocrats like himself kept fit by riding, boxing and tennis, whereas ordinary people made do with walking, or riding the newly invented bicycle. (Renoir broke his arm falling from a bicycle in 1880.) But the gentry, bourgoisie and bohème would generally meet in order to indulge their passion for rowing. Fournaise "knew all about hiring boats out to Parisians, entrusting them only to trained enthusiasts … Everyone pulled on their oars as hard as they could, trying to break records and become expert rowers."

One such expert was Gustave Caillebotte, a wealthy bachelor, here shown sitting astride a chair next to the actress Ellen Andrée. A trained engineer, he built racing boats, using them to participate in competitions. At the same time, he was an enthusiastic painter, though aware of the limitations of his talent. He was a generous man, who paid a good price for his friends' works.

Wearing the appropriately named *canotiers* – "boaters" – on their heads, and with necks and muscular arms bared, Fournaise and Caillebotte stand out among the other guests in their correct city clothes. In an era which devoted so much attention to the "decency" of clothing, a girl might easily feel embarrassed by a sportsman's bare arms, as Maupassant recounts in his *Day in the Country*: "She pretended not to notice them," whereas her

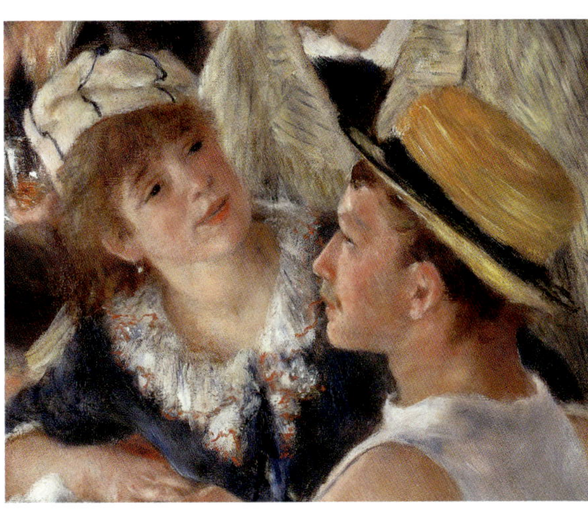

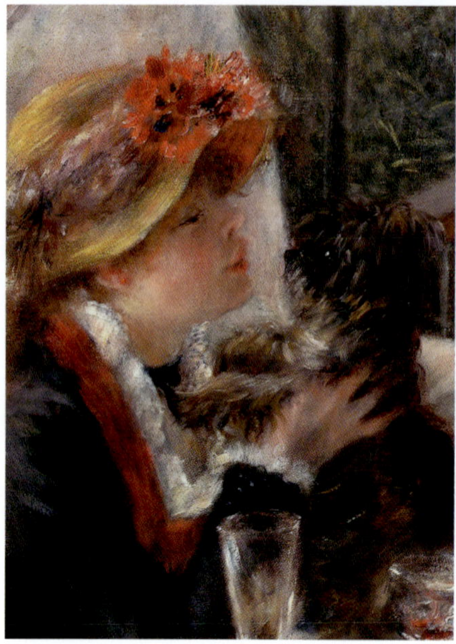

Charigot and the flower-girl Angèle, have trimmed their simple straw hats with flowers or ribbons.

Angèle, seen in Renoir's painting with a wine glass raised to her lips, was one of the many prostitutes who roamed Montmartre. This, at least, was the account Renoir gave his son. While he was working on the boating picture at Fournaise's, Angèle had managed to "pick up" a young man from a well-to-do family who married her and took her to live in the country, where he turned her into a lady with affected manners. Aline Charigot, here seen entirely engrossed in her little dog, had recently moved to Paris from her home in Burgundy. She, too, had found a serious admirer: Auguste Renoir. Since his decision to devote his life to painting, Renoir had subordinated everything to this aim, even suffering hunger or cold if need be. According to his son, he went "through life with the delicious feeling of possessing nothing" but "the hands in his pockets", avoiding serious relationships of any kind.

For "I have known painters", Renoir recalled, "who produced nothing of value because they spent their time seducing women instead of painting them." The actress Jeanne Samary, who wanted to marry him, was eventually forced to resign herself: "He was not made for marriage; with his brush he weds every woman he paints." However, what had been so easily acceptable to a young bohemian proved increasingly onerous to the 40-year-old artist: "When you are alone, the evenings are deadly dull." In 1879 he met Aline.

The young seamstress was mad about water and "adored rowing". Renoir took her with him to Chatou. During the evenings, Baron Barbier waltzed her round the terrace, while Caillebotte looked after her "as he might have done a younger sister" and Ellen Andrée was determined to "give this delightful peasant girl a bit of polish". But Aline refused to give up her Burgundian accent and "become an artificial Parisian".

She sat for Renoir, and he taught her to swim. At that time, according to Maupassant, only women who were sufficiently well-rounded dared bathe in the river. "The others, padded out with cotton-wool, shored up with stays, propped up a little here, touched up a little there, looked on in blank disdain while their sisters splashed about in the water."

Aline could show herself without fear. The 21-year-old Burgundian was "slim and yet everything in her was rounded"; she was one of those "privi-

mother, "bolder, and drawn by a feminine curiosity which may even have been desire, could not remove her eyes …"

Ideal woman in a hat

The guests gathered on the terrace had yet another thing in common: their youth. Even the solemn-looking banker Ephrussi was only 31. Caillebotte was 32, while the girls in their fashionable hats, whose healthful, rosy bloom Renoir so loved to paint, were little more than twenty years old. "Come tomorrow with a pretty summer hat," the artist wrote to one of them on 17 September 1880, "in a light dress. Wear something underneath, it's starting to get cold …"

None of the sportsmen's lady-friends would have been seen dead without a hat. The hat was an indispensable sign of respectability and social status. The actresses Ellen Andrée and Jeanne Samary, the latter of whom is shown holding her hands over her ears in the background, refusing to listen to the compliments of two admirers, wear highly fashionable headgear acquired from a milliner's. The landlord's daughter Alphonsine, leaning on the railing at the edge of the terrace, like the seamstress Aline

leged beings whom the gods have spared the horrors of acute angles." But she not only incorporated Renoir's ideal of feminine beauty; the artist felt that, with her, he was altogether in the best of hands. Aline appeared to him to be "extraordinarily gifted to succeed in an area of which men scarcely dare dream: making life bearable".

Air, light and water

Ironically, while he was painting the apparently so light-hearted and harmonious *Luncheon of the Boating Party*, Renoir's life had entered a crisis. No longer as young as he had been, the artist suffered from lack of recognition, honour and money. He had also come to a crossroads in his art: "I no longer knew what I was about."

For many years Renoir had belonged to the group of artists known as "Impressionists". Together with Frédéric Bazille, Camille Pissaro, Alfred Sisley and Claude Monet, he had left his studio in the 1860s to paint out of doors, sailing down the Seine painting and drawing with Sisley in 1865, or competing to produce the best work with Claude Monet at the "Grenouillère", near Chatou, four years later. The young artists tried "to capture the light and project it directly onto the canvas", as Monet put it. They developed new methods of reproducing the effect of light in the trees and its reflection on the surface of the water. They dissolved solid forms and revolutionized painting. At the same time, however, they met with the stern disapproval of the critics and the public, and their exhibitions of 1874 and 1876 ended

in failure, leaving them lucky if they managed to sell a painting for 50 francs. By 1878, Renoir had had enough and began to do traditional portraits of rich Paris society ladies. "I think he's sunk," wrote Pissaro in 1879. "Poverty is so hard to bear," he added sympathetically. "The problem isn't art, but a hungry stomach … and an empty purse."

However, Pissaro was doing his friend an injustice. Renoir's break with Impressionism – the group was in the process of dissolving anyway – had artistic reasons: "I had travelled as far as Impressionism could take me", he later recalled, "arriving at a point where I could no longer paint or draw … I began to notice that the paintings that came out were too complicated and that one was constantly forced to cheat."

In *The Luncheon of the Boating Party* Renoir "cheats" in virtuoso fashion once again. His reflections of light and reverberating shadows, the atmosphere of a hot summer's day spent on a riverside terrace, remain a masterpiece of Impressionist *plein-air*. The Seine landscape in the background is composed of air, light and water. The figures, however, acquire a new sense of solidity. Rigorously composed, and far from dissolving into their hazy surroundings, they attain an almost monumental stature at the centre of the canvas. They are harbingers of the new "rigorous style" that Renoir was soon to evolve under the influence of the Old Masters.

After completing the *Boating Party*, the artist – with the money from his portraits – allowed himself a trip to the South. The break had a considerable effect on his life and art. On returning to Paris in the autumn of 1881, his decision was made: he set up house with Aline, who made his "life bearable", and returned to work with renewed confidence.

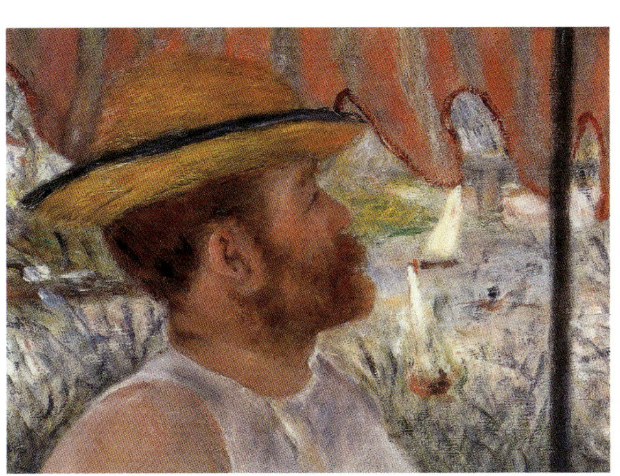

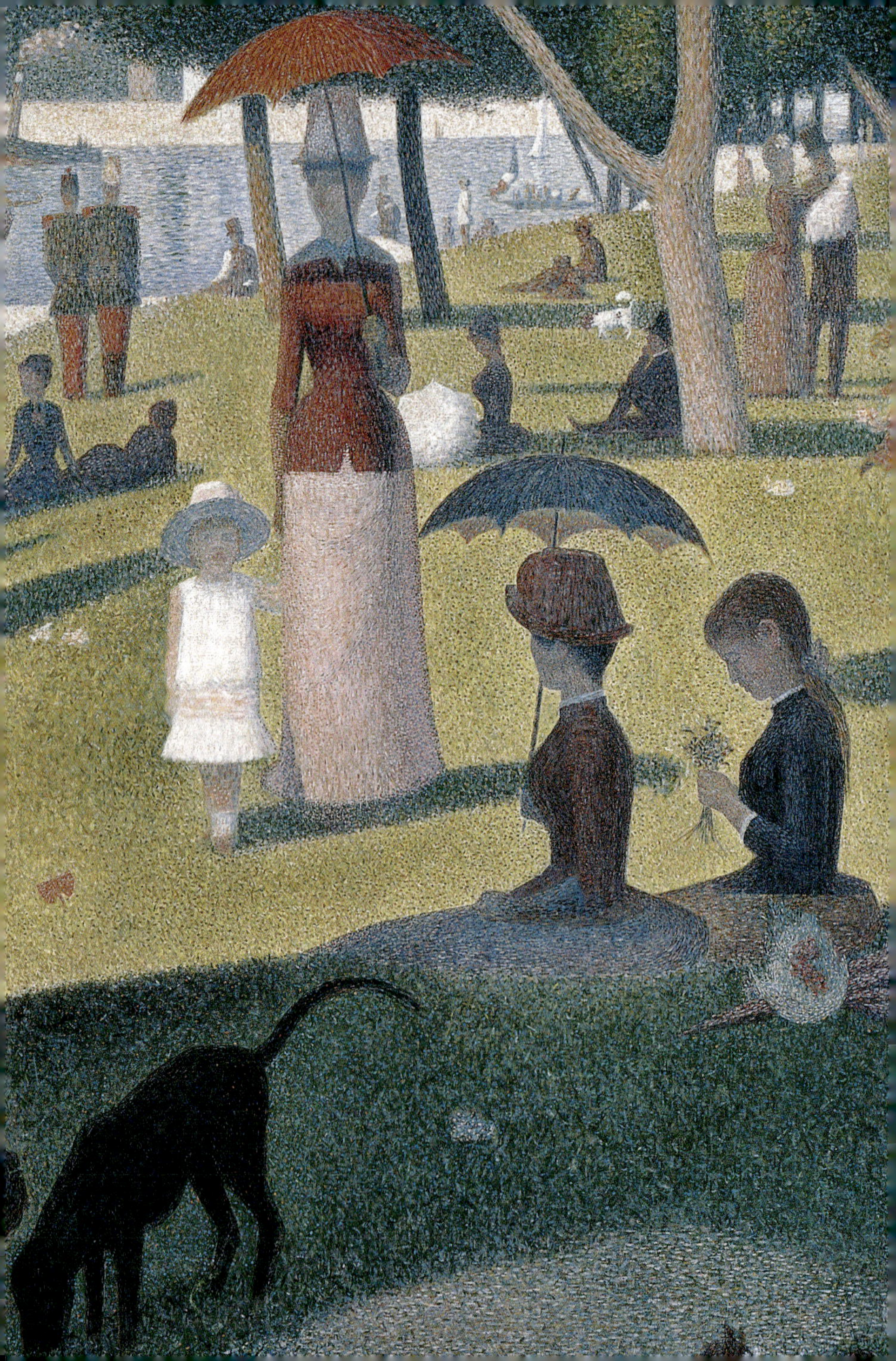

Georges Seurat (1859–1891)

In the paradise of the petite bourgeoisie, all are strangers

Sunday Afternoon on the Island of La Grande Jatte, 1884 /1886
207 x 308 cm, The Art Institute of Chicago,
Helen Bartlett Memorial Collection

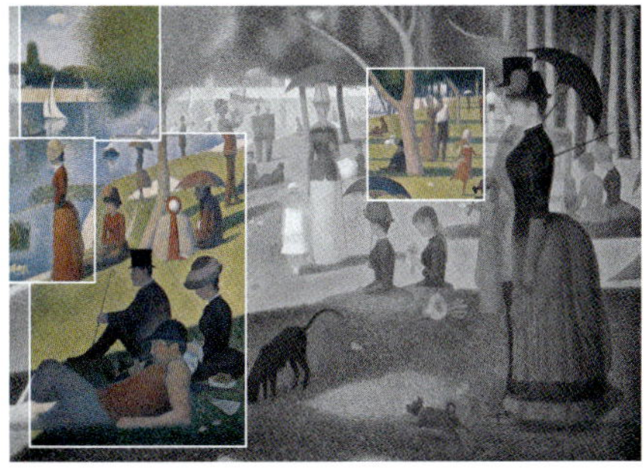

This work documents the invention of a new technique: Pointillism. Instead of mixing pigments on his palette like his predecessors, Seurat applies them to his canvas as dots of primary colour. Only when they are processed on the viewer's retina do they combine into the desired hue. The composition itself only comes into focus when viewed from several feet away.

The philosopher Ernst Bloch described the picture as a "mosaic of boredom". To the Marxist, who died in 1977, *La Grande Jatte* by Georges Seurat (1859–1891) was an image of "Sunday misery", a "landscape of painted suicide".

To the art critic Félix Fénéon, on the other hand, it was a cheerful work: "Beneath a dog-day sky, at four o'clock, the island, flanked by passing boats, alive with a fortuitously-met Sunday population happy to be out in the fresh air, amongst the trees".

Fénéon was full of admiration for *La Grande Jatte*, executed between 1884 and 1886. In his articles, he sang the praises of Seurat and his "new way of ciphering reality" – namely in a dense scatter of innumerable tiny points of light. The painting thereby documents the invention of Pointillism. The public did not share the critic's enthusiasm and the picture remained in the artist's possession until his early death in 1891. "Seurat's mother is most anxious about what will happen to his big canvases after his death," noted the painter Paul Signac in his diary. "She would like to bequeath them to a museum … but what museum would currently agree to take them?"

Nine years after Seurat's death, at his family's request, Signac and his friends held a show of Seurat's works. His drawings were priced at 10 francs unframed, or 100 francs framed. *La Grande Jatte* went for 800 francs to a member of the Paris upper middle classes. In 1911 the board of the Metropolitan Museum in New York voted against purchasing the canvas.

The wealthy Frederic Clay Bartlett displayed greater courage and better artistic judgement when he acquired the painting in Paris for 20,000 dollars. Shortly afterwards he donated it to the Art Institute of Chicago, where it is housed as a key work of European Modernism. In 1931 a French consortium tried to buy it back for 400,000 dollars. In vain.

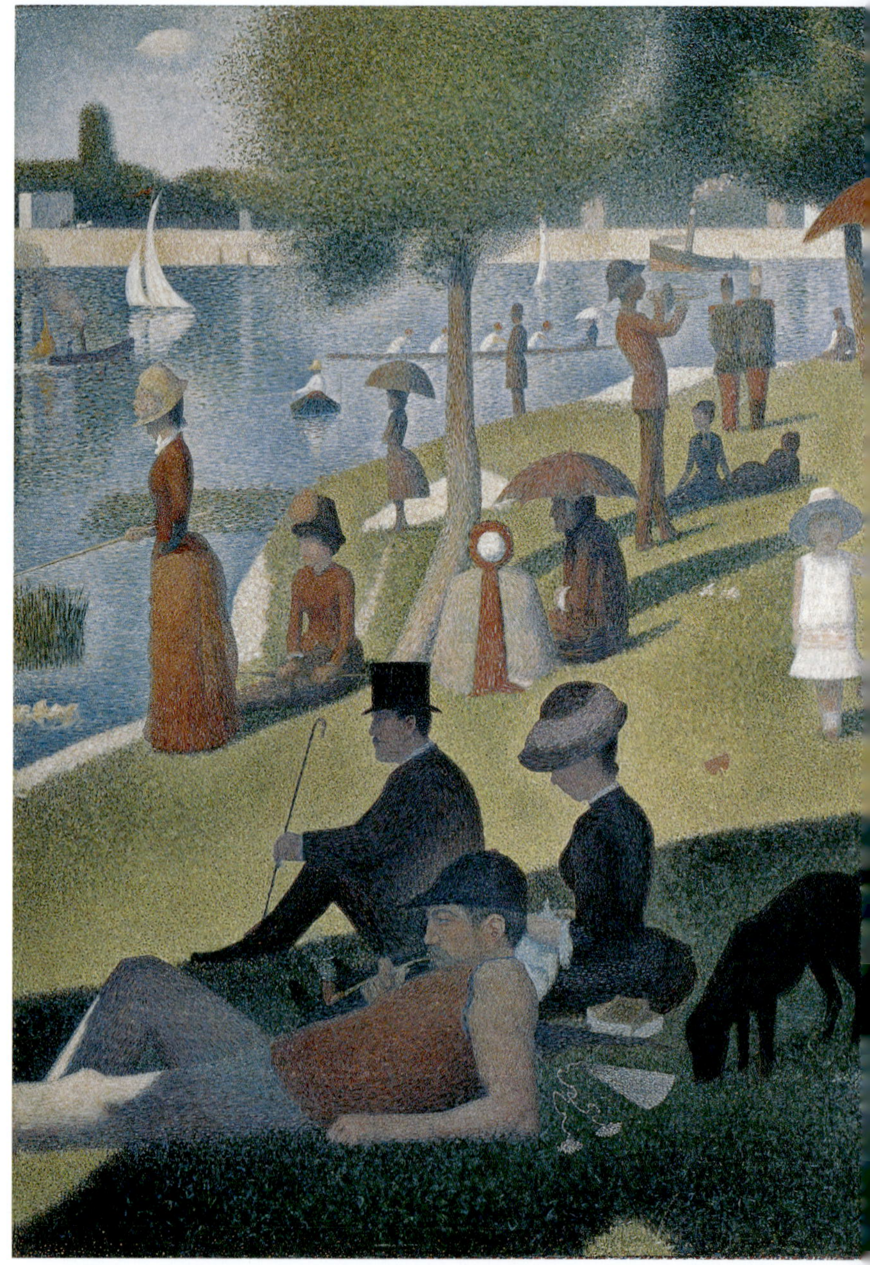

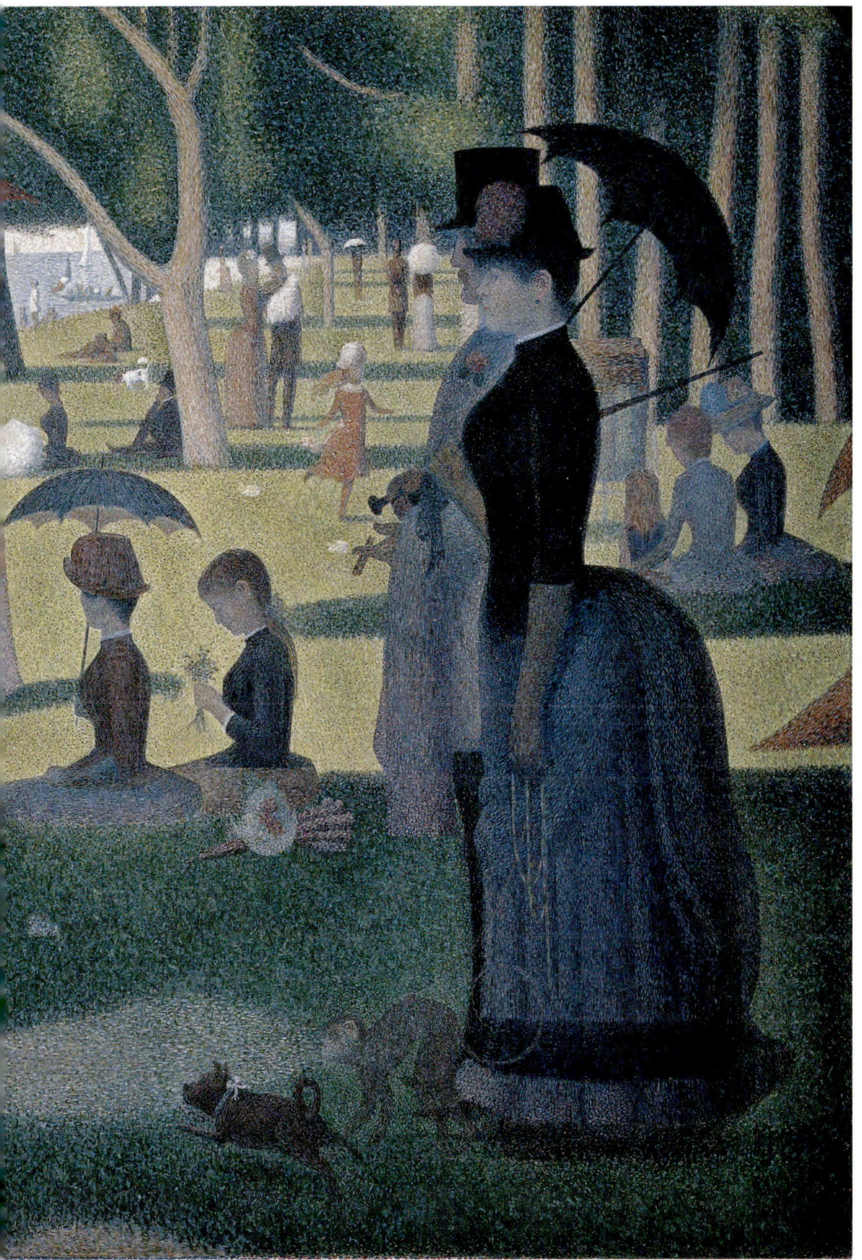

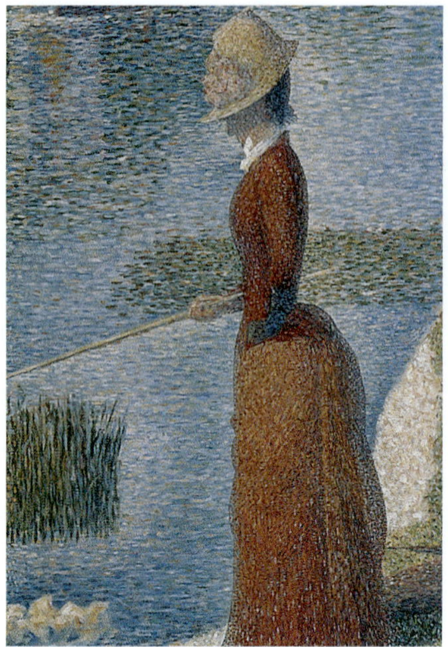

Modelled on a temple frieze

The canvas, which measures 207 by 308 centimetres, only just fitted in the studio of the 25-year-old artist. A colleague described him as "infinitely persistent", with "an energy no less extreme than his shyness". Seurat, born in 1859, could afford to indulge in artistic experimentation: he was financially supported by his father, a lawcourt official who had made a fortune in property speculation.

Seurat had left the École des Beaux-Arts when he was just 21. He wasn't interested in history painting, nor in mermaids and nymphs – and thus rejected the career path followed by conventional artists. After the "unexpected and profound shock" which he experienced upon attending the fourth Impressionist exhibition in 1879, the artist worked alone, drawing portraits and figures of ordinary people in thick black conté-crayon and painting small-format landscapes. Like the Impressionists, he liked to work *en plein air*, out of doors, and in particular beside the water.

It was particularly important to Seurat to capture the light, and nowhere did he find light more captivating than beside the Seine in Asnières, a suburb

to the north-west of Paris. His first large-scale canvas was entitled *Bathers at Asnières*; rejected by the official Salon in 1884, it drew attention at the Salon des Indépendants. It shows bathing men and boys on the banks of the Seine. They are looking across to an island in the river – La Grande Jatte, the setting for Seurat's next work.

The Impressionists, striving to capture the fleeting moment, mostly painted spontaneously out of doors. Seurat's canvas, on the other hand, was preceded by painstaking preparation. He made numerous studies on a panel, executed on site, of the riverbank, grass and trees, in part devoid of people.

These he drew in different positions in black and white sketches. He then combined his two sets of studies. Fénéon describes the some 40 figures in *La Grande Jatte* as "portrayed strictly from behind, in front or the side, sitting stiffly, lying flat, or bolt upright". Contemporaries even spoke of a "Pharaonic procession", and Seurat himself named the temple frieze by the Greek sculptor Phidias as a source of inspiration: "Phidias' Panathenaea were in procession. As in those friezes, I want to portray modern people in their essence."

A classless Sunday outing

Seurat portrays the island in the suburbs as a modern Arcadia. There are neither bottles nor picnic hampers to be seen on the well-tended grass. Invisible, too, are the restaurants, cafés, boatyards and private residences which in the 1880s already occupied two-thirds of the island. The visitors, Seurat's "modern people", are taking a genteel stroll or relaxing in the shade. No one is bathing, no one has removed their clothing.

Fénéon described them as a "fortuitously met … population", and in truth, the people who came together on the small strip of land in the Seine were drawn from various classes of society. For the modern-day viewer, however, it is hard to tell whether the reclining man with the cap and the pipe is a worker from the nearby industrial suburb of Clichy, or a Parisian watersports enthusiast dressed for the part.

For the citizens of Paris, Asnières – from where a ferry made the crossing to La Grand Jatte – was quick and easy to reach thanks to the new railway line. But technology and progress were changing the capital's suburban idylls and covering them with factories and cheap housing for the workforce.

They now became El Dorados for speculators such as Seurat's father.

Rural Asnières had doubled its population in the past few years and evolved into a dormitory town for the petite bourgeoisie – that upwardly-mobile class cultivated by the government of the Third Republic for its contribution to social stability. La Grande Jatte was now visited on a Sunday chiefly by small businessmen, shop assistants, white-collar workers and civil servants, together with their families.

Visible in the background of the painting are two soldiers and – identifiable by her white cape and her bonnet with the long ties – a nurse seen from behind, seated beside an elderly woman beneath a parasol. Everyone else has exchanged their working clothes for their Sunday best. The women in the picture are laced into tight corsets; most are wearing the fashionable *cul de Paris* beneath their full skirt, emphasizing the curves of their figure. Their outfit is completed by a hat, without which – and without a male escort – no honest woman would be seen in public.

The painting poses many questions: are the two girls at the feet of the trumpeter supposed to be easy prey for the approaching soldiers? Is the woman angler fishing for a man? The French for "to fish" (*ocher*) and "to sin" (*pêcher*) sound almost the same. And do the dog and monkey being held on a lead by the lady in the foreground signal simply fashionable extravagance, or (as traditional symbolism would have it) lewd desires?

The man accompanying this lady is wearing a top hat and monacle and carries a walking stick, all typical attributes of the upper middle classes, who usually promenaded in the Bois de Boulogne. Unlike the mixture of society found on La Grande Jatte, the Bois de Boulogne was decidedly exclusive. It would normally have been the domain of the "wellknown Parisian gentleman from the best circles", whose wife – reported the journal *Autour de Paris* in 1887 – kicked up a terrible row when she found out that he had spent the Sunday on La Grande Jatte with her chambermaid.

But Seurat tells no anecdotes. His protagonists have neither a face nor body language, neither a history nor individuality. The "modern people" whom he wanted to "portray … in their essence" are reduced to the formal attributes of top hat, cane and corset – they are characters in his frieze.

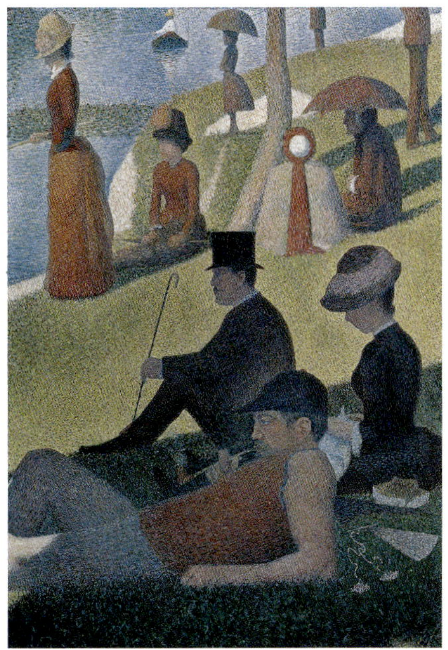

A picture of alienation?

"The secret of working-class morality lies in a Sunday day of rest." Thus ran the conclusion of an essay of 1874 which was awarded a prize by the Académie des Sciences Morales et Politiques. Instead of socializing amongst themselves, like the men in Seurat's *Bathers at Asnières*, workers were supposed to spend Sunday with their families. The government of the Third Republic similarly recommended that proletarians should avoid pubs and protest rallies and ensure order and stability through their upright behaviour. While it was usual to have one day a week free, it was not guaranteed by law until 1902 for women and children, and 1906 for men. Particularly in the 1880s, the issue was the centre of passionate debate: Seurat's subject was thus highly topical.

It is questionable whether either the workers or the petite bourgeoisie knew what to do with their prescribed "family Sunday"; there are few men on Seurat's La Grande Jatte. "Nothing but miserable inactivity" is what Ernst Bloch saw in the picture, by "puppets concentrating intensely on taking a rigid stroll". In the eyes of the Marxist, Seurat's picture spoke above all of the malaise of

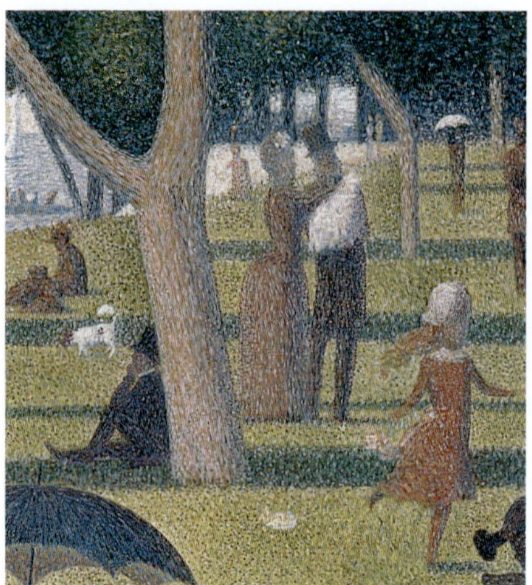

the workers and petite bourgeoisie, of alienation in an industrial society.

How different the mood in *The Luncheon of the Boating Party*, which Pierre-Auguste Renoir painted in 1882 in another Parisian suburb along the Seine. Here, the artist's friends are seated around the remains of lunch at a restaurant table, talking, flirting and laughing – a picture of relaxed conviviality. In Seurat's *La Grande Jatte*, there is virtually no eye or body contact between the protagonists; even the large couple in the foreground are strolling side by side without touching.

Marxists can draw support for their views from one of Seurat's contemporaries. In 1891, following the death of his colleague, Paul Signac wrote in the anarchist journal *La Révolte* that Seurat had a "vivid image of our transitional era", and that the work of his friend "testified to the great social conflicts between workers and capital".

The avant-garde artists in whose circles Seurat moved were fully aware of the darker side of the *belle époque*: money ruled without morality, and strikes by the exploited workforce were brutally crushed. Not a few intellectuals doubted the possibility of reform and believed that the ruling social system would have to be overthrown by force, if necessary, in order to attain a "natural harmony" between people.

Félix Fénéon for one, Seurat's friend and eminence grise of literary and artistic life in Paris.

During the day he worked as a respectable civil servant in the War Office, while at night he wrote his articles and threw bombs into an exclusive Paris restaurant. In 1894 he was only acquitted of the charge of belonging to an international conspiracy for lack of evidence.

Seurat himself left behind no tangible pointers to any political commitment. The sense of isolation and the lack of contact in *La Grande Jatte* probably reflect (amongst other things) the artist's personal problems. Paul Signac described him as a "hypocritical and jealous personality", permanently afraid that someone would contest his right to his artistic inventions.

As the youngest child, he was fussed over by his mother and aunt and taken for walks in the park. As in *La Grande Jatte*, the female element was dominant in his life. He had barely known an intact family; in 1849 his father had withdrawn into a suburban villa like a sort of religious recluse. He visited his family for dinner just once a week, on a Tuesday. The artist never dared miss this ritual; right up to his death, he slept under his mother's roof and kept secret from his family and friends the fact that he lived in his studio with a young working-class girl, with whom he had a child. Seurat lived a double life and observed the bourgeois conventions. He was only unconventional in his art.

The invention of Pointillism

La Grande Jatte was finished in the spring of 1885. Due to arguments between the organizers, however, that year's Salon des Indépendants did not take place. The painting stayed in Seurat's studio, and the artist went to the coast.

When he returned to Paris in the autumn, he turned his attention again to the picture and, over the course of the winter months, completely reworked it. He covered the entire surface with swarms of tiny dots of paint – only someone standing several feet away from the canvas could make out what it actually portrayed.

The painter thereby discovered the "optical formula" for which he had been searching, as he himself said, for as long as he had held a "brush in his hand". He had spent the summer by the Atlantic immersed in books, including *On the Law of the Simultaneous Contrasts of Colours* (1839) by the chemist Eugène Chevreul, and the *Scientific Theory of Colours* by the New York physicist Ogden

Nicholas Rood, published in France in 1881. From his reading he had learned that colours reach the eye in the form of light of varying wavelengths, and are only mixed once they get there. This in turn prompted him to rethink his own art.

Instead of mixing pigments on the palette, he applied them to the canvas as dots of primary colour. Only when these are processed on the viewer's retina do they combine to form the desired hue. Artists already knew that colours are particularly intense in their effect when perceived within a different-coloured setting; Seurat systematized the use of complementary colours and translated scientific knowledge into painstaking artistic detail.

Seurat called his new technique "divisionism"; it later became known as "pointillism". In 1886, at the eighth and last Impressionist exhibition, he presented it in the shape of *La Grande Jatte* and shocked the public. Young painters, however, such as Signac and Lucien Pissarro, followed his lead. Fénéon named the new group the Neo-Impressionists. He thereby distinguished them from the "romantic Impressionists" who had sought to capture fleeting effects of light in a more intuitive fashion. Seurat had replaced their more "arbitrary" approach with a scientific system.

The painter was addicted to order and harmony – and thereby bore an affinity with the intellectual anarchists of his day. Seurat destroyed the reigning visual conventions; he exploded the structure of colour in order to build it back up again, dot by dot. He even incorporated the frame into his striving for harmony: not wanting *La Grande Jatte* to end abruptly at a gold frame or wall, a few years later he gave it a painted frame. This narrow border brings the picture's waves of colour to a gentle conclusion.

The tranquillity and fascination exuded by the painting can be traced not simply to its colours, but also to its austere linear structure: the verticals of the trees and the strolling figures correspond to the horizontals of the shadows and the people seated and reclining.

Here too, Seurat was searching for a system and experimenting with the latest theories. The academic Charles Henry, in his Introduction to *A Scientific Aesthetic* published in 1885, had investigated the emotional expressiveness of colour and line, and had thereby distinguished between falling, constricting lines which made the viewer feel ill at ease, and rising lines which – like those of the sailing boat in the background – produced a feeling of elation and joy in the viewer. Sails such as this, with their "positive", gentle curves, are also found in a number of the later works which Seurat executed in the few years remaining to him – the signature, so to speak, of the harmony-loving art revolutionary.

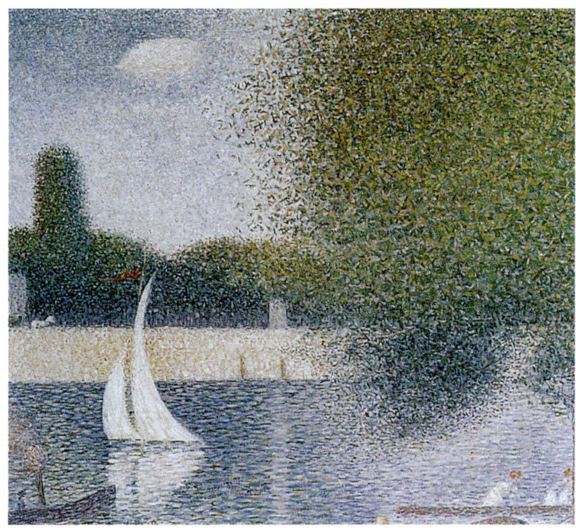

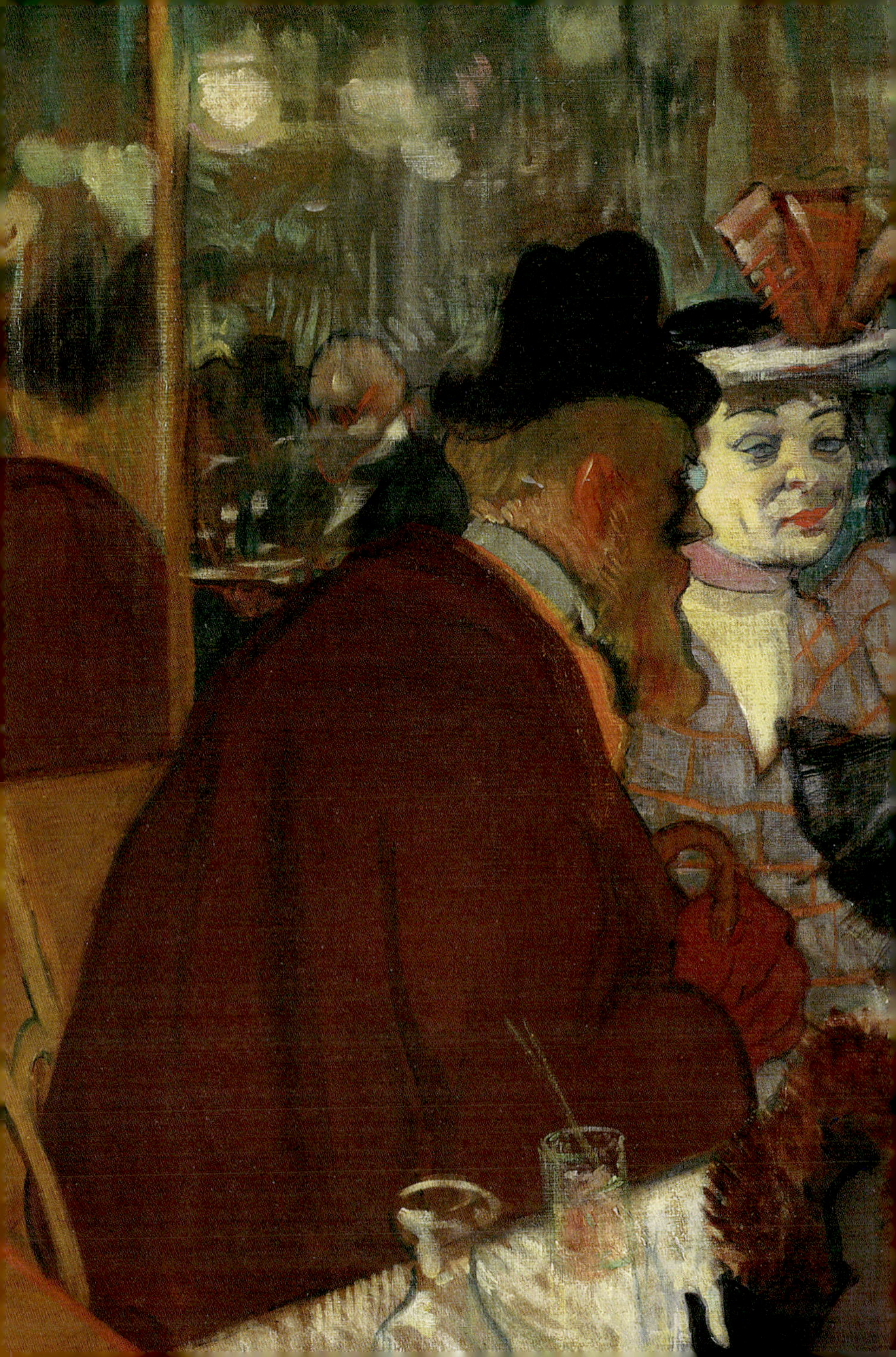

Henri de Toulouse-Lautrec (1864–1901)

Glamour and misery of the courtesans – and of the artist

At the Moulin Rouge, c. 1893
123 x 141 cm, The Art Institute of Chicago,
Helen Birch Bartlett Memorial Collection

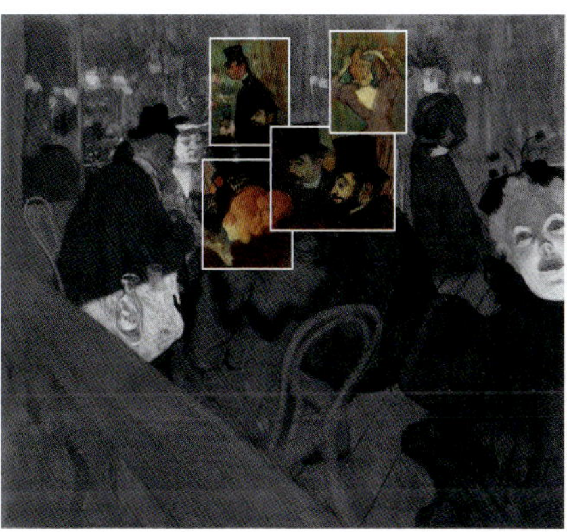

The route from the artist's apartment to his studio led past the Moulin Rouge, the red windmill that had never ground grain. Its arms were simply models and the trademark of a dance hall. It lay on Montmartre hill, on the Boulevard de Clichy, at that time the boundary between working-class district and bourgeois residential area. The Moulin Rouge thrived on the bourgeoisie's curiosity about the forms of entertainment enjoyed by the lower classes. The activity on the dance floor could be safely observed from a raised balcony running all the way round the room.

Up on the balcony right next to the railings, a small marble table was permanently reserved for Henri de Toulouse-Lautrec (1864–1901). There he drank fashionable American cocktails and passed the time in the company of his friends and the nightclub's stars. He painted them over and over again in his works from these years. In the present picture the dwarfish artist is himself visible, walking past in the background, while a dancer adjusts her hair in one of the many large mirrors.

Seated around the table in the foreground are a photographer, a champagne representative and a journalist, accompanied by two women. On the right, a cropped figure lit ghoulishly from below leans out of the picture towards the viewer. A snapshot from the heart of the Parisian entertainment industry in the *belle époque*.

A dancer causes a scandal
She was known as La Goulue, "the glutton", because she liked to drain guests' half-empty glasses and because of the voracity with which she flung

herself into life – and not least, too, because she
radiated eroticism. Even if Toulouse-Lautrec places
her in the background of the picture as here, she
is instantly recognizable from the low-cut back of
her dress and from her trademark hairstyle, her
tresses wound up into a golden knot that lent her
face – according to one contemporary – a vulgar
and attractive *air canaille*.

In a moment she will burst whooping onto
the cleared dance floor in order to perform, as she
did every night, the *quadrille naturaliste* with her
female colleagues. The star's regular partner was
Valentin "the boneless", a lawyer's assistant with a
passion for dancing. When La Goulue danced,
wrote an electrified witness, her skirts seemed
to be "virtually on fire"; "leaping like a mad goat",
she would do the splits or perform the military
port d'armes, whereby instead of arms she presented
a black-stockinged leg between white lace skirts,
kicking it high and knocking the top hats off customers' heads.

The girls jumped up onto the tables, offering
glimpses of their thighs and sometimes more. In an
epoch in which men were aroused by the mere sight
of a female ankle, this quadrille caused a scandal.
"Dancers are requested to wear underclothes," stated
a notice in the staff changing-rooms at the Moulin
Rouge. The *quadrille naturaliste* – a boisterous
variation of the can-can – had arisen in the rear
courtyards of Paris's poor districts as a spontaneous
out-burst of energy and vitality after the day's work
was done. In the 1880s, managers in the entertainment industry introduced the dance in their nightclubs as a plebeian attraction. Their female dancers
in provocative poses became a symbol of the capital
and during the Exposition Universelle of 1889 even
shunted the new Eiffel Tower off the front covers
of the city's newspapers.

La Goulue was a star who had started at the
very bottom. Born Louise Weber in the Lorraine
region of France in 1866, her family fled to Paris
from the Prussians while she was still a girl. She
scraped a living as a flower-seller and laundress
and at night danced in the dives of Montmartre.
Her audacious style drew attention and in 1886
one proprietor offered her a contract. In 1889, however, she was poached by the management of the
Moulin Rouge, who launched their new venture
with her as their star. Vulgar, brazen and always
in the spotlight, she was what we might call a

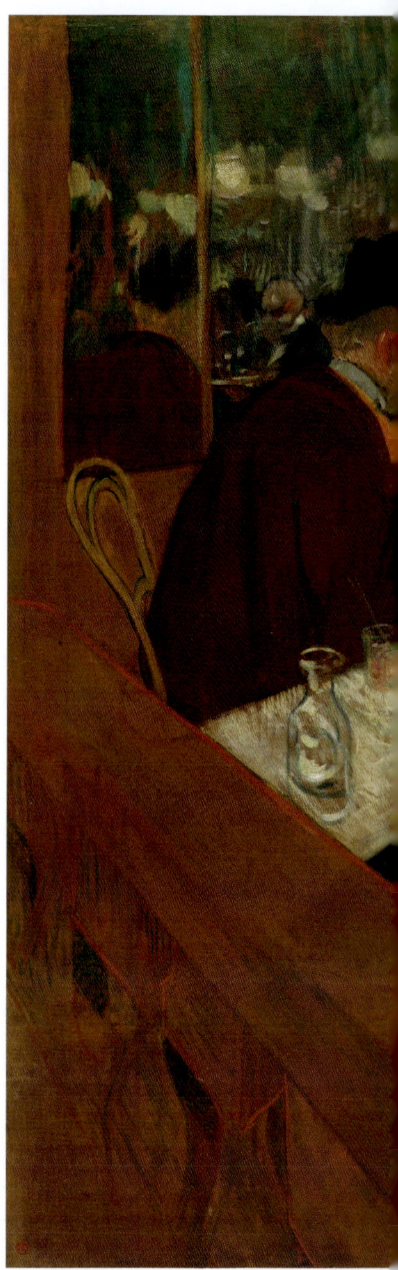

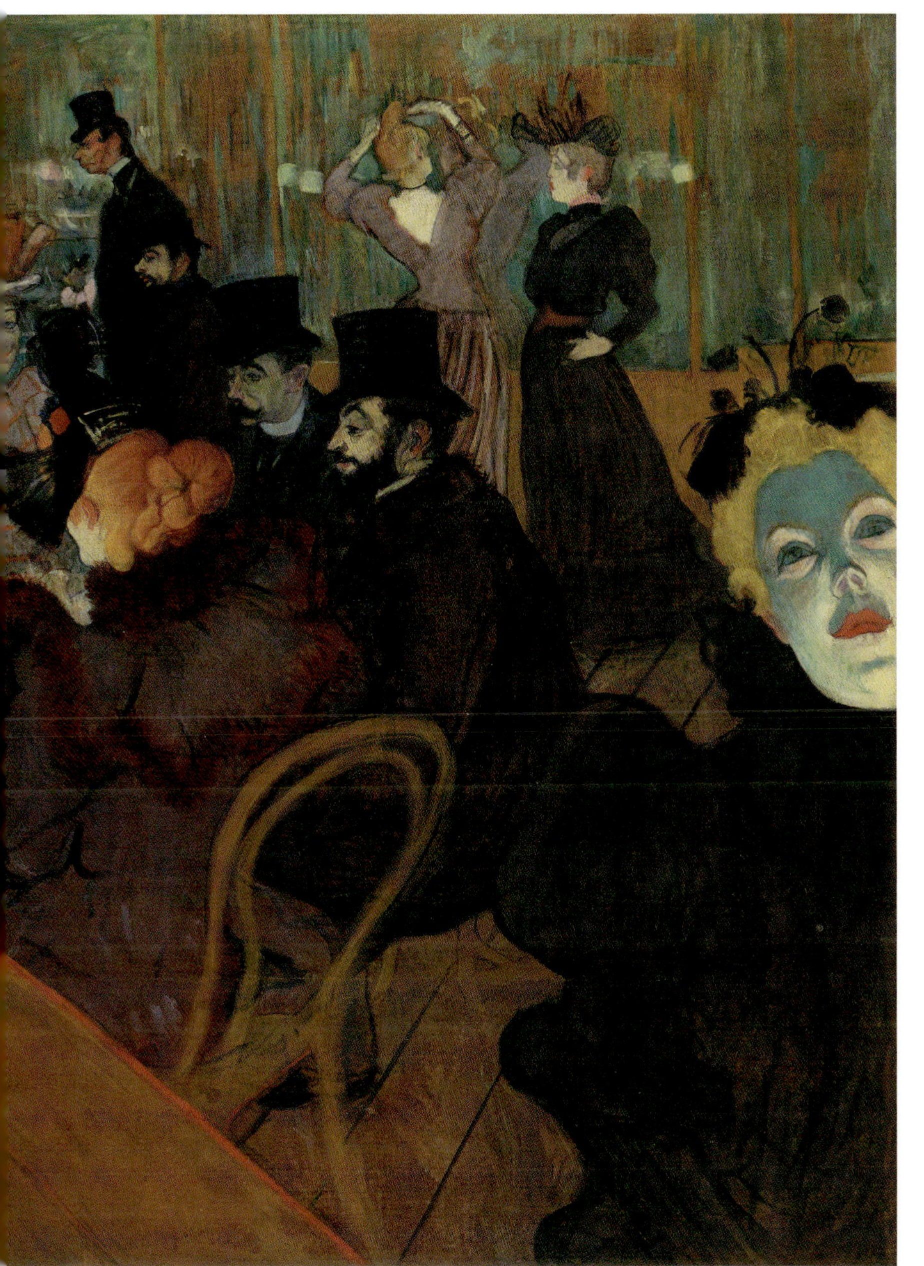

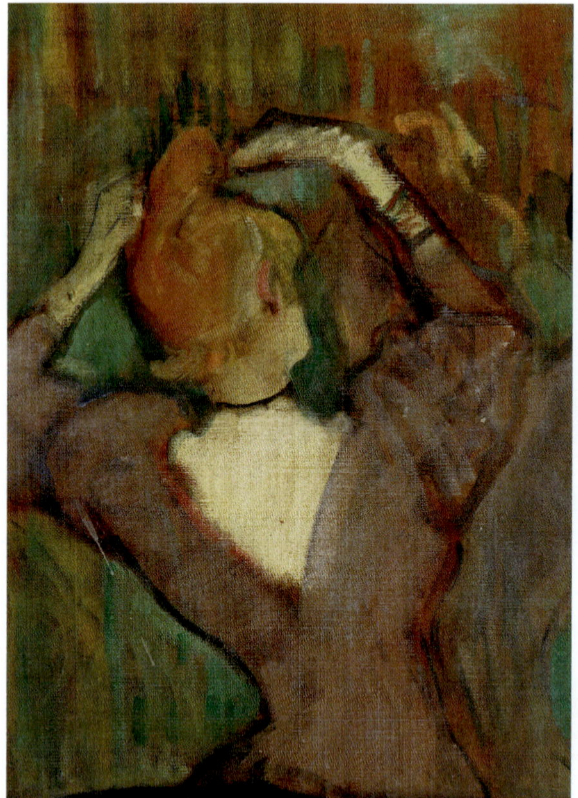

The artist's nocturnal companions

As another means of luring the curious bourgeoisie, the handbills announced that "painters, sculptors and literati… in short, all of fun-loving Paris" met at the Moulin Rouge every night. Yet to the modern-day viewer the protagonists of the painting sooner seem bored and somewhat undecided whether to stay – perhaps because they have kept their hats on their heads. In those days, however, this was entirely normal in public buildings, even in the theatre. The gentlemen are also still wearing their coats, as if they had just called in while passing. Like Toulouse-Lautrec, they all lived or worked in the vicinity of the Moulin Rouge on Montmartre.

The guest on the left, Paul Sescau, had his photographic studio very close by at 9, place Pigalle. He specialized in the reproduction of paintings and regularly photographed Toulouse-Lautrec and his works and models. Beside him is Maurice Guibert, who worked as a representative for the prestigious champagne firm of Moët et Chandon and frequented the district's restaurants and bars in a professional as well as a personal capacity. Seated further left, wearing a monocle, a soft hat, gloves and carrying a walking stick or umbrella, is the publisher Edouard Dujardin. He promoted the music of Richard Wagner and other avant-garde arts in his magazines and wrote his own Symbolist plays for the theatre. Photographer, sales agent and publisher – all three are found in other works by Toulouse-Lautrec from this same period. During the day the artist used his friends as models and at night he gathered them around his little table at the Moulin Rouge, supplying them with anecdotes and cocktails.

"celeb babe" of her time. She hauled her pimp up in front of the courts, eloped with her Portuguese lover, published love letters and even kicked the hat off the head of the heir to the English throne. Her celebrity was fuelled both by the press and by the bosses of the Moulin Rouge, who came up with entirely new ways of publicizing their nightclub. They advertised with handbills, personal invitations to VIPs and above all with large posters. When La Goulue appeared in 1891 on every wall in Paris, advertising the establishment with her skirts hoisted and her leg kicked high, not only the dancer became famous, but also the artist who had designed the poster. It was Toulouse-Lautrec's first venture into publicity lithographs.

pagne firm of Moët et Chandon and frequented the district's restaurants and bars in a professional as well as a personal capacity. Seated further left, wearing a monocle, a soft hat, gloves and carrying a walking stick or umbrella, is the publisher Edouard Dujardin. He promoted the music of Richard Wagner and other avant-garde arts in his magazines and wrote his own Symbolist plays for the theatre. Photographer, sales agent and publisher – all three are found in other works by Toulouse-Lautrec from this same period. During the day the artist used his friends as models and at night he gathered them around his little table at the Moulin Rouge, supplying them with anecdotes and cocktails.

There they sit, "the ugly mugs of doting capitalists… in the company of little whores full of insolence and malice". Thus they were characterized by another friend of the artist, the left-wing art critic Félix Fénéon. They resemble the decadent, somewhat perverse heroes of the novels by Joris Karl Huysmans. As typical representatives of the *fin de siècle*, in nightclubs such as the Moulin Rouge they probably enjoyed the sorts of charms described by Huysmans in his *Parisian Sketches* of 1880, charms such as the "exquisite and divine aroma" issuing from female armpits in the heat of the dance hall, created "to add salt and spice to the ragout of love that habit has made so indigestible and insipid", and even "to let the beast in man out of its cage".

The artist caricatures himself

The artist had a penchant for theatrical effects and liked to make his nocturnal rounds in the company of his lanky cousin Gabriel. He only reached up to the latter's waist and the contrast between them underlined his own deformity: his large head beneath a bowler hat, a normal upper body complete with proportional arms, followed by extremely short, thin legs. All of this was the result of several broken bones sustained during his childhood and above all of inbreeding within his family, who were

members of the southern French nobility. Count Henri de Toulouse-Lautrec's mother and father were first cousins and their siblings in turn were the parents of Gabriel Tapié de Céleyran. Henri and Gabriel both grew up on the family estates in the Languedoc, and when Gabriel came to Paris in the 1890s to study medicine, the painter introduced him to the city's nightlife. Gabriel was probably the only member of the aristocratic family to appreciate his cousin's art – it is largely to him that we owe the later foundation of the Musée Toulouse-Lautrec in Albi. The two young men were frowned upon within the family because they studied and painted rather than looking after their landed estates. Their forefathers, the counts of Toulouse, had distinguished themselves in particular on crusades and in hunts.

Henri vexed his father not only by his choice of profession but also by his lifestyle. In Montmartre he moved amongst fellow painters, circus artistes, dancers, alcoholics and prostitutes. It was a world in which a cripple was less conspicuous and in which he did not feel an outsider, and it was here that he sought his subjects. He portrayed not only

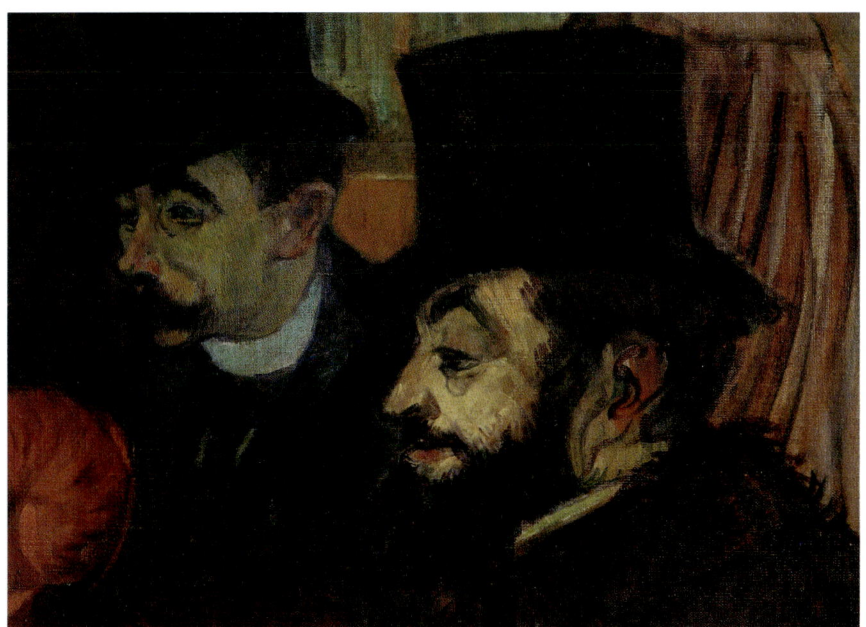

the current stars of the stage but also new dancers being "trained" for their appearance, as in an oil painting of 1889/90.

This latter picture was bought by the proprietor of the Moulin Rouge, who had it hanging in the entrance for years. In 1891 the same proprietor asked its young (and still affordable) artist to produce the preliminary design for a publicity poster. This brought Toulouse-Lautrec fame faster than any art exhibition. In the service of the entertainment business, he proceeded to produce a wealth of posters for theatres, cabarets and music halls, using the new technique of lithography. He drew easily recognizable silhouettes that were reduced to just a few typical features – almost caricatures. The two so dissimilar cousins in the Moulin Rouge picture also look like caricatures at first sight: Toulouse-Lautrec opted all his life to depict his own misshapenness, to exaggerate it and to turn himself into a figure of fun before others did. He was unsparing in his depiction of the people in his works, emphasizing the flabby faces of the *bon viveurs* and the mask-like white make-up worn by their female companions around the table.

In 1876 Auguste Renoir had taken a very different look at another of Montmartre's windmills, which

he captured in a more soft-focus Impressionist style. In his *Moulin de la Galette*, young artists are flirting with pretty milliners in the sunshine beneath the trees. Thirteen years later Toulouse-Lautrec also painted the Moulin de la Galette, but in his painting the sun does not shine: in a scene bathed in the same aquarium-green artificial light as in the Moulin Rouge, a pimp monitors deals between prostitutes and clients. Communication between the sexes seems to be entirely reduced to sex and money.

As an outsider, and as one whose family background meant that he belonged neither to the proletariat nor the bourgeoisie, the artist was able to take a distanced view of his protagonists, dancers and customers. As he said to one of his friends, he made his nightly rounds of the clubs in search for motifs like a hunter stalking his prey – in a similar fashion to his aristocratic father hunting partridge.

Redheads everywhere

Red-headed women were the painter's preferred quarry both in his life and in his art – "truly red-haired, properly red-haired!" as Toulouse-Lautrec insisted. A certain prostitute by the name of Rosa la Rouge is said to have given him the venereal disease that hastened his death. His canvases are peopled by such redheads, who pose in theatre loges, perform on cabaret floors or rustle past in the background. In this last case they are usually dressed in the style of the lady here seen in rear view, keeping the gentlemen company around the table. She wears a dark pelerine with a stand-up collar and puffed sleeves, topped by an eye-catching hat with black, transparent side flaps and a plume of ostrich feathers. In those days hats were considered an indispensable sign of female respectability and kept 2,400 milliners in work in Paris!

The faces of Toulouse-Lautrec's redheads are seldom to be seen; the artist usually depicts them in rear view, as decorative, anonymous beings. And while we know the names of his male models in this painting, we can only guess at the identities of the ladies: one might be the up-market courtesan Jane Avril, an elegant dancer who around 1892 supplanted the vulgar La Goulue as the public's favourite. The other woman at the table was known as La Macarona and was probably one of the many *petites femmes* who sought customers at the Moulin Rouge.

Like champagne, these women were a Parisian export commodity. If they knew how to warble a

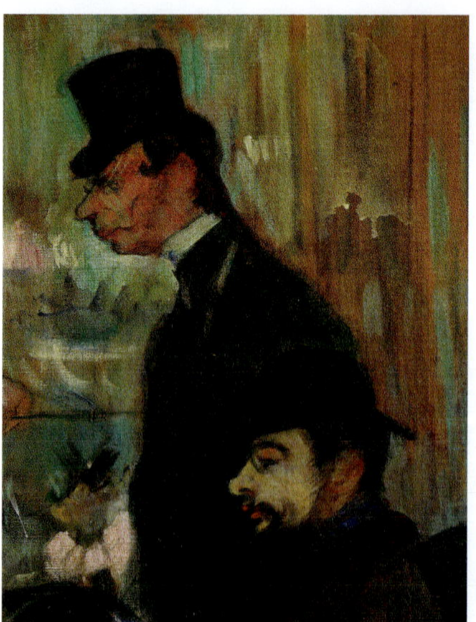

little and could kick up their legs,
they were given a third-class rail
ticket and sent off to the French
provinces or to Madrid, Russia
or Austro-Hungary. Whereas La
Goulue in her heyday was earning
up to 3,750 gold francs at month,
these beginners were paid 150
francs a month for two performances a day, with the possibility
of supplementing their salary by
keeping the guests company after
the show.

The identity of the woman on
the right-hand side of the picture,
looking up towards the viewer
with a face harshly illuminated
from below by the greenish
footlights, remains a mystery.
The gallery-owner Joyant
described her as "Nelly C". The
piece of canvas on which she is
painted is an addition, as is the
strip along the bottom, running
the full width of the canvas and
showing the wooden balustrade,
chair and black dress. This has
inspired some bizarre hypotheses.
More recent analyses have confirmed that all three sections of
canvas have the same structure.

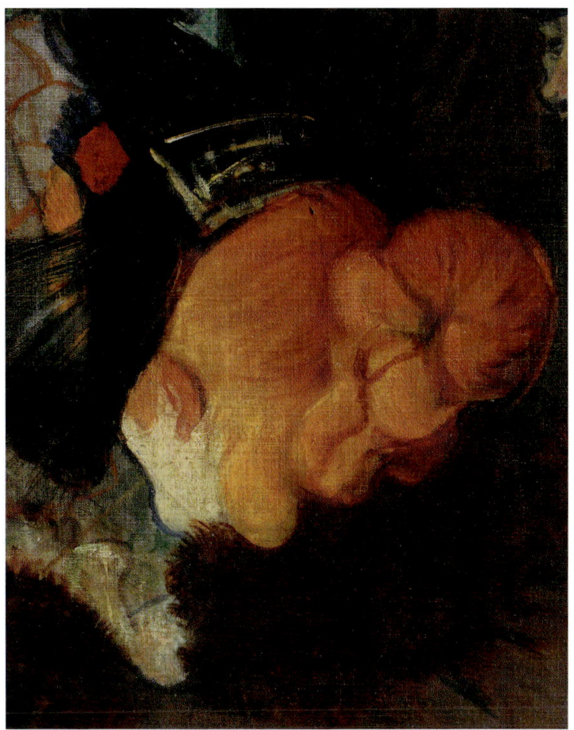

It is today assumed that Toulouse-Lautrec himself
enlarged the format in the course of his work,
on the grounds that he wished to show more than
simply a traditional group portrait and incorporate
into the picture the distinctive atmosphere of the
setting. In the resulting painting, the artist has
shifted the table away from the centre, thereby desta-
bilizing the composition. He has created a wide,
dark diagonal that starts from the bottom right-hand
corner but does not continue all the way to the top
left-hand corner. He has characterized the setting
via a host of figures yet thrusts the empty triangle
of the balustrade into the lower left-hand corner
of the picture. On the additional strip of canvas on
the right, the woman's green-lit face appears much
closer to the front than the other figures and is also
cropped in the manner of the new medium of
photography. The composition as a whole seems
disparate, is difficult to grasp: a joyless nightclub

coloured by the artist's view of life. A world in which
friends are also strangers.

After this painting the artist gradually withdrew
from the establishment on Place Blanche, which
was increasingly becoming an attraction for groups
of English tourists. He now preferred to spend his
evenings in the capital's brothels, where he found
new models – most them redheads, too, but without
hats. The 28-year-old painter had another nine years
to live. He would only return to his old material
on one other occasion, when he painted two large
decorative panels for the fairground booth of a now
overweight and seedy La Goulou. In these panels, the
well-known faces from the Moulin Rouge are assembled for one last time.

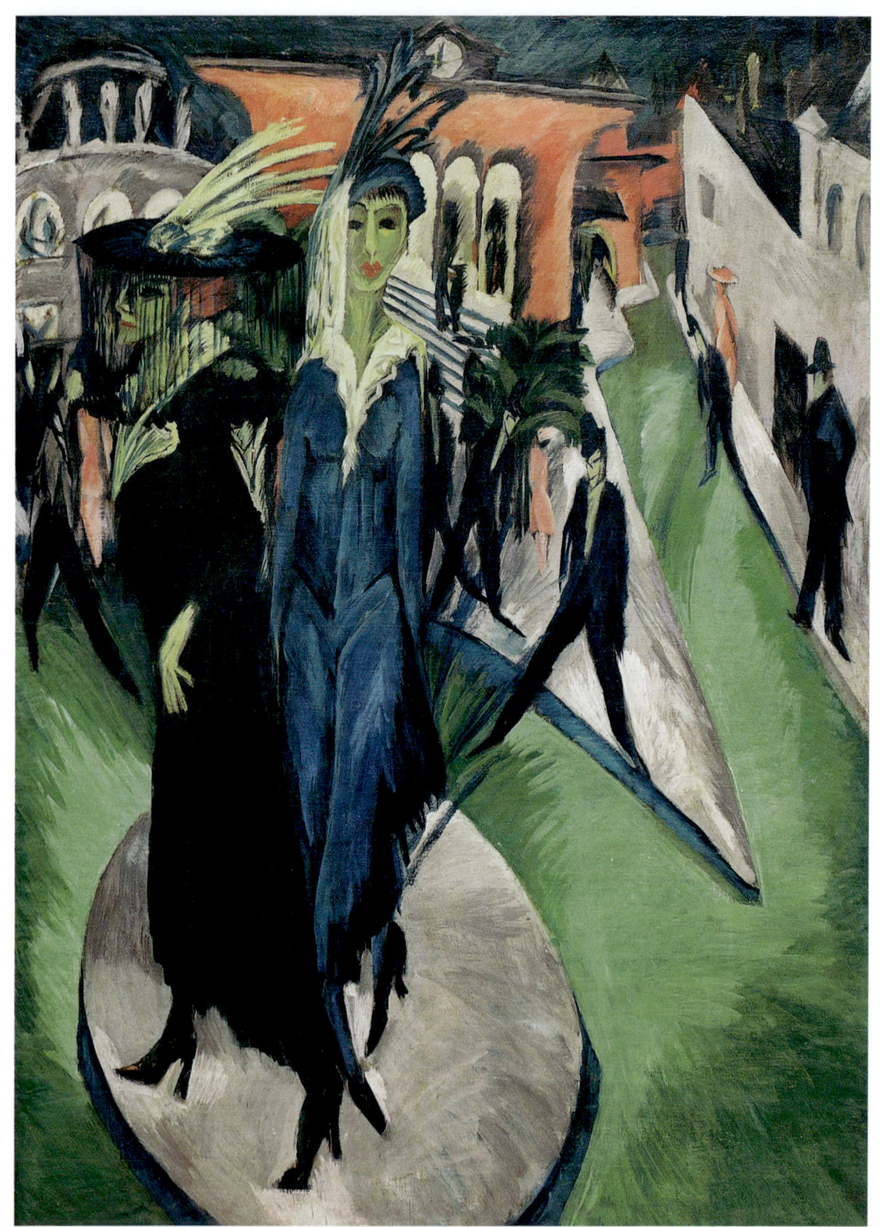

Ernst Ludwig Kirchner (1880–1938)

The world is out of joint

Potsdamer Platz, 1914
200 x 150 cm, Berlin, Staatliche Museen zu Berlin,
Neue Nationalgalerie

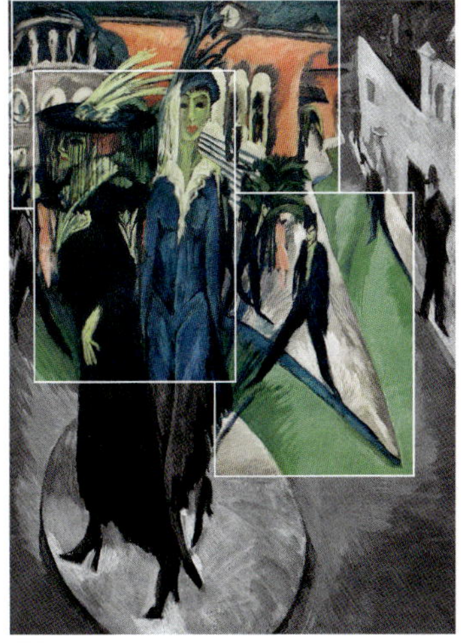

The two women in the foreground confront the
viewer in almost life size. The one in the blue dress
is walking directly towards us. The other – exiting
the painting to the left – cuts across her path. They
almost collide. The men behind them are all darkly
clad; they step out with legs apart and heads and
upper bodies bent forward at more or less the same
angle. In their uniformity, they resemble industrial
products, robots, toys.

Although, as viewers, we face the women in
this two-metre-high canvas at eye level, we see the
ground on which they are standing from a much
higher viewpoint, a dual perspective, as if the figures
are walking across a sloping floor. The pavements
and the pedestrian island are like grey slabs that have
been slid over a green road surface. The red building
at the top of the picture is crooked. The clock on
its roof says twelve. The sky is dark – midnight.
A square seems to have come out of joint.

Ernst Ludwig Kirchner painted the picture in
1914. It shows a corner of Potsdamer Platz in Berlin.
He regularly sat and sketched the square from the

pavement café opposite. This was not just any square,
but the most heavily congested in the entire city.
Five main streets and a stream of rail travellers con-
verged upon it. A guidebook of 1910 states that it was
crossed by some 5,000 trams every day. Photos from
the same era show horse-drawn omnibuses, hack-
ney carriages, handcarts, and the first automobiles
jostling alongside trams. "For foreigners, children,
women, and the elderly," warned the guidebook,
crossing Potsdamer Platz "could be hazardous to
health and life."

Nowhere in Germany had such a concentration
of people and vehicles ever been seen before, nor was
any other city home to so many people as Berlin. In
1871 the seat of the Prussian monarchy had become
the capital of the German empire. Engineering and
electrical works had made Berlin the leading centre
of German industry. In 1871 it had a population of
over 800,000; by 1914 this figure had swelled to well
over two million. Anyone who was looking for work,
who wanted to be modern, moved to Berlin – farm
labourers who had lost their jobs to agricultural

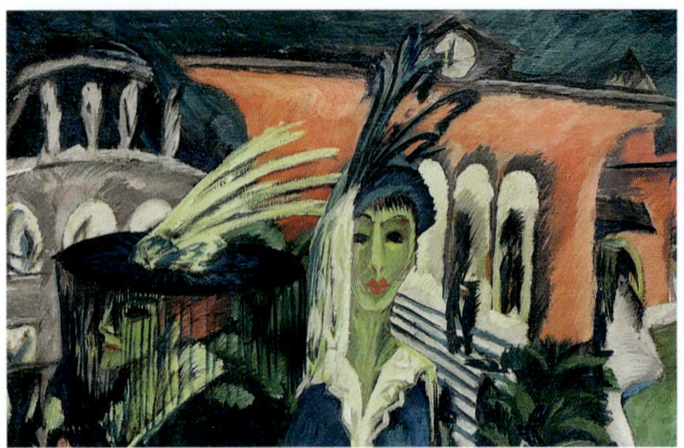

machinery, businessmen in search of better deals, journalists and artists who sensed that developments were unfolding faster here than in Dresden, Munich or Hamburg. Kirchner had been living in Berlin since 1911.

As the two hands of the clock converge vertically upon twelve, we think of midnight and the witching hour, of figures from beyond the veil or the beginning of something radically new. With the benefit of hindsight, we know that 1914 and the outbreak of the first of the catastrophic wars of the 20th century did indeed mark the start of a new era. It was something no one at that time could suspect, however, including Kirchner. As his writings reveal, he took little interest in the world of politics. He was fascinated only by what lay before his eyes, with what he experienced at first hand.

In the middle of the traffic
Railway stations in those days were hubs of activity, exerting a fascination matched at best by airports today. They were places where you could admire the latest means of high-speed transport, where guests of honour were welcomed with red carpet, a band and an armed guard, where progressive technology was lent nobility through official pomp and circumstance. Potsdam Station was the oldest in Berlin. In 1872 it had been given a new terminal building with a façade designed to recall the Italian *palazzi* of the Renaissance. Kirchner takes away its side wings and upper loggias and allows the roof to sweep out over the walls.

To the left of the station, separated only by a street, stood a large building crowned with a cupola

and statuary. It was completed in 1912, just two years before Kirchner captured it fleetingly on his canvas. A multi-purpose building, it housed a cinema, cabaret theatre, offices and – most important of all – the Café Piccadilly, "the biggest coffee house in the world", which offered seating for 2,000. Just a few steps away lay the Wertheim department store, which with its lavish interiors on several floors offered a new type of shopping experience. Everywhere new dimensions, spectacular inventions, greater numbers, fascinating for some, confusing and threatening for others.

Potsdamer Platz had evolved rather than been planned, and unlike major traffic intersections today, it was a place where many people spent time. Flower sellers plied their trade on the pavements during the day, hotel guests looked down from their balconies, and friends met in a popular pavement café, where Kirchner also sat. There were restaurants, shops, a beer garden, and of course prostitutes in large numbers – all of them together making Potsdamer Platz a centre of encounters and entertainment, especially at night.

"Ach Willy, ach Willy, um sechs im Piccadilly" ("Oh Willy, oh Willy, at six in the Piccadilly") began a light-hearted song in these increasingly dark times. It was not the Piccadilly for long. In 1914, with patriotism running high following the outbreak of war, the management changed the name to Café Vaterland (Café Fatherland). Since Kirchner began his painting in the spring and finished it in the autumn, his café could call itself by both names.

The two buildings through which Kirchner identifies his location have long since disappeared. In 1945 they were bombed and burnt out; all that remained of the cupola was its steel skeleton. The rooms beneath were used for makeshift accommodation. Now finding itself on the boundary between the Allied sectors, the Vaterland acquired a dubious reputation as a hideout for blackmarketeers.

The ruins of the Vaterland and the station were removed in the 1950s. The border dividing East and West Berlin now ran straight across Potsdamer Platz – and when it became a wall, the formerly bustling centre of urban life and transport was transformed into a wasteland. It was patrolled on one side by East German police while, on the other, the citizens of West Berlin climbed up onto a wooden platform and stared over the wall: the fate of a very German square.

The same site today shares only its geographical location and name with the Potsdamer Platz of old. Where Kirchner paints a grey wall on the righthand edge of the picture, the offices of the Daimler-Chrysler company now rise. Where platforms and tracks once lay behind the terminal building, a park is under construction. Today the jostling traffic is that of diggers and trucks.

Prostitutes are everywhere in male fantasies
The two women beneath their tall feathered hats are, in Kirchner's words, *Kokotten*, cocottes. Women appear in many of his street scenes, but where he describes them more specifically, it is only ever as "cocottes". He never mentions their male customers. In his portrayals of such women, he was evidently thinking less of their profession than of casual, changing relationships. *Kokotte – Zeitfrau* ("cocotte – temporary woman") is a phrase jotted down in one of his sketchbooks.

He was at that time living with Erna Schilling. She and her sister Gerda had fled the family home and were earning their living, it appears, as dancers in cheap cabarets. They modelled for the artist. Although the two cocottes in *Potsdamer Platz* bear a certain resemblance to Erna and Gerda, the artist stylizes them and refuses to be specific.

Visions of free, unbridled love were in those days a common feature of male fantasies, and the notion of the prostitute as an ideal partner was not exclusive to Kirchner. The Berlin neurologist and writer Alfred Döblin celebrated the cocotte as a "pioneer of socialism in a moral wasteland". For Döblin, sex within marriage was "as if you were only allowed to be hungry at mealtimes and in certain restaurants".

Kirchner (1880–1938) and Döblin (1878–1957) were almost the same age and knew each other well. Kirchner painted the doctor's portrait and in 1913 furnished the woodcuts for his short drama *Comtess Mizzi*. This strange play celebrates free love: in the countess's "academy", female pupils are prepared for a sort of erotic temple service; they "are our sacred daughters … their kissing mouths closed in prayer". At the end, the institute is stormed by the police. From here to *Berlin Alexanderplatz*, Döblin's masterpiece of 1929, it was still a long way.

Erotic fantasies such as Döblin's *Comtess Mizzi* were produced in vast quantities. Another such was called *Potsdamer Platz*, like Kirchner's painting, and was written by one Curt Corrinth. It tells the story of a young man from the provinces, who sees in Berlin's prostitutes the fairy princesses of his childhood. They become "Blessed Virgins of delight" who offer men "deliverance from the flesh". Kirchner was not unfamiliar with such sublimation of whores and the sexual act: his own cocottes reveal neither bosom nor leg nor wear a seductive smile; they walk like queens, look serious, recall temple servers at the altar, resemble hetaerae sooner than whores.

There were practical reasons for this display of severity, however. Prostitutes were required to be unobtrusive. According to a Berlin police regulation of 1911, it was forbidden "to stand or walk about in an indecent manner" or to proposition anyone directly. "Standing and sitting in doorways is also prohibited." Plain-clothed police officers made sure the city's prostitutes towed the line. Following the

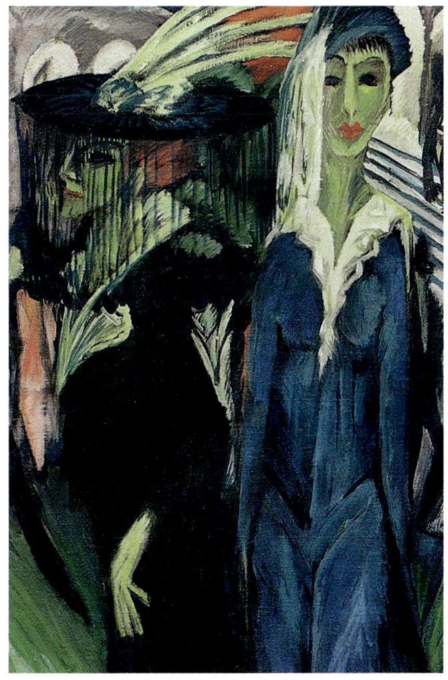

outbreak of war, it is said, many dressed themselves as widows, with a veil and black dress, in the hope that sympathy would win them extra trade.

The army maims the artist

Kirchner was called up in the spring of 1915. Military service was too much for him; he had a nervous breakdown and after a few weeks was released, "hardly able to walk". But he continued to paint. He portrayed himself as a recruit of the 75th field artillery regiment, his forehead concealed by his uniform cap, his cheeks sunken, a cigarette hanging from his lips. He would later suffer the effects of nic-otine poisoning and drug abuse. He paints himself with a bloody stump for an arm, afraid of not being able to work any more, of perhaps being impotent. What does he want with the naked woman in the background? "I myself am now like the cocottes I painted. Wiped out; next time, finished."

It is a desperate, defeatist self-portrait – painted at a time when defending the fatherland was the only

honourable activity for a man. Kirchner, the out-sider, was born on 6 May 1880 in Aschaffenburg and was 34 years old when war broke out. He had studied architecture at his father's insistence, but had secretly attended art college at the same time. In Dresden in 1905 he and a group of friends founded Die Brücke (The Bridge), an association of impoverished artists with similar aims. They wanted to turn their backs on "the well-regarded older mas-ters" and claim freedom in both their art and their lifestyles. That meant combating establishment art with their joint portfolios of graphic works and also developing their own, bohemian lifestyle. Kirchner lived with a succession of girlfriends in cave-like ateliers amongst furniture he had carved himself. His photographic series reveal a yearning for naked companionship.

In 1911, like many other painters and writers, he moved to Berlin, the new Babylon, the all-con-suming Moloch. After his military service and nervous breakdown, friends helped him find refuge in Davos. He would stay there for the rest of his life, looked after by his Berlin girlfriend Erna Schilling, permanently under the care of doctors, troubled by panic attacks and paranoia. His former urge for free-dom twisted itself into the delusion that everyone was his enemy. He felt no one understood him; his mistress lived so far beneath him that even she was unable to reach him.

Sales of his works were curtailed by external circumstances, such as the inflation which followed the end of the war, the global economic crisis of 1929 and Hitler's seizure of power in 1933. How much he nevertheless managed to sell to public collections is revealed by the number of his works impounded by the Nazis – over 600. Thirty-two of them were included in the 1937 *Degenerate Art* exhibition in Munich, where they were held up for public derision.

The following year, Kirchner shot himself. His mistress explained: "The defamation in Germany, coupled with the unsuccessful November exhibition in Basle, where he again attracted nothing but criticism, led him, on the beautiful, sunny morning of 15 November, to end his life. Thank God he shot himself clean through the heart so that he died instantly."

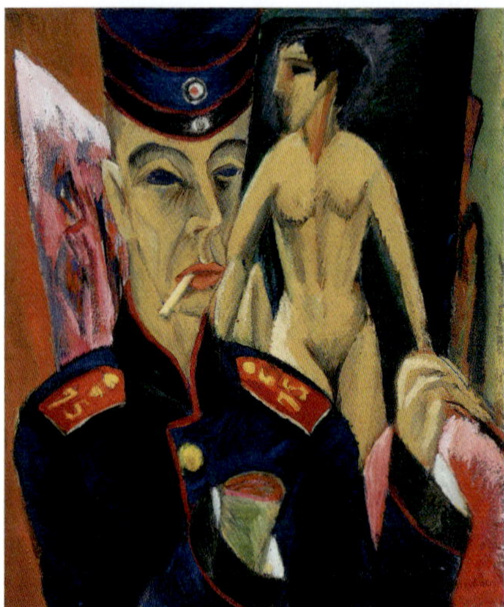

Comparative illustration:
Ernst Ludwig Kirchner
Self-portrait as a Soldier, 1915
69 x 61 cm
Oberlin, Allen Memorial Art Museum,
Oberlin College, Ohio, Charles F. Olney Fund

The Germans were late to discover the metropolis

Kirchner lived in an era during which Europe's art disintegrated. For centuries painters had oriented themselves towards objects and how they appeared to the eye. That was now over. Figure and object were distorted, splintered, compressed into geometric forms, portrayed from several sides within a single plane. They were given strange colours, lost their three-dimensional shape or disappeared entirely into an abstract surface. Each stylistic tendency had its own name. Kirchner belonged to the Expressionists.

Over and over again he said that he didn't want to portray the world as it was, but as he experienced it. He may have had a practical reason: the demand for pictures of the real world could now be satisfied by photography, whose images could be mass-produced thanks to new printing techniques. For Kirchner, the outer world was simply a starting-point: "shapes and colours spring from the imagination of the artist."

Colours in his works rarely correspond to those of the object in real life: his kerbstones are blue, the station glows red, the road surface changes from a stronger green to a mixed yellow. This liberation of colour from its object was typical not just of Expressionist painters, but also of Expressionist writers, who spoke of "black silence", "silver coolness", and "vapours in every colour of the rainbow". The idea, suggested by some, that the green street might be intended symbolically, perhaps as a reference to the banishment of Nature, does not mesh with Kirchner's aesthetic. He was concerned with expressing what life in the metropolis felt like. Judging solely by the colour combinations in *Potsdamer Platz*, there seems to be an unfriendliness, an uneasiness about the city, far removed from the feast for the eyes prepared by the Berlin Impressionists.

Dominant amongst the shapes are the circle of the pedestrian island and the pointed wedge of the pavement. Curves and acute angles are in fact repeated throughout the composition – the latter in the splayed legs of the men and the angular profile of the woman in black, the former in the arches of the building and in the face of the woman in blue. While curves suggest a pleasing, peaceful quality, acute angles are rather more aggressive, especially when pointing towards the viewer. Kirchner thereby formulates contradictory experiences.

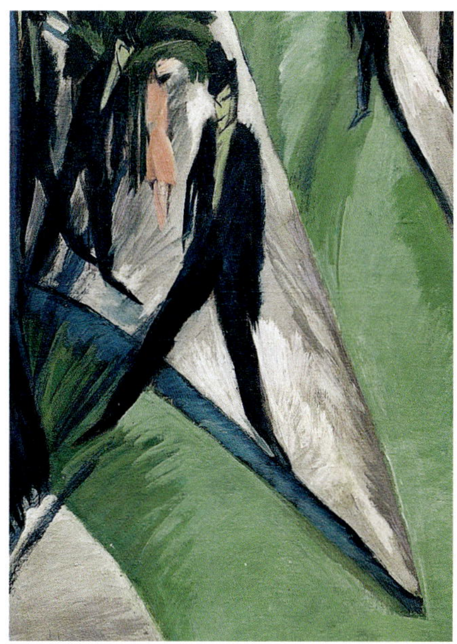

He does the same in his figures. They are hurrying to and fro, seemingly in constant motion, but pass each other with their eyes cast down or averted to one side. Their arms appear atrophied or as if grown fast to their body, and their hands are not free to touch each other. The residents of Kirchner's Berlin neither see nor feel each other; they pass each other's lives by. Perhaps the enigmatic expression on the face of the woman advancing towards the artist and viewer offers the only option, short-term happiness: "Wiped out; next time, finished." Industrialization and the metropolis were already being explored by French artists and novelists in the 19th century, while their neighbours to the east were still "lingering over sunrises and gooseherds", as Döblin put it. The Germans only woke up to such themes in the 20th century, following the explosion in Berlin's population. It is no coincidence, therefore, that the two outstanding works about the German metropolis, Döblin's *Alexanderplatz* and Kirchner's *Potsdamer Platz*, should bear the names of Berlin squares as their titles. The painting today hangs just a few hundred yards from the place after which it is named, in the Neue Nationalgalerie, Potsdamer Strasse, Berlin.

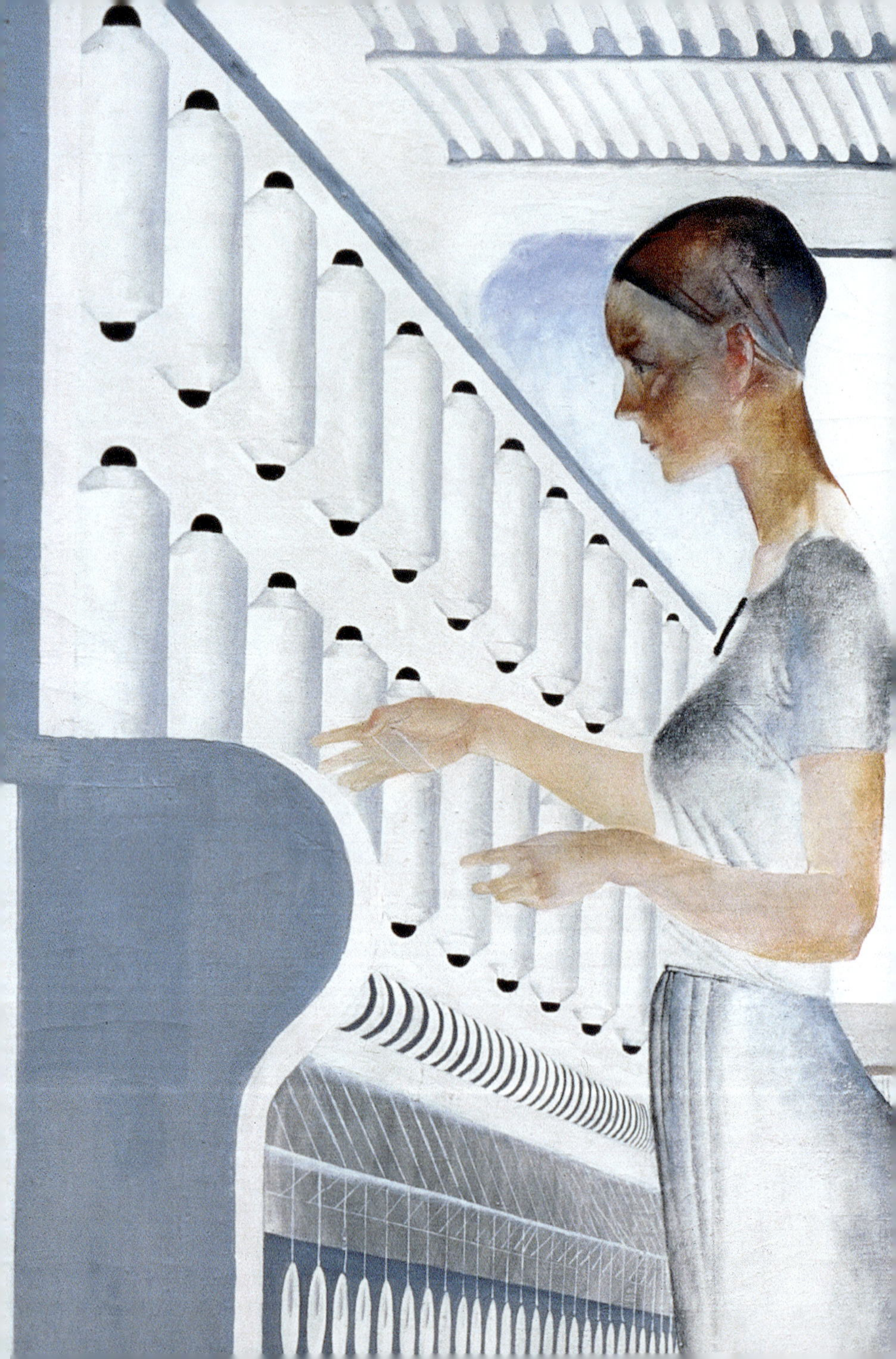

Alexander Deineka (1899–1969)

The joy of communal work

Female Textile Workers, 1927
171 x 195 cm, St Petersburg, The Russian Museum

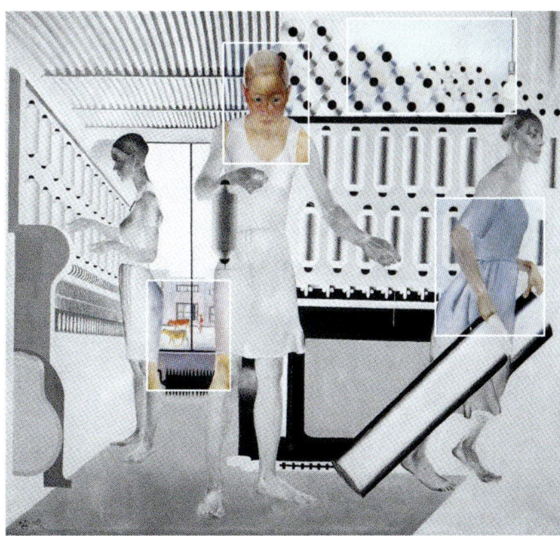

Alexander Deineka was born in Kursk, the industrial city south of Moscow. His father worked as a fitter for the railways, where the son also began an apprenticeship. He grew up amongst factories, pitheads and railway tracks. At the age of sixteen he was sent to art college in Kharkov, where he witnessed the end of tsarist Russia.

In 1918 he returned to Kursk, where he earned money as a photographer for the criminal investigation bureau and, as a nineteen-year-old, headed a Fine Arts department within the government administration. He used what he had learned in Kharkov – or some of it – to decorate railway carriages with propaganda pictures for Communist agitators. These latter travelled through the provinces attempting to explain to the peasants the benefits that revolution would bring to the rural population.

During the civil war he fought on the side of the Red Army and painted stage sets for a military travelling theatre. He thus started his artistic career battling for better living conditions for the class from which he himself originated. At the end of the civil war he went to Moscow, where he learned how to work in a range of printing techniques at the

Polygraphic Faculty of the Higher Technical-Artistic Workshops. He also drew for agitatorial magazines with titles such as *Atheist Working at the Lathe*, *Forwards* and *Searchlight*. He sought his motifs in industry, but not simply as an onlooker: "During that period I travelled a great deal. I worked in the mines in the Donets Basin and in the pits outside Moscow, I was in collective farms and saw how they were set up, I worked in Moscow plants and factories."

In the middle of the 1920s he broadened his sphere of artistic activity. He no longer painted solely for party purposes and with a political aim in mind, but began exhibiting paintings of his own composition. Their subjects were taken from the world that he knew and bore titles such as *At the Entrance to the Pit*, *Building New Factories*, and in 1927 *Female Textile Workers*.

The object withdraws

Deineka was born in 1899 under tsarist rule and grew up in the hope of a better, freer life in which the previously disadvantaged workers and peasants held the reins of power. It was to be a life in which everyone had enough to eat and enjoyed adequate living space, heating and lighting. As Lenin formulated it, "Communism equals Soviet power plus electrification".

Deineka was living in times of artistic as well as political upheaval. The art academies of tsarist society taught an Impressionistic style of realism. With the start of the 20th century, however, artists began to explore new, experimental trends: Expressionism, Cubism, Constructivism and Futurism. The Russian spectrum ranged from Marc Chagall (1887–1985), who in his village fantasies revived the pictorial forms employed by Russian illustrated broadsheets, up to Kasimir Malevich (1878–1935), who painted his *Black Square* and thereby celebrated "the liberation of art from the object". That was in 1915, during the First World War.

After the 1917 revolution, Malevich and his progressive colleagues hoped that the transformation of the social structure would accelerate these new artistic tendencies. This did not prove to be the case for abstract art – for without people and objects there could be no agitprop! Malevich's abstract works nevertheless left their mark upon politically motivated artists, as evidenced in Deineka's picture by the reels of yarn stacked beneath the ceiling: what we see are discs and circles devoid of depth and volume. The object has withdrawn from the forms. We can only deduce what is lying behind the light bulb from the context of the picture.

Lenin, too, had called for a cultural revolution, although he was not thinking of innovations in the fine arts, the theatre or the cinema. He was not concerned with aesthetics or a new "beauty" but with knowledge and education. Around 1920 only some 30 per cent of Russia's population could read and write. Within the proletariat, whose members were supposed to take over the running of the country, illiteracy was substantially more widespread than in the middle classes who were to be removed from power.

Lenin lamented the nation's "semi-Asiatic lack of culture" and concluded that "the Russian is a poor worker in comparison with the workers of the advanced nations". "Do not be lazy, do not steal," he exhorted; "observe the strictest discipline!" The Communists were concerned to ensure an elementary education for all. In 1918 one of their posters proclaimed their ambitious goal: "Every cook should be able to rule the state."

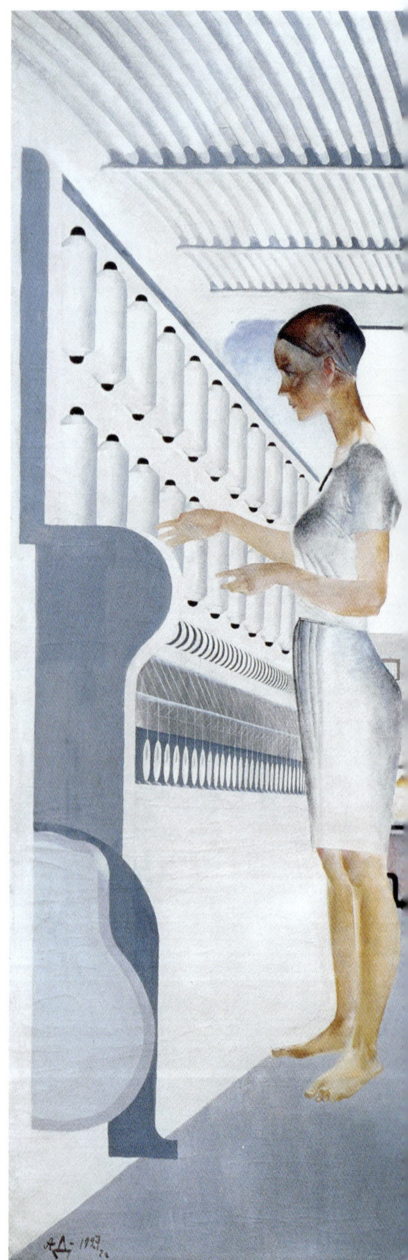

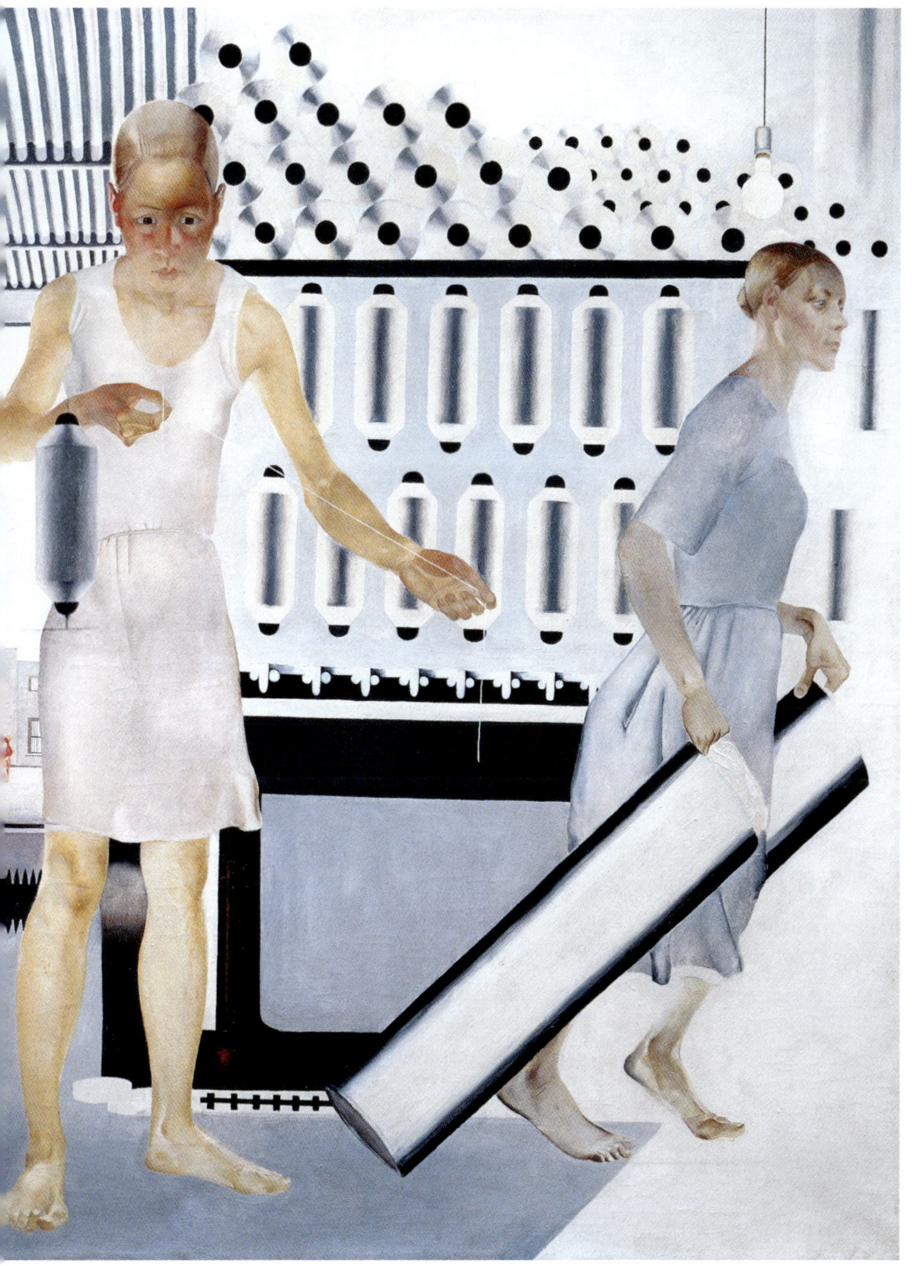

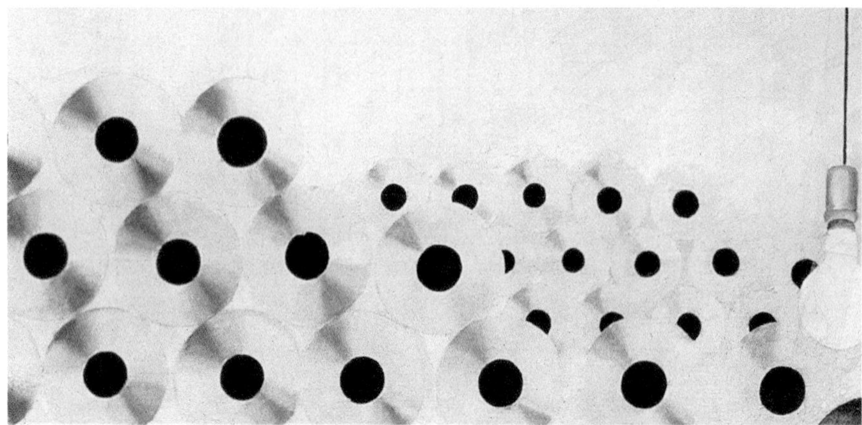

It was Deineka's duty, as he perceived it, to collaborate on the achievement of this goal. His contribution took the form of posters and journals; these were accompanied by captions and texts that carried a message. The text was an inseparable part of the picture. For a long time Deineka shied away from works without words. Perhaps, like some of his radical colleagues, he viewed the traditional "free" painting as an object to adorn a bourgeois living room and hence as an example of an art form whose existence was no longer justified. In the mid-1920s he changed his stance. His drawing board was joined by an easel, and together with a number of colleagues Deineka founded a Society of Easel Painters. These painters remained entirely committed to the Communist party, but no longer restricted their output to routine propaganda.

In the style of New Objectivity
The building on the far side of the street, visible through the windowpanes, embodies the style of New Objectivity – plain windowframes, façades devoid of decorative columns and the exterior characterized by right angles and straight lines. This ascetic architecture was new in the 1920s and was built in many countries of Europe. It was taught at the Bauhaus and developed further by Le Corbusier, the Swiss architect who in 1928 designed a council building in Moscow. The manufacturing plant in which the three women are working is probably constructed in the same style, with its focus wholly upon functionality: the large window allowing in

the natural light and its black metal frame, together with the type of radiator, all point in this direction.

This sober style, in those days still new, offered a glaring contrast to the architecture of the pre war era with its imitation of historical forms – factories concealed behind castle façades and apartment blocks in the guise of Renaissance palaces. But although many Russian architects and artists considered objectivity and functionalism as an expression of a new society, the style did not gain ground in the Soviet Union in the long term. This was probably because the country's major new buildings were commissioned by functionaries with conservative tastes, by men whose concept of power and glory was shaped by the historicizing decorative architecture of the 19th century. They would later favour the so-called "pastry cook's" style.

In the present painting, the architecture is a symbol of a better future. But in the idyll of the cattle being driven past in the background, Deineka identifies the greatest obstacle along the path: the peasants. When Marx formulated his theory of the dictatorship of the proletariat, he was basing himself on an industrial workforce such as he foresaw in the countries of the West – effective in their labour and well organized. But 80 per cent of Russians lived on the land, were for the most part unable to read and remained backward in their working methods. In 1918, after the revolution, when the large-scale landowners were dispossessed and their fields redistributed, the peasants were all in favour of the Communists. But when they were instructed to sell their products at a fixed price one year later, they boycotted the state measures. Millions of city dwellers starved. In 1927, the year Deineka painted *Female Textile Workers*, there was another shortage in supplies. The Party decided to collectivize farming, liquidizing or driving out the *kulaks* – the medium- and larger-scale farmers – and their families and forcing small-scale farmers into cooperatives.

Had Deineka wished to portray the rural economy in a positive light, he would have shown a tractor rolling down the street. The tractor was a symbol of mechanization and motorization and thus of a more efficient way of working that was only possible in the *kolkhozy*. The introduction of machines and new working methods was hindered, however, by the low level of education. To tackle the problem, "cultural brigades" were trained in the urban factories and functionaries offered themselves in a "sponsorship" role, in a mighty effort to bring agricultural production up to the level of industry or at least to install a sense of discipline amongst the workers without having to swing a *kulak's* whip.

Within the composition as a whole, with its bias towards large forms, the detailed window scene appears out of place. Deineka could have left it out or shown only the building. The reference to the rural economy was evidently important to him, however. It is possible that he wished to offer a reminder that not everyone slotted as smoothly into the new system as the three women at their work.

A German falls from the sky

The plummeting pilot whom Deineka painted in the wartime year of 1943 is a German, as indicated by the wings on his sleeve and the cross on the wing of his shot down plane. In the pilot, Deineka reworks the figure of a parachutist whom he painted in 1934, jumping against a blue sky. He thereby transforms the Soviet sporting hero who is about

to pull the ripcord into an enemy who is about to die. But his face is not the ugly mask of the enemy as demanded by propaganda, nor is it rendered anonymous beneath a flying cap. On the contrary, Deineka paints the pilot with a head of blonde hair, just as he gave many of his Russian sportsmen. He wraps his hand over his skull as if he were asleep, or as if he wanted to protect himself where no protection was possible. Like the parachutist, he has his hand on the ripcord, and the artist provides no answer to the obvious question of why the falling pilot has not pulled it.

The Russian title of the picture describes the pilot respectfully as an "ace". That, too, is remarkable, as is the large format of 283 by 188 centimetres. Does Deineka wish to honour the enemy with which his country was locked in bloody battle in 1943? The style, too, raises questions. Deineka adheres to the prescribed realism: the ruins in the background and

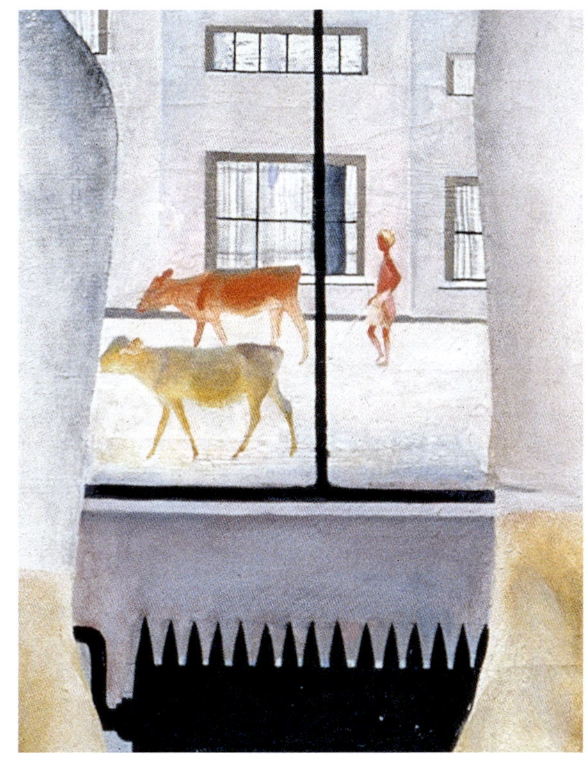

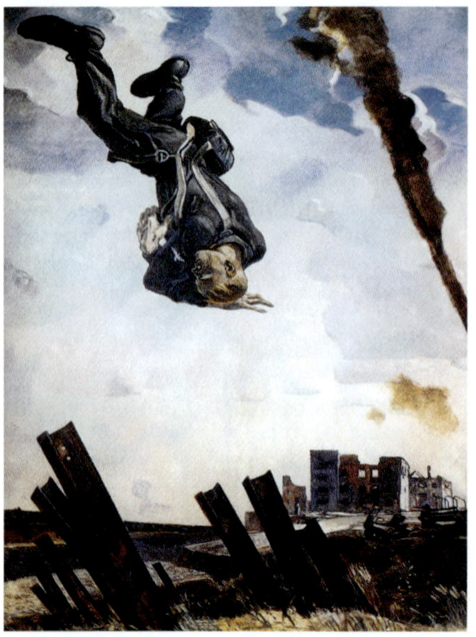

Comparative illustration:
Alexander Deineka
Air Ace Shot Down, 1943
283 x 188 cm
St Petersburg, The Russian Museum

the iron girders serving as anti tank obstacles are
painted as a spectator standing on the ground would
see them. Deineka paints the body, too, as if it were
crashing to earth right beside the viewer. But no
human eye could register this particular instant –
the body would be travelling far too fast for the eye
to follow. The realism of the scene is turned on its
head by the proximity of the body; it is almost as if
the pilot's fall has been halted shortly before his fatal
impact with the ground.

This does not fit into the ideological cliché,
and there are other questions about the artist and
his work that remain unanswered. Was Deineka
really the loyal Communist all his life, as he is portrayed in the books and articles coming out of
Russia? What did he avoid as an artist because it
was politically undesirable?

Maybe it is short sighted to interpret all his
works in terms of the agitprop of his time. If the
pilot moves us today, it is because he reminds us of
our nightmares, of our primeval fear of falling into
the abyss. Perhaps Deineka also saw, in the German
destroying Russia, a sort of Icarus who, despite all
warnings, flies too close to the sun and consequently
dies. Seen against the backdrop of this later phase
in his career, his *Female Textile Workers* also appears
in a new light. Just as Deineka knew the motif of
Icarus, so he was familiar with the famous antique
sculptural group of the three dancing Graces, the
daughters of Zeus.

If we screen out the machinery in Deineka's
picture (which is already dematerialized to such
a degree that it is impossible to tell whether this
is a spinning or a weaving plant) and concentrate
solely upon the movements and the position of the
women in relation to one another, the idea that
they are joining in a dance suggests itself very
strongly. In the antique marble the Graces are
closely intertwined, whereas with Deineka they
move freely – he seems to want to dissolve in his
painting the contradiction between work and
dance. Their lack of shoes and the colours that the
artist has chosen also suggest something like
Olympian lightness in 1927 Communist Russia.

Closely checking her own work
Pictures with industrial motifs are uncommon
in the art of the 19th and 20th century. Painters
occasionally turned their attention to factories in
the landscape and to the misery of working-class
families, and frequently to the growth of the cities
and of modes of transport – but only rarely to
work on the shop floor. The artists did not know it
at first hand, and industrial interiors were probably
not what the art buying public at large wished to
see in their living rooms.

Only under the Bolsheviks did the motif increase
in worth. In capitalism, so Marx taught, workers
are alienated both from the product of their
labour and the act of production itself, whereas
in Communism they are once again reconnected
with their work. Work becomes the cradle of the
new individual. It is this ideal, this hope for the
future, that Deineka has painted. The three young
women are neither dominated by machines nor
pressured by foremen; they are not standing by an
assembly line at which they are obliged to perform
the same repetitive movements, or in a dingy hall
thick with smoke. Lightly clad, well formed, they

appear strong and healthy. Each appears to have her own task and voluntarily slots into the larger production process.

In a preliminary study, the woman on the right wears a headscarf and the one in the middle, here checking a thread held between her fingertips, is arranging her hair. In the final painting, Deineka has standardized his figures. They all have the same hairstyle and the same skin colour; all are concentrated in the same fashion upon their work. What matters to the artist is the communal, collective dimension: individual differences are minimized and the difficult circumstances in which these female workers lived – the lack of food, living space and consumer goods – faded out.

Deineka's choice to depict the work of women in his painting of the future must also have been entirely in the spirit of the cultural revolution. There was an educational divide not only between the town and the countryside, but also between men and women. In 1920 only 20 per cent of Russia's female population could read and write, compared to 40 per cent of the male population. This situation was compounded by the traditional subordination of women, particularly in rural areas. They may have been equal before the law, but not in everyday life. In this respect, too, Deineka's painting is agitating for a new society.

Deineka left the Society of Easel Painters shortly after its major exhibition of 1927 and joined the "October" association of artists and subsequently the Russian Association of Proletarian Artists. In 1932 all artistic groupings were forcibly merged and Socialist Realism proclaimed the only approved style. To his existing range of subjects, Deineka added new ones: sport and flying. He was fascinated by bodies in motion and the bird's-eye view, and his new interests fell in line with Soviet

policy in the context of public health campaigns and the development of a Russian aviation industry. In the 1930s he painted murals for canteens, assembly chambers and gymnasiums. In 1935/36 he was granted permission to travel to the USA, France and Italy for study purposes. In 1943 he painted *Air Ace Shot Down* – a picture that shows that Deineka's art did not exhaust itself complying with an artistic doctrine even under Stalin. After the Second World War he was awarded virtually every medal and honorary title that the state had to bestow upon an artist.

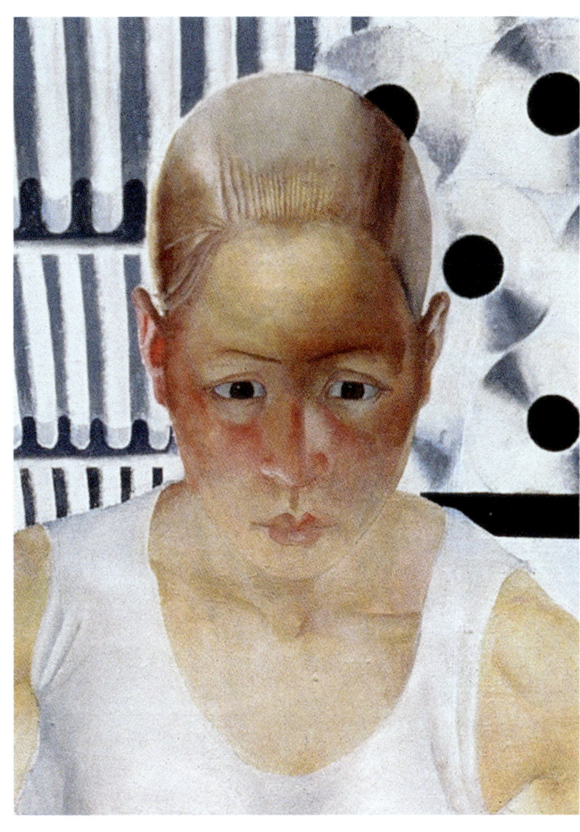

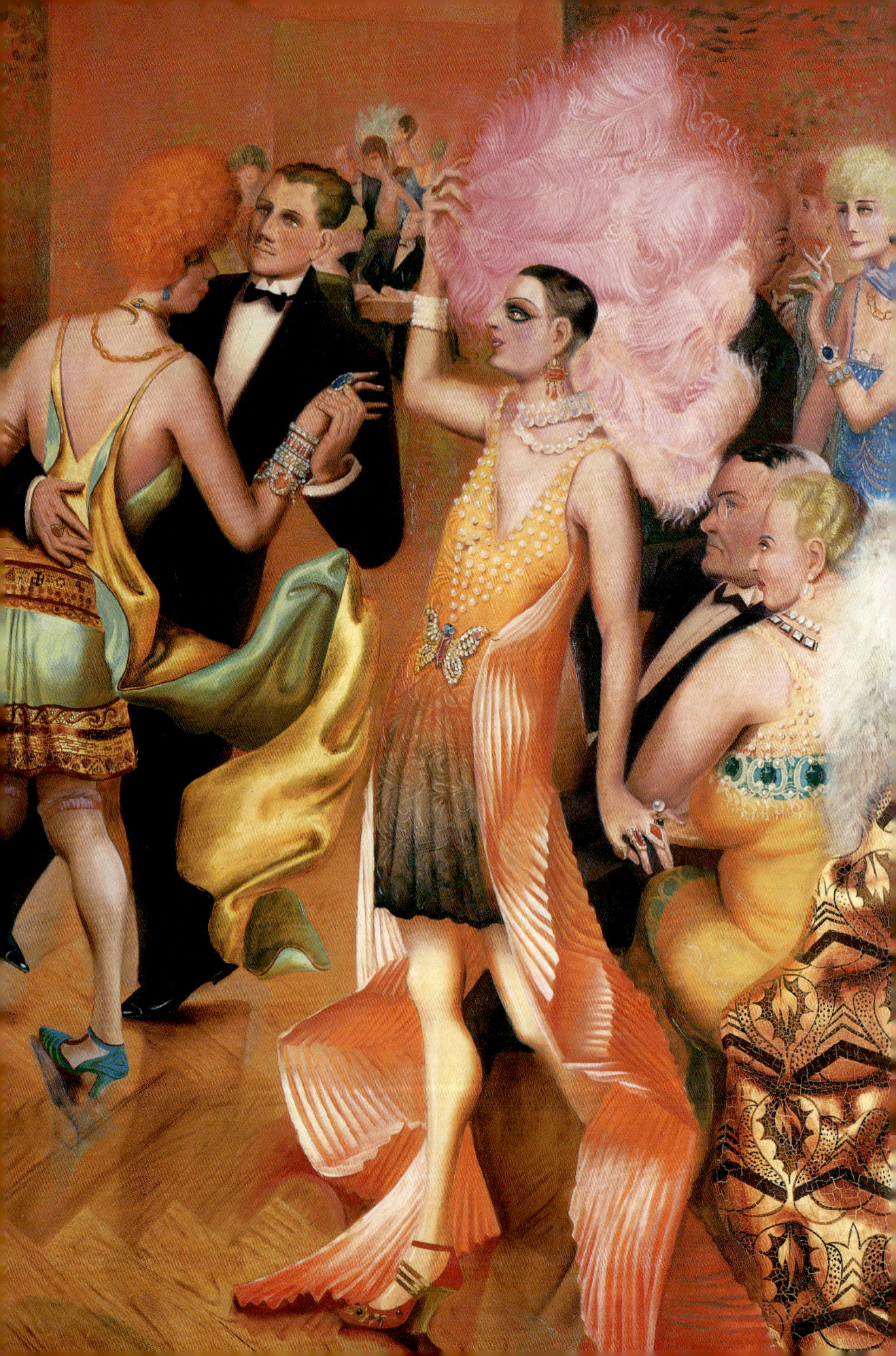

Otto Dix (1891–1969)

Not long until it bursts apart

Metropolis (Triptych), 1928
Central panel: 181 x 201 cm
Wings: each 181 x 101 cm
Kunstmuseum Stuttgart

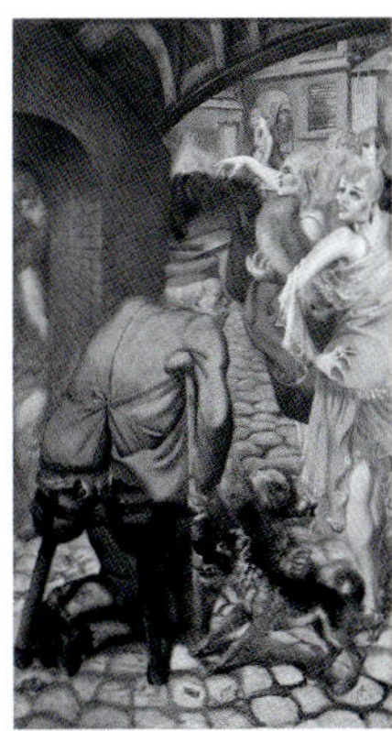
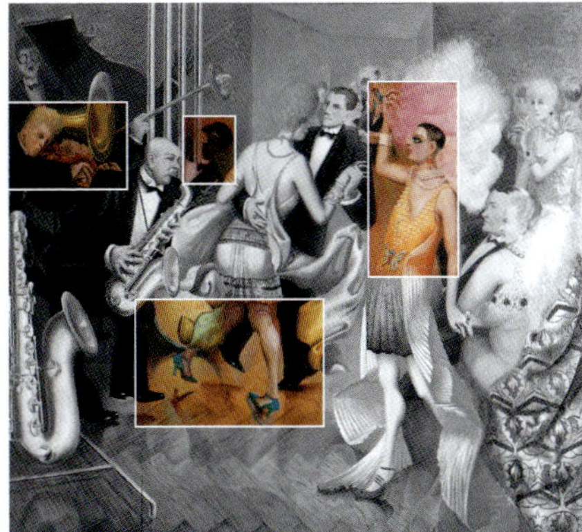
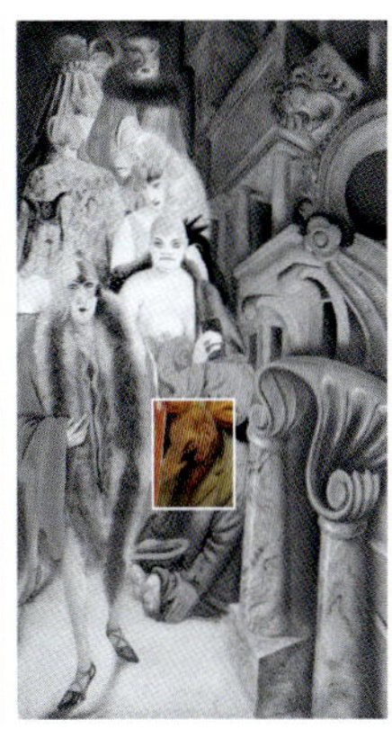

Otto Dix (1891–1969) completed his Metropolis triptych with the "roaring twenties" in full swing. Berliners danced the shimmy, the Charleston and the one-step; jazz was played even at the opera. Yet the consequences of defeat in the Great War were still conspicuous ten years after Armistice Day: begging war veterans, cripples and the victims of inflation were in sharp contrast to the hectic pace and fun-loving frenzy of the big city. Dix captures the contradictory scenes in this secular altarpiece. He, too, found it difficult to put his wartime experiences behind him.

The painter of the *Metropolis* triptych hailed from Untermhaus, a small town near Gera in Thuringia. Gera belonged to one of the smallest German states, the princedom of the Junior Branch of Reuß. Otto Dix was born "in the house next to the old Gothic church". Untermhaus was a small town in a small state, with a rigidly structured society in which everybody knew everything about everybody else and in which the upper class, even according to the proclamations of the church, was God-given. Keeping order was seen as every citizen's duty, and private charities provided the under privileged with a minimum of social security.

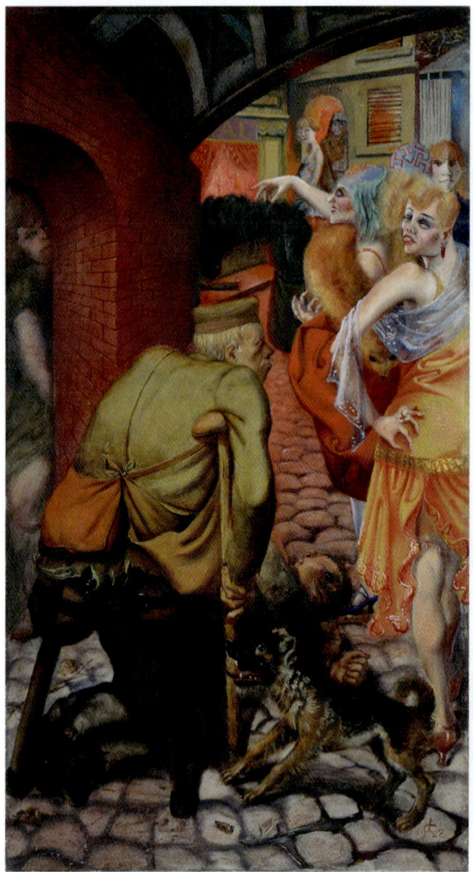

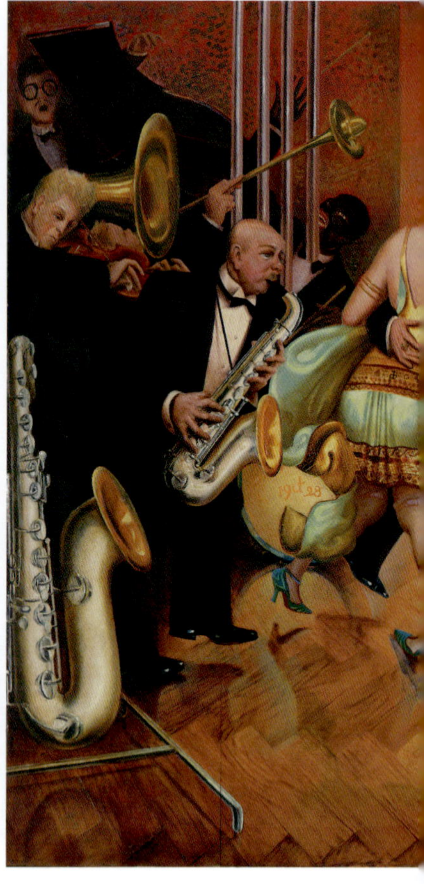

Dix's father worked as a moulder in a foundry; he was thus near the bottom of the social ladder. At the top, in distant Berlin, was the Emperor. The local ruler was Prince Henry XIV of Reuß. Dix's father was unable to pay for his son's education as a painter; the Prince stepped in to help, but only on condition that the boy learned a decent trade first. Dix left school at thirteen, apprenticing himself for four years to a decorative artist.

Finally putting the small-town atmosphere behind him, he left for Dresden, the Saxon capital and a centre of art. Here he entered the School of Arts and Crafts. In 1915 he went to war and was deeply affected by the collapse of every kind of order,

by the misery he saw at the front, by fear, mutilation and death. Never again would he be able to paint pictures that conformed to the rules of conventional aesthetics. The role of art was not to make life pleasant. Dix's paintings disillusioned their spectators; many found his manner revolting. He was twice charged with painting obscene portraits of whores and brothel scenes, and twice acquitted. In 1923, the director of an art museum bought one of Dix's war pictures, entitled *Trenches*, but was forced to remove it by the museum's governing board. One sensitive critic wrote: "Rembrandt's second anatomy lesson is charming. The Dix – excuse my language – made me want to throw up."

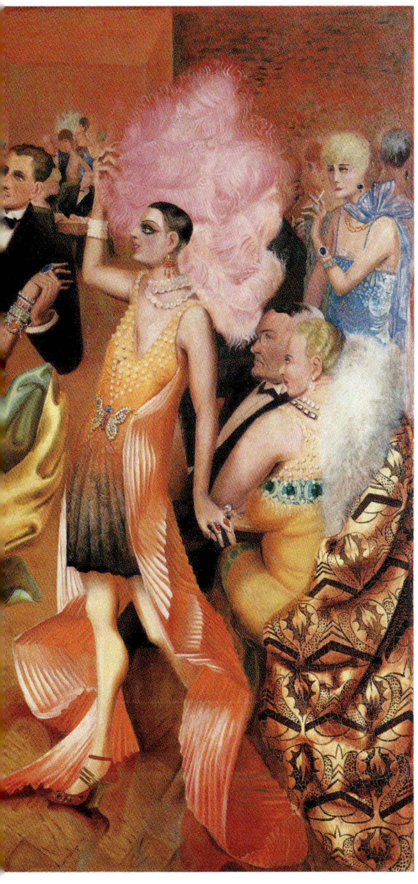 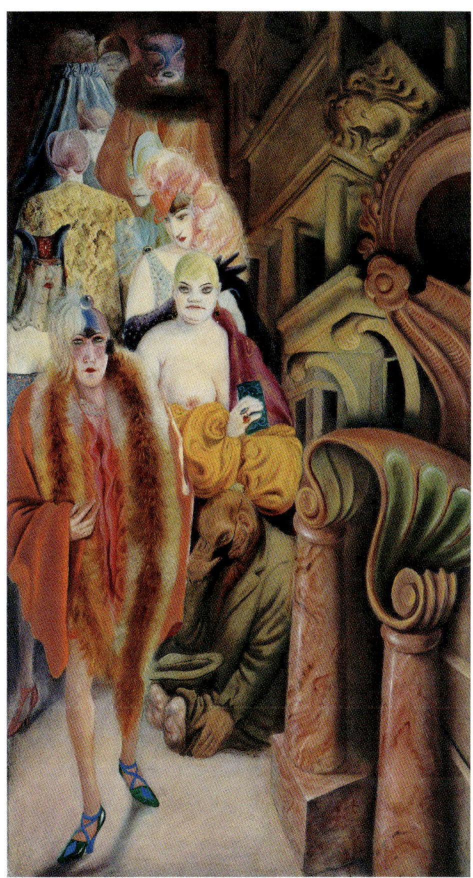

Dix painted numerous self-portraits. With his thrusting chin and provocative, even aggressive expression, he resembled the war cripple in the left panel of the triptych. Perhaps – though the artist never said so – his overpowering desire to disillusion spectators was fed by his proletarian background. He may have wanted to get his own back on the bourgoisie, with their cosy notions of beauty, security and order.

After the war, Dix lived in Dresden and Dusseldorf, then moved to Berlin, a metropolis of four million inhabitants, and became "famous". The greater part of his work now consisted of coldly realistic, large-scale portraits of doctors and artists, as well as bohemian types who frequented the Romanische Café. In 1927 he was offered a professorship at Dresden Academy, where he had graduated only five years earlier. Notwithstanding his success in Berlin, he returned to the town he knew and liked. With him, he took the preliminary studies for the *Metropolis* triptych, finally executing the painting in his quiet Academy studio on the Brühlsche Terrasse, with its broad vista over the Elbe. Full of personal experience, the work typified the mood of the 1920s.

Cripples

Though the *Metropolis* triptych was painted ten years after the Armistice, the war is still very much in

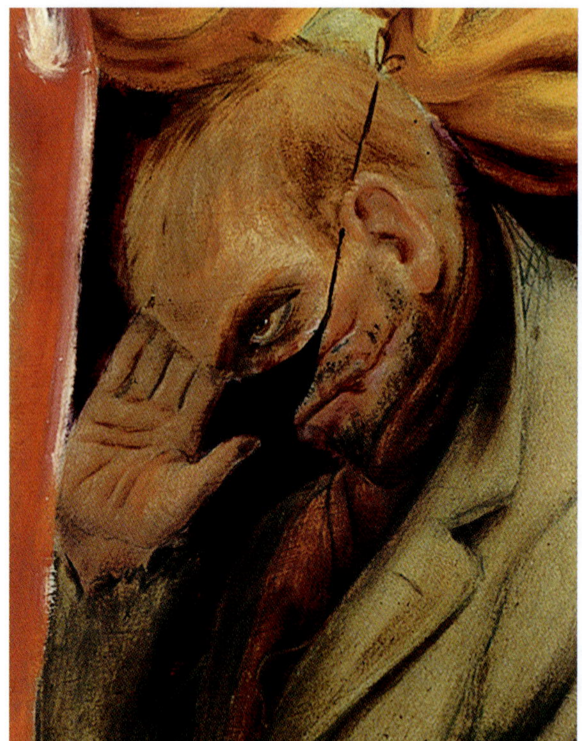

The entry also contains an *aperçu* reminiscent of the kind of contradictory scene Dix captured in the panels of his triptych, where destruction and amusement exist side by side: "The only pilgrims there now are crowds of tourists, desecrating the landscape like a revolting swarm of flies."

"War", "soldiers" and "the military" were key words in the parliamentary debates of the Weimar Republic. The Left had made Prussian militarism responsible for the disaster, while the Right blamed the ignominy of defeat on mutiny in the ranks. The Left saw the threat of a new war in the nationalist and racial politics of various right-wing groupings, while the Right saw the socialist parties plunging the country into anarchy. The election of Field Marshal Hindenburg, himself a symbol of the Prussian militarist tradition, as President of the Reich was a victory for the Right. That was in 1925, three years before Dix painted maimed soldiers in his *Metropolis* altarpiece.

It is unlikely that Dix wanted the motif to be understood as party political propaganda – at least this was not his primary intention. He was haunted by memories of horror, destruction and wartime suffering. The figure of the cripple is synonymous with these memories. This was true not only for Dix. No period in German art has produced so many paintings of cripples as the Weimar Republic. They made frequent appearances in the literature of the period, too. Erich Kästner's urban novel *Fabian* (1931) contains passages that could almost be read as a commentary on Dix's portrayal of the cripple with the botched up face whose hand is raised to his temple to salute women bent on ignoring him.

evidence: in the right panel is a man without legs, the remains of whose face suggest the effects of makeshift surgery; in the left panel a man in a field grey uniform lies on the ground behind a war cripple with artificial limbs and crutches.

The lost war still felt uncannily close, not only in Dix's paintings, but also in contemporary books, diaries and magazines. Ludwig Renn's novel *War* appeared in 1928; Erich Maria Remarque's *All Quiet on the Western Front* in 1929; and in August 1927, Harry Graf Kessler, diplomat and man of letters, noted in his diary: "Went to an American war film this evening: *What Price Glory?* – best I've seen to date …"

In August 1928 Kessler crossed the battlefields of Verdun to Rheims, where he saw "the hurt, dreadfully abused cathedral, exhausted by fire". He expressed the wish that the whole region be made sacrosanct, a mecca to pilgrims who condemned war.

Fabian, the hero of the novel, hears that "soldiers were still lying maimed in lonely hovels throughout the land: men without limbs, men with horrifically distorted faces, men without noses or mouths. And nurses who stopped at nothing would pour food through thin glass tubes, poking them through scarred, excrescent tissue into holes where these deformed creatures once had mouths – mouths capable of laughing, speaking, screaming."

The Negro

"In a bastardized, nigger-ridden world, all that we think of as human beauty and nobility … would be lost forever." A "nigger-ridden world" was the nightmare vision invoked in 1927 by a politician: Adolf Hitler, in *Mein Kampf*. Many Germans thought and felt that way. "Negroes" and Jews threatened the Germanic race and, more especially, its culture. They were enemies.

The French army of occupation in the Rhineland was also considered an enemy, partly composed as it was of black soldiers from the French colonies. For blacks to have power over Germans on German soil was deeply humiliating to many German patriots.

But public attitudes towards blacks during the Weimar Republic were determined not only by racist propaganda and the presence of black soldiers in the occupying army. Blacks, identified with America, were harbingers of a New World. Before the Great War, Europeans had viewed the United States as a kind of colony. They had looked down on Americans as the valiant but primitive colonists of a vast wilderness – especially with regard to cultural matters. For where was their music, their painting, their literature? By the end of the First World War America had unexpectedly shot to the position of number one world power. Its industry was more advanced than Europe's. Taylorism, the principle whereby manufacturing was broken down into a series of easily defined and easily executed steps (at the conveyor belt), had become the model to which European industrialists aspired. The general standard of living, industrial relations and the practical effects of democracy all seemed equally admirable or better than their equivalents in Germany. However, the most important thing to come out of America, especially as far as the cities were concerned, was its new lifestyle. "Ah, but it seems the days of old Paris are numbered: it's becoming Americanized. And it's Berlin, they say, who calls the American tune on the Continent."

This view of the contemporary scene was the subject of an article, appropriately entitled "The Americanization of Europe?" by the Swiss essayist Max Rychner. Published in the *Neue Rundschau* in 1928, the year in which Dix completed his *Metropolis*, the article lists several features Rychner considered typical of the new lifestyle: aggressive optimism, unassuming self-confidence, an unbroken faith in the goodness of the world, youth, vitality. He sees the musical expression of this temper in the music of the blacks: jazz.

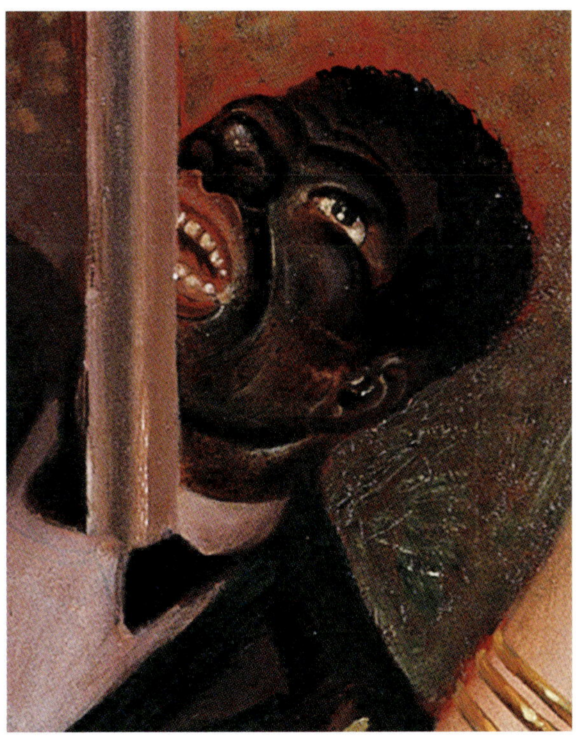

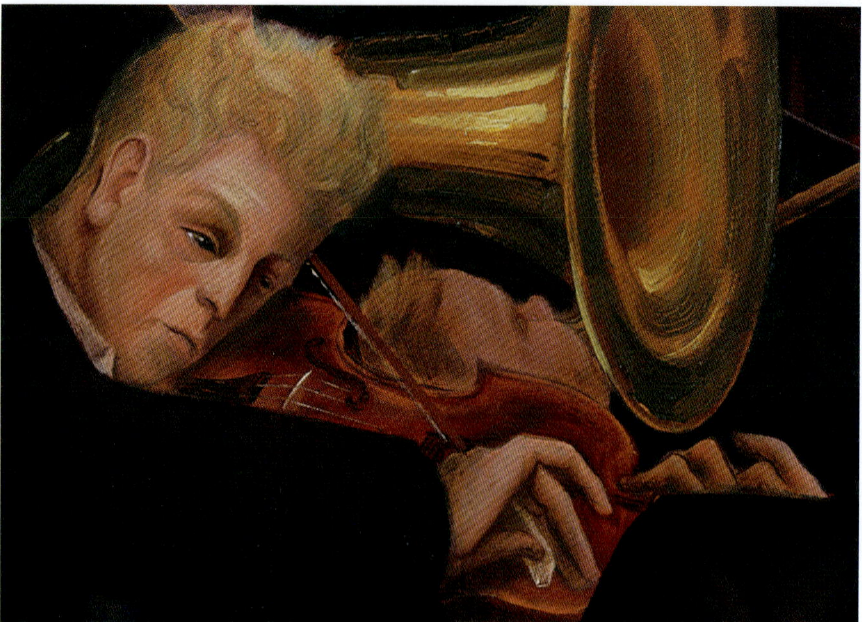

Jazz

Jazz took off in Germany in the mid-1920s. Sam Wooding and Duke Ellington toured with their bands in 1925, and a journal called *Musikblätter des Anbruchs*, in the same year, devoted an entire issue to the latest music. This contained a description of another aspect of jazz: "Revolt of the darker national instincts against a music without rhythm. Reflection of the times: chaos, machines, noise, extensity to the limit. The victory of irony, the defeat of ceremony, the wrath of the custodians of all that is precious …"

The custodians of all that was precious were those who enforced a strict division between music as entertainment and music as art. Jazz satisfied the demands of both categories: it was as popular as the commercially produced hits of the era, yet it lacked the latter's sickly-sweet superficiality. Jazz didn't fit with the assumed hierarchy of German cultural values. It was "high" culture that came from "below". Many music critics, if they took note of this kind of music at all, were left confused, their "wrath" aroused.

However, they could hardly avoid taking note when jazz musicians took to the opera stage in Ernst Krenek's *Johnny Strikes up the Band!* in 1927, with performances at 50 German theatres. Chaos, machines and noise were certainly part of the experience: telephones rang, sirens howled, machines pounded. The hero of the piece was a black jazz violinist. For the finale, the choir came in with: "A new world crosses the ocean and takes Old Europe by dance."

Charleston

Knees together, feet apart – the couple in the painting can only be dancing the shimmy or the Charleston. Both dances were new at the time, imports from the USA. Charleston was made popular in Europe by an American chorus girl called Josephine Baker. With her brown, supple body, her grand gestures and hair slicked down with pomade, she established a trend followed by many of the women who frequented bars and nightclubs.

The 1920s, especially in the big cities, were "a wild ball, sweeping along even the tired and weary", according to Walther Kiaulehn, the Berlin feature writer. Dancing took place not only in bars and clubs; people danced at home, too, thanks to the phonograph, and gramophone records, which entered mass production in 1925. In 1927 a poem published in the magazine *Weltbühne* began:

Discs in a pale lilac glow,
Violin's syrupy squeak,
Smart set's flitting shadow,
Filtered negro musique …

and ended:

For all their life's evanescent,
They live as if in a trance,
Since Heine's day incessant –
On a volcano's edge they dance.

There is much in the writing of the period to suggest a link between the dancing mania of the 1920s and the anxiety of a society teetering on the edge of a volcano, an anxiety also found in contemporary painting. In the work of artists who were interested in the portrayal of society – Max Beckmann, George Grosz, Otto Dix or Karl Hofer – bars, nightclubs and carnivalesque festivities were, like the crippled, a recurrent theme, only here the dancers seem bored rather than amused, and disturbed rather than exuberant: not one person is smiling in Dix's bar.

Flappers

Much had changed since the war, including women's fashions and hairstyles. Before and during the war women had worn ankle-length dresses with long sleeves and laced-up waists, emphasizing their hips and bosom, as well as full coiffures. In the 1920s skirts rode up above the knee; European women had never been permitted to show so much leg. Dresses were straight, while breasts, waist and hips were concealed, indeed denied. It was now deemed permissible, too, to reveal one's arms, including the shoulders, and women began to shave their armpits. Hair, which once, like the bosom and hips, had been a zone of female eroticism, was cut short, like a man's.

This departure from traditional female dress had its own reasons. Pre war society had been strongly male oriented, with the officer providing the dominant role model. While the brisk military type had determined men's notions of manliness, women had been expected to exude femininity. In 1918, however, their menfolk came back from the front. Far from basking in glory, the latter had been forced to look on as their supreme commander, the Emperor, that paragon of manly virtues, had fled the country.

Meanwhile, during the war, women had learned to fend for themselves and their families without the

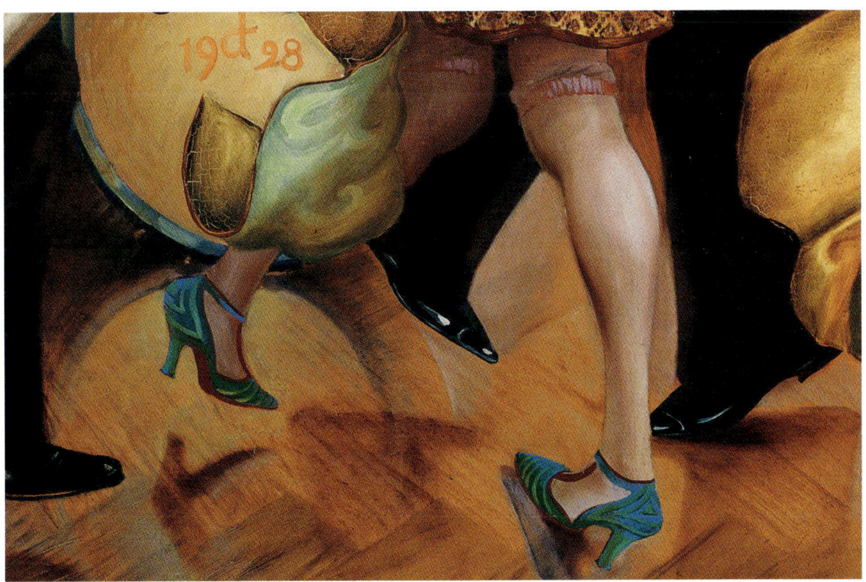

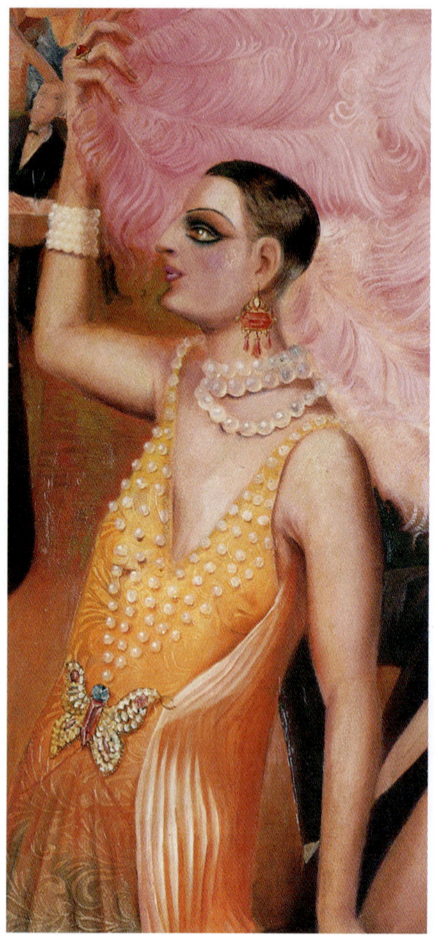

Unlike French cancan dancers, these girls did not try to whip up their audiences into an emotional frenzy. On the contrary, precisely choreographed, in long lines, they looked more like the interlocking parts of a machine. The sociologist and film critic Siegfried Kracauer had this to say: "Their lines snaking up and down the stage were an ecstatic advertisement for the merits of the conveyor belt; their quick-step sounded like: business, business; their legs, simultaneously thrown in the air, gleefully approved progress by rationalization; and their constant repetition of certain set pieces without ever breaking ranks projected upon the mind's eye the image of a never-ending line of automobiles leaving the factory for the great wide world …"

The word "girl" became synonymous with a certain female type, the "flapper": down-to-earth, neat, sporting, confident. A typical flapper was unromantic, scorning jealousy and laughing chivalry in the face. The latter was now considered part of the dead stock of the Empire, with no place in the modern world. The flapper had her counterpart, however, in the maneating "vamp", later personified by Marlene Dietrich. Essentially a later version of the *femme fatale*, there was nothing especially new about the vamp; she may not have epitomized the period to quite the same extent as the flapper, but she resembled the latter in that she, too, refused to subordinate herself to men. The large standing female figure in Dix's painting illustrates aspects of both: the ostrich plumes and eye make-up of the vamp, combined with the flapper's male hair-do, loose hanging dress and sporting legs.

Waiting room

The 1920s in Germany are referred to as the "Weimar period", after the Weimar Republic, but the period should really be known after Berlin, since it was here, in the city of four million, that the typical features of the period made themselves felt: constant political struggle, the American influence, the theatre boom, press diversity, intermingling of politics and art, the mania for entertainment. To many contemporaries, especially intellectuals and artists, the constant tension of living in Berlin was unbearable. Siegfried Kracauer said: "In the streets of Berlin it can suddenly strike you that it is unlikely to be very long until the whole lot bursts apart."

The feeling was widespread in the Weimar Republic that things were not "quite right". People

support of a husband. Gaining self-confidence, they had grown away from their traditional role as "little women". Many were war widows, and had to go to work. Women poured into the factories, staffed offices, convinced professors they could study as well as any man. In the new Republic, as opposed to the old Empire, they had won the right to vote.

Besides their debt to military defeat, changing gender roles also drew their impetus from a long, if initially weak, struggle for women's emancipation. American influence played a part, brought home to European audiences by American-style chorus girls.

did not feel at home in the world; something had to "happen". Rather than developing naturally and gradually, the new state had taken the place of the old far too abruptly when the Emperor abdicated. With the Emperor gone, the political and social head and cornerstone was missing. Deprived of their guiding star, the people had lost their bearings. There was no basic political consensus. Parliament, where more than twenty different political parties sat, proved an inadequate tool of government. The general mood was one of anticipation: something had to change. The protagonist of Erich Kästner's *Fabian* describes the mood as one imbued with the sense of the "provisional". People led a temporary existence, as if in a gigantic "waiting room".

The spaces depicted in Dix's triptych, too, with their uninviting atmosphere, are reminiscent of waiting rooms: on the right, lavishly lit, fake architecture of the grotesque sort found in movie palaces at the time; in the middle, a dance bar whose lighting alone would put most people off dancing; on the left, a gloomy bridge, with lemonade-coloured light spilling onto the cobbles from the brothels. Dix's metropolis is anything but hospitable.

Kracauer's presentiment that everything was about to burst asunder has found its way into the paintings of the triptych. Picture space appears to have come apart at the seams. On the right, pieces of architecture are meaninglessly piled on top of one another; the parquet floor in the middle slopes down to the picture plane, and the cobbles on the left are much too large in relation to the bricks of the bridge pillar. There is also something inveterately "wrong" with the painting's use of depth: the dancing couple is shown further away from the large standing figure than the lines on the parquet floor allow; the brightly dressed whore stroking the horse's head with her pointed fingers is standing next to the head of the lying man at the front of the passage, but the horse is standing at the back. The feeling is that something has gone terribly "wrong". The horse, too, with its sack of oats, looks oddly out of place.

"What was the point of his staying in this town, in this box of building bricks gone mad?" Erich Kästener asks on behalf of Fabian, the hero of his novel. "After all, he could watch Europe's decline and fall just as easily from the town where he was born." Kästner has Fabian return to his place of origin: Dresden. By coincidence, Otto Dix too returned to Dresden in 1927, when he was offered a professorship there, carrying in his portfolio the preliminary sketches for the triptych. He was travelling to a town he knew well, a place where he felt at home; he may even have felt safe there.

Degenerate

Once in Dresden, Dix increasingly turned his hand to family portraits: his wife, his children, himself as a father. More than ever before, he seems to have lived in harmony with the world around him. He began to paint biblical motifs. It was hardly coincidence that led him to tell people he had been born "next to the old Gothic church".

The *Metropolis* triptych also invites certain religious associations, and not just because of Dix's chosen form: the winged altarpiece. The vertical row of women set out of perspective in the right panel recalls the angelic hosts of medieval art. The position of the ostrich plume fan is reminiscent of a halo. The lengths of material draped over knee length dresses remind us of the trains of show stars, or of fallen angels' wings. The cripple on the left may not be nailed to a cross, but he is certainly hanging on wood. Dix might have entitled the triptych "Harlot Babylon".

Dix was one of the first to lose his position when the Nazis came to power in 1933. They demanded that art use its power to make life beautiful again and, in particular, to glorify German history and the Aryan race. The paintings that had made Dix famous did not fulfil these requirements. Instead, they were accused of "deeply offending the moral sensibility of the German people … and of undermining … the will of the German people to defend their country."

Exhibitions held in the spirit of propaganda used Dix's paintings as a method of intimidation. The exhibitions had titles like "Art as Demoralization", or "Mirrors of Corruption", or quite simply "Degenerate Art". The Nazis placed such "demoralizing" pictures in a political context, interpreting them as "mirror images" of the Weimar period.

In 1934 Dix was banned from exhibiting his work, and 260 of his paintings were confiscated in the course of that year. He retired to the country, living in Hemmenhofen on Lake Constance from 1936 until his death. *Metropolis* triptych, which remained in his estate until 1965, entered the possession of the Städtische Galerie Stuttgart in 1972, where it is now exhibited, together with the large-scale preliminary studies, to the painting's best possible advantage.

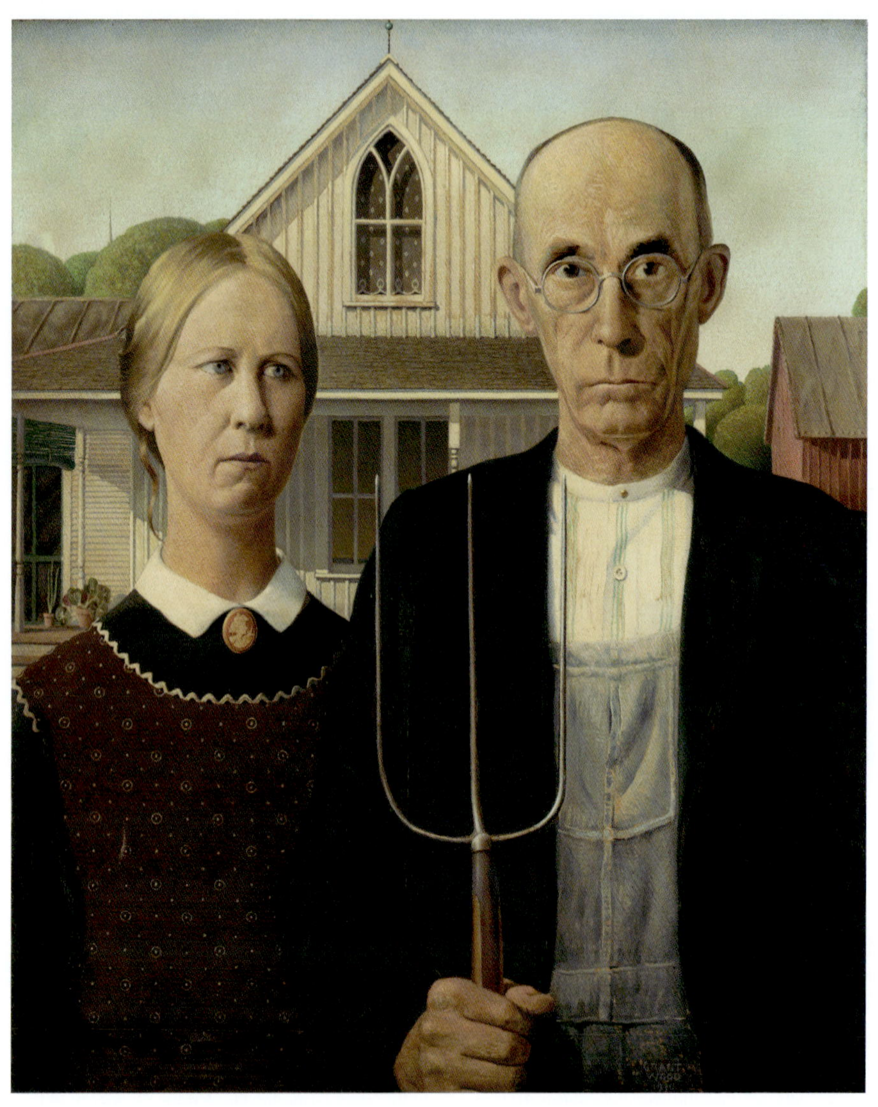

Grant Wood (1891–1942)

Guardians of the New World

American Gothic, 1930
78 x 65 cm, The Art Institute of Chicago,
Friends of American Art Collection

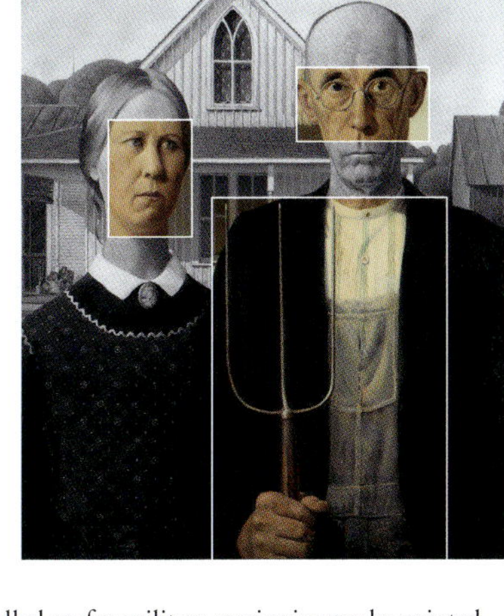

The painter of this picture grew up amongst animals, fields and people who worked with their hands. His parents' farm lay in Iowa, one of the states in the Midwest, far from America's industrial and intellectual centres. At home, the family read aloud history books such as *The Decline and Fall of the Roman Empire* and James Fenimore Cooper's *Deerslayer*, but no fairy tales. They were not "real". Grant Wood (1891–1942) was ten when his father died. His mother sold the farm and moved with her four children to Cedar Rapids, an agricultural centre with some 45,000 inhabitants. The largest employer in the town was a firm that produced rolled oats, later famous as "Quaker Oats". Grant earned pocket money as a night watchman for a small fine arts society, and the art books in the public library introduced him to pictures such as he had never seen before. He became a sort of self-made artist, availed himself of what he could and kept his head above water with his handicraft skills. In Chicago he trained under a silversmith, set up a jewellery studio and went bust. When his mother had to sell her property in 1916, Grant built a simple wooden house for her, himself and his sister Nan.

Called up for military service in 1917, he painted guns in camouflage colours. In his pictures he adopted a style popular in America at that time, a sort of Impressionism with loosely defined forms and unnatural colours. Like virtually all American artists, he made a trip to France. Back in Cedar Rapids he found an energetic patron – an undertaker. Wood decorated his funeral home and exhibited his works there. The undertaker's extensive network of connections brought Wood other commissions, including murals for hotel interiors and a stained glass window for the civic Veterans Memorial Building. The large window was constructed in Munich, and Wood spent three months in the city. There he saw the cool, critical portraits by the representatives of New Objectivity, painters the same age as himself such as Otto Dix, George Grosz, Christian Schad and Max Beckmann. In the museums he encountered the paintings of the Gothic and Early Renaissance eras, works by Hans Memling, Albrecht Dürer and Hugo van der Goes. In Germany he discovered the path that would lead him, as he said himself, to paintings such as *American Gothic* – a path that carried him away from Impressionistic transfiguration towards

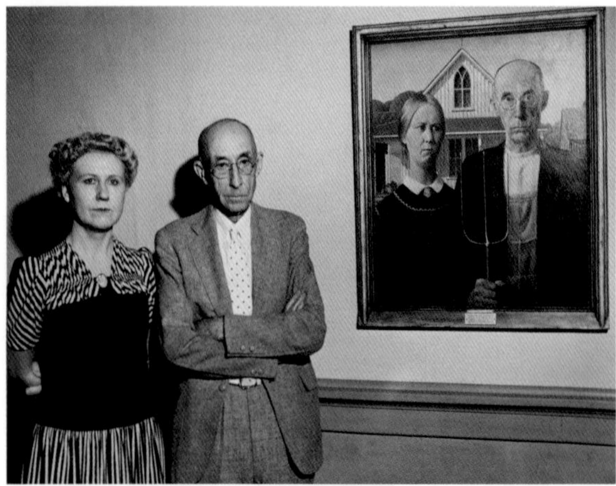

figures in hard outline, precise in their details and plastic in their modelling. From the Old Masters he adopted the custom of characterizing figures, of indicating their class or profession, by means of an object held in their hand.

The poses of the figures in Wood's painting call to mind a motif typical of early American photography: a man and woman in front of a house. Photographers were already travelling the country in the 19th century, documenting its people and their for the most part meagre possessions, but always from a distance: figures and house were to be visible from top to bottom. Wood, on the other hand, brings them up close, almost menacingly so. He painted *American Gothic* in 1930, one of the worst years in US history. On 24 October 1929, Black Friday, America's unchecked capitalism had caused the Wall Street stock exchange to crash. Many banks were forced to close and customers lost all their savings. By 1932 unemployment had risen to twelve million. On the farms, too, the situation was bad: banks called in their loans and food prices plummeted.

A dentist in overalls with a pitchfork

It all started with the house. Wood spotted it on a trip to the country – one of the wooden houses with a veranda and gable roof that were simple in design and quick to construct. The style of the window with the three pointed arches was known as "Carpenter Gothic". Fascinated by its historical European form, Wood took pencil and paper and sketched the

façade. In front of it he placed a couple, the man in a collarless shirt with a rake held vertically in his hand, the woman with a centre parting, both with narrow heads. He scribbled a dark frame around the picture and along the bottom of this fictive surround wrote the words "American Gothic".

In other words, it was not a case of seeking a background for a portrait of two people, but rather of the artist finding the right foreground for a painting of the house's façade. This was not easy in small-town Cedar Rapids, and of all the people the artist asked, the final choice boiled down to his younger sister and his dentist. Only after he had promised that he would make them unrecognizable in the finished picture did these two agree to sit for him. To their lasting annoyance, however, Wood did not keep his word, or – if he tried – did not succeed.

His sister's face, at least, he made narrower and older; she had to pull back her thick, wavy hair and fasten it tightly behind her head. Wood elongated her neck; her brooch, featuring a head seen in profile and with wild hair, was a family heirloom and had already appeared once previously in a portrait of his mother. Instead of the rake in the drawing, the man grasps a pitchfork used for hay or dung – perhaps for formal reasons, or perhaps to make it clearer that this is no amateur gardener but a man who makes his living, or at least a part of it, by the work of his hands. Wood was probably familiar with the dentist's intense stare from sitting in the surgery chair. The denim overalls that the man is wearing beneath his black jacket were the artist's everyday clothing: he wore them in his studio, when teaching, at meetings. They were comfortable and a sign that he, too, was amongst those who earned their money through physical work.

In the painting, there seem to be slight folds in the bib of the pale blue overalls, as would be natural in loose hanging fabric. The darker zones could be shadows cast by the material or alternatively shadows from the pitchfork's three prongs. There is a good argument for the latter. Wood had admired the reflections of objects in glass vases and on gleaming armour in the works of the Old Masters, and was attempting to imitate them with the shadows on the fabric. Fidelity to detail was one of his primary concerns; he considered accurately rendered details to be one of the distinguishing features of Gothic painting. Within the latter he sought a new style not just for himself but for the whole of American art. The Gothic painters, he wrote in 1932, seemed to him to be the next step. Interpreted in this light, the title of the present picture refers not just to the window in the façade. It formulates a programme.

Life in the country

In the course of the 1920s Wood made several trips to Paris, where he met Impressionists, Cubist, Surrealists, Pointillists and Dadaists. He considered himself a Bohemian and described his return to rural Iowa ironically as his "return from Bohemia". Although he had perfected his Impressionistic style, for Wood as for many American artists, Paris did not get him any further. His experience was probably similar to that of Ben Shahn (1898–1969), who concluded that what he saw in Paris was art for artists, not for people who wanted to learn something about their world. In 1931, just after Wood had completed his *American Gothic*, Shahn embarked on one of the other important paintings of 1930s America. *The Passion of Sacco and Vanzetti* documents a scandalous court case and a historic event: two open coffins, each containing one of the dead, and three men hovering over them with expressions of concern, representatives of the judiciary and society who ordered the execution of the two Italian immigrants.

Shahn's painting today hangs in the Whitney Museum of American Art in New York, Wood's *American Gothic* in the Art Institute of Chicago – two of the leading art collections in the United States. In Europe, both works were practically unknown. The only American from the first half of the last century whose works were sought after in the Old World was Edward Hopper. The fact that his art became popular beyond the bounds of the USA can be explained not least by its theme, loneliness, which needs no explanation. The paintings by Wood and Shahn, on the other hand, are often difficult to appreciate without a knowledge of American circumstances.

For these two and for many other US artists, their focus fell upon America and reality – and not, like the European avant-garde, upon new forms of expression. Roughly simplified, the difference between these artistic outlooks can be explained in historical terms. European painters had been looking at the world in ever new ways for almost two millennia. By the start of the 20th century, they – or at least some of them – wanted something completely different. They left faithful reproduction to photography, whose techniques were being increasingly perfected, and liberated forms and colours from their obligation to the object. An art revolution summed up in the name of Pablo Picasso.

Art in America in 1930, on the other hand, had little more than a century behind it. The first settlers had included Puritans, who rejected the glittering pomp of the Catholic Church and hence, by association, painting. The history of American art commenced with worthy pictures of clerics, generals and presidents, followed by scenes from the lives of the pioneers and their battles with the Native Americans, and then views of the great waterfalls and across the wide prairies. At the end of the 19th century, the bare walls of grand new residences were filled with portraits of the numerous ladies

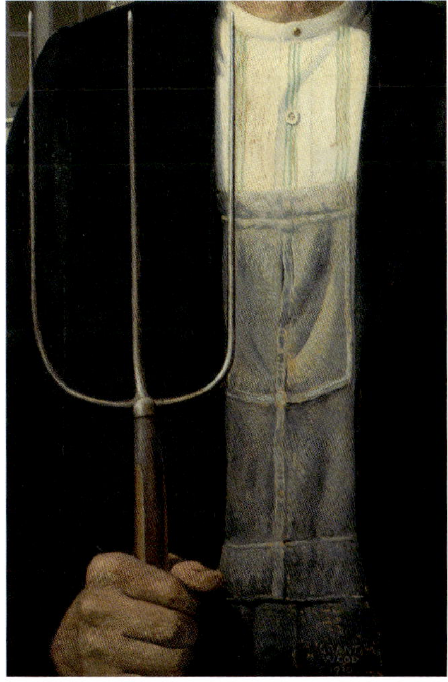

of high society. Many painters perceived themselves as reporters; some started out as press artists and would remain closely connected to their social environment in their own pictures. Men such as Shahn devoted themselves to big cities and social conflicts, artists such as Wood to life on the land and in provincial confines.

The artist's sister

In December 1934 the American magazine *Time* printed a long article on the American art market. It concluded that interest in "the French schools" was slipping, while painters "bent on portraying the US scene" were coming to the fore. "Today most top-notch US artists get their inspiration from their native land, find beauty and interest in subjects like Kansas farmers, Iowa fields, Manhattan burlesques." Grant Wood is quoted as saying that too many US artists remained in "colonial dependence" upon Europe. He called for the different regions of America to elaborate their own distinct characteristics and compete with one another "just as Old World cities competed in the building of Gothic cathedrals." The article was accompanied by a

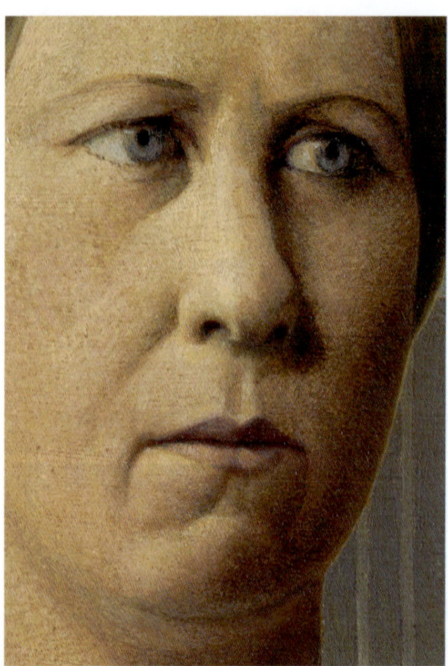

full-page illustration of *American Gothic*, of which *Time* commented: "This picture could have been painted nowhere outside the US."

This praise for the "Regionalists" in one of the most influential magazines in the United States drew protests, for example from *Art Front*, a comparatively small Marxist art journal, which bemoaned the fact that "the discoveries of Monet, Seurat, Cézanne and Picasso" were being overlooked and that "the yardsticks of art" had fallen to "the level of a Rotarians' brunch". Authors such as those writing in *Art Front* also judged art works as political statements; they supported the Communist and socialist international workers' movement and fought against "isolationism". After the First World War, successive American governments implemented protectionist measures, raising import duties, refusing to join the League of Nations, tightening immigration rules and coming down with particular severity upon socialists and immigrants such as Sacco and Vanzetti. These governments were steered by the representatives of big business – to the detriment of America's farmers, who were too scattered across the country to form themselves into an organization with political clout. Increasing numbers lost their properties. In 1930, one year after the Wall Street Crash and the year in which Grant Wood painted *American Gothic*, 42 per cent of farmers were now only leaseholders.

In 1933 Franklin D. Roosevelt took over as president and proceeded to combat unemployment with public contracts and also to provide funding for the arts. Those who profited in particular were artists whose works were able to broaden knowledge of the country and strengthen the pride of its inhabitants – artists who included the Regionalists. Although they did not consider themselves political, unless it be as opponents of the ever bigger and more powerful cities, their embrace of the rural heartland, the American interior far from the coast, brought them into line with the government's own vision. Wood became the Director of Public Art Projects in Iowa.

Paintings such as those by Wood were brought into discredit by Hitler and the "Blood and Soil" ideology of the Nazi era. The Regionalists would be able to sell their works to "any fascist or semi-fascist regime", sneered their critics. The *Time* article also included a reproduction of Wood's *Dinner for Threshers*, showing a group of men all dressed alike and seated as if in a military line around a long table. A design for a mural, a work that does not heroicize its subject but from which one might conclude that, in the countryside, all is in order. It is a picture that would have pleased Germany's ruling powers. The same cannot be said so confidently of *American Gothic*.

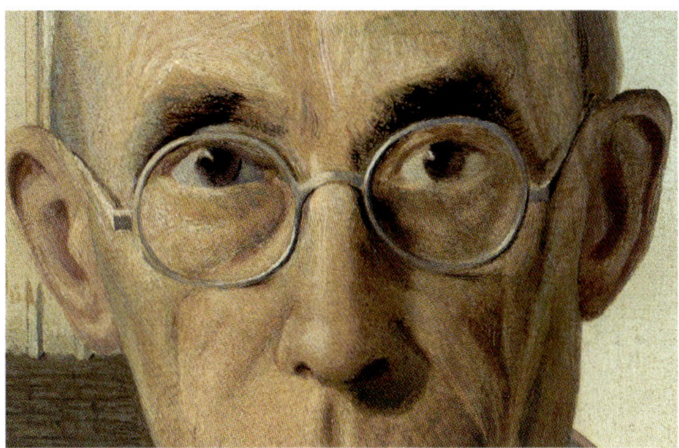

Gazing severely at the viewer

When *American Gothic* was exhibited at the Art Institute of Chicago in 1930, it sparked both interest and anger. "I received a storm of protest from Iowa farm wives because they thought I was caricaturing them", declared Wood, and elsewhere emphasized that the picture was not intended as a satire. For him, however, there is a relationship between the people and the "fake Gothic house". What sort of relationship he does not say. Did he mean a sham, superficial Christianity? Or a colonial dependency upon European architecture? Perhaps he saw this relationship in purely formal terms. One of the characteristics of Gothic cathedrals is their soaring height, and verticals dominate Wood's composition, too: the tall windows in both storeys, the ribs running down the walls, the narrow heads, the woman's elongated neck and the black selvages of the jacket. It is probably no coincidence that Wood replaced the short, horizontal prongs of the rake in the preliminary sketch with the pitchfork's long, upward-pointing prongs.

Wood does not comment on the nature of the "relationship". Ten years later, he would say of the man and woman that he had never described them as a farmer and his wife. For today's viewer, none of this matters, no more than the collapse of the stock exchange or the doctrinal disputes amongst Wood's contemporaries. Even if we approach this painting knowing nothing about it, we cannot simply pass on by. We are held fast in particular by the eyes. The woman is looking to one side – not at the man, who could be her husband or her father, but past him, it seems. She does not smile but wears a sombre, anxious expression that leaves us guessing. The man, on the other hand, looks directly at whoever is standing in front of the painting. Whether angrily, critically or severely is up to the individual to decide. Whatever the case, we experience it personally. With the eyes behind the spectacles, Wood establishes a visual axis running from picture to viewer. This axis is unpainted but psychically real. When a person – real or painted – looks at us like that, we automatically return their gaze, and we involuntarily wonder, too, what the other person wants.

And while searching for an answer, the viewer possibly also wonders whether the man and woman are to be taken entirely seriously, whether the faces are not in fact masks, exaggerated in their expressions, not caricatures but not far short of such either. And why has Wood brought the pair so far forward? Rather than giving them the distance found in traditional photographs, he constricts the space and thrusts the couple physically closer to us than would be pleasant in real life. The picture becomes uncomfortable and unsettling. It is thereby visually simple, clear and precise right down to its details and is not permitted to stray from reality in its palette, either.

A scene from Iowa on a slightly hazy day. The composition is supported by a thin, discreetly structured lattice of vertically rising lines. It is by no means simply the eyes that hold us fast, but also this tension between the way of seeing and everything bizarre and dubious that it conceals. The ability to unsettle and disturb the viewer is certainly not the first criterion for the quality of an art work, but it is one that counts.

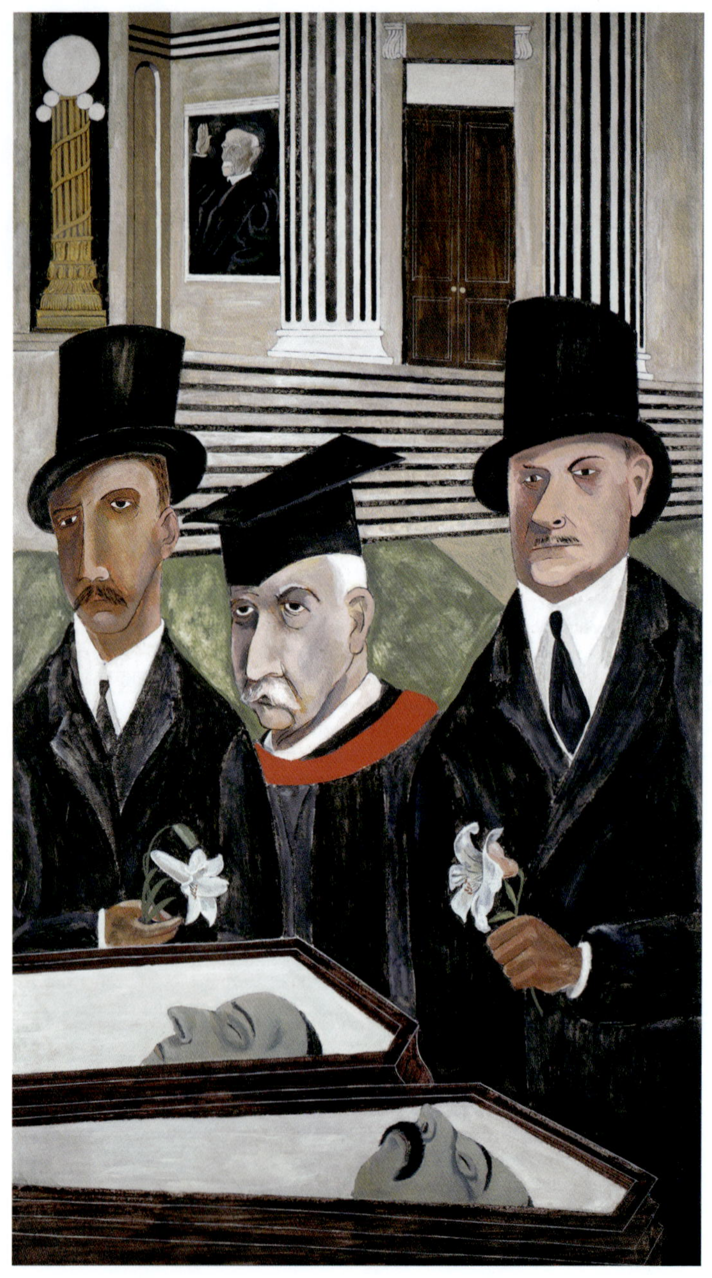

Ben Shahn (1898–1969)

Requiem for two anarchists

The Passion of Sacco and Vanzetti, 1931/1932
216 x 122 cm, New York, Whitney Museum of American Art,
Gift of Edith and Milton Lowenthal in Memory of Juliana Force

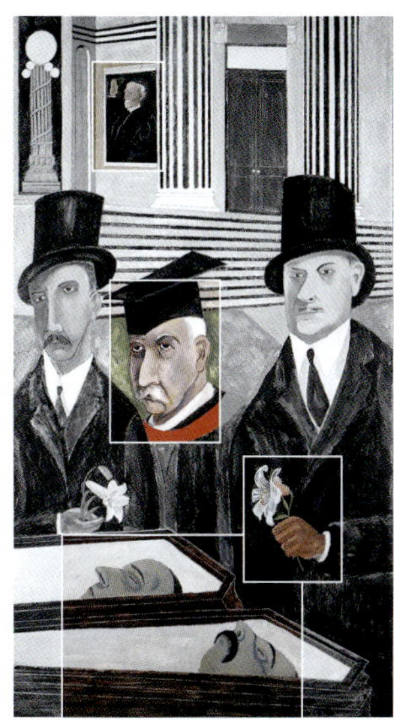

On 15 April 1920, in the American state of
Massachusetts, a paymaster and his security guard
were shot dead. The haul: 16,000 dollars. According
to witness statements, four or five men were involved
in the attack, but only two Italian immigrants were
arrested, Nicola Sacco and Bartolomeo Vanzetti.
Both swore that they were innocent. The judge presiding over the case did not seek the truth, however,
but steered the trial right from the start towards a
guilty verdict. So say his critics, who numbered not
just workers and immigrants but also prominent
individuals and highly regarded legal experts. For
seven years the hearings dragged on, for seven years
the two accused languished in prison. The provincial
court case indirectly became a national affair: the
Establishment versus immigrants, the guardians
of power versus those who wanted to improve the
social system.

On 23 August 1927 the two accused died in the
electric chair. Photos show the train of mourners
that accompanied the coffins and the vast crowds
thronging the streets all the way to the cemetery.
There were protests right across America and in
Europe too. The affair lived on in novels such as
Upton Sinclair's *Boston* (1928) and John Dos Passos'
epic *USA* (1936); films of 1960 and 1971 reached a

wide public and a ballad, written and sung by Joan
Baez, became an international protest song.

In the sphere of the fine arts, the finest tribute was
produced by Ben Shahn, himself an immigrant. He
had arrived in America with his family from Lithuania in 1906, when he was eight years old.
He later trained as a lithographer, attended design
school, married, travelled to Africa and then to Paris,
the European centre of the fine arts, where Expressionism, Cubism, Surrealism and Dadaism followed
one after the other. For Shahn it was all art for art's
sake. "The French school is not for me," he wrote.
He wanted to fathom not the possibilities of art but
the reality of his country. In the first half of the 20th
century, most of his American colleagues were doing
the same: they painted skyscrapers, automobiles, rail-
roads, the poverty of the farmers, loneliness in bars
and boxing matches complete with spectators, in a
mix that embraced both the glorification of wealth
and the criticism of social conditions. These works
barely registered in the European consciousness,
however; American art only began its triumphant
advance with what was produced after the Second
World War.

The Passion of Sacco and Vanzetti formed part of a
cycle of 24 pictures that Shahn exhibited in a New

York gallery in 1932. In a later interview he confessed that he had always wished he had "been lucky enough to be alive at a great time – when something big was going on like the Crucifixion. And suddenly I realised I was! Here I was living through another Crucifixion." By using the word "Passion" in the title, he places the two executed men in a Christian tradition. For many Americans, the picture is an icon, both a requiem for two anarchists and a warning reminder of the betrayal of national ideals.

They sought freedom

Sacco and Vanzetti, two men from Italy, one from the north, the other from the south, both from rural backgrounds. They came from farming stock and grew up within a tight-knit, Catholic society far from major cities. By local standards, both families enjoyed a degree of prosperity. As was the norm in those days, the boys were taken out of school at young age, one at nine and the other at thirteen. They went to work in their father's business or took up an apprenticeship. Further education was considered a waste of time.

It was not poverty that drove the two out of the country, but a desire to escape their cramped conditions and a youthful yearning for a new world full of undreamed of opportunities. In Vanzetti's case, the early death of his mother was another influencing factor: "I had to put the sea between me and my grief." In 1908 they both sailed for America. Bartolomeo Vanzetti, twenty years old, the man with the bushy moustache, landed in New York; the seventeen-year-old Nicola Sacco stepped onto American soil in Boston.

Both started out in the usual manner with low-paid jobs such as dishwashers or porters on construction sites. Sacco saved some money, enough to finance a short apprenticeship in a shoe factory, where he specialized in the operation of a particular machine. He was offered a permanent job, got married and had a son, and stayed in his job and with his machine until 1917. He had found his place. Not so Vanzetti. He became a sort of itinerant labourer, preferring the outdoor work to which he was accustomed but in which his cheap labour was exploited. He found it difficult to comply with authority and spent his nights with books. A homeless, impoverished man who lived in his thoughts. He read the classic European novels but also Karl Marx's *Das Kapital* and the writings of Italian anarchists.

So, too, did Sacco, who had a good job but who was also sensitive to the misery of the poor around him. Sacco hated injustice and wanted to eradicate it. He believed that the only ones who could achieve this were the anarchists, whose Utopian aims included, in his words, "no government, no police, no judges, nor bosses, no authority". Also no private ownership, but instead: "work in cooperation, distribute by need, equality, fairness, comradeship – love one other". For him, this "love one another" was the basis for a new society. The anarchists were bitterly opposed to war and consequently had no wish to join the military when the United States entered the First World War in 1917. Many escaped secretly to Mexico. It was there that Sacco and Vanzetti first met; both were living in a large cooperative that corresponded to the ideals of the anarchists. After a few months they ran out of money. Some moved on to other countries, but Sacco and Vanzetti returned to the United States and starting looking for new jobs under false names.

Defender of power and order

Nicola Sacco once again found work in a shoe factory and Bartolomeo Vanzetti became a

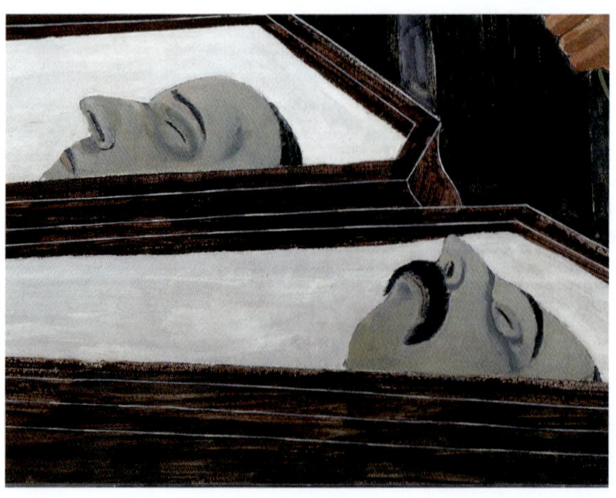

fishmonger. He bought himself a cart, some weighing scales, a bell and some knives and passed through the streets selling his fish – at last, a life outdoors without a boss. Both continued to work for the anarchists. They supported strikers, delivered speeches and collected money for colleagues awaiting trial. Both insisted they had never stolen and never killed. On 5 May 1920, just three weeks after the murder with robbery, they were arrested while moving propaganda material from one cache to another. Both were carrying revolvers on their person, but the possession of firearms was not prohibited. For the police it was sufficient that they were suspicious characters.

The trial was conducted by Judge Webster Thayer, portrayed here by Shahn as a picture within a picture on the exterior wall of the courthouse or seen inside the building through a window. Judge Thayer has raised his hand to take the oath. "I am assigning you", his superior had informed him, "to hear the most important murder case trial in Massachusetts since the last century, if not of all time." It was a pompous announcement and can only be understood against the backdrop of the social unrest of his day: America's conservative governments had permitted capitalism to grow unchecked, allowing vast fortunes to be made on the one hand, but aggravating the misery and poverty of factory workers and farmers on the other. Not until 1933 was the newly elected president Franklin D. Roosevelt able to ease the situation with his raft of New Deal reforms.

In Sacco and Vanzetti's day, America was "two nations" (Dos Passos). Property owners were gripped by Red Scare – fear of the Reds, of trade unions, of Communists and anarchists and indeed of any group wanting to enforce improved opportunities for the disadvantaged classes of society. Many anarchists considered that these ends were not to be obtained via democratic channels. They preached violence. One of their leaders wrote a guide to bomb-making, and on 1 May 1919 some 30 parcel bombs are said to have been put in the post. Some were never delivered because they bore insufficient postage. A few reached their destination but injured the housemaid, not the addressee. On 2 June 1919 bombs were detonated simultaneously outside private homes in six cities. One of them, placed outside the door of the American Attorney General, blew up the bomber. One year later a paymaster and his security guard were shot down in Massachusetts and the two Italians, Sacco and Vanzetti, arrested.

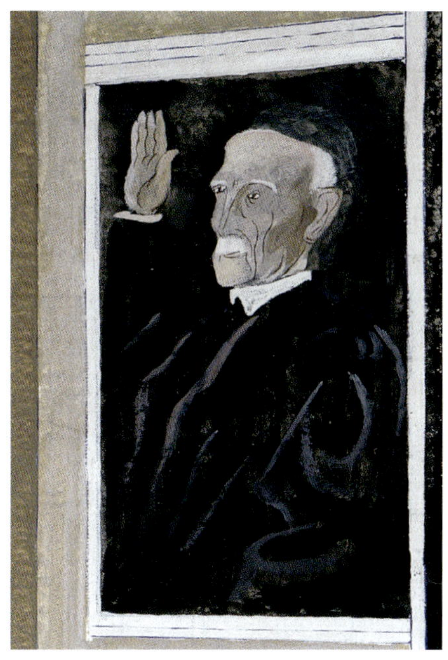

The actual damage caused by the bombs was minimal, but their emotional impact was great. Red Scare overtook politics and the press and the judicial authorities had to demonstrate that they remained in control of the situation. It became Judge Thayer's task, therefore, to convict Sacco and Vanzetti. Together with his prosecuting attorney, he concealed exonerating evidence, put pressure on witnesses and arranged for the leading police officer – who considered the accused to be innocent – to be replaced. His raised right hand in Shahn's painting can be interpreted not as his pledge to seek the truth but his obedient submission to those in power.

A highly respected figure

When Sacco and Vanzetti emigrated to America in 1908, 130,000 Italians had already preceded them. In the years leading up to the First World War, this total would reach more than one million. Most of these immigrants joined the ranks of the ever growing urban proletariat, at least at first. Those unwilling to accept low working wages in the longer term sought other ways of making money. As illegal bookmakers, for example, or by

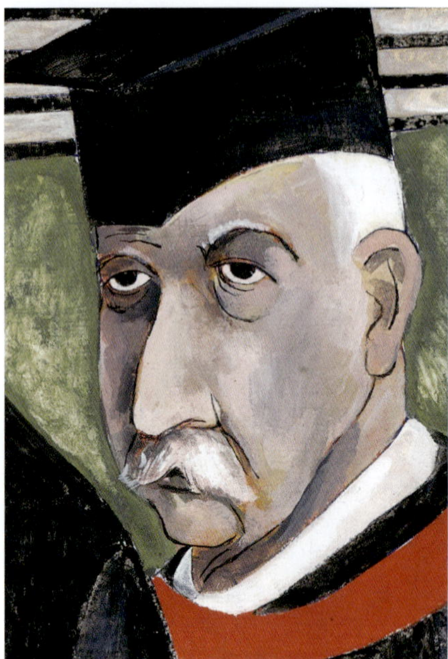

smuggling alcohol during the 1920s Prohibition. These activities, like the import of drugs, were largely in the hands of Italian "families". Even without their involvement in such shady dealings, Italians enjoyed a bad reputation amongst the long established members of American society, who considered them to be dirty and lazy. The majority of them, moreover, were Catholics and thus belonged to the Church from which the Protestant founding fathers had originally parted.

America was viewed as a crucible of nations, yet her history testifies again and again to separation, hostility and hatred. Examples range from the Ku Klux Klan and gang wars in the big cities to more subtle forms of differentiation in the upper echelons of society, where alongside fame and fortune importance was attached to a family's country of origin. Right at the top were the Anglo-Saxons, Germans, Dutch and Scandinavians, in other words the north Europeans, descendants of the Pilgrim Fathers. At the bottom in the 1920s, only just above the blacks, the former slaves, were immigrants from Eastern and Southern Europe, primarily Jews and Italians.

The three gentlemen dressed in black behind the coffins belong to the upper class. They were members of an advisory committee appointed by the Governor of Massachusetts to consider whether he should exercise his power of clemency in the Sacco–Vanzetti case. The most eminent of the three, standing in the middle, is Abbot Lawrence Lowell, after whom the committee was named. He had been president of Harvard University since 1909 and as such was the holder of one of the most respected offices in Boston society. Even his opponents considered him a man of integrity. But Lowell, too, was firmly entrenched within the hierarchical structures of his day. He made sure, for example, that the number of Jewish students admitted to Harvard was limited and that the dormitories were "racially segregated". Even if the facts of the case did not seem to him to be beyond all doubt, his class mindset and its emotion-based discriminatory attitudes led him to concur with the guilty verdict. It was the Lowell Committee that ultimately pronounced the death sentence.

The architecture in the background of the picture forms part of the courthouse in which the trial was held. Shahn shows the steps leading up to the entrance and a number of columns; the pediment above them is missing. The arrangement of spherical lamps can also be seen in photos. A broad staircase and Classical columns surmounted by a flat pediment were typical elements of an American architecture that was deliberately grandiose and which drew its inspiration from the temples of Greece and Rome. Courts, government buildings and even private houses were built in this style; their façades were intended to serve as a reminder of the origins of democracy, of equality, justice and liberty and thus of the ideals of American society. The colour white was thereby also present as a symbol of purity and innocence.

White lilies – the flowers of innocence
America's ill-regarded population of Eastern European Jews included Ben Shahn himself, and he paid tribute to the weak, to the victims of society, in many of his works. In addition to the pictures of Sacco and Vanzetti, he produced a second cycle devoted to Tom Mooney, a labour leader whose conviction was eventually overturned after lengthy hearings. He dedicated a third cycle, dating from 1960/62, to the crew of a Japanese fishing boat that was in the vicinity of the Bikini Atoll when the

United States tested its hydrogen bomb, and whose members were showered with radioactive ash that caused terrible suffering and death.

Although Shahn took part in several demonstrations in Boston protesting on behalf of Sacco and Vanzetti, he never saw either the two men or those involved in their trial in the flesh. His pictorial sources were photos from newspapers and magazines, which he magnified to a monumental scale, omitting some details, adding and altering others. In front of the columns, for example, he eliminates a chain of policemen supposed to be protecting the courthouse. The faces of the deceased are taken from a photo in which men and women, none of them carrying flowers, are filing past the coffins. Shahn replaces the mourners paying their last respects with the members of the Lowell Committee – the "judges" looking down upon their victim is his invention. The white lilies are another addition. According to reports, mourners brought – if anything at all – red roses. Red: the socialists' colour.

The lilies are taken from an altogether different tradition. In representations of the Annunciation since the Middle Ages, the Archangel Gabriel is shown holding a tall stemmed white lily as he announces to the Virgin Mary that she is to bear a child. The lily is a symbol of purity and innocence and in many parts of the world was and still is given at confirmations and funerals. According to an old popular belief in Europe, they also bloomed on the graves of those sentenced to death for a crime of which they were innocent.

The lilies provide the commentary to the collage that Shahn has compiled on the basis of press photos. How this commentary is to be read, however, remains open to debate. In 1927 George Grosz, the German painter who had emigrated to America, marked the death of Sacco and Vanzetti by drawing the Statue of Liberty and giving her an electric chair instead of a torch in her raised hand. A militant caricature, its aim is clear. This is not the case with Shahn. It is true that he has simplified the portraits of Lowell and his colleagues to the point of caricature, giving them overly long noses, sloping shoulders, a mistrustful look on the left and a top hat pulled right down to the ears on the right, and has them holding their lilies with wooden awkwardness. Shahn is condemning the representatives of class justice, that much is evident. On the other hand, the dead were members of a murderous gang and are

lent none of the venerable aura that normally surrounds martyrs. And if we take Lowell's face alone, it is not entirely certain whether Shahn has placed upon it an official mask of condolence or whether sorrow is also to be seen there – sorrow over what had to be done for reasons of state. In this case, the lilies would be more than merely hypocritical gifts for the dead, but would symbolize the three men's situation: like Pontius Pilatus, they are washing their hands as a statement of their innocence, while knowing that they will not escape the blame.

Shahn ranks amongst those artists with a critical vision and a commitment to social change. He learned much from Diego Rivera, the Mexican mural painter, and from his method of distilling a set of social circumstances into a single figure. But Rivera's large-scale mosaics have picture-book clarity and, unlike Shahn's works, leave no room for doubt. Five years after *The Passion of Sacco and Vanzetti*, Europe saw the creation of the 20th-century's most famous work of political art, at once a lament and an indictment. Unlike the work of Rivera and Shahn, it employed no real people and was set in an alien world, radical in its forms and born of artistic experiments that Shahn, in Paris, could make nothing of: Pablo Picasso's *Guernica*.

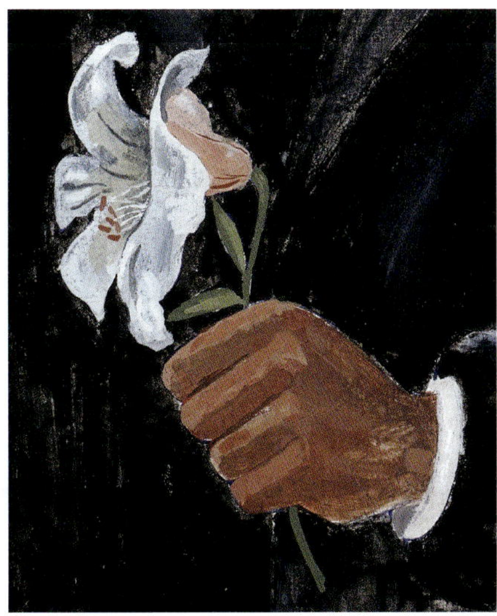

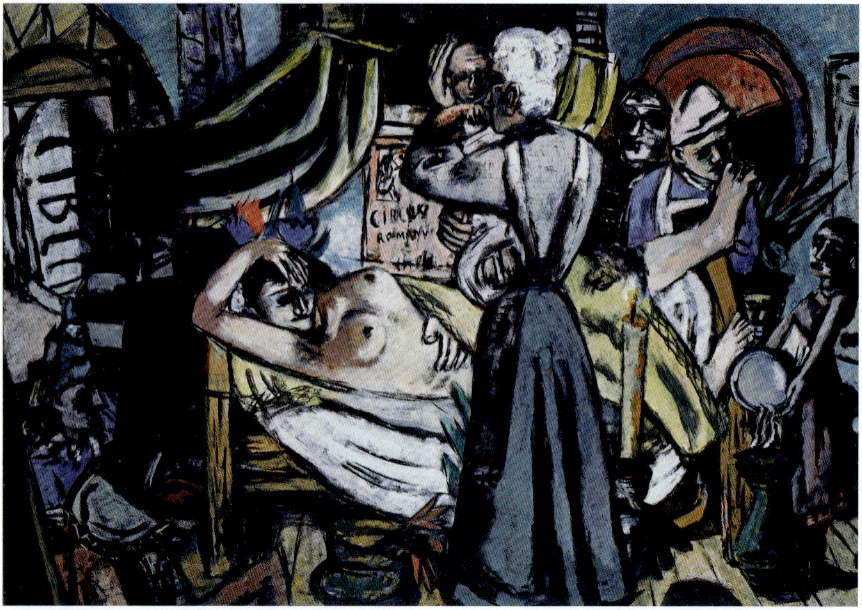

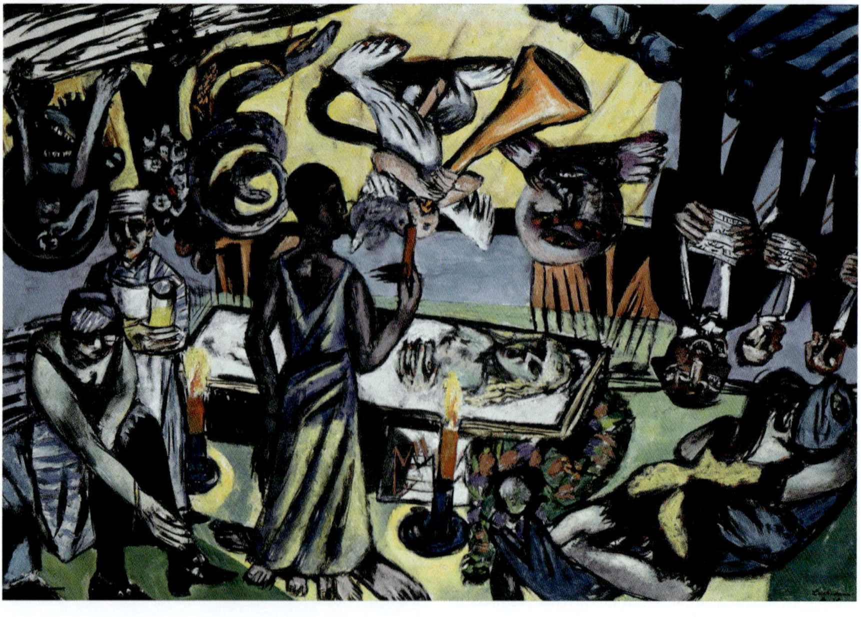

Max Beckmann (1884–1950)

The world as a circus

Birth, 1937, and *Death*, 1938
each 121 x 177 cm, Berlin, Staatliche Museen zu Berlin,
Neue Nationalgalerie

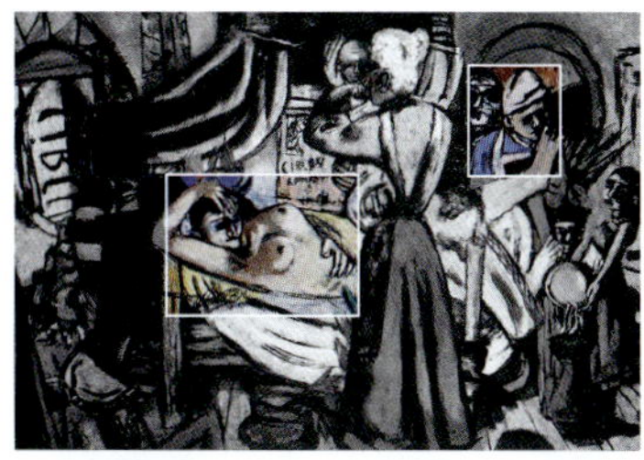

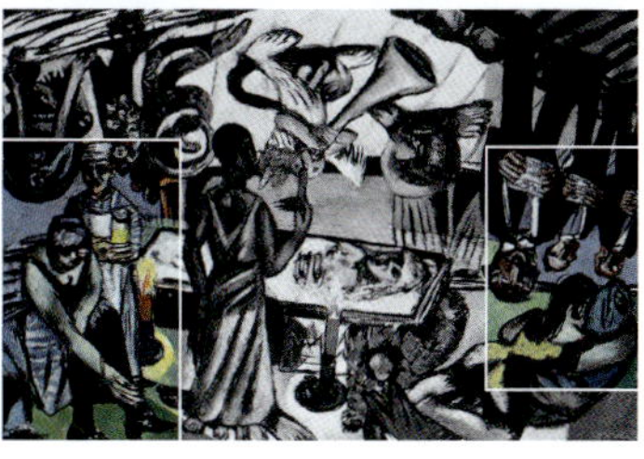

There are pictures that are accessible at first sight –
pictures with familiar motifs, inviting colours,
landscapes, people, flowers, circles. Pictures that
please the eye and do not tax the mind. Famous
paintings such as Raphael's *Sistine Madonna* and
Leonardo da Vinci's *Mona Lisa* are amongst them.
Max Beckmann's pictures of *Birth* (1937) and *Death*
(1938) are not. On the contrary: to visitors strolling
through the museum, Beckmann's images of the
beginning and end of life have the air of dingy back
rooms, confusing and crowded, as if entrance is
discouraged. Those who draw closer start to lose
their sense of orientation, for the painter draws
no clear distinction between front and back and
in *Death* he even exchanges up and down. Perhaps,
at this point, viewers will reflect wistfully upon
the splendid age of the Renaissance, when artists
invented centralized perspective, when they learned
to convey spatial depth and to assign people, objects
and even dragons belching fire to a fixed spot on
our earth.

In the work of painters such as Max Beckmann,
however, the old spatial order has dissolved. He
shows the head of the bed from the side, the foot
from above. Whether the curtain is draped over or
behind the mother, or whether the medical orderly's
face is really supposed to be as close to her foot as it
appears, are questions that remain unresolved. It is

nevertheless clear that both rooms have some sort of
rear boundary. Indeed, the birth room is positively
cramped, even if it is difficult to work out what, on
the back wall, is a window, a mirror or the top half of
a door. Immediately behind the bed hangs a poster
advertising the "Circus Romany". More letters can be
seen in mirror image further left, making up most of
the word "Circus". Beckmann suggests a circus wagon.
He gives death more room than birth: its setting
resembles a circus tent. The coffin stands in the ring;
the lilac blue band running from the left to the right-
hand edge of the painting could be the low barrier
running around the ring and the area of yellow part
of the tent roof. If we turn the picture upside down,
on the other hand, the tent roof becomes a wooden
floor on which strange figures are moving: an angel
with penis and trumpet, a spherical head on flippers,
a male voice choir and various objects that are hard
to identify. Only the corpse lies correctly regardless of
which way up it is seen.

As far as we know, none of Beckmann's contemporaries (apart perhaps from Marc Chagall)
attempted to visualize birth and death together.
The ages of man, from infancy to dotage, had been
a subject of art in earlier periods of history, but
not the act of dying beside the act of giving birth,
not the passage into and out of this earthly existence
as risked here by Beckmann.

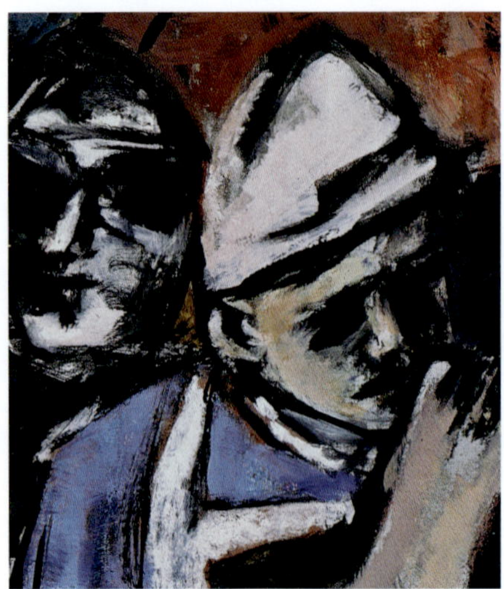

A medical orderly suffers a breakdown

Only one of the figures can be clearly recognized in both pictures, a man dressed in a blue tunic with a white apron and a white hat. In 1914 Beckmann volunteered for the German army as a medical orderly and sketched a self-portrait of himself "in my dismal nursing uniform and crazy driving goggles". Beckmann wears a similar hat in a self-portrait painted in 1926. A visitor to his studio found him "in his old medical uniform, a leftover from the War". He went off to war less in defence of his country than in search of new experiences. So at least it would seem from the tone of his letters. "Ah, this is really living again!" he exulted. "The congregations in the operating theatre, with the dark, unruly faces, the thick beards and white bandages, are splendid." And to his wife he wrote: "There is a wild, almost malevolent sense of pleasure about standing right between death and life in this way."

Beckmann would not be able to bear this "sense of pleasure" for very long. In summer 1915 he had a nervous breakdown, was granted leave and then discharged. His experience of war changed his art. The imaginary catastrophes that he had painted in the past, with subjects such as *Deluge* or *Battle*, were peopled with pseudo-realist figures, preferably nude, in the style of academic history painting. But the mangled limbs, torn flesh and bloody deaths that he had seen in the field hospitals now prohibited him from portraying naked bodies as an attractive sight in his canvases. Beckmann turned people into figures. Although not the case in his portraits, in the scenarios born of the artist's imagination faces became frozen, limbs angular, bodies doll-like. Beckmann dressed his figures as jugglers, as kings, as ungainly characters from antiquity, painted them with broad brush strokes and left them to act out their parts on a stage made of rough planks, in circus rings and carnival halls. He created a vast theatre of estrangement, constructed in order to render visible what the normal eye does not see, and thereby hoped with his pictures "to be more real than life".

All progressive artists of the 1920s sought their own reality behind external appearances, but only a fraction of the population was able or willing to follow them. It is to be suspected that most museum visitors were looking for something else, were hoping to see healthy, attractive people in an unscarred landscape, not evil mannequins, not trenches full of soldiers dying a wretched death. The *Völkischer Beobachter* newspaper, the organ of the National Socialists, lent them a voice and in 1930 wrote of the "delirium of ugliness" in modern art. "Away with these foreigners' nightmares!" it trumpeted. "Let the men conscious of their special German nature come forth! The time is ripe!"

In 1933 the day arrived. Led by Hitler, the "men conscious of their special German nature" came to power, "cleansed" museums of their incomprehensible works and staff. Beckmann lost his post as professor at the Städelsche Kunstinstitut in Frankfurt and was no longer permitted to exhibit. According to Propaganda Ministry records, a total of 590 of his paintings, drawings and prints were removed from museums and public collections. Before the opening, on 19 July 1937, of the exhibition that would denounce the creative wealth of 1920s Germany as "Degenerate Art", Beckmann left Germany and emigrated to Amsterdam and an uncertain future. It was there that he painted *Birth*. With the financial support of a few friends and gallery owners, he moved into a two-room apartment with his wife and worked in an attic studio. After the Second World War he was given one-man shows in Amsterdam, Munich and New York and was also offered teaching posts back in Germany. He decided to accept a professorship in America and in 1947 left for St Louis. He died in New York in 1950 following a stroke.

Giving birth in sinister company

Birth was followed in 1938 by *Death*. The two works bore no direct connection with the artist's emiration but were themes with which he had long been preoccupied. As astonishing as it may seem, the act of giving birth had not been a subject in Western art: the start of life remained invisible. Artists depicted the before and after, the Annunciation with Gabriel appearing to the Virgin Mary and the Nativity with the Infant Christ in his crib. St Anne appears only beneath neatly straightened bedcovers while a nursemaid washes or dresses the newborn Virgin Mary. Even the Netherlandish painting of the 16th and 17th century, with its vivid realism, only ever shows the newborn Child, never the delivery itself. Not until the 20th century, on isolated occasions within feminist-influenced art, is a baby's head to be glimpsed emerging from between parted thighs, as in the work of Frida Kahlo.

Birth and death are events of momentous significance, but although one is contingent upon the other, art practically always shows us only the end, be it on the Cross, as a martyr, in battle, on the scaffold, in bed or – particularly frequently – by suicide, as in the deaths of Cleopatra, Socrates and Seneca. The ratio is very similar in literature, which to a certain degree seems natural: only at the end is there something to say, are destinies revealed, are there characters to describe. At birth we are nobodies. In the Christian tradition, moreover, the sexual organs were considered to be possessed by the devil, and hence everything that went on in the lower body was taboo. It is also possible that the absence of birth in Western art can be traced to the fact that most artists were men. By its very nature, the process was and is less familiar to them than to their female colleagues.

Beckmann does not show the act of giving birth, but he comes closer to it than his contemporaries. The sheets have not yet been straightened and the mother's legs are still parted. She holds one hand draped across her face and rests the other on her emptied belly, her breasts resplendent in the full glare of the light. From an anatomical point of view this body is slightly distorted and dislocated, but as a metaphor for delivery, for pain, exhaustion and relief, it is something new in art. Of the proverbial "happy event", however, Beckmann offers us no

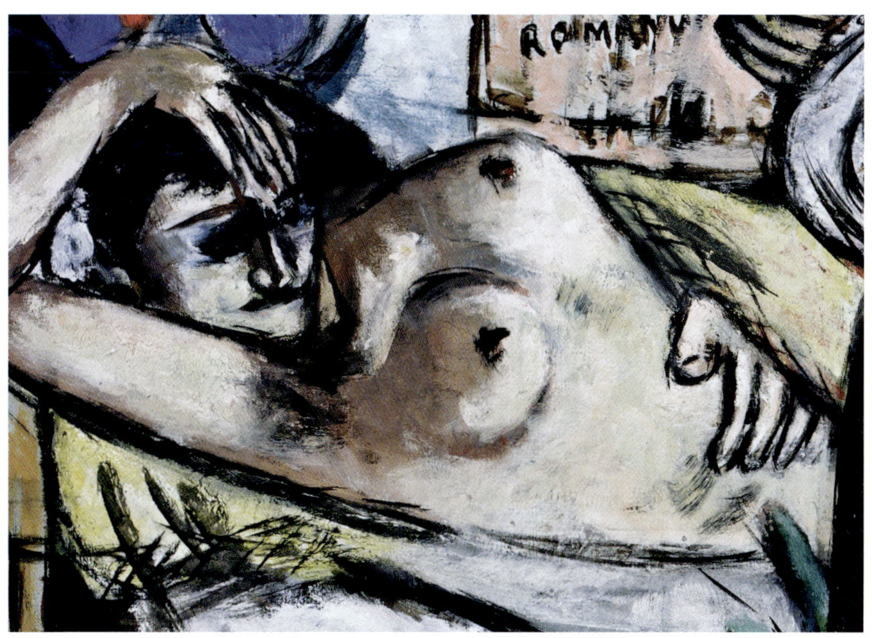

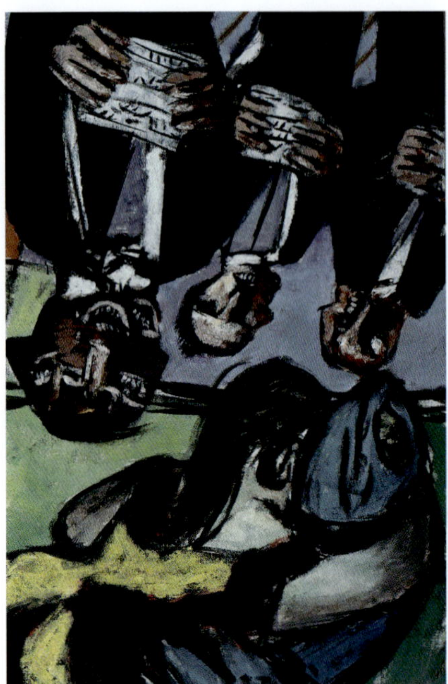

hint. The mother is looking not at her baby, not at her assistants, but downwards, perhaps because she is exhausted, but perhaps too because she does not wish to see the sort of world into which she has brought her child. The bed is too short, the surroundings too chaotic, and there are too many heads and figures making no obvious sense. The nursemaid is the only one standing as steadfast as a pillar and possessing a clear function. The child held against her shoulder has an adult and sombre air.

When up and down get confused

Death repeals all laws: up becomes down and down becomes up. Beckmann wants to show what cannot be seen, namely what is taking place inside the dying person. He plays with gravity, resorts to the myths of the Orient and antiquity and transposes them into the circus world. For example, the Lethe, the river that erases all memories from the minds of the dead. It is represented here by a band of lilac blue running from one edge of the painting to the other, bursting its banks on the right-hand side. Under Beckmann's big top, the Lethe appears as the ground adjoining

the low barrier encircling the ring, known to circus folk as the "piste".

Whether this is exactly what the painter intended is not known; he was reluctant to talk about his works and no observations about these two have come down to us. In the case of the river, perhaps he was also thinking of the Styx, which the dead cross on their way to the underworld. The entrance to Hades is guarded by Cerberus, the hound of Hell, who prevents the dead from escaping back to the realm of the living. His distinguishing characteristic was his three heads, or three faces, clearly visible in the closest of the singers. In conjunction with the two others, however, Beckmann's Hell hound might also belong to the trinity of judges who assign the arriving ghosts to their final destinations. Beckmann presents them as a trio, a vocal combination popular in his day. Whether the Lethe or the Styx, whether the hound of Hades or the three judges of the dead, trying to pin lexicological labels upon Beckmann's deliberate or merely fleeting associations will not get us very far. Detailed knowledge was not important to him, but he hoped that visitors would know "the same metaphysical code", that they would communicate with his pictures on the same wavelength.

Fish were a regular part of his repertoire and appear in several of his paintings. One is lying with a woman below the singers' heads; the woman has wrapped herself around the human-size animal and is clasping its tail fins between her legs. Slippery, cold scales against a warm female body – that must make a few viewers shudder. "The main thing is sensuality, I only want a little of the metaphysical," said Beckmann in the 1930s, albeit in a different context. The fish scene, like the male trio, has both – one side for the senses and another for what the senses cannot grasp.

What the artist associated with fishes can be deduced from his reading. He was familiar with an Indigenous deluge myth in which a fish god rescues the man whose seed then peoples the world. A fish saves humankind. Beckmann's library also included a book entitled *Urwelt, Sage and Menschheit* (*Primeval World, Myth and Mankind*), in which a pre-human creature is described, having the shape of a fish but endowed with reason. Gnostic writings speak of fishes as the "first beings" and as "primeval beings", and Beckmann probably also knew the Egyptian creation myth according to which the earth rose up out of the water, just as it appeared to the Egyptians every year as the Nile floods receded. In 1949 he painted a *Primeval Landscape* containing not only "early people" but also giant fish not dissimilar to whales. Nowhere else in his art did he demonstrate so clearly that he saw, in water, an element of creation and eternal renewal.

Protest against a world gone wrong

One of the dominant colours in Beckmann's palette is black. He uses it to draw his powerful outlines and some of his paintings give the impression that darkness is constantly present. Black is traditionally viewed as the colour of death and mourning, but also of nobility and of the dress worn in polite society. For Beckmann, however, it was probably also the matter of the cosmos, the colour that swallows all light and all order. He spoke of "the black waves of the void" and of "the black wall running all around us". Forming one of the many black zones in *Death* are the legs of the woman seated at the foot of the coffin. She has hitched her skirt up to above her knees and is fiddling with one of her shoes. Directly behind her stands the male nurse – stands Beckmann, one could say, in his fateful uniform. Both are wearing blue and white hospital uniforms and the woman has the broad cheekbones of the artist's wife.

It is possible that this group of two was inspired by an increased need for closeness in the wake of their emigration. But it also provides a counterpart to the duo in the right-hand corner of the picture, the mythical union of the woman with the primeval, fish-shaped being. And it is surely no coincidence that Beckmann has given the trumpeting gnome in the centre of the picture an erect penis, just as the Egyptians gave to their fertility god, Min. Three motifs that, for all their difference, refer to sex and procreation – grouped around a corpse that conveys the impression that it is slowly disappearing into the white palls.

But the Beckmann figure displays nothing of love or even passion. He stares darkly out across his partner. It emerges from his diary that he found sexuality an at times unbearable compulsion. "Are we never to be free from this eternal, abominable, vegetative physicality?" he asked himself in 1946. He wanted to "refuse to obey the sickening, eternally unknown laws that are imposed upon us". In painting he protested against these same eternal laws that induce men constantly to reproduce themselves in a wicked

world. According to the creation myths of Gnosticism, one of the early Christian strands of religion, the state of the world could be traced back to the Demiurge, a dull witted or malevolent inferior deity who had created the material world on behalf of his master. He had thereby built a penal colony with no possibility of escape. Beckmann rebelled in the name of humankind: "In my pictures I reproach God for everything that he has done wrong." He wrote these words at the end of the First World War, just as he was evolving his own art.

Those who step into Beckmann's paintings of the start and end of life rapidly come to realise that they have joined not a religious celebration but an organized protest. There is nothing of the joy of a birth, little of a sacrament of death. Beckmann paints instead a world that has gone wrong. In particular, he paints in protest against the fact that people continue to carry on, that they allow themselves to be compelled and seduced into constantly renewing life.

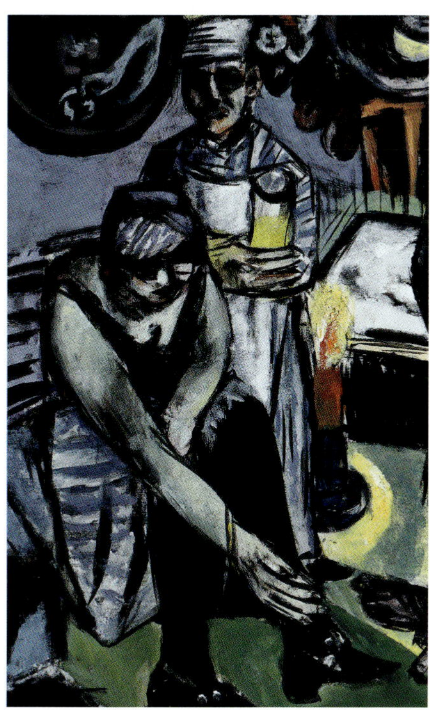

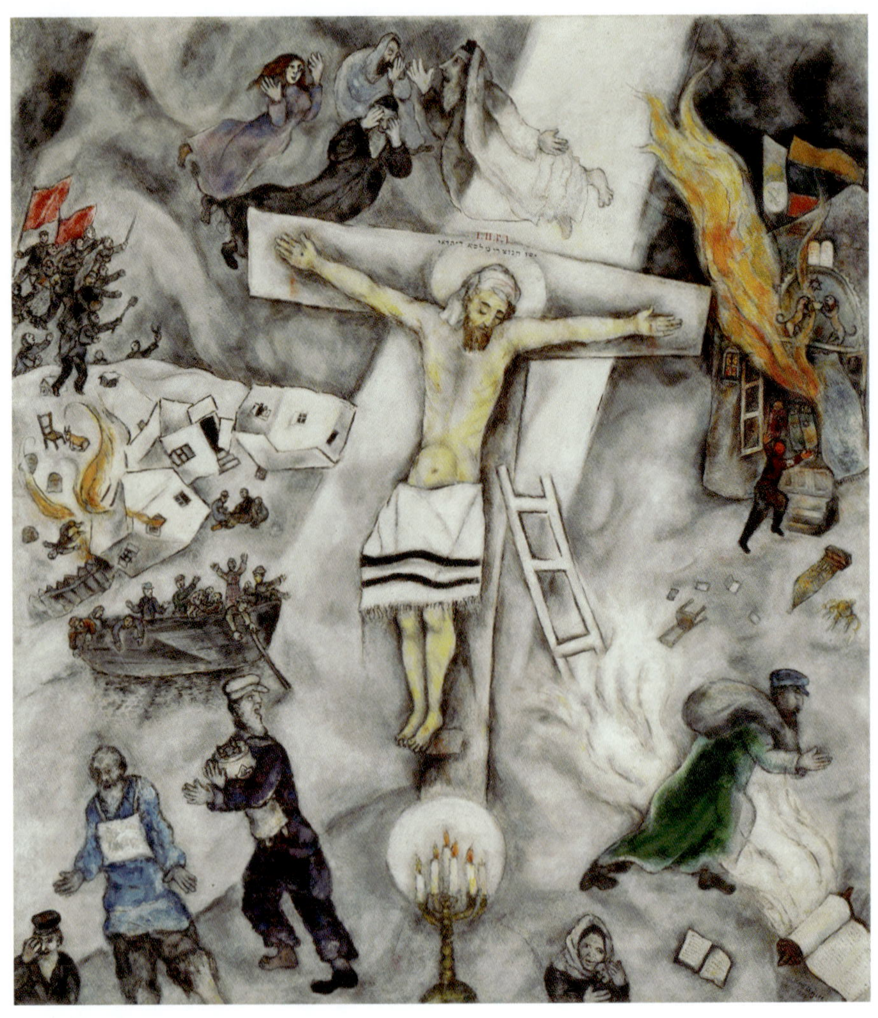

Marc Chagall (1887–1985)

The Vitebsk Man of Sorrows

White Crucifixion, 1938
155 x 139.5 cm, The Art Institute of Chicago,
Gift of Alfred S. Alschuler

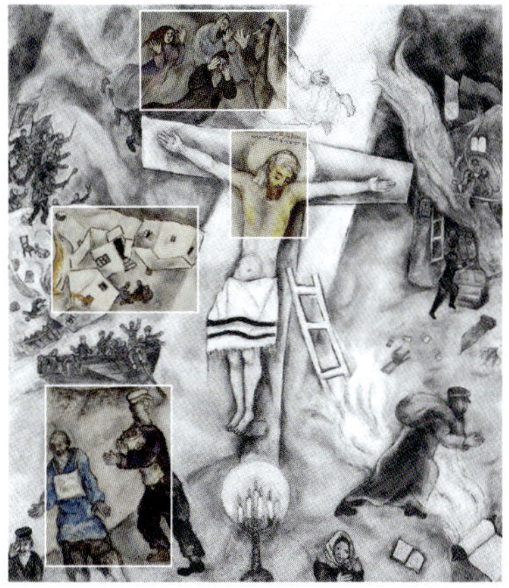

Marc Chagall died in 1985 at the age of 97. Many of his paintings plead for love and understanding between the peoples of the world, or warn of terror and violence. When the National Socialists intensified their campaign to exterminate the Jews, unleashing the "Kristallnacht" pogrom in 1938, Marc Chagall, a Jew, painted the Christian Redeemer surrounded by scenes and symbols taken from the life and beliefs of the artist's own Russian-Jewish homeland. The painting was not a work of protest. As an allegory of human suffering, it pointed to a divine order behind the misery and afflictions of this world.

In his novel *The Brothers Karamazov*, Dostoyevsky tells of a Jew who crucifies a child. The Jew, according to the story, cuts off all the four-year-old boy's fingers before nailing him to a wall and standing back to enjoy the sight.

This horrific tale epitomizes the image of Jews presented in all of Dostoyevsky's books: Jews are dishonest and malicious, exploiters, conniving hoarders of gold and silver, and perhaps – one is never quite sure – they slaughter little children at Easter.

Dostoyevsky's allegations and insinuations were a reflection of the anti-Semitic attitudes of many of his countrymen. The tsars, in tandem with the Orthodox Church, had long deprived Jews of the right even to dwell on "holy Russian" soil. This situation did not change until the 18th century when the partition of Poland paved the way for Tsarist Russia to expand west. Among the country's newly acquired subjects were a million Jews – at that time practically half the world's Jewish population.

From then on their predicament, not unlike that of Jews in many other European states, varied between periods of toleration and persecution, without their ever being fully accepted. The tsars repeatedly outlawed Jewish books and schools, attempting to coerce the "unbelievers" into accepting the Christian faith; there were pogroms, synagogues and shops were plundered, people killed. Writers like Dostoyevsky provided moral justification.

The Brothers Karamazov appeared in 1879 and 1880; not long afterwards, in 1887, Chagall was born at Vitebsk, a small town where Jews enjoyed relative freedom of movement. To visit St Petersburg, however, the capital of Tsarist Russia, special permission was required. Permits, highly coveted, were granted only to those with proof of employment: as a servant or a sign painter, or a student at one of the art academies. Chagall, each of these in succession, frequently found himself sharing cramped sleeping quarters with many of his fellow men: "I began to understand that we Jews were not the only ones to be forbidden the right to live in Russia, for there were many Russians too, all crawling over each other like lice on a head of hair."

Professional status allowed a small number of privileged Jews, most of them doctors, lawyers or bankers, to live in St Petersburg. They would often support young artists, and one paid for Chagall to visit Paris in 1910. It was a long journey – not only in kilometres. Chagall had come far: from an isolated township in provincial White Russia, via St Petersburg, to the cultural centre of Western Europe.

However, in this respect Chagall was not unique. Many artists, members of the oppressed Jewish minority, left Russia for the West in the period before the First World War, and again after the Russian Revolution. Their contribution to Western culture was both enriching and influential. They included writers like Ilya Ehrenburg, the set designer Leon Bakst, the sculptors Jacques Lipchitz and Ossip Zadkine, as well as Chaim Soutine and Issai Kulviansky, two of the many painters of whom Marc Chagall was the most famous.

Among the artists, only Chagall remained faithful to his Russian-Jewish background. His paintings return again and again to the same motifs: the small huts of Vitebsk, devout Jews with the Torah scroll, rabbis and synagogues. "I have continued the work passed on to me by my parents and by their parents in turn for thousands of years," he said. "I shall never forget the land of my birth." Thanks to Chagall's paintings, many people – even those to whom the world of the Jews otherwise means very little – have become acquainted with Jewish motifs.

Pictures of a world without pictures

The houses in Chagall's painting are depicted lying on their sides; one is on its roof, another is up in flames. The laws of motion and gravity seem no longer to apply in the world of the painting; the buildings appear to be made of folded paper, or part of a dream. In any case, they look very different from those we are used to seeing. Chagall does not attempt to copy the recognizable world, but creates a world of his own, selecting and juxtaposing otherwise disparate fragments of reality. Among these are simple houses of the kind in which he was born at Vitebsk. At the time of Chagall's birth

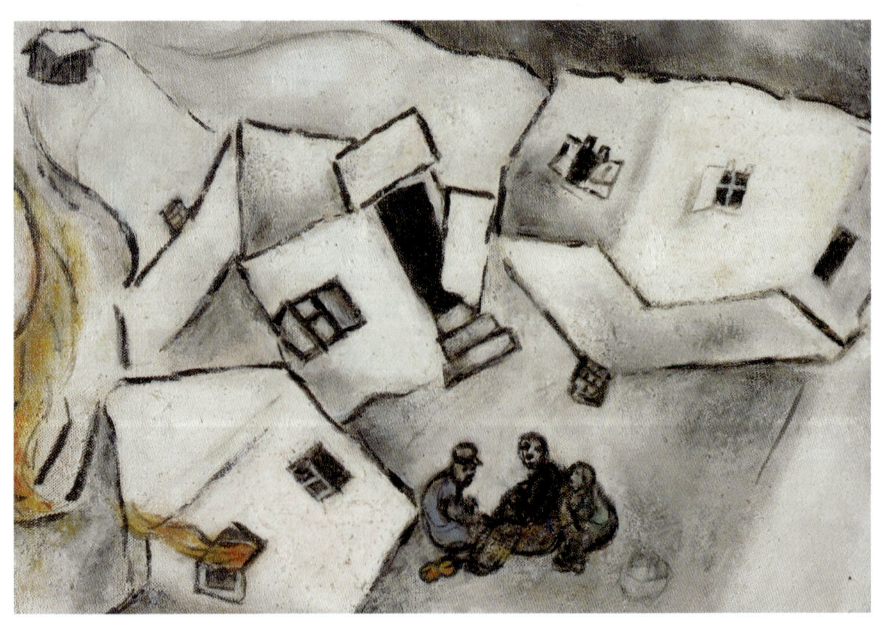

in 1887, Vitebsk, situated on the River Drina near the former Lithuanian border, had some 60,000 inhabitants, over half of them Jews. Some were tradesmen and craftsmen, or founded factories, but the majority, like the Chagalls, were poor. Chagall's father earned his living in a fishmonger's shop "hoisting heavy barrels, and I felt my heart twist like a Turkish pretzel when I saw him lift such heavy weights or go rummaging in barrels of herring with his frozen hands."

Though in material terms, standards were extremely modest, Jewish tradition made life culturally rich. The Sabbath and the different religious festivals determined the course of the year. "On Fridays, when we'd eaten the Sabbath evening meal, our father would always fall asleep at the same place in the prayer," so that Chagall's mother, he recalled, would say to her eight children: "Come on! Lets sing that song about the rabbi!" Chagall describes in his memoirs: "My mother was the eldest daughter of a grandfather who spent half his life by the stove, a quarter in the synagogue, and the rest at the butcher's shop."

"Thou shalt not make unto thee any graven image, or any likeness of any thing that is in heaven above, or that is in the earth beneath, or that is in the water under the earth." The Old Testament commandment forbidding idolatry was interpreted by Jews as a prohibition against the painting of pictures. "No picture hung on our walls, not even a print … Until 1906, in all the years I spent at Vitebsk, I had never seen a single picture." In 1906 Chagall, at nineteen years old, was permitted to take lessons from a portraitist in his home town, but his father refused to place the money for tuition in his hand, throwing it on the ground instead. As a devout Jew he did not wish to encourage painting; but neither did he wish to prevent his eldest son from doing so. Chagall recalled: "My uncle is too frightened to give me his hand. He has heard that I am a painter. What if I wanted to paint him? God forbids such things. Sin."

Not only the houses, but the scene with the prostrate woman and child, too, derive from the artist's memories of his childhood and youth. Though he had not seen these figures himself, he had been told about them, and was evidently deeply impressed. He recalled: "I no longer remember – could it have been my mother who told me? Apparently, at the very moment of my birth a great fire broke out in a little house near Vitebsk, on the road behind the

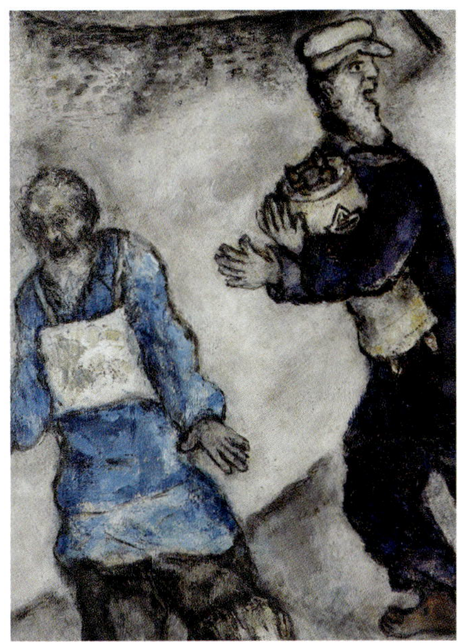

prison. The town was in flames – the poor Jewish quarter burning. They took the bed and mattress, with the mother and the baby at her feet, to a safe place on the other side of town." The artist has thus included himself in the form of an anecdote relating to the day of his birth in a great painting of fire, persecution and floating figures.

The inscription "I am a Jew" deleted

When Chagall painted these childhood memories he was over 50 years old. He had incorporated them in a picture whose subject was inspired by a misfortune of quite different proportions to that of a local fire: the persecution of the Jews by the Nazis. Chagall painted the *White Crucifixion* in 1938, the year of the "Kristallnacht" pogrom in Germany, when Hitler's Brownshirts set fire to the synagogues, plundered Jewish shops and physically abused Jewish citizens. The mass extermination of Jews in concentration camps had not yet begun, but the "Kristallnacht" and banning of Jews from German public life were stages on the way.

Only a tiny detail betrays the occasion that gave rise to Chagall's painting: in front of the burning synagogue is a figure apparently clad in the uniform of the Brownshirts. However, as if shrinking from so unequivocal a statement, the artist has avoided painting the Nazi emblem on the flags. He also later deleted an unambiguous clue from the white piece of cloth covering the chest of the man in the blue smock. It originally carried the German inscription "Ich bin Jude" (I am a Jew), as an extant preliminary sketch for the painting reveals.

But Chagall was not a political realist, nor was he interested in current affairs, or he would not have painted refugees in 1938 who, with their long beards and Russian smocks, resembled the Jews of his old home town. Moreover, the painting not only avoids precise indications of time or place, but does without aids like perspective or a recognizable horizon, both of which usually facilitate orientation. This contributes to the altogether dreamlike tenor of the work.

Torah scrolls are twice depicted in the painting: one is burning on the ground in the bottom right; the other is being rescued in the arms of a man on the left. The Torah is essentially the Jewish Bible, comprising the first five books of the Mosaic law, the Pentateuch; it is kept in the synagogue, and an excerpt is read on the Sabbath. When a boy is accepted into the community, he reads the weekly portion in Hebrew, and when a Jew dies, the Torah is brought from the synagogue to his home. The Torah forms the basis of Jewish religious practice, as well as of social cohesion in the Jewish community. Adherence to the letter of Hebrew texts in the Torah helped Jews survive through periods of persecution and exile.

It is rather more difficult to establish the exact significance of the red flags shown entering at the top left of the picture. Do the armed men belong to the oppressors, or are they liberators? Are the flags red because Chagall felt the painting needed the colour, or did he intend us to think of Communists? In fact, Chagall was a Bolshevik Commissar for Fine Art, with the task of founding an art academy at Vitebsk. He was forced to yield the post two years later, however, not because of political difficulties, but because of quarrels about art with two of the teachers he had appointed at his institute: El Lissitzky and Kasimir Malevich.

Chagall worked as a stage designer in Moscow, largely for the State Jewish Theatre, and taught at an orphanage prior to returning to the West, travelling first to Berlin and then on to Paris. There is practically no evidence to suggest he studied Marxism or Lenin's politics. Chagall saw the Revolution as

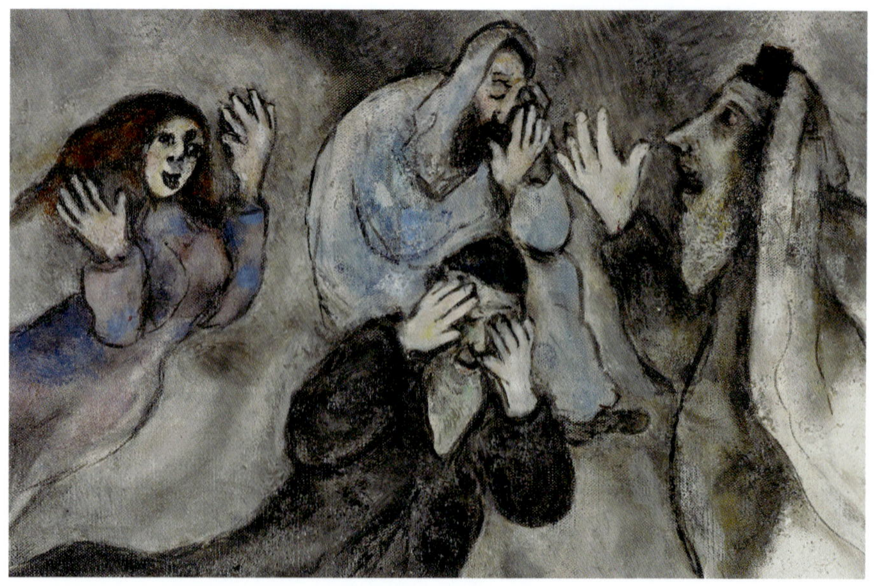

a means of releasing creative potential, a project to
which he willingly lent his support. He had no time
for political structures or ideological battles.

Joyful are those who perceive the divine purpose
The floating, birdlike figures shown wailing and
gesticulating above the Cross are evidently Jews
rather than Christian saints. Two are wearing a "tal-
lith", or prayer shawl, over their heads, and one has a
small leather box at his forehead containing parch-
ments inscribed with passages from the Old Testament. These are the "tefillin", or phylacteries, worn by
devout Jews at prayer.

Chagall, more than any other 20th-century
painter, is the artist of floating figures, figures who
appear to recline on air. Some of the figures are
dreaming; many are lovers; yet others are musicians.
These figures have in common their "heightened"
state; their bodies appear to respond to intense
emotion. The present scene possibly depicts the
exaltation of the devout. The motif is reminiscent
of a Jewish anecdote: "Sometimes, when Rabbi
Elimelech spoke the Shema on the Sabbath, he
would take out his pocket watch. This being the hour
when he felt his soul most likely to melt in sheer
bliss, he looked at his watch to keep himself locked
in the present, and thereby attached to the world."

But perhaps the artist intended to suggest not
a state of emotional intensity, but the presence of
Jewish teachers and prophets; or possibly he had
reason to mean both. In his memoirs Chagall recalls
the very real presence of the prophets in his parents'
house: "Ordering me to open the door, my father
raised his glass. Were we opening our door, the outside door, at such a late hour to let in the prophet
Elijah? A silvery sheaf of white starlight darted into
my eyes out of the blue velvet sky – and straight into
my heart. But where was Elijah and his fiery white
chariot? Perhaps he was still out there in the yard,
about to enter the house as a frail old man, or a
stooping beggar with a sack hung over his back and
a stick in his hand? 'Here I am. And where, I pray
you, is my glass of wine?'"

The story of the rabbi keeping himself in the
present by looking at his pocket watch is part
of the Chassidic tradition in which Chagall grew up.
The Chassidim, or "pious ones", aspire to the perfection of a divine purpose in reality, no matter how
imperfect, miserable or painful reality itself might
be. One who succeeds in this endeavour, even briefly

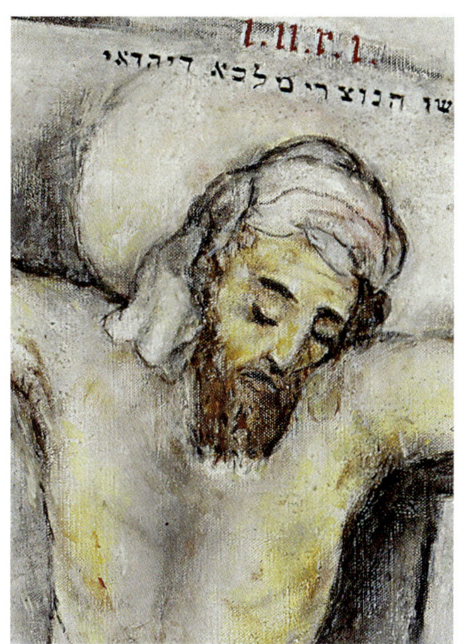

during prayer, is filled at once with joy, ecstasy,
enthusiasm. It is no coincidence that the Chassidim
are great singers and dancers.

Chassidism was originally a response to the
more intellectual discipline of Talmudism; the
"pious" held intuition and the emotions in higher
esteem than logic. Chassidism has no firm doctrine,
but is rich in tales and legends. Many concern the
right way – the pious way – to look at things. One
tells of how Rabbi Lob visited an elder, "not to
hear his teachings, but merely to see how he tied
and untied his felt shoes". Rabbi Menachem Mendel,
from Vitebsk like Chagall, is reported as saying:
"When I see a bundle of straw lying lengthways
rather than sideways on the ground, it is to me
a sign of divine presence."

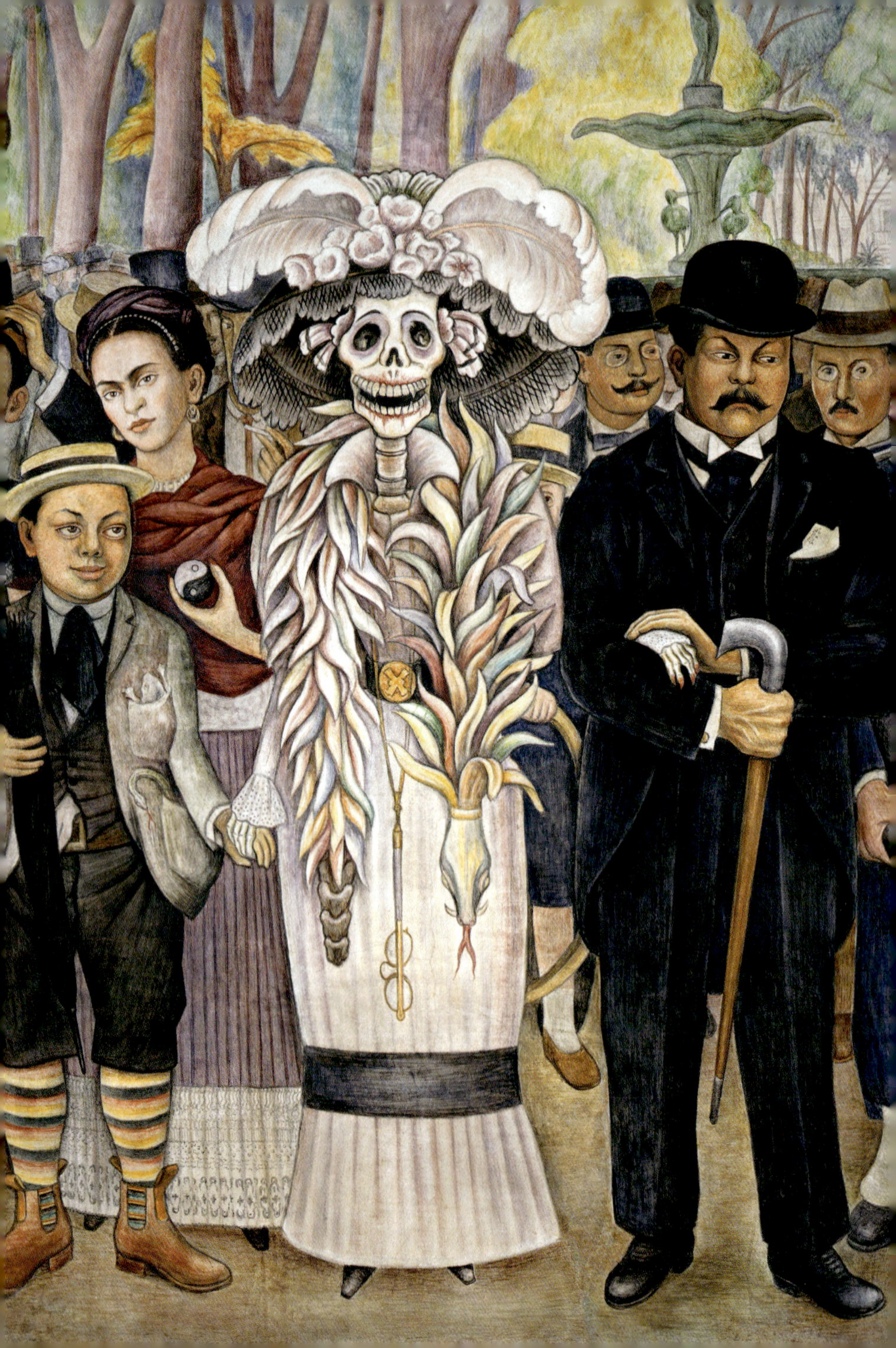

Diego Rivera (1886–1957)

Four hundred years at a glance

Dream of a Sunday Afternoon in Alameda Park, 1948
4.80 x 15 m, Mexico City, Pabellón Diego Rivera

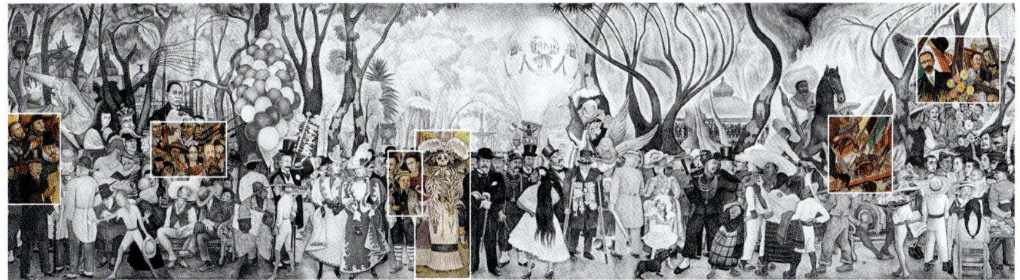

If you want to take a proper look at the whole of Diego Rivera's 4.80-metre-high mural, you'll need to take a walk – along all 15 metres of its length, and past almost 150 different characters. By European standards, the format is enormous – as enormous, indeed, as the task which the artist set himself: to bring together figures from the past 400 years into a panorama of the history of his country, set in Alameda Park. The park lies in Mexico City, and on Sunday afternoons the capital's inhabitants gather here to sit, stroll, chat and picnic. The grown-ups buy balloons and windmills for their children, and the adolescents wade in the fountain which Rivera has portrayed in the centre of his composition. He has placed well-known figures from Mexican history alongside many more who are unknown, and has also incorporated mythical figures such as angels and Death, as well as members of his own family. This is no historical record, no Social Realism, but a collage as might be experienced in a dream.

The chronology of the mural unfolds more or less logically from left to right. At the apex of three small pyramids of figures, distributed across the composition, Rivera portrays three Mexican presidents: on the left, Benito Juárez, head of state from 1858 to 1872, is holding the written constitution in his hands. Just to the right of centre is the uniformed, sleeping figure of Porfirio Díaz, who held office for over 30 years before being ousted by Francisco Madero. The latter can be seen, raising his hat in greeting, near the right-hand edge of the mural; in 1913 he was assassinated.

Beneath them, along the lower edge of the mural, are those who have no hand in politics, but who suffer its effects: ordinary citizens, Indigenous communities, agricultural workers, and the poor. The conflict between these people and those in power was one which Rivera painted many times. On the left, a thin youth is picking the pocket of a well dressed gentleman; in the middle, an Indigenous woman in a yellow dress strikes an aggressively provocative pose, while further to the right a policeman is expelling a family of Indigenous people from the park. One of the men he is threatening has already reached his hand round to the back of his belt, where he keeps his knife. Floating above all their heads is a

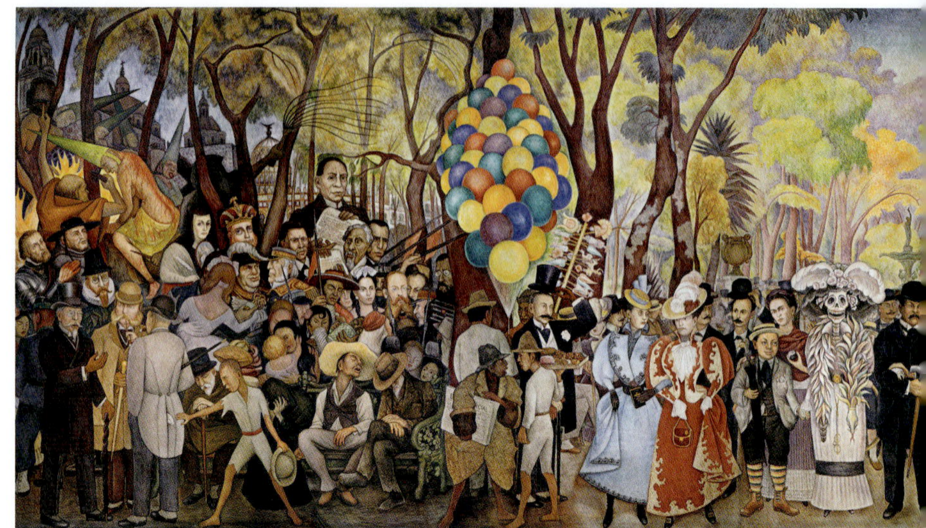

hot-air balloon – a reference to the flight made by the aeronaut Cantolla, and at the same time a symbol of hope for "RM", the Republica Mexicana.

Slaughter in the name of God

The man with the bloody hands, Hernán Cortés, is the most contentious figure in Mexican history: he conquered the country for the Spanish crown, and in so doing slaughtered countless Indigenous people and destroyed important testaments to their highly advanced culture. The history of modern Mexico thus began with death and destruction. The native population remains an underprivileged class, and the figure of the conqueror is blamed in their struggle for social justice to this day. On whose side Rivera stood can be seen from the Spaniard's hands. By the standards of his day, Cortés was an outstanding man: daring and adept at manoeuvering his small Spanish force amidst an Indigenous population of infinitely superior numbers. One of his soldiers, Bernal Díaz del Castillo, described the experience in great detail and recorded how, wherever he could, Cortés destroyed Aztec temples and erected crosses in their place. He conquered this foreign land for his God and King – not for himself.

In 1519 he set off from Cuba; in 1521 he subdued the Aztec capital once and for all. It lay on the site where Mexico City today sprawls, a city of nine million people. Cortés became the first governor of "New Spain", and Fray Juan de Zumarraga its first bishop: Rivera portrays him beside Cortés. With iron determination, seen in his own age as motivated by charity but seeming so cruel to us today, he set about converting the Indigenous to Christianity. He burned their writings – an incalculable loss as far as our understanding of ancient American culture is concerned.

From 1535, the Spanish colony was ruled by a viceroy. Rivera has painted the eighth, with glasses and ruff. The man who in 1592 created Alameda Park – not for the general public, but for the Spanish ruling classes. The execution site used by the Inquisition was later added to its grounds. Rivera shows the condemned, wearing the tall pointed hats of sinners, in front of the flames in which they will burn to death.

The undoing of an idealist

Rivera painted his dream of Mexican history for the dining room of the El Prado Hotel, beside Alameda Park. The mural was completed in 1948, but it caused an uproar and was damaged by a protester. It was subsequently concealed behind a rapidly erected wall, where it remained hidden for seven years. Only after Rivera had changed one small inscription did the hotel management put the mural back on

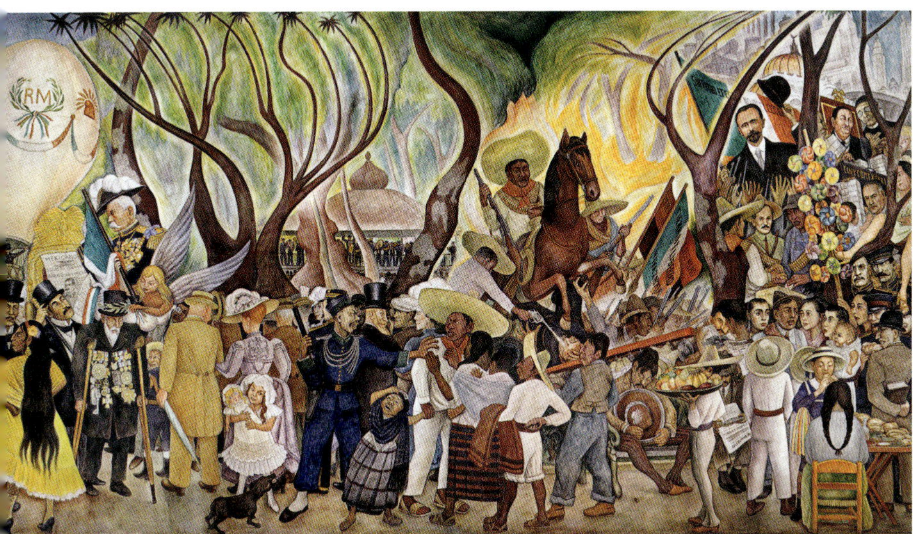

display; later, in order to satisfy the public interest, the painting was even transported – wall and all – into the reception hall. The offending words were written on the piece of paper held up by Ignacio Ramírez, the dark skinned man with the white hair. They originally read: "God does not exist".

The words visible on the sheet of paper today are: "Conference in the Academy of Letran, 1836" – a cryptic reference to an occasion when Ramirez had stated his atheist views. Not especially significant in itself, it was important only as an allusion to trends hostile to the Church and religion. The power of the Catholic Church was the subject of controversy. In the 19th century, the desire to safeguard its influence and possessions brought it to side with the Conservatives. Anyone with a liberal turn of mind was automatically its enemy. Even the unfortunate Emperor Maximilian would suffer the consequences.

Mexico's Conservatives invited the Austrian Archduke to their country almost 140 years ago. Rivera portrays him with his famous pale blue eyes and flourishing ginger beard, standing below and to the right of Ramirez. Maximilian, it was hoped, would reestablish order in a Mexico which had declared itself independent of Spain and the monarchic system of government, and which had since been ravaged by decades of civil war. In May 1864 he arrived on Mexican soil with his wife Charlotte, who was now known as Carlota. But since he neither abolished the new freedom of worship, nor returned to the Church its nationalized property, he made enemies of the very Catholic forces which had appointed him Emperor.

Maximilian, the liberal idealist and inexperienced politician, had failed. Three years after his landing, he was deposed and shot; the guns in Rivera's mural recall his execution. A few weeks before his death, his wife Carlota, portrayed next to her husband, went mad. She lived for another 60 years, dying in 1927.

Viva Zapata! Land and Freedom!

Virtually every country has an idol, a figure typifying the national characteristics of which it is most proud. In Prussia, it was the civil servant or officer – someone who placed service to the state above personal happiness. In the United States, it was and still is the cowboy: someone who prizes adventure and freedom more highly than urban civilization. In Mexico, America's southern neighbour, it is still the revolutionary: someone who fights against the exploitation of the poor and tries, by force of arms, to lessen the inequality in society. In his mural, Rivera gives particular visual emphasis to the revolutionary, placing him – like the three presidents Juárez, Díaz and

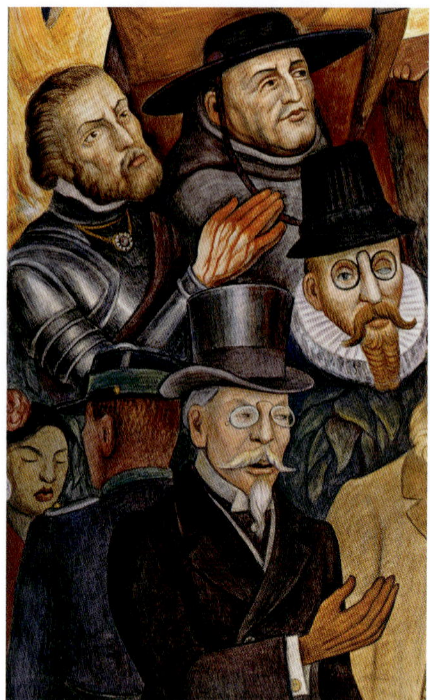

He was born in 1877 in the small Mexican village of Anenecuilco. His father was a small-scale farmer. The region, like rural Mexico as a whole, was at that time ruled by the *hacendados*, the large landowners. The haciendas in Anenecuilco dated right back to the 16th century, when they had been founded with the consent of the Spanish king. Around 1900, those Native or Indigenous villages which had managed to survive began to be squeezed out by the landowners. The railways had opened up access to the international markets, but the *hacendados* could only increase their profits by enlarging their estates. With the assistance of small private armies and a partisan judicial system, they proceeded to take away from the Mexican peasants their communal land and thus their own property. The Indigenous farmers became vassal agricultural labourers, and lost their land and their freedom – their *Tierra y Libertad*.

Emilio Zapata organized armed resistance and joined forces with rebels from other villages. Together they formed a peasants' army, were victorious on some occasions, defeated on others, and in the meantime argued amongst themselves. Zapata ultimately met the same fate as most other peasant leaders: he was betrayed and murdered. He had begun his resistance in 1909; in 1919 he met his end. For a long time, it was rumoured amongst his supporters that he had only gone underground and would return, and that the body put on display at the time was not that of Emilio Zapata at all!

Madero – at the apex of a fourth pyramid of people. In the Mexican dream and in the Mexican self-image, the revolutionary is an omnipresent point of reference, whose praises are sung in countless ballads and whose portrait – as a reprint of old photographs enlarged to poster size – hangs on many walls.

In Rivera's human panorama, the revolutionary is accompanied by an armed woman; women played an important role in the struggles of the artist's day. At the revolutionary's feet, men with guns are surging forward; one is holding a hand grenade with its fuse already lit. Their banners read *Tierra y Libertad* ("Land and Freedom") and *Viva Zapata*.

Emiliano Zapata was one of the most famous of Mexico's revolutionaries. "Hear, Señores, hear the terrible tale of how Zapata, the great rebel, was treacherously murdered in Chinameca," one folk song begins; it ends: "Restless stream, what is that carnation whispering to you? It is whispering that Zapata is not dead, he will come again!" Zapata's story is typical of that of many revolutionaries.

A repeated cycle of murder and violence

Francisco Madero, the man raising his hat in greeting, was a revolutionary like Zapata, but from a very different background. His family came from the ranks of the country's wealthy and owned haciendas, banks and industrial concerns. The two men were nevertheless united by their struggle against the ageing president Porfirio Díaz, whom Rivera portrays dozing in the middle section of his mural. Díaz held power for over 30 years. With the help of the army and the large landowners, he brought a certain stability to the country, but at the expense of the poor, the Indigenus population – and the democratic constitution. Díaz was a dictator; he suspended the article which forbade the reelection of a president after a single term in office. Madero, a liberal-minded capitalist, objected. He published a pamphlet against this violation of the law and called for universal suffrage extending to the Indigenous population. Díaz had him imprisoned. Upon his release, Madero became head of the revolutionaries. In 1911 Díaz fled the country. Madera entered Mexico City and was appointed president. His political goals are written on the banner behind him: "Universal suffrage – no reelection!" He proved unable or unwilling to realize his third declared aim, namely to give the Indigenous farmers their land back. Perhaps he had embraced this goal during the struggles more for tactical reasons than out of conviction. Had he implemented it, he would have harmed the very class from which he came. Generals of the Revolution such as Zapata, the farmer's son, immediately disassociated themselves from him and resumed fighting. Madero lost control over the country. Officers of his government placed him under arrest. On his way to prison, he was shot by his escort.

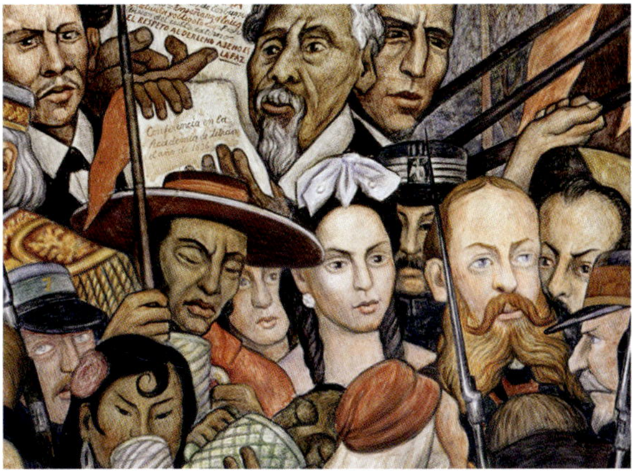

Madero was not the only president to meet an unnatural end. Murder and violence are threads running all the way through the history of Mexico, from its conquest right up to the 20th century. In Rivera's

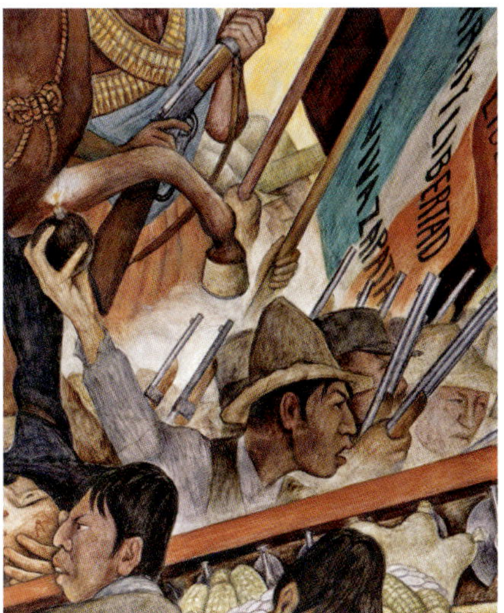

mural they are symbolized in the flames of the Inquisition's stake, as in the fires of the Revolution. There are many reasons for this bloodthirsty tradition; most can be traced back to the country's conquest by the Spaniards and to the inequality of its two cultures. Mexico's Indigenous population were unfamiliar with the European concept of individuality. Community was and still is more important than personal success. Competition played no great role. They thereby lacked the drive to learn how to survive, something which made them defenceless in the face of European aggression. Only when their misery became insufferable did they start to fight back, did they rally to the side of men like Zapata.

Through his works, Rivera wanted to contribute towards the reconciliation of Mexico's two cultures, the establishment of unity and the creation of a Mexican identity – hence his many history cycles, his championing of the oppressed Indians, the Mexican proletariat, and his criticism of the ruling Indigenous population.

Painting on walls for the Revolution

The artist who placed his talents so emphatically in the service of his people, was born in 1886. In the central section of his *Dream*, he portrays himself as he must have looked at the start of the century: in shorts and a straw boater, with a frog and a snake – living toys – in his pockets. He kept his plump figure and slightly bulging eyes all his life. Behind him stands his wife, the artist Frida Kahlo, who lays her hand protectively on the boy's shoulder.

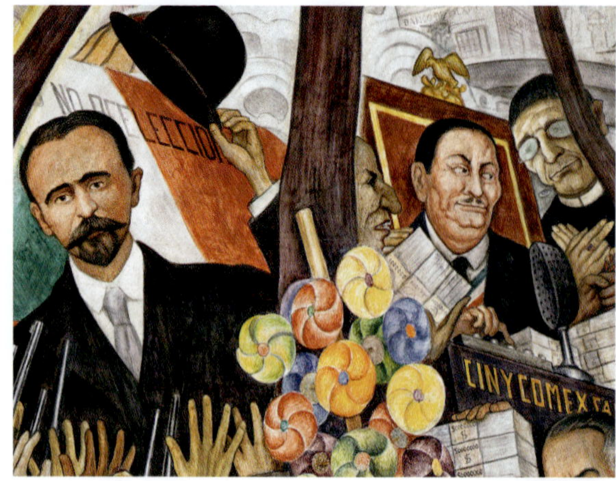

excellence, which belongs to all and is accessible to all … regained its contemporary relevance." The artists succeeded in winning over a minister to their views, and in 1923 Rivera was commissioned to decorate the former monastic cloisters in the Ministry of Education. In 1929 he embarked upon a history of Mexico in the National Palace.

Compared with the rationalistic pathos of Rivera's cycles from the 1920s and 1930s, his *Dream of a Sunday Afternoon in Alameda Park* seems more a sceptically conciliatory work of old age. Rivera was over 60 when he painted it. He now took the liberty of mixing

From 1908 to 1921 Rivera lived almost permanently in Europe, mostly in Paris, in those days the metropolis of the fine arts. He painted in the style first of the Impressionists, then of the Cubists. Later, he stated: "From 1911 onwards, my work was entirely oriented towards one day painting large-scale murals." In 1921 he realized that he wanted to fulfil this aim in Mexico; he returned home, where he proceeded to harness his talents to his social commitment. Since Rivera and other like-minded artists wanted to work not for museums and palaces, but for the broad masses of the Mexican people, uneducated in literature and art, they sought out the walls of public buildings. They thus became known as the muralists – the "wall painters". They wanted to make their message visible to all who passed by. In the Middle Ages, the walls of churches were used to teach and edify the populace. The mostly anticlerical Mexican muralists of the 20th century chose schools, assembly chambers and office buildings.

They thereby fused the Natives peoples' traditional sense of the collective with new ideas from Communist Russia. Community was important both as a statement and as a form of work. The muralists founded a syndicate in which artists and craftsmen earned the same amount.

In addition to Diego Rivera, the group included the painters José Clemente Orozco and David Alfaro Siquieros. Together these artists represent the three most important Mexican muralists. Rivera explained: "Fresco painting, the collective art *par*

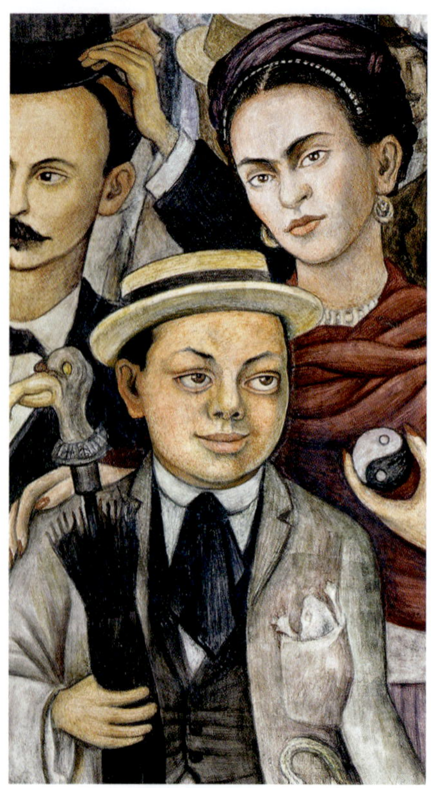

members of his family with those from history; his hopes for a happier future were no longer projected onto the Indigenous working class, but onto a gar-landed pink hot-air balloon.

Death wears a feather boa

Near the hot-air balloon, the symbol of a rosier future, stands the figure of Death, dressed up as a woman with a plumed hat and a feather boa. She is holding the hand of the young Rivera on one side, and that of José Guadalupe Posada (1852–1913) on the other. Posada was the first Mexican artist to free himself from a dependency upon European art. He executed graphic works in a folk style, illustrated song sheets and achieved special popularity with his endlessly inventive skeletons.

Rivera has incorporated one of these skeletons into his mural. The reference is undoubtedly more than simply a gesture of respect for his predecessor and source of inspiration; it is probably more, too, than simply a reference to the death and violence which had left their bloody mark on Mexico's past. The costumed skeleton symbolizes something else again: standing hand in hand between the other figures, it is a natural part of any stroll in a park on a Sunday afternoon. Those familiar with Mexico will know that this is the case not simply in Rivera's *Dream*.

Death is not excluded in Mexico in the way it is in the cultures of Western Europe and North America. It remains omnipresent, not merely as a threat or an enemy, but also as a friend and neighbour.

A visible demonstration of this can be found on All Souls' Day in every Mexican shop and apartment: they are hung full of skeletons made of card and skil-fully folded paper. Coffins are brought out in doll's houses, confectioner's shops sell marzipan coffins and sugar skulls, bakers bake loaves in the shape of bones, and the Mexicans take a trip to the cemeteries to eat and drink merrily with their dead.

The dead are thus remembered not in sorrow, but in joy. This attitude to death has its roots in Native tradition. For Mexico's native inhabitants, death was not the absolute end: it was simply another form of existence. Death was followed by rebirth, in a pro-cess watched over by a god, venerated in the shape of a feathered snake. Death and future, skeleton and balloon thus all belong together. Through rebirth, past and present are one. Rivera renders this unity visible in his Alameda *Dream* – a dream which con-tains more than simplya history of his country.

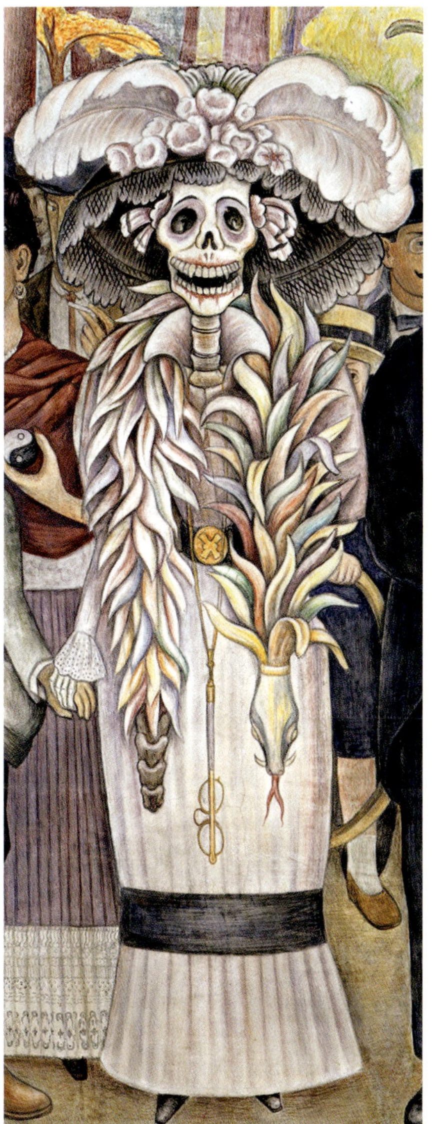

Appendix

Anonymous
**Fragment of a wall painting from the tomb of
Nebamun, Thebes, 18th Dynasty, before 1350 BC**
83 x 98 cm
London, The British Museum
Lit.: Eggebrecht, Arne (ed.): *Das alte Ägypten*,
Munich 1984. – James, T. G. H: *Egyptian Painting*,
London 1985. – Schulz, Regina/Seidel, Matthias
(eds.): *Ägypten, Die Welt der Pharaonen*, Cologne
1997. – Hagen, Rose-Marie/Hagen, Rainer: *Egypt –
People, Gods, Pharaohs*, Cologne 1999. – Hagen,
Rose-Marie/Hagen, Rainer: *Egypt Art*, Cologne 2007.

Anonymous
The Empress Theodora with her Retinue, *c.* 547
Mosaic, Ravenna, Basilica di San Vitale
Lit.: Bridge, Anthony: *Theodora, Portrait in a
Byzantine Landscape*, London 1978. – Diehl, Charles:
Théodora, Impératrice de Byzance, Paris 1904/1937. –
Diehl, Charles: *Byzance, Grandeur et Décadence*, Paris
1919. – Ebersolt, Jean: *Les arts somptuaires de Byzance*,
Paris 1923.

Gu Hongzhong (*c.* AD 910–980)
The Night Revels of Han Xizai, *c.* 960
Scroll painting (detail), 29 x 336 cm
Beijing, National Palace Museum
Lit.: Cahill, James: *Chinesische Malerei*, Geneva
1969/75. – Cahill, James: *The Painter's Practice. How
Artists Lived and Worked in Traditional China*, New
York 1994. – Van Gulik, Robert: *La vie sexuelle dans la
Chine ancienne*, Paris 1971. – Kuhn, Dieter (ed.): *Chi-
nas Goldenes Zeitalter, die Tang-Dynastie und das kul-
turelle Erbe der Seidenstraße*, Dortmund 1993. – Wang
Go Weng/Yang Boda: *Das Palastmuseum Peking – Die
Schätze der verbotenen Stadt*, Munich 1982. – Wu
Hung: *The Double Screen. Medium and Representation
in Chinese Painting*, London 1996.

Anonymous
The Bayeux Tapestry, after 1066
50 x 7034 cm
Bayeux, Centre Guillaume Le Conquérant
Lit.: Bertrand, Simone: *La tapisserie de Bayeux et la
manière de vivre au onzième siècle*, n. p. [Saint-Léger-
Vauban] 1966. – Grape, Wolfgang: *Der Teppich von
Bayeux, Triumphdenkmal der Normannen*, Munich
1995. – Parisse, Michel: *La tapisserie de Bayeux, Un
documentaire de XIe siècle*, n. p. [Paris] 1983.

Al-Wasiti (13th century)
**Two miniatures from the Maqamat of al-Hariri,
1237**
37 x 28 cm (dimensions of sheet)
Paris, Bibliothèque nationale de France
Lit.: Grabar, Oleg: *The Illustrations of the Maqamat*,
Chicago and London 1984. – Bibliothèque Nationale
de France: *L'art du livre arabe, du manuscript au livre
d'artist*, exh. cat. 2001. – Ettinghausen, R.: *Arabische
Malerei*, Geneva 1962. – Mazahéry, Aly: *So lebten die
Muselmanen im Mittelalter*, Stuttgart 1957. – Hattstein,
Markus/Delius, Peter (eds.): *Islam. Kunst und Archi-
tektur*, Cologne 2000.

Anonymous
**Miniature from Christine de Pizan's Book of the
City of Ladies,** *c.* 1405
Illumination on parchment, 12 x 18 cm
(Miniature from the *Manuscrit français* 607)
Paris, Bibliothèque nationale de France
Lit.: Walther, Ingo F./Wolf, Norbert: *Codices Illustres,
The world's Most Famous Manuscripts 400 to 1600*,
Cologne 2001. – Pernoud, Régine: *Christine de
Pisan*, Paris 1982. – Meiss, Millard: *French Painting
in the Time of Jean de Berry*, New York 1967. –
Zimmermann, Margarete: *Übersetzung und Einleitung
zu "Das Buch der Stadt der Frauen"*, Berlin 1986.
– Kottenhoff, Margarete: *"Du lebst in einer schlimmen
Zeit", Christine de Pizans Frauenstadt zwischen
Sozialkritik und Utopie*, Cologne 1994. – Moreau,
Thérèse/Hicks, Éric: *Le livre de la Cité des Dames*,
Paris 1986/2000. – Brown-Grant, Rosalind (trans.):
Christine de Pizan: The Book of the City of Ladies,
London 1999.

Upper Rhenish Master
The Little Garden of Paradise, *c.* 1410
26.3 x 33.4 cm
Frankfurt, Städel Museum
Lit.: Hennebo, Dieter/Hofmann, Alfred: *Geschichte
der deutschen Gartenkunst, Gärten des Mittelalters*,
vol. 1, Hamburg 1962. – Vetter, Ewald M.: "Das Frank-

furter Paradiesgärtlein", in: *Heidelberger Jahrbücher*, 9,
n. p. 1965. – Wolfhardt, Elisabeth: "Beiträge zur Pflan-
zensymbolik, Über die Pflanzen des Frankfurter
Paradiesgärtleins", in: *Zeitschrift für Kunstwissen-
schaft*, vol. VIII, Berlin 1954.

Robert Campin (*c.* 1375–1444)
The Mérode Triptych (*Annunciation Triptych/
Mérode Altarpiece, in which Joseph is seen making
mousetraps*), *c.* **1422/1430**
64 x 120 cm
New York, The Metropolitan Museum of Art,
The Cloisters Collection
Lit.: Châtelet, Albert: *Le maître de Flémalle,
la fascination du quotidien*, Antwerp 1996. – Lecat,
Jean-Philippe: *Quand flamboyait la Toison d'or*,
Paris 1982. – Kemperdick, Stephan: *Der Meister
von Flémalle, Die Werkstatt Robert Campins und
Rogier van der Weyden*, Turnhout 1997. – Shapiro,
Meyer: "Muscipula Diaboli, The Symbolism of the
Mérode Altarpiece", in: *The Art Bulletin*, no. 27, 1945,
pp. 182 ff. – Thürlemann, Felix: *Robert Campin, Das
Mérode-Triptychon*, Frankfurt a. M. 1997.

Jan van Eyck (*c.* 1390–1441)
The Arnolfini Marriage, 1434
82 x 60 cm
London, The National Gallery
Lit.: Calmette, Joseph: *Les Grands Ducs de Bourgogne*,
Paris 1949. – Davies, Martin: *The National Gallery,
London, Les Primitifs Flamands*, Antwerp 1954. –
Dhanens, Elisabeth: *Van Eyck*, Antwerp 1980. – Leje-
une, Jean: *Documents mémoires commissions: Jaen et
Margarethe van Eyck et le Roman des Arnolfini*, Liège
1972. – Mirot, L./Lazzareschi, E.: "Un mercante di
Lucca in Fiandra", in: *Bolletino Storico Lucchese* XII,
1940. – Panofsky, Erwin: *Early Netherlandish Painting*,
Cambridge, Mass. 1953. – Roover, Raymond de: *The
Rise and Decline of the Medici Bank*, Cambridge, Mass.
1963. – Schabacker, Peter H.: "De matrimonio ad
morganaticam contracta. Jan van Eyck's Arnolfini
portrait reconsidered", in: *The Art Quarterly*, no. 35,
1972. – Swaan, Wim: *Kunst und Kultur der Spätgotik*,
Freiburg 1978.

Paolo Uccello (1397–1475)
The Battle of San Romano, *c.* **1435**
182 x 319 cm
London, The National Gallery
Lit.: Burckhardt, Jacob: *Die Kultur der Renaissance
in Italien*, Zurich 1956. – Defourneaux, Marcelin:
La vie quotidienne au temps de Jeanne d'Arc, Paris
1957. – Griffiths, Gordon: "The Political Significance
of Uccello's Battle of San Romano", in: *Journal of
the Warburg and Courtauld Institutes*, vol. 41, 1978. –
Pope-Hennessy, John: *Paolo Uccello, Paintings and
Drawings*, London 1969. – Trease, Geoffrey: *The
Soldiers of Fortune*, New York 1971.

Fra Angelico (real name Guido di Pietro)
(*c.* 1400–1455)
St Nicholas of Bari, 1437
34 x 60 cm
Rome, Pinacoteca vaticana
Lit.: Groot, Adrian de: *Saint Nicholas, a Psychoana-
lytic Study of his History and Myth*, The Hague/Paris
1965. – Jones, Charles W.: *St Nicholas of Myra, Bari
and Manhattan. Biography of a legend*, Chicago 1978. –
Le Goff, Jacques: *Marchands et Banquiers du Moyen
Age*, Paris 1972. – Pope-Hennessy, John: *Angelico*,
London 1952.

Jean Fouquet (1420–1481)
The Melun Diptych, *c.* **1456**
Left panel: Étienne Chevalier and St Stephen
93 x 85 cm, Berlin, Staatliche Museen zu Berlin,
Gemäldegalerie
Right panel: Virgin and Child
91.8 x 83.3 cm, Antwerp, Koninklijk Museum voor
Schone Kunsten
Accompanying illustration: Enamel medallion with
self-portrait, signed "Johes Fouquet"
Paris, Musée du Louvre
Lit.: Defourneaux, Marcelin: *La vie quotidienne au
temps de Jeanne d'Arc*, Paris 1957. – Erlanger, Philippe:
Charles VII et son mystère, Paris 1945. – Huizinga,
Johan: *The Autumn of the Middle Ages*, London (?)
1919. – Schaefer, Claude: *Jean Fouquet. An der Schwelle
zur Renaissance*, Dresden 1994. – Vale, Malcolm G. A.:
Charles VII, Berkeley/Los Angeles 1974.

Antonio del Pollaiuolo (1432–1498)
Piero del Pollaiuolo (1441–1496)
Tobias and the Angel, c. 1469
188 x 119 cm
Turin, Galleria Sabauda
Lit.: Wright, Alison: *The Pollaiuolo Brothers,* New Haven/London 2005. – Vasari, Giorgio: *Leben der ausgezeichneten Maler und Baumeister,* German edn. Schorn, Ludwig/Förster, Ernst, Stuttgart/Tübingen. – Roover, Raymond de: *The Rise and Decline of the Medici Bank,* Cambridge, Mass. 1963. – Origo, Iris: *Im Namen Gottes und des Geschäfts, Lebensbild eines toskanischen Kaufmanns der Frührenaissance,* Munich 1957/85. – Larivaille, Paul: *La vie quotidienne en Italie au temps de Machiavel,* Paris 1979. – Dubreton, Lucas: *La vie quotidienne à Florence au temps des Medicis,* Paris 1958.

Andrea Mantegna (1431–1506)
Ludovico Gonzaga and His Family, c. 1470
600 x 807 cm
Mantua, Palazzo Ducale
Lit.: *Mantova e i Gonzaga nella civilità del Rinascimento,* conference proceedings, Mantua 1974. – Camesasca, Ettore: *Mantegna,* Florence 1981. – Coletti, Luigi: *La camera degli sposi del Mantegna a Mantova.* Milan 1969. – Chambers, David and Martineau, Jane: *Splendours of the Gonzaga,* exh. cat., Victoria & Albert Museum. London 1981. – Mazzoldi, Leonardo: *Mantova, La Storia.* Vol. II, Mantua 1961.

Master of the Hours of Mary of Burgundy
Window miniature, 1470/1480
Codex Vidobonensis 1857, fol. 14
22 x 16 cm
Vienna, Österreichische Nationalbibliothek
Lit.: Walther, Ingo F./Wolf, Norbert: *Codices Illustres, The World's Most Famous Manuscripts 400 to 1600,* Cologne 2001. – Unterkircher, Franz: *Burgundisches Brevier: Die schönsten Miniaturen aus dem Stundenbuch der Maria von Burgund (Codex Vindobonensis 1857),* Graz 1974. – Dumont, Georges-Henri: *Marie de Bourgogne,* Paris 1982. – Passtoureau, Michel: *Bleu, Histoire d'une Couleur,* Paris 2000.

Hugo van der Goes (c. 1440–1482)
The Portinari Altar, c. 1475
600 x 250 cm
Florence, Galleria degli Uffizi
Lit.: Hatfield Strens, Bianca: "L'arrivo del Trittico Portinari a Firenze" in: *Commentari, Rivista di Storia e di Critica d'Arte,* Rome 1968 IV. – Koch, Robert: "Flower Symbolism in the Portinari Altar", in: *The Art Bulletin,* New York 1964. – Roover, Raymond de: *The Rise and Decline of the Medici Bank,* Cambridge, Mass. 1963. – Panofsky, Erwin: *Early Netherlandish Painting,* Cambridge, Mass. 1953. – Swaan, Wim: *Kunst und Kultur der Spätgotik,* Freiburg 1978.

Sandro Botticelli (real name Alessandro di Mariano Filipepi) (1444–1510)
The Birth of Venus, c. 1486
184 x 285.5 cm
Florence, Galleria degli Uffizi
Comparative illustration:
Sandro Botticelli
Virgin and Child with Four Angels and Six Saints (detail), *c.* 1487
St Barnabas Altar, retable, main panel
268 x 280 cm, Florence, Galleria degli Uffizi
Lit.: Burke, Peter: *Culture and Society in Renaissance Italy.* London 1974. – Clark, Kenneth: *The Nude, a Study in Ideal Form.* A. W. Mellon Lectures, n. p. 1953. – Levi d'Ancona, Mirella: *Botticelli's Primavera. A Botanical Interpretation including Astrology, Alchemy and the Medici.* Florence 1983. – Lightbrown, Ronald: *Sandro Botticelli,* 2 vols. London 1978. – Uffizi, Studi e Ricerche 4: *La Nascita di Venere e l'Annunziazione del Botticelli ristaurate.* Florence 1987. – Warburg, Aby: *Sandro Botticellis "Geburt der Venus" und "Frühling". Eine Untersuchung über die Vorstellung von der Antike in der Frührenaissance.* Leipzig 1893.

Hieronymus Bosch (real name Hieronymous van Aken) (1450–1516)
The Haywain, between 1485 and 1490
135 x 100 cm
Madrid, Museo Nacional del Prado
Lit.: Dinzelbacher, Peter: "Die Realität des Teufels im Mittelalter", in: Segl, Peter (ed.): *Der Hexenhammer,*

Entstehung und Umfeld des Malleus maleficarum von 1487, Cologne/Vienna 1988. – Gibson, Walter S.: *Hieronymus Bosch*, Frankfurt/Berlin/Vienna 1974. – Hammer-Tugendhat, Daniela: *Hieronymus Bosch, eine historische Interpretation seiner Gestaltungsprinzipien*, Munich 1981. – Schuder, Rosemarie: *Hieronymus Bosch*, Wiesbaden (undated). – Tolnay, Charles de: *Hieronymus Bosch*, Baden-Baden 1973.

Ercole de' Roberti (c. 1450–1496)
Lorenzo Costa (1460–1535)
The Ship of the Argonauts, c. 1480/1490
46 x 53 cm
Padua, Musei Civici
Lit.: Chledowsky, Casimir von: *Der Hof von Ferrara*, Munich 1921. – Ferino-Pagden, Sylvia: *Isabella d'Este. La Prima Donna del Mondo*, Vienna 1994. – Gundersheimer, Werner L.: *Ferrara, The Style of a Renaissance Despotism.* Princeton 1973. – *Da Bellini al Tintoretto*, exh. cat., Musei Civici, Padua 1992. – *La Corte di Ferrara e il suo mecenatismo (The court of Ferrara and its Patronage)*, conference proceedings, Copenhagen 1990. – Lauts, Jan: *Isabella d'Este*, Hamburg 1952. – Schubring, Paul: *Truhen und Truhenbilder der italienischen Führenaissance*, Leipzig 1923.

Hans Baldung Grien (1484 or 1485–1545)
The Knight, the Maiden and Death, before 1503
35 x 30 cm
Paris, Musée du Louvre
Lit.: von der Osten, Gert: *Hans Baldung Grien, Gemälde und Dokumente*, Berlin 1983. – Sroka, Jens Joachim: *Das Pferd als Ausdrucks- und Bedeutungsträger bei Hans Baldung Grien*, Zurich 2003. – Brinkmann, Bodo: *Hexenkunst und Sündenfall, Die seltsamen Phantasien des Hans Baldung Grien*, exh. cat., Frankfurt 2007.

Albrecht Dürer (1471–1528)
Christ among the Doctors, 1506
63.4 x 80.3 cm
Madrid, Museo Thyssen-Bornemisza
Lit.: Anzelewsky, Fedja: *Dürer, Werk und Wirkung*, Erlangen 1988. – Schröder, Klaus Albrecht/Sternath, Maria Luise (eds.): *Albrecht Dürer*, Ostfildern 2003. –

Müller, Arnd: *Geschichte der Juden In Nürnberg*, Nuremberg 1968.

Michelangelo Buonarotti (1475–1564)
The Creation of Adam, 1508/1512
Section of the ceiling painting
Rome, Sistine Chapel
Lit.: Panofsky, Ernst: *Die Sixtinische Decke*, Leipzig 1921. – Vecchi, Pierluigi de: *Die Sixtinische Kapelle, Das Meisterwerk Michelangelos erstrahlt in neuem Glanz*, Munich 1996. – King, Ross: *Michelangelo und die Fresken des Papstes*, Munich 2003. – Zöllner, Frank et al. *Michelangelo Complete Works*, Cologne 2007. – Sickel, Lothar: *"Strecke deine Hand aus!" Versuch einer typologischen Deutung von Michelangelos Erschaffung Adams*, Thesis, Hamburg 1994.

Raphael (Raffaello Santi) (1483–1520)
The Sistine Madonna, 1512/1513
269.5 x 201 cm
Dresden, Gemäldegalerie Alte Meister
Lit.: Chapeaurouge, Donat de: *Raffael, Sixtinische Madonna*, Frankfurt a. M. 1993. – Brink, Claudia/Henning, Andreas (eds.): *Die Sixtinische Madonna, Geschichte und Mythos eines Meisterwerks*, Munich, Berlin 2005. – Meyer zurCapellen, Jürg: *Raphael, The Paintings*, vol. 2, *The Roman Religious Paintings*, Landshut 2005.

Matthias Grünewald (1460/1480–1528/1532)
The Isenheim Altar, 1512–1516
269 x 307 cm (Crucifixion panel)
Colmar, Musée d'Unterlinden
Lit.: Fraenger, Wilhelm: *Matthias Grünewald*, Munich 1983. – Lücking, Wolf: *Matthis, Nachforschungen über Grünewald*, Berlin 1983. – Reichenauer, Berta: *Grünewald*, Vienna 1992. – Segl, Peter (ed.): *Der Hexenhammer*, Cologne/Vienna 1988. – Seidel, Max: *Mathis Gothard Nithart Grünewald, Der Isenheimer Altar*, Stuttgart 1973.

Niklaus Manuel Deutsch (c. 1484–1530)
The Judgement of Paris, 1516/1528
223 x 160 cm
Basle, Kunstmuseum Basel

Lit.: Beerli, Conrad André: *Le peintre poète Nicolas Manuel Deutsch et l'evolution sociale de son temps*, Geneva 1953. – El-Hiemoud-Sperlich, Inge: *Das Urteil des Paris, Studien zur Bildtradition im 16.Jahrhundert*, Thesis, Munich 1977. – *Niklaus Manuel Deutsch, Maler, Dichter, Staatsmann*, exh. cat., Kunstmuseum Bern, Bern 1979.

Unknown Netherlandish Master
Lot and his Daughters, *c.* **1530**
58 x 34 cm
Paris, Musée du Louvre
Lit.: Kind, Joshua Benjamin: *The Drunken Lot and his Daughters. An iconographical study of the uses of this theme in the visual arts from 1500–1650 and its bases in exegetical and literary history*, Thesis, Columbia University 1967. – Neev, David/Emery, K. O.: *The destruction of Sodom, Gomorrah and Jericho. Geological, Climatological and Archaeological Background*, New York/Oxford 1995. – Rank, Otto: *Das Inzest-Motiv in Dichtung und Sage*, Leipzig/Vienna 1926. – Rijnaarts, Josephine: *Lots Töchter, Über den Vater-Tochter Inzest*, Düsseldorf 1988.

Albrecht Altdorfer (*c.* 1480–1538)
The Battle of Issus, 1529
158.4 x 120.3 cm
Munich, Alte Pinakothek
Lit.: Buchner, Ernst: *Die Alexanderschlacht*, Stuttgart 1956. – Krichbaum, Jörg: *Albrecht Altdorfer, Meister der Alexanderschlacht*, Cologne 1978. – Winzinger, Franz: *Albrecht Altdorfer, die Gemälde*, Munich/Zurich 1975.

Hans Holbein the Younger (1497/1498–1543)
The Ambassadors, 1533
207 x 209 cm
London, The National Gallery, reproduced by courtesy of the Trustees
Lit.: Hervey, Mary S.: *Holbein's Ambassadors. The Picture and the Men. A Historical Study*. London 1900. – Jacobs, Eberhard/de Vitray, Eva: *Heinrich VIII. von England in Augenzeugenberichten*. Düsseldorf 1969. – Pinder, Wilhelm: *Holbein der Jüngere und das Ende der altdeutschen Kunst*. Cologne 1951. – Salvini, Robert/Grohn, Hans Werner: *Das gemalte*

Gesamtwerk von Hans Holbein d. J. Milan, Lucerne 1971. – Samuel, Edgar R.: "Death in the glass – A new view of Holbein's Ambassadors". In: *The Burlington Magazine*, vol. CV, pp. 718–729, London 1963.

Titian (real name Tiziano Vecellio) (1488/1490–1576)
Pope Paul III and his Grandsons, 1545
200 x 173 cm
Naples, Museo Nazionale di Capodimonte
Lit.: *Der Glanz der Farnese*, exh. cat., Haus der Kunst, Munich 1995. – Reinhardt, Volker (ed.): *Die großen Familien Italiens*, Stuttgart 1992. – Wethey, Harold E.: *The Paintings of Titian*, complete edition, London 1971. – Zapperi, Roberto: *Tiziano, Paolo III. e i suoi nipoti*, Turin 1990. – Zapperi, Roberto: La leggenda del papa Paolo, Turin 1997.

Lucas Cranach the Elder (1472–1553)
The Fountain of Youth, 1546
121 x 184 cm
Berlin, Staatliche Museen zu Berlin, Gemäldegalerie
Lit.: Cipolla, Carlo M./Borchardt, Knut: *Die Bevölkerungsgeschichte Europas, Mittelalter bis Neuzeit*, Munich 1971. – Friedländer, Max/Rosenberg, Jakob: *Die Gemälde von Lucas Cranach*, Basle/Boston/ Stuttgart, 1979. – Hartlaub, G. F.: *Lucas Cranach d. J., Der Jungbrunnen*, Stuttgart 1958. – Koepplin, Dieter/Falk, Tilmann: *Lucas Cranach, Gemälde, Zeichnungen, Druckgraphik*, 2 vols., exh. cat., Basle/Stuttgart 1974. – Martin, Alfred: *Deutsches Badewesen in vergangenen Tagen, Nebst einem Beitrag zur Geschichte der deutschen Wasserheilkunde*, Jena 1906. – Schade, Werner: *Die Malerfamilie Cranach*, Dresden 1974.

Maerten van Heemskerck (1498–1574)
Momus Criticizes the Works of the Gods, *c.* **1561**
120 x 174 cm
Berlin, Staatliche Museen zu Berlin, Gemäldegalerie
Lit.: Cast, David: "Maerten van Heemskerck's Momus Criticizing the Works of the Gods, A Problem of Erasmian Iconography", in: *Simiolus* 1974. – Grosshans, Rainald: *Maerten van Heemskerck, Die Gemälde*, Berlin 1980. – Mander, Carel van: *Das Leben der niederländischen und deutschen Maler von 1400 bis ca. 1615*, translated by Floerke, Hans, Worms 1991.

Paolo Veronese (real name Paolo Caliari) (1528–1588)
The Marriage at Cana, 1562/1563
669 x 990 cm
Paris, Musée du Louvre
Lit.: Lebe, Reinhard: *Als Markus nach Venedig kam*. Frankfurt 1980. – Lenz, Christian: *Veroneses Bildarchitektur*. Thesis, University of Munich 1969. – Molmenti, Pompeo: *La Storia di Venezia nella Vita Privata*. Bergamo 1905–1908, Reprint Triest 1973, vol. 2. – Pignati, Terisio: *Veronese, catalogue raisonné*. Venice 1976. – Piovene, Guido: *L'Opera completa di Veronese*. Milan 1968.

Pieter Bruegel the Elder (c. 1525/1530–1569)
Hunters in the Snow, 1565
117 x 162 cm
Vienna, Kunsthistorisches Museum
Lit.: Mander, Carel van: *Das Leben der niederländischen und deutschen Maler (von 1400 bis ca. 1617)*, translated by Floerke, Hans, Worms 1991. – Jedlicka, Gotthard: *Pieter Bruegel, Der Maler in seiner Zeit*, Erlenbach/Leipzig 1938. – Stechow, Wolfgang: *Pieter Bruegel the Elder*, New York 1969. – Simson, Otto/Wiener, Matthias (eds.): *Pieter Bruegel und seine Welt. Ein Colloquium*, Berlin 1979. – Hagen, Rose-Marie/Hagen, Rainer: *Pieter Bruegel the Eder, Peasants, Fools and Demons. The Complete Paintings*, Cologne 1999. – Herold, Inge: *Pieter Bruegel d. Ä., Die Jahreszeiten*, Munich/London/New York 2002.

Tintoretto (real name Jacopo Robusti) (1518–1594)
The Origin of the Milky Way, c. 1580
148 x 165 cm
London, The National Gallery, reproduced by courtesy of the Trustees
Comparative illustration:
Jakob Hoefnagel
Origin of the Milky Way, sketch after Tintoretto, c. 1620
Berlin, Staatliche Museen zu Berlin, Kupferstich-kabinett
Lit.: Evans, Robert John Weston: *Rudolf II and his World. A Study in Intellectual History*. Oxford 1973/84. – Garas, Clara: "Le tableau du Tintoret du Musée de Budapest et le cycle peint pour l'Empereur Rodolphe II"., in: *Bulletin du Musée hongrois des Beaux-Arts* no. 30, 1967. – Gould, Cecil: "An X-ray of Tintoretto's Milky Way", in: *Arte Veneta XXXII* 1975. – *Prag um 1600, Kunst und Kultur am Hofe Rudolfs II.*, exh. cat., 2 vols., Essen/Vienna 1988.

El Greco (real name Domenikos Theotokopulos) (1541–1614)
The Burial of the Count of Orgaz, 1586
480 x 360 cm
Toledo, Santo Tomé
Lit.: Gudiol, José: *El Greco*, Geneva 1973. – Mâle, Émile: *L'art religieux de la fin du XVIe siècle, du XVIIe siècle et du XVIIIe siècle, étude sur l'iconographie après le Concile de Trente (Italie, France, Espagne, Flandres)*, Paris 1951. – Schroth, Sarah: "Burial of the Count of Orgaz", in: *Studies in the History of Art*, vol. II, National Gallery of Art, Washington, D. C. 1982.

George Gower (1540–1596)
Armada Portrait of Elizabeth I, c. 1590
105 x 133 cm
Bedfordshire, Woburn Abbey
Lit.: Jenkins, Elisabeth: *Gloriana, Queen of England*, London 1959. – Levey, Michael: *Painting at Court*, London 1971. – Lewis, Michael: *The Spanish Armada*, London 1960. – Strong, Roy: *The Cult of Elizabeth*, London 1977. – Yates, Frances A.: *Astraea, The Imperial Theme in the 16th Century*, London 1975.

Caravaggio (real name Michelangelo Merisi) (1571–1610)
Judith and Holofernes, c. 1599
145 x 195 cm
Rome, Galleria Nazionale d'Arte Antica
Lit.: Delumeau, Jean: *Vie économique et sociale de Rome dans la seconde moitié du XVI s*. Paris 1957. – Hibbard, Howard: *Caravaggio*. New York 1983. – Hinks, Roger: *Michelangelo Merisi da Caravaggio, His Life, His Legends, His Works*. London 1953. – Röttgen, Herwarth: *Il Caravaggio, ricerche e interpretazioni*, Rome 1974. – Schütze, Sebastian: *Caravaggio. The Complete Works*, Cologne 2009.

School of Fontainebleau
Gabrielle d'Estrées and One of Her Sisters, *c.* **1600**
96 x 125 cm
Paris, Musée du Louvre
Lit.: Adhémar, Hélène: *Portraits français du 15e et 16e siècle*, Musée du Louvre, Paris (undated). – Béguin, Sylvie: *L'École de Fontainebleau, le maniérisme à la cour de France*, Paris 1969. – *L'École de Fontainebleau*, exh. cat., Paris 1972. – Erlanger, Philippe: *La vie quotidienne sous Henri IV*, Paris 1958. – Hollander, Anne: *Seeing Through Clothes*, New York 1979. – Tallemant des Réaux: *Historiettes,* Paris 1961. – Vaissière, Pierre de: *Henri IV*, Paris 1928.

Artemisia Gentileschi (1593–1652)
Judith and her Maid, 1625/1627
182 x 142 cm.
Detroit Institute of Arts
Lit.: Bissell, Ward R.: *Artemisia Gentileschi and the Authority of Art, Critical Reading and Catalogue Raisonné*, Pennsylvania 1999. – Garrard, Mary D.: *Artemisia Gentileschi, The Image of the Feminine Hero in Italian Baroque Art,* Princeton 1989. – Christiansen, Keith/Mann, Judith (eds.): *Orazio e Artemisia Gentileschi*, exh. cat., Metropolitan Museum, New York 2002.

Georges de La Tour (1593–1652)
The Fortune Teller, after 1630
102 x 123 cm
New York, The Metropolitan Museum of Art, Rogers Fund, 1960
Lit.: Clébert, Jean-Paul: *Das Volk der Zigeuner*, Vienna 1964. – Erlanger, Pierre: *La vie quotidienne au siècle d'Henri IV*. Paris 1972. – *La Tour,* exh. cat., Orangerie, Paris 1972. – Nicolson, Benedict/Wright, Christopher: *Georges de La Tour*. London 1974. – Rosenberg, Pierre/Macé de Lépinay, François: *Georges de La Tour, vie et œuvre.* Fribourg 1973. – Wright, Christopher: *The Art of the Forger*, London 1984.

Claude Lorrain (1604–1682)
Seaport with the Embarkation of the Queen of Sheba, 1648
148 x 193 cm.
London, The National Gallery

Lit.: Haskell, Francis: *Maler und Auftraggeber, Kunst und Gesellschaft im italienischen Barock*, Cologne 1996. – Rötlisberger, Marcel (ed.): *Im Licht von Claude Lorrain, Landschaftsmalerei aus drei Jahrhunderten*, Munich 1983. – Schade, Werner (ed.): *Claude Lorrain, Gemälde und Zeichnungen*, Munich 1996. – Wine, Humphrey: *Claude, The Poetic Landscape*, London 1994.

Peter Paul Rubens (1577–1640)
The Love Garden, *c.* **1632/1634**
198 x 283 cm
Madrid, Museo Nacional del Prado
Lit.: Glang-Süberkrüb, Annegret: *Peter Paul Rubens, der Liebesgarten*. Thesis, Kiel 1975. – Goodman, E. L.: *Rubens "Conversatie à la mode" and the Tradition of the "Love Garden"*. Thesis, Ohio 1978. – Lessing, Erich/Schütz, Karl: *Die Niederlande. Die Geschichte in den Bildern ihrer Maler erzählt.* Munich 1985. – Warnke, Martin: *Peter Paul Rubens, Leben und Werk.* Cologne 1977. – Wedgewood, C. V.: *Rubens und seine Zeit.* Amsterdam 1973.

Nicolas Poussin (1594–1665)
The Rape of the Sabine Women, 1637/1639
159 x 206 cm
Paris, Musée du Louvre
Lit.: Arikha, Avigdor: Nicolas Poussin, *The Rape of the Sabines,* Houston 1988. – Haskell, Francis: *Patrons and Painters,* London/New York 1971. – Rosenberg, Pierre (ed.): *Nicolas Poussin*, exh. cat., Grand Palais, Paris, 1994/95. – Thuillier, Jacques: *Nicolas Poussin,* Paris, 1988.

Rembrandt (real name Rembrandt Harmensz. van Rijn) (1606–1669)
The Night Watch, 1642
359 x 438 cm
Amsterdam, Rijksmuseum
Lit.: Bauch, Kurt: *Rembrandt van Rijn, Die Nachtwache*, Stuttgart 1957. – Gerson, Horst: *Rembrandt, Gemälde, Gesamtwerk*, Wiesbaden, 1968. – Haak, Bob: *Rembrandt, Sein Leben, sein Werk, seine Zeit*, Cologne 1969. – Heiland, Susanne/Lüdecke, Heinz: *Rembrandt und die Nachwelt,* Leipzig 1960. – Hijmans, Willem/Kuiper, Luitsen/Vels Heijn, Annemarie:

Rembrandt's Nightwatch, The History of a Painting, Alphen aan den Rijn 1978. – Walser, Paul L.: *Amsterdam*, Zurich 1969. – Wilson, Charles: *Die Früchte der Freiheit, Holland und die europäische Kultur des 17. Jahrhunderts*, Munich 1968.

Jacob Jordaens (1593–1678)
The King Drinks, 1640/1645
242 x 300 cm
Vienna, Kunsthistorisches Museum
Lit.: d'Hulst, Roger Adolf: *Jacob Jordaens*. Stuttgart 1982. – Meisen, Karl: *Die Heiligen 3 Könige und ihr Festtag im volkstümlichen Glauben und Brauch*. Cologne 1949. – Pirenne, Henri: *Geschichte Belgiens*, vol. 4. Gotha 1913. – van Puyvelde, Leo: *Jordaens*. Paris/Brussels 1953. – Rooses, Max: *Jordaens, Leben und Werk*. Leipzig 1898.

Jan Steen (1626–1679)
The Burgher of Delft and his Daughter, 1655
82.5 x 68.6 cm
Amsterdam, Rijksmuseum
Lit.: Jansen, Guido M. C. (ed.): *Jan Steen, Maler und Erzähler*, exh. cat. Washington and Amsterdam 1996/97, German edn. 1996 Stuttgart/Zurich. – Muller, Sheila D.: "Jan Steen's Burgher of Delft and his Daughter, A Painting and Politics in Seventeenth-Century Holland". In: *Art History*, vol. 12, no. 3, September 1989. – Schama, Simon: *The Embarrassment of Riches, An Interpretation of Dutch Culture in the Golden Age*, New York 1987. – Spicer, Joneath: "The Renaissance Elbow" in: Bremmer, Jan/Roodenburg, Hermann (eds.): *A Cultural History of Gesture*, Ithaca/New York 1991

Diego de Silva y Velázquez (1599–1660)
Velázquez and the Royal Family (Las Meninas), 1656
318 x 276 cm
Madrid, Museo Nacional del Prado
Lit.: Defourneaux, Marcelin: *La vie quotidienne en Espagne au siècle d'or*, Paris 1964. – Gudiol, José: *Velazquez. Sa vie, son oeuvre, son évolution*, Paris/Barcelona 1975. – Hume, Martin: *The Court of Philip IV*, London 1911. – Justi, Carl: *Velazquez und sein Jahrhundert*, Munich, undated (reprint of the 2nd edn. of 1903). –

Lassaigne, Jacques: *Velazquez – Les Ménines*, Fribourg 1973. – Lopez-Rey, José: *Velazquez, catalogue raisonné*, Cologne 1996.

Johannes Vermeer (1632–1675)
The Art of Painting, 1665/1666
120 x 100 cm
Vienna, Kunsthistorisches Museum
Lit.: Asemissen, Hermann Ulrich: *Jan Vermeer, Die Malkunst*, Frankfurt a. M 1988. – Leonhard, Karin: *Das gemalte Zimmer, Zur Interieurmalerei Jan Vermeers*, Munich 2003. – Wheelock, Arthur K. Junior: *Vermeer*, Cologne 1992.

Charles Le Brun (1619–1690)
The Chancellor Séguier, after 1660
295 x 357 cm
Paris, Musée du Louvre
Comparative illustration:
François Chaveau or Charles Le Brun
From the cycle: *Chancellor Séguier at the Entry of Louis XIV into Paris*, after 1660
Stockholm, Statens Konstmuseer
Lit.: *Charles Le Brun*, exh. cat., Versailles 1963. – Erlanger, Philippe: *Louis XIV*, Paris 1965. – Gaxotte, Pierre: *Louis XIV*, Paris 1974. – Mauricheau-Beaupré, M.: "Le Portrait du Chancelier Séguier", in: *Bulletin de la Société de l'histoire de l'art Français 1941–1944*, Paris 1947.

Antoine Watteau (1684–1721)
Pilgrimage to Cythera, c. 1719
129 x 194 cm
Berlin, Schloss Charlottenburg, Stiftung Preußische Schlösser und Gärten, Berlin-Brandenburg
Lit.: Meyer, Jean: *La vie quotidienne en France au temps de la Régence*, Paris 1979. – Moureau, François/Morgan Grasselli, Margaret (eds.): *Antoine Watteau, le peintre, son temps et sa légende*, Paris/Geneva 1987 (conference proceedings, Watteau 1984). – Posner, Donald: *Antoine Watteau*, London 1984. – Rosenberg, Pierre/Morgan Grasselli, Margaret: *Watteau*, exh. cat., Washington/Paris/Berlin 1984/85. – Tomlinson, Robert: *La fête galante, Watteau et Marivaux*, Geneva/Paris 1981.

Giambattista Tiepolo (1696–1770)
The Finding of Moses, *c.* **1738**
202 x 342 cm
Edinburgh, Scottish National Gallery
Lit.: Badinter, Elisabeth: *Die Mutterliebe, Geschichte eines Gefühls vom 17. Jh. bis heute*, Munich 1981. – *Giambattista Tiepolo*, exh. cat., Ca' Rezzonico, Venice 1996/Metropolitan Museum, New York 1997. – Gemin, Massimo/Pedrocco, Filippo: *Giambattista Tiepolo, Leben und Werk*, Munich 1995. – Levey, Michael: *Giambattista Tiepolo, His Life and Art*, New Haven/London 1986. – Molmenti, Pompeo: *La Storia di Venezia nella vita privata dalle origini alla caduta della Repubblica*. 3 vols., Bergamo 1929/Triest 1973.

François Boucher (1703–1770)
The Breakfast, 1739
81.5 x 65.5 cm
Paris, Musée du Louvre
Lit.: Ananoff, Alexandrej: *François Boucher* (2 vols.), Lausanne 1976. – Ariès, Philippe: *L'Enfant et la vie familiale sous l'Ancien Régime*. Paris 1975. – Badinter, Elisabeth: *L'Amour en plus, histoire de l'aman maternel du 17e au 20e s*. Paris 1980. – Chaussinand-Nogaret, Guy: *La vie quotidienne des Français sous Louis XV*, Paris 1979. – Schivelbusch, Wolfgang: *Das Paradies, der Geschmack und die Vernunft*, Munich 1980. – Shorter, Edward: *Die Geburt der modernen Familie*, Hamburg 1977.

Thomas Gainsborough (1727–1788)
Mr and Mrs Andrews, 1749
70 x 119 cm
London, The National Gallery, reproduced by courtesy of the Trustees
Lit.: Hayes, John: *The Landscape Paintings of Thomas Gainsborough: Critical Text and Catalogue*, London 1981. – Corri, Adrienne: *The Search for Thomas Gainsborough*. London 1984. – *Thomas Gainsborough*, exh. cat., Tate Gallery, London 1980. – Mingay, G. E.: *English Landed Society in the 18th Century*, London 1963. – Makowski, Henri/Buderath, Bernhard: *Die Natur dem Menschen untertan. Ökologie im Spiegel der Landschaftsmalerei*. Munich 1983 and 1986.

William Hogarth (1697–1764)
An Election Entertainment, 1754/1755
102 x 127 cm
London, Sir John Soane's Museum
Lit.: Boehn, Max von: *England im Achtzehnten Jahrhundert*. Berlin 1920. – Fetscher, Iring: *Großbritannien – Gesellschaft, Staat, Ideologie*, Frankfurt 1968. – Gowing, Lawrence: *Hogarth*, exh. cat., Tate Gallery, London 1971. – Lindsay, Jack: *Hogarth, His Art and His World*. London 1977. – Paulson, Ronald: *The Art of Hogarth*. London 1975. – Rave, Paul Ortwin: *William Hogarth, Die Parlamentswahlen*, Berlin 1947.

Sir Joshua Reynolds (1723–1792)
George Clive with his Family and an Indian Maidservant, *c.* **1765**
140 x 171 cm
Berlin, Staatliche Museen zu Berlin, Gemäldegalerie
Lit.: Kincaid, Dennis: *British Social Life in India 1608–1937*, London/Boston 1938. – Penny, Nicolas: *Reynolds* exh. cat., Royal Academy of Arts, London 1986. – Prochno, Renate: *Joshua Reynolds*, Weinheim 1990.

Jean-Honoré Fragonard (1732–1806)
The Stolen Kiss, 1787
45 x 55 cm.
St Petersburg, The State Hermitage Museum
Comparative illustration:
Jean-Honoré Fragonard
The Bolt, c. 1778
Paris, Musée du Louvre
Lit.: Bluche, François: *La vie quotidienne au temps de Louis XVI*, Paris 1980. – Chaussinand-Nogaret, Guy: *Madame Roland, une femme en révolution*, Paris 1985. – Cuzin, Jean-Pierre: *Fragonard*, Fribourg 1987, Munich 1988. – Pastoureau, Michel: *Des Teufels Tuch*, Frankfurt am Main 1995. – Rosenberg, Pierre (ed.): *Fragonard*, exh. cat., Grand Palais, Paris and Metropolitan Museum, New York 1987/88.

Johann Heinrich Wilhelm Tischbein (1751–1821)
Goethe in the Roman Campagna, 1786/1787
164 x 206 cm
Frankfurt, Städel Museum
Comparative illustration:

Johann Heinrich Wilhelm Tischbein
Goethe at the Window of the Apartment on the Via del Corso in Rome, 1787
41.5 x 26.6 cm
Frankfurt, Freies Deutsches Hochstift, Frankfurter Goethe-Museum
Lit.: Beutler, Christian: *J. H. W Tischbein – Goethe i. d. C.* Stuttgart 1962. – Goethe: *Briefe.* Philipp Stein (ed.), vol. 3, Berlin 1902. – Goethe: *Italienische Reise.* Vol. 25/6, Munich 1962. – Goethe: *Tagebücher 1775–1809.* Vol. 43, Munich 1963. – Lenz, Christian: *J. H. W Tischbein – Goethe i. d. C.* Series: *Kleine Werkmonographie des Städelschen Kunstinstitutes,* no. 6, Frankfurt (undated). – Städelsches Kunstinstiut und Städtische Galerie Frankfurt: *Goethe gemalt von Tischbein – ein Porträt und seine Geschichte.* Frankfurt 1974. – Tischbein, Wilhelm: *Aus meinem Leben.* Lothar Brieger (ed.), Berlin 1922.

Francisco de Goya (real name Francisco José de Goya y Lucientes) (1746–1828)
The Meadow of St Isidore, 1788
44 x 94 cm
Madrid, Museo Nacional del Prado
Comparative illustration:
Francisco de Goya
Pilgrimage to St Isidore's Hermitage, 1819–1823
Wall painting, later transferred to canvas,
139 x 436 cm
Madrid, Museo Nacional del Prado
Lit.: Chastenet, Jacques: *La vie quotidienne en Espagne au temps de Goya*, Paris 1966. – Gassier, Pierre/Wilson, Juliet: *Goya,* Friburg 1971/Frankfurt a. M. 1971. – Hofmann, Werner: *Goya, vom Himmel durch die Welt zur Hölle,* Munich 2003. – Licht, Fred: *Goya, The Origin of the Modern Temper,* New York, 1979. – *Die Geburt der Moderne,* Munich 2003. – Tomlinson, Janis A. (ed.): *Goya in the Twilight of Enlightenment,* New Haven/London 1992. – *Images of women*, exh. cat., National Gallery of Art, Washington and Prado, Madrid 2002.

Jacques-Louis David (1748–1825)
The Death of Marat, 1793
165 x 128 cm
Brussels, Musées royaux des Beaux-Arts de Belgique

Lit.: Cabanès, Augustin.: *Marat inconnu, l'homme privé, le médecin, le savant.* Paris 1928. – Cordier, Stéphane: *Jean-Paul Marat.* Paris 1967. – Decours, Catherine: *Charlotte Corday.* Paris 1985. – *Goya, das Zeitalter der Revolutionen,* exh. cat., Kunsthalle Hamburg 1980. – Schnapper, Antoine: *David und seine Zeit.* Würzburg 1981.

Karl Friedrich Schinkel (1781–1841)
Cathedral Overlooking a City, 1813
94 x 126 cm
Munich, Bayerische Staatsgemäldesammlungen, Neue Pinakothek
Lit.: Bergdoll, Barry: *Karl Friedrich Schinkel, Preußens berühmtester Baumeister,* Berlin 1994. – Büchel, Wolfgang: *Karl Friedrich Schinkel,* Reinbek 1994. – Ohff, Heinz: *Karl Friedrich Schinkel oder die Schönheit in Preußen,* Munich 1997. – Zadow, Mario: *Karl Friedrich Schinkel,* Berlin 1980.

Caspar David Friedrich (1774–1840)
Chalk Cliffs on Rügen, *c.* 1818
90 x 70 cm
Winterthur, Museum Oskar Reinhart
Comparative illustration:
Caspar David Friedrich
Self-portrait at the Age of 36, c. 1810
22.8 x 18.2 cm
Berlin, Staatliche Museen zu Berlin, Kupferstichkabinett
Lit.: Arndt, Ernst Moritz: *Ein deutsches Schicksal. Aus seinen biographischen Schriften.* Berlin 1924. – Carus, Carl Gustav: *Lebenserinnerungen und Denkwürdigkeiten,* 4 Theile. Leipzig 1856/66. – Börsch-Suspan, Helmut/Jähnig, Karl Wilhelm: *C. D. F.* Munich 1973. – Hinz, Sigrid: *C. D. F in Briefen und Bekenntnissen.* Munich 1974. – Hofmann, Werner (ed.): *C. D. F. und die Nachwelt.* Frankfurt 1974. – Jensen, Jens Christian: *C. D. F.: Leben und Werk,* Cologne 1974.

Théodore Géricault (1791–1824)
The Raft of the Medusa, 1819
491 x 716 cm
Paris, Musée du Louvre
Lit.: Anthonioz, Pierre: "La véritable histoire du radeau de la Méduse", in: *L'Histoire*, no. 36, July/Au-

gust 1981. – Bellec, François: *L'affaire da la Méduse, Documentation du Musée de la Marine*, 1981. – Eitner, Lorenz: *Géricault's Raft de la Medusa*, London 1922. – Nicolson, Benedict: "The Raft from the Point of View of Subject Matter", in: *Burlington Magazine*, 1954.

Eugène Delacroix (1798–1863)
Liberty Leading the People, 1830
260 x 325 cm
Paris, Musée du Louvre
Lit.: Adhémar, Hélène: "La Liberté sur les Barricades de Delacroix", in: *Gazette des Beaux-Arts* 1954. – Archaix, Guicharnaud: *Juillet 1830*, exh. cat., Musée Carnavalet, Paris 1980. – Bory, Jean-Louis: *La Révolution de Juillet*, Paris 1972. – Huyghe, René: *Delacroix*, Munich 1967.

Ando Hiroshige (1797–1858)
Morning Mist at Mishima, c. 1833
Station no. 12 from: The 53 Stations of the Tokaido Highway
Woodcut, 25 x 38 cm
Berlin, Staatliche Museen zu Berlin, Museum für Asiatische Kunst
Lit.: Addiss, Stephen: *Tokaido, On the Road in Old Japan*, exh. cat., Spencer Museum of Art, Lawrence 1980. – Forrer, Matthi: *Hiroshige. Prints and Drawings*, exh. cat., Royal Academy of Arts, London 1997. – Jippensha, Ikku: *Hizakurige or Shank's Mare. Japan's Great Comic Novel of Travel and Ribaldry.* Vermont/Tokyo 1960. – Vaporis, Nomiko: *Breaking Barriers. Travel and the State in Early Modern Japan.* Cambridge, Mass./London 1994.

William Turner (1775–1851)
The "Fighting Temeraire" tugged to her Last Berth to be broken up, 1838, 1839
91 x 122 cm
London, The National Gallery
Comparative illustration:
William Turner, *Rain, Steam and Speed – The Great Western Railway*, 1844
London, The National Gallery
Lit.: Egerton, Judy: *Turner, The Fighting Temeraire,* London 1995. – Wilton, Andrew: *William Turner, Leben und Werk*, 2006.

Carl Spitzweg (1808–1885)
The Poor Poet, 1839
36 x 45 cm
formerly in Berlin, Schloß Charlottenburg, Stiftung Preußische Schlösser und Gärten, Berlin-Brandenburg
Comparative illustration:
Carl Spitzweg
Sketch for *The Poor Poet*, before 1839
Pencil on paper
Munich, Staatliche Graphische Sammlung
Lit.: Daxenberger, Sebastian, known as Carl Fernau: *Münchener Hundert und Eins.* No. I, Munich 1840. – Haus der Kunst Munich: *Spitzweg*, exh. cat., Munich 1985. – Jensen, Jens Christian: *Carl Spitzweg*, Cologne 1980. – Raupp, Hans-Joachim: "Carl Spitzweg – Der arme Poet", in: *Wallraf-RichartzJahrbuch*, Cologne 1985/6. – Wichmann, Siegfried: *Carl Spitzweg,* Munich 1990.

Gustave Courbet (1819–1877)
The Studio, 1855
359 x 598 cm
Paris, Musée d'Orsay
Lit.: Courthion, Pierre (ed.): Courbet, Gustave: *Raconté par lui-même et par ses amis*, Geneva 1948/50. – Fernier, Robert: *La vie et l'œuvre de Gustave Courbet*, catalogue raisonné, Lausanne/Paris 1977. – Herding, Klaus (ed.): *Realismus als Widerspruch, die Wirklichkeit in Courbets Malerei*, Frankfurt 1978. – Huyghe, René/Bazin, Germain/Adhémar, Hélène Jean: *Courbet, L'Atelier*, in the series "Monographies des Peintures du Musée du Louvre", Paris (undated). – Nicolson, Benedict: *Courbet, The Studio of the Painter*, in the series "Art in Context", London 1973.

Jean-Auguste-Dominique Ingres (1780–1867)
The Turkish Bath, 1863
108 cm diameter
Paris, Musée du Louvre
Lit.: Alazard, Jean: *Ingres et l'Ingrisme.* Paris 1950. – Ebert, Hans: *Ingres.* Berlin 1982. – *Le bain turc d'Ingres*, exh. cat., Louvre, Paris 1971. – Pach, Walter: *Ingres.* New York 1973.

Édouard Manet (1832–1883)
The Balcony, 1868/1869
169 x 125 cm
Paris, Musée d'Orsay
Lit.: *Manet*, exh. cat., Paris/New York 1983. – Crespelle, Jean-Paul: *La vie quotidienne des impressionnistes*, Paris 1981. – Jordan, David: *Die Neuerschaffung von Paris, Baron Haussmann und seine Stadt*, Frankfurt a. M. 1996. – Pfeiffer, Ingrid/Hollein, Max (eds.): *Impressionistinnen*, exh. cat., Frankfurt a. M. 2008. – Rouart, Denis (ed.) *Correspondance de Berthe Morisot avec sa famille et ses amis*, Paris 1950.

Claude Monet (1840–1926)
Camille Monet on a Garden Bench (The Bench), 1873
60.6 x 80.3 cm
New York, The Metropolitan Museum of Art, The Walter H. and Leonore Annenberg Collection
Lit.: Bailey, Colin B./Rishel, Joseph J./Rosenthal, Mark: *Masterpieces of Impressionism and Post-Impressionism. The Annenberg Collection*, cat., Philadelphia Museum of Art 1989. – Busch, Günter: *Claude Monet: Camille – Vom Realismus zum Impressionismus*, Siemens Foundation lecture, Munich 1980. – *Édouard Manet*, exh. cat., Grand Palais, Paris 1983. – Tucker, Paul Hayes: *Claude Monet, Life and Art.* New Haven/London, 1995. – Wildenstein, Daniel: *Monet or the Triumph of Impressionism*, Cologne 1996.

Edgar Degas (1834–1917)
The Rehearsal on the Stage, 1873
65 x 81 cm
Paris, Musée d'Orsay
Lit.: Browse, Lillian: *Degas' Dancers*, London 1949. – Cabanne, Pierre: *Degas*, Munich, undated (1964). – Guiral, Pierre: *La vie en France à l'âge d'or du capitalisme 1852–1879*, Paris 1976. – Merlin, Olivier: *L'Opéra de Paris*, Fribourg 1975.

Gustave Caillebotte (1848–1894)
Paris Street, Rainy Day, 1877
212 x 276 cm
The Art Institute of Chicago, Charles H. and Mary F. S. Worcester Collection

Lit.: Berhaut, Marie: *Caillebotte, catalogue raisonné des peintures et pastels*, Paris 1994. – *Gustave Caillebotte: Urban Impressionist*, exh. cat., Paris/Chicago/Los Angeles 1994/95. – Jordan, David: *Transforming Paris, The Life and Labours of Baron Haussmann.* New York 1995. – Varnedoe, Kirk: *Gustave Caillebotte*, New Haven/London 1987.

Arnold Böcklin (1827–1901)
The Isle of the Dead, 1880
111 x 155 cm
Basle, Kunstmuseum Basel, Depositum der Gottfried-Keller-Stiftung
Lit.: Andrée, Rolf: *Arnold Böcklin, Die Gemälde*, Basle/Munich 1977. – Ariès, Philippe: *L'homme devant la mort*, Paris 1977. – Centre Georges Pompidou/Staatliche Kunsthalle Berlin (eds.): *Die Welt der Bahnhöfe*, Berlin 1980. – Holle, Luise (ed.): *Im deutschen Hause, Ein Ratgeber und Helfer für das gesamte häusliche Leben der deutschen Familie*, Hanau, undated (1903). – *Arnold Böcklin*, exh. cat., Kunstmuseum Basel, Basle/Stuttgart 1977. – Lichtwark, Alfred: *Die Seele und das Kunstwerk*, Berlin 1902. – Mendelsohn, Henry: *Böcklin*, Berlin 1901.

Pierre-Auguste Renoir (1841–1919)
The Luncheon of the Boating Party, 1881
129.5 x 172.7 cm
Washington, DC, National Gallery, The Phillips Collection
Lit.: Crespelle, Jean-Paul: *La vie quotidienne des Impressionistes*, Paris 1981. – Daulte, François: *Auguste Renoir, catalogue raisonné de l'œuvre peint*, Lausanne 1971. – Goncourt, Edmond et Jules de: *Menette Salomon*, Paris 1868. – Ehrlich White, Barbara; *Renoir, His Life, Art and Letters*, New York 1984. – Maupassant, Guy de: *Une Partie de Campagne*, Paris 1881. – Renoir, Jean: *Renoir, mon père*, Paris 1962. – Vollard, Ambroise: *Auguste Renoir*, Berlin (undated).

Georges Seurat (1859–1891)
Sunday Afternoon on the Island of La Grande Jatte, 1884/1886
207 x 308 cm
The Art Institute of Chicago, Helen Bartlett Memorial Collection

Lit.: Art Institute of Chicago: *Museum Studies, Chicago*, vol. 14, no. 2, 1988/89. – Bloch, Ernst: *Das Prinzip Hoffnung*, Frankfurt 1959. – Cachin, Françoise/-Herbert, Robert L. (eds.): *Seurat*, exh. cat., Paris/New York 1991. – Halperin, Joan Ungersma: *Félix Fénéon, Aesthete and Anarchist in Fin de Siècle Paris*, New Haven/London 1988. – Russell, John: *Georges Seurat*, London 1965.

Henri de Toulouse-Lautrec (1864–1901)
At the Moulin Rouge, *c.* **1893**
123 x 141 cm,
The Art Institute of Chicago
Helen Birch Bartlett Memorial Collection
Lit.: Adriani, Götz: *Toulouse-Lautrec und das Paris um 1900*, Cologne 1978. – Arnold, Matthias: *Toulouse-Lautrec*, Reinbek 1982. – *Toulouse-Lautrec*, exh. cat., South Bank Centre, London / Musée d'Orsay, Paris 1991. – Crespelle, Jean-Paul: *La vie quotidienne à Montmartre au temps de Picasso 1900–1910*, Paris 1978. – Jando, Dominique: *Histoire mondiale du Music-Hall*, Paris 1979.

Ernst Ludwig Kirchner (1880–1938)
Potsdamer Platz, 1914
200 x 150 cm
Berlin, Staatliche Museen zu Berlin,
Neue Nationalgalerie
Comparative illustration:
Ernst Ludwig Kirchner
Self-portrait as a Soldier, 1915; 69 x 61 cm
Oberlin, Allen Memorial Art Museum, Oberlin College, Charles F. Olney Fund
Lit.: Bellmann, Günther (ed.): *Potsdamer Platz, Drehscheibe der Weltstadt*, Berlin 1997. – Döblin, Alfred: *Drama, Hörspiel, Film*, Olten/Freiburg 1983. – Flexner, Abraham: *Die Prostitution in Europa*, Berlin 1921. – Gabler, Karlheinz: *E. L. Kirchner, Dokumente*, exh. cat., Aschaffenburg 1980. – Grisebach, Lucius/Meyer zu Eissen, Annette: *Kirchner*, exh. cat., Berlin etc., Munich 1980. – Grisebach, Lothar: *Ernst Ludwig Kirchners Davoser Tagebuch*, Cologne 1968. – Kirchner, Ernst Ludwig/Schiefler, Gustav: *Briefwechsel 1910–1935/38*, Stuttgart/Zurich 1990. – März, Roland/Henkel, Katharina (eds.): *Der Potsdamer Platz, Ernst Ludwig Kirchner und der Untergang Preu-*

ßens, exh. cat., Berlin 2001. – Moeller, Magdalena M.: *Ernst Ludwig Kirchner, Die Straßenszenen 1913–1915*, Munich 1993.

Alexander Deineka (1899–1969)
Female Textile Workers, 1927
171 x 195 cm
St Petersburg, The Russian Museum
Comparative illustration:
Alexander Deineka
Air Ace Shot Down, 1943
283 x 188 cm
St Petersburg, The Russian Museum
Lit.: *Alexander Deineka, Malerei, Grafik, Plakat*, exh. cat., Kunsthalle Düsseldorf 1982. – *Alexander Deineka, Malerei, Grafik, Bildhauerkunst, Monumentalwerke und literarischer Nachlass*, Leningrad 1982. – Cullerne, Matthew (ed.): *Socialist Realist Painting*, New Haven 1998.

Otto Dix (1891–1969)
Metropolis (Triptych), 1928
Central panel: 181 x 201 cm
Wings: each 181 x 101 cm
Kunstmuseum Stuttgart
Lit.: Conzelmann, Otto: *Otto Dix*, Hannover 1959. – Giese, Fritz: *Girl-Kultur*, Munich 1925. – Hermand, Jost and Trommler, Frank: *Die Kultur der Weimarer Republik*, Munich 1978. – Kessler, Harry Graf: *Tagebücher 1918–1937*, Frankfurt a. M. 1961. – Kracauer, Siegfried: *Das Ornament der Masse*, Frankfurt a. M. 1963. – Löffler, Fritz: *Otto Dix, Leben und Werk*, Dresden 1977.

Grant Wood (1891–1942)
American Gothic, 1930
78 x 65 cm
The Art Institute of Chicago, The Friends of American Art Collection
Lit.: Hoving, Thomas: *American Gothic, The Biography of Grant Wood's American Masterpiece*, New York 2005. – Milosch, Jane C. (ed.): *Grant Wood's Studio, Birthplace of American Gothic*, New York 2005. – *Time, The Weekly Newsmagazine*, 24 December 1934, New York

Ben Shahn (1898–1969)
The Passion of Sacco and Vanzetti, 1931/1932
216 x 122 cm
New York, Whitney Museum of American Art,
Gift of Edith and Milton Lowenthal in memory of
Juliana Force
Lit.: Ben Shahn: *Malerei*, with introduction by
Thrall Soby, James, Frankfurt a. M. 1964. – Avrich,
Paul: *Sacco and Vanzetti, The Anarchist Background*,
Princeton, New Jersey 1990. – *Ben Shahn and the
Passion of Sacco and Vanzetti*, exh. cat., Jersey City
Museum, New Jersey, December 2001, organized by
Anreus, Alejandro.

Max Beckmann (1884–1950)
Birth, 1937
Death, 1938
Each 121 x 177 cm
Berlin, Staatliche Museen zu Berlin,
Neue Nationalgalerie
Lit.: Fischer, Friedrich Wilhelm: *Max Beckmann,
Symbol und Weltbild*, Munich 1972. – Spieler, Rein-
hard: *Max Beckmann, Der Weg zum Mythos*, Cologne
1994. – Reimertz, Stephan: *Max Beckmann*, Munich
2003. – Max Beckmann: *Exil in Amsterdam*, exh. cat.,
Munich 2007.

Marc Chagall (1887–1985)
White Crucifixion, 1938
155 x 139.5 cm
The Art Institute of Chicago, Gift of Alfred S.
Alschuler
Lit.: Alexander, Sidney: *Marc Chagall, Eine Biogra-
phie*, Munich 1984. – Chagall, Bella: *Erste Begegnung,
Brennende Lichter*, Hamburg 1980. – Chagall, Marc:
Ma Vie, Paris 1931. – Chagall, Marc: *Rétrospective de
l'œuvre peint*, exh. cat., Fondation Maeght, Saint-Paul
de Vence 1984.

Diego Rivera (1886–1957)
**Dream of a Sunday Afternoon in Alameda Park,
1948**
4.80 x 15 m
Mexico City, Pabellón Diego Rivera
Lit.: Bahlsen, Gerhard: *Mexiko, Aufruhr und Behar-
rung*. Stuttgart 1961. – Carillo, Rafael A.: *Mural Pain-
ting of Mexico*, Mexico City 1981. – Gonzáles, Stella
M.; Blázquez, Carmen G.: *Die Geschichte Mexikos von
der vorspanischen Zeit bis zum heutigen Tag*, Mexico
City 1980. – Paz, Octavio: *The Labyrinth of Solitude,
Life and Thought in Mexico*, New York 1961. – Rivera,
Diego: *Wort und Bekenntnis*, Zurich 1965.

Credits

438–444 © Artothek / Städel Museum,
U. Edelmann

445 © Frankfurter Goethe-Haus / Freies
Deutsches Hochstift, Frankfurt
am Main

446–452 © Museo Nacional del Prado, Madrid

453 © Museo Nacional del Prado, Madrid

454–459 © Royal Museums of Fine Arts of
Belgium, Brussels, Cussac /
Speltdoorn

460–467 © Artothek, Blauel / Gnamm

468–472 © Museum Oskar Reinhart am
Stadtgarten, Winterthur

473 © bpk / Kupferstichkabinett, Staatliche
Museen zu Berlin / Jörg P Anders

474–481 © RMN Paris, Daniel Arnaudet

482–489 © RMN Paris, Gérard Blot / Hervé
Lewandowski

490–497 © bpk / Museum für Asiatische Kunst,
Ostasiatische Kunstsammlung,
Staatliche Museen zu Berlin / Jürgen
Liepe

498–505 © National Gallery, London

506–512 © bpk / Nationalgalerie, Staatliche
Museen zu Berlin / Jörg P. Anders

513 © Staatliche Graphische Sammlung,
München

514–521 © RMN Paris, Gérard Blot / Hervé
Lewandowski

522–527 © RMN Paris, Gérard Blot /
Christian Jean

528–533 © RMN Paris, Hervé Lewandowski

534–541 © bpk Berlin / New York,
The Metropolitan Museum of Art

542–549 © RMN Paris, Hervé Lewandoswki

550–557 © The Art Institute of Chicago

558–565 © Kunstmuseum Basle,
Martin P. Bühler

566–573 © The Philips Collection, Washington

574–581 © The Art Institute of Chicago

582–589 © The Art Institute of Chicago

590–593 © bpk / Nationalgalerie, Staatliche
Museen zu Berlin / Jörg P. Anders

594 © Oberlin College, Allen Memorial Art
Museum, Oberlin

595 © bpk / Nationalgalerie, Staatliche
Museen zu Berlin / Jörg P. Anders

598–603 © 1990. Photo Scala, Florence

604–613 © Kunstmuseum Stuttgart

614–615 © The Art Institute of Chicago

616 © Cedar Rapids Museum of
Art Archives

617–619 © The Art Institute of Chicago

620–625 © Whitney Museum of American Art,
New York

626–631 © bpk / Nationalgalerie, Staatliche
Museen zu Berlin / Jörg P Anders

632–637 © The Art Institute of Chicago

638–645 © Rafael Doniz, Mexico

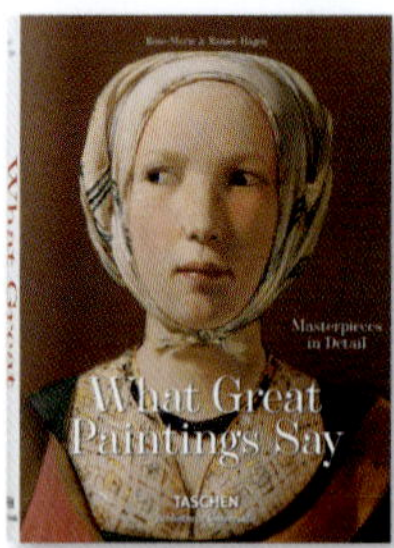

What Great Paintings Say

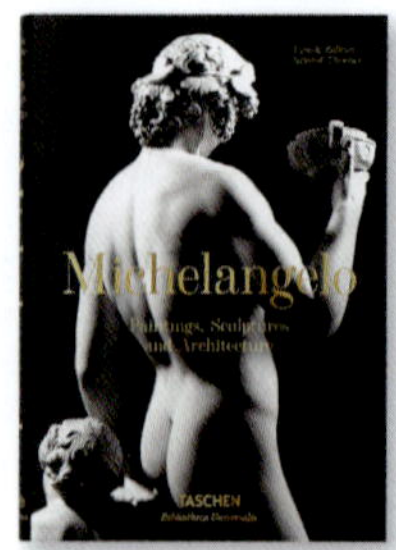

Michelangelo. Paintings,
Sculptures and Architecture

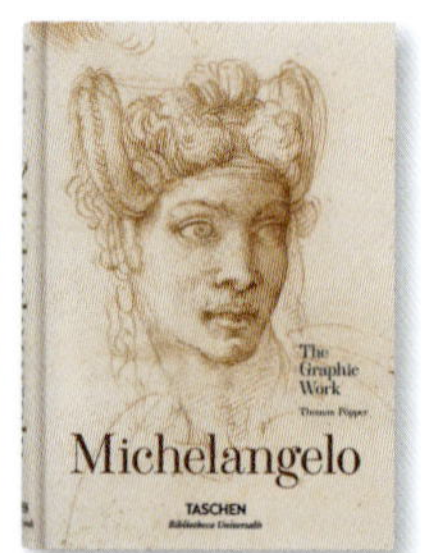

Michelangelo.
The Graphic Work

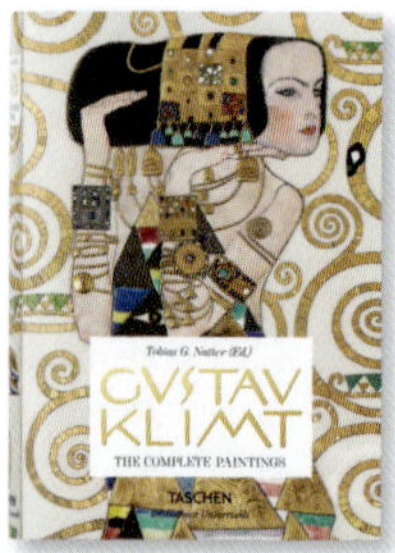

Gustav Klimt.
The Complete Paintings

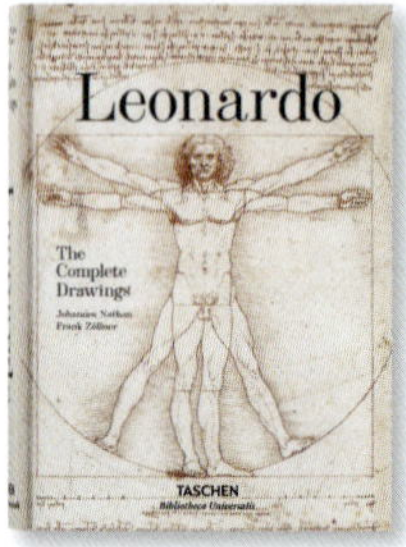

Leonardo da Vinci.
The Complete Drawings

**Bookworm's delight:
never bore, always excite!**

TASCHEN
Bibliotheca Universalis

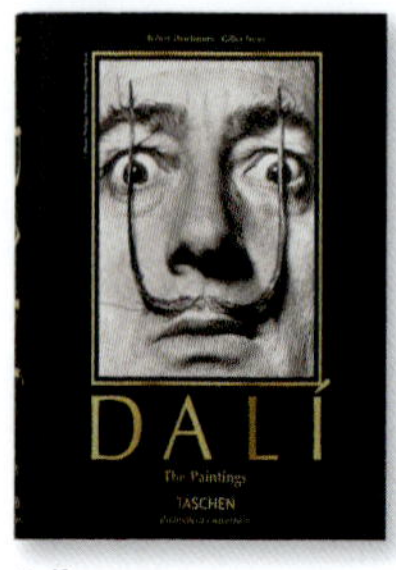

Dalí.
The Paintings

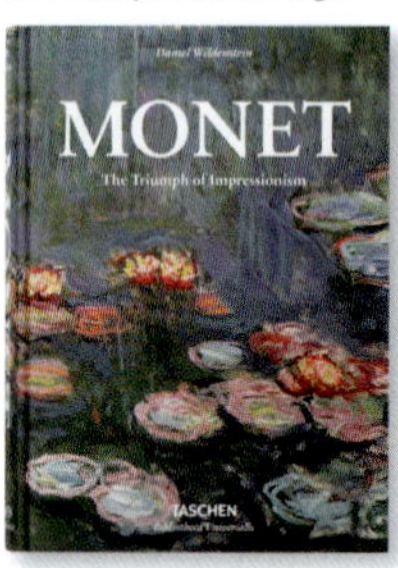

Monet

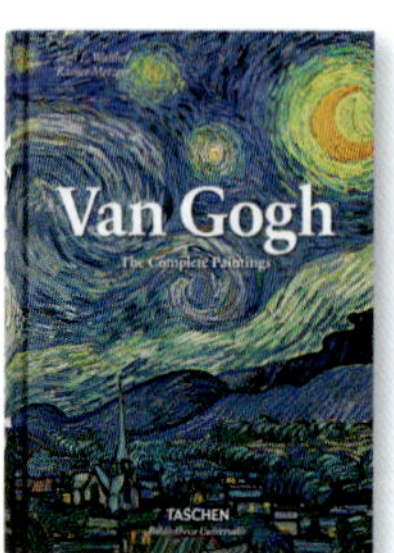

Van Gogh

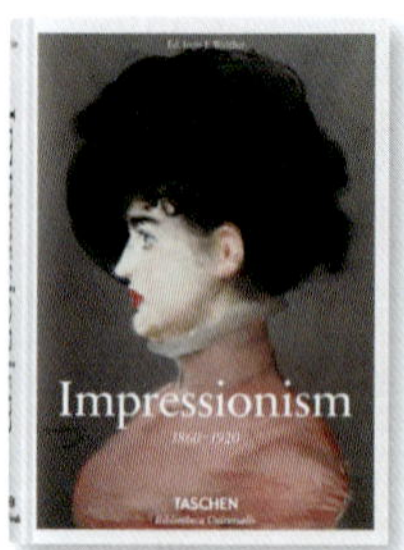

Impressionism

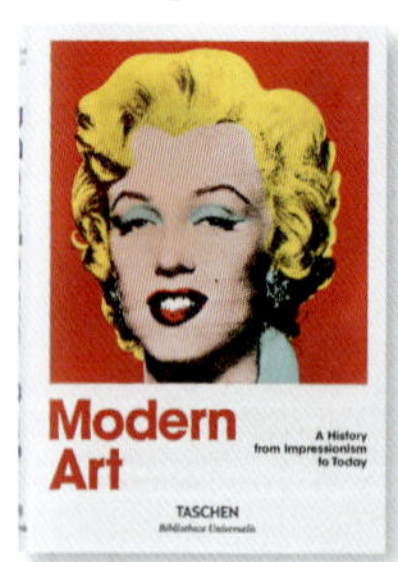

Modern Art

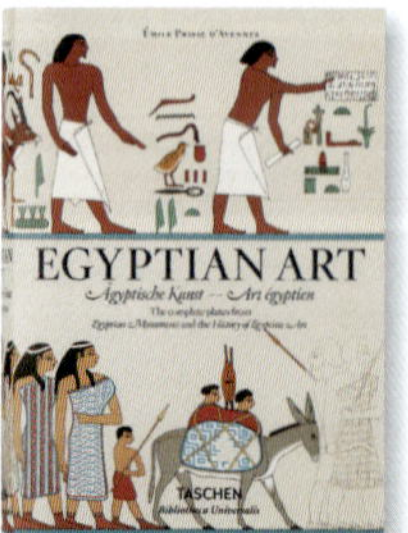

Prisse d'Avennes.
Egyptian Art

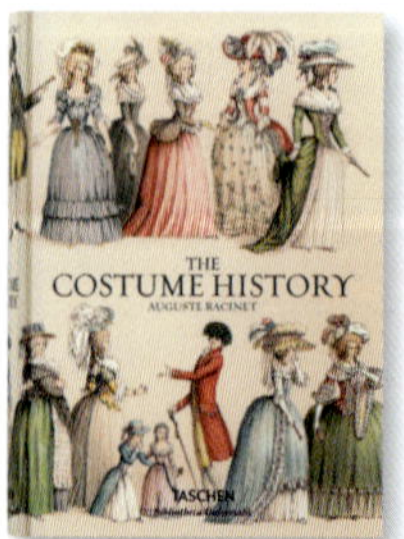

Racinet.
The Costume History

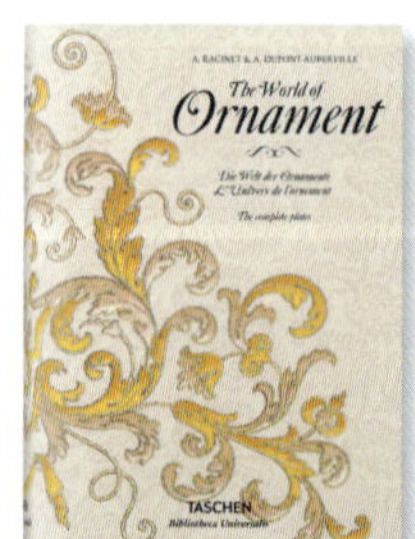

The World of Ornament

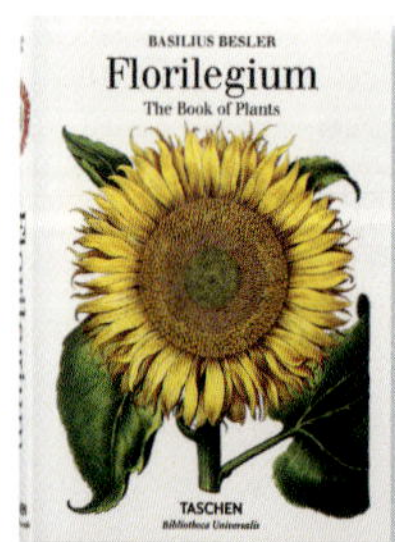

Basilius Besler's
Florilegium

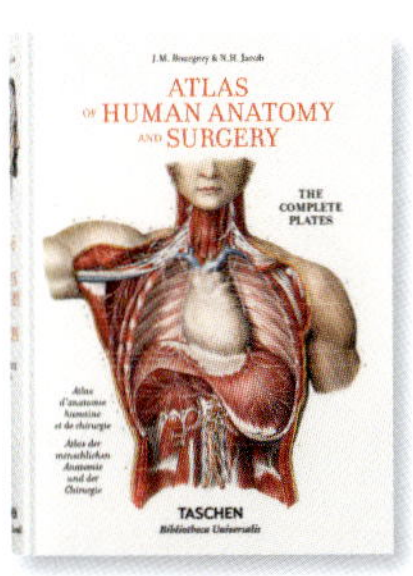

Bourgery. Atlas of
Anatomy & Surgery

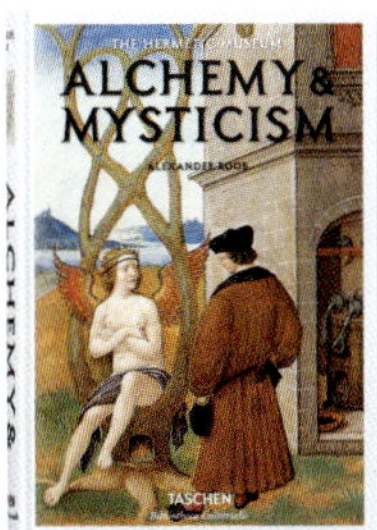

Alchemy & Mysticism

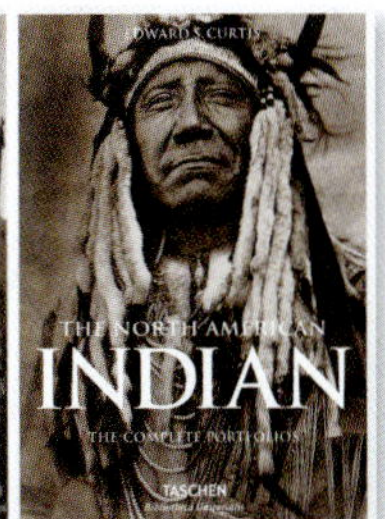

Curtis. The North
American Indian

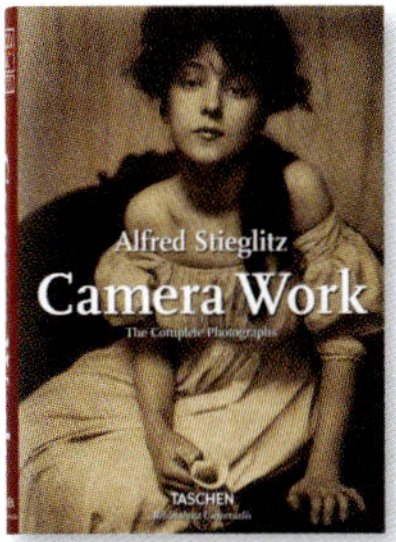

Stieglitz.
Camera Work

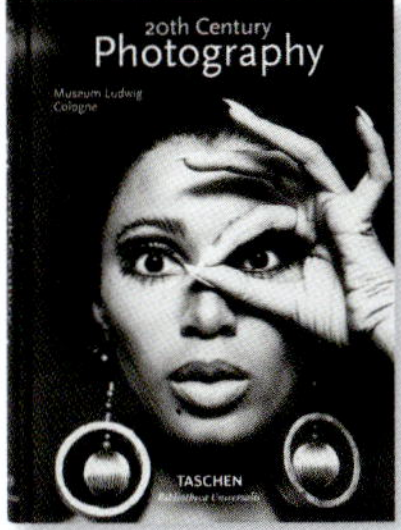

20th Century Photography

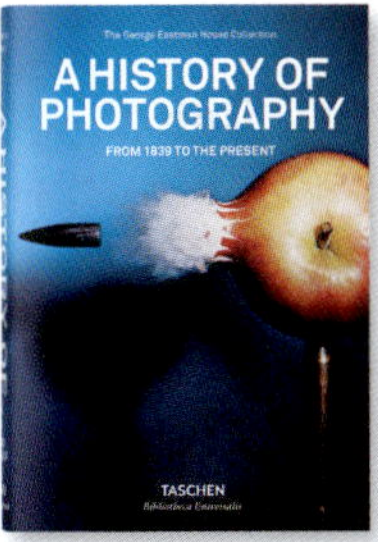

A History of Photography

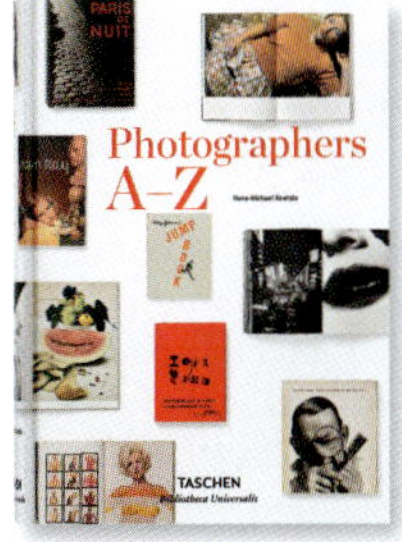

Photographers A–Z

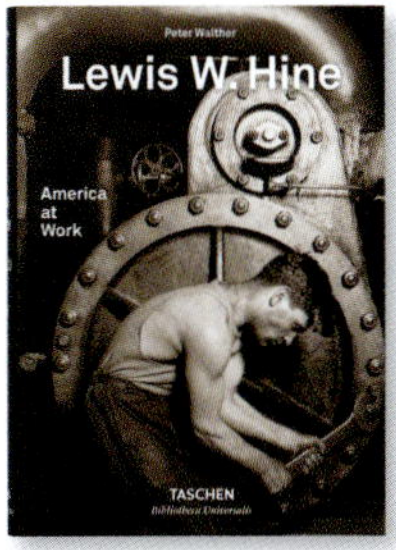

Lewis W. Hine

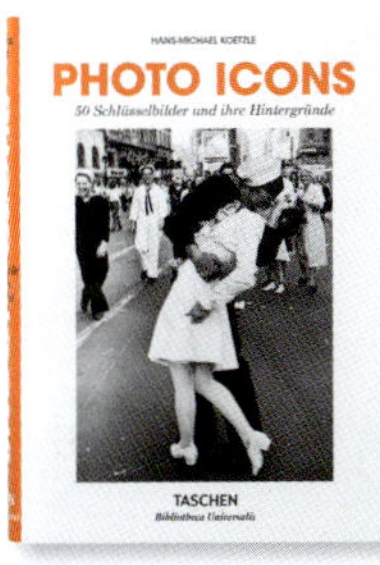

Photo Icons

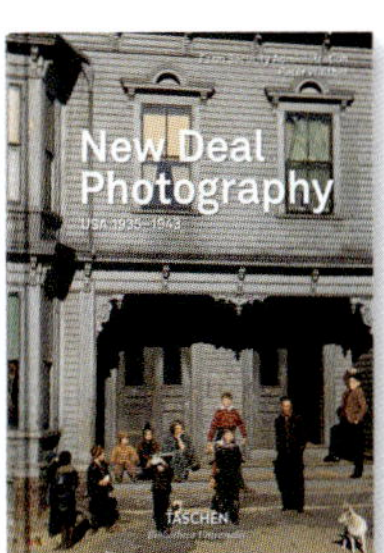

New Deal Photography

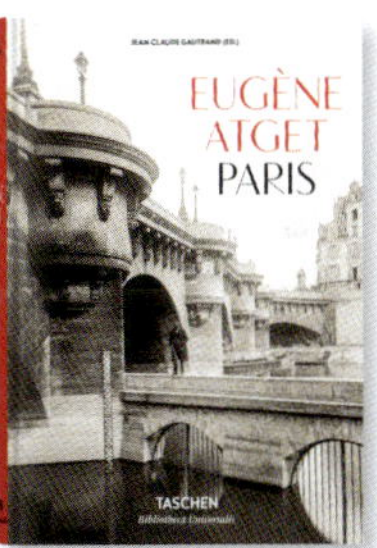

Eugène Atget. Paris

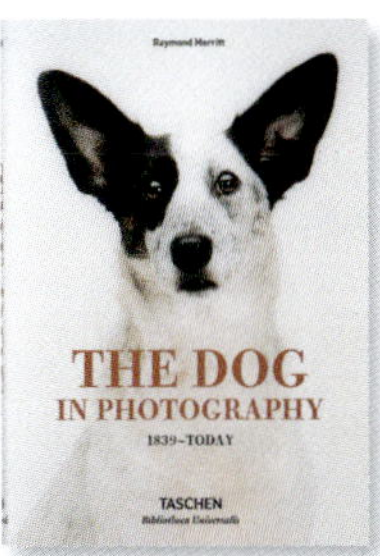

The Dog in Photography

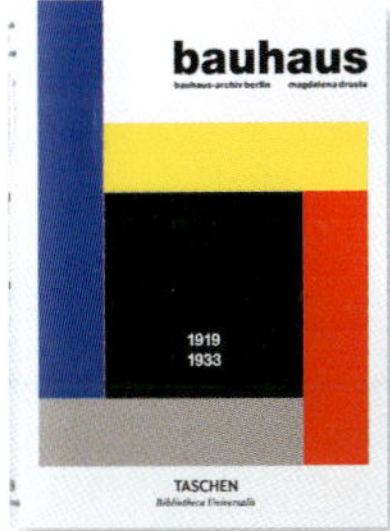

Bauhaus

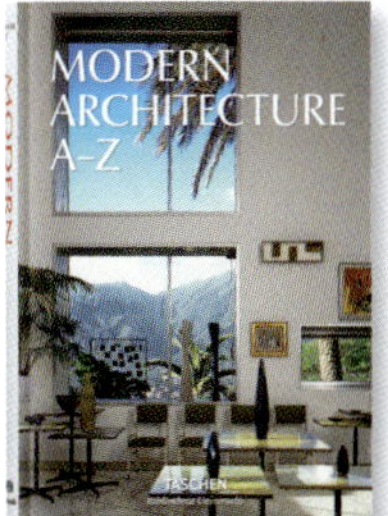

Modern
Architecture A-Z

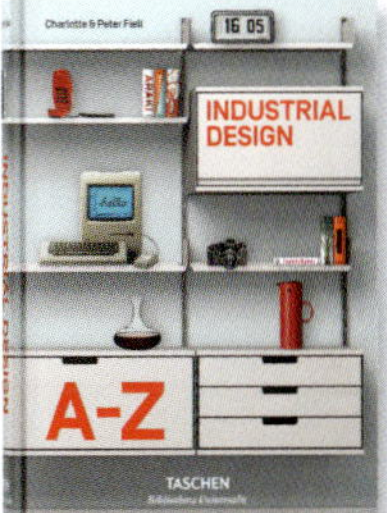

Industrial Design A–Z

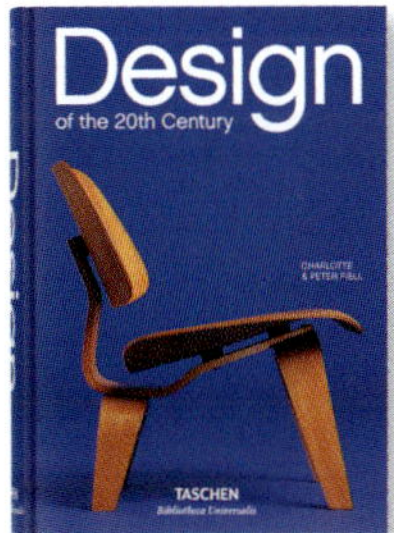

Design of the 20th Century

The authors:
Rose-Marie Hagen was born in Switzerland and studied history,
Romance languages and literature in Lausanne. After further studies
in Paris and Florence, she lectured at the American University in
Washington, D.C.
Rainer Hagen was born in Hamburg and graduated in literature
and theatre studies in Munich. He later worked for radio and TV,
most recently as chief editor of a German public broadcasting service.
Together they have collaborated on several TASCHEN titles, including
What Great Paintings Say, *Pieter Bruegel* and *Francisco de Goya*.

EACH AND EVERY TASCHEN BOOK PLANTS A SEED!
Each year, we offset our annual carbon emissions with carbon credits
at the Instituto Terra, a reforestation program in Minas Gerais, Brazil,
founded by Lélia and Sebastião Salgado. To find out more about this
ecological partnership, please check: www.taschen.com/institutoterra
Inspiration: unlimited. Carbon footprint: (almost) zero.

Want to see more? Visit taschen.com to view our current publications,
browse our latest magazine, and subscribe to our newsletter.